TYPES OF DRAMA

TYPES OF DRAMA

Plays and Essays

SYLVAN BARNET Tufts University

MORTON BERMAN Boston University

WILLIAM BURTO Lowell State College

Little, Brown and Company • *Boston*

SEVENTH PRINTING

Printed simultaneously in Canada by
Little, Brown & Company (Canada) Limited

PRINTED IN THE UNITED STATES OF AMERICA

Preface

Types of Drama is a thorough revision of our earlier collection, *Tragedy and Comedy*. Seven plays have been retained, and to them we have added eight other plays, one film script, and three critical essays on each of the three chief dramatic genres, tragedy, comedy, and modern tragicomedy. By adding works of Chekhov, O'Neill, Brecht, Miller, Bergman, Jones, and Ionesco, we have been better able to represent the twentieth century, and by adding critical essays we hope to stimulate some theoretical discussion and to provide some methods of approach. We have also added a short introductory essay on the language of drama to show (by means of reference to Eugene O'Neill's *The Emperor Jones*) the multiple ways in which a play speaks.

The PLAYS, arranged chronologically within the categories of tragedy, comedy, and tragicomedy, cover a range of years and types, but in no case were they chosen only to represent a period or a type. All were chosen because of their dramatic value. Those not written in English are represented in the best modern translations. The AFTERWORDS are relatively short. They are not attempts to explicate the plays, but they do contain some useful and relevant points, which will also be useful with other plays. For example, the afterword to *As You Like It* includes comments on two traditions of comedy, "critical" comedy and "romantic" comedy, but most of this material is relevant to other plays in the book. Similarly, the discussions of pathos, in the afterword to *Death of a Salesman*, and of three kinds of laughter, in the afterword to *Henry IV*, go beyond the plays in question. At the beginning of the book is a general introduction to basic concepts and critical terminology, but it may be best to postpone reading it until the students have carefully read at least a few plays. The ESSAYS are not analyses of particular plays, though of course they do include some specific discussions; they are fairly general, and therefore any of the essays on tragedy, for example, can be profitably read in conjunction with any of the tragedies. The GLOSSARY, drawn in part from the more detailed glossary in our *Aspects of Drama*, is a dictionary of two hundred basic critical and historical terms that are likely to come up in an introductory course. Some of these terms are discussed at length in the commentaries, but they are given again in the glossary itself; no one has to read the commentaries, unless he wants to know the dates of the plays.

Our ideas about drama have been shaped by many playwrights and many critics. Doubtless we are not aware of all of the influences upon us, but we know we are much indebted to Gerald Else, Northrop Frye, Helen Gardner, Richmond Lattimore, Konrad Lorenz, Maynard Mack, D. H. Monro, Rheinhold Niebuhr, and L. J. Potts. If other critics find they have contributed to this book, we hope that they will be as charitable as lovers in a comedy, and will accept our apologies and our thanks.

We have been fortunate in getting permission to print important modern plays and distinguished modern translations of older plays, and we are grateful to the authors, translators, and publishers who have cooperated. We are grateful, also, to Helen Willard and Jeanne T. Newlin of the Harvard Theatre Collection and to Mr. Athan Anagostopoulos and Professors Arthur Friedman and Seymour Simches for assistance in finding photographs, to Professors Oscar G. Brockett and Harry Ritchie for generously answering queries, and to Jane Aaron, Charles Christensen, Martha Davis, David Giele, Ellen Silver, and Warren Stone of Little, Brown, who have never let us get away with anything.

S.B.
M.B.
W.B.

Contents

THE NATURE OF DRAMA   1

  1. Tragedy and Comedy   3

    Imitation of an Action. Happenings and Happenings. Unity. The Tragic Hero. Hamartia. Hybris. Peripeteia. Anagnorisis. Tragic Joy. Comic Assertion. Comic Joy. Comic Isolation. Detachment and Engagement. Tragic Fate and Comic Fortune in Plots. Comic Beginnings and Endings. Self-Knowledge.

  2. Tragicomedy   14

    Tragicomedy Before 1900. Detachment and Engagement Again. Theater of the Absurd. Diminution of Man. Dissolution of Character and Plot. The Tragedy of Comedy.

THE LANGUAGE OF DRAMA   21

    Setting. Costume. Gestures. Sound Effects. Dialogue. Plot and Structure. Character. Theme.

  THE EMPEROR JONES   *Eugene O'Neill*   29

TRAGEDY   45

  OEDIPUS THE KING   *Sophocles*   47
    TRANSLATED INTO ENGLISH VERSE BY H. D. F. KITTO

  THE TRAGEDY OF KING LEAR   *William Shakespeare*   73
    EDITED BY RUSSELL FRASER

  HEDDA GABLER   *Henrik Ibsen*   139
    TRANSLATED BY OTTO REINERT

DEATH OF A SALESMAN   *Arthur Miller*   183

DUTCHMAN   *LeRoi Jones (Imamu Amiri Baraka)*   235

The Poetics   ARISTOTLE   249
TRANSLATED BY L. J. POTTS

Tragedy and the Common Man   ARTHUR MILLER   255

The Scheme of Tragedy   DOROTHEA KROOK   258

COMEDY   263

THE BIRDS   *Aristophanes*   265
TRANSLATED BY WILLIAM ARROWSMITH

AS YOU LIKE IT   *William Shakespeare*   319
EDITED BY ALBERT GILMAN

THE MISANTHROPE   *Molière*   365
ENGLISH VERSION BY RICHARD WILBUR

MAJOR BARBARA   *George Bernard Shaw*   397

The Comic Rhythm   SUSANNE K. LANGER   446

Old and New Comedy   NORTHROP FRYE   450

The Rise and Fall of the Custard Pie   RICHARD BOSTON   455

TRAGICOMEDY   461

THE CHERRY ORCHARD   *Anton Chekhov*   463
TRANSLATED BY STARK YOUNG

HENRY IV A TRAGEDY IN THREE ACTS   *Luigi Pirandello*   495
ENGLISH VERSION BY EDWARD STORER

THE GOOD WOMAN OF SETZUAN   *Bertolt Brecht*   529
TRANSLATED BY ERIC BENTLEY

WILD STRAWBERRIES   *Ingmar Bergman*   573
TRANSLATED BY LARS MALMSTRÖM AND DAVID KUSHNER

THE GAP   *Eugène Ionesco*   607
TRANSLATED BY ROSETTE LAMONT

*THE EFFECT OF GAMMA RAYS ON
MAN-IN-THE-MOON MARIGOLDS*   *Paul Zindel*   615

Comedy, Tragedy, and Tragicomedy   CYRUS HOY   636

Comedy and Tragedy Transposed   ELLEN DOUGLASS LEYBURN   643

King Lear or Endgame   JAN KOTT   648
    TRANSLATED BY BOLESLAW TABORSKI

GLOSSARY OF DRAMATIC TERMS   653

TYPES OF DRAMA

THE NATURE OF DRAMA

1. Tragedy and Comedy

Whimsical assertions that all men are Platonists or Aristotelians, or liberals or conservatives ("Nature wisely does contrive / That every boy and every gal / That's born into the world alive / Is either a little Liberal / Or else a little Conservative") reveal a tendency to divide things into two. Two is about right: peace and war, man and woman, day and night, life and death. There may be middle cases; there is the cold war, and Edmund Burke suggested that no man can point to the precise moment that divides day from night — but Burke also suggested that everyone can make the useful distinction between day and night. The distinction between comedy and tragedy may not always be easy to make, but until the twentieth century it was usually clear enough. *Hamlet,* which in Horatio's words is concerned with "woe or wonder," is a tragedy; *A Midsummer Night's Dream,* which in Puck's words is concerned with things that pleasingly "befall preposterously," is a comedy. The best plays of our century, however, are another thing, and discussion of these plays — somewhat desperately called tragicomedy — will be postponed until the end of this introduction.

What befalls — preposterous or not — is the *action of the play.* The gestures on the stage are, of course, "actions," but they are not the action of the play in the sense of Aristotle's use of *praxis* or "action" in *The Poetics,* a fragmentary treatise of the fourth century B.C. that remains the starting point for most discussions of drama. For Aristotle, drama is the imitation (i.e., representation, re-presentation, re-creation) by impersonators, of an action. In tragedy the action is serious and important, something that matters, done by people who count (e.g., King Oedipus' discovery that he has killed his father and married his mother); in comedy (for Aristotle), the action is done by unimportant laughable people who make mistakes that do not cause us pain. Commonly the tragic action is a man's perception of a great mistake he has made; he suffers intensely and perhaps dies, having exhausted all the possibilities of his life. The comic action often is the exposure of folly and the renewal rather than the exhaustion of human nature. Crabby parents, for example, find that they cannot keep young lovers apart, and so they join in the marriage festivities. Byron jocosely put the matter thus:

IMITATION OF AN ACTION

> All tragedies are finished by a death,
> All comedies are ended by a marriage.

All tragedies and all comedies do not in fact end thus, but the idea is right; tragedy has the solemnity, seriousness, and finality we often associate with death,* and comedy has the joy and fertility and suggestion of a new life we

---

* Shakespeare's tragedies all end with the death of the tragic hero, but a good many Greek tragedies do not. In *Oedipus the King* the hero remains alive, but he is blind and banished and seems to have exhausted the possibilities of his life. Some other Greek tragedies have what can reasonably be called a happy ending, i.e., some sort of joyful reconciliation. For ex-

often associate with marriage. This concept of *an action* (i.e., an underlying motif, not merely gestures) in tragedy and in comedy makes clear that comedy is not a mere matter of jokes or funny bits of business. It also makes clear what the Greek comic playwright Menander meant when he told a friend that he had composed a play, and now had only to write the dialogue: he had worked out the happenings that would embody the action, and there remained only the slighter task of providing the spirited words. The same idea is implicit in Ibsen's comment that the drafts of his plays differed "very much from each other in characterization, not in action." The action or happening dramatized in a tragedy or a comedy may be conceived of as a single course or train of events manifested on the stage by a diversity of activities. Think of such expressions as "the closing of the frontier," or "the revival of learning"; each might be said to denote an action, though such action is seen only in its innumerable manifestations. The *Iliad* announces its action in the first line: "Sing, goddess, of the wrath of Achilles." The "action" is not, of course, always explicitly announced in a literary work. Among Ibsen's preliminary notes as he worked toward *Hedda Gabler* we find such entries as "They [i.e., women] all have a leaning towards sensuality, but are afraid of the scandal," "Men and women don't belong to the same century," and "The play is to be about 'the insuperable' — the longing and striving to defy convention, to defy what people accept (including Hedda)." Clearly, Ibsen was trying to get hold of his central point and then develop a plot that would reveal it.

HAPPENINGS
AND
HAPPENINGS

A tragic playwright takes some happening, from history (for example, the assassination of Julius Caesar), or from fiction (Shakespeare derived *Othello* from an Italian short story), or from his own imagination, and he makes or shapes or arranges episodes that clarify the action. He makes (in common terminology) a *plot* that embodies the action or spiritual content. (Even when the playwright draws on history, he makes his own plot because he selects and rearranges the available historical facts.) A glance at a very different kind of drama, recently popular, helps to clarify the distinction between a plot that embodies an action or a happening, and mere unconnected activities, happenings, events. In the early 1960's there was a good deal of interest in "Events" or "Happenings" (the latter term was derived from a performance in 1959 of something called *18 Happenings in 6 Parts*), performances in which activities were not connected so as to form a coherent plot that manifested an underlying action. Sample: a girl alternately washes her feet, puts tape over her mouth, dances with a board, sprays paint from a can onto a wall, and finally disrobes. Such a performance may display wit, agility, and other virtues and skills, but it is not a play in the traditional sense, despite its playfulness. Neither would a re-enactment of everything that Julius Caesar did during his last

---

ample, in Sophocles' *Philoctetes*, the weapon which has been taken from the sick Philoctetes is returned to him, and Heracles, a messenger from Zeus, announces that Philoctetes will be healed. But these tragedies with happy endings, like those with unhappy endings, deal with "important" people, and they are about "serious" things. If there is finally joy, it is a solemn joy.

days or hours be a play with an action, for drama is not so much concerned with what in fact *happened* as with some sort of typical and coherent or unified thing that *happens*, a significant action. Sometimes, of course, history provides substantial material for drama, but even Shakespeare's *Julius Caesar* takes frequent liberties with the facts as Shakespeare knew them, and Shakespeare's source, the biographer Plutarch, doubtless had already assimilated the facts to a literary form. At most we can say that history provided Shakespeare with a man whose life lent itself well to an established literary form. Not every life does lend itself thus. We are told that Aeschylus, the earliest tragic playwright who has left us any complete plays, was killed when an eagle mistook his bald head for a rock and dropped a turtle on it to break the shell. Aeschylus' death was a great loss, but it did not have the unified significant action required of tragedy. By chance an eagle that had captured a turtle was near to Aeschylus, and Aeschylus by chance (or rather by his chemistry) was bald. There is no relation between these two circumstances; Aeschylus' death (allegedly) happened this way, and we can account for it, but the event has no intelligible unity. (A sentence from Vladimir Nabokov's *Pale Fire* comes to mind: if one is contemplating suicide, "jumping from a high bridge is not recommended even if you cannot swim, for wind and water abound in weird contingencies, and tragedy ought not to culminate in a record dive or a policeman's promotion.") In tragedy things cohere. The hero normally does some deed and suffers as a consequence. Actions have consequences in the moral world no less than in the materialistic world of the laboratory. The tragic playwright's solemn presentation of "the remorseless working of things," Alfred North Whitehead pointed out (in his *Science and the Modern World*, 1925), is "the vision possessed by science," and it cannot be accidental that the two great periods of tragic drama, fifth-century B.C. Athens and England around 1600, are periods of scientific inquiry.

This emphasis on causality means that the episodes are related, connected, and not merely contiguous. Generally the formula is to show the tragic hero moving toward committing some deed that will cause great unintended suffering, committing it, and then, by seeing the consequences, learning the true nature of his deed. The plot, that is, involves a credible character whose doings are related to his nature. For Aristotle, in the best sort of tragedy the tragic hero is an important person, almost pre-eminently virtuous, who makes some sort of great mistake that entails great suffering. Calamity does not descend upon him from above, does not happen *to* him, nor does he consciously will a destructive act; he merely makes a great mistake. The mistake is Aristotle's *hamartia*, sometimes translated as "error," sometimes as "flaw." Probably Aristotle did not mean by hamartia a trait, such as rashness or ambition, which the translation "flaw" implies, but simply meant an action based on a mental error, a sort of false step. Oedipus, erroneously thinking that Polybus and Meropê are his parents, flees from them when he hears that he will kill his father and sleep with his mother. His action is commendable, but it happens to be a great mistake because it brings him to his real parents. Nevertheless, despite the

UNITY

THE TRAGIC HERO

HAMARTIA

scholarly elucidations of Aristotle, we can sometimes feel that the erring action proceeds from a particular kind of character, that a person with different traits would not have acted in the same way. The Oedipus that we see in the play, for example, is a self-assured quick-tempered man — almost a rash man, we might say — who might well have neglected to check the facts before he fled from Corinth. There are at least times, even when reading *Oedipus the King*, when one feels with George Meredith (1828–1909) that

> in tragic life, God wot,
> No villain need be! Passions spin the plot:
> We are betrayed by what is false within.

HYBRIS

From this it is only a short step to identifying hamartia with a flaw, and the flaw most often attributed to the tragic hero is *hybris*, a word that for the Greeks meant something like "bullying," "abuse of power," but in dramatic criticism usually is translated as "overweening pride." The tragic hero forgets that (in Montaigne's words) "on the loftiest throne in the world we are still sitting only on our own rear," and he believes his actions are infallible. King Lear, for example, banishes his daughter Cordelia with "Better thou / Hadst not been born than not t' have pleased me better." Macbeth, told that he will be king of Scotland, chooses to make the prophecy come true by murdering his guest, King Duncan; Brutus decides that Rome can be saved from tyranny only by killing Caesar, and he deludes himself into thinking he is not murdering Caesar but sacrificing Caesar for the welfare of Rome.

PERIPETEIA

We have talked of hamartia and hybris in tragedy; two more Greek words, *peripeteia* and *anagnorisis*, also common in discussions of tragedy, ought to be mentioned. A peripeteia (sometimes anglicized to "peripety" or translated as "reversal") occurs when the action takes a course not intended by the doer. Aristotle gives two examples: (1) the Messenger comes to cheer up Oedipus by freeing him from fears but the message heightens Oedipus' fears; (2) Danaus (in a lost play) prosecutes a man but is himself killed. The second example, by the way, reminds one of *The Merchant of Venice*, in which Shylock, calling upon the law, in effect demands Antonio's death and finds that his own life may be lawfully taken. A few other examples may be useful: Oedipus fled from Corinth to avoid contact with his parents, but his flight brought him to them; Macbeth kills Duncan to gain the crown but his deed brings him fearful nights instead of joyful days; Lear, seeking a peaceful old age, puts himself in the hands of two daughters who maltreat him, and banishes the one daughter who later will comfort him. The Bible — especially the Old Testament — is filled with such peripeties or ironic actions. For example, the Philistines brought Samson before them to entertain them, and he performed his most spectacular feat by destroying his audience. But the archetypal tragic story is that of Adam and Eve: aiming to be like gods, they lost their immortality and the earthly paradise, and brought death to themselves.

ANAGNORISIS

The other Greek word, anagnorisis, translated as "recognition" or "discovery" or "disclosure," seems to have meant for Aristotle a clearing up of some misunderstanding, for example, the proper identification of someone or the revelation of some previously unknown fact. But later critics have given it a richer meaning and used it to describe the hero's perception of his true nature or his true plight. In the narrow sense, it is an anagnorisis or "recognition" when King Lear learns that Regan and Goneril are ungrateful and cruel. In the wider sense, the anagnorisis is in his speech in III.iv when he confesses his former ignorance and neglect:

> Poor naked wretches, wheresoe'er you are,
> That bide the pelting of this pitiless storm,
> How shall your houseless heads and unfed sides,
> Your looped and windowed raggedness, defend you
> From seasons such as these? O, I have ta'en
> Too little care of this! Take physic, pomp;
> Expose thyself to feel what wretches feel,
> That thou mayst shake the superflux to them,
> And show the heavens more just.

Similarly Hamlet's "There is special providence in the fall of a sparrow," and Othello's "one that loved not wisely, but too well," may be called recognition scenes. Here is Macbeth's recognition that his purpose has been frustrated, that his deed has been ironic:

> My way of life
> Is fall'n into the sear, the yellow leaf,
> And that which should accompany old age,
> As honor, love, obedience, troops of friends,
> I must not look to have.

THE SOCIAL WORLD OF COMEDY

"Troops of friends" abound in comedy. Where tragedy is primarily the dramatization of the single life that ripens and then can only rot, that reaches its fullest and then is destroyed, comedy is primarily the dramatization of the renewing of the self and of social relationships. The tragic figure is isolated from society, partly by his different nature, and partly by his tragic act; comedy suggests that selfhood is found not in assertion of individuality, but in joining in the fun, in becoming part of the flow of common humanity. Where tragedy suggests an incompatibility between the energy or surge of life and the laws of life or the norms of society, comedy suggests that norms are valid and necessary. The tragic hero does what he feels compelled to do; he asserts himself, and is intensely aware that he is a special person and not a member of the crowd. But that his mistake always reveals that he is hybristic is not at all certain. The Greek tragic hero is commonly set against a chorus of ordinary mortals who caution him, wring their hands, and lament his boldness, but these ordinary mortals are always aware that if they are law-abiding men, they are also less fully men than the hero. That they obey society's laws is not due to superior virtue, to the triumph of reason over will, to self-discipline; rather, their obedience is due to a lower vision, or to timidity, and indeed sometimes to a fear of what resides in their own breasts. The tragic hero is, of course, in one way inferior to those about him; his mistake costs him great suffering, and he is thus immobilized as the others are not. But his greatness remains indisputable; the anguish that at times paralyzes Hamlet also makes him greater

TRAGIC ISOLATION

than, say, Horatio and Laertes. In fact the tragic hero is circumscribed, certainly after the deed, when he is necessarily subject to the consequences (Brutus kills Caesar and finds that he brings to Rome a turmoil that makes him flee from Rome, and ultimately makes him take his own life); even before doing the tragic deed the hero is circumscribed because his action proceeds from something, either from his personality or his circumstances. Still, his action seems to him to be freely his, and indeed we feel that it is an action that a

TRAGIC
VIRTUE
lesser man could not perform. Which is almost a way of saying that it can be argued that a tragic hero may err not so much from weakness as from strength. Why can Iago so easily deceive Othello? Not because Othello is an unthinking savage, or an unsophisticated foreigner, but because (as Iago admits) Othello is of a "loving noble nature," and, again,

> The Moor is of *a free and open nature*
> *That thinks men honest* that but seem to be so;
> And will as tenderly be led by th' nose
> As asses are.

Why can Claudius see to it that Laertes murders Hamlet during a fencing match? Not because Hamlet is a poor fencer, or a coward, but because Hamlet,

> *Most generous, and free from all contriving,*
> Will not peruse the foils.

TRAGIC JOY
This is not to say that the tragic hero is faultless, or that he is quite happy with himself and with his action; but he does experience a kind of exultation even in his perception that disaster is upon him. If he grieves over his deed, we sense a glory in his grief, for he finds, like Captain Ahab, that in his topmost grief lies his topmost greatness. At last he sees everything and knows that nothing more can be experienced. He has lived his life to its limits. Othello puts it thus:

> Here is my journey's end, here is my butt,
> And very seamark of my utmost sail.

(In a comedy Shakespeare tells us that "journeys end in lovers meeting," that is, the end is a new beginning.) In "Under Ben Bulben" William Butler Yeats (1865–1939) suggests the sense of completeness that the tragic hero experiences when, under the influence of a great passion, he exhausts his nature and seems to be not a man among men but a partner (rather than a subject) of fate:

> Know that when all words are said
> And a man is fighting mad,
> Something drops from eyes long blind,
> He completes his partial mind,
> For an instant stands at ease,
> Laughs aloud, his heart at peace.
> Even the wisest man grows tense
> With some sort of violence
> Before he can accomplish fate,
> Know his work or choose his mate.

Elsewhere Yeats put his distinction between the tragic hero and the world he is up against thus: "Some Frenchman* has said that farce is the struggle against a ridiculous object, comedy against a movable object, tragedy against an immovable; and because the will, or energy, is greatest in tragedy, tragedy is the more noble; but I add that 'will or energy is eternal delight,' and when its limit is reached it may become a pure, aimless joy, though the man, the shade, still mourns his lost object." And one more passage by Yeats, this one from a play, again calling attention to the revelation of life — joyful to behold — apparent when an impassioned man expresses his fullest nature:

> I would have all know that when all falls
> In ruin, poetry calls out in joy,
> Being the scattering hand, the bursting pod,
> The victim's joy among the holy flame,
> God's laughter at the shattering of the world.

All this is to say splendidly that we sometimes feel admiration for the passionate man, for the man determined to do and to be, and we sense his superiority (as he himself senses it) to the law-abiding men who surround him, perhaps no more so than when his nobility undoes him, i.e., when we see the incompatibility between passionate self-assertion and the laws of life.

But there are contexts and times when we find passionate self-assertion funny (there are contexts and times, too, when we find it vicious, but that is another matter). Much depends on what is being asserted, and what or who the antagonist is. Recall Brunetière's opinion, or rather Yeats' version of it, that tragedy dramatizes a struggle against an immovable object, comedy a struggle against a movable one. King Lear against his tigerish daughters is a tragic figure, but a pedant against a dull schoolboy may be a comic one. The lament of the tragic hero is proportionate to the event, but the effort extended by the comic figure is absurdly disproportionate. Furthermore, as Henri Bergson (1859–1941) pointed out, the comic figure usually is a sort of mechanism, repeating his actions and catch phrases with clocklike regularity in contexts where they are inappropriate. He quotes Latin on every occasion, or he never travels without his pills, or he always wants to know how much something costs, or he is forever spying on his wife. Bergson, who suggested that the comic is "the mechanical encrusted on the living," illustrated his point by telling of the customs officers who bravely rescue the crew of a sinking vessel, and then ask, the moment the shore is reached, "Have you anything to declare?" The mechanical question, inappropriate in the situation, reveals that the officers value trivial regulations as much as they value life itself. In *The Circus* Charlie Chaplin is dusting things off; he comes upon the magician's bowl of goldfish, takes the fish out and wipes them, and then returns them to the bowl. Real life, too, affords examples of this sort of comic behavior. Emerson mentions that the biologist Camper, who had spent six months studying hairless water mammals, said he almost began to see people as narwhales, por-

COMIC ASSERTION

---

* Yeats is rather freely summarizing Ferdinand Brunetière's *La Loi du théâtre*. A translation of Brunetière's treatise is available in *European Theories of the Drama*, ed. Barrett H. Clark.

poises, and marsouins. This is whimsy, of course, but Emerson goes on to tell
of a visit to a dying friend. On his way to the friend, Emerson met the physician, who had just left the patient. The physician, Emerson says, "accosted me
in great spirits, with joy sparkling in his eyes. 'And how is my friend, the reverend Doctor?' I inquired. 'O, I saw him this morning; it is the most correct
apoplexy I have ever seen: face and hands livid, breathing stertorous, all the
symptoms perfect.' And he rubbed his hands with delight."

Emerson's doctor, valuing symptoms rather than life, nicely fulfills Bergson's formula. And in his high spirits — ludicrously out of place in the
COMIC JOY context — he inadvertently illustrates another aspect of comedy, its prevailing
high spirits. The comic world is a world of delight in variety; even its hardships
are not lasting. In *As You Like It* when Rosalind, daughter of a banished duke,
complains of the frustrations of life, "O, how full of briers is this working-day
world," Celia gives the right reply: "They are but burrs, cousin, thrown upon
thee in holiday foolery." (But if Celia were to give this answer too often she
would become laughable herself.) The comic world seems to be presided over
by a genial tolerant deity who enjoys the variety that crosses the stage. The
sketchbooks of the Japanese artist Hokusai (1760–1849) wonderfully reveal
this comic delight in humanity. There are pages of fat men, pages of thin men
(no less engagingly drawn), pages of men making funny faces, and there is a
delightful drawing of a man holding a magnifying glass in front of his face so
that his nose seems enormous. The comic playwright gives us something of
this range of types and grotesques, and he gives us also variety in language
(e.g., puns, inverted clichés, malapropisms) and variety in episodes (much
hiding behind screens, dressing in disguise). The character, then, who insists
on being himself, who mechanically holds to a formula of language or of behavior, is laughably out of place in the world of varied people who live and let
COMIC live. What comedy does not tolerate is intolerance; it regularly suggests that
ISOLATION the intolerant — for example the pedant and the ascetic — are fools and probably hypocrites. Here is the self-righteous Alceste, in Molière's *The Misanthrope*:

> Some men I hate for being rogues: the others
> I hate because they treat the rogues like brothers,
> And, lacking a virtuous scorn for what is vile,
> Receive the villain with a complaisant smile.
> Notice how tolerant people choose to be
> Toward that bold rascal who's at law with me.

Philinte genially replies, "Let's have an end of rantings and of railings, / And
show some leniency toward human failings. / This world requires a pliant
rectitude; / Too stern a virtue makes one stiff and rude." Here is the puritanical
Malvolio in *Twelfth Night*, trying to quiet down some tipsy but genial revel-
ers:

> My masters, are you mad? Or what are you? Have you no wit, manners
> nor honesty, but to gabble like tinkers at this time of night? Do ye make
> an alehouse of my lady's house? ... Is there not respect of place, per-
> sons, nor time in you?

He is aptly answered: "Art any more than a steward? Dost thou think, because thou art virtuous, there shall be no more cakes and ale?" This suspicion of a "virtue" that is opposed to cakes and ale runs through the history of comedy. In Shakespeare's *Love's Labor's Lost*, the young noblemen who vow to devote themselves to study, and to forgo the company of women, are laughed at until they accept their bodies and admit interest in those of the ladies. The celebration of the human body, or at least the good-natured acceptance of it which is present in comedy is well-put by the General in Anouilh's *The Waltz of the Toreadors*. (The life-buoy he refers to is "the ideal.")

> You're in the ocean, splashing about, doing your damndest not to drown, in spite of whirlpools and cross currents. The main thing is to do the regulation breast-stroke and if you're not a clod, never to let the life-buoy out of sight. No one expects any more than that out of you. Now if you relieve yourself in the water now and then, that's your affair. The sea is big, and if the top half of your body still looks as though it's doing the breast-stroke, nobody will say a word.

One way of distinguishing between comedy and tragedy is summarized in Horace Walpole's aphorism, "This world is a comedy to those that think, a tragedy to those that feel." Life seen thoughtfully, with considerable detachment, viewed from above, as it were, is an amusing pageant, and the comic writer gives us something of this view. With Puck we look at the antics in the forest, smile tolerantly, and say with a godlike perspective, "Lord, what fools these mortals be!" But in tragedy we are to a greater degree engaged; the tragic dramatist manages to make us in large measure identify ourselves with the hero, feel his plight as if it were our own, and value his feelings as he values them, so that with Othello we may say "The pity of it."* Yeats noticed this when he said that "character is continuously present in comedy alone," and that "tragedy must always be a drowning and breaking of the dykes that separate man from man.... It is upon these dykes comedy keeps house." And Yeats again: "Nor when the tragic reverie is at its height do we say, 'How well that man is realised, I should know him were I to meet him in the street,' for it is always ourselves that we see upon the [tragic] stage."

One consequence of this distinction between tragedy and comedy, between looking-at and feeling-with, is that the comic plot is usually more intricate than the tragic plot, and less plausible. The comic plot continues to trip up its characters, bringing them into numerous situations that allow them to display their folly over and again. The complex comic plot is often arbitrary, full of the workings of Fortune or Chance, and we delight at each new unexpected or unlikely happening. In tragedy, Fate (sometimes in the form that "character is destiny") or Necessity rules, there is the consistency and inevitability, the "remorseless working of things," that has already been mentioned. If Macbeth were struck dead by a falling roof tile while he dozed in the palace

DETACHMENT
AND
ENGAGEMENT

TRAGIC FATE
AND COMIC
FORTUNE
IN PLOTS

---

* Bergson's theory that a human being — an organism — is comical when it behaves mechanically requires, as Bergson said, a modification: feelings must be suppressed. A crippled man is not comic despite his mechanical limp, because we feel for him. Comedy requires, Bergson said, an "anesthesia of the heart."

after a good meal, instead of dying on Macduff's sword, or if Brutus were to die by slipping in his bath, instead of dying on the very sword with which he killed Caesar, we would have arbitrary happenings that violate the spirit of everything that precedes. But the unexpected letters and the long-lost relatives that often turn up at the close of a comedy are thoroughly in the spirit of the comic vision, which devalues not only rigidly consistent character but rigidity of every sort, even of plot. Tragedy usually follows a straight course, comedy a delightfully twisted one.

COMIC
BEGINNINGS
AND ENDINGS

The rigid behavior of some of comedy's laughably serious characters (e.g., misers, jealous husbands, stern fathers) is paralleled in the rigid circumstances that often are sketched at the beginning of a comedy. In *As You Like It*, the rightful duke has been banished by his usurping brother, and (a sort of parallel) an attractive young nobleman has been confined "rustically at home" by *his* brother. Gilbert and Sullivan, to draw on familiar material, afford plenty of examples of comedy's fondness for a cantankerous beginning: *The Mikado* opens with a chorus of Japanese noblemen whose code of etiquette makes them appear to be "worked by strings"; they live in a town where a law ordered that "all who flirted, leered or winked / Should forthwith be beheaded." (Comedy often begins with a society dominated by some harsh law.) Although this law has been suspended, another harsh decree is in effect: the pretty Yum-Yum is betrothed to her old guardian, Ko-Ko. We learn, too, that her appropriate wooer, Nanki-Poo, is a prince who has had to disguise himself as a humble wandering minstrel to escape his father's decree that he marry Katisha, an old and ugly lady of the court. After various doings in a comedy, a new — presumably natural, prosperous, fertile, and free — society is formed, usually centered around lovers who are going to be married. Yum-Yum and Nanki-Poo finally contrive to get married, evading Katisha and Ko-Ko, who make the best of things by marrying each other. The whole business is satisfactorily explained to the Mikado, who affably accepts, and ruffled tempers are soothed:

> The threatened cloud has passed away,
> And brightly shines the dawning day;
> What though the night may come too soon,
> We've years and years of afternoon!
>
> Then let the throng
> Our joy advance,
> With laughing song
> And merry dance,
> With joyous shout and ringing cheer,
> Inaugurate our new career!

The first four lines are sung by the young lovers, the remaining six are sung by "All," the new, or renewed, society, free from unnatural law. *H.M.S. Pinafore* begins with lovers who cannot marry because of disparity in rank, but ends with appropriate shifts in rank so that there can be "three loving pairs on the same day united."

In comedy there is often not only an improbable turn in events but an improbable (but agreeable) change in character — or at least in rank; trouble-some persons become enlightened, find their own better nature, and join in the fun, commonly a marriage-feast. Finding one's own nature is common in tragedy, too, but there self-knowledge is co-terminous with death or some death-like condition, such as blindness. *Oedipus the King* ends with a note of finality, even though Oedipus is alive at the end; the fact that twenty-five years later Sophocles decided to write a play showing Oedipus' apotheosis does not allow us to see the earlier play as less than complete. The chorus in *Oedipus the King* has the last word:

SELF-
KNOWLEDGE

> This man was Oedipus.
> That mighty King, who knew the riddle's mystery,
> Whom all the city envied, Fortune's favorite.
> Behold, in the event, the storm of his calamities,
> And, being mortal, think on that last day of death,
> Which all must see, and speak of no man's happiness
> Till, without sorrow, he hath passed the goal of life.

Or consider the irreparable loss at the end of Shakespeare's tragedies: "This was the noblest Roman of them all"; "We that are young / Shall never see so much, nor live so long"; "The rest is silence." But comedy ends with a new beginning, a newly formed society, usually a wedding party; the tragic figure commonly awakens to the fact that he has made a big mistake and his life is over, but the comic figure commonly awakens to his better nature. He usually sheds his aberration and is restored to himself and to a renewed society. In *As You Like It*, for example, Oliver is for much of the play a "most unnatu-ral brother," but he is at last converted by his brother's natural goodness and he gains a lovely wife. Alceste's refusal to change, at the end of *The Misan-thrope*, helps to push that comedy toward the borderline between comedy and tragedy. Oedipus learns that his parents were not those whom he had sup-posed, and he learns that even the mighty Oedipus can be humbled. Othello comes to see himself as a man "that loved not wisely but too well," and, hav-ing reached his journey's end, he executes justice upon himself by killing him-self. That is, at the end of the play he finds himself, but this finding of the self separates him forever from those around him, whereas the comic figure who finds himself usually does so by putting aside in some measure his individuality and by submitting himself to a partner or to the group.

Thomas Hardy, whose view of life was bleak (it has been said that in Hardy fornication always produces offspring), said:

> Tragedy is true guise,
> Comedy lies.

But the visions of comedy and tragedy are equally true and do not conflict; rather, they are different visions and represent different psychological states. And they are equally useful. The tragic vision may have more prestige, but it is no small thing to make men laugh, to call attention amusingly to the follies and joys of life, and to help develop the sense of humor — and humility — that may be indispensable to survival in a world continually threatened by aggressive ideals that demand uncritical acceptance. Infants smile easily, and children laugh often, but growing up is often attended by a frightening seriousness. True, hostile laughter, the scarcely veiled aggressiveness that manifests itself in derision, remains an adult possession, but the laughter evoked by the best comedy is good-natured while it is critical, and it is in part directed at ourselves. We look at bumbling humanity and we recall Puck's words, "Lord, what fools these mortals be." This is not to say that the comic vision is cynical; rather, it attributes to folly what less generous visions attribute to ill-will or to hopeless corruption, and when it laughs it forgives. Analyses of laughter are sometimes funny but more often they are tedious; still, they at least pay the comic spirit the compliment of recognizing it as worthy of man's best efforts.

2. Tragicomedy

The word "tragicomedy" is much newer than the words "tragedy" and "comedy"; it first appears about 186 B.C., when Plautus spoke of *tragicocomoedia* in
TRAGICOMEDY
BEFORE 1900
his *Amphitryon*, a Roman comedy in which gods assume mortal shapes in order to dupe a husband and seduce his wife. Mercury, in a joking prologue to the play, explains the author's dilemma:

> I'll make it a mixture, a tragicomedy. It wouldn't be right for me to make it all a comedy since kings and gods appear. Well, then, since there's a slave part too, I'll do as I said and make it a tragicomedy.

But the play is a traditional comedy, unalloyed with the solemnity, terror, and pity of tragedy. It shows laughable activities that finally turn out all right. It should be mentioned again, however, that although tragedy and comedy were clearly separated in the ancient world, not all ancient tragedies ended with death, or even ended unhappily. Aeschylus' trilogy, *The Oresteia*, ends with reconciliation and solemn joy (but it has been bought at the price of great suffering), and Sophocles' *Philoctetes* and Euripides' *Iphigeneia at Taurus* end with catastrophes averted. They were tragic for the Greeks because momentous issues were treated seriously, though we might say that the plots have a comic structure because they end happily. In the Renaissance there was much fussing over the meanings of tragedy, comedy, and tragicomedy, but most theoreticians inclined to the view that tragedy dealt with noble figures engaged in serious actions, was written in a lofty style, and ended unhappily; comedy dealt with humbler figures engaged in trivial actions, was written in relatively common diction, and ended happily. Tragicomedy, whether defined as some mixture (e.g., high people in trivial actions) or as a play in which, to quote Sir Philip Sidney, the writer "thrust in the clown by head and shoulders to play a part in majestical matters," was for the most part scorned by academic critics as a mongrel. It was merely additive, bits of comedy added to a tragedy. At best the advocates for tragicomedy could argue that a play without the terror of tragedy and the absurdity of comedy can cover a good deal of life and can please a good many tastes. But this sort of play, unlike modern tragicomedy, is not so much a union of tragedy and comedy as an exclusion of both, lacking, for example, the awe we associate with tragedy and the fun we associate with comedy.

In the twentieth century the word and the form have become thoroughly respectable; indeed, it is now evident that most of the best plays of our century are best described not as tragedies or as comedies but as tragicomedies — distinctive fusions (not mere aggregations) of tragedy and comedy. For a start we can take William Hazlitt's statement that "man is the only animal that laughs and weeps; for he is the only animal that is struck with the difference between what things are, and what they ought to be." This implication that the subjects of tragedy and of comedy are one rather than two has recently been amplified by Cyrus Hoy, who suggests that a single principle underlies tragedy and comedy (pp. 636–642): man has an ideal of human conduct, but circumstances and his own limitations make his belief that he can fulfill this ideal illusory. Still man persists, appearing "nobly enduring, stubbornly unyielding . . . foolishly blind," or (as in most tragicomedy) some indissoluble combination of these. Most of the best playwrights of the twentieth century have adopted the more complicated mixed view. Comedy had customarily invoked a considerable degree of detachment; in Bergson's formula (1900), already quoted, comedy requires an anesthesia of the spectator's heart as he watches folly on the stage. Tragedy, on the other hand, customarily invoked a considerable degree of involvement or sympathy; in Walpole's formula, also already quoted, "The world is a comedy to those that think, a tragedy to those that feel." But tragicomedy shows us comic characters for whom we feel deep sympathy. Pirandello in his essay *Umorismo* (1908) gives an interesting example of the phenomenon. Suppose, he says, we see an elderly woman with dyed hair and much too much make-up. We find her funny; but if we realize that she is trying to hold the attention of her husband, our sympathy is aroused. Our sense of her absurdity is not totally dissipated, but we feel for her and so our laughter is combined with pity. There are moments like this in earlier comedies, the most famous probably is Shylock's "Hath not a Jew eyes . . .? If you poison us do we not die?" in which we suddenly see Shylock not unsympathetically from the outside, as a funny-looking man with odd dietary habits but sympathetically as a man who shares our feelings. Despite such a moment, *The Merchant of Venice* is clearly a comedy, a festive play with a happy ending, and on the whole Shylock is a figure for unsympathetic laughter.

DETACHMENT AND ENGAGEMENT AGAIN

Changes in our ethical conceptions, however, have caused us to see him with increased sympathy, just as we now see madness, or the sufferings of animals, with greater sympathy than our ancestors did. Our attitudes since, say, the middle of the eighteenth century have shifted a good deal, giving us a new sense of the nature of man, and we ought briefly to look at this new sense and its background.

First, a disclaimer. There are still many different attitudes and many kinds of plays. But the theater that is vital today is not the Broadway musical, the earnest problem-play, or the well-made drawing-room comedy (though these

THEATER OF THE ABSURD

continue to be written) but a fairly unified body of drama called the absurd, whose major writers are Beckett, Genet, and Ionesco. Their theme is man's anguish, but their techniques are those of comedy: improbable situations and unheroic characters who say funny things. These writers differ, of course, and differ from play to play, but they are all preoccupied with the loneliness of man in a world without the certainties afforded by God or by optimistic rationalism. This loneliness is heightened by a sense of impotence derived partly from an awareness of man's inability to communicate in a society that has made language meaningless, and partly from an awareness of the precariousness of man's existence in an atomic age. Behind this vision are some two hundred years of thinking that have conspired to make it difficult to think of any man as a hero who confronts a mysterious cosmic order. Man, Ionesco says in *Notes and Counter Notes*, is "cut off from his religious and metaphysical roots."* One of the milestones in Western man's journey toward contemporary nihilism is the bourgeois drama of the middle of the eighteenth century, which sought to show the dignity of the common man but which, negatively put, undermined the concept of a tragic *hero*. Instead of showing a heroic yet universal man, it showed man in relation to his society, thus paving the way for Arthur Miller's Willy Loman, who apparently would have been okay, as we all would be, if our economic system allowed for early retirement. Miller's play makes no claim for Willy's grandeur or for the glory of life; it claims only that he is an ordinary man at the end of his rope in a deficient society and that he is entitled to a fair deal.

Other landmarks on the road to man's awareness of his littleness are, like bourgeois drama, developments in thinking that were thought by their builders

DIMINUTION OF MAN

to be landmarks on the road to man's progressive conquest of fear. Among these we can name Darwin's *The Origin of Species* (1859), which, in the popular phrase, seemed to record man's progress "up from apes," but which, more closely read, reduced man to the product of "accidental variations" and left God out of the picture, substituting for a cosmic order a barbaric struggle for existence. (In the second edition, 1860, Darwin spoke of life as "breathed by the creator," but the creator was not Darwin's concern and he later abandoned all religious beliefs. Probably he retained his belief that the process of "natural selection works solely by and for the good of each being," but by 1889 his disciple Huxley saw it differently. Huxley said he knew of no study "so

---

* From *Notes and Counter Notes: Writings on the Theatre* by Eugène Ionesco, p. 257. Translated from the French by Donald Watson. Copyright © 1964 by Grove Press, Inc. Reprinted by permission of the publisher, Grove Press, Inc.

unutterably saddening as that of the evolution of humanity.") Karl Marx, studying the evolution of societies at about the same time, was attributing man's sense of alienation to economic forces, thereby implying that man had no identity he could properly call his own. Moreover, Marxist thinking, like Darwinian thinking, suggested that a man could not do anything of really great importance, nor could he be blamed for his misfortunes. (Economic determinism need not lead to pessimism. Brecht, in *The Good Woman of Setzuan*, seizes joyfully on this development in thinking; since man's personality is not really his, it can be changed for the better under Communism.) At the end of the nineteenth century, and in the early twentieth century, Freud, also seeking to free man from tyranny, turned to the forces within man's mind. Ironically, the effort to chart man's unconscious drives and anarchic impulses in order to help man to know himself induced a profound distrust of the self: we can scarcely be confident of our behavior, for we know that apparently heroic behavior has unconscious unheroic motives rooted in the experiences of infancy. Tragic heroes are men with complexes, and religious codes are only wishful thinking.

The result of such developments in thought seems to be that, a "tragic sense" in the twentieth century commonly means a despairing or deeply uncertain view, something very different from what it meant in Greece and in Elizabethan England. This uncertainty, is not merely about the cosmos but even about character or identity. In 1888, in the Preface to *Miss Julie*, Strindberg called attention to the new sense of the instability of character:

DISSOLUTION OF CHARACTER AND PLOT

> I have made the people in my play fairly "characterless." The middle-class conception of a fixed character was transferred to the stage, where the middle class has always ruled. A character there came to mean an actor who was always one and the same, always drunk, always comic or always melancholy, and who needed to be characterized only by some physical defect such as a club foot, a wooden leg, or a red nose, or by the repetition of some such phrase such as, "That's capital," or "Barkis is willin'." ... Since the persons in my play are modern characters, living in a transitional era more hurried and hysterical than the previous one at least, I have depicted them as more unstable, as torn and divided, a mixture of the old and the new.

In 1902, in his preface to *A Dream Play*, he is more explicit: "Anything may happen, anything seems possible and probable. . . . The characters split, double, multiply, vanish, solidify, blur, clarify." Strindberg's view of the fluidity of character — the characterlessness of character, one might say — has continued and is apparent in O'Neill's *The Emperor Jones*, in almost all of Pirandello's work, in the underground film, and in much of the Theater of the Absurd. Ionesco, in *Fragments of a Journal*, says "I often find it quite impossible to hold an opinion about a fact, a thing or a person. Since it's all a matter of interpretation, one has to choose a particular interpretation."* (One thinks too

---

* From *Fragments of a Journal* by Eugène Ionesco, p. 131. Translated by Jean Stewart. Copyright © by Faber and Faber Ltd. Reprinted by permission of the publishers, Grove Press, Inc., and Faber and Faber Ltd.

of Dr. Borg in Bergman's *Wild Strawberries* who in effect withdrew from society because a man cannot really know his fellows.) In *Notes and Counter Notes* Ionesco said, "chance formed us," and that we would be different if we had different experiences; characteristically a few years later he said that he was no longer sure that he believed in chance.

Along with the sense of characterlessness, or at least of the mystery of character, there developed in the drama (and in the underground film and the novel) a sense of plotlessness, or fundamental untruthfulness of the traditional plot that moved by cause and effect. "Plots," Ionesco has said in *Conversations*, "are never interesting," and again he has said that a play should be able to stop at any point; it ends only because "the audience has to go home to bed. . . . It's true for real life. Why should it be different for art?"* Ionesco has treated his own plots very casually, allowing directors to make "all the cuts needed" and suggesting that endings other than those he wrote are possibilities. After all, in a meaningless world one can hardly take a dramatic plot seriously. In Ionesco's *Victims of Duty* a character defends a new kind of irrational, anti-Aristotelian drama: "The theater of my dreams would be irrationalist. . . . The contemporary theater doesn't reflect the cultural tone of our period, it's not in harmony with the general drift of the other manifestations of the modern spirit. . . . We'll get rid of the principle of identity and unity of character. . . . Personality doesn't exist." A policeman-psychologist (a materialist who demands law and order) offers an old-fashioned view: "I don't believe in the absurd, everything hangs together, everything can be comprehended . . . thanks to the achievements of human thought and science," but he is murdered by the anti-Aristotelian.†

Not surprisingly, Brecht, also an anti-Aristotelian, invites us at the end of *The Good Woman of Setzuan* to work out our own ending; he has shown us a piece of life, but he doesn't give it the joyous conclusion of a comedy or the finality of a tragedy. He leaves it open, and invites us to think of a better ending. Similarly, Beckett's *Waiting for Godot* ends — as the first act ended — without anything ending:

> VLADIMIR: Well? Shall we go?
> ESTRAGON: Yes, let's go.
>
> *They do not move.*
> *Curtain.*‡

To bring an action to a completion, as drama traditionally did, is to imply an orderly world of cause and effect, of beginnings and endings, but for the dram-

---

* From *Conversations with Eugène Ionesco* by Claude Bonnefoy, p. 82. Translated by Jan Dawson. Holt, Rinehart and Winston, 1970. Reprinted by permission of the publisher.
† From *Three Plays* by Eugène Ionesco, pp. 157–159. Translated by Donald Watson. Copyright © 1958 by John Calder (Publishers) Limited. Reprinted by permission of the publisher, Grove Press, Inc.
‡ Translated from the French by the author. Copyright © 1954 by Grove Press. Reprinted by permission of the publisher, Grove Press, Inc.

atists of the absurd, there is no such pattern. At best it is *Hamlet* as Tom Stoppard's Rosencrantz and Guildenstern see it: they are supposed to do a job they don't understand, and instead of a pattern or "order" they encounter only "Incidents! Incidents! Dear God, is it too much to expect a little sustained action?" Well, yes; it is too much to expect.

There can be no tragedy, because, as Ionesco explains in *Notes*, tragedy admits the existence of fate or destiny, which is to say it admits the existence of objective (however incomprehensible) laws ruling the universe, whereas the new comic perception of incongruity is that existence itself is absurd because there is no objective law. The new comic vision is far darker than the old tragic vision; it has nothing in it of what Yeats called "tragic joy." But what is our reaction to this joyless comedy? Let Ionesco, whose plays sometimes include meaningless babble, have the last word:

THE TRAGEDY OF COMEDY

> The fact of being astonishes us, in a world that now seems all illusion and pretense, in which all human behavior tells of absurdity and all history of absolute futility; all reality and all language appear to lose their articulation, to disintegrate and collapse, so what possible reaction is there left, when everything has ceased to matter, but laugh at it all.*

* From *Notes and Counter Notes: Writings on the Theatre* by Eugène Ionesco, p. 163. Translated from the French by Donald Watson. Copyright © 1964 by Grove Press, Inc. Reprinted by permission of the publisher, Grove Press, Inc.

THE LANGUAGE OF DRAMA

Although a play usually tells a story, "the medium of drama," as Ezra Pound shrewdly observed, "is not words, but persons moving about on a stage using words." Take Eugene O'Neill's *The Emperor Jones* as an example. The gist of the story is this: Jones, a black fugitive from a chaingang, has turned up on an island in the West Indies and established himself as Emperor. By his own admission he has tyrannized over his subjects, and he was able to get away with it because they believed that he could be killed only by a silver bullet. (This is the *antecedent action*; we learn it during the play, but it reports what happened before the play begins.) At the beginning of the play, hearing that a rebellion is in progress Jones confidently sets out to leave the island; he becomes increasingly terrified, and at the end of the play he is shot with a silver bullet.

This is moderately interesting, and not totally different from some historical episodes: President Guillaume Sam of Haiti boasted he would kill himself with a silver bullet, but he was hacked to pieces by his oppressed subjects in 1915, only five years before O'Neill wrote *The Emperor Jones*; and a century earlier, Henri Christophe, a slave who had become the merciless ruler of part of Haiti, shot himself when confronted with an insurrection. O'Neill knew these bits of history, and used them to shape *The Emperor Jones*, but even if he had not changed some facts, a play about Sam or Christophe inevitably would — if it were any good — be very different from an encyclopedia entry on them because, as Pound says, a play is made not out of words but out of "persons moving about on a stage using words."

Let's begin with the stage and its setting. When the curtain goes up on a performance of *The Emperor Jones*, the audience sees "the audience chamber in the palace of the Emperor." It is furnished solely with "one huge chair . . . painted a dazzling eye-smiting scarlet," a cushion that serves as a footstool, and two scarlet mats that go "from the foot of the throne to the two entrances." This stage, at least in the context of what follows, "says" a lot. It conveys Jones's dominance, for he alone can sit in the room, and it conveys something of his bloody career, for if the scarlet throne on which Jones sits at first suggests royalty, it also in retrospect suggests the blood that surrounds his career. Whether or not O'Neill was conscious of the fact when he was writing the play, the huge scarlet chair, which at the start is boldly emblematic of Jones both as Emperor and as murderer, is a notable contrast to the "little reddish-purple hole under his left breast" when his corpse is brought onstage at the end of the play. The imperial murderer has diminished to this.

The play uses only two other sets, and these are almost one: the edge of the Great Forest, and within the Great Forest. The Forest, again, in the context of the action, says something. O'Neill tells us, in his first description of it, that it gives an impression of "relentless immobility" and of "brooding, implacable silence." Fleeing through the forest Jones becomes terrified, and we see that the dark forest is, in part at least, the jungle of man's mind, the world of inarticulate, elemental passions that seethe beneath the fragile surface of reason. Its darkness, a strong contrast to the brightly illuminated throne room where Jones was the confident master, provides us with an example of the way in which a dramatist uses lighting — or, rather, darkness — symbolically. Not

SETTING

23

every dramatist uses his stage sets quite so obviously, but the subway setting of
LeRoi Jones's *Dutchman* is, in Jones's words, "the flying underbelly of the
city," and even a "realistic" play like *The Cherry Orchard* juxtaposes the orchard (the dying, aristocratic way of life) with telephone poles and a town
(the new, industrial way of life). In *Death of a Salesman*, Willy Loman's
"fragile-seeming home" is surrounded by "a solid vault of apartment houses,"
Miller thereby conveying the vulnerability of the individual. A bare stage, too
(much used in contemporary drama), by virtue of its barrenness says something about man's isolation or alienation. Although one frequently hears that
the Elizabethan stage was bare and that Shakespeare's plays are most effective
on a bare stage, in fact the Elizabethan stage was an elaborate piece of architecture, suggestive of a completely ordered universe, and when appropriate
the stage was decorated with banners. But it could be bleak when bleakness
was required. At the end of the second act of *King Lear* Gloucester tells us
what we are to imagine: "Alack, the night comes on, and the high winds / Do
sorely ruffle. For many miles about / There's scarce a bush." Again, this
locale says something about the impoverished people who move in it.

COSTUME

In returning to *The Emperor Jones*, and to Ezra Pound's comment on the
nature of drama, let us continue for a moment to talk about the ways in which
drama even without dialogue says something. Costumes tell us a good deal, on
the stage as in life. They do not necessarily tell the truth about their wearers,
but they tell us what the wearers want us to believe. If, on the street, we see
someone who is wearing workman's clothes, we conclude that he may be a
workman — or that for some reason (say, political or sexual) he wants us to
think that he is a workman; in any case the clothes make a statement, conscious or not. Jones at the outset is certainly making a conscious statement
through his clothes, a uniform whose blue coat is "sprayed with brass buttons,
heavy gold chevrons on his shoulders, gold braid on the collar, cuffs, etc. His
pants are bright red." The clothes say, quite as explicitly as Jones says to
Smithers, "Ain't I de Emperor?" When he begins his flight from the palace at
the end of the first scene, he goes out with imperial dignity, in full uniform
and with a Panama hat on his head. By the third scene, "he has lost his Panama hat. His face is scratched, his brilliant uniform shows several large rents."
In the fourth scene, "his uniform is ragged and torn," in the fifth he dis-
cards his worn-out shoes, in the sixth "his pants have been so torn away that
what is left of them is no better than a breech cloth." This stripping away of
Jones's clothing is clearly also a stripping away both of his external power
and of his control over himself. At the start he was "self-reliant" and coolly
calculating, but now he is a primitive bundle of inarticulate terrors. O'Neill
did not, of course, invent the use of costumes as dramatic language; it goes
back to the beginnings of drama, and one has only to think of Hamlet's "inky
cloak" or of Lear tearing off his clothing, or of the fresh clothing in which
Lear is garbed after his madness, to see how eloquently costumes can speak.
To this can be added the matter of disguises — for example Edgar's disguise
in *King Lear* and Rosalind's in *As You Like It* — which are removed near the
ends of the plays, when the truth is finally revealed and the characters can

again be fully themselves. In short, the removal of disguises *says* something.

Gestures too are part of the language of drama. When in the first scene **GESTURES** Jones knows that his role as Emperor is over, he leaves the palace — but by the front door. Somewhat needlessly he explains the gesture to Smithers, the cowardly white man: "Does you think I'd slink out de back door like a common nigger? I'se Emperor yit, ain't I? And de Emperor Jones leaves de way he comes." And in this scene, when Smithers sees Jones's hand go to his revolver, Smithers is in no doubt about the meaning of the gesture. One last example: against Jones's terrified flight, O'Neill in the final scene juxtaposes his foe Lem, who "imperturbably" squats to await Jones's inevitable death.

Although dialogue is the most conspicuous way of telling a story in plays that are also literature, first we should notice another sort of sound in *The Emperor Jones*, nonverbal sounds. The most obvious is the tom-tom, which **SOUND** "starts at a rate exactly corresponding to the normal pulse beat — seventy-two **EFFECTS** to the minute — and continues at a gradually accelerating rate from this point uninterruptedly to the very end of the play." Though this stage direction is O'Neill's, it is not quite accurate, for in the last scene another stage direction tells us that at the moment that Jones is shot "the beating of the tom-tom abruptly ceases." The tom-tom is a powerful way of working on the audience's emotions, but it is more than a gimmick, for its acceleration clearly corresponds to Jones's increasing fears that make his heart beat faster and faster, and it stops beating when a bullet causes his heart to stop beating. Other less conspicuous but no less meaningful sound effects are the moaning wind (not merely a realistic effect, but a sound related to Jones's state of mind), the "low mocking laughter like a rustling of leaves" in the second scene, the pistol shots at the ends of scenes 2, 3, 4, 5, and 7 when he seeks unsuccessfully to dispel his fears by relying on technology, and finally the shots of the rifles that bring him down. Simply to widen the canvas, we can add an example from Shakespeare: the sound of the storm in *King Lear* is a reflection of Lear's disordered kingdom, disordered family, and disordered mind. Similarly, the "scream" of the subway in LeRoi Jones's *Dutchman*, the sound of the axes cutting down the trees in *The Cherry Orchard*, and the flute ("telling of grass and trees and the horizon") in *Death of a Salesman* are not merely realism.

Dialogue is the most persistent and significant sound in a play. A good **DIALOGUE** playwright gives us not a transcript of our chaotic fragmentary sentences but language that continually reveals character and furthers plot. In the first line of *The Emperor Jones*, when Smithers grabs a black woman and says, "Easy! None o' that, me birdie. You can't wriggle out now. I got me 'ooks on yer," O'Neill reveals a good deal about Smithers: his Cockney birth, his inclination toward violence, and his contempt for blacks. And now that Jones's hours as Emperor are numbered, Smithers, though essentially a coward, is impudent and even openly angry with Jones, who recognizes the change in tone and imperiously warns, "Talk polite, white man!" Smithers, understanding the pressure in Jones's words, lapses into a cringing "No 'arm meant, old top." Within a few minutes O'Neill has let us see and hear exactly what sort of man Smithers is. The language is fully dramatic: (1) it can be spoken effectively by an actor, though the dialect is a bit tiresome in print; and (2) it seems to proceed not from O'Neill the author but from the specific characters. Notice, too, that the *amount* of dialogue is meaningful. After the first scene, the play is almost a monologue spoken by Jones, but he becomes increasingly inarticulate, so that the confident talkative Emperor of the first scene is pretty much reduced by the seventh scene to repeating a few clichés, "Oh, Lawd pertect dis sinner," "Mercy, Lawd, Mercy." What he is unable to say is as much a part of the play's meaning as what he does say.

This diminution in speech as Jones becomes increasingly terrified, and as "civilization" (e.g., the confidence and cunning by which he deceived his subjects) is peeled from him along with his uniform, works along with the play's structure, the arrangement of scenes. Three scenes of increasing terror to Jones take place in the Great Forest: First, "little formless fears," then the memory of the murder of Jeff, and then the memory of the murder of the prison guard. The next three scenes are more terrifying, and they are from sources deeper than Jones's own experience. They are racial memories of a slave auction in America, of a slave ship, and, earliest of all, of an African ceremony in which Jones is to be the sacrificial victim. We have moved backward to the very beginnings of man's experience. As the play moves forward, stripping Jones of all flimsy accretions, reducing the once proud emperor to a whimpering motionless creature face down on the ground, we learn that Jones's flight through the forest has brought him back to the very point at which he entered the forest. Smithers sees in this only the meaningless fact that Jones ran in a circle, but we can perhaps see in it a further suggestion: Jones's life had run its course; at birth he came inarticulate and naked from the dark, and at death he returns inarticulate and naked to the dark. Possibly, too, we can say that there is a sort of circularity implied in the fact that he lived by robbing his subjects of their money, and he died by money, for the natives shoot him with a silver bullet made by melting coins. No one wants to reduce the play to a neat moral, but surely in dramatic form it sets forth, among other things, the idea that there are mysterious connections in life, that if the pattern is obscure, there nevertheless is a pattern, and here the pattern suggests something like "Those who live by silver die by silver." (For further comments on this sort of tragic pattern, see the discussions of peripeteia on page 6 and of irony in the glossary, page 665.)

Finally, what sort of man *is* Jones? The best answer is that he is what the play says he is, and it says this through scenery, gestures, sound effects, dialogue, contrasting characters, arrangement of scenes, etc., in short, through everything in the play. Still, we can hazard a few rough comments. First, notice that O'Neill makes him a very specific black man, not simply a type. Among the stock dramatic types available to O'Neill in 1920, the chief were the Tom (faithful colored retainer), the Buffoon (clownish lazy servant), the Bull (villain who wants to rape white women), and the Tragic Mulatto (hovering between two races). Almost all depictions of blacks on the American stage of the time fall into these classifications. O'Neill, in a remarkable step forward in the history of American drama, and therefore in the history of American thought, used none of these stereotypes. (In *The Emperor Jones* the lazy man is not the

PLOT AND
STRUCTURE

CHARACTER

black, who diligently learned the language of the islanders and who for two years has worked hard and efficiently at his job of robbing his subjects; the lazy man is the white man, Smithers, who in ten years has not bothered to learn the language.) Today, more than fifty years after O'Neill wrote the play, inevitably we are disturbed by some racist implications in the play, but O'Neill was far ahead of most whites of his time in presenting a black whose face showed "an underlying strength of will, a hardy, self-reliant confidence," and whose eyes showed "a keen, cunning intelligence." If these words put us in mind of any type, it is, paradoxically, the rugged white individualist who was so worshipped in the nineteenth and early twentieth centuries. O'Neill gives us not a stereotyped black man (and none of the stereotypes was flattering), but a fresh conception, a black who has the virtues and faults of white society, of America as it was and is, and perhaps of mankind. (The very name "Jones" suggests Everyman — though "Brutus" adds to it both a sense of high Roman dignity and a sense of grotesque incongruity.) Jones is quite explicit about his code: his aim is to get rich in the great white man's way, by hard work and by cunning immorality on a grand scale.

> You heah what I tells you, Smithers. Dere's little stealin' like you does, and dere's big stealin' like I does. For de little stealin' dey gits you in jail soon or late. For de big stealin' dey makes you Emperor and puts you in de Hall o' Fame when you croaks. (*Reminiscently.*) If dey's one thing I learns in ten years on de Pullman ca's listenin' to de white quality talk, it's dat same fact. And when I gits a chance to use it I winds up Emperor in two years.

Smithers is no less unscrupulous or cruel than Jones is, but he simply does not have Jones's courage, perseverance, intelligence, and vision. In short, O'Neill gives us a fresh, fully realized picture of believable human beings and we should not be deceived by the funny spelling into thinking that Jones is the conventional black man of the stage up to O'Neill's time.

What does it add up to? Something has already been said about the theme or underlying idea or meaning of the play. Some critics, arguing that the concept of theme is meaningless, hold that any play gives us only an extremely detailed history of some imaginary people. But surely this view is desperate. We *can* say that we see in *The Emperor Jones* something of the savagery of our so-called civilization, and, on the other hand, something of the grandeur that may transfigure pride. (As O'Neill says in a stage direction, Jones "has a way of carrying it off," and at the end of the play Smithers grants that Jones died "in the 'eighth o' style.") To the reply that these are mere truisms, we can counter: Yes, but the truisms are presented in such a way that they take on life and become a part of us rather than remain things of which we say, "I've heard it said, and I guess it's so." And surely we are in no danger of equating the play with the theme that we sense underlies it. We never believe that our statement of the theme is really the equivalent of the play itself. The play, we recognize, presents the theme with such detail that our statement of the theme is only a wedge that helps us to enter the play so that we may more fully (in Henry James's word) "appropriate" it.

THEME

THE EMPEROR JONES

Eugene O'Neill

Eugene O'Neill (1888–1953), the son of an actor, was born in a hotel room near Broadway and spent his early years traveling with his parents throughout the United States. He entered Princeton University in 1906 but left before the end of the first year. In 1909 he traveled to Honduras looking for gold, contracted malaria, and returned to the United States in 1910. After touring briefly with his father's company, he shipped to Buenos Aires, jumped ship there, did odd jobs, shipped to South Africa, and returned to the United States in 1911. The following year he learned that he had tuberculosis. In a sanatorium he began seriously reading plays, and in 1916 he joined the Provincetown Players, who put on some of his one-act plays. *The Emperor Jones* (1920), produced by the Provincetown Players in New York, was his first major play. In time he was awarded four Pulitzer Prizes (one, posthumous, was for *A Long Day's Journey into Night*, written in 1940, but not produced until 1955), and a Nobel Prize.

CHARACTERS

BRUTUS JONES, *Emperor*	THE NEGRO CONVICTS
HENRY SMITHERS, *A Cockney Trader*	THE PRISON GUARD
AN OLD NATIVE WOMAN	THE PLANTERS
LEM, *A Native Chief*	THE AUCTIONEER
SOLDIERS, *Adherents of Lem*	THE SLAVES
THE LITTLE FORMLESS FEARS	THE CONGO WITCH-DOCTOR
JEFF	THE CROCODILE GOD

The action of the play takes place on an island in the West Indies as yet not self-determined by white Marines. The form of native government is, for the time being, an empire.

Paul Chevalier as Smithers and Habib Benglia as Jones in a 1949 production of *The Emperor Jones* in Paris. (Photograph: Bernand.)

SCENE I

Scene — The audience chamber in the palace of the Emperor — a spacious, high-ceilinged room with bare, white-washed walls. The floor is of white tiles. In the rear, to the left of center, a wide archway giving out on a portico with white pillars. The palace is evidently situated on high ground for beyond the portico nothing can be seen but a vista of distant hills, their summits crowned with thick groves of palm trees. In the right wall, center, a smaller arched doorway leading to the living quarters of the palace. The room is bare of furniture with the exception of one huge chair made of uncut wood which stands at center, its back to rear. This is very apparently the Emperor's throne. It is painted a dazzling, eye-smiting scarlet. There is a brilliant orange cushion on the seat and another smaller one is placed on the floor to serve as a footstool. Strips of matting, dyed scarlet, lead from the foot of the throne to the two entrances.

It is late afternoon but the sunlight still blazes yellowly beyond the portico and there is an oppressive burden of exhausting heat in the air.

As the curtain rises, a native Negro woman sneaks in cautiously from the entrance on the right. She is very old, dressed in cheap calico, bare-footed, a red bandana handkerchief covering all but a few stray wisps of white hair. A bundle bound in colored cloth is carried

Reprinted by permission of Random House, Inc., from *Nine Plays* by Eugene O'Neill. Copyright 1921 and renewed 1949 by Eugene O'Neill.

over her shoulder on the end of a stick. She hesitates beside the doorway, peering back as if in extreme dread of being discovered. Then she begins to glide noiselessly, a step at a time, toward the doorway in the rear. At this moment, SMITHERS *appears beneath the portico.*

SMITHERS *is a tall, stoop-shouldered man about forty. His bald head, perched on a long neck with an enormous Adam's apple, looks like an egg. The tropics have tanned his naturally pasty face with its small, sharp features to a sickly yellow, and native rum has painted his pointed nose to a startling red. His little, washy-blue eyes are red-rimmed and dart about him like a ferret's. His expression is one of unscrupulous meanness, cowardly and dangerous. He is dressed in a worn riding suit of dirty white drill, puttees, spurs, and wears a white cork helmet. A cartridge belt with an automatic revolver is around his waist. He carries a riding whip in his hand. He sees the woman and stops to watch her suspiciously. Then, making up his mind, he steps quickly on tiptoe into the room. The woman, looking back over her shoulder continually, does not see him until it is too late. When she does* SMITHERS *springs forward and grabs her firmly by the shoulder. She struggles to get away, fiercely but silently.*

SMITHERS (*tightening his grasp — roughly*): Easy! None o' that, me birdie. You can't wriggle out now. I got me 'ooks on yer.

WOMAN (*seeing the uselessness of struggling, gives way to frantic terror, and sinks to the ground, embracing his knees supplicatingly*): No tell him! No tell him, Mister!

SMITHERS (*with great curiosity*): Tell 'im? (*Then scornfully.*) Oh, you mean 'is bloomin' Majesty. What's the gaime, any 'ow? What are you sneakin' away for? Been stealin' a bit, I s'pose. (*He taps her bundle with his riding whip significantly.*)

WOMAN (*shaking her head vehemently*): No, me no steal.

SMITHERS: Bloody liar! But tell me what's up. There's somethin' funny goin' on. I smelled it in the air first thing I got up this mornin'.

You blacks are up to some devilment. This palace of 'is is like a bleedin' tomb. Where's all the 'ands?

(*The woman keeps sullenly silent.* SMITHERS *raises his whip threateningly.*)

Ow, yer won't, won't yer? I'll show yer what's what.

WOMAN (*coweringly*): I tell, Mister. You no hit. They go — all go. (*She makes a sweeping gesture toward the hills in the distance.*)

SMITHERS: Run away — to the 'ills?

WOMAN: Yes, Mister. Him Emperor — Great Father. (*She touches her forehead to the floor with a quick mechanical jerk.*) Him sleep after eat. Then they go — all go. Me old woman. Me left only. Now me go too.

SMITHERS (*his astonishment giving way to an immense, mean satisfaction*): Ow! So that's the ticket! Well, I know bloody well wot's in the air — when they runs orf to the 'ills. The tom-tom 'll be thumping out there bloomin' soon. (*With extreme vindictiveness.*) And I'm bloody glad of it, for one! Serve 'im right! Puttin' on airs, the stinkin' nigger! 'Is Majesty! Gawd blimey! I only 'opes I'm there when they takes 'im out to shoot 'im. (*Suddenly.*) 'E's still 'ere all right, ain't 'e?

WOMAN: Yes. Him sleep.

SMITHERS: 'E's bound to find out soon as 'e wakes up. 'E's cunnin' enough to know when 'is time's come.

(*He goes to the doorway on right and whistles shrilly with his fingers in his mouth. The old woman springs to her feet and runs out of the doorway, rear.* SMITHERS *goes after her, reaching for his revolver.*)

Stop or I'll shoot! (*Then stopping — indifferently.*) Pop orf then, if yer like, yer black cow. (*He stands in the doorway, looking after her.*)

JONES *enters from the right. He is a tall, powerfully-built, full-blooded Negro of middle age. His features are typically negroid, yet there is something decidedly distinctive about his face — an underlying strength of will, a hardy, self-reliant confidence in himself that inspires respect. His eyes are alive with a keen, cunning intelligence. In manner he is shrewd, suspicious, evasive. He wears a light blue uniform coat, sprayed with brass buttons, heavy gold chevrons on his shoulders, gold braid on the collar, cuffs, etc. His pants are bright red with a light blue stripe* down the side. Patent-leather laced boots with brass spurs, and a belt with a long-barreled, pearl-handled revolver in a holster complete his make up. Yet there is something not altogether ridiculous about his grandeur. He has a way of carrying it off.*)

JONES (*not seeing anyone — greatly irritated and blinking sleepily — shouts*): Who dare whistle dat way in my palace? Who dare wake up de Emperor? I'll git de hide fravled off some o' you niggers sho'!

SMITHERS (*showing himself — in a manner half-afraid and half-defiant*): It was me whistled to yer. (*As* JONES *frowns angrily.*) I got news for yer.

JONES (*putting on his suavest manner, which fails to cover up his contempt for the white man*): Oh, it's you, Mister Smithers. (*He sits down on his throne with easy dignity.*) What news you got to tell me?

SMITHERS (*coming close to enjoy his discomfiture*): Don't yer notice nothin' funny today?

JONES (*coldly*): Funny? No. I ain't perceived nothin' of de kind!

SMITHERS: Then yer ain't so foxy as I thought yer was. Where's all your court? (*Sarcastically.*) The Generals and the Cabinet Ministers and all?

JONES (*imperturbably*): Where dey mostly runs de minute I closes my eyes — drinkin' rum and talkin' big down in de town. (*Sarcastically.*) How come you don't know dat? Ain't you sousin' with 'em most every day?

SMITHERS (*stung but pretending indifference — with a wink*): That's part of the day's work. I got ter — ain't I — in my business?

JONES (*contemptuously*): Yo' business!

SMITHERS (*imprudently enraged*): Gawd blimey, you was glad enough for me ter take yer in on it when you landed here first. You didn' 'ave no 'igh and mighty airs in them days!

JONES (*his hand going to his revolver like a flash — menacingly*): Talk polite, white man! Talk polite, you heah me! I'm boss heah now, is you fergettin'? (*The Cockney seems about to challenge this last statement with the facts but something in the other's eyes holds and cows him.*)

SMITHERS (*in a cowardly whine*): No 'arm meant, old top.

JONES (*condescendingly*): I accepts yo' apology. (*Lets his hand fall from his revolver.*) No use'n you rakin' up ole times. What I was den is one thing. What I is now's another. You didn't let me in on yo' crooked work out o' no kind feelin's dat time. I done de dirty work fo' you — and most o' de brain work, too, fo' dat matter — and I was wu'th money to you, dat's de reason.

SMITHERS: Well, blimey, I give yer a start, didn't I — when no one else would. I wasn't afraid to 'ire yer like the rest was — 'count of the story about your breakin' jail back in the States.

JONES: No, you didn't have no s'cuse to look down on me fo' dat. You been in jail you'self more'n once.

SMITHERS (furiously): It's a lie! (Then trying to pass it off by an attempt at scorn.) Garn! Who told yer that fairy tale?

JONES: Dey's some tings I ain't got to be tole. I kin see 'em in folk's eyes. (Then after a pause — meditatively.) Yes, you sho' give me a start. And it didn't take long from dat time to git dese fool, woods' niggers right where I wanted dem. (With pride.) From stowaway to Emperor in two years! Dat's goin' some!

SMITHERS (with curiosity): And I bet you got yer pile o' money 'id safe some place.

JONES (with satisfaction): I sho' has! And it's in a foreign bank where no pusson don't ever git it out but me no matter what come. You didn't s'pose I was holdin' down dis Emperor job for de glory in it, did you? Sho'! De fuss and glory part of it, dat's only to turn de heads o' de low-flung, bush niggers dat's here. Dey wants de big circus show for deir money. I gives it to 'em an' I gits de money. (With a grin.) De long green, dat's me every time! (Then rebukingly.) But you ain't got no kick agin me, Smithers. I'se paid you back all you done for me many times. Ain't I pertected you and winked at all de crooked tradin' you been doin' right out in de broad day? Sho' I has — and me makin' laws to stop it at de same time! (He chuckles.)

SMITHERS (grinning): But, meanin' no 'arm, you been grabbin' right and left yourself, ain't yer? Look at the taxes you've put on 'em! Blimey! You've squeezed 'em dry!

JONES (chuckling): No, dey ain't all dry yet. I'se still heah, ain't I?

SMITHERS (smiling at his secret thought): They're dry right now, you'll find out. (Changing the subject abruptly.) And as for me breakin' laws, you've broke 'em all yerself just as fast as yer made 'em.

JONES: Ain't I de Emperor? De laws don't go for him. (Judicially.) You heah what I tells

you, Smithers. Dere's little stealin' like you does, and dere's big stealin' like I does. For de little stealin' dey gits you in jail soon or late. For de big stealin' dey makes you Emperor and puts you in de Hall o' Fame when you croaks. (Reminiscently.) If dey's one thing I learns in ten years on de Pullman ca's listenin' to de white quality talk, it's dat same fact. And when I gits a chance to use it I winds up Emperor in two years.

SMITHERS (unable to repress the genuine admiration of the small fry for the large): Yes, yer turned the bleedin' trick, all right. Blimey, I never seen a bloke 'as 'ad the bloomin' luck you 'as.

JONES (severely): Luck? What you mean — luck?

SMITHERS: I suppose you'll say as that swank about the silver bullet ain't luck — and that was what first got the fool blacks on yer side the time of the revolution, wasn't it?

JONES (with a laugh): Oh, dat silver bullet! Sho' was luck! But I makes dat luck, you heah? I loads de dice! Yessuh! When dat murderin' nigger ole Lem hired to kill me takes aim ten feet away and his gun misses fire and I shoots him dead, what you heah me say?

SMITHERS: You said yer'd got a charm so's no lead bullet'd kill yer. You was so strong only a silver bullet could kill yer, you told 'em. Blimey, wasn't that swank for yer — and plain, fat-'eaded luck?

JONES (proudly): I got brains and I uses 'em quick. Dat ain't luck.

SMITHERS: Yer know they wasn't 'ardly liable to get no silver bullets. And it was luck 'e didn't 'it you that time.

JONES (laughing): And dere all dem fool, bush niggers was kneelin' down and bumpin' deir heads on de ground like I was a miracle out o' de Bible. Oh Lawd, from dat time on I has dem all eatin' out of my hand. I cracks de whip and dey jumps through.

SMITHERS (with a sniff): Yankee bluff done it.

JONES: Ain't a man's talkin' big what makes him big — long as he makes folks believe it? Sho', I talks large when I ain't got nothin' to back it up, but I ain't talkin' wild just de same. I knows I kin fool 'em — I knows it — and dat's backin' enough fo' my game. And ain't I got to learn deir lingo and teach some of dem English befo' I kin talk to 'em? Ain't dat wuk? You ain't never learned ary word er it, Smithers, in de ten years you been heah, dough yo' knows it's money in yo' pocket tradin' wid 'em if you does. But you'se too shiftless to take de trouble.

SMITHERS (*flushing*): Never mind about me. What's this I've 'eard about yer really 'avin' a silver bullet moulded for yourself?

JONES: It's playin' out my bluff. I has de silver bullet moulded and I tells 'em when de time comes I kills myself wid it. I tells 'em dat's 'cause I'm de on'y man in de world big enuff to git me. No use'n deir tryin'. And dey falls down and bumps deir heads. (*He laughs.*) I does dat so's I kin take a walk in peace widout no jealous nigger gunnin' at me from behind de trees.

SMITHERS (*astonished*): Then you 'ad it made — 'onest?

JONES: Sho' did. Heah she be. (*He takes out his revolver, breaks it, and takes the silver bullet out of one chamber.*) Five lead an' dis silver baby at de last. Don't she shine pretty? (*He holds it in his hand, looking at it admiringly, as if strangely fascinated.*)

SMITHERS: Let me see. (*Reaches out his hand for it.*)

JONES (*harshly*): Keep yo' hands whar dey b'long, white man. (*He replaces it in the chamber and puts the revolver back on his hip.*)

SMITHERS (*snarling*): Gawd blimey! Think I'm a bleedin' thief, you would.

JONES: No, 'tain't dat. I knows you'se scared to steal from me. On'y I ain't 'lowin' nary body to touch dis baby. She's my rabbit's foot.

SMITHERS (*sneering*): A bloomin' charm, wot? (*Venomously.*) Well, you'll need all the bloody charms you 'as before long, s' 'elp me!

JONES (*judicially*): Oh, I'se good for six months yit 'fore dey gits sick o' my game. Den, when I sees trouble comin', I makes my getaway.

SMITHERS: Ho! You got it all planned, ain't yer?

JONES: I ain't no fool. I knows dis Emperor's time is sho't. Dat why I make hay when de sun shine. Was you thinkin' I'se aimin' to hold down dis job for life? No, suh! What good is gittin' money if you stays back in dis raggedy country? I wants action when I spends. And when I sees dese niggers gittin' up deir nerve to tu'n me out, and I'se got all de money in sight, I resigns on de spot and beats it quick.

SMITHERS: Where to?

JONES: None o' yo' business.

SMITHERS: Not back to the bloody States, I'll lay my oath.

JONES (*suspiciously*): Why don't I? (*Then with an easy laugh.*) You mean 'count of dat story 'bout me breakin' from jail back dere? Dat's all talk.

SMITHERS (*skeptically*): Ho, yes!

JONES (*sharply*): You ain't 'sinuatin' I'se a liar, is you?

SMITHERS (*hastily*): No, Gawd strike me! I was only thinkin' o' the bloody lies you told the blacks 'ere about killin' white men in the States.

JONES (*angered*): How come dey're lies?

SMITHERS: You'd 'ave been in jail if you 'ad, wouldn't yer then? (*With venom.*) And from what I've 'eard, it ain't 'ealthy for a black to kill a white man in the States. They burns 'em in oil, don't they?

JONES (*with cool deadliness*): You mean lynchin' 'd scare me? Well, I tells you, Smithers, maybe I does kill one white man back dere. Maybe I does. And maybe I kills another right heah 'fore long if he don't look out.

SMITHERS (*trying to force a laugh*): I was on'y spoofin' yer. Can't yer take a joke? And you was just sayin' you'd never been in jail.

JONES (*in the same tone — slightly boastful*): Maybe I goes to jail dere for gettin' in an argument wid razors ovah a crap game. Maybe I gits twenty years when dat colored man die. Maybe I gits in 'nother argument wid de prison guard was overseer ovah us when we're wukin' de roads. Maybe he hits me wid a whip and I splits his head wid a shovel and runs away and files de chain off my leg and gits away safe. Maybe I does all dat an' maybe I don't. It's a story I tells you so's you knows I'se de kind of man dat if you evah repeats one word of it, I ends yo' stealin' on dis yearth mighty damn quick!

SMITHERS (*terrified*): Think I'd peach on yer? Not me! Ain't I always been yer friend?

JONES (*suddenly relaxing*): Sho' you has — and you better be.

SMITHERS (*recovering his composure — and with it his malice*): And just to show yer I'm yer friend, I'll tell yer that bit o' news I was goin' to.

JONES: Go ahead! Shoot de piece. Must be bad news from de happy way you look.

SMITHERS (*warningly*): Maybe it's gettin' time for you to resign — with that bloomin' silver bullet, wot? (*He finishes with a mocking grin.*)

JONES (*puzzled*): What's dat you say? Talk plain.

SMITHERS: Ain't noticed any of the guards or servants about the place today, I 'aven't.

JONES (*carelessly*): Dey're all out in de garden sleepin' under de trees. When I sleeps, dey sneaks a sleep, too, and I pretends I never suspicions it. All I got to do is to ring de bell and dey come flyin', makin' a bluff dey was wukin' all de time.

SMITHERS (*in the same mocking tone*): Ring the bell now an' you'll bloody well see what I means.

JONES (*startled to alertness, but preserving the same careless tone*): Sho' I rings. (*He reaches below the throne and pulls out a big, common dinner bell which is painted the same vivid scarlet as the throne. He rings this vigorously — then stops to listen. Then he goes to both doors, rings again, and looks out.*)

SMITHERS (*watching him with malicious satisfaction, after a pause — mockingly*): The bloody ship is sinkin' an' the bleedin' rats 'as slung their 'ooks.

JONES (*in a sudden fit of anger flings the bell clattering into a corner*): Low-flung, woods' niggers! (*Then catching* SMITHERS' *eye on him, he controls himself and suddenly bursts into a low chuckling laugh.*) Reckon I overplays my hand dis once! A man can't take de pot on a bob-tailed flush all de time. Was I sayin' I'd sit in six months mo'? Well, I'se changed my mind den. I cashes in and resigns de job of Emperor right dis minute.

SMITHERS (*with real admiration*): Blimey, but you're a cool bird, and no mistake.

JONES: No use'n fussin'. When I knows de game's up I kisses it good-bye widout no long waits. Dey've all run off to de hills, ain't dey?

SMITHERS: Yes — every bleedin' man jack of 'em.

JONES: Den de revolution is at de post. And de Emperor better git his feet smokin' up de trail. (*He starts for the door in rear.*)

SMITHERS: Goin' out to look for your 'orse? Yer won't find any. They steals the 'orses first thing. Mine was gone when I went for 'im this mornin'. That's wot first give me a suspicion of wot was up.

JONES (*alarmed for a second, scratches his head, then philosophically*): Well, den I hoofs it. Feet, do yo' duty! (*He pulls out a gold watch and looks at it.*) Three-thuty. Sundown's at six-thuty or dereabouts. (*Puts his watch back — with cool confidence.*) I got plenty o' time to make it easy.

SMITHERS: Don't be so bloomin' sure of it. They'll be after you 'ot and 'eavy. Ole Lem is at the bottom o' this business an' 'e 'ates you like 'ell. 'E'd rather do for you than eat 'is dinner, 'e would!

JONES (*scornfully*): Dat fool no-count nigger! Does you think I'se scared o' him? I stands him on his thick head more'n once befo' dis, and I does it again if he come in my way ... (*Fiercely.*) And dis time I leave him a dead nigger fo' sho'!

SMITHERS: You'll 'ave to cut through the big forest — an' these blacks 'ere can sniff and follow a trail in the dark like 'ounds. You'd 'ave to 'ustle to get through that forest in twelve hours even if you knew all the bloomin' trails like a native.

JONES (*with indignant scorn*): Look-a-heah, white man! Does you think I'se a natural bo'n fool? Give me credit fo' havin' some sense, fo' Lawd's sake! Don't you s'pose I'se looked ahead and made sho' of all de chances? I'se gone out in dat big forest, pretendin' to hunt, so many times dat I knows it high an' low like a book. I could go through on dem trails wid my eyes shut. (*With great contempt.*) Think dese ign'rent bush niggers dat ain't got brains enuff to know deir own names even can catch Brutus Jones? Huh, I s'pects not! Not on yo' life! Why, man, de white men went after me wid bloodhounds whar I come from an' I jes' laughs at 'em. It's a shame to fool dese black trash around heah, dey're so easy. You watch me, man! I'll make dem look sick, I will. I'll be 'cross de plain to de edge of de forest by time dark comes. Once in de woods in de night, dey got a swell chance o' findin' dis baby! Dawn tomorrow I'll be out at de oder side and on de coast whar dat French gunboat is stayin'. She picks me up, take me to Martinique when she go dar, and dere I is safe wid a mighty big bankroll in my jeans. It's easy as rollin' off a log.

SMITHERS (*maliciously*): But s'posin' somethin' 'appens wrong an' they do nab yer?

JONES (*decisively*): Dey don't — dat's de answer.

SMITHERS: But, just for argyment's sake — what'd you do?

JONES (*frowning*): I'se got five lead bullets in dis gun good enuff fo' common bush niggers — and after dat I got de silver bullet left to cheat 'em out o' gittin' me.

SMITHERS (*jeeringly*): Ho, I was fergettin' that silver bullet. You'll bump yourself orf in style, won't yer? Blimey!

JONES (*gloomily*): You kin bet yo' whole roll on one thing, white man. Dis baby plays out his string to de end and when he quits, he quits wid a bang de way he ought. Silver bullet ain't none too good for him when he go, dat's a fac'! (*Then shaking off his nervousness — with a confident laugh.*) Sho'! What is I talkin' about? Ain't come to dat yit and I never will — not wid trash niggers like dese yer. (*Boastfully.*) Silver bullet bring me luck anyway. I kin outguess, outrun, outfight, an' outplay de whole lot o' dem all ovah de board any time o' de day er night! You watch me!

(*From the distant hills comes the faint, steady thump of a tom-tom, low and vibrating. It starts at a rate exactly corresponding to normal pulse beat — 72 to the minute — and continues at a gradually accelerating rate from this point uninterruptedly to the very end of the play.*

JONES starts at the sound. A strange look of apprehension creeps into his face for a moment as he listens. Then he asks, with an attempt to regain his most casual manner.)

What's dat drum beatin' fo'?

SMITHERS (*with a mean grin*): For you. That means the bleedin' ceremony 'as started. I've 'eard it before and I knows.

JONES: Cer'mony? What cer'mony?

SMITHERS: The blacks is 'oldin' a bloody meetin', 'avin' a war dance, gettin' their courage worked up b'fore they starts after you.

JONES: Let dem! Dey'll sho' need it!

SMITHERS: And they're there 'oldin' their 'eathen religious service — makin' no end of devil spells and charms to 'elp 'em against your silver bullet. (*He guffaws loudly.*) Blimey, but they're balmy as 'ell!

JONES (*a tiny bit awed and shaken in spite of himself*): Huh! Takes more'n dat to scare dis chicken!

SMITHERS (*scenting the other's feeling — maliciously*): Ternight when it's pitch black in the forest, they'll 'ave their pet devils and ghosts 'oundin' after you. You'll find yer bloody 'air 'll be standin' on end before termorrow mornin'. (*Seriously.*) It's a bleedin' queer place, that stinkin' forest, even in daylight. Yer don't know what might 'appen in there, it's that rotten still. Always sends the cold shivers down my back minute I gets in it.

JONES (*with a contemptuous sniff*): I an't no chicken-liver like you is. Trees an' me, we'se

friends, and dar's a full moon comin' bring me light. And let dem po' niggers make all de fool spells dey'se a min' to. Does yo' s'pect I'se silly enuff to b'lieve in ghosts an' ha'nts an' all dat ole woman's talk? G'long, white man! You ain't talkin' to me. (*With a chuckle.*) Doesn't you know dey's got to do wid a man was member in good standin' o' de Baptist Church? Sho' I was dat when I was porter on de Pullmans, befo' I gits into my little trouble. Let dem try deir heathen tricks. De Baptist Church done pertect me and land dem all in hell. (*Then with more confident satisfaction.*) And I'se got little silver bullet o' my own, don't forgit.

SMITHERS: Ho! You 'aven't give much 'eed to your Baptist Church since you been down 'ere. I've 'eard myself you 'ad turned yer coat an' was takin' up with their blarsted witch-doctors, or whatever the 'ell yer calls the swine.

JONES (*vehemently*): I pretends to! Sho' I pretends! Dat's part o' my game from de fust. If I finds out dem niggers believes dat black is white, den I yells it out louder 'n deir loudest. It don't git me nothin' to do missionary work for de Baptist Church. I'se after de coin, an' I lays my Jesus on de shelf for de time bein'. (*Stops abruptly to look at his watch — alertly.*) But I ain't got de time to waste no more fool talk wid you. I'se gwine away from heah dis secon'. (*He reaches in under the throne and pulls out an expensive Panama hat with a bright multi-colored band and sets it jauntily on his head.*) So long, white man! (*With a grin.*) See you in jail sometime, maybe!

SMITHERS: Not me, you won't. Well, I wouldn't be in yer bloody boots for no bloomin' money, but 'ere's wishin' yer luck just the same.

JONES (*contemptuously*): Yo're de frightenedest man evah I see! I tells you I'se safe's 'f I was in New York City. It takes dem niggers from now to dark to git up de nerve to start somethin'. By dat time, I'se got a head start dey never kotch up wid.

SMITHERS (*maliciously*): Give my regards to any ghosts yer meets up with.

JONES (*grinning*): If dat ghost got money, I'll tell him never ha'nt you less'n he wants to lose it.

SMITHERS (*flattered*): Garn! (*Then curiously.*) Ain't yer takin' no luggage with yer?

JONES: I travels light when I wants to move fast. And I got tinned grub buried on de edge o' de forest. (*Boastfully.*) Now say dat I don't look ahead an' use my brains! (*With a wide, liberal gesture.*) I will all dat's left in de palace to you — and you better grab all you kin sneak away wid befo' dey gits here.

SMITHERS (*gratefully*): Righto — and thanks ter yer. (*As* JONES *walks toward the door in rear — cautioningly.*) Say! Look 'ere, you ain't goin 'out that way, are yer?

JONES: Does you think I'd slink out de back door like a common nigger? I'se Emperor yit, ain't I? And de Emperor Jones leaves de way he comes, and dat black trash don't dare stop him — not yit, leastways. (*He stops for a moment in the doorway, listening to the far-off but insistent beat of the tom-tom.*) Listen to dat roll-call, will you? Must be mighty big drum carry dat far. (*Then with a laugh.*) Well, if dey ain't no whole brass band to see me off, I sho' got de drum part of it. So long, white man. (*He puts his hands in his pockets and with studied carelessness, whistling a tune, he saunters out of the doorway and off to the left.*)

SMITHERS (*looks after him with a puzzled admiration*): 'E's got 'is bloomin' nerve with 'im, s'elp me! (*Then angrily.*) Ho — the bleedin' nigger — puttin' on 'is bloody airs! I 'opes they nabs 'im an' gives 'im what's what! (*Then putting business before the pleasure of this thought, looking around him with cupidity.*) A bloke ought to find a 'ole lot in this palace that'd go for a bit of cash. Let's take a look, 'Arry, me lad. (*He starts for the doorway on right as*

THE CURTAIN FALLS

SCENE II

Scene — Nightfall. The end of the plain where the Great Forest begins. The foreground is sandy, level ground dotted by a few stones and clumps of stunted bushes covering close against the earth to escape the buffeting of the trade wind. In the rear the forest is a wall of darkness dividing the world. Only when the eye becomes accustomed to the gloom can the outlines of separate trunks of the nearest trees be made out, enormous pillars of deeper blackness. A somber monotone of wind lost in the leaves moans in the air. Yet this sound serves but to intensify the impression of the forest's relentless immobility, to form a background throwing into relief its brooding, implacable silence.

JONES *enters from the left, walking rapidly. He stops as he nears the edge of the forest, looks around him quickly, peering into the dark as if searching for some familiar landmark. Then, apparently, satisfied that he is where he ought to be, he throws himself on the ground, dog-tired.*

Well, heah I is. In de nick o' time, too! Little mo' an' it'd be blacker'n de ace of spades heahabouts. (*He pulls a bandana handkerchief from his hip pocket and mops off his perspiring face.*) Sho'! Gimme air! I'se tuckered out sho' nuff. Dat soft Emperor job ain't no trainin' fo' a long hike ovah dat plain in de brilin' sun. (*Then with a chuckle.*) Cheah up, nigger, de worst is yet to come. (*He lifts his head and stares at the forest. His chuckle peters out abruptly. In a tone of awe.*) My goodness, look at dem woods, will you? Dat no-count Smithers said dey'd be black an' he sho' called de turn. (*Turning away from them quickly and looking down at his feet, he snatches at a chance to change the subject — solicitously.*) Feet, you is holdin' up yo' end fine an' I sutinly hopes you ain't blisterin' none. It's time you git a rest. (*He takes off his shoes, his eyes studiously avoiding the forest. He feels of the soles of his feet gingerly.*) You is still in de pink — on'y a little mite feverish. Cool yo'selfs. Remember you done got a long journey yit befo' you. (*He sits in a weary attitude, listening to the rhythmic beating of the tom-tom. He grumbles in a loud tone to cover up a growing uneasiness.*) Bush niggers! Wonder dey wouldn' get sick o' beatin' dat drum. Sound louder, seem like. I wonder if dey's startin' after me? (*He scrambles to his feet, looking back across the plain.*) Couldn't see dem now, nohow, if dey was hundred feet away. (*Then shaking himself like a wet dog to get rid of these depressing thoughts.*) Sho', dey's miles an' miles behind. What you gittin' fidgety about? (*But he sits down and begins to lace up his shoes in great haste, all the time muttering reassuringly.*) You know what? Yo' belly is empty, dat's what's de matter wid you. Come time to eat! Wid nothin' but wind on yo' stumach, o' course you feels jiggedy. Well, we eats right heah an' now soon's I gits dese pesky shoes laced up! (*He finishes lacing up his shoes.*) Dere! Now le's see. (*Gets on his hands and knees and searches the ground around him with his eyes.)* White stone, white stone, where is you? (*He sees the first white stone and crawls to it — with satisfaction.*) Heah you is! I knowed dis was de right place. Box of grub, come to me. (*He turns over the stone and feels in under it — in a tone of dismay.*) Ain't heah! Gorry, is I in de right place or isn't I? Dere's 'nother stone. Guess dat's it. (*He scrambles to the next stone and turns it over.*) Ain't heah, neither! Grub, whar is you? Ain't heah. Gorry, has I got to go hungry into dem woods — all de night? (*While he is talking he scrambles from one stone to another, turning them over in frantic haste. Finally, he jumps to his feet excitedly.*) Is I lost de place? Must have! But how dat happen when I was followin' de trail across de plain in broad daylight? (*Almost plaintively.*) I'se hungry, I is! I gotta git my feed. Whar's my strength gonna come from if I doesn't? Gorry, I gotta find dat grub high an' low somehow! Why it come dark so quick like dat? Can't see nothin'. (*He scratches a match on his trousers and peers about him. The rate of the beat of the far-off tom-tom increases perceptibly as he does so. He mutters in a bewildered voice.*) How come all dese white stones come heah when I only remembers one? (*Suddenly, with a frightened gasp, he flings the match on the ground and stamps on it.*) Nigger, is you gone crazy mad? Is you lightin' matches to show dem whar you is? Fo' Lawd's sake, use yo' haid. Gorry, I'se got to be careful! (*He stares at the plain behind him apprehensively, his hand on his revolver.*) But how come all dese white stones? And whar's dat tin box o' grub I had all wrapped up in oil cloth?

(*While his back is turned, THE LITTLE FORMLESS FEARS creep out from the deeper blackness of the forest. They are black, shapeless, only their glittering little eyes can be seen. If they have any describable form at all it is that of a grubworm about the size of a creeping child. They move noiselessly, but with deliberate, painful effort, striving to raise themselves on end, failing and sinking prone again. JONES turns about to face the forest. He stares up at the tops of the trees, seeking vainly to discover his whereabouts by their conformation.*)

Can't tell nothin' from dem trees! Gorry, nothin' 'round heah look like I evah seed it

befo'. I'se done lost de place sho' 'nuff! (*With mournful foreboding.*) It's mighty queer! It's mighty queer! (*With sudden forced defiance — in an angry tone.*) Woods, is you tryin' to put somethin' ovah on me?

(*From the formless creatures on the ground in front of him comes a tiny gale of low mocking laughter like a rustling of leaves. They squirm upward toward him in twisted attitudes. JONES looks down, leaps backward with a yell of terror, yanking out his revolver as he does so — in a quavering voice.*)

What's dat? Who's dar? What is you? Git away from me befo' I shoots you up! You don't? . . .

(*He fires. There is a flash, a loud report, then silence broken only by the far-off, quickened throb of the tom-tom. The formless creatures have scurried back into the forest. JONES remains fixed in his position, listening intently. The sound of the shot, the reassuring feel of the revolver in his hand, have somewhat restored his shaken nerve. He addresses himself with renewed confidence.*)

Dey're gone. Dat shot fix 'em. Dey was only little animals — little wild pigs, I reckon. Dey've maybe rooted out yo' grub an' eat it. Sho', you fool nigger, what you think dey is — ha'nts? (*Excitedly.*) Gorry, you give de game away when you fire dat shot. Dem niggers heah dat fo' su'tin! Time you beat it in de woods widout no long waits. (*He starts for the forest — hesitates before the plunge — then urging himself in with manful resolution.*) Git in, nigger! What you skeered at? Ain't nothin' dere but de trees! Git in! (*He plunges boldly into the forest.*)

SCENE III

Scene — Nine o'clock. In the forest. The moon has just risen. Its beams, drifting through the canopy of leaves, make a barely perceptible, suffused, eerie glow. A dense low wall of underbrush and creepers is in the nearer foreground, fencing in a small triangular clearing. Beyond this is the massed blackness of the forest like an encompassing barrier. A path is dimly discerned leading down to the clearing from left, rear, and winding *away from it again toward the right. As the scene opens nothing can be distinctly made out. Except for the beating of the tom-tom, which is a trifle louder and quicker than in the previous scene, there is silence, broken every few seconds by a queer, clicking sound. Then gradually the figure of the Negro, JEFF, can be discerned crouching on his haunches at the rear of the triangle. He is middle-aged, thin, brown in color, is dressed in a Pullman porter's uniform, cap, etc. He is throwing a pair of dice on the ground before him, picking them up, shaking them, casting them out with the regular, rigid, mechanical movements of an automaton. The heavy, plodding footsteps of someone approaching along the trail from the left are heard and JONES' voice, pitched in a slightly higher key and strained in a cheering effort to overcome its own tremors.*

De moon's rizen. Does you heah dat, nigger? You gits more light from dis out. No mo' buttin' yo' fool head agin' de trunks an' scratchin' de hide off yo' legs in de bushes. Now you sees whar yo'se gwine. So cheer up! From now on you has a snap. (*He steps just to the rear of the triangular clearing and mops off his face on his sleeve. He has lost his Panama hat. His face is scratched, his brilliant uniform shows several large rents.*) What time's it gittin' to be, I wonder? I dassent light no match to find out. Phoo'. It's wa'm an' dat's a fac'! (*Wearily.*) How long I been makin' tracks in dese woods? Must be hours an' hours. Seems like fo'evah! Yit can't be, when de moon's jes' riz. Dis am a long night fo' yo', yo' Majesty! (*With a mournful chuckle.*) Majesty! Der ain't much majesty 'bout dis baby now. (*With attempted cheerfulness.*) Never min'. It's all part o' de game. Dis night come to an end like everything else. And when you gits dar safe and has dat bankroll in yo' hands you laughs at all dis. (*He starts to whistle but checks himself abruptly.*) What yo' whistlin' for, you po' dope! Want all de worl' to heah you? (*He stops talking to listen.*) Heah dat ole drum! Sho' gits nearer from de sound. Dey're packin' it along wid 'em. Time fo' me to move. (*He takes a step forward, then stops — worriedly.*) What's dat odder queer clickety sound I heah? Dere it is! Sound close! Sound like — sound like — Fo' God sake, sound like some nigger was shootin' crap! (*Frightenedly.*) I better beat it quick when I gits dem

notions. (*He walks quickly into the clear space — then stands transfixed as he sees* JEFF *— in a terrified gasp.*) Who dar? Who dat? Is dat you, Jeff? (*Starting toward the other, forgetful for a moment of his surroundings and really believing it is a living man that he sees — in a tone of happy relief.*) Jeff! I'se sho' mighty glad to see you! Dey tol' me you done died from dat razor cut I gives you. (*Stopping suddenly, bewilderedly.*) But how you come to be heah, nigger? (*He stares fascinatedly at the other who continues his mechanical play with the dice.* JONES' *eyes begin to roll wildly. He stutters.*) Ain't you gwine — look up — can't you speak to me? Is you — is you — a ha'nt? (*He jerks out his revolver in a frenzy of terrified rage.*) Nigger, I kills you dead once. Has I got to kill you again? You take it den. (*He fires. When the smoke clears away* JEFF *has disappeared.* JONES *stands trembling — then with a certain reassurance.*) He's gone, anyway. Ha'nt or no ha'nt, dat shot fix him. (*The beat of the far-off tom-tom is perceptibly louder and more rapid.* JONES *becomes conscious of it — with a start, looking back over his shoulder.*) Dey's gittin' near! Dey's comin' fast! And heah I is shootin' shots to let 'em know jes' whar I is. Oh, Gorry, I'se got to run. (*Forgetting the path he plunges wildly into the underbrush in the rear and disappears in the shadow.*)

SCENE IV

Scene — Eleven o'clock. In the forest. A wide dirt road runs diagonally from right, front, to left, rear. Rising sheer on both sides the forest walls it in. The moon is now up. Under its light the road glimmers ghastly and unreal. It is as if the forest had stood aside momentarily to let the road pass through and accomplish its veiled purpose. This done, the forest will fold in upon itself again and the road will be no more. JONES *stumbles in from the forest on the right. His uniform is ragged and torn. He looks about him with numbed surprise when he sees the road, his eyes blinking in the bright moonlight. He flops down exhaustedly and pants heavily for a while. Then with sudden anger.*

I'm meltin' wid heat! Runnin' an' runnin' an' runnin'! Damn dis heah coat! Like a straitjacket! (*He tears off his coat and flings it away* from him, revealing himself stripped to the waist.) Dere! Dat's better! Now I kin breathe! (*Looking down at his feet, the spurs catch his eye.*) And to hell wid dese high-fangled spurs. Dey're what's been a-trippin' me up an' breakin' my neck. (*He unstraps them and flings them away disgustedly.*) Dere! I gits rid o' dem frippety Emperor trappin's an' I travels lighter. Lawd! I'se tired! (*After a pause, listening to the insistent beat of the tom-tom in the distance.*) I must 'a put some distance between myself an' dem — runnin' like dat — and yit — dat damn drum sound jes' de same — nearer, even. Well, I guess I a'most holds my lead anyhow. Dey won't never catch up. (*With a sigh.*) If on'y my fool legs stands up. Oh, I'se sorry I evah went in for dis. Dat Emperor job is sho' hard to shake. (*He looks around him suspiciously.*) How'd dis road evah git heah? Good level road, too. I never remembers seein' it befo'. (*Shaking his head apprehensively.*) Dese woods is sho' full o' de queerest things at night. (*With a sudden terror.*) Lawd God, don't let me see no more o' dem ha'nts! Dey gits my goat! (*Then trying to talk himself into confidence.*) Ha'nts! You fool nigger, dey ain't no such things! Don't de Baptist parson tell you dat many time? Is you civilized, or is you like dese ign'rent black niggers heah? Sho'! Dat was all in yo' own head. Wasn't nothin' dere. Wasn't no Jeff! Know what? You jus' get seein' dem things 'cause yo' belly's empty and you's sick wid hunger inside. Hunger 'fects yo' head and yo' eyes. Any fool know dat. (*Then pleading fervently.*) But bless God, I don't come across no more o' dem, whatever dey is! (*Then cautiously.*) Rest! Don't talk! Rest! You needs it. Den you gits on yo' way again. (*Looking at the moon.*) Night's half gone a'most. You hits de coast in de mawning! Den you'se all safe.

(*From the right forward a small gang of Negroes enter. They are dressed in striped convict suits, their heads are shaven, one leg drags limpingly, shackled to a heavy ball and chain. Some carry picks, the others shovels. They are followed by a white man dressed in the uniform of a prison guard. A Winchester rifle is slung across his shoulders and he carries a heavy whip. At a signal from the* GUARD *they stop on the road opposite where* JONES *is sitting.* JONES, *who has been staring up at the sky, unmindful of their noiseless approach, suddenly looks down and sees*

them. *His eyes pop out, he tries to get to his feet and fly, but sinks back, too numbed by fright to move. His voice catches in a choking prayer.*)

Lawd Jesus!

(*The* PRISON GUARD *cracks his whip — noiselessly — and at that signal all the convicts start to work on the road. They swing their picks, they shovel, but not a sound comes from their labor. Their movements, like those of* JEFF *in the preceding scene, are those of automatons — rigid, slow, and mechanical. The* PRISON GUARD *points sternly at* JONES *with his whip, motions him to take his place among the other shovelers.* JONES *gets to his feet in a hypnotized stupor. He mumbles subserviently.*)

Yes, suh! Yes, suh! I'se comin'.

(*As he shuffles, dragging one foot, over to his place, he curses under his breath with rage and hatred.*)

God damn yo' soul, I gits even wid you yit, sometime.

(*As if there were a shovel in his hands he goes through weary, mechanical gestures of digging up dirt, and throwing it to the roadside. Suddenly the* GUARD *approaches him angrily, threateningly. He raises his whip and lashes* JONES *viciously across the shoulders with it.* JONES *winces with pain and cowers abjectly. The* GUARD *turns his back on him and walks away contemptuously. Instantly* JONES *straightens up. With arms upraised as if his shovel were a club in his hands he springs murderously at the unsuspecting* GUARD. *In the act of crashing down his shovel on the white man's skull,* JONES *suddenly becomes aware that his hands are empty. He cries despairingly.*)

Whar's my shovel? Gimme my shovel till I splits his damn head! (*Appealing to his fellow convicts.*) Gimme a shovel, one o' you, fo' God's sake!

(*They stand fixed in motionless attitudes, their eyes on the ground. The* GUARD *seems to wait expectantly, his back turned to the attacker.* JONES *bellows with baffled, terrified rage, tugging frantically at his revolver.*)

I kills you, you white debil, if it's de last thing I evah does! Ghost or debil, I kill you again!

(*He frees the revolver and fires point blank at the* GUARD's *back. Instantly the walls of the forest close in from both sides, the road and the figures of the convict gang are blotted out in an enshrouding darkness. The only sounds are a crashing in the underbrush as* JONES *leaps away in mad flight and the throbbing of the tom-tom, still far distant, but increased in volume of sound and rapidity of beat.*)

SCENE V

Scene — *One o'clock. A large circular clearing, enclosed by the serried ranks of gigantic trunks of tall trees whose tops are lost to view. In the center is a big dead stump worn by time into a curious resemblance to an auction block. The moon floods the clearing with a clear light.* JONES *forces his way in through the forest on the left. He looks wildly about the clearing with hunted, fearful glances. His pants are in tatters, his shoes cut and misshapen, flapping about his feet. He slinks cautiously to the stump in the center and sits down in a tense position, ready for instant flight. Then he holds his head in his hands and rocks back and forth, moaning to himself miserably.*

Oh Lawd, Lawd! Oh Lawd, Lawd! (*Suddenly he throws himself on his knees and raises his clasped hands to the sky* — *in a voice of agonized pleading.*) Lawd Jesus, heah my prayer! I'se a po' sinner, a po' sinner! I knows I done wrong, I knows it! When I cotches Jeff cheatin' wid loaded dice my anger overcomes me and I kills him dead! Lawd, I done wrong! When dat guard hits me wid de whip, my anger overcomes me, and I kills him dead. Lawd, I done wrong! And down heah whar dese fool bush niggers raises me up to the seat o' de mighty, I steals all I could grab. Lawd, I done wrong! I knows it! I'se sorry! Forgive me, Lawd! Forgive dis po' sinner! (*Then beseeching terrifiedly.*) And keep dem away, Lawd! Keep dem away from me! And stop dat drum soundin' in my ears! Dat begin to sound ha'nted, too. (*He gets to his feet, evidently slightly reassured by his prayer* — *with attempted confidence.*) De Lawd'll preserve me from dem ha'nts after dis. (*Sits down on the stump again.*) I ain't skeered

o' real men. Let dem come. But dem odders ... (*He shudders* — *then looks down at his feet, working his toes inside the shoes* — *with a groan.*) Oh, my po' feet! Dem shoes ain't no use no more 'ceptin' to hurt. I'se better off widout dem. (*He unlaces them and pulls them off* — *holds the wrecks of the shoes in his hands and regards them mournfully.*) You was real, A-one patin' leather, too. Look at you now. Emperor, you'se gittin' mighty low!

(*He sits dejectedly and remains with bowed shoulders, staring down at the shoes in his hands as if reluctant to throw them away. While his attention is thus occupied, a crowd of figures silently enter the clearing from all sides. All are dressed in Southern costumes of the period of the fifties of the last century. There are middle-aged men who are evidently well-to-do planters. There is one spruce, authoritative individual* — *the* AUCTIONEER. *There is a crowd of curious spectators, chiefly young belles and dandies who have come to the slave-market for diversion. All exchange courtly greetings in dumb show and chat silently together. There is something stiff, rigid, unreal, marionettish about their movements. They group themselves about the stump. Finally a batch of slaves are led in from the left by an attendant* — *three men of different ages, two women, one with a baby in her arms, nursing. They are placed to the left of the stump, beside* JONES.

The white planters look them over appraisingly as if they were cattle, and exchange judgments on each. The dandies point with their fingers and make witty remarks. The belles titter bewitchingly. All this in silence save for the ominous throb of the tom-tom. The AUCTIONEER *holds up his hand, taking his place at the stump. The group strain forward attentively. He touches* JONES *on the shoulder peremptorily, motioning for him to stand on the stump* — *the auction block.*

JONES *looks up, sees the figures on all sides, looks wildly for some opening to escape, sees none, screams and leaps madly to the top of the stump to get as far away from them as possible. He stands there, cowering, paralyzed with horror. The* AUCTIONEER *begins his silent spiel. He points to* JONES, *appeals to the planters to see for themselves. Here is a good field hand, sound in wind and limb as they can see. Very strong still in spite of his being middle-aged. Look at that back. Look at those shoulders. Look at the muscles in his arms and his sturdy legs. Capable of any amount of hard labor. Moreover, of a good disposition, intelligent and tractable. Will any gentleman start the bidding? The* PLANTERS *raise their fingers, make their bids. They are apparently all eager to possess* JONES. *The bidding is lively, the crowd interested. While this has been going on,* JONES *has been seized by the courage of desperation. He dares to look down and around him. Over his face abject terror gives way to mystification, to gradual realization — stutteringly.)*

What you all doin', white folks? What's all dis? What you all lookin' at me fo'? What you doin' wid me, anyhow? (*Suddenly convulsed with raging hatred and fear.*) Is dis a auction? Is you sellin' me like dey uster befo' de war? (*Jerking out his revolver just as the* AUCTIONEER *knocks him down to one of the planters — glaring from him to the purchaser.*) And *you* sells me? And *you* buys me? I shows you I'se a free nigger, damn yo' souls!

(*He fires at the* AUCTIONEER *and at the* PLANTER *with such rapidity that the two shots are almost simultaneous. As if this were a signal the walls of the forest fold in. Only blackness remains and silence broken by* JONES *as he rushes off, crying with fear — and by the quickened, ever louder beat of the tom-tom.*)

SCENE VI

Scene — Three o'clock. A cleared space in the forest. The limbs of the trees meet over it forming a low ceiling about five feet from the ground. The interlocked ropes of creepers reaching upward to entwine the tree trunks give an arched appearance to the sides. The space thus enclosed is like the dark, noisome hold of some ancient vessel. The moonlight is almost completely shut out and only a vague, wan light filters through. There is the noise of someone approaching from the left, stumbling and crawling through the undergrowth. JONES' *voice is heard between chattering moans.*

Oh, Lawd, what I gwine do now? Ain't got no bullet left on'y de silver one. If mo' o' dem ha'nts come after me, how I gwine skeer dem away? Oh, Lawd, on'y de silver one left — an' I gotta save dat fo' luck. If I shoots dat one I'm a goner sho'! Lawd, it's black heah! Whar's de moon? Oh, Lawd, don't dis night evah come to an end? (*By the sounds, he is feeling his way cautiously forward.*) Dere! Dis feels like a clear space. I gotta lie down an' rest. I don't care if dem niggers does cotch me. I gotta rest.

(*He is well forward now where his figure can be dimly made out. His pants have been so torn away that what is left of them is no better than a breech cloth. He flings himself full length, face downward on the ground, panting with exhaustion. Gradually it seems to grow lighter in the enclosed space and two rows of seated figures can be seen behind* JONES. *They are sitting in crumpled, despairing attitudes, hunched, facing one another with their backs touching the forest walls as if they were shackled to them. All are Negroes, naked save for loin cloths. At first they are silent and motionless. Then they begin to sway slowly forward toward each other and back again in unison, as if they were laxly letting themselves follow the long roll of a ship at sea. At the same time, a low, melancholy murmur rises among them, increasing gradually by rhythmic degrees which seem to be directed and controlled by the throb of the tom-tom in the distance, to a long, tremulous wail of despair that reaches a certain pitch, unbearably acute, then falls by slow gradations of tone into silence and is taken up again.* JONES *starts, looks up, sees the figures, and throws himself down again to shut out the sight. A shudder of terror shakes his whole body as the wail rises up about him again. But the next time, his voice, as if under some uncanny compulsion, starts with the others. As their chorus lifts he rises to a sitting posture similar to the others, swaying back and forth. His voice reaches the highest pitch of sorrow, of desolation. The light fades out, the other voices cease, and only darkness is left.* JONES *can be heard scrambling to his feet and running off, his voice sinking down the scale and receding as he moves farther and farther away in the forest. The tom-tom beats louder, quicker, with a more insistent, triumphant pulsation.*)

SCENE VII

Scene — Five o'clock. The foot of a gigantic tree by the edge of a great river. A rough structure of boulders, like an altar, is by the tree. The raised river bank is in the nearer background. Beyond this the surface of the river spreads out, brilliant and unruffled in the moonlight, blotted out and merged into a veil of bluish mist in the distance. JONES' *voice is heard from the left rising and falling in the long, despairing wail of the chained slaves, to the rhythmic beat of the tom-tom. As his voice sinks into silence, he enters the open space. The expression of his face is fixed and stony, his eyes have an obsessed glare, he moves with a strange deliberation like a sleep-walker or one in a trance. He looks around at the tree, the rough stone altar, the moonlit surface of the river beyond, and passes his hand over his head with a vague gesture of puzzled bewilderment. Then, as if in obedience to some obscure impulse, he sinks into a kneeling, devotional posture before the altar. Then he seems to come to himself partly, to have an uncertain realization of what he is doing, for he straightens up and stares about him horrifiedly — in an incoherent mumble.*

What — what is I doin'? What is — dis place? Seems like — seems like I know dat tree — an' dem stones — an' de river. I remember — seems like I been heah befo'. (*Tremblingly.*) Oh, Gorry, I'se skeered in dis place! I'se skeered! Oh, Lawd, pertect dis sinner!

(*Crawling away from the altar, he cowers close to the ground, his face hidden, his shoulders heaving with sobs of hysterical fright. From behind the trunk of the tree, as if he had sprung out of it, the figure of the* CONGO WITCH-DOCTOR *appears. He is wizened and old, naked except for the fur of some small animal tied about his waist, its bushy tail hanging down in front. His body is stained all over a bright red. Antelope horns are on each side of his head, branching upward. In one hand he carries a bone rattle, in the other a charm stick with a bunch of white cockatoo feathers tied to the end. A great number of glass beads and bone ornaments are about his neck, ears, wrists, and ankles. He struts noiselessly with a queer*

prancing step to a position in the clear ground between JONES *and the altar. Then with a preliminary, summoning stamp of his foot on the earth, he begins to dance and to chant. As if in response to his summons the beating of the tom-tom grows to a fierce, exultant boom whose throbs seem to fill the air with vibrating rhythm.* JONES *looks up, starts to spring to his feet, reaches a half-kneeling, half-squatting position and remains rigidly fixed there, paralyzed with awed fascination by this new apparition. The* WITCH-DOCTOR *sways, stamping with his foot, his bone rattle clicking the time. His voice rises and falls in a weird, monotonous croon, without articulate word divisions. Gradually his dance becomes clearly one of a narrative in pantomime, his croon is an incantation, a charm to allay the fierceness of some implacable deity demanding sacrifice. He flees, he is pursued by devils, he hides, he flees again. Ever wilder and wilder becomes his flight, nearer and nearer draws the pursuing evil, more and more the spirit of terror gains possession of him. His croon, rising to intensity, is punctuated by shrill cries.* JONES *has become completely hypnotized. His voice joins in the incantation, in the cries, he beats time with his hands and sways his body to and fro from the waist. The whole spirit and meaning of the dance has entered into him, has become his spirit. Finally the theme of the pantomime halts on a howl of despair, and is taken up again in a note of savage hope. There is a salvation. The forces of evil demand sacrifice. They must be appeased. The* WITCH-DOCTOR *points with his wand to the sacred tree, to the river beyond, to the altar, and finally to* JONES *with a ferocious command.* JONES *seems to sense the meaning of this. It is he who must offer himself for sacrifice. He beats his forehead abjectly to the ground, moaning hysterically.*)

Mercy, Oh Lawd! Mercy! Mercy on dis po' sinner.

(*The* WITCH-DOCTOR *springs to the river bank. He stretches out his arms and calls to some god within its depths. Then he starts backward slowly, his arms remaining out. A huge head of a crocodile appears over the bank and its eyes, glittering greenly, fasten upon* JONES. *He stares into them fascinatedly. The* WITCH-DOCTOR *prances up to him, touches him with his wand, motions with*) *hideous command toward the waiting monster.* JONES *squirms on his belly nearer and nearer, moaning continually.*)

Mercy, Lawd! Mercy!

(*The crocodile heaves more of his enormous bulk onto the land.* JONES *squirms toward him. The* WITCH-DOCTOR's *voice shrills out in furious exultation, the tom-tom beats madly.* JONES *cries out in a fierce, exhausted spasm of anguished pleading.*)

Lawd, save me! Lawd Jesus, heah my prayer!

(*Immediately, in answer to his prayer, comes the thought of the one bullet left him. He snatches at his hip, shouting defiantly.*)

De silver bullet! You don't git me yit!

(*He fires at the green eyes in front of him. The head of the crocodile sinks back behind the river bank, the* WITCH-DOCTOR *springs behind the sacred tree and disappears.* JONES *lies with his face to the ground, his arms outstretched, whimpering with fear as the throb of the tom-tom fills the silence about him with a somber pulsation, a baffled but revengeful power.*)

SCENE VIII

Scene — Dawn. Same as Scene II, the dividing line of forest and plain. The nearest tree trunks are dimly revealed but the forest behind them is still a mass of glooming shadows. The tom-tom seems on the very spot, so loud and continuously vibrating are its beats. LEM *enters from the left, followed by a small squad of his soldiers, and by the Cockney trader,* SMITHERS. LEM *is a heavy-set, ape-faced old savage of the extreme African type, dressed only in a loin cloth. A revolver and cartridge belt are about his waist. His soldiers are in different degrees of rag-concealed nakedness. All wear broad palm-leaf hats. Each one carries a rifle.* SMITHERS *is the same as in Scene I. One of the soldiers, evidently a tracker, is peering about keenly on the ground. He grunts and points to the spot where* JONES *entered the forest.* LEM *and* SMITHERS *come to look.*

SMITHERS (*after a glance, turns away in disgust*): That's where 'e went in right enough.

Much good it'll do yer. 'E's miles orf by this an' safe to the Coast, damn 'is 'ide! I tole yer yer'd lose 'im, didn't I? — wastin' the 'ole bloomin' night beatin' yer bloody drum and castin' yer silly spells! Gawd blimey, wot a pack!

LEM (*gutturally*): We cotch him. You see. (*He makes a motion to his soldiers who squat down on their haunches in a semicircle.*)

SMITHERS (*exasperatedly*): Well, ain't yer goin' in an' 'unt 'im in the woods? What the 'ell's the good of waitin'?

LEM (*imperturbably — squatting down himself*): We cotch him.

SMITHERS (*turning away from him contemptuously*): Aw! Garn! 'E's a better man than the lot o' you put together. I 'ates the sight o' 'im but I'll say that for 'im.

(*A sound of snapping twigs comes from the forest. The soldiers jump to their feet, cocking their rifles alertly.* LEM *remains sitting with an imperturbable expression, but listening intently. The sound from the woods is repeated.* LEM *makes a quick signal with his hand. His followers creep quickly but noiselessly into the forest, scattering so that each enters at a different spot.*)

SMITHERS (*in the silence that follows — in a contemptuous whisper*): You ain't thinkin' that would be 'im, I 'ope?

LEM (*calmly*): We cotch him.

SMITHERS: Blarsted fat 'eads! (*Then after a second's thought — wonderingly.*) Still an' all, it might 'appen. If 'e lost 'is bloody way in these stinkin' woods 'e'd likely turn in a circle without 'is knowin' it. They all does.

LEM (*peremptorily*): Sssh!

(*The reports of several rifles sound from the forest, followed a second later by savage, exultant yells. The beating of the tom-tom abruptly ceases.* LEM *looks up at the white man with a grin of satisfaction.*)

We cotch him. Him dead.

SMITHERS (*with a snarl*): 'Ow d'yer know it's 'im an' 'ow d'yer know 'e's dead?

LEM: My mens dey got 'um silver bullets. Dey kill him shore.

SMITHERS (*astonished*): They got silver bullets?

LEM: Lead bullet no kill him. He got um strong charm. I cook um money, make um silver bullet, make um strong charm, too.

SMITHERS (*light breaking upon him*): So that's wot you was up to all night, wot? You was scared to put after 'im till you'd moulded silver bullets, eh?

LEM (*simply stating a fact*): Yes. Him got strong charm. Lead no good.

SMITHERS (*slapping his thigh and guffawing*): Haw-haw! If yer don't beat all 'ell! (*Then recovering himself — scornfully.*) I'll bet yer it ain't 'im they shot at all, yer bleedin' looney!

LEM (*calmly*): Dey come bring him now.

(*The soldiers come out of the forest, carrying JONES' limp body. There is a little reddish-purple hole under his left breast. He is dead. They carry him to LEM, who examines his body with great satisfaction. SMITHERS leans over his shoulder — in a tone of frightened awe.*)

Well, they did for yer right enough, Jonsey, me lad! Dead as a 'erring! (*Mockingly.*) Where's yer 'igh an' mighty airs now, yer bloomin' Majesty? (*Then with a grin.*) Silver bullets! Gawd blimey, but yer died in the 'eighth o' style, any'ow!

(LEM *makes a motion to the soldiers to carry the body out left.* SMITHERS *speaks to him sneeringly.*)

SMITHERS: And I s'pose you think it's yer bleedin' charms and yer silly beatin' the drum that made 'im run in a circle when 'e'd lost 'imself, don't yer?

(*But* LEM *makes no reply, does not seem to hear the question, walks out left after his men.* SMITHERS *looks after him with contemptuous scorn.*)

Stupid as 'ogs, the lot of 'em! Blarsted niggers!

CURTAIN FALLS

TRAGEDY

OEDIPUS THE KING

Sophocles

Translated into English verse by H. D. F. Kitto

Sophocles (c. 495 B.C.–406 B.C.), the son of a wealthy Athenian, is one of the three Greek tragic writers whose work survives. (The other two are Aeschylus and Euripides.) Of Sophocles' more than one hundred and twenty plays, we have seven. The exact date that *Oedipus the King* was written is not known, but 430 B.C. is a reasonable guess. Some twenty-five years later, when he was almost ninety, Sophocles wrote *Oedipus at Colonus*, dramatizing Oedipus' last deeds.

DRAMATIS PERSONAE

OEDIPUS, *King of Thebes*
PRIEST OF ZEUS
CREON, *brother of Iocasta*
TEIRESIAS, *a Seer*
IOCASTA, *Queen of Thebes*
A CORINTHIAN SHEPHERD
A THEBAN SHEPHERD
A MESSENGER
CHORUS *of Theban citizens*
PRIESTS, ATTENDANTS, *etc.*

Scene: Thebes, before the royal palace.

Giant puppets of Iocasta and Oedipus, made by Remo Buffano, for a Philadelphia production of *Oedipus the King*, designed in 1931 by Robert Edmund Jones. (Photograph: Will Rapport. Harvard Theatre Collection.)

OEDIPUS:
My children, latest brood of ancient Cadmus,
What purpose brings you here, a multitude
Bearing the boughs that mark the suppliant?
Why is our air so full of frankincense,
So full of hymns and prayers and lamenta-
5   tions?
This, children, was no matter to entrust
To others: therefore I myself am come
Whose fame is known to all — I, Oedipus.
— You, Sir, are pointed out by length of years
10   To be the spokesman: tell me, what is in
Your hearts? What fear? What sorrow? Count
on all
That I can do, for I am not so hard
As not to pity such a supplication.
PRIEST:
Great King of Thebes, and sovereign Oedipus,
15   Look on us, who now stand before the altars —
Some young, still weak of wing; some bowed
with age —
The priests, as I, of Zeus; and these, the best
Of our young men; and in the market-place,
And by Athena's temples and the shrine
20   Of fiery divination, there is kneeling,
Each with his suppliant branch, the rest of
Thebes.
The city, as you see yourself, is now
Storm-tossed, and can no longer raise its head
Above the waves and angry surge of death.
25   The fruitful blossoms of the land are barren,
The herds upon our pastures, and our wives
In childbirth, barren. Last, and worst of all,
The withering god of fever swoops on us
To empty Cadmus' city and enrich
30   Dark Hades with our groans and lamentations.
No god we count you, that we bring our
prayers,
I and these children, to your palace-door,
But wise above all other men to read
Life's riddles, and the hidden ways of Heaven;
35   For it was you who came and set us free
From the blood-tribute that the cruel Sphinx
Had laid upon our city; without our aid
Or our instruction, but, as we believe,
With god as ally, you gave us back our life.
40   So now, most dear, most mighty Oedipus,
We all entreat you on our bended knees,

Come to our rescue, whether from the gods
Or from some man you can find means to
save.
For I have noted, that man's counsel is
Of best effect, who has been tried in action.   45
Come, noble Oedipus! Come, save our city.
Be well advised; for that past service given
This city calls you Savior; of your kingship
Let not the record be that first we rose
From ruin, then to ruin fell again.   50
No, save our city, let it stand secure.
You brought us gladness and deliverance
Before; now do no less. You rule this land;
Better to rule it full of living men
Than rule a desert; citadel or ship   55
Without its company of men is nothing.
OEDIPUS:
My children, what you long for, that I know
Indeed, and pity you. I know how cruelly
You suffer; yet, though sick, not one of you
Suffers a sickness half as great as mine.   60
Yours is a single pain; each man of you
Feels but his own. My heart is heavy with
The city's pain, my own, and yours together.
You come to me not as to one asleep
And needing to be wakened; many a tear   65
I have been shedding, every path of thought
Have I been pacing; and what remedy,
What single hope my anxious thought has
found
That I have tried. Creon, Menoeceus' son,
My own wife's brother, I have sent to Delphi   70
To ask in Phoebus' house what act of mine,
What word of mine, may bring deliverance.
Now, as I count the days, it troubles me
What he is doing; his absence is prolonged
Beyond the proper time. But when he comes   75
Then write me down a villain, if I do
Not each particular that the god discloses.
PRIEST:
You give us hope. — And here is more, for
they
Are signaling that Creon has returned.
OEDIPUS:
O Lord Apollo, even as Creon smiles,   80
Smile now on us, and let it be deliverance!
PRIEST:
The news is good; or he would not be wearing
That ample wreath of richly-berried laurel.
OEDIPUS:
We soon shall know; my voice will reach so
far:

85 Creon my lord, my kinsman, what response
Do you bring with you from the god of
Delphi?

[*Enter* CREON.]

CREON:

Good news! Our sufferings, if they are guided
right,
Can even yet turn to a happy issue.

OEDIPUS:

This only leaves my fear and confidence
90 In equal balance: what did Phoebus say?

CREON:

Is it your wish to hear it now, in public,
Or in the palace? I am at your service.

OEDIPUS:

Let them all hear! Their sufferings distress
Me more than if my own life were at stake.

CREON:

95 Then I will tell you what Apollo said —
And it was very clear. There is pollution
Here in our midst, long-standing. This must
we
Expel, nor let it grow past remedy.

OEDIPUS:

What has defiled us? and how are we to purge
it?

CREON:

100 By banishing or killing one who murdered,
And so called down this pestilence upon us.

OEDIPUS:

Who is the man whose death the god denounces?

CREON:

Before the city passed into your care,
My lord, we had a king called Laius.

OEDIPUS:

105 So I have often heard. — I never saw him.

CREON:

His death, Apollo clearly charges us,
We must avenge upon his murderers.

OEDIPUS:

Where are they now? And where shall we
disclose
The unseen traces of that ancient crime?

CREON:

The god said, Here. — A man who hunts with
110 care
May often find what other men will miss.

OEDIPUS:

Where was he murdered? In the palace here?
Or in the country? Or was he abroad?

CREON:

He made a journey to consult the god,
115 He said — and never came back home again.

OEDIPUS:

But was there no report? no fellow traveler
Whose knowledge might have helped you in
your search?

CREON:

All died, except one terror-stricken man,
And he could tell us nothing — next to nothing.

OEDIPUS:

And what was that? One thing might lead to
much,   120
If only we could find one ray of light.

CREON:

He said they met with brigands — not with
one,
But a whole company; they killed Laius.

OEDIPUS:

A brigand would not *dare* — unless perhaps
Conspirators in Thebes had bribed the man.   125

CREON:

There *was* conjecture; but disaster came
And we were leaderless, without our king.

OEDIPUS:

Disaster? With a king cut down like that
You did not seek the cause? Where was the
hindrance?

CREON:

The Sphinx. *Her* riddle pressed us harder still;   130
For Laius — out of sight was out of mind.

OEDIPUS:

I will begin again; I'll find the truth.
The dead man's cause has found a true
defender
In Phoebus, and in you. And I will join you
In seeking vengeance on behalf of Thebes   135
And Phoebus too; indeed, I must: if I
Remove this taint, it is not for a stranger,
But for myself: the man who murdered him
Might make the same attempt on me; and so,
Avenging him, I shall protect myself. —   140
    Now you, my sons, without delay, arise,
Take up your suppliant branches. — Someone,
go
And call the people here, for I will do
What can be done; and either, by the grace
Of God we shall be saved — or we shall fall.   145

PRIEST:

My children, we will go; the King has prom-
ised
All that we came to ask. — O Phoebus, thou
Hast given us an answer: give us too
Protection! grant remission of the plague!

[*Exeunt* CREON, PRIESTS, *etc.*
OEDIPUS *remains.*]

[*Enter the* CHORUS *representing the citizens
of Thebes.*]

STROPHE 1

CHORUS:
Sweet is the voice of the god, that
[*mainly dactyls:* $\frac{4}{4}$][1]   sounds in the
Golden shrine of Delphi.
What message has it sent to Thebes? My
    trembling
Heart is torn with anguish.
5   Thou god of Healing, Phoebus Apollo,
How do I fear! What hast thou in mind
To bring upon us now? what is to be fulfilled
From days of old?
Tell me this, O Voice divine,
10 Thou child of golden Hope.

ANTISTROPHE 1

First on the Daughter of Zeus I call for
Help, divine Athene;
And Artemis, whose throne is all the earth,
    whose
Shrine is in our city;
5   Apollo too, who shoots from afar:
Trinity of Powers, come to our defence!
If ever in the past, when ruin threatened us,
You stayed its course
And turned aside the flood of Death,
10 O then, protect us now!

STROPHE 2

[*agitated:* $\frac{3}{8}$] Past counting are the woes we
    suffer;
Affliction bears on all the city, and
Nowhere is any defence against destruction.

[1] Taking a hint from the French translators for the
Budé series I have here and there added to the lyrical
portions a quasi-musical indication of tempo or mood,
on no authority except that of common sense. These
may at least serve to remind the reader, if he needs
reminding, that the lyrics were not recited; they were
a fusion of intense poetry, music, and dancing. Of the
music we know nothing; of the dance we can at least
infer that its range extended from grave processional
movements to the expression of great excitement,
whether of joy or despair. [Kitto.]

The holy soil can bring no increase,
Our women suffer and cry in childbirth   5
But do not bring forth living children.
The souls of those who perish, one by one,
Unceasingly, swift as raging fire,
Rise and take their flight to the dark realms of
    the dead.

ANTISTROPHE 2

Past counting, those of us who perish:
They lie upon the ground, unpitied,
Unburied, infecting the air with deadly pollu-
    tion.
Young wives, and grey-haired mothers with
    them,
From every quarter approach the altars   5
And cry aloud in supplication.
The prayer for healing, the loud wail of
    lament,
Together are heard in dissonance:
O thou golden Daughter of Zeus, grant thy
    aid!

STROPHE 3

[*mainly iambic:* $\frac{3}{2}$] The fierce god of War has
    laid aside
His spear; but yet his terrible cry
Rings in our ears; he spreads death and
    destruction.
Ye gods, drive him back to his distant home!
    For what the light of day has spared,   5
    That the darkness of night destroys.
Zeus our father! All power is thine:
The lightning-flash is thine: hurl upon him
Thy thunderbolt, and quell this god of War!

ANTISTROPHE 3

We pray, Lord Apollo: draw thy bow
In our defense. Thy quiver is full of
Arrows unerring: shoot! slay the destroyer!
And thou, radiant Artemis, lend thy aid!
    Thou whose hair is bound in gold,   5
Bacchus, lord of the sacred dance,
    Theban Bacchus! Come, show thyself!
Display thy blazing torch; drive from our
    midst

The savage god, abhorred by other gods!
OEDIPUS:
Would you have answer to these prayers? Then hear
10   Then hear
My words; give heed; your help may bring
Deliverance, and the end of all our troubles.
Here do I stand before you all, a stranger
Both to the deed and to the story. — What
15 Could I have done alone, without a clue?
But I was yet a foreigner; it was later
That I became a Theban among Thebans.
So now do I proclaim to all the city:
If any Theban knows by what man's hand
20 He perished, Laius, son of Labdacus,
Him I command to tell me all he can;
And if he is afraid, let him annul
Himself the charge he fears; no punishment
Shall fall on him, save only to depart
Unharmed from Thebes. Further, if any
25   knows
The slayer to be a stranger from abroad,
Let him speak out; I will reward him, and
Besides, he will have all my gratitude.
But if you still keep silent, if any man
30 Fearing for self or friend shall disobey me,
This will I do — and listen to my words:
Whoever he may be, I do forbid
All in this realm, of which I am the King
And high authority, to shelter in their houses
35 Or speak to him, or let him be their partner
In prayers or sacrifices to the gods, or give
Him lustral water; I command you all
To drive him from your doors; for he it is
That brings this plague upon us, as the god
40 Of Delphi has but now declared to me. —
So stern an ally do I make myself
Both of the god and of our murdered king. —
And for the man that slew him, whether he
Slew him alone, or with a band of helpers,
45 I lay this curse upon him, that the wretch
In wretchedness and misery may live.
And more: if with my knowledge he be found
To share my hearth and home, then upon me
Descend that doom that I invoke on him.
50 This charge I lay upon you, to observe
All my commands: to aid myself, the god,
And this our land, so spurned of Heaven, so
     ravaged.
For such a taint we should not leave un-
     purged —
The death of such a man, and he your king —
55 Even if Heaven had not commanded us,
But we should search it out. Now, since 'tis I
That wear the crown that he had worn before
     me,

And have his Queen to wife, and common
     children
Were born to us, but that his own did perish,
And sudden death has carried him away — 60
Because of this, I will defend his cause
As if it were my father's; nothing I
Will leave undone to find the man who killed
The son of Labdacus, and offspring of
Polydorus, Cadmus, and of old Agênor. 65
On those that disobey, this is my curse:
May never field of theirs give increase, nor
Their wives have children; may our present
     plagues,
And worse, be ever theirs, for their destruction.
But for the others, all with whom my words 70
Find favour, this I pray: Justice and all
The gods be ever at your side to help you.
CHORUS-LEADER:
Your curse constrains me; therefore will I
     speak.
I did not kill him, neither can I tell
Who did. It is for Phoebus, since he laid 75
The task upon us, to declare the man.
OEDIPUS:
True; but to force the gods against their will —
That is a thing beyond all human power.
CHORUS-LEADER:
All I could say is but a second best.
OEDIPUS:
Though it were third best, do not hold it back. 80
CHORUS-LEADER:
I know of none that reads Apollo's mind
So surely as the lord Teiresias;
Consulting him you best might learn the truth.
OEDIPUS:
Not even this have I neglected: Creon
Advised me, and already I have sent 85
Two messengers. — Strange he has not come.
CHORUS-LEADER:
There's nothing else but old and idle gossip.
OEDIPUS:
And what was that? I clutch at any straw.
CHORUS-LEADER:
They said that he was killed by travelers.
OEDIPUS:
So I have heard; but no one knows a witness. 90
CHORUS-LEADER:
But if he is not proof against *all* fear
He'll not keep silent when he hears your curse.
OEDIPUS:
And will they fear a curse, who dared to kill?
CHORUS-LEADER:
Here is the one to find him, for at last
They bring the prophet here. He is inspired, 95
The only man whose heart is filled with truth.

[*Enter* TEIRESIAS, *led by a boy.*]

OEDIPUS:

Teiresias, by your art you read the signs
And secrets of the earth and of the sky;
Therefore you know, although you cannot see,
100 The plague that is besetting us; from this
No other man but you, my lord, can save us.
Phoebus has said — you may have heard already —
In answer to our question, that this plague
Will never cease unless we can discover
105 What men they were who murdered Laius,
And punish them with death or banishment.
Therefore give freely all that you have learned
From birds or other form of divination;
Save us; save me, the city, and yourself,
110 From the pollution that his bloodshed causes.
No finer task, than to give all one has
In helping others; we are in your hands.

TEIRESIAS:

Ah! what a burden knowledge is, when knowledge
Can be of·no avail! I knew this well,
115 And yet forgot, or I should not have come.

OEDIPUS:

Why, what is this? Why are you so despondent?

TEIRESIAS:

Let me go home! It will be best for you,
And best for me, if you will let me go.

OEDIPUS:

But to withhold your knowledge! This is wrong,
120 Disloyal to the city of your birth.

TEIRESIAS:

I know that what you say will lead you on
To ruin; therefore, lest the same befall me
too . . .

OEDIPUS:

No, by the gods! Say all you know, for we
Go down upon our knees, your suppliants.

TEIRESIAS:

125 Because *you* do *not* know! I never shall
Reveal my burden — I will not say *yours.*

OEDIPUS:

You know, and will not tell us? Do you wish
To ruin Thebes and to destroy us all?

TEIRESIAS:

My pain, and yours, will not be caused by me.
Why these vain questions? — for I will not
130 speak.

OEDIPUS:

You villain! — for you would provoke a stone

To anger: you'll not speak, but show yourself
So hard of heart and so inflexible?

TEIRESIAS:

You heap the blame on me; but what is yours
You do not know — therefore *I* am the villain!   135

OEDIPUS:

And who would not be angry, finding that
You treat our people with such cold disdain?

TEIRESIAS:

The truth will come to light, without *my* help.

OEDIPUS:

If it is bound to come, you ought to speak it.

TEIRESIAS:

I'll say no more, and you, if so you choose,   140
May rage and bluster on without restraint.

OEDIPUS:

Restraint? Then I'll show none! I'll tell you all
That I can see in you: I do believe
This crime was planned and carried out by
you,
All but the killing; and were you not blind   145
I'd say your hand alone had done the murder.

TEIRESIAS:

So? Then I tell you this: submit yourself
To that decree that you have made; from now
Address no word to these men nor to me:
You are the man whose crimes pollute our
city.   150

OEDIPUS:

What, does your impudence extend thus far?
And do you hope that it will go scot-free?

TEIRESIAS:

It will. I have a champion — the truth.

OEDIPUS:

Who taught you that? For it was not your art.

TEIRESIAS:

No; you! You made me speak, against my will.   155

OEDIPUS:

Speak what? Say it again, and say it clearly.

TEIRESIAS:

Was I not clear? Or are you tempting me?

OEDIPUS:

Not clear enough for me. Say it again.

TEIRESIAS:

You are yourself the murderer you seek.

OEDIPUS:

You'll not affront me twice and go unpunished!   160

TEIRESIAS:

Then shall I give you still more cause for rage?

OEDIPUS:

Say what you will; you'll say it to no purpose.

TEIRESIAS:

I know, *you* do not know, the hideous life

Of shame you lead with those most near to
    you.
OEDIPUS:

165   You'll pay most dearly for this insolence!
TEIRESIAS:
No, not if Truth is strong, and can prevail.
OEDIPUS:
It is — except in you; for you are blind
In eyes and ears and brains and everything.
TEIRESIAS:
You'll not forget these insults that you throw
170   At me, when all men throw the same at you.
OEDIPUS:
You live in darkness; you can do no harm
To me or any man who has his eyes.
TEIRESIAS:
No; I am not to bring you down, because
Apollo is enough; he'll see to it.
OEDIPUS:
175   Creon, or you? Which of you made this plot?
TEIRESIAS:
Creon's no enemy of yours; you are your own.
OEDIPUS:
O Wealth! O Royalty! whose commanding art
Outstrips all other arts in life's contentions!
How great a store of envy lies upon you,
180   If for this scepter, that the city gave
Freely to me, unasked — if now my friend,
The trusty Creon, burns to drive me hence
And steal it from me! So he has suborned
This crafty schemer here, this mountebank,
Whose purse alone has eyes, whose art is
185   blind. —
Come, prophet, show your title! When the
    Sphinx
Chanted her music here, why did not *you*
Speak out and save the city? Yet such a
    question
Was one for augury, not for mother wit.
You were no prophet then; your birds, your
190   voice
From Heaven, were dumb. But I, who came
    by chance,
I, knowing nothing, put the Sphinx to flight,
Thanks to my wit — no thanks to divination!
And now you try to drive me out; you hope
195   When Creon's king to bask in Creon's favor.
You'll expiate the curse? Ay, and repent it,
Both you and your accomplice. But that you
Seem old, I'd teach you what you gain by
    treason!
CHORUS-LEADER:
My lord, he spoke in anger; so I think,
200   Did you. What help in angry speeches? Come,

This is the task, how we can best discharge
The duty that the god has laid on us.
TEIRESIAS:
King though you are, I claim the privilege
Of equal answer. No, I have the right;
I am no slave of yours— I serve Apollo,   205
And therefore am not listed *Creon's* man.
Listen — since you have taunted me with
    blindness!
You have your sight, and yet you cannot see
Where, nor with whom, you live, nor in what
    horror.
Your parents — do you know them? or that you   210
Are enemy to your kin, alive or dead?
And that a father's and a mother's curse
Shall join to drive you headlong out of Thebes
And change the light that now you see to
    darkness?
Your cries of agony, where will they not reach?   215
Where on Cithaeron will they not re-echo?
Where you have learned what meant the
    marriage-song
Which bore you to an evil haven here
After so fair a voyage? And you are blind
To other horrors, which shall make you one   220
With your own children. Therefore, heap your
    scorn
On Creon and on me, for no man living
Will meet a doom more terrible than yours.
OEDIPUS:
What? Am I to suffer words like this from
    him?
Ruin, damnation seize you! Off at once   225
Out of our sight! Go! Get you whence you
    came!
TEIRESIAS:
Had you not called me, I should not be here.
OEDIPUS:
And had I known that you would talk such
    folly,
I'd not have called you to a house of mine.
TEIRESIAS:
To you I seem a fool, but to your parents,   230
To those who did beget you, I was wise.
OEDIPUS:
Stop! Who were they? Who *were* my parents?
    Tell me!
TEIRESIAS:
This day will show your birth and your destruc-
    tion.
OEDIPUS:
You are too fond of dark obscurities.
TEIRESIAS:
But do you not excel in reading riddles?   235

OEDIPUS:
I scorn your taunts; my skill has brought me
    glory.
TEIRESIAS:
And this success brought you to ruin too.
OEDIPUS:
I am content, if so I saved this city.
TEIRESIAS:
Then I will leave you. Come, boy, take my
    hand.
OEDIPUS:
240 Yes, let him take it. You are nothing but
Vexation here. Begone, and give me peace!
TEIRESIAS:
When I have had my say. No frown of yours
Shall frighten *me*; you cannot injure me.
Here is my message: that man whom you seek
245 With threats and proclamations for the death
Of Laius, he is living here; he's thought
To be a foreigner, but shall be found
Theban by birth — and little joy will this
Bring *him*; when, with his eyesight turned to
    blindness,
250 His wealth to beggary, on foreign soil
With staff in hand he'll tap his way along,
His children with him; and he will be known
Himself to be their father and their brother,
The husband of the mother who gave him
    birth,
255 Supplanter of his father, and his slayer.
— There! Go, and think on this; and if you
    find
That I'm deceived, say then — and not be-
    fore —
That I am ignorant in divination.
    [*Exeunt severally* TEIRESIAS *and* OEDIPUS.]

STROPHE 1

CHORUS:
The voice of god rang out in the holy cavern,
Denouncing one who has killed a King — the
    crime of crimes.
    Who is the man? Let him begone in
    Headlong flight, swift as a horse!
[*anapaests*] For the terrible god, like a warrior
5   armed,
Stands ready to strike with a lightning-flash:
    The Furies who punish crime, and never
    fail,
    Are hot in their pursuit.

ANTISTROPHE 1

The snow is white on the cliffs of high
    Parnassus.
It has flashed a message: Let every Theban
    join the hunt!
    Lurking in caves among the mountains,
    Deep in the woods — where is the man?
[*anapaests*] In wearisome flight, unresting,
    alone,   5
An outlaw, he shuns Apollo's shrine;
    But ever the living menace of the god
    Hovers around his head.

STROPHE 2

[*choriambics*] Strange, disturbing, what the
    wise
Prophet has said. What can he mean?
Neither can I believe, nor can I disbelieve;
I do not know what to say.
I look here, and there; nothing can I find —   5
No strife, either now or in the past,
Between the kings of Thebes and Corinth.
A hand unknown struck down the King;
Though I would learn who it was dealt the
    blow,
That *he* is guilty whom all revere —   10
How can I believe this with no proof?

ANTISTROPHE 2

Zeus, Apollo — they have knowledge;
They understand the ways of life.
Prophets are men, like me; that they can
    understand
More than is revealed to me —
Of that, I can find nowhere certain proof,   5
Though one man is wise, another foolish.
Until the charge is manifest
I will not credit his accusers.
I saw myself how the Sphinx challenged him:
He proved his wisdom; he saved our city;   10
Therefore how can I now condemn him?

    [*Enter* CREON]

CREON:
They tell me, Sirs, that Oedipus the King
Has made against me such an accusation

That I will not endure. For if he thinks
15 That in this present trouble I have done
Or said a single thing to do him harm,
Then let me die, and not drag out my days
With such a name as that. For it is not
One injury this accusation does me;
20 It touches my whole life, if you, my friends,
And all the city are to call me traitor.
    CHORUS-LEADER:
The accusation may perhaps have come
From heat of temper, not from sober judg-
    ment.
    CREON:
What was it made him think contrivances
25 Of mine suborned the seer to tell his lies?
    CHORUS-LEADER:
Those were his words; I do not know his
    reasons.
    CREON:
Was he in earnest, master of himself,
When he attacked me with this accusation?
    CHORUS-LEADER:
I do not closely scan what kings are doing. —
30 But here he comes in person from the palace.

[*Enter* OEDIPUS.]

    OEDIPUS:
What, *you*? You dare come here? How can
    you find
The impudence to show yourself before
My house, when you are clearly proven
To have sought my life and tried to steal my
    crown?
35 Why, do you think me then a coward, or
A fool, that you should try to lay this plot?
Or that I should not see what you were
    scheming,
And so fall unresisting, blindly, to you?
But you were mad, so to attempt the throne,
40 Poor and unaided; this is not encompassed
Without the strong support of friends and
    money!
    CREON:
This you must do: now you have had your say
Hear my reply; then yourself shall judge.
    OEDIPUS:
A ready tongue! But I am bad at listening —
To you. For I have found how much you hate
45 me.
    CREON:
One thing: first listen to what I have to say.
    OEDIPUS:
One thing: do not pretend you're not a villain.

    CREON:
If you believe it is a thing worth having,
Insensate stubbornness, then you are wrong.
    OEDIPUS:
If you believe that one can harm a kinsman 50
Without retaliation, you are wrong.
    CREON:
With this I have no quarrel; but explain
What injury you say that I have done you.
    OEDIPUS:
Did you advise, or did you not, that I
Should send a man for that most reverend
    prophet? 55
    CREON:
I did, and I am still of that advice.
    OEDIPUS:
How long a time is it since Laius . . .
    CREON:
Since Laius did *what*? How can I say?
    OEDIPUS:
Was seen no more, but met a violent death?
    CREON:
It would be many years now past and gone. 60
    OEDIPUS:
And had this prophet learned his art already?
    CREON:
Yes, his repute was great — as it is now.
    OEDIPUS:
Did he make any mention then of me?
    CREON:
He never spoke of you within my hearing.
    OEDIPUS:
Touching the murder: did you make no
    search? 65
    CREON:
No search? Of course we did; but we found
    nothing.
    OEDIPUS:
And why did this wise prophet not speak *then*?
    CREON:
Who knows? Where I know nothing I say
    nothing.
    OEDIPUS:
This much you know — and you'll do well to
    answer:
    CREON:
What is it? If I know, I'll tell you freely. 70
    OEDIPUS:
That if he had not joined with you, he'd not
Have said that I was Laius' murderer.
    CREON:
If he said this, I did not know. — But I
May rightly question you, as you have me.

OEDIPUS:

Ask what you will. You'll never prove *I* killed
75   him.

CREON:

Why then: are you not married to my sister?

OEDIPUS:

I am indeed; it cannot be denied.

CREON:

You share with her the sovereignty of Thebes?

OEDIPUS:

She need but ask, and anything is hers.

CREON:

80   And am I not myself conjoined with you?

OEDIPUS:

You are; not rebel therefore, but a traitor!

CREON:

Not so, if you will reason with yourself,
As I with you. This first: would any man,
To gain no increase of authority,
Choose kingship, with its fears and sleepless
85   nights?
Not I. What I desire, what every man
Desires, if he has wisdom, is to take
The substance, not the show, of royalty.
For now, through you, I have both power and
          ease,
90   But were I king, I'd be oppressed with cares.
Not so: while I have ample sovereignty
And rule in peace, why should I want the
          crown?
I am not yet so mad as to give up
All that which brings me honor and advantage.
95   Now, every man greets me, and I greet him;
Those who have need of you make much of
          me,
Since I can make or mar them. Why should I
Surrender this to load myself with that?
A man of sense was never yet a traitor;
100   I have no taste for that, nor could I force
Myself to aid another's treachery.
     But you can test me: go to Delphi; ask
If I reported rightly what was said.
And further: if you find that I had dealings
105   With that diviner, you may take and kill me
Not with your single vote, but yours and mine,
But not on bare suspicion, unsupported.
How wrong it is, to use a random judgment
And think the false man true, the true man
          false!
110   To spurn a loyal friend, that is no better
Than to destroy the life to which we cling.
This you will learn in time, for Time alone
Reveals the upright man; a single day
Suffices to unmask the treacherous.

CHORUS-LEADER:

My lord, he speaks with caution, to avoid   115
Grave error. Hasty judgment is not sure.

OEDIPUS:

But when an enemy is quick to plot
And strike, I must be quick in answer too.
If I am slow, and wait, then I shall find
That he has gained his end, and I am lost.   120

CREON:

What do you wish? To drive me into exile?

OEDIPUS:

No, more than exile: I will have your life.[2]

CREON:

<When will it cease, this monstrous rage of
     yours?>

OEDIPUS:

When your example shows what comes of
     envy.

CREON:

Must you be stubborn? Cannot you believe
     me?   125

OEDIPUS:

<You speak to me as if I were a fool!>

CREON:

Because I know you're wrong.

                              Right, for myself!

OEDIPUS:
CREON:

It is not right for me!

                         But you're a traitor.

OEDIPUS:
CREON:

What if your charge is false?

                               I have to govern.

OEDIPUS:
CREON:

Not govern badly!

---

[2] The next two verses, as they stand in the mss., are
impossible. Editors are agreed on this, though no
single remedy has found general acceptance. The mss.
attribute v. 624 [Oedipus' next speech] to Creon, and
v. 625 [Creon's next speech] to Oedipus. I can make
no real sense of this: the only φθόνος, "envy," that is
in question is the envy of his royal power that
Oedipus is attributing to Creon; and the words
ὑπείξων, "yield," "not to be stubborn," and πιστεύσων,
"believe," must surely be used by Creon of Oedipus,
not by Oedipus of Creon. Since a translator who
hopes to be acted must give the actors something to
say, preferably good sense, and cannot fob them off
with a row of dots, I have reconstructed the passage
by guesswork, putting my guesses within brackets. I
have assumed that two verses were lost, one after v.
623 and one after v. 625, and that the wrong attribu-
tion of vv. 624 and 625 followed almost inevitably.
[Kitto.]

130 OEDIPUS: Listen to him, Thebes!
CREON:
You're not the city! I am Theban too.
CHORUS-LEADER:
My lords, no more! Here comes the Queen,
and not
Too soon, to join you. With her help, you
must
Compose the bitter strife that now divides
you.

[*Enter* IOCASTA.]

IOCASTA:
135 You frantic men! What has aroused this wild
Dispute? Have you no shame, when such a
plague
Afflicts us, to indulge in private quarrels?
Creon, go home, I pray. You, Oedipus,
Come in; do not make much of what is
nothing.
CREON:
140 My sister: Oedipus, your husband here,
Has thought it right to punish me with one
Of two most awful dooms: exile, or death.
OEDIPUS:
I have: I have convicted him, Iocasta,
Of plotting secretly against my life.
CREON:
145 If I am guilty in a single point
Of such a crime, then may I die accursed.
IOCASTA:
O, by the gods, believe him, Oedipus!
Respect the oath that he has sworn, and have
Regard for me, and for these citizens.

[*In what follows, the parts given to the
chorus are sung, the rest, presumably, spoken. The rhythm of the music and dance is
either dochmiac, 5-time, or a combination of
3- and 5-time.*]

STROPHE

CHORUS:
My lord, I pray, give consent.
Yield to us; ponder well.
OEDIPUS:
What is it you would have me yield?
CHORUS:
Respect a man ripe in years,
5 Bound by this mighty oath he has sworn.
OEDIPUS:
Your wish is clear?

CHORUS: It is.
OEDIPUS: Then tell it me.
CHORUS:
Not to repel, and drive out of our midst a
friend,
Scorning a solemn curse, for uncertain cause.
OEDIPUS:
I tell you this: your prayer will mean for me
My banishment from Thebes, or else my
death.   10
CHORUS:
No, no! by the Sun, the chief of gods,
Ruin and desolation and all evil come upon
me
If I harbor thoughts such as these!
No; our land racked with plague breaks my
heart.
Do not now deal a new wound on Thebes
to crown the old!   15
OEDIPUS:
Then let him be, though I must die twice
over,
Or be dishonored, spurned and driven out.
It's your entreaty, and not his, that moves
My pity; he shall have my lasting hatred.
CREON:
You yield ungenerously; but when your wrath 20
Has cooled, how it will prick you! Natures
such
As yours give most vexation to themselves.
OEDIPUS:
O, let me be! Get from my sight.
CREON: I go,
Misjudged by you — but these will judge me
better [*indicating* CHORUS].
                                    [*Exit* CREON.]

ANTISTROPHE

CHORUS:
My lady, why now delay?
Let the King go in with you.
IOCASTA:
When you have told me what has passed.
CHORUS:
Suspicion came. — Random words, undeserved,
Will provoke men to wrath.   5
IOCASTA:
It was from both?
CHORUS: It was.
IOCASTA: And what was said?

CHORUS:
It is enough for me, more than enough, when I
Think of our ills, that this should rest where it
    lies.
OEDIPUS:
You and your wise advice, blunting my wrath,
10 Frustrated me — and it has come to this!
CHORUS:
This, O my King, I said, and say again:
I should be mad, distraught,
I should be a fool, and worse,
If I sought to drive you away.
15 Thebes was near sinking; you brought her safe
Through the storm. Now again we pray that
    you may save us.
IOCASTA:
In Heaven's name, my lord, I too must know
What was the reason for this blazing anger.
OEDIPUS:
There's none to whom I more defer; and so,
20 I'll tell you: Creon and his vile plot against me.
IOCASTA:
What has he done, that you are so incensed?
OEDIPUS:
He says that I am Laius' murderer.
IOCASTA:
From his own knowledge? Or has someone
    told him?
OEDIPUS:
No; that suspicion should not fall upon
25 Himself, he used a tool — a crafty prophet.
IOCASTA:
Why, have no fear of *that*. Listen to me,
And you will learn that the prophetic art
Touches our human fortunes not at all.
I soon can give you proof. — An oracle
30 Once came to Laius — from the god himself
I do not say, but from his ministers:
His fate it was, that should he have a son
By me, that son would take his father's life.
But he was killed — or so they said — by
    strangers,
35 By brigands, at a place where three ways meet.
As for the child, it was not three days old
When Laius fastened both its feet together
And had it cast over a precipice.
Therefore Apollo failed; for neither did
40 His son kill Laius, nor did Laius meet
The awful end he feared, killed by his son.
    So much for what prophetic voices uttered.
Have no regard for them. The god will bring
To light himself whatever thing he chooses.
OEDIPUS:
45 Iocasta, terror seizes me, and shakes
My very soul, at one thing you have said.

IOCASTA:
Why so? What have I said to frighten you?
OEDIPUS:
I think I heard you say that Laius
Was murdered at a place where three ways
    meet?
IOCASTA:
So it was said — indeed, they say it still.   50
OEDIPUS:
Where is the place where this encounter
    happened?
IOCASTA:
They call the country Phokis, and a road
From Delphi joins a road from Daulia.
OEDIPUS:
Since that was done, how many years have
    passed?
IOCASTA:
It was proclaimed in Thebes a little time   55
Before the city offered you the crown.
OEDIPUS:
O Zeus, what fate hast thou ordained for me?
IOCASTA:
What is the fear that so oppresses you?
OEDIPUS:
One moment yet: tell me of Laius.
What age was he? and what was his appear-
    ance?   60
IOCASTA:
A tall man, and his hair was touched with
    white;
In figure he was not unlike yourself.
OEDIPUS:
O God! Did I, then, in my ignorance,
Proclaim that awful curse against myself?
IOCASTA:
What are you saying? How you frighten me!   65
OEDIPUS:
I greatly fear that prophet was not blind.
But yet one question; that will show me more.
IOCASTA:
For all my fear, I'll tell you what I can.
OEDIPUS:
Was he alone, or did he have with him
A royal bodyguard of men-at-arms?   70
IOCASTA:
The company in all were five; the King
Rode in a carriage, and there was a Herald.
OEDIPUS:
Ah God! How clear the picture is! ... But who,
Iocasta, brought report of this to Thebes?
IOCASTA:
A slave, the only man that was not killed.   75
OEDIPUS:
And is he round about the palace now?

IOCASTA:

No, he is not. When he returned, and saw
You ruling in the place of the dead King,
He begged me, on his bended knees, to send
him
80 Into the hills as shepherd, out of sight,
As far as could be from the city here.
I sent him, for he was a loyal slave;
He well deserved this favor — and much more.

OEDIPUS:

Could he be brought back here — at once — to
see me?

IOCASTA:

85 He could; but why do you desire his coming?

OEDIPUS:

I fear I have already said, Iocasta,
More than enough; and therefore I will see
him.

IOCASTA:

Then he shall come. But, as your wife, I ask
you,
What is the terror that possesses you?

OEDIPUS:

And you shall know it, since my fears have
90 grown
So great; for who is more to me than you,
That I should speak to *him* at such a moment?
My father, then, was Polybus of Corinth;
My mother, Meropê. My station there
95 Was high as any man's — until a thing
Befell me that was strange indeed, though not
Deserving of the thought I gave to it.
A man said at a banquet — he was full
Of wine — that I was not my father's son.
100 It angered me; but I restrained myself
That day. The next I went and questioned
both
My parents. They were much incensed with
him
Who had let fall the insult. So, from them,
I had assurance. Yet the slander spread
105 And always chafed me. Therefore secretly,
My mother and my father unaware,
I went to Delphi. Phoebus would return
No answer to my question, but declared
A thing most horrible: he foretold that I
110 Should mate with my own mother, and beget
A brood that men would shudder to behold,
And that I was to be the murderer
Of my own father.
                    Therefore, back to Corinth
I never went — the stars alone have told me
115 Where Corinth lies — that I might never see
Cruel fulfillment of that oracle.
So journeying, I came to that same spot

Where, as you say, this King was killed. And
now,
This is the truth, Iocasta: when I reached
The place where three ways meet, I met a
herald,   120
And in a carriage drawn by colts was such
A man as you describe. By violence
The herald and the older man attempted
To push me off the road, I, in my rage,
Struck at the driver, who was hustling me.   125
The old man, when he saw me level with him,
Taking a double-goad, aimed at my head
A murderous blow. He paid for that, full
measure.
Swiftly I hit him with my staff; he rolled
Out of his carriage, flat upon his back.   130
I killed them all. — But if, between this
stranger
And Laius there was any bond of kinship,
Who could be in more desperate plight than I?
Who more accursèd in the eyes of Heaven?
For neither citizen nor stranger may   135
Receive me in his house, nor speak to me,
But he must bar the door. And it was none
But I invoked this curse on my own head!
And I pollute the bed of him I slew
With my own hands! Say, am I vile? Am I   140
Not all impure? Seeing I must be exiled,
And even in my exile must not go
And see my parents, nor set foot upon
My native land; or, if I do, I must
Marry my mother, and kill Polybus   145
My father, who engendered me and reared me.
If one should say it was a cruel god
Brought this upon me, would he not speak
right?
No, no, you holy powers above! Let me
Not see that day! but rather let me pass   150
Beyond the sight of men, before I see
The stain of such pollution come upon me!

CHORUS-LEADER:

My lord, this frightens me. But you must
hope,
Until we hear the tale from him that saw it.

OEDIPUS:

That is the only hope that's left to me;   155
We must await the coming of the shepherd.

IOCASTA:

What do you hope from him, when he is
here?

OEDIPUS:

I'll tell you: if his story shall be found
The same as yours, then I am free of guilt.

IOCASTA:

But what have *I* said of especial note?   160

OEDIPUS:
You said that he reported it was brigands
Who killed the King. If he still speaks of
    "men,"
It was not I; a single man, and "men,"
Are not the same. But if he says it was
165 A traveler journeying alone, why then,
The burden of the guilt must fall on me.
    IOCASTA:
But that *is* what he said, I do assure you!
He cannot take it back again! Not I
Alone, but the whole city heard him say it!
170 But even if he should revoke the tale
He told before, not even so, my lord,
Will he establish that the King was slain
According to the prophecy. For that was clear:
His son, and mine, should slay him. — He,
    poor thing,
175 Was killed himself, and never killed his father.
Therefore, so far as divination goes,
Or prophecy, I'll take no notice of it.
    OEDIPUS:
And that is wise. — But send a man to bring
The shepherd; I would not have that ne-
    glected.
    IOCASTA:
180 I'll send at once. — But come with me; for I
Would not do anything that could displease
    you.
        [*Exeunt* OEDIPUS *and* IOCASTA.]

STROPHE 1

CHORUS:
I pray that I may pass my life
[*in a steady rhythm*] In reverent holiness of
    word and deed.
For there are laws enthroned above;
Heaven created them,
5 Olympus was their father,
And mortal men had no part in their birth;
Nor ever shall their power pass from sight
In dull forgetfulness;
A god moves in them; he grows not old.

ANTISTROPHE 1

Pride makes the tyrant — pride of wealth
And power, too great for wisdom and restraint;
For Pride will climb the topmost height;
Then is the man cast down
5 To uttermost destruction.

There he finds no escape, no resource.
But high contention for the city's good
May the gods preserve.
For me — may the gods be my defense!

STROPHE 2

If there is one who walks in pride
Of word or deed, and has no fear of Justice,
No reverence for holy shrines —
May utter ruin fall on him!
So may his ill-starred pride be given its reward. 5
Those who seek dishonorable advantage
And lay violent hands on holy things
And do not shun impiety —
Who among these will secure himself from the
    wrath of God?
If deeds like these are honored, 10
Why should I join in the sacred dance?

ANTISTROPHE 2

No longer shall Apollo's shrine,
The holy center of the Earth, receive my
    worship;
No, nor his seat at Abae, nor
The temple of Olympian Zeus,
If what the god foretold does not come to
    pass. 5
Mighty Zeus — if so I should address Thee —
O great Ruler of all things, look on this!
Now are thy oracles falling into contempt, and
    men
Deny Apollo's power.
Worship of the gods is passing away. 10

    [*Enter* IOCASTA, *attended by a girl carrying a
    wreath and incense.*]

IOCASTA:
My lords of Thebes, I have bethought myself
To approach the altars of the gods, and lay
These wreaths on them, and burn this frankin-
    cense.
For every kind of terror has laid hold
On Oedipus; his judgment is distracted. 15
He will not read the future by the past
But yields himself to any who speaks fear.
Since then no words of mine suffice to calm
    him
I turn to Thee Apollo — Thou art nearest —
Thy suppliant, with these votive offerings. 20
Grant us deliverance and peace, for now

Fear is on all, when we see Oedipus,
The helmsman of the ship, so terrified.

[*A reverent silence, while* IOCASTA *lays the wreath at the altar and sets fire to the incense. The wreath will remain and the incense smoke during the rest of the play.*]
[*Enter a* SHEPHERD *from Corinth.*]

CORINTHIAN:
Might I inquire of you where I may find
25 The royal palace of King Oedipus?
Or, better, where himself is to be found?
CHORUS-LEADER:
There is the palace; himself, Sir, is within,
But here his wife and mother of his children.
CORINTHIAN:
Ever may happiness attend on her,
30 And hers, the wedded wife of such a man.
IOCASTA:
May you enjoy the same; your gentle words
Deserve no less. — Now, Sir, declare your purpose;
With what request, what message have you come?
CORINTHIAN:
With good news for your husband and his house.
IOCASTA:
What news is this? And who has sent you
35 here?
CORINTHIAN:
I come from Corinth, and the news I bring
Will give you joy, though joy be crossed with grief.
IOCASTA:
What is this, with its two-fold influence?
CORINTHIAN:
The common talk in Corinth is that they
40 Will call on Oedipus to be their king.
IOCASTA:
What? Does old Polybus no longer reign?
CORINTHIAN:
Not now, for Death has laid him in his grave.
IOCASTA:
Go quickly to your master, girl; give him
The news. — You oracles, where are you now?
45 This is the man whom Oedipus so long
Has shunned, fearing to kill him; now he's dead,
And killed by Fortune, not by Oedipus.

[*Enter* OEDIPUS, *very nervous.*]

OEDIPUS:
My dear Iocasta, tell me, my dear wife,
Why have you sent to fetch me from the palace?
IOCASTA:
Listen to *him*, and as you hear, reflect   50
What has become of all those oracles.
OEDIPUS:
Who is this man? — What has he to tell me?
IOCASTA:
He is from Corinth, and he brings you news
About your father. Polybus is dead.
OEDIPUS:
What say you, sir? Tell me the news yourself.   55
CORINTHIAN:
If you would have me first report on this,
I tell you; death has carried him away.
OEDIPUS:
By treachery? Or did sickness come to him?
CORINTHIAN:
A small mischance will lay an old man low.
OEDIPUS:
Poor Polybus! He died, then, of a sickness?   60
CORINTHIAN:
That, and the measure of his many years.
OEDIPUS:
Ah me! Why then, Iocasta, should a man
Regard the Pythian house of oracles,
Or screaming birds, on whose authority
I was to slay my father? But he is dead;   65
The earth has covered him; and here am I,
My sword undrawn — unless perchance *my* loss
Has killed him; so might I be called his slayer.
But for those oracles about my father,
Those he has taken with him to the grave   70
Wherein he lies, and they are come to nothing.
IOCASTA:
Did I not say long since it would be so?
OEDIPUS:
You did; but I was led astray by fear.
IOCASTA:
So none of this deserves another thought.
OEDIPUS:
Yet how can I not fear my mother's bed?   75
IOCASTA:
Why should we fear, seeing that man is ruled
By chance, and there is room for no clear forethought?
No; live at random, live as best one can.
So do not fear this marriage with your mother;
Many a man has suffered this before —   80
But only in his dreams. Whoever thinks
The least of this, he lives most comfortably.
OEDIPUS:
Your every word I do accept, if she

That bore me did not live; but as she does —
85 Despite your wisdom, how can I but tremble?
    IOCASTA:
Yet there is comfort in your father's death.
    OEDIPUS:
Great comfort, but still fear of her who lives.
    CORINTHIAN:
And who is this who makes you so afraid?
    OEDIPUS:
Meropê, my man, the wife of Polybus.
    CORINTHIAN:
90 And what in *her* gives cause of fear in *you*?
    OEDIPUS:
There was an awful warning from the gods.
    CORINTHIAN:
Can it be told, or must it be kept secret?
    OEDIPUS:
No secret. Once Apollo said that I
Was doomed to lie with my own mother, and
95 Defile my own hands with my father's blood.
Wherefore has Corinth been, these many years,
My home no more. My fortunes have been
    fair. —
But it is good to see a parent's face.
    CORINTHIAN:
It was for fear of *this* you fled the city?
    OEDIPUS:
100 This, and the shedding of my father's blood.
    CORINTHIAN:
Why then, my lord, since I am come in
    friendship,
I'll rid you here and now of that misgiving.
    OEDIPUS:
Be sure, your recompense would be in keeping.
    CORINTHIAN:
It was the chief cause of my coming here
That your return might bring me some advan-
105   tage.
    OEDIPUS:
Back to my parents I will never go.
    CORINTHIAN:
My son, it is clear, you know not what you
    do. . . .
    OEDIPUS:
Not know? What is this? Tell me what you
    mean.
    CORINTHIAN:
If for this reason you avoid your home.
    OEDIPUS:
110 Fearing Apollo's oracle may come true.
    CORINTHIAN:
And you incur pollution from your parents?
    OEDIPUS:
That is the thought that makes me live in
    terror.

    CORINTHIAN:
I tell you then, this fear of yours is idle.
    OEDIPUS:
How? Am I not their child, and they my
    parents?
    CORINTHIAN:
Because there's none of Polybus in you.   115
    OEDIPUS:
How can you say so? Was he not my father?
    CORINTHIAN:
I am your father just as much as he!
    OEDIPUS:
A stranger equal to the father? How?
    CORINTHIAN:
Neither did he beget you, nor did I.
    OEDIPUS:
Then for what reason did he call me son?   120
    CORINTHIAN:
He had you as a gift — from my own hands.
    OEDIPUS:
And showed such love to me? Me, not his
    own?
    CORINTHIAN:
Yes, his own childlessness so worked on him.
    OEDIPUS:
You, when you gave me: had you bought, or
    found me?
    CORINTHIAN:
I found you in the woods upon Cithaeron.   125
    OEDIPUS:
Why were you traveling in that neighborhood?
    CORINTHIAN:
I tended flocks of sheep upon the mountain.
    OEDIPUS:
You were a shepherd, then, wandering for hire?
    CORINTHIAN:
I was, my son; but that day, your preserver.
    OEDIPUS:
How so? What ailed me when you took me
    up?   130
    CORINTHIAN:
For that, your ankles might give evidence.
    OEDIPUS:
Alas! why speak of this, my life-long trouble?
    CORINTHIAN:
I loosed the fetters clamped upon your feet.
    OEDIPUS:
A pretty gift to carry from the cradle!
    CORINTHIAN:
It was for this they named you Oedipus.   135
    OEDIPUS:
Who did, my father or my mother? Tell me.
    CORINTHIAN:
I cannot; he knows more, from whom I had
    you.

OEDIPUS:
It was another, not yourself, that found me?
CORINTHIAN:
Yes, you were given me by another shepherd.
OEDIPUS:
Who? Do you know him? Can you name the
140 man?
CORINTHIAN:
They said that he belonged to Laius.
OEDIPUS:
What — him who once was ruler here in
Thebes?
CORINTHIAN:
Yes, he it was for whom this man was
shepherd.
OEDIPUS:
And is he still alive, that I can see him?
CORINTHIAN [turning to the CHORUS]:
145 You that are native here would know that best.
OEDIPUS:
Has any man of you now present here
Acquaintance with this shepherd, him he
speaks of?
Has any seen him, here, or in the fields?
Speak; on this moment hangs discovery.
CHORUS-LEADER:
150 It is, I think, the man that you have sent for,
The slave now in the country. But who should
know
The truth of this more than Iocasta here?
OEDIPUS:
The man he speaks of: do you think, Iocasta,
He is the one I have already summoned?
IOCASTA:
155 What matters who he is? Pay no regard. —
The tale is idle; it is best forgotten.
OEDIPUS:
It cannot be that I should have this clue
And then not find the secret of my birth.
IOCASTA:
In God's name stop, if you have any thought
160 For your own life! My ruin is enough.
OEDIPUS:
Be not dismayed; nothing can prove you base.
Not though I find my mother thrice a slave.
IOCASTA:
O, I beseech you, do not! Seek no more!
OEDIPUS:
You cannot move me. I will know the truth.
IOCASTA:
165 I know that what I say is for the best.
OEDIPUS:
This "best" of yours! I have no patience with it.
IOCASTA:
O may you never learn what man you are!

OEDIPUS:
Go, someone, bring the herdsman here to me,
And leave her to enjoy her pride of birth.
IOCASTA:
O man of doom! For by no other name 170
Can I address you now or evermore.
[Exit IOCASTA.]
CHORUS-LEADER:
The Queen has fled, my lord, as if before
Some driving storm of grief. I fear that from
Her silence may break forth some great disas-
ter.
OEDIPUS:
Break forth what will! My birth, however
humble, 175
I am resolved to find. But she, perhaps,
Is proud, as women will be; is ashamed
Of my low birth. But I do rate myself
The child of Fortune, giver of all good,
And I shall not be put to shame, for I 180
Am born of Her; the Years who are my
kinsmen
Distinguished my estate, now high, now low;
So born, I could not make me someone else
And not do all to find my parentage.

STROPHE 1

CHORUS:
If I have power of prophecy,
[animated rhythm] If I have judgment wise
and sure, Cithaeron
(I swear by Olympus),
Thou shalt be honored when the moon
Next is full, as mother and foster-nurse 5
And birth-place of Oedipus, with festival and
dancing,
For thou hast given great blessings to our
King.
To Thee, Apollo, now we raise our cry:
O grant our prayer find favor in thy sight!

ANTISTROPHE

Who is thy mother, O my son?
Is she an ageless nymph among the mountains,
That bore thee to Pan?
Or did Apollo father thee?
For dear to him are the pastures in the hills. 5
Or Hermes, who ruleth from the summit of
Kyllene?

Or Dionysus on the mountain-tops,
Did he receive thee from thy mother's arms,
A nymph who follows him on Helicon?
OEDIPUS:
10 If I, who never yet have met the man,
May risk conjecture, I think I see the herds-
    man
Whom we have long been seeking. In his age
He well accords; and more, I recognize
Those who are with him as of my own
    household.
15 But as for knowing, you will have advantage
Of me, if you have seen the man before.
CHORUS-LEADER:
'Tis he, for certain — one of Laius' men,
One of the shepherds whom he trusted most.

[Enter the THEBAN SHEPHERD.]

OEDIPUS:
You first I ask, you who have come from
    Corinth:
Is that the man you mean?
20 CORINTHIAN: That very man.
OEDIPUS:
Come here, my man; look at me; answer me
My questions. Were you ever Laius' man?
THEBAN:
I was; his slave — born in the house, not
    bought.
OEDIPUS:
What was your charge, or what your way of
    life?
THEBAN:
25 Tending the sheep, the most part of my life.
OEDIPUS:
And to what regions did you most resort?
THEBAN:
Now it was Cithaeron, now the country round.
OEDIPUS:
And was this man of your acquaintance there?
THEBAN:
In what employment? Which is the man you
    mean?
OEDIPUS:
30 Him yonder. Had you any dealings with him?
THEBAN:
Not such that I can quickly call to mind.
CORINTHIAN:
No wonder, Sir, but though he has forgotten
I can remind him. I am very sure,
He knows the time when, round about Cithae-
    ron,
35 He with a double flock, and I with one,
We spent together three whole summer sea-
    sons,

From spring until the rising of Arcturus.
Then, with the coming on of winter, I
Drove my flocks home, he his, to Laius' folds.
Is this the truth? or am I telling lies?   40
THEBAN:
It is true, although it happened long ago.
CORINTHIAN:
Then tell me: do you recollect a baby
You gave me once to bring up for my own?
THEBAN:
Why this? Why are you asking me this
    question?
CORINTHIAN:
My friend, here is the man who was that baby! 45
THEBAN:
O, devil take you! Cannot you keep silent?
OEDIPUS:
Here, Sir! This man needs no reproof from you.
Your tongue needs chastisement much more
    than his.
THEBAN:
O best of masters, how am I offending?
OEDIPUS:
Not telling of the child of whom he speaks.   50
THEBAN:
He? He knows nothing. He is wasting time.
OEDIPUS [threatening]:
If you'll not speak from pleasure, speak from
    pain.
THEBAN:
No, no, I pray! Not torture an old man!
OEDIPUS:
Here, someone quickly! Twist this fellow's
    arms!
THEBAN:
Why, wretched man? What would you know
    besides?   55
OEDIPUS:
That child: you gave it him, the one he speaks
    of?
THEBAN:
I did. Ah God, would I have died instead!
OEDIPUS:
And die you shall, unless you speak the truth.
THEBAN:
And if I do, then death is still more certain.
OEDIPUS:
This man, I think, is trying to delay me.   60
THEBAN:
Not I! I said I gave the child — just now.
OEDIPUS:
And got it — where? Your own? or someone
    else's?
THEBAN:
No, not my own. Someone had given it me.

OEDIPUS:
Who? Which of these our citizens? From
    what house?
THEBAN:
65 No, I implore you, master! Do not ask!
OEDIPUS:
You die if I must question you again.
THEBAN:
Then, 'twas a child of one in Laius' house.
OEDIPUS:
You mean a slave? Or someone of his kin?
THEBAN:
God! I am on the verge of saying it.
OEDIPUS:
70 And I of hearing it, but hear I must.
THEBAN:
His own, or so they said. But she within
Could tell you best — your wife — the truth of
    it.
OEDIPUS:
What, did she give you it?
THEBAN: She did, my lord.
OEDIPUS:
With what intention?
THEBAN: That I should destroy it.
OEDIPUS:
Her own? — How could she?
75 THEBAN: Frightened by oracles.
OEDIPUS:
What oracles?
THEBAN: That it would kill its parents.
OEDIPUS:
Why did you let it go to this man here?
THEBAN:
I pitied it, my lord. I thought to send
The child abroad, whence this man came. And
    he
80 Saved it, for utter doom. For if you are
The man he says, then you were born for ruin.
OEDIPUS:
Ah God! Ah God! This is the truth, at last!
O Sun, let me behold thee this once more,
I who am proved accursed in my conception,
85 And in my marriage, and in him I slew.
          [*Exeunt severally* OEDIPUS,
           CORINTHIAN, THEBAN.]

STROPHE 1

CHORUS:
Alas! you generations of men!
[*glyconics*] Even while you live you are next to
    nothing!
Has any man won for himself

More than the shadow of happiness,
A shadow that swiftly fades away?   5
Oedipus, now as I look on you,
See your ruin, how can I say that
Mortal man can be happy?

ANTISTROPHE 1

For who won greater prosperity?
Sovereignty and wealth beyond all desiring?
The crooked-clawed, riddling Sphinx,
Maiden and bird, you overcame;
You stood like a tower of strength to Thebes.   5
So you received our crown, received the
Highest honors that we could give —
King in our mighty city.

STROPHE 2

Who more wretched, more afflicted now,
With cruel misery, with fell disaster,
Your life in dust and ashes?
  O noble Oedipus!
  How could it be? to come again   5
A bridegroom of her who gave you birth!
How could such a monstrous thing
Endure so long, unknown?

ANTISTROPHE 2

Time sees all, and Time, in your despite,
Disclosed and punished your unnatural mar-
    riage —
A child, and then a husband.
  O son of Laius,
  Would I had never looked on you!   5
I mourn you as one who mourns the dead.
First you gave me back my life,
And now, that life is death.

[*Enter, from the palace, a* MESSENGER.]

MESSENGER:
My Lords, most honored citizens of Thebes,
What deeds am I to tell of, you to see!   10
What heavy grief to bear, if still remains
Your native loyalty to our line of kings.
For not the Ister, no, nor Phasis' flood.
Could purify this house, such things it hides,
Such others will it soon display to all,   15

Evils self-sought. Of all our sufferings
Those hurt the most that we ourselves inflict.
CHORUS-LEADER:
Sorrow enough — too much — in what was
    known
Already. What new sorrow do you bring?
MESSENGER:
20 Quickest for me to say and you to hear:
It is the Queen, Iocasta — she is dead.
CHORUS-LEADER:
Iocasta, dead? But how? What was the cause?
MESSENGER:
By her own hand. Of what has passed, the
    worst
Cannot be yours: that was, to see it.
25 But you shall hear, so far as memory serves,
The cruel story. — In her agony
She ran across the courtyard, snatching at
Her hair with both her hands. She made her
    way
Straight to her chamber; she barred fast the
    doors
30 And called on Laius, these long years dead,
Remembering their by-gone procreation.
"Through this did you meet death yourself,
    and leave
To me, the mother, child-bearing accursed
To my own child." She cried aloud upon
35 The bed where she had borne a double brood,
Husband from husband, children from a child.
And thereupon she died, I know not how;
For, groaning, Oedipus burst in, and we,
For watching him, saw not *her* agony
And how it ended. He, ranging through the
40   palace,
Came up to each man calling for a sword,
Calling for her whom he had called his wife,
Asking where was she who had borne them all,
Himself and his own children. So he raved.
45 And then some deity showed him the way,
For it was none of us that stood around;
He cried aloud, as if to someone who
Was leading him; he leapt upon the doors,
Burst from their sockets the yielding bars, and
    fell
50 Into the room; and there, hanged by the neck,
We saw his wife, held in a swinging cord.
He, when he saw it, groaned in misery
And loosed her body from the rope. When
    now
She lay upon the ground, awful to see
Was that which followed: from her dress he
    tore
55 The golden brooches that she had been wearing,

Raised them, and with their points struck his
    own eyes,
Crying aloud that they should never see
What he had suffered and what he had done,
But in the dark henceforth they should behold   60
Those whom they ought not; nor should
    recognize
Those whom he longed to see. To such refrain
He smote his eyeballs with the pins, not once,
Nor twice; and as he smote them, blood ran
    down
His face, not dripping slowly, but there fell   65
Showers of black rain and blood-red hail
    together.
    Not on his head alone, but on them both,
Husband and wife, this common storm has
    broken.
Their ancient happiness of early days
Was happiness indeed; but now, today,   70
Death, ruin, lamentation, shame — of all
The ills there are, not one is wanting here.
CHORUS-LEADER:
Now is there intermission in his agony?
MESSENGER:
He shouts for someone to unbar the gates,
And to display to Thebes the parricide,   75
His mother's — no, I cannot speak the words;
For, by the doom he uttered, he will cast
Himself beyond our borders, not remain
To be a curse at home. But he needs strength,
And one to guide him; for these wounds are
    greater   80
Than he can bear — as you shall see; for look!
They draw the bolts. A sight you will behold
To move the pity even of an enemy.

[*The doors open.* OEDIPUS *slowly advances.*]

CHORUS:
O horrible, dreadful sight. More dreadful far

[*These verses sung or chanted in a slow
march-time.*]

Than any I have yet seen. What cruel frenzy   85
Came over you? What spirit with superhuman
    leap
Came to assist your grim destiny?
Ah, most unhappy man!
But no! I cannot bear even to look at you,
Though there is much that I would ask and
    see and hear.   90
But I shudder at the very sight of you.
OEDIPUS [*sings in the dochmiac rhythm*]:
Alas! alas! and woe for my misery!
Where are my steps taking me?

My random voice is lost in the air.
95 O God! how hast thou crushed me!
    CHORUS-LEADER [*spoken*]:
Too terribly for us to hear or see.
    OEDIPUS [*sings*]:
O cloud of darkness abominable,
My enemy unspeakable,
In cruel onset insuperable.
100 Alas! alas! Assailed at once by pain
Of pin-points and of memory of crimes.
    CHORUS-LEADER:
In such tormenting pains you well may cry
A double grief and feel a double woe.
    OEDIPUS [*sings*]:
Ah, my friend!
105 Still at my side? Still steadfast?
Still can you endure me?
Still care for me, a blind man?
[*Speaks.*] For it is you, my friend; I know 'tis
    you;
Though all is darkness, yet I know your voice.
    CHORUS-LEADER:
110 O, to destroy your sight! How could you bring
Yourself to do it? What god incited you?
    OEDIPUS [*sings*]:
It was Apollo, friends, Apollo.
He decreed that I should suffer what I suffer;
But the hand that struck, alas! was my own,
115 And not another's.
For why should I have sight.
When sight of nothing could give me plea-
    sure?
    CHORUS:
It was even as you say.
    OEDIPUS:
What have I left, my friends, to see,
120 To cherish, whom to speak with, or
To listen to, with joy?
Lead me away at once, far from Thebes;
Lead me away, my friends!
I have destroyed; I am accursed, and, what is
    more,
125 Hateful to Heaven, as no other.
    CHORUS-LEADER [*speaks*]:
Unhappy your intention, and unhappy
Your fate. O would that I had never known
    you!
    OEDIPUS [*sings*]:
Curses on him, whoever he was,
Who took the savage fetters from my feet,
130   Snatched me from death, and saved me.
    No thanks I owe him,
    For had I died that day
Less ruin had I brought on me and mine.

    CHORUS:
That wish is my wish too.
    OEDIPUS:
I had not then come and slain my father.   135
    Nor then would men have called me
    Husband of her that bore me.
Now am I God's enemy, child of the guilty,
And she that bore me has borne too my
    children;
And if there is evil surpassing evil,   140
    That has come to Oedipus.
    CHORUS-LEADER:
How can I say that you have counseled well?
Far better to be dead than to be blind.
    OEDIPUS:
That what is done was not done for the best
Seek not to teach me: counsel me no more.   145
I know not how I could have gone to Hades
And with these eyes have looked upon my
    father
Or on my mother; such things have I done
To them, death is no worthy punishment.
Or could I look for pleasure in the sight   150
Of my own children, born as they were born?
Never! No pleasure there, for eyes of mine,
Nor in this city, nor its battlements
Nor sacred images. From these — ah, misera-
    ble! —
I, the most nobly born of any Theban   155
Am banned for ever by my own decree
That the defiler should be driven forth,
The man accursed of Heaven and Laius' house.
Was I to find such taint in me, and then
With level eyes to look *them* in the face?   160
Nay more: if for my ears I could have built
Some dam to stay the flood of sound, that I
Might lose both sight and hearing, and seal up
My wretched body — that I would have done.
How good to dwell beyond the reach of pain!   165
    Cithaeron! Why did you accept me? Why
Did you not take and kill me? Never then
Should I have come to dwell among the
    Thebans.
    O Polybus! Corinth! and that ancient home
I thought my father's — what a thing you
    nurtured!   170
How fair, how foul beneath! For I am found
Foul in myself and in my parentage.
    O you three ways, that in a hidden glen
Do meet: you narrow branching roads within
The forest — you, through my own hands, did
    drink   175
My father's blood, that was my own. — Ah! do
    you

Remember what you saw me do? And what
I did again in Thebes? You marriages!
You did beget me: then, having begotten,
180 Bore the same crop again, and brought to light
Commingled blood of fathers, brothers, sons,
Brides, mothers, wives; all that there can be
Among the human kind most horrible!
    But that which it is foul to do, it is
185 Not fair to speak of. Quick as you can, I beg,
Banish me, hide me, slay me! Throw me forth
Into the sea, where I may sink from view.
I pray you, deign to touch one so afflicted,
And do not fear: there is no man alive
190 Can bear this load of evil but myself.
    CHORUS-LEADER:
To listen to your prayers, Creon is here,
For act or guidance opportune; for he,
In your defection, is our champion.

    [*Enter* CREON.]

    OEDIPUS:
Alas! alas! How can I speak to him?
195 What word of credit find? In all my commerce
With him aforetime I am proven false.
    CREON:
No exultation, Oedipus, and no reproach
Of injuries inflicted brings me here;
But if the face of men moves not your shame,
200 Then reverence show to that all-nurturing fire,
The holy Sun, that he be not polluted
By such accursèd sight, which neither Earth
Nor rain from Heaven nor sunlight can en-
    dure.
    Take him within, and quickly: it is right
205 His kinsmen only should behold and hear
Evils that chiefly on his kinsmen fall.
    OEDIPUS:
In Heaven's name — since you cheat my expec-
    tation,
So noble towards my baseness — grant me this:
It is for you I ask it, not myself.
    CREON:
210 What is this supplication that you make?
    OEDIPUS:
Drive me at once beyond your bounds, where I
Shall be alone, and no one speak to me.
    CREON:
I would have done it; but I first desired
To ask the God what he would have me do.
    OEDIPUS:
215 No, his command was given in full, to slay
Me, the polluter and the parricide.
    CREON:
Those were his words; but in our present need
It would be wise to ask what we should do.

    OEDIPUS:
You will inquire for such a wretch as I?
    CREON:
I will; for now *you* may believe the god.   220
    OEDIPUS:
Yes; and on you I lay this charge and duty:
Give burial, as you will, to her who lies
Within — for she is yours, and this is proper;
And, while I live, let not my father's city
Endure to have me as a citizen.   225
My home must be the mountains — on Cithae-
    ron,
Which, while they lived, my parents chose to
    be
My tomb: they wished to slay me; now they
    shall.
For this I know: sickness can never kill me,
Nor any other evil; I was not saved   230
That day from death, except for some strange
    doom.
My fate must take the course it will. — Now,
    for my sons,
Be not concerned for them: they can, being
    men,
Fend for themselves, wherever they may be:
But my unhappy daughters, my two girls,   235
Whose chairs were always set beside my own
At table — they who shared in every dish
That was prepared for me — oh Creon! these
Do I commend to you. And grant me this:
To take them in my arms, and weep for them.   240
My lord! most noble Creon! could I now
But hold them in my arms, then I should
    think
I had them as I had when I could see them.
Ah! what is this?
Ah Heaven! do I not hear my dear ones,
    sobbing?   245
Has Creon, in his pity, sent to me
My darling children? Has he? Is it true?
    CREON:
It is; they have been always your delight;
So, knowing this, I had them brought to you.
    OEDIPUS:
Then Heaven reward you, and for this kind
    service   250
Protect you better than it protected me!
    Where are you, children? Where? O come
    to me!
Come, let me clasp you with a brother's arms,
These hands, which helped your father's eyes,
    once bright,
To look upon you as they see you now —   255
Your father who, not seeing, nor inquiring,
Gave you for mother her who bore himself.

See you I cannot; but I weep for you,
For the unhappiness that must be yours,
260 And for the bitter life that you must lead.
What gathering of the citizens, what festivals,
Will you have part in? Your high celebrations
Will be to go back home, and sit in tears.
And when the time for marriage comes, what man
265 Will stake upon the ruin and the shame
That *I* am to my parents and to you?
Nothing is wanting there: your father slew
His father, married her who gave him birth,
And then, from that same source whence he himself
Had sprung, got you. — With these things
270 they will taunt you;
And who will take you then in marriage? — Nobody;
But you must waste, unwedded and unfruitful.
Ah, Creon! Since they have no parent now
But you — for both of us who gave them life
275 Have perished — suffer them not to be cast out
Homeless and beggars; for they are your kin.
Have pity on them, for they are so young,
So desolate, except for you alone.
Say "Yes," good Creon! Let your hand confirm it.
280 And now, my children, for my exhortation
You are too young; but you can pray that I
May live henceforward — where I should; and you
More happily than the father who begot you.
CREON:
Now make an end of tears, and go within.
OEDIPUS:
285 Then I must go — against my will.
CREON:
There is a time for everything.
OEDIPUS:
You know what I would have you do?
CREON:
If you will tell me, I shall know.

OEDIPUS:
Send me away, away from Thebes.
CREON:
The God, not I, must grant you this. 290
OEDIPUS:
The gods hate no man more than me!
CREON:
Then what you ask they soon will give.
OEDIPUS:
You promise this?
CREON: Ah no! When I
Am ignorant, I do not speak.
OEDIPUS:
Then lead me in; I say no more. 295
CREON:
Release the children then, and come.
OEDIPUS:
What? Take these children from me? No!
CREON:
Seek not to have your way in all things:
Where you had your way before,
Your mastery broke before the end. 300

[*There was no doubt a short concluding utterance from the* CHORUS. *What stands in the mss. appears to be spurious.*][3]

[3] Few other scholars share Professor Kitto's suspicion that the concluding lines in the manuscript are spurious. The passage is translated thus by J. T. Sheppard:

CHORUS:
Look, ye who dwell in Thebes. This man was Oedipus.
That mighty King, who knew the riddle's mystery,
Whom all the city envied, Fortune's favorite.
Behold, in the event, the storm of his calamities,
And, being mortal, think on that last day of death,
Which all must see, and speak of no man's happiness
Till, without sorrow, he hath passed the goal of life.
[Eds.]

Classroom discussions of *Oedipus the King,* like discussions in books, are often mostly devoted to the problem of fate and free will. Students (who ought to be filled with youthful confidence in the freedom of the will) generally argue that Oedipus is fated; instructors (who ought to be old enough to know that the inexplicable and unwilled often comes about) generally argue that Oedipus is free and of his own accord performed the actions that fulfilled the prophecy. Prophecy or prediction or foreknowledge, instructors patiently explain, is not the same as foreordination. The physician who says that the newborn babe will never develop mentally beyond the age of six is predicting, but he is not ordaining or willing. So, the argument usually runs, the oracle who predicted that Oedipus would kill his father and marry his mother was not *causing* Oedipus to do these things but was simply, in his deep knowledge, announcing what a man like Oedipus would do. But that may be too sophisticated a reading, and a reading that derives from the much later European view of man as a creature who can shape his destiny. It is hard for us — especially if the tragedy we know best is Shakespeare's — to recognize the possibility of another sort of tragic drama which does not relate the individual's suffering to his own actions but which postulates some sort of Necessity that works within him.

Whatever the merits of these views, the spectators or readers undeniably know, when they set out to see or read the play, that Oedipus must end wretchedly. The story is known to us, fixed in Sophocles' text, and Oedipus cannot extricate himself from it. Something along these lines was suggested in the middle of the fourth century B.C. when a Greek comic dramatist complained that the comic writer's task was harder than the tragic writer's: "Tragedy has the best of it since the stories are known beforehand to the spectators even before anyone speaks; so the poet only has to remind them. For if I merely say the name Oedipus, they all know the rest — his father Laius, mother Iocasta, daughters, who his sons are, what will happen to him, what he did." In fact, it should be mentioned, the tragic writer's task was not quite so easy. First of all, we have Aristotle's statement that "even the known legends are known to only a few," and, second, we have evidence that the tragic writer could vary the details. In Homer's *Iliad* we read that Oedipus continued to rule even after his dreadful history was known, but Sophocles exiles him. And a fragment of Euripides indicates that Euripides' Oedipus was blinded by Laius' followers, but Sophocles' Oedipus blinds himself. These are details, but they are rather important ones. Probably the ancient Greeks knew the legends in a rough sort of way, as most of us know the Bible or some nuggets of Roman history. Robert Frost and Archibald MacLeish have both drawn from the Book of Job, but their works are enormously different. A writer who uses Job can scarcely omit Job's great suffering, and he can assume that his audience will know that Job had a wife and some comforters, but he is free to go on from there. Similarly, Brutus must stab Julius Caesar, but that leaves lots of room for other material in a play about Caesar. Shakespeare, by the way, could even assume that the audience that saw his *Julius Caesar* would accept a different version of the facts in his *Antony and Cleopatra*. In *Julius Caesar*, Brutus kills himself, but in *Antony and Cleopatra* Antony says (and presumably he is speaking the truth — the truth, that is, for *that* play) that Brutus died at Antony's hands.

Still, the main outline of Oedipus' life must have been fixed, and for us even the details are forever fixed in Sophocles' version. (We know that the Greeks wrote a dozen plays about Oedipus' discovery of his terrible actions, but only Sophocles' survives.) This means that as we read or watch it, each speech has for us a meaning somewhat different from the meaning it has for the speaker and the audience on the stage. Oedipus says he will hunt out the polluted man; we know, as he and the Thebans do not, that *he* is the hunted as well as the hunter. Oedipus says the killer of King Laius may well try to strike at him; we know that Oedipus will find himself out and will strike out his own eyes. A messenger from Corinth tries to allay Oedipus' fears, but he sets them going. What we are talking about, of course, is tragic irony, or Sophoclean irony, in which words and deeds have a larger meaning for the spectator than for the dramatis personae. And surely it is in part because Sophocles so persistently uses this device of giving speeches a second, awesome significance that we feel the plot is a masterpiece of construction in which Oedipus is caught. If ever a man had confidence in his will, it was Oedipus, but if ever a man moved toward a predicted point, it was Oedipus. He had solved the riddle of the sphinx (by himself, without the aid of birds, he somewhat hybristically boasts), but he did not yet know himself. That knowledge was to come later, when he commendably pursued the quest for Laius' slayer and inevitably found himself. The thing is as inevitable as the history described in the sphinx's riddle, which in J. T. Sheppard's version goes thus:

> A thing there is whose voice is one;
> Whose feet are four and two and three.
> So mutable a thing is none
> That moves in earth or sky or sea.
> When on most feet this thing doth go,
> Its strength is weakest and its pace most slow.

This is the history of man, willy-nilly. In Sophocles' time men grew from crawling infancy, through erect manhood, to bent old age supported by a stick, and so they do in our time, as the child's rhyme still claims:

> Walks on four feet,
> On two feet, on three,
> The more feet it walks on,
> The weaker it be.

There was scarcely an infant weaker than the maimed Oedipus; there was scarcely a man stronger than King Oedipus at his height; and there was scarcely a man more in need of a staff than the blind exile. However free each of his actions — and we can only feel that the man whom we see on the stage is acting freely when he abuses Teiresias and Creon — Oedipus was by fate a man, and thus the largest pattern of his life could be predicted easily enough.

THE TRAGEDY OF KING LEAR

William Shakespeare

Edited by Russell Fraser

William Shakespeare (1564–1616) was born in Stratford, England, of middle-class parents. Nothing of interest is known about his early years, but by 1590 he was acting and writing plays in London. He early worked in all three Elizabethan dramatic genres — tragedy, comedy, and history. *Romeo and Juliet*, for example, was written about 1595, the year of *Richard II*, and in the following year he wrote *A Midsummer Night's Dream*. *Julius Caesar* (1599) probably preceded *As You Like It* by one year, and *Hamlet* probably followed *As You Like It* by less than a year. Among the plays that followed *King Lear* (1605–1606) were *Macbeth* (1605–1606) and several "romances" — plays that have happy endings but that seem more meditative and closer to tragedy than such comedies as *A Midsummer Night's Dream*, *As You Like It*, and *Twelfth Night*.

[*DRAMATIS PERSONAE*

LEAR, *King of Britain*
KING OF FRANCE
DUKE OF BURGUNDY
DUKE OF CORNWALL, *husband to Regan*
DUKE OF ALBANY, *husband to Goneril*
EARL OF KENT
EARL OF GLOUCESTER
EDGAR, *son to Gloucester*
EDMUND, *bastard son to Gloucester*
CURAN, *a courtier*
OSWALD, *steward to Goneril*
OLD MAN, *tenant to Gloucester*

DOCTOR
LEAR'S FOOL
A CAPTAIN *subordinate to Edmund*
GENTLEMEN *attending on Cordelia*
A HERALD
SERVANTS *to Cornwall*
GONERIL
REGAN } *daughters to Lear*
CORDELIA
KNIGHTS *attending on Lear*, OFFICERS, MESSENGERS, SOLDIERS, ATTENDANTS

Scene: Britain]

Charles Laughton as King Lear and Ian Holm as the Fool in the Shakespeare Memorial Theatre production directed by Glen Byam Shaw at Stratford-upon-Avon, England, 1959. (Photograph: Angus McBean. Harvard Theatre Collection.)

ACT I

SCENE I. [*King* LEAR's *palace*.]

Enter KENT, GLOUCESTER, *and* EDMUND.

KENT: I thought the king had more affected°[1] the Duke of Albany° than Cornwall.

GLOUCESTER: It did always seem so to us; but now, in the division of the kingdom, it
5 appears not which of the dukes he values most, for equalities are so weighed that curiosity in neither can make choice of either's moiety.°

KENT: Is not this your son, my lord?

GLOUCESTER: His breeding,° sir, hath been at
10 my charge. I have so often blushed to acknowledge him that now I am brazed° to't.

KENT: I cannot conceive° you.

GLOUCESTER: Sir, this young fellow's mother could; whereupon she grew round-wombed,
15 and had indeed, sir, a son for her cradle ere she had a husband for her bed. Do you smell a fault?

KENT: I cannot wish the fault undone, the issue° of it being so proper.°
20 GLOUCESTER: But I have a son, sir, by order of law, some year elder than this, who yet is no dearer in my account:° though this knave° came something saucily° to the world before he was sent for, yet was his mother fair, there was
25 good sport at his making, and the whoreson° must be acknowledged. Do you know this noble gentleman, Edmund?

From *King Lear* by William Shakespeare, edited by Russell Fraser. Copyright © Russell Fraser 1963. Copyright © 1963 Sylvan Barnet. Reprinted by arrangement with The New American Library, Inc., New York, N.Y.

[1]The degree sign (°) indicates a footnote, which is keyed to the text by the line number. Text references are printed in **boldface** type; the annotation follows in lightface type. The notes are Russell Fraser's. [Eds.]
I.i.2 **affected** loved   2 **Albany** Albanacte, whose domain extended "from the river Humber to the point of Caithness" (Holinshed)   6–7 **equalities ... moiety** shares are so balanced against one another that careful examination by neither can make him wish the other's portion   9 **breeding** upbringing   11 **brazed** made brazen, hardened   12 **conceive** understand (pun follows)   19 **issue** result (child)   19 **proper** handsome   22 **account** estimation; **knave** fellow (without disapproval)   23 **saucily** (1) insolently (2) lasciviously   25 **whoreson** fellow (literally, son of a whore)

EDMUND: No, my lord.

GLOUCESTER: My Lord of Kent. Remember him hereafter as my honorable friend.   30

EDMUND: My services to your lordship.

KENT: I must love you, and sue° to know you better.

EDMUND: Sir, I shall study deserving.

GLOUCESTER: He hath been out° nine years,   35 and away he shall again. The king is coming.

(*Sound a sennet.° Enter one bearing a coronet,° then King* LEAR, *then the Dukes of* CORNWALL *and* ALBANY, *next* GONERIL, REGAN, CORDELIA, *and* ATTENDANTS.)

LEAR:
Attend the lords of France and Burgundy, Gloucester.

GLOUCESTER:
I shall, my lord.   (*Exit,* [*with* EDMUND].)

LEAR:
Meantime we shall express our darker purpose.°
Give me the map there. Know that we have   40 divided
In three our kingdom; and 'tis our fast° intent
To shake all cares and business from our age,
Conferring them on younger strengths, while we
Unburthened crawl toward death. Our son of   45 Cornwall,
And you our no less loving son of Albany,
We have this hour a constant will to publish°
Our daughters' several° dowers, that future strife
May be prevented° now. The princes, France and Burgundy,
Great rivals in our youngest daughter's love,
Long in our court have made their amorous   50 sojourn,
And here are to be answered. Tell me, my daughters
(Since now we will divest us both of rule,

32 **sue** entreat   35 **out** away, abroad   36 s.d. **sennet** set of notes played on a trumpet, signaling the entrance or departure of a procession; **coronet** small crown, intended for Cordelia   39 **darker purpose** hidden intention   41 **fast** fixed   46 **constant ... publish** fixed intention to proclaim   47 **several** separate   48 **prevented** forestalled

Interest° of territory, cares of state),
Which of you shall we say doth love us most,
55 That we our largest bounty may extend
Where nature doth with merit challenge.°
        Goneril,
Our eldest-born, speak first.
    GONERIL:
Sir, I love you more than word can wield° the
        matter;
Dearer than eyesight, space,° and liberty;
Beyond what can be valued, rich or rare;
No less than life, with grace, health, beauty,
        honor;
As much as child e'er loved, or father found;
A love that makes breath° poor, and speech
        unable:°
Beyond all manner of so much° I love you.
    CORDELIA [aside]:
What shall Cordelia speak? Love, and be
 5   silent.
    LEAR:
Of all these bounds, even from this line to
        this,
With shadowy forests, and with champains
        riched,°
With plenteous rivers, and wide-skirted
        meads,°
We make thee lady. To thine and Albany's
        issues°
Be this perpetual.° What says our second
70   daughter,
Our dearest Regan, wife of Cornwall? Speak.
    REGAN:
I am made of that self mettle° as my sister,
And prize me at her worth.° In my true heart
I find she names my very deed of love;°
75 Only she comes too short, that° I profess
Myself an enemy to all other joys
Which the most precious square of sense
        professes,°
And find I am alone felicitate°
In your dear highness' love.

53 **Interest** legal right   56 **nature ... challenge** natural affection contends with desert for (or lays claim to) bounty   58 **wield** handle   59 **space** scope   63 **breath** language; **unable** impotent   64 **Beyond ... much** beyond all these comparisons   67 **champains riched** enriched plains   68 **wide-skirted meads** extensive grasslands   69 **issues** descendants   70 **perpetual** in perpetuity   72 **self mettle** same material or temperament   73 **prize ... worth** value me the same (imperative)   74 **my ... love** what my love really is (a legalism)   75 **that** in that   77 **Which ... professes** which the choicest estimate of sense avows   78 **felicitate** made happy

CORDELIA [aside]:   Then poor Cordelia!
And yet not so, since I am sure my love's   80
More ponderous° than my tongue.
    LEAR:
To thee and thine hereditary ever
Remain this ample third of our fair kingdom,
No less in space, validity,° and pleasure
Than that conferred on Goneril. Now, our joy, 85
Although our last and least;° to whose young
        love
The vines of France and milk° of Burgundy
Strive to be interest;° what can you say to draw
A third more opulent than your sisters? Speak.
    CORDELIA:
Nothing, my lord.   90
    LEAR: Nothing?
    CORDELIA: Nothing.
    LEAR:
Nothing will come of nothing. Speak again.
    CORDELIA:
Unhappy that I am, I cannot heave
My heart into my mouth. I love your majesty   95
According to my bond,° no more nor less.
    LEAR:
How, how, Cordelia? Mend your speech a
        little,
Lest you may mar your fortunes.
    CORDELIA: Good my lord,
You have begot me, bred me, loved me. I
Return those duties back as are right fit,°   100
Obey you, love you, and most honor you.
Why have my sisters husbands, if they say
They love you all? Haply,° when I shall wed,
That lord whose hand must take my plight°
        shall carry
Half my love with him, half my care and duty. 105
Sure I shall never marry like my sisters,
To love my father all.
    LEAR:
But goes thy heart with this?
    CORDELIA: Ay, my good lord.
    LEAR:
So young, and so untender?
    CORDELIA:
So young, my lord, and true.   110
    LEAR:
Let it be so, thy truth then be thy dower!

81 **ponderous** weighty   84 **validity** value   86 **least** youngest, smallest   87 **milk** i.e., pastures   88 **interest** closely connected, as interested parties   96 **bond** filial obligation   100 **Return ... fit** i.e., am correspondingly dutiful   103 **Haply** perhaps   104 **plight** troth plight

For, by the sacred radiance of the sun,
The mysteries of Hecate° and the night,
By all the operation of the orbs°
115 From whom we do exist and cease to be,
Here I disclaim all my paternal care,
Propinquity and property of blood,°
And as a stranger to my heart and me
Hold thee from this for ever. The barbarous Scythian,°
120 Or he that makes his generation messes°
To gorge his appetite, shall to my bosom
Be as well neighbored, pitied, and relieved,
As thou my sometime° daughter.

KENT: Good my liege —

LEAR:
Peace, Kent!
125 Come not between the dragon° and his wrath.
I loved her most, and thought to set my rest°
On her kind nursery.° Hence and avoid my sight!
So be my grave my peace, as here I give
Her father's heart from her! Call France. Who stirs?'
130 Call Burgundy. Cornwall and Albany,
With my two daughters' dowers digest° the third;
Let pride, which she calls plainness, marry her.°
I do invest you jointly with my power,
Preeminence, and all the large effects
That troop with majesty.° Ourself,° by monthly
135 course,
With reservation° of an hundred knights,
By you to be sustained, shall our abode
Make with you by due turn. Only we shall retain
The name, and all th' addition° to a king. The sway,

Revènue, execution of the rest, 140
Belovèd sons, be yours; which to confirm,
This coronet° part between you.

KENT: Royal Lear,
Whom I have ever honored as my king,
Loved as my father, as my master followed,
As my great patron thought on in my prayers — 145

LEAR:
The bow is bent and drawn; make from the shaft.°

KENT:
Let it fall° rather, though the fork° invade
The region of my heart. Be Kent unmannerly
When Lear is mad. What wouldst thou do, old man?
Thinkst thou that duty shall have dread to speak 150
When power to flattery bows? To plainness honor's bound
When majesty falls to folly. Reserve thy state,°
And in thy best consideration° check
This hideous rashness. Answer my life my judgment,°
Thy youngest daughter does not love thee least, 155
Nor are those empty-hearted whose low sounds
Reverb° no hollowness.°

LEAR: Kent, on thy life, no more!

KENT:
My life I never held but as a pawn°
To wage° against thine enemies; nor fear to lose it,
Thy safety being motive.°

LEAR: Out of my sight! 160

KENT:
See better, Lear, and let me still° remain
The true blank° of thine eye.

LEAR:
Now by Apollo —

KENT: Now by Apollo, king,
Thou swear'st thy gods in vain.

---

113 **mysteries of Hecate** secret rites of Hecate (goddess of the infernal world, and of witchcraft)　114 **operation . . . orbs** astrological influence　117 **Propinquity . . . blood** relationship and common blood　119 **Scythian** type of the savage　120 **makes . . . messes** eats his own offspring　123 **sometime** former　125 **dragon** (1) heraldic device of Britain (2) emblem of ferocity　126 **set my rest** (1) stake my all (a term from the card game of primero) (2) find my rest　127 **nursery** care, nursing　131 **digest** absorb　132 **Let . . . her** Let her pride be her dowry and gain her a husband　134–135 **effects . . . majesty** accompaniments that go with kingship　135 **Ourself** the royal "we"　136 **reservation** the action of reserving a privilege (a legalism)　139 **addition** titles and honors

142 **coronet** the crown that was to have been Cordelia's　146 **make . . . shaft** avoid the arrow　147 **fall** strike; **fork** forked head of the arrow　152 **Reserve thy state** retain your kingly authority　153 **best consideration** most careful reflection　154 **Answer . . . judgment** I will stake my life on my opinion　157 **Reverb** reverberate; **hollowness** (1) emptiness (2) insincerity　158 **pawn** stake in a wager　159 **wage** (1) wager (2) carry on war　160 **motive** moving cause　161 **still** always　162 **blank** the white spot in the center of the target (at which Lear should aim)

LEAR: O vassal! Miscreant!°

[*Laying his hand on his sword.*]

165   ALBANY, CORNWALL: Dear sir, forbear!
       KENT:
       Kill thy physician, and the fee bestow
       Upon the foul disease. Revoke thy gift,
       Or, whilst I can vent clamor° from my throat,
       I'll tell thee thou dost evil.
       LEAR: Hear me, recreant!°
170   On thine allegiance,° hear me!
       That thou hast sought to make us break our
           vows,
       Which we durst never yet, and with strained°
           pride
       To come betwixt our sentence° and our power,
       Which nor our nature nor our place can bear,
175   Our potency made good,° take thy reward.
       Five days we do allot thee for provision°
       To shield thee from diseases° of the world,
       And on the sixth to turn thy hated back
       Upon our kingdom. If, on the tenth day
           following,
       Thy banished trunk° be found in our
180   dominions,
       The moment is thy death. Away! By Jupiter,
       This shall not be revoked.
       KENT:
       Fare thee well, king. Sith° thus thou wilt
           appear,
       Freedom lives hence, and banishment is here.

       [*To* CORDELIA.]

185   The gods to their dear shelter take thee, maid,
       That justly think'st, and hast most rightly said.

       [*To* REGAN *and* GONERIL.]

       And your large speeches may your deeds
           approve,°
       That good effects° may spring from words of
           love.
       Thus Kent, O princes, bids you all adieu;
190   He'll shape his old course° in a country new.
                                        (*Exit.*)

(*Flourish.*° *Enter* GLOUCESTER, *with* FRANCE *and* BURGUNDY; ATTENDANTS.)

       GLOUCESTER:
       Here's France and Burgundy, my noble lord.
       LEAR:
       My Lord of Burgundy,
       We first address toward you, who with this
           king
       Hath rivaled for our daughter. What in the
           least
       Will you require in present° dower with her,   195
       Or cease your quest of love?
       BURGUNDY: Most royal majesty,
       I crave no more than hath your highness
           offered,
       Nor will you tender° less.
       LEAR: Right noble Burgundy,
       When she was dear° to us, we did hold her so;
       But now her price is fallen. Sir, there she
           stands.   200
       If aught within that little seeming substance,°
       Or all of it, with our displeasure pieced,°
       And nothing more, may fitly like° your grace,
       She's there, and she is yours.
       BURGUNDY: I know no answer.
       LEAR:
       Will you, with those infirmities she owes,°   205
       Unfriended, new adopted to our hate,
       Dow'red with our curse, and strangered° with
           our oath,
       Take her, or leave her?
       BURGUNDY: Pardon me, royal sir.
       Election makes not up° on such conditions.
       LEAR:
       Then leave her, sir; for, by the pow'r that
           made me,   210
       I tell you all her wealth. [*To* FRANCE.] For
           you, great king,
       I would not from your love make such a stray
       To° match you where I hate; therefore
           beseech° you
       T' avert your liking a more worthier way°

190 s.d. **Flourish** trumpet fanfare   195 **present** immediate   198 **tender** offer   199 **dear** (1) beloved (2) valued at a high price   201 **little seeming substance** person who is (1) inconsiderable (2) outspoken   202 **pieced** added to it   203 **fitly like** please by its fitness   205 **owes** possesses   207 **strangered** made a stranger   209 **Election . . . up** no one can choose   212–213 **make . . . To** stray so far as to   213 **beseech** I beseech   214 **avert . . . way** turn your affections from her and bestow them on a better person

164 **vassal! Miscreant!** base wretch! Misbeliever   168 **vent clamor** utter a cry   169 **recreant** traitor   170 **On thine allegiance** to forswear, which is to commit high treason   172 **strained** forced (and so excessive)   173 **sentence** judgment, decree   175 **Our . . . good** my royal authority being now asserted   176 **for provision** for making preparation   177 **diseases** troubles   180 **trunk** body   183 **Sith** since   187 **approve** prove true   188 **effects** results   190 **shape . . . course** pursue his customary way

215 Than on a wretch whom nature is ashamed
Almost t' acknowledge hers.
    FRANCE: This is most strange,
That she whom even but now was your best
    object,°
The argument° of your praise, balm of your
    age,
The best, the dearest, should in this trice of
    time
220 Commit a thing so monstrous to dismantle°
So many folds of favor. Sure her offense
Must be of such unnatural degree
That monsters it,° or your fore-vouched°
    affection
Fall into taint;° which to believe of her
225 Must be a faith that reason without miracle
Should never plant in me.°
    CORDELIA: I yet beseech your majesty,
If for° I want that glib and oily art
To speak and purpose not,° since what I well
    intend
I'll do 't before I speak, that you make known
230 It is no vicious blot, murder, or foulness,
No unchaste action or dishonored step,
That hath deprived me of your grace and
    favor;
But even for want of that for which I am
    richer,
A still-soliciting° eye, and such a tongue
That I am glad I have not, though not to have
235   it
Hath lost° me in your liking.
    LEAR: Better thou
Hadst not been born than not t' have pleased
    me better.
    FRANCE:
Is it but this? A tardiness in nature°
Which often leaves the history unspoke°
240 That it intends to do. My Lord of Burgundy,
What say you° to the lady? Love's not love

When it is mingled with regards° that stands
Aloof from th' entire point.° Will you have her?
She is herself a dowry.
    BURGUNDY: Royal king,
Give but that portion which yourself proposed,   245
And here I take Cordelia by the hand,
Duchess of Burgundy.
    LEAR:
Nothing. I have sworn. I am firm.
    BURGUNDY:
I am sorry then you have so lost a father
That you must lose a husband.
    CORDELIA: Peace be with Burgundy.   250
Since that respects of fortune° are his love,
I shall not be his wife.
    FRANCE:
Fairest Cordelia, that art most rich being poor,
Most choice forsaken, and most loved despised,
Thee and thy virtues here I seize upon.   255
Be it lawful I take up what's cast away.
Gods, gods! 'Tis strange that from their
    cold'st neglect
My love should kindle to inflamed respect.°
Thy dow'rless daughter, king, thrown to my
    chance,°
Is queen of us, of ours, and our fair France.   260
Not all the dukes of wat'rish° Burgundy
Can buy this unprized precious° maid of me.
Bid them farewell, Cordelia, though unkind.
Thou losest here,° a better where° to find.
    LEAR:
Thou hast her, France; let her be thine, for we   265
Have no such daughter, nor shall ever see
That face of hers again. Therefore be gone,
Without our grace, our love, our benison.°
Come, noble Burgundy.
    (Flourish. Exeunt [LEAR, BURGUNDY,
        CORNWALL, ALBANY, GLOUCESTER,
            and ATTENDANTS].)
    FRANCE:
Bid farewell to your sisters.   270
    CORDELIA:
The jewels of our father,° with washed° eyes

---

217 **your best object** the one you loved most   218
argument subject   220 **dismantle** strip off   223
That monsters it as makes it monstrous, unnatural;
fore-vouched previously sworn   224 **Fall into taint**
must be taken as having been unjustified all along;
i.e., Cordelia was unworthy of your love from the first
225–226 **reason . . . me** my reason would have to be
supported by a miracle to make me believe   227 **for**
because   228 **purpose not** not mean to do what I
promise   234 **still-soliciting** always begging   236
lost ruined   238 **tardiness in nature** natural reticence   239 **leaves . . . unspoke** does not announce
the action   241 **What say you** i.e., will you have

242 **regards** considerations (the dowry)   242–243
stands . . . point have nothing to do with the essential
question (love)   251 **respects of fortune** mercenary
considerations   258 **inflamed respect** more ardent
affection   259 **chance** lot   261 **wat'rish** (1) with
many rivers (2) weak, diluted   262 **unprized precious** unappreciated by others, and yet precious   264
here in this place; **where** other place   268 **benison**
blessing   271 **The jewels . . . father** you creatures
prized by our father; **washed** (1) weeping (2)
clearsighted

Cordelia leaves you. I know you what you are,
And, like a sister,° am most loath to call
Your faults as they are named.° Love well our
      father.
275 To your professèd° bosoms I commit him.
But yet, alas, stood I within his grace,
I would prefer° him to a better place.
So farewell to you both.
      REGAN:
Prescribe not us our duty.
      GONERIL: Let your study
Be to content your lord, who hath received
280   you
At Fortune's alms.° You have obedience
      scanted,°
And well are worth the want that you have
      wanted.°
      CORDELIA:
Time shall unfold what plighted° cunning
      hides,
Who covers faults, at last shame them de-
      rides.°
Well may you prosper.
285   FRANCE: Come, my fair Cordelia.
            (Exit FRANCE and CORDELIA.)
      GONERIL: Sister, it is not little I have to say
of what most nearly appertains to us both. I
think our father will hence tonight.
      REGAN: That's most certain, and with you;
290 next month with us.
      GONERIL: You see how full of changes his
age is. The observation we have made of it
hath not been little. He always loved our sister
most, and with what poor judgment he hath
295 now cast her off appears too grossly.°
      REGAN: 'Tis the infirmity of his age; yet he
hath ever but slenderly known himself.
      GONERIL: The best and soundest of his time°
hath been but rash; then must we look from
300 his age to receive not alone the imperfections

of long-ingrafted° condition,° but therewithal°
the unruly waywardness that infirm and choleric years bring with them.
      REGAN: Such unconstant starts° are we like
to have from him as this of Kent's banish-   305
ment.
      GONERIL: There is further compliment° of
leave-taking between France and him. Pray
you, let's hit° together; if our father carry
authority with such disposition as he bears,°   310
this last surrender° of his will but offend° us.
      REGAN: We shall further think of it.
      GONERIL: We must do something, and i' th'
heat.°

                              (Exeunt.)

            SCENE II. [The Earl of GLOUCESTER's
                         castle.]

            Enter EDMUND [with a letter].

      EDMUND:
Thou, Nature,° art my goddess; to thy law
My services are bound. Wherefore should I
Stand in the plague of custom,° and permit
The curiosity° of nations to deprive me,
For that° I am some twelve or fourteen moon-
      shines°   5
Lag of° a brother? Why bastard? Wherefore
      base?
When my dimensions are as well compact,°
My mind as generous,° and my shape as true,
As honest° madam's issue? Why brand they us
With base? With baseness? Bastardy? Base?
      Base?   10
Who, in the lusty stealth of nature, take
More composition° and fierce° quality
Than doth, within a dull, stale, tired bed,
Go to th' creating a whole tribe of fops°

273 **like a sister** because I am a sister, i.e., loyal,
affectionate   274 **as ... named** by their right and
ugly names   275 **professèd** pretending to love   277
prefer recommend   281 **At Fortune's alms** as a
charitable bequest from Fortune (and so, by extension, as one beggared or cast down by Fortune);
scanted stinted   282 **worth ... wanted** deserve to
be denied, even as you have denied   283 **plighted**
pleated, enfolded   284 **Who ... derides** Those who
hide their evil are finally exposed and shamed ("He
that hideth his sins, shall not prosper")   295 **grossly**
obviously   298 **of his time** period of his life up to now

301 **long-ingrafted** implanted for a long time; **condition** disposition; **therewithal** with them   304 **uncon-
stant starts** impulsive whims   307 **compliment**
formal courtesy   309 **hit** agree   309–310 **carry ...
bears** continues, and in such frame of mind, to wield
the sovereign power   311 **last surrender** recent abdi-
cation; **offend** vex   313–314 **i' th' heat** while the iron
is hot
I.ii.1 Nature Edmund's conception of Nature accords with our description of a bastard as a natural
child   3 **Stand ... custom** respect hateful convention   4 **curiosity** nice distinctions   5 **For that** because; **moonshines** months   6 **Lag of** short of being
(in age)   7 **compact** framed   8 **generous** gallant
9 **honest** chaste   12 **composition** completeness;
fierce energetic   14 **fops** fools

15 Got° 'tween asleep and wake? Well then,
Legitimate Edgar, I must have your land.
Our father's love is to the bastard Edmund
As to th' legitimate. Fine word, "legitimate."
Well, my legitimate, if this letter speed,°
20 And my invention° thrive, Edmund the base
Shall top th' legitimate. I grow, I prosper.
Now, gods, stand up for bastards.

(*Enter* GLOUCESTER.)

GLOUCESTER:
Kent banished thus? and France in choler
    parted?
And the king gone tonight? prescribed° his
    pow'r?
25 Confined to exhibition?° All this done
Upon the gad?° Edmund, how now? What
    news?
EDMUND:
So please your lordship, none.
GLOUCESTER:
Why so earnestly seek you to put up° that
    letter?
EDMUND:
I know no news, my lord.
GLOUCESTER:
30 What paper were you reading?
EDMUND: Nothing, my lord.
GLOUCESTER: No? What needed then that
terrible dispatch° of it into your pocket? The
quality of nothing hath not such need to hide
35 itself. Let's see. Come, if it be nothing, I shall
not need spectacles.
EDMUND: I beseech you, sir, pardon me. It is
a letter from my brother that I have not all
o'er-read; and for so much as I have perused, I
40 find it not fit for your o'erlooking.°
GLOUCESTER: Give me the letter, sir.
EDMUND: I shall offend, either to detain or
give it. The contents, as in part I understand
them, are to blame.°
45 GLOUCESTER: Let's see, let's see.
EDMUND: I hope, for my brother's justification, he wrote this but as an essay or taste° of
my virtue.
GLOUCESTER (*reads*): "This policy and rev-

erence° of age makes the world bitter to the 50
best of our times;° keeps our fortunes from us
till our oldness cannot relish° them. I begin to
find an idle and fond° bondage in the oppres-
sion of aged tyranny, who sways, not as it hath
power, but as it is suffered.° Come to me, that 55
of this I may speak more. If our father would
sleep till I waked him, you should enjoy half his
revenue° for ever, and live the beloved of your
brother,

                                    Edgar." 60
Hum! Conspiracy? "Sleep till I waked him,
you should enjoy half his revenue." My son
Edgar! Had he a hand to write this? A heart
and brain to breed it in? When came you to
this? Who brought it? 65
EDMUND: It was not brought me, my lord;
there's the cunning of it. I found it thrown in
at the casement of my closet.°
GLOUCESTER: You know the character° to be
your brother's? 70
EDMUND: If the matter were good, my lord,
I durst swear it were his; but in respect of
that,° I would fain° think it were not.
GLOUCESTER: It is his.
EDMUND: It is his hand, my lord; but I hope 75
his heart is not in the contents.
GLOUCESTER: Has he never before sounded°
you in this business?
EDMUND: Never, my lord. But I have heard
him oft maintain it to be fit that, sons at 80
perfect° age, and fathers declined, the father
should be as ward to the son, and the son
manage his revenue.
GLOUCESTER: O villain, villain! His very
opinion in the letter. Abhorred villain, unnatu- 85
ral, detested,° brutish villain; worse than
brutish! Go, sirrah,° seek him. I'll apprehend
him. Abominable villain! Where is he?
EDMUND: I do not well know, my lord. If it
shall please you to suspend your indignation 90
against my brother till you can derive from
him better testimony of his intent, you should

49–50 **policy and reverence** policy of reverencing (hendiadys) 51 **best ... times** best years of our lives (i.e., our youth) 52 **relish** enjoy 53 **idle and fond** foolish 54–55 **who ... suffered** which rules, not from its own strength, but from our allowance 58 **revenue** income 68 **casement ... closet** window of my room 69 **character** handwriting 72–73 **in ... that** in view of what it is 73 **fain** prefer to 77 **sounded** sounded you out 81 **perfect** mature 86 **detested** detestable 87 **sirrah** sir (familiar form of address)

15 **Got** begot 19 **speed** prosper 20 **invention** plan 24 **prescribed** limited 25 **exhibition** an allowance or pension 26 **Upon the gad** on the spur of the moment (as if pricked by a gad or goad) 28 **put up** put away, conceal 33 **terrible dispatch** hasty putting away 40 **o'erlooking** inspection 44 **to blame** blameworthy 47 **essay or taste** test

run a certain course;° where, if you violently
proceed against him, mistaking his purpose, it
would make a great gap° in your own honor
and shake in pieces the heart of his obedience.
I dare pawn down° my life for him that he
hath writ this to feel° my affection to your
honor, and to no other pretense of danger.°

GLOUCESTER: Think you so?

EDMUND: If your honor judge it meet,° I will
place you where you shall hear us confer of
this, and by an auricular assurance° have your
satisfaction, and that without any further delay
than this very evening.

GLOUCESTER: He cannot be such a monster.

EDMUND: Nor is not, sure.

GLOUCESTER: To his father, that so tenderly
and entirely loves him. Heaven and earth!
Edmund, seek him out; wind me into him,° I
pray you; frame° the business after your own
wisdom. I would unstate myself to be in a due
resolution.°

EDMUND: I will seek him, sir, presently;°
convey° the business as I shall find means, and
acquaint you withal.°

GLOUCESTER: These late° eclipses in the sun
and moon portend no good to us. Though the
wisdom of nature° can reason° it thus and thus,
yet nature finds itself scourged by the sequent
effects.° Love cools, friendship falls off,° brothers divide. In cities, mutinies;° in countries,
discord; in palaces, treason; and the bond
cracked 'twixt son and father. This villain of
mine comes under the prediction,° there's son
against father; the king falls from bias of
nature,° there's father against child. We have
seen the best of our time.° Machinations,

hollowness,° treachery, and all ruinous disorders follow us disquietly° to our graves. Find
out this villain, Edmund; it shall lose thee
nothing.° Do it carefully. And the noble and
true-hearted Kent banished; his offense, honesty. 'Tis strange.   (Exit.)

EDMUND: This is the excellent foppery° of
the world, that when we are sick in fortune,
often the surfeits of our own behavior,° we
make guilty of our disasters the sun, the moon,
and stars; as if we were villains on° necessity;
fools by heavenly compulsion; knaves, thieves,
and treachers by spherical predominance;°
drunkards, liars, and adulterers by an enforced
obedience of planetary influence;° and all that
we are evil in, by a divine thrusting on.° An
admirable evasion of whoremaster° man, to lay
his goatish° disposition on the charge of a star.
My father compounded° with my mother
under the Dragon's Tail,° and my nativity° was
under Ursa Major,° so that it follows I am
rough and lecherous. Fut!° I should have been
that° I am, had the maidenliest star in the
firmament twinkled on my bastardizing.
Edgar —

(Enter EDGAR.)

and pat he comes, like the catastrophe° of the
old comedy. My cue is villainous melancholy,
with a sigh like Tom o' Bedlam.° — O, these
eclipses do portend these divisions. Fa, sol, la,
mi.°

EDGAR: How now, brother Edmund; what
serious contemplation are you in?

EDMUND: I am thinking, brother, of a pre-

---

93 **run ... course** proceed safely, know where you are
going 95 **gap** breach 97 **pawn down** stake 98
feel test 99 **pretense of danger** dangerous purpose
101 **meet** fit 103 **auricular assurance** proof heard
with your own ears 110 **wind ... him** insinuate
yourself into his confidence for me 111 **frame** manage 112–113 **unstate ... resolution** forfeit my earl-
dom to know the truth 114 **presently** at once 115
convey manage 116 **withal** with it 117 **late**
recent 119 **wisdom of nature** scientific learning;
reason explain 120–121 **yet ... effects** nonetheless
our world is punished with subsequent disasters 121
falls off revolts 122 **mutinies** riots 124–125 **This
... prediction** my son's villainous behavior is included in these portents, and bears them out 126–
127 **bias of nature** natural inclination (the metaphor
is from the game of bowls) 128 **best ... time** our
best days

129 **hollowness** insincerity 130 **disquietly** unquietly
131–132 **it ... nothing** you will not lose by it 135
foppery folly 137 **often ... behavior** often caused
by our own excesses 139 **on** of 141 **treachers ...
predominance** traitors because of the ascendancy of a
particular star at our birth 142–143 **by ... influence** because we had to submit to the influence of
our star 144 **divine thrusting on** supernatural
compulsion 145 **whoremaster** lecherous 146 **goat-
ish** lascivious 147 **compounded** (1) made terms (2)
formed (a child) 148 **Dragon's Tail** the constel-
lation Draco; **nativity** birthday 149 **Ursa Major**
the Great Bear 150 **Fut** 'S foot (an impatient
oath) 151 **that** what 154 **catastrophe** conclusion 155–156 **My ... Bedlam** I must be doleful, like
a lunatic beggar out of Bethlehem (Bedlam) Hospital, the London madhouse 157–158 **Fa, sol, la, mi**
Edmund's humming of the musical notes is perhaps
prompted by his use of the word *division*, which
describes a musical variation

diction I read this other day, what should
follow these eclipses.

165   EDGAR: Do you busy yourself with that?

EDMUND: I promise you, the effects he
writes of succeed° unhappily: as of unnatural-
ness° between the child and the parent, death,
dearth, dissolutions of ancient amities,° divisions in state, menaces and maledictions
170   against king and nobles, needless diffidences,°
banishment of friends, dissipation of cohorts,°
nuptial breaches, and I know not what.

EDGAR: How long have you been a sectary
astronomical?°

175   EDMUND: Come, come, when saw you my
father last?

EDGAR: Why, the night gone by.

EDMUND: Spake you with him?

EDGAR: Ay, two hours together.

180   EDMUND: Parted you in good terms? Found
you no displeasure in him by word nor countenance?°

EDGAR: None at all.

EDMUND: Bethink yourself wherein you may
185   have offended him; and at my entreaty forbear
his presence° until some little time hath quali-
fied° the heat of his displeasure, which at this
instant so rageth in him that with the mischief
of your person it would scarcely allay.°

190   EDGAR: Some villain hath done me wrong.

EDMUND: That's my fear, brother. I pray you
have a continent forbearance° till the speed of
his rage goes slower; and, as I say, retire with
me to my lodging, from whence I will fitly°
195   bring you to hear my lord speak. Pray ye, go;
there's my key. If you do stir abroad, go
armed.

EDGAR: Armed, brother?

EDMUND: Brother, I advise you to the best.
200   Go armed. I am no honest man if there be any
good meaning toward you. I have told you
what I have seen and heard; but faintly,
nothing like the image and horror° of it. Pray
you, away.

EDGAR: Shall I hear from you anon?°   205
EDMUND: I do serve you in this business.
                                    (Exit EDGAR.)
A credulous father, and a brother noble,
Whose nature is so far from doing harms
That he suspects none; on whose foolish
      honesty
My practices° ride easy. I see the business.   210
Let me, if not by birth, have lands by wit.
All with me's meet° that I can fashion fit.°
                                    (Exit.)

SCENE III. [The Duke of ALBANY's palace.]

Enter GONERIL, and [OSWALD, her] steward.

GONERIL: Did my father strike my gentle-
man for chiding of his Fool?°
OSWALD: Ay, madam.
GONERIL:
By day and night he wrongs me. Every hour
He flashes into one gross crime° or other   5
That sets us all at odds. I'll not endure it.
His knights grow riotous,° and himself up-
      braids us
On every trifle. When he returns from hunt-
      ing,
I will not speak with him. Say I am sick.
If you come slack of former services,°   10
You shall do well; the fault of it I'll answer.°

[Horns within.]

OSWALD: He's coming, madam; I hear him.
GONERIL:
Put on what weary negligence you please,
You and your fellows. I'd have it come to
      question.°
If he distaste° it, let him to my sister,   15
Whose mind and mine I know in that are one,
Not to be overruled. Idle° old man,
That still would manage those authorities
That he hath given away. Now, by my life,
Old fools are babes again, and must be used   20
With checks as flatteries, when they are seen
      abused.°
Remember what I have said.

166 **succeed** follow   166–167 **unnaturalness** unkindness   168 **amities** friendships   170 **diffidences** dis-
trusts   171 **dissipation of cohorts** falling away of
supporters   173–174 **sectary astronomical** believer in
astrology   181–182 **countenance** expression   185–
186 **forbear his presence** keep away from him   186–
187 **qualified** lessened   188–189 **with . . . allay** even
an injury to you would not appease his anger   192
have . . . forbearance be restrained and keep yourself
withdrawn   194 **fitly** at a fit time   203 **image and
horror** true horrible picture

205 **anon** in a little while   210 **practices** plots   212
meet proper; **fashion fit** shape to my purpose
I.III.2 **Fool** court jester   5 **crime** offense   7 **riotous**
dissolute   10 **come . . . services** are less serviceable
to him than formerly   11 **answer** answer for   14
come to question be discussed openly   15 **distaste**
dislike   17 **Idle** foolish   21 **With . . . abused** with
restraints as well as soothing words when they are mis-
guided

OSWALD: Well, madam.
GONERIL:
And let his knights have colder looks among
  you.
What grows of it, no matter; advise your
  fellows so.
I would breed from hence occasions, and I
25 shall,
That I may speak.° I'll write straight° to my
  sister
To hold my course. Go, prepare for dinner.
                                   (*Exeunt.*)

SCENE IV. [*A hall in the same.*]

Enter KENT [*disguised*].

KENT:
If but as well I other accents borrow
That can my speech defuse,° my good intent
May carry through itself to that full issue°
For which I razed my likeness.° Now, banished
  Kent,
5 If thou canst serve where thou dost stand
    condemned,
So may it come,° thy master whom thou lov'st
Shall find thee full of labors.

  (*Horns within.° Enter* LEAR, [KNIGHTS,] *and*
  ATTENDANTS.)

LEAR: Let me not stay° a jot for dinner; go,
get it ready. [*Exit an* ATTENDANT.] How now,
10 what art thou?
KENT: A man, sir.
LEAR: What dost thou profess?° What
wouldst thou with us?
KENT: I do profess° to be no less than I
15 seem, to serve him truly that will put me in
trust, to love him that is honest, to converse
with him that is wise and says little, to fear
judgment,° to fight when I cannot choose, and
to eat no fish.°
25 LEAR: What art thou?
KENT: A very honest-hearted fellow and as
poor as the king.

LEAR: If thou be'st as poor for a subject as
he's for a king, thou art poor enough. What
wouldst thou?   25
KENT: Service.
LEAR: Who wouldst thou serve?
KENT: You.
LEAR: Dost thou know me, fellow?
KENT: No, sir, but you have that in your   30
countenance° which I would fain° call master.
LEAR: What's that?
KENT: Authority.
LEAR: What services canst thou do?
KENT: I can keep honest counsel,° ride, run,   35
mar a curious tale in telling it,° and deliver a
plain message bluntly. That which ordinary
men are fit for, I am qualified in, and the best
of me is diligence.
LEAR: How old art thou?   40
KENT: Not so young, sir, to love a woman
for singing, nor so old to dote on her for
anything. I have years on my back forty-eight.
LEAR: Follow me; thou shalt serve me. If I
like thee no worse after dinner, I will not part 45
from thee yet. Dinner, ho, dinner! Where's
my knave?° my Fool? Go you and call my Fool
hither.   [*Exit an* ATTENDANT.]

  (*Enter* OSWALD.)

You, you, sirrah, where's my daughter?
OSWALD: So please you —   (*Exit.*)   50
LEAR: What says the fellow there? Call the
clotpoll° back. [*Exit a* KNIGHT.] Where's my
Fool? Ho, I think the world's asleep.

[*Reenter* KNIGHT.]

How now? Where's that mongrel?
KNIGHT: He says, my lord, your daughter is   55
not well.
LEAR: Why came not the slave back to me
when I called him?
KNIGHT: Sir, he answered me in the round-
est° manner, he would not.   60
LEAR: He would not?
KNIGHT: My lord, I know not what the
matter is; but to my judgment your highness is
not entertained° with that ceremonious affection as you were wont. There's a great abate-   65
ment of kindness appears as well in the general

25–26 **breed . . . speak** find in this opportunities for
speaking out   26 **straight** at once
I.iv.2 **defuse** disguise   3 **full issue** perfect result   4
razed my likeness shaved off, disguised my natural
appearance   6 **So . . . come** so may it fall out   7 s.d.
within offstage   8 **stay** wait   12 **What . . . profess**
What do you do?   14 **profess** claim   18 **judgment**
by a heavenly or earthly judge   19 **eat no fish** i.e., (1)
I am no Catholic, but a loyal Protestant (2) I am no
weakling (3) I use no prostitutes

31 **countenance** bearing; **fain** like to   35 **honest
counsel** honorable secrets   36 **mar . . . it** i.e., I
cannot speak like an affected courtier ("curious" =
elaborate, as against plain)   47 **knave** boy   52 **clot-
poll** clodpoll, blockhead   59–60 **roundest** rudest
64 **entertained** treated

dependants° as in the duke himself also and
your daughter.

LEAR: Ha? Say'st thou so?

70   KNIGHT: I beseech you pardon me, my lord,
if I be mistaken; for my duty cannot be silent
when I think your highness wronged.

LEAR: Thou but rememb'rest° me of mine
own conception.° I have perceived a most faint
75 neglect° of late, which I have rather blamed as
mine own jealous curiosity° than as a very
pretense° and purpose of unkindness. I will
look further into't. But where's my Fool? I
have not seen him this two days.

80   KNIGHT: Since my young lady's going into
France, sir, the Fool hath much pined away.

LEAR: No more of that; I have noted it well.
Go you and tell my daughter I would speak
with her. Go you, call hither my Fool.

[Exit an ATTENDANT.]

(Enter OSWALD.)

85 O, you, sir, you! Come you hither, sir. Who
am I, sir?

OSWALD: My lady's father.

LEAR: "My lady's father"? My lord's knave,
you whoreson dog, you slave, you cur!

90   OSWALD: I am none of these, my lord; I
beseech your pardon.

LEAR: Do you bandy° looks with me, you
rascal?

[Striking him.]

OSWALD: I'll not be strucken,° my lord.

95   KENT: Nor tripped neither, you base foot-
ball° player.

[Tripping up his heels.]

LEAR: I thank thee, fellow. Thou serv'st me,
and I'll love thee.

KENT: Come, sir, arise, away. I'll teach you
100 differences.° Away, away. If you will measure
your lubber's° length again, tarry; but away.
Go to!° Have you wisdom?° So.°

[Pushes OSWALD out.]

LEAR: Now, my friendly knave, I thank thee.
There's earnest° of thy service. [Giving KENT
money.]

(Enter FOOL.)

FOOL: Let me hire him too. Here's my   105
coxcomb.°

[Offering KENT his cap.]

LEAR: How now, my pretty knave? How
dost thou?

FOOL: Sirrah, you were best° take my cox-
comb.   110

KENT: Why, Fool?

FOOL: Why? For taking one's part that's out
of favor. Nay, an° thou canst not smile as the
wind sits,° thou'lt catch cold shortly. There,
take my coxcomb. Why, this fellow has ban- 115
ished° two on's daughters, and did the third a
blessing against his will. If thou follow him,
thou must needs wear my coxcomb. — How
now, nuncle?° Would I had two coxcombs and
two daughters.   120

LEAR: Why, my boy?

FOOL: If I gave them all my living,° I'd keep
my coxcombs myself. There's mine; beg another of thy daughters.

LEAR: Take heed, sirrah — the whip.   125

FOOL: Truth's a dog must to kennel; he
must be whipped out, when Lady the Brach°
may stand by th' fire and stink.

LEAR: A pestilent gall° to me.

FOOL: Sirrah, I'll teach thee a speech.   130

LEAR: Do.

FOOL: Mark it, nuncle.

Have more than thou showest,
Speak less than thou knowest,
Lend less than thou owest,°   135
Ride more than thou goest,°
Learn more than thou trowest,°
Set less than thou throwest;°
Leave thy drink and thy whore,
And keep in-a-door,   140

67 dependants servants   73 rememb'rest remindest
74 conception idea   74–75 faint neglect i.e., "weary
negligence" (I.III.13)   76 mine . . . curiosity suspicious concern for my own dignity   76–77 very pretense actual intention   92 bandy exchange insolently
(metaphor from tennis)   94 strucken struck   95–96
football a low game played by idle boys, to the scandal of sensible men   100 differences of rank   101
lubber's lout's   102 Go to expression of derisive in-
credulity; Have you wisdom i.e., Do you know what's
good for you?; So good

104 earnest money for services rendered   106 coxcomb professional fool's cap, shaped like a coxcomb
109 you were best you had better   113 an if   113–
114 smile . . . sits ingratiate yourself with those in
power   115–116 banished alienated (by making
them independent)   119 nuncle contraction of
"mine uncle"   122 living property   127 Brach
bitch   129 gall sore   135 owest ownest   136 goest
walkest   137 trowest knowest   138 Set . . . throwest
bet less than you play for (get odds from your opponent)

And thou shalt have more
Than two tens to a score.°

KENT: This is nothing, Fool.

FOOL: Then 'tis like the breath of an
145 unfee'd° lawyer — you gave me nothing for't.
Can you make no use of nothing, nuncle?

LEAR: Why, no, boy. Nothing can be made
out of nothing.

FOOL [*to* KENT]: Prithee tell him, so much
150 the rent of his land comes to; he will not
believe a fool.

LEAR: A bitter° fool.

FOOL: Dost thou know the difference, my
boy, between a bitter fool and a sweet one?

155 LEAR: No, lad; teach me.

FOOL:

That lord that counseled thee
  To give away thy land,
Come place him here by me,
  Do thou for him stand.
160 The sweet and bitter fool
  Will presently appear;
The one in motley° here,
  The other found out° there.°

LEAR: Dost thou call me fool, boy?

165 FOOL: All thy other titles thou hast given
away; that thou wast born with.

KENT: This is not altogether fool, my lord.

FOOL: No, faith; lords and great men will
not let me.° If I had a monopoly° out, they
170 would have part on't. And ladies too, they will
not let me have all the fool to myself; they'll
be snatching. Nuncle, give me an egg, and I'll
give thee two crowns.

LEAR: What two crowns shall they be?

175 FOOL: Why, after I have cut the egg i' th'
middle and eat up the meat, the two crowns of
the egg. When thou clovest thy crown i' th'
middle and gav'st away both parts, thou bor'st
thine ass on thy back o'er the dirt.° Thou hadst
180 little wit in thy bald crown when thou gav'st

thy golden one away. If I speak like myself° in
this, let him be whipped° that first finds it so.
[*Singing*.]

Fools had ne'er less grace in a year,
  For wise men are grown foppish,
And know not how their wits to wear,   185
  Their manners are so apish.°

LEAR: When were you wont to be so full of
songs, sirrah?

FOOL: I have used° it, nuncle, e'er since
thou mad'st thy daughters thy mothers; for 190
when thou gav'st them the rod, and put'st
down thine own breeches, [*Singing*.]

Then they for sudden joy did weep,
  And I for sorrow sung,
That such a king should play bo-peep°   195
  And go the fools among.

Prithee, nuncle, keep a schoolmaster that can
teach thy Fool to lie. I would fain learn to
lie.

LEAR: And° you lie, sirrah, we'll have you
whipped.   200

FOOL: I marvel what kin thou and thy
daughters are. They'll have me whipped for
speaking true; thou'lt have me whipped for
lying; and sometimes I am whipped for holding my peace. I had rather be any kind o' 205
thing than a fool, and yet I would not be thee,
nuncle: thou hast pared thy wit o' both sides
and left nothing i' th' middle. Here comes one
o' the parings.

(*Enter* GONERIL.)

LEAR: How now, daughter? What makes 210
that frontlet° on? Methinks you are too much
of late i' th' frown.

FOOL: Thou wast a pretty fellow when thou
hadst no need to care for her frowning. Now
thou art an O without a figure.° I am better 215
than thou art now: I am a fool, thou art
nothing. [*To* GONERIL.] Yes, forsooth, I will

141–142 **have . . . score** i.e., come away with more
than you had (two tens, or twenty shillings, make a
score, or one pound)   145 **unfee'd** unpaid for   152
bitter satirical   162 **motley** the drab costume of the
professional jester   163 **found out** revealed; **there**
the Fool points at Lear, as a fool in the grain   169
let me i.e., let me have all the folly to myself; **monop-
oly** James I gave great scandal by granting to his
"snatching" courtiers royal patents to deal exclusively
in some commodity   178–179 **bor'st . . . dirt** like the
foolish and unnatural countryman in Aesop's fable

181 **like myself** like a fool   182 **let . . . whipped**
i.e., let the man be whipped for a fool who thinks my
true saying to be foolish   183–186 **Fools . . . apish**
i.e., fools were never in less favor than now, and the
reason is that wise men, turning foolish, and not
knowing how to use their intelligence, imitate the
professional fools and so make them unnecessary
189 **used** practiced   195 **play bo-peep** (1) act like
a child (2) blind himself   199 **And** if   211 **frontlet**
frown (literally, ornamental band)   215 **figure** digit,
to give value to the cipher (Lear is a nought)

hold my tongue. So your face bids me, though
you say nothing. Mum, mum,

220   He that keeps nor crust nor crum,°
               Weary of all, shall want° some.

          [*Pointing to* LEAR.]

That's a shealed peascod.°
    GONERIL:
Not only, sir, this your all-licensed° Fool,
But other° of your insolent retinue
225 Do hourly carp and quarrel, breaking forth
In rank° and not-to-be-endurèd riots. Sir,
I had thought by making this well known unto
    you
To have found a safe° redress, but now grow
    fearful,
By what yourself too late° have spoke and
    done,
230 That you protect this course, and put it on
By your allowance;° which if you should, the
    fault
Would not 'scape censure, nor the redresses
    sleep,°
Which, in the tender of° a wholesome weal,°
Might in their working do you that offense,
235 Which else were shame, that then necessity
Will call discreet proceeding.°
    FOOL: For you know, nuncle,

    The hedge-sparrow fed the cuckoo° so long
    That it had it head bit off by it° young.

240 So out went the candle, and we were left
darkling.°
    LEAR: Are you our daughter?
    GONERIL:
Come, sir,
I would you would make use of your good
    wisdom
Whereof I know you are fraught° and put
245   away

These dispositions° which of late transport you
From what you rightly are.
    FOOL: May not an ass know when the cart
draws the horse? Whoop, Jug,° I love thee!
    LEAR:
Does any here know me? This is not Lear.   250
Does Lear walk thus? Speak thus? Where are
    his eyes?
Either his notion° weakens, or his discernings°
Are lethargied° — Ha! Waking? 'Tis not so.
Who is it that can tell me who I am?
    FOOL: Lear's shadow.   255
    LEAR: I would learn that; for, by the marks
of sovereignty,° knowledge, and reason, I
should be false° persuaded I had daughters.
    FOOL: Which° they will make an obedient
father.   260
    LEAR: Your name, fair gentlewoman?
    GONERIL:
This admiration,° sir, is much o' th' savor°
Of other your° new pranks. I do beseech you
To understand my purposes aright.
As you are old and reverend, should be wise.   265
Here do you keep a hundred knights and
    squires,
Men so disordered, so deboshed,° and bold,
That this our court, infected with their man-
    ners,
Shows° like a riotous inn. Epicurism° and lust
Makes it more like a tavern or a brothel   270
Than a graced° palace. The shame itself doth
    speak
For instant remedy. Be then desired°
By her, that else will take the thing she begs,
A little to disquantity your train,°
And the remainders° that shall still depend,°   275
To be such men as may besort° your age,
Which know themselves, and you.
    LEAR: Darkness and devils!
Saddle my horses; call my train together.

---

220 **crum** soft bread inside the loaf   221 **want** lack
222 **shealed peascod** empty pea pod   223 **all-
licensed** privileged to take any liberties   224 **other**
others   226 **rank** gross   228 **safe** sure   229 **too late**
lately   230–231 **put . . . allowance** promote it by
your approval   232 **redresses sleep** correction fail to
follow   233 **tender of** desire for; **weal** state   234–
236 **Might . . . proceeding** as I apply it, the correction might humiliate you; but the need to take action
cancels what would otherwise be unfilial conduct in
me   238 **cuckoo** which lays its eggs in the nests of
other birds   239 **it** its   241 **darkling** in the dark
245 **fraught** endowed

246 **dispositions** moods   249 **Jug** Joan (a quotation
from a popular song?)   252 **notion** understanding;
discernings faculties   253 **lethargied** paralyzed
256–257 **marks of sovereignty** i.e., tokens that Lear
is king, and hence father to his daughters   258
false falsely   259 **Which** whom (Lear)   262 **admiration** (affected) wonderment; **is . . . savor** smacks
much   263 **other your** others of your   267 **deboshed**
debauched   269 **Shows** appears; **Epicurism** riotous
living   271 **graced** dignified   272 **desired** re-
quested   274 **disquantity your train** reduce the number of your dependents   275 **remainders** those who
remain; **depend** attend on you   276 **besort** befit

Degenerate° bastard, I'll not trouble thee:
280 Yet have I left a daughter.
    GONERIL:
    You strike my people, and your disordered rabble
    Make servants of their betters.

    (*Enter* ALBANY.)

    LEAR:
    Woe, that too late repents. O, sir, are you come?
    Is it your will? Speak, sir. Prepare my horses.
285 Ingratitude! thou marble-hearted fiend,
    More hideous when thou show'st thee in a child
    Than the sea-monster.
    ALBANY: Pray, sir, be patient.
    LEAR:
    Detested kite,° thou liest.
    My train are men of choice and rarest parts,°
290 That all particulars of duty know,
    And, in the most exact regard,° support
    The worships° of their name. O most small fault,
    How ugly didst thou in Cordelia show!
    Which, like an engine,° wrenched my frame of nature
    From the fixed place;° drew from my heart all
295   love,
    And added to the gall.° O Lear, Lear, Lear!
    Beat at this gate that let thy folly in

    [*Striking his head.*]

    And thy dear judgment out. Go, go, my people.
    ALBANY:
    My lord, I am guiltless, as I am ignorant
    Of what hath moved you.
300   LEAR: It may be so, my lord.
    Hear, Nature, hear; dear goddess, hear:
    Suspend thy purpose if thou didst intend
    To make this creature fruitful.
    Into her womb convey sterility,
305 Dry up in her the organs of increase,°
    And from her derogate° body never spring
    A babe to honor her. If she must teem,°

Create her child of spleen,° that it may live
And be a thwart disnatured° torment to her.
Let it stamp wrinkles in her brow of youth,   310
With cadent° tears fret° channels in her cheeks,
Turn all her mother's pains and benefits°
To laughter and contempt, that she may feel
How sharper than a serpent's tooth it is
To have a thankless child. Away, away!   315
                                    (*Exit.*)
    ALBANY:
    Now, gods that we adore, whereof comes this?
    GONERIL:
    Never afflict yourself to know the cause,
    But let his disposition° have that scope
    As° dotage gives it.

    (*Enter* LEAR.)

    LEAR:
    What, fifty of my followers at a clap?°   320
    Within a fortnight?
    ALBANY: What's the matter, sir?
    LEAR:
    I'll tell thee. [*To* GONERIL.] Life and death, I am ashamed
    That thou hast power to shake my manhood° thus!
    That these hot tears, which break from me perforce,°
    Should make thee worth them. Blasts and fogs upon thee!   325
    Th' untented woundings° of a father's curse
    Pierce every sense about thee! Old fond° eyes,
    Beweep° this cause again, I'll pluck ye out
    And cast you, with the waters that you loose,°
    To temper° clay. Yea, is it come to this?   330
    Ha! Let it be so. I have another daughter,
    Who I am sure is kind and comfortable.°
    When she shall hear this of thee, with her nails
    She'll flay thy wolvish visage. Thou shalt find

---

279 **Degenerate** unnatural   288 **kite** scavenging bird of prey   289 **parts** accomplishments   291 **exact regard** strict attention to detail   292 **worships** honor   294 **engine** destructive contrivance   294–295 **wrenched … place** i.e., disorders my natural self   296 **gall** bitterness   305 **increase** childbearing   306 **derogate** degraded   307 **teem** conceive

308 **spleen** ill humor   309 **thwart disnatured** perverse unnatural   311 **cadent** falling; **fret** wear   312 **benefits** the mother's beneficent care of her child   318 **disposition** mood   319 **As** that   320 **at a clap** at one stroke   323 **shake my manhood** i.e., with tears   324 **perforce** involuntarily, against my will   326 **untented woundings** wounds too deep to be probed with a tent (a roll of lint)   327 **fond** foolish   328 **Beweep** if you weep over   329 **loose** (1) let loose (2) lose, as of no avail   330 **temper** mix with and soften   332 **comfortable** ready to comfort

That I'll resume the shape° which thou dost
335   think
I have cast off for ever.

> (*Exit* [LEAR, *with* KENT
> *and* ATTENDANTS].)

GONERIL: Do you mark that?
ALBANY:
I cannot be so partial, Goneril,
To the great love I bear you° —
GONERIL:
Pray you, content. What, Oswald, ho!

[*To the* FOOL].

You, sir, more knave than fool, after your
340   master!
    FOOL: Nuncle Lear, nuncle Lear, tarry. Take
the Fool° with thee.

    A fox, when one has caught her,
    And such a daughter,
345   Should sure to the slaughter,
    If my cap would buy a halter.°
    So the Fool follows after.°   (*Exit.*)

GONERIL:
This man hath had good counsel. A hundred
    knights!
'Tis politic° and safe to let him keep
At point° a hundred knights: yes, that on every
350   dream,
Each buzz,° each fancy, each complaint, dis-
    like,
He may enguard° his dotage with their pow'rs
And hold our lives in mercy.° Oswald, I say!
    ALBANY:
Well, you may fear too far.
    GONERIL: Safer than trust too far.
355 Let me still take away the harms I fear,
Not fear still to be taken.° I know his heart.
What he hath uttered I have writ my sister.
If she sustain him and his hundred knights,
When I have showed th' unfitness —

    (*Enter* OSWALD.)

               How now, Oswald?
360 What, have you writ that letter to my sister?
    OSWALD: Ay, madam.

GONERIL:
Take you some company,° and away to horse.
Inform her full of my particular° fear,
And thereto add such reasons of your own
As may compact° it more. Get you gone,   365
And hasten your return. [*Exit* OSWALD.] No,
    no, my lord,
This milky gentleness and course° of yours,
Though I condemn not,° yet under pardon,
You are much more attasked° for want of
    wisdom
Than praised for harmful mildness.°   370
    ALBANY:
How far your eyes may pierce I cannot tell;
Striving to better, oft we mar what's well.
    GONERIL: Nay then —
    ALBANY: Well, well, th' event.°   (*Exeunt.*)

SCENE V. [*Court before the same.*]

Enter LEAR, KENT, *and* FOOL.

    LEAR: Go you before to Gloucester with
these letters. Acquaint my daughter no further
with anything you know than comes from her
demand out of the letter.° If your diligence be
not speedy, I shall be there afore you.   5
    KENT: I will not sleep, my lord, till I have
delivered your letter.   (*Exit.*)
    FOOL: If a man's brains were in's heels,
were't° not in danger of kibes?°
    LEAR: Ay, boy.   10
    FOOL: Then I prithee be merry. Thy wit
shall not go slipshod.°
    LEAR: Ha, ha, ha.
    FOOL: Shalt° see thy other daughter will use
thee kindly;° for though she's as like this as a   15
crab's° like an apple, yet I can tell what I can
tell.
    LEAR: Why, what canst thou tell, my boy?
    FOOL: She will taste as like this as a crab

---

335 **shape** i.e., kingly role   337–338 **I cannot...
you** i.e., even though my love inclines me to you,
I must protest   342 **Fool** (1) the Fool himself (2)
the epithet or character of "fool"   346–347 **halter,
after** pronounced "hauter," "auter"   349 **politic**
good policy   350 **At point** armed   351 **buzz**
rumor   352 **enguard** protect   353 **in mercy** at his
mercy   356 **Not...taken** rather than remain fearful of being overtaken by them

362 **company** escort   363 **particular** own   365 **compact** strengthen   367 **milky ... course** mild and gentle way (hendiadys)   368 **condemn not** condemn it
not   369 **attasked** taken to task, blamed   370 **harmful mildness** dangerous indulgence   374 **th' event**
i.e., we'll see what happens
I.v.3–4 **than ... letter** than her reading of the letter
brings her to ask   9 **were't** i.e., the brains; **kibes** chilblains   11–12 **Thy ... slipshod** Your brains shall
not go in slippers (because you have no brains to be
protected from chilblains)   14 **Shalt** thou shalt   15
kindly (1) affectionately (2) after her kind or nature   16 **crab** crab apple

20 does to a crab. Thou canst tell why one's nose stands i' th' middle on's° face?

LEAR: No.

FOOL: Why, to keep one's eyes of° either side's nose, that what a man cannot smell out,
25 he may spy into.

LEAR: I did her wrong.

FOOL: Canst tell how an oyster makes his shell?

LEAR: No.
30 FOOL: Nor I neither; but I can tell why a snail has a house.

LEAR: Why?

FOOL: Why, to put's head in; not to give it away to his daughters, and leave his horns°
35 without a case.

LEAR: I will forget my nature.° So kind a father! Be my horses ready?

FOOL: Thy asses are gone about 'em. The reason why the seven stars° are no moe° than
40 seven is a pretty° reason.

LEAR: Because they are not eight.

FOOL: Yes indeed. Thou wouldst make a good fool.

LEAR: To take't again perforce!° Monster
45 ingratitude!

FOOL: If thou wert my fool, nuncle, I'd have thee beaten for being old before thy time.

LEAR: How's that?

FOOL: Thou shouldst not have been old till
50 thou hadst been wise.

LEAR:

O, let me not be mad, not mad, sweet heaven! Keep me in temper;° I would not be mad!

[*Enter* GENTLEMAN.]

How now, are the horses ready?

GENTLEMAN: Ready, my lord.
55 LEAR: Come, boy.

FOOL:

She that's a maid now, and laughs at my departure,

Shall not be a maid long, unless things be cut shorter.°

(*Exeunt.*)

ACT II

SCENE I. [*The Earl of* GLOUCESTER'S *castle.*]

Enter EDMUND *and* CURAN, *severally.*°

EDMUND: Save° thee, Curan.

CURAN: And you, sir. I have been with your father, and given him notice that the Duke of Cornwall and Regan his duchess will be here with him this night.
5
EDMUND: How comes that?

CURAN: Nay, I know not. You have heard of the news abroad? I mean the whispered ones, for they are yet but ear-kissing arguments.°

EDMUND: Not I. Pray you, what are they?
10
CURAN: Have you heard of no likely° wars toward,° 'twixt the Dukes of Cornwall and Albany?

EDMUND: Not a word.

CURAN: You may do, then, in time. Fare you
15 well, sir. (*Exit.*)

EDMUND:

The duke be here tonight? The better!° best!

This weaves itself perforce° into my business.

My father hath set guard to take my brother,

And I have one thing of a queasy question°
20 Which I must act. Briefness° and Fortune, work!

Brother, a word; descend. Brother, I say!

(*Enter* EDGAR.)

My father watches. O sir, fly this place.

Intelligence° is given where you are hid.

You have now the good advantage of the
25 night.

Have you not spoken 'gainst the Duke of Cornwall?

He's coming hither, now i' th' night, i' th' haste,°

And Regan with him. Have you nothing said

21 **on's** of his   23 **of** on   34 **horns** (1) snail's horns (2) cuckold's horns   36 **nature** paternal instincts 39 **seven stars** the Pleiades; **moe** more   40 **pretty** apt   44 **To...perforce** (1) of Goneril, who has forcibly taken away Lear's privileges; or (2) of Lear, who meditates a forcible resumption of authority 52 **in temper** sane   56–57 **She...shorter** The maid who laughs, missing the tragic implications of this quarrel, will not have sense enough to preserve her virginity ("things" = penises)

II.i.s.d. **severally** separately (from different entrances onstage)   1 **Save** God save   9 **ear-kissing arguments** subjects whispered in the ear   11 **likely** probable   12 **toward** impending   17 **The better** So much the better   18 **perforce** necessarily   20 **of... question** that requires delicate handling (to be "queasy" is to be on the point of vomiting)   21 **Briefness** speed   24 **Intelligence** information   27 **i' th' haste** in great haste

Upon his party° 'gainst the Duke of Albany?
Advise yourself.°
30 EDGAR: I am sure on't,° not a word.
EDMUND:
I hear my father coming. Pardon me:
In cunning° I must draw my sword upon you.
Draw, seem to defend yourself; now quit you°
    well.
Yield! Come before my father! Light ho,
    here!
35 Fly, brother. Torches, torches! — So farewell.
                              (*Exit* EDGAR.)
Some blood drawn on me would beget opin-
    ion°

[*Wounds his arm.*]

Of my more fierce endeavor. I have seen
    drunkards
Do more than this in sport. Father, father!
Stop, stop! No help?

    (*Enter* GLOUCESTER, *and* SERVANTS *with
    torches.*)

GLOUCESTER:
40 Now, Edmund, where's the villain?
EDMUND:
Here stood he in the dark, his sharp sword
    out,
Mumbling of wicked charms, conjuring the
    moon
To stand auspicious mistress.
GLOUCESTER: But where is he?
EDMUND:
Look, sir, I bleed.
45 GLOUCESTER: Where is the villain, Edmund?
EDMUND:
Fled this way, sir, when by no means he
    could —
GLOUCESTER:
Pursue him, ho! Go after. [*Exeunt some
SERVANTS.*] By no means what?
EDMUND:
Persuade me to the murder of your lordship;
But that I told him the revenging gods
50 'Gainst parricides did all the thunder bend;°
Spoke with how manifold and strong a bond
The child was bound to th' father. Sir, in fine,°
Seeing how loathly opposite° I stood

To his unnatural purpose, in fell° motion°
With his prepared sword he charges home   55
My unprovided° body, latched° mine arm;
But when he saw my best alarumed° spirits
Bold in the quarrel's right,° roused to th'
    encounter,
Or whether gasted° by the noise I made,
Full suddenly he fled.
GLOUCESTER: Let him fly far.   60
Not in this land shall he remain uncaught;
And found — dispatch.° The noble duke my
    master,
My worthy arch° and patron, comes tonight.
By his authority I will proclaim it,
That he which finds him shall deserve our
    thanks,   65
Bringing the murderous coward to the stake.
He that conceals him, death.°
EDMUND:
When I dissuaded him from his intent,
And found him pight° to do it, with curst°
    speech
I threatened to discover° him. He replied,   70
"Thou unpossessing° bastard, dost thou think,
If I would stand against thee, would the
    reposal°
Of any trust, virtue, or worth in thee
Make thy words faithed?° No. What I should
    deny —
As this I would, ay, though thou didst produce 75
My very character° — I'd turn it all
To thy suggestion,° plot, and damnèd prac-
    tice.°
And thou must make a dullard of the world,°
If they not thought° the profits of my death
Were very pregnant° and potential spirits°   80
To make thee seek it."
GLOUCESTER: O strange and fastened° villain!
Would he deny his letter, said he? I never got°
    him.

54 **fell** deadly; **motion** thrust (a term from fencing)   56 **unprovided** unprotected; **latched** wounded
(lanced)   57 **best alarumed** wholly aroused   58
Bold . . . right confident in the rightness of my cause
59 **gasted** struck aghast   62 **dispatch** i.e., he will
be killed   63 **arch** chief   67 **death** the same ellipti-
cal form that characterizes "dispatch," line 62   69
pight determined; **curst** angry   70 **discover** expose
71 **unpossessing** beggarly (landless)   72 **reposal**
placing   74 **faithed** believed   76 **character** handwriting   77 **suggestion** instigation; **practice** device
78 **make . . . world** think everyone stupid   79 **not
thought** did not think   80 **pregnant** teeming with
incitement; **potential spirits** powerful evil spirits   81
fastened hardened   82 **got** begot

29 **Upon his party** censuring his enmity   30 **Advise yourself** Reflect; **on't** of it   32 **In cunning** as a
pretense   33 **quit you** acquaint yourself   36 **beget
opinion** create the impression   50 **bend** aim   52 **in
fine** finally   53 **loathly opposite** bitterly opposed

(Tucket° within.)

Hark, the duke's trumpets. I know not why he
    comes.
All ports° I'll bar; the villain shall not 'scape;
The duke must grant me that. Besides, his
    picture
85 I will send far and near, that all the kingdom
May have due note of him; and of my land,
Loyal and natural° boy, I'll work the means
To make thee capable.°

(Enter CORNWALL, REGAN, *and* ATTEN-
DANTS.*)*

CORNWALL:
How now, my noble friend! Since I came
90   hither,
Which I can call but now, I have heard
    strange news.
    REGAN:
If it be true, all vengeance comes too short
Which can pursue th' offender. How dost, my
    lord?
    GLOUCESTER:
O madam, my old heart is cracked, it's
    cracked.
    REGAN:
95 What, did my father's godson seek your life?
He whom my father named, your Edgar?
    GLOUCESTER:
O lady, lady, shame would have it hid.
    REGAN:
Was he not companion with the riotous
    knights
That tended upon my father?
    GLOUCESTER:
100 I know not, madam. 'Tis too bad, too bad.
    EDMUND:
Yes, madam, he was of that consort.°
    REGAN:
No marvel then, though he were ill affected.°
'Tis they have put° him on the old man's
    death,
To have th' expense and waste° of his reve-
    nues.
105 I have this present evening from my sister
Been well informed of them, and with such
    cautions

That, if they come to sojourn at my house,
I'll not be there.
    CORNWALL: Nor I, assure thee, Regan.
Edmund, I hear that you have shown your
    father
A childlike° office.
    EDMUND: It was my duty, sir.   110
    GLOUCESTER:
He did bewray his practice,° and received
This hurt you see, striving to apprehend him.
    CORNWALL:
Is he pursued?
    GLOUCESTER:
                    Ay, my good lord.
    CORNWALL:
If he be taken, he shall never more
Be feared of doing° harm. Make your own
    purpose,   115
How in my strength you please.° For you,
    Edmund,
Whose virtue and obedience° doth this instant
So much commend itself, you shall be ours.
Natures of such deep trust we shall much
    need;
You we first seize on.
    EDMUND: I shall serve you, sir,   120
Truly, however else.
    GLOUCESTER: For him I thank your grace.
    CORNWALL:
You know not why we came to visit you?
    REGAN:
Thus out of season, threading dark-eyed night.
Occasions, noble Gloucester, of some prize,°
Wherein we must have use of your advice.   125
Our father he hath writ, so hath our sister,
Of differences,° which° I best thought it fit
To answer from° our home. The several mes-
    sengers
From hence attend dispatch.° Our good old
    friend,
Lay comforts to your bosom,° and bestow   130
Your needful° counsel to our businesses,
Which craves the instant use.°

110 **childlike** filial   111 **bewray his practice** disclose his plot   115 **of doing** because he might do
115–116 **Make ... please** Use my power freely, in
carrying out your plans for his capture   117 **virtue
and obedience** virtuous obedience   124 **prize** importance   127 **differences** quarrels; **which** referring
not to "differences," but to the letter Lear has written
128 **from** away from   129 **attend dispatch** are
waiting to be sent off   130 **Lay ... bosom** console
yourself (about Edgar's supposed treason)   131
needful needed   132 **craves ... use** demands immediate transaction

82 s.d. **Tucket** Cornwall's special trumpet call   84
ports exits, of whatever sort   88 **natural** (1) kind
(filial) (2) illegitimate   89 **capable** able to inherit
101 **consort** company   102 **ill affected** disposed to
evil   103 **put** set   104 **expense and waste** squander-
ing

GLOUCESTER: I serve you, madam.
Your graces are right welcome.
                          (*Exeunt. Flourish.*)

SCENE II. [*Before* GLOUCESTER's *castle.*]

Enter KENT *and* OSWALD, *severally.*

OSWALD: Good dawning° to thee, friend. Art
of this house?°
KENT: Ay.
OSWALD: Where may we set our horses?
5 KENT: I' th' mire.
OSWALD: Prithee, if thou lov'st me, tell me.
KENT: I love thee not.
OSWALD: Why then, I care not for thee.
KENT: If I had thee in Lipsbury Pinfold,° I
10 would make thee care for me.
OSWALD: Why dost thou use me thus? I
know thee not.
KENT: Fellow, I know thee.
OSWALD: What dost thou know me for?
15 KENT: A knave, a rascal, an eater of broken
meats;° a base, proud, shallow, beggarly, three-
suited,° hundred-pound,° filthy worsted-stock-
ing° knave; a lily-livered, action-taking,° whoreson, glass-gazing,° superserviceable,° finical°
20 rogue; one-trunk-inheriting° slave; one that
wouldst be a bawd in way of good service,° and
art nothing but the composition° of a knave,
beggar, coward, pander, and the son and heir
of a mongrel bitch; one whom I will beat into
25 clamorous whining if thou deniest the least
syllable of thy addition.°
OSWALD: Why, what a monstrous fellow art
thou, thus to rail on one that is neither known
of thee nor knows thee!
30 KENT: What a brazen-faced varlet art thou

to deny thou knowest me! Is it two days since
I tripped up thy heels and beat thee before the
king? [*Drawing his sword.*] Draw, you rogue,
for though it be night, yet the moon shines.
I'll make a sop o' th' moonshine° of you. You   35
whoreson cullionly barbermonger,° draw!
OSWALD: Away, I have nothing to do with
thee.
KENT: Draw, you rascal. You come with
letters against the king, and take Vanity the   40
puppet's° part against the royalty of her father.
Draw, you rogue, or I'll so carbonado° your
shanks. Draw, you rascal. Come your ways!°
OSWALD: Help, ho! Murder! Help!
KENT: Strike, you slave! Stand, rogue!   45
Stand, you neat° slave! Strike!

[*Beating him.*]

OSWALD: Help, ho! Murder, murder!

(*Enter* EDMUND, *with his rapier drawn,*
CORNWALL, REGAN, GLOUCESTER, SERVANTS.)

EDMUND: How now? What's the matter?
Part!
KENT: With you,° goodman boy,° if you   50
please! Come, I'll flesh° ye, come on, young
master.
GLOUCESTER: Weapons? Arms? What's the
matter here?
CORNWALL: Keep peace, upon your lives. He   55
dies that strikes again. What is the matter?
REGAN: The messengers from our sister and
the king.
CORNWALL: What is your difference?° Speak.
OSWALD: I am scarce in breath, my lord.   60
KENT: No marvel, you have so bestirred°
your valor. You cowardly rascal, nature dis-
claims in thee.° A tailor made thee.°

II.II.1 **dawning** dawn is impending, but not yet arrived   1–2 **Art . . . house** Do you live here?   9 **Lipsbury Pinfold** a pound or pen in which strayed animals
are enclosed ("Lipsbury" may denote a particular
place, or may be slang for "between my teeth")   15–
16 **broken meats** scraps of food   16–17 **three-suited**
the wardrobe permitted to a servant or "knave"   17
hundred-pound the extent of Oswald's wealth, and
thus a sneer at his aspiring to gentility   17–18
worsted-stocking worn by servants   18 **action-taking**
one who refuses a fight and goes to law instead   19
glass-gazing conceited   19 **superserviceable** sycophantic, serving without principle; **finical** overfastid-
ious   20 **one-trunk-inheriting** possessing only a
trunkful of goods   21 **bawd . . . service** pimp, to
please his master   22 **composition** compound   26
addition titles

35 **sop . . . moonshine** i.e., Oswald will admit the
moonlight, and so sop it up, through the open wounds
Kent is preparing to give him   36 **cullionly barbermonger** base patron of hairdressers (effeminate man)
40–41 **Vanity the puppet's** Goneril, here identified
with one of the personified characters in the morality
plays, which were sometimes put on as puppet shows
42 **carbonado** cut across, like a piece of meat before
cooking   43 **Come your ways** Get along!   46 **neat**
(1) foppish (2) unmixed, as in "neat wine"   50
With you i.e., the quarrel is with you; **goodman boy**
young man (peasants are "goodmen"; "boy" is a
term of contempt)   51 **flesh** introduce to blood
(term from hunting)   59 **difference** quarrel   61
bestirred exercised   62–63 **nature . . . thee** nature
renounces any part in you   63 **A tailor made thee**
from the proverb "The tailor makes the man"

CORNWALL: Thou art a strange fellow. A
65 tailor make a man?

KENT: A tailor, sir. A stonecutter or a
painter could not have made him so ill, though
they had been but two years o' th' trade.

CORNWALL:
Speak yet, how grew your quarrel?

70 OSWALD: This ancient ruffian, sir, whose life
I have spared at suit of° his gray beard —

KENT: Thou whoreson zed,° thou unnecessary letter! My lord, if you will give me leave,
I will tread this unbolted° villain into mortar
75 and daub the wall of a jakes° with him. Spare
my gray beard, you wagtail!°

CORNWALL: Peace, sirrah!
You beastly° knave, know you no reverence?

KENT:
Yes, sir, but anger hath a privilege.

CORNWALL:
80 Why art thou angry?

KENT:
That such a slave as this should wear a sword,
Who wears no honesty. Such smiling rogues as
    these,
Like rats, oft bite the holy cords° atwain
Which are too intrince° t' unloose; smooth°
    every passion
85 That in the natures of their lords rebel,
Being oil to fire, snow to the colder moods;
Renege,° affirm, and turn their halcyon beaks°
With every gale and vary° of their masters,
Knowing naught, like dogs, but following.
90 A plague upon your epileptic° visage!
Smile you° my speeches, as I were a fool?
Goose, if I had you upon Sarum Plain,°
I'd drive ye cackling home to Camelot.°

CORNWALL:
What, art thou mad, old fellow?

GLOUCESTER:
How fell you out? Say that.   95

KENT:
No contraries° hold more antipathy
Than I and such a knave.

CORNWALL:
Why dost thou call him knave? What is his
    fault?

KENT:
His countenance likes° me not.

CORNWALL:
No more perchance does mine, nor his, nor
    hers.   100

KENT:
Sir, 'tis my occupation to be plain:
I have seen better faces in my time
Than stands on any shoulder that I see
Before me at this instant.

CORNWALL: This is some fellow
Who, having been praised for bluntness, doth
    affect   105
A saucy roughness, and constrains the garb
Quite from his nature.° He cannot flatter, he;
An honest mind and plain, he must speak
    truth.
And° they will take it, so; if not, he's plain.
These kind of knaves I know, which in this
    plainness   110
Harbor more craft and more corrupter ends
Than twenty silly-ducking observants°
That stretch their duties nicely.°

KENT:
Sir, in good faith, in sincere verity,
Under th' allowance° of your great aspect,°   115
Whose influence,° like the wreath of radiant
    fire
On flick'ring Phoebus' front° —

CORNWALL: What mean'st by this?

KENT: To go out of my dialect,° which you
discommend so much. I know, sir, I am no
flatterer. He° that beguiled you in a plain   120

71 **at suit of** out of pity for   72 **zed** the letter Z,
generally omitted in contemporary dictionaries   74
unbolted unsifted, i.e., altogether a villain   75 **jakes**
privy   76 **wagtail** a bird that bobs its tail up and
down, and thus suggests obsequiousness   78 **beastly**
irrational   83 **holy cords** sacred bonds of affection
(as between husbands and wives, parents and children)   84 **intrince** entangled, intricate; **smooth** appease   87 **Renege** deny; **halcyon beaks** the halcyon
or kingfisher serves here as a type of the opportunist
because, when hung up by the tail or neck, it was
supposed to turn with the wind, like a weathervane
88 **gale and vary** varying gale (hendiadys)   90 **epi-
leptic** distorted by grinning   91 **Smile you** do you
smile at   92 **Sarum Plain** Salisbury Plain   93 **Camelot** the residence of King Arthur (presumably a particular point, now lost, is intended here)

96 **contraries** opposites   99 **likes** pleases   106–107
constrains . . . nature forces the manner of can-
did speech to be a cloak, not for candor but for
craft   109 **And** if   112 **silly-ducking observants**
ridiculously obsequious attendants   113 **nicely** punctiliously   115 **allowance** approval; **aspect** (1) appearance (2) position of the heavenly bodies   116
influence astrological power   117 **Phoebus' front**
forehead of the sun   118 **dialect** customary manner
of speaking   120 **He** i.e., the sort of candid-crafty
man Cornwall has been describing

accent was a plain knave, which, for my part, I
will not be, though I should win your displea-
sure to entreat me to't.°
CORNWALL:
What was th' offense you gave him?
OSWALD:
125 I never gave him any.
It pleased the king his master very late°
To strike at me, upon his misconstruction;°
When he, compact,° and flattering his displea-
sure,
Tripped me behind; being down, insulted,
railed,
130 And put upon him such a deal of man°
That worthied him,° got praises of the king
For him attempting who was self-subdued;°
And, in the fleshment° of this dread exploit,
Drew on me here again.
KENT: None of these rogues and cowards
But Ajax is their fool.°
135 CORNWALL: Fetch forth the stocks!
You stubborn° ancient knave, you reverent°
braggart,
We'll teach you.
KENT: Sir, I am too old to learn.
Call not your stocks for me, I serve the king,
On whose employment I was sent to you.
You shall do small respect, show too bold
140 malice
Against the grace and person° of my master,
Stocking his messenger.
CORNWALL:
Fetch forth the stocks. As I have life and
honor,
There shall he sit till noon.
REGAN:
Till noon? Till night, my lord, and all night
145 too.

KENT:
Why, madam, if I were your father's dog,
You should not use me so.
REGAN: Sir, being his knave, I will.
CORNWALL:
This is a fellow of the selfsame color°
Our sister speaks of. Come, bring away° the
stocks.

(Stocks brought out.)

GLOUCESTER:
Let me beseech your grace not to do so.   150
His fault is much, and the good king his
master
Will check° him for't. Your purposed° low
correction
Is such as basest and contemnèd'st° wretches
For pilf'rings and most common trespasses
Are punished with.   155
The king his master needs must take it ill
That he, so slightly valued in° his messenger,
Should have him thus restrained.
CORNWALL: I'll answer° that.
REGAN:
My sister may receive it much more worse,
To have her gentleman abused, assaulted, 160
For following her affairs. Put in his legs.

[KENT is put in the stocks.]

Come, my good lord, away!
        [Exeunt all but GLOUCESTER and KENT.]
GLOUCESTER:
I am sorry for thee, friend. 'Tis the duke's
pleasure,
Whose disposition° all the world well knows
Will not be rubbed° nor stopped. I'll entreat
for thee.   165
KENT:
Pray do not, sir. I have watched° and traveled
hard.
Some time I shall sleep out, the rest I'll whistle.
A good man's fortune may grow out at heels.°
Give° you good morrow.
GLOUCESTER:
The duke's to blame in this. 'Twill be ill
taken.°   (Exit.)   170

122–123 though . . . to't even if I were to succeed in
bringing your graceless person ("displeasure" personified, and in lieu of the expected form, "your grace")
to beg me to be a plain knave   126 very late recently   127 misconstruction misunderstanding   128
compact in league with the king   130 put . . . man
pretended such manly behavior   131 worthied him
made him seem heroic   132 For . . . self-subdued
for attacking a man (Oswald) who offered no resistance   133 fleshment the bloodthirstiness excited
by his first success or "fleshing"   134–135 None . . .
fool i.e., cowardly rogues like Oswald always impose
on fools like Cornwall (who is likened to Ajax: [1]
the braggart Greek-warrior [2] a jakes or privy)   136
stubborn rude; reverent old   141 grace and person
i.e., Lear as sovereign and in his personal character

148 color kind   149 away out   152 check correct;
purposed intended   153 contemnèd'st most despised
157 slightly valued in little honored in the person of
158 answer answer for   164 disposition inclination
165 rubbed diverted (metaphor from the game of
bowls)   166 watched gone without sleep   168 A
. . . heels Even a good man may have bad fortune
169 Give God give   170 taken received

KENT:

Good king, that must approve° the common
   saw,°
Thou out of heaven's benediction com'st
To the warm sun.°
Approach, thou beacon to this under globe,°
175 That by thy comfortable° beams I may
Peruse this letter. Nothing almost sees miracles
But misery.° I know 'tis from Cordelia,
Who hath most fortunately been informed
Of my obscurèd° course. And shall find time
180 From this enormous state, seeking to give
Losses their remedies.° All weary and o'er-
   watched,
Take vantage,° heavy eyes, not to behold
This shameful lodging. Fortune, good night;
Smile once more, turn thy wheel.°

(*Sleeps.*)

[SCENE III. *A wood.*]

Enter EDGAR.

EDGAR:

I heard myself proclaimed,
And by the happy° hollow of a tree
Escaped the hunt. No port is free, no place
That guard and most unusual vigilance
Does not attend my taking.° Whiles I may
5 'scape,
I will preserve myself; and am bethought°
To take the basest and most poorest shape
That ever penury, in contempt of man,
Brought near to beast;° my face I'll grime with
   filth,
10 Blanket° my loins, elf° all my hairs in knots,
And with presented° nakedness outface°

171 **approve** confirm; **saw** proverb 172–173 **Thou
. . . sun** i.e., Lear goes from better to worse, from
heaven's blessing or shelter to lack of shelter 174
beacon . . . globe i.e., the sun, whose rising Kent anticipates 175 **comfortable** comforting 176–177
Nothing . . . misery i.e., True perception belongs only
to the wretched 179 **obscurèd** disguised 179–181
shall . . . remedies a possible reading: Cordelia, away
from this monstrous state of things, will find occasion
to right the wrongs we suffer 182 **vantage** advantage
(of sleep) 184 **turn thy wheel** i.e., so that Kent,
who is at the bottom, may climb upward
II.III.2 **happy** lucky 5 **attend my taking** watch to
capture me 6 **am bethought** have decided 8–9
penury . . . beast poverty, to show how contemptible
man is, reduced to the level of a beast 10 **Blanket**
cover only with a blanket; **elf** tangle (into "elflocks,"
supposed to be caused by elves) 11 **presented** the
show of; **outface** brave

The winds and persecutions of the sky.
The country gives me proof° and precedent
Of Bedlam° beggars, who, with roaring voices,
Strike° in their numbed and mortified° bare
   arms   15
Pins, wooden pricks,° nails, sprigs of rosemary;
And with this horrible object° from low° farms,
Poor pelting° villages, sheepcotes, and mills,
Sometimes with lunatic bans,° sometime with
   prayers,
Enforce their charity. Poor Turlygod, Poor
   Tom,°   20
That's something yet: Edgar I nothing am.°
                           (*Exit.*)

[SCENE IV. *Before* GLOUCESTER'S *castle.* KENT
in the stocks.]

Enter LEAR, FOOL, *and* GENTLEMAN.

LEAR:

'Tis strange that they should so depart from
   home,
And not send back my messenger.
  GENTLEMAN: As I learned,
The night before there was no purpose° in
   them
Of this remove.°
  KENT: Hail to thee, noble master.
LEAR: Ha!   5
Mak'st thou this shame thy pastime?°
  KENT: No, my lord.
  FOOL: Ha, ha, he wears cruel° garters. Horses
are tied by the heads, dogs and bears by th'
neck, monkeys by th' loins, and men by th'
legs. When a man's overlusty at legs,° then   10
he wears wooden netherstocks.°
  LEAR:
What's he that hath so much thy place
   mistook
To set thee here?
  KENT: It is both he and she,
Your son and daughter.

13 **proof** example 14 **Bedlam** see I.II.155–156 15
Strike stick; **mortified** not alive to pain 16 **pricks**
skewers 17 **object** spectacle; **low** humble 18 **pelt-**
ing paltry 19 **bans** curses 20 **Poor . . . Tom** Edgar
recites the names a Bedlam beggar gives himself 21
That's . . . am There's a chance for me in that I am
no longer known for myself
II.IV.3 **purpose** intention 4 **remove** removal 6
Mak'st . . . pastime Are you doing this to amuse yourself? 7 **cruel** (1) painful (2) "crewel," a worsted yarn
used in garters 10 **overlusty at legs** (1) a vagabond
(2) sexually promiscuous (?) 11 **netherstocks** stockings (as opposed to knee breeches, or upperstocks)

15 LEAR: No.
    KENT: Yes.
    LEAR: No, I say.
    KENT: I say yea.
    LEAR: No, no, they would not.
20 KENT: Yes, they have.
    LEAR:
By Jupiter, I swear no!
    KENT:
By Juno, I swear ay!
    LEAR: They durst not do't;
They could not, would not do't. 'Tis worse
    than murder
To do upon respect° such violent outrage.
25 Resolve° me with all modest° haste which way
Thou mightst deserve or they impose this
    usage,
Coming from us.
    KENT: My lord, when at their home
I did commend° your highness' letters to them,
Ere I was risen from the place that showed
30 My duty kneeling, came there a reeking post,°
Stewed° in his haste, half breathless, panting
    forth
From Goneril his mistress salutations,
Delivered letters, spite of intermission,°
Which presently° they read; on° whose con-
    tents
They summoned up their meiny,° straight took
35   horse,
Commanded me to follow and attend
The leisure of their answer, gave me cold
    looks,
And meeting here the other messenger,
Whose welcome I perceived had poisoned
    mine,
40 Being the very fellow which of late
Displayed° so saucily against your highness,
Having more man than wit° about me, drew;
He raised° the house, with loud and coward
    cries.
Your son and daughter found this trespass
    worth°
45 The shame which here it suffers.

24 **upon respect** (1) on the respect due to the king
(2) deliberately 25 **Resolve** inform; **modest** becoming 28 **commend** deliver 30 **reeking post** sweating
messenger 31 **stewed** steaming 33 **spite of intermission** in spite of the interrupting of my business
34 **presently** at once; **on** on the strength of 35
meiny retinue 41 **Displayed** showed off 42 **more
. . . wit** more manhood than sense 43 **raised** aroused
44 **worth** deserving

FOOL: Winter's not gone yet, if the wild
geese fly that way.°

    Fathers that wear rags
      Do make their children blind,°
    But fathers that bear bags°   50
      Shall see their children kind.
    Fortune, that arrant whore,
      Ne'er turns the key° to th' poor.

But for all this, thou shalt have as many
dolors° for thy daughters as thou canst tell° in   55
a year.
    LEAR:
O, how this mother swells up toward my
    heart!
Hysterica passio,° down, thou climbing sorrow,
Thy element's° below. Where is this daughter?
    KENT:
With the earl, sir, here within.
    LEAR: Follow me not; 60
Stay here.   (Exit.)
    GENTLEMAN:
Made you no more offense but what you speak
    of?
    KENT: None.
How chance° the king comes with so small a
    number?
    FOOL: And° thou hadst been set i' th' stocks 65
for that question, thou'dst well deserved it.
    KENT: Why, Fool?
    FOOL: We'll set thee to school to an ant, to
teach thee there's no laboring i' th' winter.° All
that follow their noses are led by their eyes but 70
blind men, and there's not a nose among
twenty but can smell him that's stinking.° Let
go thy hold when a great wheel runs down a
hill, lest it break thy neck with following. But

46–47 **Winter's . . . way** More trouble is to come,
since Cornwall and Regan act so ("geese" is used
contemptuously, as in Kent's quarrel with Oswald,
II.ii.92–93) 49 **blind** i.e., indifferent 50 **bags**
moneybags 53 **turns the key** i.e., opens the door 55
dolors (1) sorrows (2) dollars (English name for Spanish and German coins); **tell** (1) about (2) count 57–
58 **mother . . . Hysterica passio** hysteria, causing suffocation or choking 59 **element** proper place 64
How chance how does it happen that 65 **And** if
68–69 **We'll . . . winter** in the popular fable the ant,
unlike the improvident grasshopper, anticipates the
winter when none can labor by laying up provisions in
the summer; Lear, trusting foolishly to summer days,
finds himself unprovided for, and unable to provide,
now that "winter" has come 69–72 **All . . . stinking**
i.e., all can smell out the decay of Lear's fortunes

75 the great one that goes upward, let him draw
thee after. When a wise man gives thee better
counsel, give me mine again. I would have
none but knaves follow it since a fool gives it.

That sir, which serves and seeks for gain,
80   And follows but for form,°
Will pack,° when it begins to rain,
     And leave thee in the storm.
But I will tarry; the Fool will stay,
     And let the wise man fly.
85 The knave turns Fool that runs away,
     The Fool no knave,° perdy.°

KENT: Where learned you this, Fool?
FOOL: Not i' th' stocks, fool.

(*Enter* LEAR *and* GLOUCESTER.)

LEAR:
Deny° to speak with me? They are sick, they
     are weary,
90 They have traveled all the night? Mere fetches,°
The images° of revolt and flying off!°
Fetch me a better answer.
     GLOUCESTER: My dear lord,
You know the fiery quality° of the duke,
How unremovable and fixed he is
In his own course.
95   LEAR: Vengeance, plague, death, confusion!
Fiery? What quality? Why, Gloucester,
     Gloucester,
I'd speak with the Duke of Cornwall and his
     wife.
GLOUCESTER:
Well, my good lord, I have informed them so.
     LEAR:
Informed them? Dost thou understand me,
     man?
     GLOUCESTER:
100 Ay, my good lord.
     LEAR:
The king would speak with Cornwall. The
     dear father
Would with his daughter speak, commands —
     tends° — service.

80 **form** show 81 **pack** be off 85–86 **The . . .
knave** i.e., the faithless man is the true fool, for wisdom requires fidelity; Lear's Fool, who remains faithful, is at least no knave 86 **perdy** by God (French
par Dieu) 89 **Deny** refuse 90 **fetches** subterfuges,
acts of tacking (nautical metaphor) 91 **images** exact likenesses; **flying off** desertion 93 **quality** temperament 102 **tends** attends (i.e., awaits); with,
possibly, an ironic second meaning, "tenders," or
"offers"

Are they informed of this? My breath and
     blood!
Fiery? The fiery duke, tell the hot duke that —
No, but not yet. May be he is not well.   105
Infirmity doth still neglect all office
Whereto our health is bound.° We are not
     ourselves
When nature, being oppressed, commands the
     mind
To suffer with the body. I'll forbear;
And am fallen out° with my more headier will°   110
To take the indisposed and sickly fit
For the sound man. [*Looking on* KENT.] Death
     on my state!° Wherefore
Should he sit here? This act persuades me
That this remotion° of the duke and her
Is practice° only. Give me my servant forth.°   115
Go tell the duke and's wife I'd speak with them!
Now, presently!° Bid them come forth and
     hear me,
Or at their chamber door I'll beat the drum
Till it cry sleep to death.°
     GLOUCESTER:
I would have all well betwixt you.   (*Exit.*) 120
     LEAR:
O me, my heart, my rising heart! But down!
     FOOL: Cry to it, nuncle, as the cockney° did
to the eels when she put 'em i' th' paste° alive.
She knapped° 'em o' th' coxcombs° with a
stick and cried, "Down, wantons,° down!"   125
'Twas her brother that, in pure kindness to his
horse, buttered his hay.°

(*Enter* CORNWALL, REGAN, GLOUCESTER, SER-
VANTS.)

LEAR:
Good morrow to you both.
     CORNWALL: Hail to your grace.

(KENT *here set at liberty.*)

107 **Whereto . . . bound** duties which we are required
to perform, when in health 110 **fallen out** angry;
headier will headlong inclination 112 **state** royal
condition 114 **remotion** (1) removal (2) remaining
aloof 115 **practice** pretense; **forth** i.e., out of the
stocks 117 **presently** at once 119 **cry . . . death**
follow sleep, like a cry or pack of hounds, until it kills
it 122 **cockney** Londoner (ignorant city dweller)
123 **paste** pastry pie 124 **knapped** rapped; **coxcombs** heads 125 **wantons** i.e., playful things (with
a sexual implication) 127 **buttered his hay** i.e., the
city dweller does from ignorance what the dishonest
ostler does from craft: greases the hay the traveler has
paid for, so that the horse will not eat

REGAN:
I am glad to see your highness.
LEAR:
130 Regan, I think you are. I know what reason
I have to think so. If thou shouldst not be
        glad,
I would divorce me from thy mother's tomb,
Sepulchring an adultress.° [*To* KENT.] O, are
        you free?
Some other time for that. Beloved Regan,
135 Thy sister's naught.° O Regan, she hath tied
Sharp-toothed unkindness, like a vulture, here.

        [*Points to his heart.*]

I can scarce speak to thee. Thou'lt not believe
With how depraved a quality° — O Regan!
REGAN:
I pray you, sir, take patience. I have hope
140 You less know how to value her desert
Than she to scant her duty.°
        LEAR: Say? how is that?
REGAN:
I cannot think my sister in the least
Would fail her obligation. If, sir, perchance
She have restrained the riots of your followers,
'Tis on such ground, and to such wholesome
145   end,
As clears her from all blame.
        LEAR:
My curses on her!
        REGAN: O, sir, you are old,
Nature in you stands on the very verge
Of his confine.° You should be ruled, and led
150 By some discretion that discerns your state
Better than you yourself.° Therefore I pray you
That to our sister you do make return,
Say you have wronged her.
        LEAR: Ask her forgiveness?
Do you but mark how this becomes the
        house:°
155 "Dear daughter, I confess that I am old.

        [*Kneeling.*]

Age is unnecessary. On my knees I beg
That you'll vouchsafe me raiment, bed, and
        food."
REGAN:
Good sir, no more. These are unsightly tricks.
Return you to my sister.
        LEAR [*rising*]:   Never, Regan.   160
She hath abated° me of half my train,
Looked black upon me, struck me with her
        tongue,
Most serpentlike, upon the very heart.
All the stored vengeances of heaven fall
On her ingrateful top!° Strike her young
        bones,°
You taking° airs, with lameness.
        CORNWALL: Fie, sir, fie!   165
        LEAR:
You nimble lightnings, dart your blinding
        flames
Into her scornful eyes! Infect her beauty,
You fen-sucked° fogs, drawn by the pow'rful
        sun,
To fall and blister° her pride.
        REGAN: O the blest gods!
So will you wish on me when the rash mood is
        on.   170
        LEAR:
No, Regan, thou shalt never have my curse.
Thy tender-hefted° nature shall not give
Thee o'er to harshness. Her eyes are fierce, but
        thine
Do comfort, and not burn. 'Tis not in thee
To grudge my pleasures, to cut off my train,   175
To bandy° hasty words, to scant my sizes,°
And, in conclusion, to oppose the bolt°
Against my coming in. Thou better know'st
The offices of nature, bond of childhood,°
Effects° of courtesy, dues of gratitude.   180
Thy half o' th' kingdom hast thou not forgot,
Wherein I thee endowed.
        REGAN: Good sir, to th' purpose.°

        (*Tucket within.*)

132–133 **divorce ... adultress** i.e., repudiate your dead mother as having conceived you by another man 135 **naught** wicked 138 **quality** nature 139–141 **I have ... duty** despite the double negative, the passage means, "I believe that you fail to give Goneril her due, rather than that she fails to fulfill her duty" 148–149 **Nature ... confine** i.e., you are nearing the end of your life 150–151 **some ... yourself** some discreet person who understands your condition more than you do 154 **becomes the house** suits my royal and paternal position

160 **abated** curtailed 164 **top** head; **young bones** the reference may be to unborn children, rather than to Goneril herself 165 **taking** infecting 168 **fen-sucked** drawn up from swamps by the sun 169 **fall and blister** fall upon and raise blisters 172 **tender-hefted** gently framed 176 **bandy** volley (metaphor from tennis); **scant my sizes** reduce my allowances 177 **oppose the bolt** bar the door 179 **offices ... childhood** natural duties, a child's duty to its parent 180 **Effects** manifestations 182 **to th' purpose** come to the point

LEAR:
Who put my man i' th' stocks?
CORNWALL: What trumpet's that?
REGAN:
I know't — my sister's. This approves° her letter,
That she would soon be here.

(*Enter* OSWALD.)

185   Is your lady come?
LEAR:
This is a slave, whose easy borrowed° pride
Dwells in the fickle grace° of her he follows.
Out, varlet,° from my sight.
CORNWALL: What means your grace?
LEAR:
Who stocked my servant? Regan, I have good hope
Thou didst not know on't.

(*Enter* GONERIL.)

190   Who comes here? O heavens!
If you do love old men, if your sweet sway
Allow° obedience, if you yourselves are old,
Make it° your cause. Send down, and take my part.

[*To* GONERIL.]

Art not ashamed to look upon this beard?
195 O Regan, will you take her by the hand?
GONERIL:
Why not by th' hand, sir? How have I offended?
All's not offense that indiscretion finds°
And dotage terms so.
LEAR: O sides,° you are too tough!
Will you yet hold? How came my man i' th' stocks?
CORNWALL:
200 I set him there, sir; but his own disorders°
Deserved much less advancement.°
LEAR: • You? Did you?
REGAN:
I pray you, father, being weak, seem so.°
If till the expiration of your month
You will return and sojourn with my sister,

Dismissing half your train, come then to me. 205
I am now from home, and out of that provision
Which shall be needful for your entertainment.°
LEAR:
Return to her, and fifty men dismissed?
No, rather I abjure all roofs, and choose
To wage° against the enmity o' th' air, 210
To be a comrade with the wolf and owl,
Necessity's sharp pinch.° Return with her?
Why, the hot-blooded° France, that dowerless took
Our youngest born, I could as well be brought
To knee° his throne, and, squirelike,° pension beg 215
To keep base life afoot. Return with her?
Persuade me rather to be slave and sumpter°
To this detested groom. [*Pointing at* OSWALD.]
GONERIL: At your choice, sir.
LEAR:
I prithee, daughter, do not make me mad.
I will not trouble thee, my child; farewell. 220
We'll no more meet, no more see one another.
But yet thou art my flesh, my blood, my daughter,
Or rather a disease that's in my flesh,
Which I must needs call mine. Thou art a boil,
A plague-sore, or embossèd carbuncle° 225
In my corrupted blood. But I'll not chide thee.
Let shame come when it will, I do not call it.
I do not bid the Thunder-bearer° shoot,
Nor tell tales of thee to high-judging° Jove.
Mend when thou canst, be better at thy leisure, 230
I can be patient, I can stay with Regan,
I and my hundred knights.
REGAN: Not altogether so.
I looked not for you yet, nor am provided
For your fit welcome. Give ear, sir, to my sister,
For those that mingle reason with your passion° 235

---

184 **approves** confirms 186 **easy borrowed** (1) facile and taken from another (2) acquired without anything to back it up (like money borrowed without security) 187 **grace** favor 188 **varlet** base fellow 192 **Allow** approve of 193 **it** my cause 197 **finds** judges 198 **sides** breast 200 **disorders** misconduct 201 **advancement** promotion 202 **seem so** act weak 207 **entertainment** maintenance 210 **wage** fight 212 **Necessity's sharp pinch** a summing up of the hard choice he has just announced 213 **hot-blooded** passionate 215 **knee** kneel before; **squirelike** like a retainer 217 **sumpter** pack horse 225 **embossèd carbuncle** swollen boil 228 **Thunder-bearer** Jupiter 229 **high-judging** (1) supreme (2) judging from heaven 235 **mingle . . . passion** i.e., consider your turbulent behavior coolly and reasonably

Must be content to think you old, and so —
But she knows what she does.
　　LEAR:　　　　　　Is this well spoken?
　　REGAN:
I dare avouch° it, sir. What, fifty followers?
Is it not well? What should you need of
　　more?
Yea, or so many, sith that° both charge° and
240　danger
Speak 'gainst so great a number? How in one
　　house
Should many people, under two commands,
Hold° amity? 'Tis hard, almost impossible.
　　GONERIL:
Why might not you, my lord, receive atten-
　　dance
From those that she calls servants, or from
245　mine?
　　REGAN:
Why not, my lord? If then they chanced to
　　slack° ye,
We could control them. If you will come to
　　me
(For now I spy a danger), I entreat you
To bring but five-and-twenty. To no more
250　Will I give place or notice.°
　　LEAR:
I gave you all.
　　REGAN:　　　And in good time you gave it.
　　LEAR:
Made you my guardians, my depositaries,°
But kept a reservation° to be followed
With such a number. What, must I come to
　　you
255　With five-and-twenty? Regan, said you so?
　　REGAN:
And speak't again, my lord. No more with
　　me.
　　LEAR:
Those wicked creatures yet do look well-
　　favored°
When others are more wicked; not being the
　　worst
Stands in some rank of praise.° [To GONERIL.]
　　I'll go with thee.

Thy fifty yet doth double five-and-twenty,   260
And thou art twice her love.°
　　GONERIL:　　　　Hear me, my lord.
What need you five-and-twenty? ten? or five?
To follow° in a house where twice so many
Have a command to tend you?
　　REGAN:　　　　　What need one?
　　LEAR:
O reason° not the need! Our basest beggars   265
Are in the poorest thing superfluous.°
Allow not nature more than nature needs,°
Man's life is cheap as beast's. Thou art a lady:
If only to go warm were gorgeous,
Why, nature needs not what thou gorgeous
　　wear'st,   270
Which scarcely keeps thee warm.° But, for true
　　need —
You heavens, give me that patience, patience I
　　need.
You see me here, you gods, a poor old man,
As full of grief as age, wretched in both.
If it be you that stirs these daughters' hearts   275
Against their father, fool° me not so much
To bear° it tamely; touch me with noble
　　anger,
And let not women's weapons, water drops,
Stain my man's cheeks. No, you unnatural
　　hags!
I will have such revenges on you both   280
That all the world shall — I will do such
　　things —
What they are, yet I know not; but they shall
　　be
The terrors of the earth. You think I'll weep.
No, I'll not weep.

　　(Storm and tempest.)

I have full cause of weeping, but this heart   285
Shall break into a hundred thousand flaws°
Or ere° I'll weep. O Fool, I shall go mad!
　　　　　(Exeunt LEAR, GLOUCESTER,
　　　　　　　KENT, and FOOL.)

---

238 **avouch** swear by　240 **sith that** since; **charge** expense　243 **Hold** preserve　246 **slack** neglect　250 **notice** recognition　252 **depositaries** trustees　253 **reservation** condition　257 **well-favored** handsome　258–259 **not . . . praise** i.e., that Goneril is not so bad as Regan is one thing in her favor

261 **her love** i.e., as loving as she　263 **follow** attend on you　265 **reason** scrutinize　266 **Are . . . superfluous** have some trifle not absolutely necessary　267 **needs** i.e., to sustain life　269–271 **If . . . warm** If to satisfy the need for warmth were to be gorgeous, you would not need the clothing you wear, which is worn more for beauty than warmth　276 **fool** humiliate　277 **To bear** as to make me bear　286 **flaws** (1) pieces (2) cracks (3) gusts of passion　287 **Or ere** before

CORNWALL:
Let us withdraw, 'twill be a storm.
REGAN:
This house is little; the old man and's people
290 Cannot be well bestowed.°
GONERIL:
'Tis his own blame; hath° put himself from
      rest°
And must needs taste his folly.
REGAN:
For his particular,° I'll receive him gladly,
But not one follower.
GONERIL: So am I purposed.°
295 Where is my Lord of Gloucester?
CORNWALL:
Followed the old man forth.

(*Enter* GLOUCESTER.)

                              He is returned.

GLOUCESTER:
The king is in high rage.
CORNWALL: Whither is he going?
GLOUCESTER:
He calls to horse, but will I know not whither.
CORNWALL:
'Tis best to give him way, he leads himself.°
GONERIL:
300 My lord, entreat him by no means to stay.
GLOUCESTER:
Alack, the night comes on, and the high winds
Do sorely ruffle.° For many miles about
There's scarce a bush.
REGAN: O, sir, to willful men
The injuries that they themselves procure
Must be their schoolmasters. Shut up your
305   doors.
He is attended with a desperate train,
And what they may incense° him to, being apt
To have his ear abused,° wisdom bids fear.
CORNWALL:
Shut up your doors, my lord; 'tis a wild night.
My Regan counsels well. Come out o' th'
310   storm.
                              (*Exeunt*.)

---

290 **bestowed** lodged   291 **hath** he hath; **rest** (1) place of residence (2) repose of mind   293 **his particular** himself personally   294 **purposed** determined   299 **give . . . himself** let him go; he insists on his own way   302 **ruffle** rage   307 **incense** incite   307–308 **being . . . abused** he being inclined to harken to bad counsel

---

ACT III

SCENE I. [A *heath*.]

Storm still.° Enter KENT *and a* GENTLEMAN
severally.

KENT:
Who's there besides foul weather?
GENTLEMAN:
One minded like the weather most unquietly.°
KENT:
I know you. Where's the king?
GENTLEMAN:
Contending with the fretful elements;
Bids the wind blow the earth into the sea,   5
Or swell the curlèd waters 'bove the main,°
That things might change° or cease; tears his
      white hair,
Which the impetuous blasts, with eyeless°
      rage,
Catch in their fury, and make nothing of;
Strives in his little world of man° to outscorn   10
The to-and-fro-conflicting wind and rain.
This night, wherein the cub-drawn° bear would
      couch,°
The lion, and the belly-pinchèd° wolf
Keep their fur dry, unbonneted° he runs,
And bids what will take all.°
KENT: But who is with him?   15
GENTLEMAN:
None but the Fool, who labors to outjest
His heart-struck injuries.
KENT: Sir, I do know you,
And dare upon the warrant of my note°
Commend a dear thing° to you. There is
      division,

III.1.s.d. **still** continually 2 **minded . . . unquietly** disturbed in mind, like the weather 6 **main** land 7 **change** (1) be destroyed (2) be exchanged (i.e., turned upside down) (3) change for the better 8 **eyeless** (1) blind (2) invisible 10 **little . . . man** the microcosm, as opposed to the universe or macrocosm, which it copies in little 12 **cub-drawn** sucked dry by her cubs, and so ravenously hungry; **couch** take shelter in its lair 13 **belly-pinchèd** starved 14 **unbonneted** hatless 15 **take all** like the reckless gambler, staking all he has left 18 **warrant . . . note** strength of what I have taken note (of you) 19 **Commend . . . thing** entrust important business

20 Although as yet the face of it is covered
    With mutual cunning, 'twixt Albany and
       Cornwall;
    Who have — as who have not, that° their great
       stars
    Throned° and set high? — servants, who seem
       no less,°
    Which are to France the spies and specula-
       tions
25 Intelligent° of our state. What hath been seen,
    Either in snuffs and packings° of the dukes,
    Or the hard rein which both of them hath
       borne°
    Against the old kind king, or something
       deeper,
    Whereof, perchance, these are but furnish-
       ings° —
    But, true it is, from France there comes a
30   power°
    Into this scattered° kingdom, who already,
    Wise in our negligence, have secret feet
    In some of our best ports, and are at point°
    To show their open banner. Now to you:
35 If on my credit you dare build° so far
    To° make your speed to Dover, you shall find
    Some that will thank you, making° just° report
    Of how unnatural and bemadding° sorrow
    The king hath cause to plain.°
40 I am a gentleman of blood and breeding,°
    And from some knowledge and assurance° offer
    This office° to you.
       GENTLEMAN:
    I will talk further with you.
       KENT: No, do not.
    For confirmation that I am much more
45 Than my out-wall,° open this purse and take
    What it contains. If you shall see Cordelia,
    As fear not but you shall, show her this ring,
    And she will tell you who that fellow° is

That yet you do not know. Fie on this storm!
I will go seek the king.   50
   GENTLEMAN:
Give me your hand. Have you no more to say?
   KENT:
Few words, but, to effect,° more than all yet:
That when we have found the king — in which
   your pain°
That way, I'll this — he that first lights on
   him,
Holla the other.   (Exeunt [severally].)   55

   SCENE II. [Another part of the heath.]
   Storm still. Enter LEAR and FOOL.

   LEAR:
Blow, winds, and crack your cheeks. Rage,
   blow!
You cataracts and hurricanoes,° spout
Till you have drenched our steeples, drowned
   the cocks.°
You sulph'rous and thought-executing° fires,
Vaunt-couriers° of oak-cleaving thunderbolts,   5
Singe my white head. And thou, all-shaking
   thunder,
Strike flat the thick rotundity° o' th' world,
Crack Nature's molds,° all germains spill° at
   once,
That makes ingrateful° man.
   FOOL: O nuncle, court holy-water° in a dry   10
house is better than this rain water out o'
door. Good nuncle, in; ask thy daughters
blessing. Here's a night pities neither wise man
nor fools.
   LEAR:
Rumble thy bellyful. Spit, fire. Spout, rain!   15
Nor rain, wind, thunder, fire are my daughters.
I tax° not you, you elements, with unkindness.
I never gave you kingdom, called you children,
You owe me no subscription.° Then let fall

22 **that** whom   22–23 **stars Throned** destinies have
throned   23 **seem no less** seem to be so   24–25
speculations Intelligent giving intelligence   26
snuffs and packings quarrels and plots   27 **hard . . .
borne** close and cruel control they have exercised
29 **furnishings** excuses   30 **power** army   31 **scattered** disunited   33 **at point** ready   35 **If . . . build**
if you can trust me, proceed   36 **To** as to   37
making for making; **just** accurate   38 **bemadding**
maddening   39 **plain** complain of   40 **blood and
breeding** noble family   41 **knowledge and assurance** sure and trustworthy information   42 **office**
service (i.e., the trip to Dover)   45 **out-wall** superficial appearance   48 **fellow** companion

52 **to effect** in their importance   53 **pain** labor
III.ii.2 **hurricanoes** waterspouts   3 **cocks** weather-
cocks   4 **thought-executing** (1) doing execution as
quick as thought (2) executing or carrying out the
thought of him who hurls the lightning   5 **Vaunt-
couriers** heralds, scouts who range before the main
body of the army   7 **rotundity** i.e., not only the
sphere of the globe, but the roundness of gestation
(Delius)   8 **Nature's molds** the molds or forms in
which men are made; **all germains spill** destroy the
basic seeds of life   9 **ingrateful** ungrateful   10
court holy-water flattery   17 **tax** accuse   19 **subscription** allegiance, submission

Your horrible pleasure.° Here I stand your
20 slave,
A poor, infirm, weak, and despised old man.
But yet I call you servile ministers,°
That will with two pernicious daughters join
Your high-engendered battles° 'gainst a head
25 So old and white as this. O, ho! 'tis foul.
  FOOL: He that has a house to put's head in
has a good headpiece.°

    The codpiece° that will house
      Before the head as any,
30   The head and he° shall louse:
      So beggars marry many.°
    The man that makes his toe
      What he his heart should make
    Shall of a corn cry woe,
35   And turn his sleep to wake.°

For there was never yet fair woman but she
made mouths in a glass.°

  (*Enter* KENT.)

  LEAR:
No, I will be the pattern of all patience,
I will say nothing.
40 KENT: Who's there?
  FOOL: Marry,° here's grace and a codpiece;
that's a wise man and a fool.°
  KENT:
Alas, sir, are you here? Things that love night
Love not such nights as these. The wrathful
    skies
45 Gallow° the very wanderers of the dark
And make them keep° their caves. Since I was
    man,

Such sheets of fire, such bursts of horrid°
    thunder,
Such groans of roaring wind and rain, I never
Remember to have heard. Man's nature cannot
    carry°
Th' affliction nor the fear.
  LEAR: Let the great gods   50
That keep this dreadful pudder° o'er our heads
Find out their enemies now.° Tremble, thou
    wretch,
That hast within thee undivulgèd crimes
Unwhipped of justice. Hide thee, thou bloody
    hand,
Thou perjured,° and thou simular° of virtue   55
That art incestuous. Caitiff,° to pieces shake,
That under covert and convenient seeming°
Has practiced on° man's life. Close° pent-up
    guilts,
Rive° your concealing continents° and cry
These dreadful summoners grace.° I am a man   60
More sinned against than sinning.
  KENT: Alack, bareheaded?
Gracious my lord,° hard by here is a hovel;
Some friendship will it lend you 'gainst the
    tempest.
Repose you there, while I to this hard house
(More harder than the stones whereof 'tis
    raised,   65
Which even but now, demanding after° you,
Denied me to come in) return, and force
Their scanted° courtesy.
  LEAR: My wits begin to turn.
Come on, my boy. How dost, my boy? Art cold?
I am cold myself. Where is this straw, my
    fellow?   70
The art° of our necessities is strange,
That can make vile things precious. Come,
    your hovel.
Poor Fool and knave, I have one part in my
    heart
That's sorry yet for thee.

20 **pleasure** will 22 **ministers** agents 24 **high-
engendered battles** armies formed in the heavens 27
headpiece (1) helmet (2) brain 28 **codpiece** penis
(literally, padding worn at the crotch of a man's hose)
30 **he** it 31 **many** i.e., lice 28–31 **The...many**
The man who gratifies his sexual appetites before he
has a roof over his head will end up a lousy beggar
32–35 **The...wake** The man who, ignoring the fit
order of things, elevates what is base above what is
noble, will suffer for it as Lear has, in banishing
Cordelia and enriching her sisters 37 **made...glass**
posed before a mirror (irrelevant nonsense, except
that it calls to mind the general theme of vanity and
folly) 41 **Marry** a mild oath, from "By the Virgin
Mary" 41–42 **here's...fool** Kent's question is answered: the king ("grace") is here, and the Fool —
who customarily wears an exaggerated codpiece; but
which is left ambiguous, since Lear has previously
been called a codpiece 45 **Gallow** frighten 46
keep remain inside

47 **horrid** horrible 49 **carry** endure 51 **pudder**
turmoil 52 **Find...now** i.e., discover sinners by
the terror they reveal 55 **perjured** perjurer; **simular**
counterfeiter 56 **Caitiff** wretch 57 **seeming** hypocrisy 58 **practiced on** plotted against; **Close** hidden 59 **Rive** split open; **continents** containers 59–
60 **cry...grace** beg mercy from the vengeful gods
(here figured as officers who summoned a man charged
with immorality before the ecclesiastical court) 62
Gracious my lord my gracious lord 66 **demanding
after** asking for 68 **scanted** stinted 71 **art** magic
powers of the alchemists, who sought to transmute
base metals into precious

FOOL [*Singing.*]

75 He that has and a little tiny wit,
    With heigh-ho, the wind and the rain,
    Must make content with his fortunes fit,°
    Though the rain it raineth every day.

LEAR: True, my good boy. Come, bring us
80 to this hovel.   (*Exit,* [*with* KENT].)
    FOOL: This is a brave° night to cool a
    courtesan. I'll speak a prophecy ere I go:

    When priests are more in word than matter;
    When brewers mar their malt with water;
85 When nobles are their tailors' tutors,
    No heretics burned, but wenches' suitors;°
    When every case in law is right,
    No squire in debt nor no poor knight;
    When slanders do not live in tongues;
90 Nor cutpurses come not to throngs;
    When usurers tell their gold i' th' field,°
    And bawds and whores do churches build,°
    Then shall the realm of Albion°
    Come to great confusion.
95 Then comes the time, who lives to see't,
    That going shall be used with feet.°

This prophecy Merlin° shall make, for I live
before his time.   (*Exit.*)

SCENE III. [GLOUCESTER'*s castle.*]

Enter GLOUCESTER *and* EDMUND.

GLOUCESTER: Alack, alack, Edmund, I like
not this unnatural dealing. When I desired
their leave that I might pity° him, they took
from me the use of mine own house, charged
5 me on pain of perpetual displeasure neither to

speak of him, entreat for him, or any way
sustain° him.
    EDMUND: Most savage and unnatural.
    GLOUCESTER: Go to; say you nothing. There
is division° between the dukes, and a worse°   10
matter than that. I have received a letter this
night — 'tis dangerous to be spoken° — I have
locked the letter in my closet.° These injuries
the king now bears will be revenged home;°
there is part of a power° already footed;° we   15
must incline to° the king. I will look° him and
privily° relieve him. Go you and maintain talk
with the duke, that my charity be not of° him
perceived. If he ask for me, I am ill and gone
to bed. If I die for it, as no less is threatened   20
me, the king my old master must be relieved.
There is strange things toward,° Edmund;
pray you be careful.   (*Exit.*)
    EDMUND:
This courtesy forbid° thee shall the duke
Instantly know, and of that letter too.   25
This seems a fair deserving,° and must draw
    me
That which my father loses — no less than all.
The younger rises when the old doth fall.
                              (*Exit.*)

SCENE IV. [*The heath. Before a hovel.*]

Enter LEAR, KENT, *and* FOOL.

KENT:
Here is the place, my lord. Good my lord,
    enter.
The tyranny of the open night's too rough
For nature to endure.

(*Storm still.*)

LEAR: Let me alone.
KENT:
Good my lord, enter here.
LEAR: Wilt break my heart?°
KENT:
I had rather break mine own. Good my lord,
    enter.   5

77 **Must . . . fit** must be satisfied with a fortune as tiny as his wit   81 **brave** fine   83–86 **When . . . suitors** the first four prophecies are fulfilled already, and hence "confusion" has come to England: the priest does not suit his action to his words; the brewer adulterates his beer; the nobleman is subservient to his tailor (i.e., cares only for fashion); religious heretics escape, and only those burn (i.e., suffer) who are afflicted with venereal disease   91 **tell . . . field** count their money in the open   87–92 **When . . . build** the last six prophecies, as they are Utopian, are meant ironically; they will never be fulfilled   93 **Albion** England   96 **going . . . feet** people will walk on their feet   97 **Merlin** King Arthur's great magician who, according to Holinshed's *Chronicles*, lived later than Lear
III.III.3 **pity** show pity to

7 **sustain** care for   10 **division** falling out; **worse** more serious (i.e., the French invasion)   12 **spoken** spoken of   13 **closet** room   14 **home** to the utmost   15 **power** army; **footed** landed   16 **incline to** take the side of; **look** search for   17 **privily** secretly   18 **of** by   22 **toward** impending   24 **courtesy forbid** kindness forbidden (i.e., to Lear)   26 **fair deserving** an action deserving reward
III.IV.4 **break my heart** i.e., by shutting out the storm which distracts me from thinking

LEAR:
Thou think'st 'tis much that this contentious storm
Invades us to the skin: so 'tis to thee;
But where the greater malady is fixed,°
The lesser is scarce felt. Thou'dst shun a bear;
10 But if thy flight lay toward the roaring sea,
Thou'dst meet the bear i' th' mouth.° When the mind's free,°
The body's delicate. The tempest in my mind
Doth from my senses take all feeling else,
Save what beats there. Filial ingratitude,
15 Is it not as° this mouth should tear this hand
For lifting food to't? But I will punish home.°
No, I will weep no more. In such a night
To shut me out! Pour on, I will endure.
In such a night as this! O Regan, Goneril,
Your old kind father, whose frank° heart gave
20   all —
O, that way madness lies; let me shun that.
No more of that.
KENT: Good my lord, enter here.
LEAR:
Prithee go in thyself; seek thine own ease.
This tempest will not give me leave to ponder
25 On things would hurt me more, but I'll go in.

[*To the* FOOL.]

In, boy; go first. You houseless poverty° —
Nay, get thee in. I'll pray, and then I'll sleep.
(*Exit* [FOOL].)
Poor naked wretches, wheresoe'er you are,
That bide° the pelting of this pitiless storm,
30 How shall your houseless heads and unfed sides,
Your looped and windowed° raggedness, defend you
From seasons such as these? O, I have ta'en
Too little care of this! Take physic, pomp;°
Expose thyself to feel what wretches feel,
35 That thou mayst shake the superflux° to them,
And show the heavens more just.
EDGAR [*within*]: Fathom and half, fathom and half!° Poor Tom!

(*Enter* FOOL.)

FOOL: Come not in here, nuncle, here's a spirit. Help me, help me!   40
KENT:
Give me thy hand. Who's there?
FOOL: A spirit, a spirit. He says his name's Poor Tom.
KENT:
What art thou that dost grumble there i' th' straw?
Come forth.   45

(*Enter* EDGAR [*disguised as a madman*].)

EDGAR: Away! the foul fiend follows me. Through the sharp hawthorn blows the cold wind.° Humh! Go to thy cold bed, and warm thee.°
LEAR: Didst thou give all to thy daughters?   50
And art thou come to this?
EDGAR: Who gives anything to Poor Tom? Whom the foul fiend hath led through fire and through flame, through ford and whirlpool, o'er bog and quagmire; that hath laid 55 knives under his pillow and halters in his pew,° set ratsbane° by his porridge,° made him proud of heart, to ride on a bay trotting horse over four-inched bridges,° to course° his own shadow for° a traitor. Bless thy five wits,° 60 Tom's a-cold. O, do, de, do, de, do, de. Bless thee from whirlwinds, star-blasting,° and taking.° Do Poor Tom some charity, whom the foul fiend vexes. There could I have him now — and there — and there again — and 65 there.

(*Storm still.*)

LEAR:
What, has his daughters brought him to this pass?°
Couldst thou save nothing? Wouldst thou give 'em all?

47–48 **Through . . . wind** a line from the ballad of "The Friar of Orders Gray"   48–49 **Go . . . thee** a reminiscence of *The Taming of the Shrew*, Induction, line 10, which itself is an echo of a line in Thomas Kyd's *The Spanish Tragedy*   56–57 **knives . . . halters . . . ratsbane** the fiend tempts Poor Tom to suicide 56 **pew** gallery or balcony outside a window   57 **porridge** broth   58–59 **ride . . . bridges** i.e., risk his life 59 **course** chase   60 **for** as; **five wits** common wit, imagination, fantasy, estimation, memory   62 **star-blasting** the evil caused by malignant stars   62–63 **taking** pernicious influences   67 **pass** wretched condition

---

8 **fixed** lodged (in the mind)   11 **i' th' mouth** in the teeth; **free** i.e., from care   15 **as** as if   16 **home** to the utmost   20 **frank** liberal (magnanimous)   26 **houseless poverty** the unsheltered poor, abstracted 29 **bide** endure   31 **looped and windowed** full of holes   33 **Take physic, pomp** Take medicine to cure yourselves, you great men   35 **superflux** superfluity 37–38 **Fathom and half** Edgar, because of the downpour, pretends to take soundings

FOOL: Nay, he reserved a blanket,° else we
70 had been all shamed.

LEAR:
Now all the plagues that in the pendulous° air
Hang fated o'er° men's faults light on thy
    daughters!

KENT:
He hath no daughters, sir.

LEAR:
Death, traitor; nothing could have subdued°
    nature
75 To such a lowness but his unkind daughters.
Is it the fashion that discarded fathers
Should have thus little mercy on° their flesh?
Judicious punishment — 'twas this flesh begot
Those pelican° daughters.

80   EDGAR: Pillicock sat on Pillicock Hill.° Alow,
alow, loo, loo!°

FOOL: This cold night will turn us all to
fools and madmen.

EDGAR: Take heed o' th' foul fiend; obey thy
85 parents; keep thy word's justice;° swear not;
commit not° with man's sworn spouse; set not
thy sweet heart on proud array. Tom's a-cold.

LEAR: What hast thou been?

EDGAR: A servingman, proud in heart and
90 mind; that curled my hair, wore gloves in my
cap;° served the lust of my mistress' heart, and
did the act of darkness with her; swore as
many oaths as I spake words, and broke them
in the sweet face of heaven. One that slept in
95 the contriving of lust, and waked to do it.
Wine loved I deeply, dice dearly; and in
woman out-paramoured the Turk.° False of
heart, light of ear,° bloody of hand; hog in
sloth, fox in stealth, wolf in greediness, dog in
100 madness, lion in prey.° Let not the creaking° of
shoes nor the rustling of silks betray thy poor
heart to woman. Keep thy foot out of brothels,
thy hand out of plackets,° thy pen from

lenders' books,° and defy the foul fiend. Still
through the hawthorn blows the cold wind;   105
says suum, mun, nonny.° Dolphin° my boy,
boy, sessa!° let him trot by.

(Storm still.)

LEAR: Thou wert better in a grave than to
answer° with thy uncovered body this extrem-
ity° of the skies. Is man no more than this?   110
Consider him well. Thou ow'st° the worm no
silk, the beast no hide, the sheep no wool, the
cat° no perfume. Ha! here's three on's° are
sophisticated.° Thou art the thing itself; unac-
commodated° man is no more but such a poor, 115
bare, forked° animal as thou art. Off, off, you
lendings!° Come, unbutton here.

[Tearing off his clothes.]

FOOL: Prithee, nuncle, be contented, 'tis a
naughty° night to swim in. Now a little fire in
a wild° field were like an old lecher's heart — a 120
small spark, all the rest on's° body, cold. Look,
here comes a walking fire.

(Enter GLOUCESTER with a torch.)

EDGAR: This is the foul fiend Flibbertigibbet.° He begins at curfew,° and walks till the
first cock.° He gives the web and the pin,°   125
squints° the eye, and makes the harelip; mil-
dews the white° wheat, and hurts the poor
creature of earth.

Swithold footed thrice the old;°
He met the nightmare,° and her nine fold;°   130
    Bid her alight°
    And her troth plight,°
And aroint° thee, witch, aroint thee!

---

69 **blanket** i.e., to cover his nakedness   71 **pendu-
lous** overhanging   72 **fated o'er** destined to punish
74 **subdued** reduced   77 **on** i.e., shown to   79
pelican supposed to feed on its parent's blood   80
Pillicock . . . Hill probably quoted from a nursery
rhyme, and suggested by "pelican"; "pillicock" is a
term of endearment and the phallus   80–81 **Alow
. . . loo** a hunting call, or the refrain of the song (?)
85 **keep . . . justice** i.e., do not break thy word   86
commit not i.e., adultery   90–91 **gloves . . . cap** i.e.,
as a pledge from his mistress   97 **out-paramoured
the Turk** had more concubines than the sultan   98
light of ear ready to hear flattery and slander   100
prey preying; **creaking** deliberately cultivated, as
fashionable   103 **plackets** opening in skirts

103–104 **pen . . . books** i.e., do not enter your name
in the moneylender's account book   106 **suum, mun,
nonny** the noise of the wind   106 **Dolphin** the
French dauphin (identified by the English with the
devil; Poor Tom is presumably quoting from a ballad)
107 **sessa** an interjection: "Go on!"   109 **answer**
confront, bear the brunt of   109–110 **extremity** extreme severity   111 **ow'st** have taken from   113 **cat**
civet cat, whose glands yield perfume; **on's** of us
114 **sophisticated** adulterated, made artificial   114–
115 **unaccommodated** uncivilized   116 **forked** i.e.,
two-legged   117 **lendings** borrowed garments   119
naughty wicked   120 **wild** barren   121 **on's** of his
123–124 **Flibbertigibbet** a figure from Elizabethan
demonology   124 **curfew** 9 P.M.   125 **first cock**
midnight; **web . . . pin** cataract   126 **squints** crosses
127 **white** ripening   129 **Swithold . . . old** Withold
(an Anglo-Saxon saint who subdued demons)
walked three times across the open country   130
nightmare demon; **fold** offspring   131 **alight** i.e.,
from the horse she had possessed   132 **her troth
plight** pledge her word   133 **aroint** be gone

KENT:
How fares your grace?

135 LEAR: What's he?

KENT:
Who's there? What is't you seek?

GLOUCESTER:
What are you there? Your names?

EDGAR: Poor Tom, that eats the swimming
frog, the toad, the todpole, the wall-newt and
140 the water;° that in the fury of his heart, when
the foul fiend rages, eats cow-dung for sallets,°
swallows the old rat and the ditch-dog,° drinks
the green mantle° of the standing° pool; who is
whipped from tithing° to tithing, and stocked,
145 punished, and imprisoned; who hath had three
suits to his back, six shirts to his body,

Horse to ride, and weapon to wear,
But mice and rats, and such small deer,°
Have been Tom's food for seven long year.°

150 Beware my follower!° Peace, Smulkin,° peace,
thou fiend!

GLOUCESTER:
What, hath your grace no better company?

EDGAR:
The Prince of Darkness is a gentleman.
Modo° he's called, and Mahu.°

GLOUCESTER:
155 Our flesh and blood, my lord, is grown so vile
That it doth hate what gets° it.

EDGAR: Poor Tom's a-cold.

GLOUCESTER:
Go in with me. My duty cannot suffer°
T' obey in all your daughters' hard commands.
160 Though their injunction be to bar my doors
And let this tyrannous night take hold upon
you,
Yet have I ventured to come seek you out
And bring you where both fire and food is
ready.

LEAR:
First let me talk with this philosopher.
165 What is the cause of thunder?

KENT:
Good my lord, take his offer; go into th'
house.

LEAR:
I'll talk a word with this same learnèd The-
ban.°
What is your study?°

EDGAR:
How to prevent° the fiend, and to kill vermin.

LEAR:
Let me ask you one word in private.   170

KENT:
Importune him once more to go, my lord.
His wits begin t' unsettle.

GLOUCESTER: Canst thou blame him?

(Storm still.)

His daughters seek his death. Ah, that good
Kent,
He said it would be thus, poor banished
man!
Thou say'st the king grows mad — I'll tell thee,
friend,   175
I am almost mad myself. I had a son,
Now outlawed from my blood;° he sought my
life
But lately, very late.° I loved him, friend,
No father his son dearer. True to tell thee,
The grief hath crazed my wits. What a night's
this!   180
I do beseech your grace —

LEAR: O, cry you mercy,° sir.
Noble philosopher, your company.

EDGAR: Tom's a-cold.

GLOUCESTER:
In, fellow, there, into th' hovel; keep thee
warm.

LEAR:
Come, let's in all.

KENT: This way, my lord.

LEAR: With him!   185
I will keep still with my philosopher.

KENT:
Good my lord, soothe° him; let him take the
fellow.

GLOUCESTER:
Take him you on.°

KENT:
Sirrah, come on; go along with us.

LEAR:
Come, good Athenian.°   190

139–140 **todpole . . . water** tadpole, wall lizard, water
newt   141 **sallets** salads   142 **ditch-dog** dead dog in
a ditch   143 **mantle** scum; **standing** stagnant   144
tithing a district comprising ten families   148–149
But . . . year adapted from a popular romance, "Bevis
of Hampton"   148 **deer** game   150 **follower** familiar   150–154 **Smulkin . . . Modo . . . Mahu** Elizabethan devils, from Samuel Harsnett's *Declaration*
of 1603   156 **gets** begets   158 **suffer** permit me

167 **Theban** i.e., Greek philosopher   168 **study**
particular scientific study   169 **prevent** balk   177
outlawed . . . blood disowned and tainted, like a
carbuncle in the corrupted blood   178 **late** recently
181 **cry you mercy** I beg your pardon   187 **soothe**
humor   188 **you on** with you   190 **Athenian** i.e.,
philosopher (like "Theban")

GLOUCESTER:
No words, no words! Hush.
EDGAR:
Child Rowland to the dark tower came;°
His word was still,° "Fie, foh, and fum,
I smell the blood of a British man."°
                                    (*Exeunt.*)

SCENE V. [GLOUCESTER'S *castle.*]

Enter CORNWALL *and* EDMUND.

CORNWALL: I will have my revenge ere I
depart his house.
EDMUND: How, my lord, I may be censured,°
that nature thus gives way to loyalty, some-
5 thing fears° me to think of.
CORNWALL: I now perceive it was not altogether your brother's evil disposition made him
seek his death; but a provoking merit, set
a-work by a reprovable badness in himself.°
10 EDMUND: How malicious is my fortune that
I must repent to be just! This is the letter
which he spoke of, which approves° him an
intelligent party° to the advantages° of France.
O heavens, that his treason were not! or not I
15 the detector!
CORNWALL: Go with me to the duchess.
EDMUND: If the matter of this paper be
certain, you have mighty business in hand.
CORNWALL: True or false, it hath made thee
20 Earl of Gloucester. Seek out where thy father
is, that he may be ready for our apprehension.°
EDMUND [*aside*]: If I find him comforting°
the king, it will stuff his suspicion more
fully. — I will persever° in my course of loyalty,
25 though the conflict be sore between that and
my blood.°
CORNWALL: I will lay trust upon° thee, and
thou shalt find a dearer father in my love.
                                    (*Exeunt.*)

SCENE VI. [*A chamber in a farmhouse
adjoining the castle.*]

Enter KENT *and* GLOUCESTER.

GLOUCESTER: Here is better than the open
air; take it thankfully. I will piece out the
comfort with what addition I can. I will not
be long from you.
KENT: All the power of his wits have given   5
way to his impatience.° The gods reward your
kindness.   (*Exit* [GLOUCESTER].)

(*Enter* LEAR, EDGAR, *and* FOOL.)

EDGAR: Frateretto° calls me, and tells me
Nero° is an angler in the lake of darkness.
Pray, innocent,° and beware the foul fiend.   10
FOOL: Prithee, nuncle, tell me whether a
madman be a gentleman or a yeoman.°
LEAR:
A king, a king.
FOOL: No, he's a yeoman that has a gentle-
man to his son; for he's a mad yeoman that   15
sees his son a gentleman before him.
LEAR:
To have a thousand with red burning spits
Come hizzing° in upon 'em —
EDGAR: The foul fiend bites my back.
FOOL: He's a mad that trusts in the tameness   20
of a wolf, a horse's health, a boy's love, or a
whore's oath.
LEAR:
It shall be done; I will arraign° them straight.°

[*To* EDGAR.]

Come, sit thou here, most learned justice.°

[*To the* FOOL.]

Thou, sapient° sir, sit here. Now, you she-
foxes —   25
EDGAR: Look, where he° stands and glares.
Want'st thou eyes at trial, madam?°
Come o'er the bourn,° Bessy, to me.

192 **Child . . . came** from a lost ballad (?); "child" =
a candidate for knighthood; "Rowland" was Charle-
magne's nephew, the hero of *The Song of Roland*
193 **His . . . still** his motto was always   193–194 **Fie
. . . man** a deliberately absurd linking of the chivalric
hero with the nursery tale of Jack the Giant-Killer
III.v.3 **censured** judged   4–5 **something fears** somewhat frightens   8–9 **a provoking . . . himself** a stimulating goodness in Edgar, brought into play by a
blamable badness in Gloucester   12 **approves** proves
13 **intelligent party** (1) spy (2) well-informed person; **to the advantages** on behalf of   21 **apprehension** arrest   22 **comforting** supporting (a legalism)
24 **persever** persevere   26 **blood** natural feelings
27 **lay trust upon** (1) trust (2) advance

III.vi.6 **impatience** raging   8 **Frateretto** Elizabethan
devil, from Harsnett's *Declaration*   9 **Nero** who is
mentioned by Harsnett, and whose angling is reported
by Chaucer in "The Monk's Tale"   10 **innocent** fool
12 **yeoman** farmer (just below a gentleman in rank;
the Fool asks what class of man has most indulged
his children, and thus been driven mad)   18 **hizzing**
hissing   23 **arraign** bring to trial; **straight** straightaway   24 **justice** justicer, judge   25 **sapient** wise
26 **he** i.e., a fiend   27 **Want'st . . . madam** (to
Goneril) i.e., Do you want eyes to look at you during
your trial? The fiend serves that purpose   28 **bourn**
brook (Edgar quotes from a popular ballad)

FOOL:
Her boat hath a leak,
30   And she must not speak
Why she dares not come over to thee.°
   EDGAR: The foul fiend haunts Poor Tom in
the voice of a nightingale.° Hoppedance° cries
in Tom's belly for two white herring.° Croak°
35 not, black angel; I have no food for thee.
   KENT:
How do you, sir? Stand you not so amazed.°
Will you lie down and rest upon the cushions?
   LEAR:
I'll see their trial first. Bring in their evidence.°

   [To EDGAR.]

Thou, robèd man of justice, take thy place.

   [To the FOOL.]

40 And thou, his yokefellow of equity,°
Bench° by his side. [To KENT.] You are o' th'
      commission;°
Sit you too.
   EDGAR: Let us deal justly.

Sleepest or wakest thou, jolly shepherd?
45   Thy sheep be in the corn;°
And for one blast of thy minikin° mouth
      Thy sheep shall take no harm.°

Purr, the cat is gray.°
   LEAR: Arraign her first. 'Tis Goneril, I here
50 take my oath before this honorable assembly,
she kicked the poor king her father.
   FOOL: Come hither, mistress. Is your name
Goneril?
   LEAR: She cannot deny it.
55   FOOL: Cry you mercy, I took you for a joint
stool.°

29–31 **Her . . . thee** the Fool parodies the ballad   33
nightingale i.e., the Fool's singing; **Hoppedance** Ho-
berdidance (another devil from Harsnett's *Declaration*)   34 **white herring** unsmoked (as against the
black and sulfurous devil?); **Croak** rumble (because
his belly is empty)   36 **amazed** astonished   38 **evidence** the evidence of witnesses against them   40
yokefellow of equity partner in justice   41 **Bench** sit
on the bench; **commission** those commissioned as
king's justices   44–47 **Sleepest . . . harm** probably
quoted or adapted from an Elizabethan song   45
corn wheat   46 **minikin** shrill   48 **gray** devils were
thought to assume the shape of a gray cat   55–56
Cry . . . stool proverbial and deliberately impudent
apology for overlooking a person; a joint stool was a
low stool made by a joiner, perhaps here a stage property to represent Goneril and, in line 57, Regan; "joint
stool" can also suggest the judicial bench; hence
Goneril may be identified by the Fool, ironically,
with those in power, who judge

LEAR:
And here's another, whose warped looks pro-
      claim
What store° her heart is made on. Stop her
      there!
Arms, arms, sword, fire! Corruption in the
      place!°
False justicer, why hast thou let her 'scape?   60
   EDGAR: Bless thy five wits!
   KENT:
O pity! Sir, where is the patience now
That you so oft have boasted to retain?
   EDGAR [*aside*]:
My tears begin to take his part so much
They mar my counterfeiting.°   65
   LEAR:
The little dogs and all,
Tray, Blanch, and Sweetheart — see, they bark
      at me.
   EDGAR: Tom will throw his head at them.
Avaunt, you curs.

      Be thy mouth or black or° white,   70
      Tooth that poisons if it bite;
      Mastiff, greyhound, mongrel grim,
      Hound or spaniel, brach° or lym,°
      Or bobtail tike, or trundle-tail° —
      Tom will make him weep and wail;   75
      For, with throwing° thus my head,
      Dogs leaped the hatch,° and all are fled.

Do, de, de, de. Sessa!° Come, march to wakes°
and fairs and market 'towns. Poor Tom, thy
horn° is dry.   80
   LEAR: Then let them anatomize Regan. See
what breeds about her heart.° Is there any
cause in nature that make° these hard hearts?
[*To* EDGAR.] You, sir, I entertain° for one of
my hundred;° only I do not like the fashion of   85

58 **store** stuff   59 **Corruption . . . place** bribery in the
court   65 **counterfeiting** i.e., feigned madness   70
or . . . or either . . . or   73 **brach** bitch; **lym** blood-
hound (from the liam or leash with which he was led)
74 **bobtail . . . trundle-tail** short-tailed or long-tailed
cur   76 **throwing** jerking (as a hound lifts its head
from the ground, the scent having been lost)   77
leaped the hatch leaped over the lower half of a
divided door (i.e., left in a hurry)   78 **Sessa** Be off!;
wakes feasts attending the dedication of a church   80
horn horn bottle which the Bedlam used in begging a
drink (Edgar is suggesting that he is unable to play
his role any longer)   81–82 **Then . . . heart** i.e., If
the Bedlam's horn is dry, let Regan, whose heart has
become as hard as horn, be dissected   83 **make** sub-
junctive   84 **entertain** engage   85 **hundred** i.e.,
Lear's hundred knights

your garments. You will say they are Persian;°
but let them be changed.

KENT:
Now, good my lord, lie here and rest awhile.

LEAR:
Make no noise, make no noise; draw the
   curtains.°
90 So, so. We'll go to supper i' th' morning.
FOOL: And I'll go to bed at noon.°

(*Enter* GLOUCESTER.)

GLOUCESTER:
Come hither, friend. Where is the king my
   master?

KENT:
Here, sir, but trouble him not; his wits are
   gone.

GLOUCESTER:
Good friend, I prithee take him in thy arms.
95 I have o'erheard a plot of death upon him.
There is a litter ready; lay him in't
And drive toward Dover, friend, where thou
   shalt meet
Both welcome and protection. Take up thy
   master.
If thou shouldst dally half an hour, his life,
100 With thine and all that offer to defend him,
Stand in assurèd loss. Take up, take up,
And follow me, that will to some provision°
Give thee quick conduct.°

KENT: Oppressèd nature sleeps.
This rest might yet have balmed thy broken
   sinews,°
105 Which, if convenience° will not allow,
Stand in hard cure.° [*To the* FOOL.] Come,
   help to bear thy master.
Thou must not stay behind.

GLOUCESTER: Come, come, away!
                 (*Exeunt* [*all but* EDGAR].)

EDGAR:
When we our betters see bearing our woes,
We scarcely think our miseries our foes.°
110 Who alone suffers suffers most i' th' mind,
Leaving free° things and happy shows° behind;
But then the mind much sufferance° doth
   o'erskip

When grief hath mates, and bearing fellow-
   ship.°
How light and portable° my pain seems now,
When that which makes me bend makes the
   king bow.   115
He childed as I fathered. Tom, away.
Mark the high noises,° and thyself bewray°
When false opinion, whose wrong thoughts°
   defile thee,
In thy just proof repeals and reconciles thee.°
What will hap more° tonight, safe 'scape the
   king!   120
Lurk,° lurk.   [*Exit.*]

SCENE VII. [GLOUCESTER'S *castle.*]

Enter CORNWALL, REGAN, GONERIL, EDMUND,
and SERVANTS.

CORNWALL [*to* GONERIL]: Post speedily to
my lord your husband; show him this letter.
The army of France is landed. [*To* SERVANTS.]
Seek out the traitor Gloucester.
          [*Exeunt some of the* SERVANTS.]
REGAN: Hang him instantly.   5
GONERIL: Pluck out his eyes.
CORNWALL: Leave him to my displeasure.
Edmund, keep you our sister company. The
revenges we are bound° to take upon your
traitorous father are not fit for your beholding. 10
Advise the duke where you are going, to a
most festinate° preparation. We are bound to
the like. Our posts° shall be swift and intelli-
gent° betwixt us. Farewell, dear sister; farewell,
my Lord of Gloucester.°   15

(*Enter* OSWALD.)

How now? Where's the king?

OSWALD:
My Lord of Gloucester hath conveyed him
   hence.
Some five or six and thirty of his knights,
Hot questrists° after him, met him at gate;

---

86 **Persian** gorgeous (ironically of Edgar's rags)   89
curtains Lear imagines himself in bed   91 **And . . .
noon** the Fool's last words   102 **provision** maintenance   103 **conduct** direction   104 **balmed . . . sinews** soothed thy racked nerves   105 **convenience**
fortunate occasion   106 **Stand . . . cure** will be hard
to cure   109 **our foes** enemies peculiar to ourselves
111 **free** carefree, **shows** scenes   112 **sufferance**
suffering

113 **bearing fellowship** suffering has company   114
portable able to be supported or endured   117 **Mark
. . . noises** observe the rumors of strife among those in
power; **bewray** reveal   118 **wrong thoughts** misconceptions   119 **In . . . thee** on the manifesting of your
innocence recalls you from outlawry and restores
amity between you and your father   120 **What . . .
more** whatever else happens   121 **Lurk** hide
III.VII.9 **bound** (1) forced (2) purposing to   12
festinate speedy   13 **posts** messengers   13–14 **intelligent** full of information   15 **Lord of Gloucester**
Edmund, now elevated to the title   19 **questrists**
searchers

Who, with some other of the lords depen-
20   dants,°
Are gone with him toward Dover, where they
   boast
To have well-armèd friends.
  CORNWALL: Get horses for your mistress.
                      [*Exit* OSWALD.]
  GONERIL:
Farewell, sweet lord, and sister.
  CORNWALL:
Edmund, farewell.
             [*Exeunt* GONERIL *and* EDMUND.]
          Go seek the traitor Gloucester,
25 Pinion him like a thief, bring him before us.
           [*Exeunt other* SERVANTS.]
Though well we may not pass upon° his life
Without the form of justice, yet our power
Shall do a court'sy to° our wrath, which men
May blame, but not control.

  (*Enter* GLOUCESTER, *brought in by two or
  three.*)

          Who's there, the traitor?
  REGAN:
30 Ingrateful fox, 'tis he.
  CORNWALL:
Bind fast his corky° arms.
  GLOUCESTER:
What means your graces? Good my friends,
   consider
You are my guests. Do me no foul play,
   friends.
  CORNWALL:
Bind him, I say. [SERVANTS *bind him.*]
  REGAN: Hard, hard! O filthy traitor.
  GLOUCESTER:
35 Unmerciful lady as you are, I'm none.
  CORNWALL:
To this chair bind him. Villain, thou shalt
   find —

  [REGAN *plucks his beard.*°]

  GLOUCESTER:
By the kind gods, 'tis most ignobly done
To pluck me by the beard.
  REGAN:
So white, and such a traitor?
  GLOUCESTER: Naughty° lady,

These hairs which thou dost ravish from my
  chin   40
Will quicken° and accuse thee. I am your
  host.
With robber's hands my hospitable favors°
You should not ruffle° thus. What will you do?
  CORNWALL:
Come, sir, what letters had you late° from
  France?
  REGAN:
Be simple-answered,° for we know the truth.   45
  CORNWALL:
And what confederacy have you with the
  traitors
Late footed in the kingdom?
  REGAN:
To whose hands you have sent the lunatic
  king:
Speak.
  GLOUCESTER:
I have a letter guessingly° set down,   50
Which came from one that's of a neutral
  heart,
And not from one opposed.
  CORNWALL: Cunning.
  REGAN: And false.
  CORNWALL:
Where hast thou sent the king?
  GLOUCESTER:
To Dover.
  REGAN:
Wherefore to Dover? Wast thou not charged
  at peril° —   55
  CORNWALL:
Wherefore to Dover? Let him answer that.
  GLOUCESTER:
I am tied to th' stake, and I must stand the
  course.°
  REGAN:
Wherefore to Dover?
  GLOUCESTER:
Because I would not see thy cruel nails
Pluck out his poor old eyes; nor thy fierce
  sister   60
In his anointed° flesh rash° boarish fangs.

---

20 **lords dependants** attendant lords (members of
Lear's retinue)   26 **pass upon** pass judgment on   28
do . . . to indulge   31 **corky** sapless (because old)
36 s.d. **plucks his beard** a deadly insult   39 **Naughty**
wicked

41 **quicken** come to life   42 **hospitable favors** face
of your host   43 **ruffle** tear at violently   44 **late** recently   45 **simple-answered** straight forward in answering   50 **guessingly** without certain knowledge
55 **charged at peril** ordered under penalty   57
course coursing (in which a relay of dogs baits a bull
or bear tied in the pit)   61 **anointed** holy (because
king); **rash** strike with the tusk, like a boar

The sea, with such a storm as his bare head
In hell-black night endured, would have
    buoyed° up
And quenched the stellèd° fires.
65 Yet, poor old heart, he holp° the heavens to
    rain.
If wolves had at thy gate howled that dearn°
    time,
Thou shouldst have said, "Good porter, turn
    the key."°
All cruels else subscribe.° But I shall see
The wingèd° vengeance overtake such children.
    CORNWALL:
70 See't shalt thou never. Fellows, hold the chair.
Upon these eyes of thine I'll set my foot.
    GLOUCESTER:
He that will think° to live till he be old,
Give me some help. — O cruel! O you gods!
    REGAN:
One side will mock° another. Th' other too.
    CORNWALL:
If you see vengeance —
75   FIRST SERVANT: Hold your hand, my lord!
I have served you ever since I was a child;
But better service have I never done you
Than now to bid you hold.
    REGAN: How now, you dog?
    FIRST SERVANT:
If you did wear a beard upon your chin,
I'd shake it° on this quarrel. What do you
80   mean!°
    CORNWALL: My villain!°

(Draw and fight.)

    FIRST SERVANT:
Nay, then, come on, and take the chance of
    anger.
    REGAN:
Give me thy sword. A peasant stand up thus?

(She takes a sword and runs at him behind,
kills him.)

    FIRST SERVANT:
O, I am slain! my lord, you have one eye left
To see some mischief° on him. O!   85
    CORNWALL:
Lest it see more, prevent it. Out, vile jelly.
Where is thy luster now?
    GLOUCESTER:
All dark and comfortless. Where's my son
    Edmund?
Edmund, enkindle all the sparks of nature°
To quit° this horrid act.
    REGAN: Out, treacherous villain,   90
Thou call'st on him that hates thee. It was he
That made the overture° of thy treasons to us;
Who is too good to pity thee.
    GLOUCESTER:
O my follies! Then Edgar was abused.°
Kind gods, forgive me that, and prosper him.   95
    REGAN:
Go thrust him out at gates, and let him smell
His way to Dover.
            (Exit [one], with GLOUCESTER.)
            How is't, my lord? How look you?°
    CORNWALL:
I have received a hurt. Follow me, lady.
Turn out that eyeless villain. Throw this slave
Upon the dunghill. Regan, I bleed apace.   100
Untimely comes this hurt. Give me your arm.
            (Exeunt.)
    SECOND SERVANT:
I'll never care what wickedness I do,
If this man come to good.
    THIRD SERVANT: If she live long,
And in the end meet the old course of death,°
Women will all turn monsters.   105
    SECOND SERVANT:
Let's follow the old carl, and get the Bedlam
To lead him where he would. His roguish
    madness
Allows itself to anything.°
    THIRD SERVANT:
Go thou. I'll fetch some flax and whites of
    eggs
To apply to his bleeding face. Now heaven
    help him.

                    [Exeunt severally.]

---

63 **buoyed** risen   64 **stellèd** (1) fixed (as opposed to
the planets or wandering stars) (2) starry   65 **holp**
helped   66 **dearn** dread   67 **turn the key** i.e., un-
lock the gate   68 **All . . . subscribe** All cruel creatures but man are compassionate   69 **wingèd** (1)
heavenly (2) swift   72 **will think** expects   74 **mock**
make ridiculous (because of the contrast)   80 **shake
it** an insult comparable to Regan's plucking of
Gloucester's beard; **What . . . mean** i.e., What terrible thing are you doing?   81 **villain** serf (with a suggestion of the modern meaning)

85 **mischief** injury   89 **enkindle . . . nature** fan your
natural feeling into flame   90 **quit** requite   92 **over-
ture** disclosure   93 **abused** wronged   97 **How look
you** How are you?   104 **meet . . . death** die the customary death of old age   107–108 **His . . . anything**
his lack of all self-control leaves him open to any
suggestion

ACT IV

SCENE I. [*The heath.*]

Enter EDGAR.

EDGAR:
Yet better thus, and known to be contemned,°
Than still contemned and flattered. To be
    worst,
The lowest and most dejected° thing of for-
    tune,
Stands still in esperance,° lives not in fear:
5 The lamentable change is from the best,
The worst returns to laughter.° Welcome then,
Thou unsubstantial air that I embrace!
The wretch that thou hast blown unto the
    worst
Owes° nothing to thy blasts.

    (*Enter* GLOUCESTER, *led by an* OLD MAN.)

                But who comes here?
My father, poorly led?° World, world, O
10   world!
But that thy strange mutations make us hate
    thee,
Life would not yield to age.°
OLD MAN: O, my good lord,
I have been your tenant, and your father's
    tenant,
These fourscore years.
GLOUCESTER:
15 Away, get thee away; good friend, be gone:
Thy comforts° can do me no good at all;
Thee they may hurt.°
OLD MAN: You cannot see your way.
GLOUCESTER:
I have no way and therefore want° no eyes;
I stumbled when I saw. Full oft 'tis seen,
20 Our means secure us, and our mere defects
Prove our commodities.° Oh, dear son Edgar,

The food° of thy abusèd° father's wrath!
Might I but live to see thee in° my touch,
I'd say I had eyes again!
OLD MAN: How now! Who's there?
EDGAR [*aside*]:
O gods! Who is't can say, "I am at the worst"? 25
I am worse than e'er I was.
OLD MAN: 'Tis poor mad Tom.
EDGAR [*aside*]:
And worse I may be yet: the worst is not
So long as we can say, "This is the worst."°
OLD MAN:
Fellow, where goest?
GLOUCESTER: Is it a beggar-man?
OLD MAN:
Madman and beggar too.   30
GLOUCESTER:
He has some reason,° else he could not beg.
I' th' last night's storm I such a fellow saw,
Which made me think a man a worm. My son
Came then into my mind, and yet my mind
Was then scarce friends with him. I have
    heard more since.   35
As flies to wanton° boys, are we to th' gods,
They kill us for their sport.
EDGAR [*aside*]:   How should this be?°
Bad is the trade that must play fool to sorrow,
Ang'ring° itself and others. Bless thee, master!
GLOUCESTER:
Is that the naked fellow?
OLD MAN: Ay, my lord.   40
GLOUCESTER:
Then, prithee, get thee gone: if for my sake
Thou wilt o'ertake us hence a mile or twain
I' th' way toward Dover, do it for ancient°
    love,
And bring some covering for this naked soul,
Which I'll entreat to lead me.
OLD MAN: Alack, sir, he is mad.   45
GLOUCESTER:
'Tis the time's plague,° when madmen lead the
    blind.

IV.i.1 **known ... contemned** conscious of being despised 3 **dejected** abased 4 **esperance** hope 6 **returns to laughter** changes for the better 9 **Owes** is in debt for 10 **poorly led** (1) led like a poor man, with only one attendant (2) led by a poor man 11–12 **But ... age** We should not agree to grow old and hence die, except for the hateful mutability of life 16 **comforts** ministrations 17 **hurt** injure 18 **want** require 20–21 **Our ... commodities** Our resources make us overconfident, while our afflictions make for our advantage

22 **food** i.e., the object on which Gloucester's anger fed; **abusèd** deceived 23 **in** i.e., with, by means of 27–28 **the ... worst** so long as a man continues to suffer (i.e., is still alive), even greater suffering may await him 31 **reason** faculty of reasoning 36 **wanton** (1) playful (2) reckless 37 **How ... be** i.e., How can this horror be? 39 **Ang'ring** offending 43 **ancient** (1) the love the Old Man feels, by virtue of his long tenancy (2) the love that formerly obtained between master and man 46 **time's plague** characteristic disorder of this time

Do as I bid thee, or rather do thy pleasure;°
Above the rest,° be gone.

OLD MAN:
I'll bring him the best 'parel° that I have,
50 Come on't what will.   (*Exit.*)

GLOUCESTER:
Sirrah, naked fellow —

EDGAR:
Poor Tom's a-cold. [*Aside.*] I cannot daub it°
further.

GLOUCESTER:
Come hither, fellow.

EDGAR [*aside*]:
And yet I must. — Bless thy sweet eyes, they
bleed.

GLOUCESTER:
55 Know'st thou the way to Dover?

EDGAR:
Both stile and gate, horse-way and footpath.
Poor Tom hath been scared out of his good
wits.
Bless thee, good man's son, from the foul
fiend!
Five fiends have been in Poor Tom at once; of
60 lust, as Obidicut;° Hobbididence, prince of
dumbness;° Mahu, of stealing; Modo, of murder; Flibbertigibbet, of mopping and mowing;°
who since possesses chambermaids and wait-
ing-women. So, bless thee, master!

GLOUCESTER:
Here, take this purse, thou whom the heavens'
65 plagues
Have humbled to all strokes:° that I am
wretched
Makes thee the happier. Heavens, deal so still!
Let the superfluous° and lust-dieted° man,
That slaves° your ordinance,° that will not see
Because he does not feel, feel your pow'r
70 quickly;
So distribution should undo excess,°

47 **thy pleasure** as you like it   48 **the rest** all   49
'**parel** apparel   52 **daub it** lay it on (figure from
plastering mortar)   60 **Obidicut** Hoberdicut, a devil
(like the four that follow, from Harsnett's *Declaration*)   61 **dumbness** muteness (like the crimes and
afflictions in the next lines, the result of diabolic
possession)   62 **mopping and mowing** grimacing and
making faces   66 **humbled ... strokes** brought so
low as to bear anything humbly   68 **superfluous**
possessed of superfluities; **lust-dieted** whose lust is
gratified (like Gloucester's)   69 **slaves** (1) tramples,
spurns like a slave (2) tears, rends (Old English
slaefan) (?); **ordinance** law   71 **So ... excess** Then
the man with too much wealth would distribute it
among those with too little

And each man have enough. Dost thou know
Dover?

EDGAR: Ay, master.

GLOUCESTER:
There is a cliff whose high and bending° head
Looks fearfully° in the confinèd deep:°   75
Bring me but to the very brim of it,
And I'll repair the misery thou dost bear
With something rich about me: from that
place
I shall no leading need.

EDGAR: Give me thy arm:
Poor Tom shall lead thee.   (*Exeunt.*) 80

SCENE II. [*Before the Duke of* ALBANY'S
palace.]

Enter GONERIL *and* EDMUND.

GONERIL:
Welcome, my lord: I marvel our mild husband
Not met° us on the way.

(*Enter* OSWALD.)

                        Now, where's your master?

OSWALD:
Madam, within; but never man so changed.
I told him of the army that was landed:
He smiled at it. I told him you were coming;   5
His answer was, "The worse." Of Gloucester's
treachery,
And of the loyal service of his son
When I informed him, then he called me sot,°
And told me I had turned the wrong side out:
What most he should dislike seems pleasant to
him;   10
What like,° offensive.

GONERIL [*to* EDMUND]:
Then shall you go no further.
It is the cowish° terror of his spirit,
That dares not undertake:° he'll not feel
wrongs,
Which tie him to an answer.° Our wishes on
the way   15
May prove effects.° Back, Edmund, to my
brother;

74 **bending** overhanging   75 **fearfully** occasioning
fear; **confinèd deep** the sea, hemmed in below
IV.II.2 **Not met** did not meet   8 **sot** fool   11 **What
like** what he should like   13 **cowish** cowardly   14
undertake venture   15 **tie ... answer** oblige him to
retaliate   15–16 **Our ... effects** Our desires (that
you might be my husband), as we journeyed here,
may be fulfilled

Hasten his musters° and conduct his pow'rs.°
I must change names° at home and give the
    distaff°
Into my husband's hands. This trusty servant
Shall pass between us: ere long you are like to
20 hear,
If you dare venture in your own behalf,
A mistress's° command. Wear this; spare
    speech;

[Giving a favor.]

Decline your head.° This kiss, if it durst speak,
Would stretch thy spirits up into the air:
25 Conceive,° and fare thee well.
    EDMUND:
Yours in the ranks of death.
    GONERIL: My most dear Gloucester!
                        (Exit [EDMUND].)
O, the difference of man and man!
To thee a woman's services are due:
My fool usurps my body.°
    OSWALD: Madam, here comes my lord.
                        (Exit.)

(Enter ALBANY.)

    GONERIL:
I have been worth the whistle.°
30 ALBANY: O Goneril!
You are not worth the dust which the rude
    wind
Blows in your face. I fear your disposition:°
That nature which contemns° its origin
Cannot be bordered certain in itself;°
35 She that herself will sliver and disbranch°
From her material sap,° perforce must wither
And come to deadly use.°

    GONERIL:
No more; the text° is foolish.
    ALBANY:
Wisdom and goodness to the vile seem vile:
Filths savor but themselves.° What have you
    done?   40
Tigers, not daughters, what have you per-
    formed?
A father, and a gracious agèd man,
Whose reverence even the head-lugged bear°
    would lick,
Most barbarous, most degenerate, have you
    madded.°
Could my good brother suffer you to do it?   45
A man, a prince, by him so benefited!
If that the heavens do not their visible spirits°
Send quickly down to tame these vile offenses,
It will come,
Humanity must perforce prey on itself,   50
Like monsters of the deep.
    GONERIL: Milk-livered° man!
That bear'st a cheek for blows, a head for
    wrongs;
Who hast not in thy brows an eye discerning
Thine honor from thy suffering;° that not
    know'st
Fools do those villains pity who are punished   55
Ere they have done their mischief.° Where's
    thy drum?
France spreads his banners in our noiseless°
    land,
With plumèd helm° thy state begins to threat,°
Whilst thou, a moral° fool, sits still and cries,
"Alack, why does he so?"
    ALBANY: See thyself, devil!   60
Proper° deformity seems not in the fiend
So horrid as in woman.

17 **musters** collecting of troops; **conduct his pow'rs** lead his army   18 **change names** i.e., exchange the name of "mistress" for that of "master"; **distaff** spinning stick (wifely symbol)   22 **mistress's** lover's (and also, Albany having been disposed of, lady's or wife's)   23 **Decline your head** i.e., that Goneril may kiss him   25 **Conceive** understand (with a sexual implication, that includes "stretch thy spirits," line 24; and "death," line 26: "to die," meaning "to experience sexual intercourse")   29 **My . . . body** My husband wrongfully enjoys me   30 **I . . . whistle** i.e., Once you valued me (the proverb is implied, "It is a poor dog that is not worth the whistling")   32 **disposition** nature   33 **contemns** despises   34 **bordered . . . itself** kept within its normal bounds   35 **sliver and disbranch** cut off   36 **material sap** essential and life-giving sustenance   37 **come . . . use** i.e., be as a dead branch for the burning

38 **text** i.e., on which your sermon is based   40 **Filths . . . themselves** the filthy relish only the taste of filth   43 **head-lugged bear** bear-baited by the dogs, and hence enraged   44 **madded** made mad   47 **visible spirits** avenging spirits in material form   51 **Milk-livered** lily-livered (hence cowardly, the liver being regarded as the seat of courage)   53-54 **discerning . . . suffering** able to distinguish between insults that ought to be resented and ordinary pain that is to be borne   55-56 **Fools . . . mischief** Only fools are sorry for criminals whose intended criminality is prevented by punishment   57 **noiseless** i.e., the drum, signifying preparation for war, is silent   58 **helm** helmet; **thy . . . threat** France begins to threaten Albany's realm   59 **moral** moralizing; but also with the implication that morality and folly are one   61 **Proper** (1) natural (to a fiend) (2) fair-appearing

GONERIL: O vain fool!

ALBANY:
Thou changèd and self-covered° thing, for shame,
Be-monster not thy feature.° Were't my fitness°
65 To let these hands obey my blood,°
They are apt enough to dislocate and tear
Thy flesh and bones: howe'er° thou art a fiend,
A woman's shape doth shield thee.

GONERIL:
Marry, your manhood mew° —

(*Enter a* MESSENGER.)

70 ALBANY: What news?

MESSENGER:
O, my good lord, the Duke of Cornwall's dead,
Slain by his servant, going to° put out
The other eye of Gloucester.

ALBANY: Gloucester's eyes!

MESSENGER:
A servant that he bred,° thrilled with remorse,°
75 Opposed against the act, bending his sword
To his great master, who thereat enraged
Flew on him, and amongst them felled° him dead,
But not without that harmful stroke which since
Hath plucked him after.°

ALBANY: This shows you are above,
80 You justicers,° that these our nether° crimes
So speedily can venge.° But, O poor Gloucester!
Lost he his other eye?

MESSENGER: Both, both, my lord.
This letter, madam, craves° a speedy answer;
'Tis from your sister.

GONERIL [*aside*]: One way I like this well;
85 But being widow, and my Gloucester with her,

May all the building in my fancy pluck
Upon my hateful life.° Another way,°
The news is not so tart.° — I'll read, and answer.   (*Exit.*)

ALBANY:
Where was his son when they did take his eyes?

MESSENGER:
Come with my lady hither.

ALBANY: He is not here.   90

MESSENGER:
No, my good lord; I met him back° again.

ALBANY:
Knows he the wickedness?

MESSENGER:
Ay, my good lord; 'twas he informed against him,
And quit the house on purpose, that their punishment
Might have the freer course.

ALBANY: Gloucester, I live   95
To thank thee for the love thou showed'st the king,
And to revenge thine eyes. Come hither, friend:
Tell me what more thou know'st.   (*Exeunt.*)

[SCENE III. *The French camp near Dover.*]

Enter KENT *and a* GENTLEMAN.

KENT: Why the King of France is so suddenly gone back, know you no reason?

GENTLEMAN: Something he left imperfect in the state,° which since his coming forth is thought of, which imports° to the kingdom so 5 much fear and danger that his personal return was most required and necessary.

KENT:
Who hath he left behind him general?

GENTLEMAN: The Marshal of France, Monsieur La Far.   10

KENT: Did your letters pierce° the queen to any demonstration of grief?

GENTLEMAN:
Ay, sir; she took them, read them in my presence,

63 **changèd and self-covered** i.e., transformed, by the contorting of her woman's face, on which appears the fiendish behavior she has allowed herself (Goneril has disguised nature by wickedness) 64 **Be-monster ... feature** do not change your appearance into a fiend's; **my fitness** appropriate for me 65 **blood** passion 67 **howe'er** but even if 69 **your manhood mew** (1) coop up or confine (pretended) manhood (2) molt or shed it, if that is what is supposed to "shield" me from you 72 **going to** as he was about to 74 **bred** reared; **thrilled with remorse** pierced by compassion 77 **amongst them felled** others assisting, they felled 79 **plucked him after** i.e., brought Cornwall to death with his servant 80 **justicers** judges; **nether** committed below (on earth) 81 **venge** avenge 83 **craves** demands

86–87 **May ... life** These things (line 85) may send my future hopes, my castles in air, crashing down upon the hateful (married) life I lead now 87 **Another way** looked at another way 88 **tart** sour 91 **back** going back
IV.III.3–4 **imperfect ... state** unsettled in his own kingdom 5 **imports** portends 11 **pierce** impel

And now and then an ample tear trilled° down
15 Her delicate cheek: it seemed she was a queen
Over her passion, who most rebel-like
Sought to be king o'er her.
   KENT: O, then it moved her.
   GENTLEMAN:
Not to a rage: patience and sorrow strove
Who should express her goodliest.° You have
   seen
Sunshine and rain at once: her smiles and
20   tears
Were like a better way:° those happy smilets°
That played on her ripe lip seemed not to
   know
What guests were in her eyes, which parted
   thence
As pearls from diamonds dropped. In brief,
25 Sorrow would be a rarity most belovèd,
If all could so become it.°
   KENT: Made she no verbal question?
   GENTLEMAN:
Faith, once or twice she heaved° the name of
   "father"
Pantingly forth, as if it pressed her heart;
Cried, "Sisters! Sisters! Shame of ladies!
   Sisters!
30 Kent! Father! Sisters! What, i' th' storm? i'
   th' night?
Let pity not be believed!"° There she shook
The holy water from her heavenly eyes,
And clamor moistened:° then away she started
To deal with grief alone.
   KENT: It is the stars,
35 The stars above us, govern our conditions;°
Else one self mate and make could not beget
Such different issues.° You spoke not with her
   since?
   GENTLEMAN: No.
   KENT:
Was this before the king returned?
   GENTLEMAN: No, since.

   KENT:
Well, sir, the poor distressèd Lear's i' th' town; 40
Who sometime in his better tune° remembers
What we are come about, and by no means
Will yield to see his daughter.
   GENTLEMAN: Why, good sir?
   KENT:
A sovereign° shame so elbows° him: his own
   unkindness
That stripped her from his benediction, turned
   her 45
To foreign casualties,° gave her dear rights
To his dog-hearted daughters: these things
   sting
His mind so venomously that burning shame
Detains him from Cordelia.
   GENTLEMAN: Alack, poor gentleman!
   KENT:
Of Albany's and Cornwall's powers you heard
   not? 50
   GENTLEMAN:
'Tis so;° they are afoot.
   KENT:
Well, sir, I'll bring you to our master Lear,
And leave you to attend him: some dear cause°
Will in concealment wrap me up awhile;
When I am known aright, you shall not grieve 55
Lending me this acquaintance. I pray you, go
Along with me.   [Exeunt.]

[SCENE IV. *The same. A tent.*]

Enter, with drum and colors, CORDELIA,
DOCTOR, *and* SOLDIERS.

   CORDELIA:
Alack, 'tis he: why, he was met even now
As mad as the vexed sea; singing aloud;
Crowned with rank femiter and furrow-weeds,
With hardocks, hemlock, nettles, cuckoo-
   flow'rs,
Darnel,° and all the idle weeds that grow 5

14 **trilled** trickled 19 **Who . . . goodliest** which
should give her the most becoming expression 21
Were . . . way i.e., improved on that spectacle; **smilets**
little smiles 25–26 **Sorrow . . . it** sorrow would be a
coveted jewel if it became others as it does her 27
heaved expressed with difficulty 31 **Let . . . believed** Let it not be believed for pity 33 **clamor
moistened** moistened clamor, i.e., mixed (and perhaps assuaged) her outcries with tears 35 **govern
our conditions** determine what we are 36–37 **Else
. . . issues** otherwise the same husband and wife could
not produce such different children

41 **better tune** composed, less jangled intervals 44
sovereign overpowering; **elbows** jogs his elbow (i.e.,
reminds him) 46 **casualties** chances 51 **'Tis so**
i.e., I have heard of them 53 **dear cause** important
reason
IV.iv.3–5 **femiter . . . Darnel:** *femiter* fumitory,
whose leaves and juice are bitter; *furrow-weeds* weeds
that grow in the furrow, or plowed land; *hardocks*
hoar or white docks (?), burdocks, harlocks; *hemlock*
a poison; *nettles* plants that sting and burn; *cuckoo
flow'rs* identified with a plant employed to remedy
diseases of the brain; *Darnel* tares, noisome weeds

In our sustaining corn.° A century° send forth;
Search every acre in the high-grown field,
And bring him to our eye. [*Exit an* OFFICER.]
     What can man's wisdom°
In the restoring his bereavèd° sense?
10 He that helps him take all my outward° worth.
     DOCTOR:
There is means, madam:
Our foster-nurse° of nature is repose,
The which he lacks: that to provoke° in him,
Are many simples operative,° whose power
Will close the eye of anguish.
15   CORDELIA: All blest secrets,
All you unpublished virtues° of the earth,
Spring with my tears! be aidant and remedi-
ate°
In the good man's distress! Seek, seek for him,
Lest his ungoverned rage dissolve the life
That wants the means to lead it.°
     (*Enter* MESSENGER.)
20   MESSENGER: News, madam;
The British pow'rs are marching hitherward.
     CORDELIA:
'Tis known before. Our preparation stands
In expectation of them. O dear father,
It is thy business that I go about;
25 Therefore° great France
My mourning and importuned° tears hath
pitied.
No blown° ambition doth our arms incite,
But love, dear love, and our aged father's
right:
Soon may I hear and see him!   (*Exeunt.*)

[SCENE V. GLOUCESTER's *castle*.]

Enter REGAN *and* OSWALD.

REGAN:
But are my brother's pow'rs set forth?
     OSWALD: Ay, madam.
Himself in person there?
     OSWALD: Madam, with much ado:°
Your sister is the better soldier.

6 **sustaining corn** life-maintaining wheat; **century**
sentry (?); troop of a hundred soldiers   8 **What . . .
wisdom** what can science accomplish   9 **bereavèd**
impaired   10 **outward** material   12 **foster-nurse**
fostering nurse   13 **provoke** induce   14 **simples
operative** efficacious medicinal herbs   16 **unpublished virtues** i.e., secret remedial herbs   17 **reme-
diate** remedial   20 **wants . . . it** i.e., lacks the reason
to control the rage   25 **Therefore** because of that
26 **importuned** importunate   27 **blown** puffed up
IV.v.2 **ado** bother and persuasion

REGAN:
Lord Edmund spake not with your lord at
home?
OSWALD:
No, madam.   5
REGAN:
What might import° my sister's letter to him?
OSWALD:
I know not, lady.
REGAN:
Faith, he is posted° hence on serious matter.
It was great ignorance,° Gloucester's eyes being
out,
To let him live. Where he arrives he moves   10
All hearts against us: Edmund, I think, is
gone,
In pity of his misery, to dispatch
His nighted° life; moreover, to descry
The strength o' th' enemy.
OSWALD:
I must needs after him, madam, with my
letter.   15
REGAN:
Our troops set forth tomorrow: stay with us;
The ways are dangerous.
OSWALD: I may not, madam:
My lady charged my duty° in this business.
REGAN:
Why should she write to Edmund? Might not
you
Transport her purposes° by word? Belike,°   20
Some things I know not what. I'll love thee
much,
Let me unseal the letter.
OSWALD: Madam, I had rather —
REGAN:
I know your lady does not love her husband;
I am sure of that: and at her late° being here
She gave strange eliads° and most speaking looks 25
To noble Edmund. I know you are of her
bosom.°
OSWALD: I, madam?
REGAN:
I speak in understanding: y' are; I know't:
Therefore I do advise you, take this note:°

6 **import** purport, carry as its message   8 **is posted**
has ridden speedily   9 **ignorance** folly   13 **nighted**
(1) darkened, because blinded (2) benighted   18
charged my duty ordered me as a solemn duty   20
Transport her purposes convey her intentions; **Belike**
probably   24 **late** recently   25 **eliads** amorous looks
26 **of her bosom** in her confidence   29 **take this note**
take note of this

30 My lord is dead; Edmund and I have talked;
And more convenient° is he for my hand
Than for your lady's: you may gather more.°
If you do find him, pray you, give him this;°
And when your mistress hears thus much from
    you,
35 I pray, desire her call° her wisdom to her.
So, fare you well.
If you do chance to hear of that blind traitor,
Preferment° falls on him that cuts him off.
    OSWALD:
Would I could meet him, madam! I should
    show
What party I do follow.
40   REGAN: Fare thee well. (*Exeunt.*)

[SCENE VI. *Fields near Dover.*]

Enter GLOUCESTER *and* EDGAR.

    GLOUCESTER:
When shall I come to th' top of that same
    hill?
    EDGAR:
You do climb up it now. Look, how we labor.
    GLOUCESTER:
Methinks the ground is even.
    EDGAR: Horrible steep.
Hark, do you hear the sea?
    GLOUCESTER: No, truly.
    EDGAR:
5 Why then your other senses grow imperfect
By your eyes' anguish.°
    GLOUCESTER: So may it be indeed.
Methinks thy voice is altered, and thou
    speak'st
In better phrase and matter than thou didst.
    EDGAR:
Y' are much deceived: in nothing am I changed
But in my garments.
10   GLOUCESTER: Methinks y' are better spoken.
    EDGAR:
Come on, sir; here's the place: stand still. How
    fearful
And dizzy 'tis to cast one's eyes so low!
The crows and choughs° that wing the midway
    air°
Show scarce so gross° as beetles. Half way
    down

31 **convenient** fitting   32 **gather more** surmise more
yourself   33 **this** this advice   35 **call** recall   38
Preferment promotion
IV.vi.6 **anguish** pain   13 **choughs** a kind of crow;
midway air i.e., halfway down the cliff   14 **gross**
large

Hangs one that gathers sampire,° dreadful
    trade!   15
Methinks he seems no bigger than his head.
The fishermen that walk upon the beach
Appear like mice; and yond tall anchoring°
    bark
Diminished to her cock;° her cock, a buoy
Almost too small for sight. The murmuring
    surge   20
That on th' unnumb'red idle pebble° chafes
Cannot be heard so high. I'll look no more,
Lest my brain turn and the deficient sight
Topple° down headlong.
    GLOUCESTER: Set me where you stand.
    EDGAR:
Give me your hand: you are now within a foot   25
Of th' extreme verge: for all beneath the moon
Would I not leap upright.°
    GLOUCESTER: Let go my hand.
Here, friend, 's another purse; in it a jewel
Well worth a poor man's taking. Fairies° and
    gods
Prosper it with thee! Go thou further off;   30
Bid me farewell, and let me hear thee going.
    EDGAR:
Now fare ye well, good sir.
    GLOUCESTER: With all my heart.
    EDGAR [*aside*]:
Why I do trifle thus with his despair
Is done to cure it.°
    GLOUCESTER: O you mighty gods!

(*He kneels.*)

This world I do renounce, and in your sights   35
Shake patiently my great affliction off:
If I could bear it longer and not fall
To quarrel with° your great opposeless° wills,
My snuff° and loathèd part of nature should
Burn itself out. If Edgar live, O bless him!   40
Now, fellow, fare thee well. (*He falls.*)
    EDGAR: Gone, sir, farewell.

15 **sampire** samphire, an aromatic herb associated
with Dover Cliffs   18 **anchoring** anchored   19 **cock**
cockboat, a small boat usually towed behind the ship
21 **unnumb'red idle pebble** innumerable pebbles,
moved to and fro by the waves to no purpose   23–
24 **the ... Topple** my failing sight topple me   27
upright i.e., even up in the air, to say nothing of
forward, over the cliff   29 **Fairies** who are supposed
to guard and multiply hidden treasure   33–34 **Why
... it** I play on his despair in order to cure it   37–38
fall ... with rebel against   38 **opposeless** not to be,
and not capable of being, opposed   39 **snuff** the
guttering (and stinking) wick of a burnt-out candle

And yet I know not how° conceit° may rob
The treasury of life, when life itself
Yields to° the theft. Had he been where he
    thought,
45 By this had thought been past. Alive or dead?
Ho, you sir! friend! Hear you, sir! speak!
Thus might he pass° indeed: yet he revives.
What are you, sir?
    GLOUCESTER: Away, and let me die.
    EDGAR:
Hadst thou been aught but gossamer, feathers,
    air,
50 So many fathom down precipitating,°
Thou'dst shivered like an egg: but thou dost
    breathe;
Hast heavy substance; bleed'st not; speak'st; art
    sound.
Ten masts at each° make not the altitude
Which thou hast perpendicularly fell:
55 Thy life's° a miracle. Speak yet again.
    GLOUCESTER:
But have I fall'n, or no?
    EDGAR:
From the dread summit of this chalky bourn.°
Look up a-height;° the shrill-gorged° lark so far
Cannot be seen or heard: do but look up.
    GLOUCESTER:
60 Alack, I have no eyes.
Is wretchedness deprived that benefit,
To end itself by death? 'Twas yet some
    comfort,
When misery could beguile° the tyrant's rage
And frustrate his proud will.
    EDGAR: Give me your arm.
Up, so. How is't? Feel you° your legs? You
65   stand.
    GLOUCESTER:
Too well, too well.
    EDGAR: This is above all strangeness.
Upon the crown o' th' cliff, what thing was
    that
Which parted from you?
    GLOUCESTER: A poor unfortunate beggar.
    EDGAR:
As I stood here below, methought his eyes
Were two full moons; he had a thousand
70   noses,

42 **how** but what; **conceit** imagination   44 **Yields
to** allows   47 **pass** die   50 **precipitating** falling   53
at each one on top of the other   55 **life's** survival
57 **bourn** boundary   58 **a-height** on high; **gorged**
throated, voiced   63 **beguile** cheat (i.e., by suicide)
65 **Feel you** have you any feeling in

Horns whelked° and waved like the enridgèd°
    sea:
It was some fiend; therefore, thou happy
    father,°
Think that the clearest° gods, who make them
    honors
Of men's impossibilities,° have preserved thee.
    GLOUCESTER:
I do remember now: henceforth I'll bear   75
Affliction till it do cry out itself,
"Enough, enough," and die. That thing you
    speak of,
I took it for a man; often 'twould say,
"The fiend, the fiend" — he led me to that
    place.
    EDGAR:
Bear free° and patient thoughts.

(*Enter* LEAR [*fantastically dressed with wild
flowers*].)

                 But who comes here?   80
The safer° sense will ne'er accommodate°
His master thus.
    LEAR: No, they cannot touch me for
coining;° I am the king himself.
    EDGAR:
O thou side-piercing sight!   85
    LEAR: Nature's above art in that respect.°
There's your press-money.° That fellow handles
his bow like a crow-keeper;° draw me a
clothier's yard.° Look, look, a mouse! Peace,
peace; this piece of toasted cheese will do't.   90
There's my gauntlet;° I'll prove it on° a giant.

71 **whelked** twisted; **enridgèd** i.e., furrowed into
waves   72 **happy father** fortunate old man   73
clearest purest   73–74 **who ... impossibilities** who
cause themselves to be honored and revered by performing miracles of which men are incapable   80
free i.e., emancipated from grief and despair, which
fetter the soul   81 **safer** sounder, saner; **accommodate** dress, adorn   83–84 **touch ... coining** arrest
me for minting coins (the king's prerogative)   86
Nature's ... respect i.e., a born king is superior to
legal (and hence artificial) inhibition; there is also a
glance here at the popular Renaissance debate concerning the relative importance of nature (inspiration) and art (training)   87 **press-money** paid to
conscripted soldiers   88 **crow-keeper** a farmer scar-
ing away crows   89 **clothier's yard** the standard
English arrow was a cloth-yard long; here the injunction is to draw the arrow back, like a powerful archer,
a full yard to the ear   91 **gauntlet** armored glove,
thrown down as a challenge; **prove it on** maintain
my challenge even against

Bring up the brown bills.° O, well flown,°
birds! i' th' clout, i' th' clout:° hewgh!° Give
the word.°

95   EDGAR: Sweet marjoram.°
LEAR: Pass.
GLOUCESTER:
I know that voice.
LEAR: Ha! Goneril, with a white beard!
They flattered me like a dog,° and told me I
100 had white hairs in my beard ere the black ones
were there.° To say "ay" and "no" to
everything that I said! "Ay" and "no" too was
no good divinity.° When the rain came to wet
me once and the wind to make me chatter;
105 when the thunder would not peace at my
bidding; there I found 'em, there I smelt 'em
out. Go to, they are not men o' their words:
they told me I was everything; 'tis a lie, I am
not ague-proof.°
GLOUCESTER:
110 The trick° of that voice I do well remember:
Is't not the king?
LEAR: Ay, every inch a king.
When I do stare, see how the subject quakes.
I pardon that man's life. What was thy cause?°
Adultery?
115 Thou shalt not die: die for adultery! No:
The wren goes to't, and the small gilded fly
Does lecher° in my sight.
Let copulation thrive; for Gloucester's bastard
     son
Was kinder to his father than my daughters
120 Got° 'tween the lawful sheets.
To't, luxury,° pell-mell! for I lack soldiers.°
Behold yond simp'ring dame,

Whose face between her forks presages snow,°
That minces° virtue and does shake the head
To hear of pleasure's name.°   125
The fftchew,° nor the soilèd° horse, goes to't
With a more riotous appetite.
Down from the waist they are Centaurs,°
Though women all above:
But to the girdle° do the gods inherit,°   130
Beneath is all the fiend's.
There's hell, there's darkness, there is the
sulphurous pit, burning, scalding, stench,
consumption; fie, fie, fie! pah, pah! Give me
an ounce of civet;° good apothecary, sweeten   135
my imagination: there's money for thee.
GLOUCESTER:
O, let me kiss that hand!
LEAR:
Let me wipe it first; it smells of mortality.°
GLOUCESTER:
O ruined piece of nature! This great world
Shall so wear out to nought.° Dost thou know
     me?   140
LEAR: I remember thine eyes well enough.
Dost thou squiny° at me? No, do thy worst,
blind Cupid;° I'll not love. Read thou this
challenge;° mark but the penning of it.
GLOUCESTER:
Were all thy letters suns, I could not see.   145
EDGAR:
I would not take° this from report: it is,
And my heart breaks at it.
LEAR: Read.
GLOUCESTER:
What, with the case° of eyes?
LEAR: O, ho, are you there with me?° No   150
eyes in your head, nor no money in your
purse? Your eyes are in a heavy case,° your

---

92 **brown bills** halberds varnished to prevent rust
(here the reference is to the soldiers who carry them);
well flown falconer's cry; and perhaps a reference to
the flight of the arrow   93 **clout** the target shot at;
hewgh imitating the whizzing of the arrow (?)   94
word password   95 **Sweet marjoram** herb, used as a
remedy for brain disease   99 **like a dog** as a dog
flatters   99–101 **I . . . there** I was wise before I had
even grown a beard   103 **no good divinity** bad the-
ology, because contrary to the biblical saying (II
Corinthians 1:18), "Our word toward you was not
yea and nay"; see also James 5:12, "But let your yea
be yea, and your nay, nay; lest ye fall into condemnation"; and Matthew 5:36–37   109 **ague-proof** secure against fever   110 **trick** intonation   113 **cause**
offense   117 **lecher** copulate   120 **Got** begot   121
luxury lechery; **for . . . soldiers** i.e., (1) whom copulation will supply (?) (2) and am therefore power-
less (?)

123 **Whose . . . snow** whose cold demeanor seems
to promise chaste behavior ("forks" = legs)   124
minces squeamishly pretends to   125 **pleasure's
name** the very name of sexual pleasure   126 **fitchew**
polecat (and slang for prostitute); **soilèd** put to pasture, and hence wanton with feeding   128 **Centaurs**
lustful creatures, half man and half horse   130 **girdle**
waist; **inherit** possess   135 **civet** perfume   138 **mortality** (1) death (2) existence   139–140 **This . . .
nought** i.e., The universe (macrocosm) will decay to
nothing in the same way as the little world of man
(microcosm)   142 **squiny** squint, look sideways, like
a prostitute   143 **blind Cupid** the sign hung before a
brothel   144 **challenge** a reminiscence of lines 90–
91   146 **take** believe   149 **case** empty sockets   150
are . . . me is that what you tell me   152 **heavy case**
sad plight (pun on line 149)

purse in a light,° yet you see how this world goes.

GLOUCESTER:

155 I see it feelingly.°

LEAR: What, art mad? A man may see how this world goes with no eyes. Look with thine ears: see how yond justice rails upon yond simple° thief. Hark, in thine ear: change
160 places, and, handy-dandy,° which is the justice, which is the thief? Thou hast seen a farmer's dog bark at a beggar?

GLOUCESTER: Ay, sir.

LEAR: And the creature run from the cur?
165 There thou mightst behold the great image of authority:° a dog's obeyed in office.°
Thou rascal beadle,° hold thy bloody hand!
Why dost thou lash that whore? Strip thy own back;
Thou hotly lusts to use her in that kind°
For which thou whip'st her. The usurer hangs
170 the cozener.°
Through tattered clothes small vices do appear;
Robes and furred gowns° hide all. Plate sin with gold,
And the strong lance of justice hurtless° breaks;
Arm it in rags, a pygmy's straw does pierce it.
None does offend, none, I say, none; I'll able° 'em:
175 Take that° of me, my friend, who have the power
To seal th' accuser's lips. Get thee glass eyes,°
And, like a scurvy politician,° seem
To see the things thou dost not. Now, now, now, now.
180 Pull off my boots: harder, harder: so.

---

153 **light** i.e., empty   155 **feelingly** (1) by touch (2) by feeling pain (3) with emotion   159 **simple** common, of low estate   160 **handy-dandy** i.e., choose, guess (after the children's game — "Handy-dandy, prickly prandy" — of choosing the correct hand)   165–166 **image of authority** symbol revealing the true meaning of authority   166 **a dog's . . . office** i.e., whoever has power is obeyed   167 **beadle** parish constable   169 **kind** i.e., sexual act   170 **The usurer . . . cozener** i.e., The powerful money-lender, in his role as judge, puts to death the petty cheat   172 **Robes . . . gowns** worn by a judge   173 **hurtless** i.e., without hurting the sinner   175 **able** vouch for   176 **that** the immunity just conferred (line 175)   177 **glass eyes** spectacles   178 **scurvy politician** vile politic man

EDGAR:

O, matter and impertinency° mixed!
Reason in madness!

LEAR:

If thou wilt weep my fortunes, take my eyes.
I know thee well enough; thy name is Gloucester:
Thou must be patient; we came crying hither: 185
Thou know'st, the first time that we smell the air
We wawl and cry. I will preach to thee: mark.

GLOUCESTER:

Alack, alack the day!

LEAR:

When we are born, we cry that we are come
To this great stage of fools. This'° a good block.° 190
It were a delicate° stratagem, to shoe
A troop of horse with felt: I'll put't in proof;°
And when I have stol'n upon these son-in-laws,
Then, kill, kill, kill, kill, kill, kill!

(*Enter a* GENTLEMAN, [*with* ATTENDANTS].)

GENTLEMAN:

O, here he is: lay hand upon him. Sir, 195
Your most dear daughter —

LEAR:

No rescue? What, a prisoner? I am even
The natural fool° of fortune. Use me well;
You shall have ransom. Let me have surgeons;
I am cut° to th' brains.

GENTLEMAN: You shall have anything. 200

LEAR:

No seconds?° all myself?
Why, this would make a man a man of salt,°

---

181 **matter and impertinency** sense and nonsense   190 **This** this is; **block** various meanings have been suggested, for example, the stump of a tree, on which Lear is supposed to climb; a mounting-block, which suggests "horse" (line 192); a hat (which Lear or another must be made to wear), from the block on which a felt hat is molded, and which would suggest a "felt" (line 192); the proposal here is that "block" be taken to denote the quintain, whose function is to bear blows, "a mere lifeless block" (*As You Like It*, I.II.247), an object shaped like a man and used for tilting practice; see also *Much Ado About Nothing*, II.I.231–32, "She misused me past the endurance of a block!" and, in the same passage, the associated reference, "I stood like a man at a mark [target]" (lines 237–38)   191 **delicate** subtle   192 **put't in proof** test it   198 **natural fool** born sport (with pun on "natural" = imbecile)   200 **cut** wounded   201 **seconds** supporters   202 **man of salt** i.e., all (salt) tears

To use his eyes for garden water-pots,
Ay, and laying autumn's dust.

GENTLEMAN:
205 Good sir —

LEAR:
I will die bravely,° like a smug° bridegroom.° What!
I will be jovial: come, come; I am a king;
Masters, know you that?

GENTLEMAN:
You are a royal one, and we obey you.

210 LEAR: Then there's life in't.° Come, and you get it, you shall get it by running. Sa, sa, sa, sa.°

(*Exit* [*running*; ATTENDANTS *follow*].)

GENTLEMAN:
A sight most pitiful in the meanest wretch,
Past speaking of in a king! Thou hast one daughter
215 Who redeems Nature from the general curse
Which twain have brought her to.°

EDGAR:
Hail, gentle° sir.

GENTLEMAN:
Sir, speed° you: what's your will?

EDGAR:
Do you hear aught, sir, of a battle toward?°

GENTLEMAN:
Most sure and vulgar:° every one hears that,
Which can distinguish sound.

220 EDGAR: But, by your favor,
How near's the other army?

GENTLEMAN:
Near and on speedy foot; the main descry
Stands on the hourly thought.°

EDGAR: I thank you, sir: that's all.

GENTLEMAN:
Though that the queen on special cause is here,
Her army is moved on.

225 EDGAR: I thank you, sir.

(*Exit* [GENTLEMAN].)

GLOUCESTER:
You ever-gentle gods, take my breath from me;
Let not my worser spirit° tempt me again
To die before you please.

EDGAR: Well pray you, father.

GLOUCESTER:
Now, good sir, what are you?

EDGAR:
A most poor man, made tame° to fortune's blows;   230
Who, by the art of known and feeling sorrows,°
Am pregnant° to good pity. Give me your hand,
I'll lead you to some biding.°

GLOUCESTER: Hearty thanks;
The bounty and the benison° of heaven
To boot, and boot.°

(*Enter* OSWALD.)

OSWALD:
A proclaimed prize!° Most happy!°   235
That eyeless head of thine was first framed° flesh
To raise my fortunes. Thou old unhappy traitor,
Briefly thyself remember:° the sword is out
That must destroy thee.

GLOUCESTER: Now let thy friendly° hand
Put strength enough to't. [EDGAR *interposes*.]

OSWALD: Wherefore, bold peasant,   240
Dar'st thou support a published° traitor?
Hence!
Lest that th' infection of his fortune take
Like hold on thee. Let go his arm.

EDGAR:
Chill° not let go, zir, without vurther 'casion.°

OSWALD:
Let go, slave, or thou diest!   245

EDGAR: Good gentleman, go your gait,° and

---

206 **bravely** (1) smartly attired (2) courageously; **smug** spick and span; **bridegroom** whose "brave" sexual feats are picked up in the pun on "die" 210 **there's life in't** there's still hope 211–212 **Sa . . . sa** hunting and rallying cry; also an interjection of defiance 215–216 **general . . . to** (1) universal condemnation which Goneril and Regan have made for (2) damnation incurred by the original sin of Adam and Eve 217 **gentle** noble; **speed** God speed 218 **toward** impending 219 **vulgar** common knowledge 222–223 **the main . . . thought** we expect to see the main body of the army any hour

227 **worser spirit** bad angel, evil side of my nature 230 **tame** submissive 231 **art . . . sorrows** instruction of sorrows painfully experienced 232 **pregnant** disposed 233 **biding** place of refuge 234 **benison** blessing 235 **To . . . boot** also, and in the highest degree; **proclaimed prize** i.e., one with a price on his head; **happy** fortunate (for Oswald) 236 **framed** created 238 **thyself remember** i.e., pray, think of your sins 239 **friendly** i.e., because it offers the death Gloucester covets 241 **published** proclaimed 244 **Chill** I will (Edgar speaks in rustic dialect); **vurther 'casion** further occasion 246 **gait** way

let poor volk° pass. And chud ha' bin
zwaggered° out of my life, 'twould not ha' bin
zo long as 'tis by a vortnight. Nay, come not
near th' old man; keep out, che vor' ye,° or
I'se° try whether your costard° or my ballow°
be the harder: chill be plain with you.

OSWALD: Out, dunghill!

(*They fight.*)

EDGAR: Chill pick your teeth,° zir: come; no
matter vor your foins.°

[OSWALD *falls.*]

OSWALD:
Slave, thou hast slain me. Villain, take my
purse:
If ever thou wilt thrive, bury my body,
And give the letters which thou find'st about°
me
To Edmund Earl of Gloucester; seek him out
Upon the English party.° O, untimely death!
Death!   (*He dies.*)

EDGAR:
I know thee well. A serviceable° villain,
As duteous° to the vices of thy mistress
As badness would desire.

GLOUCESTER: What, is he dead?

EDGAR:
Sit you down, father; rest you.
Let's see these pockets: the letters that he
speaks of
May be my friends. He's dead; I am only sorry
He had no other deathsman.° Let us see:
Leave,° gentle wax;° and, manners, blame us
not:
To know our enemies' minds, we rip their
hearts;
Their papers° is more lawful.

(*Reads the letter.*)

"Let our reciprocal vows be remembered. You
have many opportunities to cut him off: if
your will want not,° time and place will be

fruitfully offered. There is nothing done, if he
return the conqueror: then am I the prisoner,
and his bed my jail; from the loathed warmth
whereof deliver me, and supply the place for
your labor.
    "Your—wife, so I would° say—affectionate
servant, and for you her own for venture,°
                                    Goneril."
O indistinguished space of woman's will!°
A plot upon her virtuous husband's life;
And the exchange° my brother! Here in the
sands
Thee I'll rake up,° the post unsanctified°
Of murderous lechers; and in the mature°
time,
With this ungracious paper° strike° the sight
Of the death-practiced° duke: for him 'tis well
That of thy death and business I can tell.

GLOUCESTER:
The king is mad: how stiff° is my vile sense,°
That I stand up, and have ingenious° feeling
Of my huge sorrows! Better I were distract:°
So should my thoughts be severed from my
griefs,
And woes by wrong imaginations° lose
The knowledge of themselves.
                    (*Drum afar off.*)

EDGAR: Give me your hand:
Far off, methinks, I hear the beaten drum.
Come, father, I'll bestow° you with a friend.
                                    (*Exeunt.*)

SCENE VII. [*A tent in the French camp.*]

Enter CORDELIA, KENT, DOCTOR, *and* GENTLE-
MAN.

CORDELIA:
O thou good Kent, how shall I live and work,
To match thy goodness? My life will be too
short,
And every measure fail me.

247 **volk** folk 247–248 **And . . . zwaggered** if I
could have been swaggered 250 **che vor' ye** I warrant you 251 **I'se** I shall; **costard** head (literally,
"apple"); **ballow** cudgel 254 **Chill . . . teeth** I will
knock your teeth out 255 **foins** thrusts 258 **about**
upon 260 **party** side 262 **serviceable** ready to be
used 263 **duteous** obedient 268 **deathsman** executioner 269 **Leave** by your leave; **wax** with which
the letter is sealed 271 **Their papers** i.e., to rip their
papers 273–274 **if . . . not** if your desire (and lust)
be not lacking

280 **would** would like to 281 **and . . . venture** i.e.,
and one who holds you her own for venturing (Edmund had earlier been promised union by Goneril,
"If you dare venture in your own behalf," IV.II.21)
283 **indistinguished . . . will** unlimited range of woman's lust 285 **exchange** substitute 286 **rake up**
cover up, bury; **post unsanctified** unholy messenger
287 **mature** ripe 288 **ungracious paper** wicked letter; **strike** blast 289 **death-practiced** whose death
is plotted 291 **stiff** unbending; **vile sense** hateful
capacity for feeling 292 **ingenious** conscious 293
distract distracted, mad 295 **wrong imaginations**
delusions 298 **bestow** lodge

KENT:
To be acknowledged, madam, is o'erpaid.
5 All my reports go° with the modest truth,
Nor more nor clipped,° but so.
CORDELIA: Be better suited:°
These weeds° are memories° of those worser
    hours:
I prithee, put them off.
KENT: Pardon, dear madam;
Yet to be known shortens my made intent:°
10 My boon I make it,° that you know me not
Till time and I think meet.°
CORDELIA:
Then be't so, my good lord. [To the DOCTOR.]
    How does the king?
DOCTOR:
Madam, sleeps still.
CORDELIA:
O you kind gods!
15 Cure this great breach in his abusèd° nature.
Th' untuned and jarring senses, O, wind up°
Of this child-changèd° father.
DOCTOR: So please your majesty
That we may wake the king: he hath slept
    long.
CORDELIA:
Be governed by your knowledge, and proceed
20 I' th' sway of° your own will. Is he arrayed?

(Enter LEAR in a chair carried by
SERVANTS.)

GENTLEMAN:
Ay, madam; in the heaviness of sleep
We put fresh garments on him.
DOCTOR:
Be by good madam, when we do awake
    him;
I doubt not of his temperance.°
CORDELIA: Very well.
DOCTOR:
Please you, draw near. Louder the music
25   there!
CORDELIA:
O my dear father, restoration hang
Thy medicine on my lips, and let this kiss

Repair those violent harms that my two sisters
Have in thy reverence° made.
KENT: Kind and dear princess.
CORDELIA:
Had you not been their father, these white
    flakes°   30
Did challenge° pity of them. Was this a face
To be opposed against the warring winds?
To stand against the deep dread-bolted°
    thunder?
In the most terrible and nimble stroke
Of quick, cross° lightning to watch — poor
    perdu!° —   35
With this thin helm?° Mine enemy's dog,
Though he had bit me, should have stood that
    night
Against my fire; and wast thou fain,° poor
    father,
To hovel thee with swine and rogues° forlorn,
In short° and musty straw?° Alack, alack!   40
'Tis wonder that thy life and wits at once
Had not concluded all.° He wakes; speak to
    him.
DOCTOR:
Madam, do you; 'tis fittest.
CORDELIA:
How does my royal lord? How fares your
    majesty?
LEAR:
You do me wrong to take me out o' th' grave: 45
Thou art a soul in bliss; but I am bound
Upon a wheel of fire,° that mine own tears
Do scald like molten lead.
CORDELIA: Sir, do you know me?
LEAR:
You are a spirit, I know. Where did you die?
CORDELIA:
Still, still, far wide.°   50

29 **reverence** revered person 30 **flakes** hairs (in long strands) 31 **challenge** claim 33 **deep dread-bolted** deep-voiced and furnished with the dreadful thunderbolt 35 **cross** zigzag; **perdu** (1) sentry in a forlorn position (2) lost one 36 **helm** helmet (his scanty hair) 38 **fain** pleased 39 **rogues** vagabonds 40 **short** when straw is freshly cut, it is long, and suitable for bedding, given its flexibility and crispness; as it is used, it becomes musty, shreds into pieces, is "short"; in contemporary Maine usage, "short manure" refers to dung mixed with straw that has been broken up, "long manure" to dung mixed with coarse new straw 42 **concluded all** come to a complete end 47 **wheel of fire** torment associated by the Middle Ages with hell, where Lear thinks he is 50 **wide** i.e., of the mark (of sanity)

IV.VII.5 **go** conform 6 **clipped** curtailed; **suited** attired 7 **weeds** clothes; **memories** reminders 9 **Yet . . . intent** to reveal myself just yet interferes with the plan I have made 10 **My . . . it** I ask this reward 11 **meet** fitting 15 **abused** disturbed 16 **wind up** tune 17 **child-changèd** changed, deranged (and also, reduced to a child) by the cruelty of his children 20 **I' . . . of** according to 24 **temperance** sanity

DOCTOR:
He's scarce awake: let him alone awhile.
LEAR:
Where have I been? Where am I? Fair
   daylight?
I am mightily abused.° I should ev'n die with
   pity,
To see another thus. I know not what to say.
55 I will not swear these are my hands: let's see;
I feel this pin prick. Would I were assured
Of my condition.
   CORDELIA: O, look upon me, sir,
And hold your hand in benediction o'er me.
You must not kneel.
   LEAR: Pray, do not mock me:
60 I am a very foolish fond° old man,
Fourscore and upward, not an hour more nor
   less;
And, to deal plainly,
I fear I am not in my perfect mind.
Methinks I should know you and know this
   man,
65 Yet I am doubtful; for I am mainly° ignorant
What place this is, and all the skill I have
Remembers not these garments, nor I know
   not
Where I did lodge last night. Do not laugh at
   me,
For, as I am a man, I think this lady
To be my child Cordelia.
70 CORDELIA: And so I am, I am.
   LEAR:
Be your tears wet? Yes, faith. I pray, weep not.
If you have poison for me, I will drink it.
I know you do not love me; for your sisters
Have, as I do remember, done me wrong.
You have some cause, they have not.
75 CORDELIA: No cause, no cause.
   LEAR:
Am I in France?
   KENT: In your own kingdom, sir.
   LEAR:
Do not abuse° me.
   DOCTOR:
Be comforted, good madam: the great rage,°
You see, is killed in him: and yet it is danger
80 To make him even o'er° the time he has lost.
Desire him to go in; trouble him no more
Till further settling.°

53 **abused** deluded   60 **fond** in dotage   65 **mainly**
entirely   77 **abuse** deceive   78 **rage** frenzy   80
even o'er smooth over by filling in; and hence, "recollect"   82 **settling** calming

CORDELIA:
Will't please your highness walk?°
   LEAR: You must bear with me.
Pray you now, forget and forgive. I am old and
   foolish.
                    (*Exeunt. Mane[n]t°* KENT
                        and GENTLEMAN.)
GENTLEMAN: Holds it true, sir, that the   85
Duke of Cornwall was so slain?
KENT: Most certain, sir.
GENTLEMAN: Who is conductor of his
people?
KENT: As 'tis said, the bastard son of   90
Gloucester.
GENTLEMAN: They say Edgar, his banished
son, is with the Earl of Kent in Germany.
KENT: Report is changeable.° 'Tis time to   95
look about; the powers° of the kingdom
approach apace.
GENTLEMAN: The arbitrement° is like to be
bloody. Fare you well, sir.   [*Exit.*]
KENT:
My point and period will be throughly
   wrought,°
Or well or ill, as this day's battle's fought.   100
                              (*Exit.*)

ACT V

SCENE I. [*The British camp near Dover.*]

Enter, with drum and colors, EDMUND,
REGAN, GENTLEMEN, *and* SOLDIERS.

EDMUND:
Know° of the duke if his last purpose hold,°
Or whether since he is advised° by aught
To change the course: he's full of alteration
And self-reproving: bring his constant plea-
   sure.°
          [*To a* GENTLEMAN, *who goes out.*]
   REGAN:
Our sister's man is certainly miscarried.°   5

83 **walk** perhaps in the sense of "withdraw"   84 s.d.
Mane[n]t remain   95 **Report is changeable** rumors
are unreliable   96 **powers** armies   98 **arbitrement**
deciding encounter   99 **My . . . wrought** the aim and
end, the close of my life, will be completely worked
out
V.i.1 **Know** learn; **last purpose hold** most recent
intention (to fight) be maintained   2 **advised** induced   4 **constant pleasure** fixed (final) decision
5 **miscarried** come to grief

EDMUND:
'Tis to be doubted,° madam.

REGAN: Now, sweet lord,
You know the goodness I intend upon you:
Tell me, but truly, but then speak the truth,
Do you not love my sister?

EDMUND: In honored° love.

REGAN:
10 But have you never found my brother's way
To the forfended° place?

EDMUND: That thought abuses° you.

REGAN:
I am doubtful that you have been conjunct
And bosomed with her, as far as we call hers.°

EDMUND:
No, by mine honor, madam.

REGAN:
15 I shall never endure her: dear my lord,
Be not familiar with her.

EDMUND: Fear° me not. —
She and the duke her husband!

(Enter, with drum and colors, ALBANY,
GONERIL, [and] SOLDIERS.)

GONERIL [aside]:
I had rather lose the battle than that sister
Should loosen° him and me.

ALBANY:
20 Our very loving sister, well be-met.°
Sir, this I heard, the king is come to his
daughter,
With others whom the rigor of our state°
Forced to cry out. Where I could not be
honest,°
I never yet was valiant: for this business,
25 It touches us, as° France invades our land,
Not bolds the king, with others, whom, I fear,
Most just and heavy causes make oppose.°

EDMUND:
Sir, you speak nobly.

REGAN: Why is this reasoned?°

GONERIL:
Combine together 'gainst the enemy;

6 **doubted** feared 9 **honored** honorable 11 **for-
fended** forbidden; **abuses** (1) deceives (2) demeans,
is unworthy of 12–13 **I . . . hers** I fear that you have
united with her intimately, in the fullest possible way
16 **Fear** distrust 19 **loosen** separate 20 **be-met**
met 22 **rigor . . . state** tyranny of our government
23 **honest** honorable 25 **touches us, as** concerns me,
only in that 26–27 **Not . . . oppose** and not in that
France emboldens the king and others, who have
been led, by real and serious grievances, to take up
arms against us 28 **reasoned** argued

For these domestic and particular broils°   30
Are not the question° here.

ALBANY: Let's then determine
With th' ancient of war° on our proceeding.

EDMUND:
I shall attend you presently at your tent.

REGAN:
Sister, you'll go with us?°

GONERIL: No.   35

REGAN:
'Tis most convenient;° pray you, go with us.

GONERIL [aside]:
O, ho, I know the riddle.° — I will go.
(Exeunt both the ARMIES.)

(Enter EDGAR [disguised].)

EDGAR:
If e'er your grace had speech with man so
poor,
Hear me one word.

ALBANY [to those going out]:
I'll overtake you. [To EDGAR.] Speak.
(Exeunt [all but ALBANY and EDGAR].)

EDGAR:
Before you fight the battle, ope this letter.   40
If you have victory, let the trumpet sound
For° him that brought it: wretched though I
seem,
I can produce a champion that will prove°
What is avouchèd° there. If you miscarry,
Your business of° the world hath so an end,   45
And machination° ceases. Fortune love you.

ALBANY:
Stay till I have read the letter.

EDGAR: I was forbid it.
When time shall serve, let but the herald cry,
And I'll appear again.

ALBANY:
Why, fare thee well: I will o'erlook° thy paper. 50
(Exit [EDGAR].)

(Enter EDMUND.)

EDMUND:
The enemy's in view: draw up your powers.
Here is the guess° of their true strength and
forces

30 **particular broils** private quarrels 31 **question**
issue 32 **th' ancient of war** experienced comman-
ders 34 **us** me (rather than Edmund) 36 **convenient** fitting, desirable 37 **riddle** real reason (for
Regan's curious request) 41–42 **sound For** sum-
mon 43 **prove** i.e., by trial of combat 44 **avouchèd**
maintained 45 **of** in 46 **machination** plotting 50
o'erlook read over 52 **guess** estimate

By diligent discovery;° but your haste
Is now urged on you.

ALBANY: We will greet° the time. (*Exit.*)

EDMUND:

55 To both these sisters have I sworn my love;
Each jealous° of the other, as the stung
Are of the adder. Which of them shall I take?
Both? One? Or neither? Neither can be
     enjoyed,
If both remain alive: to take the widow
60 Exasperates, makes mad her sister Goneril;
And hardly° shall I carry out my side,°
Her husband being alive. Now then, we'll use
His countenance° for the battle; which being
     done,
Let her who would be rid of him devise
65 His speedy taking off. As for the mercy
Which he intends to Lear and to Cordelia,
The battle done, and they within our power,
Shall never see his pardon; for my state
Stands on me to defend, not to debate.°

(*Exit.*)

SCENE II. [*A field between the two camps.*]

*Alarum° within. Enter, with drum and
colors,* LEAR, CORDELIA, *and* SOLDIERS, *over
the stage; and exeunt.
Enter* EDGAR *and* GLOUCESTER.

EDGAR:

Here, father,° take the shadow of this tree
For your good host; pray that the right may
     thrive.
If ever I return to you again,
I'll bring you comfort.

GLOUCESTER: Grace go with you, sir.

(*Exit* [EDGAR].)

(*Alarum and retreat° within.* [Re]*enter*
EDGAR.)

EDGAR:

5 Away, old man; give me thy hand; away!

King Lear hath lost, he and his daughter ta'en:°
Give me thy hand; come on.

GLOUCESTER:

No further, sir; a man may rot even here.

EDGAR:

What, in ill thoughts again? Men must endure
Their going hence, even as their coming
     hither: 10
Ripeness° is all. Come on.

GLOUCESTER: And that's true too.

(*Exeunt.*)

SCENE III. [*The British camp near Dover.*]

Enter, in conquest, with drum and colors,
EDMUND; LEAR *and* CORDELIA, *as prisoners;*
SOLDIERS, CAPTAIN.

EDMUND:

Some officers take them away: good guard,°
Until their greater pleasures° first be known
That are to censure° them.

CORDELIA: We are not the first
Who with best meaning° have incurred the
     worst.
For thee, oppressèd king, I am cast down;   5
Myself could else out-frown false Fortune's
     frown.
Shall we not see these daughters and these
     sisters?

LEAR:

No, no, no, no! Come, let's away to prison:
We two alone will sing like birds i' th' cage:
When thou dost ask me blessing, I'll kneel
     down   10
And ask of thee forgiveness: so we'll live,
And pray, and sing, and tell old tales, and
     laugh
At gilded butterflies,° and hear poor rogues
Talk of court news; and we'll talk with them
     too,
Who loses and who wins, who's in, who's out;   15
And take upon's the mystery of things,
As if we were God's spies:° and we'll wear
     out,°

53 **By diligent discovery** obtained by careful recon-
noitering   54 **greet** i.e., meet the demands of   56
jealous suspicious   61 **hardly** with difficulty; **carry
. . . side** (1) satisfy my ambition (2) fulfill my bargain
(with Goneril)   63 **countenance** authority   68–69
for . . . debate my position requires me to act, not to
reason about right and wrong
V.II.s.d. **Alarum** a trumpet call to battle   1 **father**
i.e., venerable old man (Edgar has not yet revealed his
identity)   4 s.d. **retreat** signaled by a trumpet

6 **ta'en** captured   11 **Ripeness** maturity, as of fruit
that is ready to fall
V.III.1 **good guard** let them be well guarded   2
their greater pleasures the will of those in command,
the great ones   3 **censure** pass judgment on   4
meaning intentions   13 **gilded butterflies** i.e.,
gorgeously attired courtiers, fluttering after nothing
16–17 **take . . . spies** profess to read the riddle of
existence, as if endowed with divine omniscience   17
wear out outlast

In a walled prison, packs and sects of great
      ones
That ebb and flow by th' moon.°
EDMUND: Take them away.
LEAR:
20 Upon such sacrifices, my Cordelia,
The gods themselves throw incense.° Have I
      caught thee?
He that parts us shall bring a brand from heaven,
And fire us hence like foxes.° Wipe thine eyes;
The good years° shall devour them,° flesh and
      fell,°
Ere they shall make us weep. We'll see 'em
25   starved first.
Come. [Exeunt LEAR and CORDELIA, guarded.]
EDMUND:
Come hither, captain; hark.
Take thou this note: go follow them to prison:
One step I have advanced thee; if thou dost
30 As this instructs thee, thou dost make thy way
To noble fortunes: know thou this, that men
Are as the time is:° to be tender-minded
Does not become a sword:° thy great em-
      ployment
Will not bear question;° either say thou'lt do't,
Or thrive by other means.
35 CAPTAIN: I'll do't, my lord.
EDMUND:
About it; and write happy° when th' hast done.
Mark; I say, instantly, and carry it so°
As I have set it down.
CAPTAIN:
I cannot draw a cart, nor eat dried oats;
40 If it be man's work, I'll do't.   (Exit CAPTAIN.)

(Flourish. Enter ALBANY, GONERIL, REGAN
[another CAPTAIN, and] SOLDIERS.)

18–19 **packs . . . moon** intriguing and partisan cliques
of those in high station, whose fortunes change every
month   20–21 **Upon . . . incense** i.e., the gods approve our renunciation of the world   22–23 **He . . .
foxes** No human agency can separate us, but only
divine interposition, as of a heavenly torch parting us
like foxes that are driven from their place of refuge
by fire and smoke   24 **good years** plague and pestilence ("undefined malefic power or agency," Oxford
English Dictionary); **them** the enemies of Lear and
Cordelia; **fell** skin   32 **as . . . is** i.e., absolutely determined by the exigencies of the moment   33 **become a sword** befit a soldier   34 **bear question**
admit of discussion   36 **write happy** style yourself
fortunate   37 **carry it so** manage the affair in exactly that manner (as if Cordelia had taken her own
life)

ALBANY:
Sir, you have showed today your valiant strain,°
And fortune led you well: you have the
      captives
Who were the opposites of° this day's strife:
I do require them of you, so to use them
As we shall find their merits° and our safety   45
May equally determine.
EDMUND: Sir, I thought it fit
To send the old and miserable king
To some retention and appointed guard;°
Whose° age had charms in it, whose title
      more,
To pluck the common bosom on his side,°   50
And turn our impressed lances in our eyes°
Which do command them. With him I sent
      the queen:
My reason all the same; and they are ready
Tomorrow, or at further space,° t'appear
Where you shall hold your session.° At this
      time   55
We sweat and bleed: the friend hath lost his
      friend;
And the best quarrels, in the heat, are cursed
By those that feel their sharpness.°
The question of Cordelia and her father
Requires a fitter place.
ALBANY: Sir, by your patience,   60
I hold you but a subject of° this war,
Not as a brother.
REGAN: That's as we list to grace° him.
Methinks our pleasure might have been de-
      manded,
Ere you had spoke so far. He led our powers,
Bore the commission of my place and person;   65
The which immediacy may well stand up
And call itself your brother.°
GONERIL: Not so hot:

41 **strain** (1) stock (2) character   43 **opposites of**
opponents in   45 **merits** deserts   48 **retention . . .
guard** confinement under duly appointed guard   49
Whose i.e., Lear's   50 **pluck . . . side** win the sympathy of the people to himself   51 **turn . . . eyes** turn
our conscripted lancers against us   54 **further space**
a later time   55 **session** trial   57–58 **best . . . sharpness** worthiest causes may be judged badly by those
who have been affected painfully by them, and whose
passion has not yet cooled   61 **subject of** subordinate
in   62 **list to grace** wish to honor   65–67 **Bore . . .
brother** was authorized, as my deputy, to take command; his present status, as my immediate representative, entitles him to be considered your equal

In his own grace he doth exalt himself
More than in your addition.°
    REGAN: In my rights,
70 By me invested, he compeers° the best.
    GONERIL:
That were the most,° if he should husband
    you.°
    REGAN:
Jesters do oft prove prophets.
    GONERIL: Holla, holla!
That eye that told you so looked but a-squint.°
    REGAN:
Lady, I am not well; else I should answer
75 From a full-flowing stomach.° General,
Take thou my soldiers, prisoners, patrimony;°
Dispose of them, of me; the walls is thine:°
Witness the world, that I create thee here
My lord, and master.
    GONERIL: Mean you to enjoy him?
    ALBANY:
80 The let-alone° lies not in your good will.
    EDMUND:
Nor in thine, lord.
    ALBANY: Half-blooded° fellow, yes.
    REGAN [to EDMUND]:
Let the drum strike, and prove my title thine.°
    ALBANY:
Stay yet; hear reason. Edmund, I arrest thee
On capital treason; and in thy attaint°
This gilded serpent [pointing to GONERIL]. For
85   your claim, fair sister,
I bar it in the interest of my wife.
'Tis she is subcontracted° to this lord,
And I, her husband, contradict your banes.°
If you will marry, make your loves° to me;
My lady is bespoke.°
90   GONERIL: An interlude!°

69 **your addition** honors you have bestowed on him
70 **compeers** equals   71 **most** most complete invest-
ing in your rights; **husband you** become your husband   73 **a-squint** cross-eyed   75 **From . . . stomach**
angrily   76 **patrimony** inheritance   77 **walls is
thine** i.e., Regan's person, which Edmund has
stormed and won   80 **let-alone** power to prevent
81 **Half-blooded** bastard, and so only half noble   82
prove . . . thine prove by combat your entitlement to
my rights   84 **in thy attaint** as a sharer in the treason
for which you are impeached   87 **subcontracted**
pledged by a contract which is called into question
by the existence of a previous contract (Goneril's
marriage)   88 **contradict your banes** forbid your
announced intention to marry (by citing the pre-
contract)   89 **loves** love-suits   90 **bespoke** already
pledged; **interlude** play

    ALBANY:
Thou art armed, Gloucester: let the trumpet
    sound:
If none appear to prove upon thy person
Thy heinous, manifest, and many treasons,
There is my pledge° [throwing down a glove]:
    I'll make° it on thy heart,
Ere I taste bread, thou art in nothing less   95
Than I have here proclaimed thee.
    REGAN: Sick, O, sick!
    GONERIL [aside]:
If not, I'll ne'er trust medicine.°
    EDMUND [throwing down a glove]:
There's my exchange:° what in the world he is
That names me traitor, villainlike he lies:°
Call by the trumpet:° he that dares approach,   100
On him, on you — who not? — I will maintain
My truth and honor firmly.
    ALBANY:
A herald, ho!
    EDMUND: A herald, ho, a herald!
    ALBANY:
Trust to thy single virtue;° for thy soldiers,
All levied in my name, have in my name   105
Took their discharge.
    REGAN: My sickness grows upon me.
    ALBANY:
She is not well; convey her to my tent.
                     [Exit REGAN, led.]

(Enter a HERALD.)

Come hither, herald. Let the trumpet sound —
And read out this.
    CAPTAIN: Sound, trumpet!   110

(A trumpet sounds.)

HERALD (reads): "If any man of quality or
degree° within the lists° of the army will
maintain upon Edmund, supposed Earl of
Gloucester, that he is a manifold traitor, let
him appear by the third sound of the trumpet: 115
he is bold in his defense."
    EDMUND: Sound!

(First trumpet.)

HERALD: Again!

(Second trumpet.)

94 **pledge** gage; **make** prove   97 **medicine** poison
98 **exchange** technical term, denoting the glove Edmund throws down   99 **villainlike he lies** the lie
direct, a challenge to mortal combat   100 **trumpet**
trumpeter   104 **single virtue** unaided valor   111–
112 **quality or degree** rank or position   112 **lists**
rolls

HERALD: Again!

(*Third trumpet.*
    Trumpet answers within. Enter EDGAR, *at the third sound, armed, a trumpet before him.*°)

ALBANY:
120 Ask him his purposes, why he appears
Upon this call o' th' trumpet.
    HERALD: What are you?
Your name, your quality,° and why you answer
This present summons?
    EDGAR: Know, my name is lost;
By treason's tooth bare-gnawn and canker-bit:°
125 Yet am I noble as the adversary
I come to cope.°
    ALBANY: Which is that adversary?
    EDGAR:
What's he that speaks for Edmund, Earl of
    Gloucester?
    EDMUND:
Himself: what say'st thou to him?
    EDGAR: Draw thy sword,
That if my speech offend a noble heart,
130 Thy arm do thee justice: here is mine.
Behold it is my privilege,
The privilege of mine honors,
My oath, and my profession.° I protest,
Maugre° thy strength, place, youth, and emi-
    nence,
135 Despite thy victor sword and fire-new° fortune,
Thy valor and thy heart,° thou art a traitor,
False to thy gods, thy brother, and thy father,
Conspirant° 'gainst this high illustrious prince,
And from th' extremest upward° of thy head
140 To the descent and dust below thy foot,°
A most toad-spotted traitor.° Say thou "No,"
This sword, this arm and my best spirits are
    bent°

To prove upon thy heart, whereto I speak,°
Thou liest.
    EDMUND:
          In wisdom° I should ask thy name,
But since thy outside looks so fair and warlike,   145
And that thy tongue some say° of breeding
    breathes,
What safe and nicely° I might well delay°
By rule of knighthood, I disdain and spurn:
Back do I toss these treasons° to thy head;
With the hell-hated° lie o'erwhelm thy heart;   150
Which for they yet glance by and scarcely
    bruise,
This sword of mine shall give them instant
    way,
Where they shall rest for ever.° Trumpets,
    speak!

(*Alarums.* [*They*] *fight.* [EDMUND *falls.*])

ALBANY:
Save° him, save him!
    GONERIL: This is practice,° Gloucester:
By th' law of war thou wast not bound to
    answer   155
An unknown opposite;° thou art not vanquished,
But cozened and beguiled.
    ALBANY: Shut your mouth, dame,
Or with this paper shall I stop it. Hold, sir;°
Thou° worse than any name, read thine own
    evil.
No tearing, lady; I perceive you know it.   160
    GONERIL:
Say, if I do, the laws are mine, not thine:
Who can arraign me for't?
    ALBANY: Most monstrous! O!
Know'st thou this paper?
    GONERIL: Ask me not what I know.
                                   (*Exit.*)
    ALBANY:
Go after her; she's desperate; govern° her.

119 s.d. **trumpet before him** trumpeter preceding him   122 **quality** rank   124 **canker-bit** eaten by the caterpillar   126 **cope** encounter   131–133 **it . . . profession** my knighthood entitles me to challenge you, and to have my challenge accepted   134 **Maugre** despite   135 **fire-new** fresh from the forge or mint   136 **heart** courage   138 **Conspirant** conspiring, a conspirator   139 **extremest upward** the very top   140 **the . . . foot** your lowest part (sole) and the dust beneath it   141 **toad-spotted traitor** spotted with treason (and hence venomous, as the toad is allegedly marked with spots that exude venom)   142 **bent** directed

143 **whereto I speak** Edgar speaks from the heart, and speaks to the heart of Edmund   144 **wisdom** prudence (since he is not obliged to fight with one of lesser rank)   146 **say** assay (i.e., touch, sign)   147 **safe and nicely** cautiously and punctiliously; **delay** i.e., avoid   149 **treasons** accusations of treason   150 **hell-hated** hated like hell   151–153 **Which . . . ever** which accusations of treason, since as yet they do no harm, even though I have hurled them back, I now thrust upon you still more forcibly, with my sword, so that they may remain with you permanently   154 **Save** spare; **practice** trickery   156 **opposite** opponent 158 **Hold, sir** to Edmund: "Just a moment!"   159 **Thou** probably Goneril   164 **govern** control

EDMUND:

165 What you have charged me with, that have I
        done;
And more, much more; the time will bring it
        out.
'Tis past, and so am I. But what art thou
That hast this fortune on° me? If thou'rt
        noble,
I do forgive thee.

    EDGAR: Let's exchange charity.°
170 I am no less in blood° than thou art, Edmund;
If more,° the more th' hast wronged me.
My name is Edgar, and thy father's son.
The gods are just, and of our pleasant° vices
Make instruments to plague us:
175 The dark and vicious place° where thee he got°
Cost him his eyes.

    EDMUND: Th' hast spoken right, 'tis true;
The wheel is come full circle; I am here.°

    ALBANY:
Methought thy very gait did prophesy°
A royal nobleness: I must embrace thee:
180 Let sorrow split my heart, if ever I
Did hate thee or thy father!

    EDGAR: Worthy° prince, I know't.

    ALBANY:
Where have you hid yourself?
How have you known the miseries of your
        father?

    EDGAR:
By nursing them, my lord. List a brief tale;
And when 'tis told, O, that my heart would
185   burst!
The bloody proclamation to escape°
That followed me so near — O, our lives'
        sweetness,
That we the pain of death would hourly die
Rather than die at once!° — taught me to shift
190 Into a madman's rags, t' assume a semblance
That very dogs disdained: and in this habit°

---

168 **fortune on** victory over   169 **charity** forgiveness
and love   170 **blood** lineage   171 **If more** if I am
more noble (since legitimate)   173 **of our pleasant**
out of our pleasurable   175 **place** i.e., the adulterous
bed; **got** begot   177 **wheel . . . here** i.e., Fortune's
wheel, on which Edmund ascended, has now, in its
downward turning, deposited him at the bottom,
whence he began   178 **gait did prophesy** carriage
did promise   181 **Worthy** honorable   186 **to escape** (my wish) to escape the sentence of death
187–189 **O . . . once** How sweet is life, that we
choose to suffer death every hour rather than make
an end at once   191 **habit** attire

Met I my father with his bleeding rings,°
Their precious stones new lost; became his
        guide,
Led him, begged for him, saved him from
        despair;
Never — O fault! — revealed myself unto him,   195
Until some half-hour past, when I was armed,
Not sure, though hoping, of this good success,
I asked his blessing, and from first to last
Told him our pilgrimage.° But his flawed°
        heart —
Alack, too weak the conflict to support —   200
'Twixt two extremes of passion, joy and grief,
Burst smilingly.

    EDMUND:
                This speech of yours hath moved me,
And shall perchance do good: but speak you
        on;
You look as you had something more to say.

    ALBANY:
If there be more, more woeful, hold it in;   205
For I am almost ready to dissolve,°
Hearing of this.

    EDGAR: This would have seemed a period°
To such as love not sorrow; but another,
To amplify too much, would make much
        more,
And top extremity.°   210
Whilst I was big in clamor,° came there in a
        man,
Who, having seen me in my worst estate,°
Shunned my abhorred° society; but then,
        finding
Who 'twas that so endured, with his strong
        arms
He fastened on my neck, and bellowed out   215
As he'd burst heaven; threw him on my father;
Told the most piteous tale of Lear and him
That ever ear received: which in recounting
His grief grew puissant,° and the strings of life
Began to crack: twice then the trumpets
        sounded,   220
And there I left him tranced.°

    ALBANY: But who was this?

---

192 **rings** sockets   199 **our pilgrimage** of our (purga-
torial) journey; **flawed** cracked   206 **dissolve** i.e.,
into tears   207 **period** limit   208–210 **but . . . extremity** just one woe more, described too fully, would
go beyond the extreme limit   211 **big in clamor**
loud in lamentation   212 **estate** condition   213
abhorred abhorrent   219 **puissant** overmastering
221 **tranced** insensible

133

EDGAR:
Kent, sir, the banished Kent; who in disguise
Followed his enemy° king, and did him service
Improper for a slave.

(*Enter a* GENTLEMAN, *with a bloody knife.*)

GENTLEMAN:
Help, help, O, help!
EDGAR: What kind of help?
225   ALBANY: Speak, man.
EDGAR:
What means this bloody knife?
GENTLEMAN: 'Tis hot, it smokes;°
It came even from the heart of — O, she's
  dead!
ALBANY:
Who dead? Speak, man.
GENTLEMAN:
Your lady, sir, your lady: and her sister
230 By her is poisoned; she confesses it.
EDMUND:
I was contracted° to them both: all three
Now marry° in an instant.
EDGAR: Here comes Kent.
ALBANY:
Produce the bodies, be they alive or dead.
                    [*Exit* GENTLEMAN.]
This judgment of the heavens, that makes us
  tremble,
Touches us not with pity.

(*Enter* KENT.)

235   O, is this he?
The time will not allow the compliment°
Which very manners° urges.
KENT: I am come
To bid my king and master aye° good night:
Is he not here?
ALBANY: Great thing of° us forgot!
Speak, Edmund, where's the king? and where's
240   Cordelia?
See'st thou this object,° Kent?

(*The bodies of Goneril and Regan are
brought in.*)

KENT:
Alack, why thus?

EDMUND: Yet° Edmund was beloved:
The one the other poisoned for my sake,
And after slew herself.
ALBANY:
Even so. Cover their faces.   245
EDMUND:
I pant for life:° some good I mean to do,
Despite of mine own nature. Quickly send,
Be brief in it, to th' castle; for my writ°
Is on the life of Lear and on Cordelia:
Nay, send in time.
ALBANY: Run, run, O, run!   250
EDGAR:
To who, my lord? Who has the office?° Send
Thy token of reprieve.°
EDMUND:
Well thought on: take my sword,
Give it the captain.
EDGAR: Haste thee, for thy life.
                    [*Exit* MESSENGER.]
EDMUND:
He hath commission from thy wife and me   255
To hang Cordelia in the prison, and
To lay the blame upon her own despair,
That she fordid° herself.
ALBANY:
The gods defend her! Bear him hence awhile.
                  [EDMUND *is borne off.*]

(*Enter* LEAR, *with* CORDELIA *in his arms,*
[GENTLEMAN, *and others following*].)

LEAR:
Howl, howl, howl, howl! O, you are men of
  stones: 260
Had I your tongues and eyes, I'd use them so
That heaven's vault should crack. She's gone
  for ever.
I know when one is dead and when one lives;
She's dead as earth. Lend me a looking-glass;
If that her breath will mist or stain the stone,° 265
Why, then she lives.
KENT: Is this the promised end?°
EDGAR:
Or image° of that horror?
ALBANY: Fall and cease.°

223 **enemy** hostile 226 **smokes** steams 231 **contracted** betrothed 232 **marry** i.e., unite in death 236 **compliment** ceremony 237 **very manners** ordinary civility 238 **aye** forever 239 **thing of** matter by 241 **object** sight (the bodies of Goneril and Regan)

242 **Yet** in spite of all 246 **pant for life** gasp for breath 248 **writ** command (ordering the execution) 251 **office** commission 252 **token of reprieve** sign that they are reprieved 258 **fordid** destroyed 265 **stone** i.e., the surface of the crystal looking-glass 266 **promised end** doomsday 267 **image** exact likeness; **Fall and cease** i.e., Let the heavens fall, and all things finish

LEAR:
This feather stirs; she lives. If it be so,
It is a chance which does redeem° all sorrows
That ever I have felt.

270   KENT: O my good master.
LEAR:
Prithee, away.
EDGAR: 'Tis noble Kent, your friend.
LEAR:
A plague upon you, murderers, traitors all!
I might have saved her; now she's gone for
    ever.
Cordelia, Cordelia, stay a little. Ha,
What is't thou say'st? Her voice was ever

275   soft,
Gentle and low, an excellent thing in woman.
I killed the slave that was a-hanging thee.
GENTLEMAN:
'Tis true, my lords, he did.
LEAR: Did I not, fellow?
I have seen the day, with my good biting
    falchion°

280   I would have made them skip: I am old now,
And these same crosses° spoil me.° Who are
    you?
Mine eyes are not o' th' best: I'll tell you
    straight.°
KENT:
If Fortune brag of two° she loved and hated,
One of them we behold.
LEAR:
This is a dull sight.° Are you not Kent?

285   KENT: The same,
Your servant Kent. Where is your servant
    Caius?°
LEAR:
He's a good fellow, I can tell you that;
He'll strike, and quickly too: he's dead and
    rotten.
KENT:
No, my good lord; I am the very man.
LEAR:

290   I'll see that straight.°

KENT:
That from your first of difference and decay°
Have followed your sad steps.
LEAR: You are welcome hither.
KENT:
Nor no man else:° all's cheerless, dark and
    deadly.
Your eldest daughters have fordone° themselves,
And desperately° are dead.
LEAR: Ay, so I think.   295
ALBANY:
He knows not what he says, and vain is it
That we present us to him.
EDGAR: Very bootless.°

(*Enter a* MESSENGER.)

MESSENGER:
Edmund is dead, my lord.
ALBANY: That's but a trifle here.
You lords and noble friends, know our intent.
What comfort to this great decay may come°   300
Shall be applied. For us, we° will resign,
During the life of this old majesty,
To him our absolute power: [*to* EDGAR *and*
    KENT] you, to your rights;
With boot,° and such addition° as your honors
Have more than merited. All friends shall taste   305
The wages of their virtue, and all foes
The cup of their deservings. O, see, see!
LEAR:
And my poor fool° is hanged: no, no, no life?
Why should a dog, a horse, a rat, have life,
And thou no breath at all? Thou'lt come no
    more,   310
Never, never, never, never, never.
Pray you, undo this button.° Thank you, sir.
Do you see this? Look on her. Look, her
    lips,
Look there, look there. (*He dies.*)
EDGAR: He faints. My lord, my lord!
KENT:
Break, heart; I prithee, break.

269 **redeem** make good   279 **falchion** small curved
sword   281 **crosses** troubles; **spoil me** i.e., my prow-
ess as a swordsman   282 **tell you straight** recognize
you straightaway   283 **two** i.e., Lear, and some hypo-
thetical second, who is also a prime example of Fortune's inconstancy ("loved and hated")   285 **dull
sight** (1) melancholy spectacle (2) faulty eyesight
(Lear's own, clouded by weeping)   286 **Caius** Kent's
name, in disguise   290 **see that straight** attend to
that in a moment

291 **your . . . decay** beginning of your decline in
fortune   293 **Nor . . . else** no, I am not welcome, nor
is anyone else   294 **fordone** destroyed   295 **desperately** in despair   297 **bootless** fruitless   300
What . . . come whatever aid may present itself to
this great ruined man   301 **us, we** the royal "we"
304 **boot** good measure; **addition** additional titles and
rights   308 **fool** Cordelia ("fool" being a term of
endearment; but it is perfectly possible to take the
word as referring also to the Fool)   312 **undo this
button** i.e., to ease the suffocation Lear feels

315 EDGAR: Look up, my lord!
      KENT:
Vex not his ghost:° O, let him pass! He hates
        him
That would upon the rack° of this tough world
Stretch him out longer.°
      EDGAR: He is gone indeed.
      KENT:
The wonder is he hath endured so long:
320 He but usurped° his life.

316 **Vex ... ghost** do not trouble his departing spirit
317 **rack** instrument of torture, stretching the victim's
joints to dislocation   318 **longer** (1) in time (2) in
bodily length   320 **usurped** possessed beyond the
allotted term

      ALBANY:
Bear them from hence. Our present business
Is general woe. [*To* KENT *and* EDGAR.] Friends
        of my soul, you twain,
Rule in this realm and the gored state sustain.
      KENT:
I have a journey, sir, shortly to go;
My master calls me, I must not say no.   325
      EDGAR:
The weight of this sad time we must obey,°
Speak what we feel, not what we ought to say.
The oldest hath borne most: we that are
        young
Shall never see so much, nor live so long.
                    (*Exeunt, with a dead march.*)

326 **obey** submit to

The best way to understand Shakespeare's tragic vision is, of course, to see
and read the tragedies very intelligently, but some help may be gained from a
brief consideration of two speeches in *Hamlet*. In the final scene, when Fortinbras and others enter the stage looking for Claudius, they find to their amazement the corpses of Claudius, Gertrude, Laertes, and Hamlet. Horatio, Hamlet's friend, endeavors to bring the visitors up to date:

> What is it you would see?
> If aught of woe or wonder, cease your search.

Fortinbras and his associates are indeed struck with woe and wonder:

> FORTINBRAS: O proud Death,
> What feast is toward in thine eternal cell
> That thou so many princes at a shot
> So bloodily hast struck?
> AMBASSADOR: The sight is dismal.

Horatio seeks to explain: the visitors will hear

> Of carnal, bloody, and unnatural acts,
> Of accidental judgments, casual slaughters,
> Of deaths put on by cunning and forced cause,
> And, in this upshot, purposes mistook
> Fall'n on th'inventors' heads.   ·

The spectators of the play itself have indeed seen "unnatural acts," "deaths put
on by cunning," etc., and presumably these spectators have experienced the
"woe" and "wonder" that the new arrivals will experience as Horatio sets forth
the details.

Let us now look at a second passage from *Hamlet*. The speaker is the despicable Rosencrantz, and there is some flattery of King Claudius in his speech,
but the gist of his argument about the death of a king rings true, makes sense:

> The cess of majesty
> Dies not alone, but like a gulf doth draw
> What's near it with it; or it is a massy wheel
> Fixed on the summit of the highest mount,
> To whose huge spokes ten thousand lesser things
> Are mortised and adjoined, which when it falls,
> Each small annexment, petty consequence,
> Attends the boist'rous ruin. Never alone
> Did the King sigh, but with a general groan.

Surely it is understandable that the deaths of, say, Lincoln and Kennedy had a vastly greater effect upon America than the deaths of any number of men in private life. Put crudely, they mattered more.

The speeches together afford some justification of the Elizabethan view that tragedy is concerned with violence done to and by people of high rank. The fall of a man in high position evokes deeper woe and wonder than the snuffing out of a nonentity. The latter may evoke pity, but scarcely awe at the terrifying power of destructiveness or at the weakness that is at the heart of power.

Shakespeare does not merely slap the label of king or prince or general on a character and then assume that greatness has been established. His characters speak great language and perform great deeds. (And, no less important, they have the capacity to suffer greatly.) Lear, in the first scene, gives away — almost seems to create — fertile kingdoms:

> Of all these bounds, even from this line to this,
> With shadowy forests, and with champains riched,
> With plenteous rivers, and wide-skirted meads,
> We make thee lady.

Even in injustice, when he banishes his daughter, Cordelia, for speaking the truth as she sees it, he has a kind of terrible grandeur:

> Let it be so, thy truth then be thy dower!
> For, by the sacred radiance of the sun,
> The mysteries of Hecate and the night,
> By all the operation of the orbs
> From whom we do exist and cease to be,
> Here I disclaim all my paternal care,
> Propinquity and property of blood,
> And as a stranger to my heart and me
> Hold thee from this for ever.

Finally, even in his madness — "a sight most pitiful in the meanest wretch, / Past speaking of in a king" — he has grandeur. To Gloucester's "Is't not the king?" he replies:

> Ay, every inch a king.
> When I do stare, see how the subject quakes.
> I pardon that man's life. What was thy cause?
> Adultery?
> Thou shalt not die: die for adultery! No:
> The wren goes to 't, and the small gilded fly
> Does lecher in my sight.
> Let copulation thrive. . . .

We might contrast Lear's noble voice with Edmund's materialistic comment on the way of the world:

> This is the excellent foppery of the world, that when we are sick in fortune, often the surfeits of our own behavior, we make guilty of our disasters the sun, the moon, and stars; as if we were villains on necessity; fools by heavenly compulsion; knaves, thieves, and treachers by spherical predominance; drunkards, liars, and adulterers by an enforced obedience of planetary influence; and all that we are evil in, by a divine thrusting on. An admirable evasion of whoremaster man, to lay his goatish disposition on the charge of a star. . . . Fut! I should have been that I am, had the maidenliest star in the firmament twinkled on my bastardizing.

Lear seems to be displacing *Hamlet* as the play that speaks to our time. *Hamlet* was especially popular with nineteenth-century audiences, who often found in the uncertain prince an image of their own doubts in a world in which belief in a benevolent divine order was collapsing under the influence of scientific materialism and bourgeois aggressiveness. Many audiences in our age find in *Lear* — where "for many miles about / There's scarce a bush" — a play thoroughly in the spirit of Beckett's *Waiting for Godot,* where the scenery consists of a single tree. Moreover, Lear denounces the hypocrisy of the power structure and exposes the powerlessness of the disenfranchised: "Robes and furred gowns hide all. Plate sin with gold, / And the strong lance of justice hurtless breaks; / Arm it in rags, a pygmy's straw does pierce it." And what of the gods? There are several comments about their nature, but perhaps the most memorable reference to the gods is not a mere comment but one followed by an action: learning that Cordelia is in danger, Albany cries out, "The gods defend her!" and immediately his words are mocked by Lear's entrance on the stage, with the dead Cordelia in his arms.

But the interpretation of *King Lear* as a revelation of the emptiness of life fails to consider at least two things. First, there is an affirmation in those passages in which Lear comes, through heart-rending anguish, to see that he was not what he thought he was. Second, this anagnorisis or recognition is several times associated with love or charity, as when (III.iv) Lear invites the Fool to enter the hovel first and then confesses his guilt in having cared too little for humanity. And this care for humanity is seen in Cordelia, who comes — though ineffectually in the long run — to the aid of her father. It is seen, too, in the nameless servant who at the end of III.vii promises to apply medicine to Gloucester's eyeless sockets; it is seen even in the villainous Edmund, who in dying repents and says, "Some good I mean to do, / Despite mine own nature" (V.iii), and who thereupon tries, unsuccessfully, to save Cordelia. No one would say that these actions turn *King Lear* into a happy vision, but it is perverse to ignore them and to refuse to see that in this play love humanizes as surely as egoism dehumanizes. If the play dramatizes man's desolation, it also dramatizes the love that, while providing no protection against pain or death, makes man's life different from the life of "a dog, a horse, a rat."

HEDDA GABLER

Henrik Ibsen

Translated by Otto Reinert

Henrik Ibsen (1828–1906) was born in Skien, Norway, of wealthy parents who soon after his birth lost their money. Ibsen worked as a pharmacist's apprentice, but at the age of twenty-two he had written his first play, a promising melodrama entitled *Cataline*. He engaged in theater work in Norway, and then in Denmark and Germany. By 1865 his plays had won him a state pension that enabled him to settle in Rome. After writing romantic, historic, and poetic plays, he turned to realistic drama with *The League of Youth* (1869). Among the major realistic "problem plays" are *A Doll's House* (1879), *Ghosts* (1881), and *An Enemy of the People* (1882). In *The Wild Duck* (1884) he moved toward a more symbolic tragic comedy, and his last plays, written in the nineties, are highly symbolic. *Hedda Gabler* (1890) looks backward to the plays of the eighties rather than forward to the plays of the nineties.

CHARACTERS

JØRGEN TESMAN, *University Research Fellow in the History of Civilization*
HEDDA, *his wife*
MISS JULIANE TESMAN, *his aunt*

MRS. ELVSTED
JUDGE BRACK
EILERT LØVBORG
BERTE, *the Tesmans' maid*

Scene: The TESMANS' *villa in a fashionable residential section of the town.*

A note on pronunciation

The approximate Norwegian pronunciation of names likely to be difficult to a speaker of English is suggested below (the syllable in capitals is accented; the unaccented *e* is close to English *e* in *quiet*).

JØRGEN YUR-gen (*g* as in *bargain*)
EILERT LØVBORG AY-lert LUV-borg[1]

JULLE YOOL-le (short *oo*)
BERTE BAIR-te

[1] *Løvborg* means, literally, "leaf-castle" — a fact of possible bearing on the play's symbolism. [Reinert.]

Maggie Smith as Hedda Gabler in the National Theatre Company production directed by Ingmar Bergman, London, 1970. (Photograph: Dominic.)

ACT I

A spacious, handsome, tastefully furnished room. Dark décor. In the rear, a wide doorway with open portieres. Beyond is a smaller room, furnished in the same style as the front room. A door, right, leads to the front hall. Left, French doors, with portieres drawn aside, through which can be seen a part of a roofed verandah and trees with autumn foliage. Front center, an oval table covered with a cloth. Chairs around it. Front right, a wide, dark, porcelain stove, a high-backed easy chair, a footstool with a pillow, and two ottomans. In the corner far right, a sofa and a small, round table. Front left, a sofa, set out from the wall. Far left, beyond the French doors, an upright piano. On both sides of the doorway, rear center, whatnots with knickknacks. Against the rear wall of the inner room, a sofa, and in front of it a table and two chairs. Above the sofa, a portrait of a handsome, elderly man in general's uniform. Over the table hangs a lamp with milky, white glass. There are several bouquets of flowers, in vases and glasses, in various places in the front room. Others are lying on the tables. Thick carpets on the floors of both rooms. The morning sun is shining through the French doors.

MISS JULIANE TESMAN, *with hat and parasol, enters right, followed by* BERTE, *who carries a bouquet of flowers wrapped in paper.* MISS TESMAN *is a nice-looking woman of 65, of pleasant mien, neatly but not expensively dressed in a gray suit.* BERTE *is a middle-aged servant girl, of rather plain and countrified appearance.*

MISS TESMAN (*stops inside the door, listens, says in a low voice*): On my word — I don't think they are even up yet!

BERTE (*also softly*): That's what I told you, miss. When you think how late the steamer got in last night. And afterwards! — Goodness! — all the stuff she wanted unpacked before she turned in.

Hedda Gabler by Henrik Ibsen, translated by Otto Reinert. Reprinted by permission of Intext Educational Publishers.

MISS TESMAN: Well — just let them sleep. But fresh morning air — *that* we can give them when they come in here. (*Goes and opens the French doors wide.*)

BERTE (*by the table, lost, still holding the flowers*): Please, miss — I just don't see a bit of space anywhere! I think I'd better put these over here. (*Puts the flowers down on the piano.*)

MISS TESMAN: Well, well, my dear Berte. So you've got yourself a new mistress now. The good Lord knows it was hard for me to let you go.

BERTE (*near tears*): What about me, then, miss! What shall *I* say? I who have served you and Miss Rina all these blessed years.

MISS TESMAN: We shall just have to make the best of it, Berte. That's all. Jørgen can't do without you, you know. He just can't. You've looked after him ever since he was a little boy.

BERTE: Yes, but miss — I'm ever so worried about leaving Miss Rina. The poor dear lying there all helpless. With that new girl and all! She'll never learn how to make things nice and comfortable for an invalid.

MISS TESMAN: Oh yes, you'll see. I'll teach her. And of course, you know, I'll do most of it myself. So don't you worry yourself about my poor sister, Berte.

BERTE: Yes, but there's another thing, too, miss. I'm scared I won't be able to suit young Mrs. Tesman.

MISS TESMAN: Oh, well. Good heavens. So there is a thing or two — Right at first —

BERTE: For I believe she's ever so particular.

MISS TESMAN: Can you wonder? General Gabler's daughter? Just think of the kind of life she was used to when the General was alive. Do you remember when she rode by with her father? That long black riding habit she wore? And the feather in her hat?

BERTE: Oh, I remember, all right. But I'll be blessed if I ever thought she and the young master would make a pair of it.

MISS TESMAN: Nor did I. By the way, while I think of it, Berte. Jørgen has a new title now. From now on you should call him "the Doctor."

BERTE: Yes, the young mistress said something about that, too, last night. Soon as they were inside the door. Then it's really so, miss?

MISS TESMAN: It certainly is. Just think, Berte — they have made him a doctor abroad. During the trip, you know. I hadn't heard a thing about it till last night on the pier.

BERTE: Well, I daresay he could be anything he put his mind to, *he* could — smart as *he* is. But I must say I'd never thought he'd turn to doctoring people, too.

MISS TESMAN: Oh, that's not the kind of doctor he is. (*Nods significantly.*) And as far as that is concerned, there is no telling but pretty soon you may have to call him something grander yet.

BERTE: You don't say! What might that be, miss?

MISS TESMAN (*smiles*): Wouldn't you like to know! (*Moved.*) Ah yes, indeed — ! If only dear Jochum could see from his grave what has become of his little boy! (*Looking around.*) But look, Berte — what's this for? Why have you taken off all the slip covers?

BERTE: She told me to. Said she can't stand slip covers on chairs.

MISS TESMAN: Do you think they mean to make this their everyday living room, then?

BERTE: It sure sounded that way. Mrs. Tesman did, I mean. For he — the doctor — he didn't say anything.

(JØRGEN TESMAN *enters from the right side of the inner room. He is humming to himself. He carries an open, empty suitcase. He is of medium height, youthful-looking, thirty-three years old; somewhat stoutish. Round, open, cheerful face. Blond hair and beard. He wears glasses and is dressed in a comfortable, rather casual suit.*)

MISS TESMAN: Good morning, good morning, Jørgen!

TESMAN (*in the doorway*): Auntie! Dearest Aunt Julle! (*Comes forward and shakes her hand.*) All the way out here — as early as this! Hm?

MISS TESMAN: Well — I just had to drop in for a moment. To see how you are getting along, you know.

TESMAN: Even though you haven't had a good night's sleep.

MISS TESMAN: Oh, that doesn't matter at all.

TESMAN: But you did get home from the pier all right, I hope. Hm?

MISS TESMAN: Oh yes, I certainly did, thank you. The Judge was kind enough to see me all the way to my door.

TESMAN: We were so sorry we couldn't give you a ride in our carriage. But you saw for yourself — all the boxes Hedda had.

MISS TESMAN: Yes, she certainly brought quite a collection.

BERTE (*to* TESMAN): Should I go and ask Mrs. Tesman if there's anything I can help her with?

TESMAN: No, thank you, Berte — you'd better not. She said she'll ring if she wants you.

BERTE (*going right*): Well, all right.

TESMAN: But, look — you might take this suitcase with you.

BERTE (*takes it*): I'll put it in the attic. (*Exits right.*)

TESMAN: Just think, Auntie — that whole suitcase was brimful of copies of old documents. You wouldn't believe me if I told you all the things I have collected from libraries and archives all over. Quaint old items nobody has known anything about.

MISS TESMAN: Well, no, Jørgen. I'm sure you haven't wasted your time on your honeymoon.

TESMAN: No, I think I may say I have not. But take your hat off, Auntie — for goodness' sake. Here! Let me untie the ribbon for you. Hm?

MISS TESMAN (*while he does so*): Ah, God forgive me, if this isn't just as if you were still at home with us!

TESMAN (*inspecting the hat*): My, what a fine-looking hat you've got yourself!

MISS TESMAN: I bought it for Hedda's sake.

TESMAN: For Hedda's sake? Hm?

MISS TESMAN: So she won't need to feel ashamed of me if we ever go out together.

TESMAN (*patting her cheek*): If you don't think of everything, Auntie! (*Puts the hat down on a chair by the table.*) And now — over here to the sofa — we'll just sit and chat for a while till Hedda comes.

(*They seat themselves. She places her parasol in the corner by the sofa.*)

MISS TESMAN (*takes both his hands in hers and gazes at him*): What a blessing it is to have you back again, Jørgen, big as life! You — Jochum's little boy!

TESMAN: For me, too, Aunt Julle. Seeing

you again. For you have been both father and mother to me.

MISS TESMAN: Ah, yes — don't you think I know you'll always keep a spot in your heart for these two old aunts of yours!

TESMAN: So Aunt Rina isn't any better, hm?

MISS TESMAN: Oh no. We mustn't look for improvement in her case, poor dear. She is lying there just as she has been all these years. Just the same, may the good Lord keep her for me a long time yet! For else I just wouldn't know what to do with myself, Jørgen. Especially now, when I don't have you to look after any more.

TESMAN (*pats her back*): There, there, now!

MISS TESMAN (*changing tone*): And to think that you are a married man, Jørgen! And that you were the one to walk off with Hedda Gabler. The lovely Hedda Gabler. Just think! As many admirers as she had!

TESMAN (*hums a little, smiles complacently*): ·Yes, I daresay I have quite a few good friends here in town who'd gladly be in my shoes, hm?

MISS TESMAN: And such a long and lovely honeymoon you had! More than five — almost six months!

TESMAN: Well, you know — for me it has been a kind of study tour as well. All the collections I had to go through. And the books I had to read!

MISS TESMAN: Yes, I suppose. (*More confidentially, her voice lowered a little.*) But listen, Jørgen — haven't you got something — something special to tell me?

TESMAN: About the trip?

MISS TESMAN: Yes.

TESMAN: No — I don't know of anything besides what I wrote in my letters. They gave me a doctor's degree down there — but I told you that last night; I'm sure I did.

MISS TESMAN: Well, yes, that sort of thing — What I mean is — don't you have certain — certain — expectations?

TESMAN: Expectations?

MISS TESMAN: Ah for goodness' sake, Jørgen! I am your old Auntie, after all!

TESMAN: Certainly I have expectations.

MISS TESMAN: Well!!

TESMAN: I fully expect to be made a ' professor one of these days.

MISS TESMAN: Professor — oh yes —

TESMAN: I may even say I am quite certain of it. But dear Aunt Julle — you know this just as well as I do!

MISS TESMAN (*laughing a little*): Of course I do. You're quite right. (*Changing topic.*) But about the trip. It must have cost a great deal of money — hm, Jørgen?

TESMAN: Well, now; you know that large stipend went quite a long way.

MISS TESMAN: I just don't see how you made it do for both of you, though.

TESMAN: No, I suppose that's not so easy to understand, hm?

MISS TESMAN: Particularly with a lady along. For I have always heard that is ever so much more expensive.

TESMAN: Well, yes, naturally. That *is* rather more expensive. But Hedda had to have this trip, Auntie! She really had to. Nothing less would do.

MISS TESMAN: No, I daresay. For a wedding journey is quite the thing these days. But now tell me — have you had a chance to look around here yet?

TESMAN: I certainly have. I have been up and about ever since dawn.

MISS TESMAN: And what do you think of it all?

TESMAN: Delightful! Perfectly delightful! The only thing is I don't see what we are going to do with the two empty rooms between the second sitting room in there and Hedda's bedroom.

MISS TESMAN (*with a chuckle*): Oh my dear Jørgen — you may find them useful enough — when the time comes!

TESMAN: Of course, you're right, Auntie! As my library expands, hm?

MISS TESMAN: Quite so, my dear boy. It was your library I was thinking of.

TESMAN: But I'm really most happy on Hedda's behalf. For you know, before we were engaged she used to say she wouldn't care to live anywhere but in Secretary Falk's house.

MISS TESMAN: Yes, just think — wasn't that a lucky coincidence, that it was up for sale right after you had left?

TESMAN: Yes, Aunt Julle. We've certainly been lucky. Hm?

MISS TESMAN: But it will be expensive, my dear Jørgen. Terribly expensive — all this.

TESMAN (*looks at her, a bit crestfallen*): Yes, I daresay it will, Auntie.

MISS TESMAN: Heavens, yes!

TESMAN: How much, do you think? Roughly. Hm?

MISS TESMAN: No, I couldn't possibly say till all the bills arrive.

TESMAN: Well, anyway, Judge Brack managed to get very reasonable terms for us. He said so himself in a letter to Hedda.

MISS TESMAN: Yes, and I won't have you uneasy on that account, Jørgen. Besides, I have given security for the furniture and the carpets.

TESMAN: Security? You? But dear Aunt Julle — what kind of security could you give?

MISS TESMAN: The annuity.

TESMAN (jumps up): What! Your and Aunt Rina's annuity?

MISS TESMAN: Yes. I didn't know what else to do, you see.

TESMAN (standing before her): But are you clear out of your mind, Auntie! That annuity — that's all the two of you have to live on!

MISS TESMAN: Oh well, there's nothing to get so excited about, I'm sure. It's all just a matter of form, you know. That's what the Judge said, too. For he was kind enough to arrange the whole thing for me. Just a matter of form — those were his words.

TESMAN: That's all very well. Still —

MISS TESMAN: For now you'll have your own salary, you know. And, goodness — what if we do have a few expenses — Help out a bit right at first — ? That would only be a joy for us —

TESMAN: Oh, Auntie! When will you ever stop making sacrifices for my sake!

MISS TESMAN (gets up, puts her hands on his shoulders): But what other happiness do I have in this world than being able to smooth your way a little, my own dear boy? Orphan as you were, with no one to lean on but us? And now the goal is in sight, Jørgen. Things may have looked black at times. But heaven be praised; now you've arrived!

TESMAN: Yes, it's really quite remarkable the way things have worked out.

MISS TESMAN: Yes — and those who were against you — who tried to block your way — now they are tasting defeat. They are down, Jørgen! He, the most dangerous of them all, his fall was the greatest! He made his bed, and now he is lying in it — poor, lost wretch that he is!

TESMAN: Have you had any news about Eilert? Since I went away, I mean?

MISS TESMAN: Just that he is supposed to have published a new book.

TESMAN: What? Eilert Løvborg? Recently? Hm?

MISS TESMAN: That's what they say. But I wonder if there can be much to it. What do you think? Ah — but when your new book comes, that will be something quite different, Jørgen! What is it going to be about?

TESMAN: It deals with the domestic industries of Brabant during the Middle Ages.

MISS TESMAN: Just think — being able to write about something like that!

TESMAN: But as far as that is concerned, it may be quite some time before it is ready. I have all these collections to put in order first, you see.

MISS TESMAN: Yes, collecting and putting things in order — you certainly know how to do that. In that you are your father's own son.

TESMAN: Well, I must say I am looking forward to getting started. Particularly now, that I've got my own delightful home to work in.

MISS TESMAN: And most of all now that you have the one your heart desired, dear Jørgen.

TESMAN (embracing her): Oh yes, yes, Aunt Jule! Hedda — she is the most wonderful part of it all! (Looks toward the doorway.) There — I think she is coming now, hm?

*HEDDA enters from the left side of the inner room. She is twenty-nine years old. Both features and figure are noble and elegant. Pale, ivory complexion. Steel-gray eyes, expressive of cold, clear calm. Beautiful brown hair, though not particularly ample. She is dressed in a tasteful, rather loose-fitting morning costume.)

MISS TESMAN (going toward her): Good morning, my dear Hedda! A very happy morning to you!

HEDDA (giving her hand): Good morning, dear Miss Tesman! So early a call? That is most kind.

MISS TESMAN (seems slightly embarrassed): And — has the little lady of the house slept well the first night in her new home?

HEDDA: Passably, thank you.

TESMAN (laughs): Passably! You are a good one, Hedda! You were sleeping like a log when I got up.

HEDDA: Fortunately. And then, of course, Miss Tesman, it always takes time to get used to new surroundings. That has to come gradually. (Looks left.) Oh dear. The maid has left the verandah doors wide open. There's a veritable flood of sunlight in here.

MISS TESMAN (toward the doors): Well, then, we'll just close them.

HEDDA: No, no, not that. Tesman, dear, please pull the curtains. That will give a softer light.

TESMAN (*over by the French doors*): Yes, dear. There, now! Now you have both shade and fresh air, Hedda.

HEDDA: We certainly can use some air in here. Such loads of flowers — but, Miss Tesman, please — won't you be seated?

MISS TESMAN: No thanks. I just wanted to see if everything was all right — and so it is, thank goodness. I had better get back to Rina. I know she is waiting for me, poor thing.

TESMAN: Be sure to give her my love, Auntie. And tell her I'll be around to see her later today.

MISS TESMAN: I'll certainly do that! — Oh my! I almost forgot! (*Searches the pocket of her dress.*) I have something for you, Jørgen. Here.

TESMAN: What's that, Auntie? Hm?

MISS TESMAN (*pulls out a flat parcel wrapped in newspaper and gives it to him*): Here you are, dear.

TESMAN (*opens the parcel*): Well, well, well! So you took care of them for me, Aunt Julle! Hedda! Now, isn't that sweet, hm?

HEDDA (*by the whatnot, right*): If you'd tell me what it is —

TESMAN: My old slippers! You know!

HEDDA: Oh really? I remember you often talked about them on the trip.

TESMAN: Yes, for I missed them so. (*Walks over to her.*) Here — now you can see what they're like, Hedda.

HEDDA (*crosses toward stove*): Thanks. I don't know that I really care.

TESMAN (*following*): Just think — Aunt Rina embroidered these slippers for me. Ill as she was. You can't imagine how many memories they hold for me!

HEDDA (*by the table*): Hardly for me.

MISS TESMAN: That's true, you know, Jørgen.

TESMAN: Yes, but — I just thought that now that she's one of the family —

HEDDA (*interrupting*): I don't think we'll get on with that maid, Tesman.

MISS TESMAN: Not get on with Berte?

TESMAN: Whatever makes you say that, dear? Hm?

HEDDA (*points*): Look — she has left her old hat on the chair over there.

TESMAN (*appalled, drops the slippers*): But Hedda — !

HEDDA: What if somebody were to come and see it!

TESMAN: No, no, Hedda — that's Aunt Julle's hat!

HEDDA: Oh?

MISS TESMAN (*picking up the hat*): Yes, indeed it is. And it isn't old either, my dear young lady.

HEDDA: I really didn't look that closely —

MISS TESMAN (*tying the ribbons*): I want you to know that this is the first time I have had it on my head. On my word it is!

TESMAN: And very handsome it is, too. Really a splendid-looking hat!

MISS TESMAN: Oh, I don't know that it is anything so special, Jørgen. (*Looks around.*) My parasol — ? Ah, here it is. (*Picks it up.*) For that is mine, too. (*Mutters.*) Not Berte's.

TESMAN: New hat and new parasol! What do you think of that, Hedda!

HEDDA: Very nice indeed.

TESMAN: Yes, don't you think so? Hm? But, Auntie, take a good look at Hedda before you leave. See how pretty and blooming she looks.

MISS TESMAN: Dear me, Jørgen; that's nothing new. Hedda has been lovely all her days. (*She nods and walks right.*)

TESMAN (*following*): Yes, but have you noticed how full-figured and healthy she looks after the trip? How she has filled out?

HEDDA (*crossing*): Oh — stop it!

MISS TESMAN (*halts, turns around*): Filled out?

TESMAN: Yes, Aunt Julle. You can't see it so well now when she wears that dress. But I, who have the opportunity —

HEDDA (*by the French doors, impatiently*): Oh, you haven't any opportunities at all!

TESMAN: It must be the mountain air in Tyrol.

HEDDA (*curtly interrupting*): I am just as I was when I left.

TESMAN: Yes, so you say. I just don't think you're right. What do you think, Auntie?

MISS TESMAN (*has folded her hands, gazes at HEDDA*): Lovely — lovely — lovely; that is what Hedda is. (*Goes over to her, inclines her head forward with both her hands, and kisses her hair.*) God bless and keep Hedda Tesman. For Jørgen's sake.

HEDDA (*gently freeing herself*): There, there. Now let me go.

MISS TESMAN (*in quiet emotion*): Every single day I'll be over and see you two.

TESMAN: Yes, please do, Auntie. Hm?

MISS TESMAN: Goodbye, goodbye!

(*She leaves through door, right.* TESMAN *sees her out. The door remains ajar.* TESMAN *is heard repeating his greetings for Aunt Rina and his thanks for the slippers. In the meantime,* HEDDA *paces up and down, raises her arms, clenching her fists, as in quiet rage. Opens the curtains by the French doors and stands looking out. In a few moments,* TESMAN *re-enters and closes the door behind him.*)

TESMAN (*picking up the slippers*): What are you looking at, Hedda?

HEDDA (*once again calm and controlled*): Just the leaves. They are so yellow. And withered.

TESMAN (*wrapping the slippers in their paper, putting the parcel down on the table*): Well, you know — we're in September now.

HEDDA (*again restless*): Yes — just think. It's already — September.

TESMAN: Don't you think Aunt Julle acted strange, Hedda? Almost solemn. I wonder why. Hm?

HEDDA: I hardly know her, you see. Isn't she often like that?

TESMAN: Not the way she was today.

HEDDA (*turning away from the French doors*): Do you think she minded that business with the hat?

TESMAN: Oh, I don't think so. Not much. Perhaps a little bit right at the moment —

HEDDA: Well, I'm sorry, but I must say it strikes me as very odd — putting her hat down here in the living room. One just doesn't do that.

TESMAN: Well, you may be sure Aunt Julle won't ever do it again.

HEDDA: Anyway, I'll make it up to her, somehow.

TESMAN: Oh yes, Hedda; if only you would!

HEDDA: When you go over there today, why don't you ask her over for tonight?

TESMAN: I'll certainly do that. And then there is one other thing you could do that she'd appreciate ever so much.

HEDDA: What?

TESMAN: If you could just bring yourself to call her Auntie. For my sake, Hedda, hm?

HEDDA: No, Tesman, no. You really mustn't ask me to do that. I have already told you I can't. I'll try to call her Aunt Juliane. That will have to do.

TESMAN: All right, if you say so. I just thought that now that you're in the family —

HEDDA: Hmmm — I don't know about that — (*She walks toward the doorway.*)

TESMAN (*after a brief pause*): Anything the matter, Hedda? Hm?

HEDDA: I'm just looking at my old piano. It doesn't quite go with the other furniture in here.

TESMAN: As soon as I get my first pay check we'll have it traded in.

HEDDA: No — I don't want to do that. I want to keep it. But let's put it in this inner room and get another one for out here. Whenever it's convenient. I mean.

TESMAN (*a little taken back*): Well — yes — we could do that —

HEDDA (*picks up the bouquet from the piano*): These flowers weren't here last night.

TESMAN: I suppose Aunt Julle brought them for you.

HEDDA (*looking at the flowers*): There's a card here. (*Takes it out and reads.*) "Will be back later." Can you guess who it's from?

TESMAN: No. Who? Hm?

HEDDA: Thea Elvsted.

TESMAN: No, really? Mrs. Elvsted! Miss Rysing that was.

HEDDA: That's right. The one with that irritating head of hair she used to show off with. An old flame of yours, I understand.

TESMAN (*laughs*): Well, now — that didn't last long! Anyway, that was before I knew you, Hedda. Just think — her being in town.

HEDDA: Strange, that she'd call on us. I have hardly seen her since we went to school together.

TESMAN: As far as that goes, I haven't seen her either for — God knows how long. I don't see how she can stand living in that out-of-the-way place. Hm?

HEDDA (*suddenly struck by a thought*): Listen, Tesman — isn't it some place near there that he lives — what's his name — Eilert Løvborg?

TESMAN: Yes, that's right. He is up there, too.

(BERTE *enters right.*)

BERTE: Ma'am, she's here again, that lady who brought those flowers a while back. (*Pointing.*) The flowers you're holding in your hand, ma'am.

HEDDA: Ah, she is? Well, show her in, please.

(BERTE *opens the door for* MRS. ELVSTED *and exits.* MRS. ELVSTED *is of slight build, with a pretty, soft face. Her eyes are light blue, large, round, rather prominent, of a timid and querying expression. Her hair is strikingly light in color, almost whitish, and unusually rich and wavy. She is a couple of years younger than* HEDDA. *She is dressed in a dark visiting dress, tasteful, but not quite in the most recent fashion.*)

HEDDA (*walks toward her. Friendly*): Good morning, my dear Mrs. Elvsted. How very nice to see you again.

MRS. ELVSTED (*nervous, trying not to show it*): Well, yes, it is quite some time since we met.

TESMAN (*shaking hands*): And we, too. Hm?

HEDDA: Thank you for your lovely flowers —

MRS. ELVSTED: Please, don't — I would have come here yesterday afternoon. But I was told you were still traveling —

TESMAN: You've just arrived in town, hm?

MRS. ELVSTED: I got here yesterday, at noon. Oh, I was quite desperate when I learned you weren't home.

HEDDA: Desperate? But why?

TESMAN: But my dear Mrs. Rysing — I mean Mrs. Elvsted —

HEDDA: There is nothing wrong, I hope?

MRS. ELVSTED: Yes there is. And I don't know a single soul other than you that I can turn to here.

HEDDA (*putting the flowers down on the table*): Come — let's sit down here on the sofa.

MRS. ELVSTED: Oh, I'm in no mood to sit!

HEDDA: Of course you are. Come on. (*She pulls* MRS. ELVSTED *over to the sofa and sits down next to her.*)

TESMAN: Well, now, Mrs. — ? Exactly what — ?

HEDDA: Has something — special happened at home?

MRS. ELVSTED: Well, yes — and no. Oh, but I am so afraid you won't understand!

HEDDA: In that case, it seems to me you ought to tell us exactly what has happened, Mrs. Elvsted.

TESMAN: After all, that's why you are here. Hm?

MRS. ELVSTED: Yes, yes, of course. Well, then, maybe you already know — Eilert Løvborg is in town.

HEDDA: Is Løvborg — !

TESMAN: No! You don't say! Just think, Hedda — Løvborg's back!

HEDDA: All right. I can hear.

MRS. ELVSTED: He has been here a week already. Imagine — a whole week! In this dangerous place. Alone! With all that bad company around.

HEDDA: But my dear Mrs. Elvsted — why is he a concern of yours?

MRS. ELVSTED (*with an apprehensive look at her, says quickly*): He tutored the children.

HEDDA: Your children?

MRS. ELVSTED: My husband's. I don't have any.

HEDDA: In other words, your stepchildren.

MRS. ELVSTED: Yes.

TESMAN (*with some hesitation*): But was he — I don't quite know how to put this — was he sufficiently — regular — in his way of life to be thus employed? Hm?

MRS. ELVSTED: For the last two years, there hasn't been a thing to object to in his conduct.

TESMAN: No, really? Just think, Hedda!

HEDDA: I hear.

MRS. ELVSTED: Not the least little bit, I assure you! Not in any respect. And yet — knowing he's here — in the big city — And with all that money, too! I'm scared to death!

TESMAN: But in that case, why didn't he remain with you and your husband? Hm?

MRS. ELVSTED: After his book came out, he was too restless to stay.

TESMAN: Ah yes, that's right. Aunt Julle said he has published a new book.

MRS. ELVSTED: Yes, a big new book, about the course of civilization in general. It came out about two weeks ago. And since it has had such big sales and been discussed so much and made such a big splash —

TESMAN: It has, has it? I suppose this is something he has had lying around from better days?

MRS. ELVSTED: You mean from earlier?

TESMAN: Yes.

MRS. ELVSTED: No; it's all been written since he came to stay with us. During this last year.

TESMAN: Well, now! That's very good news, Hedda! Just think!

MRS. ELVSTED: Yes, if it only would last!

HEDDA: Have you seen him since you came to town?

MRS. ELVSTED: No, not yet. I had a great deal of trouble finding his address. But this morning I finally tracked him down.

HEDDA (*looks searchingly at her*): Isn't it rather odd that your husband — hm —

MRS. ELVSTED (*with a nervous start*): My husband! What about him?

HEDDA: That he sends you to town on such an errand? That he doesn't go and look after his friend himself?

MRS. ELVSTED: Oh, no, no — my husband doesn't have time for things like that. Besides, I have some — some shopping to do, anyway.

HEDDA (*with a slight smile*): Well, in that case, of course —

MRS. ELVSTED (*getting up, restlessly*): And now I beg of you, Mr. Tesman — won't you please receive Eilert Løvborg nicely if he calls on you? And I am sure he will. After all — Such good friends as you two used to be. And then you both do the same kind of work — the same field of study, as far as I know.

TESMAN: We used to, at any rate.

MRS. ELVSTED: Yes. And that's why I implore you to please, please, try to keep an eye on him — you too. You'll do that, Mr. Tesman, won't you? Promise?

TESMAN: With the greatest pleasure, Mrs. Rysing.

HEDDA: Elvsted.

TESMAN: I'll gladly do as much for Eilert as I possibly can. You may certainly count on that.

MRS. ELVSTED: Oh, how good and kind you are! (*Clasps his hands.*) Thank you, thank you, thank you! (*Nervously.*) You see, my husband is so very fond of him.

HEDDA (*getting up*): You ought to write him a note, Tesman. Maybe he won't come without an invitation.

TESMAN: Yes, I suppose that would be the right thing to do, Hedda. Hm?

HEDDA: The sooner the better. Right away, I think.

MRS. ELVSTED (*pleadingly*): If only you would!

TESMAN: I'll write this minute. Do you have his address, Mrs. — Mrs. Elvsted?

MRS. ELVSTED: Yes. (*Pulls a slip of paper from her bag and gives it to him.*) Here it is.

TESMAN: Very good. Well, then, if you'll excuse me — (*Looks around.*) By the way — the slippers? Ah, here we are. (*Leaving with the parcel.*)

HEDDA: Be sure you write a nice, warm, friendly letter, Tesman. And a long one, too.

TESMAN: Certainly, certainly.

MRS. ELVSTED: But not a word that it is I who — !

TESMAN: No, that goes without saying, I should think. Hm? (*Goes out right through inner room.*)

HEDDA (*goes over to* MRS. ELVSTED, *smiles, says in a low voice*): There! We just killed two birds with one stone.

MRS. ELVSTED: What do you mean?

HEDDA: Didn't you see I wanted him out of the room?

MRS. ELVSTED: Yes, to write that letter —

HEDDA: And to speak to you alone.

MRS. ELVSTED (*flustered*): About this same thing?

HEDDA: Exactly.

MRS. ELVSTED (*anxious*): But there *is* nothing more, Mrs. Tesman! Really, there isn't!

HEDDA: Oh yes, there is. There is considerably more. I can see that much. Over here — We are going to have a real, nice, confidential talk, you and I. (*She forces* MRS. ELVSTED *down in the easy chair and seats herself on one of the ottomans.*)

MRS. ELVSTED (*worried, looks at her watch*): But my dear Mrs. Tesman — I had really thought I would be on my way now.

HEDDA: Oh I am sure there is no rush. Now, then. Tell me about yourself. How are things at home?

MRS. ELVSTED: That is just what I don't want to talk about.

HEDDA: But to me — ! After all, we are old schoolmates.

MRS. ELVSTED: But you were a year ahead of me. And I used to be so scared of you!

HEDDA: Scared of me?

MRS. ELVSTED: Terribly. For when we met on the stairs, you always ruffled my hair.

HEDDA: Did I really?

MRS. ELVSTED: Yes. And once you said you were going to burn it off.

HEDDA: Oh, but you know — I wasn't serious!

MRS. ELVSTED: No, but I was such a silly, then. Anyway, afterwards we drifted far apart. Our circles are so very different, you know.

HEDDA: All the more reason for getting close again. Listen. In school we called each other by our first names.

MRS. ELVSTED: Oh I'm sure you're wrong —

HEDDA: I'm sure I'm not! I remember it quite clearly. And now we want to be open with one another, just the way we used to. (*Moves the ottoman closer.*) There, now! (*Kisses her cheek.*) You call me Hedda.

MRS. ELVSTED (*seizes her hands*): Oh you are so good and kind! I'm not used to that.

HEDDA: There, there! And I'll call you my dear Thora, just as in the old days.

MRS. ELVSTED: My name is Thea.

HEDDA: So it is. Of course. I meant Thea. (*Looks at her with compassion.*) So you're not much used to goodness and kindness, Thea? Not in your own home?

MRS. ELVSTED: If I even had a home! But I don't. I never have had one.

HEDDA (*looks at her for a moment*): I thought there might be something like this.

MRS. ELVSTED (*helplessly, looking straight ahead*): Yes — yes — yes —

HEDDA: I ' am not sure if I quite remember — Didn't you first come to your husband as his housekeeper?

MRS. ELVSTED: I was really hired as governess. But his wife — his first wife — was ailing already then and practically bedridden. So I had to take charge of the household as well.

HEDDA: But in the end you became his wife.

MRS. ELVSTED (*dully*): So I did.

HEDDA: Let's see. How long ago is that?

MRS. ELVSTED: Since my marriage?

HEDDA: Yes.

MRS. ELVSTED: About five years.

HEDDA: Right. It must be that long.

MRS. ELVSTED: Oh, those five years! Or mostly the last two or three! Oh, Mrs. Tesman — if you could just imagine!

HEDDA (*slaps her hand lightly*): Mrs. Tesman? Shame on you!

MRS. ELVSTED: Oh yes; all right, I'll try. Yes — if you could just — conceive — understand —

HEDDA (*casually*): And Eilert Løvborg has been living near you for some three years or so, hasn't he?

MRS. ELVSTED (*looks at her uncertainly*): Eilert Løvborg? Yes — he has.

HEDDA: Did you know him before? Here in town?

MRS. ELVSTED: Hardly at all. That is, of course I did in a way. I mean, I knew *of* him.

HEDDA: But up there — You saw a good deal of him; did you?

MRS. ELVSTED: Yes, he came over to us every day. He was supposed to tutor the children, you see. For I just couldn't do it all by myself.

HEDDA: Of course not. And your husband — ? I suppose he travels quite a bit.

MRS. ELVSTED: Well, yes, Mrs. Tes — Hedda — as a public magistrate, you know, he very often has to travel all over his district.

HEDDA (*leaning against the armrest on the easy chair*): Thea — poor, sweet Thea — now you have to tell me everything — just as it is.

MRS. ELVSTED: You'd better ask me, then.

HEDDA: How *is* your husband, Thea? I mean — you know — *really*? To be with. What kind of person is he? Is he good to you?

MRS. ELVSTED (*evasively*): I believe he thinks he does everything for the best.

HEDDA: But isn't he altogether too old for you? He is more than twenty years older, isn't he?

MRS. ELVSTED (*with irritation*): Yes, there is that, too. But there isn't just one thing. Every single little thing about him repels me! We don't have a thought in common, he and I. Not a thing in the world!

HEDDA: But isn't he fond of you all the same? I mean in his own way?

MRS. ELVSTED: I don't know. I think I am just useful to him. And I don't use much money. I am inexpensive.

HEDDA: That is foolish of you.

MRS. ELVSTED (*shakes her head*): Can't be changed. Not with him. I don't think he cares for anybody much except himself. Perhaps the children a little.

HEDDA: And Eilert Løvborg, Thea.

MRS. ELVSTED (*looks at her*): Eilert Løvborg? What makes you think that?

HEDDA: Well, it seems to me that when he sends you all the way to town to look after him. (*With an almost imperceptible smile.*) Besides, you said so yourself. To Tesman.

MRS. ELVSTED (*with a nervous twitch*): Did I? I suppose I did. (*With a muted outburst.*) No! I might as well tell you now as later. For it's bound to come out, anyway.

HEDDA: But my dear Thea — ?

MRS. ELVSTED: All right. My husband doesn't know I've gone!

HEDDA: What! He doesn't know?

MRS. ELVSTED: He wasn't even home. He's away again. Oh, I just couldn't take it any longer, Hedda! It had become utterly impossible. All alone as I was.

HEDDA: So what did you do?

MRS. ELVSTED: I packed some of my things. Just the most necessary. Without telling anybody. And left.

HEDDA: Just like that?

MRS. ELVSTED: Yes. And took the next train to town.

HEDDA: But dearest Thea — how did you dare to do a thing like that!

MRS. ELVSTED (*rises, walks*): What else could I do?

HEDDA: But what do you think your husband will say when you go back?

MRS. ELVSTED (*by the table; looks at her*): Go back to him?

HEDDA: Yes!

MRS. ELVSTED: I'll never go back.

HEDDA (*rises, approaches her slowly*): So you have really, seriously — left everything?

MRS. ELVSTED: Yes. It seemed to me there was nothing else I could do.

HEDDA: And quite openly, too.

MRS. ELVSTED: You can't keep a thing like that secret, anyway.

HEDDA: But what do you think people will say, Thea?

MRS. ELVSTED: In God's name, let them say whatever they like. (*Sits down on the sofa, dully, tired.*) For I have only done what I had to do.

HEDDA (*after a brief silence*): And what do you plan to do with yourself? What sort of work will you do?

MRS. ELVSTED: I don't know yet. I only know I have to live where Eilert Løvborg is. If I am to live at all.

HEDDA (*moves a chair from the table closer to* MRS. ELVSTED, *sits down, strokes her hands*): Thea — tell me. How did this — this friendship between you and Eilert — how did it begin?

MRS. ELVSTED: Oh, it grew little by little. I got some sort of power over him.

HEDDA: Oh?

MRS. ELVSTED: He dropped his old ways. Not because I asked him to. I never dared to do that. But I think he must have noticed how I felt about that kind of life. So he changed.

HEDDA (*quickly suppresses a cynical smile*): So you have — rehabilitated him, as they say. Haven't you, Thea?

MRS. ELVSTED: At least, that's what *he* says. On the other hand, he has turned me into a real human being. Taught me to think — and understand — all sorts of things.

HEDDA: Maybe he tutored you, too?

MRS. ELVSTED: No, not tutored exactly. But he talked to me. About so many, many things. And then came that lovely, lovely time when I could share his work with him. He let me help him!

HEDDA: He did?

MRS. ELVSTED: Yes! Whatever he wrote, he wanted us to be together about it.

HEDDA: Just like two good comrades.

MRS. ELVSTED (*with animation*): Comrades! — that's it! Imagine, Hedda — that's just what he called it, too. Oh, I really ought to feel so happy. But I can't. For you see, I don't know if it will last.

HEDDA: You don't trust him any more than that?

MRS. ELVSTED (*heavily*): The shadow of a woman stands between Eilert Løvborg and me.

HEDDA (*tensely, looks at her*): Who?

MRS. ELVSTED: I don't know. Somebody or other from — his past. I don't think he has ever really forgotten her.

HEDDA: What has he told you about it?

MRS. ELVSTED: He has mentioned it only once — just casually.

HEDDA: And what did he say?

MRS. ELVSTED: He said that when they parted she was going to kill him with a gun.

HEDDA (*cold, controlled*): Oh, nonsense. People don't do that sort of thing here.

MRS. ELVSTED: No, I know. And that is why I think it must be that red-headed singer he used to —

HEDDA: Yes, I suppose so.

MRS. ELVSTED: For I remember people said she carried a loaded gun.

HEDDA: Well, then I'm sure it's she.

MRS. ELVSTED (*wringing her hands*): Yes, but just think, Hedda — now I hear that she — that singer — that she's here in town again, too! Oh, I'm just desperate — !

HEDDA (*with a glance toward the inner room*): Shhh! Here's Tesman. (*Rises and whispers.*) Not a word about all this to anybody, Thea!

MRS. ELVSTED (*jumps up*): No, no. For God's sake — !

(TESMAN, *carrying a letter, enters from the right side of the inner room.*)

TESMAN: There now — here's the missive, all ready to go!

HEDDA: Good. But I believe Mrs. Elvsted wants to be on her way. Wait a moment. I'll see you to the garden gate.

TESMAN: Say, Hedda — do you think Berte could take care of this?

HEDDA (*takes the letter*): I'll tell her.

(BERTE *enters right.*)

BERTE: Judge Brack is here and wants to know if you're receiving.

HEDDA: Yes, ask the Judge please to come in. And — here — drop this in a mailbox, will you?

BERTE (*takes the letter*): Yes, ma'am.

(*She opens the door for* JUDGE BRACK *and exits. The* JUDGE *is forty-five years of age. Rather thickset, but well-built and with brisk athletic movements. Roundish face, aristocratic profile. His hair is short, still almost completely black, very neatly dressed. Lively, sparkling eyes. Thick eyebrows and mustache with cut-off points. He is dressed in an elegant suit, a trifle youthful for his age. He wears pince-nez glasses, attached to a string, and lets them drop from time to time.*)

JUDGE BRACK (*hat in hand, salutes*): May one pay one's respects as early as this?

HEDDA: One certainly may.

TESMAN (*shaking his hand*): You are always welcome. (*Introducing.*) Judge Brack — Miss Rysing —

(HEDDA *groans.*)

BRACK (*bowing*): Delighted!

HEDDA (*looks at him, laughs*): How nice it is to see you in daylight, Judge!

BRACK: You find me changed, perhaps?

HEDDA: A bit younger, I think.

BRACK: Much obliged.

TESMAN: But what do you think of Hedda? Hm? Did you ever see her in such bloom? She positively —

HEDDA: Will you please leave me out of this? You had better thank the Judge for all the trouble he has taken.

BRACK: Oh, nonsense. It's been a pleasure.

HEDDA: Yes, you are indeed a faithful soul. But my friend here is dying to be off. Don't leave, Judge. I'll be back in a minute.

(*Mutual goodbyes.* MRS. ELVSTED *and* HEDDA *exit, right.*)

BRACK: Well, now — your wife — is she tolerably satisfied?

TESMAN: Yes, indeed, and we really can't thank you enough. That is, I understand there will have to be some slight changes made here and there. And there are still a few things — just a few trifles — we'll have to get.

BRACK: Oh? Really?

TESMAN: But we certainly don't want to bother you with that. Hedda said she's going to take care of it herself. But do sit down, hm?

BRACK: Thanks. Maybe just for a moment — (*Sits down by the table.*) There's one thing I'd like to talk to you about, my dear Tesman.

TESMAN: Oh? Ah, I see! (*Sits down.*) I suppose it's the serious part of the festivities that's beginning now. Hm?

BRACK: Oh — there's no great rush as far as the money is concerned. Though I must say I wish we could have established ourselves a trifle more economically.

TESMAN: Out of the question, my dear fellow! Remember, it's all for Hedda! You, who know her so well — ! After all, I couldn't put her up like any little middle-class housewife —

BRACK: No, I suppose — That's just it.

TESMAN: Besides — fortunately — it can't be long now before I receive my appointment.

BRACK: Well, you know — things like that have a way of hanging fire.

TESMAN: Perhaps you have heard something? Something definite? Hm?

BRACK: No, nothing certain — (*Interrupting himself.*) But that reminds me. I have some news for you.

TESMAN: Oh?

BRACK: Your old friend Eilert Løvborg is back in town.

TESMAN: I know that already.

BRACK: So? Who told you?

TESMAN: The lady who just left.

BRACK: I see. What did you say her name was again? I didn't quite catch —

TESMAN: Mrs. Elvsted.

BRACK: Ah yes — the Commissioner's wife. Yes, it's up in her part of the country that Løvborg has been staying, too.

TESMAN: And just think. I am so glad to hear it. He is quite respectable again.

BRACK: Yes, so they say.

TESMAN: And he has published a new book, hm?

BRACK: Oh yes.

TESMAN: Which is making quite a stir.

BRACK: Quite an unusual stir.

TESMAN: Just think! Isn't that just wonderful! He — with his remarkable gifts. And I was so sure he'd gone under for good.

BRACK: That seems to have been the general opinion.

TESMAN: What I don't understand, though, is what he is going to do with himself. What sort of living can he make? Hm?

(*During the last remark* HEDDA *re-enters, right.*)

HEDDA (*to* BRACK, *with a scornful little laugh*): Tesman is forever worrying about how people are going to make a living.

TESMAN: Well, you see, we are talking about poor Eilert Løvborg, Hedda.

HEDDA (*with a quick look at him*): You are? (*Sits down in the easy chair by the stove and asks casually.*) What is the matter with him?

TESMAN: Well, you see, I believe he's run through his inheritance a long time ago. And I don't suppose he can write a new book every year. Hm? So I really must ask how he is going to make out.

BRACK: Maybe I could help you answer that.

TESMAN: Yes?

BRACK: Remember, he has relatives with considerable influence.

TESMAN: Ah — unfortunately, those relatives have washed their hands of him long ago.

BRACK: Just the same, they used to call him the hope of the family.

TESMAN: Yes, before! But he has ruined all that.

HEDDA: Who knows? (*With a little smile.*) I hear the Elvsteds have rehabilitated him.

BRACK: And then this book —

TESMAN: Well, I certainly hope they will help him to find something or other. I just wrote him a letter. Hedda, dear, I asked him to come out here tonight.

BRACK: Oh dear, I am sorry. Don't you remember — you're supposed to come to my little stag dinner tonight? You accepted last night on the pier, you know.

HEDDA: Had you forgotten, Tesman?

TESMAN: So I had.

BRACK: Oh well. I'm sure he won't come, so it doesn't really make any difference.

TESMAN: Why is that? Hm?

BRACK (*gets up somewhat hesitantly, rests his hands on the back of the chair*): Dear Tesman — and you, too, Mrs. Tesman — I cannot in good conscience let you remain in ignorance of something, which — which —

TESMAN: Something to do with Eilert?

BRACK: With both you and him.

TESMAN: But my dear Judge, do speak!

BRACK: You must be prepared to find that your appointment will not come through as soon as you hope and expect.

TESMAN (*jumps up, nervously*): Something's happened? Hm?

BRACK: It may conceivably be made contingent upon the result of a competition.

TESMAN: Competition! Just think, Hedda!

HEDDA (*leaning farther back in her chair*): Ah — I see, I see — !

TESMAN: But with whom? Don't tell me with — ?

BRACK: Precisely. With Eilert Løvborg.

TESMAN (*claps his hands together*): No, no! This can't be! It is unthinkable! Quite impossible! Hm?

BRACK: All the same, that's the way it may turn out.

TESMAN: No, but Judge, this would amount to the most incredible callousness toward me! (*Waving his arms.*) For just think — I'm a married man! We married on the strength of these prospects, Hedda and I. Got ourselves deep in debt. Borrowed money from Aunt Julle, too. After all, I had practically been promised the post, you know. Hm?

BRACK: Well, well. I daresay you'll get it in the end. If only after a competition.

HEDDA (*motionless in her chair*): Just think, Tesman. It will be like a kind of contest.

TESMAN: But dearest Hedda, how can you be so unconcerned!

HEDDA (*still without moving*): I'm not at all unconcerned. I'm dying to see who wins.

BRACK: In any case, Mrs. Tesman, I'm glad you know the situation as it is. I mean — before you proceed to make the little additional purchases I understand you threaten us with.

HEDDA: This makes no difference as far as that is concerned.

BRACK: Really? Well, in that case, of course — Goodbye! (*To* TESMAN.) I'll pick you up on my afternoon walk.

TESMAN: What? Oh yes, yes, of course. I'm sorry; I'm just all flustered.

HEDDA (*without getting up, gives her hand*): Goodbye, Judge. Come back soon.

BRACK: Thanks. Goodbye, goodbye.

TESMAN (*sees him to the door*): Goodbye, my dear Judge. You really must excuse me —

(JUDGE BRACK *exits, right.*)

TESMAN (*pacing the floor*): Oh, Hedda, Hedda! One should never venture into fairyland. Hm?

HEDDA (*looks at him, smiles*): Do you do that?

TESMAN: Well, yes — it can't be denied — it was most venturesome of me to rush into marriage and set up a home on the strength of mere prospects.

HEDDA: Well, maybe you're right.

TESMAN: Anyway — we do have our own nice, comfortable home, now. Just think, Hedda — the very home both of us dreamed about. Set our hearts on, I may almost say. Hm?

HEDDA (*rises, slowly, tired*): The agreement was that we were to maintain a certain position — entertain —

TESMAN: Don't I know it! Dearest Hedda — I have been so looking forward to seeing you as hostess in a select circle! Hm? Well, well, well! In the meantime, we'll just have to be content with one another. See Aunt Julle once in a while. Nothing more. And you were meant for such a different kind of life, altogether!

HEDDA: I suppose a footman is completely out of the question.

TESMAN: I'm afraid so. Under the circumstances, you see — we couldn't possibly —

HEDDA: And as for getting my own riding horse —

TESMAN (*aghast*): Riding horse!

HEDDA: I suppose I mustn't even think of that.

TESMAN: Good heavens, no! That goes without saying, I hope!

HEDDA (*walking*): Well — at least I have one thing to amuse myself with in the meantime.

TESMAN (*overjoyed*): Oh thank goodness for that! And what *is* that, Hedda, hm?

HEDDA (*in the doorway, looks at him with suppressed scorn*): My guns — Jørgen!

TESMAN (*in fear*): Your guns!

HEDDA (*with cold eyes*): General Gabler's guns. (*She exits left, through the inner room.*)

TESMAN (*runs up to the doorway, calls after her*): But Hedda! Good gracious! Hedda, dear! Please don't touch those dangerous things! For my sake, Hedda! Hm?

ACT II

The same room at the TESMANS'. *The piano has been moved out and replaced by an elegant little writing desk. A small table has been placed near the sofa, left. Most of the flowers have been removed.* MRS. ELVSTED'S *bouquet is on the big table front center. Afternoon.*

HEDDA, *dressed to receive callers, is alone. She is standing near the open French doors, loading a revolver. Its mate is lying in an open case on the desk.*

HEDDA (*looking down into the garden, calls*): Hello there, Judge! Welcome back!

JUDGE BRACK (*off stage*): Thanks, Mrs. Tesman!

HEDDA (*raises the gun, sights*): I am going to shoot you, Judge Brack!

BRACK (*calls off stage*): No — no — no! Don't point the gun at me like that!

HEDDA: That's what you get for sneaking in the back door! (*Fires.*)

BRACK (*closer*): Are you out of your mind — !

HEDDA: Oh dear — did I hit you?

BRACK (*still off stage*): Stop that nonsense!

HEDDA: Come on in, then.

(JUDGE BRACK, *dressed for dinner, enters, left. He carries a light overcoat over his arm.*)

BRACK: Dammit! Do you still fool around with that thing? What are you shooting at, anyway?

HEDDA: Oh — just firing off into blue air.

BRACK (*gently but firmly taking the gun away from her*): With your permission, Mrs. Tesman. (*Looks at it.*) Ah yes, I remember this gun very well. (*Looks around.*) Where is the case? Ah, here we are. (*Puts the gun in the case and closes it.*) That's enough of that silliness for today.

HEDDA: But in the name of heaven, what do you expect me to do with myself?

BRACK: No callers?

HEDDA (*closing the French doors*): Not a soul. All my close friends are still out of town, it seems.

BRACK: And Tesman is out, too, perhaps?

HEDDA (*by the desk, puts the gun case in a drawer*): Yes. He took off for the aunts' right after lunch. He didn't expect you so early.

BRACK: I should have thought of that. That was stupid of me.

HEDDA (*turns her head, looks at him*): Why stupid?

BRACK: I would have come a little — sooner.

HEDDA (*crossing*): If you had, you wouldn't have found anybody home. For I have been in my room ever since lunch, changing my clothes.

BRACK: And isn't there the tiniest little opening in the door for negotiations?

HEDDA: You forgot to provide one.

BRACK: Another stupidity.

HEDDA: So we'll have to stay in here. And wait. For I don't think Tesman will be back for some time.

BRACK: By all means. I'll be very patient.

(HEDDA *sits on the sofa in the corner.* BRACK *puts his overcoat over the back of the nearest chair and sits down, keeping his hat in his hand. Brief silence. They look at one another.*)

HEDDA: Well?

BRACK (*in the same tone*): Well?

HEDDA: I said it first.

BRACK (*leans forward a little*): All right. Let's have a nice little chat, Mrs. Tesman.

HEDDA (*leans back*): Don't you think it's an eternity since last time we talked! I don't count last night and this morning. That was nothing.

BRACK: You mean — just the two of us?

HEDDA: Mmm. If you like.

BRACK: There hasn't been a day I haven't wished you were back again.

HEDDA: My feelings, exactly.

BRACK: Yours? Really, Mrs. Tesman? And I have been assuming you were having such a wonderful time.

HEDDA: I'd say!

BRACK: All Tesman's letters said so.

HEDDA: Oh yes, he! He's happy just poking through old collections of books. And copying old parchments — or whatever they are.

BRACK (*with a touch of malice*): Well, that's his calling, you know. Partly, anyway.

HEDDA: Yes, so it is. And in that case I suppose — But I! Oh, Judge! You've no idea how bored I've been.

BRACK (*with sympathy*): Really? You're serious?

HEDDA: Surely you can understand that? For a whole half year never to see anyone who knows even a little bit about our circle? And talks our language?

BRACK: Yes, I think I would find that trying, too.

HEDDA: And then the most unbearable thing of all —

BRACK: Well?

HEDDA: — everlastingly to be in the company of the same person —

BRACK (*nods in agreement*): Both early and late — yes. I can imagine — at all possible times —

HEDDA: I said everlastingly.

BRACK: All right. Still, it seems to me that with as excellent a person as our Tesman, it ought to be possible —

HEDDA: My dear Judge — Tesman is a specialist.

BRACK: Granted.

HEDDA: And specialists are not at all entertaining travel companions. Not in the long run, at any rate.

BRACK: Not even — the specialist — one happens to love?

HEDDA: Bah! That nauseating word!

BRACK (*puzzled*): Really, now, Mrs. Tesman — ?

HEDDA (*half laughing, half annoyed*): You ought to try it some time! Listening to talk about the history of civilization, early and late —

BRACK: Everlastingly —

HEDDA: All right. And then this business about the domestic industry in the Middle Ages — ! That's the ghastliest part of it all!

BRACK (*looking searchingly at her*): But in that case — tell me — how am I to explain — ?

HEDDA: That Jørgen Tesman and I made a pair of it, you mean?

BRACK: If you want to put it that way — yes.

HEDDA: Come now. Do you really find that so strange?

BRACK: Both yes and no — Mrs. Tesman.

HEDDA: I had danced myself tired, my dear

Judge? My season was over — (*Gives a slight start.*) No, no — I don't really mean that. Won't think it, either!

BRACK: Nor do you have the slightest reason to, I am sure.

HEDDA: Oh — as far as reasons are concerned — (*Looks at him as if trying to read his mind.*) And, after all, Jørgen Tesman must be said to be a most proper young man in all respects.

BRACK: Both proper and substantial. Most certainly.

HEDDA: And one can't say there is anything exactly comical about him. Do you think there is?

BRACK: Comical? No — o. I wouldn't say that —

HEDDA: All right, then. And he is a most assiduous collector. Nobody can deny that. I think it is perfectly possible he may go quite far, after all.

BRACK (*looks at her rather uncertainly*): I assumed that you, like everybody else, thought he'll in time become an exceptionally eminent man?

HEDDA (*with a weary expression*): Yes, I did. And then, you see — there he was, wanting so desperately to be allowed to provide for me — I don't know why I shouldn't have accepted?

BRACK: No, certainly. From that point of view —

HEDDA: For you know, Judge, that was considerably more than my other admirers were willing to do.

BRACK (*laughs*): Well! Of course I can't answer for all the others. But as far as I am concerned, I have always had a certain degree of — respect for the bonds of matrimony. You know — as a general proposition, Mrs. Tesman.

HEDDA (*lightly*): Well, I never really counted very heavily on *you* —

BRACK: All I want is a nice, confidential circle, in which I can be of service, both in deed and in counsel. Be allowed to come and go like a true and trusted friend —

HEDDA: You mean, of the master of the house — ?

BRACK (*with a slight bow*): To be perfectly frank — rather of the mistress. But by all means — the master, too, of course. Do you know, that kind of — shall I say, triangular? — relationship can really be a great comfort to all parties involved.

HEDDA: Yes, many were the times I missed a second travel companion. To be twosome in the compartment — brrr!

BRACK: Fortunately, the wedding trip is over.

HEDDA (*shakes her head*): There's a long journey ahead. I've just arrived at a station on the way.

BRACK: Well, at the station one gets out and moves around a bit, Mrs. Tesman.

HEDDA: I never get out.

BRACK: Really?

HEDDA: No. For there's always someone around, who —

BRACK (*laughs*): — looks at one's legs; is that it?

HEDDA: Exactly.

BRACK: Oh well, really, now —

HEDDA (*with a silencing gesture*): I won't have it! Rather stay in my seat — once I'm seated. Twosome and all.

BRACK: I see. But what if a third party were to join the couple?

HEDDA: Well, now — *that* would be something altogether different!

BRACK: A proven, understanding friend —

HEDDA: — entertaining in all sorts of lively ways —

BRACK: — and not at all a specialist!

HEDDA (*with audible breath*): Yes, that would indeed be a comfort.

BRACK (*hearing the front door open, looking at her*): The triangle is complete.

HEDDA (*half aloud*): And the train goes on.

(TESMAN, *in gray walking suit and soft hat, enters, right. He carries a pile of paperbound books under his arm. Others are stuffed in his pockets.*)

TESMAN (*as he walks up to the table in front of the corner sofa*): Puuhh — ! Quite some load to carry, all this — and in this heat, too. (*Puts the books down.*) I am positively perspiring, Hedda. Well, well. So you're here already, my dear Judge. Hm? And Berte didn't tell me.

BRACK (*rises*): I came through the garden.

HEDDA: What are all those books?

TESMAN (*leafing through some of them*): Just some new publications in my special field.

HEDDA: Special field, hm?

BRACK: Ah yes — professional publications, Mrs. Tesman.

(BRACK *and* HEDDA *exchange knowing smiles.*)

HEDDA: Do you still need more books?

TESMAN: Yes, my dear. There is no such thing as having too many books in one's special field. One has to keep up with what is being written and published, you know.

HEDDA: I suppose.

TESMAN (*searching among the books*): And look. Here is Eilert Løvborg's new book, too. (*Offers it to her.*) Want to take a look at it, Hedda? Hm?

HEDDA: No — thanks just the same. Or perhaps later.

TESMAN: I glanced at it on my way home.

BRACK: And what do you think of it? As a specialist yourself?

TESMAN: It is remarkable for its sobriety. He never wrote like that before. (*Gathers up all the books.*) I just want to take these into my study. I am so much looking forward to cutting them open! And then I'll change. (*To* BRACK.) I assume there's no rush to be off, is there?

BRACK: Not at all. We have plenty of time.

TESMAN: In that case, I think I'll indulge myself a little. (*On his way out with the books he halts in the doorway and turns.*) By the way, Hedda — Aunt Julle won't be out to see you tonight, after all.

HEDDA: No? Is it that business with the hat, do you think?

TESMAN: Oh, no — not at all. How can you believe a thing like that about Aunt Julle! Just think! No, it's Aunt Rina. She's feeling very poorly.

HEDDA: Isn't she always?

TESMAN: Yes, but it's especially bad today, poor thing.

HEDDA: Well, in that case I suppose she ought to stay home. I shall have to put up with it; that's all.

TESMAN: And you have no idea how perfectly delighted Aunt Julle was, even so. Because of how splendid you look after the trip, Hedda!

HEDDA (*half aloud, rising*): Oh, these everlasting aunts!

TESMAN: Hm?

HEDDA (*walks over to the French doors*): Nothing.

TESMAN: No? All right. Well, excuse me. (*Exits right, through inner room.*)

BRACK: What is this about a hat?

HEDDA: Oh, something with Miss Tesman this morning. She had put her hat down on the chair over there. (*Looks at him, smiles.*) So I pretended to think it was the maid's.

BRACK (*shakes his head*): But my dear Mrs. Tesman — how could you do a thing like that! And to that excellent old lady, too!

HEDDA (*nervously pacing the floor*): Well, you see — something just takes hold of me at times. And then I can't help myself — (*Throws herself down in the easy chair near the stove.*) Oh I can't explain it even to myself.

BRACK (*behind her chair*): You aren't really happy — that's the trouble.

HEDDA (*staring into space*): I don't know any reason why I should be. Do you?

BRACK: Well, yes — partly because you've got the home you've always wanted.

HEDDA (*looks up at him and laughs*): So you too believe that story about my great wish?

BRACK: You mean, there is nothing to it?

HEDDA: Well, yes; there is *something* to it.

BRACK: Well?

HEDDA: There is this much to it, that last summer I used Tesman to see me home from evening parties.

BRACK: Unfortunately — my route was in quite a different direction.

HEDDA: True. You walked on other roads last summer.

BRACK (*laughs*): Shame on you, Mrs. Tesman! So, all right — you and Tesman — ?

HEDDA: One evening we passed by here. And Tesman, poor thing, was practically turning himself into knots trying to find something to talk about. So I felt sorry for all that erudition —

BRACK (*with a doubting smile*): You did? Hm —

HEDDA: I really did. So, just to help him out of his misery, I happened to say that I'd like to live in this house.

BRACK: Just that?

HEDDA: That was all — *that* evening.

BRACK: But afterwards — ?

HEDDA: Yes, my frivolity had consequences, Judge.

BRACK: Unfortunately — that's often the way with frivolities. It happens to all of us, Mrs. Tesman.

HEDDA: Thanks! So in our common enthusiasm for Mr. Secretary Falk's villa Tesman and I found each other, you see! The result was engagement and wedding and honeymoon abroad and all the rest of it. Well, yes, my dear Judge — I've made my bed — I almost said.

BRACK: But this is priceless! And you didn't really care for the house at all?

HEDDA: Certainly not.

BRACK: Not even now? After all, we've set up quite a comfortable home for you here, haven't we?

HEDDA: Oh — it seems to me I smell lavender and rose sachets in all the rooms. But maybe that's a smell Aunt Julle brought with her.

BRACK (*laughs*): My guess is rather the late lamented Secretary's wife.

HEDDA: It smells of mortality, whoever it is. Like corsages — the next day. (*Clasps her hands behind her neck, leans back, looks at him.*) Judge, you have no idea how dreadfully bored I'll be — out here.

BRACK: But don't you think life may hold some task for you, too, Mrs. Tesman?

HEDDA: A task? With any kind of appeal?

BRACK: Preferably that, of course.

HEDDA: Heaven knows what kind of task that might be. There are times when I wonder if — (*Interrupts herself.*) No; I'm sure that wouldn't work, either.

BRACK: Who knows? Tell me.

HEDDA: It has occurred to me that maybe I could get Tesman to enter politics.

BRACK (*laughs*): Tesman! No, really — I must confess that — politics doesn't strike me as being exactly Tesman's line.

HEDDA: I agree. But suppose I were to prevail on him, all the same?

BRACK: What satisfaction could you possibly find in that? If he can't succeed — why do you want him even to try?

HEDDA: Because I am bored, I tell you! (*After a brief pause.*) So you think it's quite out of the question that Tesman could ever become prime minister?

BRACK: Well, you see, Mrs. Tesman — to do that he'd first of all have to be a fairly wealthy man.

HEDDA (*getting up, impatiently*): Yes! There we are! These shabby circumstances I've married into! (*Crosses the floor.*) That's what makes life so mean. So — so — ridiculous! For that's what it is, you know.

BRACK: Personally I believe something else is to blame.

HEDDA: What?

BRACK: You've never been through anything that's really stirred you.

HEDDA: Something serious, you mean?

BRACK: If you like. But maybe it's coming now.

HEDDA (*with a toss of her head*): You are thinking of that silly old professorship! That's Tesman's business. I refuse to give it a thought.

BRACK: As you wish. But now — to put it in the grand style — now when a solemn challenge of responsibility is being posed? Demands made on you? (*Smiles.*) New demands, Mrs. Tesman.

HEDDA (*angry*): Quiet! You'll never see anything of the kind.

BRACK (*cautiously*): We'll talk about this a year from now — on the outside.

HEDDA (*curtly*): I'm not made for that sort of thing, Judge! No demands for me!

BRACK: But surely you, like most women, are made for a duty, which —

HEDDA (*over by the French doors*): Oh, do be quiet! Often it seems to me there's only one thing in the world that I am made for.

BRACK (*coming close*): And may I ask what that is?

HEDDA (*looking out*): To be bored to death. Now you know. (*Turns, looks toward the inner room, laughs.*) Just as I thought. Here comes the professor.

BRACK (*warningly, in a low voice*): Steady, now, Mrs. Tesman!

(TESMAN, *dressed for a party, carrying his hat and gloves, enters from the right side of the inner room.*)

TESMAN: Hedda, any word yet from Eilert Løvborg that he isn't coming, hm?

HEDDA: No.

TESMAN: In that case, I wouldn't be a bit surprised if we have him here in a few minutes.

BRACK: You really think he'll come?

TESMAN: I am almost certain he will. For I'm sure it's only idle gossip that you told me this morning.

BRACK: Oh?

TESMAN: Anyway, that's what Aunt Julle said. She doesn't for a moment believe he'll stand in my way. Just think!

BRACK: I'm very glad to hear that.

TESMAN (*puts his hat and his gloves down*

on a chair, right): But you must let me wait for him as long as possible.

BRACK: By all means. We have plenty of time. Nobody will arrive at my place before seven — seven-thirty, or so.

TESMAN: And in the meantime we can keep Hedda company. Take our time. Hm?

HEDDA (*carrying* BRACK's *hat and coat over to the sofa in the corner*): And if worst comes to worst, Mr. Løvborg can stay here with me.

BRACK (*trying to take the things away from her*): Let me, Mrs. Tesman — What do you mean — "if worst comes to worst"?

HEDDA: If he doesn't want to go with you and Tesman.

TESMAN (*looks dubiously at her*): But, dearest Hedda — do you think that will quite do? He staying here with you? Hm? Remember, Aunt Julle won't be here.

HEDDA: No, but Mrs. Elvsted will. The three of us will have a cup of tea together.

TESMAN: Oh yes; *that* will be perfectly all right!

BRACK (*with a smile*): And perhaps the wiser course of action for him.

HEDDA: What do you mean?

BRACK: Begging your pardon, Mrs. Tesman — you've often enough looked askance at my little stag dinners. It's been your opinion that only men of the firmest principles ought to attend.

HEDDA: I should think Mr. Løvborg is firm-principled enough now. A reformed sinner —

(BERTE *appears in door, right.*)

BERTE: Ma'am — there's a gentleman here who asks if —

HEDDA: Show him in, please.

TESMAN (*softly*): I'm sure it's he! Just think!

(EILERT LØVBORG *enters, right. He is slim, gaunt. Of* TESMAN's *age, but he looks older and somewhat dissipated. Brown hair and beard. Pale, longish face, reddish spots on the cheekbones. Dressed for visiting in elegant, black, brand-new suit. He carries a silk hat and dark gloves in his hand. He remains near the door, makes a quick bow. He appears a little embarrassed.*)

TESMAN (*goes over to him, shakes his hand*): My dear Eilert — at last we meet again!

EILERT LØVBORG (*subdued voice*): Thanks for your note, Jørgen! (*Approaching* HEDDA.) Am I allowed to shake your hand, too, Mrs. Tesman?

HEDDA (*accepting his proffered hand*): I am very glad to see you, Mr. Løvborg. (*With a gesture.*) I don't know if you two gentlemen —

LØVBORG (*with a slight bow*): Judge Brack, I believe.

BRACK (*also bowing lightly*): Certainly. Some years ago —

TESMAN (*to* LØVBORG, *both hands on his shoulders*): And now I want you to feel quite at home here, Eilert! Isn't that right, Hedda? For you plan to stay here in town, I understand. Hm?

LØVBORG: Yes, I do.

TESMAN: Perfectly reasonable. Listen — I just got hold of your new book, but I haven't had a chance to read it yet.

LØVBORG: You may save yourself the trouble.

TESMAN: Why do you say that?

LØVBORG: There's not much to it.

TESMAN: Just think — you saying that!

BRACK: Nevertheless, people seem to have very good things to say about it.

LØVBORG: That's exactly why I wrote it — so everybody would like it.

BRACK: Very wise of you.

TESMAN: Yes, but Eilert — !

LØVBORG: For I am trying to rebuild my position. Start all over again.

TESMAN (*with some embarrassment*): Yes, I suppose you are, aren't you? Hm?

LØVBORG (*smiles, puts his hat down, pulls a parcel out of his pocket*): When *this* appears — Jørgen Tesman — this you must read. For this is the real thing. This is me.

TESMAN: Oh really? And what is it?

LØVBORG: The continuation.

TESMAN: Continuation? Of what?

LØVBORG: Of the book.

TESMAN: Of the new book?

LØVBORG: Of course.

TESMAN: But Eilert — you've carried the story all the way up to the present!

LØVBORG: So I have. And this is about the future.

TESMAN: The future! But, heavens — we don't know a thing about the future!

LØVBORG: No, we don't. But there are a couple of things to be said about it all the same. (*Unwraps the parcel.*) Here, let me show you —

TESMAN: But that's not your handwriting.

LØVBORG: I have dictated it. (*Leafs through portions of the manuscript.*) It's in two parts. The first is about the forces that will shape the civilization of the future. And the second (*riffling through more pages*) — about the course which that future civilization will take.

TESMAN: How remarkable! It would never occur to me to write anything like that.

HEDDA (*over by the French doors, her fingers drumming the pane*): Hmm — I dare say —

LØVBORG (*replacing the manuscript in its wrappings and putting it down on the table*): I brought it along, for I thought maybe I'd read parts of it aloud to you this evening.

TESMAN: That's very good of you, Eilert. But this evening — ? (*Looks at BRACK.*) I'm not quite sure how to arrange that —

LØVBORG: Some other time, then. There's no hurry.

BRACK: You see, Mr. Løvborg, there's a little get-together over at my house tonight. Mainly for Tesman, you know —

LØVBORG (*looking for his hat*): In that case, I certainly won't —

BRACK: No, listen. Won't you do me the pleasure to join us?

LØVBORG (*firmly*): No, I won't. But thanks all the same.

BRACK: Oh come on! Why don't you do that? We'll be a small, select circle. And I think I can promise you a fairly lively evening, as Hed — as Mrs. Tesman would say.

LØVBORG: I don't doubt that. Nevertheless —

BRACK: And you may bring your manuscript along and read aloud to Tesman over at my house. I have plenty of room.

TESMAN: Just think, Eilert! Wouldn't that be nice, hm?

HEDDA (*intervening*): But can't you see that Mr. Løvborg doesn't want to? I'm sure he would rather stay here and have supper with me.

LØVBORG (*looks at her*): With you, Mrs. Tesman?

HEDDA: And with Mrs. Elvsted.

LØVBORG: Ah — ! (*Casually.*) I ran into her at noon today.

HEDDA: Oh? Well, she'll be here tonight. So you see your presence is really required, Mr. Løvborg. Otherwise she won't have anybody to see her home.

LØVBORG: True. All right, then, Mrs. Tesman — I'll stay, thank you.

HEDDA: Good. I'll just tell the maid. (*She rings for BERTE over by the door, right.*)

(BERTE *appears just off stage.* HEDDA *talks with her in a low voice, points toward the inner room.* BERTE *nods and exits.*)

TESMAN (*while* HEDDA *and* BERTE *are talking, to* LØVBORG): Tell me, Eilert — is it this new subject — about the future — is that what you plan to lecture on?

LØVBORG: Yes.

TESMAN: For the bookseller told me you have announced a lecture series for this fall.

LØVBORG: Yes, I have. I hope you won't mind too much.

TESMAN: Of course not! But —

LØVBORG: For of course I realize it is rather awkward for you.

TESMAN (*unhappily*): Oh well — I certainly can't expect — that just for my sake —

LØVBORG: But I will wait till you receive your appointment.

TESMAN: Wait? But — but — but — you mean you aren't going to compete with me? Hm?

LØVBORG: No. Just triumph over you. In people's opinion.

TESMAN: Oh, for goodness' sake! Then Aunt Julle was right, after all! I knew it all the time. Hedda! Do you hear that! Just think — Eilert Løvborg isn't going to stand in our way after all.

HEDDA (*tersely*): Our? I have nothing to do with this.

(HEDDA *walks into the inner room, where* BERTE *is bringing in a tray with decanters and glasses.* HEDDA *nods her approval and comes forward again.*)

TESMAN (*during the foregoing business*): How about that, Judge? What do you say to this? Hm?

BRACK: I say that moral victory and all that — hm — may be glorious enough and beautiful enough —

TESMAN: Oh, I agree. All the same —

HEDDA (*looks at* TESMAN *with a cold smile*): You look thunderstruck.

TESMAN: Well, I am — pretty much — I really believe —

BRACK: After all, Mrs. Tesman, that was quite a thunderstorm that just passed over.

HEDDA (*points to the inner room*): How about a glass of cold punch, gentlemen?

BRACK (*looks at his watch*): A stirrup cup. Not a bad idea.

TESMAN: Splendid, Hedda. Perfectly splendid. In such a lighthearted mood as I am now —

HEDDA: Please. You, too, Mr. Løvborg.

LØVBORG (*with a gesture of refusal*): No, thanks. Really. Nothing for me.

BRACK: Good heavens, man! Cold punch isn't poison, you know!

LØVBORG: Perhaps not for everybody.

HEDDA: I'll keep Mr. Løvborg company in the meantime.

TESMAN: All right, Hedda. You do that.

(*He and* BRACK *go into the inner room, sit down, drink punch, smoke cigarettes, and engage in lively conversation during the next scene.* EILERT LØVBORG *remains standing near the stove.* HEDDA *walks over to the desk.*)

HEDDA (*her voice a little louder than usual*): I'll show you some pictures, if you like. You see — Tesman and I, we took a trip through Tyrol on our way back.

(*She brings an album over to the table by the sofa. She sits down in the far corner of the sofa.* LØVBORG *approaches, stops, looks at her. He takes a chair and sits down at her left, his back toward the inner room.*)

HEDDA (*opens the album*): Do you see these mountains, Mr. Løvborg? They are the Ortler group. Tesman has written their name below. Here it is: "The Ortler group near Meran."

LØVBORG (*has looked steadily at her all this time. Says slowly*): Hedda — Gabler!

HEDDA (*with a quick glance sideways*): Not that! Shhh!

LØVBORG (*again*): Hedda Gabler!

HEDDA (*looking at the album*): Yes, that used to be my name. When — when we two knew each other.

LØVBORG: And so from now on — for the whole rest of my life — I must get used to never again saying Hedda Gabler.

HEDDA (*still occupied with the album*): Yes, you must. And you might as well start right now. The sooner the better, I think.

LØVBORG (*with indignation*): Hedda Gabler married? And married to — Jørgen Tesman!

HEDDA: Yes — that's the way it goes.

LØVBORG: Oh, Hedda, Hedda — how could you throw yourself away like that!

HEDDA (*with a fierce glance at him*): What's this? I won't have any of that!

LØVBORG: What do you mean?

(TESMAN *enters from the inner room.*)

HEDDA (*hears him coming and remarks casually*): And this here, Mr. Løvborg, this is from somewhere in the Ampezzo valley. Just look at those peaks over there. (*With a kindly look at* TESMAN.) What did you say those peaks were called, dear?

TESMAN: Let me see. Oh, they — they are the Dolomites.

HEDDA: Right. Those are the Dolomites, Mr. Løvborg.

TESMAN: Hedda, I thought I'd just ask you if you don't want me to bring you some punch, after all? For you, anyway? Hm?

HEDDA: Well, yes; thanks. And a couple of cookies, maybe.

TESMAN: No cigarettes?

HEDDA: No.

TESMAN: All right.

(*He returns to the inner room, then turns right.* BRACK *is in there, keeping an eye on* HEDDA *and* LØVBORG *from time to time.*)

LØVBORG (*still in a low voice*): Answer me, Hedda. How could you do a thing like that?

HEDDA (*apparently engrossed in the album*): If you keep on using my first name I won't talk to you.

LØVBORG: Not even when we're alone?

HEDDA: No. You may think it, but you must not say it.

LØVBORG: I see. It offends your love for — Jørgen Tesman.

HEDDA (*glances at him, smiles*): Love? That's a good one!

LØVBORG: Not love, then.

HEDDA: But no infidelities, either! I won't have it.

LØVBORG: Hedda — answer me just one thing —

HEDDA: Shhh!

(TESMAN *enters with a tray from the inner room.*)

TESMAN: Here! Here are the goodies. (*Puts the tray down.*)

HEDDA: Why don't you get Berte to do it?

TESMAN (*pouring punch*): Because I think it's so much fun waiting on you, Hedda.

HEDDA: But you've filled both glasses. And Mr. Løvborg didn't want any —

TESMAN: I know, but Mrs. Elvsted will soon be here, won't she?

HEDDA: That's right. So she will.

TESMAN: Had you forgotten about her? Hm?

HEDDA: We've been so busy looking at this. (*Shows him a picture.*) Remember that little village?

TESMAN: That's the one just below the Brenner Pass, isn't it? We spent the night there —

HEDDA: — and ran into that lively crowd of summer guests.

TESMAN: Right! Just think — if we only could have had you with us, Eilert! Oh well.

(*Returns to the inner room, sits down, and resumes his conversation with* BRACK.)

LØVBORG: Just tell me this, Hedda —

HEDDA: What?

LØVBORG: Wasn't there love in your feelings for me, either? Not a touch — not a shimmer of love? Wasn't there?

HEDDA: I wonder. To me, we seemed to be simply two good comrades. Two close friends. (*Smiles.*) You, particularly, were very frank.

LØVBORG: You wanted it that way.

HEDDA: And yet — when I look back upon it now, there was something beautiful, something thrilling, something brave, I think, about the secret frankness — that comradeship that not a single soul so much as suspected.

LØVBORG: Yes, wasn't there, Hedda? Wasn't there? When I called on your father in the afternoons — And the General sat by the window with his newspapers — his back turned —

HEDDA: And we two in the sofa in the corner —

LØVBORG: — always with the same illustrated magazine —

HEDDA: — for want of an album, yes —

LØVBORG: Yes, Hedda — and then when I confessed to you — ! Told you all about myself, things the others didn't know. Sat and told you about my orgies by day and night. Dissipation day in and day out! Oh, Hedda — what sort of power in you was it that forced me to tell you things like that?

HEDDA: You think there was some power in me?

LØVBORG: How else can I explain it? And all those veiled questions you asked —

HEDDA: — which you understood so perfectly well —

LØVBORG: That you could ask such questions! With such complete frankness!

HEDDA: *Veiled,* if you please.

LØVBORG: But frankly all the same. All about — that!

HEDDA: And to think that you answered, Mr. Løvborg!

LØVBORG: Yes, that's just what I can't understand — now, afterwards. But tell me, Hedda; wasn't love at the bottom of our whole relationship? Didn't you feel some kind of urge to — purify me — when I came to you in confession? Wasn't that it?

HEDDA: No, not quite.

LØVBORG: Then what made you do it?

HEDDA: Do you find it so very strange that a young girl — when she can do so, without anyone knowing —

LØVBORG: Yes — ?

HEDDA: — that she wants to take a peek into a world which —

LØVBORG: — which — ?

HEDDA: — she is not supposed to know anything about?

LØVBORG: So that was it!

HEDDA: That, too. That, too — I think —

LØVBORG: Companionship in the lust for life. But why couldn't *that* at least have continued?

HEDDA: That was your own fault.

LØVBORG: You were the one who broke off.

HEDDA: Yes, when reality threatened to enter our relationship. Shame on you, Eilert Løvborg! How could you want to do a thing like that to your frank and trusting comrade!

LØVBORG (*clenching his hands*): Oh, why didn't you do it! Why didn't you shoot me down, as you said you would!

HEDDA: Because I'm scared of scandal.

LØVBORG: Yes, Hedda. You are really a coward.

HEDDA: A terrible coward. (*Changing her tone.*) But that was your good luck, wasn't it? And now the Elvsteds have healed your broken heart very nicely.

LØVBORG: I know what Thea has told you.

HEDDA: Perhaps you have told her about us?

LØVBORG: Not a word. She is too stupid to understand.

HEDDA: Stupid?

LØVBORG: In things like that.

HEDDA: And I'm a coward. (*Leans forward, without looking in his eyes, whispers.*) But now I am going to confess something to *you.*

LØVBORG (*tense*): What?

HEDDA: That I didn't dare to shoot —

LØVBORG: Yes — ?

HEDDA: — that was not the worst of my cowardice that night.

LØVBORG (*looks at her a moment, understands, whispers passionately*): Oh, Hedda! Hedda Gabler! Now I begin to see what was behind the companionship! You and I! So it *was* your lust for life — !

HEDDA (*in a low voice, with an angry glance*): Take care! Don't you believe it!

(*Darkness is falling. The door, right, is opened, and* BERTE *enters.*)

HEDDA (*closing the album, calls out, smiling*): At last! So there you are, dearest Thea! Come in!

(MRS. ELVSTED *enters. She is dressed for a party.* BERTE *exits, closing the door behind her.*)

HEDDA (*on the sofa, reaching out for* MRS. ELVSTED): Sweetest Thea, you have no idea how I've waited for you.

(*In passing,* MRS. ELVSTED *exchanges quick greetings with* TESMAN *and* BRACK *in the inner room. She walks up to the table and shakes* HEDDA'S *hand.* EILERT LØVBORG *rises. He and* MRS. ELVSTED *greet one another with a silent nod.*)

MRS. ELVSTED: Shouldn't I go in and say hello to your husband?

HEDDA: No, never mind that. Leave them alone. They're soon leaving, anyway.

MRS. ELVSTED: Leaving?

HEDDA: They're going out to drink.

MRS. ELVSTED (*quickly, to* LØVBORG): Not you?

LØVBORG: No.

HEDDA: Mr. Løvborg stays here with us.

MRS. ELVSTED (*pulls up a chair, is about to sit down next to* LØVBORG): Oh, how wonderful it is to be here!

HEDDA: Oh no, little Thea. Not that. Not there. Over here by me, please. *I* want to be in the middle.

MRS. ELVSTED: Just as you like. (*She walks in front of the table and seats herself on the*

sofa, on HEDDA'S *right.* LØVBORG *sits down again on his chair.*)

LØVBORG (*after a brief pause, to* HEDDA): Isn't she lovely to look at?

HEDDA (*gently stroking her hair*): Just to look at?

LØVBORG: Yes. For you see — she and I — we are real comrades. We have absolute faith in one another. And we can talk together in full freedom.

HEDDA: Unveiled, Mr. Løvborg?

LØVBORG: Well —

MRS. ELVSTED (*in a low voice, clinging to* HEDDA): Oh, I am so happy, Hedda! For just think — he also says I have inspired him!

HEDDA (*looks at her with a smile*): No, really! He says that?

LØVBORG: And she has such courage, Mrs. Tesman! Such courage of action.

MRS. ELVSTED: Oh, my God — courage — ! I!

LØVBORG: Infinite courage — when it concerns the comrade.

HEDDA: Yes, courage — if one only had that.

LØVBORG: What then?

HEDDA: Then maybe life would be tolerable, after all. (*Changing her tone.*) But now, dearest Thea, you want a glass of nice, cold punch.

MRS. ELVSTED: No, thanks. I never drink things like that.

HEDDA: Then what about you, Mr. Løvborg?

LØVBORG: Thanks. Nothing for me, either.

MRS. ELVSTED: No, nothing for him, either.

HEDDA (*looks firmly at him*): If I say so?

LØVBORG: Makes no difference.

HEDDA (*laughs*): Oh dear! So I have no power over you at all. Is that it?

LØVBORG: Not in that respect.

HEDDA: Seriously, though; I really think you should. For your own sake.

MRS. ELVSTED: No, but Hedda — !

LØVBORG: Why so?

HEDDA: Or rather for people's sake.

LØVBORG: Oh?

HEDDA: For else they might think you don't really trust yourself — That you lack self-confidence —

MRS. ELVSTED (*softly*): Don't, Hedda!

LØVBORG: People may think whatever they like for all I care — for the time being.

MRS. ELVSTED (*happy*): Exactly!

HEDDA: I could easily tell from watching Judge Brack just now.

LØVBORG: Tell what?

HEDDA: He smiled so contemptuously when you didn't dare to join them in there.

LØVBORG: Didn't I dare to! It's just that I'd much rather stay here and talk with you!

MRS. ELVSTED: But that's only natural, Hedda.

HEDDA: The Judge had no way of knowing that. And I also noticed he smiled and looked at Tesman when you didn't dare to go to his silly old party.

LØVBORG: Didn't dare! Are you saying I didn't dare?

HEDDA: *I* am not. But that's how Judge Brack understood it.

LØVBORG: Let him.

HEDDA: So you're not going?

LØVBORG: I'm staying here with you and Thea.

MRS. ELVSTED: Of course, he is, Hedda!

HEDDA (*smiles, nods approvingly*): That's what I call firm foundations. Principled forever; that's the way a man ought to be! (*Turning to* MRS. ELVSTED, *stroking her cheek.*) What did I tell you this morning — when you came here, quite beside yourself — ?

LØVBORG (*puzzled*): Beside herself?

MRS. ELVSTED (*in terror*): Hedda — Hedda — don't!

HEDDA: Now do you see? There was no need at all for that mortal fear of yours — (*Interrupting herself.*) There, now! Now we can all three relax and enjoy ourselves.

LØVBORG (*startled*): What's all this, Mrs. Tesman?

MRS. ELVSTED: Oh, God, Hedda — what are you saying? What are you doing?

HEDDA: Please be quiet. That horrible Judge is looking at you.

LØVBORG: In mortal fear? So that's it. For my sake.

MRS. ELVSTED (*softly, wailing*): Oh, Hedda — if you only knew how utterly miserable you have made me!

LØVBORG (*stares at her for a moment. His face is distorted*): So that was the comrade's happy confidence in me!

MRS. ELVSTED: Oh, my dearest friend — listen to me first — !

LØVBORG (*picks up one of the glasses of punch, raises it, says hoarsely*): Here's to you, Thea! (*Empties the glass, puts it down, picks up the other one.*)

MRS. ELVSTED (*softly*): Hedda, Hedda — why did you want to do this?

HEDDA: Want to! I! Are you mad?

LØVBORG: And here's to you, too, Mrs. Tesman! Thanks for telling me the truth. Long live the truth! (*He drains the glass and is about to fill it again.*)

HEDDA (*restrains him*): That's enough for now. Remember you are going to a party.

MRS. ELVSTED: No, no, no!

HEDDA: Shhh! They are looking at you.

LØVBORG (*puts his glass down*): Listen, Thea — tell me the truth —

MRS. ELVSTED: I will, I will!

LØVBORG: Did your husband know you were coming after me?

MRS. ELVSTED (*wringing her hands*): Oh, Hedda — do you hear what he's asking?

LØVBORG: Did the two of you agree that you were to come here and look after me? Maybe it was his idea, even? Did he send you? Ah, I know what it was — he missed me in the office, didn't he? Or was it at the card table?

MRS. ELVSTED (*softly, in agony*): Oh, Løvborg, Løvborg!

LØVBORG (*grabs a glass and is about to fill it*): Here's to the old Commissioner, too!

HEDDA (*stops him*): No more now. You're supposed to read aloud for Tesman tonight — remember?

LØVBORG (*calm again, puts the glass down*): This was silly of me, Thea. I'm sorry. Taking it this way. Please, don't be angry with me. You'll see — both you and all those others — that even if I have been down — ! With your help, Thea — dear comrade.

MRS. ELVSTED (*beaming*): Oh, thank God — !

(*In the meantime,* BRACK *has looked at his watch. He and* TESMAN *get up and come forward.*)

BRACK (*picking up his coat and hat*): Well, Mrs. Tesman; our time is up.

HEDDA: I suppose it is.

LØVBORG (*rising*): Mine, too, Judge.

MRS. ELVSTED (*softly, pleadingly*): Oh, Løvborg — don't do it!

HEDDA (*pinches her arm*): They can hear you!

MRS. ELVSTED (*with a soft exclamation*): Ouch!

LØVBORG (*to* BRACK): You were good enough to ask me —

BRACK: So you're coming, after all?

LØVBORG: If I may.

BRACK: I'm delighted.

LØVBORG (*picks up his manuscript and says*

to TESMAN): For there are a couple of things here I'd like to show you before I send it off.

TESMAN: Just think! Isn't that nice! But — dearest Hedda — ? In that case, how are you going to get Mrs. Elvsted home? Hm?

HEDDA: We'll manage somehow.

LØVBORG (*looking at the two women*): Mrs. Elvsted? I'll be back to pick her up, of course. (*Coming closer.*) About ten o'clock, Mrs. Tesman? Is that convenient?

HEDDA: Certainly. That will be fine.

TESMAN: Then everything is nice and settled. But don't expect me that early, Hedda.

HEDDA: You just stay as long as — as long as you want to, dear.

MRS. ELVSTED (*in secret fear*): I'll be waiting for you here, then, Mr. Løvborg.

LØVBORG (*hat in hand*): Of course, Mrs. Elvsted.

BRACK: All aboard the pleasure train, gentlemen! I hope we'll have a lively evening — as a certain fair lady would say.

HEDDA: Ah — if only the fair lady could be present. Invisibly.

BRACK: Why invisibly?

HEDDA: To listen to some of your unadulterated liveliness, Judge.

BRACK (*laughs*): I shouldn't advise the fair lady to do that!

TESMAN (*also laughing*): You're a good one, Hedda! Just think!

BRACK: Well — good night, ladies!

LØVBORG (*with a bow*): Till about ten, then.

(BRACK, LØVBORG, *and* TESMAN *go out, right. At the same time* BERTE *enters from the inner room with a lighted lamp, which she places on the table, front center. She goes out the same way.*)

MRS. ELVSTED (*has risen and paces restlessly up and down*): Hedda, Hedda — how do you think all this will end?

HEDDA: At ten o'clock he'll be here. I see him already. With vine leaves in his hair. Flushed and confident.

MRS. ELVSTED: I only hope you're right.

HEDDA: For then, you see, he'll have mastered himself. And be a free man for all the days of his life.

MRS. ELVSTED: Dear God — how I hope you are right! That he'll come back like that.

HEDDA: That is the way he will come. No other way. (*She rises and goes closer to* MRS. ELVSTED.) *You* may doubt as long as you like. I believe in him. And now we'll see —

MRS. ELVSTED: There is something behind all this, Hedda. Some hidden purpose.

HEDDA: Yes, there is! For once in my life I want to have power over a human destiny.

MRS. ELVSTED: But don't you already?

HEDDA: I don't and I never have.

MRS. ELVSTED: But your husband — ?

HEDDA: You think that's worth the trouble? Oh, if you knew how poor I am! And you got to be so rich! (*Embraces her passionately.*) I think I'll have to burn your hair off, after all!

MRS. ELVSTED: Let me go! Let me go! You scare me, Hedda!

BERTE (*in the doorway*): Supper is served, ma'am.

HEDDA: Good. We're coming.

MRS. ELVSTED: No, no, no! I'd rather go home by myself! Right now!

HEDDA: Nonsense! You'll have your cup of tea first, you little silly. And then — at ten o'clock — Eilert Løvborg comes — with vine leaves in his hair! (*She almost pulls* MRS. ELVSTED *toward the doorway.*)

ACT III

The same room at the TESMANS'. *The doorway and the French windows both have their portieres closed. The lamp, turned half down, is still on the table. The stove is open. Some dying embers can be seen.* MRS. ELVSTED, *wrapped in a big shawl, is in the easy chair near the stove, her feet on a footstool.* HEDDA, *also dressed, is lying on the sofa, covered by a blanket.*

MRS. ELVSTED (*after a while suddenly sits up, listens anxiously; then she wearily sinks back in her chair, whimpers softly*): Oh my God, my God — not yet!

(BERTE *enters cautiously, right, carrying a letter.*)

MRS. ELVSTED (*turns and whispers tensely*): Well — has anybody been here?

BERTE (*in a low voice*): Yes. Just now there was a girl with this letter.

MRS. ELVSTED (*quickly, reaches for it*): A letter! Give it to me.

BERTE: No, ma'am. It's for the Doctor.

MRS. ELVSTED: I see.

BERTE: Miss Tesman's maid brought it. I'll leave it here on the table.

MRS. ELVSTED: All right.

BERTE (*puts the letter down*): I'd better put out the lamp. It just reeks.

MRS. ELVSTED: Yes, do that. It must be daylight soon, anyway.

BERTE (*putting out the lamp*): It's light already, ma'am.

MRS. ELVSTED: Light already! And still not back!

BERTE: No, so help us. Not that I didn't expect as much —

MRS. ELVSTED: You did?

BERTE: Yes, when I saw a certain character was back in town. Taking them off with him. We sure heard enough about him in the old days!

MRS. ELVSTED: Not so loud. You are waking up Mrs. Tesman.

BERTE (*looks toward the sofa, sighs*): God forbid —! Let her sleep, poor thing. Do you want me to get the fire going again?

MRS. ELVSTED: Not on my account, thank you.

BERTE: All right. (*Exits quietly, right.*)

HEDDA (*awakened by the closing door*): What's that?

MRS. ELVSTED: Just the maid.

HEDDA (*looks around*): Why in here —? Oh, I remember! (*Sits up, rubs her eyes, stretches.*) What time is it, Thea?

MRS. ELVSTED (*looks at her watch*): Past seven.

HEDDA: When did Tesman get home?

MRS. ELVSTED: He didn't.

HEDDA: Not home yet!

MRS. ELVSTED (*getting up*): Nobody's come.

HEDDA: And we waited till four!

MRS. ELVSTED (*wringing her hands*): And how we waited!

HEDDA (*her hand covering a yawn*): We — ll. We could have saved ourselves that trouble.

MRS. ELVSTED: Did you get any sleep at all?

HEDDA: Yes, I slept pretty well, I think. Didn't you?

MRS. ELVSTED: Not a wink. I just couldn't, Hedda! It was just impossible.

HEDDA (*rises, walks over to her*): Well, now! There's nothing to worry about, for heaven's sake. I know exactly what's happened.

MRS. ELVSTED: Then tell me please. Where do you think they are?

HEDDA: Well, first of all, I'm sure they were terribly late leaving the Judge's —

MRS. ELVSTED: Dear, yes. I'm sure you're right. Still —

HEDDA: — and so Tesman didn't want to wake us up in the middle of the night. (*Laughs.*) Maybe he didn't want us to see him, either — after a party like that.

MRS. ELVSTED: But where do you think he has gone?

HEDDA: To the aunts', of course. His old room is still there, all ready for him.

MRS. ELVSTED: No, he can't be there. Just a few minutes ago there came a letter for him from Miss Tesman. It's over there.

HEDDA: Oh? (*Looks at the envelope.*) So it is — Auntie Julle herself. In that case, I suppose he's still at Brack's. And there's Eilert Løvborg, too — reading aloud, with vine leaves in his hair.

MRS. ELVSTED: Oh Hedda — you're only saying things you don't believe yourself.

HEDDA: My, what a little imbecile you really are, Thea!

MRS. ELVSTED: Yes, I suppose I am.

HEDDA: And you look dead tired, too.

MRS. ELVSTED: I *am* dead tired.

HEDDA: Why don't you do as I say. Go into my room and lie down.

MRS. ELVSTED: No, no — I wouldn't be able to go to sleep, anyway.

HEDDA: Of course, you would.

MRS. ELVSTED: And your husband is bound to be home any minute now. And I have to know right away.

HEDDA: I'll let you know as soon as he gets here.

MRS. ELVSTED: You promise me that, Hedda?

HEDDA: I do. You just go to sleep.

MRS. ELVSTED: Thanks. At least I'll try. (*Exits through inner room.*)

(HEDDA *goes to the French doors, opens the portieres. The room is now in full daylight. She picks up a little hand mirror from the desk, looks at herself, smooths her hair. Walks over to door, right, rings the bell for the maid.* BERTE *presently appears.*)

BERTE: You want something, ma'am?

HEDDA: Yes. You'll have to start the fire again. I'm cold.

BERTE: Yes, ma'am! I'll get it warm in no time. (*Rakes the embers together and puts in another piece of wood. Then she suddenly listens.*) There's the doorbell, ma'am.

HEDDA: All right. See who it is. I'll take care of the stove myself.

BERTE: You'll have a nice blaze going in a minute. (*Exits right.*)

(HEDDA *kneels on the footstool and puts in more pieces of wood. Presently* TESMAN *enters, right. He looks tired and somber. He tiptoes toward the doorway and is about to disappear between the portieres.*)

HEDDA (*by the stove, without looking up*): Good morning.

TESMAN (*turning*): Hedda! (*Comes closer.*) For heaven's sake — you up already! Hm?

HEDDA: Yes, I got up very early this morning.

TESMAN: And I was sure you'd still be sound asleep! Just think!

HEDDA: Not so loud. Mrs. Elvsted is asleep in my room.

TESMAN: Mrs. Elvsted stayed here all night?

HEDDA: Yes. Nobody came for her, you know.

TESMAN: No, I suppose —

HEDDA (*closes the stove, rises*): Well, did you have a good time at the Judge's?

TESMAN: Were you worried about me? Hm?

HEDDA: I'd never dream of worrying about you. I asked if you had a good time.

TESMAN: Yes, indeed. Nice for a change anyway. But I think I liked it best early in the evening. For then Eilert read to me. Just think — we were more than an hour early! And Brack, of course, had things to see to. So Eilert read.

HEDDA (*sits down at the right side of the table*): So? Tell me all about it.

TESMAN (*sits down on an ottoman near the stove*): Oh Hedda, you'll never believe what a book that will be! It must be just the most remarkable thing ever written! Just think!

HEDDA: Yes, but I don't really care about that —

TESMAN: I must tell you, Hedda — I have a confession to make. As he was reading — something ugly came over me —

HEDDA: Ugly?

TESMAN: I sat there envying Eilert for being able to write like that! Just think, Hedda!

HEDDA: All right. I'm thinking!

TESMAN: And yet, with all his gifts — he's incorrigible, after all.

HEDDA: I suppose you mean he has more courage for life than the rest of you?

TESMAN: No, no — I don't mean that. I mean that he's incapable of exercising moderation in his pleasures.

HEDDA: What happened — in the end?

TESMAN: Well — I would call it bacchanal, Hedda.

HEDDA: Did he have vine leaves in his hair?

TESMAN: Vine leaves? No, I didn't notice any vine leaves. But he gave a long, muddled speech in honor of the woman who had inspired him in his work. Those were his words.

HEDDA: Did he mention her name?

TESMAN: No, he didn't. But I'm sure it must be Mrs. Elvsted. You just wait and see if I'm not right!

HEDDA: And where did you and he part company?

TESMAN: On the way back to town. We left — the last of us did — at the same time. And Brack came along, too, to get some fresh air. Then we decided we'd better see Eilert home. You see, he had had altogether too much to drink!

HEDDA: I can imagine.

TESMAN: But then the strangest thing of all happened, Hedda! Or maybe I should say the saddest. I'm almost ashamed — on Eilert's behalf — even talking about it.

HEDDA: Well — ?

TESMAN: You see, on the way back I happened to be behind the others a little. Just for a minute or two — you know —

HEDDA: All right, all right — !

TESMAN: And when I hurried to catch up with them, can you guess what I found by the roadside? Hm?

HEDDA: How can I possibly — ?

TESMAN: You mustn't tell this to a living soul, Hedda! Do you hear! Promise me that, for Eilert's sake. (*Pulls a parcel out of his coat pocket.*) Just think — I found this!

HEDDA: Isn't that what he had with him here yesterday?

TESMAN: Yes! It's his whole, precious, irreplaceable manuscript! And he had dropped it — just like that! Without even noticing! Just think, Hedda! Isn't that awfully sad?

HEDDA: But why didn't you give it back to him?

TESMAN: In the condition he was in! Dear — I just didn't dare to.

HEDDA: And you didn't tell any of the others that you had found it, either?

TESMAN: Of course not. I didn't want to, for Eilert's sake — don't you see?

HEDDA: So nobody knows that you have Eilert Løvborg's papers?

TESMAN: Nobody. And nobody must know, either.

HEDDA: And what did you and he talk about afterwards?

TESMAN: I didn't have a chance to talk to him at all after that. For when we came into town, he and a couple of the others simply vanished. Just think!

HEDDA: Oh? I expect they took him home.

TESMAN: I suppose that must be it. And Brack took off on his own, too.

HEDDA: And what have you been doing with yourself since then?

TESMAN: Well, you see, I and some of the others went home with one of the younger fellows and had a cup of early morning coffee. Or night coffee maybe, rather. Hm? And now, after I've rested a bit and poor Eilert's had some sleep, I'll take this back to him.

HEDDA (reaches for the parcel): No — don't do that! Not right away, I mean. Let me look at it first.

TESMAN: Dearest Hedda — honestly, I just don't dare to.

HEDDA: Don't you dare to?

TESMAN: No, for I'm sure you realize how utterly desperate he'll be when he wakes up and finds that the manuscript is gone. For he hasn't a copy, you know. He said so himself.

HEDDA (looks searchingly at him): But can't a thing like that be written over again?

TESMAN: Hardly. I really don't think so. For, you see — the inspiration —

HEDDA: Yes, I daresay that's the main thing. (Casually.) By the way, here's a letter for you.

TESMAN: Imagine!

HEDDA (gives it to him): It came early this morning.

TESMAN: It's from Aunt Julle, Hedda! I wonder what it can be. (Puts the manuscript down on the other ottoman, opens the letter, skims the content, jumps up.) Oh Hedda! She says here that poor Aunt Rina is dying!

HEDDA: You know we had to expect that.

TESMAN: And if I want to see her again I had better hurry. I'll rush over right away.

HEDDA (suppressing a smile): You'll rush?

TESMAN: Dearest Hedda of mine — if only you could bring yourself to come along! Hm?

HEDDA (rises, weary, with an air of refusal): No, no. You mustn't ask me that. I don't want to look at death and disease. I don't want anything to do with ugliness.

TESMAN: Well, all right — (Rushing around.) My hat? My coat? Oh — out here in the hall. I just hope I won't be too late, Hedda. Hm?

HEDDA: Oh I'm sure that if you rush —

(BERTE appears in the door, right.)

BERTE: Judge Brack is here and wants to know if he may see you.

TESMAN: At this hour! No, no. I can't possibly see him now!

HEDDA: But I can. (To BERTE.) Tell the Judge please to come in.

(BERTE exits.)

HEDDA (with a quick whisper): Tesman! The package! (She grabs it from the ottoman.)

TESMAN: Yes! Give it to me!

HEDDA: No, no. I'll hide it for you till later.

(She walks over to the desk and sticks the parcel in among the books on the shelf. In his hurry TESMAN is having difficulties getting his gloves on. JUDGE BRACK enters, right.)

HEDDA (nods to him): If you aren't an early bird —

BRACK: Yes, don't you think so? (To TESMAN.) You're going out, too?

TESMAN: Yes, I must go and see the aunts. Just think, the invalid — she's dying!

BRACK: Oh, I'm terribly sorry! In that case, don't let me keep you. At such a moment —

TESMAN: Yes, I really must run. Goodbye, goodbye! (Hurries out, right.)

HEDDA (approaching BRACK): It appears that things were quite lively last night over at your house.

BRACK: Indeed, Mrs. Tesman — I didn't get to bed at all.

HEDDA: You didn't either?

BRACK: As you see. But tell me — what has Tesman told you about the night's adventures?

HEDDA: Just some tiresome story about having coffee with somebody someplace —

BRACK: I believe I know all about that coffee. Eilert Løvborg wasn't one of them, was he?

HEDDA: No, they had taken him home first.

BRACK: Tesman, too?

HEDDA: No. Some of the others, he said.

BRACK (*smiles*): Jørgen Tesman is really an ingenuous soul, you know.

HEDDA: He certainly is. But why do you say that? Is there something more to all this?

BRACK: Yes, there is.

HEDDA: Well! In that case, why don't we make ourselves comfortable, Judge. You'll tell your story better, too.

(*She sits down at the left side of the table,* BRACK *near her at the adjacent side.*)

HEDDA: All right?

BRACK: For reasons of my own I wanted to keep track of my guests' movements last night. Or, rather — some of my guests.

HEDDA: Eilert Løvborg was one of them, perhaps?

BRACK: As a matter of fact — he was.

HEDDA: Now you are really making me curious.

BRACK: Do you know where he and a couple of the others spent the rest of the night, Mrs. Tesman?

HEDDA: No — tell me. If it can be told.

BRACK: Oh, certainly. They turned up at an exceptionally gay early morning gathering.

HEDDA: Of the lively kind?

BRACK: Of the liveliest.

HEDDA: A little more about this, Judge.

BRACK: Løvborg had been invited beforehand. I knew about that. But he had declined. He is a reformed character, you know.

HEDDA: As of his stay with the Elvsteds — yes. But he went after all?

BRACK: Well, yes, you see, Mrs. Tesman — unfortunately, the spirit moved him over at my house last evening.

HEDDA: Yes, I understand he became inspired.

BRACK: Quite violently inspired. And that, I gather, must have changed his mind. You know, we men don't always have as much integrity as we ought to have.

HEDDA: Oh, I'm sure you're an exception, Judge Brack. But about Løvborg — ?

BRACK: To make a long story short — he ended up at Miss Diana's establishment.

HEDDA: Miss Diana's?

BRACK: She was the hostess at this gathering — a select circle of intimate friends, male and female.

HEDDA: Is she a redhead, by any chance?

BRACK: That's correct.

HEDDA: And a singer — of sorts?

BRACK: Yes — that, too. And a mighty huntress — of men, Mrs. Tesman. You seem to have heard of her. Eilert Løvborg used to be one of her most devoted protectors in his more affluent days.

HEDDA: And how did it all end?

BRACK: Not in a very friendly fashion, apparently. It seems that after the tenderest reception Miss Diana resorted to brute force —

HEDDA: Against Løvborg?

BRACK: Yes. He accused her or her women friends of having stolen something of his. Said his wallet was gone. And other things, too. In brief, he's supposed to have started a pretty wicked row.

HEDDA: And — ?

BRACK: Well — there was a general free-for-all — men and women both. Fortunately, the police stepped in —

HEDDA: The police — !

BRACK: Yes. But I'm afraid this will be an expensive escapade for Eilert Løvborg, crazy fool that he is.

HEDDA: Well!

BRACK: It appears that he made quite violent objection — struck an officer in the car and tore his coat. So they had to take him along.

HEDDA: How do you know all this?

BRACK: From the police.

HEDDA (*staring straight ahead*): So that's how it was. No vine leaves in his hair.

BRACK: Vine leaves, Mrs. Tesman?

HEDDA (*changing her tone*): But tell me, Judge Brack — why did you keep such a close watch on Eilert Løvborg?

BRACK: Well — for one thing, it is obviously of some concern to me if he testifies that he came straight from my party.

HEDDA: So you think there will be an investigation?

BRACK: Naturally. But I suppose that doesn't really matter too much. However, as a friend of the house I considered it my duty to give you and Tesman a full account of his nighttime exploits.

HEDDA: Yes, but why?

BRACK: Because I very strongly suspect that he intends to use you as a kind of screen.

HEDDA: Really! Why do you think that?

BRACK: Oh, come now, Mrs. Tesman! We can use our eyes, can't we? This Mrs. Elvsted — she isn't leaving town right away you know.

HEDDA: Well, even if there should be something going on between those two, I'd think there would be plenty of other places they could meet.

BRACK: But no home. After last night, every respectable house will once again be closed to Eilert Løvborg.

HEDDA: And so should mine, you mean?

BRACK: Yes. I admit I would find it more than embarrassing if the gentleman were to become a daily guest here, Mrs. Tesman. If he, as an outsider — a highly dispensable outsider — if he were to intrude himself —

HEDDA: — into the triangle?

BRACK: Precisely. It would amount to homelessness for me.

HEDDA (smiling): Sole cock-o'-the-walk — so, that's your goal, is it, Judge?

BRACK (nods slowly, lowers his voice): Yes. That is my goal. And for that I will fight with every means at my disposal.

HEDDA (her smile fading): You're really a dangerous person, you know — when you come right down to it.

BRACK: You think so?

HEDDA: Yes. I am beginning to think so now. And I must say I am exceedingly glad you don't have any kind of hold on me.

BRACK (with a noncommittal laugh): Well, well, Mrs. Tesman! Maybe there is something to what you are saying, at that. Who knows what I might do if I did.

HEDDA: Really, now, Judge Brack! Are you threatening me?

BRACK (rising): — Nonsense! For the triangle, you see — is best maintained on a voluntary basis.

HEDDA: My sentiments, exactly.

BRACK: Well, I have said what I came to say. And now I should get back to town. Goodbye, Mrs. Tesman! (Walks toward the French doors.)

HEDDA (rises): You're going through the garden?

BRACK: Yes. For me that's a short cut.

HEDDA: Yes, and then it's a back way.

BRACK: Quite true. I have nothing against back ways. There are times when they are most intriguing.

HEDDA: You mean when real ammunition is used?

BRACK (in the doorway, laughs back at her): Oh good heavens! I don't suppose one shoots one's tame roosters!

HEDDA (laughs also): No — not if one has only one — !

(They nod to each other, both still laughing. He leaves. She closes the door behind him. For a few moments she remains by the door, quite serious now, looking into the garden. Then she walks over to the doorway and opens the portieres wide enough to look into the inner room. Goes to the desk, pulls LØVBORG's manuscript from the bookshelf and is about to read it when BERTE's voice, very loud, is heard from the hall, right. HEDDA turns around, listens. She hurriedly puts the manuscript into the drawer of the desk and puts the key down on its top. EILERT LØVBORG, wearing his coat and with his hat in his hand, flings open the door, right. He looks somewhat confused and excited.)

LØVBORG (turned toward the invisible BERTE in the hall): — And I say I must! You can't stop me! (He closes the door, turns, sees HEDDA, immediately controls himself, greets her.)

HEDDA (by the desk): Well, well, Mr. Løvborg — aren't you a trifle late coming for Thea?

LØVBORG: Or a trifle early for calling on you. I apologize.

HEDDA: How do you know she is still here?

LØVBORG: The people she is staying with told me she's been gone all night.

HEDDA (walks over to the table): Did they seem — strange — when they said it?

LØVBORG (puzzled): Strange?

HEDDA: I mean, did they seem to find it a little — unusual?

LØVBORG (suddenly understands): Ah, I see what you mean! Of course! I'm dragging her down with me. No, as a matter of fact, I didn't notice anything. I suppose Tesman isn't up yet?

HEDDA: I — I don't think so —

LØVBORG: When did he get home?

HEDDA: Very late.

LØVBORG: Did he tell you anything?

HEDDA: Yes, he said you'd all had quite a time over at Brack's.

LØVBORG: Just that?

HEDDA: I think so. But I was so awfully sleepy —

(MRS. ELVSTED enters through portieres in the rear.)

MRS ELVSTED (toward him): Oh, Løvborg! At last!

LØVBORG: Yes, at last. And too late.

MRS. ELVSTED (in fear): What is too late?

LØVBORG: Everything is too late now. It's all over with me.

MRS. ELVSTED: Oh no, no! Don't say things like that!

LØVBORG: You'll say the same yourself when you hear —

MRS. ELVSTED: I don't want to hear — !

HEDDA: Maybe you'd rather talk with her alone? I'll leave.

LØVBORG: No stay — you, too. I beg you to.

MRS. ELVSTED: But I don't want to listen, do you hear?

LØVBORG: It isn't last night I want to talk about.

MRS. ELVSTED: What about, then?

LØVBORG: We'll have to part, Thea.

MRS. ELVSTED: Part!

HEDDA (involuntarily): I knew it!

LØVBORG: For I don't need you any more.

MRS. ELVSTED: And you can stand there and tell me a thing like that! Don't need me! Why can't I help you the way I did before? Aren't we going to keep on working together?

LØVBORG: I don't intend to work any more.

MRS. ELVSTED (desperately): What am I going to do with my life, then?

LØVBORG: You'll have to try to live your life as if you'd never known me.

MRS. ELVSTED: But I can't do that!

LØVBORG: Try, Thea. Go back home.

MRS. ELVSTED (agitated): Never again! Where you are I want to be! And you can't chase me away just like that! I want to stay right here! Be with you when the book appears.

HEDDA (in a tense whisper): Ah — yes — the book!

LØVBORG (looks at her): My book — and Thea's. For that's what it is.

MRS. ELVSTED: That's what I feel, too. And that's why I have the right to be with you when it comes out. I want to see all the honor and all the fame you'll get. And the joy — I want to share the joy, too.

LØVBORG: Thea, our book is never going to come out.

HEDDA: Ah!

MRS. ELVSTED: It won't!

LØVBORG: Can't ever appear.

MRS. ELVSTED (with fearful suspicion): Løvborg, what have you done with the manuscript?

HEDDA (watching him tensely): Yes — what about the manuscript?

MRS. ELVSTED: Where is it?

LØVBORG: Oh Thea — please, don't ask me about that!

MRS. ELVSTED: Yes, yes — I want to be told! I have the right to know — right now!

LØVBORG: All right. I've torn it to pieces.

MRS. ELVSTED (screams): Oh, no! No!

HEDDA (involuntarily): But that's not — !

LØVBORG (looks at her): Not true, you think?

HEDDA (composing herself): Well, of course, if you say so. You should know. It just sounds so — so unbelievable.

LØVBORG: All the same, it's true.

MRS. ELVSTED (hands clenched): Oh God — Oh God, Hedda. He has torn his own work to pieces!

LØVBORG: I have torn my whole life to pieces, so why not my life's work as well?

MRS. ELVSTED: And that's what you did last night?

LØVBORG: Yes, I tell you! In a thousand pieces. And scattered them in the fjord. Far out — where the water is clean and salty. Let them drift there, with wind and current. Then they'll sink. Deep, deep down. Like me, Thea.

MRS. ELVSTED: Do you know, Løvborg — this thing you've done to the book — all the rest of my life I'll think of it as killing a little child.

LØVBORG: You are right. It is like murdering a child.

MRS. ELVSTED: But then, how could you? For the child was mine, too!

HEDDA (almost soundlessly): The child —

MRS. ELVSTED (with a deep sigh): So it's all over. I'll go now, Hedda.

HEDDA: But you aren't leaving town?

MRS. ELVSTED: Oh, I don't know myself what I'll do. There's only darkness before me. (Exits, right.)

HEDDA (waits for a moment): Aren't you going to see her home, Mr. Løvborg?

LØVBORG: I? Through the streets? Letting people see her with me?

HEDDA: Of course, I don't know what else may have happened last night. But is it really so absolutely irreparable — ?

LØVBORG: Last night is not the end of it. That I know. And yet, I don't really care for that kind of life any more. Not again. She has broken all the courage for life and all the defiance that was in me.

HEDDA (*staring ahead*): So that sweet little goose has had her hand in a human destiny. (*Looks at him.*) But that you could be so heartless, even so!

LØVBORG: Don't tell me I was heartless!

HEDDA: To ruin everything that's filled her soul for such a long time! You don't call that heartless!

LØVBORG: Hedda — to you I can tell the truth.

HEDDA: The truth?

LØVBORG: But first promise me — give me your word you'll never let Thea know what I'm going to tell you now.

HEDDA: You have it.

LØVBORG: All right. It isn't true, what I just told her.

HEDDA: About the manuscript?

LØVBORG: Yes. I have not torn it up. Not thrown it in the sea, either.

HEDDA: But then — where is it?

LØVBORG: I've destroyed it just the same. Really, I have, Hedda!

HEDDA: I don't understand.

LØVBORG: Thea said that what I had done seemed to her like murdering a child.

HEDDA: Yes — she did.

LØVBORG: But killing a child, that's not the worst thing a father can do to it.

HEDDA: No?

LØVBORG: No. And the worst is what I don't want Thea to know.

HEDDA: What *is* the worst?

LØVBORG: Hedda — suppose a man, say, early in the morning, after a stupid, drunken night — suppose he comes home to his child's mother and says: Listen, I've been in such and such a place. I've been here — and I've been there. And I had our child with me. In all those places. And the child is lost. Gone. Vanished. I'll be damned if I know where it is. Who's got hold of it —

HEDDA: Yes — but when all is said and done — it is only a book, you know.

LØVBORG: Thea's pure soul was in that book.

HEDDA: I realize that.

LØVBORG: Then you surely also realize that she and I can have no future together.

HEDDA: Where do you go from here?

LØVBORG: Nowhere. Just finish everything off. The sooner the better.

HEDDA (*a step closer*): Listen — Eilert Løvborg — Couldn't you make sure it's done beautifully?

LØVBORG: Beautifully? (*Smiles.*) With vine leaves in the hair, as you used to say.

HEDDA: Oh no. I don't believe in vine leaves any more. But still beautifully! For once. Goodbye. Go now. And don't come back.

LØVBORG: Goodbye, Mrs. Tesman. Give my regards to Jørgen Tesman. (*He is about to leave.*)

HEDDA: Wait! I want to give you something — a remembrance. (*Goes to the desk, opens the drawer, takes out the gun case. Returns to* LØVBORG *with one of the revolvers.*)

LØVBORG: The gun? That's the remembrance?

HEDDA (*nods slowly*): Do you recognize it? It was pointed at you once.

LØVBORG: You should have used it then.

HEDDA: Take it! *You* use it.

LØVBORG (*pockets the gun*): Thanks!

HEDDA: And beautifully, Eilert Løvborg! That's all I ask!

LØVBORG: Goodbye, Hedda Gabler. (*Exits, right.*)

(HEDDA *listens by the door for a moment. Then she crosses to the desk, takes out the manuscript, glances inside the cover, pulls some of the pages halfway out and looks at them. Carries the whole manuscript over to the chair by the stove. She sits down with the parcel in her lap. After a moment she opens the stove and then the manuscript.*)

HEDDA (*throws a bundle of sheets into the fire, whispers*): Now I'm burning your child, Thea. You — curlyhead! (*Throws more sheets in.*) Your and Eilert Løvborg's child. (*Throws all the rest of the manuscript into the stove.*) I am burning — I am burning your child.

ACT IV

The same rooms at the TESMANS'. *Evening. The front room is dark. The inner room is lighted by the ceiling lamp over the table. Portieres cover the French doors.*

HEDDA, *in black, is walking up and down in the dark of the front room. She goes into the inner room, turning left in the doorway. She is heard playing a few bars on the piano. She reappears and comes forward again.* BERTE *enters from the right side of the inner room. She carries a lighted lamp, which she puts down on the table in front of the corner sofa. Her eyes show signs of weeping; she wears black ribbons on her uniform. She exits quietly, right.* HEDDA *goes over to the French windows, looks between the portieres into the dark. Presently* MISS TESMAN, *in mourning, with hat and veil, enters, right.* HEDDA *walks over to meet her, gives her her hand.*

MISS TESMAN: Yes, my dearest Hedda — here you see me in my garb of grief. For now at last my poor sister has fought her fight to the end.

HEDDA: I already know — as you see. Tesman sent word.

MISS TESMAN: Yes, he promised he'd do that. But I thought that to you, Hedda — here in the house of life — I really ought to bring you the tidings of death myself.

HEDDA: That is very kind of you.

MISS TESMAN: Ah, but Rina shouldn't have died just now. There should be no mourning in Hedda's house at this time.

HEDDA (*changing the topic*): I understand she had a very quiet end.

MISS TESMAN: Oh so beautiful, so peaceful! She left us so quietly! And then the unspeakable happiness of seeing Jørgen one more time! To say goodbye to him to her heart's content! Isn't he back yet?

HEDDA: No. He wrote I mustn't expect him back very soon. But do sit down.

MISS TESMAN: No — no, thanks, my dear, blessed Hedda. Not that I wouldn't like to. But I don't have much time. I must go back and prepare her as best I can. I want her to look right pretty when she goes into her grave.

HEDDA: Is there anything I can help you with?

MISS TESMAN: I won't have you as much as think of it! That's not for Hedda Tesman to lend a hand to. Or lend thoughts to either. Not now, of all times!

HEDDA: Oh — thoughts! We can't always control our thoughts —

MISS TESMAN (*still preoccupied*): Ah yes — such is life. At home we're making a shroud for Rina. And here, too, there'll be sewing to do soon, I expect. But of quite a different kind, thank God!

(TESMAN *enters, right.*)

HEDDA: Finally!

TESMAN: You here, Aunt Julle? With Hedda? Just think!

MISS TESMAN: I am just about to leave, Jørgen dear. Well — did you do all the things you promised me you'd do?

TESMAN: No, I'm afraid I forgot half of them, Auntie. I'd better run in again tomorrow. I'm all confused today. I can't seem to keep my thoughts together.

MISS TESMAN: But dearest Jørgen — you mustn't take it this way!

TESMAN: Oh, I mustn't? How do you mean?

MISS TESMAN: You ought to be joyful in the midst of your sorrow. Glad for what's happened. The way I am.

TESMAN: Oh yes, of course. You're thinking of Aunt Rina.

HEDDA: You're going to feel lonely now, Miss Tesman.

MISS TESMAN: The first few days, yes. But I hope that won't last long. Dear Rina's little parlor won't be empty for long, if I can help it!

TESMAN: Oh? And who do you want to move in there? Hm?

MISS TESMAN: Ah — it's not very hard to find some poor soul who needs nursing and comfort.

HEDDA: And you really want to take on such a burden all over again?

MISS TESMAN: Heavens! God forgive you, child — burden? It has not been a burden to me.

HEDDA: Still — a stranger, who —

MISS TESMAN: Oh, it's easy to make friends with sick people. And I need somebody to live for, too. Well, the Lord be praised, maybe soon there'll be a thing or two an old aunt can turn her hand to here.

HEDDA: Oh, never mind us —

TESMAN: Yes, just think — how lovely it would be for the three of us, if only —

HEDDA: If only — ?

TESMAN (*uneasy*): Oh, nothing. I daresay it will all work out. Let's hope it will, hm?

MISS TESMAN: Well, well. I can see that you two have something to talk about. (*With a smile.*) And perhaps Hedda has something to tell you, Jørgen! Goodbye! I'm going home to Rina, now. (*Turns round in the door.*) Dear, dear — how strange to think — Now Rina is both with me and with Jochum!

TESMAN: Yes, just think, Aunt Julle! Hm?

(MISS TESMAN *exits, right.*)

HEDDA (*coldly scrutinizing* TESMAN): I wouldn't be at all surprised if you aren't more affected by this death than she is.

TESMAN: Oh, it isn't just Aunt Rina's death, Hedda. It's Eilert I worry about.

HEDDA (*quickly*): Any news about him?

TESMAN: I went over to his room this afternoon to tell him the manuscript is safe.

HEDDA: Well? And didn't you see him?

TESMAN: No. He wasn't home. But I ran into Mrs. Elvsted and she told me he'd been here early this morning.

HEDDA: Yes, right after you'd left.

TESMAN: And he said he'd torn up the manuscript? Did he really say that?

HEDDA: Yes. So he claimed.

TESMAN: But dear God — in that case he really must have been out of his mind! So I assume you didn't give it to him either, hm, Hedda?

HEDDA: No. He didn't get it.

TESMAN: But you told him we had it, of course?

HEDDA: No. (*Quickly.*) Did you tell Mrs. Elvsted?

TESMAN: No, I didn't want to. But you ought to have told him, Hedda. Just think — what if he does something rash — something to hurt himself! Give me the manuscript, Hedda! I want to rush down to him with it right this minute. Where is it?

HEDDA (*cold motionless, one arm resting on the chair*): I haven't got it any more.

TESMAN: You haven't got it! What do you mean by that?

HEDDA: I burned it — the whole thing.

TESMAN (*jumps up*): Burned it! Burned Eilert's book!

HEDDA: Don't shout. The maid might hear you.

TESMAN: Burned it? But good God — no, no, no — ! This can't be — !

HEDDA: It is, all the same.

TESMAN: But do you realize what you've done, Hedda? It's illegal! Willful destruction of lost property! You just ask Judge Brack! He'll tell you!

HEDDA: You'd better not talk about this to anyone — the Judge or anybody else.

TESMAN: But how could you do a thing like that! I never heard anything like it! What came over you? What can possibly have been going on in your head? Answer me! Hm?

HEDDA (*suppresses an almost imperceptible smile*): I did it for your sake, Jørgen.

TESMAN: For my sake!

HEDDA: When you came back this morning and told me he had read aloud to you —

TESMAN: Yes, yes! What then?

HEDDA: You admitted you were jealous of him for having written such a book.

TESMAN: But good gracious — ! I didn't mean it as seriously as all that!

HEDDA: All the same. I couldn't stand the thought that somebody else was to overshadow you.

TESMAN (*in an outburst of mingled doubt and joy*): Hedda — oh Hedda! Is it true what you're saying. But — but — but — I never knew you loved me like that! Just think!

HEDDA: In that case, I might as well tell you — that — just at this time — (*Breaks off, vehemently.*) No, no! You can ask Aunt Julle. She'll tell you.

TESMAN: I almost think I know what you mean, Hedda! (*Claps his hands.*) For goodness' sake! Can that really be so! Hm?

HEDDA: Don't shout so! The maid can hear you.

TESMAN (*laughing with exuberant joy*): The maid! Well, if you don't take the prize, Hedda! The maid — but that's Berte! I'm going to tell Berte myself this very minute!

HEDDA (*her hands clenched in despair*): Oh I'll die — I'll die, in all this!

TESMAN: In what, Hedda? Hm?

HEDDA (*cold and composed*): In all this — ludicrousness, Jørgen.

TESMAN: Ludicrous? That I'm so happy? Still — maybe I oughtn't to tell Berte, after all.

HEDDA: Oh, go ahead. What difference does it make?

TESMAN: No, not yet. But on my word — Aunt Julle must be told. And that you've started to call me "Jørgen," too! Just think! She'll be ever so happy — Aunt Julle will!

HEDDA: Even when you tell her that I have burned Eilert Løvborg's papers?

TESMAN: No, oh no! That's true! That about the manuscript — nobody must know about that. But to think that you'd burn for me, Hedda — I certainly want to tell *that* to Aunt Julle! I wonder now — is that sort of thing usual with young wives, hm?

HEDDA: Why don't you ask Aunt Julle about that, too?

TESMAN: I shall — I certainly shall, when I get the chance. (*Looks uneasy and disturbed again.*) But the manuscript! Good God — I don't dare to think what this is going to do to poor Eilert!

(MRS. ELVSTED, *dressed as on her first visit wearing hat and coat, enters, right.*)

MRS. ELVSTED (*gives a hurried greeting, is obviously upset*): Oh Hedda, you must forgive me for coming here again!

HEDDA: What has happened, Thea?

TESMAN: Something to do with Eilert Løvborg again? Hm?

MRS. ELVSTED: Yes, yes — I'm so terribly afraid something's happened to him.

HEDDA (*seizing her arm*): Ah — you think so?

TESMAN: Oh dear — why do you think that, Mrs. Elvsted?

MRS. ELVSTED: I heard them talking about him in the boarding house, just as I came in. And people are saying the most incredible things about him today.

TESMAN: Yes, imagine! I heard that, too! And I can testify that he went straight home to bed! Just think!

HEDDA: And what did they say in the boarding house?

MRS. ELVSTED: Oh, I didn't find out anything. Either they didn't know any details or — They all became silent when they saw me. And I didn't dare to ask.

TESMAN (*pacing the floor uneasily*): We'll just have to hope — to hope that you heard wrong, Mrs. Elvsted!

MRS. ELVSTED: No, no. I'm sure it was he they were talking about. And somebody said something about the hospital or —

TESMAN: The hospital — !

HEDDA: Surely, that can't be so!

MRS. ELVSTED: I got so terribly frightened! So I went up to his room and asked for him there.

HEDDA: Could you bring yourself to do that, Thea?

MRS. ELVSTED: What else could I do? For I felt I just couldn't stand the uncertainty any longer.

TESMAN: But I suppose you didn't find him in, either, did you? Hm?

MRS. ELVSTED: No. And the people there didn't know anything about him. He hadn't been home since yesterday afternoon, they said.

TESMAN: Yesterday! Just think! How could they say that!

MRS. ELVSTED: I don't know what else to think — something bad must have happened to him!

TESMAN: Hedda, dear — ? What if I were to walk downtown and ask around for him — ?

HEDDA: No, no — don't you go and get mixed up in all this.

(JUDGE BRACK, *hat in hand, enters through the door, right, which* BERTE *opens and closes for him. He looks serious and greets the others in silence.*)

TESMAN: So here you are, Judge, hm?

BRACK: Yes. I had to see you this evening.

TESMAN: I can see you have got Aunt Julle's message.

BRACK: That, too — yes.

TESMAN: Isn't it sad, though?

BRACK: Well, my dear Tesman — that depends on how you look at it.

TESMAN (*looks at him uncertainly*): Has something else happened?

BRACK: Yes.

HEDDA (*tense*): Something sad, Judge Brack?

BRACK: That, too, depends on how you look at it, Mrs. Tesman.

MRS. ELVSTED (*bursting out*): Oh, I'm sure it has something to do with Eilert Løvborg!

BRACK (*looks at her for a moment*): Why do you think that, Mrs. Elvsted? Maybe you already know something — ?

MRS. ELVSTED (*confused*): No, no; not at all. It's just —

TESMAN: For heaven's sake, Brack, out with it!

BRACK (*shrugging his shoulders*): Well — unfortunately, Eilert Løvborg's in the hospital. Dying.

MRS. ELVSTED (*screams*): Oh God, oh God!

TESMAN: In the hospital! And dying!

HEDDA (*without thinking*): So soon — !

MRS. ELVSTED (*wailing*): And we didn't even part as friends, Hedda!

HEDDA (*whispers*): Thea, Thea — for heaven's sake — !

MRS. ELVSTED (*paying no attention to her*): I want to see him! I want to see him alive!

BRACK: Won't do you any good, Mrs. Elvsted. Nobody can see him.

MRS. ELVSTED: Then tell me what's happened to him! What?

TESMAN: For, surely, he hasn't himself — !

HEDDA: I'm sure he has.

TESMAN: Hedda! How can you — !

BRACK (*observing her all this time*): I am sorry to say that your guess is absolutely correct, Mrs. Tesman.

MRS. ELVSTED: Oh, how awful!

TESMAN: Did it himself! Just think!

HEDDA: Shot himself!

BRACK: Right again, Mrs. Tesman.

MRS. ELVSTED (*trying to pull herself together*): When did this happen, Judge?

BRACK: This afternoon. Between three and four.

TESMAN: But dear me — where can he have done a thing like that? Hm?

BRACK (*a little uncertain*): Where? Well — I suppose in his room. I don't really know —

MRS. ELVSTED: No, it can't have been there. For I was up there sometime between six and seven.

BRACK: Well, then, some other place. I really can't say. All I know is that he was found. He had shot himself — in the chest.

MRS. ELVSTED: Oh, how horrible to think! That he was to end like that!

HEDDA (*to* BRACK): In the chest?

BRACK: Yes — as I just told you.

HEDDA: Not the temple?

BRACK: In the chest, Mrs. Tesman.

HEDDA: Well, well — the chest is a good place, too.

BRACK: How is that, Mrs. Tesman?

HEDDA: (*turning him aside*): Oh — nothing.

TESMAN: And you say the wound is fatal? Hm?

BRACK: No doubt about it — absolutely fatal. He's probably dead already.

MRS. ELVSTED: Yes, yes! I feel you're right! It's over! It's all over! Oh, Hedda!

TESMAN: But tell me — how do *you* know all this?

BRACK (*tersely*): A man on the force told me. One I had some business with.

HEDDA (*loudly*): At last a deed!

TESMAN (*appalled*): Oh dear — what are you saying, Hedda!

HEDDA: I am saying there is beauty in this.

BRACK: Well, now — Mrs. Tesman —

TESMAN: Beauty — ! Just think!

MRS. ELVSTED: Oh, Hedda — how can you talk about beauty in a thing like this!

HEDDA: Eilert Løvborg has settled his account with himself. He has had the courage to do — what had to be done.

MRS. ELVSTED: But you mustn't believe it happened that way! He did it when he was not himself!

TESMAN: In despair! That's how!

HEDDA: He did not. I am certain of that.

MRS. ELVSTED: Yes he did! He was not himself! That's the way he tore up the book, too!

BRACK (*puzzled*): The book? You mean the manuscript? Has he torn it up?

MRS. ELVSTED: Yes, last night.

TESMAN (*whispers*): Oh, Hedda — we'll never get clear of all this!

BRACK: That is strange.

TESMAN (*walking the floor*): To think that this was to be the end of Eilert! Not to leave behind him anything that would have preserved his name —

MRS. ELVSTED: Oh, if only it could be put together again!

TESMAN: Yes, if only it could. I don't know what I wouldn't give —

MRS. ELVSTED: Maybe it can, Mr. Tesman.

TESMAN: What do you mean?

MRS. ELVSTED (*searching her dress pocket*): Look. I have kept these little slips he dictated from.

HEDDA (*a step closer*): Ah — !

TESMAN: You've kept them, Mrs. Elvsted? Hm?

MRS. ELVSTED: Yes. Here they are. I took them with me when I left. And I've had them in my pocket ever since —

TESMAN: Please, let me see —

MRS. ELVSTED (*gives him a pile of small paper slips*): But it's such a mess. Without any kind of system or order — !

TESMAN: But just think if we could make sense out of them, all the same! Perhaps if we helped each other —

MRS. ELVSTED: Oh yes! Let's try, anyway!

TESMAN: It will work! It *has* to work! I'll stake my whole life on this!

HEDDA: You, Jørgen? Your life?

TESMAN: Yes, or at any rate all the time I can set aside. My own collections can wait. Hedda, you understand — don't you? Hm? This is something I owe Eilert's memory.

HEDDA: Maybe so.

TESMAN: And now, my dear Mrs. Elvsted, we want to get to work. Good heavens, there's no point brooding over what's happened. Hm? We'll just have to acquire sufficient peace of mind to —

MRS. ELVSTED: All right, Mr. Tesman. I'll try to do my best.

TESMAN: Very well, then. Come over here. Let's look at these slips right away. Where can we sit? Here? No, it's better in the other room. If you'll excuse us, Judge! Come along, Mrs. Elvsted.

MRS. ELVSTED: Oh dear God — if only it were possible — !

(TESMAN *and* MRS. ELVSTED *go into the inner room. She takes off her hat and coat. Both sit down at the table under the hanging lamp and absorb themselves in the slips.* HEDDA *walks over toward the stove and sits down in the easy chair. After a while,* BRACK *walks over to her.*)

HEDDA (*in a low voice*): Ah, Judge — what a liberation there is in this thing with Eilert Løvborg!

BRACK: Liberation, Mrs. Tesman? Well, yes, for him perhaps one may say there was liberation of a kind —

HEDDA: I mean for me. There is liberation in knowing that there is such a thing in the world as an act of free courage. Something which becomes beautiful by its very nature.

BRACK (*smiles*): Well — dear Mrs. Tesman —

HEDDA: Oh I know what you're going to say! For you see — you really are a kind of specialist, too!

BRACK (*looks at her fixedly*): Eilert Løvborg has meant more to you than perhaps you're willing to admit, even to yourself. Or am I wrong?

HEDDA: I won't answer such questions. All I know is that Eilert Løvborg had the courage to live his own life. And then now — this — magnificence! The beauty of it! Having the strength and the will to get up and leave life's feast — so early —

BRACK: Believe me, Mrs. Tesman, this pains me, but I see it is necessary that I destroy a pretty illusion —

HEDDA: An illusion?

BRACK: Which could not have been maintained for very long, anyway.

HEDDA: And what is that?

BRACK: He didn't shoot himself — of his own free will.

HEDDA: Not of his own — !

BRACK: No. To tell the truth, the circumstances of Eilert Løvborg's death aren't exactly what I said they were.

HEDDA (*tense*): You've held something back? What?

BRACK: For the sake of poor Mrs. Elvsted I used a few euphemisms.

HEDDA: What?

BRACK: First — he is already dead.

HEDDA: In the hospital.

BRACK: Yes. And without regaining consciousness.

HEDDA: What else haven't you told?

BRACK: That fact that it didn't happen in his room.

HEDDA: Well, does that really make much difference?

BRACK: Some. You see — Eilert Løvborg was found shot in Miss Diana's bedroom.

HEDDA (*is about to jump up, but sinks back*): That's impossible, Judge Brack! He can't have been there again today!

BRACK: He was there this afternoon. He came to claim something he said they had taken from him. Spoke some gibberish about a lost child —

HEDDA: So that's why — !

BRACK: I thought maybe he meant his manuscript. But now I hear he has destroyed that himself. So I suppose it must have been something else.

HEDDA: I suppose. So it was there — so they found him there?

BRACK: Yes. With a fired gun in his pocket. Mortally wounded.

HEDDA: Yes — in the chest.

BRACK: No — in the guts.

HEDDA (*looks at him with an expression of disgust*): That, too! What is this curse that turns everything I touch into something ludicrous and low!

BRACK: There is something else, Mrs. Tesman. Something I'd call — nasty.

HEDDA: And what is that.

BRACK: The gun they found —

HEDDA (*breathless*): What about it?

BRACK: He must have stolen it.

HEDDA (*jumps up*): Stolen! That's not true! He didn't!

BRACK: Anything else is impossible. He *must* have stolen it. — Shhh!

(TESMAN *and* MRS. ELVSTED *have risen from the table and come forward into the front room.*)

TESMAN (*with papers in both hands*): D'you know, Hedda — you can hardly see in there with that lamp! Just think!

HEDDA: I am thinking.

TESMAN: I wonder if you'd let us use your desk, hm?

HEDDA: Certainly, if you like. (*Adds quickly.*) Wait a minute, though! Let me clear it off a bit first.

TESMAN: Ah, there's no need for that, Hedda. There's plenty of room.

HEDDA: No, no. I want to straighten it up. I'll carry all this in here. I'll put it on top of the piano for the time being.

(*She has pulled an object, covered by note paper, out of the bookcase. She puts several other sheets of paper on top of it and carries the whole pile into the left part of the inner room.* TESMAN *puts the papers down on the desk and moves the lamp from the corner table over to the desk. He and* MRS. ELVSTED *sit down and resume their work.* HEDDA *returns.*)

HEDDA (*behind* MRS. ELVSTED's *chair, softly ruffling her hair*): Well, little Thea — how is Eilert Løvborg's memorial coming along?

MRS. ELVSTED (*looks up at her, discouraged*): Oh God — I'm sure it's going to be terribly hard to make anything out of all this.

TESMAN: But we have to. We just don't have a choice. And putting other people's papers in order — that's just the thing for me.

(HEDDA *walks over to the stove and sits down on one of the ottomans.* BRACK *stands over her, leaning on the easy chair.*)

HEDDA (*whispers*): What were you saying about the gun?

BRACK (*also softly*): That he must have stolen it.

HEDDA: Why, necessarily?

BRACK: Because any other explanation ought to be out of the question, Mrs. Tesman.

HEDDA: Oh?

BRACK (*looks at her for a moment*): Eilert Løvborg was here this morning, of course. Isn't that so?

HEDDA: Yes.

BRACK: Were you alone with him?

HEDDA: Yes, for a while.

BRACK: You didn't leave the room while he was here?

HEDDA: No.

BRACK: Think. Not at all? Not even for a moment?

HEDDA: Well — maybe just for a moment — out in the hall.

BRACK: And where was the gun case?

HEDDA: In the —

BRACK: Mrs. Tesman?

HEDDA: On the desk.

BRACK: Have you looked to see if both guns are still there?

HEDDA: No.

BRACK: You needn't bother. I saw the gun they found on Løvborg, and I knew it immediately. From yesterday — and from earlier occasions, too.

HEDDA: Perhaps you have it?

BRACK: No, the police do.

HEDDA: What are the police going to do with it?

BRACK: Try to find the owner.

HEDDA: Do you think they will?

BRACK (*leans over her, whispers*): No, Hedda Gabler — not as long as I keep quiet.

HEDDA (*with a hunted look*): And if you don't?

BRACK (*shrugs his shoulders*): Of course, there's always the chance that the gun was stolen.

HEDDA (*firmly*): Rather die!

BRACK (*smiles*): People *say* things like that. They don't *do* them.

HEDDA (*without answering*): And if the gun was not stolen — and if they find the owner — then what happens?

BRACK: Well, Hedda — then comes the scandal!

HEDDA: The scandal!

BRACK: Yes — the scandal. That you are so afraid of. You will of course be required to testify. Both you and Miss Diana. Obviously, she'll have to explain how the whole thing happened. Whether it was accidental or homicide. Did he try to pull the gun out of his pocket to threaten her? And did it fire accidentally? Or did she grab the gun away from him, shoot him, and put it back in his pocket? She might just possibly have done that. She's a pretty tough girl — Miss Diana.

HEDDA: But this whole disgusting mess has nothing to do with me.

BRACK: Quite so. But you'll have to answer the question: Why did you give Eilert Løvborg the gun? And what inferences will be drawn from the fact that you did?

HEDDA (*lowers her head*): That's true. I hadn't thought of that.

BRACK: Well — luckily, there's nothing to worry about as long as I don't say anything.

HEDDA (*looks up at him*): So then I'm in your power, Judge. From now on you can do anything you like with me.

BRACK (*in an even softer whisper*): Dearest Hedda — believe me, I'll not misuse my position.

HEDDA: In your power, all the same. Dependent on your will. Servant to your demands. Not free. Not free! (*Rises suddenly.*) No — I can't stand that thought! Never!

BRACK (*looks at her, half mockingly*): Most people submit to the inevitable.

HEDDA (*returning his glance*): Perhaps. (*Walks over to the desk. Suppresses a smile and mimics* TESMAN's *way of speaking.*) Well? Do you think you can do it, Jørgen? Hm?

TESMAN: Lord knows, Hedda. Anyway, I can already see it will take months.

HEDDA (*still mimicking*): Just think! (*Runs her hands lightly through* MRS. ELVSTED's *hair.*) Doesn't this seem strange to you, Thea? Sitting here with Tesman — just the way you used to with Eilert Løvborg?

MRS. ELVSTED: Oh dear — if only I could inspire your husband, too!

HEDDA: Oh, I'm sure that will come — in time.

TESMAN: Well, yes — do you know, Hedda? I really think I begin to feel something of the kind. But why don't you go and talk to the Judge again.

HEDDA: Isn't there anything you two can use me for?

TESMAN: No, not a thing, dear. (*Turns around.*) From now on, you must be good enough to keep Hedda company, my dear Judge!

BRACK (*glancing at* HEDDA): I'll be only too delighted.

HEDDA: Thank you. But I'm tired tonight. I think I'll go and lie down for a while.

TESMAN: Yes, you do that, dear; why don't you? Hm?

(HEDDA *goes into the inner room, closes the portieres behind her. Brief pause. Suddenly, she is heard playing a frenzied dance tune on the piano.*)

MRS. ELVSTED (*jumps up*): Oh God! What's that!

TESMAN (*running to the doorway*): But dearest Hedda — you mustn't play dance music tonight, for goodness' sake! Think of Aunt Rina! And Eilert, too!

HEDDA (*peeks in from between the portieres*): And Aunt Julle. And everybody. I'll be quiet. (*She pulls the portieres shut again.*)

TESMAN (*back at the desk*): I don't think it's good for her to see us at such a melancholy task. I'll tell you what, Mrs. Elvsted. You move in with Aunt Julle, and then I'll come over in the evenings. Then we can sit and work over there. Hm?

MRS. ELVSTED: Maybe that would be better —

HEDDA (*from inner room*): I hear every word you're saying, Tesman. And how am I going to spend my evenings?

TESMAN (*busy with the papers*): Oh, I'm sure Judge Brack will be good enough to come out and see you, anyway.

BRACK (*in the easy chair, calls out gaily*): Every single night, as far as I'm concerned, Mrs. Tesman! I'm sure we're going to have a lovely time, you and I!

HEDDA (*loud and clear*): Yes, don't you think that would be nice, Judge Brack? You — sole cock-o'-the-walk —

(A *shot is heard from the inner room,* TESMAN, MRS. ELVSTED, *and* JUDGE BRACK *all jump up.*)

TESMAN: There she is, fooling with those guns again.

(He *pulls the portieres apart and runs inside.* MRS. ELVSTED *also.* HEDDA, *lifeless, is lying on the sofa. Cries and confusion,* BERTE, *flustered, enters, right.*)

TESMAN (*shouts to* BRACK): She's shot herself! In the temple! Just think!

BRACK (*half stunned in the easy chair*): But, merciful God — ! One just doesn't *do* that!

Before he was forty Ibsen had written two masterpieces of poetic drama, *Brand* (1866) and *Peer Gynt* (1867). But a few years later he came to feel, along with many others, that the future of dramatic literature was not in poetic language, but in language that closely resembled ordinary speech.* He devoted his subsequent efforts to prose drama, and we find him, in his letters, occasionally prophesying that poetic drama has no future, and warning his translators to avoid all expressions that depart from "everyday speech." In the 1870's and 1880's he wrote the so-called "problem plays" (including *A Doll's House*, *Ghosts*, and *An Enemy of the People*) that for the next seventy-five years made his name familiar to the English-speaking world. A problem play, or "play of ideas," or *pièce à thèse,* is concerned with some troublesome social institution, its author hoping to arouse the audience to do something about the problem (for example, to modify the divorce laws, to extend the ballot, to alter the tax structure). The more successful the play, the more it insures its own demise, for when the social institutions have been altered and the problem has been solved, the play has no relevance to experience; it is merely a thing of historical importance, a museum curio. The violent reviews that *Ghosts* and some of Ibsen's other plays engendered are evidence that more was at stake than aesthetic matters; discussions of the plays inevitably became discussions of divorce, venereal disease, incest, etc. Almost a century has passed, and readers have found that Ibsen has something more to offer than thoughts on how to improve society.

In December 1890, a few weeks after he finished *Hedda Gabler,* Ibsen made the point that "it was not really my intention to deal in this play with so-called problems. What I principally wanted to do was to depict human beings, human emotions, and human destinies, upon a groundwork of certain of the social conditions and principles of the present day." We get some idea of what Ibsen meant by "the social conditions and principles of the present day" from another jotting he made while he was getting the play into shape: "Tesman represents propriety. Hedda represents *ennui.* Mrs. R. [i.e., Mrs. Elvsted] modern nervousness and hysteria. Brack the representative of bourgeois society." This early summary does not, of course, correspond exactly to the finished play, but it gives us some idea of the direction Ibsen was taking. "Propriety," "*ennui,*" "nervousness and hysteria," and even "bourgeois society" are not problems that can be solved by legislation or by any other form of tinkering. The play, after all, is not about a society that foolishly restrains energetic women from putting their energy to use — though it is in part about the

---

* Prose, and indeed prose clearly imitative of speech, had, of course, been occasionally used much earlier, even during the Renaissance, but prose tragedy with its middle-class figures was for a long while a poor relation of poetic tragedy. With the increasing power of the middle class and the rise of science (which not only helped to enlarge the middle class but also helped to popularize the view that all matter is equally interesting and presumably equally fit for literature), the days of "heroic" tragedy were numbered. Probably Darwin's *Origin of Species* (1859) was the *coup de grâce;* one could hardly take a very high view of creatures that had survived because accidental variations made them more suited to their environment than other creatures.

social conventions (especially aristocratic pride) that Hedda cannot abandon. The other jottings show even more clearly that Ibsen was concerned with unchanging experiences rather than with transitory problems. Here are two of them:

> They aren't all created to be mothers.
> The daemon in Hedda is that she wants to influence another human being, but once that has happened, she despises him.

Hedda wishes to influence someone, to shape a human destiny. Her own destiny, like everyone else's, has been partly shaped by the circumstances of her birth. She is the daughter of an aristocrat, General Gabler (in a letter Ibsen called attention to the fact that the play is entitled *Hedda Gabler*, and not, despite her marriage to Jørgen Tesman, *Hedda Tesman*). Her aristocratic background has given her leisure but no direction, energy but no channel for it, and we see her becoming increasingly desperate. Having married rashly, she now feels her identity is threatened. The point is obvious, but it is worth quoting Ibsen's own description, from a letter: "Jørgen Tesman, his old aunts, and the faithful servant Berte together form a picture of complete unity. They think alike, they share the same memories and have the same outlook on life. To Hedda they appear like a strange and hostile power, aimed at her very being." Tesman is a bore, scarcely worth shaping, and the aunt and the maid are no challenge. Yet this family group frightens Hedda because (she thinks) it would lessen her identity if it absorbed her. Her distress at the thought of having a child is a further indication that although she yearns to shape a human destiny, she does not want to become involved in any sort of relationship in which she herself may be shaped; that is, she evades responsibilities. Presumably when she rejected Eilert Løvborg's overtures, she did so not only because she feared scandal, but also because she feared the relationship itself. Now she seeks to fulfill herself by controlling Løvborg's life to the point that he will be a Dionysian figure who will kill himself "beautifully." Hedda apparently has in mind something of the romantic view of Greek tragedy that Ibsen himself had held twenty-five years earlier, when he rhapsodized over a statue of "the Tragic Muse," with its "laurel-crowned head with something supernaturally exuberant and bacchantic about it."

In Ibsen's world, as everywhere, people impinge upon each other and relationships are necessarily established. Miss Tesman's life, for example, is intertwined with the invalid Aunt Rina's, and when Rina dies, a replacement must be found: "Ah — it's not very hard to find some poor soul who needs nursing and comfort." To Hedda's question, "And you really want to take on such a burden all over again?" Miss Tesman replies, "Heavens! God forgive you, child — burden? It has not been a burden to me." Similarly, Mrs. Elvsted and Løvborg require each other, and are shaped by each other as they shape each other, and Tesman is at his best when he is bringing to completion someone else's work. The play is built on a groundwork of "social conditions and principles" of nineteenth-century Norwegian life, but these conditions themselves, as

Ibsen presents them, are rooted in elementary facts of life and are not out-moded institutions that needlessly create problems. (In *Peer Gynt* Ibsen had earlier represented this matter of interrelationships with a brilliant image. Peer wishes "to be himself," but he finds he has no individuality when apart from others. He peels an onion, to get at the core, and finds that after all layers — or relationships — are removed, there is nothing left.) Hedda seeks power divorced from responsibility, which means that finally her power must be directed against herself. The attempt to have Løvborg do some "beautiful" deed in defiance of society fails because she cannot have full power over Løvborg unless she gives something of herself to him. When Løvborg is dead, and Tesman and Mrs. Elvsted are occupied with each other, and Hedda is at Judge Brack's mercy, Hedda releases her energy against herself, killing herself "beautifully." Judge Brack's final comment, "One just doesn't *do* that!" is the sort of scandalized remark that Hedda had feared all her life, the voice of society, a society that does not know the depths of Hedda's anguish, a society that holds itself together by dull virtues, petty vices, and all sorts of dodges. But society does help men to survive, and to reject it is to annihilate oneself.

DEATH OF A SALESMAN

Certain private conversations in two acts and a requiem

Arthur Miller

Arthur Miller was born in New York in 1915. In 1938 he graduated from the University of Michigan, where he won several prizes for drama. Six years later he had his first Broadway production, *The Man Who Had All the Luck*, but the play was unlucky and closed after four days. By the time of his first commercial success, *All My Sons* (1947), he had already written eight or nine plays. In 1949 he won a Pulitzer prize with *Death of a Salesman* and achieved an international reputation. Among his other works are an adaptation (1950) of Ibsen's *Enemy of the People* and a play about the Salem witch trials, *The Crucible* (1953), both containing political implications, and *The Misfits* (1961, a screen-play), *After the Fall* (1964), and *Incident at Vichy* (1965).

The action takes place in WILLY LOMAN's house and yard and in various places he visits in the New York and Boston of today.

Throughout the play, in the stage directions, left and right mean stage left and stage right.

Design for Act I of *Death of a Salesman*. Painting by Jo Mielziner. (Photograph: Peter A. Juley & Sons.)

ACT I

A melody is heard, played upon a flute. It is small and fine, telling of grass and trees and the horizon. The curtain rises.

Before us is the Salesman's house. We are aware of towering, angular shapes behind it, surrounding it on all sides. Only the blue light of the sky falls upon the house and forestage; the surrounding area shows an angry glow of orange. As more light appears, we see a solid vault of apartment houses around the small, fragile-seeming home. An air of the dream clings to the place, a dream rising out of reality. The kitchen at center seems actual enough, for there is a kitchen table with three chairs, and a refrigerator. But no other fixtures are seen. At the back of the kitchen there is a draped entrance, which leads to the living-room. To the right of the kitchen, on a level raised two feet, is a bedroom furnished only with a brass bedstead and a straight chair. On a shelf over the bed a silver athletic trophy stands. A window opens onto the apartment house at the side.

Behind the kitchen, on a level raised six and a half feet, is the boys' bedroom, at present barely visible. Two beds are dimly seen, and at the back of the room a dormer window. (This bedroom is above the unseen living-room.) At the left a stairway curves up to it from the kitchen.

The entire setting is wholly or, in some places, partially transparent. The roof-line of the house is one-dimensional; under and

over it we see the apartment buildings. Before the house lies an apron, curving beyond the forestage into the orchestra. This forward area serves as the back yard as well as the locale of all WILLY's imaginings and of his city scenes. Whenever the action is in the present the actors observe the imaginary wall-lines, entering the house only through its door at the left. But in the scenes of the past these boundaries are broken, and characters enter or leave a room by stepping "through" a wall onto the forestage.

From the right, WILLY LOMAN, the Salesman, enters, carrying two large sample cases. The flute plays on. He hears but is not aware of it. He is past sixty years of age, dressed quietly. Even as he crosses the stage to the doorway of the house, his exhaustion is apparent. He unlocks the door, comes into the kitchen, and thankfully lets his burden down, feeling the soreness of his palms. A word-sigh escapes his lips — it might be "Oh, boy, oh, boy." He closes the door, then carries his cases out into the living-room, through the draped kitchen doorway. LINDA, his wife, has stirred in her bed at the right. She gets out and puts on a robe, listening. Most often jovial, she has developed an iron repression of her exceptions to WILLY's behavior — she more than loves him, she admires him, as though his mercurial nature, his temper, his massive dreams and little cruelties, served her only as sharp reminders of the turbulent longings within him, longings which she shares but lacks the temperament to utter and follow to their end.

LINDA (hearing WILLY outside the bedroom, calls with some trepidation): Willy!

WILLY: It's all right. I came back.

LINDA: Why? What happened? (Slight pause.) Did something happen, Willy?

WILLY: No, nothing happened.

LINDA: You didn't smash the car, did you?

WILLY (with casual irritation): I said nothing happened. Didn't you hear me?

LINDA: Don't you feel well?

WILLY: I am tired to the death. (The flute

has faded away. He sits on the bed beside her, a little numb.) I couldn't make it. I just couldn't make it, Linda.

LINDA (*very carefully, delicately*): Where were you all day? You look terrible.

WILLY: I got as far as a little above Yonkers. I stopped for a cup of coffee. Maybe it was the coffee.

LINDA: What?

WILLY (*after a pause*): I suddenly couldn't drive any more. The car kept going off onto the shoulder, y'know?

LINDA (*helpfully*): Oh. Maybe it was the steering again. I don't think Angelo knows the Studebaker.

WILLY: No, it's me, it's me. Suddenly I realize I'm goin' sixty miles an hour and I don't remember the last five minutes. I'm — I can't seem to — keep my mind to it.

LINDA: Maybe it's your glasses. You never went for your new glasses.

WILLY: No, I see everything. I came back ten miles an hour. It took me nearly four hours from Yonkers.

LINDA (*resigned*): Well, you'll just have to take a rest, Willy, you can't continue this way.

WILLY: I just got back from Florida.

LINDA: But you didn't rest your mind. Your mind is overactive, and the mind is what counts, dear.

WILLY: I'll start out in the morning. Maybe I'll feel better in the morning. (*She is taking off his shoes.*) These goddam arch supports are killing me.

LINDA: Take an aspirin. Should I get you an aspirin? It'll soothe you.

WILLY (*with wonder*): I was driving along, you understand? And I was fine. I was even observing the scenery. You can imagine, me looking at scenery, on the road every week of my life. But it's so beautiful up there, Linda, the trees are so thick, and the sun is warm. I opened the windshield and just let the warm air bathe over me. And then all of a sudden I'm goin' off the road! I'm tellin' ya, I absolutely forgot I was driving. If I'd've gone the other way over the white line I might've killed somebody. So I went on again — and five minutes later I'm dreamin' again, and I nearly — (*He presses two fingers against his eyes.*) I have such thoughts, I have such strange thoughts.

LINDA: Willy, dear. Talk to them again.

There's no reason why you can't work in New York.

WILLY: They don't need me in New York. I'm the New England man. I'm vital in New England.

LINDA: But you're sixty years old. They can't expect you to keep traveling every week.

WILLY: I'll have to send a wire to Portland. I'm supposed to see Brown and Morrison tomorrow morning at ten o'clock to show the line. Goddammit, I could sell them! (*He starts putting on his jacket.*)

LINDA (*taking the jacket from him*): Why don't you go down to the place tomorrow and tell Howard you've simply got to work in New York? You're too accommodating, dear.

WILLY: If old man Wagner was alive I'd a been in charge of New York now! That man was a prince, he was a masterful man. But that boy of his, that Howard, he don't appreciate. When I went north the first time, the Wagner Company didn't know where New England was!

LINDA: Why don't you tell those things to Howard, dear?

WILLY (*encouraged*): I will, I definitely will. Is there any cheese?

LINDA: I'll make you a sandwich.

WILLY: No, go to sleep. I'll take some milk. I'll be up right away. The boys in?

LINDA: They're sleeping. Happy took Biff on a date tonight.

WILLY (*interested*): That so?

LINDA: It was so nice to see them shaving together, one behind the other, in the bathroom. And going out together. You notice? The whole house smells of shaving lotion.

WILLY: Figure it out. Work a lifetime to pay off a house. You finally own it, and there's nobody to live in it.

LINDA: Well, dear, life is a casting off. It's always that way.

WILLY: No, no, some people — some people accomplish something. Did Biff say anything after I went this morning?

LINDA: You shouldn't have criticized him, Willy, especially after he just got off the train. You mustn't lose your temper with him.

WILLY: When the hell did I lose my temper? I simply asked him if he was making any money. Is that a criticism?

LINDA: But, dear, how could he make any money?

WILLY (*worried and angered*): There's such an undercurrent in him. He became a moody man. Did he apologize when I left this morning?

LINDA: He was crestfallen, Willy. You know how he admires you. I think if he finds himself, then you'll both be happier and not fight any more.

WILLY: How can he find himself on a farm? Is that a life? A farmhand? In the beginning, when he was young, I thought, well, a young man, it's good for him to tramp around, take a lot of different jobs. But it's more than ten years now and he has yet to make thirty-five dollars a week!

LINDA: He's finding himself, Willy.

WILLY: Not finding yourself at the age of thirty-four is a disgrace!

LINDA: Shh!

WILLY: The trouble is he's lazy, goddammit!

LINDA: Willy, please!

WILLY: Biff is a lazy bum!

LINDA: They're sleeping. Get something to eat. Go on down.

WILLY: Why did he come home? I would like to know what brought him home.

LINDA: I don't know. I think he's still lost, Willy. I think he's very lost.

WILLY: Biff Loman is lost. In the greatest country in the world a young man with such — personal attractiveness, gets lost. And such a hard worker. There's one thing about Biff — he's not lazy.

LINDA: Never.

WILLY (*with pity and resolve*): I'll see him in the morning; I'll have a nice talk with him. I'll get him a job selling. He could be big in no time. My God! Remember how they used to follow him around in high school? When he smiled at one of them their faces lit up. When he walked down the street . . . (*He loses himself in reminiscences.*)

LINDA (*trying to bring him out of it*): Willy, dear, I got a new kind of American-type cheese today. It's whipped.

WILLY: Why do you get American when I like Swiss?

LINDA: I just thought you'd like a change —

WILLY: I don't want a change! I want Swiss cheese. Why am I always being contradicted?

LINDA (*with a covering laugh*): I thought it would be a surprise.

WILLY: Why don't you open a window in here, for God's sake?

LINDA (*with infinite patience*): They're all open, dear.

WILLY: The way they boxed us in here. Bricks and windows, windows and bricks.

LINDA: We should've bought the land next door.

WILLY: The street is lined with cars. There's not a breath of fresh air in the neighborhood. The grass don't grow any more, you can't raise a carrot in the back yard. They should've had a law against apartment houses. Remember those two beautiful elm trees out there? When I and Biff hung the swing between them?

LINDA: Yeah, like being a million miles from the city.

WILLY: They should've arrested the builder for cutting those down. They massacred the neighborhood. (*Lost.*) More and more I think of those days, Linda. This time of year it was lilac and wisteria. And then the peonies would come out, and the daffodils. What fragrance in this room!

LINDA: Well, after all, people had to move somewhere.

WILLY: No, there's more people now.

LINDA: I don't think there's more people. I think —

WILLY: There's more people! That's what's ruining this country! Population is getting out of control. The competition is maddening! Smell the stink from that apartment house! And another one on the other side . . . How can they whip cheese?

(*On* WILLY's *last line,* BIFF *and* HAPPY *raise themselves up in their beds, listening.*)

LINDA: Go down, try it. And be quiet.

WILLY (*turning to* LINDA, *guiltily*): You're not worried about me, are you, sweetheart?

BIFF: What's the matter?

HAPPY: Listen!

LINDA: You've got too much on the ball to worry about.

WILLY: You're my foundation and my support, Linda.

LINDA: Just try to relax, dear. You make mountains out of molehills.

WILLY: I won't fight with him any more. If he wants to go back to Texas, let him go.

LINDA: He'll find his way.

WILLY: Sure. Certain men just don't get started till later in life. Like Thomas Edison, I think. Or B. F. Goodrich. One of them was deaf. (*He starts for the bedroom doorway.*) I'll put my money on Biff.

LINDA: And Willy — if it's warm Sunday we'll drive in the country. And we'll open the windshield, and take lunch.

WILLY: No, the windshields don't open on the new cars.

LINDA: But you opened it today.

WILLY: Me? I didn't. (*He stops.*) Now isn't that peculiar! Isn't that a remarkable — (*He breaks off in amazement and fright as the flute is heard distantly.*)

LINDA: What, darling?

WILLY: That is the most remarkable thing.

LINDA: What, dear?

WILLY: I was thinking of the Chevvy. (*Slight pause.*) Nineteen twenty-eight . . . when I had that red Chevvy — (*Breaks off.*) That funny? I coulda sworn I was driving that Chevvy today.

LINDA: Well, that's nothing. Something must've reminded you.

WILLY: Remarkable. Ts. Remember those days? The way Biff used to simonize that car? The dealer refused to believe there was eighty thousand miles on it. (*He shakes his head.*) Heh! (*To Linda.*) Close your eyes, I'll be right up. (*He walks out of the bedroom.*)

HAPPY (*to* BIFF): Jesus, maybe he smashed up the car again!

LINDA (*calling after* WILLY): Be careful on the stairs, dear! The cheese is on the middle shelf! (*She turns, goes over to the bed, takes his jacket, and goes out of the bedroom.*)

(*Light has risen on the boys' room. Unseen,* WILLY *is heard talking to himself, "Eighty thousand miles," and a little laugh.* BIFF *gets out of bed, comes downstage a bit, and stands attentively.* BIFF *is two years older than his brother* HAPPY, *well built, but in these days bears a worn air and seems less self-assured. He has succeeded less, and his dreams are stronger and less acceptable than* HAPPY's. HAPPY *is tall, powerfully made. Sexuality is like a visible color on him, or a scent that many women have discovered. He, like his brother, is lost, but in a different way, for he has never allowed himself to turn his face toward defeat and is thus more confused and hard-skinned, although seemingly more content.*)

HAPPY (*getting out of bed*): He's going to get his license taken away if he keeps that up.

I'm getting nervous about him, y'know, Biff?

BIFF: His eyes are going.

HAPPY: No, I've driven with him. He sees all right. He just doesn't keep his mind on it. I drove into the city with him last week. He stops at a green light and then it turns red and he goes. (*He laughs.*)

BIFF: Maybe he's color-blind.

HAPPY: Pop? Why he's got the finest eye for color in the business. You know that.

BIFF (*sitting down on his bed*): I'm going to sleep.

HAPPY: You're not still sour on Dad, are you, Biff?

BIFF: He's all right, I guess.

WILLY (*underneath them, in the living-room*): Yes, sir, eighty thousand miles — eighty-two thousand!

BIFF: You smoking?

HAPPY (*holding out a pack of cigarettes*): Want one?

BIFF (*taking a cigarette*): I can never sleep when I smell it.

WILLY: What a simonizing job, heh!

HAPPY (*with deep sentiment*): Funny, Biff, y'know? Us sleeping in here again? The old beds. (*He pats his bed affectionately.*) All the talk that went across those two beds, huh? Our whole lives.

BIFF: Yeah. Lotta dreams and plans.

HAPPY (*with a deep and masculine laugh*): About five hundred women would like to know what was said in this room.

(*They share a soft laugh.*)

BIFF: Remember that big Betsy something — what the hell was her name — over on Bushwick Avenue?

HAPPY (*combing his hair*): With the collie dog!

BIFF: That's the one. I got you in there, remember?

HAPPY: Yeah, that was my first time — I think. Boy, there was a pig! (*They laugh, almost crudely.*) You taught me everything I know about women. Don't forget that.

BIFF: I bet you forgot how bashful you used to be. Especially with girls.

HAPPY: Oh, I still am, Biff.

BIFF: Oh, go on.

HAPPY: I just control it, that's all. I think I got less bashful and you got more so. What happened, Biff? Where's the old humor, the old confidence? (*He shakes* BIFF's *knee.* BIFF

gets up and moves restlessly about the room.)
What's the matter?

BIFF: Why does Dad mock me all the time?

HAPPY: He's not mocking you, he —

BIFF: Everything I say there's a twist of mockery on his face. I can't get near him.

HAPPY: He just wants you to make good, that's all. I wanted to talk to you about Dad for a long time, Biff. Something's — happening to him. He — talks to himself.

BIFF: I noticed that this morning. But he always mumbled.

HAPPY: But not so noticeable. It got so embarrassing I sent him to Florida. And you know something? Most of the time he's talking to you.

BIFF: What's he say about me?

HAPPY: I can't make it out.

BIFF: What's he say about me?

HAPPY: I think the fact that you're not settled, that you're still kind of up in the air . . .

BIFF: There's one or two other things depressing him, Happy.

HAPPY: What do you mean?

BIFF: Never mind. Just don't lay it all to me.

HAPPY: But I think if you just got started — I mean — is there any future for you out there?

BIFF: I tell ya, Hap, I don't know what the future is. I don't know — what I'm supposed to want.

HAPPY: What do you mean?

BIFF: Well, I spent six or seven years after high school trying to work myself up. Shipping clerk, salesman, business of one kind or another. And it's a measly manner of existence. To get on that subway on the hot mornings in summer. To devote your whole life to keeping stock, or making phone calls, or selling or buying. To suffer fifty weeks of the year for the sake of a two-week vacation, when all you really desire is to be outdoors, with your shirt off. And always to have to get ahead of the next fella. And still — that's how you build a future.

HAPPY: Well, you really enjoy it on a farm? Are you content out there?

BIFF (*with rising agitation*): Hap, I've had twenty or thirty different kinds of jobs since I left home before the war, and it always turns out the same. I just realized it lately. In Nebraska when I herded cattle, and the Da-

kotas, and Arizona, and now in Texas. It's why I came home now, I guess, because I realized it. This farm I work on, it's spring there now, see? And they've got about fifteen new colts. There's nothing more inspiring or — beautiful than the sight of a mare and a new colt. And it's cool there now, see? Texas is cool now, and it's spring. And whenever spring comes to where I am, I suddenly get the feeling, my God, I'm not gettin' anywhere! What the hell am I doing, playing around with horses, twenty-eight dollars a week! I'm thirty-four years old, I oughta be makin' my future. That's when I come running home. And now, I get here, and I don't know what to do with myself. (*After a pause.*) I've always made a point of not wasting my life, and everytime I come back here I know that all I've done is to waste my life.

HAPPY: You're a poet, you know that, Biff? You're a — you're an idealist!

BIFF: No, I'm mixed up very bad. Maybe I oughta get married. Maybe I oughta get stuck into something. Maybe that's my trouble. I'm like a boy. I'm not married, I'm not in business, I just — I'm like a boy. Are you content, Hap? You're a success, aren't you? Are you content?

HAPPY: Hell, no!

BIFF: Why? You're making money, aren't you?

HAPPY (*moving about with energy, expressiveness*): All I can do now is wait for the merchandise manager to die. And suppose I get to be merchandise manager? He's a good friend of mine, and he just built a terrific estate on Long Island. And he lived there about two months and sold it, and now he's building another one. He can't enjoy it once it's finished. And I know that's just what I would do. I don't know what the hell I'm workin' for. Sometimes I sit in my apartment — all alone. And I think of the rent I'm paying. And it's crazy. But then, it's what I always wanted. My own apartment, a car, and plenty of women. And still, goddammit, I'm lonely.

BIFF (*with enthusiasm*): Listen, why don't you come out West with me?

HAPPY: You and I, heh?

BIFF: Sure, maybe we could buy a ranch. Raise cattle, use our muscles. Men built like we are should be working out in the open.

HAPPY (*avidly*): The Loman Brothers, heh?

BIFF (*with vast affection*): Sure, we'd be known all over the counties!

HAPPY (*enthralled*): That's what I dream about, Biff. Sometimes I want to just rip my clothes off in the middle of the store and outbox that goddam merchandise manager. I mean I can outbox, outrun, and outlift anybody in that store, and I have to take orders from those common, petty sons-of-bitches till I can't stand it any more.

BIFF: I'm tellin' you, kid, if you were with me I'd be happy out there.

HAPPY (*enthused*): See, Biff, everybody around me is so false that I'm constantly lowering my ideals . . .

BIFF: Baby, together we'd stand up for one another, we'd have someone to trust.

HAPPY: If I were around you —

BIFF: Hap, the trouble is we weren't brought up to grub for money. I don't know how to do it.

HAPPY: Neither can I!

BIFF: Then let's go!

HAPPY: The only thing is — what can you make out there?

BIFF: But look at your friend. Builds an estate and then hasn't the peace of mind to live in it.

HAPPY: Yeah, but when he walks into the store the waves part in front of him. That's fifty-two thousand dollars a year coming through the revolving door, and I got more in my pinky finger than he's got in his head.

BIFF: Yeah, but you just said —

HAPPY: I gotta show some of those pompous, self-important executives over there that Hap Loman can make the grade. I want to walk into the store the way he walks in. Then I'll go with you, Biff. We'll be together yet, I swear. But take those two we had tonight. Now weren't they gorgeous creatures?

BIFF: Yeah, yeah, most gorgeous I've had in years.

HAPPY: I get that any time I want, Biff. Whenever I feel disgusted. The only trouble is, it gets like bowling or something. I just keep knockin' them over and it doesn't mean anything. You still run around a lot?

BIFF: Naa. I'd like to find a girl — steady, somebody with substance.

HAPPY: That's what I long for.

BIFF: Go on! You'd never come home.

HAPPY: I would! Somebody with character, with resistance! Like Mom, y'know? You're gonna call me a bastard when I tell you this. That girl Charlotte I was with tonight is engaged to be married in five weeks. (*He tries on his new hat.*)

BIFF: No kiddin'!

HAPPY: Sure, the guy's in line for the vice-presidency of the store. I don't know what gets into me, maybe I just have an overdeveloped sense of competition or something, but I went and ruined her, and furthermore I can't get rid of her. And he's the third executive I've done that to. Isn't that a crummy characteristic? And to top it all, I go to their weddings! (*Indignantly, but laughing.*) Like I'm not supposed to take bribes. Manufacturers offer me a hundred-dollar bill now and then to throw an order their way. You know how honest I am, but it's like this girl, see. I hate myself for it. Because I don't want the girl, and, still, I take it and — I love it!

BIFF: Let's go to sleep.

HAPPY: I guess we didn't settle anything, heh?

BIFF: I just got one idea that I think I'm going to try.

HAPPY: What's that?

BIFF: Remember Bill Oliver?

HAPPY: Sure, Oliver is very big now. You want to work for him again?

BIFF: No, but when I quit he said something to me. He put his arm on my shoulder, and he said, "Biff, if you ever need anything, come to me."

HAPPY: I remember that. That sounds good.

BIFF: I think I'll go to see him. If I could get ten thousand or even seven or eight thousand dollars I could buy a beautiful ranch.

HAPPY: I bet he'd back you. 'Cause he thought highly of you, Biff. I mean, they all do. You're well liked, Biff. That's why I say to come back here, and we both have the apartment. And I'm tellin' you, Biff, any babe you want . . .

BIFF: No, with a ranch I could do the work I like and still be something. I just wonder though. I wonder if Oliver still thinks I stole that carton of basketballs.

HAPPY: Oh, he probably forgot that long ago. It's almost ten years. You're too sensitive. Anyway, he didn't really fire you.

BIFF: Well, I think he was going to. I think that's why I quit. I was never sure whether he knew or not. I know he thought the world of me, though. I was the only one he'd let lock up the place.

WILLY (*below*): You gonna wash the engine, Biff?

HAPPY: Shh!

(BIFF *looks at* HAPPY, *who is gazing down, listening.* WILLY *is mumbling in the parlor.*)

HAPPY: You hear that?

(*They listen.* WILLY *laughs warmly.*)

BIFF (*growing angry*): Doesn't he know Mom can hear that?

WILLY: Don't get your sweater dirty, Biff!

(*A look of pain crosses* BIFF's *face.*)

HAPPY: Isn't that terrible? Don't leave again, will you? You'll find a job here. You gotta stick around. I don't know what to do about him, it's getting embarrassing.

WILLY: What a simonizing job!

BIFF: Mom's hearing that!

WILLY: No kiddin', Biff, you got a date? Wonderful!

HAPPY: Go on to sleep. But talk to him in the morning, will you?

BIFF (*reluctantly getting into bed*): With her in the house. Brother!

HAPPY (*getting into bed*): I wish you'd have a good talk with him.

(*The light on their room begins to fade.*)

BIFF (*to himself in bed*): That selfish, stupid . . .

HAPPY: Sh . . . Sleep, Biff.

(*Their light is out. Well before they have finished speaking,* WILLY's *form is dimly seen below in the darkened kitchen. He opens the refrigerator, searches in there, and takes out a bottle of milk. The apartment houses are fading out, and the entire house and surroundings become covered with leaves. Music insinuates itself as the leaves appear.*)

WILLY: Just wanna be careful with those girls, Biff, that's all. Don't make any promises. No promises of any kind. Because a girl, y'know, they always believe what you tell 'em, and you're very young, Biff, you're too young to be talking seriously to girls.

(*Light rises on the kitchen.* WILLY, *talking, shuts the refrigerator door and comes downstage to the kitchen table. He pours milk into a glass. He is totally immersed in himself, smiling faintly.*)

WILLY: Too young entirely, Biff. You want to watch your schooling first. Then when you're all set, there'll be plenty of girls for a boy like you. (*He smiles broadly at a kitchen chair.*) That so? The girls pay for you? (*He laughs.*) Boy, you must really be makin' a hit.

(WILLY *is gradually addressing — physically — a point offstage, speaking through the wall of the kitchen, and his voice has been rising in volume to that of a normal conversation.*)

WILLY: I been wondering why you polish the car so careful. Ha! Don't leave the hubcaps, boys. Get the chamois to the hubcaps. Happy, use newspaper on the windows, it's the easiest thing. Show him how to do it, Biff! You see, Happy? Pad it up, use it like a pad. That's it, that's it, good work. You're doin' all right, Hap. (*He pauses, then nods in approbation for a few seconds, then looks upward.*) Biff, first thing we gotta do when we get time is clip that big branch over the house. Afraid it's gonna fall in a storm and hit the roof. Tell you what. We get a rope and sling her around, and then we climb up there with a couple of saws and take her down. Soon as you finish the car, boys, I wanna see ya. I got a surprise for you, boys.

BIFF (*offstage*): Whatta ya got, Dad?

WILLY: No, you finish first. Never leave a job till you're finished — remember that. (*Looking toward the "big trees."*) Biff, up in Albany I saw a beautiful hammock. I think I'll buy it next trip, and we'll hang it right between those two elms. Wouldn't that be something? Just swingin' there under those branches. Boy, that would be . . .

(YOUNG BIFF *and* YOUNG HAPPY *appear from the direction* WILLY *was addressing.* HAPPY *carries rags and a pail of water.* BIFF, *wearing a sweater with a block "S," carries a football.*)

BIFF (*pointing in the direction of the car offstage*): How's that, Pop, professional?

WILLY: Terrific. Terrific job, boys. Good work, Biff.

HAPPY: Where's the surprise, Pop?

WILLY: In the back seat of the car.

HAPPY: Boy! (*He runs off.*)

BIFF: What is it, Dad? Tell me, what'd you buy?

WILLY (*laughing, cuffs him*): Never mind, something I want you to have.

BIFF (*turns and starts off*): What is it, Hap?

HAPPY (*offstage*): It's a punching bag!

BIFF: Oh, Pop!

WILLY: It's got Gene Tunney's signature on it!

(HAPPY *runs onstage with a punching bag.*)

BIFF: Gee, how'd you know we wanted a punching bag?

WILLY: Well, it's the finest thing for the timing.

HAPPY (*lies down on his back and pedals with his feet*): I'm losing weight, you notice, Pop?

WILLY (*to* HAPPY): Jumping rope is good too.

BIFF: Did you see the new football I got?

WILLY (*examining the ball*): Where'd you get a new ball?

BIFF: The coach told me to practice my passing.

WILLY: That so? And he gave you the ball, heh?

BIFF: Well, I borrowed it from the locker room. (*He laughs confidentially.*)

WILLY (*laughing with him at the theft*): I want you to return that.

HAPPY: I told you he wouldn't like it!

BIFF (*angrily*): Well, I'm bringing it back!

WILLY (*stopping the incipient argument, to* HAPPY): Sure, he's gotta practice with a regulation ball, doesn't he? (*To* BIFF.) Coach'll probably congratulate you on your initiative.

BIFF: Oh, he keeps congratulating my initiative all the time, Pop.

WILLY: That's because he likes you. If somebody else took that ball there'd be an uproar. So what's the report, boys, what's the report?

BIFF: Where'd you go this time, Dad? Gee we were lonesome for you.

WILLY (*pleased, puts an arm around each boy and they come down to the apron*): Lonesome, heh?

BIFF: Missed you every minute.

WILLY: Don't say? Tell you a secret, boys.

Don't breathe it to a soul. Someday I'll have my own business, and I'll never have to leave home any more.

HAPPY: Like Uncle Charley, heh?

WILLY: Bigger than Uncle Charley! Because Charley is not — liked. He's liked, but he's not — well liked.

BIFF: Where'd you go this time, Dad?

WILLY: Well, I got on the road, and I went north to Providence. Met the Mayor.

BIFF: The Mayor of Providence!

WILLY: He was sitting in the hotel lobby.

BIFF: What'd he say?

WILLY: He said, "Morning!" And I said, "You got a fine city here, Mayor." And then he had coffee with me. And then I went to Waterbury. Waterbury is a fine city. Big clock city, the famous Waterbury clock. Sold a nice bill there. And then Boston — Boston is the cradle of the Revolution. A fine city. And a couple of other towns in Mass., and on to Portland and Bangor and straight home!

BIFF: Gee, I'd love to go with you sometime, Dad.

WILLY: Soon as summer comes.

HAPPY: Promise?

WILLY: You and Hap and I, and I'll show you all the towns. America is full of beautiful towns and fine, upstanding people. And they know me, boys, they know me up and down New England. The finest people. And when I bring you fellas up, there'll be open sesame for all of us, 'cause one thing, boys: I have friends. I can park my car in any street in New England, and the cops protect it like their own. This summer, heh?

BIFF AND HAPPY (*together*): Yeah! You bet!

WILLY: We'll take our bathing suits.

HAPPY: We'll carry your bags, Pop!

WILLY: Oh, won't that be something! Me comin' into the Boston stores with you boys carryin' my bags. What a sensation!

(BIFF *is prancing around, practicing passing the ball.*)

WILLY: You nervous, Biff, about the game?

BIFF: Not if you're gonna be there.

WILLY: What do they say about you in school, now that they made you captain?

HAPPY: There's a crowd of girls behind him everytime the classes change.

BIFF (*taking* WILLY'*s hand*): This Saturday, Pop, this Saturday — just for you, I'm going to break through for a touchdown.

HAPPY: You're supposed to pass.

BIFF: I'm takin' one play for Pop. You watch me, Pop, and when I take off my helmet, that means I'm breakin' out. Then you watch me crash through that line!

WILLY (*kisses* BIFF): Oh, wait'll I tell this in Boston!

(BERNARD *enters in knickers. He is younger than* BIFF, *earnest and loyal, a worried boy.*)

BERNARD: Biff, where are you? You're supposed to study with me today.

WILLY: Hey, looka Bernard. What're you lookin' so anemic about, Bernard?

BERNARD: He's gotta study, Uncle Willy. He's got Regents next week.

HAPPY (*tauntingly, spinning* BERNARD *around*): Let's box, Bernard!

BERNARD: Biff! (*He gets away from* HAPPY.) Listen, Biff, I heard Mr. Birnbaum say that if you don't start studyin' math he's gonna flunk you, and you won't graduate. I heard him!

WILLY: You better study with him, Biff. Go ahead now.

BERNARD: I heard him!

BIFF: Oh, Pop, you didn't see my sneakers! (*He holds up a foot for* WILLY *to look at.*)

WILLY: Hey, that's a beautiful job of printing!

BERNARD (*wiping his glasses*): Just because he printed University of Virginia on his sneakers doesn't mean they've got to graduate him, Uncle Willy!

WILLY (*angrily*): What're you talking about? With scholarships to three universities they're gonna flunk him?

BERNARD: But I heard Mr. Birnbaum say —

WILLY: Don't be a pest, Bernard! (*To his boys.*) What an anemic!

BERNARD: Okay, I'm waiting for you in my house, Biff.

(*Bernard goes off.* THE LOMANS *laugh.*)

WILLY: Bernard is not well liked, is he?

BIFF: He's liked, but he's not well liked.

HAPPY: That's right, Pop.

WILLY: That's just what I mean. Bernard can get the best marks in school, y'understand, but when he gets out in the business world, y'understand, you are going to be five times ahead of him. That's why I thank Almighty God you're both built like Adonises. Because the man who makes an appearance in the business world, the man who creates personal interest, is the man who gets ahead. Be liked and you will never want. You take me, for instance. I never have to wait in line to see a buyer. "Willy Loman is here!" That's all they have to know, and I go right through.

BIFF: Did you knock them dead, Pop?

WILLY: Knocked 'em cold in Providence, slaughtered 'em in Boston.

HAPPY (*on his back, pedaling again*): I'm losing weight, you notice, Pop?

(LINDA *enters, as of old, a ribbon in her hair, carrying a basket of washing.*)

LINDA (*with youthful energy*): Hello, dear!

WILLY: Sweetheart!

LINDA: How'd the Chevvy run?

WILLY: Chevrolet, Linda, is the greatest car ever built. (*To the boys.*) Since when do you let your mother carry wash up the stairs?

BIFF: Grab hold there, boy!

HAPPY: Where to, Mom?

LINDA: Hang them up on the line. And you better go down to your friends, Biff. The cellar is full of boys. They don't know what to do with themselves.

BIFF: Ah, when Pop comes home they can wait!

WILLY (*laughs appreciatively*): You better go down and tell them what to do, Biff.

BIFF: I think I'll have them sweep out the furnace room.

WILLY: Good work, Biff.

BIFF (*goes through wall-line of kitchen to doorway at back and calls down*): Fellas! Everybody sweep out the furnace room! I'll be right down!

VOICES: All right! Okay, Biff.

BIFF: George and Sam and Frank, come out back! We're hangin' up the wash! Come on, Hap, on the double! (*He and* HAPPY *carry out the basket.*)

LINDA: The way they obey him!

WILLY: Well, that's training, the training. I'm tellin' you, I was sellin' thousands and thousands, but I had to come home.

LINDA: Oh, the whole block'll be at that game. Did you sell anything?

WILLY: I did five hundred gross in Providence and seven hundred gross in Boston.

LINDA: No! Wait a minute, I've got a pencil. (*She pulls pencil and paper out of her apron pocket.*) That makes your commission . . . Two hundred — my God! Two hundred and twelve dollars!

WILLY: Well, I didn't figure it yet, but . . .

LINDA: How much did you do?

WILLY: Well, I — I did — about a hundred and eighty gross in Providence. Well, no — it came to — roughly two hundred gross on the whole trip.

LINDA (*without hesitation*): Two hundred gross. That's . . . (*She figures.*)

WILLY: The trouble was that three of the stores were half closed for inventory in Boston. Otherwise I woulda broke records.

LINDA: Well, it makes seventy dollars and some pennies. That's very good.

WILLY: What do we owe?

LINDA: Well, on the first there's sixteen dollars on the refrigerator —

WILLY: Why sixteen?

LINDA: Well, the fan belt broke, so it was a dollar eighty.

WILLY: But it's brand new.

LINDA: Well, the man said that's the way it is. Till they work themselves in, y'know.

(*They move through the wall-line into the kitchen.*)

WILLY: I hope we didn't get stuck on that machine.

LINDA: They got the biggest ads of any of them!

WILLY: I know, it's a fine machine. What else?

LINDA: Well, there's nine-sixty for the washing machine. And for the vacuum cleaner there's three and a half due on the fifteenth. Then the roof, you got twenty-one dollars remaining.

WILLY: It don't leak, does it?

LINDA: No, they did a wonderful job. Then you owe Frank for the carburetor.

WILLY: I'm not going to pay that man! That goddam Chevrolet, they ought to prohibit the manufacture of that car!

LINDA: Well, you owe him three and a half. And odds and ends, comes to around a hundred and twenty dollars by the fifteenth.

WILLY: A hundred and twenty dollars! My God, if business don't pick up I don't know what I'm gonna do!

LINDA: Well, next week you'll do better.

WILLY: Oh, I'll knock 'em dead next week. I'll go to Hartford. I'm very well liked in Hartford. You know, the trouble is, Linda, people don't seem to take to me.

(*They move onto the forestage.*)

LINDA: Oh, don't be foolish.

WILLY: I know it when I walk in. They seem to laugh at me.

LINDA: Why? Why would they laugh at you? Don't talk that way, Willy.

(WILLY *moves to the edge of the stage.* LINDA *goes into the kitchen and starts to darn stockings.*)

WILLY: I don't know the reason for it, but they just pass me by. I'm not noticed.

LINDA: But you're doing wonderful, dear. You're making seventy to a hundred dollars a week.

WILLY: But I gotta be at it ten, twelve hours a day. Other men — I don't know — they do it easier. I don't know why — I can't stop myself — I talk too much. A man oughta come in with a few words. One thing about Charley. He's a man of few words, and they respect him.

LINDA: You don't talk too much, you're just lively.

WILLY (*smiling*): Well, I figure, what the hell, life is short, a couple of jokes. (*To himself.*) I joke too much! (*The smile goes.*)

LINDA: Why? You're —

WILLY: I'm fat. I'm very — foolish to look at, Linda. I didn't tell you, but Christmas time I happened to be calling on F. H. Stewarts, and a salesman I know, as I was going in to see the buyer I heard him say something about — walrus. And I — I cracked him right across the face. I won't take that. I simply will not take that. But they do laugh at me. I know that.

LINDA: Darling . . .

WILLY: I gotta overcome it. I know I gotta overcome it. I'm not dressing to advantage, maybe.

LINDA: Willy, darling, you're the handsomest man in the world —

WILLY: Oh, no, Linda.

LINDA: To me you are. (*Slight pause.*) The handsomest.

(*From the darkness is heard the laughter of a woman.* WILLY *doesn't turn to it, but it continues through* LINDA's *lines.*)

LINDA: And the boys, Willy. Few men are idolized by their children the way you are.

(*Music is heard as behind a scrim, to the left of the house,* THE WOMAN, *dimly seen, is dressing.*)

WILLY (*with great feeling*): You're the best there is, Linda, you're a pal, you know that? On the road — on the road I want to grab you sometimes and just kiss the life outa you.

(*The laughter is loud now, and he moves into a brightening area at the left, where* THE WOMAN *has come from behind the scrim and is standing, putting on her hat, looking into a "mirror" and laughing.*)

WILLY: 'Cause I get so lonely — especially when business is bad and there's nobody to talk to. I get the feeling that I'll never sell anything again, that I won't make a living for you, or a business, a business for the boys. (*He talks through* THE WOMAN'S *subsiding laughter;* THE WOMAN *primps at the "mirror."*) There's so much I want to make for —

THE WOMAN: Me? You didn't make me, Willy. I picked you.

WILLY (*pleased*): You picked me?

THE WOMAN (*who is quite proper-looking,* WILLY'S *age*): I did. I've been sitting at that desk watching all the salesmen go by, day in, day out. But you've got such a sense of humor, and we do have such a good time together, don't we?

WILLY: Sure, sure. (*He takes her in his arms.*) Why do you have to go now?

THE WOMAN: It's two o'clock . . .

WILLY: No, come on in! (*He pulls her.*)

THE WOMAN: . . . my sisters'll be scandalized. When'll you be back?

WILLY: Oh, two weeks about. Will you come up again?

THE WOMAN: Sure thing. You do make me laugh. It's good for me. (*She squeezes his arm, kisses him.*) And I think you're a wonderful man.

WILLY: You picked me, heh?

THE WOMAN: Sure. Because you're so sweet. And such a kidder.

WILLY: Well, I'll see you next time I'm in Boston.

THE WOMAN: I'll put you right through to the buyers.

WILLY (*slapping her bottom*): Right. Well, bottoms up!

THE WOMAN (*slaps him gently and laughs*): You just kill me, Willy. (*He suddenly grabs her and kisses her roughly.*) You kill me. And thanks for the stockings. I love a lot of stockings. Well, good night.

WILLY: Good night. And keep your pores open!

THE WOMAN: Oh, Willy!

(THE WOMAN *bursts out laughing, and* LINDA's *laughter blends in.* THE WOMAN *disappears into the dark. Now the area at the kitchen table brightens.* LINDA *is sitting where she was at the kitchen table, but now is mending a pair of her silk stockings.*)

LINDA: You are, Willy. The handsomest man. You've got no reason to feel that —

WILLY (*coming out of* THE WOMAN's *dimming area and going over to* LINDA): I'll make it all up to you, Linda, I'll —

LINDA: There's nothing to make up, dear. You're doing fine, better than —

WILLY (*noticing her mending*): What's that?

LINDA: Just mending my stockings. They're so expensive —

WILLY (*angrily, taking them from her*): I won't have you mending stockings in this house! Now throw them out!

(LINDA *puts the stockings in her pocket.*)

BERNARD (*entering on the run*): Where is he? If he doesn't study!

WILLY (*moving to the forestage, with great agitation*): You'll give him the answers!

BERNARD: I do, but I can't on a Regents! That's a state exam! They're liable to arrest me!

WILLY: Where is he? I'll whip him, I'll whip him!

LINDA: And he'd better give back that football, Willy, it's not nice.

WILLY: Biff! Where is he? Why is he taking everything?

LINDA: He's too rough with the girls, Willy. All the mothers are afraid of him!

WILLY: I'll whip him!

BERNARD: He's driving the car without a license!

(THE WOMAN's *laugh is heard.*)

WILLY: Shut up!

LINDA: All the mothers —

WILLY: Shut up!

BERNARD (*backing quietly away and out*): Mr. Birnbaum says he's stuck up.

WILLY: Get outa here!

BERNARD: If he doesn't buckle down he'll flunk math! (*He goes off.*)

LINDA: He's right, Willy, you've gotta —

WILLY (*exploding at her*): There's nothing the matter with him! You want him to be a worm like Bernard? He's got spirit, personality . . .

(*As he speaks,* LINDA, *almost in tears, exits into the living-room.* WILLY *is alone in the kitchen, wilting and staring. The leaves are gone. It is night again, and the apartment houses look down from behind.*)

WILLY: Loaded with it. Loaded! What is he stealing? He's giving it back, isn't he? Why is he stealing? What did I tell him? I never in my life told him anything but decent things.

(HAPPY *in pajamas has come down the stairs;* WILLY *suddenly becomes aware of* HAPPY's *presence.*)

HAPPY: Let's go now, come on.

WILLY (*sitting down at the kitchen table*): Huh! Why did she have to wax the floors herself? Everytime she waxes the floors she keels over. She knows that!

HAPPY: Shh! Take it easy. What brought you back tonight?

WILLY: I got an awful scare. Nearly hit a kid in Yonkers. God! Why didn't I go to Alaska with my brother Ben that time! Ben! That man was a genius, that man was success incarnate! What a mistake! He begged me to go.

HAPPY: Well, there's no use in —

WILLY: You guys! There was a man started with the clothes on his back and ended up with diamond mines!

HAPPY: Boy, someday I'd like to know how he did it.

WILLY: What's the mystery? The man knew what he wanted and went out and got it! Walked into a jungle, and comes out, the age of twenty-one, and he's rich! The world is an oyster, but you don't crack it open on a mattress!

HAPPY: Pop, I told you I'm gonna retire you for life.

WILLY: You'll retire me for life on seventy goddam dollars a week? And your women and your car and your apartment, and you'll retire me for life! Christ's sake, I couldn't get past Yonkers today! Where are you guys, where are you? The woods are burning! I can't drive a car!

(CHARLEY *has appeared in the doorway. He is a large man, slow of speech, laconic, immovable. In all he says, despite what he says, there is pity, and, now,* trepidation. *He has a robe over pajamas, slippers on his feet. He enters the kitchen.*)

CHARLEY: Everything all right?

HAPPY: Yeah, Charley, everything's . . .

WILLY: What's the matter?

CHARLEY: I heard some noise. I thought something happened. Can't we do something about the walls? You sneeze in here, and in my house hats blow off.

HAPPY: Let's go to bed, Dad. Come on.

(CHARLEY *signals to* HAPPY *to go.*)

WILLY: You go ahead, I'm not tired at the moment.

HAPPY (*to* WILLY): Take it easy, huh? (*He exits.*)

WILLY: What're you doin' up?

CHARLEY (*sitting down at the kitchen table opposite* WILLY): Couldn't sleep good. I had a heartburn.

WILLY: Well, you don't know how to eat.

CHARLEY: I eat with my mouth.

WILLY: No, you're ignorant. You gotta know about vitamins and things like that.

CHARLEY: Come on, let's shoot. Tire you out a little.

WILLY (*hesitantly*): All right. You got cards?

CHARLEY (*taking a deck from his pocket*): Yeah, I got them. Someplace. What is it with those vitamins?

WILLY (*dealing*): They build up your bones. Chemistry.

CHARLEY: Yeah, but there's no bones in a heartburn.

WILLY: What are you talkin' about? Do you know the first thing about it?

CHARLEY: Don't get insulted.

WILLY: Don't talk about something you don't know anything about.

(*They are playing. Pause.*)

CHARLEY: What're you doin' home?

WILLY: A little trouble with the car.

CHARLEY: Oh. (*Pause.*) I'd like to take a trip to California.

WILLY: Don't say.

CHARLEY: You want a job?

WILLY: I got a job, I told you that. (*After a slight pause.*) What the hell are you offering me a job for?

CHARLEY: Don't get insulted.

WILLY: Don't insult me.

CHARLEY: I don't see no sense in it. You don't have to go on this way.

WILLY: I got a good job. (*Slight pause.*) What do you keep comin' in here for?

CHARLEY: You want me to go?

WILLY (*after a pause, withering*): I can't understand it. He's going back to Texas again. What the hell is that?

CHARLEY: Let him go.

WILLY: I got nothin' to give him, Charley, I'm clean, I'm clean.

CHARLEY: He won't starve. None a them starve. Forget about him.

WILLY: Then what have I got to remember?

CHARLEY: You take it too hard. To hell with it. When a deposit bottle is broken you don't get your nickel back.

WILLY: That's easy enough for you to say.

CHARLEY: That ain't easy for me to say.

WILLY: Did you see the ceiling I put up in the living-room?

CHARLEY: Yeah, that's a piece of work. To put up a ceiling is a mystery to me. How do you do it?

WILLY: What's the difference?

CHARLEY: Well, talk about it.

WILLY: You gonna put up a ceiling?

CHARLEY: How could I put up a ceiling?

WILLY: Then what the hell are you bothering me for?

CHARLEY: You're insulted again.

WILLY: A man who can't handle tools is not a man. You're disgusting.

CHARLEY: Don't call me disgusting, Willy.

(UNCLE BEN, *carrying a valise and an umbrella, enters the forestage from around the right corner of the house. He is a stolid man, in his sixties, with a mustache and an authoritative air. He is utterly certain of his destiny, and there is an aura of far places about him. He enters exactly as* WILLY *speaks.*)

WILLY: I'm getting awfully tired, Ben.

(BEN's *music is heard.* BEN *looks around at everything.*)

CHARLEY: Good, keep playing; you'll sleep better. Did you call me Ben?

(BEN *looks at his watch.*)

WILLY: That's funny. For a second there you reminded me of my brother Ben.

BEN: I only have a few minutes. (*He strolls, inspecting the place.* WILLY *and* CHARLEY *continue playing.*)

CHARLEY: You never heard from him again, heh? Since that time?

WILLY: Didn't Linda tell you? Couple of weeks ago we got a letter from his wife in Africa. He died.

CHARLEY: That so.

BEN (*chuckling*): So this is Brooklyn, eh?

CHARLEY: Maybe you're in for some of his money.

WILLY: Naa, he had seven sons. There's just one opportunity I had with that man . . .

BEN: I must make a train, William. There are several properties I'm looking at in Alaska.

WILLY: Sure, sure! If I'd gone with him to Alaska that time, everything would've been totally different.

CHARLEY: Go on, you'd froze to death up there.

WILLY: What're you talking about?

BEN: Opportunity is tremendous in Alaska, William. Surprised you're not up there.

WILLY: Sure, tremendous.

CHARLEY: Heh?

WILLY: There was the only man I ever met who knew the answers.

CHARLEY: Who?

BEN: How are you all?

WILLY (*taking a pot, smiling*): Fine, fine.

CHARLEY: Pretty sharp tonight.

BEN: Is Mother living with you?

WILLY: No, she died a long time ago.

CHARLEY: Who?

BEN: That's too bad. Fine specimen of a lady, Mother.

WILLY (*to* CHARLEY): Heh?

BEN: I'd hoped to see the old girl.

CHARLEY: Who died?

BEN: Heard anything from Father, have you?

WILLY (*unnerved*): What do you mean, who died?

CHARLEY (*taking a pot*): What're you talkin' about?

BEN (*looking at his watch*): William, it's half-past eight!

WILLY (*as though to dispel his confusion he*

angrily stops CHARLEY's *hand*): That's my build!

CHARLEY: I put the ace —

WILLY: If you don't know how to play the game I'm not gonna throw my money away on you!

CHARLEY (*rising*): It was my ace, for God's sake!

WILLY: I'm through, I'm through!

BEN: When did Mother die?

WILLY: Long ago. Since the beginning you never knew how to play cards.

CHARLEY (*picks up the cards and goes to the door*): All right! Next time I'll bring a deck with five aces.

WILLY: I don't play that kind of game!

CHARLEY (*turning to him*): You ought to be ashamed of yourself!

WILLY: Yeah?

CHARLEY: Yeah! (*He goes out.*)

WILLY (*slamming the door after him*): Ignoramus!

BEN (*as* WILLY *comes toward him through the wall-line of the kitchen*): So you're William.

WILLY (*shaking* BEN's *hand*): Ben! I've been waiting for you so long! What's the answer? How did you do it?

BEN: Oh, there's a story in that.

(LINDA *enters the forestage, as of old, carrying the wash basket.*)

LINDA: Is this Ben?

BEN (*gallantly*): How do you do, my dear.

LINDA: Where've you been all these years? Willy's always wondered why you —

WILLY (*pulling* BEN *away from her impatiently*): Where is Dad? Didn't you follow him? How did you get started?

BEN: Well, I don't know how much you remember.

WILLY: Well, I was just a baby, of course, only three or four years old —

BEN: Three years and eleven months.

WILLY: What a memory, Ben!

BEN: I have many enterprises, William, and I have never kept books.

WILLY: I remember I was sitting under the wagon in — was it Nebraska?

BEN: It was South Dakota, and I gave you a bunch of wild flowers.

WILLY: I remember you walking away down some open road.

BEN (*laughing*): I was going to find Father in Alaska.

WILLY: Where is he?

BEN: At that age I had a very faulty view of geography, William. I discovered after a few days that I was heading due south, so instead of Alaska, I ended up in Africa.

LINDA: Africa!

WILLY: The Gold Coast!

BEN: Principally diamond mines.

LINDA: Diamond mines!

BEN: Yes, my dear. But I've only a few minutes —

WILLY: No! Boys! Boys! (YOUNG BIFF *and* HAPPY *appear.*) Listen to this. This is your Uncle Ben, a great man! Tell my boys, Ben!

BEN: Why, boys, when I was seventeen I walked into the jungle, and when I was twenty-one I walked out. (*He laughs.*) And by God I was rich.

WILLY (*to the boys*): You see what I been talking about? The greatest things can happen!

BEN (*glancing at his watch*): I have an appointment in Ketchikan Tuesday week.

WILLY: No, Ben! Please tell about Dad. I want my boys to hear. I want them to know the kind of stock they spring from. All I remember is a man with a big beard, and I was in Mamma's lap, sitting around a fire, and some kind of high music.

BEN: His flute. He played the flute.

WILLY: Sure, the flute, that's right!

(*New music is heard, a high, rollicking tune.*)

BEN: Father was a very great and a very wild-hearted man. We would start in Boston, and he'd toss the whole family into the wagon, and then he'd drive the team right across the country; through Ohio, and Indiana, Michigan, Illinois, and all the Western states. And we'd stop in the towns and sell the flutes that he'd made on the way. Great inventor, Father. With one gadget he made more in a week than a man like you could make in a lifetime.

WILLY: That's just the way I'm bringing them up, Ben — rugged, well liked, all-around.

BEN: Yeah? (*To* BIFF.) Hit that, boy — hard as you can. (*He pounds his stomach.*)

BIFF: Oh, no, sir!

BEN (*taking boxing stance*): Come on, get to me! (*He laughs.*)

WILLY: Go to it, Biff! Go ahead, show him!

BIFF: Okay! (*He cocks his fists and starts in.*)

LINDA (*to* WILLY): Why must he fight, dear?

BEN (*sparring with* BIFF): Good boy! Good boy!

WILLY: How's that, Ben, heh?

HAPPY: Give him the left, Biff!

LINDA: Why are you fighting?

BEN: Good boy! (*Suddenly comes in, trips* BIFF, *and stands over him, the point of his umbrella poised over* BIFF's *eye.*)

LINDA: Look out, Biff!

BIFF: Gee!

BEN (*patting* BIFF's *knee*): Never fight fair with a stranger, boy. You'll never get out of the jungle that way. (*Taking* LINDA's *hand and bowing.*) It was an honor and a pleasure to meet you, Linda.

LINDA (*withdrawing her hand coldly, frightened*): Have a nice — trip.

BEN (*to* WILLY): And good luck with your — what do you do?

WILLY: Selling.

BEN: Yes. Well . : . (*He raises his hand in farewell to all.*)

WILLY: No, Ben, I don't want you to think . . . (*He takes* BEN's *arm to show him.*) It's Brooklyn, I know, but we hunt too.

BEN: Really, now.

WILLY: Oh, sure, there's snakes and rabbits and — that's why I moved out here. Why, Biff can fell any one of these trees in no time! Boys! Go right over to where they're building the apartment house and get some sand. We're gonna rebuild the entire front stoop right now! Watch this, Ben!

BIFF: Yes, sir! On the double, Hap!

HAPPY (*as he and* BIFF *run off*): I lost weight, Pop, you notice?

(CHARLEY *enters in knickers, even before the boys are gone.*)

CHARLEY: Listen, if they steal any more from that building the watchman'll put the cops on them!

LINDA (*to* WILLY): Don't let Biff . . .

(BEN *laughs lustily.*)

WILLY: You shoulda seen the lumber they brought home last week. At least a dozen six-by-tens worth all kinds a money.

CHARLEY: Listen, if that watchman —

WILLY: I gave them hell, understand. But I got a couple of fearless characters there.

CHARLEY: Willy, the jails are full of fearless characters.

BEN (*clapping* WILLY *on the back, with a laugh at* CHARLEY): And the stock exchange, friend!

WILLY (*joining in* BEN's *laughter*): Where are the rest of your pants?

CHARLEY: My wife bought them.

WILLY: Now all you need is a golf club and you can go upstairs and go to sleep. (*To* BEN.) Great athlete! Between him and his son Bernard they can't hammer a nail!

BERNARD (*rushing in*): The watchman's chasing Biff!

WILLY (*angrily*): Shut up! He's not stealing anything!

LINDA (*alarmed, hurrying off left*): Where is he? Biff, dear! (*She exits.*)

WILLY (*moving toward the left, away from* BEN): There's nothing wrong. What's the matter with you?

BEN: Nervy boy. Good!

WILLY (*laughing*): Oh, nerves of iron, that Biff!

CHARLEY: Don't know what it is. My New England man comes back and he's bleedin', they murdered him up there.

WILLY: It's contacts, Charley, I got important contacts!

CHARLEY (*sarcastically*): Glad to hear it, Willy. Come in later, we'll shoot a little casino. I'll take some of your Portland money. (*He laughs at* WILLY *and exists.*)

WILLY (*turning to* BEN): Business is bad, it's murderous. But not for me, of course.

BEN: I'll stop by on my way back to Africa.

WILLY (*longingly*): Can't you stay a few days? You're just what I need, Ben, because I — I have a fine position here, but I — well, Dad left when I was such a baby and I never had a chance to talk to him and I still feel — kind of temporary about myself.

BEN: I'll be late for my train.

(*They are at opposite ends of the stage.*)

WILLY: Ben, my boys — can't we talk? They'd go into the jaws of hell for me, see, but I —

BEN: William, you're being first-rate with your boys. Outstanding, manly chaps!

WILLY (*hanging on to his words*): Oh, Ben, that's good to hear! Because sometimes I'm afraid that I'm not teaching them the right kind of — Ben, how should I teach them?

BEN (*giving great weight to each word, and with a certain vicious audacity*): William, when I walked into the jungle, I was seventeen. When I walked out I was twenty-one. And, by God, I was rich! (*He goes off into darkness around the right corner of the house.*)

WILLY: . . . was rich! That's just the spirit I want to imbue them with! To walk into a jungle! I was right! I was right! I was right!

(BEN *is gone, but* WILLY *is still speaking to him as* LINDA, *in nightgown and robe, enters the kitchen, glances around for* WILLY, *then goes to the door of the house, looks out and sees him. Comes down to his left. He looks at her.*)

LINDA: Willy, dear? Willy?

WILLY: I was right!

LINDA: Did you have some cheese? (*He can't answer.*) It's very late, darling. Come to bed, heh?

WILLY (*looking straight up*): Gotta break your neck to see a star in this yard.

LINDA: You coming in?

WILLY: Whatever happened to that diamond watch fob? Remember? When Ben came from Africa that time? Didn't he give me a watch fob with a diamond in it?

LINDA: You pawned it, dear. Twelve, thirteen years ago. For Biff's radio correspondence course.

WILLY: Gee, that was a beautiful thing. I'll take a walk.

LINDA: But you're in your slippers.

WILLY (*starting to go around the house at the left*): I was right! I was! (*Half to* LINDA, *as he goes, shaking his head.*) What a man! There was a man worth talking to. I was right!

LINDA (*calling after* WILLY): But in your slippers, Willy!

(WILLY *is almost gone when* BIFF, *in his pajamas, comes down the stairs and enters the kitchen.*)

BIFF: What is he doing out there?

LINDA: Sh!

BIFF: God Almighty, Mom, how long has he been doing this?

LINDA: Don't, he'll hear you.

BIFF: What the hell is the matter with him?

LINDA: It'll pass by morning.

BIFF: Shouldn't we do anything?

LINDA: Oh, my dear, you should do a lot of things, but there's nothing to do, so go to sleep.

(HAPPY *comes down the stairs and sits on the steps.*)

HAPPY: I never heard him so loud, Mom.

LINDA: Well, come around more often; you'll hear him. (*She sits down at the table and mends the lining of* WILLY's *jacket.*)

BIFF: Why didn't you ever write me about this, Mom?

LINDA: How would I write to you? For over three months you had no address.

BIFF: I was on the move. But you know I thought of you all the time. You know that, don't you, pal?

LINDA: I know, dear, I know. But he likes to have a letter. Just to know that there's still a possibility for better things.

BIFF: He's not like this all the time, is he?

LINDA: It's when you come home he's always the worst.

BIFF: When I come home?

LINDA: When you write you're coming, he's all smiles, and talks about the future, and — he's just wonderful. And then the closer you seem to come, the more shaky he gets, and then, by the time you get here, he's arguing, and he seems angry at you. I think it's just that maybe he can't bring himself to — to open up to you. Why are you so hateful to each other? Why is that?

BIFF (*evasively*): I'm not hateful, Mom.

LINDA: But you no sooner come in the door than you're fighting!

BIFF: I don't know why. I mean to change. I'm tryin', Mom, you understand?

LINDA: Are you home to stay now?

BIFF: I don't know. I want to look around, see what's doin'.

LINDA: Biff, you can't look around all your life, can you?

BIFF: I just can't take hold, Mom. I can't take hold of some kind of a life.

LINDA: Biff, a man is not a bird, to come and go with the springtime.

BIFF: Your hair . . . (*He touches her hair.*) Your hair got so gray.

LINDA: Oh, it's been gray since you were in high school. I just stopped dyeing it, that's all.

BIFF: Dye it again, will ya? I don't want my pal looking old. (*He smiles.*)

LINDA: You're such a boy! You think you can go away for a year and . . . You've got to get it into your head now that one day you'll knock on this door and there'll be strange people here —

BIFF: What are you talking about? You're not even sixty, Mom.

LINDA: But what about your father?

BIFF (*lamely*): Well, I meant him too.

HAPPY: He admires Pop.

LINDA: Biff, dear, if you don't have any feeling for him, then you can't have any feeling for me.

BIFF: Sure I can, Mom.

LINDA: No. You can't just come to see me, because I love him. (*With a threat, but only a threat, of tears.*) He's the dearest man in the world to me, and I won't have anyone making him feel unwanted and low and blue. You've got to make up your mind now, darling, there's no leeway any more. Either he's your father and you pay him that respect, or else you're not to come here. I know he's not easy to get along with — nobody knows that better than me — but . . .

WILLY (*from the left, with a laugh*): Hey, hey, Biffo!

BIFF (*starting to go out after* WILLY): What the hell is the matter with him? (HAPPY *stops him.*)

LINDA: Don't — don't go near him!

BIFF: Stop making excuses for him! He always, always wiped the floor with you. Never had an ounce of respect for you.

HAPPY: He's always had respect for —

BIFF: What the hell do you know about it?

HAPPY (*surlily*): Just don't call him crazy!

BIFF: He's got no character — Charley wouldn't do this. Not in his own house — spewing out that vomit from his mind.

HAPPY: Charley never had to cope with what he's got to.

BIFF: People are worse off than Willy Loman. Believe me, I've seen them!

LINDA: Then make Charley your father, Biff. You can't do that, can you? I don't say he's a great man. Willy Loman never made a lot of money. His name was never in the paper. He's not the finest character that ever lived. But he's a human being, and a terrible thing is happening to him. So attention must be paid. He's not to be allowed to fall into his grave like an old dog. Attention, attention must be finally paid to such a person. You called him crazy —

BIFF: I didn't mean —

LINDA: No, a lot of people think he's lost his — balance. But you don't have to be very smart to know what his trouble is. The man is exhausted.

HAPPY: Sure!

LINDA: A small man can be just as exhausted as a great man. He works for a company thirty-six years this March, opens up unheard-of territories to their trademark, and now in his old age they take his salary away.

HAPPY (*indignantly*): I didn't know that, Mom.

LINDA: You never asked, my dear! Now that you get your spending money someplace else you don't trouble your mind with him.

HAPPY: But I gave you money last —

LINDA: Christmas time, fifty dollars! To fix the hot water it cost ninety-seven fifty! For five weeks he's been on straight commission, like a beginner, an unknown!

BIFF: Those ungrateful bastards!

LINDA: Are they any worse than his sons? When he brought them business, when he was young, they were glad to see him. But now his old friends, the old buyers that loved him so and always found some order to hand him in a pinch — they're all dead, retired. He used to be able to make six, seven calls a day in Boston. Now he takes his valises out of the car and puts them back and takes them out again and he's exhausted. Instead of walking he talks now. He drives seven hundred miles, and when he gets there no one knows him any more, no one welcomes him. And what goes through a man's mind, driving seven hundred miles home without having earned a cent? Why shouldn't he talk to himself? Why? When he has to go to Charley and borrow fifty dollars a week and pretend to me that it's his pay? How long can that go on? How long? You see what I'm sitting here and waiting for? And you tell me he has no character? The man who never worked a day but for your benefit? When does he get the medal for that? Is this his reward — to turn around at the age of sixty-three and find his sons, who he loved better than his life, one a philandering bum —

HAPPY: Mom!

LINDA: That's all you are, my baby! (*To* BIFF.) And you! What happened to the love you had for him? You were such pals! How you used to talk to him on the phone every night! How lonely he was till he could come home to you!

BIFF: All right, Mom. I'll live here in my room, and I'll get a job. I'll keep away from him, that's all.

LINDA: No, Biff. You can't stay here and fight all the time.

BIFF: He threw me out of this house, remember that.

LINDA: Why did he do that? I never knew why.

BIFF: Because I know he's a fake and he doesn't like anybody around who knows!

LINDA: Why a fake? In what way? What do you mean?

BIFF: Just don't lay it all at my feet. It's between me and him — that's all I have to say. I'll chip in from now on. He'll settle for half my pay check. He'll be all right. I'm going to bed. (*He starts for the stairs.*)

LINDA: He won't be all right.

BIFF (*turning on the stairs, furiously*): I hate this city and I'll stay here. Now what do you want?

LINDA: He's dying, Biff.

(HAPPY *turns quickly to her, shocked.*)

BIFF (*after a pause*): Why is he dying?

LINDA: He's been trying to kill himself.

BIFF (*with great horror*): How?

LINDA: I live from day to day.

BIFF: What're you talking about?

LINDA: Remember I wrote you that he smashed up the car again? In February?

BIFF: Well?

LINDA: The insurance inspector came. He said that they have evidence. That all these accidents in the last year — weren't — weren't — accidents.

HAPPY: How can they tell that? That's a lie.

LINDA: It seems there's a woman ... (*She takes a breath as —*)

{ BIFF (*sharply but contained*): What woman?
{ LINDA (*simultaneously*): . . . and this woman ...

LINDA: What?

BIFF: Nothing. Go ahead.

LINDA: What did you say?

BIFF: Nothing. I just said what woman?

HAPPY: What about her?

LINDA: Well, it seems she was walking down the road and saw his car. She says that he wasn't driving fast at all, and that he didn't

skid. She says he came to that little bridge, and then deliberately smashed into the railing, and it was only the shallowness of the water that saved him.

BIFF: Oh, no, he probably just fell asleep again.

LINDA: I don't think he fell asleep.

BIFF: Why not?

LINDA: Last month ... (*With great difficulty.*) Oh, boys, it's so hard to say a thing like this! He's just a big stupid man to you, but I tell you there's more good in him than in many other people. (*She chokes, wipes her eyes.*) I was looking for a fuse. The lights blew out, and I went down the cellar. And behind the fuse box — it happened to fall out — was a length of rubber pipe — just short.

HAPPY: No kidding?

LINDA: There's a little attachment on the end of it. I knew right away. And sure enough, on the bottom of the water heater there's a new little nipple on the gas pipe.

HAPPY (*angrily*): That — jerk.

BIFF: Did you have it taken off?

LINDA: I'm — I'm ashamed to. How can I mention it to him? Every day I go down and take away that little rubber pipe. But, when he comes home, I put it back where it was. How can I insult him that way? I don't know what to do. I live from day to day, boys. I tell you, I know every thought in his mind. It sounds so old-fashioned and silly, but I tell you he put his whole life into you and you've turned your backs on him. (*She is bent over in the chair, weeping, her face in her hands.*) Biff, I swear to God! Biff, his life is in your hands!

HAPPY (*to* BIFF): How do you like that damned fool!

BIFF (*kissing her*): All right, pal, all right. It's all settled now. I've been remiss. I know that, Mom. But now I'll stay, and I swear to you, I'll apply myself. (*Kneeling in front of her, in a fever of self-reproach.*) It's just — you see, Mom, I don't fit in business. Not that I won't try. I'll try, and I'll make good.

HAPPY: Sure you will. The trouble with you in business was you never tried to please people.

BIFF: I know, I —

HAPPY: Like when you worked for Harrison's. Bob Harrison said you were tops, and then you go and do some damn fool thing like whistling whole songs in the elevator like a comedian.

BIFF (*against* HAPPY): So what? I like to whistle sometimes.

HAPPY: You don't raise a guy to a responsible job who whistles in the elevator!

LINDA: Well, don't argue about it now.

HAPPY: Like when you'd go off and swim in the middle of the day instead of taking the line around.

BIFF (*his resentment rising*): Well, don't you run off? You take off sometimes, don't you? On a nice summer day?

HAPPY: Yeah, but I cover myself!

LINDA: Boys!

HAPPY: If I'm going to take a fade the boss can call any number where I'm supposed to be and they'll swear to him that I just left. I'll tell you something that I hate to say, Biff, but in the business world some of them think you're crazy.

BIFF (*angered*): Screw the business world!

HAPPY: All right, screw it! Great, but cover yourself!

LINDA: Hap, Hap!

BIFF: I don't care what they think! They've laughed at Dad for years, and you know why? Because we don't belong in this nut-house of a city! We should be mixing cement on some open plain, or — or carpenters. A carpenter is allowed to whistle!

(WILLY *walks in from the entrance of the house, at left.*)

WILLY: Even your grandfather was better than a carpenter. (*Pause. They watch him.*) You never grew up. Bernard does not whistle in the elevator, I assure you.

BIFF (*as though to laugh* WILLY *out of it*): Yeah, but you do, Pop.

WILLY: I never in my life whistled in an elevator! And who in the business world thinks I'm crazy?

BIFF: I didn't mean it like that, Pop. Now don't make a whole thing out of it, will ya?

WILLY: Go back to the West! Be a carpenter, a cowboy, enjoy yourself!

LINDA: Willy, he was just saying —

WILLY: I heard what he said!

HAPPY (*trying to quiet* WILLY): Hey, Pop, come on now . . .

WILLY (*continuing over* HAPPY'S *line*): They laugh at me, heh? Go to Filene's, go to the Hub, go to Slattery's, Boston. Call out the name Willy Loman and see what happens! Big shot!

BIFF: All right, Pop.

WILLY: Big!

BIFF: All right!

WILLY: Why do you always insult me?

BIFF: I didn't say a word. (*To* LINDA.) Did I say a word?

LINDA: He didn't say anything, Willy.

WILLY (*going to the doorway of the living-room*): All right, good night, good night.

LINDA: Willy, dear, he just decided . . .

WILLY (*to* BIFF): If you get tired hanging around tomorrow, paint the ceiling I put up in the living-room.

BIFF: I'm leaving early tomorrow.

HAPPY: He's going to see Bill Oliver, Pop.

WILLY (*interestedly*): Oliver? For what?

BIFF (*with reserve, but trying, trying*): He always said he'd stake me. I'd like to go into business, so maybe I can take him up on it.

LINDA: Isn't that wonderful?

WILLY: Don't interrupt. What's wonderful about it? There's fifty men in the City of New York who'd stake him. (*To* BIFF.) Sporting goods?

BIFF: I guess so. I know something about it and —

WILLY: He knows something about it! You know sporting goods better than Spalding, for God's sake! How much is he giving you?

BIFF: I don't know, I didn't even see him yet, but —

WILLY: Then what're you talkin' about?

BIFF (*getting angry*): Well, all I said was I'm gonna see him, that's all!

WILLY (*turning away*): Ah, you're counting your chickens again.

BIFF (*starting left for the stairs*): Oh, Jesus, I'm going to sleep!

WILLY (*calling after him*): Don't curse in this house!

BIFF (*turning*): Since when did you get so clean?

HAPPY (*trying to stop them*): Wait a . . .

WILLY: Don't use that language to me! I won't have it!

HAPPY (*grabbing* BIFF, *shouts*): Wait a minute! I got an idea. I got a feasible idea. Come here, Biff, let's talk this over now, let's talk some sense here. When I was down in Florida last time, I thought of a great idea to sell sporting goods. It just came back to me. You and I, Biff — we have a line, the Loman Line. We train a couple of weeks, and put on a couple of exhibitions, see?

WILLY: That's an idea!

HAPPY: Wait! We form two basketball teams, see? Two water-polo teams. We play each other. It's a million dollars' worth of publicity. Two brothers, see? The Loman Brothers. Displays in the Royal Palms — all the hotels. And banners over the ring and the basketball court: "Loman Brothers." Baby, we could sell sporting goods!

WILLY: That is a one-million-dollar idea!

LINDA: Marvelous!

BIFF: I'm in great shape as far as that's concerned.

HAPPY: And the beauty of it is, Biff, it wouldn't be like a business. We'd be out playin' ball again . . .

BIFF (*enthused*): Yeah, that's . . .

WILLY: Million-dollar . . .

HAPPY: And you wouldn't get fed up with it, Biff. It'd be the family again. There'd be the old honor, and comradeship, and if you wanted to go off for a swim or somethin' — well, you'd do it! Without some smart cooky gettin' up ahead of you!

WILLY: Lick the world! You guys together could absolutely lick the civilized world.

BIFF: I'll see Oliver tomorrow. Hap, if we could work that out . . .

LINDA: Maybe things are beginning to —

WILLY (*wildly enthused, to* LINDA): Stop interrupting! (*To* BIFF.) But don't wear sport jacket and slacks when you see Oliver.

BIFF: No, I'll —

WILLY: A business suit, and talk as little as possible, and don't crack any jokes.

BIFF: He did like me. Always liked me.

LINDA: He loved you!

WILLY (*to* LINDA): Will you stop! (*To* BIFF.) Walk in very serious. You are not applying for a boy's job. Money is to pass. Be quiet, fine, and serious. Everybody likes a kidder, but nobody lends him money.

HAPPY: I'll try to get some myself, Biff. I'm sure I can.

WILLY: I see great things for you kids, I think your troubles are over. But remember, start big and you'll end big. Ask for fifteen. How much you gonna ask for?

BIFF: Gee, I don't know —

WILLY: And don't say "Gee." "Gee" is a boy's word. A man walking in for fifteen thousand dollars does not say "Gee!"

BIFF: Ten, I think, would be top though.

WILLY: Don't be so modest. You always started too low. Walk in with a big laugh. Don't look worried. Start off with a couple of your good stories to lighten things up. It's not what you say, it's how you say it — because personality always wins the day.

LINDA: Oliver always thought the highest of him —

WILLY: Will you let me talk?

BIFF: Don't yell at her, Pop, will ya?

WILLY (*angrily*): I was talking, wasn't I?

BIFF: I don't like you yelling at her all the time, and I'm tellin' you, that's all.

WILLY: What're you, takin' over this house?

LINDA: Willy —

WILLY (*turning on her*): Don't take his side all the time, goddammit!

BIFF (*furiously*): Stop yelling at her!

WILLY (*suddenly pulling on his cheek, beaten down, guilt ridden*): Give my best to Bill Oliver — he may remember me. (*He exits through the living-room doorway.*)

LINDA (*her voice subdued*): What'd you have to start that for? (BIFF *turns away.*) You see how sweet he was as soon as you talked hopefully? (*She goes over to* BIFF.) Come up and say good night to him. Don't let him go to bed that way.

HAPPY: Come on, Biff, let's buck him up.

LINDA: Please, dear. Just say good night. It takes so little to make him happy. Come. (*She goes through the living-room doorway, calling upstairs from within the living-room.*) Your pajamas are hanging in the bathroom, Willy!

HAPPY (*looking toward where* LINDA *went out*): What a woman! They broke the mold when they made her. You know that, Biff?

BIFF: He's off salary. My God, working on commission!

HAPPY: Well, let's face it: he's no hot-shot selling man. Except that sometimes, you have to admit, he's a sweet personality.

BIFF (*deciding*): Lend me ten bucks, will ya? I want to buy some new ties.

HAPPY: I'll take you to a place I know. Beautiful stuff. Wear one of my striped shirts tomorrow.

BIFF: She got gray. Mom got awful old. Gee, I'm gonna go in to Oliver tomorrow and knock him for a —

HAPPY: Come on up. Tell that to Dad. Let's give him a whirl. Come on.

BIFF (*steamed up*): You know, with ten thousand bucks, boy!

HAPPY (*as they go into the living-room*): That's the talk, Biff, that's the first time I've heard the old confidence out of you! (*From within the living-room, fading off.*) You're gonna live with me, kid, and any babe you want just say the word . . . (*The last lines are hardly heard. They are mounting the stairs to their parents' bedroom.*)

LINDA (*entering her bedroom and addressing* WILLY, *who is in the bathroom. She is straightening the bed for him*): Can you do anything about the shower? It drips.

WILLY (*from the bathroom*): All of a sudden everything falls to pieces! Goddam plumbing, oughta be sued, those people. I hardly finished putting it in and the thing . . . (*His words rumble off.*)

LINDA: I'm just wondering if Oliver will remember him. You think he might?

WILLY (*coming out of the bathroom in his pajamas*): Remember him? What's the matter with you, you crazy? If he'd've stayed with Oliver he'd be on top by now! Wait'll Oliver gets a look at him. You don't know the average caliber any more. The average young man today — (*he is getting into bed*) — is got a caliber of zero. Greatest thing in the world for him was to bum around.

(BIFF *and* HAPPY *enter the bedroom. Slight pause.*)

WILLY (*stops short, looking at* BIFF): Glad to hear it, boy.

HAPPY: He wanted to say good night to you, sport.

WILLY (*to* BIFF): Yeah. Knock him dead, boy. What'd you want to tell me?

BIFF: Just take it easy, Pop. Good night. (*He turns to go.*)

WILLY (*unable to resist*): And if anything falls off the desk while you're talking to him — like a package or something — don't you pick it up. They have office boys for that.

LINDA: I'll make a big breakfast —

WILLY: Will you let me finish? (*To* BIFF.) Tell him you were in the business in the West. Not farm work.

BIFF: All right, Dad.

LINDA: I think everything —

WILLY (*going right through her speech*): And don't undersell yourself. No less than fifteen thousand dollars.

BIFF (*unable to bear him*): Okay. Good night, Mom. (*He starts moving.*)

WILLY: Because you got a greatness in you, Biff, remember that. You got all kinds a greatness . . . (*He lies back, exhausted.* BIFF *walks out.*)

LINDA (*calling after* BIFF): Sleep well, darling!

HAPPY: I'm gonna get married, Mom. I wanted to tell you.

LINDA: Go to sleep, dear.

HAPPY (*going*): I just wanted to tell you.

WILLY: Keep up the good work. (HAPPY *exits.*) God . . . remember that Ebbets Field game? The championship of the city?

LINDA: Just rest. Should I sing to you?

WILLY: Yeah. Sing to me. (LINDA *hums a soft lullaby.*) When that team came out — he was the tallest, remember?

LINDA: Oh, yes. And in gold.

(BIFF *enters the darkened kitchen, takes a cigarette, and leaves the house. He comes downstage into a golden pool of light. He smokes, staring at the night.*)

WILLY: Like a young god. Hercules — something like that. And the sun, the sun all around him. Remember how he waved to me? Right up from the field, with the representatives of three colleges standing by? And the buyers I brought, and the cheers when he came out — Loman, Loman, Loman! God Almighty, he'll be great yet. A star like that, magnificent, can never really fade away!

(*The light on* WILLY *is fading. The gas heater begins to glow through the kitchen wall, near the stairs, a blue flame beneath red coils.*)

LINDA (*timidly*): Willy dear, what has he got against you?

WILLY: I'm so tired. Don't talk any more.

(BIFF *slowly returns to the kitchen. He stops, stares toward the heater.*)

LINDA: Will you ask Howard to let you work in New York?

WILLY: First thing in the morning. Everything'll be all right.

(BIFF *reaches behind the heater and draws out a length of rubber tubing. He is horrified and turns his head toward* WILLY's *room, still dimly lit, from which the strains of* LINDA's *desperate but monotonous humming rise.*)

WILLY (*staring through the window into the*

moonlight): Gee, look at the moon moving between the buildings!

(BIFF *wraps the tubing around his hand and quickly goes up the stairs.*)

CURTAIN

ACT II

Music is heard, gay and bright. The curtain rises as the music fades away. WILLY, *in shirt sleeves, is sitting at the kitchen table, sipping coffee, his hat in his lap.* LINDA *is filling his cup when she can.*

WILLY: Wonderful coffee. Meal in itself.

LINDA: Can I make you some eggs?

WILLY: No. Take a breath.

LINDA: You look so rested, dear.

WILLY: I slept like a dead one. First time in months. Imagine, sleeping till ten on a Tuesday morning. Boys left nice and early, heh?

LINDA: They were out of here by eight o'clock.

WILLY: Good work!

LINDA: It was so thrilling to see them leaving together. I can't get over the shaving lotion in this house!

WILLY (*smiling*): Mmm —

LINDA: Biff was very changed this morning. His whole attitude seemed to be hopeful. He couldn't wait to get downtown to see Oliver.

WILLY: He's heading for a change. There's no question, there simply are certain men that take longer to get — solidified. How did he dress?

LINDA: His blue suit. He's so handsome in that suit. He could be a — anything in that suit!

(WILLY *gets up from the table.* LINDA *holds his jacket for him.*)

WILLY: There's no question, no question at all. Gee, on the way home tonight I'd like to buy some seeds.

LINDA (*laughing*): That'd be wonderful. But not enough sun gets back there. Nothing'll grow any more.

WILLY: You wait, kid, before it's all over we're gonna get a little place out in the country, and I'll raise some vegetables, a couple of chickens . . .

LINDA: You'll do it yet, dear.

(WILLY *walks out of his jacket.* LINDA *follows him.*)

WILLY: And they'll get married, and come for a weekend. I'd build a little guest house. 'Cause I got so many fine tools, all I'd need would be a little lumber and some peace of mind.

LINDA (*joyfully*): I sewed the lining . . .

WILLY: I could build two guest houses, so they'd both come. Did he decide how much he's going to ask Oliver for?

LINDA (*getting him into the jacket*): He didn't mention it, but I imagine ten or fifteen thousand. You going to talk to Howard today?

WILLY: Yeah. I'll put it to him straight and simple. He'll just have to take me off the road.

LINDA: And Willy, don't forget to ask for a little advance, because we've got the insurance premium. It's the grace period now.

WILLY: That's a hundred . . . ?

LINDA: A hundred and eight, sixty-eight. Because we're a little short again.

WILLY: Why are we short?

LINDA: Well, you had the motor job on the car . . .

WILLY: That goddam Studebaker!

LINDA: And you got one more payment on the refrigerator . . .

WILLY: But it just broke again!

LINDA: Well, it's old, dear.

WILLY: I told you we should've bought a well-advertised machine. Charley bought a General Electric and it's twenty years old and it's still good, that son-of-a-bitch.

LINDA: But, Willy —

WILLY: Whoever heard of a Hastings refrigerator? Once in my life I would like to own something outright before it's broken! I'm always in a race with the junkyard! I just finished paying for the car and it's on its last legs. The refrigerator consumes belts like a goddam maniac. They time those things. They time them so when you finally paid for them, they're used up.

LINDA (*buttoning up his jacket as he unbuttons it*): All told, about two hundred dollars would carry us, dear. But that includes the last payment on the mortgage. After this payment, Willy, the house belongs to us.

WILLY: It's twenty-five years!

LINDA: Biff was nine years old when we bought it.

WILLY: Well, that's a great thing. To weather a twenty-five year mortgage is —

LINDA: It's an accomplishment.

WILLY: All the cement, the lumber, the reconstruction I put in this house! There ain't a crack to be found in it any more.

LINDA: Well, it served its purpose.

WILLY: What purpose? Some stranger'll come along, move in, and that's that. If only Biff would take this house, and raise a family ... (*He starts to go.*) Good-by, I'm late.

LINDA (*suddenly remembering*): Oh, I forgot! You're supposed to meet them for dinner.

WILLY: Me?

LINDA: At Frank's Chop House on Forty-eighth near Sixth Avenue.

WILLY: Is that so! How about you?

LINDA: No, just the three of you. They're gonna blow you to a big meal!

WILLY: Don't say! Who thought of that?

LINDA: Biff came to me this morning, Willy, and he said, "Tell Dad, we want to blow him to a big meal." Be there six o'clock. You and your two boys are going to have dinner.

WILLY: Gee whiz! That's really somethin'. I'm gonna knock Howard for a loop, kid. I'll get an advance, and I'll come home with a New York job. Goddammit, now I'm gonna do it!

LINDA: Oh, that's the spirit, Willy!

WILLY: I will never get behind a wheel the rest of my life!

LINDA: It's changing, Willy, I can feel it changing!

WILLY: Beyond a question. G'by, I'm late. (*He starts to go again.*)

LINDA (*calling after him as she runs to the kitchen table for a handkerchief*): You got your glasses?

WILLY (*feels for them, then comes back in*): Yeah, yeah, got my glasses.

LINDA (*giving him the handkerchief*): And a handkerchief.

WILLY: Yeah, handkerchief.

LINDA: And your saccharine?

WILLY: Yeah, my saccharine.

LINDA: Be careful on the subway stairs.

(*She kisses him, and a silk stocking is seen hanging from her hand. WILLY notices it.*)

WILLY: Will you stop mending stockings? At least while I'm in the house. It gets me nervous. I can't tell you. Please.

(LINDA *hides the stocking in her hand as she follows* WILLY *across the forestage in front of the house.*)

LINDA: Remember, Frank's Chop House.

WILLY (*passing the apron*): Maybe beets would grow out there.

LINDA (*laughing*): But you tried so many times.

WILLY: Yeah. Well, don't work hard today. (*He disappears around the right corner of the house.*)

LINDA: Be careful!

(*As* WILLY *vanishes,* LINDA *waves to him. Suddenly the phone rings. She runs across the stage and into the kitchen and lifts it.*)

LINDA: Hello? Oh, Biff! I'm so glad you called, I just ... Yes, sure, I just told him. Yes, he'll be there for dinner at six o'clock, I didn't forget. Listen, I was just dying to tell you. You know that little rubber pipe I told you about? That he connected to the gas heater? I finally decided to go down the cellar this morning and take it away and destroy it. But it's gone! Imagine? He took it away himself, it isn't there! (*She listens.*) When? Oh, then you took it. Oh — nothing, it's just that I'd hoped he'd taken it away himself. Oh, I'm not worried, darling, because this morning he left in such high spirits, it was like the old days! I'm not afraid any more. Did Mr. Oliver see you? ... Well, you wait there then. And make a nice impression on him, darling. Just don't perspire too much before you see him. And have a nice time with Dad. He may have big news too! ... That's right, a New York job. And be sweet to him tonight, dear. Be loving to him. Because he's only a little boat looking for a harbor. (*She is trembling with sorrow and joy.*) Oh, that's wonderful, Biff, you'll save his life. Thanks, darling. Just put your arm around him when he comes into the restaurant. Give him a smile. That's the boy ... Good-by, dear.... You got your comb? ... That's fine. Good-by, Biff dear.

(*In the middle of her speech,* HOWARD WAGNER, *thirty-six, wheels on a small typewriter table on which is a wire-recording machine and proceeds to plug it in. This is on the left forestage. Light slowly fades on* LINDA *as it 'rises on* HOWARD. HOWARD *is intent on threading the machine and only glances over his shoulder as* WILLY *appears.*)

WILLY: Pst! Pst!

HOWARD: Hello, Willy, come in.

WILLY: Like to have a little talk with you, Howard.

HOWARD: Sorry to keep you waiting. I'll be with you in a minute.

WILLY: What's that, Howard?

HOWARD: Didn't you ever see one of these? Wire recorder.

WILLY: Oh. Can we talk a minute?

HOWARD: Records things. Just got delivery yesterday. Been driving me crazy, the most terrific machine I ever saw in my life. I was up all night with it.

WILLY: What do you do with it?

HOWARD: I bought it for dictation, but you can do anything with it. Listen to this. I had it home last night. Listen to what I picked up. The first one is my daughter. Get this. (*He flicks the switch and "Roll out the Barrel" is heard being whistled.*) Listen to that kid whistle.

WILLY: That is lifelike, isn't it?

HOWARD: Seven years old. Get that tone.

WILLY: Ts, ts. Like to ask a little favor if you . . .

(*The whistling breaks off, and the voice of* HOWARD'S DAUGHTER *is heard.*)

HIS DAUGHTER: "Now you, Daddy."

HOWARD: She's crazy for me! (*Again the same song is whistled.*) That's me! Ha! (*He winks.*)

WILLY: You're very good!

(*The whistling breaks off again. The machine runs silent for a moment.*)

HOWARD: Sh! Get this now, this is my son.

HIS SON: "The capital of Alabama is Montgomery; the capital of Arizona is Phoenix; the capital of Arkansas is Little Rock; the capital of California is Sacramento . . ." (*And on, and on.*)

HOWARD (*holding up five fingers*): Five years old, Willy!

WILLY: He'll make an announcer some day!

HIS SON (*continuing*): "The capital . . ."

HOWARD: Get that — alphabetical order! (*The machine breaks off suddenly.*) Wait a minute. The maid kicked the plug out.

WILLY: It certainly is a —

HOWARD: Sh, for God's sake!

HIS SON: "It's nine o'clock, Bulova watch time. So I have to go to sleep."

WILLY: That really is —

HOWARD: Wait a minute! The next is my wife.

(*They wait.*)

HOWARD'S VOICE: "Go on, say something." (*Pause.*) "Well, you gonna talk?"

HIS WIFE: "I can't think of anything."

HOWARD'S VOICE: "Well, talk — it's turning."

HIS WIFE (*shyly, beaten*): "Hello." (*Silence.*) "Oh, Howard, I can't talk into this . . ."

HOWARD (*snapping the machine off*): That was my wife.

WILLY: That is a wonderful machine. Can we —

HOWARD: I tell you, Willy, I'm gonna take my camera, and my bandsaw, and all my hobbies, and out they go. This is the most fascinating relaxation I ever found.

WILLY: I think I'll get one myself.

HOWARD: Sure, they're only a hundred and a half. You can't do without it. Supposing you wanna hear Jack Benny, see? But you can't be at home at that hour. So you tell the maid to turn the radio on when Jack Benny comes on, and this automatically goes on with the radio . . .

WILLY: And when you come home you . . .

HOWARD: You can come home twelve o'clock, one o'clock, any time you like, and you get yourself a Coke and sit yourself down, throw the switch, and there's Jack Benny's program in the middle of the night!

WILLY: I'm definitely going to get one. Because lots of time I'm on the road, and I think to myself, what I must be missing on the radio!

HOWARD: Don't you have a radio in the car?

WILLY: Well, yeah, but who ever thinks of turning it on?

HOWARD: Say, aren't you supposed to be in Boston?

WILLY: That's what I want to talk to you about, Howard. You got a minute? (*He draws a chair in from the wing.*)

HOWARD: What happened? What're you doing here?

WILLY: Well . . .

HOWARD: You didn't crack up again, did you?

WILLY: Oh, no. No . . .

HOWARD: Geez, you had me worried there for a minute. What's the trouble?

WILLY: Well, tell you the truth, Howard. I've come to the decision that I'd rather not travel any more.

HOWARD: Not travel! Well, what'll you do?

WILLY: Remember, Christmas time, when you had the party here? You said you'd try to think of some spot for me here in town.

HOWARD: With us?

WILLY: Well, sure.

HOWARD: Oh, yeah, yeah. I remember. Well, I couldn't think of anything for you, Willy.

WILLY: I tell ya, Howard. The kids are all grown up, y'know. I don't need much any more. If I could take home — well, sixty-five dollars a week, I could swing it.

HOWARD: Yeah, but Willy, see I —

WILLY: I tell ya why, Howard. Speaking frankly and between the two of us, y'know — I'm just a little tired.

HOWARD: Oh, I could understand that, Willy. But you're a road man, Willy, and we do a road business. We've only got a half-dozen salesmen on the floor here.

WILLY: God knows, Howard, I never asked a favor of any man. But I was with the firm when your father used to carry you in here in his arms.

HOWARD: I know that, Willy, but —

WILLY: Your father came to me the day you were born and asked me what I thought of the name of Howard, may he rest in peace.

HOWARD: I appreciate that, Willy, but there just is no spot here for you. If I had a spot I'd slam you right in, but I just don't have a single solitary spot.

(*He looks for his lighter.* WILLY *has picked it up and gives it to him. Pause.*)

WILLY (*with increasing anger*): Howard, all I need to set my table is fifty dollars a week.

HOWARD: But where am I going to put you, kid?

WILLY: Look, it isn't a question of whether I can sell merchandise, is it?

HOWARD: No, but it's a business, kid, and everybody's gotta pull his own weight.

WILLY (*desperately*): Just let me tell you a story, Howard —

HOWARD: 'Cause you gotta admit, business is business.

WILLY (*angrily*): Business is definitely business, but just listen for a minute. You don't understand this. When I was a boy — eighteen, nineteen — I was already on the road. And there was a question in my mind as to whether selling had a future for me. Because in those days I had a yearning to go to Alaska. See, there were three gold strikes in one month in Alaska, and I felt like going out. Just for the ride, you might say.

HOWARD (*barely interested*): Don't say.

WILLY: Oh, yeah, my father lived many years in Alaska. He was an adventurous man. We've got quite a little streak of self-reliance in our family. I thought I'd go out with my older brother and try to locate him, and maybe settle in the North with the old man. And I was almost decided to go, when I met a salesman in the Parker House. His name was Dave Singleman. And he was eighty-four years old, and he'd drummed merchandise in thirty-one states. And old Dave, he'd go up to his room, y'understand, put on his green velvet slippers — I'll never forget — and pick up his phone and call the buyers, and without ever leaving his room, at the age of eighty-four, he made his living. And when I saw that, I realized that selling was the greatest career a man could want. 'Cause what could be more satisfying than to be able to go, at the age of eighty-four, into twenty or thirty different cities, and pick up a phone, and be remembered and loved and helped by so many different people? Do you know? when he died — and by the way he died the death of a salesman, in his green velvet slippers in the smoker of the New York, New Haven and Hartford, going into Boston — when he died, hundreds of salesmen and buyers were at his funeral. Things were sad on a lotta trains for months after that. (*He stands up.* HOWARD *has not looked at him.*) In those days there was personality in it, Howard. There was respect, and comradeship, and gratitude in it. Today, it's all cut and dried, and there's no chance for bringing friendship to bear — or personality. You see what I mean? They don't know me any more.

HOWARD (*moving away, to the right*): That's just the thing, Willy.

WILLY: If I had forty dollars a week — that's all I'd need. Forty dollars, Howard.

HOWARD: Kid, I can't take blood from a stone, I —

WILLY (*desperation is on him now*): Howard, the year Al Smith was nominated, your father came to me and —

HOWARD (*starting to go off*): I've got to see some people, kid.

WILLY (*stopping him*): I'm talking about your father! There were promises made across this desk! You mustn't tell me you've got people to see — I put thirty-four years into this firm, Howard, and now I can't pay my insurance! You can't eat the orange and throw the peel away — a man is not a piece of fruit! (*After a pause.*) Now pay attention. Your father — in 1928 I had a big year. I averaged a hundred and seventy dollars a week in commissions.

HOWARD (*impatiently*): Now, Willy, you never averaged —

WILLY (*banging his hand on the desk*): I averaged a hundred and seventy dollars a week in the year of 1928! And your father came to me — or rather, I was in the office here — it was right over this desk — and he put his hand on my shoulder —

HOWARD (*getting up*): You'll have to excuse me, Willy, I gotta see some people. Pull yourself together. (*Going out.*) I'll be back in a little while.

(*On* HOWARD's *exit, the light on his chair grows very bright and strange.*)

WILLY: Pull myself together! What the hell did I say to him? My God, I was yelling at him! How could I! (WILLY *breaks off, staring at the light, which occupies the chair, animating it. He approaches this chair, standing across the desk from it.*) Frank, Frank, don't you remember what you told me that time? How you put your hand on my shoulder, and Frank . . . (*He leans on the desk and as he speaks the dead man's name he accidentally switches on the recorder, and instantly —*)

HOWARD'S SON: ". . . of New York is Albany. The capital of Ohio is Cincinnati, the capital of Rhode Island is . . ." (*The recitation continues.*)

WILLY (*leaping away with fright, shouting*): Ha! Howard! Howard! Howard!

HOWARD (*rushing in*): What happened?

WILLY (*pointing at the machine, which continues nasally, childishly, with the capital cities*): Shut it off! Shut it off!

HOWARD (*pulling the plug out*): Look, Willy . . .

WILLY (*pressing his hands to his eyes*): I gotta get myself some coffee. I'll get some coffee . . .

(WILLY *starts to walk out.* HOWARD *stops him.*)

HOWARD (*rolling up the cord*): Willy, look . . .

WILLY: I'll go to Boston.

HOWARD: Willy, you can't go to Boston for us.

WILLY: Why can't I go?

HOWARD: I don't want you to represent us. I've been meaning to tell you for a long time now.

WILLY: Howard, are you firing me?

HOWARD: I think you need a good long rest, Willy.

WILLY: Howard —

HOWARD: And when you feel better, come back, and we'll see if we can work something out.

WILLY: But I gotta earn money, Howard. I'm in no position to —

HOWARD: Where are your sons? Why don't your sons give you a hand?

WILLY: They're working on a very big deal.

HOWARD: This is no time for false pride, Willy. You go to your sons and you tell them that you're tired. You've got two great boys, haven't you?

WILLY: Oh, no question, no question, but in the meantime . . .

HOWARD: Then that's that, heh?

WILLY: All right, I'll go to Boston tomorrow.

HOWARD: No, no.

WILLY: I can't throw myself on my sons. I'm not a cripple!

HOWARD: Look, kid, I'm busy this morning.

WILLY (*grasping* HOWARD's *arm*): Howard, you've got to let me go to Boston!

HOWARD (*hard, keeping himself under control*): I've got a line of people to see this morning. Sit down, take five minutes, and pull yourself together, and then go home, will ya? I need the office, Willy. (*He starts to go, turns, remembering the recorder, starts to push off the table holding the recorder.*) Oh, yeah. Whenever you can this week, stop by and drop off the samples. You'll feel better, Willy, and then come back and we'll talk. Pull yourself together, kid, there's people outside.

(HOWARD *exits, pushing the table off left.* WILLY *stares into space, exhausted. Now the music is heard —* BEN's *music — first distantly, then closer, closer. As* WILLY *speaks,* BEN *enters from the right. He carries valise and umbrella.*)

WILLY: Oh, Ben, how did you do it? What

is the answer? Did you wind up the Alaska deal already?

BEN: Doesn't take much time if you know what you're doing. Just a short business trip. Boarding ship in an hour. Wanted to say good-by.

WILLY: Ben, I've got to talk to you.

BEN (*glancing at his watch*): Haven't the time, William.

WILLY (*crossing the apron to* BEN): Ben, nothing's working out. I don't know what to do.

BEN: Now, look here, William. I've bought timberland in Alaska and I need a man to look after things for me.

WILLY: God, timberland! Me and my boys in those grand outdoors!

BEN: You've a new continent at your doorstep, William. Get out of these cities, they're full of talk and time payments and courts of law. Screw on your fists and you can fight for a fortune up there.

WILLY: Yes, yes! Linda, Linda!

(LINDA *enters as of old, with the wash.*)

LINDA: Oh, you're back?

BEN: I haven't much time.

WILLY: No, wait! Linda, he's got a proposition for me in Alaska.

LINDA: But you've got — (*To* BEN.) He's got a beautiful job here.

WILLY: But in Alaska, kid, I could —

LINDA: You're doing well enough, Willy!

BEN (*to* LINDA): Enough for what, my dear?

LINDA (*frightened of* BEN *and angry at him*): Don't say those things to him! Enough to be happy right here, right now. (*To* WILLY, *while* BEN *laughs.*) Why must everybody conquer the world? You're well liked, and the boys love you, and someday — (*to* BEN) — why, old man Wagner told him just the other day that if he keeps it up he'll be a member of the firm, didn't he, Willy?

WILLY: Sure, sure. I am building something with this firm, Ben, and if a man is building something he must be on the right track, mustn't he?

BEN: What are you building? Lay your hand on it. Where is it?

WILLY (*hesitantly*): That's true, Linda, there's nothing.

LINDA: Why? (*To* BEN.) There's a man eighty-four years old —

WILLY: That's right, Ben, that's right. When I look at that man I say, what is there to worry about?

BEN: Bah!

WILLY: It's true, Ben. All he has to do is go into any city, pick up the phone, and he's making his living and you know why?

BEN (*picking up his valise*): I've got to go.

WILLY (*holding* BEN *back*): Look at this boy!

(BIFF, *in his high school sweater, enters carrying suitcase.* HAPPY *carries* BIFF's *shoulder guards, gold helmet, and football pants.*)

WILLY: Without a penny to his name, three great universities are begging for him, and from there the sky's the limit, because it's not what you do, Ben. It's who you know and the smile on your face! It's contacts, Ben, contacts! The whole wealth of Alaska passes over the lunch table at the Commodore Hotel, and that's the wonder, the wonder of this country, that a man can end with diamonds here on the basis of being liked! (*He turns to* BIFF.) And that's why when you get out on that field today it's important. Because thousands of people will be rooting for you and loving you. (*To* BEN, *who has again begun to leave.*) And Ben! when he walks into a business office his name will sound out like a bell and all the doors will open to him! I've seen it, Ben, I've seen it a thousand times! You can't feel it with your hand like timber, but it's there!

BEN: Good-by, William.

WILLY: Ben, am I right? Don't you think I'm right? I value your advice.

BEN: There's a new continent at your doorstep, William. You could walk out rich. Rich! (*He is gone.*)

WILLY: We'll do it here, Ben! You hear me? We're gonna do it here!

(YOUNG BERNARD *rushes in. The gay music of the boys is heard.*)

BERNARD: Oh, gee, I was afraid you left already!

WILLY: Why? What time is it?

BERNARD: It's half-past one!

WILLY: Well, come on, everybody! Ebbets Field next stop! Where's the pennants? (*He rushes through the wall-line of the kitchen and out into the living-room.*)

LINDA (*to* BIFF): Did you pack fresh underwear?

BIFF (*who has been limbering up*): I want to go!

BERNARD: Biff, I'm carrying your helmet, ain't I?

HAPPY: No, I'm carrying the helmet.

BERNARD: Oh, Biff, you promised me.

HAPPY: I'm carrying the helmet.

BERNARD: How am I going to get in the locker room?

LINDA: Let him carry the shoulder guards. (*She puts her coat and hat on in the kitchen.*)

BERNARD: Can I, Biff? 'Cause I told everybody I'm going to be in the locker room.

HAPPY: In Ebbets Field it's the clubhouse.

BERNARD: I meant the clubhouse. Biff!

HAPPY: Biff!

BIFF (*grandly, after a slight pause*): Let him carry the shoulder guards.

HAPPY (*as he gives* BERNARD *the shoulder guards*): Stay close to us now.

(WILLY *rushes in with the pennants.*)

WILLY (*handing them out*): Everybody wave when Biff comes out on the field. (HAPPY *and* BERNARD *run off.*) You set now, boy?

(*The music has died away.*)

BIFF: Ready to go, Pop. Every muscle is ready.

WILLY (*at the edge of the apron*): You realize what this means?

BIFF: That's right, Pop.

WILLY (*feeling* BIFF's *muscles*): You're comin' home this afternoon captain of the All-Scholastic Championship Team of the City of New York.

BIFF: I got it, Pop. And remember, pal, when I take off my helmet, that touchdown is for you.

WILLY: Let's go! (*He is starting out, with his arm around* BIFF, *when* CHARLEY *enters, as of old, in knickers.*) I got no room for you, Charley.

CHARLEY: Room? For what?

WILLY: In the car.

CHARLEY: You goin' for a ride? I wanted to shoot some casino.

WILLY (*furiously*): Casino! (*Incredulously.*) Don't you realize what today is?

LINDA: Oh, he knows, Willy. He's just kidding you.

WILLY: That's nothing to kid about!

CHARLEY: No, Linda, what's goin' on?

LINDA: He's playing in Ebbets Field.

CHARLEY: Baseball in this weather?

WILLY: Don't talk to him. Come on, come on! (*He is pushing them out.*)

CHARLEY: Wait a minute, didn't you hear the news?

WILLY: What?

CHARLEY: Don't you listen to the radio? Ebbets Field just blew up.

WILLY: You go to hell! (CHARLEY *laughs. Pushing them out.*) Come on, come on! We're late.

CHARLEY (*as they go*): Knock a homer, Biff, knock a homer!

WILLY (*the last to leave, turning to* CHARLEY): I don't think that was funny, Charley. This is the greatest day of his life.

CHARLEY: Willy, when are you going to grow up?

WILLY: Yeah, heh? When this game is over, Charley, you'll be laughing out of the other side of your face. They'll be calling him another Red Grange. Twenty-five thousand a year.

CHARLEY (*kidding*): Is that so?

WILLY: Yeah, that's so.

CHARLEY: Well, then, I'm sorry, Willy. But tell me something.

WILLY: What?

CHARLEY: Who is Red Grange?

WILLY: Put up your hands. Goddam you, put up your hands!

(CHARLEY, *chuckling, shakes his head and walks away, around the left corner of the stage.* WILLY *follows him. The music rises to a mocking frenzy.*)

WILLY: Who the hell do you think you are, better than everybody else? You don't know everything, you big, ignorant, stupid . . . Put up your hands!

(*Light rises, on the right side of the forestage, on a small table in the reception room of* CHARLEY's *office. Traffic sounds are heard.* BERNARD, *now mature, sits whistling to himself. A pair of tennis rackets and an overnight bag are on the floor beside him.*)

WILLY (*offstage*): What are you walking away for? Don't walk away! If you're going to say something say it to my face! I know you laugh at me behind my back. You'll laugh out of the other side of your goddam face after this game. Touchdown! Touchdown! Eighty thousand people! Touchdown! Right between the goal posts.

(BERNARD *is a quiet, earnest, but self-assured young man.* WILLY's *voice is coming from right upstage now.* BERNARD *lowers his feet off the table and listens.* JENNY, *his father's secretary, enters.*)

JENNY (*distressed*): Say, Bernard, will you go out in the hall?

BERNARD: What is that noise? Who is it?

JENNY: Mr. Loman. He just got off the elevator.

BERNARD (*getting up*): Who's he arguing with?

JENNY: Nobody. There's nobody with him. I can't deal with him any more, and your father gets all upset everytime he comes. I've got a lot of typing to do, and your father's waiting to sign it. Will you see him?

WILLY (*entering*): Touchdown! Touch — (*He sees* JENNY.) Jenny, Jenny, good to see you. How're ya? Workin'? Or still honest?

JENNY: Fine. How've you been feeling?

WILLY: Not much any more, Jenny. Ha, ha! (*He is surprised to see the rackets.*)

BERNARD: Hello, Uncle Willy.

WILLY (*almost shocked*): Bernard! Well, look who's here! (*He comes quickly, guiltily, to* BERNARD *and warmly shakes his hand.*)

BERNARD: How are you? Good to see you.

WILLY: What are you doing here?

BERNARD: Oh, just stopped by to see Pop. Get off my feet till my train leaves. I'm going to Washington in a few minutes.

WILLY: Is he in?

BERNARD: Yes, he's in his office with the accountant. Sit down.

WILLY (*sitting down*): What're you going to do in Washington?

BERNARD: Oh, just a case I've got there, Willy.

WILLY: That so? (*Indicating the rackets.*) You going to play tennis there?

BERNARD: I'm staying with a friend who's got a court.

WILLY: Don't say. His own tennis court. Must be fine people, I bet.

BERNARD: They are, very nice. Dad tells me Biff's in town.

WILLY (*with a big smile*): Yeah, Biff's in. Working on a very big deal, Bernard.

BERNARD: What's Biff doing?

WILLY: Well, he's been doing very big things in the West. But he decided to establish himself here. Very big. We're having dinner. Did I hear your wife had a boy?

BERNARD: That's right. Our second.

WILLY: Two boys! What do you know!

BERNARD: What kind of a deal has Biff got?

WILLY: Well, Bill Oliver — very big sporting-goods man — he wants Biff very badly. Called him in from the West. Long distance, carte blanche, special deliveries. Your friends have their own private tennis court?

BERNARD: You still with the old firm, Willy?

WILLY (*after a pause*): I'm — I'm overjoyed to see how you made the grade, Bernard, overjoyed. It's an encouraging thing to see a young man really — really — Looks very good for Biff — very — (*He breaks off, then.*) Bernard — (*He is so full of emotion, he breaks off again.*)

BERNARD: What is it, Willy?

WILLY (*small and alone*): What — what's the secret?

BERNARD: What secret?

WILLY: How — how did you? Why didn't he ever catch on?

BERNARD: I wouldn't know that, Willy.

WILLY (*confidentially, desperately*): You were his friend, his boyhood friend. There's something I don't understand about it. His life ended after that Ebbets Field game. From the age of seventeen nothing good ever happened to him.

BERNARD: He never trained himself for anything.

WILLY: But he did, he did. After high school he took so many correspondence courses. Radio mechanics; television; God knows what, and never made the slightest mark.

BERNARD (*taking off his glasses*): Willy, do you want to talk candidly?

WILLY (*rising, faces* BERNARD): I regard you as a very brilliant man, Bernard. I value your advice.

BERNARD: Oh, the hell with the advice, Willy. I couldn't advise you. There's just one thing I've always wanted to ask you. When he was supposed to graduate, and the math teacher flunked him —

WILLY: Oh, that son-of-a-bitch ruined his life.

BERNARD: Yeah, but, Willy, all he had to do was go to summer school and make up that subject.

WILLY: That's right, that's right.

BERNARD: Did you tell him not to go to summer school?

WILLY: Me? I begged him to go. I ordered him to go!

BERNARD: Then why wouldn't he go?

WILLY: Why? Why! Bernard, that question has been trailing me like a ghost for the last fifteen years. He flunked the subject, and laid down and died like a hammer hit him!

BERNARD: Take it easy, kid.

WILLY: Let me talk to you — I got nobody to talk to. Bernard, Bernard, was it my fault? Y'see? It keeps going around in my mind, maybe I did something to him. I got nothing to give him.

BERNARD: Don't take it so hard.

WILLY: Why did he lay down? What is the story there? You were his friend!

BERNARD: Willy, I remember, it was June, and our grades came out. And he'd flunked math.

WILLY: That son-of-a-bitch!

BERNARD: No, it wasn't right then. Biff just got very angry, I remember, and he was ready to enroll in summer school.

WILLY (surprised): He was?

BERNARD: He wasn't beaten by it at all. But then, Willy, he disappeared from the block for almost a month. And I got the idea that he'd gone up to New England to see you. Did he have a talk with you then?

(WILLY stares in silence.)

BERNARD: Willy?

WILLY (with a strong edge of resentment in his voice): Yeah, he came to Boston. What about it?

BERNARD: Well, just that when he came back — I'll never forget this, it always mystifies me. Because I'd thought so well of Biff, even though he'd always taken advantage of me. I loved him, Willy, y'know? And he came back after that month and took his sneakers — remember those sneakers with "University of Virginia" printed on them? He was so proud of those, wore them every day. And he took them down in the cellar, and burned them up

in the furnace. We had a fist fight. It lasted at least half an hour. Just the two of us, punching each other down the cellar, and crying right through it. I've often thought of how strange it was that I knew he'd given up his life. What happened in Boston, Willy?

(WILLY looks at him as at an intruder.)

BERNARD: I just bring it up because you asked me.

WILLY (angrily): Nothing. What do you mean, "What happened?" What's that got to do with anything?

BERNARD: Well, don't get sore.

WILLY: What are you trying to do, blame it on me? If a boy lays down is that my fault?

BERNARD: Now, Willy, don't get —

WILLY: Well, don't — don't talk to me that way! What does that mean, "What happened?"

(CHARLEY enters. He is in his vest, and he carries a bottle of bourbon.)

CHARLEY: Hey, you're going to miss that train. (He waves the bottle.)

BERNARD: Yeah, I'm going. (He takes the bottle.) Thanks, Pop. (He picks up his rackets and bag.) Good-by, Willy, and don't worry about it. You know, "If at first you don't succeed . . ."

WILLY: Yes, I believe in that.

BERNARD: But sometimes, Willy, it's better for a man just to walk away.

WILLY: Walk away?

BERNARD: That's right.

WILLY: But if you can't walk away?

BERNARD (after a slight pause): I guess that's when it's tough. (Extending his hand.) Good-by, Willy.

WILLY (shaking BERNARD's hand): Good-by, boy.

CHARLEY (an arm on BERNARD's shoulder): How do you like this kid? Gonna argue a case in front of the Supreme Court.

BERNARD (protesting): Pop!

WILLY (genuinely shocked, pained, and happy): No! The Supreme Court!

BERNARD: I gotta run. 'By, Dad!

CHARLEY: Knock 'em dead, Bernard!

(BERNARD goes off.)

WILLY (as CHARLEY takes out his wallet): The Supreme Court! And he didn't even mention it!

CHARLEY (*counting out money on the desk*): He don't have to — he's gonna do it.

WILLY: And you never told him what to do, did you? You never took any interest in him.

CHARLEY: My salvation is that I never took any interest in anything. There's some money — fifty dollars. I got an accountant inside.

WILLY: Charley, look . . . (*With difficulty.*) I got my insurance to pay. If you can manage it — I need a hundred and ten dollars.

(CHARLEY *doesn't reply for a moment; merely stops moving.*)

WILLY: I'd draw it from my bank but Linda would know, and I . . .

CHARLEY: Sit down, Willy.

WILLY (*moving toward the chair*): I'm keeping an account of everything, remember. I'll pay every penny back. (*He sits.*)

CHARLEY: Now listen to me, Willy.

WILLY: I want you to know I appreciate . . .

CHARLEY (*sitting down on the table*): Willy, what're you doin'? What the hell is goin' on in your head?

WILLY: Why? I'm simply . . .

CHARLEY: I offered you a job. You can make fifty dollars a week. And I won't send you on the road.

WILLY: I've got a job.

CHARLEY: Without pay? What kind of a job is a job without pay? (*He rises.*) Now, look, kid, enough is enough. I'm no genius but I know when I'm being insulted.

WILLY: Insulted!

CHARLEY: Why don't you want to work for me?

WILLY: What's the matter with you? I've got a job.

CHARLEY: Then what're you walkin' in here every week for?

WILLY (*getting up*): Well, if you don't want me to walk in here —

CHARLEY: I am offering you a job.

WILLY: I don't want your goddam job!

CHARLEY: When the hell are you going to grow up?

WILLY (*furiously*): You big ignoramus, if you say that to me again I'll rap you one! I don't care how big you are! (*He's ready to fight.*)

(*Pause.*)

CHARLEY (*kindly, going to him*): How much do you need, Willy?

WILLY: Charley, I'm strapped. I'm strapped. I don't know what to do. I was just fired.

CHARLEY: Howard fired you?

WILLY: That snotnose. Imagine that? I named him. I named him Howard.

CHARLEY: Willy, when're you gonna realize that them things don't mean anything? You named him Howard, but you can't sell that. The only thing you got in this world is what you can sell. And the funny thing is that you're a salesman, and you don't know that.

WILLY: I've always tried to think otherwise, I guess. I always felt that if a man was impressive, and well liked, that nothing —

CHARLEY: Why must everybody like you? Who liked J. P. Morgan? Was he impressive? In a Turkish bath he'd look like a butcher. But with his pockets on he was very well liked. Now listen, Willy, I know you don't like me, and nobody can say I'm in love with you, but I'll give you a job because — just for the hell of it, put it that way. Now what do you say?

WILLY: I — I just can't work for you, Charley.

CHARLEY: What're you, jealous of me?

WILLY: I can't work for you, that's all, don't ask me why.

CHARLEY (*angered, takes out more bills*): You been jealous of me all your life, you damned fool! Here, pay your insurance. (*He puts the money in* WILLY'S *hand.*)

WILLY: I'm keeping strict accounts.

CHARLEY: I've got some work to do. Take care of yourself. And pay your insurance.

WILLY (*moving to the right*): Funny, y'know? After all the highways, and the trains, and the appointments, and the years, you end up worth more dead than alive.

CHARLEY: Willy, nobody's worth nothin' dead. (*After a slight pause.*) Did you hear what I said?

(WILLY *stands still, dreaming.*)

CHARLEY: Willy!

WILLY: Apologize to Bernard for me when you see him. I didn't mean to argue with him. He's a fine boy. They're all fine boys, and they'll end up big — all of them. Someday they'll all play tennis together. Wish me luck, Charley. He saw Bill Oliver today.

CHARLEY: Good luck.

WILLY (*on the verge of tears*): Charley, you're the only friend I got. Isn't that a remarkable thing? (*He goes out.*)

CHARLEY: Jesus!

(CHARLEY *stares after him a moment and follows. All light blacks out. Suddenly raucous music is heard, and a red glow rises behind the screen at right.* STANLEY, *a young waiter, appears, carrying a table, followed by* HAPPY, *who is carrying two chairs.*)

STANLEY (*putting the table down*): That's all right, Mr. Loman, I can handle it myself. (*He turns and takes the chairs from* HAPPY *and places them at the table.*)

HAPPY (*glancing around*): Oh, this is better.

STANLEY: Sure, in the front there you're in the middle of all kinds a noise. Whenever you got a party, Mr. Loman, you just tell me and I'll put you back here. Y'know, there's a lotta people they don't like it private, because when they go out they like to see a lotta action around them because they're sick and tired to stay in the house by theirself. But I know you, you ain't from Hackensack. You know what I mean?

HAPPY (*sitting down*): So how's it coming, Stanley?

STANLEY: Ah, it's a dog's life. I only wish during the war they'd a took me in the Army. I coulda been dead by now.

HAPPY: My brother's back, Stanley.

STANLEY: Oh, he come back, heh? From the Far West.

HAPPY: Yeah, big cattle man, my brother, so treat him right. And my father's coming too.

STANLEY: Oh, your father too!

HAPPY: You got a couple of nice lobsters?

STANLEY: Hundred per cent, big.

HAPPY: I want them with the claws.

STANLEY: Don't worry, I don't give you no mice. (HAPPY *laughs.*) How about some wine? It'll put a head on the meal.

HAPPY: No. You remember, Stanley, that recipe I brought you from overseas? With the champagne in it?

STANLEY: Oh, yeah, sure. I still got it tacked up yet in the kitchen. But that'll have to cost a buck apiece anyways.

HAPPY: That's all right.

STANLEY: What'd you, hit a number or somethin'?

HAPPY: No, it's a little celebration. My brother is — I think he pulled off a big deal today. I think we're going into business together.

STANLEY: Great! That's the best for you. Because a family business, you know what I mean? — that's the best.

HAPPY: That's what I think.

STANLEY: 'Cause what's the difference? Somebody steals? It's in the family. Know what I mean? (*Sotto voce.*) Like this bartender here. The boss is goin' crazy what kinda leak he's got in the cash register. You put it in but it don't come out.

HAPPY (*raising his head*): Sh!

STANLEY: What?

HAPPY: You notice I wasn't lookin' right or left, was I?

STANLEY: No.

HAPPY: And my eyes are closed.

STANLEY: So what's the — ?

HAPPY: Strudel's comin'.

STANLEY (*catching on, looks around*): Ah, no, there's no —

(*He breaks off as a furred, lavishly dressed* GIRL *enters and sits at the next table. Both follow her with their eyes.*)

STANLEY: Geez, how'd ya know?

HAPPY: I got radar or something. (*Staring directly at her profile.*) Oooooooo . . . Stanley.

STANLEY: I think that's for you, Mr. Loman.

HAPPY: Look at that mouth. Oh, God. And the binoculars.

STANLEY: Geez, you got a life, Mr. Loman.

HAPPY: Wait on her.

STANLEY (*going to* THE GIRL'*s table*): Would you like a menu, ma'am?

GIRL: I'm expecting someone, but I'd like a —

HAPPY: Why don't you bring her — excuse me, miss, do you mind? I sell champagne, and I'd like you to try my brand. Bring her a champagne, Stanley.

GIRL: That's awfully nice of you.

HAPPY: Don't mention it. It's all company money. (*He laughs.*)

GIRL: That's a charming product to be selling, isn't it?

HAPPY: Oh, gets to be like everything else. Selling is selling, y'know.

GIRL: I suppose.

HAPPY: You don't happen to sell, do you?

GIRL: No, I don't sell.

HAPPY: Would you object to a compliment from a stranger? You ought to be on a magazine cover.

GIRL (*looking at him a little archly*): I have been.

(STANLEY *comes in with a glass of champagne.*)

HAPPY: What'd I say before, Stanley? You see? She's a cover girl.

STANLEY: Oh, I could see, I could see.

HAPPY (to THE GIRL): What magazine?

GIRL: Oh, a lot of them. (She takes the drink.) Thank you.

HAPPY: You know what they say in France, don't you? "Champagne is the drink of the complexion" — Hya, Biff!

(BIFF has entered and sits with HAPPY.)

BIFF: Hello, kid. Sorry I'm late.

HAPPY: I just got here. Uh, Miss — ?

GIRL: Forsythe.

HAPPY: Miss Forsythe, this is my brother.

BIFF: Is Dad here?

HAPPY: His name is Biff. You might've heard of him. Great football player.

GIRL: Really? What team?

HAPPY: Are you familiar with football?

GIRL: No, I'm afraid I'm not.

HAPPY: Biff is quarterback with the New York Giants.

GIRL: Well, that is nice, isn't it? (She drinks.)

HAPPY: Good health.

GIRL: I'm happy to meet you.

HAPPY: That's my name. Hap. It's really Harold, but at West Point they called me Happy.

GIRL (now really impressed): Oh, I see. How do you do? (She turns her profile.)

BIFF: Isn't Dad coming?

HAPPY: You want her?

BIFF: Oh, I could never make that.

HAPPY: I remember the time that idea would never come into your head. Where's the old confidence, Biff?

BIFF: I just saw Oliver —

HAPPY: Wait a minute. I've got to see that old confidence again. Do you want her? She's on call.

BIFF: Oh, no. (He turns to look at THE GIRL.)

HAPPY: I'm telling you. Watch this. (Turning to THE GIRL.) Honey? (She turns to him.) Are you busy?

GIRL: Well, I am ... but I could make a phone call.

HAPPY: Do that, will you, honey? And see if you can get a friend. We'll be here for a while. Biff is one of the greatest football players in the country.

GIRL (standing up): Well, I'm certainly happy to meet you.

HAPPY: Come back soon.

GIRL: I'll try.

HAPPY: Don't try, honey, try hard.

(THE GIRL exits. STANLEY follows, shaking his head in bewildered admiration.)

HAPPY: Isn't that a shame now? A beautiful girl like that? That's why I can't get married. There's not a good woman in a thousand. New York is loaded with them, kid!

BIFF: Hap, look —

HAPPY: I told you she was on call!

BIFF (strangely unnerved): Cut it out, will ya? I want to say something to you.

HAPPY: Did you see Oliver?

BIFF: I saw him all right. Now look, I want to tell Dad a couple of things and I want you to help me.

HAPPY: What? Is he going to back you?

BIFF: Are you crazy? You're out of your goddam head, you know that?

HAPPY: Why? What happened?

BIFF (breathlessly): I did a terrible thing today, Hap. It's been the strangest day I ever went through. I'm all numb, I swear.

HAPPY: You mean he wouldn't see you?

BIFF: Well, I waited six hours for him, see? All day. Kept sending my name in. Even tried to date his secretary so she'd get me to him, but no soap.

HAPPY: Because you're not showin' the old confidence, Biff. He remembered you, didn't he?

BIFF (stopping HAPPY with a gesture): Finally, about five o'clock, he comes out. Didn't remember who I was or anything. I felt like such an idiot, Hap.

HAPPY: Did you tell him my Florida idea?

BIFF: He walked away. I saw him for one minute. I got so mad I could've torn the walls down! How the hell did I ever get the idea I was a salesman there? I even believed myself that I'd been a salesman for him! And then he gave me one look and — I realized what a ridiculous lie my whole life has been! We've been talking in a dream for fifteen years. I was a shipping clerk.

HAPPY: What'd you do?

BIFF (with great tension and wonder): Well, he left, see. And the secretary went out. I was all alone in the waiting-room. I don't know what came over me, Hap. The next thing I know I'm in his office — paneled walls, everything. I can't explain it. I — Hap, I took his fountain pen.

HAPPY: Geez, did he catch you?

BIFF: I ran out. I ran down all eleven flights. I ran and ran and ran.

HAPPY: That was an awful dumb — what'd you do that for?

BIFF (*agonized*): I don't know, I just — wanted to take something, I don't know. You gotta help me, Hap, I'm gonna tell Pop.

HAPPY: You crazy? What for?

BIFF: Hap, he's got to understand that I'm not the man somebody lends that kind of money to. He thinks I've been spiting him all these years and it's eating him up.

HAPPY: That's just it. You tell him something nice.

BIFF: I can't.

HAPPY: Say you got a lunch date with Oliver tomorrow.

BIFF: So what do I do tomorrow?

HAPPY: You leave the house tomorrow and come back at night and say Oliver is thinking it over. And he thinks it over for a couple of weeks, and gradually it fades away and nobody's the worse.

BIFF: But it'll go on forever!

HAPPY: Dad is never so happy as when he's looking forward to something!

(WILLY *enters*.)

HAPPY: Hello, scout!

WILLY: Gee, I haven't been here in years!

(STANLEY *has followed* WILLY *in and sets a chair for him.* STANLEY *starts off but* HAPPY *stops him.*)

HAPPY: Stanley!

(STANLEY *stands by, waiting for an order.*)

BIFF (*going to* WILLY *with guilt, as to an invalid*): Sit down, Pop. You want a drink?

WILLY: Sure, I don't mind.

BIFF: Let's get a load on.

WILLY: You look worried.

BIFF: N-no. (*To* STANLEY.) Scotch all around. Make it doubles.

STANLEY: Doubles, right. (*He goes.*)

WILLY: You had a couple already, didn't you?

BIFF: Just a couple, yeah.

WILLY: Well, what happened, boy?

(*Nodding affirmatively, with a smile.*) Everything go all right?

BIFF (*takes a breath, then reaches out and grasps* WILLY's *hand*): Pal ... (*He is smiling bravely, and* WILLY *is smiling too.*) I had an experience today.

HAPPY: Terrific, Pop.

WILLY: That so? What happened?

BIFF (*high, slightly alcoholic, above the earth*): I'm going to tell you everything from first to last. It's been a strange day. (*Silence. He looks around, composes himself as best he can, but his breath keeps breaking the rhythm of his voice.*) I had to wait quite a while for him, and —

WILLY: Oliver?

BIFF: Yeah, Oliver. All day, as a matter of cold fact. And a lot of — instances — facts, Pop, facts about my life came back to me. Who was it, Pop? Who ever said I was a salesman with Oliver?

WILLY: Well, you were.

BIFF: No, Dad, I was a shipping clerk.

WILLY: But you were practically —

BIFF (*with determination*): Dad, I don't know who said it first, but I was never a salesman for Bill Oliver.

WILLY: What're you talking about?

BIFF: Let's hold on to the facts tonight, Pop. We're not going to get anywhere bullin' around. I was a shipping clerk.

WILLY (*angrily*): All right, now listen to me —

BIFF: Why don't you let me finish?

WILLY: I'm not interested in stories about the past or any crap of that kind because the woods are burning, boys, you understand? There's a big blaze going on all around. I was fired today.

BIFF (*shocked*): How could you be?

WILLY: I was fired, and I'm looking for a little good news to tell your mother, because the woman has waited and the woman has suffered. The gist of it is that I haven't got a story left in my head, Biff. So don't give me a lecture about facts and aspects. I am not interested. Now what've you got to say to me?

(STANLEY *enters with three drinks. They wait until he leaves.*)

WILLY: Did you see Oliver?

BIFF: Jesus, Dad!

WILLY: You mean you didn't go up there?

HAPPY: Sure he went up there.

BIFF: I did. I — saw him. How could they fire you?

WILLY (*on the edge of his chair*): What kind of a welcome did he give you?

BIFF: He won't even let you work on commission?

WILLY: I'm out! (*Driving.*) So tell me, he gave you a warm welcome?

HAPPY: Sure, Pop, sure!

BIFF (*driven*): Well, it was kind of —

WILLY: I was wondering if he'd remember you. (*To* HAPPY.) Imagine, man doesn't see him for ten, twelve years and gives him that kind of a welcome!

HAPPY: Damn right!

BIFF (*trying to return to the offensive*): Pop, look —

WILLY: You know why he remembered you, don't you? Because you impressed him in those days.

BIFF: Let's talk quietly and get this down to the facts, huh?

WILLY (*as though* BIFF *had been interrupting*): Well, what happened? It's great news, Biff. Did he take you into his office or'd you talk in the waiting-room?

BIFF: Well, he came in, see, and —

WILLY (*with a big smile*): What'd he say? Betcha he threw his arm around you.

BIFF: Well, he kinda —

WILLY: He's a fine man. (*To* HAPPY.) Very hard man to see, y'know.

HAPPY (*agreeing*): Oh, I know.

WILLY (*to* BIFF): Is that where you had the drinks?

BIFF: Yeah, he gave me a couple of — no, no!

HAPPY (*cutting in*): He told him my Florida idea.

WILLY: Don't interrupt. (*To* BIFF.) How'd he react to the Florida idea?

BIFF: Dad, will you give me a minute to explain?

WILLY: I've been waiting for you to explain since I sat down here! What happened? He took you into his office and what?

BIFF: Well — I talked. And — and he listened, see.

WILLY: Famous for the way he listens, y'know. What was his answer?

BIFF: His answer was — (*He breaks off, suddenly angry.*) Dad, you're not letting me tell you what I want to tell you!

WILLY (*accusing, angered*): You didn't see him, did you?

BIFF: I did see him!

WILLY: What'd you insult him or something? You insulted him, didn't you?

BIFF: Listen, will you let me out of it, will you just let me out of it!

HAPPY: What the hell!

WILLY: Tell me what happened!

BIFF (*to* HAPPY): I can't talk to him!

(*A single trumpet note jars the ear. The light of green leaves stains the house, which holds the air of night and a dream.* YOUNG BERNARD *enters and knocks on the door of the house.*)

YOUNG BERNARD (*frantically*): Mrs. Loman, Mrs. Loman!

HAPPY: Tell him what happened!

BIFF (*to* HAPPY): Shut up and leave me alone!

WILLY: No, no! You had to go and flunk math!

BIFF: What math? What're you talking about?

YOUNG BERNARD: Mrs. Loman, Mrs. Loman!

(LINDA *appears in the house, as of old.*)

WILLY (*wildly*): Math, math, math!

BIFF: Take it easy, Pop!

YOUNG BERNARD: Mrs. Loman!

WILLY (*furiously*): If you hadn't flunked you'd've been set by now!

BIFF: Now, look, I'm gonna tell you what happened, and you're going to listen to me.

YOUNG BERNARD: Mrs. Loman!

BIFF: I waited six hours —

HAPPY: What the hell are you saying?

BIFF: I kept sending in my name but he wouldn't see me. So finally he . . . (*He continues unheard as light fades low on the restaurant.*)

YOUNG BERNARD: Biff flunked math!

LINDA: No!

YOUNG BERNARD: Birnbaum flunked him! They won't graduate him!

LINDA: But they have to. He's gotta go to the university. Where is he? Biff! Biff!

YOUNG BERNARD: No, he left. He went to Grand Central.

LINDA: Grand — You mean he went to Boston!

YOUNG BERNARD: Is Uncle Willy in Boston?

LINDA: Oh, maybe Willy can talk to the teacher. Oh, the poor, poor boy!

(*Light on house area snaps out.*)

BIFF (*at the table, now audible, holding up a gold fountain pen*): . . . so I'm washed up with Oliver, you understand? Are you listening to me?

WILLY (*at a loss*): Yeah, sure. If you hadn't flunked —

BIFF: Flunked what? What're you talking about?

WILLY: Don't blame everything on me! I didn't flunk math — you did! What pen?

HAPPY: That was awful dumb, Biff, a pen like that is worth —

WILLY (*seeing the pen for the first time*): You took Oliver's pen?

BIFF (*weakening*): Dad, I just explained it to you.

WILLY: You stole Bill Oliver's fountain pen!

BIFF: I didn't exactly steal it! That's just what I've been explaining to you!

HAPPY: He had it in his hand and just then Oliver walked in, so he got nervous and stuck it in his pocket!

WILLY: My God, Biff!

BIFF: I never intended to do it, Dad!

OPERATOR'S VOICE: Standish Arms, good evening!

WILLY (*shouting*): I'm not in my room!

BIFF (*frightened*): Dad, what's the matter? (*He and* HAPPY *stand up.*)

OPERATOR: Ringing Mr. Loman for you!

WILLY: I'm not there, stop it!

BIFF (*horrified, gets down on one knee before* WILLY): Dad, I'll make good, I'll make good. (WILLY *tries to get to his feet.* BIFF *holds him down.*) Sit down now.

WILLY: No, you're no good, you're no good for anything.

BIFF: I am, Dad, I'll find something else, you understand? Now don't worry about anything. (*He holds up* WILLY's *face.*) Talk to me, Dad.

OPERATOR: Mr. Loman does not answer. Shall I page him?

WILLY (*attempting to stand, as though to rush and silence the* OPERATOR): No, no, no!

HAPPY: He'll strike something, Pop.

WILLY: No, no . . .

BIFF (*desperately, standing over* WILLY): Pop, listen! Listen to me! I'm telling you

something good. Oliver talked to his partner about the Florida idea. You listening? He — he talked to his partner, and he came to me . . . I'm going to be all right, you hear? Dad, listen to me, he said it was just a question of the amount!

WILLY: Then you . . . got it?

HAPPY: He's gonna be terrific, Pop!

WILLY (*trying to stand*): Then you got it, haven't you? You got it! You got it!

BIFF (*agonized, holds* WILLY *down*): No, no. Look, Pop. I'm supposed to have lunch with them tomorrow. I'm just telling you this so you'll know that I can still make an impression, Pop. And I'll make good somewhere, but I can't go tomorrow, see?

WILLY: Why not? You simply —

BIFF: But the pen, Pop!

WILLY: You give it to him and tell him it was an oversight!

HAPPY: Sure, have lunch tomorrow!

BIFF: I can't say that —

WILLY: You were doing a crossword puzzle and accidentally used his pen!

BIFF: Listen, kid, I took those balls years ago, now I walk in with his fountain pen? That clinches it, don't you see? I can't face him like that! I'll try elsewhere.

PAGE'S VOICE: Paging Mr. Loman!

WILLY: Don't you want to be anything?

BIFF: Pop, how can I go back?

WILLY: You don't want to be anything, is that what's behind it?

BIFF (*now angry at* WILLY *for not crediting his sympathy*): Don't take it that way! You think it was easy walking into that office after what I'd done to him? A team of horses couldn't have dragged me back to Bill Oliver!

WILLY: Then why'd you go?

BIFF: Why did I go? Why did I go! Look at you! Look at what's become of you!

(*Off left,* THE WOMAN *laughs.*)

WILLY: Biff, you're going to go to that lunch tomorrow, or —

BIFF: I can't go. I've got no appointment!

HAPPY: Biff, for . . . !

WILLY: Are you spiting me?

BIFF: Don't take it that way! Goddammit!

WILLY (*strikes* BIFF *and falters away from the table*): You rotten little louse! Are you spiting me?

THE WOMAN: Someone's at the door, Willy!

BIFF: I'm no good, can't you see what I am?

HAPPY (*separating them*): Hey, you're in a restaurant! Now cut it out, both of you! (THE GIRLS *enter*.) Hello, girls, sit down.

(THE WOMAN *laughs, off left*.)

MISS FORSYTHE: I guess we might as well. This is Letta.

THE WOMAN: Willy, are you going to wake up?

BIFF (*ignoring* WILLY): How're ya, miss, sit down. What do you drink?

MISS FORSYTHE: Letta might not be able to stay long.

LETTA: I gotta get up very early tomorrow. I got jury duty. I'm so excited! Were you fellows ever on a jury?

BIFF: No, but I been in front of them! (THE GIRLS *laugh*.) This is my father.

LETTA: Isn't he cute? Sit down with us, Pop.

HAPPY: Sit him down, Biff!

BIFF (*going to him*): Come on, slugger, drink us under the table. To hell with it! Come on, sit down, pal.

(*On* BIFF's *last insistence,* WILLY *is about to sit*.)

THE WOMAN (*now urgently*): Willy, are you going to answer the door!

(THE WOMAN's *call pulls* WILLY *back. He starts right, befuddled*.)

BIFF: Hey, where are you going?

WILLY: Open the door.

BIFF: The door?

WILLY: The washroom . . . the door . . . where's the door?

BIFF (*leading* WILLY *to the left*): Just go straight down.

(WILLY *moves left*.)

THE WOMAN: Willy, Willy, are you going to get up, get up, get up, get up?

(WILLY *exits left*.)

LETTA: I think it's sweet you bring your daddy along.

MISS FORSYTHE: Oh, he isn't really your father!

BIFF (*at left, turning to her resentfully*): Miss Forsythe, you've just seen a prince walk by. A fine, troubled prince. A hard-working, unappreciated prince. A pal, you understand? A good companion. Always for his boys.

LETTA: That's so sweet.

HAPPY: Well, girls, what's the program? We're wasting time. Come on, Biff. Gather round. Where would you like to go?

BIFF: Why don't you do something for him?

HAPPY: Me!

BIFF: Don't you give a damn for him, Hap?

HAPPY: What're you talking about? I'm the one who —

BIFF: I sense it, you don't give a good goddam about him. (*He takes the rolled-up hose from his pocket and puts it on the table in front of* HAPPY.) Look what I found in the cellar, for Christ's sake. How can you bear to let it go on?

HAPPY: Me? Who goes away? Who runs off and —

BIFF: Yeah, but he doesn't mean anything to you. You could help him — I can't! Don't you understand what I'm talking about? He's going to kill himself, don't you know that?

HAPPY: Don't I know it! Me!

BIFF: Hap, help him! Jesus . . . help him . . . Help me, help me, I can't bear to look at his face! (*Ready to weep, he hurries out, up right*.)

HAPPY (*starting after him*): Where are you going?

MISS FORSYTHE: What's he so mad about?

HAPPY: Come on, girls, we'll catch up with him.

MISS FORSYTHE (*as* HAPPY *pushes her out*): Say, I don't like that temper of his!

HAPPY: He's just a little overstrung, he'll be all right!

WILLY (*off left, as* THE WOMAN *laughs*): Don't answer! Don't answer!

LETTA: Don't you want to tell your father —

HAPPY: No, that's not my father. He's just a guy. Come on, we'll catch Biff, and, honey, we're going to paint this town! Stanley, where's the check! Hey, Stanley!

(*They exit.* STANLEY *looks toward left*.)

STANLEY (*calling to* HAPPY *indignantly*): Mr. Loman! Mr. Loman!

(STANLEY *picks up a chair and follows them off. Knocking is heard off left.* THE WOMAN *enters, laughing.* WILLY *follows her. She is in a black slip; he is buttoning his shirt. Raw, sensuous music accompanies their speech*.)

WILLY: Will you stop laughing? Will you stop?

THE WOMAN: Aren't you going to answer the door? He'll wake the whole hotel.

WILLY: I'm not expecting anybody.

THE WOMAN: Whyn't you have another drink, honey, and stop being so damn self-centered?

WILLY: I'm so lonely.

THE WOMAN: You know you ruined me, Willy? From now on, whenever you come to the office, I'll see that you go right through to the buyers. No waiting at my desk any more, Willy. You ruined me.

WILLY: That's nice of you to say that.

THE WOMAN: Gee, you are self-centered! Why so sad? You are the saddest self-centeredest soul I ever did see-saw. (*She laughs. He kisses her.*) Come on inside, drummer boy. It's silly to be dressing in the middle of the night. (*As knocking is heard.*) Aren't you going to answer the door?

WILLY: They're knocking on the wrong door.

THE WOMAN: But I felt the knocking. And he heard us talking in here. Maybe the hotel's on fire!

WILLY (*his terror rising*): It's a mistake.

THE WOMAN: Then tell him to go away!

WILLY: There's nobody there.

THE WOMAN: It's getting on my nerves, Willy. There's somebody standing out there and it's getting on my nerves!

WILLY (*pushing her away from him*): All right, stay in the bathroom here, and don't come out. I think there's a law in Massachusetts about it, so don't come out. It may be that new room clerk. He looked very mean. So don't come out. It's a mistake, there's no fire.

(*The knocking is heard again. He takes a few steps away from her, and she vanishes into the wing. The light follows him, and now he is facing* YOUNG BIFF, *who carries a suitcase.* BIFF *steps toward him. The music is gone.*)

BIFF: Why didn't you answer?

WILLY: Biff! What are you doing in Boston?

BIFF: Why didn't you answer? I've been knocking for five minutes, I called you on the phone —

WILLY: I just heard you. I was in the bathroom and had the door shut. Did anything happen home?

BIFF: Dad — I let you down.

WILLY: What do you mean?

BIFF: Dad . . .

WILLY: Biffo, what's this about? (*Putting his arm around* BIFF.) Come on, let's go downstairs and get you a malted.

BIFF: Dad, I flunked math.

WILLY: Not for the term?

BIFF: The term. I haven't got enough credits to graduate.

WILLY: You mean to say Bernard wouldn't give you the answers?

BIFF: He did, he tried, but I only got a sixty-one.

WILLY: And they wouldn't give you four points?

BIFF: Birnbaum refused absolutely. I begged him, Pop, but he won't give me those points. You gotta talk to him before they close the school. Because if he saw the kind of man you are, and you just talked to him in your way, I'm sure he'd come through for me. The class came right before practice, see, and I didn't go enough. Would you talk to him? He'd like you, Pop. You know the way you could talk.

WILLY: You're on. We'll drive right back.

BIFF: Oh, Dad, good work! I'm sure he'll change it for you!

WILLY: Go downstairs and tell the clerk I'm checkin' out. Go right down.

BIFF: Yes, sir! See, the reason he hates me, Pop — one day he was late for class so I got up at the blackboard and imitated him. I crossed my eyes and talked with a lithp.

WILLY (*laughing*): You did? The kids like it?

BIFF: They nearly died laughing!

WILLY: Yeah? What'd you do?

BIFF: The thquare root of thixthy twec is . . . (WILLY *bursts out laughing;* BIFF *joins him.*) And in the middle of it he walked in!

(WILLY *laughs and* THE WOMAN *joins in offstage.*)

WILLY (*without hesitation*): Hurry downstairs and —

BIFF: Somebody in there?

WILLY: No, that was next door.

(THE WOMAN *laughs offstage.*)

BIFF: Somebody got in your bathroom!

WILLY: No, it's the next room, there's a party —

THE WOMAN (*enters, laughing. She lisps*

this): Can I come in? There's something in the bathtub, Willy, and it's moving!

(WILLY *looks at* BIFF, *who is staring open-mouthed and horrified at* THE WOMAN.)

WILLY: Ah — you better go back to your room. They must be finished painting by now. They're painting her room so I let her take a shower here. Go back, go back . . . (*He pushes her.*)

THE WOMAN (*resisting*): But I've got to get dressed, Willy, I can't —

WILLY: Get out of here! Go back, go back . . . (*Suddenly striving for the ordinary.*) This is Miss Francis, Biff, she's a buyer. They're painting her room. Go back, Miss Francis, go back . . .

THE WOMAN: But my clothes, I can't go out naked in the hall!

WILLY (*pushing her offstage*): Get outa here! Go back, go back!

(BIFF *slowly sits down on his suitcase as the argument continues offstage.*)

THE WOMAN: Where's my stockings? You promised me stockings, Willy!

WILLY: I have no stockings here!

THE WOMAN: You had two boxes of size nine sheers for me, and I want them!

WILLY: Here, for God's sake, will you get outa here!

THE WOMAN (*enters holding a box of stockings*): I just hope there's nobody in the hall. That's all I hope. (*To* BIFF.) Are you football or baseball?

BIFF: Football.

THE WOMAN (*angry, humiliated*): That's me too. G'night. (*She snatches her clothes from* WILLY, *and walks out.*)

WILLY (*after a pause*): Well, better get going. I want to get to the school first thing in the morning. Get my suits out of the closet. I'll get my valise. (BIFF *doesn't move.*) What's the matter? (BIFF *remains motionless, tears falling.*) She's a buyer. Buys for J. H. Simmons. She lives down the hall — they're painting. You don't imagine — (*He breaks off. After a pause.*) Now listen, pal, she's just a buyer. She sees merchandise in her room and they have to keep it looking just so . . . (*Pause. Assuming command.*) All right, get my suits. (BIFF *doesn't move.*) Now stop crying and do as I say. I gave you an order. Biff, I gave you an order! Is that what you do when I give you

an order? How dare you cry! (*Putting his arm around* BIFF.) Now look, Biff, when you grow up you'll understand about these things. You mustn't — you mustn't overemphasize a thing like this. I'll see Birnbaum first thing in the morning.

BIFF: Never mind.

WILLY (*getting down beside* BIFF): Never mind! He's going to give you those points. I'll see to it.

BIFF: He wouldn't listen to you.

WILLY: He certainly will listen to me. You need those points for the U. of Virginia.

BIFF: I'm not going there.

WILLY: Heh? If I can't get him to change that mark you'll make it up in summer school. You've got all summer to —

BIFF (*his weeping breaking from him*): Dad . . .

WILLY (*infected by it*): Oh, my boy . . .

BIFF: Dad . . .

WILLY: She's nothing to me, Biff. I was lonely, I was terribly lonely.

BIFF: You — you gave her Mama's stockings! (*His tears break through and he rises to go.*)

WILLY (*grabbing for* BIFF): I gave you an order!

BIFF: Don't touch me, you — liar!

WILLY: Apologize for that!

BIFF: You fake! You phony little fake! You fake! (*Overcome, he turns quickly and weeping fully goes out with his suitcase.* WILLY *is left on the floor on his knees.*)

WILLY: I gave you an order! Biff, come back here or I'll beat you! Come back here! I'll whip you!

(STANLEY *comes quickly in from the right and stands in front of* WILLY.)

WILLY (*shouts at* STANLEY): I gave you an order . . .

STANLEY: Hey, let's pick it up, pick it up, Mr. Loman. (*He helps* WILLY *to his feet.*) Your boys left with the chippies. They said they'll see you home.

(A *second waiter watches some distance away.*)

WILLY: But we were supposed to have dinner together.

(*Music is heard,* WILLY's *theme.*)

STANLEY: Can you make it?

WILLY: I'll — sure, I can make it. (*Suddenly*

concerned about his clothes.) Do I — I look all right?

STANLEY: Sure, you look all right. (*He flicks a speck off* WILLY's *lapel.*)

WILLY: Here — here's a dollar.

STANLEY: Oh, your son paid me. It's all right.

WILLY (*putting it in* STANLEY's *hand*): No, take it. You're a good boy.

STANLEY: Oh, no, you don't have to . . .

WILLY: Here — here's some more, I don't need it any more. (*After a slight pause.*) Tell me — is there a seed store in the neighborhood?

STANLEY: Seeds? You mean like to plant?

(*As* WILLY *turns,* STANLEY *slips the money back into his jacket pocket.*)

WILLY: Yes. Carrots, peas . . .

STANLEY: Well, there's hardware stores on Sixth Avenue, but it may be too late now.

WILLY (*anxiously*): Oh, I'd better hurry. I've got to get some seeds. (*He starts off to the right.*) I've got to get some seeds, right away. Nothing's planted. I don't have a thing in the ground.

(WILLY *hurries out as the light goes down.* STANLEY *moves over to the right after him, watches him off. The other waiter has been staring at* WILLY.)

STANLEY (*to the waiter*): Well, whatta you looking at?

(*The waiter picks up the chairs and moves off right.* STANLEY *takes the table and follows him. The light fades on this area. There is a long pause, the sound of the flute coming over. The light gradually rises on the kitchen, which is empty.* HAPPY *appears at the door of the house, followed by* BIFF. HAPPY *is carrying a large bunch of long-stemmed roses. He enters the kitchen, looks around for* LINDA. *Not seeing her, he turns to* BIFF, *who is just outside the house door, and makes a gesture with his hands, indicating "Not here, I guess." He looks into the living-room and freezes. Inside,* LINDA, *unseen, is seated,* WILLY's *coat on her lap. She rises ominously and quietly and moves toward* HAPPY, *who backs up into the kitchen, afraid.*)

HAPPY: Hey, what're you doing up? (LINDA *says nothing but moves toward him impla-*

cably.) Where's Pop? (*He keeps backing to the right, and now* LINDA *is in full view in the doorway to the living-room.*) Is he sleeping?

LINDA: Where were you?

HAPPY (*trying to laugh it off*): We met two girls, Mom, very fine types. Here, we brought you some flowers. (*Offering them to her.*) Put them in your room, Ma.

(*She knocks them to the floor at* BIFF's *feet. He has now come inside and closed the door behind him. She stares at* BIFF, *silent.*)

HAPPY: Now what'd you do that for? Mom, I want you to have some flowers —

LINDA (*cutting* HAPPY *off, violently to* BIFF): Don't you care whether he lives or dies?

HAPPY (*going to the stairs*): Come upstairs, Biff.

BIFF (*with a flare of disgust, to* HAPPY): Go away from me! (*To* LINDA.) What do you mean, lives or dies? Nobody's dying around here, pal.

LINDA: Get out of my sight! Get out of here!

BIFF: I wanna see the boss.

LINDA: You're not going near him!

BIFF: Where is he? (*He moves into the living-room and* LINDA *follows.*)

LINDA (*shouting after* BIFF): You invite him for dinner. He looks forward to it all day — (BIFF *appears in his parents' bedroom, looks around, and exits*) — and then you desert him there. There's no stranger you'd do that to!

HAPPY: Why? He had a swell time with us. Listen, when I — (LINDA *comes back into the kitchen*) — desert him I hope I don't outlive the day!

LINDA: Get out of here!

HAPPY: Now look, Mom . . .

LINDA: Did you have to go to women tonight? You and your lousy rotten whores!

(BIFF *re-enters the kitchen.*)

HAPPY: Mom, all we did was follow Biff around trying to cheer him up! (*To* BIFF.) Boy, what a night you gave me!

LINDA: Get out of here, both of you, and don't come back! I don't want you tormenting him any more. Go on now, get your things together! (*To* BIFF.) You can sleep in his apartment. (*She starts to pick up the flowers and stops herself.*) Pick up this stuff, I'm not your maid any more. Pick it up, you bum, you!

(HAPPY *turns his back to her in refusal.* BIFF *slowly moves over and gets down on his knees, picking up the flowers.*)

LINDA: You're a pair of animals! Not once, not another living soul would have had the cruelty to walk out on that man in a restaurant!

BIFF (*not looking at her*): Is that what he said?

LINDA: He didn't have to say anything. He was so humiliated he nearly limped when he came in.

HAPPY: But, Mom, he had a great time with us —

BIFF (*cutting him off violently*): Shut up!

(*Without another word,* HAPPY *goes upstairs.*)

LINDA: You! You didn't even go in to see if he was all right!

BIFF (*still on the floor in front of* LINDA, *the flowers in his hand; with self-loathing*): No. Didn't. Didn't do a damned thing. How do you like that, heh? Left him babbling in a toilet.

LINDA: You louse. You . . .

BIFF: Now you hit it on the nose! (*He gets up, throws the flowers in the wastebasket.*) The scum of the earth, and you're looking at him!

LINDA: Get out of here!

BIFF: I gotta talk to the boss, Mom. Where is he?

LINDA: You're not going near him. Get out of this house!

BIFF (*with absolute assurance, determination*): No. We're gonna have an abrupt conversation, him and me.

LINDA: You're not talking to him!

(*Hammering is heard from outside the house, off right.* BIFF *turns toward the noise.*)

LINDA (*suddenly pleading*): Will you please leave him alone?

BIFF: What's he doing out there?

LINDA: He's planting the garden!

BIFF (*quietly*): Now? Oh, my God!

(BIFF *moves outside,* LINDA *following. The light dies down on them and comes up on the center of the apron as* WILLY *walks into it. He is carrying a flashlight, a hoe, and a handful of seed packets. He raps the top of the hoe sharply to fix it firmly, and then moves to the left, measuring off the distance with his foot. He holds the flashlight to look at the seed packets, reading off the instructions. He is in the blue of night.*)

WILLY: Carrots . . . quarter-inch apart. Rows . . . one-foot rows. (*He measures it off.*) One foot. (*He puts down a package and measures off.*) Beets. (*He puts down another package and measures again.*) Lettuce. (*He reads the package, puts it down.*) One foot — (*He breaks off as* BEN *appears at the right and moves slowly down to him.*) What a proposition, ts, ts. Terrific, terrific. 'Cause she's suffered, Ben, the woman has suffered. You understand me? A man can't go out the way he came in, Ben, a man has got to add up to something. You can't, you can't — (*Ben moves toward him as though to interrupt.*) You gotta consider, now. Don't answer so quick. Remember, it's a guaranteed twenty-thousand-dollar proposition. Now look, Ben, I want you to go through the ins and outs of this thing with me. I've got nobody to talk to, Ben, and the woman has suffered, you hear me?

BEN (*standing still, considering*): What's the proposition?

WILLY: It's twenty thousand dollars on the barrelhead. Guaranteed, gilt-edged, you understand?

BEN: You don't want to make a fool of yourself. They might not honor the policy.

WILLY: How can they dare refuse? Didn't I work like a coolie to meet every premium on the nose? And now they don't pay off? Impossible!

BEN: It's called a cowardly thing, William.

WILLY: Why? Does it take more guts to stand here the rest of my life ringing up a zero?

BEN (*yielding*): That's a point, William. (*He moves, thinking, turns.*) And twenty thousand — that *is* something one can feel with the hand, it is there.

WILLY (*now assured, with rising power*): Oh, Ben, that's the whole beauty of it! I see it like a diamond, shining in the dark, hard and rough, that I can pick up and touch in my hand. Not like — like an appointment! This would not be another damned-fool appointment, Ben, and it changes all the aspects.

Because he thinks I'm nothing, see, and so he spites me. But the funeral — (*Straightening up.*) Ben, that funeral will be massive! They'll come from Maine, Massachusetts, Vermont, New Hampshire! All the old-timers with the strange license plates — that boy will be thunder-struck, Ben, because he never realized — I am known! Rhode Island, New York, New Jersey — I am known, Ben, and he'll see it with his eyes once and for all. He'll see what I am, Ben! He's in for a shock, that boy!

BEN (*coming down to the edge of the garden*): He'll call you a coward.

WILLY (*suddenly fearful*): No, that would be terrible.

BEN: Yes. And a damned fool.

WILLY: No, no, he mustn't, I won't have that! (*He is broken and desperate.*)

BEN: He'll hate you, William.

(*The gay music of the boys is heard.*)

WILLY: Oh, Ben, how do we get back to all the great times? Used to be so full of light, and comradeship, the sleigh-riding in winter, and the ruddiness on his cheeks. And always some kind of good news coming up, always something nice coming up ahead. And never even let me carry the valises in the house, and simonizing, simonizing that little red car! Why, why can't I give him something and not have him hate me?

BEN: Let me think about it. (*He glances at his watch.*) I still have a little time. Remarkable proposition, but you've got to be sure you're not making a fool of yourself.

(*BEN drifts off upstage and goes out of sight. BIFF comes down from the left.*)

WILLY (*suddenly conscious of BIFF, turns and looks up at him, then begins picking up the packages of seeds in confusion*): Where the hell is that seed? (*Indignantly.*) You can't see nothing out here! They boxed in the whole goddam neighborhood!

BIFF: There are people all around here. Don't you realize that?

WILLY: I'm busy. Don't bother me.

BIFF (*taking the hoe from WILLY*): I'm saying good-by to you, Pop. (*WILLY looks at him, silent, unable to move.*) I'm not coming back any more.

WILLY: You're not going to see Oliver tomorrow?

BIFF: I've got no appointment, Dad.

WILLY: He put his arm around you, and you've got no appointment?

BIFF: Pop, get this now, will you? Everytime I've left it's been a fight that sent me out of here. Today I realized something about myself and I tried to explain it to you and I — I think I'm just not smart enough to make any sense out of it for you. To hell with whose fault it is or anything like that. (*He takes WILLY's arm.*) Let's just wrap it up, heh? Come on in, we'll tell Mom. (*He gently tries to pull WILLY to left.*)

WILLY (*frozen, immobile, with guilt in his voice*): No, I don't want to see her.

BIFF: Come on! (*He pulls again, and WILLY tries to pull away.*)

WILLY (*highly nervous*): No, no, I don't want to see her.

BIFF (*tries to look into WILLY's face, as if to find the answer there*): Why don't you want to see her?

WILLY (*more harshly now*): Don't bother me, will you?

BIFF: What do you mean, you don't want to see her? You don't want them calling you yellow, do you? This isn't your fault; it's me, I'm a bum. Now come inside! (*WILLY strains to get away.*) Did you hear what I said to you?

(*WILLY pulls away and quickly goes by himself into the house. BIFF follows.*)

LINDA (*to WILLY*): Did you plant, dear?

BIFF (*at the door, to LINDA*): All right, we had it out. I'm going and I'm not writing any more.

LINDA (*going to WILLY in the kitchen*): I think that's the best way, dear. 'Cause there's no use drawing it out, you'll just never get along.

(*WILLY doesn't respond.*)

BIFF: People ask where I am and what I'm doing, you don't know, and you don't care. That way it'll be off your mind and you can start brightening up again. All right? That clears it, doesn't it? (*WILLY is silent, and BIFF goes to him.*) You gonna wish me luck, scout? (*He extends his hand.*) What do you say?

LINDA: Shake his hand, Willy.

WILLY (*turning to her, seething with hurt*): There's no necessity to mention the pen at all, y'know.

BIFF (*gently*): I've got no appointment, Dad.

WILLY (*erupting fiercely*): He put his arm around . . . ?

BIFF: Dad, you're never going to see what I am, so what's the use of arguing? If I strike oil I'll send you a check. Meantime forget I'm alive.

WILLY (*to* LINDA): Spite, see?

BIFF: Shake hands, Dad.

WILLY: Not my hand.

BIFF: I was hoping not to go this way.

WILLY: Well, this is the way you're going. Good-by.

(BIFF *looks at him a moment, then turns sharply and goes to the stairs.*)

WILLY (*stops him with*): May you rot in hell if you leave this house!

BIFF (*turning*): Exactly what is it that you want from me?

WILLY: I want you to know, on the train, in the mountains, in the valleys, wherever you go, that you cut down your life for spite!

BIFF: No, no.

WILLY: Spite, spite, is the word of your undoing! And when you're down and out, remember what did it. When you're rotting somewhere beside the railroad tracks, remember, and don't you dare blame it on me!

BIFF: I'm not blaming it on you!

WILLY: I won't take the rap for this, you hear?

(HAPPY *comes down the stairs and stands on the bottom step, watching.*)

BIFF: That's just what I'm telling you!

WILLY (*sinking into a chair at the table, with full accusation*): You're trying to put a knife in me — don't think I don't know what you're doing!

BIFF: All right, phony! Then let's lay it on the line. (*He whips the rubber tube out of his pocket and puts it on the table.*)

HAPPY: You crazy —

LINDA: Biff! (*She moves to grab the hose, but* BIFF *holds it down with his hand.*)

BIFF: Leave it there! Don't move it!

WILLY (*not looking at it*): What is that?

BIFF: You know goddam well what that is.

WILLY (*caged, wanting to escape*): I never saw that.

BIFF: You saw it. The mice didn't bring it into the cellar! What is this supposed to do, make a hero out of you? This supposed to make me sorry for you?

WILLY: Never heard of it.

BIFF: There'll be no pity for you, you hear it? No pity!

WILLY (*to* LINDA): You hear the spite!

BIFF: No, you're going to hear the truth — what you are and what I am!

LINDA: Stop it!

WILLY: Spite!

HAPPY (*coming down toward* BIFF): You cut it now!

BIFF (*to* HAPPY): The man don't know who we are! The man is gonna know! (*To* WILLY.) We never told the truth for ten minutes in this house!

HAPPY: We always told the truth!

BIFF (*turning on him*): You big blow, are you the assistant buyer? You're one of the two assistants to the assistant, aren't you?

HAPPY: Well, I'm practically —

BIFF: You're practically full of it! We all are! And I'm through with it. (*To* WILLY.) Now hear this, Willy, this is me.

WILLY: I know you!

BIFF: You know why I had no address for three months? I stole a suit in Kansas City and I was in jail. (*To* LINDA, *who is sobbing.*) Stop crying. I'm through with it.

(LINDA *turns away from them, her hands covering her face.*)

WILLY: I suppose that's my fault!

BIFF: I stole myself out of every good job since high school!

WILLY: And whose fault is that?

BIFF: And I never got anywhere because you blew me so full of hot air I could never stand taking orders from anybody! That's whose fault it is!

WILLY: I hear that!

LINDA: Don't, Biff!

BIFF: It's goddam time you heard that! I had to be boss big shot in two weeks, and I'm through with it!

WILLY: Then hang yourself! For spite, hang yourself!

BIFF: No! Nobody's hanging himself, Willy! I ran down eleven flights with a pen in my hand today. And suddenly I stopped, you hear me? And in the middle of that office building, do you hear this? I stopped in the middle of that building and I saw — the sky. I saw the things that I love in this world. The work and the food and time to sit and smoke. And I looked at the pen and said to myself, what the hell am I grabbing this for? Why am I trying to become what I don't want to be? What am I doing in an office, making a contemptuous, begging fool of myself, when all I want is out there, waiting for me the minute I say I know who I am! Why can't I say that, Willy? (*He tries to make* WILLY *face him, but* WILLY *pulls away and moves to the left.*)

WILLY (*with hatred, threateningly*): The door of your life is wide open!

BIFF: Pop! I'm a dime a dozen, and so are you!

WILLY (*turning on him now in an uncontrolled outburst*): I am not a dime a dozen! I am Willy Loman, and you are Biff Loman!

(BIFF *starts for* WILLY, *but is blocked by* HAPPY. *In his fury,* BIFF *seems on the verge of attacking his father.*)

BIFF: I am not a leader of men, Willy, and neither are you. You were never anything but a hard-working drummer who landed in the ash can like all the rest of them! I'm one dollar an hour, Willy! I tried seven states and couldn't raise it. A buck an hour! Do you gather my meaning? I'm not bringing home any prizes any more, and you're going to stop waiting for me to bring them home!

WILLY (*directly to* BIFF): You vengeful, spiteful mut!

(BIFF *breaks from* HAPPY. WILLY, *in fright, starts up the stairs.* BIFF *grabs him.*)

BIFF (*at the peak of his fury*): Pop, I'm nothing! I'm nothing, Pop. Can't you understand that? There's no spite in it any more. I'm just what I am, that's all.

(BIFF'*s fury has spent itself, and he breaks down, sobbing, holding on to* WILLY, *who dumbly fumbles for* BIFF'*s face.*)

WILLY (*astonished*): What're you doing? What're you doing? (*To* LINDA.) Why is he crying?

BIFF (*crying, broken*): Will you let me go, for Christ's sake? Will you take that phony dream and burn it before something happens? (*Struggling to contain himself, he pulls away and moves to the stairs.*) I'll go in the morning. Put him — put him to bed. (*Exhausted,* BIFF *moves up the stairs to his room.*)

WILLY (*after a long pause, astonished, ele-*vated): Isn't that — isn't that remarkable? Biff — he likes me!

LINDA: He loves you, Willy!

HAPPY (*deeply moved*): Always did, Pop.

WILLY: Oh, Biff! (*Staring wildly.*) He cried! Cried to me. (*He is choking with his love, and now cries out his promise.*) That boy — that boy is going to be magnificent!

(BEN *appears in the light just outside the kitchen.*)

BEN: Yes, outstanding, with twenty thousand behind him.

LINDA (*sensing the racing of his mind, fearfully, carefully*): Now come to bed, Willy. It's all settled now.

WILLY (*finding it difficult not to rush out of the house*): Yes, we'll sleep. Come on. Go to sleep, Hap.

BEN: And it does take a great kind of a man to crack the jungle.

(*In accents of dread,* BEN'*s idyllic music starts up.*)

HAPPY (*his arm around* LINDA): I'm getting married, Pop, don't forget it. I'm changing everything. I'm gonna run that department before the year is up. You'll see, Mom. (*He kisses her.*)

BEN: The jungle is dark but full of diamonds, Willy.

(WILLY *turns, moves, listening to* BEN.)

LINDA: Be good. You're both good boys, just act that way, that's all.

HAPPY: 'Night, Pop. (*He goes upstairs.*)

LINDA (*to* WILLY): Come, dear.

BEN (*with greater force*): One must go in to fetch a diamond out.

WILLY (*to* LINDA, *as he moves slowly along the edge of the kitchen, toward the door*): I just want to get settled down, Linda. Let me sit alone for a little.

LINDA (*almost uttering her fear*): I want you upstairs.

WILLY (*taking her in his arms*): In a few minutes, Linda. I couldn't sleep right now. Go on, you look awful tired. (*He kisses her.*)

BEN: Not like an appointment at all. A diamond is rough and hard to the touch.

WILLY: Go on now. I'll be right up.

LINDA: I think this is the only way, Willy.

WILLY: Sure, it's the best thing.

BEN: Best thing!

WILLY: The only way. Everything is gonna be — go on, kid, get to bed. You look so tired.

LINDA: Come right up.

WILLY: Two minutes.

(LINDA *goes into the living-room, then reappears in her bedroom.* WILLY *moves just outside the kitchen door.*)

WILLY: Loves me. (*Wonderingly.*) Always loved me. Isn't that a remarkable thing? Ben, he'll worship me for it!

BEN (*with promise*): It's dark there, but full of diamonds.

WILLY: Can you imagine that magnificence with twenty thousand dollars in his pocket?

LINDA (*calling from her room*): Willy! Come up!

WILLY (*calling into the kitchen*): Yes! Yes. Coming! It's very smart, you realize that, don't you, sweetheart? Even Ben sees it. I gotta go, baby. 'By! 'By! (*Going over to* BEN, *almost dancing.*) Imagine? When the mail comes he'll be ahead of Bernard again!

BEN: A perfect proposition all around.

WILLY: Did you see how he cried to me? Oh, if I could kiss him, Ben!

BEN: Time, William, time!

WILLY: Oh, Ben, I always knew one way or another we were gonna make it, Biff and I!

BEN (*looking at his watch*): The boat. We'll be late. (*He moves slowly off into the darkness.*)

WILLY (*elegiacally, turning to the house*): Now when you kick off, boy, I want a seventy-yard boot, and get right down the field under the ball, and when you hit, hit low and hit hard, because it's important, boy. (*He swings around and faces the audience.*) There's all kinds of important people in the stands, and the first thing you know ... (*Suddenly realizing he is alone.*) Ben! Ben, where do I ...? (*He makes a sudden movement of search.*) Ben, how do I ...?

LINDA (*calling*): Willy, you coming up?

WILLY (*uttering a gasp of fear, whirling about as if to quiet her*): Sh! (*He turns around as if to find his way; sounds, faces, voices, seem to be swarming in upon him and he flicks at them, crying*) Sh! Sh! (*Suddenly music, faint and high, stops him. It rises in intensity, almost to an unbearable scream. He goes up and down on his toes, and rushes off around the house.*) Shhh!

LINDA: Willy?

(*There is no answer.* LINDA *waits.* BIFF *gets up off his bed. He is still in his clothes.* HAPPY *sits up.* BIFF *stands listening.*)

LINDA (*with real fear*): Willy, answer me! Willy!

(*There is the sound of a car starting and moving away at full speed.*)

LINDA: No!

BIFF (*rushing down the stairs*): Pop!

(*As the car speeds off, the music crashes down in a frenzy of sound, which becomes the soft pulsation of a single cello string.* BIFF *slowly returns to his bedroom. He and* HAPPY *gravely don their jackets.* LINDA *slowly walks out of her room. The music has developed into a dead march. The leaves of day are appearing over everything.* CHARLEY *and* BERNARD, *somberly dressed, appear and knock on the kitchen door.* BIFF *and* HAPPY *slowly descend the stairs to the kitchen as* CHARLEY *and* BERNARD *enter. All stop a moment when* LINDA, *in clothes of mourning, bearing a little bunch of roses, comes through the draped doorway into the kitchen. She goes to* CHARLEY *and takes his arm. Now all move toward the audience, through the wall-line of the kitchen. At the limit of the apron,* LINDA *lays down the flowers, kneels, and sits back on her heels. All stare down at the grave.*)

REQUIEM *for a salesman*

CHARLEY: It's getting dark, Linda.

(LINDA *doesn't react. She stares at the grave.*)

BIFF: How about it, Mom? Better get some rest, heh? They'll be closing the gate soon.

(LINDA *makes no move. Pause.*)

HAPPY (*deeply angered*): He had no right to do that. There was no necessity for it. We would've helped him.

CHARLEY (*grunting*): Hmmm.

BIFF: Come along, Mom.

LINDA: Why didn't anybody come?

CHARLEY: It was a very nice funeral.

LINDA: But where are all the people he knew? Maybe they blame him.

CHARLEY: Naa. It's a rough world, Linda. They wouldn't blame him.

LINDA: I can't understand it. At this time especially. First time in thirty-five years we were just about free and clear. He only needed a little salary. He was even finished with the dentist.

CHARLEY: No man only needs a little salary.

LINDA: I can't understand it.

BIFF: There were a lot of nice days. When he'd come home from a trip; or on Sundays, making the stoop; finishing the cellar; putting on the new porch; when he built the extra bathroom; and put up the garage. You know something, Charley, there's more of him in that front stoop than in all the sales he ever made.

CHARLEY: Yeah. He was a happy man with a batch of cement.

LINDA: He was so wonderful with his hands.

BIFF: He had the wrong dreams. All, all, wrong.

HAPPY (almost ready to fight BIFF): Don't say that!

BIFF: He never knew who he was.

CHARLEY (stopping HAPPY's movement and reply. To BIFF): Nobody dast blame this man. You don't understand: Willy was a salesman. And for a salesman, there is no rock bottom to the life. He don't put a bolt to a nut, he don't tell you the law or give you medicine. He's a man way out there in the blue, riding on a smile and a shoeshine. And when they start not smiling back — that's an earthquake. And then you get yourself a couple of spots on your hat, and you're finished. Nobody dast blame this man. A salesman is got to dream, boy. It comes with the territory.

BIFF: Charley, the man didn't know who he was.

HAPPY (infuriated): Don't say that!

BIFF: Why don't you come with me, Happy?

HAPPY: I'm not licked that easily. I'm staying right in this city, and I'm gonna beat this racket! (He looks at BIFF, his chin set.) The Loman Brothers!

BIFF: I know who I am, kid.

HAPPY: All right, boy. I'm gonna show you and everybody else that Willy Loman did not die in vain. He had a good dream. It's the only dream you can have — to come out number-one man. He fought it out here, and this is where I'm gonna win it for him.

BIFF (with a hopeless glance at HAPPY, bends toward his mother): Let's go, Mom.

LINDA: I'll be with you in a minute. Go on, Charley. (He hesitates.) I want to, just for a minute. I never had a chance to say good-by.

(CHARLEY moves away, followed by HAPPY. BIFF remains a slight distance up and left of LINDA. She sits there, summoning herself. The flute begins, not far away, playing behind her speech.)

LINDA: Forgive me, dear. I can't cry. I don't know what it is, but I can't cry. I don't understand it. Why did you ever do that? Help me, Willy, I can't cry. It seems to me that you're just on another trip. I keep expecting you. Willy, dear, I can't cry. Why did you do it? I search and search and I search, and I can't understand it, Willy. I made the last payment on the house today. Today, dear. And there'll be nobody home. (A sob rises in her throat.) We're free and clear. (Sobbing more fully, released.) We're free. (BIFF comes slowly toward her.) We're free ... We're free ...

(BIFF lifts her to her feet and moves out up right with her in his arms. LINDA sobs quietly. BERNARD and CHARLEY come together and follow them, followed by HAPPY. Only the music of the flute is left on the darkening stage as over the house the hard towers of the apartment buildings rise into sharp focus, and —)

THE CURTAIN FALLS

For the ancient Greeks, at least for Aristotle, *pathos* was the destructive or painful act common in tragedy; but in English "pathos" refers to an element in art or life that evokes tenderness or sympathetic pity. Modern English critical usage distinguishes between tragic figures and pathetic figures by recognizing some element either of strength or of regeneration in the former that is not in the latter. The tragic protagonist perhaps acts so that he brings his destruction upon himself, or if his destruction comes from outside, he resists it, and in either case he comes to at least a partial understanding of the causes of his suffering. The pathetic figure, however, is largely passive, an unknowing and unresisting innocent. In such a view Macbeth is tragic, Duncan pathetic; Lear is tragic, Cordelia pathetic; Othello is tragic, Desdemona pathetic; Hamlet is tragic (the situation is not of his making, but he does what he can to alter it), Ophelia pathetic. (Note, by the way, that of the four pathetic figures named, the first is old and the remaining three are women. Pathos is more likely to be evoked by persons assumed to be relatively defenseless than by the able-bodied.)

The guardians of critical terminology, then, have tended to insist that "tragedy" be reserved for a play showing action that leads to suffering which in turn leads to knowledge. They get very annoyed when a newspaper describes as a tragedy the death of a promising high school football player in an automobile accident, and they insist that such a death is pathetic not tragic; it is unexpected, premature, and deeply regrettable, but it does not give us a sense of man's greatness achieved through understanding the sufferings that a sufferer has at least in some degree chosen. Probably critics hoard the term "tragedy" because it is also a word of praise: to call a play a comedy or a problem play is not to imply anything about its merits, but to call a play a tragedy is tantamount to calling it an important or even a great play. In most of the best-known Greek tragedies the protagonist either does some terrible deed, or resists mightily. But Greek drama has its pathetic figures too, figures who do not so much act as suffer. Euripides' *The Trojan Women* is perhaps the greatest example of a play which does not allow its heroes to choose and to act but only to undergo, to be in agony. When we think of pathetic figures in Greek drama, however, we probably think chiefly of the choruses, groups of rather commonplace persons who do not perform a tragic deed but who suffer in sympathy with the tragic hero, who lament the hardness of the times, and who draw the spectators into the range of the hero's suffering.

That the spectators were not themselves heroic figures seems to have been assumed by the Greeks and by the Elizabethans; at least there are usually these lesser choral figures, nameless citizens, who interpret the action and call attention to the fact that even highly placed great heroes are not exempt from pain: indeed, high place and strenuous activity invite pain: the lofty pine tree, or the mariner who ventures far from the coast, is more likely to meet destruction than the lowly shrub or the fair-weather sailor. For Greeks of the fifth century B.C., and for Elizabethans, high place was not a mere matter of rank, but of worth. In both ages, it was of course known that a king may be unkingly, but it was assumed that kingship required a special nature — though that nature was not always forthcoming. Put it this way: tragedy deals with kings not because they are men with a certain title (though of course the title does give them special power), but because they are men with a certain nature. This nature is an extraordinary capacity for action and for feeling; when they make an error its consequences are enormous, and they themselves feel it as lesser people would not. When Oedipus is polluted, all of Thebes feels it. Arthur Miller is somewhat misleading when he argues (p. 255) that because Oedipus has given his name to a complex that the common man may have, the common man is therefore "as apt a subject for tragedy." It is not Oedipus' "complex" but his unique importance that is the issue in the play. Moreover, even if one argues that a man of no public importance may suffer as much as a man of public importance (and surely no one doubts this), one may be faced with the fact that the unimportant man by his ordinariness is not particularly good material for drama, and we are here concerned with drama rather than with life. In *Death of a Salesman* Willy Loman's wife says, rightly, "A small man can be just as exhausted as a great man." Yes, but is his exhaustion itself interesting, and do his activities (and this includes the words he utters) before his exhaustion have interesting dramatic possibilities? Isn't there a colorlessness that may weaken the play, an impoverishment of what John Milton called "gorgeous tragedy"?

Inevitably the rise of the bourgeoisie brought about the rise of bourgeois drama, and in the eighteenth century we get a fair number of tragedies with prologues that insist that characters like ourselves deserve our *pity*:

> No fustian hero rages here tonight,
> No armies fall, to fix a tyrant's right.
> From lower life we draw our scene's distress:
> — Let not your equals move your pity less.
>
> George Lillo, *Fatal Curiosity* (1733)

Note the deflation of older tragedy, the implication that its heroes were "fustian" (bombastic, pretentious) rather than genuinely heroic persons of deep feelings and high aspirations. Or, to put it differently, older tragedy in the bourgeois view dealt with persons of high rank, but rank (in this view) is not significant; therefore one may as well show persons of middle rank with whom the middle-class audience may readily identify. At the same time, the dismissal of heroic activities ("no fustian hero *rages*," "no armies *fall*") and the substitution of "distress" indicates that we are well on the road to The Hero As Victim.

And we have kept on that road. As early as the sixteenth century Copernicus had shown that man and his planet were not the center of the universe, but the thought did not distress the bulk of men until much later. In 1859 Darwin published *The Origin of Species,* arguing that man was not a special creation but a creature that had evolved because "accidental variations" had aided him in the struggle for survival. At about the same time, Marx (who wished to dedicate *Capital* to Darwin) argued that economic forces guided men's lives. Early in the twentieth century Freud seemed to argue that men are conditioned by infantile experiences and are enslaved by the dark forces of the id. All in all, by the time of the Depression of the 1930's, it was difficult to have much confidence in man's ability to shape his destiny. The human condition was a sorry one; man was an insignificant lust-ridden, soulless creature in a terrifying materialistic universe. He was no Oedipus whose moral pollution infected a great city, no Brutus whose deed might bring civil war to Rome. He was really not much of anything, except perhaps to a few who immediately depended upon him.

Arthur Miller accurately noted (*Theatre Arts*, October, 1953) that American drama "has been a steady year by year documentation of the frustration of man," and it is evident that Miller has set out to restore a sense of importance if not greatness to the individual. In "Tragedy and the Common Man," published in the same year that *Death of a Salesman* was produced and evidently a defense of the play, he argues on behalf of the common man as a tragic figure and he insists that tragedy and pathos are very different: "Pathos truly is the mode of the pessimist.... The plays we revere, century after century, are the tragedies. In them, and in them alone, lies the belief — optimistic, if you will — in the perfectibility of man." Elsewhere (*Harper's*, August 1958) he has said that pathos is an oversimplification and therefore is the "counterfeit of meaning." Curiously, however, many spectators and readers find that by Miller's own terms Willy Loman fails to be a tragic figure; he seems to them pathetic rather than tragic, a victim rather than a man who acts and who wins our esteem. True, he is partly the victim of his own actions (although he could have chosen to be a carpenter, he chose to live by the bourgeois code that values a white collar), but he seems in larger part to be a victim of the system itself, a system of ruthless competition that has no place for the man who can no longer produce. (Here is an echo of the social-realist drama of the 'thirties.) Willy had believed in this system; and although his son Biff comes to the realization that Willy "had the wrong dreams," Willy himself seems not to achieve this insight. Of course he knows that he is out of a job, that the system does not value him any longer, but he still seems not to question the values he had subscribed to. Even in the last minutes of the play, when he is planning his suicide in order to provide money for his family — really for Biff — he says such things as "Can you imagine his magnificence with twenty thousand dollars in his pocket?" and "When the mail comes he'll be ahead of Bernard again." In the preface to his *Collected Plays* Miller comments on the "exultation" with which Willy faces the end, but it is questionable whether an audience shares it. Many people find that despite the gulf in rank, they can share King Lear's feelings more easily than Willy's.

Perhaps, however, tradition has been too arbitrary in its use of the word "tragedy." Perhaps we should be as liberal as the ancient Greeks were, who did not withhold it from any play that was serious and dignified.

DUTCHMAN

LeRoi Jones (Imamu Amiri Baraka)

LeRoi Jones (born in 1934), who has taken the name Imamu Amiri Baraka, was born in Newark, N.J., attended Rutgers, and graduated from Howard University. After his graduation he served for three years in the United States Air Force, and then did graduate work at the New School for Social Research and at Columbia. In addition to writing plays, poems, stories, essays, and a book on black music, he founded the Black Arts Repertory Theatre/School. *Dutchman*, produced off Broadway in 1964, was made into a film in 1967. During the Newark riots of 1967, Jones was arrested and charged with illegal possession of weapons. He was convicted in 1968 and was sentenced to two and one-half to three years in jail but he appealed and his appeal was upheld. He continues to be active as a writer and an educator in Newark.

CHARACTERS

CLAY, *twenty-year-old Negro*
LULA, *thirty-year-old white woman*
RIDERS OF COACH, *white and black*
YOUNG NEGRO
CONDUCTOR

In the flying underbelly of the city. Steaming hot, and summer on top, outside. Underground. The subway heaped in modern myth.

Opening scene is a man sitting in a subway seat, holding a magazine but looking vacantly just above its wilting pages. Occasionally he looks blankly toward the window on his right. Dim lights and darkness whistling by against the glass. (Or paste the lights, as admitted props, right on the subway windows. Have them move, even dim and flicker. But give the sense of speed. Also stations, whether the train is stopped or the glitter and activity of these stations merely flashes by the windows.)

The man is sitting alone. That is, only his seat is visible, though the rest of the car is outfitted as a complete subway car. But only his seat is shown. There might be, for a time, as the play begins, a loud

Calvin Lockhart as Clay and Tony Robbins as Lula in the Hampstead Theatre Club production directed by Charles Jarrott, London, 1967. (Photograph: © 1972 John Haynes.)

scream of the actual train. And it can recur throughout the play, or continue on a lower key once the dialogue starts.

The train slows after a time, pulling to a brief stop at one of the stations. The man looks idly up, until he sees a woman's face staring at him through the window; when it realizes that the man has noticed the face, it begins very premeditatedly to smile. The man smiles too, for a moment, without a trace of self-consciousness. Almost an instinctive though undesirable response. Then a kind of awkwardness or embarrassment sets in, and the man makes to look away, is further embarrassed, so he brings back his eyes to where the face was, but by now the train is moving again, and the face would seem to be left behind by the way the man turns his head to look back through the other windows at the slowly fading platform. He smiles then; more comfortably confident, hoping perhaps that his memory of this brief encounter will be pleasant. And then he is idle again.

SCENE I

Train roars. Lights flash outside the windows.

LULA *enters from the rear of the car in bright, skimpy summer clothes and sandals. She carries a net bag full of paper books, fruit, and other anonymous articles. She is wearing sunglasses, which she pushes up on her forehead from time to time.* LULA *is a tall, slender, beautiful woman with long red hair hanging straight down her back, wearing only loud lipstick in somebody's good taste. She is eating an apple, very daintily. Coming down the car toward* CLAY.

She stops beside CLAY's *seat and hangs languidly from the strap, still managing to eat the apple. It is apparent that she is going to sit in the seat next to* CLAY, *and that she is only waiting for him to notice her before she sits.*

CLAY *sits as before, looking just beyond his magazine, now and again pulling the magazine slowly back and forth in front of his face in a hopeless effort to fan himself. Then he sees the woman hanging there beside him and he looks up into her face, smiling quizzically.*

LULA: Hello.
CLAY: Uh, hi're you?
LULA: I'm going to sit down. . . . O.K.?

From *The Dutchman and The Slave* by LeRoi Jones. Copyright © 1964 by LeRoi Jones. Reprinted by permission of The Sterling Lord Agency, Inc.

CLAY: Sure.
LULA (*swings down onto the seat, pushing her legs straight out as if she is very weary*): Oooof! Too much weight.
CLAY: Ha, doesn't look like much to me. (*Leaning back against the window, a little surprised and maybe stiff.*)
LULA: It's so anyway.

(*And she moves her toes in the sandals, then pulls her right leg up on the left knee, better to inspect the bottoms of the sandals and the back of her heel. She appears for a second not to notice that* CLAY *is sitting next to her or that she has spoken to him just a second before.* CLAY *looks at the magazine, then out the black window. As he does this, she turns very quickly toward him.*)

Weren't you staring at me through the window?
CLAY (*wheeling around and very much stiffened*): What?
LULA: Weren't you staring at me through the window? At the last stop?
CLAY: Staring at you? What do you mean?
LULA: Don't you know what staring means?
CLAY: I saw you through the window . . . if that's what it means. I don't know if I was staring. Seems to me you were staring through the window at me.
LULA: I was. But only after I'd turned around and saw you staring through that

window down in the vicinity of my ass and legs.

CLAY: Really?

LULA: Really. I guess you were just taking those idle potshots. Nothing else to do. Run your mind over people's flesh.

CLAY: Oh boy. Wow, now I admit I was looking in your direction. But the rest of that weight is yours.

LULA: I suppose.

CLAY: Staring through train windows is weird business. Much weirder than staring very sedately at abstract asses.

LULA: That's why I came looking through the window . . . so you'd have more than that to go on. I even smiled at you.

CLAY: That's right.

LULA: I even got into this train, going some other way than mine. Walked down the aisle . . . searching you out.

CLAY: Really? That's pretty funny.

LULA: That's pretty funny. . . . God, you're dull.

CLAY: Well, I'm sorry, lady, but I really wasn't prepared for party talk.

LULA: No, you're not. What are you prepared for? (Wrapping the apple core in a Kleenex and dropping it on the floor.)

CLAY (takes her conversation as pure sex talk. He turns to confront her squarely with this idea): I'm prepared for anything. How about you?

LULA (laughing loudly and cutting it off abruptly): What do you think you're doing?

CLAY: What?

LULA: You think I want to pick you up, get you to take me somewhere and screw me, huh?

CLAY: Is that the way I look?

LULA: You look like you been trying to grow a beard. That's exactly what you look like. You look like you live in New Jersey with your parents and are trying to grow a beard. That's what. You look like you've been reading Chinese poetry and drinking lukewarm sugarless tea. (Laughs, uncrossing and recrossing her legs.) You look like death eating a soda cracker.

CLAY (cocking his head from one side to the other, embarrassed and trying to make some comeback, but also intrigued by what the woman is saying . . . even the sharp city coarseness of her voice, which is still a kind of gentle sidewalk throb): Really? I look like all that?

LULA: Not all of it. (She feints a seriousness to cover an actual somber tone.) I lie a lot. (Smiling.) It helps me control the world.

CLAY (relieved and laughing louder than the humor): Yeah, I bet.

LULA: But it's true, most of it, right? Jersey? Your bumpy neck?

CLAY: How'd you know all that? Huh? Really, I mean about Jersey . . . and even the beard. I met you before? You know Warren Enright?

LULA: You tried to make it with your sister when you were ten.

(CLAY leans back hard against the back of the seat, his eyes opening now, still trying to look amused.)

But I succeeded a few weeks ago. (She starts to laugh again.)

CLAY: What're you talking about? Warren tell you that? You're a friend of Georgia's?

LULA: I told you I lie. I don't know your sister. I don't know Warren Enright.

CLAY: You mean you're just picking these things out of the air?

LULA: Is Warren Enright a tall skinny black boy with a phony English accent?

CLAY: I figured you knew him.

LULA: But I don't. I just figured you would know somebody like that. (Laughs.)

CLAY: Yeah, yeah.

LULA: You're probably on your way to his house now.

CLAY: That's right.

LULA (putting her hand on CLAY's closest knee, drawing it from the knee up to the thigh's hinge, then removing it, watching his face very closely, and continuing to laugh, perhaps more gently than before): Dull, dull, dull. I bet you think I'm exciting.

CLAY: You're O.K.

LULA: Am I exciting you now?

CLAY: Right. That's not what's supposed to happen?

LULA: How do I know? (She returns her hand, without moving it, then takes it away and plunges it in her bag to draw out an apple.) You want this?

CLAY: Sure.

LULA (she gets one out of the bag for herself): Eating apples together is always the first step. Or walking up uninhabited Seventh Avenue in the twenties on weekends. (Bites *and giggles, glancing at* CLAY *and speaking in loose sing-song.*) Can get you involved . . . boy! Get us involved. Um-huh. (*Mock seriousness.*) Would you like to get involved with me, Mister Man?

switch in 70's

CLAY (*trying to be as flippant as* LULA, *whacking happily at the apple*): Sure. Why not? A beautiful woman like you. Huh, I'd be a fool not to.

LULA: And I bet you're sure you know what you're talking about. (*Taking him a little roughly by the wrist, so he cannot eat the apple, then shaking the wrist.*) I bet you're sure of almost everything anybody ever asked you about . . . right? (*Shakes his wrist harder.*) Right?

CLAY: Yeah, right. . . . Wow, you're pretty strong, you know? Whatta you, a lady wrestler or something?

LULA: What's wrong with lady wrestlers? And don't answer because you never knew any. Huh. (*Cynically.*) That's for sure. They don't have any lady wrestlers in that part of Jersey. That's for sure.

CLAY: Hey, you still haven't told me how you know so much about me.

LULA: I told you I didn't know anything about *you* . . . you're a well-known type.

CLAY: Really?

LULA: Or at least I know the type very well. And your skinny English friend too.

CLAY: Anonymously?

LULA (*settles back in seat, single-mindedly finishing her apple and humming snatches of rhythm and blues song*): What?

CLAY: Without knowing us specifically?

LULA: Oh boy. (*Looking quickly at* CLAY.) What a face. You know, you could be a handsome man.

CLAY: I can't argue with you.

LULA (*vague, off-center response*): What?

CLAY (*raising his voice, thinking the train noise has drowned part of his sentence*): I can't argue with you.

LULA: My hair is turning gray. A gray hair for each year and type I've come through.

CLAY: Why do you want to sound so old?

LULA: But it's always gentle when it starts. (*Attention drifting.*) Hugged against tenements, day or night.

CLAY: What?

LULA (*refocusing*): Hey, why don't you take me to that party you're going to?

CLAY: You must be a friend of Warren's to know about the party.

LULA: Wouldn't you like to take me to the party? (*Imitates clinging vine.*) Oh, come on, ask me to your party.

CLAY: Of course I'll ask you to come with me to the party. And I'll bet you're a friend of Warren's.

LULA: Why not be a friend of Warren's? Why not? (*Taking his arm.*) Have you asked me yet?

CLAY: How can I ask you when I don't know your name?

LULA: Are you talking to my name?

CLAY: What is it, a secret?

LULA: I'm Lena the Hyena.

CLAY: The famous woman poet?

LULA: Poetess! The same!

CLAY: Well, you know so much about me . . . what's my name?

LULA: Morris the Hyena.

CLAY: The famous woman poet?

LULA: The same. (*Laughing and going into her bag.*) You want another apple?

CLAY: Can't make it, lady. I only have to keep one doctor away a day.

LULA: I bet your name is . . . something like . . . uh, Gerald or Walter. Huh?

CLAY: God, no.

LULA: Lloyd, Norman? One of those hopeless colored names creeping out of New Jersey. Leonard? Gag. . . .

CLAY: Like Warren?

LULA: Definitely. Just exactly like Warren. Or Everett.

CLAY: Gag. . . .

LULA: Well, for sure, it's not Willie.

CLAY: It's Clay.

LULA: Clay? Really? Clay what?

CLAY: Take your pick. Jackson, Johnson, or Williams.

LULA: Oh, really? Good for you. But it's got to be Williams. You're too pretentious to be a Jackson or Johnson.

CLAY: Thass right.

LULA: But Clay's O.K.

CLAY: So's Lena.

LULA: It's Lula.

CLAY: Oh?

LULA: Lula the Hyena.

CLAY: Very good.

acting grand or glorious

LULA (*starts laughing again*): Now you say to me, "Lula, Lula, why don't you go to this party with me tonight?" It's your turn, and let those be your lines.

CLAY: Lula, why don't you go to this party with me tonight, huh?

LULA: Say my name twice before you ask, and no huh's.

CLAY: Lula, Lula, why don't you go to this party with me tonight?

LULA: I'd like to go, Clay, but how can you ask me to go when you barely know me?

CLAY: That is strange, isn't it?

LULA: What kind of reaction is that? You're supposed to say, "Aw, come on, we'll get to know each other better at the party."

CLAY: That's pretty corny.

LULA: What are you into anyway? (*Looking at him half sullenly but still amused.*) What thing are you playing at, Mister? Mister Clay Williams? (*Grabs his thigh, up near the crotch.*) What are you thinking about?

CLAY: Watch it now, you're gonna excite me for real.

LULA (*taking her hand away and throwing her apple core through the window*): I bet. (*She slumps in the seat and is heavily silent.*)

CLAY: I thought you knew everything about me? What happened?

(LULA *looks at him, then looks slowly away, then over where the other aisle would be. Noise of the train. She reaches in her bag and pulls out one of the paper books. She puts it on her leg and thumbs the pages listlessly.* CLAY *cocks his head to see the title of the book. Noise of the train.* LULA *flips pages and her eyes drift. Both remain silent.*)

Are you going to the party with me, Lula?

LULA (*bored and not even looking*): I don't even know you.

CLAY: You said you know my type.

LULA (*strangely irritated*): Don't get smart with me, Buster. I know you like the palm of my hand.

CLAY: The one you eat the apples with?

LULA: Yeh. And the one I open doors late Saturday evening with. That's my door. Up at the top of the stairs. Five flights. Above a lot of Italians and lying Americans. And scrape carrots with. Also ... (*looks at him*) the same hand I unbutton my dress with, or let my skirt fall down. Same hand. Lover.

CLAY: Are you angry about anything? Did I say something wrong?

LULA: Everything you say is wrong. (*Mock smile.*) That's what makes you so attractive. Ha. In that funnybook jacket with all the buttons. (*More animate, taking hold of his jacket.*) What've you got that jacket and tie

on in all this heat for? And why're you wearing a jacket and tie like that? Did your people ever burn witches or start revolutions over the price of tea? Boy, those narrow-shoulder clothes come from a tradition you ought to feel oppressed by. A three-button suit. What right do you have to be wearing a three-button suit and striped tie? Your grandfather was a slave, he didn't go to Harvard.

CLAY: My grandfather was a night watchman.

LULA: And you went to a colored college where everybody thought they were Averell Harriman.

CLAY: All except me.

LULA: And who did you think you were? Who do you think you are now?

CLAY (*laughs as if to make light of the whole trend of the conversation*): Well, in college I thought I was Baudelaire. But I've slowed down since.

LULA: I bet you never once thought you were a black nigger.

(*Mock serious, then she howls with laughter.* CLAY *is stunned but after initial reaction, he quickly tries to appreciate the humor.* LULA *almost shrieks.*)

A black Baudelaire.

CLAY: That's right.

LULA: Boy, are you corny. I take back what I said before. Everything you say is not wrong. It's perfect. You should be on television.

CLAY: You act like you're on television already.

LULA: That's because I'm an actress.

CLAY: I thought so.

LULA: Well, you're wrong. I'm no actress. I told you I always lie. I'm nothing, honey, and don't you ever forget it. (*Lighter.*) Although my mother was a Communist. The only person in my family ever to amount to anything.

CLAY: My mother was a Republican.

LULA: And your father voted for the man rather than the party.

CLAY: Right!

LULA: Yea for him. Yea, yea for him.

CLAY: Yea!

LULA: And yea for America where he is free to vote for the mediocrity of his choice! Yea!

CLAY: Yea!

LULA: And yea for both your parents who even though they differ about so crucial a matter as the body politic still forged a union of love and sacrifice that was destined to flower at the birth of the noble Clay . . . what's your middle name?

CLAY: Clay.

LULA: A union of love and sacrifice that was destined to flower at the birth of the noble Clay Clay Williams. Yea! And most of all yea yea for you, Clay Clay. The Black Baudelaire! Yes! (*And with knifelike cynicism.*) My Christ. My Christ.

CLAY: Thank you, ma'am.

LULA: May the people accept you as a ghost of the future. And love you, that you might not kill them when you can.

CLAY: What?

LULA: You're a murderer, Clay, and you know it. (*Her voice darkening with significance.*) You know goddamn well what I mean.

CLAY: I do?

LULA: So we'll pretend the air is light and full of perfume.

CLAY (*sniffing at her blouse*): It is.

LULA: And we'll pretend the people cannot see you. That is, the citizens. And that you are free of your own history. And I am free of my history. We'll pretend that we are both anonymous beauties smashing along through the city's entrails. (*She yells as loud as she can.*) GROOVE!

BLACK

SCENE II

Scene is the same as before, though now there are other seats visible in the car. And throughout the scene other people get on the subway. There are maybe one or two seated in the car as the scene opens, though neither CLAY nor LULA notices them. CLAY's tie is open. LULA is hugging his arm.

CLAY: The party!

LULA: I know it'll be something good. You can come in with me, looking casual and significant. I'll be strange, haughty, and silent, and walk with long slow strides.

CLAY: Right.

LULA: When you get drunk, pat me once, very lovingly on the flanks, and I'll look at you cryptically, licking my lips.

CLAY: It sounds like something we can do.

LULA: You'll go around talking to young men about your mind, and to old men about your plans. If you meet a very close friend who is also with someone like me, we can stand together, sipping our drinks and exchanging codes of lust. The atmosphere will be slithering in love and half-love and very open moral decision.

CLAY: Great. Great.

LULA: And everyone will pretend they don't know your name, and then . . . (*she pauses heavily*) later, when they have to, they'll claim a friendship that denies your sterling character.

CLAY (*kissing her neck and fingers*): And then what?

LULA: Then? Well, then we'll go down the street, late night, eating apples and winding very deliberately toward my house.

CLAY: Deliberately?

LULA: I mean, we'll look in all the shopwindows, and make fun of the queers. Maybe we'll meet a Jewish Buddhist and flatten his conceits over some very pretentious coffee.

CLAY: In honor of whose God?

LULA: Mine.

CLAY: Who is . . . ?

LULA: Me . . . and you?

CLAY: A corporate Godhead.

LULA: Exactly. Exactly. (*Notices one of the other people entering.*)

CLAY: Go on with the chronicle. Then what happens to us?

LULA (*a mild depression, but she still makes her description triumphant and increasingly direct*): To my house, of course.

CLAY: Of course.

LULA: And up the narrow steps of the tenement.

CLAY: You live in a tenement?

LULA: Wouldn't live anywhere else. Reminds me specifically of my novel form of insanity.

CLAY: Up the tenement stairs.

LULA: And with my apple-eating hand I push open the door and lead you, my tender big-eyed prey, into my . . . God, what can I call it . . . into my hovel.

CLAY: Then what happens?

LULA: After the dancing and games, after the long drinks and long walks, the real fun begins.

CLAY: Ah, the real fun. (*Embarrassed, in spite of himself.*) Which is . . . ?

LULA (*laughs at him*): Real fun in the dark house. Hah! Real fun in the dark house, high up above the street and the ignorant cowboys. I lead you in, holding your wet hand gently in my hand . . .

CLAY: Which is not wet?

LULA: Which is dry as ashes.

CLAY: And cold?

LULA: Don't think you'll get out of your responsibility that way. It's not cold at all. You Fascist! Into my dark living room. Where we'll sit and talk endlessly, endlessly.

CLAY: About what?

LULA: About what? About your manhood, what do you think? What do you think we've been talking about all this time?

CLAY: Well, I didn't know it was that. That's for sure. Every other thing in the world but that. (*Notices another person entering, looks quickly, almost involuntarily up and down the car, seeing the other people in the car.*) Hey, I didn't even notice when those people got on.

LULA: Yeah, I know.

CLAY: Man, this subway is slow.

LULA: Yeah, I know.

CLAY: Well, go on. We were talking about my manhood.

LULA: We still are. All the time.

CLAY: We were in your living room.

LULA: My dark living room. Talking endlessly.

CLAY: About my manhood.

LULA: I'll make you a map of it. Just as soon as we get to my house.

CLAY: Well, that's great.

LULA: One of the things we do while we talk. And screw.

CLAY (*trying to make his smile broader and less shaky*): We finally got there.

LULA: And you'll call my rooms black as a grave. You'll say, "This place is like Juliet's tomb."

CLAY (*laughs*): I might.

LULA: I know. You've probably said it before.

CLAY: And is that all? The whole grand tour?

LULA: Not all. You'll say to me very close to my face, many, many times, you'll say, even whisper, that you love me.

CLAY: Maybe I will.

LULA: And you'll be lying.

CLAY: I wouldn't lie about something like that.

LULA: Hah. It's the only kind of thing you

will lie about. Especially if you think it'll keep me alive.

CLAY: Keep you alive? I don't understand.

LULA (*bursting out laughing, but too shrilly*): Don't understand? Well, don't look at me. It's the path I take, that's all. Where both feet take me when I set them down. One in front of the other.

CLAY: Morbid. Morbid. You sure you're not an actress? All that self-aggrandizement.

LULA: Well, I told you I wasn't an actress . . . but I also told you I lie all the time. Draw your own conclusions.

CLAY: Morbid. Morbid. You sure you're not an actress? All scribed? There's no more?

LULA: I've told you all I know. Or almost all.

CLAY: There's no funny parts?

LULA: I thought it was all funny.

CLAY: But you mean peculiar, not ha-ha.

LULA: You don't know what I mean.

CLAY: Well, tell me the almost part then. You said almost all. What else? I want the whole story.

LULA (*searching aimlessly through her bag. She begins to talk breathlessly, with a light and silly tone*): All stories are whole stories. All of 'em. Our whole story . . . nothing but change. How could things go on like that forever? Huh? (*Slaps him on the shoulder, begins finding things in her bag, taking them out and throwing them over her shoulder into the aisle.*) Except I do go on as I do. Apples and long walks with deathless intelligent lovers. But you mix it up. Look out the window, all the time. Turning pages. Change change change. Till, shit, I don't know you. Wouldn't, for that matter. You're too serious. I bet you're even too serious to be psychoanalyzed. Like all those Jewish poets from Yonkers, who leave their mothers looking for other mothers, or others' mothers, on whose baggy tits they lay their fumbling heads. Their poems are always funny, and all about sex.

CLAY: They sound great. Like movies.

LULA: But you change. (*Blankly.*) And things work on you till you hate them.

(*More people come into the train. They come closer to the couple, some of them not sitting, but swinging drearily on the straps, staring at the two with uncertain interest.*)

CLAY: Wow. All these people, so suddenly. They must all come from the same place.

LULA: Right. That they do.

CLAY: Oh? You know about them too?

LULA: Oh yeah. About them more than I know about you. Do they frighten you?

CLAY: Frighten me? Why should they frighten me?

LULA: 'Cause you're an escaped nigger.

CLAY: Yeah?

LULA: 'Cause you crawled through the wire and made tracks to my side.

CLAY: Wire?

LULA: Don't they have wire around plantations?

CLAY: You must be Jewish. All you can think about is wire. Plantations didn't have any wire. Plantations were big open white-washed places like heaven, and everybody on 'em was grooved to be there. Just strummin' and hummin' all day.

LULA: Yes, yes.

CLAY: And that's how the blues was born.

LULA: Yes, yes. And that's how the blues was born. (*Begins to make up a song that becomes quickly hysterical. As she sings she rises from her seat, still throwing things out of her bag into the aisle, beginning a rhythmical shudder and twistlike wiggle, which she continues up and down the aisle, bumping into many of the standing people and tripping over the feet of those sitting. Each time she runs into a person she lets out a very vicious piece of profanity, wiggling and stepping all the time.*) And that's how the blues was born. Yes. Yes. Son of a bitch, get out of the way. Yes. Quack. Yes. Yes. And that's how the blues was born. Ten little niggers sitting on a limb, but none of them ever looked like him. (*Points to* CLAY, *returns toward the seat, with her hands extended for him to rise and dance with her.*) And that's how blues was born. Yes. Come on, Clay. Let's do the nasty. Rub bellies. Rub bellies.

CLAY (*waves his hands to refuse. He is embarrassed, but determined to get a kick out of the proceedings*): Hey, what was in those apples? Mirror, mirror on the wall, who's the fairest one of all? Snow White, baby, and don't you forget it.

LULA (*grabbing for his hands, which he draws away*): Come on, Clay. Let's rub bellies on the train. The nasty. The nasty. Do the gritty grind, like your ol' rag-head mammy. Grind till you lose your mind. Shake it, shake it, shake it, shake it! OOOOweeee! Come on,

Clay. Let's do the choochoo train shuffle, the navel scratcher.

CLAY: Hey, you coming on like the lady who smoked up her grass skirt.

LULA (*becoming annoyed that he will not dance, and becoming more animated as if to embarrass him still further*): Come on, Clay ... let's do the thing. Uhh! Uhh! Clay! Clay! You middle-class black bastard. Forget your social-working mother for a few seconds and let's knock stomachs. Clay, you liver-lipped white man. You would-be Christian. You ain't no nigger, you're just a dirty white man. Get up, Clay. Dance with me, Clay.

CLAY: Lula! Sit down, now. Be cool.

LULA (*mocking him, in wild dance*): Be cool. Be cool. That's all you know ... shaking that wildroot cream-oil on your knotty head, jackets buttoning up to your chin, so full of white man's words. Christ. God. Get up and scream at these people. Like scream meaningless shit in these hopeless faces. (*She screams at people in train, still dancing.*) Red trains cough Jewish underwear for keeps! Expanding smells of silence. Gravy snot whistling like sea birds. Clay. Clay, you got to break out. Don't sit there dying the way they want you to die. Get up.

CLAY: Oh, sit the fuck down. (*He moves to restrain her.*) Sit down, goddamn it.

LULA (*twisting out of his reach*): Screw yourself, Uncle Tom. Thomas Woolly-Head. (*Begins to dance a kind of jig, mocking* CLAY *with loud forced humor.*) There is Uncle Tom ... I mean, Uncle Thomas Woolly-Head. With old white matted mane. He hobbles on his wooden cane. Old Tom. Old Tom. Let the white man hump his ol' mama, and he jes' shuffle off in the woods and hide his gentle gray head. Ol' Thomas Woolly-Head.

(*Some of the other riders are laughing now. A drunk gets up and joins* LULA *in her dance, singing, as best he can, her "song."* CLAY *gets up out of his seat and visibly scans the faces of the other riders.*)

CLAY: Lula! Lula!

(*She is dancing and turning, still shouting as loud as she can. The drunk too is shouting, and waving his hands wildly.*)

Lula ... you dumb bitch. Why don't you stop it? (*He rushes half stumbling from his seat, and grabs one of her flailing arms.*)

If its not black ← business ≠ white

LULA: Let me go! You black son of a bitch. (*She struggles against him.*) Let me go! Help!

(CLAY *is dragging her toward her seat, and the drunk seeks to interfere. He grabs* CLAY *around the shoulders and begins wrestling with him.* CLAY *clubs the drunk to the floor without releasing* LULA, *who is still screaming.* CLAY *finally gets her to the seat and throws her into it.*)

CLAY: Now you shut the hell up. (*Grabbing her shoulders.*) Just shut up. You don't know what you're talking about. You don't know anything. So just keep your stupid mouth closed.

LULA: You're afraid of white people. And your father was. Uncle Tom Big Lip!

CLAY (*slaps her as hard as he can, across the mouth.* LULA's *head bangs against the back of the seat. When she raises it again,* CLAY *slaps her again*): Now shut up and let me talk.

(*He turns toward the other riders, some of whom are sitting on the edge of their seats. The drunk is on one knee, rubbing his head, and singing softly the same song. He shuts up too when he sees* CLAY *watching him. The others go back to newspapers or stare out the windows.*)

Shit, you don't have any sense, Lula, nor feelings either. I could murder you now. Such a tiny ugly throat. I could squeeze it flat, and watch you turn blue, on a humble. For dull kicks. And all these weak-faced ofays squatting around here, staring over their papers at me. Murder them too. Even if they expected it. That man there . . . (*Points to well-dressed man.*) I could rip that *Times* right out of his hand, as skinny and middle-classed as I am, I could rip that paper out of his hand and just as easily rip out his throat. It takes no great effort. For what? To kill you soft idiots? You don't understand anything but luxury.

LULA: You fool!

CLAY (*pushing her against the seat*): I'm not telling you again, Tallulah Bankhead! Luxury. In your face and your fingers. You telling me what I ought to do. (*Sudden scream frightening the whole coach.*) Well, don't! Don't you tell me anything! If I'm a middle-class fake white man . . . let me be. And let me be in the way I want. (*Through his teeth.*) I'll rip your lousy breasts off! Let me be who I feel

like being. Uncle Tom. Thomas. Whoever. It's none of your business. You don't know anything except what's there for you to see. An act. Lies. Device. Not the pure heart, the pumping black heart. You don't ever know that. And I sit here, in this buttoned-up suit, to keep myself from cutting all your throats. I mean wantonly. You great liberated whore! You fuck some black man, and right away you're an expert on black people. What a lotta shit that is. The only thing you know is that you come if he bangs you hard enough. And that's all. The belly rub? You wanted to do the belly rub? Shit, you don't even know how. You don't know how. That ol' dipty-dip shit you do, rolling your ass like an elephant. That's not my kind of belly rub. Belly rub is not Queens. Belly rub is dark places, with big hats and overcoats held up with one arm. Belly rub hates you. Old bald-headed four-eyed ofays popping their fingers . . . and don't know yet what they're doing. They say, "I love Bessie Smith." And don't even understand that Bessie Smith is saying, "Kiss my ass, kiss my black unruly ass." Before love, suffering, desire, anything you can explain, she's saying, and very plainly, "Kiss my black ass." And if you don't know that, it's you that's doing the kissing. Charlie Parker? Charlie Parker. All the hip white boys scream for Bird. And Bird saying, "Up your ass, feeble-minded ofay! Up your ass." And they sit there talking about the tortured genius of Charlie Parker. Bird would've played not a note of music if he just walked up to East Sixty-seventh Street and killed the first ten white people he saw. Not a note! And I'm the great would-be poet. Yes. That's right! Poet. Some kind of bastard literature . . . all it needs is a simple knife thrust. Just let me bleed you, you loud whore, and one poem vanished. A whole people of neurotics, struggling to keep from being sane. And the only thing that would cure the neurosis would be your murder. Simple as that. I mean if I murdered you, then other white people would begin to understand me. You understand? No. I guess not. If Bessie Smith had killed some white people she wouldn't have needed that music. She could have talked very straight and plain about the world. No metaphors. No grunts. No wiggles in the dark of her soul. Just straight two and two are four. Money. Power. Luxury. Like that. All of them. Crazy niggers turning their backs on sanity.

what conquests — in a white world

but he isn't it safe with big words in a white man's world

When all it needs is that simple act. Murder. Just murder! Would make us all sane.

(*Suddenly weary.*) Ahhh. Shit. But who needs it? I'd rather be a fool. Insane. Safe with my words, and no deaths, and clean, hard thoughts, urging me to new conquests. My people's madness. Hah! That's a laugh. My people. They don't need me to claim them. They got legs and arms of their own. Personal insanities. Mirrors. They don't need all those words. They don't need any defense. But listen, though, one more thing. And you tell this to your father, who's probably the kind of man who needs to know at once. So he can plan ahead. Tell him not to preach so much rationalism and cold logic to these niggers. Let them alone. Let them sing curses at you in code and see your filth as simple lack of style. Don't make the mistake, through some irresponsible surge of Christian charity, of talking too much about the advantages of Western rationalism, or the great intellectual legacy of the white man, or maybe they'll begin to listen. And then, maybe one day, you'll find they actually do understand exactly what you are talking about, all these fantasy people. All these blues people. And on that day, as sure as shit, when you really believe you can "accept" them into your fold, as half-white trusties late of the subject peoples. With no more blues, except the very old ones, and not a watermelon in sight, the great missionary heart will have triumphed, and all of those ex-coons will be stand-up Western men, with eyes, for clean hard useful lives, sober, pious and sane, and they'll murder you. They'll murder you, and have very rational explanations. Very much like your own. They'll cut your throats, and drag you out to the edge of your cities so the flesh can fall away from your bones, in sanitary isolation.

prejudiced

LULA (*her voice takes on a different, more businesslike quality*): I've heard enough.

CLAY (*reaching for his books*): I bet you have. I guess I better collect my stuff and get off this train. Looks like we won't be acting out that little pageant you outlined before.

LULA: No. We won't. You're right about that, at least. (*She turns to look quickly around the rest of the car.*) All right!

(*The others respond.*)

CLAY (*bending across the girl to retrieve his belongings*): Sorry, baby, I don't think we could make it.

(*As he is bending over her, the girl brings up a small knife and plunges it into* CLAY's *chest. Twice. He slumps across her knees, his mouth working stupidly.*)

LULA: Sorry is right. (*Turning to the others in the car who have already gotten up from their seats.*) Sorry is the rightest thing you've said. Get this man off me! Hurry, now!

(*The others come and drag* CLAY's *body down the aisle.*)

Open the door and throw his body out.

(*They throw him off.*)

And all of you get off at the next stop.

(LULA *busies herself straightening her things. Getting everything in order. She takes out a notebook and makes a quick scribbling note. Drops it in her bag. The train apparently stops and all the others get off, leaving her alone in the coach.*

Very soon a young Negro of about twenty comes into the coach, with a couple of books under his arm. He sits a few seats in back of* LULA. *When he is seated she turns and gives him a long slow look. He looks up from his book and drops the book on his lap. Then an old Negro conductor comes into the car, doing a sort of restrained soft shoe, and half mumbling the words of some song. He looks at the young man, briefly, with a quick greeting.*)

CONDUCTOR: Hey, brother!
YOUNG MAN: Hey.

(*The conductor continues down the aisle with his little dance and the mumbled song.* LULA *turns to stare at him and follows his movements down the aisle. The conductor tips his hat when he reaches her seat, and continues out the car.*)

CURTAIN

Near the end of the nineteenth century, Joseph Conrad wrote:

> My task which I am trying to achieve is, by the power of the written
> word, to make you hear, to make you feel — it is, before all, to make you
> see. That — and no more, and it is everything.

To make an audience see has been the aim of many writers, but LeRoi Jones
argues, in several essays in a collection entitled *Home*, that the black writer,
such as Jones, who by his very status as outsider may be equipped to see American society with special clarity, will inevitably be opposed by the white Establishment, which regularly demands that writers see only what glorifies the
Establishment. Not surprisingly, Jones has been harassed by public officials
who claim that his revolutionary vision is a threat to public morality.

Jones admits the charge. Several quotations from "The Revolutionary
Theatre" (included in *Home*) will give the gist of his position:

> The Revolutionary Theatre should force change; it should be change.
> . . . The Revolutionary Theatre must EXPOSE! Show up the insides of
> these humans, look into black skulls. White men will cower before this
> theatre because it hates them. Because they themselves have been trained
> to hate.

> The Revolutionary Theatre must take dreams and give them a reality. . . .
> It must be food for all those who need food, and daring propaganda for
> the beauty of the Human Mind. It is a political theatre, a weapon to help
> in the slaughter of these dim-witted fatbellied white guys who somehow
> believe that the rest of the world is here for them to slobber on.

> Our theatre will show victims so that their brothers in the audience will
> be better able to understand that they are the brothers of victims, and
> that they themeslves are victims if they are blood brothers.*

Finally, here is a passage from the short essay that concludes *Home*:

> The Black Artist's role in America is to aid in the destruction of America
> as he knows it. His role is to report and reflect so precisely the nature of
> the society, that other men will be moved by the exactness of his render-
> ing and, if they are black men, grow strong through this moving, having
> seen their own strength, and weakness; and if they are white men, trem-
> ble, curse, and go mad, because they will be drenched with the filth of
> their evil.

Jones thus assumes that art is enormously potent, and in so doing he takes his
place in a tradition that can be traced back to Chekhov (who said that he
wrote his plays in order to make people see that their lives were dreary and to
make them create a better life for themselves), back to Shakespeare (whose
Hamlet had heard that "guilty creatures sitting at a play" may see their own
image on the stage and may be moved to "proclaim" their malefactions), and
finally back to Plato, who in the fourth century B.C. argued that the tragic

---

* The four extracts on this page and the one on page 246 are reprinted from LeRoi Jones's
Home, pages 210–11, 211–12, 213, 251, and 188, by permission of The Sterling Lord Agency,
Inc. Copyright © 1961, 1962, 1963, 1964, 1965, 1966 by LeRoi Jones.

dramatists should be barred from the ideal commonwealth precisely because they have the power to stir up pity and terror in men and thus to obscure men's rational faculty. For Plato the emotional effect of dramatic art is harmful. People ought not to be stirred by such emotions. (If this seems hopelessly old fashioned, one can reflect that probably some such thinking plays a part in our own prohibition of such entertainments as bull fighting and public executions.) Aristotle apparently tried to reply to Plato by arguing that the playwrights arouse pity and terror for the sake of moral well-being. There is a good deal of uncertainty about the meaning of Aristotle's remarks on the catharsis of pity and terror, but perhaps he meant that spectators were educated by being shown on the stage the proper objects of these emotions, or perhaps he meant that these emotions are expended harmlessly in the theater and thus the spectators are healthier when they leave the theater — rather as a boxing match or a prize fight may drain off the aggressions of the spectators who otherwise might expend their aggression outside of the stadium. In any case, the doctrine of catharsis, though much disputed, tends to be seen as counter-revolutionary; it stimulates the passions in order to diminish them, making spectators more willing to accept the affairs of the daily world.

Acceptance of the daily world is intolerable to Jones, for whom psychic health depends not on calm acceptance but on drastically changed social conditions. So Jones shows us an intolerable society, and in *Dutchman* he does this not by abstract preaching (though his essays are full of such preaching) but by vividly setting forth on the stage characters engaged in a human relationship. Jones has denied that Clay and Lula are symbols: they are, he says, real people in a real world. At the same time, however, he admits that these characters are not only individuals but are recognizable human types:

> Lula, for all her alleged insanity, just barely reflects the insanity of this hideous place. And Clay is a young boy trying desperately to become a man. *Dutchman* is about the difficulty of becoming a man in America. It is very difficult, to be sure, if you are black, but I think it is now much harder to become one if you're white. In fact, you will find very few white American males with the slightest knowledge of what manhood involves. They are too busy running the world, or running from it.

Let us begin with Lula. Jones presents her in such a way that we see her, we know her, and he does this as a dramatist must, by endowing the character with gestures and with language that ring true. Early in the play we see her as a vivid rendition of a fairly common type, someone whose precise kind of vulgarity is especially revealed in pretentiousness. She says that Clay was staring "in the vicinity of my ass" (not "at my ass"), and before she tosses her apple core onto the floor of the subway car she wraps it in a Kleenex. Through such bits of dialogue and such gestures a very real human being is rendered visible to us — but our perception of her reality is partly indebted to our recognition of her as a type. Moreover, she is not just one of millions of people whose special sort of coarseness reveals itself in ludicrous attempts at being genteel: she is also a *femme fatale*, a woman who seeks out victims, an Eve tempting Adam with her apple — specifically, the white woman who, surrounded by a myth of purity, lures black men to their destruction. Early in her conversation with Clay, Lula admits that she sought him out, and that she often lies because "it helps me to control the world." We can say that Lula — while never ceasing to be a specific woman who encounters a specific man on the subway — at least in part stands for, or, perhaps better, embodies the white society that Jones sees as enslaving all blacks.

And what of Clay, the black man? Jones said that "Clay is a young boy trying desperately to become a man." Just because Jones said so in an essay does not make it true in the play, but when we return to the play we can see ample evidence. Lula immediately sees Clay's effort to mature: "You look like you live in New Jersey with your parents and are trying to grow a beard." Again the specific details embody a type. She knows him well because he is, as she says, "a well-known type," and she later calls to Clay's attention that they have all the while been talking (however indirectly) about his manhood. The kind of man Clay wants to be is clear to Lula and to us, from his clothing:

> Boy, those narrow-shoulder clothes come from a tradition you ought to
> feel oppressed by. A three-button suit. What right do you have to be
> wearing a three-button suit and striped tie? Your grandfather was a slave,
> he didn't go to Harvard.

Clay is, Lula says, a "middle-class black bastard. . . . You ain't no nigger, you're just a dirty white man." Clay half knows that he is trying to surrender his black identity, and he also knows that he embodies the slave's murderous impulses toward his white oppressor. But Clay's bourgeois aspirations enslave him, and rather than achieve manhood by murdering his oppressor (so Jones seems to see it) Clay makes the mistake of thinking that murder can be avoided. "I sit here, in this buttoned-up suit, to keep myself from cutting your throats." Clay, self-imprisoned in the white man's clothes, thinks he is achieving manhood but he is ensuring his own destruction. The white oppressor, having none of Clay's illusions, knows that in white America the whites must murder the blacks (deprive them of "manhood") or the whites will be murdered by the blacks.

This commentary has become increasingly abstract, and a reader does well to remember that the play is about individuals as well as about ideas. But ideas are not antithetical to individuals and to realities, and the individuals and the realistic details that fill the play are endowed with metaphoric implications that insistently point beyond themselves. The very first line of the first stage direction is metaphoric: the play is set "in the flying underbelly of the city." The subway is the belly, the guts, of the city, invisible to the eye that dwells on the surface but real and teeming, like the passions that churn within an individual and like the political, social, and economic structures that, though invisible to many, dominate men's lives. The stage direction also tells that from time to time there is "a loud scream" of a train. Such screams are not only bits of realism, representations of trains; the title forces us, on reflection, toward a symbolic reading.

There is no Dutchman in the play; in fact the word is never used within the play. But, in conjunction with the description of the locale — "the *flying* underbelly of the city . . . the subway heaped in modern *myth*" — is it fanciful to see the endlessly shuttling subway as a modern version of the ship of the mythical flying Dutchman, who was condemned to sail the stormy seas until redeemed by the love of a pure woman? Both Lula and Clay are condemned to restlessness; Clay thinks he can find peace in the white man's world but he finds only the loss of identity; Lula's fate is that she is condemned to go on riding the subway, murdering one black after another.

The Poetics

Aristotle

Translated by L. J. Potts

It is no exaggeration to say that the history of tragic criticism is a series of footnotes to Aristotle. In a fragmentary treatise usually called the *Poetics*, Aristotle (384–322 B.C.) raises almost all the points that have subsequently been argued, such as the nature of the hero, the emotional effect on the spectator, the coherence of the plot. Whether or not he gave the right answers, it has seemed for more than two thousand years that he asked the right questions.

[ART IS IMITATION]

Let us talk of the art of poetry as a whole, and its different species with the particular force of each of them; how the fables must be put together if the poetry is to be well formed; also what are its elements and their different qualities; and all other matters pertaining to the subject.

To begin in the proper order, at the beginning. The making of epics and of tragedies, and also comedy, and the art of the dithyramb, and most flute and lyre art, all have this in common, that they are imitations. But they differ from one another in three respects: the different kinds of medium in which they imitate, the different objects they imitate, and the different manner in which they imitate (when it does differ).... When the imitators imitate the doings of people, the people in the imitation must be either high or low; the characters almost always follow this line exclusively, for all men differ in character according to their degree of goodness or badness. They must therefore be either above our norm, or below it, or normal; as, in painting, Polygnōtus depicted superior, Pauson inferior, and Dionysius normal, types. It is clear that each variant of imitation

Reprinted from *Aristotle on the Art of Fiction* by L. J. Potts by permission of the publisher, Cambridge University Press.

that I have mentioned will have these differences, and as the object imitated varies in this way so the works will differ. Even in the ballet, and in flute and lyre music, these dissimilarities can occur; and in the art that uses prose, or verse without music.... This is the difference that marks tragedy out from comedy; comedy is inclined to imitate persons below the level of our world, tragedy persons above it.

[ORIGINS OF POETRY]

There seem to be two causes that gave rise to poetry in general, and they are natural. The impulse to imitate is inherent in man from his childhood; he is distinguished among the animals by being the most imitative of them, and he takes the first steps of his education by imitating. Everyone's enjoyment of imitation is also inborn. What happens with works of art demonstrates this: though a thing itself is disagreeable to look at, we enjoy contemplating the most accurate representations of it — for instance, figures of the most despicable animals, or of human corpses. The reason for this lies in another fact: learning is a great pleasure, not only to philosophers but likewise to everyone else, however limited his gift for it may be. He enjoys looking at these representations, because in the act of studying them he is learning — identifying the object by an inference (for instance, recognizing who is the original of a portrait); since, if he happens not to have already seen the object depicted, it will not be the imitation as such that is giving him pleasure, but the finish of the workmanship, or the colouring, or some such other cause.

And just as imitation is natural to us, so also are music and rhythm (metres, clearly, are constituent parts of rhythms). Thus, from spontaneous beginnings, mankind developed poetry by a series of mostly minute changes out of these improvisations.

[THE ELEMENTS OF TRAGEDY]

Let us now discuss tragedy, having first picked up from what has been said the definition of its essence that has so far emerged. Tragedy, then, is an imitation of an action of high importance, complete and of some amplitude; in language enhanced by distinct and varying beauties; acted not narrated; by means of pity and fear effecting its purgation of these emotions. By the beauties enhancing the language I mean rhythm and melody; by "distinct and varying" I mean that some are produced by metre alone, and others at another time by melody.

Now since the imitating is done by actors, it would follow of necessity that one element in a tragedy must be the *Mise en scène*. Others are Melody and Language, for these are the media in which the imitating is done. By Language, I mean the component parts of the verse, whereas Melody has an entirely sensuous effect. Again, since the object imitated is an action, and doings are done by persons, whose individuality will be determined by their Character and their Thought (for these are the factors we have in mind when we define the quality of their doings), it follows that there are two natural causes of these doings, Thought and Character; and these causes determine the good or ill fortune of everyone. But the Fable is the imitation of the action; and by the Fable I mean the whole structure of the incidents. By Character I mean the factor that enables us to define the particular quality of the people involved in the doings; and Thought is shown in everything they say when they are demonstrating a fact or disclosing an opinion. There are therefore necessarily six elements in every tragedy, which give it its quality; and they are the Fable, Character, Language, Thought, the *Mise en scène*, and Melody. Two of these are the media in which the imitating is done, one is the manner of imitation, and three are its objects; there is

no other element besides these. Numerous poets have turned these essential components to account; all of them are always present — the *Mise en scene*, Character, the Fable, Language, Melody, and Thought.

The chief of these is the plotting of the incidents; for tragedy is an imitation not of men but of doings, life, happiness; unhappiness is located in doings, and our end is a certain kind of doing, not a personal quality; it is their characters that give men their quality, but their doings that make them happy or the opposite. So it is not the purpose of the actors to imitate character, but they include character as a factor in the doings. Thus it is the incidents (that is to say the Fable) that are the end for which tragedy exists; and the end is more important than anything else. Also, without an action there could not be a tragedy, but without Character there could. (In fact, the tragedies of most of the moderns are non-moral, and there are many non-moral poets of all periods; this also applies to the paintings of Zeuxis, if he is compared with Polygnōtus, for whereas Polygnōtus is a good portrayer of character the painting of Zeuxis leaves it out.) Again, if any one strings together moral speeches with the language and thought well worked out, he will be doing what is the business of tragedy; but it will be done much better by a tragedy that handles these elements more weakly, but has a fable with the incidents connected by a plot. Further, the chief means by which tragedy moves us, Irony of events and Disclosure, are elements in the Fable. A pointer in the same direction is that beginners in the art of poetry are able to get the language and characterization right before they can plot their incidents, and so were almost all the earliest poets.

So the source and as it were soul of tragedy is the Fable; and Character comes next. For, to instance a parallel from the art of painting, the most beautiful colours splashed on anyhow would not be as pleasing as a recognizable picture in black and white. Tragedy is an imitation of an action, and it is chiefly for this reason that it imitates the persons involved.

Third comes Thought: that is, the ability to say what circumstances allow and what is appropriate to them. It is the part played by social morality and rhetoric in making the dialogue: the old poets made their characters talk like men of the world, whereas our contemporaries make them talk like public speakers. Character is what shows a man's disposition — the kind of things he chooses or rejects when his choice is not obvious. Accordingly those speeches where the speaker shows no preferences or aversions whatever are non-moral. Thought, on the other hand, is shown in demonstrating a matter of fact or disclosing a significant opinion.

Fourth comes the Language. By Language I mean, as has already been said, words used semantically. It has the same force in verse as in prose.

Of the remaining elements, Melody is the chief of the enhancing beauties. The *Mise en scène* can excite emotion, but it is the crudest element and least akin to the art of poetry; for the force of tragedy exists even without stage and actors; besides, the fitting out of a *Mise en scène* belongs more to the wardrobe-master's art than to the poet's.

[THE TRAGIC FABLE]

So much for analysis. Now let us discuss in what sort of way the incidents should be plotted, since that is the first and chief consideration in tragedy. Our data are that tragedy is an imitation of a whole and complete action of some amplitude (a thing can be whole and yet quite lacking in amplitude). Now a whole is that which has a beginning, a middle, and an end. A beginning is that which does not itself necessarily follow anything else, but which leads naturally to another event or development; an end is the opposite, that which itself naturally (either of necessity or most commonly) follows something else, but nothing else comes after it; and a middle is that which itself follows something else and is followed by another thing. So, well-plotted fables must not begin or end casually, but must follow the pattern here described.

But, besides this, a picture, or any other composite object, if it is to be beautiful, must not only have its parts properly arranged, but be of an appropriate size; for beauty depends on size and structure. Accordingly, a minute picture cannot be beautiful (for when our vision has almost lost its sense of time it becomes confused); nor can an immense one (for we cannot take it all in together, and so our vision loses its unity and wholeness) — imagine a picture a thousand miles long! So, just as there is a proper size for bodies and pictures (a size that can be well surveyed), there is also a proper amplitude for fables (what can be kept well in one's mind). The length of the performance on the stage has nothing to do with art; if a hundred tragedies had to be produced, the length of the production would be settled by the clock, as the story goes that another kind of performance once was. But as to amplitude, the invariable rule dictated by the nature of the action is the fuller the more beautiful so long as the outline remains clear; and for a simple rule of size, the number of happenings that will make a chain of probability (or necessity) to change a given situation from misfortune to good fortune or from good fortune to misfortune is the minimum.

[UNITY]

Unity in a fable does not mean, as some think, that it has one man for its subject. To any one man many things happen — an infinite number — and some of them do not make any sort of unity; and in the same way one man has many doings which cannot be made into a unit of action. . . . Accordingly, just as in the other imitative arts the object of each imitation is a unit, so, since the fable is an imitation of an action, that action must be a complete unit, and the events of which it is made up must be so plotted that if any of these elements is moved or removed the whole is altered and upset. For when a thing can be included or not included without making any noticeable difference, that thing is no part of the whole.

[PROBABILITY]

From what has been said it is also clear that it is not the poet's business to tell what has happened, but the kind of things that would happen — what is possible according to probability or necessity. The difference between the historian and the poet is not the difference between writing in verse or prose; the work of Herodotus could be put into verse, and it would be just as much a history in verse as it is in prose. The difference is that the one tells what has happened, and the other the kind of things that would happen. It follows therefore that poetry is more philosophical and of higher value than history; for poetry unifies more, whereas history aggregates. To unify is to make a man of a certain description say or do the things that suit him, probably or necessarily, in the circumstances (this is the point of the descriptive proper names in poetry); what Alcibiades did or what happened to him is an aggregation. In comedy this has now become clear. They first plot the fable on a base of probabilities, and then find imaginary names for the people — unlike the lampooners, whose work was an aggregation of personalities. But in tragedy they keep to the names of real people. This is because possibility depends on conviction; if a thing has not happened we are not yet convinced that it is possible, but if it has happened it is clearly possible, for it would not have happened if it were impossible. Even tragedies, however, sometimes have all their persons fictitious except for one or two known names; and sometimes they have not a single known name, as in the *Anthos* of Agathon, in which both the events and the names are equally fictitious, without in the least reducing the delight it gives. It is not, therefore, requisite at all costs to keep to the traditional fables from which our tragedies draw their subject-matter. It would be absurd to insist on that, since even the known legends are known only to a few, and yet the delight is shared by every one. . . .

[SIMPLE AND COMPLEX FABLES]

The action imitated must contain incidents that evoke fear and pity, besides being a complete action; but this effect is accentuated when these incidents occur logically as well as unexpectedly, which will be more sensational than if they happen arbitrarily, by chance. Even when events are accidental the sensation is greater if they appear to have a purpose, as when the statue of Mitys at Argos killed the man who had caused his death, by falling on him at a public entertainment. Such things appear not to have happened blindly. Inevitably, therefore, plots of this sort are finer.

Some fables are simple, others complex: for the obvious reason that the original actions imitated by the fables are the one or the other. By a simple action I mean one that leads to the catastrophe in the way we have laid down, directly and singly, without Irony of events or Disclosure.

An action is complex when the catastrophe involves Disclosure, or Irony, or both. But these complications should develop out of the very structure of the fable, so that they fit what has gone before, either necessarily or probably. To happen after something is by no means the same as to happen because of it.

[IRONY]

Irony is a reversal in the course of events, of the kind specified, and, as I say, in accordance with probability or necessity. Thus in the *Oedipus* the arrival of the messenger, which was expected to cheer Oedipus up by releasing him from his fear about his mother, did the opposite by showing him who he was; and in the *Lynceus* [Abas], who was awaiting sentence of death, was acquitted, whereas his prosecutor Dănaüs was killed, and all this arose out of what had happened previously.

A Disclosure, as the term indicates, is a change from ignorance to knowledge; if the people are marked out for good fortune it leads to affection, if for misfortune, to enmity. Disclosure produces its finest effect when it is connected with Irony, as the disclosure in the *Oedipus* is. There are indeed other sorts of Disclosure: the process I have described can even apply to inanimate objects of no significance, and mistakes about what a man has done or not done can be cleared up. But the sort I have specified is more a part of the fable and of the action than any other sort; for this coupling of Irony and Disclosure will carry with it pity or fear, which we have assumed to be the nature of the doings tragedy imitates; and further, such doings will constitute good or ill fortune. Assuming then that it is a disclosure of the identity of persons, it may be of one person only, to the other, when the former knows who the latter is; or sometimes both have to be disclosed — for instance, the sending of the letter led Orestes to the discovery of Iphigeneia, and there had to be another disclosure to make him known to her.

This then is the subject-matter of two elements in the Fable, Irony and Disclosure. A third element is the Crisis of feeling. Irony and Disclosure have been defined; the Crisis of feeling is a harmful or painful experience, such as deaths in public, violent pain, physical injuries, and everything of that sort.

[THE TRAGIC PATTERN]

Following the proper order, the next subject to discuss after this would be: What one should aim at and beware of in plotting fables; that is to say, What will produce the tragic effect. Since, then, tragedy, to be at its finest, requires a complex, not a simple, structure, and its structure should also imitate fearful and pitiful events (for that is the peculiarity of this sort of imitation), it is clear: first, that decent people must not be shown passing from good fortune to misfortune (for that is not fearful or pitiful but disgusting); again, vicious people must not be shown passing from misfortune to good fortune (for that is the most untragic situation possible — it has none of the requisites, it is neither humane, nor pitiful, nor fearful); nor again should an utterly evil man fall from good fortune into misfortune (for though a plot of that kind would be humane, it would not induce pity or fear — pity is induced by undeserved misfortune, and fear by the misfortunes of normal people, so that this situation will be neither pitiful nor fearful). So we are left with the man between these extremes: that is to say, the kind of man who neither is distinguished for excellence and virtue, nor comes to grief on account of baseness and vice, but on account of some error; a man of great reputation and prosperity, like Oedipus and Thyestes and conspicuous people of such families as theirs. So, to be well informed, a fable must be single rather than (as some say) double — there must be no change from misfortune to good fortune, but only the opposite, from good fortune to misfortune; the cause must not be vice, but a great error; and the man must be either of the type specified or better, rather than worse. This is borne out by the practice of poets; at first they picked a fable at random and made an inventory of its contents, but now the finest tragedies are plotted, and concern a few families — for example, the tragedies about Alcmeon, Oedipus, Orestes, Mĕlĕăger, Thyestes, Tēlĕphus, and any others whose lives were attended by terrible experiences or doings.

This is the plot that will produce the technically finest tragedy. Those critics are therefore wrong who censure Euripides on this very ground — because he does this in his tragedies, and many of them end in misfortune; for it is, as I have said, the right thing to do. This is clearly demonstrated on the stage in the competitions, where such plays, if they succeed, are the most tragic, and Euripides, even if he is inefficient in every other respect, still shows himself the most tragic of our poets. The next best plot, which is said by some people to be the best, is the tragedy with a double plot, like the *Odyssey*, ending in one way for the better people and in the opposite way for the worse. But it is the weakness of theatrical performances that gives priority to this kind; when poets write what the audience would like to happen, they are in leading strings. This is not the pleasure proper to tragedy, but rather to comedy, where the greatest enemies in the fable, say Orestes and Aegisthus, make friends

and go off at the end, and nobody is killed by anybody.

[THE TRAGIC EMOTIONS]

The pity and fear can be brought about by the *Mise en scène*; but they can also come from the mere plotting of the incidents, which is preferable, and better poetry. For, without seeing anything, the fable ought to have been so plotted that if one heard the bare facts, the chain of circumstances would make one shudder and pity. That would happen to anyone who heard the fable of the *Oedipus*. To produce this effect by the *Mise en scène* is less artistic and puts one at the mercy of the technician; and those who use it not to frighten but merely to startle have lost touch with tragedy altogether. We should not try to get all sorts of pleasure from tragedy, but the particular tragic pleasure. And clearly, since this pleasure coming from pity and fear has to be produced by imitation, it is by his handling of the incidents that the poet must create it.

Let us, then, take next the kind of circumstances that seem terrible or lamentable. Now, doings of that kind must be between friends, or enemies, or neither. If an enemy injures an enemy, there is no pity either beforehand or at the time, except on account of the bare fact; nor is there if they are neutral; but when sufferings are engendered among the affections — for example, if murder is done or planned, or some similar outrage is committed, by brother on brother, or son on father, or mother on son, or son on mother — that is the thing to aim at.

Though it is not permissible to ruin the traditional fables — I mean, such as the killing of Clytemnestra by Orestes, or Erĭphyle by Alcmeon — the poet should use his own invention to refine on what has been handed down to him. Let me explain more clearly what I mean by "refine." The action may take place, as the old poets used to make it, with the knowledge and understanding of the participants; this was how Euripides made Medea kill her children. Or they may do it, but in ignorance of the horror of the deed, and then afterwards discover the tie of affection, like the Oedipus of Sophocles; his act was outside the play, but there are examples where it is inside the tragedy itself — Alcmeon in the play by Astydămas, or Tēlĕgŏnus in *The Wounded Odysseus*. Besides these, there is a third possibility: when a man is about to do some fatal act in ignorance, but is enlightened before he does it. These are the only possible alternatives. One must either act or not act, and either know or not know. Of these alternatives, to know, and to be about to act, and then not to act, is thoroughly bad — it is disgusting without being tragic, for there is no emotional crisis; accordingly poets only rarely create such situations, as in the *Antigone*, when Haemon fails to kill Creon. Next in order is to act; and if the deed is done in ignorance and its nature is disclosed afterwards, so much the better — there is no bad taste in it, and the revelation is overpowering. But the last is best; I mean, like Mĕrŏpe in the *Cresphontes*, intending to kill her son, but recognizing him and not killing him; and the brother and sister in the *Iphigeneia*; and in the *Helle*, the son recognizing his mother just as he was going to betray her. — This is the reason for what was mentioned earlier: that the subject-matter of our tragedies is drawn from a few families. In their search for matter they discovered this recipe in the fables, not by cunning but by luck. So they are driven to have recourse to those families where such emotional crises have occurred. . . .

[CHARACTER]

And in the characterization, as in the plot-

ting of the incidents, the aim should always be either necessity or probability: so that they say or do such things as it is necessary or probable that they would, being what they are; and that for this to follow that is either necessary or probable. . . . As for extravagant incidents, there should be none in the story, or if there are they should be kept outside the tragedy, as is the one in the *Oedipus* of Sophocles.

Since tragedy is an imitation of people above the normal, we must be like good portrait-painters, who follow the original model closely, but refine on it; in the same way the poet, in imitating people whose character is choleric or phlegmatic, and so forth, must keep them as they are and at the same time make them attractive. So Homer made Achilles noble, as well as a pattern of obstinacy. . . .

[CHORUS]

Treat the chorus as though it were one of the actors; it should be an organic part of the play and reinforce it, not as it is in Euripides, but as in Sophocles. In their successors the songs belong no more to the fable than to that of any other tragedy. This has led to the insertion of borrowed lyrics, an innovation for which Agathon was responsible.

Tragedy and the Common Man

Arthur Miller

> Arthur Miller's "Tragedy and the Common Man" was written while his *Death of a Salesman* was running on Broadway. Implicitly a defense of his play, the essay's assertions about the nature of the tragic hero have implications for other plays about middle-class figures and even for earlier tragedies with heroes of high rank.

In this age few tragedies are written. It has often been held that the lack is due to a paucity of heroes among us, or else that modern man has had the blood drawn out of his organs of belief by the skepticism of science, and the heroic attack on life cannot feed on an attitude of reserve and circumspection. For one reason or another, we are often held to be below tragedy — or tragedy above us. The inevitable conclusion is, of course, that the tragic mode is archaic, fit only for the very highly placed, the kings or the kingly, and where this admission is not made in so many words it is most often implied.

I believe that the common man is as apt a subject for tragedy in its highest sense as kings were. On the face of it this ought to be obvious in the light of modern psychiatry, which bases its analysis upon classific formulations, such as the Oedipus and Orestes complexes, for instance, which were enacted by royal beings, but which apply to everyone in similar emotional situations.

More simply, when the question of tragedy in art is not at issue, we never hesitate to attribute to the well-placed and the exalted the very same mental processes as the lowly. And finally, if the exaltation of tragic action were truly a property of the high-bred character alone, it is inconceivable that the mass of mankind should cherish tragedy above all other forms, let alone be capable of understanding it.

As a general rule, to which there may be exceptions unknown to me, I think the tragic feeling is evoked in us when we are in the presence of a character who is ready to lay down his life, if need be, to secure one thing — his sense of personal dignity. From Orestes to Hamlet, Medea to Macbeth, the underlying struggle is that of the individual attempting to gain his "rightful" position in his society.

Sometimes he is one who has been displaced from it, sometimes one who seeks to attain it for the first time, but the fateful wound from which the inevitable events spiral is the wound of indignity, and its dominant force is indignation. Tragedy, then, is the consequence of a man's total compulsion to evaluate himself justly.

In the sense of having been initiated by the hero himself, the tale always reveals what has been called his "tragic flaw," a failing that is not peculiar to grand or elevated characters. Nor is it necessarily a weakness. The flaw, or crack in the character, is really nothing — and need be nothing — but his inherent unwillingness to remain passive in the face of what he conceives to be a challenge to his dignity, his image of his rightful status. Only the passive, only those who accept their lot without active retaliation, are "flawless." Most of us are in that category.

But there are among us today, as there always have been, those who act against the scheme of things that degrades them, and in the process of action, everything we have accepted out of fear or insensitivity or ignorance is shaken before us and examined, and from this total onslaught by an individual against the seemingly stable cosmos surrounding us — from this total examination of the "unchangeable" environment — comes the terror and the fear that is classically associated with tragedy.

More important, from this total questioning of what has been previously unquestioned, we learn. And such a process is not beyond the common man. In revolutions around the world, these past thirty years, he has demonstrated again and again this inner dynamic of all tragedy.

Insistence upon the rank of the tragic hero, or the so-called nobility of his character, is really but a clinging to the outward forms of tragedy. If rank or nobility of character was indispensable, then it would follow that the problems of those with rank were the particular problems of tragedy. But surely the right of one monarch to capture the domain from another no longer raises our passions, nor are our concepts of justice what they were to the mind of an Elizabethan king.

The quality in such plays that does shake us, however, derives from the underlying fear of being displaced, the disaster inherent in being torn away from our chosen image of what and who we are in this world. Among us today this fear is as strong, and perhaps stronger, than it ever was. In fact, it is the common man who knows this fear best.

Now, if it is true that tragedy is the consequence of a man's total compulsion to evaluate himself justly, his destruction in the attempt posits a wrong or an evil in his environment. And this is precisely the morality of tragedy and its lesson. The discovery of the moral law, which is what the enlightenment of tragedy consists of, is not the discovery of some abstract or metaphysical quantity.

The tragic right is a condition of life, a condition in which the human personality is able to flower and realize itself. The wrong is the condition which suppresses man, perverts the flowing out of his love and creative instinct. Tragedy enlightens — and it must, in that it points the heroic finger at the enemy of man's freedom. The thrust for freedom is the quality in tragedy which exalts. The revolutionary questioning of the stable environment is what terrifies. In no way is the common man debarred from such thoughts or such actions.

Seen in this light, our lack of tragedy may be partially accounted for by the turn which modern literature has taken toward the purely psychiatric view of life, or the purely sociological. If all our miseries, our indignities, are born and bred within our minds, then all action, let alone the heroic action, is obviously impossible.

And if society alone is responsible for the cramping of our lives, then the protagonist must needs be so pure and faultless as to force us to deny his validity as a character. From neither of these views can tragedy derive, simply because neither represents a balanced concept of life. Above all else, tragedy requires the finest appreciation by the writer of cause and effect.

No tragedy can therefore come about when its author fears to question absolutely everything, when he regards any institution, habit or custom as being either everlasting, immutable or inevitable. In the tragic view the need of man to wholly realize himself is the only fixed star, and whatever it is that hedges his nature and lowers it is ripe for attack and examination. Which is not to say that tragedy must preach revolution.

The Greeks could probe the very heavenly origin of their ways and return to confirm the rightness of laws. And Job could face God in anger, demanding his right, and end in submission. But for a moment everything is in suspension, nothing is accepted, and in this stretching and tearing apart of the cosmos, in the very action of so doing, the character gains "size," the tragic stature which is spuriously attached to the royal or the high born in our minds. The commonest of men may take on that stature to the extent of his willingness to throw all he has into the contest, the battle to secure his rightful place in his world.

There is a misconception of tragedy with which I have been struck in review after review, and in many conversations with writers and readers alike. It is the idea that tragedy is of necessity allied to pessimism. Even the dictionary says nothing more about the word than that it means a story with a sad or unhappy ending. This impression is so firmly fixed that I almost hesitate to claim that in truth tragedy implies more optimism in its author than does comedy, and that its final result ought to be the reinforcement of the onlooker's brightest opinions of the human animal.

For, if it is true to say that in essence the tragic hero is intent upon claiming his whole due as a personality, and if this struggle must be total and without reservation, then it automatically demonstrates the indestructible will of man to achieve his humanity.

The possibility of victory must be there in tragedy. Where pathos rules, where pathos is finally derived, a character has fought a battle he could not possibly have won. The pathetic is achieved when the protagonist is, by virtue of his witlessness, his insensitivity, or the very air he gives off, incapable of grappling with a much superior force.

Pathos truly is the mode for the pessimist.

But tragedy requires a nicer balance between what is possible and what is impossible. And it is curious, although edifying, that the plays we revere, century after century, are the tragedies. In them, and in them alone, lies the belief — optimistic, if you will — in the perfectibility of man.

It is time, I think, that we who are without kings, took up this bright thread of our history and followed it to the only place it can possibly lead in our time — the heart and spirit of the average man.

The Scheme of Tragedy

Dorothea Krook

In the following essay Professor Krook indicates what she takes to be the four universal elements of tragedy: the act of shame or horror, consequent intense suffering, then an increase in knowledge, and finally a reaffirmation of the value of life. All of these were more or less bundled together in Aristotle's *mythos* or fable or plot or action. The reader may be interested to know that in the book from which this essay is taken Mrs. Krook goes on to examine, among other plays *King Oedipus, Hedda Gabler,* and *The Cherry Orchard.*

The four elements are easily named. The first I call *the act of shame or horror*[1] and define as that act or series of acts (or in some modern drama, the situation or condition) which directly precipitates the central spectacle of suffering in the drama. The second of the universal elements of tragedy is the *suffering* itself. This is properly tragic if and only if it generates knowledge, in the sense of insight into, understanding of, man's fundamental nature or the fundamental human condition. *Knowledge* in this sense is therefore the third universal element of tragedy. But the knowledge is not properly tragic unless it issues in some kind of affirmation, or reaffirmation, of the dignity of the human spirit and the worthwhileness of human life. This *affirmation* or *reaffirmation* is accordingly the fourth and last of the universal elements of tragedy.

It will be seen that the elements are so closely involved in each other that it is impossible to define one without reference to the rest. The reason is obvious: they are separable in analysis but not in experience. In our actual experience, they are organically interrelated, inter-

Reprinted by permission of Yale University Press from *Elements of Tragedy* by Dorothea Krook. Copyright © 1969 by Yale University.

[1] I owe this striking phrase to my friend Professor David Wilkinson, who first used it in a paper on Greek tragedy.

fused parts or aspects of that single, indivisible whole which Aristotle called the *mythos*, that is, the fable or plot conceived of as an action subject to an order or design; and as such they are both coeval and contemporaneous. The basic pattern of the experience of tragedy proposed here may therefore be schematized as act of shame-suffering-knowledge-affirmation, the hyphens indicating the mutual inseparability of the elements; or (on the principle of the house that Jack built) as "the act of shame which precipitates the suffering which generates the knowledge which issues in the affirmation."

These bare definitions of the elements can be immediately extended by a few preliminary elucidations.

In Greek tragedy and the tragedy of Shakespeare (but not always in modern tragedy) what I have called the act of shame or horror is generally self-evident and self-explanatory. In *Oedipus Rex*, it is two single, simple acts: the murder of a father by a son and the subsequent marriage of the son to the mother. In *King Lear*, it is a series of acts — the wanton division of a kingdom, leading to a father's rejection of a loving daughter and a loyal friend, and culminating in the rejection of the father by two pelican daughters and the betrayal of another father by a bastard son. The act of shame may but need not be committed by the tragic hero or heroine, the principal vessel of the tragic suffering (in *Macbeth* it is, in *Hamlet* it is not);

and it need not be actually committed but may be merely intended or imagined (as in T. S. Eliot's *The Family Reunion*, where the adultery of Agatha and Harry's father is intended not enacted, and the death of Harry's wife is likewise imagined and intended but not, or not certainly, enacted).

What is vital to the definition, however, is, first, that the act of shame shall be an objective act or series of acts, or an objective situation or condition — for instance, in *A Doll's House* the degrading (shameful) situation created for Nora by her marriage, or in *The Cherry Orchard* the helpless, hopeless, self-annihilating, and in that sense "shameful," condition of Russian society. What it must not be is merely a subjective attitude or state of mind, or a merely passive disposition of character and temperament; as Aristotle puts it, it must be "a certain kind of activity, not a quality."[2] Second, the shameful act, or situation or condition of shame, must directly precipitate the spectacle of suffering in the drama. Consequently, where there is a doubt or difficulty about identifying the act of shame[3] in a particular play (as there is in much modern drama), the question to ask oneself is *not* "What is shameful or horrible in this drama?" (there may be a dozen things which are), but "What is the act or situation here that directly precipitates the central spectacle of suffering?" The answer to this question is the act of shame which is the first defining element of tragedy.

There are two more preliminary things to be noted about the act of shame in tragedy. The first is that to be properly tragic it must be in a special sense representative. It must be the kind of act that men are constitutionally liable to commit: an act expressing the fundamental nature of man, or arising out of the fundamental human condition. For in being thus representative such acts are necessarily universal, that is, permanently valid and meaningful, exemplary and instructive.

The second point is that the most shameful of these representative acts of shame appear to belong to the category of acts of betrayal or rejection. It is for this reason, one may suppose,

that murder, adultery, and usurpation are among the most frequently recurring acts of shame in tragedy from the earliest times to the present day. Murder, in particular murder of one's kin — as in the *Oresteia*, *Oedipus Rex*, *Hamlet*, *Macbeth*; adultery, either actual or potential — actual in *Agamemnon*, *The White Devil*, *Anna Karenina*, *The Golden Bowl*, potential in the *Hippolytus* of Euripides and *The Family Reunion*; usurpation — as in *Hamlet*, *Macbeth*, *The Tempest*: these, exhibited as acts of betrayal or rejection of those closest to one, may be seen as archetypal acts of shame in tragedy. And this it seems is what Aristotle had in mind when he remarked that the kind of "tragic deed" that strikes us as most "horrible" is that "done within the family — when murder or the like is done or meditated by brother on brother, by son on father, by mother on son, or son on mother."[4] So interpreted, his suggestion has certainly been confirmed by the practice of tragic dramatists from Aeschylus to Henry James.

The elements of suffering and knowledge can scarcely be discussed separately, for as I have indicated, what makes the suffering properly tragic depends intimately on the kind and quality of the knowledge it yields. What can be said about the suffering in separation from the knowledge is simple and self-explanatory. First, it must be felt to be intense and real. It must attain, in the given circumstances, the furthest reach of human suffering; and it must be real both in the ordinary sense of being completely genuine or sincere (not false, assumed, affected, in whatever degree) and also in the more important sense of being commensurate with its cause, the act of shame or horror. (It is in this sense that Hamlet's suffering — in despite of T. S. Eliot — is real, and Hedda Gabler's is not.) Second, the suffering must be felt to be fatally undermining or destructive, involving absolute loss and deprivation for the human vessel of the suffering, and therefore generally (though not invariably) culminating in death, the ultimate form of loss and deprivation in human experience. Third, it must be conscious. A blind, dumb, inarticulate — that is, not fully conscious — suffering may be pitiful and heart-rending, as all intense human suffering is, but it cannot be tragic. However, it need not be more than conscious; and the consciousness

[2] *Poetics*, 1450a, 15.
[3] I use here and subsequently the abbreviated formula "act of shame" to avoid the clumsy repetition of the full formula, "the act or situation or condition of shame or horror."

[4] Aristotle, *Poetics*, 1453b, 20.

may but need not be (like Hamlet's) analytical — exploratory, reflective, discursive in a specifically intellectual way: it may be somewhat intuitive, imperfectly analyzed and incompletely understood, and yet serve perfectly as the consciousness that makes suffering properly tragic. This feature of the tragic suffering, however, already involves the element of knowledge, about which I want to make just one preliminary observation.

I have already suggested that the knowledge which springs from suffering in tragedy must be a knowledge that has the property of illuminating some fundamental aspect of man's nature or the human condition. The qualification I want to add at this point is that it may but need not take the form of self-knowledge. There is point in stressing this because in the tragedy of Shakespeare and of most modern writers the form the knowledge takes is in fact generally self-knowledge, and by extrapolation from these classic cases (*King Lear* and *Hamlet*, Nora in *A Doll's House*, Nina in *The Seagull*, Harry in *The Family Reunion*), we have come to regard self-knowledge as the only proper form of the knowledge that illuminates and redeems in tragedy. It is easy to see, however, that Greek tragedy does not bear out this generalization. In a comparatively Shakespearean tragedy like *Oedipus Rex*, the knowledge of an Oedipus is perhaps equivalent to, or approximates, the self-knowledge of a King Lear. But this is distinctly not the case in, say, the *Agamemnon* or Sophocles' *Antigone* or *Electra*. Consequently, if it is the universal and permanent elements of tragedy we are after, self-knowledge cannot be one of them, and that is why I have proposed knowledge plain and unadorned as that which the tragic suffering yields.

The important implication here is that what matters in tragedy is not that the tragic hero, the vessel of the tragic suffering, shall receive the knowledge issuing from the suffering, but that we, the readers or audience, shall receive it. And if this view is correct, it follows that even when the knowledge takes the form of self-knowledge, it is not because it illuminates the self of the tragic hero that it is tragic, but because, in and through the representative self of the tragic hero, it illuminates for us some fundamental aspect of man's nature or the human condition. . . .

A convenient way of approaching the fourth and last of the elements of tragedy I have isolated is by way of Aristotle's doctrine of catharsis. What the Aristotelian theory chiefly emphasizes in our experience of great tragedy is the paradoxical nature of its final effect. With a play like *King Lear* in mind, this paradox is evident enough. Having been exposed to a spectacle of suffering as terrible as any we have ever witnessed, we would expect to feel — as in such a situation we would feel in life — intolerably depressed and oppressed; heavy with the sense of the helplessness of man and the hopelessness of the human condition; bitter, angry, and in despair about the seemingly wanton cruelty of it all. In fact, what we feel is something quite different. We feel, extraordinarily, liberated from pain and fear (Aristotle's "purgation" of the emotions of pity and terror); not depressed or oppressed, but in a curious way exhilarated; not angry and bitter but somehow reconciled; our faith in man and the human condition not destroyed or undermined but restored, fortified, reaffirmed. This is the psychological fact of our final response to tragedy; and the reason behind it is what I have named as the fourth universal element of tragedy — the affirmation or reaffirmation of the dignity of man and the worthwhileness of human life, which in great tragedy issues from the spectacle of suffering itself and the knowledge the suffering yields.

This bare statement, however, obviously does not answer the question, "*Why* do the suffering and knowledge in great tragedy yield such a reaffirmation?" To give the answer, it is necessary to extend the scope of the inquiry into a further dimension. This, by enlarging the framework of our analysis, will explain more fully the element of affirmation and provide a more inclusive context — the most inclusive, I believe — for the whole scheme I have proposed.

In the greatest tragedy, I suggest, what is in the end affirmed is something more than the dignity of man and the value of human life. We are made to feel that, through the affirmation of man and the life of man, there is at the same time being affirmed an order of values transcending the values of the human order. This order of values is not, or is not felt to be, a mere projection of the human mind: it is felt to have a real, objective existence — an existence independent of, other than, and antecedent to man and the life of man. At the same time, however, it has the closest bearing on the life of man, in particular on the conduct of men; therefore, it is properly described as moral — a moral order, in the most inclusive sense of the term.

An objective moral order which at once incorporates the human and transcends it: this, I am suggesting, is what is finally affirmed in great tragedy. That this is true of classical Greek tragedy can hardly be contested.[5] There the transcendent order is most often palpably manifest in the shape of the gods and goddesses, the oracles and prophecies, which play a vital part in the tragic action. And even when the supernatural powers are not present as dramatis personae (as in Sophocles' *Antigone* or *Electra* or *Philoctetes*), the transcendent order is nevertheless openly and explicitly invoked through the direct reference to a moral law — the moral law that in *Antigone* is violated by Creon and affirmed by Antigone — presented as eternal, immutable, and absolutely binding.

In the tragedy of Shakespeare, by contrast, the reference to an order of this kind generally is not open, explicit, and palpable: it is rather intimated — suggested, hinted at, obliquely invoked. The plays show a wide range of variation in this respect: in the history plays and the middle plays it tends to be open and explicit (Ulysses' famous speech on degree is a case in point); in the mature tragedies — *King Lear* and *Macbeth*, for instance — it tends more and more to be only intimated, in and through the developed Shakespearean imagery. Whether or not it is specifically Christian need not be inquired; the point for the present argument is that the reference to an objective moral order is there in Shakespeare as positively and significantly as in the Greek drama.

This is the vital common ground that links Shakespeare with the classical Greeks and sep-

[5] By "classical Greek tragedy" I mean, here and elsewhere, the tragedy of Aeschylus and Sophocles. I exclude Euripides (even though Aristotle thought him "the most tragic certainly of the dramatists") for reasons that I hope will be generally recognized as valid. He is a "modern," at least as modern as Ibsen; and for my analysis of tragedy at any rate he raises all, or almost all, the problems of modern naturalistic drama. These for obvious reasons I have chosen to discuss mainly in the works of Ibsen; but I could almost as well have chosen Euripides. For a parallel reason, I have omitted to treat separately French neoclassical tragedy. The tragedies of Racine and Corneille I found presented no problems essentially different from those of classical Greek tragedy, which could therefore I felt be used to serve for both.

arates both from the moderns (Ibsen and after). Taking Ibsen's drama as the exemplary case, what we will find there, I suggest, is a seeking, an aspiration, to affirm an order of values transcending the human, but no actual affirmation, either explicit or by intimation; and this unfulfilled aspiration after that which in tragedy is always present and is always in the end affirmed does much, I believe, to account for those mysteries, obscurities, and ambiguities of some of Ibsen's best dramas — in particular such late plays as *Rosmersholm*, *The Master Builder*, and *When We Dead Awaken* — which raise grave and interesting doubts about their claim to be tragedies. . . .

If, as I have suggested, there is always in tragedy a reference to something in the nature of an objective order of values which incorporates the human and transcends it, the four elements of tragedy I have proposed can be seen to derive both their objective validity and their internal, organic unity from their connection with it. The primary "act of shame" is then seen to be shameful and horrible because it is a violation of a moral order which is objectively real and absolutely binding. The "suffering" precipitated by the act of shame is seen to be not merely arbitrary but objectively necessary, and thus necessary because *expiatory*. For in relation to the transcendent moral order the suffering in tragedy is always and essentially expiatory: an act of shame which violates the moral order having been committed, this act of violation has to be expiated in order that the moral order may be restored; and the way of expiation for human creatures being the way of suffering, the more shameful the violation, the more intense and awful the expiatory suffering. Again, what the "knowledge" that issues from the suffering illuminates, renders intelligible, is precisely the necessity of the suffering, as expiatory in the sense explained. And the final "affirmation" of tragedy springs from our reconciliation to, or acceptance of, the necessity of the suffering rendered intelligible by the knowledge: by illuminating the necessity of the suffering, the knowledge reconciles us to it; by being reconciled to ("accepting") the suffering as necessary, we reaffirm the supremacy of the universal moral order; and by this act of recognition of and submission to the universal moral order, which the reaffirmation of its supremacy implies, we express and affirm the dignity of man and the value of human life. From this it also follows that the final affirmation of the greatness of the human spirit and the worthwhileness of human life in tragedy is effected not directly but indirectly — as a *consequence* of the restoration and reaffirmation of the universal moral order by the suffering and knowledge of the human agent.

Finally, in the light of this objectivist, quasi-religious view, the cathartic effect of great tragedy may be seen to admit of an objective, non-psychological explanation. If we are in the end not oppressed but emotionally liberated by the spectacle of human suffering in tragedy, if as Aristotle says, a catharsis by pity and terror is effected, the liberation is due to our sense that the moral law, the moral order, have been powerfully restored and reaffirmed by the capacity of man for expiatory suffering and redemptive knowledge. What a piece of work is man, we may well exclaim, that weak and wretched as he is he should yet possess the power by his suffering perpetually to reaffirm and restore the eternal moral order itself, as it is violated by the acts of shame or horror that he is perpetually liable to commit.

COMEDY

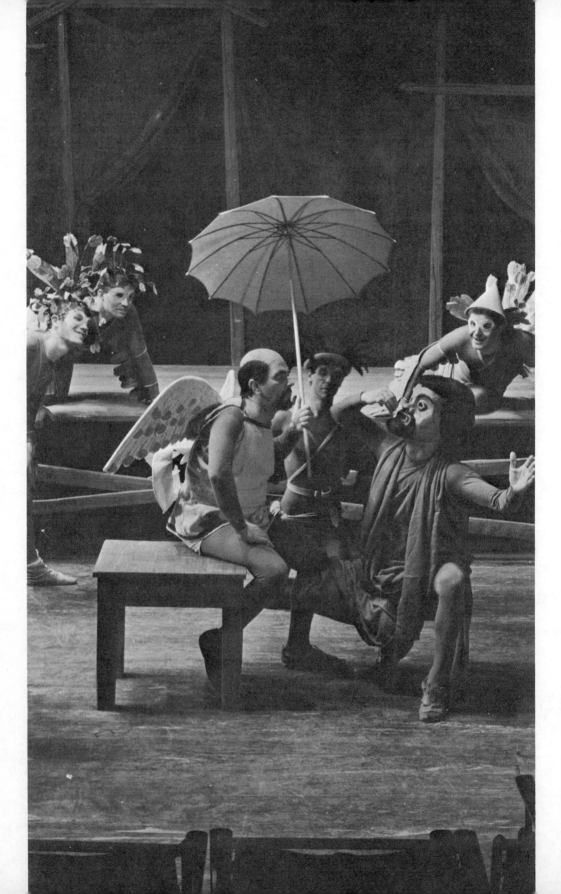

THE BIRDS

Aristophanes

Translated by William Arrowsmith

Nothing of much interest is known about Aristophanes (c. 450 B.C.–
c. 385 B.C.). An Athenian, he competed for about forty years in the annual
festivals of comic drama to which three playwrights each contributed one
play. His first play was produced in 427 B.C., his last extant play in 388 B.C.,
but he is known to have written two comedies after this date. Of the forty
or so plays he wrote, eleven survive. *The Birds*, widely regarded as his masterpiece, won second prize in 414 B.C.

CHARACTERS OF THE PLAY

EUELPIDES (*i.e., Hopeful*), *an Athenian*
PISTHETAIROS (*i.e., Plausible*), *an Athenian*
SANDPIPER, *servant of Epops the Hoopoe*
EPOPS, OR HOOPOE, *otherwise known as Tereus*
CHORUS OF BIRDS
KORYPHAIOS
PRIEST
POET
PROPHET
METON
INSPECTOR
LEGISLATOR

FIRST MESSENGER
SENTRY
IRIS
HERALD
DELINQUENT
KINESIAS, *a dithyrambic poet*
INFORMER
PROMETHEUS
POSEIDON
TRIBALLOS
HERAKLES
SECOND MESSENGER

Prometheus, with the aid of his umbrella, protects himself from Zeus, in a
modern Greek production directed by Karolos Koun. (Photograph: Elite.)

Scene: A desolate wilderness.°1 *In the background is a single tree and the sheer rock-face of a cliff. Enter, in the last stages of exhaustion,* EUELPIDES *and* PISTHETAIROS. *On his arm* EUELPIDES *carries a* MAGPIE; PISTHETAIROS *holds a* CROW. *They are followed by slaves with their luggage, consisting mostly of kitchen equipment, cauldrons, pots, spits, etc.*

EUELPIDES (*to his* MAGPIE):
Straight ahead, croaker? Over by that tree?
PISTHETAIROS:
Damn this cracked Crow! He keeps cawing
    me backwards.
EUELPIDES:
Look, halfwit, what's the point of hiking these
    hills?
If we don't stop this zigzagging pretty soon,
I'm through.
PISTHETAIROS:
5   I must have been mad — trusting a Crow
to go trudging off on this hundred-mile hike.
EUELPIDES: *Y*ou're mad?
Look at me, man — hitched to a Magpie
and my toenails worn away right down to the
    nub.
PISTHETAIROS:
I'll be damned if I know where we are.
EUELPIDES: Say,
do you suppose we could find our way back
10   home from
here?
PISTHETAIROS:
Friend, even Exekestides couldn't do *that.*°

EUELPIDES (*stumbling*):   Hell.
PISTHETAIROS:
That's just where we're headed now, old man.
EUELPIDES: You know,
that birdseller Philokrates who sold us these
    damn Birds
was a filthy fraud, that's what. Swearing up
    and down   15
that these two Birds here would lead us to the
    Hoopoe,
old Tereus the Bird who used to be a man,°
and swindling us with this stinking, jabbering
    Magpie here°
for two bits and that cluckhead Crow of yours
    for six!
And what do they do but nip our fingers off?   20

(*To the* MAGPIE.)

Well, what are you gaping at, imbecile?
    Where?
Straight into the cliff? But there's no road
    there, idiot.
PISTHETAIROS:
A *road*? Sweet gods, there isn't even a track!
EUELPIDES:
Say, isn't your Crow croaking something about
    a road?
PISTHETAIROS:
You know, now that you mention it, I think
    he *is* croaking   25
in a different key.
EUELPIDES:
                Something about a road, isn't it?

From *The Birds* by Aristophanes, translated by William Arrowsmith. Copyright © 1961 by William Arrowsmith. Reprinted by arrangement with The New American Library, Inc., New York, N.Y.
[1] The degree sign (°) indicates a footnote, which is keyed to the text by the line number. Text references are printed in **boldface** type; the annotation follows in lightface type. The notes are William Arrowsmith's. [Eds.]
s.d. **A desolate wilderness:** The locale of the Hoopoe's nest belongs, of course, to the same fabulous geography as Cloudcuckooland itself. Since in mythology Tereus was the king of the Daulians, a Thracian people, the scene may be laid "somewhere in Thrace" — an extremely imprecise designation.
12 **even Exekestides couldn't do *that*:** Cf. Glossary, EXEKESTIDES. From the frequent allusions in the play to men who, technically ineligible, had somehow managed to get themselves enrolled as Athenian citizens, it is tempting to believe that proposals to revise the citizenship lists were in the air or had recently been carried out. The climax of these allusions comes in the final scene of the play, in which Pisthetairos attempts to prove that Herakles is technically a bastard (and hence cannot inherit Zeus' estate) because his mother was an ordinary mortal, i.e., of foreign stock.
17 **old Tereus the bird who used to be a man:** Cf. Glossary, TEREUS.
Despite the violent story which tells how Tereus became the Hoopoe, Prokne the Nightingale, and Philomela the Swallow, Aristophanes' Tereus and Prokne live happily together in marital bliss.
18 **this stinking, jabbering Magpie here:** In the Greek, the Magpie is actually called "son of Tharraleides." According to the Scholiast, Tharraleides' son was Asopodoros, a diminutive man commonly ridiculed as a runt. There may also be a pun on the word ϑαρραλέος, loquacious or impudent.

PISTHETAIROS:

Naw, he's cawing he'll gnaw my fingers off.

EUELPIDES:

It's a filthy shame, that's what. Think of it, man:

here we are dying to go tell it to the Birds,°

30 and then, by god, we can't even find the way.

(*To the Audience.*)

Yes, dear people, we confess we're completely mad.

But it's not like Sakas'° madness. Not a bit.

For he, poor dumb foreigner, wants in, while we,

born and bred Athenians both, true blue,

35 true citizens, not afraid of any man,

want out.

Yes, we've spread our little feet

and taken off. Not that we hate Athens —

heavens, no. And not that dear old Athens

isn't grand, that blessed land where men are free —

to pay their taxes.°

40 No, look to the locust

who, one month or two, drones and shrills

among the little thickets, while the men of Athens,

perched upon the thorny thickets of the law, sit

shrilling out their three score years and ten.

Because of legal locusts,° gentlemen, we have

45 left,

lugging these baskets and pots and boughs of myrtle,

looking for some land of soft and lovely leisure°

where a man may loaf and play and settle down

for good. Tereus the Hoopoe is our journey's end.

From him we hope to learn if he has seen 50

in all his many travels such a place

on earth.

47 soft and lovely leisure: Pisthetairos and Euelpides are looking, that is, for a place that offers them what Athens does not: release from the tortured, nervous, frenetic restlessness of Athenian life.

In Greek this quality of Athenian national restlessness was called πολυπραγμοσύνη, and its lexical meanings include "officiousness," "meddling," and "the activities of the busybody." Translated to social and political life, the word connotes those national characteristics which made the Athenians at once the wonder and the bane of the Greek world: national enterprise and energy vs. a spirit of unsatisfied restlessness; adventurous daring of action and intellect as against a spirit that seemed destructive of tradition and the life of rural peace; hunger for innovation and change undercut by the inability to temporize or be still. The word, in short, expresses precisely those qualities — daring, energy, ingenuity, strain, dynamic action, restlessness, ambition for acquisition and conquest, glory in change — that typify the Athens of the fifth century. It was these qualities that had made Athens great; they also made Athens imperial and thereby propagated themselves; they were responsible for the senseless protraction of the Peloponnesian War and they would, Aristophanes believed, eventually destroy Athens as they had already destroyed the countryside of Attika and the virtue it fostered: ἀπραγμοσύνη, the contented leisure of traditional order and the rural conservatism of peaceful life.

The word is, of course, crucial to the play. For if Aristophanes shows us in Pisthetairos here an Athenian exhausted by years of national restlessness and in search of ἀπραγμοσύνη among the Birds, it is precisely his point that no Athenian can escape his origin. And once arrived among the Birds, Pisthetairos promptly exhibits the national quality from which he is trying to escape. He is daring, acquisitive, ruthlessly energetic, inventive, and a thorough-paced imperialist. And finally, in the apotheosis that closes the play, he arrives at his logical destination — divinity. For πολυπραγμοσύνη, as Aristophanes ironically observed, is moved by nothing less than man's divine discontent with his condition, and the hunger of the Athenians to be supreme, and therefore god.

29 dying to go tell it to the Birds: Literally, the Greek says "dying to go to the crows," a common Athenian imprecation, and roughly equivalent to "go to perdition" or "go to hell" in English. Pisthetairos and Euelpides propose merely to follow the imprecation in its literal meaning — only to get lost en route.

32 Sakas': Cf. Glossary, SAKAS and the note on *even Exekestides,* above.

40 to pay their taxes: A slight modernization of the Greek which says: "to pay fines."

45 Because of legal locusts: Aristophanes' favorite complaint against Athens, and one to which the entire *Wasps* is devoted. But although Aristophanes here develops Athens' love of litigation as the major source of dissatisfaction, elsewhere throughout the play the other grievances emerge: the restless and mischievous Athenian character (called πολυπραγμοσύνη); the plague of informers; the victimization of the Allies; the ambition for power, an ambition which knows no limits and whose only goal is World Mastery (βασιλεία).

PISTHETAIROS:
Pssst! Hey!
EUELPIDES: What's up?
PISTHETAIROS: Look at my Crow
staring up in the air.
EUELPIDES: And my Magpie's gaping too.
It looks as though he's pointing his beak at the
    sky.
I'll bet that means there's Birds somewhere
55   hereabouts.
We'll find out soon enough if we make a ruckus.
PISTHETAIROS:
I know. Try kicking the side of the cliff with
    your foot.°
EUELPIDES:
Go bash it with your head. You'll make more
    noise.
PISTHETAIROS:
Pick up a rock and pound.
EUELPIDES: Good idea. I'll try.

(*He picks up a rock and pounds on the
cliff, shouting.*)

Boy! Hey, boy!
PISTHETAIROS:
60   Don't call old Hoopoe "boy."
You'd better say, "Ho, Hoopoe!" or "Hey,
    Epops!"
EUELPIDES:
Hey, Hoopoe!

(*No answer.*)

            Hmmm. Shall I try him again?
Yoohoo, Hoopoe!

(*A concealed door in the cliff suddenly
swings open and a* SANDPIPER *with an enormous curved beak peers out, almost spitting*
PISTHETAIROS.)

SANDPIPER: What are you whooping about?
EUELPIDES:
Apollo help us! What a beak on the Bird!

(*In his fright he lets go of his* MAGPIE *who
flaps off.* PISTHETAIROS *falls backward, losing
his* CROW, *while the* SANDPIPER *retreats in
horror.*)

SANDPIPER:
Halp!
        Nest-robbers! Egg-stealers! Bird-catchers!
65   Halp!

57 **Try kicking the side of the cliff with your
foot:** As the Scholiast explains it, this line is an echo
of a children's jingle: "Kick the rock with your foot,
and the birds will fall down."

EUELPIDES:
You hear that? His bark is worse than his beak.
SANDPIPER:
Mortals, you die!
EUELPIDES: But we're not men.
SANDPIPER: What are you?
EUELPIDES:
Me? I'm *turdus turdus*. An African migrant.°
SANDPIPER:
What nonsense.
EUELPIDES:
            Not nonsense, crap. Look at my feet.
SANDPIPER (*indicating* PISTHETAIROS):
And that bird over there? What's his species?
PISTHETAIROS: Me? 70
Brown-tailed Smellyrump. Quail family.
EUELPIDES (*to* SANDPIPER):   Say,
what about you, Birdie? What the hell are you?
SANDPIPER:
I'm a Slavebird.°
EUELPIDES:
            I see. Some bantam thrash you
in a scrap?
SANDPIPER:
            No, but when the boss got himself
    changed
into a Hoopoe, I put in my application for
    feathers too   75
so I could stay in his service, doing odd jobs
    and buttling.
EUELPIDES:
And since when have our Birds been having
    butlers?
SANDPIPER:
He gets the habit, I think, from having once
    been human.
But suppose he wants some sardines. Up I
    jump,
dash down with a dish and catch him some
    fish.   80
If it's soup he wants, I grab a little ladle
and skitter to the kettle.
EUELPIDES: Quite the runner, eh?
Tell you what, runner-bird: just skitter inside
and fetch your master out.

68 **I'm *turdus turdus*. An African migrant:** I have
taken a liberty here in an attempt to make English
of the Greek which literally says: "I'm a Scared-
stifflet. A Libyan species." *Turdus turdus* (the scientific name of the thrush) seemed to introduce the
right scientific note, as well as to accommodate the
obscenity which follows.
73 **I'm a Slavebird:** Cock-fighting cant. Greeks
called the loser in a cock-fight the "slave" of the
winner.

SANDPIPER: But he's napping now.
He gorged himself silly on a mess of midges
85   and myrtle.
EUELPIDES:
His nap be damned. Go wake him.
SANDPIPER: I warn you:
He'll be grumpy. But just for a favor I'll do it.

(*Exit* SANDPIPER.)

PISTHETAIROS:
And then drop dead.

(*To* EUELPIDES.)

              — Whoosh, I'm still shaking.
EUELPIDES:
Me too. And guess what. My Magpie's gone,
got clear away.
PISTHETAIROS:
90   *Got away?* Why you big baby,
were you so scared you dropped your load?
EUELPIDES: Well,
what about you? Where's your bird?
PISTHETAIROS: Where's my bird?
Right here in my hand.°
EUELPIDES: Right where?
PISTHETAIROS: Well, he was here.
EUELPIDES:
And where were you? Holding on for dear life?
HOOPOE (*from within*):
CLEAR THE COPSE, I SAY, AND WHEEL
95   ME OUT!

(*The eccyclema wheels out the* HOOPOE,
*sitting on a pile of brush and peering out
from a thicket. Except for his huge crest and
beak and a few bedraggled feathers here and
there, the* HOOPOE *is human.*)

EUELPIDES:
Holy Herakles! That's no Bird, it's a freak.
Get a load of that plumage! What a tiara!
HOOPOE:
Who *are* you?
EUELPIDES:
           Birdie, you looked bedraggled.
I'll bet the gods° gave you some nasty knocks.

HOOPOE:
You dare sneer at my plumage? I, strangers,   100
was once a man.
EUELPIDES: Oh, we're not laughing at you.
HOOPOE:
Then, what's so funny?
EUELPIDES: Your beak. It tickles me.
HOOPOE:
I am dressed as the poet Sophokles disfigures
    me°
in that atrocious tragedy of his entitled *Tereus*.
EUELPIDES: Gee,
you're Tereus in person?
                Are you Bird or Peacock?   105
HOOPOE (*with ferocious dignity*):
I am a Bird.
EUELPIDES:
Then what happened to your feathers, Bird?
HOOPOE:
They've fallen out.
EUELPIDES: Caught the mange, I suppose?
HOOPOE:
I'll ignore that remark.
              All Birds moult in winter,°
and then in spring we grow fresh feathers back.
Now then, suppose you tell me who *you* are.
EUELPIDES: Mortals.   110
HOOPOE:
Country?
EUELPIDES:
      Athens, land of lovely — warships.
HOOPOE:
Then you must be jurymen.°
EUELPIDES: No, just the reverse:
we're non-jurymen.
HOOPOE:
    I thought that species had become extinct
in Athens.

---

93 **Right here in my hand:** If, as I suspect — contrary to the belief of most scholars — the phallus was worn in Aristophanic comedy, these words have a point that is otherwise lacking. Pisthetairos, having let his bird escape, finds himself holding his own phallus in terror. It is good fun based on good observation.

99 **I'll bet the gods:** The Greek introduces the official *Twelve* Gods here, probably for emphasis. I have omitted them for clarity's sake.

103 **as the poet Sophokles disfigures me:** Sophokles had produced a tragedy called *Tereus* (lost) in which he may have described Tereus' metamorphosis into a Hoopoe. In the Aristophanic play, Tereus is obviously only slightly — and rather shabbily — metamorphosed, and he ascribes his shabbiness to his Sophoklean origins.

In appearance the European Hoopoe is a stunning and unusual bird, with brilliant black and white wing pattern and pink plumage and splendid black-tipped erectile crest.

108 **All Birds moult in winter:** With this statement the Hoopoe realistically accounts for his bedraggled plumage in March, when the play was performed.

112 **Then you must be jurymen:** The familiar taunt: everybody in Athens is on a jury.

EUELPIDES:
You can still find a few growing wild —°
if you look hard enough.

HOOPOE:
115 But what brings you here, gentlemen?

EUELPIDES:
Your assistance and advice.

HOOPOE: My advice? About what?

EUELPIDES:
You were mortal once as we are mortal now.
You once were plagued with creditors, and
we're plagued now.
You welshed on your debts; we welsh on our
debts now.
But though you were mortal once, you became
120 a Bird
and flew the circuit of the spreading earth and
sea;
yet both as Bird and Man you understand.
And so we come to you, to ask your help,
bearing our hope that you may know some
land,
125 some country like a blanket, soft and snug,°
between whose folds two tired men might flop.

HOOPOE:
And Athens won't do? You want something
more . . . splendid?

EUELPIDES:
It wasn't exactly splendor we had in mind. No,
130 we wanted a country that was made for just *us*.

HOOPOE:
Ah, something more exclusive? An Aristocracy
perhaps?

EUELPIDES:
Ugh. Can't abide that Aristokrates.

HOOPOE: But my dear fellow,
what *do* you want?

EUELPIDES: Oh, the sort of country
where the worst trouble I could have would be
135 friends trooping to my door bright and early
in the morning to pester me with invitations
to dinner:
"C'mon, old boy, I'm throwing a big celebration.
So fresh up, give your kiddies a bath,

and come on over. And don't go standing me up,
or I won't turn to you when I'm in trouble." 140

HOOPOE:
Zeus, you like your troubles pleasant, don't you?

(*To* PISTHETAIROS.)

And you?

PISTHETAIROS:
I like pleasant troubles too.

HOOPOE: For instance?

PISTHETAIROS:
For instance, this. Some pretty little boy's old
man
comes up, really peeved, giving me hell:
"Fine way you treat my son, you old stinker! 145
You met the boy coming home from the baths
and never fondled him, never even kissed him
or tickled his balls. And *you*, his daddy's pal!"

HOOPOE:
Poor old bastard, you *are* in love with trouble.
Well, I've got just the place to please you
both. 150
Now, down on the Red Sea —

EUELPIDES: Sweet gods, not the sea!
No, sir. I don't want any court-officials with
summons°
and subpoenas showing up on ships at the
crack of dawn.
Look here, don't you know of some city in
Hellas?

HOOPOE:
Well now, there's always Lepreus? How would
that suit you? 155

EUELPIDES:
Lepreus? Never heard of it. Offhand, I'd say
no.
Smacks of old Melanthios. He's leprous.

HOOPOE: Hmmm.
Well, how about Opous then?

EUELPIDES: Count me out.
If Opountios comes from Opous,° then Opous
isn't for me. You couldn't pay me to live there. 160

---

114 **You can still find a few growing wild:** Aristophanes means that the only Athenians still un-
touched by the national disease of litigation were
countrymen. The countryside breeds ἀπραγμοσύνη;
the city, πολυπραγμοσύνη which finds expression in
the suits brought by informers, etc.

125 **some country like a blanket, soft and snug:**
ἀπραγμοσύνη again.

152 **court-officials with summons:** Euelpides is
terrified by the thought of officials with summonses
who may show up *anywhere* near the sea, even the
Red Sea. The Greek mentions the "Salaminia," the
galley used in Athens for official business, the
very vessel which had, a few months earlier, been
despatched to Sicily with orders for the recall of
Alkibiades to Athens to stand trial.

159 **If Opountios comes from Opous:** The pun
here is untranslatable. Opountios was a one-eyed
Athenian informer; Opous was a town in Lokris,
and the word Oupountios designates an inhabitant
of Opous as well as the Athenian informer.

But look here, what kind of life do you Birds
   lead?
You should know. You've lived here long
   enough.
HOOPOE:
Life among the Birds? Not bad. And you don't
   need cash.
EUELPIDES:
Well that's the worst of life's big swindles
   disposed of.
HOOPOE:
165 We scour the gardens for food, pecking mint,
scrabbling for poppyseed, sesame and myrtle-
   berries . . .
EUELPIDES:
Gods alive, that's not life! That's a honey-
   moon!°
PISTHETAIROS (*suddenly illuminated*):
WAIT!
             WONDERFUL!
                        I'VE GOT IT!
                              WHAT A SCHEME!
If you Birds will just do what I say, we'll make
   it succeed.
HOOPOE:
Do what?
PISTHETAIROS:
170   First, take my advice. For instance,
stop flapping around with your beaks hanging
   open.
It looks undignified and people jeer at the
   Birds.
In Athens whenever we see some silly ass,
we ask, "Hey, who's that Bird?" and people say,°
175 "Oh, *him*? He's a real bat, dumb as a dodo,
booby, that's what, hasn't got the brains of a
   Bird."
HOOPOE:
A palpable hit. And we deserve it too.
But what remedy do you suggest?
PISTHETAIROS: Found your own city.
HOOPOE:
Found *our own city*? But who ever heard
of a City of Birds?
PISTHETAIROS:
180   O Hebetude, thy name is Hoopoe!
Look down there.

167 **That's a honeymoon!:** Poppyseed was used in
making wedding cakes, and myrtle berries were used
for wedding wreaths.
   174 **and people say:** In the manuscript it is Teleas
— and not people — who sneers at the Birds. Teleas
was evidently an extremely flighty and silly Athenian
official and Aristophanes' point is the obvious one:
it takes a Bird to recognize a Bird.

HOOPOE: I'm looking.
PISTHETAIROS: Now look up there.
HOOPOE:
I'm looking.
PISTHETAIROS:
             Way up. Crane your neck.
HOOPOE: By Zeus,
I'll be a helluva sight if I sprain my neck look-
   ing.
PISTHETAIROS:
See anything?
HOOPOE:
             Nothing but clouds and a mess of sky.
PISTHETAIROS:
Precisely. That mess of sky is the sphere of the
   Birds.   185
HOOPOE:
Sphere? How do you mean?
PISTHETAIROS: Habitat, as it were.
The heavens, you see, revolve upon a kind of
   pole°
or axis, whence we call the sky a sphere.
Well then, you settle in your sphere, you build
   your walls,
and from this sphere of yours a city will appear.   190
And then, my friend, you'll be lords of all
   mankind
as once you were merely lords of locusts and
   bugs.
As for the gods, if they object or get in your
   way,
you can wipe them all out by starvation.°
HOOPOE: Wipe them out?
But *how*?

187 **The heavens, you see, revolve upon a kind
of pole:** This line and the three that follow it involve a series of untranslatable puns and some difficult scientific jargon. The Greek for "the vault of
the heavens" is πόλος, which leads naturally to
πολεῖται (revolves), which resembles πολῖται (citizens), which in turn yields πόλις (city). The argument is a fine specimen of sophistic doubletalk.
   194 **wipe them all out by starvation:** The manuscript says literally, "wipe them out with a Melian
famine." The year before the performance of *The
Birds*, the small neutral island of Melos had been
blockaded by an Athenian fleet and reduced by slow
starvation. When finally captured, the entire male
population was put to the sword and the women
and children enslaved.
   It is, of course, a deliberate part of Aristophanes'
general ironic design that the tactics used by Pisthetairos against the gods are, in fact, the brutal military tactics of Athenian imperialism. However fantastic the play may seem, its purpose is the relentless
satirical equation of Athens and Cloudcuckooland.

PISTHETAIROS:
Your air is the boundary between
earth and heaven.
Now just as we, when we make a trip to Delphi,
are required to secure a visa from the Theban government,
so you, when men propose a sacrifice to heaven,
impose a boycott, refusing your passport to these offerings
and forbidding any transit through your land,
until the gods agree to pay you tribute.

HOOPOE: By Earth!
Holy Snares! Sweep Springes and Nets!
A trickier gimmick I never heard of yet!
We'll put it to a vote. A referendum. We'll enlist your help
and build our city, provided the Birds agree.

PISTHETAIROS:
But who will make the motion?

HOOPOE: You, of course.
Don't worry. They don't twitter nonsense any more.
They used to chirp, but now I've taught them Greek.

PISTHETAIROS:
But can we muster a quorum?

HOOPOE: Nothing simpler.
I'll just step behind this little thicket here
and wake my sleeping wife, my lovely Nightingale.
We'll do a small duet and whistle them here.
They'll all come flocking in when they hear our song.

PISTHETAIROS:
Hoopoe, old Bird, you're wonderful!
But hurry. Quick.
Go wake your sleeping Nightingale and sing your song.

(The HOOPOE retires and begins to sing.)

HOOPOE:
Awake from sleep, my love!
Sing, O tawnythroat,
bird with honeyed tongue!
Awake and sing
your song and mine,
Itys, Itys!

(From the thicket the flute begins its obbligato in imitation of the song of the Nightingale at her most melancholy.)

Pure sound of sorrow!
Hear it rise,
a grief that goes,
Itys, Itys!

from the ivy's dark,
the tangled leaves,
and climbs and soars,
Itys, Itys!
till lord Apollo hears,
god with golden hair,
and sweeps his lovely lyre
in echo of your song,
Itys, Itys!
and throats that cannot die
sing the sorrow back,
Itys! Itys! Itys!

(There is a short coda by the flute, accompanied now by the distant sweeping of the lyre.)

EUELPIDES:
Holy Zeus, just hear the little Birdie's song!
A sound like honey streaming through the woods . . .

PISTHETAIROS: Pssst.
Hush.

EUELPIDES:
Hush? But why?

PISTHETAIROS: Shush.

EUELPIDES: But why?

PISTHETAIROS:
The Hoopoe is preening to sing another song.

HOOPOE (singing, with flute obbligato):
Epopopopopopopopoi!
Popopopopopopoi!
Io! Io! Io!
Hear ye ye ye ye ye ye ye!

(Calling first to the landbirds.)

O Birds of fellow feather come!
Come, you Birds who graze, who feed
over the farmers' fresh-sown fields!
Barley-eating tribes, in thousands come!
O peckers after seeds, hungry nations,
swift of wing! Come, O chirrupers!
All you who flitter in the furrows,
who throng, who flock the new-turned sod,
who sing your chirrup, chirrup-song,
tio tio tio tio tio tio tio!

All you who in the gardens nest,
who perch beneath the ivy's leaves!
O rangers on the mountain, come,
arbutus-stealers, olive-thieves!
Flock, fly to my call! Come, O come!
trio trio trio totobrix!

(To the Birds of marsh and meadow.)

O Birds of swamp and river, come!

You whose beaks snap up the whining gnats,
who splash in water where the earth is wet
or skim the meadows over Marathon!
265   O Birds of blazoned feather, come!

(*To the Seabirds.*)

Come, Birds who soar upon the sea
where the kingfisher swoops!
O Birds with delicate necks,
O taper-throated, come!
270   Come and see the world remade!
Come and see the Birds reborn!

Lo, a MAN has come, of skill and craft,
    whose wit cuts like a knife,
and to the Birds he brings the Word
275   of more abundant life.

Hear ye, hear ye, hear ye!
Come to council, come!
Hither, hither, hither!

    Toro toro toro tix
280   *kikka bau, kikka bau*
    toro toro toro li
        li lix!

PISTHETAIROS:
Hey, seen any Birds yet?
EUELPIDES: Not a sign of one.
And my neck's damn near broken from looking
    too.
PISTHETAIROS:
The way it looks to me, the Hoopoe hopped
285   in
and whooped himself hoarse, and all for noth-
    ing.
HOOPOE:
            Toro tix! Toro tix!

(*As the* HOOPOE's *call ends, the first member of the* CHORUS *enters. He is dressed as a
Flamingo and is shortly followed by other
members, each costumed in broad representation of some bird.*)

PISTHETAIROS:
Pssst. Euelpides! Look over there! There's a
    Bird coming in!
EUELPIDES:
By Zeus, it *is* a Bird! What do you suppose he
    is? A
290   Peacock?

(*Enter* HOOPOE.)

PISTHETAIROS:
The Hoopoe will tell us.
            — Say, what sort of Bird is that?

HOOPOE:
That, my friend, is a rare marshbird. Not the
    sort of Bird you run into every day.
EUELPIDES: Golly, what a flaming red!
HOOPOE:
Exactly. That Bird's a Flamingo.
EUELPIDES: Oooh. Look.
PISTHETAIROS: What is it?
EUELPIDES:
That Bird.

(*Enter a second bird, dressed in gorgeous
Persian costume, with a magnificent strut.*)

PISTHETAIROS:
            Say, he's exotic. Like something out of
    Aischylos.°   295
Prithee, sir,
how is yon strange and mountain-ranging man-
    tic Bird
yclept?
HOOPOE:
We call him the Bedouin Bird.
PISTHETAIROS: You don't say? The Bedouin   300
Bird! But how could a Bedouin Bird get to
    Greece without
a Camel Bird?
EUELPIDES:
And look there! There comes another Bird
    with a
whopping crest.

    (*Enter a* HOOPOE.)

PISTHETAIROS:
Say, that's odd. You mean you aren't the only
    Hoopoe   305
going? Is he a Hoopoe too?
HOOPOE: Yes indeed, he's a Hoopoe too.
But he's the son of the Hoopoe in Philokles'
    tragedy of
Tereus.° I'm his grandpa, and he's my name-
    sake,

295 **Like something out of Aischylos:** The line
which follows is a quotation from the (lost)
Edonoi of Aischylos.
307–308 **the son of the Hoopoe in Philokles' tragedy of** *Tereus:* The passage is a complicated one. But
its basis seems to be an elaborate comparison between three generations of Hoopoes and three generations of the family of Kallias, and its point is
surely (1) a charge of plagiarism against the tragedian Philokles and (2) the charge of profligacy
against the younger Kallias.
    There are three *Hoopoes:* (1) Hoopoe *grandpère*
(the Hoopoe who married Prokne and the hero of
Sophokles' *Tereus*); (2) Hoopoe *père* (the Hoopoe
of Philokles' *Tereus,* a plagiarism of — and therefore descended from — Sophokles' play); and (3)

Hoopoe Jr. — You know the pattern, the way Kallias calls
his son Hipponikos, and then these Hipponi-
310   koses call all
their sons Kalliases.

EUELPIDES:
So this is the Kallias Hoopoe. Well, he sure looks plucked.

HOOPOE:
He's quite the bird about town, so parasites strip him bare
and the chorus girls keep yanking his pretty feathers out.

(*Enter a dazzlingly brilliant bird with an enormous crest and a great protruding belly.*)

EUELPIDES:
Sweet Poseidon! Look at that gorgeous Birdie
315   strutting in!
What's he called?

HOOPOE:
That one? He's the Crested Guzzleguzzle.

EUELPIDES:
The Guzzleguzzle, eh? I thought that was our boy
Kleonymos.°

PISTHETAIROS:
No, this Bird has a crest. Our man is crestfallen now.
Don't you remember how he ditched his
320   helmet and ran
away?

EUELPIDES:
Look, Hoopoe, what's the point of all this crestwork on the
Birds?° Dress parade?

Hoopoe *fils*, the dissolute and bedraggled Hoopoe of the Chorus. To these correspond: (1) Kallias *grandpère*, a distinguished Athenian; (2) Hipponikos, son of Kallias (1), and also distinguished; and (3) Kallias *fils*, the unworthy and profligate scion of a distinguished line. (The family was evidently addicted to alternating names with each generation: Kallias, Hipponikos, Kallias, Hipponikos, etc.)
317–318 **our boy Kleonymos:** Kleonymos was a notorious glutton and an equally notorious coward. Since cowards have lost their crests (by throwing away their helmets on the battlefield), the Crested Guzzleguzzle should not be confused with Kleonymos.
322–323 **this crestwork on the Birds:** This joke depends upon a pun on the word λόφος, which means: (1) the crest of a bird, (2) the summit — or crest — of a hill.

HOOPOE: No. Partly self-defence, partly sanitation.
Some towns are built on crests of hills, others in the passes.   325
So some Birds sport their plumes on top, but others on their asses.

PISTHETAIROS:
What an ungodly crowd of Birds! It gives me the jitters.

(*The rest of the* CHORUS, *birds of every size and description, now stream into the orchestra.*)

Look, Birds everywhere!

EUELPIDES: Apollo, what a bevy of Birds!
Why, when they lift up their wings, they block out the
entrance.   330

PISTHETAIROS:
Look, there's the Partridge!

EUELPIDES:
And here's the Hooded Ptarmigan!

PISTHETAIROS:
And there's a Widgeon, I think.

EUELPIDES: Here comes a female Plover.
But who's that Bird on her tail?

PISTHETAIROS:
Her lover. The Horny Pecker.°

EUELPIDES:
What does her husband say?

PISTHETAIROS:
He's a queer Bird and doesn't care.

HOOPOE:
Here's the Owl.

PISTHETAIROS:
Now there's a thought! Bringing Owls to Athens.°   335

HOOPOE:
And Jay and Pigeon. Lark, Wren, Wheatear, and
Turtledove. Ringdove, Stockdove, Cuckoo, and Hawk.
Firecrest and Wren, Rail and Kestrel and Gull, Waxwing,
Woodpecker, and Vulture . . .

---

333 **Her lover. The Horny Pecker:** This is Arrowsmith, not Aristophanes, and so too is the following line. But the lines seemed to me utterly untranslatable since they involved an impossible pun on the word κειρύλος (which means both "kingfisher" and "barber") and an obscure barber by the name of Sporgilos. In the circumstances it seemed better to betray the letter than the spirit.
335 **Bringing Owls to Athens:** The Athenian equivalent of "bringing coals to Newcastle."

(In one last surge the remaining members of the CHORUS *stream into the orchestra, ruffling their feathers and chirping and hissing.)*

PISTHETAIROS:
Birds, Birds, billions of Birds!

EUELPIDES *(indicating the Audience)*:
340   But most of them Cuckoos and Geese.

PISTHETAIROS:
What a skittering and cackling!

EUELPIDES: Unless I'm much mistaken,
I detect a note of menace.°

PISTHETAIROS:
             They *do* seem somewhat peeved.
You know, I think they're glaring at *us*.

EUELPIDES: Damn right they are.

KORYPHAIOS:
Who-oo-chee-who-chee-who-oo-oo-oo
345 who-oo-chee-oo-oo has summoned me?

HOOPOE:
Me, that's who. Your old friend Hoopoe.

KORYPHAIOS:
Spea-pea-pea-pea-speak, Hoopopopopopoi.

HOOPOE:
Listen. Great news! Glorious news!
News of Profit, gravy for all!
350 Two brilliant men have come to call
on me.

KORYPHAIOS:
On YOU?
             But HOW?
                          And WHO?

HOOPOE:
But I'm trying to tell you.
             Two old men have come to call,
two old refugees who have renounced the
human race for good

342 **I detect a note of menace:** The effect of the entire following scene depends upon our understanding of the *natural* hostility between Birds and Man (cf. l. 360). In a country policed by the bird-loving vigilantes of the Audubon Society, Aristophanes' Birds might seem unreasonably hostile and suspicious of human motives. But anyone who has ever seen a Mediterranean bird-market or been offered pickled thrushes or *uccellini con polenta* will understand. Those who do not are advised to read closely the second Parabasis(l. 1281) and to ponder Pisthetairos' little poem at l. 606. Seen in the light of this total hostility, Pisthetairos' persuasion of the Birds is an extraordinary feat, designed, I believe, in order to exhibit his characteristic Athenian resourcefulness and eloquence and cunning.

and who bring us a glorious scheme, a Plan of
fantastic proportions,
gigantic, sublime, colossal —

KORYPHAIOS:
             Colossal's the word for your blunder. 355
Have you lost your mind?

HOOPOE: Wait, listen . . .

KORYPHAIOS: Explain. And fast.

HOOPOE:
Listen. I welcomed two old men. Harmless
ornithologists,
infatuated with the Birds. They want to live
with their
Feathered Friends.

KORYPHAIOS:
What? You welcomed TWO MEN?

HOOPOE: What's more, I'd do it again. 360

KORYPHAIOS:
You mean they're *here*? In our midst?

HOOPOE: As much as I. Look.

(He raises his wings, revealing the two men cowering behind him.)

CHORUS:
— O Treachery!
             O Treason!
                          — O!
BAD Hoopoe, to betray us so!
To think that you, the Birdies' friend,
could come to such a wicked end! 365
To think that I should one day see
the Bird who pecked the corn with me
             dishonor and disgrace
the MAGNA CARTA of our race,
             and sell us to our foe! 370
— O Treachery!
             O Treason!
                          — O!

KORYPHAIOS:
All right, we'll settle accounts with this treacherous Hoopoe later.
As for these venerable old fools, we'll settle
with them right now.
We'll shred them into tatters.

PISTHETAIROS:
             Gods, they're shredding us to tatters!

EUELPIDES:
Well, it's all your fault. This whole damn trip
was your idea. 375
Why in god's name did you lead me here?

PISTHETAIROS: To bring up my rear.

EUELPIDES:
It's so hopeless I could cry.

PISTHETAIROS:
             Fat chance you'll have of crying.

Once those Birds are through with you, you
    won't have any
eyes.

CHORUS:
380   Advance the wings and charge the flanks!
       The Rooster shrills ATTACK!
     Aerial squadrons, take to the air!
       Beat your enemy back.

     These men are spies, their lives are lies,
385   so kill without regrets!
     The skill to kill lies in your bills.
       Your beaks are bayonets.

     No cloud exists, no breaker is,
       no fog on mountain peaks,
390   quite big or thick or black enough
       to save them from our beaks!

KORYPHAIOS:
Mount the attack!
       Charge them, Birds! Bite them, tear them!
On the double!
          Captain on the right! Advance
     your wing and charge!

(*The* CHORUS *wheels in massed formation
toward the stage.* EUELPIDES *in terror starts
to run.*)

EUELPIDES:
They're charging! Where can we run?
    PISTHETAIROS: Run, man? Stand and fight!
EUELPIDES:
And get torn to tatters?
PISTHETAIROS:
395   What good's running? *They*'re flying.
EUELPIDES:
But what should I do?
PISTHETAIROS:
         Listen to me and follow my orders.
First pick up that platter and use it as a shield.
    Now HOLD THAT LINE!
EUELPIDES:
But what good's a platter?
PISTHETAIROS:
         Birds are skittish of platters.°
         They'll scatter.

---

398 **Birds are skittish of platters:** In the Greek it
is owls who are said to be skittish of platters. The
reason for this skittishness is not known; it may be
because owls are sacred to Athena and Athena was
supposed to have invented the art of pottery. I preferred in the circumstances to emphasize the Birds'
terror of becoming a meal.

EUELPIDES:
Yeah? Well, what about that vulture there?
    PISTHETAIROS: Snatch up a skewer.   400
Now stick it out front like a spear.
    EUELPIDES: But what about my eyes?
PISTHETAIROS:
Jam a jug on your head. Now cover your eyes
    with saucers.
EUELPIDES:
What a kitchen tactician! What crockery-
    strategy! Gee,
old Nikias is tricky, but he can't compare with
    you.
KORYPHAIOS:
FORWARD!
    Spit them with your beaks! At 'em, Birds!
                CHARGE!   405
Rip 'em, scratch 'em, flay 'em, bite! BUT
    BREAK THAT
POT!
HOOPOE (*intervening*):
Truce, truce.
         No more of this bitterness. You
    Birds should be ashamed.
Why should you kill these men? What harm
    have they done to you?
Somewhat more to the point, they're both
    closely related to my wife.°   410
KORYPHAIOS:
Why spare these men any more than wolves?
    What worse
enemy than men do we Birds have?
    HOOPOE: Enemies by nature, I admit.
But these men are exceptions to the rule. They
    come to you as friends.
Moreover, they bring a scheme from which we
    Birds stand to profit.
KORYPHAIOS:
Are you suggesting that Birds should take
    advice from men?
What can *we* learn from men?   415
    HOOPOE:
         If wise men learn from their enemies,
then why not you?
         Remember the advantage of
    keeping an open mind.
Preparedness, after all, is not a lesson taught us
    by our friends
but by our enemies. It is our enemies, not our
    friends, who teach us to survive.

---

410 **closely related to my wife:** Tereus' wife
Prokne was Athenian and all Athenians regarded
themselves as related by virtue of the very kinship-
structure of the city.

I might cite the case of cities: was it from
their friends or their foes
that mankind first learned to build walls and
ships in self-defence?
But that one lesson still preserves us all and all
we have.

KORYPHAIOS:
There's something in what you say.
                    Perhaps we'd better hear them.

PISTHETAIROS (*to* EUELPIDES):
They're beginning to show signs of reason.
Don't say a word.

HOOPOE (*to the* CHORUS):
That's better, friends. You're doing right, and
you'll thank
me for it later.

KORYPHAIOS:
We've never disobeyed your advice before.

PISTHETAIROS:
                    They seem more peaceful now.
So you can ground the pan
and put the platter down.
But stand your ground
and keep that spit on hand,
while I look round
our little camp of crocks
and see how matters stand
by peeking over pots.

EUELPIDES:
Chief, suppose we die
in combat?

PISTHETAIROS:
                    Then we'll lie
in Athens at public cost.°
They'll give us hero's honors
and bury us like gods
when we say our lives were lost
fighting foreign soldiers
at very heavy odds.
In fact, I'll use those very words
(omitting, for effect, of course
any reference to Birds.)°

KORYPHAIOS:
All right, you Birds, FALL IN!

438 **in Athens at public cost:** Soldiers who fell on
the battlefield for Athens were buried at public
expense in the Kerameikos outside the city.
446 **any reference to Birds:** Literally, the Greek
says, "we will say that we died fighting the enemy
at Orneai." "At Orneai" in the Greek is a pun on
ὄρνις (bird), i.e., "at Birdland," and the town of
Orneai which lay between Korinth and Sikyon and
which, in 416, underwent a bloodless one-day
siege.

The war's over.
                    AT EASE!
You there, quiet!
                    QUIET, PLEASE!

(*The* CHORUS *returns to its normal position
in the orchestra. Much whispering, nodding,
and shuffling. Then silence.*)

Now we have to inquire
who these strangers are
and why they've come.
Look here, Hoopoe.

HOOPOE: Um?

KORYPHAIOS:
Who are these fellows?

HOOPOE:
Two humans from Hellas
where genius grows greener than grass.

KORYPHAIOS:
But why have they come?
What do they hope to get from the Birds?

HOOPOE:
Their motive is Love.
Love is the burden of all their words.
Love of your life
and Love of you,
to live with you
in Love always.

KORYPHAIOS:
Is *that* what they say?
But what is the gist of their scheme?

HOOPOE:
They envisage a vision of glory,
a dream so fantastic
it staggers the sensible mind.

KORYPHAIOS:
Well, it doesn't stagger mine.
What's in it for them?
Who are they trying to stick?

HOOPOE:
No one.
                    This is no trick.
What this means is bliss.
Believe me, utter bliss. Sheer
and absolute.
                    Viz.
all shall be yours,
whatever is,
here or there,
far or near,
all, everywhere.
And this they swear.

KORYPHAIOS:
Crackpots, eh?

HOOPOE:

485
  Right as rain.
  Foxes, not men.
  Boxes of slyness,
  brimming with brain.

KORYPHAIOS:

Then let them talk! We're all in a twitter to
 hear.

HOOPOE:

So be it, then.
    — Men, take these weapons inside
the house and hang them up beside the
490 blazing hearth
where the god of fire presides. They'll bring us
 luck.

(Servants pick up the pots and plates and
skewers and carry them inside. The HOOPOE
turns to PISTHETAIROS.)

Pisthetairos, you have the floor. Proceed with
 your case.
Explain your proposal.

PISTHETAIROS:

    By Apollo, only on condition
that you Birds agree to swear a solemn truce
 with me
like the truce which that armor-making ba-
495 boon — you know who I mean — °
signed with his wife: no biting, scratching, or
 cutting,
no hauling around by the balls, no shoving
 things —

EUELPIDES (bending over):

— Up there?

PISTHETAIROS:

    In my eyes, I was going to say.

KORYPHAIOS:

We accept your terms.

PISTHETAIROS:

    First you have to swear to them.

KORYPHAIOS:

We swear it then, but on this one condition
500 only:
that you guarantee that this comedy of ours
 will win First
Prize by completely unanimous vote of the
 Judges.

PISTHETAIROS:

  Agreed.

495 **you know who I mean:** "The armor-making
baboon" seems to have been a certain knife-maker
called Panaitios who was married to an extremely
promiscuous shrew. They managed to arrive at a
marital *modus vivendi* only by making a formal
compact of truce.

KORYPHAIOS:

Splendid. If, however, we Birds should break
 the truce,
we agree to forfeit, say, forty-nine per cent
of the votes.

HOOPOE (to the CHORUS):

  Fall out!
    Pick up your weapons, men 505
and return at once to your quarters. On the
 double!
Company Assignments will be posted on the
 bulletin boards.

CHORUS:

— Man by nature is a liar made.
 He plays a double game.
— Dishonesty's his stock-in-trade. 510
 Deception is his name.
— We say no more.
    — But it may be
 your canny mortal brain may see
 what our poor feeble wits cannot —
— some gift of noble intellect 515
 we once possessed and then forgot
 as our race declined;
— some genius of the will
 or wisdom of the mind,
— grown rusty with neglect, 520
 but fusting in us still.
— It seems to us fantastic.
— But still, it *could* be true.
— And, of course, we'd split the profits —
— if any such accrue. 525

KORYPHAIOS:

Pisthetairos, proceed. You may say whatever
 you wish. With impunity.
We pledge you our words as Birds: we won't
 renege on the truce.

PISTHETAIROS:

By god, I'm wild to begin!
    The dough of my vision has risen,
and there's nothing now but the kneading.
    — Boy, bring me a wreath.
Someone fetch water for my hands.°

EUELPIDES: Hey, we going to a feast? 530

PISTHETAIROS:

A dinner of words, a fat and succulent haunch
 of speech,
a meal to shiver the soul.
    — Unhappy Birds, I grieve for you,
you who once were kings —

530 **Someone fetch water for my hands:** An
orator put on a crown of myrtle before beginning
his speech, but the wreath and the washing of hands
are the customary preparations for a feast; hence
Euelpides' question.

KORYPHAIOS: — Kings? Of what?
PISTHETAIROS: Kings of everything.
Kings of creation. My kings. This man's kings.
     Kings of king Zeus.
More ancient than Kronos. Older than Titans.
535   Older than Earth.
KORYPHAIOS:
Older than Earth?
PISTHETAIROS:
                Older than Earth.
KORYPHAIOS:
               And to think I never suspected!
PISTHETAIROS:
Because you're a lazy Bird° and you haven't
     reread your Aesop.
For Aesop states that the Lark is the oldest
     thing in the world,
older than Earth. So ancient, in fact, that
     when her father died,
she couldn't find him a grave, for the Earth
540   hadn't yet been made,
and therefore couldn't be dug. So what on
     earth could she do?
Well, the little Lark was stumped. Then
     suddenly she had it!
She laid her daddy out and buried him under
     her tail.
EUELPIDES:
She did for a fact.
          And that's how Asbury got its name.°
PISTHETAIROS:
Hence my argument stands thus: if the Birds
545   are older than Earth,
and therefore older than gods, then the Birds
     are the heirs of the world.
For the oldest always inherits.
     EUELPIDES: It stands to reason, friends.
So pack some bone in your bills and hone
     them down to a point.

537 **Because you're a lazy Bird:** In the Greek
κοὐ πολυπράγμων, uninquisitive, not on one's toes,
sluggish, without curiosity. The Birds' fallen estate
and decadence is directly traceable to their lack of
πολυπραγμοσύνη, Pisthetairos' most outstanding
trait. Cf. note on p. 267, *soft and lovely leisure.*

544 **And that's how Asbury got its name:** A
complicated bit of foolery crowned by Euelpides'
elaborate pun, which I have freely altered for the
effect. Pisthetairos actually says that, according to
"Aesop," the Lark buried her father in her own
head. The word for "head" in Greek is κεφαλή,
which is also the name of an Athenian deme. Hence
Euelpides' crack: the father of the Lark is buried
at κεφαλή.

Old Zeus won't rush to resign and let the
     Woodpeckers reign.°
PISTHETAIROS:
Think of it, the springtime of the world!
                         The Age of the Birds!   550
Primal lords of Creation! Absolute masters of
     man!
But the gods are mere upstarts and usurpers of
     very recent date.
And proof abounds.
               Let me adduce, for instance,
     the case of the Rooster.
Aeons and aeons ago, ages before the age of
     Darius,
the kingdom of Persia lay prostrate beneath
     the sway of the Rooster   555
And the Rooster, ever since, has been called
     the Persian Red.
EUELPIDES:
And that's why, even now, he swaggers and
     struts like a king
and keeps a harem of hens. And, unique
     among the Birds,
he wears the royal red tiara of the ancient
     Persian kings.
PISTHETAIROS:
And talk of power!
          Why, even now its memory remains,   560
enshrined in habit. For when the Cock his
     matins crows,
mankind goes meekly off to work — bakers,
     smiths, and potters,
tanners and merchants and musical-instrument
     makers.
And when he crows at dusk, the night-shift
     goes.
EUELPIDES:
          I'll vouch for that.
It was thanks to his night-shift crowing that I
     lost my warmest coat.   565
I'd gone downtown to dinner, see, in honor of
     a birth.
Well, after a while I'd had five or six and
     passed out cold,
when that blasted Rooster started to crow.
     Needless to say,
I thought it was dawn, jumped into my clothes
     and tore off to work.
But just outside the gate, somebody conked
     me with a club   570

549 **and let the woodpeckers reign:** Since the oak
tree was sacred to Zeus and the woodpeckers
attacked the oaks, Zeus would be particularly unwilling to yield his sceptre to the Woodpecker.

and I passed out cold again. And when I came
    to, no coat!
PISTHETAIROS:
What's more, once upon a time the Kites were
    the kings of
Hellas
KORYPHAIOS:
The *kings* of Hellas?
PISTHETAIROS:
    Right. The Kites were the kings of Hellas.
And it was during their reign that the custom
    began in Greece
575
of falling flat on your face whenever you saw a
    Kite.°
EUELPIDES:
You know, I once spotted a Kite and went
    down on the ground —
so damn hard I swallowed my money° and two
    of my teeth.
I damn near starved.
PISTHETAIROS:
    And once the Cuckoo was king of Egypt.
And when the call of the Cuckoo was heard in
    the land, every Egyptian
580
grabbed his scythe and ran to the fields to reap.
EUELPIDES: That's a fact.
And that's why, even today, we still call the
    Egyptians
cuckoo.°
PISTHETAIROS:
Why, so great was the power of the Birds that
    even the greatest kings —
Agamemnon and Menelaos, to name only two
585
of the greatest —
had their sceptres tipped with Birds, and the
    Birds got a cut in the take.
EUELPIDES:
So *that's* it. That explains all that funny
    business in the plays
I never understood before — where Priam, for
    instance, walks in,

and there on his sceptre, large as life, some
    Bird is perching.
I used to think he was there to keep an eye
    peeled down below   590
on the rows where the politicians sit,° to see
    where our money goes.
PISTHETAIROS:
But the crowning proof is this: the present
    incumbent, Zeus,
wears an Eagle upon his helmet as the symbol
    of royal power.
Athena uses the Owl, and Apollo, as aide to
    Zeus, a Hawk.
EUELPIDES:
By Demeter, they do! But why do the gods use
    these Birds   595
as emblems?
PISTHETAIROS:
An unconscious admission of the Birds' an-
    cient power and supremacy.
That's why when men sacrifice to the gods, the
    Birds swoop down and snatch the food,
thereby beating out the gods, and so asserting
    their old priority.
Again, no one ever swore by the gods, but
    always by the Birds.   600
EUELPIDES:
Doctors still swear by the Duck.° That's why
    we call them quacks.
PISTHETAIROS:
But these were the honors you held in the days
    of your
greatness.

Whereas now you've been downgraded.
You're the slaves, not lords, of men.   605
They call you brainless or crazy.
They kill you whenever they can.

The temples are no protection:
the hunters are lying in wait
with traps and nooses and nets   610
and little limed twigs and bait.

576 **falling flat on your face whenever you saw
a Kite:** The Kite was a harbinger of Spring, according to the Scholiast, and one which was evidently
welcomed with almost religious joy.
578 **I swallowed my money:** It was common in
antiquity for people to carry their coins in their
mouth, probably as a precaution against theft.
582–583 **we still call the Egyptians cuckoo:** The
cuckoo's call was in Egypt a call to reap, as
Pisthetairos explains. To this Euelpides replies with
a proverbial expression whose meaning is obscure —
though almost certainly obscene. Since I could not
translate what I could not understand, I have tried
to make Euelpides' reply consistent with his zaniness
elsewhere.

591 **on the rows where the politicians sit:** Literally, the Greek says that the birds on sceptres were
keeping an eye on Lysikrates, to see whether he was
bribed. Lysikrates was an Athenian general of a
dishonest and corrupt character.
601 **Doctors still swear by the Duck:** A deliberate
improvisation of my own to circumvent the com-
plexity of the Greek. Literally, the line reads:
"Lampon swears by the Goose when he's trying to
cheat you." Lampon was a notorious soothsayer, but
evidently superstitious enough that he tried to miti-
gate his perjury when fleecing a victim: instead of
swearing an oath by Zeus (Ζῆνα), he swore by the
Goose (Χῆνα).

And when you're taken, they sell you
as tiny *hors d'oeuvres* for a lunch.
And you're not even sold alone,
615 but lumped and bought by the bunch.

And buyers come crowding around
and pinch your breast and your rump,
to see if your fleshes are firm
and your little bodies are plump.

620 Then, as if this weren't enough,
they refuse to roast you whole,
but dump you down in a dish
and call you a *casserôle*.

They grind up cheese and spices
625 with some oil and other goo,
and they take this slimy gravy
and they pour it over you!

Yes, they pour it over you!

It's like a disinfectant,
630 and they pour it piping hot,
as though your meat were putrid,
to sterilize the rot!

Yes, to sterilize the rot!

(As PISTHETAIROS *finishes, a long low susur-
rus of grief runs through the* CHORUS *and
the Birds sigh, weep, and beat their breasts
with their wings.*)

CHORUS:
Stranger, forgive us if we cry,
635 reliving in your words
those years of cowardice that brought
disaster to the Birds: —
that tragic blunder
and our fathers' crime,
640 complacency whose cost
was greatness and our name,
as dignity went under
in a chicken-hearted time,
and all was lost.

645 But now, by luck,
or heaven-sent,
a Man has come
to pluck us from disgrace.

Hail, Pisthetairos!
650 Hail, Savior of the Birds,
Redeemer of our Race!
To you we now commit:
ourselves,
our nests,
655 our chicks,
et cet.

KORYPHAIOS:
Sir, you have the floor once more. Proceed
with your
explanation. Until our power is restored, life
means less
than nothing to the Birds.
PISTHETAIROS: My Plan, in gist, is this
— a city of the Birds,
whose walls and ramparts shall include the
atmosphere of the world   660
within their circuit. But make the walls of
brick, like Babylon.
EUELPIDES:
A Babylon of the Birds!° What a whopping,
jumbo-size city!
PISTHETAIROS:
The instant your walls are built, reclaim your
sceptre from Zeus.
If he shilly-shallies or fobs you off with a lot of
excuses,
proclaim a Holy War, a Great Crusade against
the gods.   665
Then slap embargoes on their lust, forbidding
any gods
in manifest state of erection to travel through
your sky
on amatory errands down to Earth to lay their
women —
their Semeles, Alkmenes, and so forth. Then,
if they attempt to ignore
your warning, place their offending peckers
under bond   670
as contraband and seal them shut. That will
stop their fun,
I think.
        Second, appoint some Bird as your
official ambassador
to men, and serve them formal notice that the
Birds demand priority
in all their sacrifices. The leftovers, of course,
will go to the gods.
But for the future, even when they offer
sacrifices to the gods,   675
each Bird must be paired with a god° —
whichever one seems most apt.

662 **A Babylon of the Birds!:** Cf. Glossary,
BABYLON.
676 **each Bird must be paired with a god:** These
pairs depend upon similarity in character or upon
puns, and I have altered several of them accordingly.
Thus in the manuscript Aphrodite is paired with
the phalarope (which is suggested by *phallos*);
Poseidon, god of the sea, is matched by a seabird;
the glutton Herakles by the cormorant; and Zeus,
king of the gods, by the wren, king of the birds.

Thus, if Aphrodite is offered a cake, the Wagtail will get one too.

When Poseidon gets his sheep, the Seagull must have his wheat.

Greedy Herakles shall eat — when the glutton Jay is fed.

And as for Zeus, why, Zeus must wait his turn until the Kinglet, [680]

lord of all the Birds, receives his sacrificial gnat.

EUELPIDES:

I *like* that gnat. Old has-been Zeus can rumble with rage!

KORYPHAIOS:

But why should men believe we're gods and not just shabby

Birds? These wings are a giveaway.

PISTHETAIROS:

Rubbish. Hermes is a god, isn't he?

But he goes flapping around on wings. And so do loads of gods. [685]

There's Victory on "gildered wings," and don't forget the god of Love.

And Homer says that Iris looks like a dove with the jitters.

EUELPIDES:

And lightning too, that's got wings. Hey, what if lightning

fell on us?

KORYPHAIOS:

And what if men are blind and go on truckling to Olympos [690]

and refuse to worship the Birds?

PISTHETAIROS:

Then swarms of starving Sparrows

shall descend on their fields in millions and gobble up their seeds.

They'll damn well go hungry. We'll see then if Demeter will feed them.

EUELPIDES:

If I know that Demeter, she'll have plenty of excuses ready.

PISTHETAIROS:

Then we'll muster the Crows and Ravens and send them down in droves [695]

to peck out the eyes of the oxen and make the sheep go blind.

Dr. Apollo can cure them — but I'd hate to pay the fee.

EUELPIDES:

Give me the nod when you're ready. I want to unload my

OX.

PISTHETAIROS:

If, on the other hand, mankind accepts you as their gods, [700]

their manifest Poseidon, their Earth, their Principle of Life,

all their wishes shall come true.

KORYPHAIOS:

All their wishes? For instance?

PISTHETAIROS:

Why, enormous plagues of locusts will not infest their vines:

a single regiment of our Owls will wipe the locusts out.

And the gallfly and the mite will no longer blight their figs [705]

since we'll send down troops of Thrushes to annihilate the bugs.

KORYPHAIOS:

But what about money? Money's Man's dominant passion.

PISTHETAIROS:

Duck soup for you. Your oracles will tell them what they

want — the whereabouts of the richest mines, when the

market is right to make a killing, and so forth. And no [710]

more shipwrecks either.

KORYPHAIOS:

No more shipwrecks?

PISTHETAIROS:

No shipwrecks. You take your omens, you see,

and some Bird pipes up, "Bad weather brewing" or "Forecast: fair."

EUELPIDES:

To hell with the Birds! A ship for me! I'm off to sea! [715]

PISTHETAIROS:

You'll show them buried treasure; you'll tell them where to find gold.

For Birds know all the answers, or so the saying goes —

"A little Bird told me." People are always saying that.

EUELPIDES:

The hell with the sea! A shovel for me! I'm off to dig for

gold! [720]

KORYPHAIOS:

But how will we give them health? That lies in the hands of

the gods.

PISTHETAIROS:

Give them wealth, you give them health. They're really

much the same.

EUELPIDES:
And that's a fact. The man who's sick is always
725   doing badly.
KORYPHAIOS:
But longevity and old age also lie in the hands
of the gods.
How will a man grow old if the gods refuse
him Old Age?
Will he die in childhood?
PISTHETAIROS:
                    Die? The Birds will add to his life
three centuries at least.
KORYPHAIOS: But how?
PISTHETAIROS:
                    From their own lives, of course.
What doth the poet say?
730   "Five lives of men the cawing Crow
outliveth."°
EUELPIDES:
                    Long live the Birds! Down with Zeus!
PISTHETAIROS: I'm with you there,
and think of the money we'll save!

For Birds won't want any shrines;
    marble just leaves them cold.
735   They don't give a hoot for temples
    with doors of beaten gold.

They'll live in woodses and copses —
    that's plenty of shrine for them.
And the social-register swells
740   can strut on an olive limb.°

And we'll go no more to Delphi!
    To hell with Ammon's seat!
We'll amble out under the olives
    and toss them bits of wheat,

745   and hold up our paws to heaven
    and make the Birds a prayer,
and the Birds will grant all our wishes
    for cutting them a share.

And we won't be out of pocket.
750   No, the only dough we'll need
is a little loaf of barley
    and a tiny pinch of seed.
KORYPHAIOS:
The Birds' best friend! And to think how we
    misjudged you
once, most generous of men!
            Ask us what you will. It shall be done.

730–731 "Five lives of men the cawing Crow
outliveth": A garbled echo of Hesiod, frag. 50.
    740 can strut on an olive limb: The olive was
sacred to Athena and hence should be acceptable
even to aristocratic birds.

CHORUS:
Amen, we say.   755

And now, presuming you concur,
    we Birds propose an oath
of mutual assistance, sir,
    and binding on us both.

Arm to wing, we'll soar to war!   760
    Our cause needs no excuse.
We'll storm up Mt. Olympos, friend,
    and make a pulp of Zeus!
KORYPHAIOS:
We await your orders, sir. Tasks that need
    mere brawn and muscle
we Birds can do. The complicated mental stuff
    we leave to you.   765
HOOPOE:
Action, dammit, action! That's what we need.
Strike while the iron's hot. No dawdling around
like slowpoke Nikias.
                    — Dear me, I nearly forgot.
You two gentlemen must see my little nest,
my trash of sticks and straw and kickshaw stuff.   770
And good heavens! We haven't been formally
    introduced.
PISTHETAIROS:
Pisthetairos here.
HOOPOE: Ah. And this gentleman?
EUELPIDES: Euelpides.
From Athens.
HOOPOE:
                    Enchanted, I'm sure.
PISTHETAIROS: The pleasure's ours.
HOOPOE:
Please come in.
PISTHETAIROS:
                    No, after you.
HOOPOE: This way, gentlemen.

(The HOOPOE begins to flap his wings to
flutter into his nest.)

PISTHETAIROS:
Hey, you!
            Damn it, stop! Back water, blast you!   775
Look here, what sort of partnership is this
    supposed to be
if you start taking off when we can't even fly?
HOOPOE:
Does it matter?
PISTHETAIROS:
                    Remember what old Aesop tells us°

778 Remember what old Aesop tells us: According to the Scholiast, the fable should be ascribed to
Archilochos rather than Aesop. But the gist of the
fable seems to be as follows. The Fox and the Eagle

in his fable of the Eagle and the Fox in business
who couldn't get along? The Fox got swindled
780   by the Eagle.
    HOOPOE:
Don't be nervous. I know of a wonderful
    magic roôt.
Merely nibble on it and you'll sprout a set of
    wings.
    PISTHETAIROS:
Splendid. Then let's go in.
              — You there, Xanthias.
Hey, Manodorus! Bring our luggage inside the
    house.
    KORYPHAIOS:
One moment, please, Hoopoe, when you go
    inside . . .
785   HOOPOE: Yes?
    KORYPHAIOS:
By all means take your human guests and feast
    them well.
But first do one little favor for the Chorus,
    please.
Bring out your wife, your lovely Nightingale,
the bird with honeyed tongue, the Muses'
    love,
790 and let the Chorus play with her a little while.
    PISTHETAIROS:
I add my entreaty to theirs. In the name of
    heaven,
bring her out from the bed of rushes where she
    hides.
    EUELPIDES:
Please, please do. Bring the pretty Birdie out.
I've never met a Nightingale before.
    HOOPOE: With all my heart.
I'd be delighted, gentlemen.

    (*Calling inside.*)

795   Oh Prokne! Prokne.
Please come out, my dear, and meet our visitors.

(*A lovely well-rounded young* FLUTEGIRL
*shyly appears. She is dressed in the rich
gold-encrusted robes of a young Athenian
matron of high birth. On her head she wears
the mask of the Nightingale.*)

    PISTHETAIROS:
Almighty Zeus! Gosh, what a baby of a Birdie!
What curves! What grace! What a looker!

---

swore lasting friendship and built their homes close
together: the Eagle up in the tree, the Fox at the
foot. During the Fox's absence one day, the Eagle
swooped down, carried off the Fox's cubs, and
proceeded to make a meal of them. The Fox, unable
to climb the tree, could not take vengeance.

    EUELPIDES: Gee! By god,
I'd like to bounce between her thighs right
    now!
    PISTHETAIROS:
And what a shimmer of gold! Just like a bride.   800
    EUELPIDES:
By god, I've got half a mind to kiss her!
    PISTHETAIROS: Look out,
you old lecher, her beak's a pair of skewers.
    EUELPIDES: Very well.
Then I'll treat her like an egg and peel her
    shell.
I'll lift her little mask and kiss her — so.
    HOOPOE:
Harrumph. This way.
    PISTHETAIROS:
        And may good fortune go with us.   805

(*Exeunt* PISTHETAIROS, EUELPIDES, *and*
HOOPOE, *followed by the slaves with the
luggage.*)

    CHORUS:
        O love,
            tawny throat!
        Sweet nightingale,
        musician of the Birds
        Come and sing,
            honey-throated one!   810
        Come, O love,
            flutist of the Spring,
        accompany our song.

(*The* CHORUS *turns sharply and faces the
audience,° while the* FLUTEGIRL *begins the
song of the nightingale at its most mournful. The flute obbligato accompanies the*
CHORUS *throughout.*)

813 s.d. **The** CHORUS **turns sharply and faces the
audience:** The Parabasis (or Digression), that part
of an Aristophanic comedy in which the Chorus
steps forth and addresses the audience directly,
usually on behalf of the poet. In this play the Parabasis is linked with unusual coherence to the action,
whereas in most comedies the Chorus employs the
Parabasis to expound the topical social and political
views of the comedian.
    The opening anapestic section of the Parabasis is
devoted to what might be called an Avine Cosmogony, a splendid and eloquent exposition of the
origins of the world and the creation of the Birds
and the gods. This defense of the antiquity of the
Birds then passes into an overtly humorous bid for
support, as though the Birds were campaigning for
the votes which will make them gods. This is followed by a lovely lyric strophe ("O woodland
Muse") which is succeeded by the *epirrhema* in
a more topical and satirical vein; then the lyric

O suffering mankind,
>   lives of twilight,
>   race feeble and fleeting,
like the leaves scattered!
>   Pale generations,
815
>   creatures of clay,
the wingless, the fading!
>   Unhappy mortals,
>   shadows in time,
flickering dreams!
>   Hear us now,
>   the ever-living Birds,
the undying,
>   the ageless ones,
>   scholars of eternity.
Hear and learn from us
>   the truth
>   of all there is to know —
what we are,
>   and how the gods began,
820
>   of Chaos and Dark.
(And when you know
>   tell Prodikos to go
>   hang:° he's had it!)
There was Chaos at first
>   and Night and Space
>   and Tartaros.
There was no Earth.
>   No Heaven was.
>   But sable-wingèd Night
laid her wind-egg there°
>   in the boundless lap
>   of infinite Dark.

---

antistrophe ("And so the swans") and the farcical *antepirrhema* ("You haven't really lived till you've tried a set of FEATHERS!").

The relevance of the opening cosmogony to the theme of the play has been questioned, but unreasonably I think. If Cloudcuckooland is an Athenian Utopia, the meaning of Utopia is scored when Pisthetairos achieves his apotheosis in the finale. He has built Utopia by becoming god, and escaping his human condition. It is to the reality and sadness of man's condition that the cosmogony of the blessed Birds is addressed, and these lovely opening lines ("O suffering mankind, lives of twilight, race feeble and fleeting") are intended as a tragic counterweight to the crazy comic dream of mankind with which the play closes.

821 **tell Prodikos to go hang:** Prodikos was a sophist whom Aristophanes seems to have respected. The point here is that, wise as Prodikos may be, as a teacher of truth he is not to be compared with the Birds.

824 **laid her wind-egg there:** A wind-egg is an unfertilized pullet's egg.

And from that egg,
>   in the seasons' revolving,
>   Love was born,   825
the graceful, the golden,
>   the whirlwind Love
>   on gleaming wings.
And there in the waste
>   of Tartaros,
>   Love with Chaos lay
and hatched the Birds.
>   We come from Love.
>   Love brought us to the light.
There were no gods
>   till Love had married
>   all the world in love.
Then the world was made.
>   Blue Heaven stirred,
>   and Ocean,   830
the Earth and ageless gods,
>   the blessèd ones
>   who do not die.
But we came first.
>   We Birds were born
>   the first-born sons of Love,
in proof whereof
>   we wear Love's wings,
>   we help his lovers.
How many pretty boys,
>   their prime not past,
>   abjuring Love,
have opened up their thighs
>   and yielded,
>   overborne by us,   835
bribed by a Bird,
>   a Coot, a Goose,
>   a little Persian Cock!
Think of the services
>   we Birds perform
>   for all mankind.
We mark your seasons off,
>   summer, spring,
>   winter, fall.
When for Africa
>   the screaming Crane departs,
>   you sow your fields.
And then the sailor
>   takes his ease
>   and hangs his rudder up,   840
and thief Orestes
>   weaves himself a cloak
>   and robs no man.
And then the Kite appears,
>   whose coming says
>   the Spring is here,
the time has come
>   to shear the sheep.

And so the Swallow
brings his summer,
     when mankind lays
         its winter weeds away.
And we are Ammon
     and Dodona.
845   We are your Apollo,
that prophetic voice
     to whom you turn
        in everything you do —
practical affairs,
     commerce and trade,
        and marriage too.
Birds are your signs,
     and all your omens
        are governed by Birds:
words are omens
     sent by the Birds.
        And the same for sneezes,
meetings, asses, voices:
     all are omens,
850   and omens are Birds.
Who are we then
     if we are not
        your prophetic Apollo?

(*The obbligato of the flute ceases as the* CHORUS *now shifts to a lighter vein and a quicker tempo.*)

So elect us as your gods
and we, in turn, shall be
your weathervane and Muse,
855 your priests of prophecy,
  foretelling all,
winter, summer, spring, and fall.

Furthermore, we promise we'll
give mankind an honest deal.
860 Unlike our smug opponent, Zeus,
we'll stop corruption and abuse.
NO ABSENTEE ADMINISTRATION!
NO PERMANENT VACATION
IN THE CLOUDS!
        And we promise
865 to be scrupulously honest.

Last of all, we guarantee
to every single soul on earth,
his sons and their posterity:
     HEALTH
870   WEALTH
     HAPPINESS
     YOUTH
     LONG LIFE
     LAUGHTER
875   PEACE

     DANCING
     and
     LOTS TO EAT!
We'll mince no words.
Your lives shall be   880
the milk of the Birds!
     We guarantee
     you'll all be
     revoltingly
     RICH!   885

O woodland Muse
with lovely throat,
tio tio tio tinx!
who with me sing
whenas in glade or mountain, I,   890
perched upon the ashtree cry,
tio tio tio tinx!
my tawny-throated song of praise,
to call the Mother to the dance,
a song of joy for blessed Pan,   895
  totototototototinx!
whence, like a bee,
the poet stole his honeyed song,°
my ravished cry,
tio tio tio tinx!   900

Do *you* suffer pangs of conscience?
              Nervous?
              Jumpy?
              Scared?
Need a hideout from the law? Some cozy place
  to pass the time? Well, step right up,
  friend!
     We'll get you a berth with the Birds.
We do things differently up here.
        What your laws condemn,
the things that you think shady or immoral are
  compulsory with us.
Consider the case, for instance, of a boy who
  beats up his dad.   905
Admit it: you're shocked. The idea! But *we*
  call it courage
when some bantam twirps, "C'mon, old Bird,
  put up your spurs and fight!"
Or suppose you've deserted. You're a runaway,
  branded with shame.
Hell, come and live with us! We'll call you a
  Yellow Chicken.
Or perhaps you happen to come from some
  foppish hole in Asia?   910
Come on up, you fairy fop, and be an Asiatic
  Finch.

898 **the poet stole his honied song:** i.e., the tragic poet, Phrynichos, famous for his lyric sweetness.

Or suppose you're a slave from Krete, like our
  friend Exekestides —
We'll call you little Cuckoo and pawn you off
  as our own.
Was Peisias your father?
                Are you a future traitor too?
Hell, make like a Partridge then. That's what
915   your Daddy did.
And who are we Birds to fuss at shamming
  hurt and partridge tricks?

    And so the swans
    their clamor cry,
    tio tio tio tinx!
920   and beating wings
    and bursting throats
    lord Apollo sing,
    tio tio tio tinx!
by Hebros' waters, swarming, crying,
925   *tio tio tio tinx!*
And every living thing is still.
On bird, on beast, the hush of awe.
The windless sea lies stunned when —
    totototototinx!
930   All Olympos rings,
and wonder breaks upon the gods,
and echoing, the Graces sing,
and lovely Muses raise the cry,
    tio tio tio tinx!

Friends, you haven't really lived till you've
935   tried a set of FEATHERS!
Think, spectators.
    Imagine yourselves with a pair of wings!
The sheer joy of it! Not having to sit those
  tragedies out!
No getting bored. You merely flap your little
  wings and fly off home.
You have a snack, then make it back to catch
  the COMIC play.
Or again, suppose you're overtaken by a sud-
940   den need to crap.
Do you do it in your pants?
                Not a bit.
                You just zoom off,
fart and shit to your heart's content and whizz
  right back.
Or perhaps you're having an affair — I won't
  name any names.
You spot the lady's husband attending some
  meeting or other.
Up you soar, flap your wings, through the
945   window and into bed!
You make it a quickie, of course, then flutter
  back to your seat.
So what do you say?

Aren't wings just the most *wonderful* things?
Look at Dieitrephes, our vulgar Ikaros of
  trade,°
who started life on wicker wings but rose to
  captain's rank,   950
and now, still riding high, is colonel of a wing
  of horse.
From horse's ass to Pegasos! But *that's* what
  wings can do!

(*The* CHORUS *now turns and faces the stage
as* PISTHETAIROS *and* EUELPIDES *return. Both
of them now sport tiny wings, a few feathers, and outsize beaks.*)

PISTHETAIROS:
Well, here we are.
EUELPIDES: Sweet gods, in all my days,
I've never seen a sillier sight than you!
PISTHETAIROS: Yeah,
what's so damn funny?
EUELPIDES: You and those baby wings.   955
They tickle me. You know what you look like,
  don't you?
PISTHETAIROS:
You look like an abstraction of a Goose.
EUELPIDES: Yeah?
Well, if you're supposed to be a Blackbird, boy,
somebody botched the job. You're more bare
  than Bird.
PISTHETAIROS:
We made the choice that gave these barbs
  their bite.   960
Remember the poor Birds in that Aischylos
  play° —
"Shot down by shafts of their own feathers
  made?"
EUELPIDES:
What's the next move?
PISTHETAIROS: First, we'll give our city
some highfalutin' name. Then a special sacrifice
to our new gods.
EUELPIDES: A special sacrifice? Yummy.   965
KORYPHAIOS:
To work, men. How do you propose to name
  our city?

949 **Dieitrephes, our vulgar Ikaros of trade:** For
Dieitrephes, see Glossary. Aristophanes, like most
conservatives, is a convinced snob, and he almost
never forgives a man his business background, especially if the man has succeeded, as Dieitrephes had,
in making his way into the *élite* ranks of the chivalry.
961 **the poor Birds in that Aischylos play:** A
reference to, followed by a quotation from, the lost
Myrmidones of Aischylos.

PISTHETAIROS:
How about Sparta? That's a grand old name
with a fine pretentious ring.
EUELPIDES: Great Herakles,
call my city Sparta? I wouldn't even insult
my mattress by giving it a name like Sparta.°
970   PISTHETAIROS: Well,
what do you suggest instead?
EUELPIDES: Something big, smacking
of the clouds. A pinch of fluff and rare air.
A swollen sound.
PISTHETAIROS:
                    I've got it! Listen —
                    CLOUDCUCKOOLAND!
KORYPHAIOS:
That's it! The perfect name. And it's a *big*
word too.
EUELPIDES:
CLOUDCUCKOOLAND!
975   Imagination's happy home,
where Theogenes builds castles in the air, and
Aischines
becomes a millionaire.
PISTHETAIROS: Better yet, here we have
the plain of Phlegra, that windy battlefield of
blah and bluff,
where the gabbling gods outbragged the wordy
giants.
KORYPHAIOS:
A suave and splendid city.
980   — But which of the gods
should we designate as patron and protector?
EUELPIDES: Why not Athena?
PISTHETAIROS:
But it's bound to seem a bit odd, isn't it? I
mean,
a female goddess protecting our walls with a
spear
while men like Kleisthenes sit home with their
knitting?
KORYPHAIOS:
And, come to think of it, who will guard our
985   Storkade?°

969–970 **insult my mattress by giving it a name
like Sparta:** A pun on Σπάρτη (Sparta and σπάρτη,
a kind of broom from which rope and bed-cording
were made). Euelpides detests Sparta so much that
he wouldn't attach σπάρτη to his bed.
985 **who will guard our Storkade?:** The wall
which surrounded the Akropolis of Athens was
usually called the Pelasgic Wall but sometimes the
Pelargic Wall, both related forms. Aristophanes here
uses Pelargic Wall, fancifully deriving it from
πελαργός ("stork"). "Storkade" is B. B. Rogers'
trouvaille and one which I gratefully adopt here.

PISTHETAIROS:
A Bird.
KORYPHAIOS:
            One of us, you mean?
PISTHETAIROS: Why not the Rooster?
They're terrible scrappers and famous fighting
Birds.
Little chicks of Ares.
EUELPIDES: Little Corporal Cock!
He's the perfect Bird for protecting our rock.
PISTHETAIROS (*to* EUELPIDES):
Hop it, man!°
                    Quick, up the rigging of the air!   990
Hurry! Done? Now supervise the workers on
the wall.
Run the rubble up!
                    Quick, mix the mortar, man!
Up the ladder with your hod — and then fall
down!
Don't stop!
            Post the sentries!
                    Bank the furnace!
Now the watchman's round.
                    All right, catch two winks.   995
Rise and shine!
                    Now send your heralds off,
one to the gods above, one to the mortals
below.
Then scurry back.
EUELPIDES:
                    As for you, just stay right here —
and I hope you choke.
PISTHETAIROS: Obey your orders, friend.
Unless you do your share, we shan't get done.   1000

(*Exit* EUELPIDES.)

Now, let me see.
                    First, a priest to supervise
our sacrifice.
            — Boy!

(*An* ACOLYTE *appears.*)

                    Boy, go fetch me a priest.
And when you're finished, bring me a basket
and a laver.

(*Exit* ACOLYTE.)

CHORUS:
            The Birds agree
            most heartily.   1005
            You're absolutely right.

990 **Hop it, man!:** Pisthetairos' officiousness with
Euelpides here is a stunning example of πολυπραγμοσύνη.

Hymns and laud
are dear to god,
    but dinner's their delight.

Yes, gratitude
is shown with food,
    so rise and offer up,

in witness of
our shrunken love,
    one miserable lamp chop!

KORYPHAIOS:
Flutist, come in.°
Now let our sacrifice begin.

(*Enter the* FLUTIST, *a Raven whose beak is
an enormous flute which is strapped to his
mouth by means of a leather harness. After
strenuous huffing, he manages to produce
what are unmistakably caws.*)

PISTHETAIROS:
Stop that raucous Rook!
                In the name of god,
what are you anyway?
                I've seen some weird sights,
but this is the first time in my life I ever saw
a Blackbird propping his beak with a leather
belt.°

(*Exit* FLUTIST. *Enter* PRIEST, *followed by the*
ACOLYTE *with the paraphernalia of the sacrifice.*)

At last.
      — Eminence, you may begin the inau-
gural sacrifice.
PRIEST:
Your humble servant, sir.
               — But where's my acolyte?

(*The* ACOLYTE *steps forward. The* PRIEST
*raises his hands and begins the Bidding
Prayer of the Birds.*°)

1016 **Flutist, come in:** At these words the flutist
Chairis, dressed as a Blackbird or a Crow, steps forward. Chairis' music seems to have grated intolerably
on Aristophanes' ears; he is a *bête noire* in *The
Acharnians* (425 B.C.) and still obnoxious by the
time of *The Birds* eleven years later.
1021 **propping his beak with a leather belt:**
Evidently a mouth band or flutist's lip protector.
1023 s.d. **the Bidding Prayer of the Birds:** This entire prayer is a parody of the customary invocation of
the gods, in each case, by pun or burlesqued attributes
or cult titles, linking a god with a bird. Because of the
elaborateness of the puns and the obscurities of cult
titles, literal translation is out of the question, and
I have tried to make my own puns where I could

Now let us pray —
PRAY TO THE HESTIA OF NESTS,   1025
TO THE HOUSEHOLDING HARRIER
    HAWK,
TO ALL THE OLYMPIAN COCKS AND
    COQUETTES,
TO THE SWOOPING STORK OF THE
    SEA —
PISTHETAIROS:
ALL HAIL, THE STORK! HAIL, POSEI-
DON OF PINIONS!
PRIEST:
TO THE SWEETSINGER OF DELOS,   1030
THE APOLLONIAN SWAN,
TO LETO THE QUEEN OF THE
    QUAIL,
TO ARTEMIS THE PHOEBE —
PISTHETAIROS:
HAIL TO THE PHOEBE, VIRGIN SIS-
TER OF PHOIBOS!
PRIEST:
PRAY TO WOODPECKER PAN,   1035
TO DOWITCHER KYBELE,
MOTHER OF MORTALS AND GODS —
PISTHETAIROS:
HAIL, DOWAGER QUEEN, GREAT
    MOTHER OF BUSTARDS!
PRIEST:
PRAY THAT THEY GRANT US
HEALTH AND LENGTH OF LIFE,   1040
PRAY THAT THEY PROTECT US,
pray for the Chians too° —
PISTHETAIROS:
You know, I like the way he tacks those Chians
    on.
PRIEST:
COME, ALL HERO BIRDS,
ALL HEROINE HENS AND PULLETS!   1045
COME, O GALLINULE!
BRING DICKYBIRD AND DUNNOCK,
COME, CROSSBILL AND BUNTING!
ON DIPPER, ON DIVER,
ON WHIMBREL AND FINCH!   1050
COME CURLEW AND CREEPER,

not re-create the Greek — as I rarely could. Thus
my Artemis is not a Finch but an American Phoebe,
an appropriate name, I thought, for the sister of
Phoibos; Kybele, Mother of Gods and Men, is not
an Ostrich, as she is in the Greek, but a Dowitcher,
a bird which suggested "dowager," and the Great
Mother of Bustards. Those who are interested in
discussion of the literal Greek should consult
Rogers' commentary on the passage.
1042 **pray for the Chians too:** Cf. Glossary,
CHIANS.

ON PIPIT, ON PARROT,
COME VULTURE, COME TIT —
PISTHETAIROS:
Stop it, you fool! Stop that rollcall of the
    Birds!
Are you utterly daft, man, inviting Vultures
1055   and Eagles
and suchlike to our feast? Or weren't you
    aware
one single beak could tuck it all away?
Clear out, and take your blasted ribands with
    you.
So help me, I'll finish this sacrifice myself.

(*Exit* PRIEST.)

CHORUS:
1060   Again we raise
    the hymn of praise
      and pour the sacred wine.

    With solemn rite
    we now invite
1065   the blessed gods to dine.

    But don't *all* come —
    perhaps just one,
      and maybe then again,

    there's not enough
1070   (besides, it's tough),
      so stay away. Amen.
PISTHETAIROS:
Let us pray to the pinion'd gods —

(*Enter a hungry, ragged* POET, *chanting.*)

POET:
In all thy songs, O Muse,
    let one city
1075   praisèd be —
CLOUDCUCKOOLAND THE LOVELY!
PISTHETAIROS:
Who spawned this spook?
        — Look here, who are you?
POET:
One of the tribe of dulcet tongue and tripping
    speech —
    "the slave of Poesy,
1080   whose ardent soul
    the Muses hold in thrall,"
    as Homer hath it.°
PISTHETAIROS:
Judging from your clothes, friend, your Muses
    must be

1082 **as Homer hath it:** Everything about this
poet is begged, borrowed, or stolen. Here he attributes lines to Homer which either are not Homeric
or Homer so muddled as to be unrecognizable.

bankrupt. Tell me, bard, what ill wind plopped
    you here?
POET:
I've been composing poems in honor of your
    new city —   1085
oodles of little odes, some dedication-anthems,
songs for soprano voice, a lyric or two
à la Simonides —
PISTHETAIROS:
        How long has your little poetic mill
been grinding out this chaff?
POET: Why, simply ages.
Long, long since my Muse commenced to sing 1090
Cloudcuckooland in all her orisons.
PISTHETAIROS: Long ago?
But that's impossible. This city's still a baby.
I just now gave birth. I just baptised her.
POET:
Ah, but swift are the mouths of the Muses,
more swift than steeds the galloping news 1095
    of the Muses!

(*He turns to the altar and with outstretched*
hands invokes it in Pindaric parody.)

    O Father,
      Founder of Etna,°
    of thy bounty give,
    O Hiero, O Homonym,
    Great Hero of the Fire,   1100
    just one slender sliv-
    -er to my desire,
    some tidbit to savor,
    some token of favor —
PISTHETAIROS:
You know, I think we'd better bribe this
    beggar bard   1105
to leave before we die of doggerel.

(*To the* ACOLYTE.)

        —You there,
strip and let the beggar poet have your over-
    coat.

(*He hands the coat to the* POET.)

Dress.
    Why, you poor poet, you're shivering with
    cold.
POET:
    My Muse accepts with thanks
    this modest donation.   1110

1097 **O Father, Founder of Etna:** This whole
passage is evidently a hideously garbled and atro-
ciously adapted burlesque of Pindar's ode dedicated
to the Syracusan tyrant Hiero on the founding of
the town of Etna.

But first, before I leave,
one brief quotation,
a snatch of Pindar
you might ponder —

POET:

PISTHETAIROS:
Gods above, will this poor man's Pindar never
1115　　leave?

POET:
Undressed amidst the nomad Skyths,°
the Frozen Poet fareth,
as Beastly Cold as Bard may be,
who Next-to-Nothing weareth.

1120　Genius, ah, hath deck'd his Song,
but oh, th' Ingratitude!
Whilst other Blokes be warm as Toast,
the Poet's damn near Nude.

You catch my drift?

PISTHETAIROS:　　Yes, I catch your drift.
You want some underwear.

(To the ACOLYTE.)

1125　　　　　　　All right, off with it, lad.
We can't allow our delicate poets to freeze to
death.
And now clear out, will you?

POET:　　　　　　I go, I go,
but first my final valediction to this little
village —

(Singing.)

O Muse on golden throne,
1130　Muse with chattering teeth
sing this capitol of cold,
this frigorifical city!

I have been where the glebe is frozen with
frore.
I have traipsed where the furrows are sown
with snow.
Alalai!
Alalai!
1135　　　　　　　　　　　　G'bye.

(Exit POET.)

PISTHETAIROS:
Well, how do you like that? Griping about the
cold
after making off with an entire new winter
outfit!

1116 Undressed amidst the nomad Skyths: More
Pindar, perhaps quoted almost verbatim, but dog-
gerelized deliberately by me since no contemporary
reader could be expected to recognize the Pindaric
manner or its incongruous humor in this particular
context.

And how in the name of heaven did that
poetic plague
discover us so fast?

(To the naked and shivering ACOLYTE.)

　　　　　— You there, to work again.
Take up your laver and circle the altar, boy,　1140
and we'll resume our inaugural sacrifice once
again.
Quiet now, everyone.

(As PISTHETAIROS approaches the altar with
the sacrificial knife, an itinerant PROPHET
with a great open tome of oracles makes his
appearance.)

PROPHET:　　　　　HALT! Forbear, I say!
Let no one touch the victim.

PISTHETAIROS:　　　　Who the hell are you,
may I ask?

PROPHET:
　　　　　I am a Prophet, sir, in person.

PISTHETAIROS:　　　　　　Then beat it.

PROPHET:
Ah, the naughty wee scamp.
　　　　　　　　But we mustn't scoff.　1145
Friend, I have brought you an oracle of the
prophet Bakis,
transparently alluding to the city of Cloudcuckooland.

PISTHETAIROS:
Why did you wait till after I founded my city
before disgorging this revelation of yours?

PROPHET:　　　　　　　　　Alas,
I could not come. The Inner Voice said No.　1150

PISTHETAIROS:
I suppose we'll have to hear you expound
your oracle.

PROPHET:　　Listen —
LO, IN THAT DAY WHEN THE WOLF
AND THE
CROW DO FOREGATHER AND COM-
PANION,
AND DOMICILE IN THE AIR, AT THAT
POINT
WHERE　　KORINTH　　KISSETH
SIKYON° —　　　　　　　　　　　　1155

1155 WHERE KORINTH KISSETH SIKYON:
That is, at Orneai. Cf. note on p. 277, any reference to Birds. Itinerant prophets in Athens could
live well by supplying ambiguous predictions of
conquest and victory to the ambitious Athenians.
This particular prophet may very well be quoting
from an actual oracle which predicted the sack of
Orneai and thereby prompted the expedition; he
then attempts to resell the same article, differently
interpreted, to Cloudcuckooland.

PISTHETAIROS:
Look here, what has Korinth got to do with me?

PROPHET:
Why,
it's ambiguous, of course. Korinth signifies "air."

(*Resuming.*)

PRESENT, I SAY, A WHITE SHEEP TO PANDORA,
BUT TO THE SEER WHO BRINGS MY BEHEST:
1160   IN PRIMIS, A WARM WINTER COAT PLUS A PAIR OF SANDALS (THE BEST) —

PISTHETAIROS:
The *best* sandals, eh?

PROPHET: Yup. Look in the book.

(*Resuming.*)

ITEM, A GOBLET OF WINE,
ITEM, A GIBLET OF GOAT —

PISTHETAIROS:
Giblet? It says giblet?

1165   PROPHET: Yup. Look in the book.

(*Resuming.*)

IF, O BLESSÈD YOUTH, THOU DOST AS I ENJOIN,
REGAL EAGLE WINGS THIS VERY DAY ARE THINE.°
NOT SO MUCH AS PIGEON FLUFF, IF THOU DECLINE.

PISTHETAIROS:
It really says that?

PROPHET: Yup. Look in the book.

PISTHETAIROS (*drawing out a huge tome from under his cloak*):
You know, your oracles somehow don't mesh
1170   with mine,
and I got these from Apollo's mouth.
                        Listen —
LO, IF IT CHANCE THAT SOME FAKER INTRUDE,
TROUBLING   THY   WORSHIP   AND SCROUNGING FOR FOOD,
LET HIS RIBS BE BASHED
1175   AND HIS TESTICLES MASHED —

PROPHET:
I suspect you're bluffing.

1167 **REGAL EAGLE WINGS THIS VERY DAY ARE THINE:** This is said to have been the favorite prediction of the Athenian Demos (cf. *Knights,* 1013). The Eagle, of course, symbolized supremacy and conquest.

PISTHETAIROS: Nope. Look in the book.

(*Resuming.*)

SMITE ON, I SAY, IF ANY PROPHET SHOULD COME,
YEA, THOUGH HE SOARETH LIKE THE SWALLOW.
FOR THE GREATER THE FAKER,° THE HARDER HIS BUM
SHOULD BE BATTERED.
                GOOD LUCK.
                    Signed,
                    APOLLO.   1180

PROPHET:
Honest? It says that?

PISTHETAIROS: Yup. Look in the book.

(*Suddenly throwing his tome at him and beating him.*)

Take that!
        And that!
                And that!

PROPHET: Ouch. Help!

PISTHETAIROS:
Scat. Go hawk your prophecies somewhere else.

(*Exit* PROPHET. *From the other side enters the geometrician and surveyor* METON,° *his arms loaded with surveying instruments.*)

METON:
The occasion that hath hied me hither —

PISTHETAIROS: Not another!
State your business, stranger. What's your racket?   1185
What tragic error brings you here?

METON: My purpose here
is a geodetic survey of the atmosphere of Cloudcuckooland
and the immediate allocation of all this aerial area
into cubic acres.

PISTHETAIROS:
                Who are *you*?

METON: Who am *I*?
Why, Meton, of course. Who else could *I* be?   1190
Geometer to Hellas by special appointment.
Also Kolonos.

PISTHETAIROS:
                And those tools?

1179 **FOR THE GREATER THE FAKER:** The manuscript specifies by name two of these fakers. The first is Lampon, Athens' most renowned soothsayer; the second, Diopeithes, the accuser of the philosopher Anaxagoras.
1183 s.d. **METON:** Cf. Glossary.

METON: Celestial rules,
of course.
              Now attend, sir.
                        Taken *in extenso*,
our welkin resembles a cosmical charcoal-oven°
or potbellied stove worked by the convection
      principle,
though vaster. Now then, with the flue as my
      base,
and twirling the calipers thus, I obtain the
      azimuth,
whence, by calibrating the arc or radial sine —
you follow me, friend?
    PISTHETAIROS:
                    No, I don't follow you.
    METON:
No matter. Now then, by training the theodo-
      lite here
on the vectored zenith tangent to the Apex A,
I deftly square the circle, whose conflux, or C,
I designate as the center or axial hub of
      Cloudcuckooland,
whence, like global spokes or astral radii,
broad boulevards diverge centrifugally, forming,
as it were —
    PISTHETAIROS:
                Why, this man's a regular Thales!

(*Whispering confidentially*.)

Pssst. Meton.
    METON: Sir?
    PISTHETAIROS:
                    I've taken quite a shine to you.
Take my advice, friend, and decamp while
      there's still time.
    METON:
You anticipate danger, you mean?
    PISTHETAIROS: The kind of danger
one meets in Sparta. You know, nasty little riots,
a few foreigners beaten up or murdered, knif-
      ings,
fighting in the streets and so on.
    METON: Dear me, you mean
there might actually be revolution?
    PISTHETAIROS: I certainly hope not.
    METON:
Then what *is* the trouble?

1195, 1200, 1205, 1210 in margins

PISTHETAIROS: The new law. You see,
attempted fraud is now punishable by thrashing. 1215
    METON:
Er, perhaps I'd best be going.
    PISTHETAIROS: I'm half afraid
you're just a bit too late.
                  Yes!
                      Look out!
Here comes your thrashing!

(*He batters* METON *with a surveying rod*.)

    METON: HALP! MURDER!
    PISTHETAIROS:
I warned you. Go survey some other place, will
      you?

(*Exit* METON. *From the other side enters an*
INSPECTOR,° *dressed in a magnificent military uniform and swaggering imperiously*.)

    INSPECTOR:
Fetch me the Mayor, yokel.
    PISTHETAIROS: Who's this popinjay? 1220
    INSPECTOR:
Inspector-general of Cloudcuckooland County,
      sir,
invested, I might add, with plenary powers —
    PISTHETAIROS: Invested?
On whose authority?
    INSPECTOR: Why, the powers vested in me
by virtue of this piddling piece of paper here
signed by one Teleas of Athens.
    PISTHETAIROS: Look. Let me propose 1225
a little deal, friend. I'll pay you off right now,
provided you leave the city.
    INSPECTOR: A capital suggestion.
As it so happens, my presence is urgently re-
      quired
at home. They're having one of their Great
      Debates.
The Persian crisis, you know.°
    PISTHETAIROS: Really? Splendid. 1230
I'll pay you off right now.

1194 **our welkin resembles a cosmical charcoal-
oven:** Meton's whole lecture is an elaborate spoof
of technical "scientific" jargon of the age. But because Greek scientific jargon is almost chaste compared to our splendid modern proliferations, I have
worked it up in order to create an effect analogous
to that intended for Greek ears.

1219 s.d. **enters an INSPECTOR:** The Inspector, or
Commissioner, was a regular Athenian official sent
out from Athens to supervise subject states or to organize newly founded colonies. Their salaries seem
to have been paid by the colonies they supervised,
and some of them, like the Inspector here, had
become rich men in the course of their careers.
1230 **The Persian crisis, you know:** A free rendering. In the original the Inspector alludes loftily
to his negotiations with the Persian satrap Phar-
nakes; he is needed at home for consultation about
these weighty negotiations. Persia at this time, however, was more and more becoming a crucial factor
in Greek political life.

(Violently beating the INSPECTOR.)

Take that!
And that!

INSPECTOR:
What does this outrage mean?
PISTHETAIROS: The payoff. Round One
of the Great Debate.
INSPECTOR:
          But this is mutiny! Insubordination!

(To the CHORUS.)

Gentlemen, I call on you Birds to bear me
     witness
that this man wilfully assaulted an Inspector.

1235   PISTHETAIROS: Shoo, fellow,
and take your ballot boxes with you° when
     you go.

(Exit INSPECTOR.)

What confounded gall! Sending us one of
     their Inspectors
before we've even finished the Inaugural Serv-
     ice.

(Enter an itinerant LEGISLATOR° *reading
from a huge volume of laws.)*

LEGISLATOR:
BE IT HEREBY PROVIDED THAT IF
     ANY CLOUD-
CUCKOOLANDER SHALL WILFULLY
1240   INJURE OR
WRONG ANY CITIZEN OF ATHENS —
PISTHETAIROS:
Gods, what now? Not *another* bore with a
     book?
LEGISLATOR:
A seller of laws and statutes, sir, at your service.
Fresh shipment of by-laws on special sale
for only —
PISTHETAIROS:
          Perhaps you'd better demonstrate
1245   your wares.

1236 **and take your ballot boxes with you:**
Wherever Athenian inspectors are found, there will
also be ballot boxes, the typical device of Athenian
democracy, and arbitrarily instituted throughout
the empire.
1238 s.d. **Enter an itinerant** LEGISLATOR: During
the war the Athenian Assembly had passed so many
decrees, regulations, etc., that it became virtually
impossible for the subject-cities and colonies to
keep abreast of them. In the circumstances the
practice of peddling the latest crop of statutes became a flourishing trade.

LEGISLATOR *(reading)*:
BE IT HEREBY PROVIDED BY LAW
     THAT FROM THE DATE SPECI-
     FIED BELOW
THE WEIGHTS AND MEASURES OF
THE CLOUDCUCKOOLANDERS ARE TO
     BE ADJUSTED
TO THOSE IN EFFECT AMONG THE
     OLOPHYXIANS —
PISTHETAIROS *(pummelling him)*:
By god, I'll Olo-phyx you!
LEGISLATOR: Hey, mister, stop!   1250
PISTHETAIROS:
Get lost, you and your laws, or I'll carve mine
on the skin of your tail.

(Exit LEGISLATOR. *Enter* INSPECTOR.)

INSPECTOR:
          I summon the defendant Pisthetairos
to stand trial in court on charges of assault and
     battery
not later than April.
PISTHETAIROS:
          Good gods, are *you* back too?

(He thrashes INSPECTOR *who runs off. Re-
enter* LEGISLATOR.)

LEGISLATOR:
IF ANY MAN, EITHER BY WORD OR
     ACTION, DO IMPEDE OR RESIST   1255
A MAGISTRATE IN THE PROSECUTION
     OF HIS OFFICIAL DUTIES, OR RE-
     FUSE
TO WELCOME HIM WITH THE COUR-
     TESY PRESCRIBED BY LAW —
PISTHETAIROS:
Great thundery Zeus, are *you* back here too?

(He drives the LEGISLATOR *away. Re-enter*
INSPECTOR.)

INSPECTOR:
I'll have you sacked. What's more, I'm suing
     you
for a fat two thousand.
PISTHETAIROS: By Zeus, I'll fix you   1260
and your blasted ballot boxes once and for all!

(Exit INSPECTOR *under a barrage of blows.
Re-enter* LEGISLATOR.)

LEGISLATOR:
Remember that evening when you crapped in
     court?
PISTHETAIROS:
          Dammit.
Someone arrest that pest!

(*Exit* LEGISLATOR.)

And this time stay away!
But enough's enough.

We'll take our goat inside
1265 and finish this sacrifice in peace and privacy.

(*Exit* PISTHETAIROS *into house, followed by*
ACOLYTE *with basket and slaves with the*
sacrifice.)

CHORUS° (*wheeling sharply and facing the*
audience):
Praise Ye the Birds, O Mankind!
Our sway is over all.
The eyes of the Birds observe you:
we see if any fall.

1270 We watch and guard all growing green,
protecting underwing
this lavish lovely life of earth,
its birth and harvesting.

We smite the mite, we slay the pest,
1275 all ravagers that seize
the good that burgeons in your buds
or ripens on your trees.

Whatever makes contagion come,
whatever blights or seeks
1280 to raven in this green shall die,
devoured by our beaks.

KORYPHAIOS:
You know, gentlemen, that proclamation that's
posted everywhere in town —
WANTED, DEAD OR ALIVE! DIAGORAS
OF MELOS.
ONE TALENT'S REWARD FOR ANY
MAN WHO KILLS THE TYRANT!
Well, we Birds have published our own public
1285 proclamation: —
"HEAR YE!
WANTED DEAD OR ALIVE!
PHILOKRATES THE BIRDSELLER!
DEAD, 1 TALENT'S REWARD. 4 TAL-
ENTS IF
TAKEN ALIVE,
BUT PROCEED WITH
CAUTION. THIS MAN IS DANGER-
OUS.
WANTED FOR MURDER AND CRU-
ELTY TO BIRDS ON THE FOLLOW-
ING COUNTS: —

1266 s.d. CHORUS: The second Parabasis: The Birds
eulogize themselves and the blessings they bring,
issue their own proclamation, and explain to the
Judges the advantages of awarding *The Birds* the
first prize.

For the Spitting of Finches, seven to a
skewer;   1290
item, for Disfiguring Thrushes by means of
inflation;
item, for Insertion of Feathers in Blackbirds'
nostrils;
item, for Unlawful Detention of Pigeons in
Cages;
item, for Felonious Snaring of Innocent
Pigeons;
item, for Flagrant Misuse of Traps and
Decoy-devices."   1295
So much for Philokrates.
But as for you, dear spectators,
we give you solemn warning.
If any boy in this audience
has as his hobby the keeping of Birds in
captivity or cages,
we urgently suggest that you let your pets go
free. Disobey,
and we'll catch *you* and lock you up in a
wicker cage   1300
or stake you out to a snare as a little decoy
boy!

CHORUS:
How blessèd is our breed of Bird,
dressed in fluff and feather,
that, when hard winter holds the world,
wears no clothes whatever.   1305

And blazoned summer hurts no Bird,
for when the sun leaps high,
and, priestly in that hellish light,
the chaunting crickets cry,

the Birds keep cool among the leaves   1310
or fan themselves with flight;
while winter days we're snug in caves
and nest with nymphs at night.

But Spring is joy, when myrtle blooms
and Graces dance in trio,   1315
and quiring Birds cantatas sing
vivace e con brio.

KORYPHAIOS:
Finally, gentlemen, a few brief words about
the First Prize
and the striking advantages of casting your
vote for *THE BIRDS* of Aristophanes —
advantages compared to which that noble
prince,   1320
poor Paris of Troy, was very shabbily bribed
indeed.
First on our list of gifts comes a little item
that every judge's greedy heart must be panting to possess.

I refer, of course, to those lovely little owls of Laurium,
sometimes called the coin of the realm.
1325   Yes, gentlemen,
these lovely owls, we promise, will flock to you by the
thousand, settle down in your wallets for good and hatch
you a brood of nice little nest eggs.
                          Secondly, gentlemen, we promise
to redesign your houses.
                    See, the sordid tenements vanish,
while in their place rise splendid shrines whose dizzy
1330
heights, like Eagle-eyries,° hang in heaven.
                                  Are you perhaps
a politician faced with the vexing problem of insufficient
plunder? Friend, your problems are over. Accept as our gift
to you a pair of Buzzard claws designed with special hooks
for more efficient grafting.
1335   As for heavy eaters,
those suffering from biliousness, heartburn, acid indigestion
or other stomach ailments and upsets, we proudly present them
with special lifetime Bird-crops, guaranteed to be virtually
indestructible.
                    If, however, gentlemen, you with-hold your vote,
you'd better do as the statues do and wear a
1340   metal lid
against our falling guano.
                          I repeat.
                    Vote against THE BIRDS,
and every Bird in town will cover you with — vituperation!

(*The* CHORUS *turns and faces the stage. Enter* PISTHETAIROS.)

PISTHETAIROS:
Birds, the omens are favorable. Our sacrifice has been
auspicious. But I wonder where in the world our messenger
is with news about our wall.

(A *sound of furious panting offstage.*)

                              Aha. There he is now.   1345
I'd recognize that awful huffing and puffing anywhere.
Those are the true Olympic pants and puffs I hear.

(*Enter* MESSENGER, *panting.*)

MESSENGER:
Where anh where hoo where uh where can he be?
Where is Pisthetairos hanh?
    PISTHETAIROS: Here hunh here.
MESSENGER:
Whew, the wall's all up! The wall's done!
    PISTHETAIROS: Splendid!   1350
MESSENGER:
What a wonderful, whopping, well-built wall! Whew!
Why, that wall's so wide that if you hitched up
four Trojan Horses to two huge chariots
with those braggarts Proxenides in one and Theogenes in the other,
they could pass head-on. *That's* the width of your wall!   1355
PISTHETAIROS:
Wow, what a width!
    MESSENGER:
            And what a height! Measured it myself.
Six hundred feet high!
    PISTHETAIROS: Poseidon, what a height!
Who in the world could have built a wall like that?
    MESSENGER:
The Birds.
        Nobody but Birds.
                        Not one Egyptian.
No bricklayers. No carpenters. Or masons.   1360
Only the Birds. I couldn't credit my eyes.
What a sight it was:
                    Thirty thousand Cranes
whose crops were all loaded with boulders and stones,°
while the Rails with their beaks blocked out the rocks
and thousands of Storks came bringing up bricks   1365

1330–1331 **shrines whose dizzy heights, like Eagle-eyries:** In Greek the word ἀετός meant (1) an Eagle, and (2) the triangular pediment which crowned the pillars.

1362–1363 **Thirty thousand Cranes whose crops were all loaded with boulders and stones:** Cranes were believed to use stones to ballast themselves; the ballast was held in the crop.

and Plovers and Terns and seabirds by billions
transported the water right up to the sky!

PISTHETAIROS: Heavens!
But which Birds hauled the mortar up?

MESSENGER: Herons,
in hods.

PISTHETAIROS:
         But how was the mortar heaped in
         the hods?

MESSENGER:
Gods, now *that* was a triumph of engineering
1370   skill!
Geese burrowed their feet like shovels beneath
and heaved it over their heads to the hods.

PISTHETAIROS: They did?
Ah Feet! Ah, Feet! O incredible feat!°
What can compete with a pair of feet?

MESSENGER: And, sir,
you should have seen the Ducks with their
1375   aprons on
go hauling the bricks! And how the Swallows
         came
swooping, dangling their trowels behind them
         like boys,
and darting and dipping with mouthfuls of
         mortar!

PISTHETAIROS:
                  Why,
if this is true, then human labor is obsolete.
But what happened next? Who finished off
1380   the job?
Who did the woodwork on the wall?

MESSENGER: Mastercraftsmen birds.
It was Pelicans, like carpenters, with handy
         hatchet-beaks
who hewed the gates, and what with the racket
         and hubbub
of all that hacking and chopping and hewing
         and banging,
sir, you'd have sworn it was a shipyard down at
1385   the docks.
Or so it sounded to me.
                        But the gates are done,
the bolts shot home, watchbirds make their
         rounds
with clanging bells, the guards patrol their
         beats
and every tower along the circuit of the wall
blazes with its watchfire. And in three words,
1390   sir,
all is well.

1373 **Ah Feet! Ah, Feet! O incredible feat!:**
This is a common proverb with the word "feet"
substituted for "hands."

But I must go and wash my face.
My job is done. The rest is up to you.

(*Exit* MESSENGER.)

KORYPHAIOS: Well,
wasn't it a wonder the way that wall of ours
         shot up?

PISTHETAIROS:
A damn sight too wonderful. If you're asking
         me,
I think it's all a lie.
                        — But look what's coming: 1395
another messenger, and a sentry judging by his
         looks.

(*Enter* SENTRY, *whirling on stage in the
wild steps of a military dance.*°)

— What are you, fellow? A soldier or a balle-
         rina?

SENTRY:
ALAS! ALACKADAY!
                              OCHONE!
                                    WOE IS ME!

PISTHETAIROS:
Well, what's troubling y*ou*?

SENTRY: Sir, we are diddled
and undone.
                  Some god has given us the slip,   1400
I wot not which. Carommed through the gates
out into territorial air. The Daws on guard
never spotted him.

PISTHETAIROS: Gad. A national scandal.
Which god?

SENTRY:
              We couldn't tell. But he was wear-
         ing wings,
that much we know.

PISTHETAIROS: Were Pursuitbirds sent up   1405
to intercept him?

SENTRY: Everything we had took off, sir.
The Sparrowhawk Reserve, thirty thousand
         Falcons,
every claw-carrying Harrier we could throw
in the sky: — Kestrels, Buzzards, Owls, Eagles,
Vultures, you name it.
                        Why, the whole atmosphere   1410
is throbbing and buzzing with the whirr of
         beating wings
as they comb the clouds for that sneaky little
         god.

1396 s.d. **the wild steps of a military dance:** The
pyrrhichē danced in full armor. Actually, the sentry
is not dancing; the dancing is in his eyes, i.e.,
ablaze with martial ardor.

If you're asking me, he's not so far away either.
He's hereabouts. I'm sure.

(*Exit* SENTRY.)

PISTHETAIROS: Where's my bow?
Bring me my sling!
1415   Archerbirds, fall in!
Now shoot to kill.
                Dammit, where's my sling?

CHORUS:
            Now words are weak
            and ACTIONS speak
                ineffably of War.

1420   Let every Bird
            for battle gird:
                the gods are at our door:

            Rise up, defend
            your native land!
1425   Go mobilize the Air!

            Immortal spies
            now prowl our skies.
                And saboteurs. Take care.

KORYPHAIOS:
Quiet.
        I hear the whirr of beating wings.
Listen. Some god comes whizzing through our
1430   air.

(*With a loud whoosh and a burst of
baroque movement and color,* IRIS *descends
in the machine. She is a young girl with
golden wings and billowing rainbow-colored
robes. From her dress and hair, in gracious
and extravagant loops of color, pennants and
ribbons and streamers trail out behind.*)

PISTHETAIROS:
Ship ahoy!
        Belay!
                Where are you cruising?
Down anchors!
                And stop luffing those wings.
Now who are you? Home Port? Purpose of
    voyage?
IRIS:
I am Iris the fleet.
PISTHETAIROS: Clippership or sloop?
IRIS:
What does this mean?
1435   PISTHETAIROS: Some Buzzard flap up
and arrest that bitch.
    IRIS: You dare arrest *me*?
What sort of joke is this?
    PISTHETAIROS: You'll see, sister.

IRIS:
But I must be dreaming. This can't be real.
    PISTHETAIROS:
What gate did you enter by? Answer, you slut.
    IRIS:
Gates? What would a goddess know about
    gates?   1440
    PISTHETAIROS:
A glib little piece. Just listen to those lies.
— Well, did you report to the Daw on duty at
    the gate?
Mum, eh?
            Where's your Storkpass?
    IRIS: I must be mad.
    PISTHETAIROS:
What? You never even applied?
    IRIS: *You* must be mad.
    PISTHETAIROS:
Was your form filled out by Colonel Cock   1445
and properly punched?
    IRIS: Just let him try!
Why, the very idea!
    PISTHETAIROS: So that's your game, is it?
To sneak in here, infiltrate our territorial air,
spy on our city —
    IRIS: But where can a poor god go?
    PISTHETAIROS:
How should I know? But not here, by god!   1450
You're trespassing. What's more, it would
    serve you right
if I ordered you put to death this very instant.
If ever a god deserved to die, that god is you.
    IRIS:
But I *can't* die.
    PISTHETAIROS:
                Well, you damn well should.
A pretty pickle it would be if the whole world   1455
obeyed the Birds while you gods got uppity
and defied your betters.
                Now then, you aerial yacht,
state your business here.
    IRIS: *My* business? Why,
I am bearing the following message from my
    father Zeus
to mankind:
                "LET HOLOCAUSTS MAKE
        GLAD THY   1460
GODS AND MUTTON BARBECUES ON
    BEEFY
ALTARS TOAST, YEA, TILL EVERY
    STREET DOTH
REEK WITH ROAST AMBROSIALLY."
    PISTHETAIROS:
                Hmm. I think he wants a sacrifice.
But to which gods?

IRIS: To *which* gods? To *us*, of course.
Who else could he mean?
1465   PISTHETAIROS: But that's quite absurd.
You, gods? I mean, really!
IRIS: Name me any other gods.
PISTHETAIROS:
Why, the Birds, madam. Birds are now the
    gods.
Men worship Birds, not gods. Good gods, no!
    IRIS (*in the high tragic manner°*):
Then beware, O Mole, lest thou court the
    choler
of the gallèd gods, and Justice with the angry
1470   pick
of peevèd Zeus prise up thy pedestals
and topple all thy people, leaving not a smitch;
yea, and forkèd levin sear thee to a crisp,
lambasted low amongst thy mortal porticoes
by lightnings blunderbuss'd, yea —
1475   PISTHETAIROS: Listen, lady,
stow that tragic guff. You're starting to slob-
    ber.
And kindly stop twitching.
    What do you think I am?
Some poor Lydian or Phrygian slave° you can
    browbeat
with that bogey-talk?
    Go back and tell your Zeus
if he messes around with me, I'll fry him to a
1480   cinder!
What doth the poet say?°
    Aye, with eagles belching levin,
    I shall scorch the halls of heav'n,
    till Zeus doth frizzle in his juice
1485   *and Amphion, e'en Amphion —*
    — But what am I saying?
How does Amphion fit in here?
    Well, no matter.
But you tell your Zeus that if he crosses me,
    by god,
I'll send six hundred Porphyrions up against
    him,
and every Bird-Jack of the lot tricked out as a
1490   panther.

1469 s.d. **in the high tragic manner:** Iris' tragic ful-
mination is probably a pastiche of all the tragedi-
ans, patched out with some Aristophanic inventions.
1478 **Some poor Lydian or Phrygian slave:** A
direct quotation from Euripides' *Alkestis*, 675.
1481 **What doth the poet say?:** A quotation
from the lost *Niobe* of Aischylos, incongruously
incorporated into the passage without alteration. In
order to clarify the deliberate incongruity (the mention of Amphion), I have intruded the line which
follows the quotation.

I'd like to see his face. I remember the time
when one poor piddling little Porphyrion
was one too many for Zeus.
    But as for *you*,
Miss Messenger Iris, sail my way once more
and I'll lay my course right up your lovely legs,   1495
and board you at the top.
    Mark my words:
you'll be one flabbergasted little goddess
when you feel the triple ram on this old hulk.
    IRIS:
What a disgusting way to talk.
    PISTHETAIROS: Skedaddle, slut.
    IRIS:
Just you wait till my Father hears about this.   1500
    PISTHETAIROS:
Heaven defend me from this flying flirt. Beat
    it!
Go singe some youngster with your lechery,
    will you?

(*Exit* IRIS *in the machine.*)

CHORUS:
The gods' attack
has been rolled back,
    rebuffed by our Blockade.   1505

Let god and man
now heed our ban:
    NO TRANSETHEREAL TRADE!

No more, no more
do victuals soar;   1510
    no savory ascends;

and chops and stew
are now taboo:
    the party's over, friends!

PISTHETAIROS:
You know, it's rather odd about that other
    messenger   1515
we despatched to earth. He should be back by
    now.

(*Enter* HERALD *in great haste. He throws
himself to the ground at* PISTHETAIROS' *feet
and salaams profoundly.*)

HERALD:
O Pisthetairos! O Paragon! O Pink!
Thou Apogee of Genius! Sweet Flower of
    Finesse!
O Phoenix of Fame! Flimflam's Non-Pareil!
O of every noble attribute the Plus!   1520
O Happy Happy Chap! O Blest! O Most!
O Best! —
    oh, balls.

PISTHETAIROS:
           You were about to say, my friend,
when you so rudely interrupted yourself?
    HERALD (*rising and crowning* PISTHETAI-
       ROS):
Deign, my lord, to accept this crown of solid
       gold,
proffered in honor of your glorious wisdom and
1525   chicane
by an adoring world.
    PISTHETAIROS: I am deeply honored, sir.
But why should man's election fall on me?
    HERALD:
O fabulous founder of great Cloudcuckooland,
how can you ask such a question? Have you
      not heard
that Pisthetairos has become the darling of the
1530   mortal world,
a name to conjure with? That all mankind
has gone Cloudcuckoolandophile,
madly, utterly?
           And yet, only yesterday,
before your dispensation in the skies became a
      fact,
1535   the Spartan craze had swept the faddish world.
Why, men went mad with mimicry of
      Sokrates,°
affected long hair, indifferent food,
rustic walking sticks, total bathlessness,
and led, in short, what I can only call
a Spartan existence.
1540   But then suddenly, overnight,
the Birds became the vogue, the *dernier cri*
of human fashion.° And men immediately
      began
to feather their own nests; to cluck and brood;
play ducks and drakes; grub for chickenfeed;
1545   hatch deals, and being rooked or gulled,
to have their little gooses cooked. But if they
      grouse,

1536 **mimicry of Sokrates:** A gibe at the Spartan
affectations of the Socratic circle and especially
Sokrates' personal uncleanliness. To some extent
this may be merely an exploitation of the common
man's stereotype of the intellectual and philosopher.
I remember a Princeton landlady telling me that
Einstein never took a bath; this was her revenge
on his genius. As for Sokrates, who knows?
1541–1542 **the *dernier cri* of human fashion:**
The examples of the avine vogue which follow are
all of my own invention. The Greek cannot be
literally translated into English because it is based
upon an untranslatable pun (νομός, meaning both
"law" and "pasture" or "feeding-place"), designed
to parody, in avine terms, the Athenian love of
litigation.

they still are game.
           In sum, the same old life,
but feathered over with the faddish thrills of
      being
chic.
      But the latest word in Birds is names.
The gimpy peddler is tagged Old Partridge
      now;   1550
Menippos is called Cuckoo; Opountios, Stool
      Pigeon;
Philokles is the Lark; Theogenes, the Pseudo-
      Goose;
Lykourgos, Lame Duck; Chairephon is Bats;
Syrakosios, of course, is called the Jaybird,
and as for Meidias, why, he's the Sitting
      Duck —   1555
and judging from that ugly clobbered beak of
      his,
no man ever missed.
           And that's not all.
Mankind has gone so utterly batty over Birds
that all the latest songs are filled with them —
Swallows, Pigeons, Ducks, Geese, you name it.   1560
Any tune with feathers in it or a pinch or fluff
becomes a hit.
           And that's how matters stand
below.
      But one last point before I leave.
Vast swarms and coveys of men are on the
      move,
all migrating here to Cloudcuckooland in quest
      of wings   1565
and the Feathered Way of Life. Somehow, sir,
you'll have to wing these mortal immigrants.

    (*Exit* HERALD.)

PISTHETAIROS: Gad!
We'd best get busy.

    (*To a* SLAVE.)

           — You there.
                 Run inside.
Stuff every hamper you can find with sets of
      wings
and tell Manes to bring them out. I'll stay
      here   1570
to give my greeting to these wingless refugees
      in person.

    (*Exit* SLAVE.)

CHORUS:
      Upon thy head, Cloudcuckooland,
         the crown of praise we set:
      O Beautiful for Swarming Skies —
PISTHETAIROS:
      — Don't count your chickens yet.   1575

CHORUS:
> This feather'd isle, this pinion'd place,
>   where martyr-Birds have bled,
> where men aspire on wings of fluff —

(*Enter* MANES, *slowly and empty-handed.*)

PISTHETAIROS:
> — Their legs are made of lead.

(*Exit* MANES.)

CHORUS:
> 1580   What greater bliss can men require?
> Here the lovely Graces go,
>   and Wisdom strolls with sweet Desire,
> and Peace comes tripping slow.

(*Enter* MANES *carrying two wings.*)

PISTHETAIROS:
> She's miles ahead of Manes.
>   — Dammit, blockhead, move!

CHORUS:
> 1585   To work, dull clod! Heave-ho the wings!

(*Exit* MANES. *To* PISTHETAIROS.)

> Now show him you're the master.
> Flog him, thrash him —

(*Enter* MANES *with two more wings.*)

PISTHETAIROS: — What's the use?
> A mule could manage faster.

(*Exit* MANES.)

CHORUS:
> Now sort the wings in pinion-piles
> 1590   by order of professions:
> Seabirds' wings for nautical types,
>   Warblers' for musicians —

(*Enter* MANES *with three wings.*)

PISTHETAIROS:
> — So help me, Kestrels, if I don't bash your
> head to a pulp, you lazy, stupid, bungling
> ass!

(*Beats him.* MANES *scurries off, instantly reappearing with crates and hampers of wings which he quickly dumps and sorts into the appropriate piles. Suddenly from offstage is heard the tenor voice of* DELINQUENT, *singing:*)

> If I had the wings of an Eagle,°
> 1595   o'er this barren blue brine I would fly . . .

1594 **If I had the wings of an Eagle:** A quotation, according to the Scholiast, from the lost *Oinomaos* of Sophokles.

PISTHETAIROS:
> That messenger of ours was telling the truth,
>   by god.
> Here comes someone crooning Eagle-ballads.

(*Enter* DELINQUENT,° *a strapping boy in his teens.*)

DELINQUENT:
Some kicks!
There's nothin' on earth like flyin'! Whee!
                                        Chee,
Cloudcuckooland's the roost for me! Hey,
    man,   1600
I'm bats about the Birds! I'm with it chum!
I wanna be a Bird! I want your way of life!

PISTHETAIROS:
Which way? We Birds have bushels of ways.

DELINQUENT:
If it's strictly for the Birds, then it's for me,
    man.
But best of all I like that splendid custom
    you've got   1605
that permits a little Bird to choke his daddy
    dead.

PISTHETAIROS:
True. We think it very manly of a young Bird
if he walks up and takes a poke at his old man.

DELINQUENT: That's it, Dad.
Exactly why I'm here. I want to throttle
the old man and inherit his jack.

PISTHETAIROS: One moment.   1610
We Birds observe another custom older still.
You'll find it preserved in the Scrolls of the
    Storks. I quote:
"ONCE THE AGED STORK HATH
    REARED HIS BROOD
AND HIS CHICKS HAVE MADE THEIR
    MAIDEN FLIGHT ALONE,
THEY MUST IN TURN SUPPORT THEIR
    FATHER IN HIS AGE."   1615

DELINQUENT:
A fat lot of good I've got from coming here,
    chum,
if I have to go back home and support the old
    man.

PISTHETAIROS:
I tell you what. You seem a decent lad,
and I'll adopt you as our city's official Mascot-
    Bird.

1597 s.d. DELINQUENT: The Greek is πατϱολοίας, a word which it is usual to translate as "parricide," although it means merely "father-beater." Since our young man merely *wants* to murder his father, I have made him an adolescent punk and called him Delinquent.

8

But first some good advice I received as a
1620   toddler
at my mother's knee:
                    Don't drub your dad.
Take this wing instead.
                    With your other hand,
accept this spur. Here, your helmet is this
        crest.
Now march off, rookie. Drill, stand your guard,
1625   live on your pay and let your father be.
You look aggressive: flutter off to Thrace.
There's fighting there.
        DELINQUENT: By god, I think you're right.
What's more, I'm game.
        PISTHETAIROS: You damn well better be.

(*Exit* DELINQUENT. *From the other side
enters the dithyrambic poet* KINESIAS. *His
splay-footed galumphing entrance is in sharp
contrast to his aerial pretensions.*)

        KINESIAS:
                On gossamer I go,
1630   *delicately wending,*°
                up, up, up the airy stairs
                of Poesy ascending —
        PISTHETAIROS:
By god, we'll need a boatload of wings at least
to get this limping poet off the ground!
        KINESIAS:
1635   *— forth through the Vast Unknown,*
                original, alone —
        PISTHETAIROS:
Welcome, Kinesias, bard of balsa-wood!
What made you whirl your splay-foot hither,
        bard?
        KINESIAS:
                I yearn, I burn, thou know'st it well,
1640   *to be a lilting Philomel.*
        PISTHETAIROS:
A little less lilt, please. Could you stoop to
        prose?
        KINESIAS:
Wings, dull wight, wings!
                    Vouchsafe me wings
to percolate amidst the churning scud and rack
of yon conceited clouds from which I'll pluck
        and cull
1645   tornado similes of blizzard speech.
        PISTHETAIROS:
You mean you plagiarize the clouds?

        KINESIAS: Ah, my dear sir,
but our poet's craft depends completely on the
        clouds.°
Why, the most resplendent poem is but the
        insubstantial
shimmer refracted from that blue and bubbled
        murk of
froth, that featherfillip'd air.
                    Judge for yourself.   1650
        PISTHETAIROS:
I won't.
        KINESIAS:
        Ah, but you shall, dear boy, you shall.
I'll do my Aerial Aria, and just for you.
                                Ready?

(*Singing.*)
                Now wingèd wraiths
                of the hovering Plover
                over yon Ether rove —   1655
        PISTHETAIROS:
GALE WARNINGS POSTED! STAND BY,
        ALL SHIPS AT SEA!
        KINESIAS:
                — over the billows pillow'd aloft,
                in the buffeting gust of the gathered gale —
        PISTHETAIROS:
By god, I'll give you some buffets you won't
        like!

(*He snatches a pair of large wings from a
pile and beats* KINESIAS *who runs about, still
spouting.*)

        KINESIAS:
                — now north, now south,   1660
                and where they fare, fare I,
                cutting my wake
                on the harborless lake
                of the featherfillip'd sky.
Get that, old boy? A catchy figure, what?   1665
        PISTHETAIROS: (*lashing him again*):
Get that? What? No taste for featherfillips,
        poet?
        KINESIAS:
What a beastly way to welcome a poetic
        genius
for whose services the entire civilized world
        competes!

1629–1630 **On gossamer I go, delicately wending:** According to the Scholiast, a parody of
Anakreon.

1647 **our poet's craft depends completely on
the clouds:** For the Clouds as patron goddesses of
dithyrambic poets, cf. *Clouds*, 335 ff. Poets whose
compositions are a characteristic blend of obscurity,
turbid emptiness and inflated language naturally
depend upon the Murky Muse for inspiration.

PISTHETAIROS:
Then stay with us. You can train an All-Bird Chorus. Leotrophides will conduct his own
1670   compositions.
He likes the delicate stuff.

KINESIAS: Durst despise me, sir?
Know then, I ne'er shall cease from Poesy
until with wings I waltz upon Cloudcuckooland.
       Farewell.

(*Exit* KINESIAS. *Enter an* INFORMER *in a tattered coat, singing.*)

INFORMER:
   What suspicious Birds are these°
1675   *that own no clothes and house in trees?*
   O Cuckoo, Cuckoo, tell me true!

PISTHETAIROS:
We've passed the nuisance stage. This is crisis.
Here comes a warbler humming treason-trills.

INFORMER: Ho!
Again I cry:
1680   *O Cuckoo, Cuckoo, tell me true!*

PISTHETAIROS:
I think it must be an epigram on his tattered
   coat.
He's so cold he's calling the Cuckoo to bring
   the Spring.°
Poets are always talking out loud to Cuckoos
   in April.

INFORMER:
You there. Where's the guy who's handing out
   the wings?

PISTHETAIROS:
You're looking at him now. What do *you*
1685   want, friend?

INFORMER:
Wings, fellow, wings! Got it?

PISTHETAIROS: I get it:
to hide the holes in your coat.°

INFORMER: Listen, Buster:
my business is the indictment of islands for
   subversive

activities.° You see in me a professional informer.

PISTHETAIROS:
       A splendid calling.

INFORMER:
Also an *agent provocateur* of lawsuits and
1690   investigations.
That's why I want the wings. They'd come in
   handy
for whizzing around the islands delivering my
   indictments
and handing out subpoenas in person.

PISTHETAIROS: I see. And these wings
would increase your efficiency?

INFORMER: Increase my efficiency?
Impossible. But they'd help me dodge the
1695   pirates I meet
en route. Then, coming home, I'd load the
   crops of the
Cranes with writs and suits for ballast.

PISTHETAIROS: And *that's* your trade?
A husky lad like yourself earning his liveli-
   hood
by indicting foreigners?

INFORMER: But what am I supposed to do?
I don't know how to dig.

PISTHETAIROS: Great Zeus Almighty, 1700
Aren't there enough honest means of earning a
   living
without this dirty little dodge of hatching
   suits?

INFORMER:
Listen, mister: it's wings I want, not words.

PISTHETAIROS:
But my words *are* wings.

INFORMER: Your words are *wings?*

PISTHETAIROS:
But of course. How else do you think mankind
   won its 1705
wings if not from words?

INFORMER: From words?

PISTHETAIROS: Wings from words.
You know the old men, how they loll around
   at the barbershop°

1674 **What suspicious Birds are these:** Adapted from a poem by Alkaios.

1682 **he's calling the Cuckoo to bring the Spring:** In the Greek it is the Swallow who brings the Informer's Spring.

1687 **to hide the holes in your coat:** Literally the manuscript has Pisthetairos say: "Are you planning to fly to Pellene?" Pellene was famous for its heavy woolen clothing, offered as prizes in the contests celebrated there.

1688–1689 **the indictment of islands for subversive activities:** By "islands" is meant the subject-states of the Athenian Empire, very largely comprised of the Aegean islands. Since the islanders were compelled to refer their more important lawsuits to the verdict of Athenian juries, they were therefore in a disadvantageous position and easily victimized by professional informers.

1707 **they loll around at the barbershop:** The barbershop was *par excellence* the nerve center of Athenian gossip, rumor, and political speculation.

grousing and bitching about the younger generation? —

"Thanks to that damned Dieitrephes° and his damned

advice," growls one, "my boy has flown the
1710   family nest

to take a flier on the horses."

                    "Hell,"

pipes another, "you should see that kid of mine:

he's gone so damn batty over those tragic plays,

he flies into fits of ecstasy and gets goose-bumps

all over."

INFORMER:
                    And *that's* how words give wings?
1715   PISTHETAIROS: Right.

Through dialectic the mind of man takes wing and soars;

he is morally and spiritually uplifted. And so I hoped

with words of good advice to wing you on your way

toward some honest trade.

INFORMER: It just won't work.

PISTHETAIROS:
But why won't it?

INFORMER:
1720   I can't disgrace the family name.

We've been informers now for several generations,

you see.

                    So give me wings — Hawk's or Kestrel's

will suit me fine, but anything's all right by me
provided they're fast and light. I'll slip them on,

dart out to the islands with stacks of sub-
1725   poenas and

summons, whizz back home to defend the case in court,

then zip right back to the islands again.

PISTHETAIROS: I get it.

When they arrive, they find their case is lost by default;

they've been condemned *in absentia*.

INFORMER: You've got it.

PISTHETAIROS:
And while they're coming here, you're going
1730   there

to confiscate their property? Right?

1709 **that damned Dieitrephes:** Cf. Glossary,
DIEITREPHES. Dieitrephes was a notorious horse-racing enthusiast and hence in high favor with the wastrels among the Athenian *jeunesse dorée.*

INFORMER: You've got it.
I'll whirr around like a top.

PISTHETAIROS: Right. I've got it:

you're a top. And guess what I've got here for you:

a lovely little set of Korkyrean wings.

(*He pulls out a whip.*)

INFORMER:
Hey, that's a whip!

PISTHETAIROS: Not a whip, it's wings   1735

to make your little top go round.

(*He lashes* INFORMER *with the whip.*)

                    Got it?

INFORMER:
Ouch! Owwooooo!

PISTHETAIROS: Flap your wings, Birdie!

That's it, old top, wobble on your way!

                    By god,

I'll make this legal whirligig go round!

(*Exit* INFORMER *under the lash.* PISTHETAI-
ROS *signals to his slaves to pick up the piles
of wings.*)

                    — Hey,

you there. Gather up the wings and bring
them inside.   1740

(*Exeunt* PISTHETAIROS *and* ATTENDANTS *with
the hampers of wings.*)

CHORUS:°
Many the marvels I have seen,
    the wonders on land and sea;
but the strangest sight I ever saw
    was the weird KLEONYMOS-tree.

1741 s.d. CHORUS: With this strophe Aristophanes commences a series of brief Travelogues by the Birds: strange sights and marvels which their world-traveling has enabled them to visit. Actually, of course, all of the wonders are merely fabulized versions of familiar Athenian institutions and personages: the coward-sycophant Kleonymos, the thief Orestes, the psychagogue Sokrates and his accomplice Chairephon, the incredible tongue-worship of the wondrous men of Athens.

In this strophe Kleonymos is compared to a tree which grows enormous in the Spring and in winter sheds, not leaves, but shields. The Spring was the banner season for informers and sycophants, when men like Kleonymos (physically fat to begin with) were bloated with the profits of their trade. In winter the Kleonymos-tree sheds its shields, an allusion to Kleonymos' cowardice in battle (i.e., throwing down his shield and running away).

The second part of the strophe deals with the notorious footpad Orestes and concludes with a play on the name: (1) the Athenian thief, (2) his

1745 It grows in faraway places;
    its lumber looks quite stout,
but the wood is good for nothing,
    for the heart is rotten out.

In Spring it grows gigantic
1750   with sycophantic green,
and bitter buds of slander
    on every bough are seen.

But when, like war, cold winter comes,
    this strange KLEONYMOS yields,
1755 instead of leaves like other trees,
    a crop of coward's shields.

And far away (but not so far),
    we saw a second wonder,
a place of awful, dismal dark —
1760   when the sun goes under.

And there by day dead heroes come
    and talk with living men,
and while it's light no ghost will hurt,
    but when it's dark again,

1765 then thieves and ghosts take common shape,
    and who knows which is which?
So wise men dodge that dive at night —
    but most of all the rich.

For any man who ventures in
1770   may meet ORESTES there,
the ghost who paralyzes men,
    the thief who strips them bare.

(*Enter* PROMETHEUS,° *so muffled in blankets as to be completely unrecognizable. His every motion is furtive, but his furtiveness is hampered by an immense umbrella which he carries underneath his blankets. He speaks in a whisper.*)

PROMETHEUS:
Easy does it. I hope old Zeus can't see me.

(*To a* BIRD.)

Psst. Where's Pisthetairos?
    PISTHETAIROS: What in the world is *this*?
— Who are you, blanket?

---

famous legendary predecessor, the son of Agamemnon. The point seems to be that those who venture out in Athens at night may meet Orestes the thief (who stripped his victims) or Orestes the heroic ghost (who paralyzed his victims — a power possessed by heroes, according to the Scholiast).
    1772 s.d. **Enter** PROMETHEUS: Mankind's greatest champion and arch foe of Zeus makes his ridiculously furtive entrance on still another philanthropic mission: to warn Pisthetairos of Zeus' plans and secrets. Needless to say, he is extremely anxious to avoid observation by the gods.

PROMETHEUS: Shh. Are there any gods 1775
on my trail?
    PISTHETAIROS:
        Gods? No, not a god in sight.
Who *are* you?
    PROMETHEUS:
        What's the time? Is it dark yet?
    PISTHETAIROS:
You want the time? It's still early afternoon.
Look, who the hell *are* you?
    PROMETHEUS: Is it milking-time, or later?
    PISTHETAIROS:
Look, you stinking bore —
    PROMETHEUS: What's the weather doing? 1780
How's the visibility? Clear skies? Low ceiling?
    PISTHETAIROS (*raising his stick*):   By God,
if you won't talk —
    PROMETHEUS:
        Dark, eh? Good. I'm coming out.

(*Uncovers.*)

PISTHETAIROS:
Hullo: it's Prometheus!
    PROMETHEUS: Shh. Don't make a sound.
    PISTHETAIROS:
What's the matter?
    PROMETHEUS:
        Shh. Don't even whisper my name.
If Zeus spots me here, he'll cook my goose but
    good. 1785
Now then, if you want to learn the lay of the
    land
in heaven, kindly open up this umbrella here
and hold it over my head while I'm talking.
Then the gods won't see me.

(PISTHETAIROS *takes the umbrella, opens it up, and holds it over* PROMETHEUS.)

PISTHETAIROS: Say, that's clever.
Prometheus all over.°
        — All right. Pop underneath 1790
and give us your news.
    PROMETHEUS: Brace yourself.
    PISTHETAIROS: Shoot.
    PROMETHEUS:
Zeus has had it.
    PISTHETAIROS:
        Since when?
    PROMETHEUS: Since the moment
you founded the city of Cloudcuckooland.
    Since that day

1789–1790 **Say, that's clever. Prometheus all over:** Pisthetairos is impressed by the ingenuity of Prometheus' umbrella, and compliments him as deserving of his name (Prometheus meant "Foresight").

not a single sacrifice, not even a whiff of smoke,
1795 no savories, no roast, nothing at all
has floated up to heaven. In consequence, my
      friend,
Olympos is starving to death. And that's not
      the worst of it.
All the Stone Age gods° from the hill country
have gone wild with hunger, screaming and
      gibbering away
like a lot of savages. And what's more, they've
1800   threatened
war unless Zeus succeeds in getting your Bird-
      embargo lifted
and the tidbit shipments back on the move
      once more.
    PISTHETAIROS:
You mean to say there are *other* gods in
      Heaven?
Stone Age gods?
    PROMETHEUS:
            Stone Age gods for Stone Age people.
Exekestides must have something to worship.
1805   PISTHETAIROS: Heavens,
they *must* be savages. But what do you call
      them?
    PROMETHEUS:
We call them Triballoi.
    PISTHETAIROS:
                Triballoi? From the same root
as our word "trouble," I suppose.
    PROMETHEUS: Very probably, I think.
But give me your attention. At present these
      Triballoi gods
have joined with Zeus to send an official
1810   embassy
to sue for peace. Now here's the policy you
      must follow:
flatly reject any offers of peace they make you
until Zeus agrees to restore his sceptre to the
      Birds
and consents to give you Miss Universe° as
      your wife.

1798 **All the Stone Age gods:** A free — but I
thought plausible — rendering of the "barbarian
gods" of the text. If Triballos is a representative of
the barbarian gods, then the divinities meant are
not merely uncivilized but Neolithic.
1814 **Miss Universe:** The Greek gives βασιλεία,
which means "sovereignty," "empire," "supreme
power." Because she is an unfamiliar abstraction
and not a genuine Olympian at all, I have felt free
to turn her into a "sort of Beauty Queen" and to
gloss her in the text as "the symbol of divine supremacy." In this play she symbolizes the logical
conclusion of the Athenian (or the Birds') struggle
for domination and universal supremacy. She is

    PISTHETAIROS:
But who's Miss Universe?
    PROMETHEUS: A sort of Beauty Queen,   1815
the sign of Empire and the symbol of divine
      supremacy.
It's she who keeps the keys to Zeus' thunder-
      bolts
and all his other treasures — Divine Wisdom,
Good Government, Common Sense, Naval
      Bases,
Slander, Libel, Political Graft, Sops to the
      Voters —   1820
    PISTHETAIROS:
And *she* keeps the keys?
    PROMETHEUS: Take it from me, friend.
Marry Miss Universe and the world is yours.
                        — You understand
why I had to tell you this? As Prometheus,
      after all,
my philanthropy is proverbial.
    PISTHETAIROS: Yes, we worship you
as the inventor of the barbecue.°
    PROMETHEUS: Besides, I loathe the gods.   1825
    PISTHETAIROS:
The loathing's mutual, I know.
    PROMETHEUS: Just call me Timon:
I'm a misanthrope of gods.
                — But I must be running along.
Give me my parasol. If Zeus spots me now,
he'll think I'm an ordinary one-god procession.
    I'll pretend
to be the girl behind the boy behind the
      basket.   1830
    PISTHETAIROS:
Here — take this stool and watch yourself
      march by.

(*Exit* PROMETHEUS *in solemn procession,
draped in his blanket, the umbrella in one
hand, the stool in the other.* PISTHETAIROS
and the ATTENDANTS *retire.*)

CHORUS:°
There lies a marsh in Webfoot Land,
    the Swamp of Dismal Dread,
and there we saw foul SOKRATES
    come calling up the dead.   1835

what Thoukydides called ἀρχή ("empire," "domination") and what I believe Euripides everywhere
in his tragedies meant by the figure of Helen: the
prize for which the (Peloponnesian) War was
fought.
1825 **the inventor of the barbecue:** Because
Prometheus gave fire to man.
1832 s.d. CHORUS: The second installment of the
Birds' Travelogue. The subject is Sokrates as psychagogue or psychopomp, the guide of the soul, engaged

And there that cur PEISANDROS came
to see if he could see
the soul he'd lost while still alive
by dying cowardly.

1840 He brought a special sacrifice,
a little camel lamb;
then, like Odysseus, slit its throat —
he slit its throat and ran!

And then a phantom shape flew down,
1845 a specter cold and wan,
and on the camel's blood he pounced —
the vampire CHAIREPHON!

(*Enter the Peace Delegation from Olympos:
first,* POSEIDON, *a god of immense and avun-
cular dignity, carrying a trident; then* HERA-
KLES *with lion skin and club, a god with the
character and build of a wrestler and an
appetite to match; and finally* TRIBALLOS,
*hopelessly tangled up in the unfamiliar robes
of Olmpian civilization.*)

POSEIDON:
Here we are. And there before us, ambassadors,
lies Cloudcuckooland.

(TRIBALLOS, *by now hopelessly snarled up in
his robes, trips and falls flat on his face.*)

— Damn you! Back on your feet,
1850 you hulking oaf. Look, you've got your robes
all twisted up.
No. Screw them around to the right.
This way. Where's your dignity, you heavenly
hick?
O Democracy, I fear your days are numbered
if Heaven's diplomatic corps is recruited like
this!
1855 Dammit, stop twitching! Gods, I've never seen

---

in calling up spirits from the dead in a little sacrifice
which resembles that of Odysseus in Book XI of
the *Odyssey.* Sokrates' Stygian assistant is his cadav-
erous colleague of Athenian life, Chairephon.
    The scene takes place in the land of Shadowfeet
(according to Ktesias, a curious web-footed tribe
which lived in Libya; when they lay down for a
nap, they held up their huge webfeet as awnings
against the sun. To this the Scholiast adds that they
had four legs, three of which were used for walking,
and the fourth as a tentpole for their tentlike feet).
Here, beside a Stygian swamp, haunted by terror,
Sokrates summons the soul of Peisandros, an Athenian coward in search of his *psyche* (i.e., courage),
by means of sacrifice; but so faint-hearted is
Sokrates that he runs away in terror, leaving the
bloody victim to the spectral vampire Chairephon.

a gawkier god than you!
— Look here, Herakles,
how should we proceed in your opinion?
HERAKLES: You hoid me,
Poseidon. If I had my way, I'd throttle the
guy,
any guy, what dared blockade the gods.
POSEIDON: My dear nephew,
have you forgotten that the purpose of our
mission here   1860
is to treat for peace?
HERAKLES: I'd throttle him all the more.

(*Enter* PISTHETAIROS, *followed by* ATTEND-
ANTS *with cooking utensils. He pointedly
ignores the presence of the Divine Delegation.*)

PISTHETAIROS (*to* ATTENDANTS):
Hand me the cheese grater. Vinegar, please.
All right,
now the cheese. Poke up that fire, somebody.
POSEIDON:
Mortal, three immortal gods give you greeting.

(*Dead silence.*)

Mortal, three immortal —
PISTHETAIROS: Shush: I'm slicing pickles.   1865
HERAKLES:
Hey, what kind of meat is dat?
PISTHETAIROS: Those are jailbirds
sentenced to death on the charge of High
Treason
against the Sovereign Birds.
HERAKLES: And dat luscious gravy
gets poured on foist?
PISTHETAIROS (*looking up for the first time*):
Why hullo there: it's Herakles!
What do you want?
POSEIDON: Mortal, as the official spokesman   1870
for the Divine Delegation, I venture to suggest
that —
PISTHETAIROS (*holding up an empty bottle*):
Drat it. We're out of oil.
HERAKLES: Out of oil?
Say, dat's a shame. Boids should be basted
good.
POSEIDON:
— As I was on the point of saying, official
Olympos
regards the present hostilities as utterly point-
less.   1875
Further, I venture to observe that you Birds
have a great deal to gain from a kindlier
Olympos.
I might mention, for instance, a supply of
clean rainwater

for your Birdbaths and a perpetual run, say,
1880 of halcyon days. On some such terms as these
we are formally empowered by Zeus to sign the articles
of peace.

PISTHETAIROS:
Poseidon, you forget: it was not the Birds
who began this war. Moreover, peace is our desire
as much as yours. And if you gods stand prepared
to treat in good faith, I see no obstacle to
1885 peace.
None whatsoever. Our sole demand is this:
Zeus must restore his royal sceptre to the Birds.
If this one trifling concession seems agreeable to you,
I invite you all to dinner.

HERAKLES: Youse has said enough.
I vote Yes.

POSEIDON:
1890   You contemptible, idiotic glutton!
Would you dethrone your own Father?

PISTHETAIROS: I object, Poseidon.
Look at it in this light.
                    Can you gods be unaware
that you actually stand to increase, not diminish your power,
by yielding your present supremacy to the Birds? Why,
1895 as things stand now, men go skulking around
under cover of the clouds, with impunity committing perjury
and in your name too. But conclude alliance with the Birds,
gentlemen, and your problems are over forever. How?
Suppose, for instance, some man swears a solemn oath
by Zeus and the Raven and then breaks his
1900   word. Suddenly
down swoops a Raven when he's least suspecting it
and pecks out his eyes!

POSEIDON: Holy Poseidon! You know,
I think you've got something there.

HERAKLES: Youse is so right.

POSEIDON (to TRIBALLOS):
                    What do you say?

TRIBALLOS:
Fapple gleep.

HERAKLES:
Dat's Stone Age for Yeah.°

1904 **Dat's Stone Age for Yeah:** Cf. note on
p. 306, *All the Stone Age gods.*

PISTHETAIROS: And that's not all.
Suppose some fellow vows to make a sacrifice
to the gods   1905
and then later changes his mind or tries to procrastinate,
thinking, *The mills of the gods grind slow; well, so do mine.*
                We Birds, I can promise you,
will put a stop to sophistry like that.

POSEIDON: Stop it? But how?

PISTHETAIROS:
Someday our man will be busily counting up his cash   1910
or lolling around in the tub, singing away,
and a Kite will dive down like a bolt from the blue,
snatch up two of his sheep or a wad of cash
and whizz back up to the gods with the loot.

HERAKLES: Friend,
youse is right. Zeus should give dat sceptre   1915
back to the Boids.

POSEIDON: What do *you* think, Triballos?

HERAKLES (threatening him with his club):
Vote Yes, bub, or I'll drub youse.

TRIBALLOS: Schporckl nu?
Momp gapa birdschmoz kluk.

HERAKLES: See? He votes wid me.

POSEIDON:
If you both see eye to eye, I'll have to go along.

HERAKLES:
Dat does it. Hey, youse. The sceptre's yours.   1920

PISTHETAIROS:
Dear me, I nearly forgot one trifling condition.
We Birds willingly waive any claim we might have to Hera:
Zeus can have her. We don't object in the slightest.
But I must have Miss Universe as my wife. On that demand
I stand absolutely firm.

POSEIDON: Then you won't have peace.   1925
Good afternoon.

(*The Delegation prepares to leave,* HERAKLES *with great reluctance.*)

PISTHETAIROS:
                It's all the same to me.
                — Oh chef:
make the gravy thick.

HERAKLES:
                God alive, Poseidon, where in the
world is youse going? Are we going to war for the sake of a
dame?

POSEIDON:
What alternative would you suggest?

1930 HERAKLES: Peace, peace!
POSEIDON:
You poor fool, don't you realize that you're
   being tricked?
What's more, you're only hurting yourself.
                           Listen here:
if Zeus should abdicate his throne in favor of
   the Birds
and then die, you'd be left a pauper. Whereas
   now
1935 you're the legal heir of Zeus. Heir, in fact,
to everything he owns.
   PISTHETAIROS: Watch your step, Herakles.
You're being hoodwinked.

(*Taking* HERAKLES *by the arm and withdrawing a little.*)

          — Now, just step aside with me.
I have something to tell you.
             Look, you poor chump,
your uncle's pulling a fast one. Not one cent
1940 of Zeus' enormous estate will ever come to you
You see, my friend, you're a bastard.
   HERAKLES: What's dat, fella?
I'm a bastard?
   PISTHETAIROS:
         Of course you're a bastard — by Zeus.
Your mother, you see, was an ordinary mortal
   woman,
not a goddess. In other words, she comes
of foreign stock. Which makes you legally a
1945 bastard,°
pure and simple.
         Moreover, Pallas Athene
is normally referred to as The Heiress.° That's
   her title.
But how in the name of Zeus could Athene be
   an heiress
if Zeus had any legitimate sons?
   HERAKLES: Maybe.
Youse could be right. But what if the Old
1950 • Man
swears I'm his son?
   PISTHETAIROS: The law still says No.
In any case, Poseidon here, who's been egging
   you on,

1945 **Which makes you legally a bastard:** According to Athenian laws on citizenship, citizens
must be born of Athenian fathers and mothers.
Herakles, as the son of Zeus (a *bona fide* Olympian) and Alkmene (an ordinary woman, i.e., a
foreigner) would be both illegitimate and ineligible
for citizenship — according to Athenian law.
1946–1947 **Pallas Athene is normally referred
to as The Heiress:** Because Athens was Athena's
"portion," she was officially called The Heiress.

would be the first person to challenge the will
   in court.
As your father's brother, he's the next-of-kin,
   and hence
the legal heir.
   Let me read you the provisions of the law. 1955

(*He draws a lawbook from his robes.*)

In the words of Solon himself:
SO LONG AS LEGITIMATE ISSUE SHALL
SURVIVE THE DECEASED, NO BAS-
TARD SHALL INHERIT. IN THE CASE
THAT NO LEGITIMATE ISSUE SUR- 1960
VIVES, THE ESTATE SHALL PASS TO
THE NEXT OF KIN.
   HERAKLES:
Youse mean to say I won't inherit a damn
   thing
from the Old Man?
   PISTHETAIROS: Not a smitch. By the way,
has your Father ever had your birth legally
   recorded 1965
or had you registered in court as his official
   heir?
   HERAKLES:
No, never. I always thought there was some-
   thing fishy.
   PISTHETAIROS:
Come, my boy, chin up. Don't pout at heaven
with that sullen glare. Join us. Come in with
   the Birds.
We'll set you on a throne and you can guzzle
   pigeon's milk 1970
the rest of your endless days.
   HERAKLES: You know, fella,
I been thinking about that dame you want so
   bad.
Well, I vote youse can have her.
   PISTHETAIROS: Splendid.
What do you say, Poseidon?
   POSEIDON: No. A resounding No.
   PISTHETAIROS:
Then it rests with Triballos.
          — What's your verdict, my friend? 1975
   TRIBALLOS:
*Gleep? Schnoozer skirt wotta twatch snock!
Birdniks pockle. Ugh.*
   HERAKLES: He said she's for the Boids.
I hoid him.
   POSEIDON:
   And I distinctly heard him say the opposite:
A firm No — with a few choice obscenities
   added.
   HERAKLES:
The poor dumb sap never said a doity word. 1980
All he said was: *Give 'er to the Boids.*

POSEIDON: I yield.
You two can come to terms together as you
    please.
Since you seem to be agreed on everything, I'll
    just abstain.
    HERAKLES (*to* PISTHETAIROS):
Man, youse is getting everything youse wants.
1985 Fly up to Heaven wid us, and get your missus
and anything else your little heart desires.
    PISTHETAIROS:
And we're in luck. This feast of poultry I've
    prepared
will grace our wedding supper.
    HERAKLES: Youse guys push along.
I'll stay here and watch the barbecue.
    POSEIDON: Not on your life.
You'd guzzle grill and all. You'd better come
1990   along
with us, my boy.
    HERAKLES:
        Aw, Unc, but it woulda tasted so good.
    PISTHETAIROS (*to* ATTENDANTS):
— You there, servants.
            Bring my wedding clothes along.

(*Exeunt* PISTHETAIROS, *the gods and* AT-
TENDANTS.)

    CHORUS:°
Beneath the clock in a courtroom,
    down in the land of Gab,
1995 We saw a weird race of people,
    earning their bread by blab.

Their name is the Claptraptummies.
    Their only tool is talk.
They sow and reap and shake the figs
2000   by dexterous yakkity-yak.

Their tongues and twaddle mark them off,
    barbarians every one;
but the worst of all are in the firm
    of GORGIAS & SON.°

2005 But from this bellyblabbing tribe,
    one custom's come to stay:
in Athens, when men sacrifice,
    they cut the tongue away.

1993 s.d. CHORUS: The concluding section of the
Birds' Travelogue, a pointed satire on the Athenian
worship of the Clacking Money-Making Tongue in
thin anthropological disguise.
2004 of GORGIAS & SON: To Gorgias the manuscript adds the name of Philippos, son or disciple
of Gorgias the sophist. It was believed that the per-
suasive tongue of Gorgias served to stimulate the
disastrous interest in Sicily among Athenians which
culminated in the Sicilian Expedition.

(*Enter a* MESSENGER.)

    MESSENGER:
O blessèd, blessèd, blessèd breed of Bird,
more happy than human tongue can tell: 2010
welcome your lord and King as he ascends to
    heaven!
Attend him now!
                Praise him, whose glory glisters
more brightly than the rising stars at dusk
flare their loveliness upon the golden evening
    air,
purer than the blazoned sun!
                    He comes, he comes,   2015
and with him comes the splendid glory of a
    bride
whose beauty has no peer. In his hand he
    shakes
the wingèd thunderbolt at Zeus, the flash of
    lightning.
Unspeakably sweet, a fragrance ascends to
    heaven
and curls of incense trace their lovely spirals   2020
on the drinking air.
                He comes!
            Greet your King with song!
Raise the wedding song the lovely Muses sing!

(*Re-enter* PISTHETAIROS, *gorgeously attired,°
his long golden train carried by the three
gods. Beside him, dressed in the magnificent
golden robes of a bride, walks the veiled
figure of* MISS UNIVERSE.)

    KORYPHAIOS:
Make way! Make way!
                Fall back for the dancers!
Welcome your King with beating wings!
Dance, dance!
            Praise this happy Prince!   2025
sing the loveliness of brides!
Weave with circling feet, weave and dance
in honor of the King, in honor of his bride!
Now let the Golden Age of Birds begin
    by lovely marriage ushered in,   2030
        Hymen Hymenaios O!

2022 s.d. **Re-enter** PISTHETAIROS, **gorgeously attired:** The culmination of the play in the apotheosis
of Pisthetairos and the marriage with Miss Universe.
Man's comic dream is completed; by building
Cloudcuckooland and winning Miss Universe, Man
becomes supreme, escapes his mortal condition, and
achieves divinity. It would be blasphemous if it
were not so terribly ironic a wish-fulfillment of the
god-intoxicated Athenian Dream.

CHORUS:

> To such a song as this,
> the weaving Fates once led
> the universal King,
> Zeus, the lord of all,
> to lovely Hera's bed.
>   *O Hymen! Hymenaios O!*

2035

> And blooming Love was there,
> Love with shimmering wings,
> Love the charioteer!
> Love once held the reins,
> Love drove the happy pair!
>   *O Hymen! Hymenaios O!*

2040

PISTHETAIROS:

I thank you for your songs and dance. Thank
    you, thank you,
one and all.

KORYPHAIOS:

2045
    Now praise the lightnings of your King!
Sing his thunders crashing on the world!
Sing the blazing bolts of Zeus, praise the man
who hurls them!
        Sing the flare of lightning;
praise, praise the crashing of its awful fire!

CHORUS:

2050
> O Lightning, flash of livid fire,
> O javelin of Zeus,
>   everliving light!

(A great low roll of thunder is heard.)

O thunders breaking on this lovely world,
rumble majestic that runs before the rain!
O Lightning and Thunders,
            bow low, bow down,
2055 bow before this man, bow to the lord of all!

(Another great crack of thunder.)

He wields the thunder as his very own.
Lightnings flare at the touch of his hand,
            winning, achieving
the Bride of Heaven and the Crown of God!
        O Hymen! Hymenaios O!   2060

PISTHETAIROS:

Now follow our bridal party, one and all.
Soar on high, you happy breed of Birds,
to the halls of Zeus, to the bed of love!

*(He extends his hand to his bride and
together they dance toward the waiting
machine.)*

> Reach me your hand, dear bride.
> Now take me by my wings,   2065
> oh my lovely,
>   my sweet,
> and let me lift you up,
> and soar beside you
> through the buoyant air!

*(PISTHETAIROS and his bride dance toward
the waiting machine. With slowly beating
wings they rise gradually heavenward. The
gods and ATTENDANTS bow down in homage,
the CHORUS divides and flocks triumphantly
toward the exits, chanting as they go.)*

CHORUS:

> *Alalalai!*
>   *Io!*
>   *Paion!*   2070
> *O greatest of the gods!*
> *Tenella Kallinikos O!*

GLOSSARY

AESCHYLUS, AISCHYLOS: The great Athenian
tragedian (525–456 B.C.).

AESOP, AISOPOS: A writer of fables, perhaps
legendary himself. He was reputed a native of
Samos who flourished in the sixth century B.C.

AGAMEMNON: In mythology, commander-in-
chief of the Greek forces at the siege of Troy.

AISCHINES: An indigent Athenian braggart,
much given to boasting about his fabulous
estates, as imaginary as Cloudcuckooland.

AKESTOR: An Athenian tragic poet. See
SAKAS.

ALKMENE: Wife of Amphitryon and mistress
of Zeus by whom she became the mother of
Herakles.

ALOPE: Mortal woman beloved by Poseidon.

AMMON: A celebrated shrine and oracle of
Zeus in Libya.

AMPHION: Musician and husband of Niobe;
at the touch of his lyre the stones rose from

the ground and formed themselves together to make the ramparts of Thebes.

APHRODITE: Goddess of beauty and sexual love.

APOLLO: God of prophecy, music, healing, and light; his two chief shrines were at Delphoi (q.v.) and Delos (q.v.).

ARES: God of War.

ARISTOKRATES: Son of Skellias; a prominent Athenian politician of conservative persuasion. In 421 B.C. he was one of the signers of the Peace of Nikias between Athens and Sparta. In 411 he joined the moderate conservative Theramenes in setting up the government of the Four Hundred, but later withdrew.

ARTEMIS: Goddess of chastity, childbirth, and the hunt; sister of Apollo.

ATHENE, ATHENA: Patron goddess of Athens, commonly called "owl-eyed." Although a virgin goddess, she was also a goddess of war.

BABYLON: Ancient capital of Mesopotamia, situated on the Euphrates River. It was one of the largest cities of the ancient world, and among its wonders were its great brick walls, described by the historian Herodotos.

BAKIS: A famous prophet of Boiotia, whose oracles were delivered in hexameter verse. In Aristophanes' comedies, the seers who cite Bakis are usually charlatans.

BASILEIA: The personification of Empire and Sovereign Power; in the present version she appears as Miss Universe.

CHAIREPHON: Friend and disciple of the philosopher Sokrates. His utter devotion to philosophy and the studious life and his striking pallor and emaciation made him a popular image of The Philosopher. Hence his nickname, The Bat or The Vampire.

CHAOS: The nothingness or vacancy which existed before the creation of the world. In mythology Chaos was the mother of Erebos and Night.

CHIANS: Inhabitants of the island of Chios, a state closely allied to Athens during the early Peloponnesian War and whose fidelity to the Athenian cause was rewarded by inclusion in the Athenian prayers for prosperity and success.

DARIUS, DAREIOS: King of Persia (ruled 521–486 B.C.).

DELOS: Small Aegean island sacred to Apollo.

DELPHOI, DELPHI: A town in Phokis, celebrated for its great temple and oracle of Apollo.

DEMETER: The Earth Mother; goddess of grain, agriculture, and the harvest, worshipped at her shrine at Eleusis in Attika.

DIAGORAS: Poet and philosopher of Melos. Charged with atheism in Athens and condemned to death, he fled the city.

DIEITREPHES: A notorious social climber. Of doubtful Athenian origin, he began his public career as a worker in wicker and a basketmaker, and gradually made his way upward in the military hierarchy. In 413 a detachment of Thracians under his command went amok and massacred a school full of children at Mykalessos.

DODONA: An ancient oracle of Zeus in the mountains of Epiros.

EPOPS: The Hoopoe, Tereus (q.v.).

ETNA, AITNA: A city situated on a spur of the Sicilian mountain of the same name, founded by Hiero of Syracuse.

EXEKESTIDES: Evidently a foreign slave of Karian extraction who succeeded in passing himself off as an Athenian citizen, i.e., the sort of man who would be at home anywhere.

GORGIAS: Of Leontini, a noted sophist and teacher of rhetoric.

HEBROS: A river of Thrace.

HERA: Consort of Zeus.

HERAKLES: Hero and demigod, son of Zeus and Alkmene, renowned for his great labors, prodigious strength, and equally prodigious appetite. Because Herakles is *par excellence* the monster-killer, it is particularly appropriate to swear by him when confronted by the 'monstrous, prodigious, freakish, or strange.

HERMES: The messenger god of Olympos; also god of thieves and the guide of the underworld.

HESTIA: Goddess of the hearth (and among Birds, goddess of the nest).

HIERO: Famous tyrant of Syracuse in Sicily, celebrated by the poet Pindar.

HIPPONIKOS: A common name in a wealthy and aristocratic Athenian family.

HOMER: The great epic poet of Greece, author of the *Iliad* and *Odyssey*.

HYMEN: God of marriage.

IKAROS: Son of the craftsman Daidalos, who escaped from Krete with his father by means of homemade wings of wax and feathers. But when Ikaros flew too high, the sun melted the wax, his wings dissolved, and he fell to his death in the sea.

IRIS: Messenger of the gods; in the earlier poets represented as a virgin.

ITYS: The son of Tereus and Prokne (q.v.),

murdered by his mother in revenge for Tereus' rape and mutilation of Philomela. To the Greek ear, the name Itys seemed to form part of the refrain of the mourning nightingale.

KALLIAS: Common name in a wealthy and aristocratic Athenian family. The Kallias singled out here was a notorious profligate and spendthrift.

KINESIAS: A clubfooted dithyrambic poet of great pretensions but little ability.

KLEISTHENES: A notorious Athenian homosexual and one of Aristophanes' favorite butts.

KLEONYMOS: A corpulent glutton and part-time informer; he is Aristophanes' commonest representative of cowardice (i.e., throwing one's shield away).

KOLONOS: Small town on a hill near Athens; here the astronomer Meton (q.v.) had evidently constructed a complicated piece of engineering or clockwork.

KORINTH: Greek city allied to Sparta during the Peloponnesian War; situated on the strategic Isthmus of Korinth.

KORKYRA: Modern Corfu, a large island off the western coast of Greece. "Korkyrean wings" means "whip."

KRONOS: Father of Zeus.

KYBELE: A Phrygian Mother Goddess, worshipped as The Great Mother, "mother of gods and men."

LAURIUM, LAUREION: In southeastern Attika, famous for its silver mines. Athenian silver coins, stamped with the owl of Athena, were commonly called "owls of Laureion."

LEOTROPHIDES: An extremely fragile, delicate, and unsubstantial poet.

LEPREUS, LEPREUM: A town in Elis; it recovered its independence from Elis during the Peloponnesian War.

LETO: Mother of Artemis and Apollo.

LYDIA: A region in Western Asia Minor which provided Athens with a large number of slaves.

LYKOURGOS: An Athenian of sufficient distinction and/or oddity of appearance to have won the nickname of The Ibis. In this translation, however, he appears as The Lame Duck.

MANES: A lazy slave.

MANODOROS: A slave.

MARATHON: A plain in the eastern part of Attika; site of the famous battle (490 B.C.) in which the Athenian forces under Miltiades crushingly defeated the first Persian invasion of Hellas.

MEIDIAS: A venal and corrupt Athenian informer, evidently also a quail-breeder in his own right, whence his nickname, The Quail. For Aristophanes the propriety of the name is confirmed by Meidias' habitually dazed expression, like that of a freshly stunned quail.

MELANTHIOS: Son of Philokles and, like his father, an atrocious tragedian. Afflicted with leprosy, he seems to have been also a noted glutton (cf. Peace, 804).

MENELAOS: Mythological king of Sparta and brother of Agamemnon.

MENIPPOS: An Athenian horse-raiser, nicknamed The Swallow (from a pun on the word chelidon which means both "swallow" and the tender "hollow" in a horse's hoof).

METON: An Athenian astronomer, geometrician, and city-planner of considerable notoriety (see KOLONOS). According to Plutarch, Meton objected to the Sicilian expedition and pretended madness in order to keep his son at home.

NIKIAS: Prominent Athenian general during the Peloponnesian War. Enormously respected at Athens during his lifetime, Nikias' caution, slowness to move, stiffness, and superstitious piety were among the chief causes for the defeat of the Sicilian expedition. But as a cautious strategist and tactician, he had no equal among the Athenian generals.

ODYSSEUS: Hero of the Odyssey of Homer.

OLOPHYXIANS: Inhabitants of Olophyxos, a small town on the peninsula of Akte in Thrace.

OLYMPOS: A mountain in Thessaly, covered at the peak with perpetual snow and regarded by the Greeks as the abode of the gods.

OPOUNTIOS: A notorious one-eyed sycophant nicknamed The Crow.

OPOUS: A town in Lokris, whose inhabitants were called the Opuntian Lokrians.

ORESTES: A notorious burglar and highwayman; not to be confused with the heroic son of Agamemnon.

PAIAN: Manifestation of Apollo as god of healing.

PAN: Rural Arcadian god of the flocks and the woodlands.

PANDORA: Mother Earth, the giver of all gifts (pan, all; dora, gifts); not to be confused with the mythological mischief-maker and her box of human troubles.

PARIS: Prince of Troy; in the famous judgment of Paris, he was offered the most beautiful woman in the world by Aphrodite in return for awarding her the prize for beauty.

PEGASOS: The famous winged horse of mythology.

PEISANDROS: A notorious Athenian coward.

PEISIAS: Otherwise unknown, but evidently a noted traitor in his day.

PHILOKLES: Athenian tragic poet and nephew of Aischylos; among his lost plays was one which treated the story of Tereus and was evidently plagiarized from Sophokles' play of the same name. His nickname was The Lark because, according to the Scholiast, his head tapered like the pointed crest of that bird.

PHILOKRATES: An Athenian bird-seller.

PHLEGRA: A plain in Thrace said to have been the site of the great battle between the Gods and the Giants.

PHOIBOS: Apollo.

PHRYGIA: A country in central Asia Minor.

PINDAR: Great lyric poet of Thebes (518–438 B.C.).

PORPHYRION: Name of one of the Titans who fought against Zeus in the Battle of the Gods and the Giants; it is also the name of a bird, the Purple Waterhen.

POSEIDON: Brother of Zeus and god of the sea. As sea-god, he girdles the earth and has it in his power as Poseidon Earth-Shaker to cause earthquakes. In still another manifestation he is Poseidon Hippios, patron god of horses and horsemen.

PRIAM: King of Troy.

PRODIKOS: Of Keos, a famous sophist.

PROKNE: The nightingale, wife of Tereus (q.v.).

PROMETHEUS: The great Titan who championed the cause of mankind against Zeus. Because he stole fire from heaven and gave it to men, he was regarded by the gods as a traitor to Olympos. His name means Foresight and his cleverness and philanthropy were both proverbial.

PROXENIDES: An Athenian braggart and blowhard.

SAKAS: The nickname of the Athenian tragic poet Akestor (q.v.). The word Sakas seems to be a pejorative for "Skyth" and presumably Akestor, like Exekestides, was a foreigner who had managed, or was reputed to have managed, to get his name entered on the citizenship rolls of Athens.

SEMELE: Daughter of Kadmos of Thebes and mistress of Zeus, by whom she became the mother of Dionysos.

SIKYON: Greek city situated on the northeast of the Peloponnesos, adjacent to Korinth.

SIMONIDES: Of Keos, a lyric and elegiac poet (ca. 556–468 B.C.).

SKYTHS: Savage nomadic inhabitants of Skythia, a region lying roughly between the Carpathians and the river Don.

SOKRATES: The famous Athenian philosopher, ridiculed by Aristophanes for his long hair, bathlessness, and other philosophical traits.

SOLON: Greatest of Athenian lawgivers (ca. 640–561 B.C.).

SOPHOKLES: Athenian tragic poet (495–404 B.C.).

SYRAKOSIOS: An extremely garrulous Athenian orator whose loquacity earned him the sobriquet of The Jaybird.

TARTAROS: The great abyss which opened underneath Hades in the classical underworld.

TELEAS: Flighty and irresponsible Athenian bureaucrat; secretary to the Committee in charge of the Parthenon treasury.

TEREUS: In mythology, a son of Ares and king of the Daulians in Thrace. According to the legend, Pandion, king of Athens, had two daughters, Prokne and Philomela. Prokne was married to Tereus, by whom she became the mother of a son, Itys. Tereus, however became infatuated with Prokne's sister Philomela, raped her, and cut out her tongue to keep her from informing Prokne. But Philomela managed to embroider her story in needlework and sent it to Prokne who, in retaliation against her husband, murdered her son Itys and served him up to Tereus for dinner. When he discovered the truth, Tereus pursued Prokne and Philomela but, before he could catch them, he was transformed into a Hoopoe, Prokne into a Nightingale, and Philomela into the Swallow. (In the better known but less appropriate Latin version of the myth, Philomela is the nightingale and Prokne the swallow.)

The story of Tereus was tragically treated by both Sophokles and Philokles.

THALES: Of Miletos, one of the Seven Sages of antiquity; renowned for his scientific genius and for having predicted an eclipse of the sun (ca. 636–546 B.C.).

THEBES: The principal city of Boiotia; during the Peloponnesian War an ally of Sparta.

THEOGENES: An Athenian braggart; probably took part with Kleon in the blockade of Sphakteria and was one of the signers of the Peace of Nikias in 421 B.C.

TIMON: The misanthrope *par excellence*.

TITANS: The race of pre-Olympian deities, born of Heaven and Earth. After the coming of the Olympians, the Titans rebelled against Zeus and were vanquished in the Battle of the Gods and the Giants at Phlegra.

TRIBALLOI: A savage people of Thrace. The name Triballos is merely an eponym of this people.

ZEUS: Chief god of the Olympian pantheon; son of Kronos, brother of Poseidon, and father of Athena. As the supreme ruler of the world, he is armed with thunder and lightning and creates storms and tempests.

Of the hundreds of ancient Greek comedies that were written, only eleven by Aristophanes and four by Menander (c. 342 B.C.–299 B.C.) are extant, and three of Menander's four survive only in long fragments. Aristophanes seems to have written about 40 plays, Menander more than twice as many. Hundreds of other men wrote comedies in ancient Greece, but they are mere names, or names attached to brief fragments. This means that when we talk about Greek comedy we are really talking about a fraction of Aristophanes' work, and an even smaller fraction of Menander's.

Greek comedy is customarily divided into three kinds: Old Comedy (486 B.C., when comedy was first given official recognition at the festival called the City Dionysia, to 404 B.C., the end of the Peloponnesian War, when Athens was humbled and freedom of speech was curtailed); Middle Comedy (404 B.C., to 336 B.C., the accession of Alexander, when Athens was no longer free); and New Comedy (336 B.C., to c. 250 B.C., the approximate date of the last fragments). Of Old Comedy, there are Aristophanes' plays; of Middle Comedy, there is *Plutus*, one of Aristophanes' last plays; of New Comedy, there are Menander's fragments and his recently discovered *Dyskolos* (*The Disagreeable Man*).

Old Comedy is a curious combination of obscenity, farce, political allegory, satire, and lyricism. Puns, literary allusions, phallic jokes, political jibes, etc. periodically give way to joyful song; Aristophanes seems to have been something of a combination of Joyce, Swift, and Shelley. Normally his plays have the following structure:

1. *Prologos*, prologue or exposition. Someone has a bright idea, and sets it forth either in monologue or dialogue. In *The Birds* the prologue consists of lines 1–287, in which Pisthetairos suggests that the birds unite to regain their sovereignty over the universe by intercepting sacrificial smoke and thus starving the gods into submission.

2. *Parodos*, entrance of the fantastically dressed chorus. The twenty-four or so members of the chorus express their opinion of the idea. (The *koryphaios* or leader of the chorus perhaps sang some lines by himself.) *The Birds* is unusual in devoting part of the parodos (lines 288–488) to the lyrics of Epops instead of entirely to choral songs.

3. *Agon*, or debate. In lines 489–805 Pisthetairos persuades the chorus of birds to accept his idea. Aristophanes now adds a short song (lines 806–813)

introducing the nightingale, which gets the actors (as distinguished from the chorus) off the stage.

4. *Parabasis* (lines 814–952), an elaborate composition in which the leader of the chorus ordinarily sheds his dramatic character and addresses the audience on the poet's behalf, the other actors having briefly retired. (Its parts are the *kommation*, or introductory song; the parabasis itself, or "coming forward"; the *makron* or *pnigos*, lines to be recited at one breath; the *strophe* or *ode*; the *epirrhema*; the *antistrophe* or *antode*; and the *antepirrhema*.) In *The Birds*, atypically, the chorus retains its identity during the parabasis. Also atypical is the second parabasis, lines 1266–1342, full of warnings to men who maltreat birds.

5. *Epeisodia*, scenes or episodes (lines 1343–1740, 1773–1831, 1848–1992), briefly separated by choral songs. These episodes have to do with putting the original idea into practice. In *The Birds*, they are devoted to talk of building the new city, and to fending off various intruders. After the second parabasis the episodes set forth further problems having to do with Cloudcuckooland.

6. *Exodos* or final scene (lines 2009–2072), customarily of rejoicing. There is often talk of a wedding and a feast. In this play the chorus sings in honor of the marriage of Pisthetairos and Miss Universe ("Sovereign Power"), and then marches out joyfully.

Perhaps all Old Comedy was rather like this, but it should be remembered that even Aristophanes' eleven plays do not all follow the pattern exactly. *The Birds*, for example, is unusual in having the chorus retain its identity during the parabasis, in having a second parabasis, and in the sparseness of its obscenity. But *The Birds* is typical in its fantasy, in its variety, in its political concern, and in its revelry. It is joyous and extravagant, it touches on serious themes (What ought a city to be?), and it follows the usual comic formula of ending with a newly unified society. It begins with Pisthetairos and Euelpides complaining of the frustrating life in Athens, and it ends with talk of a *gamos* (sexual union) in a new city where men live among birds. Pisthetairos is wed to Zeus' daughter, Miss Universe, in the city of his whim. The *polos* (pole, sky, heaven) has paradoxically become a *polis* (city), a city of wind, a city of nothingness, and yet a city that is rather like an Athens ruled by Pisthetairos — who had left Athens because he longed for a quieter life. It should be noted that this new society is not conspicuously more moral than the Athens abandoned by Pisthetairos. If Aristophanes was voicing a criticism of Athens at the outset, he did not follow it with a depiction of an ideal city. Pisthetairos is as much rascal as reformer, and scholarly attempts to see in his city some sort of allegory furnishing a blueprint for reforming Athens are unconvincing. Utopia as well as Athens is satirized. What is celebrated is not so much a vision of a new Athens as a vision of the powers of fantasy. Aristophanes toys with ideas, turns them around and around, holds them up and laughs at them; they are soap bubbles or smoke rings, clever and attractive things that the creator delights in and yet demolishes with no less delight. Something of this double vision, this playing seriously with an idea that one doesn't believe, and treating playfully something one does believe, can be neatly seen in Matthew Arnold's, "Poor Mathias," a poem on the death of a pet canary. Arnold, recalling Aristophanes' celebration of birds as superior to men, in his elegy for the canary included a passage that (although devoid of bawdry and exuberance) is Aristophanic in its lyricism and in the play of mind it reveals:

> Was it, as the Grecian sings,
> Birds were born the first of things,
> Before the sun, before the wind,
> Before the gods, before mankind,
> Airy, ante-mundane throng —
> Witness their unworldly song!
> Proof they give, too, primal powers,
> Of a prescience more than ours —
> Teach us, while they come and go,
> When to sail, and when to sow.
> Cuckoo calling from the hill,
> Swallow skimming by the mill,
> Swallows trooping in the sedge,
> Starlings swirling from the hedge,
> Mark the seasons, map our year,
> As they show and disappear.
> But, with all this travail sage
> Brought from that anterior age,
> Goes an unreversed decree
> Whereby strange are they and we,
> Making want of theirs, and plan,
> Indiscernible by man.

A few words should be said about Middle Comedy and New Comedy. Middle Comedy is a convenient label to apply to the lost plays that must have marked the transition from Old Comedy to New Comedy. In New Comedy, written when Athens' political greatness was gone, and when political invective was impossible, the chorus has dwindled to musicians and dancers who perform intermittently, characters tend to be types (the young lover, the crabby old father, etc.), and the plot is regularly a young man's wooing of a maid. The personal satire and obscenity of Old Comedy are gone, and in their place is a respectably conducted tale showing how, after humorous difficulties, the young man achieves his goal. The happy ending is the thing toward which the plot steadily moves, and it is far more integral than the more or less elusive allegoric (or metaphoric) union at the end of *The Birds*. It was New Comedy that influenced Rome (which could scarcely have imitated the political satire of Old Comedy), and through Rome modern Europe. Shakespeare, for example, whose comedies have been described as obstacle races to the altar, was a descendant of Menander though he knew nothing of Menander's work first-hand.

AS YOU LIKE IT

William Shakespeare

Edited by Albert Gilman

William Shakespeare (1564–1616) was born in Stratford, England, of middle-class parents. Nothing of interest is known about his early years, but by 1590 he was acting and writing plays in London. He early worked in all three Elizabethan dramatic genres — tragedy, comedy, and history. *Romeo and Juliet,* for example, was written about 1595, the year of *Richard II,* and in the following year he wrote *A Midsummer Night's Dream. Julius Caesar* (1599) probably preceded *As You Like It* by one year, and *Hamlet* probably followed *As You Like It* by less than a year. Among the plays that followed *King Lear* (1605–1606) were *Macbeth* (1605–1606) and several "romances" — plays that have happy endings but that seem more meditative and closer to tragedy than such comedies as *A Midsummer Night's Dream, As You Like It,* and *Twelfth Night.*

[DRAMATIS PERSONAE

DUKE SENIOR, *in banishment in the Forest of Arden*
DUKE FREDERICK, *his brother, usurper of the Dukedom*
AMIENS ⎱
JAQUES ⎰ *lords attending on Duke Senior*
LE BEAU, *a courtier*
CHARLES, *a wrestler*
OLIVER ⎱
JAQUES ⎰ *sons of Sir Rowland de Boys*
ORLANDO ⎰
ADAM ⎱
DENNIS ⎰ *servants to Oliver*
TOUCHSTONE, *a clown*

SIR OLIVER MAR-TEXT, *a vicar*
CORIN ⎱
SILVIUS ⎰ *shepherds*
WILLIAM, *a country fellow*
HYMEN
ROSALIND, *daughter to Duke Senior*
CELIA, *daughter to Duke Frederick*
PHEBE, *a shepherdess*
AUDREY, *a country girl*
LORDS, PAGES, FORESTERS.
    and ATTENDANTS

Scene: OLIVER's *house; the court; the Forest of Arden.*]

ACT I

Scene I. [*Orchard of* OLIVER'*s house.*]

Enter ORLANDO *and* ADAM.

ORLANDO: As I remember, Adam, it was
upon this fashion bequeathed me by will but
poor a°¹ thousand crowns, and, as thou say'st,
charged my brother on his blessing to breed
5 me well; and there begins my sadness. My
brother Jaques he keeps at school, and report
speaks goldenly of his profit.° For my part, he
keeps me rustically° at home or, to speak more
properly, stays me here at home unkept;° for
10 call you that keeping for a gentleman of my
birth that differs not from the stalling of an
ox? His horses are bred better, for, besides that
they are fair° with their feeding, they are
taught their manage,° and to that end riders
15 dearly hired; but I, his brother, gain nothing
under him but growth, for the which his
animals on his dunghills are as much bound to
him as I. Besides this nothing that he so
plentifully gives me, the something that nature
20 gave me his countenance° seems to take from
me. He lets me feed with his hinds,° bars me
the place of a brother, and, as much as in him
lies, mines my gentility° with my education.
This is it, Adam, that grieves me; and the
25 spirit of my father, which I think is within me,
begins to mutiny against this servitude. I will
no longer endure it, though yet I know no
wise remedy how to avoid it.

(*Enter* OLIVER.)

ADAM: Yonder comes my master, your
30 brother.

ORLANDO: Go apart, Adam, and thou shalt
hear how he will shake me up.°
OLIVER: Now, sir, what make you° here?
ORLANDO: Nothing. I am not taught to
make anything.   35
OLIVER: What mar you then, sir?
ORLANDO: Marry,° sir, I am helping you to
mar that which God made, a poor unworthy
brother of yours, with idleness.
OLIVER: Marry, sir, be better employed, and   40
be naught awhile.°
ORLANDO: Shall I keep your hogs and eat
husks with them? What prodigal portion have
I spent° that I should come to such penury?
OLIVER: Know you where° you are, sir?   45
ORLANDO: O, sir, very well. Here in your
orchard.
OLIVER: Know you before whom, sir?
ORLANDO: Ay, better than him I am before
knows me. I know you are my eldest brother,   50
and in the gentle condition of blood° you
should so know me. The courtesy of nations°
allows you my better in that you are the first
born, but the same tradition takes not away
my blood were there twenty brothers betwixt   55
us. I have as much of my father in me as you,
albeit I confess your coming before me is
nearer to his reverence.°
OLIVER: What, boy! [*Strikes him.*]
ORLANDO: Come, come, elder brother, you   60
are too young in this. [*Seizes him.*]
OLIVER: Wilt thou lay hands on me, villain?°
ORLANDO: I am no villain. I am the youngest
son of Sir Rowland de Boys; he was my father,   65

¹ The degree sign (°) indicates a footnote, which
is keyed to the text by line number. Text references
are printed in **boldface** type; the annotation follows
in lightface type. The notes are Albert Gilman's.
[Eds.] I.i.3 **poor a** a mere   7 **goldenly of his profit**
glowingly of his progress   8 **keeps me rustically** supports me like a peasant   9 **unkept** uncared for   13
fair handsome   14 **manage** paces   20 **countenance**
behavior   21 **hinds** farm hands   23 **mines my gentility** undermines my good birth

32 **shake me up** berate me   33 **make you** are
you doing (in the next line Orlando pretends to
take the phrase to mean "accomplish")   37 **Marry**
(an expletive, from "By the Virgin Mary")   41 **be
naught awhile** i.e., don't bother me   42–44 **Shall
I ... spent** (an allusion to the story of the Prodigal
Son. See Luke 15:11–32)   45 **where** i.e., in whose
presence (Orlando pretends to take it literally)   51
in the gentle condition of blood i.e., of the same
good blood   52 **courtesy of nations** i.e., sanctioned
custom of primogeniture   57–58 **your coming ...
reverence** i.e., as the eldest son you are head of the
family and therefore entitled to respect   62–63 **villain** (Oliver uses it in the sense of "wicked person,"
but Orlando plays on its other meaning, "low-born
person")

and he is thrice a villain that says such a father begot villains. Wert thou not my brother, I would not take this hand from thy throat till this other had pulled out thy tongue for saying so. Thou hast railed on thyself.

ADAM: Sweet masters, be patient. For your father's remembrance, be at accord.

OLIVER: Let me go, I say.

ORLANDO: I will not till I please. You shall hear me. My father charged you in his will to give me good education. You have trained me like a peasant, obscuring and hiding from me all gentlemanlike qualities.° The spirit of my father grows strong in me, and I will no longer endure it. Therefore allow me such exercises° as may become a gentleman, or give me the poor allottery° my father left me by testament; with that I will go buy my fortunes.

OLIVER: And what wilt thou do? Beg when that is spent? Well, sir, get you in. I will not long be troubled with you. You shall have some part of your will. I pray you leave me.

ORLANDO: I will no further offend you than becomes me for my good.

OLIVER: Get you with him, you old dog.

ADAM: Is "old dog" my reward? Most true, I have lost my teeth in your service. God be with my old master; he would not have spoke such a word.

(*Exeunt* ORLANDO, ADAM.)

OLIVER: Is it even so? Begin you to grow upon me?° I will physic your rankness° and yet give no thousand crowns neither. Holla, Dennis!

(*Enter* DENNIS.)

DENNIS: Calls your worship?

OLIVER: Was not Charles, the Duke's wrestler, here to speak with me?

DENNIS: So please you, he is here at the door and importunes access to you.

OLIVER: Call him in. [*Exit* DENNIS.] 'Twill be a good way; and tomorrow the wrestling is.

(*Enter* CHARLES.)

CHARLES: Good morrow to your worship.

OLIVER: Good Monsieur Charles, what's the new news at the new court?

CHARLES: There's no news at the court, sir, but the old news. That is, the old Duke° is banished by his younger brother the new Duke, and three or four loving lords have put themselves into voluntary exile with him, whose lands and revenues enrich the new Duke; therefore he gives them good leave to wander.

OLIVER: Can you tell if Rosalind, the Duke's daughter, be banished with her father?

CHARLES: O, no; for the Duke's daughter, her cousin, so loves her, being ever from their cradles bred together, that she would have followed her exile, or have died to stay behind her. She is at the court, and no less beloved of her uncle than his own daughter, and never two ladies loved as they do.

OLIVER: Where will the old Duke live?

CHARLES: They say he is already in the Forest of Arden,° and a many merry men with him; and there they live like the old Robin Hood of England. They say many young gentlemen flock to him every day, and fleet the time carelessly° as they did in the golden world.°

OLIVER: What, you wrestle tomorrow before the new Duke?

CHARLES: Marry, do I, sir; and I came to acquaint you with a matter. I am given, sir, secretly to understand that your younger brother, Orlando, hath a disposition to come in disguised against me to try a fall.° Tomorrow, sir, I wrestle for my credit, and he that escapes me without some broken limb shall acquit him well. Your brother is but young and tender, and for your love I would be loath to foil° him, as I must for my own honor if he come in. Therefore, out of my love to you, I came hither to acquaint you withal, that either you might stay him from his intendment, or brook° such disgrace well as he shall run into, in that it is a thing of his own search and altogether against my will.

OLIVER: Charles, I thank thee for thy love to me, which thou shalt find I will most kindly requite. I had myself notice of my brother's

---

110 **old Duke** i.e., Duke Senior   128 **Forest of Arden** Ardennes (in France; though Shakespeare may also have had in mind the Forest of Arden near his birthplace)   131–132 **fleet the time carelessly** pass the time at ease   132–133 **golden world** the Golden Age of classical mythology, when men were free of sin, want, and care)   140 **fall** bout   145 **foil** throw, defeat   149 **brook** endure

77 **qualities** accomplishments   80 **exercises** occupations   82 **allottery** share   95–96 **grow upon me** i.e., usurp my place   96 **physic your rankness** purge your overgrowth

155 purpose herein and have by underhand means°
labored to dissuade him from it; but he is
resolute. I'll tell thee, Charles, it is the stub-
bornest young fellow of France; full of ambition, an envious emulator° of every man's good
160 parts,° a secret and villainous contriver against
me his natural° brother. Therefore use thy
discretion. I had as lief° thou didst break his
neck as his finger. And thou wert best look
to't; for if thou dost him any slight disgrace, or
165 if he do not mightily grace himself on thee,°
he will practice° against thee by poison, entrap
thee by some treacherous device, and never
leave thee till he hath ta'en thy life by some
indirect means or other; for, I assure thee, and
170 almost with tears I speak it, there is not one so
young and so villainous this day living. I speak
but brotherly of him, but should I anatomize°
him to thee as he is, I must blush and weep,
and thou must look pale and wonder.
175   CHARLES: I am heartily glad I came hither to
you. If he come tomorrow, I'll give him his
payment. If ever he go alone° again, I'll never
wrestle for prize more. And so God keep your
worship.   (Exit.)
180   OLIVER: Farewell, good Charles. Now will I
stir this gamester.° I hope I shall see an end of
him; for my soul, yet I know not why, hates
nothing more than he. Yet he's gentle,° never
schooled and yet learned, full of noble device,°
185 of all sorts° enchantingly beloved; and indeed
so much in the heart of the world, and
especially of my own people, who best know
him, that I am altogether misprized.° But it
shall not be so long; this wrestler shall clear
190 all.° Nothing remains but that I kindle the boy
thither, which now I'll go about.   (Exit.)

SCENE II. [The DUKE's palace.]

Enter ROSALIND and CELIA.

CELIA: I pray thee, Rosalind, sweet my coz,°
be merry.

ROSALIND: Dear Celia, I show more mirth
than I am mistress of, and would you yet I
were merrier? Unless you could teach me to 5
forget a banished father, you must not learn°
me how to remember any extraordinary pleasure.
CELIA: Herein I see thou lov'st me not with
the full weight that I love thee. If my uncle, 10
thy banished father, had banished thy uncle,
the Duke my father, so° thou hadst been still
with me, I could have taught my love to take
thy father for mine. So wouldst thou, if the
truth of thy love to me were so righteously 15
tempered° as mine is to thee.
ROSALIND: Well, I will forget the condition
of my estate° to rejoice in yours.
CELIA: You know my father hath no child
but I, nor none is like to have; and truly, when 20
he dies, thou shalt be his heir; for what he
hath taken away from thy father perforce,° I
will render thee again in affection. By mine
honor, I will, and when I break that oath, let
me turn monster. Therefore, my sweet Rose, 25
my dear Rose, be merry.
ROSALIND: From henceforth I will, coz, and
devise sports. Let me see, what think you of
falling in love?
CELIA: Marry, I prithee, do, to make sport 30
withal; but love no man in good earnest, nor
no further in sport neither than with safety of
a pure° blush thou mayst in honor come off°
again.
ROSALIND: What shall be our sport then? 35
CELIA: Let us sit and mock the good
housewife° Fortune from her wheel,° that her
gifts may henceforth be bestowed equally.
ROSALIND: I would we could do so, for her
benefits are mightily misplaced, and the boun- 40
tiful blind woman doth most mistake in her
gifts to women.
CELIA: 'Tis true, for those that she makes
fair,° she scarce makes honest° and those that
she makes honest, she makes very ill-favoredly.° 45
ROSALIND: Nay, now thou goest from For-

155 by underhand means indirectly 159 envious
emulator malicious rival 160 parts abilities 161
natural blood 162 lief soon 165 grace himself
on thee gain credit at your expense 166 practice
plot 172 anatomize fully describe 177 go alone
i.e., walk without crutches 181 gamester athlete,
sportsman 183 gentle endowed with the qualities
of a gentleman 184 noble device gentleman-like
purposes 185 all sorts all kinds of people 188 misprized scorned 189–190 clear all settle matters
I.II.1 sweet my coz my sweet cousin

6 learn teach 12 so provided that 15–16 righteously tempered perfectly composed 18 estate fortune 22 perforce forcibly 33 pure mere; come off
get away 37 housewife (1) woman of the house
(with a spinning wheel) (2) inconstant hussy; wheel
(the wheel turned by Fortune, blind goddess who
distributed her favors at random, elevated some men
and hurled others down) 44 fair beautiful; honest
chaste 45 ill-favoredly ugly

tune's office° to Nature's. Fortune reigns in gifts of the world,° not in the lineaments of Nature.°

(*Enter* [TOUCHSTONE, *the*] *Clown.*)

50 CELIA: No; when Nature hath made a fair creature, may she not by Fortune fall into the fire? Though Nature hath given us wit to flout at Fortune, hath not Fortune sent in this fool to cut off the argument?

55 ROSALIND: Indeed, there is Fortune too hard for Nature when Fortune makes Nature's natural° the cutter-off of Nature's wit.

CELIA: Peradventure° this is not Fortune's work neither, but Nature's, who perceiveth our 60 natural wits too dull to reason of such goddesses and hath sent this natural for our whetstone. For always the dullness of the fool is the whetstone of the wits. How now, wit; whither wander you?

65 TOUCHSTONE: Mistress, you must come away to your father.

CELIA: Were you made the messenger?

TOUCHSTONE: No, by mine honor, but I was bid to come for you.

70 ROSALIND: Where learned you that oath, fool?

TOUCHSTONE: Of a certain knight that swore by his honor they were good pancakes, and swore by his honor the mustard was naught.° 75 Now I'll stand to it,° the pancakes were naught, and the mustard was good, and yet was not the knight forsworn.°

CELIA: How prove you that in the great heap of your knowledge?

80 ROSALIND: Ay, marry, now unmuzzle your wisdom.

TOUCHSTONE: Stand you both forth now. Stroke your chins, and swear by your beards that I am a knave.

85 CELIA: By our beards, if we had them, thou art.

TOUCHSTONE: By my knavery, if I had it, then I were; but if you swear by that that is not, you are not forsworn; no more was this 90 knight, swearing by his honor, for he never had any; or if he had, he had sworn it away

before ever he saw those pancakes or that mustard.

CELIA: Prithee, who is't that thou mean'st?

TOUCHSTONE: One that old Frederick, your 95 father, loves.

CELIA: My father's love is enough to honor him enough. Speak no more of him; you'll be whipped for taxation° one of these days.

TOUCHSTONE: The more pity that fools may 100 not speak wisely what wise men do foolishly.

CELIA: By my troth,° thou sayest true, for since the little wit that fools have was silenced, the little foolery that wise men have makes a great show. Here comes Monsieur Le Beau. 105

(*Enter* LE BEAU.)

ROSALIND: With his mouth full of news.

CELIA: Which he will put° on us as pigeons feed their young.

ROSALIND: Then shall we be news-crammed.

CELIA: All the better; we shall be the more 110 marketable. Bon jour, Monsieur Le Beau, what's the news?

LE BEAU: Fair princess, you have lost much good sport.

CELIA: Sport? Of what color?° 115

LE BEAU: What color, madam? How shall I answer you?

ROSALIND: As wit and fortune° will.

TOUCHSTONE: Or as the Destinies decrees.°

CELIA: Well said; that was laid on with a 120 trowel.

TOUCHSTONE: Nay, if I keep not my rank —

ROSALIND: Thou losest thy old smell.

LE BEAU: You amaze° me, ladies. I would have told you of good wrestling, which you 125 have lost the sight of.°

ROSALIND: Yet tell us the manner of the wrestling.

LE BEAU: I will tell you the beginning; and if it please your ladyships, you may see the 130 end, for the best is yet to do,° and here, where you are, they are coming to perform it.

CELIA: Well, the beginning that is dead and buried.

LE BEAU: There comes an old man and his 135 three sons —

---

47 **office** function   48 **gifts of the world** e.g., wealth, power   48–49 **lineaments of Nature** e.g., virtue, intelligence   56–57 **natural** born fool, halfwit   58 **Peradventure** perhaps   74 **naught** worthless   75 **stand to it** swear   77 **forsworn** perjured

99 **taxation** slander   102 **troth** faith   107 **put** force   115 **color** sort   118 **fortune** good luck   119 **decrees** (the ending *s* was a common variant in the third person plural)   124 **amaze** confuse   126 **lost the sight of** missed   131 **do** be done

CELIA: I could match this beginning with an old tale.°

LE BEAU: Three proper° young men, of ex-
140 cellent growth and presence.

ROSALIND: With bills° on their necks, "Be it known unto all men by these presents."°

LE BEAU: The eldest of the three wrestled with Charles, the Duke's wrestler; which
145 Charles in a moment threw him and broke three of his ribs, that there is little hope of life in him. So he served the second, and so the third. Yonder they lie, the poor old man, their father, making such pitiful dole° over them
150 that all the beholders take his part with weeping.

ROSALIND: Alas!

TOUCHSTONE: But what is the sport, mon-sieur, that the ladies have lost?

155 LE BEAU: Why, this that I speak of.

TOUCHSTONE: Thus men may grow wiser every day. It is the first time that ever I heard breaking of ribs was sport for ladies.

CELIA: Or I, I promise thee.

160 ROSALIND: But is there any° else longs to see this broken music° in his sides? Is there yet another dotes upon rib-breaking? Shall we see this wrestling, cousin?

LE BEAU: You must, if you stay here, for
165 here is the place appointed for the wrestling, and they are ready to perform it.

CELIA: Yonder sure they are coming. Let us now stay and see it.

(*Flourish.*° *Enter* DUKE [FREDERICK], LORDS, ORLANDO, CHARLES, *and* ATTENDANTS.)

DUKE FREDERICK: Come on. Since the youth
170 will not be entreated, his own peril on his forwardness.

ROSALIND: Is yonder the man?

LE BEAU: Even he, madam.

CELIA: Alas, he is too young; yet he looks
175 successfully.°

DUKE FREDERICK: How now, daughter and

cousin; are you crept hither to see the wres-tling?

ROSALIND: Ay, my liege, so please you give us leave.   180

DUKE FREDERICK: You will take little delight in it, I can tell you, there is such odds in the man.° In pity of the challenger's youth I would fain° dissuade him, but he will not be en-treated. Speak to him, ladies; see if you can   185 move him.

CELIA: Call him hither, good Monsieur Le Beau.

DUKE FREDERICK: Do so. I'll not be by.

LE BEAU: Monsieur the challenger, the prin- 190 cess calls for you.

ORLANDO: I attend them with all respect and duty.

ROSALIND: Young man, have you challenged Charles the wrestler?   195

ORLANDO: No, fair princess. He is the general challenger; I come but in as others do, to try with him the strength of my youth.

CELIA: Young gentleman, your spirits are too bold for your years. You have seen cruel proof 200 of this man's strength; if you saw yourself with your eyes or knew yourself with your judg-ment, the fear of your adventure would coun-sel you to a more equal enterprise. We pray you for your own sake to embrace your own   205 safety and give over this attempt.

ROSALIND: Do, young sir. Your reputation shall not therefore be misprized;° we will make it our suit to the Duke that the wrestling might not go forward.   210

ORLANDO: I beseech you, punish me not with your hard thoughts, wherein I confess me much guilty to deny so fair and excellent ladies anything. But let your fair eyes and gentle wishes go with me to my trial; wherein if I be 215 foiled,° there is but one shamed that was never gracious;° if killed, but one dead that is willing to be so. I shall do my friends no wrong, for I have none to lament me; the world no injury, for in it I have nothing. Only in the world I°   220 fill up a place, which may be better supplied when I have made it empty.

ROSALIND: The little strength that I have, I would it were with you.

138 **old tale** (Le Beau's story has a "Once upon a time" beginning)   139 **proper** fine   141 **bills** no-tices   142 **by these presents** (part of the opening formula of many legal documents. Rosalind puns on Le Beau's use of "presence," meaning "bearing")   149 **dole** lamentation   160 **any** anyone   161 **broken music** music arranged in parts for different instru-ments   168 s.d. **Flourish** trumpet fanfare   175 **suc-cessfully** able to succeed

182–183 **such odds in the man** i.e., the odds are all in Charles' favor   184 **fain** like to   208 **misprized** despised   216 **foiled** thrown   217 **gracious** graced by Fortune   220 **Only in the world I** in the world I only

225 CELIA: And mine to eke° out hers.

ROSALIND: Fare you well. Pray heaven I be deceived in you!°

CELIA: Your heart's desires be with you!

CHARLES: Come, where is this young gallant
230 that is so desirous to lie with his mother earth?

ORLANDO: Ready, sir; but his will hath in it a more modest working.°

DUKE FREDERICK: You shall try but one fall.

CHARLES: No, I warrant your Grace you
235 shall not entreat him to a second that have so mightily persuaded him from a first.

ORLANDO: You mean to mock me after. You should not have mocked me before. But come your ways.°

240 ROSALIND: Now Hercules be thy speed,° young man!

CELIA: I would I were invisible, to catch the strong fellow by the leg.

(*Wrestle.*)

ROSALIND: O excellent young man!

245 CELIA: If I had a thunderbolt in mine eye, I can tell who should down.

([CHARLES *is thrown.*] *Shout.*)

DUKE FREDERICK: No more, no more.

ORLANDO: Yes, I beseech your Grace; I am not yet well breathed.°

250 DUKE FREDERICK: How dost thou, Charles?

LE BEAU: He cannot speak, my lord.

DUKE FREDERICK: Bear him away. What is thy name, young man?

ORLANDO: Orlando, my liege, the youngest
255 son of Sir Rowland de Boys.

DUKE FREDERICK:
I would thou hadst been son to some man else.
The world esteemed thy father honorable,
But I did find him still° mine enemy.
Thou shouldst have better pleased me with this deed
260 Hadst thou descended from another house.
But fare thee well; thou art a gallant youth;
I would thou hadst told me of another father.

(*Exit* DUKE, [*with* TRAIN].)

CELIA:
Were I my father, coz, would I do this?

ORLANDO:
I am more proud to be Sir Rowland's son,
His youngest son, and would not change that calling°   265
To be adopted heir to Frederick.

ROSALIND:
My father loved Sir Rowland as his soul,
And all the world was of my father's mind.
Had I before known this young man his son,
I should have given him tears unto° entreaties   270
Ere he should thus have ventured.

CELIA: Gentle cousin,
Let us go thank him and encourage him.
My father's rough and envious disposition
Sticks° me at heart. Sir, you have well deserved;
If you do keep your promises in love   275
But justly° as you have exceeded all promise,
Your mistress shall be happy.

ROSALIND: Gentleman, [*gives chain*]
Wear this for me, one out of suits° with fortune,
That could° give more but that her hand lacks means.
Shall we go, coz?

CELIA: Ay. Fare you well, fair gentleman.   280

ORLANDO:
Can I not say "I thank you"? My better parts°
Are all thrown down, and that which here stands up
Is but a quintain,° a mere lifeless block.

ROSALIND:
He calls us back. My pride fell with my fortunes;
I'll ask him what he would. Did you call, sir?   285
Sir, you have wrestled well, and overthrown
More than your enemies.

CELIA: Will you go, coz?

ROSALIND:
Have with you.° Fare you well.

(*Exit* [*with* CELIA].)

ORLANDO:
What passion° hangs these weights upon my tongue?

---

225 **eke** stretch   227 **deceived in you** i.e., wrong in my estimation of your strength   232 **modest working** humble aim   238–239 **come your ways** i.e., let's get started   240 **Hercules be thy speed** may Hercules help you   249 **well breathed** fully warmed up   258 **still** always

265 **calling** name   270 **unto** as well as   274 **Sticks** pains   276 **justly** exactly   278 **out of suits** in disfavor   279 **could** would   281 **parts** qualities   283 **quintain** wooden post (used for tilting practice) 288 **Have with you** I'm coming   289 **passion** strong feeling

290 I cannot speak to her, yet she urged conference.°

(*Enter* LE BEAU.)

O poor Orlando, thou art overthrown!
Or Charles or something weaker masters thee.

LE BEAU:
Good sir, I do in friendship counsel you
To leave this place. Albeit you have deserved
295 High commendation, true applause, and love,
Yet such is now the Duke's condition
That he misconsters° all that you have done.
The Duke is humorous.° What he is, indeed,
More suits you to conceive° than I to speak of.

ORLANDO:
300 I thank you, sir; and pray you, tell me this:
Which of the two was daughter of the Duke,
That here was at the wrestling?

LE BEAU:
Neither his daughter, if we judge by manners,
But yet indeed the taller° is his daughter,
305 The other is daughter to the banished Duke,
And here detained by her usurping uncle
To keep his daughter company, whose loves
Are dearer than the natural bond of sisters.
But I can tell you that of late this Duke
310 Hath ta'en displeasure 'gainst his gentle niece,
Grounded upon no other argument°
But that the people praise her for her virtues
And pity her for her good father's sake;
And, on my life, his malice 'gainst the lady
315 Will suddenly break forth. Sir, fare you well.
Hereafter, in a better world° than this,
I shall desire more love and knowledge of you.

ORLANDO:
I rest much bounden° to you. Fare you well.
[*Exit* LE BEAU.]
Thus must I from the smoke into the smother,°
320 From tyrant Duke unto a tyrant brother.
But heavenly Rosalind! (*Exit.*)

SCENE III. [*The palace.*]

Enter CELIA *and* ROSALIND.

CELIA: Why cousin, why, Rosalind! Cupid have mercy, not a word?

290 **conference** conversation   297 **misconsters** misinterprets   298 **humorous** moody   299 **conceive** understand   304 **taller** (unless "taller" is a printer's slip for "smaller," Shakespeare here erred. Rosalind is later said to be taller)   311 **argument** basis   316 **a better world** better times   318 **bounden** indebted   319 **smother** smothering smoke (the idea is: "Out of the frying pan into the fire")

ROSALIND: Not one to throw at a dog.

CELIA: No, thy words are too precious to be cast away upon curs; throw some of them at 5 me; come, lame me with reasons.

ROSALIND: Then there were two cousins laid up, when the one should be lamed with reasons and the other mad° without any.

CELIA: But is all this for your father? 10

ROSALIND: No, some of it is for my child's father.° O, how full of briers is this working-day world!

CELIA: They are but burrs, cousin, thrown upon thee in holiday foolery; if we walk not in 15 the trodden paths, our very petticoats will catch them.

ROSALIND: I could shake them off my coat; these burrs are in my heart.

CELIA: Hem° them away. 20

ROSALIND: I would try, if I could cry "hem,"° and have him.

CELIA: Come, come, wrestle with thy affections.°

ROSALIND: O, they take the part of a better 25 wrestler than myself!

CELIA: O, a good wish upon you! You will try° in time, in despite of a fall. But turning these jests out of service,° let us talk in good earnest. Is it possible on such a sudden you 30 should fall into so strong a liking with old Sir Rowland's youngest son?

ROSALIND: The Duke my father loved his father dearly.

CELIA: Doth it therefore ensue that you 35 should love his son dearly? By this kind of chase,° I should hate him, for my father hated his father dearly; yet I hate not Orlando.

ROSALIND: No, faith, hate him not, for my sake. 40

CELIA: Why should I not? Doth he not deserve well?°

(*Enter* DUKE [FREDERICK], *with* LORDS.)

ROSALIND: Let me love him for that,° and do

I.III.9 **mad** melancholy   11–12 **child's father** i.e., future husband, Orlando   20 **Hem** (1) cough (2) tuck   21–22 **cry "hem"** clear my throat (with a pun on "him")   23–24 **affections** feelings   28 **try** i.e., chance a bout   28–29 **turning...service** to stop joking   37 **chase** pursuit (of the argument)   42 **deserve well** i.e., deserve to be hated (if Rosalind's reasoning is valid, it follows that Celia should hate Orlando)   43 **for that** i.e., for his virtues (Rosalind takes "deserve well" in its usual sense)

you love him because I do. Look, here comes
45 the Duke.

CELIA: With his eyes full of anger.

DUKE FREDERICK:
Mistress, dispatch you with your safest haste
And get you from our court.

ROSALIND: Me, uncle?

DUKE FREDERICK: You, cousin.°
Within these ten days if that thou beest found
50 So near our public court as twenty miles,
Thou diest for it.

ROSALIND: I do beseech your Grace
Let me the knowledge of my fault bear with
    me.
If with myself I hold intelligence°
Or have acquaintance with mine own desires,
55 If that I do not dream or be not frantic,°
As I do trust I am not; then, dear uncle,
Never so much as in a thought unborn
Did I offend your Highness.

DUKE FREDERICK: Thus do all traitors.
60 If their purgation° did consist in words,
They are as innocent as grace° itself.
Let it suffice thee that I trust thee not.

ROSALIND:
Yet your mistrust cannot make me a traitor.
Tell me whereon the likelihoods° depends.

DUKE FREDERICK:
Thou art thy father's daughter, there's enough.
65 ROSALIND:
So was I when your Highness took his dukedom;
So was I when your Highness banished him.
Treason is not inherited, my lord,
Or if we did derive it from our friends,°
70 What's that to me? My father was no traitor.
Then, good my liege, mistake me not so much
To think my poverty is treacherous.

CELIA:
Dear sovereign, hear me speak.

DUKE FREDERICK:
Ay, Celia. We stayed° her for your sake,
Else had she with her father ranged° along.
75 CELIA:
I did not then entreat to have her stay;
It was your pleasure and your own remorse.°
I was too young that time to value her,
But now I know her. If she be a traitor,

Why, so am I. We still° have slept together,
Rose at an instant, learned, played, eat° to-
    gether;
And wheresoe'er we went, like Juno's swans,
Still we went coupled and inseparable.   80

DUKE FREDERICK:
She is too subtile° for thee; and her smooth-
    ness,
Her very silence and her patience,
Speak to the people, and they pity her.   85
Thou art a fool. She robs thee of thy name,
And thou wilt show more bright and seem
    more virtuous°
When she is gone. Then open not thy lips.
Firm and irrevocable is my doom°
Which I have passed upon her; she is ban-
    ished.   90

CELIA:
Pronounce that sentence then on me, my liege;
I cannot live out of her company.

DUKE FREDERICK:
You are a fool. You, niece, provide yourself;
If you outstay the time, upon mine honor,
And in the greatness° of my word, you die.   95

(Exit DUKE, &c.)

CELIA:
O my poor Rosalind, whither wilt thou go?
Wilt thou change fathers? I will give thee
    mine.
I charge thee be not thou more grieved than I
    am.

ROSALIND:
I have more cause.

CELIA: Thou hast not, cousin.
Prithee be cheerful. Know'st thou not the
    Duke   100
Hath banished me, his daughter?

ROSALIND: That he hath not.

CELIA:
No? Hath not? Rosalind lacks then the love
Which teacheth thee that thou and I am one.
Shall we be sund'red, shall we part, sweet girl?
No, let my father seek another heir.   105
Therefore devise with me how we may fly,
Whither to go, and what to bear with us;
And do not seek to take your change° upon
    you,
To bear your griefs yourself and leave me out;

48 **cousin** kinsman   53 **hold intelligence** communicate   55 **frantic** insane   59 **purgation** clearance
60 **grace** virtue   63 **likelihoods** possibilities   68
friends relatives   73 **stayed** kept   74 **ranged** wandered   76 **remorse** pity

79 **still** always   80 **eat** eaten   83 **subtile** crafty   87
virtuous full of good qualities   89 **doom** sentence
95 **greatness** power   108 **change** i.e., change of
fortune

110 For, by this heaven, now at our sorrows pale,°
     Say what thou canst, I'll go along with thee.
          ROSALIND:
     Why, whither shall we go?
          CELIA:
     To seek my uncle in the Forest of Arden.
          ROSALIND:
     Alas, what danger will it be to us,
115 Maids as we are, to travel forth so far!
     Beauty provoketh thieves sooner than gold.
          CELIA:
     I'll put myself in poor and mean° attire
     And with a kind of umber° smirch my face;
     The like do you; so shall we pass along
     And never stir assailants.
120   ROSALIND: Were it not better,
     Because that I am more than common° tall,
     That I did suit me all points° like a man?
     A gallant curtle-ax° upon my thigh,
     A boar-spear in my hand; and, in my heart
125 Lie there what hidden woman's fear there will,
     We'll have a swashing° and a martial outside,
     As many other mannish cowards have
     That do outface° it with their semblances.°
          CELIA:
     What shall I call thee when thou art a man?
          ROSALIND:
     I'll have no worse a name than Jove's own
130   page,
     And therefore look you call me Ganymede.
     But what will you be called?
          CELIA:
     Something that hath a reference to my state:
     No longer Celia, but Aliena.°
          ROSALIND:
135 But, cousin, what if we assayed° to steal
     The clownish fool out of your father's court;
     Would he not be a comfort to our travel?
          CELIA:
     He'll go along o'er the wide world with me;
     Leave me alone to woo° him. Let's away
140 And get our jewels and our wealth together,
     Devise the fittest time and safest way
     To hide us from pursuit that will be made

After my flight. Now go in we content
To liberty, and not to banishment.   (*Exeunt.*)

ACT II

SCENE I. [*The Forest of Arden.*]

Enter DUKE SENIOR, AMIENS, *and two or
three* LORDS, *like Foresters.*

     DUKE SENIOR:
Now, my co-mates and brothers in exile,°
Hath not old custom made this life more sweet
Than that of painted pomp? Are not these
     woods
More free from peril than the envious court?
Here feel we not° the penalty of Adam;°   5
The seasons' difference, as° the icy fang
And churlish° chiding of the winter's wind,
Which, when it bites and blows upon my body
Even till I shrink with cold, I smile and say
"This is no flattery; these are counselors   10
That feelingly° persuade me what I am."
Sweet are the uses of adversity,
Which, like the toad, ugly and venomous,
Wears yet a precious jewel° in his head;
And this our life, exempt from public haunt,°   15
Finds tongues in trees, books in the running
     brooks,
Sermons in stones, and good in everything.
     AMIENS:
I would not change it; happy is your Grace   20
That can translate the stubbornness° of fortune
Into so quiet and so sweet a style.
     DUKE SENIOR:
Come, shall we go and kill us venison?
And yet it irks me the poor dappled fools,°
Being native burghers° of this desert° city,
Should, in their own confines, with forkèd
     heads°
Have their round haunches gored.
     FIRST LORD: Indeed, my lord,   25
The melancholy Jaques° grieves at that,

---

110 **now at our sorrows pale** now pale at our sorrows
117 **mean** lowly   118 **umber** reddish-brown color
121 **common** usually   122 **suit me at all points**
dress myself entirely   123 **curtle-ax** cutlass   126
swashing blustering   128 **outface** bluff; **semblances**
appearances (of bravery)   134 **Aliena** (Latin: the
estranged one)   135 **assayed** attempted   139 **woo**
coax

II.i.1 **exile** (accent on second syllable)   5 **feel we not**
we do not feel (some editors emend "not" to "but");
penalty of Adam loss of Eden   6 **as** for example   7
churlish harsh   11 **feelingly** (1) through the senses
(2) with intensity   14 **a precious jewel** (the fabled
toadstone)   15 **public haunt** society   19 **stubbornness** hardness   22 **fools** simple creatures   23 **bur-
ghers** citizens; **desert** deserted   24 **forkèd heads**
arrows   26 **Jaques** (dissyllabic, pronounced "Jā' kis")

And in that kind° swears you do more usurp
Than doth your brother that hath banished
    you.
Today my Lord of Amiens and myself
30 Did steal behind him as he lay along°
Under an oak, whose antique root peeps out
Upon the brook that brawls° along this wood;
To the which place a poor sequest'red° stag
That from the hunter's aim had ta'en a hurt
35 Did come to languish; and indeed, my lord,
The wretched animal heaved forth such
    groans
That their discharge did stretch his leathern
    coat
Almost to bursting, and the big round tears
Coursed one another down his innocent nose
40 In piteous chase; and thus the hairy fool,
Much markèd of° the melancholy Jaques,
Stood on th' extremest verge of the swift
    brook,
Augmenting it with tears.
  DUKE SENIOR: But what said Jaques?
Did he not moralize° this spectacle?
  FIRST LORD:
45 O, yes, into a thousand similes.
First, for his weeping into the needless°
    stream:
"Poor deer," quoth he, "thou mak'st a tes-
    tament
As worldlings do, giving thy sum of more
To that which had too much." Then, being
    there alone,
50 Left and abandoned of his velvet° friend:
" 'Tis right," quoth he, "thus misery doth part
The flux° of company." Anon a careless° herd,
Full of the pasture, jumps along by him
And never stays to greet him; "Ay," quoth
    Jaques,
55 "Sweep on, you fat and greasy citizens,
'Tis just the fashion; wherefore do you look°
Upon that poor and broken bankrupt there?"
Thus most invectively he pierceth through
The body of the country, city, court,

Yea, and of this our life, swearing that we   60
Are mere usurpers, tyrants, and what's worse,
To fright the animals and to kill them up
In their assigned° and native dwelling place.
  DUKE SENIOR:
And did you leave him in this contemplation?
  SECOND LORD:
We did, my lord, weeping and commenting   65
Upon the sobbing deer.
  DUKE SENIOR: Show me the place.
I love to cope° him in these sullen fits,
For then he's full of matter.
  FIRST LORD:
I'll bring you to him straight.°   (Exeunt.)

SCENE II. [The palace.]

Enter DUKE [FREDERICK], with LORDS.

  DUKE FREDERICK:
Can it be possible that no man saw them?
It cannot be; some villains of my court
Are of consent and sufferance° in this.
  FIRST LORD:
I cannot hear of any that did see her.   5
The ladies, her attendants of her chamber,
Saw her abed, and in the morning early
They found the bed untreasured of their
    mistress.
  SECOND LORD:
My lord, the roynish° clown at whom so oft
Your Grace was wont to laugh is also missing. 10
Hisperia, the princess' gentlewoman,
Confesses that she secretly o'erheard
Your daughter and her cousin much commend
The parts and graces° of the wrestler
That did but lately foil the sinewy Charles,   15
And she believes, wherever they are gone,
That youth is surely in their company.
  DUKE FREDERICK:
Send to his brother, fetch that gallant hither;
If he be absent, bring his brother to me;
I'll make him find him. Do this suddenly,°   20
And let not search and inquisition quail°
To bring again these foolish runaways.
                  (Exeunt.)

27 **kind** way 30 **along** stretched out 32 **brawls** makes noise 33 **sequest'red** separated 41 **markèd of** noted by 44 **moralize** sermonize 46 **needless** i.e., needing no more water 50 **velvet** i.e., courtier-like (the furry skin on the antlers, or the sleek hide, makes the deer resemble a velvet-clad courtier) 52 **flux** stream; **Anon a careless** soon an untroubled 56 **wherefore do you look** why should you bother looking

63 **assigned** allotted (by nature) 67 **cope** encounter 69 **straight** at once II.ii.3 **Are of consent and sufferance** approved and helped 8 **roynish** scurvy 13 **parts and graces** good qualities and manner 19 **suddenly** immediately 20 **quail** fail

Scene III. [OLIVER's *house*.]

Enter ORLANDO *and* ADAM.

ORLANDO:
Who's there?

ADAM:
What, my young master, O my gentle master,
O my sweet master, O you memory
Of old Sir Rowland, why, what make you°
here?
Why are you virtuous? Why do people love
5   you?
And wherefore are you gentle, strong, and
valiant?
Why would you be so fond° to overcome
The bonny prizer° of the humorous° Duke?
Your praise is come too swiftly home before
you.
10   Know you not, master, to some kind of men
Their graces serve them but as enemies?
No more° do yours. Your virtues, gentle mas-
ter,
Are sanctified and holy traitors to you°
O, what a world is this, when what is comely
15   Envenoms him that bears it!

ORLANDO:
Why, what's the matter?

ADAM: O unhappy youth,
Come not within these doors; within this roof
The enemy of all your graces lives.
20   Your brother — no, no brother, yet the son —
Yet not the son, I will not call him son,
Of him I was about to call his father —
Hath heard your praises, and this night he
means
To burn the lodging where you use° to lie
And you within it. If he fail of that,
25   He will have other means to cut you off.
I overheard him, and his practices;°
This is no place, this house is but a butchery;°
Abhor it, fear it, do not enter it!

ORLANDO:
Why, whither, Adam, wouldst thou have me
go?

ADAM:
30   No matter whither, so you come not here.

ORLANDO:
What, wouldst thou have me go and beg my
food,
Or with a base and boist'rous° sword enforce
A thievish living on the common road?°
This I must do, or know not what to do;
Yet this I will not do, do how I can.   35
I rather will subject me to the malice
Of a diverted° blood and bloody brother.

ADAM:
But do not so. I have five hundred crowns,
The thrifty hire I saved° under your father,
Which I did store to be my foster nurse   40
When service should in my old limbs lie lame
And unregarded age in corners thrown.
Take that, and he that doth the ravens feed,
Yea, providently caters for the sparrow,°
Be comfort to my age. Here is the gold;   45
All this I give you. Let me be your servant;
Though I look old, yet I am strong and lusty,
For in my youth I never did apply
Hot and rebellious° liquors in my blood,
Nor did not with unbashful forehead° woo   50
The means of weakness and debility;
Therefore my age is as a lusty winter,
Frosty, but kindly. Let me go with you;
I'll do the service of a younger man
In all your business and necessities.   55

ORLANDO:
O good old man, how well in thee appears
The constant° service of the antique world,°
When service sweat for duty, not for meed!°
Thou art not for the fashion of these times,
Where none will sweat but for promotion,   60
And having that, do choke their service up
Even with the having; it is not so with thee.
But, poor old man, thou prun'st a rotten tree
That cannot so much as a blossom yield
In lieu of° all thy pains and husbandry.   65
But come thy ways, we'll go along together,
And ere we have thy youthful wages spent,
We'll light upon some settled low content.°

ADAM:
Master, go on, and I will follow thee

II.III.4 **make you** are you doing   7 **fond** foolish   8
bonny prizer stout fighter; **humorous** moody, tem-
peramental   12 **No more** no better   12–13 **Your virtues . . . traitors to you** i.e., Orlando's blessed virtues
have worked against him   23 **use** are accustomed
26 **practices** plots   27 **butchery** slaughterhouse
32 **base and boist'rous** low and swaggering   33 **common road** highway   37 **diverted** estranged   39
thrifty hire I saved wages I carefully saved   43–44
he that . . . the sparrow (see Psalms 147:9, Luke
12:6)   49 **rebellious** i.e., causing the flesh to rebel
50 **unbashful forehead** bold face   57 **constant**
faithful; **the antique world** the past   58 **meed** reward   65 **In lieu of** in return for   68 **low content**
humble way of life

70 To the last gasp with truth and loyalty.
From seventeen years till now almost fourscore
Here livèd I, but now live here no more;
At seventeen years many their fortunes seek,
But at fourscore it is too late a week;°
75 Yet fortune cannot recompense me better.
Than to die well and not my master's debtor.

(Exeunt.)

Scene iv. [*The Forest of Arden.*]

Enter ROSALIND *for Ganymede,* CELIA *for
Aliena, and Clown, alias* TOUCHSTONE.

ROSALIND: O Jupiter, how weary are my
spirits!

TOUCHSTONE: I care not for my spirits if my
legs were not weary.

5 ROSALIND: I could find in my heart to
disgrace my man's apparel and to cry like a
woman; but I must comfort the weaker vessel,
as doublet and hose° ought to show itself
courageous to petticoat. Therefore, courage,
10 good Aliena!

CELIA: I pray you bear with me; I cannot go
no further.

TOUCHSTONE: For my part, I had rather bear
with you than bear you; yet I should bear no
15 cross° if I did bear you, for I think you have
no money in your purse.

ROSALIND: Well, this is the Forest of Arden.

TOUCHSTONE: Ay, now am I in Arden, the
more fool I. When I was at home, I was in a
20 better place, but travelers must be content.

(Enter CORIN *and* SILVIUS.)

ROSALIND: Ay, be so, good Touchstone.
Look you, who comes here, a young man and
an old in solemn talk.

CORIN:
That is the way to make her scorn you still.

SILVIUS:
25 O Corin, that thou knew'st how I do love her!

CORIN:
I partly guess, for I have loved ere now.

SILVIUS:
No, Corin, being old, thou canst not guess,
Though in thy youth thou wast as true a
    lover
As ever sighed upon a midnight pillow.

But if thy love were ever like to mine,   30
As sure I think did never man love so,
How many actions most ridiculous
Hast thou been drawn to by thy fantasy?°

CORIN:
Into a thousand that I have forgotten.

SILVIUS:
O, thou didst then never love so heartily!   35
If thou rememb'rest not the slightest folly
That ever love did make thee run into,
Thou hast not loved.
Or if thou hast not sat as I do now,
Wearing° thy hearer in thy mistress' praise,   40
Thou hast not loved.
Or if thou hast not broke from company
Abruptly, as my passion now makes me,
Thou has not loved.
O Phebe, Phebe, Phebe!   *(Exit.)*   45

ROSALIND: Alas, poor shepherd! Searching
of° thy wound, I have by hard adventure°
found mine own.

TOUCHSTONE: And I mine. I remember,
when I was in love I broke my sword upon a   50
stone and bid him take that for coming a-night
to Jane Smile; and I remember the kissing of
her batler,° and the cow's dugs that her pretty
chopt° hands had milked; and I remember the
wooing of a peascod° instead of her, from   55
whom I took two cods, and giving her them
again, said with weeping tears, "Wear these for
my sake." We that are true lovers run into
strange capers; but as all is mortal in nature, so
is all nature in love mortal in folly.°   60

ROSALIND: Thou speak'st wiser than thou art
ware° of.

TOUCHSTONE: Nay, I shall ne'er be ware of
mine own wit° till I break my shins against it.

ROSALIND:
Jove, Jove! This shepherd's passion   65
Is much upon my fashion.

TOUCHSTONE:
And mine, but it grows something stale with
    me.

CELIA:
I pray you, one of you question yond man

---

74 **week** time
II.iv.8 **doublet and hose** jacket and breeches 15
cross (1) trouble (2) coin stamped with a cross

33 **fantasy** love (and all its fancies)   40 **Wearing**
exhausting   46–47 **Searching of** probing   47 **hard
adventure** bad luck   53 **batler** wooden paddle (used
in washing clothes)   54 **chopt** chapped   55 **peascod**
peapod   59–60 **as all is mortal . . . folly** just as everything that lives must die, so all who love inevitably
do foolish things   62 **art ware** know   64 **wit**
wisdom

If he for gold will give us any food.
70 I faint almost to death.
TOUCHSTONE:
Holla, you clown!°
ROSALIND:
Peace, fool! He's not thy kinsman.
CORIN:
Who calls?
TOUCHSTONE:
Your betters, sir.
CORIN: Else are they very wretched.
ROSALIND:
75 Peace, I say! Good even to you, friend.
CORIN:
And to you, gentle sir, and to you all.
ROSALIND:
I prithee, shepherd, if that love or gold
Can in this desert place buy entertainment,°
Bring us where we may rest ourselves and feed.
Here's a young maid with travel much op-
80   pressed,
And faints for succor.
CORIN: Fair sir, I pity her
And wish, for her sake more than for mine own,
My fortunes were more able to relieve her;
But I am shepherd to another man
85 And do not shear the fleeces that I graze.
My master is of churlish° disposition
And little recks° to find the way to heaven
By doing deeds of hospitality.
Besides, his cote,° his flocks, and bounds of
     feed°
90 Are now on sale, and at our sheepcote now,
By reason of his absence, there is nothing
That you will feed on; but what is, come see,
And in my voice° most welcome shall you be.
ROSALIND:
What is he that shall buy his flock and pasture?
CORIN:
That young swain that you saw here but
95   erewhile,°
That little cares for buying anything.
ROSALIND:
I pray thee, if it stand° with honesty,
Buy thou the cottage, pasture, and the flock,
And thou shalt have° to pay for it of us.

CELIA:
And we will mend° thy wages. I like this
     place   100
And willingly could waste° my time in it.
CORIN:
Assuredly the thing is to be sold.
Go with me; if you like upon report
The soil, the profit, and this kind of life,
I will your very faithful feeder° be   105
And buy it with your gold right suddenly.
                                        (Exeunt.)

SCENE V. [The forest.]

Enter AMIENS, JAQUES, and others.

Song.
AMIENS:
     Under the greenwood tree
          Who loves to lie with me,
     And turn° his merry note
          Unto the sweet bird's throat,
     Come hither, come hither, come hither.   5
          Here shall he see no enemy
     But winter and rough weather.

JAQUES: More, more, I prithee more!
AMIENS: It will make you melancholy, Monsieur Jaques.   10
JAQUES: I thank it. More, I prithee
more! I can suck melancholy out of a
song as a weasel sucks eggs. More, I prithee
more!
AMIENS: My voice is ragged. I know I can-   15
not please you.
JAQUES: I do not desire you to please me; I do
desire you to sing. Come, more, another
stanzo! Call you 'em stanzos?
AMIENS: What you will, Monsieur Jaques.   20
JAQUES: Nay, I care not for their names;
they owe me nothing.° Will you sing?
AMIENS: More at your request than to please
myself.
JAQUES: Well then, if ever I thank any man,   25
I'll thank you. But that they call compliment°
is like th' encounter of two dog-apes,° and
when a man thanks me heartily, methinks I
have given him a penny and he renders me the

---

71 **clown** (1) rustic (2) fool 78 **entertainment**
food and shelter 86 **churlish** miserly 87 **recks**
thinks 89 **cote** cottage; **bounds of feed** pastures
93 **in my voice** as far as my position allows 95
erewhile a short while ago 97 **stand** be consistent
99 **have** i.e., have the money

100 **mend** improve 101 **waste** spend 105 **feeder**
servant
II.v.3 **turn** attune, adapt 21–22 **names . . . nothing**
(Jaques plays on the word "name," a term for the
borrower's signature on a loan) 26 **compliment**
politeness 27 **dog-apes** baboons

30 beggarly thanks.° Come, sing; and you that will
not, hold your tongues.

AMIENS: Well, I'll end the song. Sirs, cover
the while;° the Duke will drink under this tree.
He hath been all this day to look you.

35 JAQUES: And I have been all this day to
avoid him. He is too disputable for my company. I think of as many matters as he, but I
give heaven thanks and make no boast of
them. Come, warble, come.

Song.

(All together here.)

40 Who doth ambition shun
      And loves to live i' th' sun,
   Seeking the food he eats,
   And pleased with what he gets,
Come hither, come hither, come hither.
45   Here shall he see no enemy
      But winter and rough weather.

JAQUES: I'll give you a verse to this note°
that I made yesterday in despite of my invention.°

AMIENS: And I'll sing it.

50 JAQUES: Thus it goes.

   If it do come to pass
   That any man turn ass,
   Leaving his wealth and ease
   A stubborn will to please,
55 Ducdame,° ducdame, ducdame,
   Here shall he see gross fools as he,
   And if° he will come to me.

AMIENS: What's that "ducdame"?

JAQUES: 'Tis a Greek° invocation to call
60 fools into a circle. I'll go sleep, if I can; if I cannot, I'll rail against all the first-born of Egypt.°

27–30 **and when . . . beggarly thanks** i.e., the hearty
thanks of polite society are no more sincere than the
extravagant gratitude of a beggar given a small coin
32–33 **cover the while** lay the table in the meantime
47 **note** tune   48 **in despite of my invention** without using my imagination   55 **Ducdame** (various
derivations have been suggested: Romany *dukrā mē*
["I tell fortunes"]; Welsh *dewch 'da mi* ["come with
me"]; Latin *duc ad me* ["bring (him) to me"]; Italian
Duc' da mè ["duke by myself" or "duke without a
dukedom"]. Probably the word is nonsense)   57
An if if only   59 **Greek** unintelligible   61 **first-born
of Egypt** (perhaps "persons of high rank," but perhaps an allusion to life in the Forest of Arden. Exodus
11, 12 reports that when the first-born of Egypt died,
the Israelites were sent into the wilderness)

AMIENS: And I'll go seek the Duke. His ban-
quet° is prepared.   (*Exeunt.*)

SCENE VI. [*The forest.*]

Enter ORLANDO *and* ADAM.

ADAM: Dear master, I can go no further. O,
I die for food. Here lie I down and measure
out my grave. Farewell, kind master.

ORLANDO: Why, how now, Adam? No
greater heart in thee? Live a little, comfort° a   5
little, cheer thyself a little. If this uncouth°
forest yield anything savage, I will either be
food for it or bring it for food to thee. Thy
conceit° is nearer death than thy powers. For
my sake be comfortable; hold death awhile at   10
the arm's end. I will here be with thee presently,° and if I bring thee not something to eat,
I will give thee leave to die; but if thou diest
before I come, thou art a mocker of my labor.
Well said; thou look'st cheerly, and I'll be with   15
thee quickly. Yet thou liest in the bleak air.
Come, I will bear thee to some shelter, and
thou shalt not die for lack of a dinner if there
live anything in this desert. Cheerly, good
Adam.   (*Exeunt.*)   20

SCENE VII. [*The forest.*]

Enter DUKE SENIOR, *and* LORDS, *like Out-
laws.*

DUKE SENIOR:
I think he be transformed into a beast,
For I can nowhere find him like a man.

FIRST LORD:
My lord, he is but even now gone hence;
Here was he merry, hearing of a song.

DUKE SENIOR:
If he, compact of jars,° grow musical,   5
We shall have shortly discord in the spheres.°
Go seek him; tell him I would speak with him.

(*Enter* JAQUES.)

FIRST LORD:
He saves my labor by his own approach.

DUKE SENIOR:
Why, how now, monsieur, what life is this,

62–63 **banquet** light meal
II.vi.5 **comfort** take comfort   6 **uncouth** wild   9
conceit thought   11–12 **presently** at once
II.vii.5 **compact of jars** made up of discord   6 **discord in the spheres** (Ptolemaic astronomy taught
that the planetary spheres produced a ravishing harmony as they revolved)

That your poor friends must woo your com-
10   pany?
What, you look merrily.
   JAQUES:
A fool, a fool! I met a fool i' th' forest,
A motley° fool! A miserable world!
As I do live by food, I met a fool
Who laid him down and basked him in the
15   sun
And railed on Lady Fortune in good terms,
In good set terms,° and yet a motley fool.
"Good morrow, fool," quoth I. "No, sir,"
   quoth he,
"Call me not fool till heaven hath sent me
   fortune."°
20 And then he drew a dial from his poke,°
And looking on it with lack-luster eye,
Says very wisely, "It is ten o'clock.
Thus we may see," quoth he, "how the world
   wags.°
'Tis but an hour ago since it was nine,
25 And after one hour more 'twill be eleven;
And so, from hour to hour,° we ripe and ripe,
And then, from hour to hour, we rot and rot;
And thereby hangs a tale." When I did hear
The motley fool thus moral° on the time,
30 My lungs began to crow like chanticleer°
That fools should be so deep contemplative;
And I did laugh sans intermission°
An hour by his dial. O noble fool,
A worthy fool! Motley's the only wear.
   DUKE SENIOR:
35 What fool is this?
   JAQUES:
O worthy fool! One that hath been a courtier,
And says, if ladies be but young and fair,
They have the gift to know it. And in his
   brain,
Which is as dry as the remainder biscuit°
40 After a voyage, he hath strange places crammed
With observation, the which he vents°

In mangled forms. O that I were a fool!
I am ambitious for a motley coat.
   DUKE SENIOR:
Thou shalt have one.
   JAQUES: It is my only suit,°
Provided that you weed your better judgments 45
Of all opinion that grows rank° in them
That I am wise. I must have liberty
Withal, as large a charter° as the wind,
To blow on whom I please, for so fools have.
And they that are most gallèd° with my folly, 50
They most must laugh. And why, sir, must
   they so?
The why is plain as way to parish church:
He that a fool doth very wisely hit
Doth very foolishly, although he smart,
Not to seem senseless of the bob.° If not, 55
The wise man's folly is anatomized°
Even by the squand'ring glances° of the fool.
Invest° me in my motley, give me leave
To speak my mind, and I will through and
   through
Cleanse the foul body of th' infected world, 60
If they will patiently receive my medicine.
   DUKE SENIOR:
Fie on thee! I can tell what thou wouldst do.
   JAQUES:
What, for a counter,° would I do but good?
   DUKE SENIOR:
Most mischievous foul sin, in chiding sin.
For thou thyself hast been a libertine, 65
As sensual as the brutish sting° itself;
And all th' embossèd° sores and headed evils
That thou with license of free foot° hast
   caught,
Wouldst thou disgorge into the general world.
   JAQUES:
Why, who cries out on pride 70
That can therein tax any private party?°
Doth it not flow as hugely as the sea
Till that the weary very means do ebb?°
What woman in the city do I name

13 **motley** garbed in the multicolored costume of the court fool (a motley costume is commonly thought to be checkered or patched; Leslie Hotson, in *Shakespeare's Motley*, argues it was of varicolored threads but drab, like a tweed)   17 **set terms** precise phrases   19 **Call me ... fortune** (fortune proverbially favors fools)   20 **dial from his poke** sundial from his pocket   23 **wags** goes   26 **hour to hour** (perhaps with a pun on "whore")   29 **moral** moralize   30 **chanticleer** (traditional name for a rooster)   32 **sans intermission** without stop   39 **remainder biscuit** leftover hardtack   41 **vents** gives forth

44 **suit** (1) garment (2) petition   46 **rank** luxuriant   48 **large a charter** liberal license   50 **gallèd** chafed   55 **senseless of the bob** unaware of the hit   56 **anatomized** revealed   57 **squand'ring glances** chance hits   58 **Invest** clothe   63 **counter** worthless coin   66 **the brutish sting** lust   67 **embossèd** swollen   68 **license of free foot** complete freedom   71 **tax any private party** criticize any particular person   73 **weary very means do ebb** (perhaps: "ostentation eventually exhausts the wealth that makes it possible." Some editors emend "weary" to "wearer's")

75 When that I say the city woman bears
The cost° of princes on unworthy shoulders?
Who can come in and say that I mean her,
When such a one as she, such is her neighbor?
Or what is he of basest function°
80 That says his bravery is not on my cost,°
Thinking that I mean him, but therein suits
His folly to the mettle of my speech?°
There then, how then, what then? Let me see
wherein
My tongue hath wronged him. If it do him
right,
85 Then he hath wronged himself. If he be free,°
Why, then my taxing like a wild goose flies
Unclaimed of any man. But who comes here?

(*Enter* ORLANDO [*with his sword drawn*].)

ORLANDO:
Forebear, and eat no more!
JAQUES: Why, I have eat none yet.
ORLANDO:
Nor shalt not, till necessity be served.
JAQUES:
90 Of what kind° should this cock come of?
DUKE SENIOR:
Art thou thus boldened, man, by thy distress,
Or else a rude despiser of good manners,
That in civility thou seem'st so empty?
ORLANDO:
You touched my vein at first.° The thorny
point
95 Of bare distress hath ta'en from me the show
Of smooth civility; yet am I inland bred°
And know some nurture.° But forbear, I say!
He dies that touches any of this fruit
Till I and my affairs are answerèd.°
JAQUES:
An° you will not be answered with reason,° I
100 must die.
DUKE SENIOR:
What would you have? Your gentleness shall
force
More than your force move us to gentleness.

76 **cost** wealth 79 **function** position 80 **his
bravery . . . cost** his fine dress is not paid for by me
(and therefore is not my business) 81–82 **suits . . .
my speech** matches his folly to the substance of my
words 85 **free** innocent 90 **kind** breed 94 **You
touched . . . first** i.e., the Duke's first supposition is
correct 96 **inland bred** brought up in civilized society 97 **nurture** good breeding 99 **answerèd** provided for 100 **An** if; **reason** (perhaps Jaques puns,
eating a raisin [grape])

ORLANDO:
I almost die for food, and let me have it!
DUKE SENIOR:
Sit down and feed, and welcome to our table.
ORLANDO:
Speak you so gently? Pardon me, I pray you. 105
I thought that all things had been savage
here,
And therefore put I on the countenance
Of stern commandment. But whate'er you are
That in this desert inaccessible,
Under the shade of melancholy boughs,   110
Lose and neglect the creeping hours of time;
If ever you have looked on better days,
If ever been where bells have knolled° to
church,
If ever sat at any good man's feast,
If ever from your eyelids wiped a tear   115
And know what 'tis to pity and be pitied,
Let gentleness my strong enforcement° be;
In the which hope I blush, and hide my
sword.
DUKE SENIOR:
True is it that we have seen better days,
And have with holy bell been knolled to
church,   120
And sat at good men's feasts, and wiped our
eyes
Of drops that sacred pity hath engend'red;
And therefore sit you down in gentleness,
And take upon command° what help we have
That to your wanting° may be minist'red.   125
ORLANDO:
Then but forbear your food a little while,
Whiles, like a doe, I go to find my fawn
And give it food. There is an old poor man
Who after me hath many a weary step
Limped in pure love. Till he be first sufficed, 130
Oppressed with two weak evils,° age and hunger,
I will not touch a bit.
DUKE SENIOR: Go find him out,
And we will nothing waste° till you return.
ORLANDO:
I thank ye, and be blest for your good
comfort!   [*Exit.*]
DUKE SENIOR:
Thou seest we are not all alone unhappy: 135
This wide and universal theater

113 **knolled** rung 117 **enforcement** support 124
upon command as you wish 125 **wanting** need
131 **weak evils** evils causing weakness 133 **waste**
consume

Presents more woeful pageants° than the scene
Wherein we play in.
    JAQUES: All the world's a stage,
And all the men and women merely players;
140 They have their exits and their entrances,
And one man in his time plays many parts,
His acts being seven ages.° At first, the in-
    fant,
Mewling° and puking in the nurse's arms.
Then the whining schoolboy, with his satchel
And shining morning face, creeping like
145   snail
Unwillingly to school. And then the lover,
Sighing like furnace, with a woeful ballad
Made to his mistress' eyebrow. Then a soldier,
Full of strange oaths and bearded like the
    pard,°
Jealous° in honor, sudden° and quick in quar-
150   rel,
Seeking the bubble reputation
Even in the cannon's mouth. And then the
    justice,
In fair round belly with good capon lined,°
With eyes severe and beard of formal cut,
155 Full of wise saws° and modern instances;°
And so he plays his part. The sixth age shifts
Into the lean and slippered pantaloon,°
With spectacles on nose and pouch on side;
His youthful hose,° well saved, a world too
    wide
For his shrunk shank, and his big manly
160   voice,
Turning again toward childish treble, pipes
And whistles in his° sound. Last scene of all,
That ends this strange eventful history,
Is second childishness and mere° oblivion,
Sans teeth, sans eyes, sans taste, sans every-
165   thing.

    (*Enter* ORLANDO, *with* ADAM.)

137 **pageants** scenes   142 **seven ages** (for a survey in art and literature of the image of man's life divided into ages, see Samuel C. Chew, " 'This Strange Eventful History,' " in *John Quincy Adams Memorial Studies,* ed. James G. McManaway *et al.*)   143 **Mewling** bawling   149 **pard** leopard   150 **Jealous** touchy; **sudden** rash   153 **capon lined** (perhaps an allusion to the practice of bribing a judge with a capon)   155 **saws** sayings; **modern instances** commonplace examples   157 **pantaloon** ridiculous old man (from Pantalone, a stock figure in Italian comedy)   159 **hose** breeches   162 **his** its   164 **mere** utter

DUKE SENIOR:
Welcome. Set down your venerable burden
And let him feed.
    ORLANDO:
I thank you most for him.
    ADAM: So had you need.
I scarce can speak to thank you for myself.
    DUKE SENIOR:
Welcome, fall to. I will not trouble you   170
As yet to question you about your fortunes.
Give us some music; and, good cousin, sing.

Song.

    AMIENS:
Blow, blow, thou winter wind,
Thou art not so unkind°
    As man's ingratitude: 175
Thy tooth is not so keen,
Because thou art not seen,
    Although thy breath be rude.
Heigh-ho, sing heigh-ho, unto the green
    holly.
Most friendship is faining,° most loving mere
    folly: 180
    Then, heigh-ho, the holly.
    This life is most jolly.

Freeze, freeze, thou bitter sky
That dost not bite so nigh
    As benefits forgot: 185
Though thou the waters warp,°
Thy sting is not so sharp
    As friend rememb'red not.
Heigh-ho, sing, &c.
    DUKE SENIOR:
If that you were the good Sir Rowland's
    son,   190
As you have whispered faithfully you were,
And as mine eye doth his effigies° witness
Most truly limned° and living in your face,
Be truly welcome hither. I am the Duke
That loved your father. The residue of your
    fortune   195
Go to my cave and tell me. Good old man,
Thou art right welcome, as thy master is.
Support him by the arm. Give me your
    hand,
And let me all your fortunes understand.
                       (*Exeunt.*)

174 **unkind** unnatural   180 **faining** longing (perhaps with a pun on "feigning" [pretending])   186 **warp** turn (into ice)   192 **effigies** likeness (accent on second syllable)   193 **limned** depicted

ACT III

SCENE I. [*The palace.*]

Enter DUKE [FREDERICK], LORDS, *and* OLIVER.

DUKE FREDERICK:
Not see him since? Sir, sir, that cannot be.
But were I not the better part made mercy,°
I should not seek an absent argument°
Of my revenge, thou present. But look to it:
5 Find out thy brother, wheresoe'er he is;
Seek him with candle; bring him dead or living
Within this twelvemonth, or turn° thou no
    more
To seek a living in our territory.
Thy lands, and all things that thou dost call
    thine
10 Worth seizure, do we seize into our hands
Till thou canst quit° thee by thy brother's
    mouth°
Of what we think against thee.

OLIVER:
O that your Highness knew my heart in this!
I never loved my brother in my life.

DUKE FREDERICK:
More villain thou. Well, push 'him out of
15   doors,
And let my officers of such a nature°
Make an extent upon° his house and lands.
Do this expediently° and turn him going.
                    (*Exeunt.*)

SCENE II. [*The forest.*]

Enter ORLANDO [*with a paper*].

ORLANDO:
Hang there, my verse, in witness of my love;
And thou, thrice-crownèd Queen of Night,°
    survey
With thy chaste eye, from thy pale sphere above,
Thy huntress' name° that my full life doth
    sway.

O Rosalind! These trees shall be my books,   5
And in their barks my thoughts I'll charac-
    ter,°
That every eye which in this forest looks
Shall see thy virtue witnessed° everywhere.
Run, run, Orlando, carve on every tree
The fair, the chaste, and unexpressive she.°   10
                      (*Exit.*)

(*Enter* CORIN *and* [TOUCHSTONE, *the*] *Clown.*)

CORIN: And how like you this shepherd's
life, Master Touchstone?
TOUCHSTONE: Truly, shepherd, in respect of
itself, it is a good life; but in respect that it is
a shepherd's life, it is naught.° In respect that   15
it is solitary, I like it very well; but in respect
that it is private,° it is a very vile life. Now in
respect it is in the fields, it pleaseth me well;
but in respect it is not in the court, it is
tedious. As it is a spare° life, look you, it fits   20
my humor° well; but as there is no more
plenty in it, it goes much against my stomach.
Hast any philosophy° in thee, shepherd?
CORIN: No more, but that I know the more
one sickens, the worse at ease he is; and that   25
he that wants° money, means, and content is
without three good friends; that the property
of rain is to wet and fire to burn; that good
pasture makes fat sheep, and that a great cause
of the night is lack of the sun; that he that   30
hath learned no wit by nature nor art° may
complain° of good breeding, or comes of a very
dull kindred.
TOUCHSTONE: Such a one is a natural philosopher.° Wast ever in court, shepherd?   35
CORIN: No, truly.
TOUCHSTONE: Then thou art damned.
CORIN: Nay, I hope.
TOUCHSTONE: Truly thou art damned, like
an ill-roasted egg, all on one side.   40
CORIN: For not being at court? Your reason.
TOUCHSTONE: Why, if thou never wast at
court, thou never saw'st good manners;° if thou
never saw'st good manners, then thy manners

III.i.2 **the better part made mercy** so merciful 3
argument object (i.e., Orlando) 7 **turn** return 11
quit acquit; **mouth** testimony 16 **of such a nature**
i.e., appropriate 17 **Make an extent upon** seize by
writ 18 **expediently** speedily
III.ii.2 **thrice-crownèd Queen of Night** Diana (goddess of the moon, the hunt, and of chastity) 4 **Thy
huntress' name** i.e., Rosalind, who, because she is
chaste, serves Diana

6 **character** write 8 **virtue witnessed** power attested
to 10 **unexpressive she** i.e., woman beyond description 15 **naught** worthless 17 **private** lonely 20
spare frugal 21 **humor** disposition 23 **philosophy**
learning 26 **wants** lacks 31 **by nature nor art**
by birth or education 32 **complain** cry the lack
34–35 **a natural philosopher** (1) wise by nature
(2) a wise idiot 43 **manners** (1) behavior (2)
morals

45 must be wicked; and wickedness is sin, and sin
is damnation. Thou art in a parlous° state,
shepherd.

CORIN: Not a whit, Touchstone. Those that
are good manners at the court are as ridiculous
50 in the country as the behavior of the country is
most mockable at the court. You told me you
salute not at the court but you kiss° your
hands. That courtesy would be uncleanly if
courtiers were shepherds.

55 TOUCHSTONE: Instance,° briefly. Come, instance.

CORIN: Why, we are still° handling our
ewes, and their fells° you know are greasy.

TOUCHSTONE: Why, do not your courtier's
60 hands sweat? And is not the grease of a
mutton as wholesome as the sweat of a man?
Shallow, shallow. A better instance, I say.
Come.

CORIN: Besides, our hands are hard.

65 TOUCHSTONE: Your lips will feel them the
sooner. Shallow again. A more sounder instance, come.

CORIN: And they are often tarred over with
the surgery° of our sheep, and would you have
70 us kiss tar? The courtier's hands are perfumed
with civet.°

TOUCHSTONE: Most shallow man! Thou
worms' meat° in respect of° a good piece of
flesh indeed! Learn of the wise, and perpend.°
75 Civet is of a baser birth than tar, the very
uncleanly flux° of a cat. Mend the instance,°
shepherd.

CORIN: You have too courtly a wit for me;
I'll rest.

80 TOUCHSTONE: Wilt thou rest damned? God
help thee, shallow man! God make incision in
thee!° Thou art raw.°

CORIN: Sir, I am a true laborer; I earn that°
I eat, get that I wear, owe no man hate, envy
85 no man's happiness, glad of other men's good,

content with my harm;° and the greatest of my
pride is to see my ewes graze and my lambs suck.

TOUCHSTONE: That is another simple sin in
you: to bring the ewes and the rams together
and to offer to get your living by the copula- 90
tion of cattle, to be bawd to a bell-wether° and
to betray a she-lamb of a twelve-month to a
crookèd-pated° old cuckoldly° ram, out of all
reasonable match. If thou beest not damned for
this, the devil himself will have no shepherds; 95
I cannot see else how thou shouldst 'scape.

CORIN: Here comes young Master Ganymede, my new mistress' brother.

(*Enter* ROSALIND [*reading a paper*].)

ROSALIND:
"From the east to western Ind,
No jewel is like Rosalind.   100
Her worth, being mounted on the wind,
Through all the world bears Rosalind.
All the pictures fairest lined°
Are but black to Rosalind.
Let no face be kept in mind   105
But the fair° of Rosalind."

TOUCHSTONE: I'll rhyme you so eight years
together, dinners and suppers and sleeping
hours excepted. It is the right butterwomen's
rank to market.°   110

ROSALIND: Out, fool!

TOUCHSTONE: For a taste:

If a hart do lack a hind,
Let him seek out Rosalind.
If the cat will after kind,°   115
So be sure will Rosalind.
Wintred° garments must be lined,°
So must slender Rosalind.
They that reap must sheaf and bind,
Then to cart° with Rosalind.   120
Sweetest nut hath sourest rind,
Such a nut is Rosalind.
He that sweetest rose will find
Must find love's prick, and Rosalind.

---

46 **parlous** dangerous   52 **but you kiss** without kissing   55 **Instance** proof   57 **still** always   58 **fells**
fleeces   68–69 **tarred . . . surgery** (shepherds used
tar as an ointment)   71 **civet** perfume obtained
from the civet cat   73 **worms' meat** food for worms;
respect of comparison with   74 **perpend** consider
76 **flux** secretion; **Mend the instance** give a better
example   81–82 **make incision in thee** let your
blood (a common cure, here for folly)   82 **raw** (1)
inexperienced (2) sore   83 **that** what

86 **content with my harm** bear with my troubles   91
bell-wether (the leading sheep of a flock carries a
bell)   93 **crookèd-pated** i.e., with crooked horns;
cuckoldy (because horned)   103 **lined** drawn   106
fair lovely face   109–110 **right butterwomen's rank
to market** i.e., the verses jog along exactly like a procession of women riding to market   115 **kind** its own
kind   117 **Wintred** i.e., prepared for winter; **lined**
stuffed   120 **to cart** (perhaps an allusion not only to
the harvest but to the custom of transporting prostitutes to jail in a cart)

125 This is the very false gallop of verses. Why do you infect yourself with them?

ROSALIND: Peace, you dull fool! I found them on a tree.

TOUCHSTONE: Truly the tree yields bad fruit.

130 ROSALIND: I'll graff° it with you and then I shall graff it with a medlar.° Then it will be the earliest fruit i' th' country; for you'll be rotten ere you be half ripe, and that's the right virtue° of the medlar.

135 TOUCHSTONE: You have said; but whether wisely or no, let the forest judge.

(*Enter* CELIA, *with a writing.*)

ROSALIND: Peace! Here comes my sister reading; stand aside.

CELIA:
"Why should this a desert be?
    For° it is unpeopled? No.
140
Tongues I'll hang on every tree
    That shall civil sayings° show:
Some, how brief the life of man
    Runs his erring pilgrimage,
145 That the stretching of a span°
    Buckles in° his sum of age;
Some, of violated vows
    'Twixt the souls of friend and friend;
But upon the fairest boughs,
    Or at every sentence end,
150
Will I 'Rosalinda' write,
    Teaching all that read to know
The quintessence of every sprite°
    Heaven would in little° show.
155 Therefore heaven Nature charged
    That one body should be filled
With all graces wide-enlarged.
    Nature presently° distilled
Helen's cheek, but not her heart,°
160
    Cleopatra's majesty,
Atalanta's better part,°
    Sad° Lucretia's° modesty.

130 **graff** graft   131 **medlar** (1) an applelike fruit, not ready to eat until it is almost rotten (2) interferer 133–134 **right virtue** true quality   140 **For** because 142 **civil sayings** civilized maxims   145 **stretching of a span** span of an open hand   146 **Buckles in** limits   153 **sprite** soul   154 **in little** in miniature (i.e., the microcosm)   158 **presently** thereupon 159 **cheek . . . heart** i.e., Helen's beauty but not her false heart   161 **Atalanta's better part** i.e., Rosalind has the gracefulness but not the cruelty of Atalanta, a huntress famed in Greek mythology for her fleetness 162 **Sad** dignified; **Lucretia** (a Roman matron who killed herself rather than live dishonored)

Thus Rosalind of many parts
    By heavenly synod° was devised,
Of many faces, eyes, and hearts,   165
    To have the touches° dearest prized.
Heaven would that she these gifts should have,
And I to live and die her slave."

ROSALIND: O most gentle pulpiter, what tedious homily of love have you wearied your   170 parishioners withal, and never cried, "Have patience, good people"!

CELIA: How now? Back, friends. Shepherd, go off a little. Go with him, sirrah.

TOUCHSTONE: Come, shepherd, let us make   175 an honorable retreat; though not with bag and baggage, yet with scrip and scrippage.°

                    (*Exit* [*with* CORIN].)

CELIA: Didst thou hear these verses?

ROSALIND: O, yes, I heard them all, and more too; for some of them had in them more   180 feet° than the verses would bear.

CELIA: That's no matter. The feet might bear the verses.

ROSALIND: Ay, but the feet were lame, and could not bear themselves without the verse,   185 and therefore stood lamely in the verse.

CELIA: But didst thou hear without wondering how thy name should be hanged and carved upon these trees?

ROSALIND: I was seven of the nine days° out   190 of the wonder before you came; for look here what I found on a palm tree. I was never so berhymed since Pythagoras'° time that° I was an Irish rat,° which I can hardly remember.

CELIA: Trow° you who hath done this?   195

ROSALIND: Is it a man?

CELIA: And a chain that you once wore, about his neck. Change you color?

ROSALIND: I prithee who?

CELIA: O Lord, Lord, it is a hard matter for   200 friends to meet; but mountains may be removed with earthquakes, and so encounter.

ROSALIND: Nay, but who is it?

CELIA: Is it possible?

164 **synod** council   166 **touches** features   177 **scrip and scrippage** shepherd's pouch and its contents   181 **feet** metrical units   190 **seven of the nine days** (cf. the phrase "nine days' wonder")   193 **Pythagoras** (Greek philosopher who taught the doctrine of the transmigration of souls); **that** when   194 **Irish rat** (it was believed that Irish sorcerers could kill rats with rhymed spells)   195 **Trow** know

205 ROSALIND: Nay, I prithee now with most petitionary vehemence,° tell me who it is.

CELIA: O wonderful, wonderful, and most wonderful wonderful, and yet again wonderful, and after that, out of all hooping!°

210 ROSALIND: Good my complexion!° Dost thou think, though I am caparisoned° like a man, I have a doublet and hose in my disposition! One inch of delay more is a South Sea of discovery.° I prithee tell me who is it 215 quickly, and speak apace.° I would thou couldst stammer, that thou mightst pour this concealed man out of thy mouth as wine comes out of a narrow-mouthed bottle; either too much at once, or none at all. I prithee take 220 the cork out of thy mouth, that I may drink thy tidings.

CELIA: So you may put a man in your belly.

ROSALIND: Is he of God's making? What manner of man? Is his head worth a hat? Or 225 his chin worth a beard?

CELIA: Nay, he hath but a little beard.

ROSALIND: Why, God will send more, if the man will be thankful. Let me stay° the growth of his beard, if thou delay me not the knowl-230 edge of his chin.

CELIA: It is young Orlando, that tripped up the wrestler's heels and your heart both in an instant.

ROSALIND: Nay, but the devil take mocking! 235 Speak sad brow and true maid.°

CELIA: I' faith, coz, 'tis he.

ROSALIND: Orlando?

CELIA: Orlando.

ROSALIND: Alas the day! What shall I do 240 with my doublet and hose? What did he when thou saw'st him? What said he? How looked he? Wherein went he?° What makes he here? Did he ask for me? Where remains he? How parted he with thee? And when shalt thou see 245 him again? Answer me in one word.

CELIA: You must borrow me Gargantua's°

mouth first; 'tis a word too great for any mouth of this age's size. To say "ay" and "no" to these particulars is more than to answer in a catechism. 250

ROSALIND: But doth he know that I am in this forest, and in man's apparel? Looks he as freshly° as he did the day he wrestled?

CELIA: It is as easy to count atomies° as to resolve the propositions° of a lover; but take a 255 taste of my finding him, and relish it with good observance.° I found him under a tree, like a dropped acorn.

ROSALIND: It may well be called Jove's tree° when it drops forth fruit. 260

CELIA: Give me audience,° good madam.

ROSALIND: Proceed.

CELIA: There lay he stretched along like a wounded knight.

ROSALIND: Though it be pity to see such a 265 sight, it well becomes the ground.

CELIA: Cry "holla"° to the tongue, I prithee; it curvets° unseasonably. He was furnished° like a hunter.

ROSALIND: O, ominous! He comes to kill 270 my heart.°

CELIA: I would sing my song without a burden.° Thou bring'st me out of tune.

ROSALIND: Do you not know I am a woman? When I think, I must speak. Sweet, say on. 275

(*Enter* ORLANDO *and* JAQUES.)

CELIA: You bring me out. Soft. Comes he not here?

ROSALIND: 'Tis he! Slink by, and note him.

JAQUES: I thank you for your company; but, good faith, I had as lief have been myself alone. 280

ORLANDO: And so had I; but yet for fashion sake I thank you too for your society.

JAQUES: God b' wi' you; let's meet as little as we can.

ORLANDO: I do desire we may be better 285 strangers.

JAQUES: I pray you mar no more trees with writing love songs in their barks.

ORLANDO: I pray you mar no moe° of my verses with reading them ill-favoredly.° 290

205–206 **with most petitionary vehemence** i.e., I beg you 209 **out of all hooping** beyond all measure 210 **Good my complexion** (a mild expletive) 211 **caparisoned** dressed 213–214 **One inch ... discovery** i.e., another minute more will seem as long as it takes to voyage to the South Seas 215 **apace** quickly 228 **stay** wait for 235 **sad brow and true maid** i.e., seriously and truthfully 242 **Wherein went he** how was he dressed 246 **Gargantua** (a giant in Rabelais and other writers)

253 **freshly** handsome 254 **atomies** motes 255 **resolve the propositions** answer the questions 257 **good observance** close attention 259 **Jove's tree** (the oak, sacred to Jove) 261 **Give me audience** listen 267 **holla** whoa 268 **curvets** frolics; **furnished** dressed 271 **heart** (pun on "hart") 273 **burden** refrain 289 **moe** more 290 **ill-favoredly** badly

JAQUES: Rosalind is your love's name?

ORLANDO: Yes, just.

JAQUES: I do not like her name.

ORLANDO: There was no thought of pleasing
295 you when she was christened.

JAQUES: What stature is she of?

ORLANDO: Just as high as my heart.

JAQUES: You are full of pretty answers. Have
you not been acquainted with goldsmiths'
300 wives, and conned them out of rings?°

ORLANDO: Not so; but I answer you right
painted cloth,° from whence you have studied
your questions.

JAQUES: You have a nimble wit; I think
305 'twas made of Atalanta's heels.° Will you sit
down with me, and we two will rail against our
mistress the world and all our misery.

ORLANDO: I will chide no breather° in the
world but myself, against whom I know most
310 faults.

JAQUES: The worst fault you have is to be in
love.

ORLANDO: 'Tis a fault I will not change for
your best virtue. I am weary of you.

315 JAQUES: By my troth, I was seeking for a
fool when I found you.

ORLANDO: He is drowned in the brook. Look
but in and you shall see him.

JAQUES: There I shall see mine own figure.

320 ORLANDO: Which I take to be either a fool
or a cipher.°

JAQUES: I'll tarry no longer with you. Farewell, good Signior Love.

ORLANDO: I am glad of your departure. Adieu,
325 good Monsieur Melancholy.   [*Exit* JAQUES.]

ROSALIND: I will speak to him like a saucy
lackey, and under that habit° play the knave
with him. Do you hear, forester?

ORLANDO: Very well. What would you?

330 ROSALIND: I pray you, what is't o'clock?

ORLANDO: You should ask me, what time o'
day. There's no clock in the forest.

ROSALIND: Then there is no true lover in the
forest, else sighing every minute and groaning
335 every hour would detect° the lazy foot of Time
as well as a clock.

ORLANDO: And why not the swift foot of
Time? Had not that been as proper?

ROSALIND: By no means, sir. Time travels in
divers paces with divers persons. I'll tell you   340
who Time ambles withal, who Time trots
withal, who Time gallops withal, and who he
stands still withal.

ORLANDO: I prithee, who doth he trot
withal?   345

ROSALIND: Marry, he trots hard with a young
maid between the contract of her marriage°
and the day it is solemnized. If the interim be
but a se'nnight,° Time's pace is so hard that it
seems the length of seven year.   350

ORLANDO: Who ambles Time withal?

ROSALIND: With a priest that lacks Latin
and a rich man that hath not the gout; for the
one sleeps easily because he cannot study, and
the other lives merrily because he feels no   355
pain; the one lacking the burden of lean and
wasteful° learning, the other knowing no burden of heavy tedious penury. These Time
ambles withal.

ORLANDO: Who doth he gallop withal?   360

ROSALIND: With a thief to the gallows; for
though he go as softly° as foot can fall, he
thinks himself too soon there.

ORLANDO: Who stays it still withal?

ROSALIND: With lawyers in the vacation; for   365
they sleep between term° and term, and then
they perceive not how time moves.

ORLANDO: Where dwell you, pretty youth?

ROSALIND: With this shepherdess, my sister;
here in the skirts of the forest, like fringe upon 370
a petticoat.

ORLANDO: Are you native of this place?

ROSALIND: As the cony° that you see dwell
where she is kindled.°

ORLANDO: Your accent is something finer   375
than you could purchase° in so removed° a
dwelling.

ROSALIND: I have been told so of many. But
indeed an old religious° uncle of mine taught
me to speak, who was in his youth an inland°   380
man; one that knew courtship° too well, for

300 **conned them out of rings** i.e., memorized the
sentimental sayings inscribed in rings   302 **painted
cloth** (cheap substitute for tapestry, on which were
painted pictures with trite sayings)   305 **Atalanta's
heels** (Atalanta was a symbol of speed)   308
breather creature   321 **cipher** zero   327 **habit** guise
335 **detect** show

347 **contract of her marriage** betrothal   349 **a
se'nnight** seven days, a week   357 **wasteful** i.e.,
causing one to waste away   362 **softly** slowly   366
term court session   373 **cony** rabbit   374 **kindled**
born   376 **purchase** acquire; **removed** remote   379
religious i.e., a member of a religious order   380 **inland** city   381 **courtship** (1) court manners (2)
wooing

there he fell in love. I have heard him read
many lectures against it; and I thank God I am
not a woman, to be touched° with so many
385 giddy° offenses as he hath generally taxed their
whole sex withal.

ORLANDO: Can you remember any of the
principal evils that he laid to the charge of
women?

390 ROSALIND: There were none principal. They
were all like one another as halfpence are,
every one fault seeming monstrous till his
fellow fault came to match it.

ORLANDO: I prithee recount some of them.
395 ROSALIND: No, I will not cast away my
physic but on those that are sick. There is a
man haunts the forest that abuses our young
plants with carving "Rosalind" on their barks,
hangs odes upon hawthorns, and elegies on
400 brambles; all, forsooth, deifying the name of
Rosalind. If I could meet that fancy-monger,° I
would give him some good counsel, for he
seems to have the quotidian° of love upon
him.

405 ORLANDO: I am he that is so love-shaked. I
pray tell me your remedy.

ROSALIND: There is none of my uncle's
marks upon you. He taught me how to know a
man in love; in which cage of rushes° I am
410 sure you are not prisoner.

ORLANDO: What were his marks?

ROSALIND: A lean cheek, which you have
not; a blue eye° and sunken, which you have
not; an unquestionable° spirit, which you have
415 not; a beard neglected, which you have
not — but I pardon you for that, for simply
your having° in beard is a younger brother's
revenue.° Then your hose should be ungar-
tered, your bonnet unbanded, your sleeve un-
420 buttoned, your shoe untied, and everything
about you demonstrating a careless desolation.°
But you are no such man: you are rather
point-device in your accouterments,° as loving
yourself than seeming the lover of any other.

ORLANDO: Fair youth, I would I could make   425
thee believe I love.

ROSALIND: Me believe it? You may as soon
make her that you love believe it, which I
warrant she is apter to do than to confess she
does; that is one of the points in the which   430
women still give the lie to their consciences. But
in good sooth, are you he that hangs the verses
on the trees wherein Rosalind is so admired?

ORLANDO: I swear to thee, youth, by the
white hand of Rosalind, I am that he, that   435
unfortunate he.

ROSALIND: But are you so much in love as
your rhymes speak?

ORLANDO: Neither rhyme nor reason can
express how much.   440

ROSALIND: Love is merely° a madness, and, I
tell you, deserves as well a dark house and a
whip° as madmen do; and the reason why they
are not so punished and cured is that the
lunacy is so ordinary that the whippers are in   445
love too. Yet I profess curing it by counsel.

ORLANDO: Did you ever cure any so?

ROSALIND: Yes, one, and in this manner. He
was to imagine me his love, his mistress; and I
set him every day to woo me. At which time   450
would I, being but a moonish° youth, grieve,
be effeminate, changeable, longing and liking,
proud, fantastical,° apish, shallow, inconstant,
full of tears, full of smiles; for every passion
something and for no passion truly anything,   455
as boys and women are for the most part cattle
of this color; would now like him, now loathe
him; then entertain him, then forswear him;
now weep for him, then spit at him; that I
drave my suitor from his mad humor° of love   460
to a living° humor of madness, which was, to
forswear the full stream of the world and to
live in a nook merely monastic. And thus I
cured him; and this way will I take upon me to
wash your liver° as clean as a sound sheep's heart,   465
that there shall not be one spot of love in't.

ORLANDO: I would not be cured, youth.

ROSALIND: I would cure you, if you would
but call me Rosalind and come every day to
my cote and woo me.   470

ORLANDO: Now, by the faith of my love, I
will. Tell me where it is.

384 **touched** tainted   385 **giddy** frivolous   401
fancy-monger dealer in love   403 **quotidian** daily
fever   409 **cage of rushes** i.e., prison easy to escape
from   413 **a blue eye** i.e., dark circles under the
eyes   414 **unquestionable** averse to conversation
416–417 **simply your having** truthfully what you
have   417–418 **a younger brother's revenue** i.e., a
small portion   421 **a careless desolation** indifferent
despondency   423 **point-device in your accouterments** precise in your dress

441 **merely** completely   442–443 **a dark house and
a whip** (the usual treatment of the insane in Shakespeare's day)   451 **moonish** changeable   453 **fantastical** capricious   460 **humor** condition   461 **living** real   465 **liver** (thought to be the seat of love)

ROSALIND: Go with me to it, and I'll show it you; and by° the way you shall tell me where in the forest you live. Will you go?

ORLANDO: With all my heart, good youth.

475 ROSALIND: Nay, you must call me Rosalind. Come sister, will you go?   (*Exeunt.*)

SCENE III. [*The forest.*]

Enter [TOUCHSTONE, *the*] *Clown*, AUDREY; *and* JAQUES [*apart*].

TOUCHSTONE: Come apace,° good Audrey. I will fetch up your goats, Audrey. And how, Audrey, am I the man yet? Doth my simple feature° content you?

5 AUDREY: Your features, Lord warrant° us! What features?

TOUCHSTONE: I am here with thee and thy goats, as the most capricious poet, honest Ovid, was among the Goths.°

10 JAQUES [*aside*]: O knowledge ill-inhabited,° worse than Jove in a thatched house!

TOUCHSTONE: When a man's verses cannot be understood, nor a man's good wit seconded with° the forward child, understanding, it 15 strikes a man more dead than a great reckoning in a little room.° Truly, I would the gods had made thee poetical.

AUDREY: I do not know what poetical is. Is it honest in deed and word? Is it a true thing?

20 TOUCHSTONE: No, truly; for the truest poetry is the most feigning, and lovers are given to poetry, and what they swear in poetry may be said as lovers they do feign.°

AUDREY: Do you wish then that the gods 25 had made me poetical?

TOUCHSTONE: I do truly; for thou swear'st to me thou art honest. Now, if thou wert a poet, I might have some hope thou didst feign.

AUDREY: Would you not have me honest?

TOUCHSTONE: No, truly, unless thou wert hard-favored;° for honesty coupled to beauty is 30 to have honey a sauce to sugar.

JAQUES [*aside*]: A material° fool.

AUDREY: Well, I am not fair, and therefore I pray the gods make me honest.

TOUCHSTONE: Truly, and to cast away hon- 35 esty upon a foul slut were to put good meat into an unclean dish.

AUDREY: I am not a slut, though I thank the gods I am foul.

TOUCHSTONE: Well, praised be the gods for 40 thy foulness! Sluttishness may come hereafter. But be it as it may be, I will marry thee; and to that end I have been with Sir° Oliver Mar-text, the vicar of the next village, who hath promised to meet me in this place of the 45 forest and to couple us.

JAQUES [*aside*]: I would fain see this meeting.

AUDREY: Well, the gods give us joy!

TOUCHSTONE: Amen. A man may, if he were 50 of a fearful heart, stagger° in this attempt; for here we have no temple but the wood, no assembly but horn-beasts.° But what though? Courage! As horns are odious, they are necessary.° It is said, "Many a man knows no end of 55 his goods." Right! Many a man has good horns and knows no end of them. Well, that is the dowry of his wife, 'tis none of his own getting. Horns? Even so, poor men aione. No, no; the noblest deer hath them as huge as the 60 rascal.° Is the single man therefore blessed? No; as a walled town is more worthier than a village, so is the forehead of a married man more honorable than the bare brow of a bachelor; and by how much defense° is better 65 than no skill, by so much is a horn more precious than to want.°

(*Enter* SIR OLIVER MAR-TEXT.)

Here comes Sir Oliver. Sir Oliver Mar-text, you are well met. Will you dispatch us° here under 70 this tree, or shall we go with you to your chapel?

474 **by** along
III.iii.1 **apace** swiftly   4 **feature** appearance   5 **warrant** save   8–9 **capricious . . . Goths** (the Roman poet Ovid was exiled among the Goths — pronounced in Elizabethan England the same as "goats" — for the immorality of his verses. Touchstone plays on the words "honest" [chaste] and "capricious" [derived from Latin *caper*, male goat])   10 **ill-inhabited** ill-housed   14 **with** by   15–16 **great reckoning . . . room** large bill for poor accommodations   23 **feign** (1) pretend (2) desire (a pun on "fain")

31 **hard-favored** ugly   33 **material** full of good matter   44 **Sir** (an old form of address for a priest)   52 **stagger** tremble   54 **horn-beasts** (1) horned animals (2) cuckolds   55–56 **necessary** inevitable   62 **rascal** inferior deer   66 **defense** the art of defense   68 **want** i.e., lack horns   70 **dispatch us** finish our business

OLIVER MAR-TEXT: Is there none here to give the woman?

75   TOUCHSTONE: I will not take her on gift of any man.

OLIVER MAR-TEXT: Truly, she must be given, or the marriage is not lawful.

JAQUES [comes forward]: Proceed, proceed;
80   I'll give her.

TOUCHSTONE: Good even, good Master What-ye-call't.° How do you, sir? You are very well met. God 'ield you for your last company;° I am very glad to see you. Even a toy°
85   in hand here, sir. Nay, pray be covered.°

JAQUES: Will you be married, motley?

TOUCHSTONE: As the ox hath his bow,° sir, the horse his curb, and the falcon her bells, so man hath his desires; and as pigeons bill, so
90   wedlock would be nibbling.

JAQUES: And will you, being a man of your breeding, be married under a bush like a beggar? Get you to church, and have a good priest that can tell you what marriage is. This
95   fellow will but join you together as they join wainscot;° then one of you will prove a shrunk panel, and like green timber warp, warp.

TOUCHSTONE [aside]: I am not in the mind but° I were better to be married of him than
100   of another; for he is not like to marry me well; and not being well married,° it will be a good excuse for me hereafter to leave my wife.

JAQUES: Go thou with me and let me counsel thee.

TOUCHSTONE:
105   Come, sweet Audrey.
We must be married, or we must live in
        bawdry.
Farewell, good Master Oliver: not
        O sweet Oliver,
        O brave Oliver,
110   Leave me not behind thee;
but
        Wind° away,
        Be gone, I say;
        I will not to wedding with thee.

OLIVER MAR-TEXT: 'Tis no matter. Ne'er a   115
fantastical° knave of them all shall flout me
out of my calling.   (Exeunt.)

SCENE IV. [The forest.]

Enter ROSALIND and CELIA.

ROSALIND: Never talk to me; I will weep.

CELIA: Do, I prithee; but yet have the grace to consider that tears do not become a man.

ROSALIND: But have I not cause to weep?

CELIA: As good cause as one would desire;   5
therefore weep.

ROSALIND: His very hair is of the dissembling color.°

CELIA: Something browner than Judas'. Marry, his kisses are Judas' own children.   10

ROSALIND: I' faith, his hair is of a good color.

CELIA: An excellent color. Your chestnut was ever the only color.

ROSALIND: And his kissing is as full of   15
sanctity as the touch of holy bread.°

CELIA: He hath bought a pair of cast° lips of Diana.° A nun of winter's sisterhood° kisses not more religiously; the very ice of chastity is in them.   20

ROSALIND: But why did he swear he would come this morning, and comes not?

CELIA: Nay, certainly there is no truth in him.

ROSALIND: Do you think so?   25

CELIA: Yes; I think he is not a pickpurse nor a horse-stealer, but for his verity in love, I do think him as concave° as a covered goblet or a worm-eaten nut.

ROSALIND: Not true in love?   30

CELIA: Yes, when he is in, but I think he is not in.

ROSALIND: You have heard him swear downright he was.

CELIA: "Was" is not "is." Besides, the oath   35
of a lover is no stronger than the word of a tapster;° they are both the confirmer of false reckonings. He attends here in the forest on the Duke your father.

81–82 **Master What-ye-call't** (Touchstone delicately avoids the name "Jaques," which could be pronounced "jakes," a privy) 83–84 **God 'ield . . . company** God reward you for the last time we met 84 **toy** trifle 85 **pray be covered** (Jaques has removed his hat) 87 **bow** yoke 96 **wainscot** wood paneling 98–99 **I am not in the mind but** I am not sure but that 101 **well married** (1) legally married (2) happily married (3) married into wealth 112 **Wind** turn

116 **fantastical** odd
III.iv.7–8 **dissembling color** i.e., red, like the hair of Judas 16 **holy bread** (not the sacramental wafer, but bread brought to church to be blessed and then distributed to the poor) 17 **cast** (1) molded (2) castoff 18 **Diana** goddess of chastity; **winter's sisterhood** i.e., the most rigorous chastity 28 **concave** hollow 37 **tapster** waiter in a tavern

40 ROSALIND: I met the Duke yesterday and had much question° with him. He asked me of what parentage I was. I told him, of as good as he; so he laughed and let me go. But what talk we of fathers when there is such a man as
45 Orlando?

CELIA: O, that's a brave° man; he writes brave verses, speaks brave words, swears brave oaths, and breaks them bravely, quite traverse,° athwart the heart of his lover, as a puisny°
50 tilter, that spurs his horse but on one side, breaks his staff like a noble goose. But all's brave that youth mounts and folly guides. Who comes here?

(*Enter* CORIN.)

CORIN: Mistress and master, you have oft enquired
55 After the shepherd that complained° of love, Who you saw sitting by me on the turf, Praising the proud disdainful shepherdess That was his mistress.

CELIA: Well, and what of him?

CORIN: If you will see a pageant° truly played
60 Between the pale complexion of true love And the red glow of scorn and proud disdain, Go hence a little, and I shall conduct you, If you will mark it.

ROSALIND: O, come, let us remove: The sight of lovers feedeth those in love.
65 Bring us to this sight, and you shall say I'll prove a busy actor in their play. (*Exeunt.*)

SCENE V. [*The forest.*]

Enter SILVIUS *and* PHEBE.

SILVIUS: Sweet Phebe, do not scorn me; do not, Phebe! Say that you love me not, but say not so In bitterness. The common executioner Whose heart th' accustomed sight of death makes hard,
5 Falls° not the ax upon the humbled neck But first begs pardon. Will you sterner be Than he that dies and lives° by bloody drops?

(*Enter [apart]* ROSALIND, CELIA, *and* CORIN.)

PHEBE: I would not be thy executioner. I fly thee, for I would not injure thee. Thou tell'st me there is murder in mine eye: 10 'Tis pretty, sure, and very probable That eyes, that are the frail'st and softest things, Who shut their coward gates on atomies,° Should be called tyrants, butchers, murderers. Now I do frown on thee with all my heart,   15 And if mine eyes can wound, now let them kill thee. Now counterfeit to swound,° why, now fall down; Or if thou canst not, O, for shame, for shame, Lie not, to say mine eyes are murderers. Now show the wound mine eye hath made in thee;   20 Scratch thee but with a pin, and there remains Some scar of it; lean upon a rush, The cicatrice and capable impressure° Thy palm some moment keep; but now mine eyes, Which I have darted at thee, hurt thee not,   25 Nor I am sure there is no force in eyes That can do hurt.

SILVIUS: O dear Phebe, If ever, as that ever may be near,° You meet in some fresh cheek the power of fancy,° Then shall you know the wounds invisible   30 That love's keen arrows make.

PHEBE: But till that time Come thou not near me; and when that time comes, Afflict me with thy mocks, pity me not, As till that time I shall not pity thee.

ROSALIND: And why, I pray you? Who might be your mother,   35 That you insult, exult, and all at once, Over the wretched? What though you have no beauty (As, by my faith, I see no more in you Than without candle may go dark to bed°)

41 **question** talk   46 **brave** fine   48 **traverse** at an angle (instead of head-on)   49 **puisny** inexperienced 55 **complained** lamented   59 **pageant** scene, show III.v.5 **Falls** lets fall   7 **dies and lives** earns his living

13 **atomies** motes   17 **counterfeit to swound** pretend to swoon   23 **cicatrice and capable impressure** mark and visible impression   28 **as that ever may be near** and may the time be soon   29 **fancy** love   39 **Than . . . to bed** i.e., your beauty is not so dazzling as to light up the room

40 Must you be therefore proud and pitiless?
Why, what means this? Why do you look on
    me?
I see no more in you than in the ordinary
Of nature's sale-work.° 'Od's° my little life,
I think she means to tangle my eyes too!

45 No, faith, proud mistress, hope not after it;
'Tis not your inky brows, your black silk hair,
Your bugle° eyeballs, nor your cheek of cream
That can entame my spirits to your worship.
You foolish shepherd, wherefore do you follow
    her,

50 Like foggy south,° puffing with wind and rain?
You are a thousand times a properer° man
Than she a woman. 'Tis such fools as you
That makes the world full of ill-favored chil-
    dren.
'Tis not her glass,° but you, that flatters her,

55 And out of you she sees herself more proper
Than any of her lineaments can show her.
But mistress, know yourself. Down on your
    knees,
And thank heaven, fasting, for a good man's
    love;
For I must tell you friendly in your ear,

60 Sell when you can, you are not for all markets.
Cry the man mercy,° love him, take his offer;
Foul° is most foul, being foul to be a scoffer;
So take her to thee, shepherd. Fare you well.
        PHEBE:
Sweet youth, I pray you chide a year together;
I had rather hear you chide than this man

65   woo.
        ROSALIND [aside]: He's fall'n in love with
your foulness, and she'll fall in love with my
anger. If it be so, as fast as she answers thee
with frowning looks, I'll sauce her with bitter

70 words. [To PHEBE.] Why look you so upon
me?
        PHEBE:
For no ill will I bear you.
        ROSALIND:
I pray you do not fall in love with me,
For I am falser than vows made in wine.
Besides, I like you not. If you will know my

75   house,
'Tis at the tuft of olives, here hard° by.

Will you go, sister? Shepherd, ply her hard.
Come, sister. Shepherdess, look on him better
And be not proud. Though all the world could
    see,
None could be so abused° in sight as he.   80
Come, to our flock.
                    (Exit [with CELIA and CORIN].)
        PHEBE:
Dead shepherd, now I find thy saw° of might,
"Who ever loved that loved not at first
    sight?"°
        SILVIUS:
Sweet Phebe.
        PHEBE: Ha! What say'st thou, Silvius?
        SILVIUS:
Sweet Phebe, pity me.   85
        PHEBE:
Why, I am sorry for thee, gentle Silvius.
        SILVIUS:
Wherever sorry is, relief would be.
If you do sorrow at my grief in love,
By giving love your sorrow and my grief
Were both extermined.°   90
        PHEBE:
Thou hast my love. Is not that neighborly?°
        SILVIUS:
I would have you.
        PHEBE: Why, that were covetousness.
Silvius, the time was that I hated thee;
And yet it is not that I bear thee love,
But since that thou canst talk of love so well, 95
Thy company, which erst° was irksome to me,
I will endure; and I'll employ thee too;
But do not look for further recompense
Than thine own gladness that thou art em-
    ployed.
        SILVIUS:
So holy and so perfect is my love,   100
And in such a poverty of grace,°
That I shall think it a most plenteous crop
To glean the broken ears after the man
That the main harvest reaps. Loose now and
    then
A scatt'red° smile, and that I'll live upon.   105

42–43 **ordinary Of nature's sale-work** usual product of nature's manufacture   43 **'Od's** God save   47 **bugle** black and glassy   50 **south** south wind   51 **properer** more handsome   54 **glass** mirror   61 **Cry the man mercy** ask the man's forgiveness   62 **Foul** (1) ugliness (2) wickedness   76 **hard** near

80 **abused** deceived   82 **saw** saying   83 **Who ever . . . sight** (a line from Christopher Marlowe's poem *Hero and Leander*, published in 1598. The "Dead shepherd" is Marlowe, who died in 1593)   90 **extermined** ended   91 **neighborly** friendly (perhaps alluding to the commandment to love one's neighbor)   96 **erst** formerly   101 **a poverty of grace** small favor   105 **scatt'red** stray

PHEBE:
Know'st thou the youth that spoke to me
  erewhile?°

SILVIUS:
Not very well, but I have met him oft,
And he hath bought the cottage and the
  bounds
That the old carlot° once was master of.

PHEBE:
110 Think not I love him, though I ask for him;
'Tis but a peevish boy; yet he talks well.
But what care I for words? Yet words do well
When he that speaks them pleases those that
  hear.
It is a pretty youth. Not very pretty.
But sure he's proud. And yet his pride becomes
115 him.
He'll make a proper man. The best thing in
  him
Is his complexion. And faster than his tongue
Did make offense, his eye did heal it up.
He is not very tall. Yet for his years he's tall.
120 His leg is but so so. And yet 'tis well.
There was a pretty redness in his lip,
A little riper and more lusty red
Than that mixed in his cheek. 'Twas just the
  difference
Betwixt the constant° red and mingled da-
  mask.°
There be some women, Silvius, had they
125 marked him
In parcels° as I did, would have gone near
To fall in love with him; but, for my part,
I love him not nor hate him not. And yet
I have more cause to hate him than to love
  him;
130 For what had he to do to chide at me?
He said mine eyes were black and my hair
  black;
And, now I am rememb'red,° scorned at me.
I marvel why I answered not again.
But that's all one: omittance is no quittance.°
135 I'll write to him a very taunting letter,
And thou shalt bear it. Wilt thou, Silvius?

SILVIUS:
Phebe, with all my heart.

PHEBE: I'll write it straight;°
The matter's in my head and in my heart;
I will be bitter with him and passing short.°
Go with me, Silvius.   (*Exeunt.*)   140

ACT IV

Scene I. [*The forest.*]

Enter ROSALIND *and* CELIA *and* JAQUES.

JAQUES: I prithee, pretty youth, let me be
better acquainted with thee.

ROSALIND: They say you are a melancholy
fellow.

JAQUES: I am so; I do love it better than   5
laughing.

ROSALIND: Those that are in extremity of°
either are abominable fellows, and betray
themselves to every modern censure° worse
than drunkards.   10

JAQUES: Why, 'tis good to be sad and say
nothing.

ROSALIND: Why then, 'tis good to be a post.

JAQUES: I have neither the scholar's melancholy, which is emulation;° nor the musician's, 15
which is fantastical; nor the courtier's, which is
proud; nor the soldier's, which is ambitious;
nor the lawyer's, which is politic;° nor the
lady's, which is nice;° nor the lover's, which is
all these: but it is a melancholy of mine own, 20
compounded of many simples,° extracted from
many objects, and indeed the sundry contemplation of my travels, in which my often
rumination° wraps me in a most humorous
sadness.   25

ROSALIND: A traveler! By my faith, you have
great reason to be sad. I fear you have sold
your own lands to see other men's. Then to
have seen much and to have nothing is to have
rich eyes and poor hands.   30

JAQUES: Yes, I have gained my experience.

(*Enter* ORLANDO.)

ROSALIND: And your experience makes you

---

106 **erewhile** a short time ago   109 **carlot** countryman   124 **constant** uniform; **mingled damask** pink
and white   126 **In parcels** piece by piece   132 **rememb'red** reminded   134 **omittance is no quittance**
i.e., the fact that I did not reply does not mean I will
not do so later

137 **straight** at once   139 **passing short** very curt
IV.i.7 **are in extremity of** go to extremes in   9 **every
modern censure** i.e., the average man's disapproval
15 **emulation** envy   18 **politic** i.e., put on to seem
grave   19 **nice** fastidious   21 **simples** ingredients
23–24 **often rumination** constant reflection

sad. I had rather have a fool to make me merry than experience to make me sad — and to
35 travel° for it too.

ORLANDO: Good day and happiness, dear Rosalind.

JAQUES: Nay then, God b'wi'you, an° you talk in blank verse.   [*Exit.*]

40 ROSALIND: Farewell, Monsieur Traveler. Look you lisp° and wear strange suits, disable° all the benefits of your own country, be out of love with your nativity,° and almost chide God for making you that countenance you are; or I
45 will scarce think you have swam in a gundello.° Why, how now, Orlando, where have you been all this while? You a lover? An you serve me such another trick, never come in my sight more.

50 ORLANDO: My fair Rosalind, I come within an hour of my promise.

ROSALIND: Break an hour's promise in love? He that will divide a minute into a thousand parts and break but a part of the thousand part
55 of a minute in the affairs of love, it may be said of him that Cupid hath clapped° him o' th' shoulder, but I'll warrant him heart-whole.

ORLANDO: Pardon me, dear Rosalind.

ROSALIND: Nay, an you be so tardy, come no
60 more in my sight. I had as lief be wooed of a snail.

ORLANDO: Of a snail?

ROSALIND: Ay, of a snail; for though he comes slowly, he carries his house on his head;
65 a better jointure,° I think, than you make a woman. Besides, he brings his destiny with him.

ORLANDO: What's that?

ROSALIND: Why, horns; which such as you
70 are fain to be beholding to your wives for; but he comes armed° in his fortune and prevents° the slander of his wife.

ORLANDO: Virtue is no horn-maker, and my Rosalind is virtuous.

75 ROSALIND: And I am your Rosalind.

CELIA: It pleases him to call you so; but he hath a Rosalind of a better leer° than you.

ROSALIND: Come, woo me, woo me; for now

I am in a holiday humor and like enough to consent. What would you say to me now, an I
80 were your very very Rosalind?

ORLANDO: I would kiss before I spoke.

ROSALIND: Nay, you were better speak first, and when you were graveled for lack of matter,° you might take occasion to kiss. Very
85 good orators, when they are out,° they will spit; and for lovers, lacking — God warn° us! — matter. the cleanliest shift is to kiss.

ORLANDO: How if the kiss be denied?

ROSALIND: Then she puts you to entreaty,
90 and there begins new matter.

ORLANDO: Who could be out, being before his beloved mistress?

ROSALIND: Marry, that should you, if I were your mistress, or I should think my honesty
95 ranker° than my wit.

ORLANDO: What, of my suit?

ROSALIND: Not out of your apparel, and yet out of your suit.° Am not I your Rosalind?

ORLANDO: I take some joy to say you are,
100 because I would be talking of her.

ROSALIND: Well, in her person, I say I will not have you.

ORLANDO: Then, in mine own person, I die.

ROSALIND: No faith, die by attorney.° The
105 poor world is almost six thousand years old, and in all this time there was not any man died in his own person,° videlicet,° in a love cause. Troilus° had his brains dashed out with a Grecian club; yet he did what he could to
110 die before, and he is one of the patterns of love. Leander,° he would have lived many a fair year though Hero had turned nun, if it had not been for a hot midsummer night; for, good youth, he went but forth to wash him in
115 the Hellespont, and being taken with the cramp, was drowned; and the foolish chroniclers of that age found° it was "Hero of Sestos." But these are all lies. Men have died

84–85 **graveled for lack of matter** hard put for something to say   86 **out** i.e., out of material   87 **warn** protect (warrant)   95–96 **honesty ranker** virtue fouler   99 **suit** (1) apparel (2) entreaty   105 **attorney** proxy   108 **in his own person** in real life (as opposed to fiction); **videlicet** that is to say   109 **Troilus** (Priam's son, betrayed in love by Cressida and killed by the spear of Achilles. "As true as Troilus" became a proverbial expression)   112 **Leander** (a prototype of dedicated love, who swam the Hellespont nightly to see his mistress, Hero of Sestos)   118 **found** gave the verdict

35 **travel** (pun on "travail")   38 **an** if   41 **lisp** speak affectedly; **disable** disparage   43 **nativity** birthplace   45 **gundello** gondola   56 **clapped** touched   65 **jointure** marriage settlement   71 **armed** i.e., with horns; **prevents** (1) forestalls (2) anticipates (?)   77 **leer** face

120 from time to time, and worms have eaten them, but not for love.

ORLANDO: I would not have my right Rosalind of this mind, for I protest her frown might kill me.

125 ROSALIND: By this hand, it will not kill a fly. But come, now I will be your Rosalind in a more coming-on disposition; and ask me what you will, I will grant it.

ORLANDO: Then love me, Rosalind.

130 ROSALIND: Yes, faith, will I, Fridays and Saturdays and all.

ORLANDO: And wilt thou have me?

ROSALIND: Ay, and twenty such.

ORLANDO: What sayest thou?

135 ROSALIND: Are you not good?

ORLANDO: I hope so.

ROSALIND: Why then, can one desire too much of a good thing? Come, sister, you shall be the priest and marry us. Give me your 140 hand, Orlando. What do you say, sister?

ORLANDO: Pray thee marry us.

CELIA: I cannot say the words.

ROSALIND: You must begin, "Will you, Orlando —"

145 CELIA: Go to.° Will you, Orlando, have to wife this Rosalind?

ORLANDO: I will.

ROSALIND: Ay, but when?

ORLANDO: Why now, as fast as she can 150 marry us.

ROSALIND: Then you must say, "I take thee, Rosalind, for wife."

ORLANDO: I take thee, Rosalind, for wife.

ROSALIND: I might ask you for your commis- 155 sion;° but I do take thee, Orlando, for my husband. There's a girl goes before° the priest, and certainly a woman's thought runs before her actions.

ORLANDO: So do all thoughts; they are 160 winged.

ROSALIND: Now tell me how long you would have her after you have possessed her.

ORLANDO: For ever and a day.

ROSALIND: Say "a day," without the "ever." 165 No, no, Orlando. Men are April when they woo, December when they wed. Maids are May when they are maids, but the sky changes when they are wives. I will be more jealous of

thee than a Barbary cock-pigeon° over his hen, more clamorous than a parrot against° rain, 170 more newfangled° than an ape, more giddy° in my desires than a monkey. I will weep for nothing, like Diana in the fountain,° and I will do that when you are disposed to be merry; I will laugh like a hyen, and that when thou art 175 inclined to sleep.

ORLANDO: But will my Rosalind do so?

ROSALIND: By my life, she will do as I do.

ORLANDO: O, but she is wise.

ROSALIND: Or else she could not have the 180 wit to do this; the wiser, the waywarder. Make° the doors upon a woman's wit, and it will out at the casement; shut that, and 'twill out at the keyhole; stop that, 'twill fly with the smoke out at the chimney. 185

ORLANDO: A man that had a wife with such a wit, he might say, "Wit, whither wilt?"°

ROSALIND: Nay, you might keep that check° for it till you met your wife's wit going to your neighbor's bed. 190

ORLANDO: And what wit could wit have to excuse that?

ROSALIND: Marry, to say she came to seek you there. You shall never take her without her answer unless you take her without her 195 tongue. O, that woman that cannot make her fault her husband's occasion,° let her never nurse her child herself, for she will breed it like a fool.

ORLANDO: For these two hours, Rosalind, I 200 will leave thee.

ROSALIND: Alas, dear love, I cannot lack thee two hours!

ORLANDO: I must attend the Duke at dinner. By two o'clock I will be with thee again. 205

ROSALIND: Ay, go your ways, go your ways; I knew what you would prove. My friends told me as much, and I thought no less. That flattering tongue of yours won me. 'Tis but one cast away,° and so, come death! Two 210 o'clock is your hour?

169 **Barbary cock-pigeon** Barb pigeon ("Barbary" suggests jealousy) 170 **against** before 171 **new-fangled** given to novelty; **giddy** changeable 173 **like Diana in the fountain** i.e., steadily (Diana was a popular subject for fountain statuary) 181 **Make** shut 187 **Wit, whither wilt** i.e., where are your senses 188 **check** rebuke 196–197 **make . . . occasion** i.e., turn defense of her own actions into an accusation of her husband's 210 **one cast away** i.e., one girl deserted

145 **Go to** that's enough 154–155 **commission** license 156 **goes before** runs ahead (Rosalind has not waited for Celia to say, "Will you, Rosalind, have to husband")

ORLANDO: Ay, sweet Rosalind.

ROSALIND: By my troth, and in good earnest, and so God mend me, and by all pretty oaths
215 that are not dangerous, if you break one jot of your promise or come one minute behind your hour, I will think you the most pathetical° break-promise, and the most hollow lover, and the most unworthy of her you call Rosalind,
220 that may be chosen out of the gross° band of the unfaithful. Therefore beware my censure and keep your promise.

ORLANDO: With no less religion° than if thou wert indeed my Rosalind. So adieu.
225 ROSALIND: Well, Time is the old justice that examines all such offenders, and let Time try. Adieu.   (Exit [ORLANDO].)

CELIA: You have simply misused° our sex in your loveprate. We must have your doublet
230 and hose plucked over your head, and show the world what the bird hath done to her own nest.

ROSALIND: O coz, coz, coz, my pretty little coz, that thou didst know how many fathom
235 deep I am in love! But it cannot be sounded. My affection hath an unknown bottom, like the Bay of Portugal.

CELIA: Or rather, bottomless, that as fast as you pour affection in, it runs out.
240 ROSALIND: No, that same wicked bastard of Venus° that was begot of thought,° conceived of spleen,° and born of madness, that blind rascally boy that abuses every one's eyes because his own are out, let him be judge how
245 deep I am in love. I'll tell thee, Aliena, I cannot be out of the sight of Orlando. I'll go find a shadow, and sigh till he come.

CELIA: And I'll sleep.   (Exeunt.)

SCENE II. [The forest.]

Enter JAQUES; and LORDS, [like] Foresters.

JAQUES: Which is he that killed the deer?
LORD: Sir, it was I.
JAQUES: Let's present him to the Duke like a Roman conqueror; and it would do well to
5 set the deer's horns upon his head for a branch of victory. Have you no song, forester, for this purpose?
ANOTHER LORD: Yes, sir.

JAQUES: Sing it. 'Tis no matter how it be in tune, so it make noise enough.   10

(Music.)

Song.

What shall he have that killed the deer?
His leather skin and horns to wear:
   Then sing him home. The rest shall bear
     This burden.°

Take thou no scorn° to wear the horn,   15
It was a crest ere thou wast born,
   Thy father's father wore it,
   And thy father bore it.
The horn, the horn, the lusty horn,
Is not a thing to laugh to scorn.°   20
                                          (Exeunt.)

SCENE III. [The forest.]

Enter ROSALIND and CELIA.

ROSALIND: How say you now, is it not past two o'clock? And here much° Orlando!

CELIA: I warrant you, with pure love and troubled brain, he hath ta'en his bow and arrows and is gone forth to sleep.   5

(Enter SILVIUS.)

Look who comes here.

SILVIUS:
My errand is to you, fair youth.
My gentle Phebe bid me give you this.
I know not the contents, but, as I guess
By the stern brow and waspish action   10
Which she did use as she was writing of it,
It bears an angry tenor. Pardon me;
I am but as a guiltless messenger.

ROSALIND:
Patience herself would startle at this letter
And play the swaggerer. Bear this, bear all!   15
She says I am not fair, that I lack manners;
She calls me proud, and that she could not
   love me,

217 **pathetical** (1) pitiful (2) passionate (?)   220 **gross** large   223 **religion** faith   228 **simply misused** completely abused   240–241 **bastard of Venus** Cupid   241 **thought** despondency   242 **spleen** sheer impulse

IV.II.13–14 **The rest shall bear This burden** i.e., not only the forester who killed the deer but all men will wear the horns of cuckoldry (many editors read the line as a stage direction: the other foresters ["the rest"] are to join in the refrain ["burden"] after one forester has sung the first three lines of the song. If the Folio version — here followed — is correct, it is likely that all sing the song from the beginning)   15 **Take thou no scorn** do not be ashamed   20 **laugh to scorn** ridicule
IV.III.2 **much** i.e., not much

Were man as rare as phoenix.° 'Od's my will!
Her love is not the hare that I do hunt.
Why writes she so to me? Well, shepherd,
20   well,
This is a letter of your own device.

SILVIUS:
No, I protest, I know not the contents.
Phebe did write it.

ROSALIND: Come, come, you are a fool,
And turned into the extremity° of love.
25 I saw her hand. She has a leathern hand.
A freestone-colored° hand. I verily did think
That her old gloves were on, but 'twas her
    hands.
She has a housewife's hand; but that's no
    matter:
I say she never did invent° this letter;
30 This is a man's invention and his hand.

SILVIUS:
Sure it is hers.

ROSALIND:
Why, 'tis a boisterous and a cruel style,
A style for challengers. Why, she defies me
Like Turk to Christian. Women's gentle brain
35 Could not drop forth such giant-rude° inven-
    tion,
Such Ethiop words, blacker in their effect
Than in their countenance. Will you hear the
    letter?

SILVIUS:
So please you, for I never heard it yet;
Yet heard too much of Phebe's cruelty.

ROSALIND:
40 She Phebes me.° Mark how the tyrant writes.

(*Read.*)

    "Art thou god, to shepherd turned,
      That a maiden's heart hath burned?"

Can a woman rail thus?

SILVIUS:
Call you this railing?

ROSALIND:

(*Read.*)

45   "Why, thy godhead laid apart,°
      Warr'st thou with a woman's heart?"

Did you ever hear such railing?

    "Whiles the eye of man did woo me,
      That could do no vengeance° to me."

Meaning me a beast.   50

    "If the scorn of your bright eyne°
      Have power to raise such love in mine,
    Alack, in me what strange effect
    Would they work in mild aspect!°
    Whiles you chid me, I did love;   55
    How then might your prayers move!
    He that brings this love to thee
    Little knows this love in me;
    And by him seal up thy mind,°
    Whether that thy youth and kind°   60
    Will the faithful offer take
    Of me and all that I can make,°
    Or else by him my love deny,
    And then I'll study how to die."

SILVIUS:
Call you this chiding?   65

CELIA: Alas poor shepherd!

ROSALIND: Do you pity him? No, he deserves
no pity. Wilt thou love such a woman? What,
to make thee an instrument,° and play false
strains upon thee? Not to be endured! Well, 70
go your way to her, for I see love hath made
thee a tame snake,° and say this to her: that if
she love me, I charge her to love thee; if she
will not, I will never have her unless thou
entreat for her. If you be a true lover, hence, 75
and not a word; for here comes more company.
                  (*Exit* SILVIUS.)

(*Enter* OLIVER.)

OLIVER:
Good morrow, fair ones. Pray you, if you
    know,
Where in the purlieus° of this forest stands
A sheepcote, fenced about with olive trees?

CELIA:
West of this place, down in the neighbor
    bottom.°   80
The rank of osiers° by the murmuring stream
Left on your right hand brings you to the
    place.

---

18 **phoenix** (a legendary bird, of which there was
only one in the world at any time) 24 **turned into the
extremity** became the very essence 26 **freestone-
colored** i.e., yellowish-brown 29 **invent** compose
35 **giant-rude** incredibly rude 40 **She Phebes me**
i.e., she writes with her customary disdain 45 **thy
godhead laid apart** i.e., having assumed human form

49 **vengeance** harm 51 **eyne** eyes 54 **aspect** (1)
look (2) planetary influence 59 **seal up thy mind**
i.e., tell your feelings in a letter 60 **youth and kind**
youthful nature 62 **make** give 69 **make thee an
instrument** use you 72 **tame snake** poor worm 78
purlieus borders 80 **neighbor bottom** nearby valley
81 **rank of osiers** row of willows

But at this hour the house doth keep itself;
There's none within.

OLIVER:

85 If that an eye may profit by a tongue,
Then should I know you by description,
Such garments and such years: "The boy is
   fair,
Of female favor,° and bestows° himself
Like a ripe sister;° the woman low,°
90 And browner than her brother." Are not you
The owner of the house I did enquire for?

CELIA:

It is no boast, being asked, to say we are.

OLIVER:

Orlando doth commend him to you both,
And to that youth he calls his Rosalind
95 He sends this bloody napkin.° Are you he?

ROSALIND:

I am. What must we understand by this?

OLIVER:

Some of my shame, if you will know of me
What man I am, and how and why and where
This handkercher was stained.

CELIA: I pray you tell it.

OLIVER:

When last the young Orlando parted from
100   you,
He left a promise to return again
Within an hour; and pacing through the
   forest,
Chewing the food of sweet and bitter fancy,°
Lo, what befell. He threw his eye aside,
105 And mark what object did present itself:
Under an old oak, whose boughs were mossed
   with age
And high top bald with dry antiquity,
A wretched ragged man, o'ergrown with hair,
Lay sleeping on his back; about his neck
110 A green and gilded snake had wreathed itself,
Who with her head, nimble in threats, ap-
   proached
The opening of his mouth; but suddenly,
Seeing Orlando, it unlinked itself
And with indented° glides did slip away
115 Into a bush, under which bush's shade
A lioness, with udders all drawn dry,
Lay couching,° head on ground, with catlike
   watch

When that the sleeping man should stir; for
   'tis
The royal disposition of that beast
To prey on nothing that doth seem as dead.   120
This seen, Orlando did approach the man
And found it was his brother, his elder
   brother.

CELIA:

O, I have heard him speak of that same
   brother,
And he did render° him the most unnatural
That lived amongst men.

OLIVER: And well he might so do,   125
For well I know he was unnatural.

ROSALIND:

But, to Orlando: did he leave him there,
Food to the sucked and hungry lioness?

OLIVER:

Twice did he turn his back and purposed so;
But kindness,° nobler ever than revenge,   130
And nature, stronger than his just occasion,°
Made him give battle to the lioness,
Who quickly fell before him; in which hur-
   tling
From miserable slumber I awaked.

CELIA:

Are you his brother?

ROSALIND: Was't you he rescued?   135

CELIA:

Was't you that did so oft contrive° to kill
   him?

OLIVER:

'Twas I. But 'tis not I. I do not shame
To tell you what I was, since my conversion
So sweetly tastes, being the thing I am.

ROSALIND:

But, for the bloody napkin?

OLIVER: By and by.°   140
When from the first to last, betwixt us two,
Tears our recountments° had most kindly
   bathed,
As how I came into that desert place:
In brief, he led me to the gentle Duke,
Who gave me fresh array and entertain-
   ment,°   145
Committing me unto my brother's love,
Who led me instantly unto his cave,

88 **favor** features; **bestows** carries   89 **ripe sister**
grown-up woman (some editors emend "sister" to
"forester"); **low** short   95 **napkin** handkerchief
103 **fancy** love   114 **indented** serpentine   117
couching crouching

124 **render** describe   130 **kindness** familial affection
131 **occasion** opportunity   136 **contrive** plot   140
By and by soon   142 **recountments** recital (of our
adventures since we last met)   145 **entertainment**
hospitality

There stripped himself, and here upon his arm
The lioness had torn some flesh away,
Which all this while had bled; and now he
150   fainted,
And cried, in fainting, upon Rosalind.
Brief, I recovered° him, bound up his wound;
And after some small space, being strong at
     heart,
He sent me hither, stranger as I am,
155 To tell this story, that you might excuse
His broken promise, and to give this napkin,
Dyed in his blood, unto the shepherd youth
That he in sport doth call his Rosalind.

[ROSALIND *swoons.*]

CELIA:
Why, how now, Ganymede, sweet Ganymede!
OLIVER:
160 Many will swoon when they do look on blood.
CELIA:
There is more in it. Cousin Ganymede!
OLIVER:
Look, he recovers.
ROSALIND:
I would I were at home.
CELIA: We'll lead you thither.
I pray you, will you take him by the arm?
165 OLIVER: Be of good cheer, youth. You a
man! You lack a man's heart.
ROSALIND: I do so, I confess it. Ah, sirrah, a
body would think this was well counterfeited.°
I pray you tell your brother how well I
170 counterfeited. Heigh-ho!
OLIVER: This was not counterfeit. There is
too great testimony in your complexion that it
was a passion of earnest.°
ROSALIND: Counterfeit, I assure you.
175 OLIVER: Well then, take a good heart and
counterfeit to be a man.
ROSALIND: So I do; but, i' faith, I should
have been a woman by right.
CELIA: Come, you look paler and paler. Pray
180 you draw homewards. Good sir, go with us.
OLIVER: That will I, for I must bear answer
back how you excuse my brother, Rosalind.
ROSALIND: I shall devise something. But I
pray you commend my counterfeiting to him.
185 Will you go?

(*Exeunt.*)

---

152 **recovered** revived   168 **counterfeited** pretended
173 **passion of earnest** real emotion

ACT V

SCENE I. [*The forest.*]

Enter [TOUCHSTONE, *the*] *Clown and* AUDREY.

TOUCHSTONE: We shall find a time, Audrey.
Patience, gentle Audrey.
AUDREY: Faith, the priest was good enough,
for all the old gentleman's saying.
TOUCHSTONE: A most wicked Sir Oliver, 5
Audrey, a most vile Mar-text. But, Audrey,
there is a youth here in the forests lays claim
to you.
AUDREY: Ay, I know who 'tis. He hath no
interest in me in the world. Here comes the 10
man you mean.

(*Enter* WILLIAM.)

TOUCHSTONE: It is meat and drink to me to
see a clown;° by my troth, we that have good
wits have much to answer for. We shall be
flouting;° we cannot hold.° 15
WILLIAM: Good ev'n, Audrey.
AUDREY: God ye° good ev'n, William.
WILLIAM: And good ev'n to you, sir.
TOUCHSTONE: Good ev'n, gentle friend.
Cover thy head,° cover thy head. Nay, prithee 20
be covered. How old are you, friend?
WILLIAM: Five-and-twenty, sir.
TOUCHSTONE: A ripe° age. Is thy name
William?
WILLIAM: William, sir. 25
TOUCHSTONE: A fair name. Wast born i' th'
forest here?
WILLIAM: Ay, sir, I thank God.
TOUCHSTONE: "Thank God." A good answer.
Art rich? 30
WILLIAM: Faith, sir, so so.
TOUCHSTONE: "So so" is good, very good,
very excellent good; and yet it is not, it is but
so so. Art thou wise?
WILLIAM: Ay, sir, I have a pretty wit. 35
TOUCHSTONE: Why, thou say'st well. I do
now remember a saying, "The fool doth think
he is wise, but the wise man knows himself to
be a fool." The heathen philosopher, when he
had a desire to eat a grape, would open his lips 40

V.i.13 **clown** yokel 15 **flouting** mocking; **hold** i.e.,
keep from mocking 17 **God ye** God give you 20
Cover thy head (William has removed his hat) 23
ripe fine

when he put it into his mouth, meaning thereby that grapes were made to eat and lips to open. You do love this maid?

WILLIAM: I do, sir.

45   TOUCHSTONE: Give me your hand. Art thou learned?

WILLIAM: No, sir.

TOUCHSTONE: Then learn this of me: to have is to have; for it is a figure° in rhetoric 50 that drink, being poured out of a cup into a glass, by filling the one doth empty the other; for all your writers do consent that *ipse*° is he. Now, you are not *ipse*, for I am he.

WILLIAM: Which he, sir?

55   TOUCHSTONE: He, sir, that must marry this woman. Therefore, you clown, abandon — which is in the vulgar, leave — the society — which in the boorish is, company — of this female — which in the common is, woman. 60 Which together is, abandon the society of this female, or, clown, thou perishest; or, to thy better understanding, diest; or, to wit, I kill thee, make thee away, translate thy life into death, thy liberty into bondage. I will deal in 65 poison with thee, or in bastinado,° or in steel; I will bandy with thee in faction;° I will o'errun thee with policy;° I will kill thee a hundred and fifty ways. Therefore tremble and depart.

70   AUDREY: Do, good William.

WILLIAM: God rest you merry, sir.   (*Exit.*)

(*Enter* CORIN.)

CORIN: Our master and mistress seeks you. Come away, away!

TOUCHSTONE: Trip, Audrey, trip, Audrey. I 75 attend,° I attend.   (*Exeunt.*)

SCENE II. [*The forest.*]

Enter ORLANDO *and* OLIVER.

ORLANDO: Is't possible that on so little acquaintance you should like her? That but seeing, you should love her? And loving, woo? And wooing, she should grant? And will you 5 persever to enjoy her?

OLIVER: Neither call the giddiness° of it in question, the poverty of her, the small acquaintance, my sudden wooing, nor her sudden consenting; but say with me, I love Aliena; say with her that she loves me; consent with both 10 that we may enjoy each other. It shall be to your good; for my father's house, and all the revenue that was old Sir Rowland's, will I estate° upon you, and here live and die a shepherd.   15

(*Enter* ROSALIND.)

ORLANDO: You have my consent. Let your wedding be tomorrow: thither will I invite the Duke and all's contented followers. Go and prepare Aliena; for look you, here comes my Rosalind.   20

ROSALIND: God save you, brother.

OLIVER: And you, fair sister.   [*Exit.*]

ROSALIND: O my dear Orlando, how it grieves me to see thee wear thy heart in a scarf!°   25

ORLANDO: It is my arm.

ROSALIND: I thought thy heart had been wounded with the claws of a lion.

ORLANDO: Wounded it is, but with the eyes of a lady.   30

ROSALIND: Did your brother tell you how I counterfeited to sound° when he showed me your handkercher?

ORLANDO: Ay, and greater wonders than that.   35

ROSALIND: O, I know where you are! Nay, 'tis true. There was never anything so sudden but the fight of two rams and Caesar's thrasonical° brag of "I came, saw, and overcame"; for your brother and my sister no sooner met but 40 they looked; no sooner looked but they loved; no sooner loved but they sighed; no sooner sighed but they asked one another the reason; no sooner knew the reason but they sought the remedy: and in these degrees° have they made 45 a pair of stairs to marriage, which they will climb incontinent, or else be incontinent° before marriage: they are in the very wrath of love, and they will together; clubs cannot part them.   50

ORLANDO: They shall be married tomorrow, and I will bid the Duke to the nuptial. But,

---

49 **figure** figure of speech   52 *ipse* he himself (Latin)
65 **bastinado** cudgeling   66 **bandy with thee in faction** i.e., argue with you as do politicians   67 **o'errun thee with policy** overwhelm you with craft   75 **attend** come
V.ii.6 **giddiness** suddenness

14 **estate** settle   25 **scarf** sling   32 **sound** swoon
38–39 **thrasonical** boastful (after the braggart soldier Thraso in Terence's comedy *Eunuchus*)   45 **degrees** (a pun on the literal meaning, "steps")   47 **incontinent . . . incontinent** with all haste . . . unchaste

O, how bitter a thing it is to look into happiness through another man's eyes! By so
55 much the more shall I tomorrow be at the height of heart-heaviness, by how much I shall think my brother happy in having what he wishes for.

ROSALIND: Why then, tomorrow I cannot
60 serve your turn for Rosalind?

ORLANDO: I can live no longer by thinking.

ROSALIND: I will weary you then no longer with idle talking. Know of me then, for now I speak to some purpose, that I know you are a
65 gentleman of good conceit.° I speak not this that you should bear a good opinion of my knowledge, insomuch I say I know you are; neither do I labor for a greater esteem than may in some little measure draw a belief from
70 you, to do yourself good, and not to grace me.° Believe then, if you please, that I can do strange things. I have, since I was three year old, conversed° with a magician, most profound in his art and yet not damnable.° If you
75 do love Rosalind so near the heart as your gesture° cries it out, when your brother marries Aliena shall you marry her. I know into what straits of fortune she is driven; and it is not impossible to me, if it appear not inconve-
80 nient° to you, to set her before your eyes tomorrow, human as she is,° and without any danger.

ORLANDO: Speak'st thou in sober meanings?

ROSALIND: By my life, I do, which I tender
85 dearly,° though I say I am a magician.° Therefore put you in your best array, bid your friends; for if you will be married tomorrow, you shall; and to Rosalind, if you will.

(*Enter* SILVIUS *and* PHEBE.)

Look, here comes a lover of mine and a lover
90 of hers.

PHEBE:
Youth, you have done me much ungentleness
To show the letter that I writ to you.

ROSALIND:
I care not if I have. It is my study°

To seem despiteful° and ungentle to you.
You are there followed by a faithful shepherd: 95
Look upon him, love him; he worships you.

PHEBE:
Good shepherd, tell this youth what 'tis to
   love.

SILVIUS:
It is to be all made of sighs and tears;
And so am I for Phebe.

PHEBE:
And I for Ganymede. 100

ORLANDO:
And I for Rosalind.

ROSALIND:
And I for no woman.

SILVIUS:
It is to be all made of faith and service;
And so am I for Phebe.

PHEBE:
And I for Ganymede. 105

ORLANDO:
And I for Rosalind.

ROSALIND:
And I for no woman.

SILVIUS:
It is to be all made of fantasy,°
All made of passion, and all made of wishes,
All adoration, duty, and observance,° 110
All humbleness, all patience, and impatience,
All purity, all trial, all observance;°
And so am I for Phebe.

PHEBE:
And so am I for Ganymede.

ORLANDO:
And so am I for Rosalind. 115

ROSALIND:
And so am I for no woman.

PHEBE:
If this be so, why blame you me to love you?

SILVIUS:
If this be so, why blame you me to love you?

ORLANDO:
If this be so, why blame you me to love you?

ROSALIND: Why do you speak too,° "Why 120
blame you me to love you?"

ORLANDO:
To her that is not here, nor doth not hear.

ROSALIND: Pray you, no more of this; 'tis
like the howling of Irish wolves against the

---

65 **conceit** understanding   70 **to grace me** to do credit to myself   73 **conversed** spent time   74 **and yet not damnable** (because he practices white, not black, magic)   76 **gesture** conduct   79–80 **inconvenient** unfitting   81 **human as she is** i.e., Rosalind herself, not a spirit   84–85 **tender dearly** hold precious   85 **though . . . magician** (a magician could be punished with death)   93 **study** intention

94 **despiteful** scornful   108 **fantasy** fancy   110 **observance** devoted attention   112 **observance** (some editors emend to "obedience")   120 **Why do you speak too** (some editors emend to "Who do you speak to")

125 moon. [*To* SILVIUS.] I will help you if I can. [*To* PHEBE.] I would love you if I could. Tomorrow meet me all together. [*To* PHEBE.] I will marry you if ever I marry woman, and I'll be married tomorrow. [*To* ORLANDO.] I will
130 satisfy you if ever I satisfied man, and you shall be married tomorrow. [*To* SILVIUS.] I will content you if what pleases you contents you, and you shall be married tomorrow. [*To* ORLANDO.] As you love Rosalind, meet. [*To*
135 SILVIUS.] As you love Phebe, meet. And as I love no woman, I'll meet. So fare you well. I have left you commands.

SILVIUS: I'll not fail if I live.

PHEBE: Nor I.

140 ORLANDO: Nor I.   (*Exeunt.*)

SCENE III. [*The forest.*]

Enter [TOUCHSTONE, *the*] *Clown and* AU-DREY.

TOUCHSTONE: Tomorrow is the joyful day, Audrey; tomorrow will we be married.

AUDREY: I do desire it with all my heart; and I hope it is no dishonest desire to desire to
5 be a woman of the world.° Here come two of the banished Duke's pages.

(*Enter two* PAGES.)

FIRST PAGE: Well met, honest° gentleman.

TOUCHSTONE: By my troth, well met. Come, sit, sit, and a song!

10 SECOND PAGE: We are for you. Sit i' th' middle.

FIRST PAGE: Shall we clap into't roundly,° without hawking or spitting or saying we are hoarse, which are the only° prologues to a bad
15 voice?

SECOND PAGE: I'faith, i'faith! and both in a tune,° like two gypsies on a horse.

Song.

It was a lover and his lass,
   With a hey, and a ho, and a hey nonino,
20 That o'er the green cornfield° did pass
   In springtime, the only pretty ringtime,°
When birds do sing, hey ding a ding, ding.
Sweet lovers love the spring.

Between the acres° of the rye,
   With a hey, and a ho, and a hey nonino,   25
These pretty country folks would lie
   In springtime, &c.

This carol they began that hour,
   With a hey, and a ho, and a hey nonino,
How that a life was but a flower   30
   In springtime, &c.

And therefore take° the present time,
   With a hey, and a ho, and a hey nonino,
For love is crownèd with the prime°
   In springtime, &c.   35

TOUCHSTONE: Truly, young gentlemen, though there was no great matter in the ditty,° yet the note° was very untuneable.

FIRST PAGE: You are deceived, sir. We kept time, we lost not our time.   40

TOUCHSTONE: By my troth, yes; I count it but time lost to hear such a foolish song. God b' wi' you, and God mend your voices. Come, Audrey.   (*Exeunt.*)

SCENE IV. [*The forest.*]

Enter DUKE SENIOR, AMIENS, JAQUES, OR-LANDO, OLIVER, CELIA.

DUKE SENIOR:
Dost thou believe, Orlando, that the boy
Can do all this that he hath promisèd?

ORLANDO:
I sometimes do believe, and sometimes do not,
As those that fear they hope,° and know they
   fear.

(*Enter* ROSALIND, SILVIUS, *and* PHEBE.)

ROSALIND:
Patience once more, whiles our compact is
   urged.°   5
You say, if I bring in your Rosalind.
You will bestow her on Orlando here?

DUKE SENIOR:
That would I, had I kingdoms to give with
   her.

ROSALIND:
And you say you will have her when I bring
   her?

V.III.5 **a woman of the world** i.e., (1) married (2) fashionable 7 **honest** honorable 12 **clap into't roundly** begin directly 14 **the only** merely the 16–17 **in a tune** in unison 20 **cornfield** wheatfield 21 **ringtime** i.e., the time for giving marriage rings

24 **Between the acres** i.e., in the strips of unploughed land 32 **take** seize 34 **prime** spring 37 **ditty** words of the song 38 **note** melody
V.IV.4 **hope** i.e., hope in vain 5 **compact is urged** agreement is restated

ORLANDO:
10 That would I, were I of all kingdoms king.
ROSALIND:
You say you'll marry me, if I be willing?
PHEBE:
That will I, should I die the hour after.
ROSALIND:
But if you do refuse to marry me,
You'll give yourself to this most faithful shep-
herd?
PHEBE:
15 So is the bargain.
ROSALIND:
You that you'll have Phebe, if she will?
SILVIUS:
Though to have her and death were both one
thing.
ROSALIND:
I have promised to make all this matter even.°
Keep you your word, O Duke, to give your
daughter;
20 You yours, Orlando, to receive his daughter;
Keep you your word, Phebe, that you'll marry
me,
Or else, refusing me, to wed this shepherd;
Keep your word, Silvius, that you'll marry her
If she refuse me; and from hence I go,
25 To make these doubts all even.
(Exit ROSALIND and CELIA.)
DUKE SENIOR:
I do remember in this shepherd boy
Some lively° touches of my daughter's favor.°
ORLANDO:
My lord, the first time that I ever saw him
Methought he was a brother to your daughter.
30 But, my good lord, this boy is forest-born,
And hath been tutored in the rudiments
Of many desperate° studies by his uncle,
Whom he reports to be a great magician,
Obscurèd° in the circle of this forest.

(Enter [TOUCHSTONE, the] Clown and AU-
DREY.)

35 JAQUES: There is, sure, another flood toward,° and these couples are coming to the
ark.° Here comes a pair of very strange beasts,
which in all tongues are called fools.

TOUCHSTONE: Salutation and greeting to you
all! 40
JAQUES: Good my lord, bid him welcome.
This is the motley-minded gentleman that I
have so often met in the forest. He hath been
a courtier, he swears.
TOUCHSTONE: If any man doubt that, let 45
him put me to my purgation.° I have trod a
measure;° I have flattered a lady; I have been
politic° with my friend, smooth with mine
enemy; I have undone° three tailors; I have
had four quarrels, and like to have fought one.° 50
JAQUES: And how was that ta'en up?°
TOUCHSTONE: Faith, we met, and found the
quarrel was upon the seventh cause.
JAQUES: How seventh cause? Good my lord,
like this fellow. 55
DUKE SENIOR: I like him very well.
TOUCHSTONE: God 'ield° you, sir; I desire you
of the like.° I press in here, sir, amongst the
rest of the country copulatives,° to swear and
to forswear, according as marriage binds and 60
blood breaks.° A poor virgin, sir, an ill-favored
thing, sir, but mine own; a poor humor° of
mine, sir, to take that that no man else will.
Rich honesty° dwells like a miser, sir, in a poor
house, as your pearl in your foul oyster. 65
DUKE SENIOR: By my faith, he is very swift
and sententious.°
TOUCHSTONE: According to the fool's bolt,°
sir, and such dulcet diseases.°
JAQUES: But, for the seventh cause. How 70
did you find the quarrel on the seventh cause?
TOUCHSTONE: Upon a lie seven times removed — bear your body more seeming,° Audrey — as thus, sir. I did dislike the cut of a
certain courtier's beard. He sent me word, if I 75
said his beard was not cut well, he was in the
mind it was: this is called the Retort Courteous. If I sent him word again it was not well
cut, he would send me word he cut it to please

18 **make all this matter even** straighten out everything 27 **lively** living; **favor** features 32 **desperate**
dangerous 34 **Obscurèd** hidden 35–36 **toward** approaching 36–37 **couples are coming to the ark**
(cf. Genesis 7:2, "and of beasts that are not clean by
two, the male and his female")

46 **put me to my purgation** test me 47 **measure**
stately dance 48 **politic** crafty 49 **undone** ruined
(by not paying his bills) 50 **like to have fought
one** almost fought over one 51 **ta'en up** settled 57
God 'ield God reward 57–58 **I desire you of the
like** may I return the compliment 59 **copulatives**
couples soon to be wed 61 **blood breaks** sexual interest wanes 62 **humor** whim 64 **honesty** virtue
66–67 **swift and sententious** quick-witted and pithy
68 **According to the fool's bolt** (cf. the proverb "A
fool's bolt [arrow] is soon shot") 69 **dulcet diseases**
pleasing weaknesses 73 **seeming** becomingly

80 himself: this is called the Quip Modest.° If
again, it was not well cut, he disabled° my
judgment: this is called the Reply Churlish. If
again, it was not well cut, he would answer I
spake not true: this is called the Reproof
85 Valiant. If again, it was not well cut, he would
say I lie: this is called the Countercheck°
Quarrelsome: and so to the Lie Circumstan-
tial° and the Lie Direct.

JAQUES: And how oft did you say his beard
90 was not well cut?

TOUCHSTONE: I durst go no further than the
Lie Circumstantial, nor he durst not give me
the Lie Direct; and so we measured swords° and
parted.

95 JAQUES: Can you nominate° in order now
the degrees of the lie?

TOUCHSTONE: O sir, we quarrel in print, by
the book,° as you have books for good manners. I will name you the degrees. The first,
100 the Retort Courteous; the second, the Quip
Modest; the third, the Reply Churlish; the
fourth, the Reproof Valiant; the fifth, the
Countercheck Quarrelsome; the sixth, the Lie
with Circumstance; the seventh, the Lie Di-
105 rect. All these you may avoid but the Lie
Direct, and you may avoid that too, with an If.
I knew when seven justices could not take up°
a quarrel, but when the parties were met
themselves, one of them thought but of an If:
110 as, "If you said so, then I said so"; and they
shook hands and swore brothers. Your If is the
only peace-maker. Much virtue in If.

JAQUES: Is not this a rare fellow, my lord?
He's as good at anything, and yet a fool.
115 DUKE SENIOR: He uses his folly like a
stalking horse,° and under the presentation° of
that he shoots his wit.

(*Enter* HYMEN,° ROSALIND, *and* CELIA. *Still°
music.*)

HYMEN:
Then is there mirth in heaven
When earthly things made even°
120   Atone together.°

80 **Modest** moderate 81 **disabled** did not value
86 **Countercheck** contradiction 87–88 **Circumstantial** indirect 93 **measured swords** (swords were
measured before a duel) 95 **nominate** name 97–
98 **by the book** according to the rules 107 **take up**
settle 116 **stalking horse** (any object under cover of
which a hunter pursues his game); **presentation** protection 117 s.d. **Hymen** god of marriage; **Still** soft
119 **made even** i.e., reconciled 120 **Atone together**
are set at one

Good Duke, receive thy daughter;
Hymen from heaven brought her,
    Yea, brought her hither,
That thou mightst join her hand with his
Whose heart within his bosom is.   125
ROSALIND [*to* DUKE]:
To you I give myself, for I am yours.

[*To* ORLANDO.]

To you I give myself, for I am yours.
DUKE SENIOR:
If there be truth in sight, you are my daugh-
ter.
ORLANDO:
If there be truth in sight, you are my Rosa-
lind.
PHEBE:
If sight and shape be true,   130
Why then, my love adieu!
ROSALIND [*to* DUKE]:
I'll have no father, if you be not he.

[*To* ORLANDO.]

I'll have no husband, if you be not he.

[*To* PHEBE.]

Nor ne'er wed woman, if you be not she.
HYMEN:
Peace ho! I bar confusion: 135
'Tis I must make conclusion
    Of these most strange events.
Here's eight that must take hands
To join in Hymen's bands,
    If truth holds true contents.°   140

[*To* ORLANDO *and* ROSALIND.]

You and you no cross° shall part.

[*To* OLIVER *and* CELIA.]

You and you are heart in heart.

[*To* PHEBE.]

You to his love must accord,°
Or have a woman to your lord.

[*To* TOUCHSTONE *and* AUDREY.]

You and you are sure together°   145
As the winter to foul weather.

[*To all.*]

Whiles a wedlock hymn we sing,
Feed yourselves with questioning,

140 **If truth . . . contents** if the truth is true 141
cross quarrel 143 **accord** agree 145 **sure together**
securely bound

That reason wonder may diminish
150 How thus we met, and these things finish.

Song.

Wedding is great Juno's crown,
    O blessèd bond of board and bed!
'Tis Hymen peoples every town;
    High° wedlock then be honorèd.
155 Honor, high honor, and renown
    To Hymen, god of every town!

DUKE SENIOR:
O my dear niece, welcome thou art to me,
Even daughter,° welcome, in no less degree!
PHEBE [*to* SILVIUS]:
I will not eat my word, now thou art mine;
160 Thy faith my fancy to thee doth combine.°

(*Enter* SECOND BROTHER [*Jaques de Boys*].)

SECOND BROTHER:
Let me have audience for a word or two.
I am the second son of old Sir Rowland
That bring these tidings to this fair assembly.
Duke Frederick, hearing how that every day
165 Men of great worth resorted to this forest,
Addressed a mighty power,° which were on
    foot
In his own conduct,° purposely to take
His brother here and put him to the sword;
And to the skirts of this wild wood he came,
170 Where, meeting with an old religious man,°
After some question° with him, was converted
Both from his enterprise and from the world,
His crown bequeathing to his banished
    brother,
And all their lands restored to them again
175 That were with him exiled. This to be true
I do engage° my life.
DUKE SENIOR: Welcome, young man.
Thou offer'st fairly° to thy brothers' wedding:
To one, his lands withheld; and to the other,
A land itself at large, a potent° dukedom.
180 First, in this forest let us do those ends°
That here were well begun and well begot;
And after, every° of this happy number

That have endured shrewd° days and nights
    with us
Shall share the good of our returnèd fortune,
According to the measure° of their states.   185
Meantime forget this new-fall'n° dignity
And fall into our rustic revelry.
Play, music, and you brides and bridegrooms
    all,
With measure heaped in joy, to th' measures°
    fall.
JAQUES:
Sir, by your patience. If I heard you rightly,   190
The Duke hath put on a religious life
And thrown into neglect the pompous court.°
SECOND BROTHER:
He hath.
JAQUES:
To him will I. Out of these convertites°
There is much matter to be heard and learned.   195

[*To* DUKE.]

You to your former honor I bequeath;
Your patience and your virtue well deserves it.

[*To* ORLANDO.]

You to a love that your true faith doth merit;

[*To* OLIVER.]

You to your land and love and great allies;

[*To* SILVIUS.]

You to a long and well-deservèd bed;   200

[*To* TOUCHSTONE.]

And you to wrangling, for thy loving voyage
Is but for two months victualled. So, to your
    pleasures:
I am for other than for dancing measures.
DUKE SENIOR:
Stay, Jaques, stay.
JAQUES:
To see no pastime I. What you would have   205
I'll stay to know at your abandoned cave.
                                        (*Exit.*)
DUKE SENIOR:
Proceed, proceed. We will begin these rites.
As we do trust they'll end, in true delights.
                        (*Exit* [*after the dance*].)

154 **High** solemn   158 **Even daughter** i.e., even as a
daughter   160 **combine** unite   166 **Addressed a
mighty power** prepared a mighty army   167 **conduct**
leadership   170 **old religious man** (a hermit?)   171
question talk   176 **engage** pledge   177 **offer'st
fairly** bring a good gift   179 **potent** powerful   180
do those ends complete those purposes   182 **every**
each one

183 **shrewd** hard   185 **measure** rank   186 **new-
fall'n** newly acquired   189 **measures** dance steps
192 **thrown into . . . court** given up the ceremonious
life of the court   194 **convertites** converts

[Epilogue]

ROSALIND: It is not the fashion to see the lady the epilogue, but it is no more unhandsome° than to see the lord the prologue. If it be true that good wine needs no bush,° 'tis
5 true that a good play needs no epilogue; yet to good wine they do use good bushes, and good plays prove the better by the help of good epilogues. What a case am I in then, that am neither a good epilogue, nor cannot insinuate
10 with you° in the behalf of a good play! I am not furnished° like a beggar; therefore to beg will not become me. My way is to conjure°

you, and I'll begin with the women. I charge you, O women, for the love you bear to men, to like as much of this play as please you; and 15 I charge you, O men, for the love you bear to women — as I perceive by your simpering none of you hates them — that between you and the women the play may please. If I were a woman,° I would kiss as many of you as had 20 beards that pleased me, complexions that liked° me, and breaths that I defied° not; and I am sure, as many as have good beards, or good faces, or sweet breaths, will, for my kind offer, when I make curtsy, bid me farewell.° (*Exit.*) 25

FINIS

EPILOGUE 2–3 **unhandsome** unbecoming   4 **no bush** no advertisement (in Shakespeare's time vintners used an ivy bush as a sign)   9–10 **insinuate with you** slyly get your approval   11 **furnished** dressed   12 **conjure** (1) solemnly entreat (2) charm (by magic)

19–20 **If I were a woman** (Rosalind, of course, was played by a boy)   22 **liked** pleased; **defied** disliked   25 **bid me farewell** i.e., applaud

Shakespeare is today perhaps most highly valued for his tragedies, but this is because somehow we glumly rank tragedy above comedy; other generations have realized that his comedies represent no less an achievement. Shakespeare is the only playwright who wrote great works in both genres, and he seems to have written them more or less simultaneously. The romantic view that Shakespeare suffered a depression and wrote tragedies, and then pulled out of it to write comedies is refuted by the facts: *As You Like It* (1599–1600), for example, intervened between *Julius Caesar* (1599) and *Hamlet* (1600).

Following his usual practice, Shakespeare borrowed the gist of his story, this time from Thomas Lodge's prose romance, *Rosalynde* (1590). Like Shakespeare's other great comedies, *As You Like It* is a play about love, dominated by a heroine who is no less witty and charming because she is in love. She spoofs love ("Men have died from time to time, and worms have eaten them, but not for love") and she spoofs lovers ("I must tell you friendly in your ear, / Sell when you can, you are not for all markets"), but she herself is "many fathom deep . . . in love," which makes her spoofing the more engaging. And sometimes Shakespeare spoofs her, as when he contrives a plot that by chance brings her, disguised in male attire, into the forest that contains her beloved Orlando:

What shall I do with my doublet and hose? What did he when thou saw'st him? What said he? How looked he? Wherein went he? What makes he here? Did he ask for me? Where remains he? How parted he with thee? And when shalt thou see him again? Answer me in one word.

Though in love, Rosalind never loses her wits more than momentarily, and she pulls the strings of the plot, but even she, "out of suits with fortune," is subject to Fortune and is at times helpless and absurd. Her father was banished by a usurper before the play began; in I.iii Rosalind is banished too. Fortune's gifts "are mightily misplaced." But in Shakespeare's comic world, despite appearances, a benevolent deity (which we may call Nature) reigns, and banishment to the Forest of Arden is scarcely a hard fate; it is in Arden, rather than in "the envious court," that the benevolent powers (sometimes seen in rather pagan terms, sometimes seen in more biblical terms, such as "He that doth the ravens feed") can most effectively operate. The Forest of Arden is a place where "merry men . . . fleet the time carelessly [i.e., without care] as they did in the golden world," but it should be noted that Arden is not a utopia. It has its icy winter (though an icy winter about which one sings so exquisitely cannot be very bad), and even its detractors, Touchstone ("When I was at home, I was in a better place") and Jaques ("Here shall he see gross fools as he"). Still, in the fifth act spring comes to Arden:

> It was a lover and his lass,
>   With a hey, and a ho, and a hey nonino,
> That o'er the green cornfield did pass
>   In springtime, the only pretty ringtime,
> When birds do sing, hey ding a ding, ding,
> Sweet lovers love the spring.

It is in the Forest of Arden that lovers meet, tyrants reform, good Fortune returns to the outcasts, the corrupt return to their better selves, and those who wish can return to their proper place in the city to constitute a happy and renewed society. Nature and Fortune, that is, are joined in bounty. Joy and forgiveness triumph in this as in most of Shakespeare's comedies; if men are fools and sinners and no one is wholly exempt from comic exposure, still, no one is denied redemption. All are offered the possibility of a new life of "true delights," and the last speech of the play, Rosalind's epilogue, assumes a delighted audience and explicitly asks the audience to extend its goodwill to the performers.

Speaking broadly, there are in the Renaissance two comic traditions, which may be called "critical comedy" (or "bitter comedy") and "romantic comedy" (or "sweet comedy"). The former claims, in Hamlet's words, that the "purpose of playing . . . is to hold, as 'twere, the mirror up to nature; to show virtue her own feature, scorn her own image, and the very age and body of the time his form and pressure." Because it aims to hold a mirror up to the audience, its dramatis personae are usually urban citizens — jealous husbands, foolish merchants, and the like. These are ultimately punished, at times merely by exposure, at times by imprisonment or fines or some such thing. The second kind of comedy, romantic comedy, seeks less to correct than to delight with scenes of pleasant behavior. It does not hold a mirror to the audience; rather, it leads the audience into an elegant dream world where charming gentlefolk live a timeless existence. Thomas Heywood, who claimed to have collaborated often with Shakespeare, briefly set forth the characteristics of both traditions in *An Apology for Actors* (1612). A comedy, he said,

> is pleasantly contrived with merry accidents, and intermixed with apt and witty jests. . . . And what then is the subject of this harmless mirth? Either in the shape of a clown to show others their slovenly behavior, that they may reform that simplicity in themselves, which others make their sport, . . . or to refresh such weary spirits as are tired with labors or study, to moderate the cares and heaviness of the mind, that they may return to their trades and faculties with more zeal and earnestness, after some small soft and pleasant retirement.

When we think of *As You Like It*, we think of "harmless mirth," "sport," and the refreshing of weary spirits. But even *As You Like It* has its touches of critical comedy, its elements that, in Heywood's words, "may reform" by holding up a mirror to unsocial behavior. There is some satire — spoken not only by Jaques, but *of* Jaques — but mostly the play is pervaded by genial spirits and a humane vision that make it moral without moralizing. Not every reader will agree with Dr. Johnson that "by hastening to the end of his work Shakespeare suppressed the dialogue between the usurper and the hermit, and lost an opportunity of exhibiting a moral lesson in which he might have found matter worthy of his highest powers." It is enough that the usurper met "an old religious man" who dwells in the forest. We do not need the hermit's speech, because we have already found "sermons in stones, and good in everything."

Le Misantrope.

THE MISANTHROPE

Molière

English version by Richard Wilbur

Jean Baptiste Poquelin (1622–1673), who took the name Molière, was born into a prosperous middle-class family. For a while he studied law and philosophy, but by 1643 he was acting. He became the head of a theatrical company which had its initial difficulties and later, thanks largely to Molière's comedies, its great successes. In 1662 he married Armande Béjart. The marriage apparently was unhappy, but the capricious and flirtatious Armande proved to be an accomplished actress. Molière continued to act, with great success in comedy, until his death. In one of those improbable things that happen in real life but that are too strange for art, Molière died of a hemorrhage that he suffered while playing the title role in his comedy *The Hypochondriac*. The early plays are highly farcical; among the later and greater plays are *The Highbrow Ladies* (1659), *Tartuffe* (1664), *Don Juan* (1665), *The Misanthrope* (1666), and *The Miser* (1668).

CHARACTERS

ALCESTE, *in love with* Célimène
PHILINTE, *Alceste's friend*
ORONTE, *in love with* Célimène
CÉLIMÈNE, *Alceste's beloved*
ÉLIANTE, *Célimène's cousin*
ARSINOÉ, *a friend of Célimène's*
ACASTE } *Marquesses*
CLITANDRE
BASQUE, *Célimène's servant*
A GUARD *of the Marshalsea*
DUBOIS, *Alceste's valet*

The Scene throughout is in Célimène's house at Paris.

ACT I

Molière's *The Misanthrope*, translated by Richard
Wilbur. Copyright © 1954, 1955, by Richard
Wilbur. Reprinted by permission of Harcourt Brace
Jovanovich, Inc.
Caution: Professionals and amateurs are hereby warned that this translation, being fully protected
under the copyright laws of the United States of
America, the British Empire, including the Dominion
of Canada, and all other countries which are signa-
tories to the Universal Copyright Convention and
the International Copyright Union, is subject to
royalty. All rights, including professional, amateur,
motion picture, recitation, lecturing, public reading,
radio broadcasting, and television, are strictly reserved. Particular emphasis is laid on the question
of readings, permission for which must be secured
from the author's agent in writing. Inquiries on professional rights (except for amateur rights) should
be addressed to Mr. Gilbert Parker, Curtis Brown,
Ltd., 60 East 56th Street, New York, N.Y. 10022;
inquiries on translation rights should be addressed to
Harcourt Brace Jovanovich, Inc., 757 Third Avenue,
New York, N.Y. 10017. The amateur acting rights
are controlled exclusively by the Dramatists Play
Service, Inc., 440 Park Avenue South, New York,
N.Y. 10016. No amateur performance of the play
may be given without obtaining in advance the written permission of the Dramatists Play Service, Inc.,
and paying the requisite fee.

SCENE I. [PHILINTE, ALCESTE.]

PHILINTE:
Now, what's got into you?
    ALCESTE (*seated*):   Kindly leave me alone.
    PHILINTE:
Come, come, what is it? This lugubrious
    tone . . .
    ALCESTE:
Leave me, I said; you spoil my solitude.
    PHILINTE:
Oh, listen to me, now, and don't be rude.
    ALCESTE:
I choose to be rude, Sir, and to be hard of
    hearing.
    PHILINTE:
These ugly moods of yours are not endearing;
Friends though we are, I really must insist . . .
    ALCESTE (*abruptly rising*):
Friends? Friends, you say? Well, cross me off
    your list.

I've been your friend till now, as you well
    know;
But after what I saw a moment ago
I tell you flatly that our ways must part.
I wish no place in a dishonest heart.
    PHILINTE:
Why, what have I done, Alceste? Is this quite
    just?
    ALCESTE:
My God, you ought to die of self-disgust.
I call your conduct inexcusable, Sir,
And every man of honor will concur.
I see you almost hug a man to death,
Exclaim for joy until you're out of breath,
And supplement these loving demonstrations
With endless offers, vows, and protestations;
Then when I ask you "Who was that?" I find
That you can barely bring his name to mind!
Once the man's back is turned, you cease to
    love him,
And speak with absolute indifference of him!
By God, I say it's base and scandalous
To falsify the heart's affections thus;
If I caught myself behaving in such a way,
I'd hang myself for shame, without delay.
    PHILINTE:
It hardly seems a hanging matter to me;
I hope that you will take it graciously
If I extend myself a slight reprieve,
And live a little longer, by your leave.
    ALCESTE:
How dare you joke about a crime so grave?
    PHILINTE:
What crime? How else are people to behave?
    ALCESTE:
I'd have them be sincere, and never part
With any word that isn't from the heart.
    PHILINTE:
When someone greets us with a show of
    pleasure,
It's but polite to give him equal measure,
Return his love the best that we know how,
And trade him offer for offer, vow for vow.
    ALCESTE:
No, no, this formula you'd have me follow,
However fashionable, is false and hollow,
And I despise the frenzied operations
Of all these barterers of protestations,
These lavishers of meaningless embraces,
These utterers of obliging commonplaces,

Who court and flatter everyone on earth
And praise the fool no less than the man of
    worth.
Should you rejoice that someone fondles you,
50 Offers his love and service, swears to be true,
And fills your ears with praises of your name,
When to the first damned fop he'll say the
    same?
No, no: no self-respecting heart would dream
Of prizing so promiscuous an esteem;
55 However high the praise, there's nothing worse
Than sharing honors with the universe.
Esteem is founded on comparison:
To honor all men is to honor none.
Since you embrace this indiscriminate vice,
60 Your friendship comes at far too cheap a price;
I spurn the easy tribute of a heart
Which will not set the worthy man apart:
I choose, Sir, to be chosen; and in fine,
The friend of mankind is no friend of mine.
    PHILINTE:
65 But in polite society, custom decrees
That we show certain outward courtesies. . . .
    ALCESTE:
Ah, no! we should condemn with all our force
Such false and artificial intercourse.
Let men behave like men; let them display
70 Their inmost hearts in everything they say;
Let the heart speak, and let our sentiments
Not mask themselves in silly compliments.
    PHILINTE:
In certain cases it would be uncouth
And most absurd to speak the naked truth;
75 With all respect for your exalted notions,
It's often best to veil one's true emotions.
Wouldn't the social fabric come undone
If we were wholly frank with everyone?
Suppose you met with someone you couldn't
    bear;
80 Would you inform him of it then and there?
    ALCESTE:
Yes.
    PHILINTE:
        Then you'd tell old Emilie it's pathetic
The way she daubs her features with cosmetic
And plays the gay coquette at sixty-four?
    ALCESTE:
I would.
    PHILINTE:
        And you'd call Dorilas a bore,
85 And tell him every ear at court is lame
From hearing him brag about his noble name?
    ALCESTE:
Precisely.

    PHILINTE:
    Ah, you're joking.
    ALCESTE: *Au contraire:*
In this regard there's none I'd choose to spare.
All are corrupt; there's nothing to be seen
In court or town but aggravates my spleen.   90
I fall into deep gloom and melancholy
When I survey the scene of human folly,
Finding on every hand base flattery,
Injustice, fraud, self-interest, treachery. . . .
Ah, it's too much; mankind has grown so base, 95
I mean to break with the whole human race.
    PHILINTE:
This philosophic rage is a bit extreme;
You've no idea how comical you seem;
Indeed, we're like those brothers in the play
Called *School for Husbands*, one of whom was
    prey . . .   100
    ALCESTE:
Enough, now! None of your stupid similes.
    PHILINTE:
Then let's have no more tirades, if you please.
The world won't change, whatever you say or
    do;
And since plain speaking means so much to
    you,
I'll tell you plainly that by being frank   105
You've earned the reputation of a crank,
And that you're thought ridiculous when you
    rage
And rant against the manners of the age.
    ALCESTE:
So much the better; just what I wish to hear.
No news could be more grateful to my ear. 110
All men are so detestable in my eyes,
I should be sorry if they thought me wise.
    PHILINTE:
Your hatred's very sweeping, is it not?
    ALCESTE:
Quite right: I hate the whole degraded lot.
    PHILINTE:
Must all poor human creatures be embraced, 115
Without distinction, by your vast distaste?
Even in these bad times, there are surely a
    few . . .
    ALCESTE:
No, I include all men in one dim view:
Some men I hate for being rogues: the others
I hate because they treat the rogues like
    brothers,   120
And, lacking a virtuous scorn for what is vile,
Receive the villain with a complaisant smile.
Notice how tolerant people choose to be
Toward that bold rascal who's at law with me.

125 His social polish can't conceal his nature;
One sees at once that he's a treacherous creature;
No one could possibly be taken in
By those soft speeches and that sugary grin.
The whole world knows the shady means by which
130 The low-brow's grown so powerful and rich,
And risen to a rank so bright and high
That virtue can but blush, and merit sigh.
Whenever his name comes up in conversation,
None will defend his wretched reputation;
Call him knave, liar, scoundrel, and all the
135 rest,
Each head will nod, and no one will protest.
And yet his smirk is seen in every house,
He's greeted everywhere with smiles and bows,
And when there's any honor that can be got
140 By pulling strings, he'll get it, like as not.
My God! It chills my heart to see the ways
Men come to terms with evil nowadays;
Sometimes, I swear, I'm moved to flee and find
Some desert land unfouled by humankind.
    PHILINTE:
145 Come, let's forget the follies of the times
And pardon mankind for its petty crimes;
Let's have an end of rantings and of railings,
And show some leniency toward human failings.
This world requires a pliant rectitude;
150 Too stern a virtue makes one stiff and rude;
Good sense views all extremes with detestation,
And bids us to be noble in moderation.
The rigid virtues of the ancient days
Are not for us; they jar with all our ways
155 And ask of us too lofty a perfection.
Wise men accept their times without objection,
And there's no greater folly, if you ask me,
Than trying to reform society.
Like you, I see each day a hundred and one
160 Unhandsome deeds that might be better done,
But still, for all the faults that meet my view,
I'm never known to storm and rave like you.
I take men as they are, or let them be,
And teach my soul to bear their frailty;
And whether in court or town, whatever the
165 scene,
My phlegm's as philosophic as your spleen.
    ALCESTE:
This phlegm which you so eloquently commend,

Does nothing ever rile it up, my friend?
Suppose some man you trust should treacherously
Conspire to rob you of your property, 170
And do his best to wreck your reputation?
Wouldn't you feel a certain indignation?
    PHILINTE:
Why, no. These faults of which you so complain
Are part of human nature, I maintain,
And it's no more a matter for disgust 175
That men are knavish, selfish and unjust,
Than that the vulture dines upon the dead,
And wolves are furious, and apes ill-bred.
    ALCESTE:
Shall I see myself betrayed, robbed, torn to bits,
And not . . . Oh, let's be still and rest our wits. 180
Enough of reasoning, now. I've had my fill.
    PHILINTE:
Indeed, you would do well, Sir, to be still.
Rage less at your opponent, and give some thought
To how you'll win this lawsuit that he's brought.
    ALCESTE:
I assure you I'll do nothing of the sort. 185
    PHILINTE:
Then who will plead your case before the court?
    ALCESTE:
Reason and right and justice will plead for me.
    PHILINTE:
Oh, Lord. What judges do you plan to see?
    ALCESTE:
Why, none. The justice of my cause is clear.
    PHILINTE:
Of course, man; but there's politics to fear. . . . 190
    ALCESTE:
No, I refuse to lift a hand. That's flat.
I'm either right, or wrong.
    PHILINTE: Don't count on that.
    ALCESTE:
No, I'll do nothing.
    PHILINTE: Your enemy's influence
Is great, you know . . .
    ALCESTE: That makes no difference.
    PHILINTE:
It will; you'll see.
    ALCESTE: Must honor bow to guile? 195
If so, I shall be proud to lose the trial.
    PHILINTE:
Oh, really . . .
    ALCESTE: I'll discover by this case

Whether or not men are sufficiently base
And impudent and villainous and perverse
200 To do me wrong before the universe.
    PHILINTE:
What a man!
    ALCESTE:
            Oh, I could wish, whatever the cost,
Just for the beauty of it, that my trial were
    lost.
    PHILINTE:
If people heard you talking so, Alceste,
They'd split their sides. Your name would be a
    jest.
    ALCESTE:
So much the worse for jesters.
205 PHILINTE: May I enquire
Whether this rectitude you so admire,
And these hard virtues you're enamored of
Are qualities of the lady whom you love?
It much surprises me that you, who seem
210 To view mankind with furious disesteem,
Have yet found something to enchant your
    eyes
Amidst a species which you so despise.
And what is more amazing, I'm afraid,
Is the most curious choice your heart has
    made.
215 The honest Éliante is fond of you,
Arsinoé, the prude, admires you too;
And yet your spirit's been perversely led
To choose the flighty Célimène instead,
Whose brittle malice and coquettish ways
220 So typify the manners of our days.
How is it that the traits you most abhor
Are bearable in this lady you adore?
Are you so blind with love that you can't find
    them?
Or do you contrive, in her case, not to mind
    them?
    ALCESTE:
225 My love for that young widow's not the kind
That can't perceive defects; no, I'm not blind.
I see her faults, despite my ardent love,
And all I see I fervently reprove.
And yet I'm weak; for all her falsity,
230 That woman knows the art of pleasing me,
And though I never cease complaining of her,
I swear I cannot manage not to love her.
Her charm outweighs her faults; I can but aim
To cleanse her spirit in my love's pure flame.
    PHILINTE:
235 That's no small task; I wish you all success.
You think then that she loves you?
    ALCESTE: Heavens, yes!

I wouldn't love her did she not love me.
    PHILINTE:
Well, if her taste for you is plain to see,
Why do these rivals cause you such despair?
    ALCESTE:
True love, Sir, is possessive, and cannot bear   240
To share with all the world. I'm here today
To tell her she must send that mob away.
    PHILINTE:
If I were you, and had your choice to make,
Éliante, her cousin, would be the one I'd
    take;
That honest heart, which cares for you alone,   245
Would harmonize far better with your own.
    ALCESTE:
True, true: each day my reason tells me so;
But reason doesn't rule in love, you know.
    PHILINTE:
I fear some bitter sorrow is in store;
This love . . .

SCENE II. [ORONTE, ALCESTE, PHILINTE.]

ORONTE (to ALCESTE):
                The servants told me at the door
That Éliante and Célimène were out,
But when I heard, dear Sir, that you were
    about,
I came to say, without exaggeration,
That I hold you in the vastest admiration,   5
And that it's always been my dearest desire
To be the friend of one I so admire.
I hope to see my love of merit requited,
And you and I in friendship's bond united.
I'm sure you won't refuse — if I may be
    frank —   10
A friend of my devotedness — and rank.

(During this speech of ORONTE'S ALCESTE is
abstracted, and seems unaware that he is
being spoken to. He only breaks off his
reverie when ORONTE says:)

It was for you, if you please, that my words
    were intended.
    ALCESTE:
For me, Sir?
    ORONTE:
                Yes, for you. You're not offended?
    ALCESTE:
By no means. But this much surprises me. . . .
The honor comes most unexpectedly. . . .   15
    ORONTE:
My high regard should not astonish you;
The whole world feels the same. It is your due.

ALCESTE:
Sir . . .

ORONTE:
        Why, in all the State there isn't one
Can match your merits; they shine, Sir, like
    the sun.

ALCESTE:
Sir . . .

ORONTE:
20   You are higher in my estimation
Than all that's most illustrious in the nation.

ALCESTE:
Sir . . .

ORONTE:
        If I lie, may heaven strike me dead!
To show you that I mean what I have said,
Permit me, Sir, to embrace you most sincerely,
And swear that I will prize our friendship
25   dearly.
Give me your hand. And now, Sir, if you
    choose,
We'll make our vows.

ALCESTE: Sir . . .

ORONTE: What! You refuse?

ALCESTE:
Sir, it's a very great honor you extend:
But friendship is a sacred thing, my friend;
30 It would be profanation to bestow
The name of friend on one you hardly know.
All parts are better played when well-rehearsed;
Let's put off friendship, and get acquainted
    first.
We may discover it would be unwise
35 To try to make our natures harmonize.

ORONTE:
By heaven! You're sagacious to the core;
This speech has made me admire you even
    more.
Let time, then, bring us closer day by day;
Meanwhile, I shall be yours in every way.
40 If, for example, there should be anything
You wish at court, I'll mention it to the King.
I have his ear, of course; it's quite well known
That I am much in favor with the throne.
In short, I am your servant. And now, dear
    friend,
45 Since you have such fine judgment, I intend
To please you, if I can, with a small sonnet
I wrote not long ago. Please comment on it,
And tell me whether I ought to publish it.

ALCESTE:
You must excuse me, Sir; I'm hardly fit
To judge such matters.

ORONTE: Why not?

ALCESTE: I am, I fear,   50
Inclined to be unfashionably sincere.

ORONTE:
Just what I ask; I'd take no satisfaction
In anything but your sincere reaction.
I beg you not to dream of being kind.

ALCESTE:
Since you desire it, Sir, I'll speak my mind.   55

ORONTE:
Sonnet. It's a sonnet. . . . *Hope* . . . The poem's
    addressed
To a lady who wakened hopes within my
    breast.
Hope . . . this is not the pompous sort of thing,
Just modest little verses, with a tender ring.

ALCESTE:
Well, we shall see.

ORONTE: *Hope* . . . I'm anxious to hear   60
Whether the style seems properly smooth and
    clear,
And whether the choice of words is good or
    bad.

ALCESTE:
We'll see, we'll see.

ORONTE: Perhaps I ought to add
That it took me only a quarter-hour to write it.

ALCESTE:
The time's irrelevant, Sir: kindly recite it.   65

ORONTE (*reading*):
    Hope comforts us awhile, 'tis true,
    Lulling our cares with careless laughter,
    And yet such joy is full of rue,
    My Phyllis, if nothing follows after.

PHILINTE:
I'm charmed by this already; the style's de-
    lightful.   70

ALCESTE (*sotto voce, to* PHILINTE):
How can you say that? Why, the thing is
    frightful.

ORONTE:
    Your fair face smiled on me awhile,
    But was it kindness so to enchant me?
    'Twould have been fairer not to smile,
    If hope was all you meant to grant me.   75

PHILINTE:
What a clever thought! How handsomely you
    phrase it!

ALCESTE (*sotto voce, to* PHILINTE):
You know the thing is trash. How dare you
    praise it?

ORONTE:
    If it's to be my passion's fate
    Thus everlastingly to wait,
    Then death will come to set me free: 80

For death is fairer than the fair;
Phyllis, to hope is to despair
When one must hope eternally.

PHILINTE:
The close is exquisite — full of feeling and
    grace.

ALCESTE (*sotto voce, aside*):
Oh, blast the close; you'd better close your
    face
Before you send your lying soul to hell.

PHILINTE:
I can't remember a poem I've liked so well.

ALCESTE (*sotto voce, aside*):
Good Lord!

ORONTE (*to* PHILINTE):
                    I fear you're flattering me a bit.

PHILINTE:
Oh, no!

ALCESTE (*sotto voce, aside*):
        What else d'you call it, you hypocrite?

ORONTE (*to* ALCESTE):
But you, Sir, keep your promise now: don't
    shrink
From telling me sincerely what you think.

ALCESTE:
Sir, these are delicate matters; we all desire
To be told that we've the true poetic fire.
But once, to one whose name I shall not
    mention,
I said, regarding some verse of his invention,
That gentlemen should rigorously control
That itch to write which often afflicts the soul;
That one should curb the heady inclination
To publicize one's little avocation;
And that in showing off one's works of art
One often plays a very clownish part.

ORONTE:
Are you suggesting in a devious way
That I ought not ...

ALCESTE: Oh, that I do not say.
Further, I told him that no fault is worse
Than that of writing frigid, lifeless verse,
And that the merest whisper of such a shame
Suffices to destroy a man's good name.

ORONTE:
D'you mean to say my sonnet's dull and trite?

ALCESTE:
I don't say that. But I went on to cite
Numerous cases of once-respected men
Who came to grief by taking up the pen.

ORONTE:
And am I like them? Do I write so poorly?

ALCESTE:
I don't say that. But I told this person, "Surely

You're under no necessity to compose;
Why you should wish to publish, heaven
    knows.
There's no excuse for printing tedious rot
Unless one writes for bread, as you do not.
Resist temptation, then, I beg of you;
Conceal your pastimes from the public view;
And don't give up, on any provocation,
Your present high and courtly reputation,
To purchase at a greedy printer's shop
The name of silly author and scribbling fop."
These were the points I tried to make him see.

ORONTE:
I sense that they are also aimed at me;
But now — about my sonnet — I'd like to be
    told ...

ALCESTE:
Frankly, that sonnet should be pigeonholed.
You've chosen the worst models to imitate.
The style's unnatural. Let me illustrate:
For example, *Your fair face smiled on me*
    awhile,
Followed by, *'Twould have been fairer not to*
    smile!
Or this: *such joy is full of rue;*
Or this: *For death is fairer than the fair;*
Or, *Phyllis, to hope is to despair*
    When one must hope eternally!
This artificial style, that's all the fashion,
Has neither taste, nor honesty, nor passion;
It's nothing but a sort of wordy play,
And nature never spoke in such a way.
What, in this shallow age, is not debased?
Our fathers, though less refined, had better
    taste;
I'd barter all that men admire today
For one old love song I shall try to say:
    If the King had given me for my own
    Paris, his citadel,
    And I for that must leave alone
    Her whom I love so well,
    I'd say then to the Crown,
    Take back your glittering town;
    My darling is more fair, I swear,
    My darling is more fair.
The rhyme's not rich, the style is rough and
    old,
But don't you see that it's the purest gold
Beside the tinsel nonsense now preferred,
And that there's passion in its every word?
    If the King had given me for my own
    Paris, his citadel,
    And I for that must leave alone
    Her whom I love so well,

160   *I'd say then to the Crown,*
    Take back your glittering town;
    My darling is more fair, I swear,
    My darling is more fair.
There speaks a loving heart. (To PHILINTE.)
    You're laughing, eh?
165 Laugh on, my precious wit. Whatever you say,
I hold that song's worth all the bibelots
That people hail today with ah's and oh's.
    ORONTE:
And I maintain my sonnet's very good.
    ALCESTE:
It's not at all surprising that you should.
You have your reasons; permit me to have
170   mine
For thinking that you cannot write a line.
    ORONTE:
Others have praised my sonnet to the skies.
    ALCESTE:
I lack their art of telling pleasant lies.
    ORONTE:
You seem to think you've got no end of wit.
    ALCESTE:
175 To praise your verse, I'd need still more of it.
    ORONTE:
I'm not in need of your approval, Sir.
    ALCESTE:
That's good; you couldn't have it if you were.
    ORONTE:
Come now, I'll lend you the subject of my
    sonnet;
I'd like to see you try to improve upon it.
    ALCESTE:
I might, by chance, write something just as
180   shoddy;
But then I wouldn't show it to everybody.
    ORONTE:
You're most opinionated and conceited.
    ALCESTE:
Go find your flatterers, and be better treated.
    ORONTE:
Look here, my little fellow, pray watch your
    tone.
    ALCESTE:
My great big fellow, you'd better watch your
185   own.
    PHILINTE (*stepping between them*):
Oh, please, please, gentlemen! This will never
    do.
    ORONTE:
The fault is mine, and I leave the field to you.
I am your servant, Sir, in every way.
    ALCESTE:
And I, Sir, am your most abject valet.

SCENE III. [PHILINTE, ALCESTE.]

    PHILINTE:
Well, as you see, sincerity in excess
Can get you into a very pretty mess;
Oronte was hungry for appreciation. . . .
    ALCESTE:
Don't speak to me.
    PHILINTE: What?
    ALCESTE: No more conversation.
    PHILINTE:
Really, now . . .
    ALCESTE: Leave me alone.
    PHILINTE: If I . . .
    ALCESTE: Out of my sight!   5
    PHILINTE:
But what . . .
    ALCESTE: I won't listen.
    PHILINTE: But . . .
    ALCESTE: Silence!
    PHILINTE: Now, is it polite . . .
    ALCESTE:
By heaven, I've had enough. Don't follow me.
    PHILINTE:
Ah, you're just joking. I'll keep you company.

ACT II

SCENE I. [ALCESTE, CÉLIMÈNE.]

    ALCESTE:
Shall I speak plainly, Madam? I confess
Your conduct gives me infinite distress,
And my resentment's grown too hot to
    smother.
Soon, I foresee, we'll break with one another.
If I said otherwise, I should deceive you;   5
Sooner or later, I shall be forced to leave you,
And if I swore that we shall never part,
I should misread the omens of my heart.
    CÉLIMÈNE:
You kindly saw me home, it would appear,
So as to pour invectives in my ear.   10
    ALCESTE:
I've no desire to quarrel. But I deplore
Your inability to shut the door
On all these suitors who beset you so.
There's what annoys me, if you care to know.
    CÉLIMÈNE:
Is it my fault that all these men pursue me?   15
Am I to blame if they're attracted to me?
And when they gently beg an audience,

Ought I to take a stick and drive them hence?
ALCESTE:
Madam, there's no necessity for a stick;
20 A less responsive heart would do the trick.
Of your attractiveness I don't complain;
But those your charms attract, you then detain
By a most melting and receptive manner,
And so enlist their hearts beneath your banner.
25 It's the agreeable hopes which you excite
That keep these lovers round you day and
    night;
Were they less liberally smiled upon,
That sighing troop would very soon be gone.
But tell me, Madam, why it is that lately
30 This man Clitandre interests you so greatly?
Because of what high merits do you deem
Him worthy of the honor of your esteem?
Is it that your admiring glances linger
On the splendidly long nail of his little finger?
35 Or do you share the general deep respect
For the blond wig he chooses to affect?
Are you in love with his embroidered hose?
Do you adore his ribbons and his bows?
Or is it that this paragon bewitches
Your tasteful eye with his vast German
40   breeches?
Perhaps his giggle, or his falsetto voice,
Makes him the latest gallant of your choice?
CÉLIMÈNE:
You're much mistaken to resent him so.
Why I put up with him you surely know:
45 My lawsuit's very shortly to be tried,
And I must have his influence on my side.
ALCESTE:
Then lose your lawsuit, Madam, or let it drop;
Don't torture me by humoring such a fop.
CÉLIMÈNE:
You're jealous of the whole world, Sir.
ALCESTE: That's true,
50 Since the whole world is well-received by you.
CÉLIMÈNE:
That my good nature is so unconfined
Should serve to pacify your jealous mind;
Were I to smile on one, and scorn the rest,
Then you might have some cause to be
    distressed.
ALCESTE:
55 Well, if I mustn't be jealous, tell me, then,
Just how I'm better treated than other men.
CÉLIMÈNE:
You know you have my love. Will that not
    do?
ALCESTE:
What proof have I that what you say is true?

CÉLIMÈNE:
I would expect, Sir, that my having said it
Might give the statement a sufficient credit.   60
ALCESTE:
But how can I be sure that you don't tell
The selfsame thing to other men as well?
CÉLIMÈNE:
What a gallant speech! How flattering to me!
What a sweet creature you make me out to be!
Well then, to save you from the pangs of
    doubt,   65
All that I've said I hereby cancel out;
Now, none but yourself shall make a monkey
    of you:
Are you content?
ALCESTE:
                Why, why am I doomed to love you?
I swear that I shall bless the blissful hour
When this poor heart's no longer in your
    power!   70
I make no secret of it: I've done my best
To exorcise this passion from my breast;
But thus far all in vain; it will not go;
It's for my sins that I must love you so.
CÉLIMÈNE:
Your love for me is matchless, Sir; that's clear. 75
ALCESTE:
Indeed, in all the world it has no peer;
Words can't describe the nature of my passion,
And no man ever loved in such a fashion.
CÉLIMÈNE:
Yes, it's a brand-new fashion, I agree:
You show your love by castigating me,   80
And all your speeches are enraged and rude.
I've never been so furiously wooed.
ALCESTE:
Yet you could calm that fury, if you chose.
Come, shall we bring our quarrels to a close?
Let's speak with open hearts, then, and
    begin . . .   85

SCENE II. [CÉLIMÈNE, ALCESTE, BASQUE.]

CÉLIMÈNE:
What is it?
BASQUE: Acaste is here.
CÉLIMÈNE: Well, send him in.

SCENE III. [CÉLIMÈNE, ALCESTE.]

ALCESTE:
What! Shall we never be alone at all?
You're always ready to receive a call,
And you can't bear, for ten ticks of the clock,

Not to keep open house for all who knock.
CÉLIMÈNE:
5 I couldn't refuse him: he'd be most put out.
  ALCESTE:
Surely that's not worth worrying about.
  CÉLIMÈNE:
Acaste would never forgive me if he guessed
That I consider him a dreadful pest.
  ALCESTE:
If he's a pest, why bother with him then?
  CÉLIMÈNE:
10 Heavens! One can't antagonize such men;
Why, they're the chartered gossips of the court,
And have a say in things of every sort.
One must receive them, and be full of charm;
They're no great help, but they can do you
    harm,
15 And though your influence be ever so great,
They're hardly the best people to alienate.
  ALCESTE:
I see, dear lady, that you could make a case
For putting up with the whole human race;
These friendships that you calculate so
    nicely . . .

SCENE IV. [ALCESTE, CÉLIMÈNE, BASQUE.]

  BASQUE:
Madam, Clitandre is here as well.
  ALCESTE: Precisely.
  CÉLIMÈNE:
Where are you going?
  ALCESTE: Elsewhere.
  CÉLIMÈNE: Stay.
  ALCESTE: No, no.
  CÉLIMÈNE:
Stay, Sir.
  ALCESTE:
          I can't.
  CÉLIMÈNE: I wish it.
  ALCESTE: No, I must go.
I beg you, Madam, not to press the matter;
5 You know I have no taste for idle chatter.
  CÉLIMÈNE:
Stay. I command you.
  ALCESTE: No, I cannot stay.
  CÉLIMÈNE:
Very well; you have my leave to go away.

SCENE V. [ÉLIANTE, PHILINTE, ACASTE,
CLITANDRE, ALCESTE, CÉLIMÈNE, BASQUE.]

  ÉLIANTE (to CÉLIMÈNE):
The Marquesses have kindly come to call.
Were they announced?

  CÉLIMÈNE:
                Yes. Basque, bring chairs for all.
(BASQUE provides the chairs, and exits.)
(To ALCESTE.) You haven't gone?
  ALCESTE: No; and I shan't depart
Till you decide who's foremost in your heart.
  CÉLIMÈNE:
Oh, hush.
  ALCESTE:
          It's time to choose; take them, or me.   5
  CÉLIMÈNE:
You're mad.
  ALCESTE:
            I'm not, as you shall shortly see.
  CÉLIMÈNE:
Oh?
  ALCESTE:
      You'll decide.
  CÉLIMÈNE: You're joking now, dear friend.
  ALCESTE:
No, no; you'll choose; my patience is at an
    end.
  CLITANDRE:
Madam, I come from court, where poor
    Cléonte
Behaved like a perfect fool, as is his wont.   10
Has he no friend to counsel him, I wonder,
And teach him less unerringly to blunder?
  CÉLIMÈNE:
It's true, the man's a most accomplished
    dunce;
His gauche behavior charms the eye at once;
And every time one sees him, on my word,   15
His manner's grown a trifle more absurd.
  ACASTE:
Speaking of dunces, I've just now conversed
With old Damon, who's one of the very worst;
I stood a lifetime in the broiling sun
Before his dreary monologue was done.   20
  CÉLIMÈNE:
Oh, he's a wondrous talker, and has the power
To tell you nothing hour after hour:
If, by mistake, he ever came to the point,
The shock would put his jawbone out of
    joint.
  ÉLIANTE (to PHILINTE):
The conversation takes its usual turn,   25
And all our dear friends' ears will shortly burn.
  CLITANDRE:
Timante's a character, Madam.
  CÉLIMÈNE: Isn't he, though?
A man of mystery from top to toe,
Who moves about in a romantic mist
On secret missions which do not exist.   30

His talk is full of eyebrows and grimaces;
How tired one gets of his momentous faces;
He's always whispering something confidential
Which turns out to be quite inconsequential;
35   Nothing's too slight for him to mystify;
He even whispers when he says "good-by."

ACASTE:
Tell us about Géralde.

CÉLIMÈNE: That tiresome ass.
He mixes only with the titled class,
And fawns on dukes and princes, and is bored
40   With anyone who's not at least a lord.
The man's obsessed with rank, and his dis-
     courses
Are all of hounds and carriages and horses;
He uses Christian names with all the great,
And the word Milord, with him, is out of date.

CLITANDRE:
45   He's very taken with Bélise, I hear.

CÉLIMÈNE:
She is the dreariest company, poor dear.
Whenever she comes to call, I grope about
To find some topic which will draw her out,
But, owing to her dry and faint replies,
50   The conversation wilts, and droops, and dies.
In vain one hopes to animate her face
By mentioning the ultimate commonplace;
But sun or shower, even hail or frost
Are matters she can instantly exhaust.
55   Meanwhile her visit, painful though it is,
Drags on and on through mute eternities,
And though you ask the time, and yawn, and
     yawn,
She sits there like a stone and won't be gone.

ACASTE:
Now for Adraste.

CÉLIMÈNE: Oh, that conceited elf
60   Has a gigantic passion for himself;
He rails against the court, and cannot bear it
That none will recognize his hidden merit;
All honors given to others give offense
To his imaginary excellence.

CLITANDRE:
65   What about young Cléon? His house, they say,
Is full of the best society, night and day.

CÉLIMÈNE:
His cook has made him popular, not he:
It's Cléon's table that people come to see.

ÉLIANTE:
He gives a splendid dinner, you must admit.

CÉLIMÈNE:
70   But must he serve himself along with it?
For my taste, he's a most insipid dish
Whose presence sours the wine and spoils the
     fish.

PHILINTE:
Damis, his uncle, is admired no end.
What's your opinion, Madam?

CÉLIMÈNE: Why, he's my friend.

PHILINTE:
He seems a decent fellow, and rather clever.   75

CÉLIMÈNE:
He works too hard at cleverness, however.
I hate to see him sweat and struggle so
To fill his conversation with bons mots.
Since he's decided to become a wit
His taste's so pure that nothing pleases it;   80
He scolds at all the latest books and plays,
Thinking that wit must never stoop to praise,
That finding fault's a sign of intellect,
That all appreciation is abject,
And that by damning everything in sight   85
One shows oneself in a distinguished light.
He's scornful even of our conversations:
Their trivial nature sorely tries his patience;
He folds his arms, and stands above the battle,
And listens sadly to our childish prattle.   90

ACASTE:
Wonderful, Madam! You've hit him off pre-
     cisely.

CLITANDRE:
No one can sketch a character so nicely.

ALCESTE:
How bravely, Sirs, you cut and thrust at all
These absent fools, till one by one they fall:
But let one come in sight, and you'll at once   95
Embrace the man you lately called a dunce,
Telling him in a tone sincere and fervent
How proud you are to be his humble servant.

CLITANDRE:
Why pick on us? *Madame's* been speaking,
     Sir.
And you should quarrel, if you must, with her.   100

ALCESTE:
No, no, by God, the fault is yours, because
You lead her on with laughter and applause,
And make her think that she's the more de-
     lightful
The more her talk is scandalous and spiteful.
Oh, she would stoop to malice far, far less   105
If no such claque approved her cleverness.
It's flatterers like you whose foolish praise
Nourishes all the vices of these days.

PHILINTE:
But why protest when someone ridicules
Those you'd condemn, yourself, as knaves or
     fools?   110

CÉLIMÈNE:
Why, Sir? Because he loves to make a fuss.
You don't expect him to agree with us,

When there's an opportunity to express
His heaven-sent spirit of contrariness?
115 What other people think, he can't abide;
Whatever they say, he's on the other side;
He lives in deadly terror of agreeing;
'Twould make him seem an ordinary being.
Indeed, he's so in love with contradiction,
He'll turn against his most profound convic-
120   tion
And with a furious eloquence deplore it,
If only someone else is speaking for it.

ALCESTE:

Go on, dear lady, mock me as you please;
You have your audience in ecstasies.

PHILINTE:

125 But what she says is true: you have a way
Of bridling at whatever people say;
Whether they praise or blame, your angry
      spirit
Is equally unsatisfied to hear it.

ALCESTE:

Men, Sir, are always wrong, and that's the
      reason
130 That righteous anger's never out of season;
All that I hear in all their conversation
Is flattering praise or reckless condemnation.

CÉLIMÈNE:

But . . .

ALCESTE:

          No, no, Madam, I am forced to state
That you have pleasures which I deprecate,
And that these others, here, are much to
135   blame
For nourishing the faults which are your
      shame.

CLITANDRE:

I shan't defend myself, Sir; but I vow
I'd thought this lady faultless until now.

ACASTE:

I see her charms and graces, which are many;
140 But as for faults, I've never noticed any.

ALCESTE:

I see them, Sir; and rather than ignore them,
I strenuously criticize her for them.
The more one loves, the more one should
      · object
To every blemish, every least defect.
145 Were I this lady, I would soon get rid
Of lovers who approved of all I did,
And by their slack indulgence and applause
Endorsed my follies and excused my flaws.

CÉLIMÈNE:

If all hearts beat according to your measure,
The dawn of love would be the end of plea-
150   sure;

And love would find its perfect consummation
In ecstasies of rage and reprobation.

ÉLIANTE:

Love, as a rule, affects men otherwise,
And lovers rarely love to criticize.
They see their lady as a charming blur,   155
And find all things commendable in her.
If she has any blemish, fault, or shame,
They will redeem it by a pleasing name.
The pale-faced lady's lily-white, perforce;
The swarthy one's a sweet brunette, of course;   160
The spindly lady has a slender grace;
The fat one has a most majestic pace;
The plain one, with her dress in disarray,
They classify as *beauté négligée*;
The hulking one's a goddess in their eyes,   165
The dwarf, a concentrate of Paradise;
The haughty lady has a noble mind;
The mean one's witty, and the dull one's
      kind;
The chatterbox has liveliness and verve,
The mute one has a virtuous reserve.   170
So lovers manage, in their passion's cause,
To love their ladies even for their flaws.

ALCESTE:

But I still say . . .

CÉLIMÈNE: I think it would be nice
To stroll around the gallery once or twice.
What! You're not going, Sirs?

CLITANDRE *and* ACASTE: No, Madam, no.   175

ALCESTE:

You seem to be in terror lest they go.
Do what you will, Sirs; leave, or linger on,
But I shan't go till after you are gone.

ACASTE:

I'm free to linger, unless I should perceive
Madame is tired, and wishes me to leave.   180

CLITANDRE:

And as for me, I needn't go today
Until the hour of the King's *coucher*.

CÉLIMÈNE (*to* ALCESTE):

You're joking, surely?

ALCESTE: Not in the least; we'll see
Whether you'd rather part with them, or me.

SCENE VI. [ALCESTE, CÉLIMÈNE, ÉLIANTE,
    ACASTE, PHILINTE, CLITANDRE, BASQUE.]

BASQUE (*to* ALCESTE):

Sir, there's a fellow here who bids me state
That he must see you, and that it can't wait.

ALCESTE:

Tell him that I have no such pressing affairs.

BASQUE:
It's a long tailcoat that this fellow wears,
With gold all over.
    CÉLIMÈNE (*to* ALCESTE):
5   You'd best go down and see.
Or — have him enter.

    SCENE VII. [ALCESTE, CÉLIMÈNE, ÉLIANTE,
    ACASTE, PHILINTE, CLITANDRE, GUARD.]

    ALCESTE (*confronting the* GUARD):
          Well, what do you want with me?
Come in, Sir.
    GUARD: I've a word, Sir, for your ear.
    ALCESTE:
Speak it aloud, Sir; I shall strive to hear.
    GUARD:
The Marshals have instructed me to say
5 You must report to them without delay.
    ALCESTE:
Who? Me, Sir?
    GUARD: Yes, Sir; you.
    ALCESTE: But what do they want?
    PHILINTE (*to* ALCESTE):
To scotch your silly quarrel with Oronte.
    CÉLIMÈNE (*to* PHILINTE):
What quarrel?
    PHILINTE: Oronte and he have fallen out
Over some verse he spoke his mind about;
10 The Marshals wish to arbitrate the matter.
    ALCESTE:
Never shall I equivocate or flatter!
    PHILINTE:
You'd best obey their summons; come, let's go.
    ALCESTE:
How can they mend our quarrel, I'd like to
    know?
Am I to make a cowardly retraction,
15 And praise those jingles to his satisfaction?
I'll not recant; I've judged that sonnet rightly.
It's bad.
    PHILINTE:
        But you might say so more politely....
    ALCESTE:
I'll not back down; his verses make me sick.
    PHILINTE:
If only you could be more politic!
But come, let's go.
20   ALCESTE: I'll go, but I won't unsay
A single word.
    PHILINTE: Well, let's be on our way.
    ALCESTE:
Till I am ordered by my lord the King
To praise that poem, I shall say the thing

Is scandalous, by God, and that the poet
Ought to be hanged for having the nerve to
    show it.   25

    (*To* CLITANDRE *and* ACASTE, *who are laugh-
ing.*)

By heaven, Sirs, I really didn't know
That I was being humorous.
    CÉLIMÈNE: Go, Sir, go;
Settle your business.
    ALCESTE: I shall, and when I'm through,
I shall return to settle things with you.

ACT III

SCENE I. [CLITANDRE, ACASTE.]

    CLITANDRE:
Dear Marquess, how contented you appear;
All things delight you, nothing mars your
    cheer.
Can you, in perfect honesty, declare
That you've a right to be so debonair?
    ACASTE:
By Jove, when I survey myself, I find   5
No cause whatever for distress of mind.
I'm young and rich; I can in modesty
Lay claim to an exalted pedigree;
And owing to my name and my condition
I shall not want for honors and position.   10
Then as to courage, that most precious trait,
I seem to have it, as was proved of late
Upon the field of honor, where my bearing,
They say, was very cool and rather daring.
I've wit, of course; and taste in such perfection 15
That I can judge without the least reflection,
And at the theater, which is my delight,
Can make or break a play on opening night,
And lead the crowd in hisses or bravos,
And generally be known as one who knows. 20
I'm clever, handsome, gracefully polite;
My waist is small, my teeth are strong and
    white;
As for my dress, the world's astonished eyes
Assure me that I bear away the prize.
I find myself in favor everywhere,   25
Honored by men, and worshiped by the fair;
And since these things are so, it seems to me
I'm justified in my complacency.
    CLITANDRE:
Well, if so many ladies hold you dear,
Why do you press a hopeless courtship here? 30

ACASTE:
Hopeless, you say? I'm not the sort of fool
That likes his ladies difficult and cool.
Men who are awkward, shy, and peasantish
May pine for heartless beauties, if they wish,
35 Grovel before them, bear their cruelties,
Woo them with tears and sighs and bended knees,
And hope by dogged faithfulness to gain
What their poor merits never could obtain.
For men like me, however, it makes no sense
40 To love on trust, and foot the whole expense.
Whatever any lady's merits be,
I think, thank God, that I'm as choice as she;
That if my heart is kind enough to burn
For her, she owes me something in return;
45 And that in any proper love affair
The partners must invest an equal share.
CLITANDRE:
You think, then, that our hostess favors you?
ACASTE:
I've reason to believe that that is true.
CLITANDRE:
How did you come to such a mad conclusion?
You're blind, dear fellow. This is sheer delu-
50 sion.
ACASTE:
All right, then: I'm deluded and I'm blind.
CLITANDRE:
Whatever put the notion in your mind?
ACASTE:
Delusion.
CLITANDRE:
What persuades you that you're right?
ACASTE:
I'm blind.
CLITANDRE:
But have you any proofs to cite?
ACASTE:
I tell you I'm deluded.
55 CLITANDRE: Have you, then,
Received some secret pledge from Célimène?
ACASTE:
Oh, no: she scorns me.
CLITANDRE: Tell me the truth, I beg.
ACASTE:
She just can't bear me.
CLITANDRE: Ah, don't pull my leg.
Tell me what hope she's given you, I pray.
ACASTE:
60 I'm hopeless, and it's you who win the day.
She hates me thoroughly, and I'm so vexed
I mean to hang myself on Tuesday next.

CLITANDRE:
Dear Marquess, let us have an armistice
And make a treaty. What do you say to this?
If ever one of us can plainly prove 65
That Célimène encourages his love,
The other must abandon hope, and yield,
And leave him in possession of the field.
ACASTE:
Now, there's a bargain that appeals to me;
With all my heart, dear Marquess, I agree. 70
But hush.

SCENE II. [CÉLIMÈNE, ACASTE, CLITANDRE.]

CÉLIMÈNE:
Still here?
CLITANDRE: 'Twas love that stayed our feet.
CÉLIMÈNE:
I think I heard a carriage in the street.
Whose is it? D'you know?

SCENE III. [CÉLIMÈNE, ACASTE, CLITANDRE, BASQUE.]

BASQUE: Arsinoé is here,
Madame.
CÉLIMÈNE:
Arsinoé, you say? Oh, dear.
BASQUE:
Éliante is entertaining her below.
CÉLIMÈNE:
What brings the creature here, I'd like to know?
ACASTE:
They say she's dreadfully prudish, but in fact 5
I think her piety . . .
CÉLIMÈNE: It's all an act.
At heart she's worldly, and her poor success
In snaring men explains her prudishness.
It breaks her heart to see the beaux and gallants
Engrossed by other women's charms and talents, 10
And so she's always in a jealous rage
Against the faulty standards of the age.
She lets the world believe that she's a prude
To justify her loveless solitude,
And strives to put a brand of moral shame 15
On all the graces that she cannot claim.
But still she'd love a lover; and Alceste
Appears to be the one she'd love the best.

His visits here are poison to her pride;
She seems to think I've lured him from her
20   side;
And everywhere, at court or in the town,
The spiteful, envious woman runs me down.
In short, she's just as stupid as can be,
Vicious and arrogant in the last degree,
25 And . . .

SCENE IV. [ARSINOÉ, CÉLIMÈNE, CLITANDRE,
ACASTE.]

CÉLIMÈNE:
        Ah! What happy chance has brought
you here?
I've thought about you ever so much, my dear.
ARSINOÉ:
I've come to tell you something you should
know.
CÉLIMÈNE:
How good of you to think of doing so!

(CLITANDRE and ACASTE go out, laughing.)

SCENE V. [ARSINOÉ, CÉLIMÈNE.]

ARSINOÉ:
It's just as well those gentlemen didn't tarry.
CÉLIMÈNE:
Shall we sit down?
ARSINOÉ   That won't be necessary.
Madam, the flame of friendship ought to burn
Brightest in matters of the most concern,
And as there's nothing which concerns us
5   more
Than honor, I have hastened to your door
To bring you, as your friend, some informa-
       tion
About the status of your reputation.
I visited, last night, some virtuous folk,
And, quite by chance, it was of you they
10   spoke;
There was, I fear, no tendency to praise
Your light behavior and your dashing ways.
The quantity of gentlemen you see
And your by now notorious coquetry
15 Were both so vehemently criticized
By everyone, that I was much surprised.
Of course, I needn't tell you where I stood;
I came to your defense as best I could,
Assured them you were harmless, and declared
20 Your soul was absolutely unimpaired.

But there are some things, you must realize,
One can't excuse, however hard one tries,
And I was forced at last into conceding
That your behavior, Madam, is misleading,
That it makes a bad impression, giving rise   25
To ugly gossip and obscene surmise,
And that if you were more *overtly* good,
You wouldn't be so much misunderstood.
Not that I think you've been unchaste — no!
       no!
The saints preserve me from a thought so low! 30
But mere good conscience never did suffice:
One must avoid the outward show of vice.
Madam, you're too intelligent, I'm sure,
To think my motives anything but pure
In offering you this counsel — which I do   35
Out of a zealous interest in you.
CÉLIMÈNE:
Madam, I haven't taken you amiss;
I'm very much obliged to you for this;
And I'll at once discharge the obligation
By telling you about *your* reputation.   40
You've been so friendly as to let me know
What certain people say of me, and so
I mean to follow your benign example
By offering you a somewhat similar sample.
The other day, I went to an affair   45
And found some most distinguished people
       there
Discussing piety, both false and true.
The conversation soon came round to you.
Alas! Your prudery and bustling zeal
Appeared to have a very slight appeal.   50
Your affectation of a grave demeanor,
Your endless talk of virtue and of honor,
The aptitude of your suspicious mind
For finding sin where there is none to find,
Your towering self-esteem, that pitying face   55
With which you contemplate the human race,
Your sermonizings and your sharp aspersions
On people's pure and innocent diversions —
All these were mentioned, Madam, and, in fact,
Were roundly and concertedly attacked.   60
"What good," they said, "are all these outward
       shows,
When everything belies her pious pose?
She prays incessantly; but then, they say,
She beats her maids and cheats them of their
       pay;
She shows her zeal in every holy place,   65
But still she's vain enough to paint her face;
She holds that naked statues are immoral,
But with a naked *man* she'd have no quarrel."

Of course, I said to everybody there
70 That they were being viciously unfair;
But still they were disposed to criticize you,
And all agreed that someone should advise you
To leave the morals of the world alone,
And worry rather more about your own.
They felt that one's self-knowledge should be
75   great
Before one thinks of setting others straight;
That one should learn the art of living well
Before one threatens other men with hell,
And that the Church is best equipped, no
    doubt,
80 To guide our souls and root our vices out.
Madam, you're too intelligent, I'm sure,
To think my motives anything but pure
In offering you this counsel — which I do
Out of a zealous interest in you.
    ARSINOÉ:
85 I dared not hope for gratitude, but I
Did not expect so acid a reply;
I judge, since you've been so extremely tart,
That my good counsel pierced you to the
    heart.
    CÉLIMÈNE:
Far from it, Madam. Indeed, it seems to me
90 We ought to trade advice more frequently.
One's vision of oneself is so defective
That it would be an excellent corrective.
If you are willing, Madam, let's arrange
Shortly to have another frank exchange
95 In which we'll tell each other, *entre nous*,
What you've heard tell of me, and I of you.
    ARSINOÉ:
Oh, people never censure you, my dear;
It's me they criticize. Or so I hear.
    CÉLIMÈNE:
Madam, I think we either blame or praise
100 According to our taste and length of days.
There is a time of life for coquetry,
And there's a season, too, for prudery.
When all one's charms are gone, it is, I'm
    sure,
Good strategy to be devout and pure:
105 It makes one seem a little less forsaken.
Some day, perhaps, I'll take the road you've
    taken:
Time brings all things. But I have time
    aplenty,
And see no cause to be a prude at twenty.
    ARSINOÉ:
You give your age in such a gloating tone
110 That one would think I was an ancient crone;
We're not so far apart, in sober truth,

That you can mock me with a boast of youth!
Madam, you baffle me. I wish I knew
What moves you to provoke me as you do.
    CÉLIMÈNE:
For my part, Madam, I should like to know   115
Why you abuse me everywhere you go.
Is it my fault, dear lady, that your hand
Is not, alas, in very great demand?
If men admire me, if they pay me court
And daily make me offers of the sort   120
You'd dearly love to have them make to you,
How can I help it? What would you have me
    do?
If what you want is lovers, please feel free
To take as many as you can from me.
    ARSINOÉ:
Oh, come. D'you think the world is losing
    sleep   125
Over the flock of lovers which you keep,
Or that we find it difficult to guess
What price you pay for their devotedness?
Surely you don't expect us to suppose
Mere merit could attract so many beaux?   130
It's not your virtue that they're dazzled by;
Nor is it virtuous love for which they sigh.
You're fooling no one, Madam; the world's not
    blind;
There's many a lady heaven has designed
To call men's noblest, tenderest feelings out, 135
Who has no lovers dogging her about;
From which it's plain that lovers nowadays
Must be acquired in bold and shameless ways,
And only pay one court for such reward
As modesty and virtue can't afford.   140
Then don't be quite so puffed up, if you
    please,
About your tawdry little victories;
Try, if you can, to be a shade less vain,
And treat the world with somewhat less dis-
    dain.
If one were envious of your amours,   145
One soon could have a following like yours;
Lovers are no great trouble to collect
If one prefers them to one's self-respect.
    CÉLIMÈNE:
Collect them then, my dear; I'd love to see
You demonstrate that charming theory;   150
Who knows, you might . . .
    ARSINOÉ: Now, Madam, that will do;
It's time to end this trying interview.
My coach is late in coming to your door,
Or I'd have taken leave of you before.
    CÉLIMÈNE:
Oh, please don't feel that you must rush away; 155

I'd be delighted, Madam, if you'd stay.
However, lest my conversation bore you,
Let me provide some better company for you;
This gentleman, who comes most apropos,
160 Will please you more than I could do, I know.

SCENE VI. [ALCESTE, CÉLIMÈNE, ARSINOÉ.]

CÉLIMÈNE:
Alceste, I have a little note to write
Which simply must go out before tonight;
Please entertain *Madame*; I'm sure that she
Will overlook my incivility.

SCENE VII. [ALCESTE, ARSINOÉ.]

ARSINOÉ:
Well, Sir, our hostess graciously contrives
For us to chat until my coach arrives;
And I shall be forever in her debt
For granting me this little tête-à-tête.
5 We women very rightly give our hearts
To men of noble character and parts,
And your especial merits, dear Alceste,
Have roused the deepest sympathy in my
    breast.
Oh, how I wish they had sufficient sense
10 At court, to recognize your excellence!
They wrong you greatly, Sir. How it must hurt
    you
Never to be rewarded for your virtue!
ALCESTE:
Why, Madam, what cause have I to feel
    aggrieved?
What great and brilliant thing have I
    achieved?
15 What service have I rendered to the King
That I should look to him for anything?
ARSINOÉ:
Not everyone who's honored by the State
Has done great services. A man must wait
Till time and fortune offer him the chance.
20 Your merit, Sir, is obvious at a glance,
And . . .
ALCESTE:
    Ah, forget my merit; I am not neglected.
The court, I think, can hardly be expected
To mine men's souls for merit, and unearth
Our hidden virtues and our secret worth.
ARSINOÉ:
Some virtues, though, are far too bright to
25   hide;
Yours are acknowledged, Sir, on every side.

Indeed, I've heard you warmly praised of late
By persons of considerable weight.
ALCESTE:
This fawning age has praise for everyone,
And all distinctions, Madam, are undone.   30
All things have equal honor nowadays,
And no one should be gratified by praise.
To be admired, one only need exist,
And every lackey's on the honors list.
ARSINOÉ:
I only wish, Sir, that you had your eye   35
On some position at court, however high;
You'd only have to hint at such a notion
For me to set the proper wheels in motion;
I've certain friendships I'd be glad to use
To get you any office you might choose.   40
ALCESTE:
Madam, I fear that any such ambition
Is wholly foreign to my disposition.
The soul God gave me isn't of the sort
That prospers in the weather of a court.
It's all too obvious that I don't possess   45
The virtues necessary for success.
My one great talent is for speaking plain;
I've never learned to flatter or to feign;
And anyone so stupidly sincere
Had best not seek a courtier's career.   50
Outside the court, I know, one must dispense
With honors, privilege, and influence;
But still one gains the right, foregoing these,
Not to be tortured by the wish to please.
One needn't live in dread of snubs and slights,   55
Nor praise the verse that every idiot writes,
Nor humor silly Marquesses, nor bestow
Politic sighs on Madam So-and-So.
ARSINOÉ:
Forget the court, then; let the matter rest.
But I've another cause to be distressed   60
About your present situation, Sir.
It's to your love affair that I refer.
She whom you love, and who pretends to love
    you,
Is, I regret to say, unworthy of you.
ALCESTE:
Why, Madam? Can you seriously intend   65
To make so grave a charge against your friend?
ARSINOÉ:
Alas, I must. I've stood aside too long
And let that lady do you grievous wrong;
But now my debt to conscience shall be paid:
I tell you that your love has been betrayed.   70
ALCESTE:
I thank you, Madam; you're extremely kind.
Such words are soothing to a lover's mind.

ARSINOÉ:

Yes, though she *is* my friend, I say again
You're very much too good for Célimène.
75 She's wantonly misled you from the start.

ALCESTE:

You may be right; who knows another's heart?
But ask yourself if it's the part of charity
To shake my soul with doubts of her sincerity.

ARSINOÉ:

Well, if you'd rather be a dupe than doubt
her,
80 That's your affair. I'll say no more about her.

ALCESTE:

Madam, you know that doubt and vague
suspicion
Are painful to a man in my position;
It's most unkind to worry me this way
Unless you've some real proof of what you say.

ARSINOÉ:

85 Sir, say no more: all doubts shall be removed,
And all that I've been saying shall be proved.
You've only to escort me home, and there
We'll look into the heart of this affair.
I've ocular evidence which will persuade you
Beyond a doubt, that Célimène's betrayed
90 you.
Then, if you're saddened by that revelation,
Perhaps I can provide some consolation.

ACT IV

SCENE I. [ÉLIANTE, PHILINTE.]

PHILINTE:

Madam, he acted like a stubborn child;
I thought they never would be reconciled;
In vain we reasoned, threatened, and appealed;
He stood his ground and simply would not
yield.
5 The Marshals, I feel sure, have never heard
An argument so splendidly absurd.
"No, gentlemen," said he, "I'll not retract.
His verse is bad: extremely bad, in fact.
Surely it does the man no harm to know it.
10 Does it disgrace him, not to be a poet?
A gentleman may be respected still,
Whether he writes a sonnet well or ill.
That I dislike his verse should not offend him;
In all that touches honor, I commend him;
15 He's noble, brave, and virtuous — but I fear
He can't in truth be called a sonneteer.

I'll gladly praise his wardrobe; I'll endorse
His dancing, or the way he sits a horse;
But, gentlemen, I cannot praise his rhyme.
In fact, it ought to be a capital crime   20
For anyone so sadly unendowed
To write a sonnet, and read the thing aloud."
At length he fell into a gentler mood
And, striking a concessive attitude,
He paid Oronte the following courtesies: 25
"Sir, I regret that I'm so hard to please,
And I'm profoundly sorry that your lyric
Failed to provoke me to a panegyric."
After these curious words, the two embraced,
And then the hearing was adjourned — in
haste.   30

ÉLIANTE:

His conduct has been very singular lately;
Still, I confess that I respect him greatly.
The honesty in which he takes such pride
Has — to my mind — it's noble, heroic side.
In this false age, such candor seems outra-
geous;   35
But I could wish that it were more contagious.

PHILINTE:

What most intrigues me in our friend Alceste
Is the grand passion that rages in his breast.
The sullen humors he's compounded of
Should not, I think, dispose his heart to love;   40
But since they do, it puzzles me still more
That he should choose your cousin to adore.

ÉLIANTE:

It does, indeed, belie the theory
That love is born of gentle sympathy,
And that the tender passion must be based   45
On sweet accords of temper and of taste.

PHILINTE:

Does she return his love, do you suppose?

ÉLIANTE:

Ah, that's a difficult question, Sir. Who knows?
How can we judge the truth of her devotion?
Her heart's a stranger to its own emotion.   50
Sometimes it thinks it loves, when no love's
there;
At other times it loves quite unaware.

PHILINTE:

I rather think Alceste is in for more
Distress and sorrow than he's bargained for;
Were he of my mind, Madam, his affection   55
Would turn in quite a different direction,
And we would see him more responsive to
The kind regard which he receives from you.

ÉLIANTE:

Sir, I believe in frankness, and I'm inclined,

60 In matters of the heart, to speak my mind.
I don't oppose his love for her; indeed,
I hope with all my heart that he'll succeed,
And were it in my power, I'd rejoice
In giving him the lady of his choice.
65 But if, as happens frequently enough
In love affairs, he meets with a rebuff —
If Célimène should grant some rival's suit —
I'd gladly play the role of substitute;
Nor would his tender speeches please me less
70 Because they'd once been made without suc-
    cess.
PHILINTE:
Well, Madam, as for me, I don't oppose
Your hopes in this affair; and heaven knows
That in my conversations with the man
I plead your cause as often as I can.
75 But if those two should marry, and so remove
All chance that he will offer you his love,
Then I'll declare my own, and hope to see
Your gracious favor pass from him to me.
In short, should you be cheated of Alceste,
80 I'd be most happy to be second best.
ÉLIANTE:
Philinte, you're teasing.
PHILINTE: Ah, Madam, never fear;
No words of mine were ever so sincere,
And I shall live in fretful expectation
Till I can make a fuller declaration.

SCENE II. [ALCESTE, ÉLIANTE, PHILINTE.]

ALCESTE:
Avenge me, Madam! I must have satisfaction,
Or this great wrong will drive me to distrac-
    tion!
ÉLIANTE:
Why, what's the matter? What's upset you so?
ALCESTE:
Madam, I've had a mortal, mortal blow.
5 If Chaos repossessed the universe,
I swear I'd not be shaken any worse.
I'm ruined....I can say no more....My
    soul ...
ÉLIANTE:
Do try, Sir, to regain your self-control.
ALCESTE:
Just heaven! Why were so much beauty and
    grace
10 Bestowed on one so vicious and so base?
ÉLIANTE:
Once more, Sir, tell us. . . .
ALCESTE: My world has gone to wrack;

I'm — I'm betrayed; she's stabbed me in the
    back:
Yes, Célimène (who would have thought it of
    her?)
Is false to me, and has another lover.
ÉLIANTE:
Are you quite certain? Can you prove these
    things?   15
PHILINTE:
Lovers are prey to wild imaginings
And jealous fancies. No doubt there's some
    mistake. . . .
ALCESTE:
Mind your own business, Sir, for heaven's sake.
(To ÉLIANTE.) Madam, I have the proof that
    you demand
Here in my pocket, penned by her own hand.   20
Yes, all the shameful evidence one could want
Lies in this letter written to Oronte —
Oronte! whom I felt sure she couldn't love,
And hardly bothered to be jealous of.
PHILINTE:
Still, in a letter, appearances may deceive;   25
This may not be so bad as you believe.
ALCESTE:
Once more I beg you, Sir, to let me be;
Tend to your own affairs; leave mine to me.
ÉLIANTE:
Compose yourself; this anguish that you
    feel . . .
ALCESTE:
Is something, Madam, you alone can heal.   30
My outraged heart, beside itself with grief,
Appeals to you for comfort and relief.
Avenge me on your cousin, whose unjust
And faithless nature has deceived my trust;
Avenge a crime your pure soul must detest.   35
ÉLIANTE:
But how, Sir?
ALCESTE:
       Madam, this heart within my breast
Is yours; pray take it; redeem my heart from
    her,
And so avenge me on my torturer.
Let her be punished by the fond emotion,
The ardent love, the bottomless devotion,   40
The faithful worship which this heart of mine
Will offer up to yours as to a shrine.
ÉLIANTE:
You have my sympathy, Sir, in all you suffer;
Nor do I scorn the noble heart you offer;
But I suspect you'll soon be mollified,   45
And this desire for vengeance will subside.

When some belovèd hand has done us wrong
We thirst for retribution — but not for long;
However dark the deed that she's committed,
50 A lovely culprit's very soon acquitted.
Nothing's so stormy as an injured lover,
And yet no storm so quickly passes over.
      ALCESTE:
No, Madam, no — this is no lovers' spat;
I'll not forgive her; it's gone too far for that;
55 My mind's made up; I'll kill myself before
I waste my hopes upon her any more.
Ah, here she is. My wrath intensifies.
I shall confront her with her tricks and lies,
And crush her utterly, and bring you then
60 A heart no longer slave to Célimène.

      SCENE III. [CÉLIMÈNE, ALCESTE.]

      ALCESTE (aside):
Sweet heaven, help me to control my passion.
      CÉLIMÈNE (aside):
Oh, Lord. (To ALCESTE.) Why stand there
      staring in that fashion?
And what d'you mean by those dramatic sighs,
And that malignant glitter in your eyes?
      ALCESTE:
I mean that sins which cause the blood to
5   freeze
Look innocent beside your treacheries;
That nothing Hell's or Heaven's wrath could
      do
Ever produced so bad a thing as you.
      CÉLIMÈNE:
Your compliments were always sweet and
      pretty.
      ALCESTE:
10 Madam, it's not the moment to be witty.
No, blush and hang your head; you've ample
      reason,
Since I've the fullest evidence of your treason.
Ah, this is what my sad heart prophesied;
Now all my anxious fears are verified;
15 My dark suspicion and my gloomy doubt
Divined the truth, and now the truth is out.
For all your trickery, I was not deceived;
It was my bitter stars that I believed.
But don't imagine that you'll go scot-free;
20 You shan't misuse me with impunity.
I know that love's irrational and blind;
I know the heart's not subject to the mind,
And can't be reasoned into beating faster;
I know each soul is free to choose its master;
25 Therefore had you but spoken from the heart,

Rejecting my attention from the start,
I'd have no grievance, or at any rate
I could complain of nothing but my fate.
Ah, but so falsely to encourage me —
That was a treason and a treachery   30
For which you cannot suffer too severely,
And you shall pay for that behavior dearly.
Yes, now I have no pity, not a shred;
My temper's out of hand; I've lost my head;
Shocked by the knowledge of your double-deal-
      ings,   35
My reason can't restrain my savage feelings;
A righteous wrath deprives me of my senses,
And I won't answer for the consequences.
      CÉLIMÈNE:
What does this outburst mean? Will you
      please explain?
Have you, by any chance, gone quite insane?   40
      ALCESTE:
Yes, yes, I went insane the day I fell
A victim to your black and fatal spell,
Thinking to meet with some sincerity
Among the treacherous charms that beckoned
      me.
      CÉLIMÈNE:
Pooh. Of what treachery can you complain?   45
      ALCESTE:
How sly you are, how cleverly you feign!
But you'll not victimize me any more.
Look: here's a document you've seen before.
This evidence, which I acquired today,
Leaves you, I think, without a thing to say.   50
      CÉLIMÈNE:
Is this what sent you into such a fit?
      ALCESTE:
You should be blushing at the sight of it.
      CÉLIMÈNE:
Ought I to blush? I truly don't see why.
      ALCESTE:
Ah, now you're being bold as well as sly;
Since there's no signature, perhaps you'll
      claim ...   55
      CÉLIMÈNE:
I wrote it, whether or not it bears my name.
      ALCESTE:
And you can view with equanimity
This proof of your disloyalty to me!
      CÉLIMÈNE:
Oh, don't be so outrageous and extreme.
      ALCESTE:
You take this matter lightly, it would seem.   60
Was it no wrong to me, no shame to you,
That you should send Oronte this billet-doux?

CÉLIMÈNE:
Oronte! Who said it was for him?
ALCESTE: Why, those
Who brought me this example of your prose.
But what's the difference? If you wrote the
65   letter
To someone else, it pleases me no better.
My grievance and your guilt remain the same.
CÉLIMÈNE:
But need you rage, and need I blush for
    shame,
If this was written to a *woman* friend?
ALCESTE:
70   Ah! Most ingenious. I'm impressed no end;
And after that incredible evasion
Your guilt is clear. I need no more persuasion.
How dare you try so clumsy a deception?
D'you think I'm wholly wanting in perception?
75   Come, come, let's see how brazenly you'll try
To bolster up so palpable a lie:
Kindly construe this ardent closing section
As nothing more than sisterly affection!
Here, let me read it. Tell me, if you dare to,
That this is for a woman . . .
80   CÉLIMÈNE: I don't care to.
What right have you to badger and berate me,
And so highhandedly interrogate me?
ALCESTE:
Now, don't be angry; all I ask of you
Is that you justify a phrase or two . . .
CÉLIMÈNE:
85   No, I shall not. I utterly refuse,
And you may take those phrases as you choose.
ALCESTE:
Just show me how this letter could be meant
For a woman's eyes, and I shall be content.
CÉLIMÈNE:
No, no, it's for Oronte; you're perfectly right.
90   I welcome his attentions with delight,
I prize his character and his intellect,
And everything is just as you suspect.
Come, do your worst now; give your rage free
    rein;
But kindly cease to bicker and complain.
ALCESTE (*aside*):
95   Good God! Could anything be more inhuman?
Was ever a heart so mangled by a woman?
When I complain of how she has betrayed me,
She bridles, and commences to upbraid me!
She tries my tortured patience to the limit;
100   She won't deny her guilt; she glories in it!
And yet my heart's too faint and cowardly
To break these chains of passion, and be free,

To scorn her as it should, and rise above
This unrewarded, mad, and bitter love.
(*To* CÉLIMÈNE.) Ah, traitress, in how confident
    a fashion   105
You take advantage of my helpless passion,
And use my weakness for your faithless charms
To make me once again throw down my arms!
But do at least deny this black transgression;
Take back that mocking and perverse confes-
    sion;   110
Defend this letter and your innocence,
And I, poor fool, will aid in your defense.
Pretend, pretend, that you are just and true,
And I shall make myself believe in you.
CÉLIMÈNE:
Oh, stop it. Don't be such a jealous dunce,   115
Or I shall leave off loving you at once.
Just why should I *pretend*? What could impel
    me
To stoop so low as that? And kindly tell me
Why, if I loved another, I shouldn't merely
Inform you of it, simply and sincerely!   120
I've told you where you stand, and that admis-
    sion
Should altogether clear me of suspicion;
After so generous a guarantee,
What right have you to harbor doubts of me?
Since women are (from natural reticence)   125
Reluctant to declare their sentiments,
And since the honor of our sex requires
That we conceal our amorous desires,
Ought any man for whom such laws are
    broken
To question what the oracle has spoken?   130
Should he not rather feel an obligation
To trust that most obliging declaration?
Enough, now. Your suspicions quite disgust
    me;
Why should I love a man who doesn't trust
    me?
I cannot understand why I continue,   135
Fool that I am, to take an interest in you.
I ought to choose a man less prone to doubt,
And give you something to be vexed about.
ALCESTE:
Ah, what a poor enchanted fool I am;
These gentle words, no doubt, were all a sham,   140
But destiny requires me to entrust
My happiness to you, and so I must.
I'll love you to the bitter end, and see
How false and treacherous you dare to be.
CÉLIMÈNE:
No, you don't really love me as you ought.   145

ALCESTE:
I love you more than can be said or thought;
Indeed, I wish you were in such distress
That I might show my deep devotedness.
Yes, I could wish that you were wretchedly
    poor,
150 Unloved, uncherished, utterly obscure;
That fate had set you down upon the earth
Without possessions, rank, or gentle birth;
Then, by the offer of my heart, I might
Repair the great injustice of your plight;
155 I'd raise you from the dust, and proudly prove
The purity and vastness of my love.
CÉLIMÈNE:
This is a strange benevolence indeed!
God grant that I may never be in need. . . .
Ah, here's Monsieur Dubois, in quaint dis-
    guise.

SCENE IV. [CÉLIMÈNE, ALCESTE, DUBOIS.]

ALCESTE:
Well, why this costume? Why those fright-
    ened eyes?
What ails you?
DUBOIS:
          Well, Sir, things are most mysterious.
ALCESTE:
What do you mean?
DUBOIS: I fear they're very serious.
ALCESTE:
What?
DUBOIS:
    Shall I speak more loudly?
ALCESTE: Yes; speak out.
DUBOIS:
Isn't there someone here, Sir?
5   ALCESTE: Speak, you lout!
Stop wasting time.
DUBOIS: Sir, we must slip away.
ALCESTE:
How's that?
DUBOIS: We must decamp without delay.
ALCESTE:
Explain yourself.
DUBOIS: I tell you we must fly.
ALCESTE:
What for?
DUBOIS:
          We mustn't pause to say good-by.
ALCESTE:
Now what d'you mean by all of this, you
10   clown?

DUBOIS:
I mean, Sir, that we've got to leave this town.
ALCESTE:
I'll tear you limb from limb and joint from
    joint
If you don't come more quickly to the point.
DUBOIS:
Well, Sir, today a man in a black suit,
Who wore a black and ugly scowl to boot,   15
Left us a document scrawled in such a hand
As even Satan couldn't understand.
It bears upon your lawsuit, I don't doubt;
But all hell's devils couldn't make it out.
ALCESTE:
Well, well, go on. What then? I fail to see   20
How this event obliges us to flee.
DUBOIS:
Well, Sir, an hour later, hardly more,
A gentleman who's often called before
Came looking for you in an anxious way.
Not finding you, he asked me to convey   25
(Knowing I could be trusted with the same)
The following message. . . . Now, what *was* his
    name?
ALCESTE:
Forget his name, you idiot. What did he say?
DUBOIS:
Well, it was one of your friends, Sir, anyway.
He warned you to begone, and he suggested   30
That if you stay, you may well be arrested.
ALCESTE:
What? Nothing more specific? Think, man,
    think!
DUBOIS:
No, Sir. He had me bring him pen and ink,
And dashed you off a letter which, I'm sure,
Will render things distinctly less obscure.   35
ALCESTE:
Well — let me have it!
CÉLIMÈNE: What *is* this all about?
ALCESTE:
God knows; but I have hopes of finding out.
How long am I to wait, you blitherer?
DUBOIS (*after a protracted search for the
    letter*):
I must have left it on your table, Sir.
ALCESTE:
I ought to . . .
CÉLIMÈNE:
          No, no, keep your self-control;   40
Go find out what's behind his rigmarole.
ALCESTE:
It seems that fate, no matter what I do,

Has sworn that I may not converse with you;
But, Madam, pray permit your faithful lover
45   To try once more before the day is over.

ACT V

SCENE I. [ALCESTE, PHILINTE.]

ALCESTE:
No, it's too much. My mind's made up, I tell
    you.
PHILINTE:
Why should this blow, however hard, compel
    you . . .
ALCESTE:
No, no, don't waste your breath in argument;
Nothing you say will alter my intent;
5   This age is vile, and I've made up my mind
To have no further commerce with mankind.
Did not truth, honor, decency, and the laws
Oppose my enemy and approve my cause?
My claims were justified in all men's sight;
10   I put my trust in equity and right;
Yet, to my horror and the world's disgrace,
Justice is mocked, and I have lost my case!
A scoundrel whose dishonesty is notorious
Emerges from another lie victorious!
15   Honor and right condone his brazen fraud,
While rectitude and decency applaud!
Before his smirking face, the truth stands
    charmed,
And virtue conquered, and the law disarmed!
His crime is sanctioned by a court decree!
20   And not content with what he's done to me,
The dog now seeks to ruin me by stating
That I composed a book now circulating,
A book so wholly criminal and vicious
That even to speak its title is seditious!
25   Meanwhile Oronte, my rival, lends his credit
To the same libelous tale, and helps to spread
    it!
Oronte! a man of honor and of rank,
With whom I've been entirely fair and frank;
Who sought me out and forced me, willy-nilly,
30   To judge some verse I found extremely silly;
And who, because I properly refused
To flatter him, or see the truth abused,
Abets my enemy in a rotten slander!
There's the reward of honesty and candor!
35   The man will hate me to the end of time
For failing to commend his wretched rhyme!

And not this man alone, but all humanity
Do what they do from interest and vanity;
They prate of honor, truth, and righteousness,
But lie, betray, and swindle nonetheless.   40
Come then: man's villainy is too much to
    bear;
Let's leave this jungle and this jackal's lair.
Yes! treacherous and savage race of men,
You shall not look upon my face again.
PHILINTE:
Oh, don't rush into exile prematurely;   45
Things aren't as dreadful as you make them,
    surely.
It's rather obvious, since you're still at large,
That people don't believe your enemy's charge.
Indeed, his tale's so patently untrue
That it may do more harm to him than you.   50
ALCESTE:
Nothing could do that scoundrel any harm:
His frank corruption is his greatest charm,
And, far from hurting him, a further shame
Would only serve to magnify his name.
PHILINTE:
In any case, his bald prevarication   55
Has done no injury to your reputation,
And you may feel secure in that regard.
As for your lawsuit, it should not be hard
To have the case reopened, and contest
This judgment . . .
ALCESTE: No, no, let the verdict rest.   60
Whatever cruel penalty it may bring,
I wouldn't have it changed for anything.
It shows the times' injustice with such clarity
That I shall pass it down to our posterity
As a great proof and signal demonstration   65
Of the black wickedness of this generation.
It may cost twenty thousand francs; but I
Shall pay their twenty thousand, and gain
    thereby
The right to storm and rage at human evil,
And send the race of mankind to the devil.   70
PHILINTE:
Listen to me . . .
ALCESTE:
           Why? What can you possibly say?
Don't argue, Sir; your labor's thrown away.
Do you propose to offer lame excuses
For men's behavior and the times' abuses?
PHILINTE:
No, all you say I'll readily concede: 75
This is a low, conniving age indeed;
Nothing but trickery prospers nowadays,
And people ought to mend their shabby ways.

Yes, man's a beastly creature; but must we then
80 Abandon the society of men?
Here in the world, each human frailty
Provides occasion for philosophy,
And that is virtue's noblest exercise;
If honesty shone forth from all men's eyes,
85 If every heart were frank and kind and just.
What could our virtues do but gather dust
(Since their employment is to help us bear
The villainies of men without despair)?
A heart well-armed with virtue can endure. . . .
    ALCESTE:
90 Sir, you're a matchless reasoner, to be sure;
Your words are fine and full of cogency;
But don't waste time and eloquence on me.
My reason bids me go, for my own good.
My tongue won't lie and flatter as it should;
God knows what frankness it might next
95   commit,
And what I'd suffer on account of it.
Pray let me wait for Célimène's return
In peace and quiet. I shall shortly learn,
By her response to what I have in view,
100 Whether her love for me is feigned or true.
    PHILINTE:
Till then, let's visit Éliante upstairs.
    ALCESTE:
No, I am too weighed down with somber cares.
Go to her, do; and leave me with my gloom
Here in the darkened corner of this room.
    PHILINTE:
105 Why, that's no sort of company, my friend;
I'll see if Éliante will not descend.

SCENE II. [CÉLIMÈNE, ORONTE, ALCESTE.]

    ORONTE:
Yes, Madam, if you wish me to remain
Your true and ardent lover, you must deign
To give me some more positive assurance.
All this suspense is quite beyond endurance.
5 If your heart shares the sweet desires of mine,
Show me as much by some convincing sign;
And here's the sign I urgently suggest:
That you no longer tolerate Alceste,
But sacrifice him to my love, and sever
10 All your relations with the man forever.
    CÉLIMÈNE:
Why do you suddenly dislike him so?
You praised him to the skies not long ago.
    ORONTE:
Madam, that's not the point. I'm here to find
Which way your tender feelings are inclined.

Choose, if you please, between Alceste and me, 15
And I shall stay or go accordingly.
    ALCESTE (*emerging from the corner*):
Yes, Madam, choose; this gentleman's demand
Is wholly just, and I support his stand.
I too am true and ardent; I too am here
To ask you that you make your feelings clear. 20
No more delays, now; no equivocation;
The time has come to make your declaration.
    ORONTE:
Sir, I've no wish in any way to be
An obstacle to your felicity.
    ALCESTE:
Sir, I've no wish to share her heart with you; 25
That may sound jealous, but at least it's true.
    ORONTE:
If, weighing us, she leans in your direction . . .
    ALCESTE:
If she regards you with the least affection . . .
    ORONTE:
I swear I'll yield her to you there and then.
    ALCESTE:
I swear I'll never see her face again. 30
    ORONTE:
Now, Madam, tell us what we've come to hear.
    ALCESTE:
Madam, speak openly and have no fear.
    ORONTE:
Just say which one is to remain your lover.
    ALCESTE:
Just name one name, and it will all be over.
    ORONTE:
What! Is it possible that you're undecided? 35
    ALCESTE:
What! Can your feelings possibly be divided?
    CÉLIMÈNE:
Enough: this inquisition's gone too far:
How utterly unreasonable you are!
Not that I couldn't make the choice with ease;
My heart has no conflicting sympathies; 40
I know full well which one of you I favor,
And you'd not see me hesitate or waver.
But how can you expect me to reveal
So cruelly and bluntly what I feel?
I think it altogether too unpleasant 45
To choose between two men when both are present;
One's heart has means more subtle and more kind
Of letting its affections be divined,
Nor need one be uncharitably plain
To let a lover know he loves in vain. 50
    ORONTE:
No, no, speak plainly; I for one can stand it.
I beg you to be frank.

ALCESTE: And I demand it.
The simple truth is what I wish to know,
And there's no need for softening the blow.
55 You've made an art of pleasing everyone,
But now your days of coquetry are done:
You have no choice now, Madam, but to choose,
For I'll know what to think if you refuse;
I'll take your silence for a clear admission
60 That I'm entitled to my worst suspicion.
     ORONTE:
I thank you for this ultimatum, Sir,
And I may say I heartily concur.
     CÉLIMÈNE:
Really, this foolishness is very wearing:
Must you be so unjust and overbearing?
65 Haven't I told you why I must demur?
Ah, here's Éliante; I'll put the case to her.

     SCENE III. [ÉLIANTE, PHILINTE, CÉLIMÈNE,
         ORONTE, ALCESTE.]

     CÉLIMÈNE:
Cousin, I'm being persecuted here
By these two persons, who, it would appear,
Will not be satisfied till I confess
Which one I love the more, and which the less,
5 And tell the latter to his face that he
Is henceforth banished from my company.
Tell me, has ever such a thing been done?
     ÉLIANTE:
You'd best not turn to me; I'm not the one
To back you in a matter of this kind:
10 I'm all for those who frankly speak their mind.
     ORONTE:
Madam, you'll search in vain for a defender.
     ALCESTE:
You're beaten, Madam, and may as well sur-
     render.
     ORONTE:
Speak, speak, you must; and end this awful
     strain.
     ALCESTE:
Or don't, and your position will be plain.
     ORONTE:
15 A single word will close this painful scene.
     ALCESTE:
But if you're silent, I'll know what you mean.

     SCENE IV. [ARSINOÉ, CÉLIMÈNE, ÉLIANTE,
       ALCESTE, PHILINTE, ACASTE, CLITANDRE,
         ORONTE.]

     ACASTE (to CÉLIMÈNE):
Madam, with all due deference, we two
Have come to pick a little bone with you.

CLITANDRE (to ORONTE and ALCESTE):
I'm glad you're present, Sirs, as you'll soon
     learn,
Our business here is also your concern.
     ARSINOÉ (to CÉLIMÈNE):
Madam, I visit you so soon again   5
Only because of these two gentlemen,
Who came to me indignant and aggrieved
About a crime too base to be believed.
Knowing your virtue, having such confidence
     in it,
I couldn't think you guilty for a minute,   10
In spite of all their telling evidence;
And, rising above our little difference,
I've hastened here in friendship's name to see
You clear yourself of this great calumny.
     ACASTE:
Yes, Madam, let us see with what composure   15
You'll manage to respond to this disclosure.
You lately sent Clitandre this tender note.
     CLITANDRE:
And this one, for Acaste, you also wrote.
     ACASTE (to ORONTE and ALCESTE):
You'll recognize this writing, Sirs, I think;
The lady is so free with pen and ink   20
That you must know it all too well, I fear.
But listen: this is something you should hear.

     "How absurd you are to condemn my light-
heartedness in society, and to accuse me of
being happiest in the company of others.   25
Nothing could be more unjust; and if you do
not come to me instantly and beg pardon for
saying such a thing, I shall never forgive you as
long as I live. Our big bumbling friend the
Viscount . . ."   30

What a shame that he's not here.

     "Our big bumbling friend the Viscount,
whose name stands first in your complaint, is
hardly a man to my taste; and ever since the
day I watched him spend three-quarters of an   35
hour spitting into a well, so as to make circles
in the water, I have been unable to think
highly of him. As for the little Marquess . . ."

In all modesty, gentlemen, that is I.

     "As for the little Marquess, who sat squeez-   40
ing my hand for such a long while yesterday, I
find him in all respects the most trifling
creature alive; and the only things of value
about him are his cape and his sword. As for
the man with the green ribbons . . ."   45

(To ALCESTE.) It's your turn now, Sir.

"As for the man with the green ribbons, he
amuses me now and then with his bluntness
and his bearish ill-humor; but there are many
50 times indeed when I think him the greatest
bore in the world. And as for the sonneteer . . ."

(*To* ORONTE.) Here's your helping.

"And as for the sonneteer, who has taken it
55 into his head to be witty, and insists on being
an author in the teeth of opinion, I simply
cannot be bothered to listen to him, and his
prose wearies me quite as much as his poetry.
Be assured that I am not always so well-enter-
60 tained as you suppose; that I long for your
company, more than I dare to say, at all these
entertainments to which people drag me; and
that the presence of those one loves is the true
and perfect seasoning to all one's pleasures."

65   CLITANDRE: And now for me.

"Clitandre, whom you mention, and who so
pesters me with his saccharine speeches, is the
last man on earth for whom I could feel any
affection. He is quite mad to suppose that I
70 love him, and so are you, to doubt that you are
loved. Do come to your senses; exchange your
suppositions for his; and visit me as often as
possible, to help me bear the annoyance of his
unwelcome attentions."

75 It's sweet character that these letters show,
And what to call it, Madam, you well know.
Enough. We're off to make the world ac-
        quainted
With this sublime self-portrait that you've
        painted.
    ACASTE:
Madam, I'll make you no farewell oration;
80 No, you're not worthy of my indignation.
Far choicer hearts than yours, as you'll dis-
        cover,
Would like this little Marquess for a lover.

SCENE V. [CÉLIMÈNE, ÉLIANTE, ARSINOÉ, ALCESTE, ORONTE, PHILINTE.]

    ORONTE:
So! After all those loving letters you wrote,
You turn on me like this, and cut my throat!
And your dissembling, faithless heart, I find,
Has pledged itself by turns to all mankind!
5 How blind I've been! But now I clearly see;
I thank you, Madam, for enlightening me.
My heart is mine once more, and I'm content;

The loss of it shall be your punishment.
(*To* ALCESTE.) Sir, she is yours; I'll seek no
        more to stand
Between your wishes and this lady's hand.   10

SCENE VI. [CÉLIMÈNE, ÉLIANTE, ARSINOÉ, ALCESTE, PHILINTE.]

    ARSINOÉ (*to* CÉLIMÈNE):
Madam, I'm forced to speak. I'm far too
        stirred
To keep my counsel, after what I've heard.
I'm shocked and staggered by your want of
        morals.
It's not my way to mix in others' quarrels;
But really, when this fine and noble spirit,   5
This man of honor and surpassing merit,
Laid down the offering of his heart before you,
How *could* you . . .
    ALCESTE:
                Madam, permit me, I implore you,
To represent myself in this debate.
Don't bother, please, to be my advocate.   10
My heart, in any case, could not afford
To give your services their due reward;
And if I chose, for consolation's sake,
Some other lady, 'twould not be you I'd take.
    ARSINOÉ:
What makes you think you could, Sir? And
        how dare you   15
Imply that I've been trying to ensnare you?
If you can for a moment entertain
Such flattering fancies, you're extremely vain.
I'm not so interested as you suppose
In Célimène's discarded gigolos.   20
Get rid of that absurd illusion, do.
Women like me are not for such as you.
Stay with this creature, to whom you're so
        attached;
I've never seen two people better matched.

SCENE VII. [CÉLIMÈNE, ÉLIANTE, ALCESTE, PHILINTE.]

    ALCESTE (*to* CÉLIMÈNE):
Well, I've been still throughout this exposé,
Till everyone but me has said his say.
Come, have I shown sufficient self-restraint?
And may I now . . .
    CÉLIMÈNE: Yes, make your just complaint.
Reproach me freely, call me what you will;   5
You've every right to say I've used you ill.
I've wronged you, I confess it; and in my
        shame

I'll make no effort to escape the blame.
The anger of those others I could despise;
10 My guilt toward you I sadly recognize.
Your wrath is wholly justified, I fear;
I know how culpable I must appear,
I know all things bespeak my treachery,
And that, in short, you've grounds for hating
    me.
Do so; I give you leave.
15   ALCESTE: Ah, traitress — how,
How should I cease to love you, even now?
Though mind and will were passionately bent
On hating you, my heart would not consent.
(*To* ÉLIANTE *and* PHILINTE.) Be witness to my
    madness, both of you;
20 See what infatuation drives one to;
But wait; my folly's only just begun,
And I shall prove to you before I'm done
How strange the human heart is, and how far
From rational we sorry creatures are.
(*To* CÉLIMÈNE.) Woman, I'm willing to for-
25   get your shame,
And clothe your treacheries in a sweeter name;
I'll call them youthful errors, instead of crimes,
And lay the blame on these corrupting times.
My one condition is that you agree
30 To share my chosen fate, and fly with me
To that wild, trackless, solitary place
In which I shall forget the human race.
Only by such a course can you atone
For those atrocious letters; by that alone
35 Can you remove my present horror of you,
And make it possible for me to love you.
      CÉLIMÈNE:
What! *I* renounce the world at my young age,
And die of boredom in some hermitage?
      ALCESTE:
Ah, if you really loved me as you ought,
You wouldn't give the world a moment's
40   thought;
Must you have me, and all the world beside?
      CÉLIMÈNE:
Alas, at twenty one is terrified
Of solitude. I fear I lack the force
And depth of soul to take so stern a course.
45 But if my hand in marriage will content you,

Why, there's a plan which I might well
    consent to,
And . . .
      ALCESTE:
      No, I detest you now. I could excuse
Everything else, but since you thus refuse
To love me wholly, as a wife should do,
And see the world in me, as I in you,   50
Go! I reject your hand, and disenthrall
My heart from your enchantments, once for
    all.

SCENE VIII. [ÉLIANTE, ALCESTE, PHILINTE.]

      ALCESTE (*to* ÉLIANTE):
Madam, your virtuous beauty has no peer;
Of all this world you only are sincere;
I've long esteemed you highly, as you know;
Permit me ever to esteem you so,
And if I do not now request your hand,   5
Forgive me, Madam, and try to understand.
I feel unworthy of it; I sense that fate
Does not intend me for the married state,
That I should do you wrong by offering you
My shattered heart's unhappy residue,   10
And that in short . . .
      ÉLIANTE: Your argument's well taken:
Nor need you fear that I shall feel forsaken.
Were I to offer him this hand of mine,
Your friend Philinte, I think, would not
    decline.
      PHILINTE:
Ah, Madam, that's my heart's most cherished
    goal,   15
For which I'd gladly give my life and soul.
      ALCESTE (*to* ÉLIANTE *and* PHILINTE):
May you be true to all you now profess,
And so deserve unending happiness.
Meanwhile, betrayed and wronged in every-
    thing,
I'll flee this bitter world where vice is king, 20
And seek some spot unpeopled and apart
Where I'll be free to have an honest heart.
      PHILINTE:
Come, Madam, let's do everything we can
To change the mind of this unhappy man.

The introduction to this volume (pp. 9–10) makes the rather obvious point that in both tragedy and comedy we have characters who are motivated by some ideal, and that (for example) the tragic hero who hunts out the polluted man in Thebes or who kills his wife because he thinks she is unfaithful is neither more nor less impassioned than the comic lover who writes sonnets to his mistress' eyebrow. Whether the passion is noble or comic depends not on its depth, or its persistence, but on its context, and especially on its object.

The passion for honesty that drives Molière's misanthrope, Alceste, is said by the equable Éliante to have "its noble, heroic side," and her view has found wide acceptance among audiences and readers. Alceste is sometimes seen as a tragic figure caught in a comic world, and the play is sometimes said to be a sort of tragic comedy. Alceste demands honesty, and he fulminates against flattery and other forms of insincerity that apparently compose the entire life of the other figures. Surrounded by trimmers and gossips and worse, he alone (if we except the gentle Éliante) seems to hold to a noble ideal. The only other ideal given much prominence is Philinte's, a code of such easy tolerance that it is at times almost indistinguishable from mere passive acceptance of everything.

What case can be made that Alceste is comic, not tragic? A few points suggest themselves. First, this champion of honesty is in love (or thinks he is) with a coquette. What can be more comic than the apostle of plain-dealing being himself in the power of the irrational, especially when this power deposits him at the feet of Célimène, a woman who employs all the devices that in others infuriate him? Second, his demand for honesty is indiscriminate; he is as offended at trivial courtesies as at the law's injustice. Philinte "ought to die of self-disgust" for his "crime" of effusively greeting a casual acquaintance whose name he cannot even recall. So disproportionate is Alceste's passion that when he pops onstage in IV.II, saying to Éliante, "Avenge me, Madam," he is funny, though the words in themselves are scarcely amusing. It is worth comparing a few other lines in this scene with some roughly similar lines in *Othello*. Alceste (still talking to Éliante about Célimène's letter to a rival suitor) says, "My world has gone to wrack" ("Ah! tout est ruiné!"). When, early in the play, Brabantio had cautioned Othello that Desdemona might deceive him, Othello had said, "My life upon her faith," and, in the middle of the play "Perdition catch my soul / But I do love thee! And when I love thee not, / Chaos is come again." Later, poisoned by Iago's insinuations, he believes Desdemona is faithless, and chaos comes again as he calls her a devil, banishes her from his sight, and finally suffocates her. But Othello is "the noble Moor," whose nobility is demonstrated early in the play by his language and his actions. And Desdemona, "the divine Desdemona," "the grace of heaven," and "the sweetest innocent / That e'er did lift up eye," demonstrates her worth in every line and deed. On the other hand, Alceste, lacking all sense of proportion, is at the outset surly and evidently funny. In the very first scene his tirade against Philinte's "loving demonstrations" offered to one who is almost a stranger evokes Philinte's good-natured

> It hardly seems a hanging matter to me;
> I hope that you will take it graciously
> If I extend myself a slight reprieve,
> And live a little longer, by your leave;

but this droll reply acerbates Alceste:

> How dare you joke about a crime so grave?

Alceste is thus laughably introduced; his passion is comic because it is disproportionate — and also because it leads to no action; Othello is heroically introduced (after an initial scene in which he is slandered), and his passion is tragic because it is frightening and pitiable, especially because it leads him to murder an innocent woman who, as he has said, is the center of his being.

Alceste's remark about joking provides a thread that may be followed usefully. He cannot take a joke. Whenever he is laughed at, he becomes indignant, but indignation (when motivated by a desire to protect the self from criticism) itself evokes further laughter because of the gap between the indignant man's presentation of himself and his real worth. Comedy does not allow people to strike attitudes. The man who protests that his argument *is* valid, dammit, or that he *has* a sense of humor, or that his opponent is a fool, is likely to evoke laughter by his monolithic insistence on his merit. When Philinte laughs at the old poem Alceste quotes, Alceste resorts to bitter irony, and when told that his frankness has made him ridiculous, he irritably replies:

> So much the better; just what I wish to hear.
> No news could be more grateful to my ear.
> All men are so detestable in my eyes.
> I should be sorry if they thought me otherwise.

He hopes that he will lose his lawsuit, just to prove that the world *is* as bad as he thinks it is. (An odd psychological state, resembling Master Ford's in Shakespeare's *Merry Wives of Windsor*, whose "God be praised for my jealousy" reveals the comic figure's infatuation with his abnormality.) And when Alceste is told that his hope that he will lose his lawsuit would reduce all hearers to laughter and would make his name a jest, he ill-humoredly replies, "So much the worse for jesters." When his persistent refusal to praise a trivial poem moves two auditors to laughter, he again employs frigid irony, and concludes the scene ominously:

> By heaven, Sirs, I really didn't know
> That I was being humorous.
> CÉLIMÈNE: Go, Sir; go;
> Settle your business.
> ALCESTE: I shall, and when I'm through,
> I shall return to settle things with you.

Alceste, unable to laugh at the folly of others, cannot, of course, tolerate laughter at himself. When Philinte puts into practice the frankness Alceste stormily advocates, Alceste's response is the indignation we have been commenting on. A sense of humor (as distinct from derisive laughter) involves the ability to laugh at what one values, and among the things one values is the self. Children can laugh at surprises and at the distress of other children, but they cannot laugh at themselves because they cannot see themselves in perspective, at a distance, as it were. The mature man can laugh at (for example) mimicry of himself, but the child or the immature adult will, like Alceste, sulk or fly into a rage.

In *The Misanthrope* it is entirely possible that Molière is in some degree mimicking himself. In 1662 Molière at forty married Armande Béjart, a woman less than half his age. The marriage seems to have been unhappy, apparently because his wife enjoyed attracting the attentions of other men. Some critics, pressing this point, assume that if the play is autobiographical, Alceste must be expressing Molière's point of view, and therefore he cannot be a comic figure. If anything, the autobiographic origin shows only that Molière had (which no one has doubted) a sense of humor. He could laugh at himself. Alceste's courtship of Célimène may in some degree represent Molière's unhappy marriage to a flirtatious and unappreciative woman, but the point is that Molière apparently could stand back and laugh at his own exasperation, which Alceste cannot do. (Molière subtitled the play "The Atrabilious Man in Love"; one cannot hear Alceste speaking thus of himself.) Alceste can only, rather childishly, try to maintain his way, and demand that his special merit be noted and rewarded:

> However high the praise, there's nothing worse
> Than sharing honors with the universe.
> Esteem is founded on comparison:
> To honor all men is to honor none.
> Since you embrace this indiscriminate vice,
> Your friendship comes at far too cheap a price;
> I spurn the easy tribute of a heart
> Which will not set the worthy man apart:
> I choose, Sir, to be chosen; and in fine,
> The friend of mankind is no friend of mine.

Once or twice, when he confesses that his love for Célimène is irrational, he seems to have some perspective, but mostly the scenes of Alceste as lover serve to reveal again and again his consuming egotism. His love is so great, he tells Célimène, that he wishes she were in some peril so that he could prove his love by saving her. Célimène aptly replies that Alceste's is "a strange benevolence indeed."

The argument thus far has tried to make the point that Alceste is funny — funny because (among other things) his anger is indiscriminate and disproportionate, because he is a sort of philosopher and yet is in love, and because his *idée fixe*, frankness, when turned against him, exasperates him. But when we return to Éliante's reference to his "noble, heroic side," and we recall his passion for honesty and his passionate desire to be himself, and when we see the hollowness all about him, the comic figure begins to take on a tragic aspect; and when at the end he departs from the stage unrepentant and bitter, banishing himself from the company of men, we feel that the usual comic plot too has taken on a tragic aspect. But this is hardly to say that Alceste is tragic and *The Misanthrope* a tragedy. One cannot, for example, imagine Alceste committing suicide. He is not an Othello.

MAJOR BARBARA

George Bernard Shaw

George Bernard Shaw (1856–1950), later famous as Bernard Shaw, was born in Dublin of Anglo-Irish stock. His father drank too much, his mother — something of an Ibsenite "new woman" — went to London to make her way as singer and voice teacher. Shaw worked in a Dublin real estate office for a while (he did not attend a college or university), and then followed his mother to London, where he wrote critical reviews, and five novels (1879–1883) before turning playwright. His first play, begun with William Archer (playwright and translator of Ibsen), was abandoned in 1885, and then entirely revised by Shaw into *Widowers' Houses* (1892). He had already shown, in a critical study entitled *The Quintessence of Ibsenism* (1891), that he regarded the stage as a pulpit and soap box; before the nineteenth century was over, he wrote nine more plays, in order (he said) to espouse socialism effectively. *Major Barbara* (1905) is his comic masterpiece, but at least a dozen of his plays have established themselves in the repertoire, including one tragedy, *Saint Joan* (1924).

Undershaft (Brewster Mason) visits Lady Britomart (Elizabeth Spriggs) to meet Sara (Lisa Harrow) and Barbara (Judi Dench) in the Royal Shakespeare Company production of *Major Barbara* directed by Clifford Williams and designed by Ralph Koltai, Aldwych, 1970. (Photograph: Patrick Eagar.)

ACT I

It is after dinner in January 1906, in the library in LADY BRITOMART UNDERSHAFT'S *house in Wilton Crescent. A large and comfortable settee is in the middle of the room, upholstered in dark leather. A person sitting on it (it is vacant at present) would have, on his right,* LADY BRITOMART'S *writing table, with the lady herself busy at it; a smaller writing table behind him on his left; the door behind him on* LADY BRITOMART'S *side; and a window with a window seat directly on his left. Near the window is an armchair.*

LADY BRITOMART *is a woman of fifty or thereabouts, well dressed and yet careless of her dress, well bred and quite reckless of her breeding, well mannered and yet appallingly outspoken and indifferent to the opinion of her interlocutors, amiable and yet peremptory, arbitrary, and high-tempered to the last bearable degree, and withal a very typical managing matron of the upper class, treated as a naughty child until she grew into a scolding mother, and finally settling down with plenty of practical ability and worldly experience, limited in the oddest way with domestic and class limitations, conceiving the universe exactly as if it were a large house in Wilton Crescent, though handling her corner of it very effectively on that assumption, and being quite enlightened and liberal as to the books in the library, the pictures on the walls, and the music in the portfolios, and the articles in the papers.*

Her son, STEPHEN, *comes in. He's a gravely correct young man under 25, taking himself very seriously, but still in some awe of his mother, from childish habit and bachelor shyness rather than from any weakness of character.*

STEPHEN: Whats the matter?

LADY BRITOMART: Presently, Stephen.

(STEPHEN *submissively walks to the settee*

Major Barbara by George Bernard Shaw. Copyright 1907, 1913, 1930, 1941, George Bernard Shaw. Copyright 1957, The Public Trustee as Executor of the Estate of George Bernard Shaw. Reprinted by permission of Dodd, Mead & Company, Inc., and The Society of Authors for the Estate of Bernard Shaw.

and sits down. He takes up a Liberal weekly called The Speaker.)

LADY BRITOMART: Dont begin to read, Stephen. I shall require all your attention.

STEPHEN: It was only while I was waiting —

LADY BRITOMART: Dont make excuses, Stephen. (*He puts down* The Speaker.) Now! (*She finishes her writing; rises; and comes to the settee.*) I have not kept you waiting very long, I think.

STEPHEN: Not at all, mother.

LADY BRITOMART: Bring me my cushion. (*He takes the cushion from the chair at the desk and arranges it for her as she sits down on the settee.*) Sit down. (*He sits down and fingers his tie nervously.*) Don't fiddle with your tie, Stephen: there is nothing the matter with it.

STEPHEN: I beg your pardon. (*He fiddles with his watch chain instead.*)

LADY BRITOMART: Now are you attending to me, Stephen?

STEPHEN: Of course, mother.

LADY BRITOMART: No: it's not of course. I want something much more than your everyday matter-of-course attention. I am going to speak to you very seriously, Stephen. I wish you would let that chain alone.

STEPHEN (*hastily relinquishing the chain*): Have I done anything to annoy you, mother? If so, it was quite unintentional.

LADY BRITOMART (*astonished*): Nonsense! (*With some remorse.*) My poor boy, did you think I was angry with you?

STEPHEN: What is it, then, mother? You are making me very uneasy.

LADY BRITOMART (*squaring herself at him rather aggressively*): Stephen: may I ask how soon you intend to realize that you are a grown-up man, and that I am only a woman?

STEPHEN (*amazed*): Only a —

LADY BRITOMART: Dont repeat my words, please: it is a most aggravating habit. You must learn to face life seriously, Stephen. I really cannot bear the whole burden of our family affairs any longer. You must advise me: you must assume the responsibility.

STEPHEN: I!

LADY BRITOMART: Yes, you, of course. You

were 24 last June. Youve been at Harrow and Cambridge. Youve been to India and Japan. You must know a lot of things, now; unless you have wasted your time most scandalously. Well, advise me.

STEPHEN (*much perplexed*): You know I have never interfered in the household —

LADY BRITOMART: No: I should think not. I dont want you to order the dinner.

STEPHEN: I mean in our family affairs.

LADY BRITOMART: Well, you must interfere now; for they are getting quite beyond me.

STEPHEN (*troubled*): I have thought sometimes that perhaps I ought; but really, mother, I know so little about them; and what I do know is so painful! it is so impossible to mention some things to you — (*He stops, ashamed.*)

LADY BRITOMART: I suppose you mean your father.

STEPHEN (*almost inaudibly*): Yes.

LADY BRITOMART: My dear: we cant go on all our lives not mentioning him. Of course you were quite right not to open the subject until I asked you to; but you are old enough now to be taken into my confidence, and to help me to deal with him about the girls.

STEPHEN: But the girls are all right. They are engaged.

LADY BRITOMART (*complacently*): Yes: I have made a very good match for Sarah. Charles Lomax will be a millionaire at 35. But that is ten years ahead and in the meantime his trustees cannot under the terms of his father's will allow him more than £800 a year.

STEPHEN: But the will says also that if he increases his income by his own exertions, they may double the increase.

LADY BRITOMART: Charles Lomax's exertions are much more likely to decrease his income than to increase it. Sarah will have to find at least another £800 a year for the next ten years; and even then they will be as poor as church mice. And what about Barbara? I thought Barbara was going to make the most brilliant career of all of you. And what does she do? Joins the Salvation Army; discharges her maid; lives on a pound a week; and walks in one evening with a professor of Greek whom she has picked up in the street, and who pretends to be a Salvationist, and actually plays the big drum for her in public because he has fallen head over ears in love with her.

STEPHEN: I was certainly rather taken aback when I heard they were engaged. Cusins is a very nice fellow, certainly: nobody would ever guess that he was born in Australia; but —

LADY BRITOMART: Oh, Adolphus Cusins will make a very good husband. After all, nobody can say a word against Greek: it stamps a man at once as an educated gentleman. And my family, thank Heaven, is not a pig-headed Tory one. We are Whigs, and believe in liberty. Let snobbish people say what they please: Barbara shall marry, not the man they like, but the man I like.

STEPHEN: Of course I was thinking only of his income. However, he is not likely to be extravagant.

LADY BRITOMART: Dont be too sure of that, Stephen. I know your quiet, simple, refined, poetic people like Adolphus: quite content with the best of everything! They cost more than your extravagant people, who are always as mean as they are second rate. No: Barbara will need at least £2000 a year. You see it means two additional households. Besides, my dear, you must marry soon. I dont approve of the present fashion of philandering bachelors and late marriages; and I am trying to arrange something for you.

STEPHEN: It's very good of you, mother; but perhaps I had better arrange that for myself.

LADY BRITOMART: Nonsense! you are much too young to begin matchmaking: you would be taken in by some pretty little nobody. Of course I dont mean that you are not to be consulted: you know that as well as I do. (STEPHEN *closes his lips and is silent.*) Now dont sulk, Stephen.

STEPHEN: I am not sulking, mother. What has all this got to do with — with — my father?

LADY BRITOMART: My dear Stephen: where is the money to come from? It is easy enough for you and the other children to live on my income as long as we are in the same house; but I cant keep four families in four separate houses. You know how poor my father is: he has barely seven thousand a year now; and really, if he were not the Earl of Stevenage, he would have to give up society. He can do nothing for us. He says, naturally enough, that it is absurd that he should be asked to provide for the children of a man who is rolling in money. You see, Stephen, your father must be fabulously wealthy, because there is always a war going on somewhere.

STEPHEN: You need not remind me of that, mother. I have hardly ever opened a newspaper in my life without seeing our name in it. The Undershaft torpedo! The Undershaft quick firers! The Undershaft ten inch! the Undershaft disappearing rampart gun! the Undershaft submarine! and now the Undershaft aerial battleship! At Harrow they called me the Woolwich Infant. At Cambridge it was the same. A little brute at King's who was always trying to get up revivals, spoilt my Bible — your first birthday present to me — by writing under my name, 'Son and heir to Undershaft and Lazarus, Death and Destruction Dealers: address Christendom and Judea.' But that was not so bad as the way I was kowtowed to everywhere because my father was making millions by selling cannons.

LADY BRITOMART: It is not only the cannons, but the war loans that Lazarus arranges under cover of giving credit for the cannons. You know, Stephen, it's perfectly scandalous. Those two men, Andrew Undershaft and Lazarus, positively have Europe under their thumbs. That is why your father is able to behave as he does. He is above the law. Do you think Bismarck or Gladstone or Disraeli could have openly defied every social and moral obligation all their lives as your father has? They simply wouldnt have dared. I asked Gladstone to take it up. I asked The Times to take it up. I asked the Lord Chamberlain to take it up. But it was just like asking them to declare war on the Sultan. They wouldnt. They said they couldnt touch him. I believe they were afraid.

STEPHEN: What could they do? He does not actually break the law.

LADY BRITOMART: Not break the law! He is always breaking the law. He broke the law when he was born: his parents were not married.

STEPHEN: Mother! Is that true?

LADY BRITOMART: Of course it's true: that was why we separated.

STEPHEN: He married without letting you know this!

LADY BRITOMART (rather taken aback by this inference): Oh no. To do Andrew justice, that was not the sort of thing he did. Besides, you know the Undershaft motto: Unashamed. Everybody knew.

STEPHEN: But you said that was why you separated.

LADY BRITOMART: Yes, because he was not content with being a foundling himself: he wanted to disinherit you for another foundling. That was what I couldnt stand.

STEPHEN (ashamed): Do you mean for — for — for —

LADY BRITOMART: Dont stammer, Stephen. Speak distinctly.

STEPHEN: But this is so frightful to me, mother. To have to speak to you about such things!

LADY BRITOMART: It's not pleasant for me, either, especially if you are still so childish that you must make it worse by a display of embarrassment. It is only in the middle classes, Stephen, that people get into a state of dumb helpless horror when they find that there are wicked people in the world. In our class, we have to decide what is to be done with wicked people; and nothing should disturb our self-possession. Now ask your question properly.

STEPHEN: Mother: have you no consideration for me? For Heaven's sake either treat me as a child, as you always do, and tell me nothing at all; or tell me everything and let me take it as best I can.

LADY BRITOMART: Treat you as a child! What do you mean? It is most unkind and ungrateful of you to say such a thing. You know I have never treated any of you as children. I have always made you my companions and friends, and allowed you perfect freedom to do and say whatever you liked, so long as you liked what I could approve of.

STEPHEN (desperately): I daresay we have been the very imperfect children of a very perfect mother; but I do beg you to let me alone for once, and tell me about this horrible business of my father wanting to set me aside for another son.

LADY BRITOMART (amazed): Another son! I never said anything of the kind. I never dreamt of such a thing. This is what comes of interrupting me.

STEPHEN: But you said —

LADY BRITOMART (cutting him short): Now be a good boy, Stephen, and listen to me patiently. The Undershafts are descended from a foundling in the parish of St Andrew Undershaft in the city. That was long ago, in the reign of James the First. Well this foundling was adopted by an armorer and gun-maker. In the course of time the foundling succeeded to the business; and from some notion of gratitude, or some vow or something, he adopted another foundling, and left the business to him. And that foundling did the same. Ever since that, the cannon business has always been left to an adopted foundling named Andrew Undershaft.

STEPHEN: But did they never marry? Were there no legitimate sons?

LADY BRITOMART: Oh yes: they married just as your father did; and they were rich enough to buy land for their own children and leave them well provided for. But they always adopted and trained some foundling to succeed them in the business; and of course they always quarrelled with their wives furiously over it. Your father was adopted in that way; and he pretends to consider himself bound to keep up the tradition and adopt somebody to leave the business to. Of course I was not going to stand that. There may have been some reason for it when the Undershafts could only marry women in their own class, whose sons were not fit to govern great estates. But there could be no excuse for passing over my son.

STEPHEN (*dubiously*): I am afraid I should make a poor hand of managing a cannon foundry.

LADY BRITOMART: Nonsense! you could easily get a manager and pay him a salary.

STEPHEN: My father evidently had no great opinion of my capacity.

LADY BRITOMART: Stuff, child! you were only a baby: it had nothing to do with your capacity. Andrew did it on principle, just as he did every perverse and wicked thing on principle. When my father remonstrated, Andrew actually told him to his face that history tells us of only two successful institutions: one the Undershaft firm, and the other the Roman Empire under the Antonines. That was because the Antonine emperors all adopted their successors. Such rubbish! The Stevenages are as good as the Antonines, I hope; and you are a Stevenage. But that was Andrew all over. There you have the man! Always clever and unanswerable when he was defending nonsense and wickedness: always awkward and sullen when he had to behave sensibly and decently!

STEPHEN: Then it was on my account that your home life was broken up, mother. I am sorry.

LADY BRITOMART: Well, dear, there were other differences. I really cannot bear an immoral man. I am not a Pharisee, I hope; and I should not have minded his merely doing wrong things: we are none of us perfect. But your father didnt exactly do wrong things: he said them and thought them: that was what was so dreadful. He really had a sort of religion of wrongness. Just as one doesnt mind men practising immorality so long as they own that they are in the wrong by preaching morality; so I couldn't forgive Andrew for preaching immorality while he practised morality. You would all have grown up without principles, without any knowledge of right and wrong, if he had been in the house. You know, my dear, your father was a very attractive man in some ways. Children did not dislike him; and he took advantage of it to put the wickedest ideas into their heads, and make them quite unmanageable. I did not dislike him myself: very far from it; but nothing can bridge over moral disagreement.

STEPHEN: All this simply bewilders me, mother. People may differ about matters of opinion, or even about religion; but how can they differ about right and wrong? Right is right; and wrong is wrong; and if a man cannot distinguish them properly, he is either a fool or a rascal: thats all.

LADY BRITOMART (*touched*): Thats my own boy (*she pats his cheek*)! Your father never could answer that: he used to laugh and get out of it under cover of some affectionate nonsense. And now that you understand the situation, what do you advise me to do?

STEPHEN: Well, what can you do?

LADY BRITOMART: I must get the money somehow.

STEPHEN: We cannot take money from him. I had rather go and live in some cheap place like Bedford Square or even Hampstead than take a farthing of his money.

LADY BRITOMART: But after all, Stephen, our present income comes from Andrew.

STEPHEN (*shocked*): I never knew that.

LADY BRITOMART: Well, you surely didnt suppose your grandfather had anything to give me. The Stevenages could not do everything for you. We gave you social position. Andrew had to contribute something. He had a very good bargain, I think.

STEPHEN (*bitterly*): We are utterly dependent on him and his cannons, then?

LADY BRITOMART: Certainly not: the money is settled. But he provided it. So you see it is not a question of taking money from him or not: it is simply a question of how much. I don't want any more for myself.

STEPHEN: Nor do I.

LADY BRITOMART: But Sarah does; and Barbara does. That is, Charles Lomax and Adolphus Cusins will cost them more. So I must put my pride in my pocket and ask for it, I suppose. That is your advice, Stephen, is it not?

STEPHEN: No.

LADY BRITOMART (sharply): Stephen!

STEPHEN: Of course if you are determined —

LADY BRITOMART: I am not determined: I ask your advice; and I am waiting for it. I will not have all the responsibility thrown on my shoulders.

STEPHEN (obstinately): I would die sooner than ask him for another penny.

LADY BRITOMART (resignedly): You mean that I must ask him. Very well, Stephen: it shall be as you wish. You will be glad to know that your grandfather concurs. But he thinks I ought to ask Andrew to come here and see the girls. After all, he must have some natural affection for them.

STEPHEN: Ask him here!!!

LADY BRITOMART: Do not repeat my words, Stephen. Where else can I ask him?

STEPHEN: I never expected you to ask him at all.

LADY BRITOMART: Now dont tease, Stephen. Come! you see that it is necessary that he should pay us a visit, dont you?

STEPHEN (reluctantly): I suppose so, if the girls cannot do without his money.

LADY BRITOMART: Thank you, Stephen: I knew you would give me the right advice when it was properly explained to you. I have asked your father to come this evening. (STEPHEN bounds from his seat.) Dont jump, Stephen: it fidgets me.

STEPHEN (in utter consternation): Do you mean to say that my father is coming here tonight — that he may be here at any moment?

LADY BRITOMART (looking at her watch): I said nine. (He gasps. She rises.) Ring the bell, please. (STEPHEN goes to the smaller writing table; presses a button on it; and sits at it with his elbows on the table and his head in his hands, outwitted and overwhelmed.) It is ten minutes to nine yet; and I have to prepare the girls. I asked Charles Lomax and Adolphus to dinner on purpose that they might be here.

Andrew had better see them in case he should cherish any delusions as to their being capable of supporting their wives. (The butler enters: LADY BRITOMART goes behind the settee to speak to him.) Morrison: go up to the drawing room and tell everybody to come down here at once. (MORRISON withdraws. LADY BRITOMART turns to STEPHEN.) Now remember, Stephen: I shall need all your countenance and authority. (He rises and tries to recover some vestige of these attributes.) Give me a chair, dear. (He pushes a chair forward from the wall to where she stands, near the smaller writing table. She sits down; and he goes to the armchair, into which he throws himself.) I dont know how Barbara will take it. Ever since they made her a major in the Salvation Army she has developed a propensity to have her own way and order people about which quite cows me sometimes. It's not ladylike: I'm sure I dont know where she picked it up. Anyhow, Barbara shant bully me; but still it's just as well that your father should be here before she has time to refuse to meet him or make a fuss. Dont look nervous, Stephen: it will only encourage Barbara to make difficulties. I am nervous enough, goodness knows; but I dont shew it.

(SARAH and BARBARA come in with their respective young men, CHARLES LOMAX and ADOLPHUS CUSINS. SARAH is slender, bored, and mundane. BARBARA is robuster, jollier, much more energetic. SARAH is fashionably dressed: BARBARA is in Salvation Army uniform. LOMAX, a young man about town, is like many other young men about town. He is afflicted with a frivolous sense of humor which plunges him at the most inopportune moments into paroxysms of imperfectly suppressed laughter. CUSINS is a spectacled student, slight, thin haired, and sweet voiced, with a more complex form of LOMAX's complaint. His sense of humor is intellectual and subtle, and is complicated by an appalling temper. The lifelong struggle of a benevolent temperament and a high conscience against impulses of inhuman ridicule and fierce impatience has set up a chronic strain which has visibly wrecked his constitution. He is a most implacable, determined, tenacious, intolerant person who by mere force of character presents himself as — and indeed actually is — considerate, gentle, ex-

planatory, even mild and apologetic, capable possibly of murder, but not of cruelty or coarseness. By the operation of some instinct which is not merciful enough to blind him with the illusions of love, he is obstinately bent on marrying BARBARA. LOMAX *likes* SARAH *and thinks it will be rather a lark to marry her. Consequently he has not attempted to resist* LADY BRITOMART'S *arrangements to that end.*

All four look as if they had been having a good deal of fun in the drawing room. The girls enter first, leaving the swains outside. SARAH *comes to the settee.* BARBARA *comes in after her and stops at the door.*)

BARBARA: Are Cholly and Dolly to come in?

LADY BRITOMART (*forcibly*): Barbara: I will not have Charles called Cholly: the vulgarity of it positively makes me ill.

BARBARA: It's all right, mother: Cholly is quite correct nowadays. Are they to come in?

LADY BRITOMART: Yes, if they will behave themselves.

BARBARA (*through the door*): Come in, Dolly; and behave yourself.

(BARBARA *comes to her mother's writing table.* CUSINS *enters smiling, and wanders towards* LADY BRITOMART.)

SARAH (*calling*): Come in, Cholly. (LOMAX *enters, controlling his features very imperfectly, and places himself vaguely between* SARAH *and* BARBARA.)

LADY BRITOMART (*peremptorily*): Sit down, all of you. (*They sit.* CUSINS *crosses to the window and seats himself there.* LOMAX *takes a chair.* BARBARA *sits at the writing table and* SARAH *on the settee.*) I dont in the least know what you are laughing at, Adolphus. I am surprised at you, though I expected nothing better from Charles Lomax.

CUSINS (*in a remarkably gentle voice*): Barbara has been trying to teach me the West Ham Salvation March.

LADY BRITOMART: I see nothing to laugh at in that; nor should you if you are really converted.

CUSINS (*sweetly*): You were not present. It was really funny, I believe.

LOMAX: Ripping.

LADY BRITOMART: Be quiet, Charles. Now listen to me, children. Your father is coming here this evening.

(*General stupefaction.* LOMAX, SARAH, *and* BARBARA *rise:* SARAH *scared, and* BARBARA *amused and expectant.*)

LOMAX (*remonstrating*): Oh I say!

LADY BRITOMART: You are not called on to say anything, Charles.

SARAH: Are you serious, mother?

LADY BRITOMART: Of course I am serious. It is on your account, Sarah, and also on Charles's. (*Silence.* SARAH *sits, with a shrug.* CHARLES *looks painfully unworthy.*) I hope you are not going to object, Barbara.

BARBARA: I! why should I? My father has a soul to be saved like anybody else. He's quite welcome as far as I am concerned. (*She sits on the table, and softly whistles 'Onward, Christian Soldiers.'*)

LOMAX (*still remonstrant*): But really, dont you know! Oh I say!

LADY BRITOMART (*frigidly*): What do you wish to convey, Charles?

LOMAX: Well, you must admit that this is a bit thick.

LADY BRITOMART (*turning with ominous suavity to* CUSINS): Adolphus: you are a professor of Greek. Can you translate Charles Lomax's remarks into reputable English for us?

CUSINS (*cautiously*): If I may say so, Lady Brit, I think Charles has rather happily expressed what we all feel. Homer, speaking of Autolycus, uses the same phrase. πυκινὸν δόμον ἐλθεῖν means a bit thick.

LOMAX (*handsomely*): Not that I mind, you know, if Sarah dont. (*He sits.*)

LADY BRITOMART (*crushingly*): Thank you. Have I your permission, Adolphus, to invite my own husband to my own house?

CUSINS (*gallantly*): You have my unhesitating support in everything you do.

LADY BRITOMART: Tush! Sarah: have you nothing to say?

SARAH: Do you mean that he is coming regularly to live here?

LADY BRITOMART: Certainly not. The spare room is ready for him if he likes to stay for a day or two and see a little more of you; but there are limits.

SARAH: Well, he cant eat us, I suppose. I dont mind.

LOMAX (*chuckling*): I wonder how the old man will take it.

LADY BRITOMART: Much as the old woman will, no doubt, Charles.

LOMAX (*abashed*): I didnt mean — at least —

LADY BRITOMART: You didnt think, Charles. You never do; and the result is, you never mean anything. And now please attend to me, children. Your father will be quite a stranger to us.

LOMAX: I suppose he hasnt seen Sarah since she was a little kid.

LADY BRITOMART: Not since she was a little kid, Charles, as you express it with that elegance of diction and refinement of thought that seem never to desert you. Accordingly — er — (*Impatiently.*) Now I have forgotten what I was going to say. That comes of your provoking me to be sarcastic, Charles. Adolphus: will you kindly tell me where I was.

CUSINS (*sweetly*): You were saying that as Mr Undershaft has not seen his children since they were babies, he will form his opinion of the way you have brought them up from their behavior tonight, and that therefore you wish us all to be particularly careful to conduct ourselves well, especially Charles.

LADY BRITOMART (*with emphatic approval*): Precisely.

LOMAX: Look here, Dolly: Lady Brit didnt say that.

LADY BRITOMART (*vehemently*): I did, Charles. Adolphus's recollection is perfectly correct. It is most important that you should be good; and I do beg you for once not to pair off into opposite corners and giggle and whisper while I am speaking to your father.

BARBARA: All right, mother. We'll do you credit. (*She comes off the table, and sits in her chair with ladylike elegance.*)

LADY BRITOMART: Remember, Charles, that Sarah will want to feel proud of you instead of ashamed of you.

LOMAX: Oh I say! theres nothing to be exactly proud of, dont you know.

LADY BRITOMART: Well, try and look as if there was.

(MORRISON, *pale and dismayed, breaks into the room in unconcealed disorder.*)

MORRISON: Might I speak a word to you, my lady?

LADY BRITOMART: Nonsense! Shew him up.

MORRISON: Yes, my lady. (*He goes.*)

LOMAX: Does Morrison know who it is?

LADY BRITOMART: Of course. Morrison has always been with us.

LOMAX: It must be a regular corker for him, dont you know.

LADY BRITOMART: Is this a moment to get on my nerves, Charles, with your outrageous expressions?

LOMAX: But this is something out of the ordinary, really —

MORRISON (*at the door*): The — er — Mr Undershaft. (*He retreats in confusion.*)

(ANDREW UNDERSHAFT *comes in. All rise.* LADY BRITOMART *meets him in the middle of the room behind the settee.*

ANDREW *is, on the surface, a stoutish, easy-going elderly man, with kindly patient manners, and an engaging simplicity of character. But he has a watchful, deliberate, waiting, listening face, and formidable reserves of power, both bodily and mental, in his capacious chest and long head. His gentleness is partly that of a strong man who has learnt by experience that his natural grip hurts ordinary people unless he handles them very carefully, and partly the mellowness of age and success. He is also a little shy in his present very delicate situation.*)

LADY BRITOMART: Good evening, Andrew.

UNDERSHAFT: How d'ye do, my dear.

LADY BRITOMART: You look a good deal older.

UNDERSHAFT (*apologetically*): I am somewhat older. (*Taking her hand with a touch of courtship.*) Time has stood still with you.

LADY BRITOMART (*throwing away his hand*): Rubbish! This is your family.

UNDERSHAFT (*surprised*): Is it so large? I am sorry to say my memory is failing very badly in some things. (*He offers his hand with paternal kindness to* LOMAX.)

LOMAX (*jerkily shaking his hand*): Ahdedoo.

UNDERSHAFT: I can see you are my eldest. I am very glad to meet you again, my boy.

LOMAX (*remonstrating*): No, but look here dont you know — (*Overcome.*) Oh I say!

LADY BRITOMART (*recovering from momentary speechlessness*): Andrew: do you mean to say that you dont remember how many children you have?

UNDERSHAFT: Well, I am afraid I —. They have grown so much — er. Am I making any ridiculous mistake? I may as well confess: I recollect only one son. But so many things have happened since, of course — er —

LADY BRITOMART (*decisively*): Andrew: you

are talking nonsense. Of course you have only one son.

UNDERSHAFT: Perhaps you will be good enough to introduce me, my dear.

LADY BRITOMART: That is Charles Lomax, who is engaged to Sarah.

UNDERSHAFT: My dear sir, I beg your pardon.

LOMAX: Notatall. Delighted, I assure you.

LADY BRITOMART: This is Stephen.

UNDERSHAFT (bowing): Happy to make your acquaintance, Mr Stephen. Then (going to CUSINS) you must be my son. (Taking CUSINS' hands in his.) How are you, my young friend? (To LADY BRITOMART.) He is very like you, my love.

CUSINS: You flatter me, Mr Undershaft. My name is Cusins: engaged to Barbara. (Very explicitly.) That is Major Barbara Undershaft, of the Salvation Army. That is Sarah, your second daughter. This is Stephen Undershaft, your son.

UNDERSHAFT: My dear Stephen, I beg your pardon.

STEPHEN: Not at all.

UNDERSHAFT: Mr Cusins: I am much indebted to you for explaining so precisely. (Turning to SARAH.) Barbara, my dear —

SARAH (prompting him): Sarah.

UNDERSHAFT: Sarah, of course. (They shake hands. He goes over to BARBARA.) Barbara — I am right this time, I hope?

BARBARA: Quite right. (They shake hands.)

LADY BRITOMART (resuming command): Sit down, all of you. Sit down, Andrew. (She comes forward and sits on the settee. CUSINS also brings his chair forward on her left. BARBARA and STEPHEN resume their seats. LOMAX gives his chair to SARAH and goes for another.)

UNDERSHAFT: Thank you, my love.

LOMAX (conversationally, as he brings a chair forward between the writing table and the settee, and offers it to UNDERSHAFT): Takes you some time to find out exactly where you are, dont it?

UNDERSHAFT (accepting the chair, but remaining standing): That is not what embarrasses me, Mr Lomax. My difficulty is that if I play the part of a father, I shall produce the effect of an intrusive stranger; and if I play the part of a discreet stranger, I may appear a callous father.

LADY BRITOMART: There is no need for you to play any part at all, Andrew. You had much better be sincere and natural.

UNDERSHAFT (submissively): Yes, my dear: I daresay that will be best. (He sits down comfortably.) Well, here I am. Now what can I do for you all?

LADY BRITOMART: You need not do anything, Andrew. You are one of the family. You can sit with us and enjoy yourself.

(A painfully conscious pause. BARBARA makes a face at LOMAX, whose too long suppressed mirth immediately explodes in agonized neighings.)

LADY BRITOMART (outraged): Charles Lomax: if you can behave yourself, behave yourself. If not, leave the room.

LOMAX: I'm awfully sorry, Lady Brit; but really you know, upon my soul! (He sits on the settee between LADY BRITOMART and UNDERSHAFT, quite overcome.)

BARBARA: Why dont you laugh if you want to, Cholly? It's good for your inside.

LADY BRITOMART: Barbara: you have had the education of a lady. Please let your father see that; and dont talk like a street girl.

UNDERSHAFT: Never mind me, my dear. As you know, I am not a gentleman; and I was never educated.

LOMAX (encouragingly): Nobody'd know it, I assure you. You look all right, you know.

CUSINS: Let me advise you to study Greek, Mr Undershaft. Greek scholars are privileged men. Few of them know Greek; and none of them know anything else; but their position is unchallengeable. Other languages are the qualifications of waiters and commercial travellers: Greek is to a man of position what the hallmark is to silver.

BARBARA: Dolly: dont be insincere. Cholly: fetch your concertina and play something for us.

LOMAX (jumps up eagerly, but checks himself to remark doubtfully to UNDERSHAFT): Perhaps that sort of thing isnt in your line, eh?

UNDERSHAFT: I am particularly fond of music.

LOMAX (delighted): Are you? Then I'll get it. (He goes upstairs for the instrument.)

UNDERSHAFT: Do you play, Barbara?

BARBARA: Only the tambourine. But Cholly's teaching me the concertina.

UNDERSHAFT: Is Cholly also a member of the Salvation Army?

BARBARA: No: he says it's bad form to be a dissenter. But I dont despair of Cholly. I made him come yesterday to a meeting at the dock gates, and take the collection in his hat.

UNDERSHAFT (*looks whimsically at his wife*): !!

LADY BRITOMART: It is not my doing, Andrew. Barbara is old enough to take her own way. She has no father to advise her.

BARBARA: Oh yes she has. There are no orphans in the Salvation Army.

UNDERSHAFT: Your father there has a great many children and plenty of experience, eh?

BARBARA (*looking at him with quick interest and nodding*): Just so. How did you come to understand that? (LOMAX *is heard at the door trying the concertina.*)

LADY BRITOMART: Come in, Charles. Play us something at once.

LOMAX: Righto! (*He sits down in his former place, and preludes.*)

UNDERSHAFT: One moment, Mr Lomax. I am rather interested in the Salvation Army. Its motto might be my own: Blood and Fire.

LOMAX (*shocked*): But not your sort of blood and fire, you know.

UNDERSHAFT: My sort of blood cleanses: my sort of fire purifies.

BARBARA: So do ours. Come down tomorrow to my shelter — the West Ham shelter — and see what we're doing. We're going to march to a great meeting in the Assembly Hall at Mile End. Come and see the shelter and then march with us: it will do you a lot of good. Can you play anything?

UNDERSHAFT: In my youth I earned pennies, and even shillings occasionally, in the streets and in public house parlors by my natural talent for stepdancing. Later on, I became a member of the Undershaft orchestral society, and performed passably on the tenor trombone.

LOMAX (*scandalized — putting down the concertina*): Oh I say!

BARBARA: Many a sinner has played himself into heaven on the trombone, thanks to the Army.

LOMAX (*to* BARBARA, *still rather shocked*): Yes; but what about the cannon business, dont you know? (*To* UNDERSHAFT.) Getting into heaven is not exactly in your line, is it?

LADY BRITOMART: Charles!!!

LOMAX: Well; but it stands to reason, dont it? The cannon business may be necessary and all that: we cant get on without cannons; but it isnt right, you know. On the other hand, there may be a certain amount of tosh about the Salvation Army — I belong to the Established Church myself — but still you cant deny that it's religion; and you cant go against religion, can you? At least unless youre downright immoral, dont you know.

UNDERSHAFT: You hardly appreciate my position, Mr Lomax —

LOMAX (*hastily*): I'm not saying anything against you personally —

UNDERSHAFT: Quite so, quite so. But consider for a moment. Here I am, a profiteer in mutilation and murder. I find myself in a specially amiable humor just now because, this morning, down at the foundry, we blew twenty-seven dummy soldiers into fragments with a gun which formerly destroyed only thirteen.

LOMAX (*leniently*): Well, the more destructive war becomes, the sooner it will be abolished, eh?

UNDERSHAFT: Not at all. The more destructive war becomes the more fascinating we find it. No, Mr Lomax: I am obliged to you for making the usual excuse for my trade; but I am not one of those men who keep their morals and their business in watertight compartments. All the spare money my trade rivals spend on hospitals, cathedrals, and other receptacles for conscience money, I devote to experiments and researches in improved methods of destroying life and property. I have always done so; and I always shall. Therefore your Christmas card moralities of peace on earth and goodwill among men are of no use to me. Your Christianity, which enjoins you to resist not evil, and to turn the other check, would make me a bankrupt. My morality — my religion — must have a place for cannons and torpedoes in it.

STEPHEN (*coldly — almost sullenly*): You speak as if there were half a dozen moralities and religions to choose from, instead of one true morality and one true religion.

UNDERSHAFT: For me there is only one true morality; but it might not fit you, as you do not manufacture aerial battleships. There is only one true morality for every man; but every man has not the same true morality.

LOMAX (*overtaxed*): Would you mind saying that again? I didnt quite follow it.

CUSINS: It's quite simple. As Euripides says, one man's meat is another man's poison morally as well as physically.

UNDERSHAFT: Precisely.

LOMAX: Oh, that! Yes, yes, yes. True. True.

STEPHEN: In other words, some men are honest and some are scoundrels.

BARBARA: Bosh! There are no scoundrels.

UNDERSHAFT: Indeed? Are there any good men?

BARBARA: No. Not one. There are neither good men nor scoundrels: there are just children of one Father; and the sooner they stop calling one another names the better. You neednt talk to me: I know them. Ive had scores of them through my hands: scoundrels, criminals, infidels, philanthropists, missionaries, county councillors, all sorts. Theyre all just the same sort of sinner; and theres the same salvation ready for them all.

UNDERSHAFT: May I ask have you ever saved a maker of cannons?

BARBARA: No. Will you let me try?

UNDERSHAFT: Well, I will make a bargain with you. If I go to see you tomorrow in your Salvation Shelter, will you come the day after to see me in my cannon works?

BARBARA: Take care. It may end in your giving up the cannons for the sake of the Salvation Army.

UNDERSHAFT: Are you sure it will not end in your giving up the Salvation Army for the sake of the cannons?

BARBARA: I will take my chance of that.

UNDERSHAFT: And I will take my chance of the other. (*They shake hands on it.*) Where is your shelter?

BARBARA: In West Ham. At the sign of the cross. Ask anybody in Canning Town. Where are your works?

UNDERSHAFT: In Perivale St Andrews. At the sign of the sword. Ask anybody in Europe.

LOMAX: Hadnt I better play something?

BARBARA: Yes. Give us Onward, Christian Soldiers.

LOMAX: Well, thats rather a strong order to begin with, dont you know. Suppose I sing Thourt passing hence, my brother. It's much the same tune.

BARBARA: It's too melancholy. You get saved, Cholly; and youll pass hence, my brother, without making such a fuss about it.

LADY BRITOMART: Really, Barbara, you go on as if religion were a pleasant subject. Do have some sense of propriety.

UNDERSHAFT: I do not find it an unpleasant subject, my dear. It is the only one that capable people really care for.

LADY BRITOMART (*looking at her watch*): Well, if you are determined to have it, I insist on having it in a proper and respectable way. Charles: ring for prayers.

(*General amazement.* STEPHEN *rises in dismay.*)

LOMAX (*rising*): Oh I say!

UNDERSHAFT (*rising*): I am afraid I must be going.

LADY BRITOMART: You cannot go now, Andrew: it would be most improper. Sit down. What will the servants think?

UNDERSHAFT: My dear: I have conscientious scruples. May I suggest a compromise? If Barbara will conduct a little service in the drawing room, with Mr Lomax as organist, I will attend it willingly. I will even take part, if a trombone can be procured.

LADY BRITOMART: Dont mock, Andrew.

UNDERSHAFT (*shocked — to* BARBARA): You dont think I am mocking, my love, I hope.

BARBARA: No, of course not; and it wouldnt matter if you were: half the Army came to their first meeting for a lark. (*Rising.*) Come along. (*She throws her arm round her father and sweeps him out, calling to the others from the threshold.*) Come, Dolly. Come, Cholly.

(CUSINS *rises.*)

LADY BRITOMART: I will not be disobeyed by everybody. Adolphus: sit down. (*He does not.*) Charles: you may go. You are not fit for prayers: you cannot keep your countenance.

LOMAX: Oh I say! (*He goes out.*)

LADY BRITOMART (*continuing*): But you, Adolphus, can behave yourself if you choose to. I insist on your staying.

CUSINS: My dear Lady Brit: there are things in the family prayer book that I couldnt bear to hear you say.

LADY BRITOMART: What things, pray?

CUSINS: Well, you would have to say before all the servants that we have done things we ought not to have done, and left undone things we ought to have done, and that there is no health in us. I cannot bear to hear you doing yourself such an injustice, and Barbara such an injustice. As for myself, I flatly deny it: I have done my best. I shouldnt dare to marry Barbara — I couldnt look you in the face — if it were true. So I must go to the drawing room.

LADY BRITOMART (*offended*): Well, go. (*He starts for the door.*) And remember this, Adolphus (*he turns to listen*): I have a very strong suspicion that you went to the Salvation Army to worship Barbara and nothing else. And I quite appreciate the very clever way in which you systematically humbug me. I have found you out. Take care Barbara doesnt. Thats all.

CUSINS (*with unruffled sweetness*): Dont tell on me. (*He steals out.*)

LADY BRITOMART: Sarah: if you want to go, go. Anything's better than to sit there as if you wished you were a thousand miles away.

SARAH (*languidly*): Very well, mamma. (*She goes.*)

(*LADY BRITOMART, with a sudden flounce, gives way to a little gust of tears.*)

STEPHEN (*going to her*): Mother: whats the matter?

LADY BRITOMART (*swishing away her tears with her handkerchief*): Nothing. Foolishness. You can go with him, too, if you like, and leave me with the servants.

STEPHEN: Oh, you mustnt think that, mother. I — I dont like him.

LADY BRITOMART: The others do. That is the injustice of a woman's lot. A woman has to bring up her children; and that means to restrain them, to deny them things they want, to set them tasks, to punish them when they do wrong, to do all the unpleasant things. And then the father, who has nothing to do but pet them and spoil them, comes in when all her work is done and steals their affection from her.

STEPHEN: He has not stolen our affection from you. It is only curiosity.

LADY BRITOMART (*violently*): I wont be consoled, Stephen. There is nothing the matter with me. (*She rises and goes towards the door.*)

STEPHEN: Where are you going, mother?

LADY BRITOMART: To the drawing room, of course. (*She goes out. Onward, Christian Soldiers, on the concertina, with tambourine accompaniment, is heard when the door opens.*) Are you coming, Stephen?

STEPHEN: No. Certainly not. (*She goes. He sits down on the settee, with compressed lips and an expression of strong dislike.*)

ACT II

The yard of the West Ham shelter of the Salvation Army is a cold place on a January morning. The building itself, an old warehouse, is newly whitewashed. Its gabled end projects into the yard in the middle, with a door on the ground floor, and another in the loft above it without any balcony or ladder, but with a pulley rigged over it for hoisting sacks. Those who come from this central gable end into the yard have the gateway leading to the street on their left, with a stone horse-trough just beyond it, and, on the right, a penthouse shielding a table from the weather. There are forms at the table; and on them are seated a man and a woman, both much down on their luck, finishing a meal of bread (one thick slice each, with margarine and golden syrup) and diluted milk.

The man, a workman out of employment, is young, agile, a talker, a poser, sharp enough to be capable of anything in reason except honesty or altruistic considerations of any kind. The woman is a commonplace old bundle of poverty and hard-worn humanity. She looks sixty and probably is forty-five. If they were rich people, gloved and muffed and well wrapped up in furs and overcoats, they would be numbed and miserable; for it is a grindingly cold raw January day; and a glance at the background of grimy warehouses and leaden sky visible over the whitewashed walls of the yard would drive any idle rich person straight to the Mediterranean. But these two, being no more troubled with visions of the Mediterranean than of the moon, and being compelled to keep more of their clothes in the pawnshop, and less on their persons, in winter than in summer, are not depressed by the cold: rather are they stung into vivacity, to which their meal has just now given an almost jolly turn. The man takes a pull at his mug, and then gets up and moves about the yard with his hands deep in his pockets, occasionally breaking into a stepdance.

THE WOMAN: Feel better arter your meal, sir?

THE MAN: No. Call that a meal! Good enough for you, praps; but wot is it to me, an intelligent workin man.

THE WOMAN: Workin man! Wot are you?

THE MAN: Painter.

THE WOMAN (*sceptically*): Yus, I dessay.

THE MAN: Yus, you dessay! I know. Every loafer that cant do nothink calls isself a painter. Well, I'm a real painter: grainer, finisher, thirty-eight bob a week when I can get it.

THE WOMAN: Then why dont you go and get it?

THE MAN: I'll tell you why. Fust: I'm intelligent — fffff! it's rotten cold here (*he dances a step or two*) — yes: intelligent beyond the station o life into which it has pleased the capitalists to call me; and they dont like a man that sees through em. Second, an intelligent bein needs a doo share of appiness; so I drink somethink cruel when I get the chawnce. Third, I stand by my class and do as little as I can so's to leave arf the job for me fellow workers. Fourth, I'm fly enough to know wots inside the law and wots outside it; and inside it I do as the capitalists do: pinch wot I can lay me ands on. In a proper state of society I am sober, industrious and honest: in Rome, so to speak, I do as the Romans do. Wots the consequence? When trade is bad — and it's rotten bad just now — and the employers az to sack arf their men, they generally start on me.

THE WOMAN: Whats your name?

THE MAN: Price. Bronterre O'Brien Price. Usually called Snobby Price, for short.

THE WOMAN: Snobby's a carpenter, aint it? You said you was a painter.

PRICE: Not that kind of snob, but the genteel sort. I'm too uppish, owing to my intelligence, and my father being a Chartist and a reading, thinking man: a stationer, too. I'm none of your common hewers of wood and drawers of water; and dont you forget it. (*He returns to his seat at the table, and takes up his mug.*) Wots your name?

THE WOMAN: Rummy Mitchens, sir.

PRICE (*quaffing the remains of his milk to her*): Your elth, Miss Mitchens.

RUMMY (*correcting him*): Missis Mitchens.

PRICE: Wot! Oh Rummy, Rummy! Respectable married woman, Rummy, gittin rescued by the Salvation Army by pretendin to be a bad un. Same old game!

RUMMY: What am I to do? I cant starve. Them Salvation lasses is dear good girls; but the better you are, the worse they likes to think you were before they rescued you. Why shouldnt they av a bit o credit, poor loves? theyre worn to rags by their work. And where would they get the money to rescue us if we was to let on we're no worse than other people? You know what ladies and gentlemen are.

PRICE: Thievin swine! Wish I ad their job, Rummy, all the same. Wot does Rummy stand for? Pet name praps?

RUMMY: Short for Romola.

PRICE: For wot!?

RUMMY: Romola. It was out of a new book. Somebody me mother wanted me to grow up like.

PRICE: We're companions in misfortune, Rummy. Both on us got names that nobody cawnt pronounce. Consequently I'm Snobby and youre Rummy because Bill and Sally wasnt good enough for our parents. Such is life!

RUMMY: Who saved you, Mr Price? Was it Major Barbara?

PRICE: No: I come here on my own. I'm going to be Bronterre O'Brien Price, the converted painter. I know wot they like. I'll tell em how I blasphemed and gambled and wopped my poor old mother —

RUMMY (*shocked*): Used you to beat your mother?

PRICE: Not likely. She used to beat me. No matter: you come and listen to the converted painter, and youll hear how she was a pious woman that taught me me prayers at er knee, an how I used to come home drunk and drag her out o bed be er snow white airs, an lam into er with the poker.

RUMMY: Thats whats so unfair to us women. Your confessions is just as big lies as ours: you dont tell what you really done no more than us; but you men can tell your lies right out at the meetins and be made much of for it; while the sort o confessions we az to make az to be wispered to one lady at a time. It ain't right, spite of all their piety.

PRICE: Right! Do you spose the Army'd be allowed if it went and did right? Not much. It combs our air and makes us good little blokes to be robbed and put upon. But I'll play the game as good as any of em. I'll see somebody struck by lightnin, or hear a voice sayin 'Snobby Price: where will you spend eternity?' I'll av a time of it, I tell you.

RUMMY: You wont be let drink, though.

PRICE: I'll take it out in gorspellin, then. I dont want to drink if I can get fun enough any other way.

(JENNY HILL, *a pale, overwrought, pretty Salvation lass of 18, comes in through the yard gate, leading* PETER SHIRLEY, *a half hardened, half worn-out elderly man, weak with hunger.*)

JENNY (*supporting him*): Come! pluck up. I'll get you something to eat. Youll be all right then.

PRICE (*rising and hurrying officiously to take the old man off* JENNY'S *hands*): Poor old man! Cheer up, brother: youll find rest and peace and appiness ere. Hurry up with the food, miss: e's fair done. (JENNY *hurries into the shelter.*) Ere, buck up, daddy! she's fetchin y'a thick slice o breadn treacle, an a mug o skyblue. (*He seats him at the corner of the table.*)

RUMMY (*gaily*): Keep up your old art! Never say die!

SHIRLEY: I'm not an old man. I'm only 46. I'm as good as ever I was. The grey patch come in my hair before I was thirty. All it wants is three pennorth o hair dye: am I to be turned on the streets to starve for it? Holy God! Ive worked ten to twelve hours a day since I was thirteen, and paid my way all through; and now am I to be thrown into the gutter and my job given to a young man that can do it no better than me because Ive black hair that goes white at the first change?

PRICE (*cheerfully*): No good jawrin about it. Youre ony a jumped-up, jerked-off, orspittle-turned-out incurable of an ole workin man: who cares about you? Eh? Make the thievin swine give you a meal: theyve stole many a one from you. Get a bit o your own back. (JENNY *returns with the usual meal.*) There you are, brother. Awsk a blessin an tuck that into you.

SHIRLEY (*looking at it ravenously but not touching it, and crying like a child*): I never took anything before.

JENNY (*petting him*): Come, come! the Lord sends it to you: he wasnt above taking bread from his friends; and why should you be? Besides, when we find you a job you can pay us for it if you like.

SHIRLEY (*eagerly*): Yes, yes: thats true. I can pay you back: it's only a loan. (*Shivering.*) Oh Lord! oh Lord! (*He turns to the table and attacks the meal ravenously.*)

JENNY: Well, Rummy, are you more comfortable now?

RUMMY: God bless you, lovely! youve fed my body and saved my soul, havnt you? (JENNY, *touched, kisses her.*) Sit down and rest a bit: you must be ready to drop.

JENNY: Ive been going hard since morning. But theres more work than we can do. I mustnt stop.

RUMMY: Try a prayer for just two minutes. Youll work all the better after.

JENNY (*her eyes lighting up*): Oh isnt it wonderful how a few minutes prayer revives you! I was quite lightheaded at twelve o'clock, I was so tired; but Major Barbara just sent me to pray for five minutes; and I was able to go on as if I had only just begun. (*To* PRICE.) Did you have a piece of bread?

PRICE (*with unction*): Yes, miss; but Ive got the piece that I value more; and thats the peace that passeth hall hannerstennin.

RUMMY (*fervently*): Glory Hallelujah!

(BILL WALKER, *a rough customer of about 25, appears at the yard gate and looks malevolently at* JENNY.)

JENNY: That makes me so happy. When you say that, I feel wicked for loitering here. I must get to work again.

(*She is hurrying to the shelter, when the new-comer moves quickly up to the door and intercepts her. His manner is so threatening that she retreats as he comes at her truculently, driving her down the yard.*)

BILL: Aw knaow you. Youre the one that took awy maw girl. Youre the one that set er agen me. Well, I'm gowin to ev er aht. Not that Aw care a carse for er or you: see? Bat Aw'll let er knaow; and Aw'll let you knaow. Aw'm gowing to give her a doin thatll teach er to cat awy from me. Nah in wiv you and tell er to cam aht afore Aw cam in and kick er aht. Tell er Bill Walker wants er. She'll knaow wot thet means; and if she keeps me witin itll be worse. You stop to jawr beck at me; and Aw'll stawt on you: d'ye eah? Theres your wy. In you gow. (*He takes her by the arm and slings her towards the door of the shelter. She falls on her hand and knee.* RUMMY *helps her up again.*)

PRICE (*rising, and venturing irresolutely towards* BILL): Easy there, mate. She aint doin you no arm.

BILL: Oo are you callin mite? (*Standing

over him threateningly.) Youre gowing to stend ap for er, aw yer? Put ap your ends.

RUMMY (*running indignantly to him to scold him*): Oh, you great brute — (*He instantly swings his left hand back against her face. She screams and reels back to the trough, where she sits down, covering her bruised face with her hands and rocking herself and moaning with pain.*)

JENNY (*going to her*): Oh, God forgive you! How could you strike an old woman like that?

BILL (*seizing her by the hair so violently that she also screams, and tearing her away from the old woman*): You Gawd forgimme again an Aw'll Gawd forgive you one on the jawr thetll stop you pryin for a week. (*Holding her and turning fiercely on* PRICE.) Ev you ennything to sy agen it?

PRICE (*intimidated*): No, matey: she aint anything to do with me.

BILL: Good job for you! Aw'd pat two meals into you and fawt you with one finger arter, you stawved cur. (*To* JENNY.) Nah are you gowin to fetch aht Mog Ebbijem; or em Aw to knock your fice off you and fetch her meself?

JENNY (*writhing in his grasp*): Oh please someone go in and tell Major Barbara — (*She screams again as he wrenches her head down; and* PRICE *and* RUMMY *flee into the shelter.*)

BILL: You want to gow in and tell your Mijor of me, do you?

JENNY: Oh please dont drag my hair. Let me go.

BILL: Do you or downt you? (*She stifles a scream.*) Yus or nao?

JENNY: God give me strength —

BILL (*striking her with his fist in the face*): Gow an shaow her thet, and tell her if she wants one lawk it to cam and interfere with me. (JENNY, *crying with pain, goes into the shed. He goes to the form and addresses the old man.*) Eah: finish your mess; an git aht o maw wy.

SHIRLEY (*springing up and facing him fiercely, with the mug in his hand*): You take a liberty with me, and I'll smash you over the face with the mug and cut your eye out. Aint you satisfied — young whelps like you — with takin the bread out o the mouths of your elders that have brought you up and slaved for you, but you must come shovin and cheekin and bullyin in here, where the bread o charity is sickenin in our stummicks?

BILL (*contemptuously, but backing a little*):

Wot good are you, you aold palsy mag? Wot good are you?

SHIRLEY: As good as you and better. I'll do a day's work agen you or any fat young soaker of your age. Go and take my job at Horrockses where I worked for ten year. They want young men there: they cant afford to keep men over forty-five. Theyre very sorry — give you a character and happy to help you to get anything suited to your years — sure a steady man wont be long out of a job. Well, let em try you. Theyll find the differ. What do you know? Not as much as how to beeyave yourself — laying your dirty fist across the mouth of a respectable woman!

BILL: Downt provowk me to ly it acrost yours: d'ye eah?

SHIRLEY (*with blighting contempt*): Yes: you like an old man to hit, dont you, when youve finished with the women. I aint seen you hit a young one yet.

BILL (*stung*): You loy, you aold soupkitchener, you. There was a yang menn eah. Did Aw offer to itt him or did Aw not?

SHIRLEY: Was he starvin or was he not? Was he a man or only a crosseyed thief an a loafer? Would you hit my son-in-law's brother?

BILL: Oo's ee?

SHIRLEY: Todger Fairmile o Balls Pond. Him that won £20 off the Japanese wrastler at the music hall by standin out 17 minutes 4 seconds agen him.

BILL (*sullenly*): Aw'm nao music awl wrastler. Ken he box?

SHIRLEY: Yes: an you cant.

BILL: Wot! Aw cawnt, cawnt Aw? Wots thet you sy (*threatening him*)?

SHIRLEY (*not budging an inch*): Will you box Todger Fairmile if I put him on to you? Say the word.

BILL (*subsiding with a slouch*): Aw'll stend ap to enny menn alawy, if he was ten Todger Fairmawls. But Aw dont set ap to be a perfeshnal.

SHIRLEY (*looking down on him with unfathomable disdain*): You box! Slap an old woman with the back o your hand! You hadnt even the sense to hit her where a magistrate couldnt see the mark of it, you silly young lump of conceit and ignorance. Hit a girl in the jaw and ony make her cry! If Todger Fairmile'd done it, she wouldnt a got up inside o ten minutes, no more than you would if he got on to you. Yah! I'd set about you myself if I had a week's feedin in me instead o two months' starvation. (*He turns his back on him and sits down moodily at the table.*)

BILL (*following him and stooping over him to drive the taunt in*): You loy! youve the bread and treacle in you that you cam eah to beg.

SHIRLEY (*bursting into tears*): Oh God! it's true: I'm only an old pauper on the scrap heap. (*Furiously.*) But youll come to it yourself; and then youll know. Youll come to it sooner than a teetotaller like me, fillin yourself with gin at this hour o the mornin!

BILL: Aw'm nao gin drinker, you oald lawr; bat wen Aw want to give my girl a bloomin good awdin Aw lawk to ev a bit o devil in me: see? An eah Aw emm, talkin to a rotten aold blawter like you sted o givin her wot for. (*Working himself into a rage.*) Aw'm gowin in there to fetch her aht. (*He makes vengefully for the shelter door.*)

SHIRLEY: Youre going to the station on a stretcher, more likely; and theyll take the gin and the devil out of you there when they get you inside. You mind what youre about: the major here is the Earl o Stevenage's granddaughter.

BILL (*checked*): Garn!

SHIRLEY: Youll see.

BILL (*his resolution oozing*): Well, Aw aint dan nathin to er.

SHIRLEY: Spose she said you did! who'd believe you?

BILL (*very uneasy, skulking back to the corner of the penthouse*): Gawd! theres no jastice in this cantry. To think wot them people can do! Aw'm as good as er.

SHIRLEY: Tell her so. It's just what a fool like you would do.

(*BARBARA, brisk and businesslike, comes from the shelter with a note book, and addresses herself to* SHIRLEY. BILL, *cowed, sits down in the corner of a form, and turns his back on them.*)

BARBARA: Good morning.

SHIRLEY (*standing up and taking off his hat*): Good morning, miss.

BARBARA: Sit down: make yourself at home. (*He hesitates; but she puts a friendly hand on his shoulder and makes him obey.*) Now then! since youve made friends with us, we want to know all about you. Names and addresses and trades.

SHIRLEY: Peter Shirley. Fitter. Chucked out two months ago because I was too old.

BARBARA (*not at all surprised*): Youd pass still. Why didnt you dye your hair?

SHIRLEY: I did. Me age come out at a coroner's inquest on me daughter.

BARBARA: Steady?

SHIRLEY: Teetotaller. Never out of a job before. Good worker. And sent to the knackers like an old horse!

BARBARA: No matter: if you did your part God will do his.

SHIRLEY (*suddenly stubborn*): My religion's no concern of anybody but myself.

BARBARA (*guessing*): I know. Secularist?

SHIRLEY (*hotly*): Did I offer to deny it?

BARBARA: Why should you? My own father's a Secularist, I think. Our Father — yours and mine — fulfills himself in many ways; and I daresay he knew what he was about when he made a Secularist of you. So buck up, Peter! we can always find a job for a steady man like you. (SHIRLEY, *disarmed and a little bewildered, touches his hat. She turns from him to* BILL.) Whats your name?

BILL (*insolently*): Wots thet to you?

BARBARA (*calmly making a note*): Afraid to give his name. Any trade?

BILL: Oo's afride to give is nime? (*Doggedly, with a sense of heroically defying the House of Lords in the person of Lord Stevenage.*) If you want to bring a chawge agen me, bring it. (*She waits, unruffled.*) Moy nime's Bill Walker.

BARBARA (*as if the name were familiar: trying to remember how*): Bill Walker? (*Recollecting.*) Oh, I know: youre the man that Jenny Hill was praying for inside just now. (*She enters his name in her note book.*)

BILL: Oo's Jenny Ill? And wot call as she to pry for me?

BARBARA: I dont know. Perhaps it was you that cut her lip.

BILL (*defiantly*): Yus, it was me that cat her lip. Aw aint afride o you.

BARBARA: How could you be, since youre not afraid of God? Youre a brave man, Mr Walker. It takes some pluck to do our work here; but none of us dare lift our hand against a girl like that, for fear of her father in heaven.

BILL (*sullenly*): I want nan o your kentin jawr. I spowse you think Aw cam eah to beg from you, like this demmiged lot eah. Not me. Aw downt want your bread and scripe and ketlep. Aw dont blieve in your Gawd, no more than you do yourself.

BARBARA (*sunnily apologetic and ladylike, as*

on a new footing with him): Oh, I beg your pardon for putting your name down, Mr Walker. I didnt understand. I'll strike it out.

BILL (*taking this as a slight, and deeply wounded by it*): Eah! you let maw nime alown. Aint it good enaff to be in your book?

BARBARA (*considering*): Well, you see, theres no use putting down your name unless I can do something for you, is there? Whats your trade?

BILL (*still smarting*): Thets nao concern o yours.

BARBARA: Just so. (*Very businesslike.*) I'll put you down as (*writing*) the man who — struck — poor little Jenny Hill — in the mouth.

BILL (*rising threateningly*): See eah. Awve ed enaff o this.

BARBARA (*quite sunny and fearless*): What did you come to us for?

BILL: Aw cam for maw gel, see? Aw cam to tike her aht o this and to brike er jawr for er.

BARBARA (*complacently*): You see I was right about your trade. (BILL, *on the point of retorting furiously, finds himself, to his great shame and terror, in danger of crying instead. He sits down again suddenly.*) Whats her name?

BILL (*dogged*): Er nime's Mog Ebbijem: thets wot her nime is.

BARBARA: Mog Habbijam! Oh, she's gone to Canning Town, to our barracks there.

BILL (*fortified by his resentment of Mog's perfidy*): Is she? (*Vindictively.*) Then Aw'm gowing to Kennintahn arter her. (*He crosses to the gate; hesitates; finally comes back at* BARBARA.) Are you loyin to me to git shat o me?

BARBARA: I dont want to get shut of you. I want to keep you here and save your soul. Youd better stay: youre going to have a bad time today, Bill.

BILL: Oo's gowing to give it to me? You, preps?

BARBARA: Someone you dont believe in. But youll be glad afterwards.

BILL (*slinking off*): Aw'll gow to Kennintahn to be aht o reach o your tangue. (*Suddenly turning on her with intense malice.*) And if Aw downt fawnd Mog there, Aw'll cam beck and do two years for you, selp me Gawd if Aw downt!

BARBARA (*a shade kindlier, if possible*): It's no use, Bill. She's got another bloke.

BILL: Wot!

BARBARA: One of her own converts. He fell

in love with her when he saw her with her soul saved, and her face clean, and her hair washed.

BILL (*surprised*): Wottud she wash it for, the carroty slat? It's red.

BARBARA: It's quite lovely now, because she wears a new look in her eyes with it. It's a pity youre too late. The new bloke has put your nose out of joint, Bill.

BILL: Aw'll put his nowse aht o joint for him. Not that Aw care a carse for er, mawnd thet. But Aw'll teach her to drop me as if Aw was dirt. And Aw'll teach him to meddle with maw judy. Wots iz bleedin nime?

BARBARA: Sergeant Todger Fairmile.

SHIRLEY (*rising with grim joy*): I'll go with him, miss. I want to see them two meet. I'll take him to the infirmary when it's over.

BILL (*to* SHIRLEY, *with undissembled misgiving*): Is thet im you was speakin on?

SHIRLEY: Thats him.

BILL: Im that wrastled in the music awl?

SHIRLEY: The competitions at the National Sportin Club was worth nigh a hundred a year to him. He's gev em up now for religion; so he's a bit fresh for want of the exercise he was accustomed to. He'll be glad to see you. Come along.

BILL: Wots is wight?

SHIRLEY: Thirteen four. (BILL'S *last hope expires.*)

BARBARA: Go and talk to him, Bill. He'll convert you.

SHIRLEY: He'll convert your head into a mashed potato.

BILL (*sullenly*): Aw aint afride of im. Aw aint afride of ennybody. Bat e can lick me. She's dan me. (*He sits down moodily on the edge of the horse trough.*)

SHIRLEY: You aint going. I thought not. (*He resumes his seat.*)

BARBARA (*calling*): Jenny!

JENNY (*appearing at the shelter door with a plaster on the corner of her mouth*): Yes, Major.

BARBARA: Send Rummy Mitchens out to clear away here.

JENNY: I think she's afraid.

BARBARA (*her resemblance to her mother flashing out for a moment*): Nonsense! she must do as she's told.

JENNY (*calling into the shelter*): Rummy: the Major says you must come.

(JENNY *comes to* BARBARA, *purposely keeping on the side next* BILL, *lest he should suppose that she shrank from him or bore malice.*)

BARBARA: Poor little Jenny! Are you tired? (*Looking at the wounded cheek.*) Does it hurt?

JENNY: No: it's all right now. It was nothing.

BARBARA (*critically*): It was as hard as he could hit, I expect. Poor Bill! You dont feel angry with him, do you?

JENNY: Oh no, no, no: indeed I dont, Major, bless his poor heart!

(BARBARA *kisses her; and she runs away merrily into the shelter.* BILL *writhes with an agonizing return of his new and alarming symptoms, but says nothing.* RUMMY MITCHENS *comes from the shelter.*)

BARBARA (*going to meet* RUMMY): Now Rummy, bustle. Take in those mugs and plates to be washed; and throw the crumbs about for the birds.

RUMMY *takes the three plates and mugs; but* SHIRLEY *takes back his mug from her, as there is still some milk left in it.*)

RUMMY: There aint any crumbs. This aint a time to waste good bread on birds.

PRICE (*appearing at the shelter door*): Gentleman come to see the shelter, Major. Says he's your father.

BARBARA: All right. Coming. (SNOBBY *goes back into the shelter, followed by* BARBARA.)

RUMMY (*stealing across to* BILL *and addressing him in a subdued voice, but with intense conviction*): I'd av the lor of you, you flat eared pignosed potwalloper, if she'd let me. Youre no gentleman, to hit a lady in the face. (BILL, *with greater things moving in him, takes no notice.*)

SHIRLEY (*following her*): Here! in with you and dont get yourself into more trouble by talking.

RUMMY (*with hauteur*): I aint ad the pleasure o being hintroduced to you, as I can remember. (*She goes into the shelter with the plates.*)

SHIRLEY: Thats the —

BILL (*savagely*): Downt you talk to me, d'ye eah? You lea me alown, or Aw'll do you a mischief. Aw'm not dirt under your feet, ennywy.

SHIRLEY (*calmly*): Dont you be afeerd. You

aint such prime company that you need expect to be sought after. (*He is about to go into the shelter when* BARBARA *comes out, with* UNDERSHAFT *on her right.*)

BARBARA: Oh, there you are, Mr Shirley! (*Between them.*) This is my father: I told you he was a Secularist, didn't I? Perhaps youll be able to comfort one another.

UNDERSHAFT (*startled*): A Secularist! Not the least in the world: on the contrary, a confirmed mystic.

BARBARA: Sorry, I'm sure. By the way, papa, what is your religion? in case I have to introduce you again.

UNDERSHAFT: My religion? Well, my dear, I am a Millionaire. That is my religion.

BARBARA: Then I'm afraid you and Mr Shirley wont be able to comfort one another after all. Youre not a Millionaire, are you, Peter?

SHIRLEY: No; and proud of it.

UNDERSHAFT (*gravely*): Poverty, my friend, is not a thing to be proud of.

SHIRLEY (*angrily*): Who made your millions for you? Me and my like. Whats kep us poor? Keepin you rich. I wouldnt have your conscience, not for all your income.

UNDERSHAFT: I wouldnt have your income, not for all your conscience, Mr Shirley. (*He goes to the penthouse and sits down on a form.*)

BARBARA (*stopping* SHIRLEY *adroitly as he is about to retort*): You wouldnt think he was my father, would you, Peter? Will you go into the shelter and lend the lasses a hand for a while: we're worked off our feet.

SHIRLEY (*bitterly*): Yes: I'm in their debt for a meal, aint I?

BARBARA: Oh, not because youre in their debt, but for love of them, Peter, for love of them. (*He cannot understand, and is rather scandalized.*) There! dont stare at me. In with you; and give that conscience of yours a holiday. (*Bustling him into the shelter.*)

SHIRLEY (*as he goes in*): Ah! it's a pity you never was trained to use your reason, miss. Youd have been a very taking lecturer on Secularism.

(BARBARA *turns to her father.*)

UNDERSHAFT: Never mind me, my dear. Go about your work; and let me watch it for a while.

BARBARA: All right.

UNDERSHAFT: For instance, whats the matter with that outpatient over there?

BARBARA (*looking at* BILL, *whose attitude has never changed, and whose expression of brooding wrath has deepened*): Oh, we shall cure him in no time. Just watch. (*She goes over to* BILL *and waits. He glances up at her and casts his eyes down again, uneasy, but grimmer than ever.*) It would be nice to just stamp on Mog Habbijam's face, wouldnt it, Bill?

BILL (*starting up from the trough in consternation*): It's a loy: Aw never said so. (*She shakes her head.*) Oo taold you wot was in moy mawnd?

BARBARA: Only your new friend.

BILL: Wot new friend?

BARBARA: The devil, Bill. When he gets round people they get miserable, just like you.

BILL (*with a heartbreaking attempt at devil-may-care cheerfulness*): Aw aint miserable. (*He sits down again, and stretches his legs in an attempt to seem indifferent.*)

BARBARA: Well, if youre happy, why dont you look happy, as we do?

BILL (*his legs curling back in spite of him*): Aw'm eppy enaff, Aw tell you. Woy cawnt you lea me alown? Wot ev I dan to you? Aw aint smashed your fice, ev Aw?

BARBARA (*softly: wooing his soul*): It's not me thats getting at you, Bill.

BILL: Oo else is it?

BARBARA: Somebody that doesnt intend you to smash women's faces, I suppose. Somebody or something that wants to make a man of you.

BILL (*blustering*): Mike a menn o me! Aint Aw a menn? eh? Oo sez Aw'm not a menn?

BARBARA: Theres a man in you somewhere, I suppose. But why did he let you hit poor little Jenny Hill? That wasnt very manly of him, was it?

BILL (*tormented*): Ev dan wiv it, Aw tell you. Chack it. Aw'm sick o your Jenny Ill and er silly little fice.

BARBARA: Then why do you keep thinking about it? Why does it keep coming up against you in your mind? Youre not getting converted, are you?

BILL (*with conviction*): Not ME. Not lawkly.

BARBARA: Thats right, Bill. Hold out against it. Put out your strength. Dont lets get you cheap. Todger Fairmile said he wrestled for

three nights against his salvation harder than he ever wrestled with the Jap at the music hall. He gave in to the Jap when his arm was going to break. But he didnt give in to his salvation until his heart was going to break. Perhaps youll escape that. You havnt any heart, have you?

BILL: Wot d'ye mean? Woy aint Aw got a awt the sime as ennybody else?

BARBARA: A man with a heart wouldnt have bashed poor little Jenny's face, would he?

BILL (*almost crying*): Ow, will you lea me alown? Ev Aw ever offered to meddle with you, that you cam neggin and provowkin me lawk this? (*He writhes convulsively from his eyes to his toes.*)

BARBARA (*with a steady soothing hand on his arm and a gentle voice that never lets him go*): It's your soul thats hurting you, Bill, and not me. Weve been through it all ourselves. Come with us, Bill. (*He looks wildly round.*) To brave manhood on earth and eternal glory in heaven. (*He is on the point of breaking down.*) Come. (*A drum is heard in the shelter; and* BILL, *with a gasp, escapes from the spell as* BARBARA *turns quickly.* ADOLPHUS *enters from the shelter with a big drum.*) Oh! there you are, Dolly. Let me introduce a new friend of mine, Mr Bill Walker. This is my bloke, Bill: Mr Cusins. (*CUSINS salutes with his drumstick.*)

BILL: Gowin to merry im?

BARBARA: Yes.

BILL (*fervently*): Gawd elp im! Gaw-aw-aw-awd elp im!

BARBARA: Why? Do you think he wont be happy with me?

BILL: Awve aony ed to stend it for a mawnin: e'll ev to stend it for a lawftawm.

CUSINS: That is a frightful reflection, Mr Walker. But I cant tear myself away from her.

BILL: Well, Aw ken. (*To* BARBARA.) Eah! do you knaow where Aw'm gowin to, and wot Aw'm gowin to do?

BARBARA: Yes: youre going to heaven; and youre coming back here before the week's out to tell me so.

BILL: You loy. Aw'm gowin to Kennintahn, to spit in Todger Fairmawl's eye. Aw beshed Jenny Ill's fice; an nar Aw'll git me aown fice beshed and cam beck and shaow it to er. Ee'll itt me ardern Aw itt her. Thatll mike us square. (*To* ADOLPHUS.) Is thet fair or is it not? Youre a genlmn: you oughter knaow.

BARBARA: Two black eyes wont make one white one, Bill.

BILL: Aw didnt awst you. Cawnt you never keep your mahth shat? Oy awst the genlmn.

CUSINS (*reflectively*): Yes: I think youre right, Mr Walker. Yes: I should do it. It's curious: it's exactly what an ancient Greek would have done.

BARBARA: But what good will it do?

CUSINS: Well, it will give Mr Fairmile some exercise; and it will satisfy Mr Walker's soul.

BILL: Rot! there aint nao sach a thing as a saoul. Ah kin you tell wevver Awve a saoul or not? You never seen it.

BARBARA: Ive seen it hurting you when you went against it.

BILL (*with compressed aggravation*): If you was maw gel and took the word aht o me mahth lawk thet, Aw'd give you sathink youd feel urtin, Aw would. (*To* ADOLPHUS.) You tike maw tip, mite. Stop er jawr; or youll doy afoah your tawm (*With intense expression.*) Wore aht: thets wot youll be: wore aht. (*He goes away through the gate.*)

CUSINS (*looking after him*): I wonder!

BARBARA: Dolly! (*indignant, in her mother's manner*).

CUSINS: Yes, my dear, it's very wearing to be in love with you. If it lasts, I quite think I shall die young.

BARBARA: Should you mind?

CUSINS: Not at all. (*He is suddenly softened, and kisses her over the drum, evidently not for the first time, as people cannot kiss over a big drum without practice.* UNDERSHAFT *coughs.*)

BARBARA: It's all right, papa, weve not forgotten you. Dolly: explain the place to papa: I havnt time. (*She goes busily into the shelter.*)

(UNDERSHAFT *and* ADOLPHUS *now have the yard to themselves.* UNDERSHAFT, *seated on a form, and still keenly attentive, looks hard at* ADOLPHUS. ADOLPHUS *looks hard at him.*)

UNDERSHAFT: I fancy you guess something of what is in my mind, Mr Cusins. (CUSINS *flourishes his drumsticks as if in the act of beating a lively rataplan, but makes no sound.*) Exactly so. But suppose Barbara finds you out!

CUSINS: You know, I do not admit that I am imposing on Barbara. I am quite genuinely interested in the views of the Salvation Army. The fact is, I am a sort of collector of religions; and the curious thing is that I find I

can believe them all. By the way, have you any religion?

UNDERSHAFT: Yes.

CUSINS: Anything out of the common?

UNDERSHAFT: Only that there are two things necessary to Salvation.

CUSINS (*disappointed, but polite*): Ah, the Church Catechism. Charles Lomax also belongs to the Established Church.

UNDERSHAFT: The two things are —

CUSINS: Baptism and —

UNDERSHAFT: No. Money and gunpowder.

CUSINS (*surprised, but interested*): That is the general opinion of our governing classes. The novelty is in hearing any man confess it.

UNDERSHAFT: Just so.

CUSINS: Excuse me: is there any place in your religion for honor, justice, truth, love, mercy and so forth?

UNDERSHAFT: Yes: they are the graces and luxuries of a rich, strong, and safe life.

CUSINS: Suppose one is forced to choose between them and money or gunpowder?

UNDERSHAFT: Choose money and gunpowder; for without enough of both you cannot afford the others.

CUSINS: That is your religion?

UNDERSHAFT: Yes.

(*The cadence of this reply makes a full close in the conversation,* CUSINS *twists his face dubiously and contemplates* UNDERSHAFT. UNDERSHAFT *contemplates him.*)

CUSINS: Barbara wont stand that. You will have to choose between your religion and Barbara.

UNDERSHAFT: So will you, my friend. She will find out that that drum of yours is hollow.

CUSINS: Father Undershaft: you are mistaken: I am a sincere Salvationist. You do not understand the Salvation Army. It is the army of joy, of love, of courage: it has banished the fear and remorse and despair of the old hell-ridden evangelical sects: it marches to fight the devil with trumpet and drum, with music and dancing, with banner and palm, as becomes a sally from heaven by its happy garrison. It picks the waster out of the public house and makes a man of him: it finds a worm wriggling in a back kitchen, and lo! a woman! Men and women of rank too, sons and daughters of the Highest. It takes the poor professor of Greek, the most artificial and self-suppressed of human creatures, from his meal of roots, and lets loose the rhapsodist in him; reveals the true worship of Dionysos to him; sends him down the public street drumming dithyrambs. (*He plays a thundering flourish on the drum.*)

UNDERSHAFT: You will alarm the shelter.

CUSINS: Oh, they are accustomed to these sudden ecstasies. However, if the drum worries you — (*He pockets the drumsticks; unhooks the drum; and stands it on the ground opposite the gateway.*)

UNDERSHAFT: Thank you.

CUSINS: You remember what Euripides says about your money and gunpowder?

UNDERSHAFT: No.

CUSINS (*declaiming*):

One and another
In money and guns may outpass his brother;
And men in their millions float and flow
And seethe with a million hopes as leaven;
And they win their will; or they miss their will;
And their hopes are dead or are pined for still;
   But who'er can know
   As the long days go
That to live is happy, has found his heaven.

My translation: what do you think of it?

UNDERSHAFT: I think, my friend, that if you wish to know, as the long days go, that to live is happy, you must first acquire money enough for a decent life, and power enough to be your own master.

CUSINS: You are damnably discouraging. (*He resumes his declamation.*)

   Is it so hard a thing to see
   That the spirit of God — whate'er it be —
The law that abides and changes not, ages long,
The Eternal and Nature-born: these things be strong?
What else is Wisdom? What of Man's endeavor,
Or God's high grace so lovely and so great?
To stand from fear set free? to breathe and wait?
To hold a hand uplifted over Fate?
And shall not Barbara be loved for ever?

UNDERSHAFT: Euripides mentions Barbara, does he?

CUSINS: It is a fair translation. The word means Loveliness.

UNDERSHAFT: May I ask — as Barbara's father — how much a year she is to be loved for ever on?

CUSINS: As for Barbara's father, that is more your affair than mine. I can feed her by teaching Greek: that is about all.

UNDERSHAFT: Do you consider it a good match for her?

CUSINS (*with polite obstinacy*): Mr Undershaft: I am in many ways a weak, timid, ineffectual person; and my health is far from satisfactory. But whenever I feel that I must have anything, I get it, sooner or later. I feel that way about Barbara. I dont like marriage: I feel intensely afraid of it; and I dont know what I shall do with Barbara or what she will do with me. But I feel that I and nobody else must marry her. Please regard that as settled. — Not that I wish to be artibrary; but why should I waste your time in discussing what is inevitable?

UNDERSHAFT: You mean that you will stick at nothing: not even the conversion of the Salvation Army to the worship of Dionysos.

CUSINS: The business of the Salvation Army is to save, not to wrangle about the name of the pathfinder. Dionysos or another: what does it matter?

UNDERSHAFT (*rising and approaching him*): Professor Cusins: you are a young man after my own heart.

CUSINS: Mr Undershaft: you are, as far as I am able to gather, a most infernal old rascal; but you appeal very strongly to my sense of ironic humor.

(UNDERSHAFT *mutely offers his hand. They shake.*)

UNDERSHAFT (*suddenly concentrating himself*): And now to business.

CUSINS: Pardon me. We are discussing religion. Why go back to such an uninteresting and unimportant subject as business?

UNDERSHAFT: Religion is our business at present, because it is through religion alone that we can win Barbara.

CUSINS: Have you, too, fallen in love with Barbara?

UNDERSHAFT: Yes, with a father's love.

CUSINS: A father's love for a grown-up daughter is the most dangerous of all infatuations. I apologize for mentioning my own pale, coy, mistrustful fancy in the same breath with it.

UNDERSHAFT: Keep to the point. We have to win her; and we are neither of us Methodists.

CUSINS: That doesnt matter. The power Barbara wields here — the power that wields Barbara herself — is not Calvinism, not Presbyterianism, not Methodism —

UNDERSHAFT: Not Greek Paganism either, eh?

CUSINS: I admit that. Barbara is quite original in her religion.

UNDERSHAFT (*triumphantly*): Aha! Barbara Undershaft would be. Her inspiration comes from within herself.

CUSINS: How do you suppose it got there?

UNDERSHAFT (*in towering excitement*): It is the Undershaft inheritance. I shall hand on my torch to my daughter. She shall make my converts and preach my gospel —

CUSINS: What! Money and gunpowder!

UNDERSHAFT: Yes, money and gunpowder. Freedom and power. Command of life and command of death.

CUSINS (*urbanely: trying to bring him down to earth*): This is extremely interesting, Mr Undershaft. Of course you know that you are mad.

UNDERSHAFT (*with redoubled force*): And you?

CUSINS: Oh, mad as a hatter. You are welcome to my secret since I have discovered yours. But I am astonished. Can a madman make cannons?

UNDERSHAFT: Would anyone else than a madman make them? And now (*with surging energy*) question for question. Can a sane man translate Euripides?

CUSINS: No.

UNDERSHAFT (*seizing him by the shoulder*): Can a sane woman make a man of a waster or a woman of a worm?

CUSINS (*reeling before the storm*): Father Colossus — Mammoth Millionaire —

UNDERSHAFT (*pressing him*): Are there two mad people or three in this Salvation shelter today?

CUSINS: You mean Barbara is as mad as we are?

UNDERSHAFT (*pushing him lightly off and resuming his equanimity suddenly and completely*): Pooh, Professor! let us call things by their proper names. I am a millionaire; you are a poet: Barbara is a savior of souls. What have we three to do with the common mob of slaves and idolators? (*He sits down again with a shrug of contempt for the mob.*)

CUSINS: Take care! Barbara is in love with the common people. So am I. Have you never felt the romance of that love?

UNDERSHAFT (*cold and sardonic*): Have you ever been in love with Poverty, like St Francis? Have you ever been in love with Dirt, like St Simeon! Have you ever been in love with disease and suffering, like our nurses and philanthropists? Such passions are not virtues, but the most unnatural of all the vices. This love of the common people may please an earl's granddaughter and a university professor; but I have been a common man and a poor man; and it has no romance for me. Leave it to the poor to pretend that poverty is a blessing: leave it to the coward to make a religion of his cowardice by preaching humility: we know better than that. We three must stand together above the common people: how else can we help their children to climb up beside us? Barbara must belong to us, not to the Salvation Army.

CUSINS: Well, I can only say that if you think you will get her away from the Salvation Army by talking to her as you have been talking to me, you don't know Barbara.

UNDERSHAFT: My friend: I never ask for what I can buy.

CUSINS (*in a white fury*): Do I understand you to imply that you can buy Barbara?

UNDERSHAFT: No; but I can buy the Salvation Army.

CUSINS: Quite impossible.

UNDERSHAFT: You shall see. All religious organizations exist by selling themselves to the rich.

CUSINS: Not the Army. That is the Church of the poor.

UNDERSHAFT: All the more reason for buying it.

CUSINS: I don't think you quite know what the Army does for the poor.

UNDERSHAFT: Oh yes I do. It draws their teeth: that is enough for me as a man of business.

CUSINS: Nonsense! It makes them sober —

UNDERSHAFT: I prefer sober workmen. The profits are larger.

CUSINS: — honest —

UNDERSHAFT: Honest workmen are the most economical.

CUSINS: — attached to their homes —

UNDERSHAFT: So much the better: they will put up with anything sooner than change their shop.

CUSINS: — happy —

UNDERSHAFT: An invaluable safeguard against revolution.

CUSINS: — unselfish —

UNDERSHAFT: Indifferent to their own interests, which suits me exactly.

CUSINS: — with their thoughts on heavenly things —

UNDERSHAFT (*rising*): And not on Trade Unionism nor Socialism. Excellent.

CUSINS (*revolted*): You really are an infernal old rascal.

UNDERSHAFT (*indicating* PETER SHIRLEY, *who has just come from the shelter and strolled dejectedly down the yard between them*): And this is an honest man!

SHIRLEY: Yes; and what av I got by it? (*He passes on bitterly and sits on the form, in the corner of the penthouse.*)

(SNOBBY PRICE, *beaming sactimoniously, and* JENNY HILL, *with a tambourine full of coppers, come from the shelter and go to the drum, on which* JENNY *begins to count the money.*)

UNDERSHAFT (*replying to* SHIRLEY): Oh, your employers must have got a good deal by it from first to last. (*He sits on the table, with one foot on the side form.* CUSINS, *overwhelmed, sits down on the same form nearer the shelter.* BARBARA *comes from the shelter to the middle of the yard. She is excited and a little overwrought.*)

BARBARA: Weve just had a splendid experience meeting at the other gate in Cripps's lane. I've hardly ever seen them so much moved as they were by your confession, Mr Price.

PRICE: I could almost be glad of my past wickedness if I could believe that it would elp to keep hathers straight.

BARBARA: So it will, Snobby. How much, Jenny?

JENNY: Four and tenpence, Major.

BARBARA: Oh Snobby, if you had given your poor mother just one more kick, we should have got the whole five shillings!

PRICE: If she heard you say that, miss, she'd be sorry I didnt. But I'm glad. Oh what a joy it will be to her when she hears I'm saved!

UNDERSHAFT: Shall I contribute the odd twopence, Barbara? The millionaire's mite, eh? (*He takes a couple of pennies from his pocket.*)

BARBARA: How did you make that twopence?

UNDERSHAFT: As usual. By selling cannons, torpedoes, submarines, and my new patent Grand Duke hand grenade.

BARBARA: Put it back in your pocket. You cant buy your salvation here for twopence: you must work it out.

UNDERSHAFT: Is twopence not enough? I can afford a little more, if you press me.

BARBARA: Two million millions would not be enough. There is bad blood on your hands; and nothing but good blood can cleanse them. Money is no use. Take it away. (*She turns to* CUSINS.) Dolly: you must write another letter for me to the papers. (*He makes a wry face.*) Yes: I know you dont like it; but it must be done. The starvation this winter is beating us: everybody is unemployed. The General says we must close this shelter if we cant get more money. I force the collections at the meetings until I am ashamed: dont I, Snobby?

PRICE: It's a fair treat to see you work it, miss. The way you got them up from three-and-six to four-and-ten with that hymn, penny by penny and verse by verse, was a caution. Not a Cheap Jack on Mile End Waste could touch you at it.

BARBARA: Yes; but I wish we could do without it. I am getting at last to think more of the collection than of the people's souls. And what are those hatfuls of pence and halfpence? We want thousands! tens of thousands! hundreds of thousands! I want to convert people, not to be always begging for the Army in a way I'd die sooner than beg for myself.

UNDERSHAFT (*in profound irony*): Genuine unselfishness is capable of anything, my dear.

BARBARA (*unsuspectingly, as she turns away to take the money from the drum and put it in a cash bag she carries*): Yes, isnt it? (UNDERSHAFT *looks sardonically at* CUSINS.)

CUSINS (*aside to* UNDERSHAFT): Mephistopheles! Machiavelli!

BARBARA (*tears coming into her eyes as she ties the bag and pockets it*): How are we to feed them? I cant talk religion to a man with bodily hunger in his eyes. (*Almost breaking down.*) It's frightful.

JENNY (*running to her*): Major, dear —

BARBARA (*rebounding*): No: dont comfort

me. It will be all right. We shall get the money.

UNDERSHAFT: How?

JENNY: By praying for it, of course. Mrs Baines says she prayed for it last night; and she has never prayed for it in vain: never once. (*She goes to the gate and looks out into the street.*)

BARBARA (*who has dried her eyes and regained her composure*): By the way, dad, Mrs Baines has come to march with us to our big meeting this afternoon; and she is very anxious to meet you, for some reason or other. Perhaps she'll convert you.

UNDERSHAFT: I shall be delighted, my dear.

JENNY (*at the gate: excitedly*): Major! Major! heres that man back again.

BARBARA: What man?

JENNY: The man that hit me. Oh, I hope he's coming back to join us.

(BILL WALKER, *with frost on his jacket, comes through the gate, his hands deep in his pockets and his chin sunk between his shoulders, like a cleaned-out gambler. He halts between* BARBARA *and the drum.*)

BARBARA: Hullo, Bill! Back already!

BILL (*nagging at her*): Bin talkin ever sence, ev you?

BARBARA: Pretty nearly. Well, has Todger paid you out for poor Jenny's jaw?

BILL: Nao e aint.

BARBARA: I thought your jacket looked a bit snowy.

BILL: Sao it is snaowy. You want to knaow where the snaow cam from, downt you?

BARBARA: Yes.

BILL: Well, it cam from orf the grahnd in Pawkinses Corner in Kennintahn. It got rabbed orf be maw shaoulders: see?

BARBARA: Pity you didnt rub some off with your knees, Bill! That would have done you a lot of good.

BILL (*with sour mirthless humor*): Aw was sivin anather menn's knees at the tawm. E was kneelin on moy ed, e was.

JENNY: Who was kneeling on your head?

BILL: Todger was. E was pryin for me: pryin camfortable wiv me as a cawpet. Sow was Mog. Sao was the aol bloomin meetin. Mog she sez 'Ow Lawd brike is stabborn sperrit; bat downt urt is dear art.' Thet was wot she said. 'Downt urt is dear art'! An er blowk — thirteen stun

four! — kneelin wiv all is wight on me. Fanny, aint it?

JENNY: Oh no. We're so sorry, Mr Walker.

BARBARA (*enjoying it frankly*): Nonsense! of course it's funny. Served you right, Bill! You must have done something to him first.

BILL (*doggedly*): Aw did wot Aw said Aw'd do. Aw spit in is eye. E looks ap at the skoy and sez, 'Ow that Aw should be fahnd worthy to be spit upon for the gospel's sike!' e sez; an Mog sez 'Glaory Allelloolier!'; an then e called me Braddher, an dahned me as if Aw was a kid and e was me mather worshin me a Setterda nawt. Aw ednt jast nao shaow wiv im at all. Arf the street pryed; an the tather arf larfed fit to split theirselves. (*To* BARBARA.) There! are you settisfawd nah?

BARBARA (*her eyes dancing*): Wish I'd been there, Bill.

BILL: Yus: youd a got in a hextra bit o talk on me, wouldnt you?

JENNY: I'm so sorry, Mr Walker.

BILL (*fiercely*): Downt you gow being sorry for me: youve no call. Listen eah. Aw browk your jawr.

JENNY: No, it didn't hurt me: indeed it didnt, except for a moment. It was only that I was frightened.

BILL: Aw downt want to be forgive be you, or be ennybody. Wot Aw did Aw'll py for. Aw trawd to gat me aown jawr browk to settisfaw you —

JENNY (*distressed*): Oh no —

BILL (*impatiently*): Tell y' Aw did: cawnt you listen to wots bein taold you? All Aw got be it was bein mide a sawt of in the pablic street for me pines. Well, if Aw cawnt settisfaw you one way, Aw ken anather. Listen eah! Aw ed two quid sived agen the frost; an Awve a pahnd of it left. A mite o mawn last week ed words with the judy e's gowing to merry. E give er wot-for; an e's bin fawnd fifteen bob. E ed a rawt to itt er cause they was gowin to be merrid; but Aw ednt nao rawt to itt you! sao put anather fawy bob on an call it a pahnd's worth. (*He produces a sovereign.*) Eahs the manney. Tike it; and lets ev no more o your forgivin an prying and your Mijor jawrin me. Let wot Aw dan be dan an pide for; and let there be a end of it.

JENNY: Oh, I couldnt take it, Mr Walker. But if you would give a shilling or two to poor Rummy Mitchens! you really did hurt her; and she's old.

BILL (*contemptuously*): Not lawkly. Aw'd give her anather as soon as look at er. Let her ev the lawr o me as she threatened! She aint forgiven me: not mach. Wot Aw dan to cr is not on me mawnd — wot she (*indicating* BAR-BARA) mawt call on me conscience — no more than stickin a pig. It's this Christian gime o yours that Aw wownt ev plyed agen me: this bloomin forgivin an neggin an jawrin that mikes a menn thet sore that iz lawf's a burdn to im. Aw wownt ev it, Aw tell you; sao tike your manney and stop thraowin your silly beshed fice hap agen me.

JENNY: Major: may I take a little of it for the Army?

BARBARA: No: the Army is not to be bought. We want your soul, Bill; and we'll take nothing less.

BILL (*bitterly*): Aw knaow. Me an maw few shillins is not good enaff for you. Youre a earl's grendorter, you are. Nathink 'less than a an-dered pahnd for you.

UNDERSHAFT: Come Barbara! you could do a great deal of good with a hundred pounds. If you will set this gentleman's mind at ease by taking his pound, I will give the other ninety-nine.

(BILL, *dazed by such opulence, instinctively touches his cap.*)

BARBARA: Oh, youre too extravagant, papa. Bill offers twenty pieces of silver. All you need offer is the other ten. That will make the standard price to buy anybody who's for sale. I'm not; and the Army's not. (*To* BILL.) Youll never have another quiet moment, Bill, until you come round to us. You cant stand out against your salvation.

BILL (*sullenly*): Aw cawnt stend aht agen music awl wrastlers and awtful tangued women. Awve offered to py. Aw can do no more. Tike it or leave it. There it is. (*He throws the sovereign on the drum, and sits down on the horse-trough. The coin fascinates SNOBBY PRICE, who takes an early opportunity of dropping his cap on it.*)

(MRS BAINES *comes from the shelter. She is dressed as a Salvation Army Commissioner. She is an earnest looking woman of about 40, with a caressing, urgent voice, and an appealing manner.*)

BARBARA: This is my father, Mrs Baines. (UNDERSHAFT *comes from the table, taking his hat off with marked civility*). Try what you can do with him. He wont listen to me, because he remembers what a fool I was when I was a baby. (*She leaves them together and chats with* JENNY.)

MRS BAINES: Have you been shewn over the shelter, Mr Undershaft? You know the work we're doing, of course.

UNDERSHAFT (*very civilly*): The whole nation knows it, Mrs Baines.

MRS BAINES: No, sir: the whole nation does not know it, or we should not be crippled as we are for want of money to carry our work through the length and breadth of the land. Let me tell you that there would have been rioting this winter in London but for us.

UNDERSHAFT: You really think so?

MRS BAINES: I know it. I remember 1886, when you rich gentlemen hardened your hearts against the cry of the poor. They broke the windows of your clubs in Pall Mall.

UNDERSHAFT (*gleaming with approval of their method*): And the Mansion House Fund went up next day from thirty thousand pounds to seventy-nine thousand! I remember quite well.

MRS BAINES: Well, wont you help me to get at the people? They wont break windows then. Come here, Price. Let me shew you to this gentleman. (*Price comes to be inspected.*) Do you remember the window breaking?

PRICE: My ole father thought it was the revolution, maam.

MRS BAINES: Would you break windows now?

PRICE: Oh no, maam. The windows of caven av bin opened to me. I know now that the rich man is a sinner like myself.

RUMMY (*appearing above at the loft door*): Snobby Price!

SNOBBY: Wot is it?

RUMMY: Your mother's askin for you at the other gate in Cripps's Lane. She's heard about your confession. (*Price turns pale.*)

MRS BAINES: Go, Mr Price; and pray with her.

JENNY: You can go through the shelter, Snobby.

PRICE (*to* MRS BAINES): I couldnt face her now, maam, with all the weight of my sins fresh on me. Tell her she'll find her son at ome, waitin for her in prayer. (*He skulks off through the gate, incidentally stealing the sovereign on his way out by picking up his cap from the drum.*)

MRS BAINES (*with swimming eyes*): You see how we take the anger and the bitterness against you out of their hearts, Mr Undershaft.

UNDERSHAFT: It is certainly most convenient and gratifying to all large employers of labor, Mrs Baines.

MRS BAINES: Barbara: Jenny: I have good news: most wonderful news. (JENNY *runs to her.*) My prayers have been answered. I told you they would, Jenny, didnt I?

JENNY: Yes, yes.

BARBARA (*moving nearer to the drum*): Have we got money enough to keep the shelter open?

MRS BAINES: I hope we shall have enough to keep all the shelters open. Lord Saxmundham has promised us five thousand pounds —

BARBARA: Hooray!

JENNY: Glory!

MRS BAINES: — if —

BARBARA: 'If!' If what?

MRS BAINES: — if five other gentlemen will give a thousand each to make it up to ten thousand.

BARBARA: Who is Lord Saxmundham? I never heard of him.

UNDERSHAFT (*who has pricked up his ears at the peer's name, and is now watching* BARBARA *curiously*): A new creation, my dear. You have heard of Sir Horace Bodger?

BARBARA: Bodger! Do you mean the distiller? Bodger's whiskey!

UNDERSHAFT: That is the man. He is one of the greatest of our public benefactors. He restored the cathedral at Hakington. They made him a baronet for that. He gave half a million to the funds of his party: they made him a baron for that.

SHIRLEY: What will they give him for the five thousand?

UNDERSHAFT: There is nothing left to give him. So the five thousand, I should think, is to save his soul.

MRS BAINES: Heaven grant it may! O Mr Undershaft, you have some very rich friends. Cant you help us towards the other five thousand? We are going to hold a great meeting this afternoon at the Assembly Hall in the Mile End Road. If I could only announce that one gentleman had come forward to support Lord Saxmundham, others would follow. Dont you know somebody? couldnt you? wouldn't you? (*her eyes fill with tears*) oh,

think of those poor people, Mr Undershaft: think of how much it means to them, and how little to a great man like you.

UNDERSHAFT (*sardonically gallant*): Mrs Baines: you are irresistible. I cant disappoint you; and I cant deny myself the satisfaction of making Bodger pay up. You shall have your five thousand pounds.

MRS BAINES: Thank God!

UNDERSHAFT: You dont thank me?

MRS BAINES: Oh sir, dont try to be cynical: dont be ashamed of being a good man. The Lord will bless you abundantly; and our prayers will be like a strong fortification round you all the days of your life. (*With a touch of caution.*) You will let me have the cheque to shew at the meeting, wont you? Jenny: go in and fetch a pen and ink. (JENNY *runs to the shelter door.*)

UNDERSHAFT: Do not disturb Miss Hill: I have a fountain pen (JENNY *halts. He sits at the table and writes the cheque.* CUSINS *rises to make room for him. They all watch him silently.*)

BILL (*cynically, aside to* BARBARA, *his voice and accent horribly debased*): Wot prawce selvytion nah?

BARBARA: Stop. (UNDERSHAFT *stops writing: they all turn to her in surprise.*) Mrs Baines: are you really going to take this money?

MRS BAINES (*astonished*): Why not, dear?

BARBARA: Why not! Do you know what my father is? Have you forgotten that Lord Saxmundham is Bodger the whisky man? Do you remember how we implored the County Council to stop him from writing Bodger's Whisky in letters of fire against the sky; so that the poor drink-ruined creatures on the Embankment could not wake up from their snatches of sleep without being reminded of their deadly thirst by that wicked sky sign? Do you know that the worst thing I have had to fight here is not the devil, but Bodger, Bodger, Bodger, with his whisky, his distilleries, and his tied houses? Are you going to make our shelter another tied house for him, and ask me to keep it?

BILL: Rotten dranken whisky it is too.

MRS BAINES: Dear Barbara: Lord Saxmundham has a soul to be saved like any of us. If heaven has found the way to make a good use of his money, are we to set ourselves up against the answer to our prayers?

BARBARA: I know he has a soul to be saved. Let him come down here; and I'll do my best to help him to his salvation. But he wants to send his cheque down to buy us, and go on being as wicked as ever.

UNDERSHAFT (*with a reasonableness which* CUSINS *alone perceives to be ironical*): My dear Barbara: alcohol is a very necessary article. It heals the sick —

BARBARA: It does nothing of the sort.

UNDERSHAFT: Well, it assists the doctor: that is perhaps a less questionable way of putting it. It makes life bearable to millions of people who could not endure their existence if they were quite sober. It enables Parliament to do things at eleven at night that no sane person would do at eleven in the morning. Is it Bodger's fault that this inestimable gift is deplorably abused by less than one per cent of the poor? (*He turns again to the table; signs the cheque; and crosses it.*)

MRS BAINES: Barbara: will there be less drinking or more if all those poor souls we are saving come tomorrow and find the doors of our shelters shut in their faces? Lord Saxmundham gives us the money to stop drinking — to take his own business from him.

CUSINS (*impishly*): Pure self-sacrifice on Bodger's part, clearly! Bless dear Bodger! (BARBARA *almost breaks down as* ADOLPHUS, *too, fails her.*)

UNDERSHAFT (*tearing the cheque and pocketing the book as he rises and goes past* CUSINS *to* MRS BAINES): I also, Mrs Baines, may claim a little disinterestedness. Think of my business! think of the widows and orphans! the men and lads torn to pieces with shrapnel and poisoned with lyddite! (MRS BAINES *shrinks; but he goes on remorselessly*) the oceans of blood, not one drop of which is shed in a really just cause! the ravaged crops! the peaceful peasants forced, women and men, to till their fields under the fire of opposing armies on pain of starvation! the bad blood of the fierce little cowards at home who egg on others to fight for the gratification of their national vanity! All this makes money for me: I am never richer, never busier than when the papers are full of it. Well, it is your work to preach peace on earth and good will to men. (MRS BAINES's *face lights up again.*) Every convert you make is a vote against war. (*Her lips move in prayer.*) Yet I give you this money to help you to hasten my own commercial ruin. (*He gives her the cheque.*)

CUSINS (*mounting the form in an ecstasy of mischief*): The millennium will be inaugurated by the unselfishness of Undershaft and Bodger. Oh be joyful! (*He takes the drumsticks from his pocket and flourishes them.*)

MRS BAINES (*taking the cheque*): The longer I live the more proof I see that there is an Infinite Goodness that turns everything to the work of salvation sooner or later. Who would have thought that any good could have come out of war and drink? And yet their profits are brought today to the feet of salvation to do its blessed work. (*She is affected to tears.*)

JENNY (*running to* MRS BAINES *and throwing her arms around her*): Oh dear! how blessed, how glorious it all is!

CUSINS (*in a convulsion of irony*): Let us seize this unspeakable moment. Let us march to the great meeting at once. Excuse me just an instant. (*He rushes into the shelter.* JENNY *takes her tambourine from the drum head.*)

MRS BAINES: Mr Undershaft: have you ever seen a thousand people fall on their knees with one impulse and pray? Come with us to the meeting. Barbara shall tell them that the Army is saved, and saved through you.

CUSINS (*returning impetuously from the shelter with a flag and a trombone, and coming between* MRS BAINES *and* UNDERSHAFT): You shall carry the flag down the first street, Mrs Baines (*he gives her the flag*). Mr Undershaft is a gifted trombonist: he shall intone an Olympian diapason to the West Ham Salvation March. (*Aside to* UNDERSHAFT, *as he forces the trombone on him.*) Blow, Machiavelli, blow.

UNDERSHAFT (*aside to him, as he takes the trombone*): The trumpet in Zion! (CUSINS *rushes to the drum, which he takes up and puts on.* UNDERSHAFT *continues, aloud.*) I will do my best. I could vamp a bass if I knew the tune.

CUSINS: It is a wedding chorus from one of Donizetti's operas; but we have converted it. We convert everything to good here, including Bodger. You remember the chorus. 'For thee immense rejoicing — immenso giubilo — immenso giubilo.' (*With drum obbligato.*) Rum tum ti tum tum, tum tum ti ta —

BARBARA: Dolly: you are breaking my heart.

CUSINS: What is a broken heart more or less here? Dionysos Undershaft has descended. I am possessed.

MRS BAINES: Come, Barbara: I must have my dear Major to carry the flag with me.

JENNY: Yes, yes, Major darling.

CUSINS (*snatches the tambourine out of* JENNY's *hand and mutely offers it to* BARBARA).

BARBARA (*coming forward a little as she puts the offer behind her with a shudder, whilst* CUSINS *recklessly tosses the tambourine back to* JENNY *and goes to the gate*): I cant come.

JENNY: Not come!

MRS BAINES (*with tears in her eyes*): Barbara: do you think I am wrong to take the money?

BARBARA (*impulsively going to her and kissing her*): No, no: God help you, dear, you must: you are saving the Army. Go; and may you have a great meeting!

JENNY: But arnt you coming?

BARBARA: No. (*She begins taking off the silver S brooch from her collar.*)

MRS BAINES: Barbara: what are you doing?

JENNY: Why are you taking your badge off? You cant be going to leave us, Major.

BARBARA (*quietly*): Father: come here.

UNDERSHAFT (*coming to her*): My dear! (*Seeing that she is going to pin the badge on his collar, he retreats to the penthouse in some alarm.*)

BARBARA (*following him*): Dont be frightened. (*She pins the badge on and steps back towards the table, shewing him to the others.*) There! It's not much for £5000, is it?

MRS BAINES: Barbara: if you wont come and pray with us, promise me you will pray for us.

BARBARA: I cant pray now. Perhaps I shall never pray again.

MRS BAINES: Barbara!

JENNY: Major!

BARBARA (*almost delirious*): I cant bear any more. Quick march!

CUSINS (*calling to the procession in the street outside*): Off we go. Play up, there! Immenso giubilo. (*He gives the time with his drum; and the band strikes up the march, which rapidly becomes more distant as the procession moves briskly away.*)

MRS BAINES: I must go, dear. Youre overworked: you will be all right tomorrow. We'll never lose you. Now Jenny: step out with the old flag. Blood and Fire! (*She marches out through the gate with her flag.*)

JENNY: Glory Hallelujah! (*flourishing her tambourine and marching*).

UNDERSHAFT (*to* CUSINS, *as he marches out past him easing the slide of his trombone*): 'My ducats and my daughter'!

CUSINS (*following him out*): Money and gunpowder!

BARBARA: Drunkenness and Murder! My God: why hast thou forsaken me?

(*She sinks on the form with her face buried in her hands. The march passes away into silence.* BILL WALKER *steals across to her.*)

BILL (*taunting*): Wot prawce selvytion nah?

SHIRLEY: Dont you hit her when she's down.

BILL: She itt me wen aw wiz dahn. Waw shouldnt Aw git a bit o me aown beck?

BARBARA (*raising her head*): I didnt take your money, Bill.

(*She crosses the yard to the gate and turns her back on the two men to hide her face from them.*)

BILL (*sneering after her*): Naow, it warnt cnaff for you. (*Turning to the drum, he misses the money.*) Ellow! If you aint took it sammun else ez. Weres it gorn? Bly me if Jenny Ill didnt tike it arter all!

RUMMY (*screaming at him from the loft*): You lie, you dirty blackguard! Snobby Price pinched it off the drum when he took up his cap. I was up here all the time an see im do it.

BILL: Wot! Stowl maw manney! Waw didnt you call thief on him, you silly aold macker you?

RUMMY: To serve you aht for ittin me acrost the ficc. It's cost y'pahnd, that az. (*Raising a pæan of squalid triumph.*) I done you. I'm even with you. Uve ad it aht o y — (BILL *snatches up* SHIRLEY's *mug and hurls it at her. She slams the loft door and vanishes. The mug smashes against the door and falls in fragments.*)

BILL (*beginning to chuckle*): Tell us, aol menn, wot o'clock this mawnin was it wen im as they call Snobby Prawce was sived?

BARBARA (*turning to him more composedly, and with unspoiled sweetness*): About half past twelve, Bill. And he pinched your pound at a quarter to two. I know. Well, you cant afford to lose it. I'll send it to you.

BILL (*his voice and accent suddenly improv-*

ing): Not if Aw wiz to stawve for it. Aw aint to be bought.

SHIRLEY: Aint you? Youd sell yourself to the devil for a pint o' beer; only there aint no devil to make the offer.

BILL (*unashamed*): Sao Aw would, mite, and often ev, cheerful. But she cawnt baw me. (*Approaching* BARBARA.) You wanted maw saoul, did you? Well, you aint got it.

BARBARA: I nearly got it, Bill. But weve sold it back to you for ten thousand pounds.

SHIRLEY: And dear at the money!

BARBARA: No, Peter: it was worth more than money.

BILL (*salvationproof*): It's nao good: you cawnt get rahnd me nah. Aw downt blieve in it; and Awve seen tody that Aw was rawt. (*Going.*) Sao long, aol soupkitchener! Ta, ta, Mijor Earl's Grendorter! (*Turning at the gate.*) Wot prawce selvytion nah? Snobby Prawce! Ha! ha!

BARBARA (*offering her hand*): Goodbye, Bill.

BILL (*taken aback, half plucks his cap off; then shoves it on again defiantly*): Git aht. (BARBARA *drops her hand, discouraged. He has a twinge of remorse.*) But thets aw rawt, you knaow. Nathink pasnl. Naow mellice. Sao long, Judy. (*He goes.*)

BARBARA: No malice. So long, Bill.

SHIRLEY (*shaking his head*): You make too much of him, miss, in your innocence.

BARBARA (*going to him*): Peter: I'm like you now. Cleaned out, and lost my job.

SHIRLEY: Youve youth an hope. Thats two better than me.

BARBARA: I'll get you a job, Peter. Thats hope for you: the youth will have to be enough for me. (*She counts her money.*) I have just enough left for two teas at Lockharts, a Rowton doss for you, and my tram and bus home. (*He frowns and rises with offended pride. She takes his arm.*) Dont be proud, Peter: it's sharing between friends. And promise me youll talk to me and not let me cry. (*She draws him towards the gate.*)

SHIRLEY: Well, I'm not accustomed to talk to the like of you —

BARBARA (*urgently*): Yes, yes: you must talk to me. Tell me about Tom Paine's books and Bradlaugh's lectures. Come along.

SHIRLEY: Ah, if you would only read Tom Paine in the proper spirit, miss! (*They go out through the gate together.*)

ACT III

Next day after lunch LADY BRITOMART *is writing in the library in Wilton Crescent.* SARAH *is reading in the armchair near the window.* BARBARA, *in ordinary fashionable dress, pale and brooding, is on the settee.* CHARLES LOMAX *enters. He starts on seeing* BARBARA *fashionably attired and in low spirits.*

LOMAX: Youve left off your uniform!

(BARBARA *says nothing; but an expression of pain passes over her face.*)

LADY BRITOMART (*warning him in low tones to be careful*): Charles!

LOMAX (*much concerned, coming behind the settee and bending sympathetically over* BARBARA): I'm awfully sorry, Barbara. You know I helped you all I could with the concertina and so forth. (*Momentously.*) Still, I have never shut my eyes to the fact that there is a certain amount of tosh about the Salvation Army. Now the claims of the Church of England —

LADY BRITOMART: Thats enough, Charles. Speak of something suited to your mental capacity.

LOMAX: But surely the Church of England is suited to all our capacities.

BARBARA (*pressing his hand*): Thank you for your sympathy, Cholly. Now go and spoon with Sarah.

LOMAX (*dragging a chair from the writing table and seating himself affectionately by* SARAH's *side*): How is my ownest today?

SARAH: I wish you wouldnt tell Cholly to do things, Barbara. He always comes straight and does them. Cholly: we're going to the works this afternoon.

LOMAX: What works?

SARAH: The cannon works.

LOMAX: What? your governor's shop!

SARAH: Yes.

LOMAX: Oh I say!

(CUSINS *enters in poor condition. He also starts visibly when he sees* BARBARA *without her uniform.*)

BARBARA: I expected you this morning, Dolly. Didnt you guess that?

CUSINS (*sitting down beside her*): I'm sorry. I have only just breakfasted.

SARAH: But weve just finished lunch.

BARBARA: Have you had one of your bad nights?

CUSINS: No: I had rather a good night: in fact, one of the most remarkable nights I have ever passed.

BARBARA: The meeting?

CUSINS: No: after the meeting.

LADY BRITOMART: You should have gone to bed after the meeting. What were you doing?

CUSINS: *Drinking*.

LADY BRITOMART.	Adolphus!
SARAH.	Dolly!
BARBARA.	Dolly!
LOMAX.	Oh I say!

LADY BRITOMART: What were you drinking, may I ask?

CUSINS: A most devilish kind of Spanish burgundy, warranted free from added alcohol: a Temperance burgundy in fact. Its richness in natural alcohol made any addition superfluous.

BARBARA: Are you joking, Dolly?

CUSINS (*patiently*): No. I have been making a night of it with the nominal head of this household: that is all.

LADY BRITOMART: Andrew made you drunk!

CUSINS: No: he only provided the wine. I think it was Dionysos who made me drunk. (*To* BARBARA.) I told you I was possessed.

LADY BRITOMART: Youre not sober yet. Go home to bed at once.

CUSINS: I have never before ventured to reproach you, Lady Brit; but how could you marry the Prince of Darkness?

LADY BRITOMART: It was much more excusable to marry him than to get drunk with him. That is a new accomplishment of Andrew's, by the way. He usent to drink.

CUSINS: He doesnt now. He only sat there and completed the wreck of my moral basis, the rout of my convictions, the purchase of my soul. He cares for you, Barbara. That is what makes him so dangerous to me.

BARBARA: That has nothing to do with it, Dolly. There are larger loves and diviner dreams than the fireside ones. You know that, dont you?

CUSINS: Yes: that is our understanding. I know it. I hold to it. Unless he can win me on that holier ground he may amuse me for a while; but he can get no deeper hold, strong as he is.

BARBARA: Keep to that; and the end will be right. Now tell me what happened at the meeting?

CUSINS: It was an amazing meeting. Mrs Baines almost died of emotion. Jenny Hill simply gibbered with hysteria. The Prince of Darkness played his trombone like a madman: its brazen roarings were like the laughter of the damned. 117 conversions took place then and there. They prayed with the most touching sincerity and gratitude for Bodger, and for the anonymous donor of the £5000. Your father would not let his name be given.

LOMAX: That was rather fine of the old man, you know. Most chaps would have wanted the advertisement.

CUSINS: He said all the charitable institutions would be down on him like kites on a battle-field if he gave his name.

LADY BRITOMART: Thats Andrew all over. He never does a proper thing without giving an improper reason for it.

CUSINS: He convinced me that I have all my life been doing improper things for proper reasons.

LADY BRITOMART: Adolphus: now that Barbara has left the Salvation Army, you had better leave it too. I will not have you playing that drum in the streets.

CUSINS: Your orders are already obeyed, Lady Brit.

BARBARA: Dolly: were you ever really in earnest about it? Would you have joined if you had never seen me?

CUSINS (*disingenuously*): Well — er — well, possibly, as a collector of religious —

LOMAX (*cunningly*): Not as a drummer, though, you know. You are a very clearheaded brainy chap, Dolly; and it must have been apparent to you that there is a certain amount of tosh about —

LADY BRITOMART: Charles: if you must drivel, drivel like a grown-up man and not like a schoolboy.

LOMAX (*out of countenance*): Well, drivel is drivel, dont you know, whatever a man's age.

LADY BRITOMART: In good society in England, Charles, men drivel at all ages by repeating silly formulas with an air of wisdom. Schoolboys make their own formulas out of slang, like you. When they reach your age, and get political private secretaryships and thing of that sort, they drop slang and get their formulas out of The Spectator or The Times. You had better confine yourself to The Times. You will find that there is a certain amount of tosh about The Times; but at least its language is reputable.

LOMAX (*overwhelmed*): You are so awfully strong-minded, Lady Brit —

LADY BRITOMART: Rubbish! (MORRISON *comes in.*) What is it?

MORRISON: If you please, my lady, Mr Undershaft has just drove up to the door.

LADY BRITOMART: Well, let him in. (MORRISON *hesitates.*) Whats the matter with you?

MORRISON: Shall I announce him, my lady; or is he at home here, so to speak, my lady?

LADY BRITOMART: Announce him.

MORRISON: Thank you, my lady. You wont mind my asking, I hope. The occasion is in a manner of speaking new to me.

LADY BRITOMART: Quite right. Go and let him in.

MORRISON: Thank you, my lady. (*He withdraws.*)

LADY BRITOMART: Children: go and get ready. (SARAH *and* BARBARA *go upstairs for their out-of-door wraps.*) Charles: go and tell Stephen to come down here in five minutes: you will find him in the drawing room. (CHARLES *goes.*) Adolphus: tell them to send round the carriage in about fifteen minutes. (ADOLPHUS *goes.*)

MORRISON (*at the door*): Mr Undershaft.

(UNDERSHAFT *comes in.* MORRISON *goes out.*)

UNDERSHAFT: Alone! How fortunate!

LADY BRITOMART (*rising*): Dont be sentimental, Andrew. Sit down. (*She sits on the settee: he sits beside her, on her left. She comes to the point before he has time to breathe.*) Sarah must have £800 a year until Charles Lomax comes into his property. Barbara will need more, and need it permanently, because Adolphus hasnt any property.

UNDERSHAFT (*resignedly*): Yes, my dear: I will see to it. Anything else? for yourself, for instance?

LADY BRITOMART: I want to talk to you about Stephen.

UNDERSHAFT (*rather wearily*): Dont, my dear. Stephen doesnt interest me.

LADY BRITOMART: He does interest me. He is our son.

UNDERSHAFT: Do you really think so? He has induced us to bring him into the world; but he chose his parents very incongruously, I think. I see nothing of myself in him, and less of you.

LADY BRITOMART: Andrew: Stephen is an excellent son, and a most steady, capable, highminded young man. You are simply trying to find an excuse for disinheriting him.

UNDERSHAFT: My dear Biddy: the Undershaft tradition disinherits him. It would be dishonest of me to leave the cannon foundry to my son.

LADY BRITOMART: It would be most unnatural and improper of you to leave it to anyone else, Andrew. Do you suppose this wicked and immoral tradition can be kept up for ever? Do you pretend that Stephen could not carry on the foundry just as well as all the other sons of the big business houses?

UNDERSHAFT: Yes: he could learn the office routine without understanding the business, like all the other sons; and the firm would go on by its own momentum until the real Undershaft — probably an Italian or a German — would invent a new method and cut him out.

LADY BRITOMART: There is nothing that any Italian or German could do that Stephen could not do. And Stephen at least has breeding.

UNDERSHAFT: The son of a foundling! Nonsense!

LADY BRITOMART: My son, Andrew! And even you may have good blood in your veins for all you know.

UNDERSHAFT: True. Probably I have. That is another argument in favor of a foundling.

LADY BRITOMART: Andrew: dont be aggravating. And dont be wicked. At present you are both.

UNDERSHAFT: This conversation is part of the Undershaft tradition, Biddy. Every Undershaft's wife has treated him to it ever since the house was founded. It is mere waste of breath. If the tradition be ever broken it will be for an abler man than Stephen.

LADY BRITOMART (*pouting*): Then go away.

UNDERSHAFT (*deprecatory*): Go away!

LADY BRITOMART: Yes: Go away. If you will do nothing for Stephen, you are not wanted here. Go to your foundling, whoever he is; and look after him.

UNDERSHAFT: The fact is, Biddy —

LADY BRITOMART: Dont call me Biddy. I dont call you Andy.

UNDERSHAFT: I will not call my wife Britomart: it is not good sense. Seriously, my love, the Undershaft tradition has landed me in a difficulty. I am getting on in years; and my partner Lazarus has at last made a stand and insisted that the succession must be settled one way or the other; and of course he is quite right. You see, I havent found a fit successor yet.

LADY BRITOMART (obstinately): There is Stephen.

UNDERSHAFT: Thats just it: all the foundlings I can find are exactly like Stephen.

LADY BRITOMART: Andrew!

UNDERSHAFT: I want a man with no relations and no schooling: that is, a man who would be out of the running altogether if he were not a strong man. And I cant find him. Every blessed foundling nowadays is snapped up in his infancy by Barnardo homes, or School Board officers, or Boards of Guardians; and if he shews the least ability he is fastened on by schoolmasters; trained to win scholarships like a racehorse; crammed with second-hand ideas; drilled and disciplined in docility and what they call good taste; and lamed for life so that he is fit for nothing but teaching. If you want to keep the foundry in the family, you had better find an eligible foundling and marry him to Barbara.

LADY BRITOMART: Ah! Barbara! Your pet! You would sacrifice Stephen to Barbara.

UNDERSHAFT: Cheerfully. And you, my dear, would boil Barbara to make soup for Stephen.

LADY BRITOMART: Andrew: this is not a question of our likings and dislikings: it is a question of duty. It is your duty to make Stephen your successor.

UNDERSHAFT: Just as much as it is your duty to submit to your husband: Come, Biddy! these tricks of the governing class are of no use with me. I am one of the governing class myself; and it is waste of time giving tracts to a missionary. I have the power in this matter; and I am not to be humbugged into using it for your purposes.

LADY BRITOMART: Andrew: you can talk my head off; but you cant change wrong into right. And your tie is all on one side. Put it straight.

UNDERSHAFT (disconcerted): It wont stay unless it's pinned (he fumbles at it with childish grimaces) —

(STEPHEN comes in.)

STEPHEN (at the door): I beg your pardon (about to retire).

LADY BRITOMART: No: come in, Stephen. (STEPHEN comes forward to his mother's writing table.)

UNDERSHAFT (not very cordially): Good afternoon.

STEPHEN (coldly): Good afternoon.

UNDERSHAFT (to LADY BRITOMART): He knows all about the tradition, I suppose?

LADY BRITOMART: Yes. (To STEPHEN.) It is what I told you last night, Stephen.

UNDERSHAFT (sulkily): I understand you want to come into the cannon business.

STEPHEN: I go into the trade! Certainly not.

UNDERSHAFT (opening his eyes, greatly eased in mind and manner): Oh! in that case —

LADY BRITOMART: Cannons are not trade, Stephen. They are enterprise.

STEPHEN: I have no intention of becoming a man of business in any sense. I have no capacity for business and no taste for it. I intend to devote myself to politics.

UNDERSHAFT (rising): My dear boy: this is an immense relief to me. And I trust it may prove an equally good thing for the country. I was afraid you would consider yourself disparaged and slighted. (He moves towards STEPHEN as if to shake hands with him.)

LADY BRITOMART (rising and interposing): Stephen: I cannot allow you to throw away an enormous property like this.

STEPHEN (stiffly): Mother: there must be an end of treating me as a child, if you please. (LADY BRITOMART recoils, deeply wounded by his tone.) Until last night I did not take your attitude seriously, because I did not think you meant it seriously. But I find now that you left me in the dark as to matters which you should have explained to me years ago. I am extremely hurt and offended. Any further discussion of my intentions had better take place with my father, as between one man and another.

LADY BRITOMART: Stephen! (She sits down again, her eyes filling with tears.)

UNDERSHAFT (with grave compassion): You see, my dear, it is only the big men who can be treated as children.

STEPHEN: I am sorry, mother, that you have forced me —

UNDERSHAFT (*stopping him*): Yes, yes, yes, yes: thats all right, Stephen. She wont interfere with you any more: your independence is achieved: you have won your latchkey. Dont rub it in; and above all, dont apologize. (*He resumes his seat.*) Now what about your future, as between one man and another — I beg your pardon, Biddy: as between two men and a woman.

LADY BRITOMART (*who has pulled herself together strongly*): I quite understand, Stephen. By all means go your own way if you feel strong enough. (STEPHEN *sits down magisterially in the chair at the writing table with an air of affirming his majority.*)

UNDERSHAFT: It is settled that you do not ask for the succession to the cannon business.

STEPHEN: I hope it is settled that I repudiate the cannon business.

UNDERSHAFT: Come, come! dont be so devilishly sulky: it's boyish. Freedom should be generous. Besides, I owe you a fair start in life in exchange for disinheriting you. You cant become prime minister all at once. Havnt you a turn for something? What about literature, art, and so forth?

STEPHEN: I have nothing of the artist about me, either in faculty or character, thank Heaven!

UNDERSHAFT: A philosopher, perhaps? Eh?

STEPHEN: I make no such ridiculous pretension.

UNDERSHAFT: Just so. Well, there is the army, the navy, the Church, the Bar. The Bar requires some ability. What about the Bar?

STEPHEN: I have not studied law. And I am afraid I have not the necessary push — I believe that is the name barristers give to their vulgarity — for success in pleading.

UNDERSHAFT: Rather a difficult case, Stephen. Hardly anything left but the stage, is there? (STEPHEN *makes an impatient movement.*) Well, come! is there anything you know or care for?

STEPHEN (*rising and looking at him steadily*): I know the difference between right and wrong.

UNDERSHAFT (*hugely tickled*): You dont say so! What! no capacity for business, no knowledge of law, no sympathy with art, no pretension to philosophy; only a simple knowledge of the secret that has puzzled all the philosophers, baffled all the lawyers, muddled all the men of business, and ruined most of the artists: the secret of right and wrong. Why, man, youre a genius, a master of masters, a god! At twentyfour, too!

STEPHEN (*keeping his temper with difficulty*): You are pleased to be facetious. I pretend to nothing more than any honorable English gentleman claims as his birthright (*he sits down angrily*).

UNDERSHAFT: Oh, thats everybody's birthright. Look at poor little Jenny Hill, the Salvation lassie! she would think you were laughing at her if you asked her to stand up in the street and teach grammar or geography or mathematics or even drawing room dancing; but it never occurs to her to doubt that she can teach morals and religion. You are all alike, you respectable people. You cant tell me the bursting strain of a ten-inch gun, which is a very simple matter; but you all think you can tell me the bursting strain of a man under temptation. You darent handle high explosives; but youre all ready to handle honesty and truth and justice and the whole duty of man, and kill one another at that game. What a country! What a world!

LADY BRITOMART (*uneasily*): What do you think he had better do, Andrew?

UNDERSHAFT: Oh, just what he wants to do. He knows nothing and he thinks he knows everything. That points clearly to a political career. Get him a private secretaryship to someone who can get him an Under Secretaryship; and then leave him alone. He will find his natural and proper place in the end on the Treasury Bench.

STEPHEN (*springing up again*): I am sorry, sir, that you force me to forget the respect due to you as my father. I am an Englishman and I will not hear the Government of my country insulted. (*He thrusts his hands in his pockets, and walks angrily across to the window.*)

UNDERSHAFT (*with a touch of brutality*): The government of your country! *I* am the government of your country: I, and Lazarus. Do you suppose that you and half a dozen amateurs like you, sitting in a row in that foolish gabble shop, can govern Undershaft and Lazarus? No, my friend: you will do what pays us. You will make war when it suits us, and keep peace when it doesnt. You will find out that trade requires certain measures when we have decided on those measures. When I want anything to keep my dividends up, you will discover that my want is a national need. When other people want something to keep my dividends down, you will call out the police and military. And in return you shall have the support and applause of my newspapers, and the delight of imagining that you are a great statesman. Government of your country! Be off with you, my boy, and play with your caucuses and leading articles and historical parties and great leaders and burning questions and the rest of your toys. I am going back to my counting-house to pay the piper and call the tune.

STEPHEN (*actually smiling, and putting his hand on his father's shoulder with indulgent patronage*): Really, my dear father, it is impossible to be angry with you. You dont know how absurd all this sounds to me. You are very properly proud of having been industrious enough to make money; and it is greatly to your credit that you have made so much of it. But it has kept you in circles where you are valued for your money and deferred to for it, instead of in the doubtless very old-fashioned and behind-the-times public school and university where I formed my habits of mind. It is natural for you to think that money governs England; but you must allow me to think I know better.

UNDERSHAFT: And what does govern England, pray?

STEPHEN: Character, father, character.

UNDERSHAFT: Whose character? Yours or mine?

STEPHEN: Neither yours nor mine, father, but the best elements in the English national character.

UNDERSHAFT: Stephen: Ive found your profession for you. Youre a born journalist. I'll start you with a high-toned weekly review. There!

(*Before* STEPHEN *can reply* SARAH, BARBARA, LOMAX, *and* CUSINS *come in ready for walking.* BARBARA *crosses the room to the window and looks out.* CUSINS *drifts amiably to the armchair.* LOMAX *remains near the door, whilst* SARAH *comes to her mother.*

STEPHEN *goes to the smaller writing table and busies himself with his letters.*)

SARAH: Go and get ready, mamma: the carriage is waiting. (LADY BRITOMART *leaves the room.*)

UNDERSHAFT (*to* SARAH): Good day, my dear. Good afternoon, Mr Lomax.

LOMAX (*vaguely*): Ahdedoo.

UNDERSHAFT (*to* CUSINS): Quite well after last night, Euripides, eh?

CUSINS: As well as can be expected.

UNDERSHAFT: Thats right. (*To* BARBARA.) So you are coming to see my death and devastation factory, Barbara?

BARBARA (*at the window*): You came yesterday to see my salvation factory. I promised you a return visit.

LOMAX (*coming forward between* SARAH *and* UNDERSHAFT): Youll find it awfully interesting. Ive been through the Woolwich Arsenal; and it gives you a ripping feeling of security, you know, to think of the lot of beggars we could kill if it came to fighting. (*To* UNDERSHAFT, *with sudden solemnity.*) Still, it must be rather an awful reflection for you, from the religious point of view as it were. Youre getting on, you know, and all that.

SARAH: You dont mind Cholly's imbecility, papa, do you?

LOMAX (*much taken aback*): Oh I say!

UNDERSHAFT: Mr Lomax looks at the matter in a very proper spirit, my dear.

LOMAX: Just so. Thats all I meant, I assure you.

SARAH: Are you coming, Stephen?

STEPHEN: Well, I am rather busy — er — (*Magnanimously.*) Oh well, yes: I'll come. That is, if there is room for me.

UNDERSHAFT: I can take two with me in a little motor I am experimenting with for field use. You wont mind its being rather unfashionable. It's not painted yet; but it's bullet proof.

LOMAX (*appalled at the prospect of confronting Wilton Crescent in an unpainted motor*): Oh I say!

SARAH: The carriage for me, thank you. Barbara doesnt mind what she's seen in.

LOMAX: I say, Dolly, old chap: do you really mind the car being a guy? Because of course if you do I'll go in it. Still —

CUSINS: I prefer it.

LOMAX: Thanks awfully, old man. Come, my ownest. (*He hurries out to secure his seat in the carriage.* SARAH *follows him.*)

CUSINS (*moodily walking across to* LADY BRITOMART's *writing table*): Why are we two coming to this Works Department of Hell? that is what I ask myself.

BARBARA: I have always thought of it as a sort of pit where lost creatures with blackened faces stirred up smoky fires and were driven and tormented by my father? Is it like that, dad?

UNDERSHAFT (*scandalized*): My dear! It is a spotlessly clean and beautiful hillside town.

CUSINS: With a Methodist chapel? Oh do say theres a Methodist chapel.

UNDERSHAFT: There are two: a Primitive one and a sophisticated one. There is even an Ethical Society; but it is not much patronized, as my men are all strongly religious. In the High Explosives Sheds they object to the presence of Agnostics as unsafe.

CUSINS: And yet they dont object to you!

BARBARA: Do they obey all your orders?

UNDERSHAFT: I never give them any orders. When I speak to one of them it is 'Well, Jones, is the baby doing well? and has Mrs Jones made a good recovery?' 'Nicely, thank you, sir.' And thats all.

CUSINS: But Jones has to be kept in order. How do you maintain discipline among your men?

UNDERSHAFT: I dont. They do. You see, the one thing Jones wont stand is any rebellion from the man under him, or any assertion of social equality between the wife of the man with 4 shillings a week less than himself, and Mrs Jones! Of course they all rebel against me, theoretically. Practically, every man of them keeps the man just below him in his place. I never meddle with them. I never bully them. I dont even bully Lazarus. I say that certain things are to be done; but I dont order anybody to do them. I dont say, mind you, that there is no ordering about and snubbing and even bullying. The men snub the boys and order them about; the carmen snub the sweepers; the artisans snub the unskilled laborers; the foremen drive and bully both the laborers and artisans; the assistant engineers find fault with the foremen; the chief engineers drop on the assistants; the departmental managers worry the chiefs; and the clerks have tall hats and hymnbooks and keep up the social tone by refusing to associate on equal terms with anybody. The result is a colossal profit, which comes to me.

CUSINS (*revolted*): You really are a — well, what I was saying yesterday.

BARBARA: What was he saying yesterday?

UNDERSHAFT: Never mind, my dear. He thinks I have made you unhappy. Have I?

BARBARA: Do you think I can be happy in this vulgar silly dress? I! who have worn the uniform. Do you understand what you have done to me? Yesterday I had a man's soul in my hand. I set him in the way of life with his face to salvation. But when we took your money he turned back to drunkenness and derision. (*With intense conviction.*) I will never forgive you that. If I had a child, and you destroyed its body with your explosives — if you murdered Dolly with your horrible guns — I could forgive you if my forgiveness would open the gates of heaven to you. But to take a human soul from me, and turn it into the soul of a wolf! that is worse than any murder.

UNDERSHAFT: Does my daughter despair so easily? Can you strike a man to the heart and leave no mark on him?

BARBARA (*her face lighting up*): Oh, you are right: he can never be lost now: where was my faith?

CUSINS: Oh, clever clever devil!

BARBARA: You may be a devil; but God speaks through you sometimes. (*She takes her father's hands and kisses them.*) You have given me back my happiness; I feel it deep down now, though my spirit is troubled.

UNDERSHAFT: You have learnt something. That always feels at first as if you had lost something.

BARBARA: Well, take me to the factory of death; and let me learn something more. There must be some truth or other behind all this frightful irony. Come, Dolly. (*She goes out.*)

CUSINS: My guardian angel! (*To* UNDER-SHAFT.) Avaunt! (*He follows* BARBARA.)

STEPHEN (*quietly, at the writing table*): You must not mind Cusins, father. He is a very amiable good fellow; but he is a Greek scholar and naturally a little eccentric.

UNDERSHAFT: Ah, quite so. Thank you, Stephen. Thank you. (*He goes out.*)

(STEPHEN *smiles patronizingly; buttons his coat responsibly; and crosses the room to the door.* LADY BRITOMART, *dressed for out-of-doors, opens it before he reaches it. She looks round for others; looks at* STEPHEN; *and turns to go without a word.*)

STEPHEN (*embarrassed*): Mother —

LADY BRITOMART: Dont be apologetic, Stephen. And dont forget that you have outgrown your mother. (*She goes out.*)

(*Perivale St Andrews lies between two Middlesex hills, half climbing the northern one. It is an almost smokeless town of white walls, roofs of narrow green slates or red tiles, tall trees, domes, campaniles, and slender chimney shafts, beautifully situated and beautiful in itself. The best view of it is obtained from the crest of a slope about half a mile to the east, where the high explosives are dealt with. The foundry lies hidden in the depths between, the tops of its chimneys sprouting like huge skittles into the middle distance. Across the crest runs an emplacement of concrete, with a firestep, and a parapet which suggests a fortification, because there is a huge cannon of the obsolete Woolwich Infant pattern peering across it at the town. The cannon is mounted on an experimental gun carriage: possibly the original model of the Undershaft disappearing rampart gun alluded to by* STEPHEN. *The firestep, being a convenient place to sit, is furnished here and there with straw disc cushions; and at one place there is the additional luxury of a fur rug.*

BARBARA *is standing on the firestep, looking over the parapet towards the town. On her right is the cannon; on her left the end of a shed raised on piles, with a ladder of three or four steps up to the door, which opens outwards and has a little wooden landing at the threshold, with a fire bucket in the corner of the landing. Several dummy soldiers more or less mutilated, with straw protruding from their gashes, have been shoved out of the way under the landing. A few others are nearly upright against the shed; and one has fallen forward and lies, like a grotesque corpse, on the emplacement. The parapet stops short of the shed, leaving a gap which is the beginning of the path down the hill through the foundry to the town. The rug is on the firestep near this gap. Down on the emplacement behind the cannon is a trolley carrying a huge conical bombshell with a red band painted on it. Further to the right is the door of an office, which, like the sheds, is of the lightest possible construction.*

CUSINS *arrives by the path from the town.*)

BARBARA: Well?

CUSINS: Not a ray of hope. Everything perfect! wonderful! real! It only needs a cathedral to be a heavenly city instead of a hellish one.

BARBARA: Have you found out whether they have done anything for old Peter Shirley?

CUSINS: They have found him a job as gatekeeper and timekeeper. He's frightfully miserable. He calls the time-keeping brainwork, and says he isnt used to it; and his gate lodge is so splendid that he's ashamed to use the rooms, and skulks in the scullery.

BARBARA: Poor Peter!

(STEPHEN *arrives from the town. He carries a fieldglass.*)

STEPHEN (*enthusiastically*): Have you two seen the place? Why did you leave us?

CUSINS: I wanted to see everything I was not intended to see; and Barbara wanted to make the men talk.

STEPHEN: Have you found anything discreditable?

CUSINS: No. They call him Dandy Andy and are proud of his being a cunning old rascal; but it's all horribly, frightfully, immorally, unanswerably perfect.

(SARAH *arrives.*)

SARAH: Heavens! what a place! (*She crosses to the trolley.*) Did you see the nursing home!? (*She sits down on the shell.*)

STEPHEN: Did you see the libraries and schools!?

SARAH: Did you see the ball room and the banqueting chamber in the Town Hall!?

STEPHEN: Have you gone into the insurance fund, the pension fund, the building society, the various applications of cooperation!?

(UNDERSHAFT *comes from the office, with a sheaf of telegrams in his hand.*)

UNDERSHAFT: Well, have you seen everything? I'm sorry I was called away. (*Indicating the telegrams.*) Good news from Manchuria.

STEPHEN: Another Japanese victory?

UNDERSHAFT: Oh, I don't know. Which side wins does not concern us here. No: the good news is that the aerial battleship is a tremendous success. At the first trial it has wiped out a fort with three hundred soldiers in it.

CUSINS (*from the platform*): Dummy soldiers?

UNDERSHAFT (*striding across to* STEPHEN *and kicking the prostrate dummy brutally out of his way*): No: the real thing.

(CUSINS *and* BARBARA *exchange glances. Then* CUSINS *sits on the step and buries his face in his hands.* BARBARA *gravely lays her hand on his shoulder. He looks up at her in whimsical desperation.*)

UNDERSHAFT: Well, Stephen, what do you think of the place?

STEPHEN: Oh, magnificent. A perfect triumph of modern industry. Frankly, my dear father, I have been a fool: I had no idea of what it all meant: of the wonderful forethought, the power of organization, the administrative capacity, the financial genius, the colossal capital it represents. I have been repeating to myself as I came through your streets 'Peace hath her victories no less renowned than War.' I have only one misgiving about it all.

UNDERSHAFT: Out with it.

STEPHEN: Well, I cannot help thinking that all this provision for every want of your workmen may sap their independence and weaken their sense of responsibility. And greatly as we enjoyed our tea at that splendid restaurant — how they gave us all that luxury and cake and jam and cream for threepence I really cannot imagine! — still you must remember that restaurants break up home life. Look at the continent, for instance! Are you sure so much pampering is really good for the men's characters?

UNDERSHAFT: Well you see, my dear boy, when you are organizing civilization you have to make up your mind whether trouble and anxiety are good things or not. If you decide that they are, then, I take it, you simply dont organize civilization; and there you are, with trouble and anxiety enough to make us all angels! But if you decide the other way, you may as well go through with it. However, Stephen, our characters are safe here. A sufficient dose of anxiety is always provided by the fact that we may be blown to smithereens at any moment.

SARAH: By the way, papa, where do you make the explosives?

UNDERSHAFT: In separate little sheds, like that one. When one of them blows up, it costs very little; and only the people quite close to it are killed.

(STEPHEN, *who is quite close to it, looks at it rather scaredly, and moves away quickly to the cannon. At the same moment the door of the shed is thrown abruptly open; and a foreman in overalls and list slippers comes out on the little landing and holds the door for* LOMAX, *who appears in the doorway.*)

LOMAX (*with studied coolness*): My good fellow: you neednt get into a state of nerves. Nothing's going to happen to you; and I suppose it wouldnt be the end of the world if anything did. A little bit of British pluck is what you want, old chap. (*He descends and strolls across to* SARAH.)

UNDERSHAFT (*to the foreman*): Anything wrong, Bilton?

BILTON (*with ironic calm*): Gentleman walked into the high explosives shed and lit a cigaret, sir: thats all.

UNDERSHAFT: Ah, quite so. (*Going over to* LOMAX.) Do you happen to remember what you did with the match?

LOMAX: Oh come! I'm not a fool. I took jolly good care to blow it out before I chucked it away.

BILTON: The top of it was red hot inside, sir.

LOMAX: Well, suppose it was! I didnt chuck it into any of your messes.

UNDERSHAFT: Think no more of it, Mr Lomax. By the way, would you mind lending me your matches.

LOMAX (*offering his box*): Certainly.

UNDERSHAFT: Thanks. (*He pockets the matches.*)

LOMAX (*lecturing to the company generally*): You know, these high explosives dont go off like gunpowder, except when theyre in a gun. When theyre spread loose, you can put a match to them without the least risk: they just burn quietly like a bit of paper. (*Warming to the scientific interest of the subject.*) Did you know that, Undershaft? Have you ever tried?

UNDERSHAFT: Not on a large scale, Mr Lomax. Bilton will give you a sample of gun cotton when you are leaving if you ask him. You can experiment with it at home. (BILTON *looks puzzled.*)

SARAH: Bilton will do nothing of the sort, papa. I suppose it's your business to blow up the Russians and Japs; but you might really stop short of blowing up poor Cholly. (BILTON *gives it up and retires into the shed.*)

LOMAX: My ownest, there is no danger. (*He sits beside her on the shell.*)

(LADY BRITOMART *arrives from the town with a bouquet.*)

LADY BRITOMART (*impetuously*): Andrew: you shouldnt have let me see this place.

UNDERSHAFT: Why, my dear?

LADY BRITOMART: Never mind why: you shouldnt have: thats all. To think of all that (*indicating the town*) being yours! and that you have kept it to yourself all these years!

UNDERSHAFT: It does not belong to me. I belong to it. It is the Undershaft inheritance.

LADY BRITOMART: It is not. Your ridiculous cannons and that noisy banging foundry may be the Undershaft inheritance; but all that plate and linen, all that furniture and those houses and orchards and gardens belong to us. They belong to me: they are not a man's business. I wont give them up. You must be out of your senses to throw them all away; and if you persist in such folly, I will call in a doctor.

UNDERSHAFT (*stooping to smell the bouquet*): Where did you get the flowers, my dear?

LADY BRITOMART: Your men presented them to me in your William Morris Labor Church.

CUSINS: Oh! It needed only that. A Labor Church! (*He mounts the firestep distractedly, and leans with his elbows on the parapet, turning his back to them.*)

LADY BRITOMART: Yes, with Morris's words in mosaic letters ten feet high round the dome. NO MAN IS GOOD ENOUGH TO BE ANOTHER MAN'S MASTER. The cynicism of it!

UNDERSHAFT: It shocked the men at first, I am afraid. But now they take no more notice of it than of the ten commandments in church.

LADY BRITOMART: Andrew: you are trying to put me off the subject of the inheritance by profane jokes. Well, you shant. I dont ask it any longer for Stephen: he has inherited far too much of your perversity to be fit for it. But Barbara has rights as well as Stephen. Why should not Adolphus succeed to the inheritance? I could manage the town for him; and he can look after the cannons, if they are really necessary.

UNDERSHAFT: I should ask nothing better if Adolphus were a foundling. He is exactly the sort of new blood that is wanted in English business. But he's not a foundling; and theres an end of it. (*He makes for the office door.*)

CUSINS (*turning to them*): Not quite. (*They all turn and stare at him.*) I think— Mind! I am not committing myself in any way as to my future course—but I think the foundling difficulty can be got over. (*He jumps down to the emplacement.*)

UNDERSHAFT (*coming back to him*): What do you mean?

CUSINS: Well, I have something to say which is in the nature of a confession.

SARAH:
LADY BRITOMART: } Confession!
BARBARA:
STEPHEN:

LOMAX: Oh I say!

CUSINS: Yes, a confession. Listen, all. Until I met Barbara I thought myself in the main an honorable, truthful man, because I wanted the approval of my conscience more than I wanted anything else. But the moment I saw Barbara, I wanted her far more than the approval of my conscience.

LADY BRITOMART: Adolphus!

CUSINS: It is true. You accused me yourself, Lady Brit, of joining the Army to worship Barbara; and so I did. She bought my soul like a flower at a street corner; but she bought it for herself.

UNDERSHAFT: What! Not for Dionysos or another?

CUSINS: Dionysos and all the others are in herself. I adored what was divine in her, and was therefore a true worshipper. But I was romantic about her too. I thought she was a woman of the people, and that a marriage with a professor of Greek would be far beyond the wildest social ambitions of her rank.

LADY BRITOMART: Adolphus!!

LOMAX: Oh I say!!!

CUSINS: When I learnt the horrible truth—

LADY BRITOMART: What do you mean by the horrible truth, pray?

CUSINS: That she was enormously rich; that her grandfather was an earl; that her father was the Prince of Darkness—

UNDERSHAFT: Chut!

CUSINS: —and that I was only an adventurer trying to catch a rich wife, then I stooped to deceive her about my birth.

BARBARA (*rising*): Dolly!

LADY BRITOMART: Your birth! Now Adolphus, dont dare to make up a wicked story for the sake of these wretched cannons. Remember: I have seen photographs of your parents; and the Agent General for South Western Australia knows them personally and has assured me that they are most respectable married people.

CUSINS: So they are in Australia; but here they are outcasts. Their marriage is legal in Australia, but not in England. My mother is my father's deceased wife's sister; and in this island I am consequently a foundling. (*Sensation.*)

BARBARA: Silly! (*She climbs to the cannon, and leans, listening, in the angle it makes with the parapet.*)

CUSINS: Is the subterfuge good enough, Machiavelli?

UNDERSHAFT (*thoughtfully*): Biddy: this may be a way out of the difficulty.

LADY BRITOMART: Stuff! A man cant make cannons any the better for being his own cousin instead of his proper self. (*She sits down on the rug with a bounce that expresses her downright contempt for their casuistry.*)

UNDERSHAFT (*to* CUSINS): You are an educated man. That is against the tradition.

CUSINS: Once in ten thousand times it happens that the schoolboy is a born master of what they try to teach him. Greek has not destroyed my mind: it has nourished it. Besides, I did not learn it at an English public school.

UNDERSHAFT: Hm! Well, I cannot afford to be too particular: you have cornered the foundling market. Let it pass. You are eligible, Euripides: you are eligible.

BARBARA: Dolly: yesterday morning, when Stephen told us all about the tradition, you became very silent; and you have been strange and excited ever since. Were you thinking of your birth then?

CUSINS: When the finger of Destiny suddenly points at a man in the middle of his breakfast, it makes him thoughtful.

UNDERSHAFT: Aha! You have had your eye on the business, my young friend, have you?

CUSINS: Take care! There is an abyss of moral horror between me and your accursed aerial battleships.

UNDERSHAFT: Never mind the abyss for the present. Let us settle the practical details and leave your final decision open. You know that you will have to change your name. Do you object to that?

CUSINS: Would any man named Adolphus — any man called Dolly! — object to be called something else?

UNDERSHAFT: Good. Now, as to money! I propose to treat you handsomely from the beginning. You shall start at a thousand a year.

CUSINS (*with sudden heat, his spectacles twinkling with mischief*): A thousand! You dare offer a miserable thousand to the son-in-law of a millionaire! No, by Heavens, Machiavelli! you shall not cheat me. You cannot do without me; and I can do without you. I must have two thousand five hundred a year for two years. At the end of that time, if I am a failure, I go. But if I am a success, and stay on, you must give me the other five thousand.

UNDERSHAFT: What other five thousand?

CUSINS: To make the two years up to five thousand a year. The two thousand five hundred is only half pay in case I should turn out a failure. The third year I must have ten per cent on the profits.

UNDERSHAFT (*taken aback*): Ten per cent! Why, man, do you know what my profits are?

CUSINS: Enormous, I hope: otherwise I shall require twenty-five per cent.

UNDERSHAFT: But, Mr Cusins, this is a serious matter of business. You are not bringing any capital into the concern.

CUSINS: What! no capital! Is my mastery of Greek no capital? Is my access to the subtlest thought, the loftiest poetry yet attained by humanity, no capital? My character! my intellect! my life! my career! what Barbara calls my soul! are these no capital? Say another word; and I double my salary.

UNDERSHAFT: Be reasonable —

CUSINS (*peremptorily*): Mr Undershaft: you have my terms. Take them or leave them.

UNDERSHAFT (*recovering himself*): Very well. I note your terms; and I offer you half.

CUSINS (*disgusted*): Half!

UNDERSHAFT (*firmly*): Half.

CUSINS: You call yourself a gentleman; and you offer me half!!

UNDERSHAFT: I do not call myself a gentleman; but I offer you half.

CUSINS: This to your future partner! your successor! your son-in-law!

BARBARA: You are selling your own soul,

Dolly, not mine. Leave me out of the bargain, please.

UNDERSHAFT: Come! I will go a step further for Barbara's sake. I will give you three fifths; but that is my last word.

CUSINS: Done!

LOMAX: Done in the eye! Why, I get only eight hundred, you know.

CUSINS: By the way, Mac, I am a classical scholar, not an arithmetical one. Is three fifths more than half or less?

UNDERSHAFT: More, of course.

CUSINS: I would have taken two hundred and fifty. How you can succeed in business when you are willing to pay all that money to a University don who is obviously not worth a junior clerk's wages! — well! What will Lazarus say?

UNDERSHAFT: Lazarus is a gentle romantic Jew who cares for nothing but string quartets and stalls at fashionable theatres. He will be blamed for your rapacity in money matters, poor fellow! as he has hitherto been blamed for mine. You are a shark of the first order, Euripides. So much the better for the firm!

BARBARA: Is the bargain closed, Dolly? Does your soul belong to him now?

CUSINS: No: the price is settled: that is all. The real tug of war is still to come. What about the moral question?

LADY BRITOMART: There is no moral question in the matter at all, Adolphus. You must simply sell cannons and weapons to people whose cause is right and just, and refuse them to foreigners and criminals.

UNDERSHAFT (determined): No: None of that. You must keep the true faith of an Armorer, or you dont come in here.

CUSINS: What on earth is the true faith of an Armorer?

UNDERSHAFT: To give arms to all men who offer an honest price for them, without respect of persons or principles: to aristocrat and republican, to Nihilist and Tsar, to Capitalist and Socialist, to Protestant and Catholic, to burglar and policeman, to black man, white man and yellow man, to all sorts and conditions, all nationalities, all faiths, all follies, all causes and all crimes. The first Undershaft wrote up in his shop IF GOD GAVE THE HAND, LET NOT MAN WITHHOLD THE SWORD. The second wrote up ALL HAVE THE RIGHT TO FIGHT: NONE HAVE THE RIGHT TO JUDGE. The

third wrote up TO MAN THE WEAPON: TO HEAVEN THE VICTORY. The fourth had no literary turn; so he did not write up anything; but he sold cannons to Napoleon under the nose of George the Third. The fifth wrote up PEACE SHALL NOT PREVAIL SAVE WITH A SWORD IN HER HAND. The sixth, my master, was the best of all. He wrote up NOTHING IS EVER DONE IN THIS WORLD UNTIL MEN ARE PREPARED TO KILL ONE ANOTHER IF IT IS NOT DONE. After that, there was nothing left for the seventh to say. So he wrote up, simply, UNASHAMED.

CUSINS: My good Machiavelli, I shall certainly write something up on the wall; only, as I shall write it in Greek, you wont be able to read it. But as to your Armorer's faith, if I take my neck out of the noose of my own morality I am not going to put it into the noose of yours. I shall sell cannons to whom I please and refuse them to whom I please. So there!

UNDERSHAFT: From the moment when you become Andrew Undershaft, you will never do as you please again. Dont come here lusting for power, young man.

CUSINS: If power were my aim I should not come here for it. You have no power.

UNDERSHAFT: None of my own, certainly.

CUSINS: I have more power than you, more will. You do not drive this place: it drives you. And what drives the place?

UNDERSHAFT (enigmatically): A will of which I am a part.

BARBARA (startled): Father! Do you know what you are saying; or are you laying a snare for my soul?

CUSINS: Dont listen to his metaphysics, Barbara. The place is driven by the most rascally part of society, the money hunters, the pleasure hunters, the military promotion hunters; and he is their slave.

UNDERSHAFT: Not necessarily. Remember the Armorer's Faith. I will take an order from a good man as cheerfully as from a bad one. If you good people prefer preaching and shirking to buying my weapons and fighting the rascals, dont blame me. I can make cannons: I cannot make courage and conviction. Bah! you tire me, Euripides, with your morality mongering. Ask Barbara: she understands. (He suddenly reaches up and takes BARBARA's hands, looking powerfully into her eyes.) Tell him, my love, what power really means.

BARBARA (hypnotized): Before I joined the

Salvation Army, I was in my own power; and the consequence was that I never knew what to do with myself. When I joined it, I had not time enough for all the things I had to do.

UNDERSHAFT (*approvingly*): Just so. And why was that, do you suppose?

BARBARA: Yesterday I should have said, because I was in the power of God. (*She resumes her self-possession, withdrawing her hands from his with a power equal to his own.*) But you came and shewed me that I was in the power of Bodger and Undershaft. Today I feel — oh! how can I put it into words? Sarah: do you remember the earthquake at Cannes, when we were little children? — how little the surprise of the first shock mattered compared to the dread and horror of waiting for the second? That is how I feel in this place today. I stood on the rock I thought eternal; and without a word of warning it reeled and crumbled under me. I was safe with an infinite wisdom watching me, an army marching to Salvation with me; and in a moment, at a stroke of your pen in a cheque book, I stood alone; and the heavens were empty. That was the first shock of the earthquake: I am waiting for the second.

UNDERSHAFT: Come, come, my daughter! dont make too much of your tinpot tragedy. What do we do here when we spend years of work and thought and thousands of pounds of solid cash on a new gun or an aerial battleship that turns out just a hairsbreadth wrong after all? Scrap it. Scrap it without wasting another hour or another pound on it. Well, you have made for yourself something that you call a morality or a religion or what not. It doesn't fit the facts. Well, scrap it. Scrap it and get one that does fit. That is what is wrong with the world at present. It scraps its obsolete steam engines and dynamos; but it wont scrap its old prejudices and its old moralities and its old religions and its old political constitutions. Whats the result? In machinery it does very well; but in morals and religion and politics it is working at a loss that brings it nearer bankruptcy every year. Dont persist in that folly. If your old religion broke down yesterday, get a newer and a better one for tomorrow.

BARBARA: Oh how gladly I would take a better one to my soul! But you offer me a worse one. (*Turning on him with sudden vehe-*

mence.) Justify yourself: shew me some light through the darkness of this dreadful place, with its beautifully clean workshops, and respectable workmen, and model homes.

UNDERSHAFT: Cleanliness and respectability do not need justification, Barbara: they justify themselves. I see no darkness here, no dreadfulness. In your Salvation shelter I saw poverty, misery, cold and hunger. You gave them bread and treacle and dreams of heaven. I give from thirty shillings a week to twelve thousand a year. They find their own dreams; but I look after the drainage.

BARBARA: And their souls?

UNDERSHAFT: I save their souls just as I saved yours.

BARBARA (*revolted*): You saved my soul! What do you mean?

UNDERSHAFT: I fed you and clothed you and housed you. I took care that you should have money enough to live handsomely — more than enough; so that you could be wasteful, careless, generous. That saved your soul from the seven deadly sins.

BARBARA (*bewildered*): The seven deadly sins!

UNDERSHAFT: Yes, the deadly seven. (*Counting on his fingers.*) Food, clothing, firing, rent, taxes, respectability and children. Nothing can lift those seven millstones from Man's neck but money; and the spirit cannot soar until the millstones are lifted. I lifted them from your spirit. I enabled Barbara to become Major Barbara; and I saved her from the crime of poverty.

CUSINS: Do you call poverty a crime?

UNDERSHAFT: The worst of crimes. All the other crimes are virtues beside it: all the other dishonors are chivalry itself by comparison. Poverty blights whole cities; spreads horrible pestilences; strikes dead the very souls of all who come within sight, sound, or smell of it. What you call crime is nothing: a murder here and a theft there, a blow now and a curse then: what do they matter? they are only the accidents and illnesses of life: there are not fifty genuine professional criminals in London. But there are millions of poor people, abject people, dirty people, ill fed, ill clothed people. They poison us morally and physically: they kill the happiness of society: they force us to do away with our own liberties and to organize unnatural cruelties for fear they should rise against us and drag us down into their abyss. Only fools fear crime: we all fear poverty. Pah! (turning on BARBARA) you talk of your half-saved ruffian in West Ham: you accuse me of dragging his soul back to perdition. Well, bring him to me here; and I will drag his soul back again to salvation for you. Not by words and dreams; but by thirtyeight shillings a week, a sound house in a handsome street, and a permanent job. In three weeks he will have a fancy waistcoat; in three months a tall hat and a chapel sitting; before the end of the year he will shake hands with a duchess at a Primrose League meeting, and join the Conservative Party.

BARBARA: And will he be the better for that?

UNDERSHAFT: You know he will. Dont be a hypocrite, Barbara. He will be better fed, better housed, better clothed, better behaved; and his children will be pounds heavier and bigger. That will be better than an American cloth mattress in a shelter, chopping firewood, eating bread and treacle, and being forced to kneel down from time to time to thank heaven for it: knee drill, I think you call it. It is cheap work converting starving men with a Bible in one hand and a slice of bread in the other. I will undertake to convert West Ham to Mahometanism on the same terms. Try your hand on my men: their souls are hungry because their bodies are full.

BARBARA: And leave the east end to starve?

UNDERSHAFT (his energetic tone dropping into one of bitter and brooding remembrance): I was an east ender. I moralized and starved until one day I swore that I would be a full-fed free man at all costs; that nothing should stop me except a bullet, neither reason nor morals nor the lives of other men. I said 'Thou shalt starve ere I starve'; and with that word I became free and great. I was a dangerous man until I had my will: now I am a useful, beneficent, kindly person. That is the history of most self-made millionaires, I fancy. When it is the history of every Englishman we shall have an England worth living in.

LADY BRITOMART: Stop making speeches, Andrew. This is not the place for them.

UNDERSHAFT (punctured): My dear: I have no other means of conveying my ideas.

LADY BRITOMART: Your ideas are nonsense. You got on because you were selfish and unscrupulous.

UNDERSHAFT: Not at all. I had the strongest scruples about poverty and starvation. Your moralists are quite unscrupulous about both: they make virtues of them. I had rather be a thief than a pauper. I had rather be a murderer than a slave. I dont want to be either; but if you force the alternative on me, then, by Heaven, I'll choose the braver and more moral one. I hate poverty and slavery worse than any other crimes whatsoever. And let me tell you this. Poverty and slavery have stood up for centuries to your sermons and leading articles: they will not stand up to my machine guns. Dont preach at them: dont reason with them. Kill them.

BARBARA: Killing. Is that your remedy for everything?

UNDERSHAFT: It is the final test of conviction, the only lever strong enough to overturn a social system, the only way of saying Must. Let six hundred and seventy fools loose in the streets; and three policemen can scatter them. But huddle them together in a certain house in Westminster; and let them go through certain ceremonies and call themselves certain names until at last they get the courage to kill; and your six hundred and seventy fools become a government. Your pious mob fills up ballot papers and imagines it is governing its masters; but the ballot paper that really governs is the paper that has a bullet wrapped up in it.

CUSINS: That is perhaps why, like most intelligent people, I never vote.

UNDERSHAFT: Vote! Bah! When you vote, you only change the names of the cabinet. When you shoot, you pull down governments, inaugurate new epochs, abolish old orders and set up new. Is that historically true, Mr Learned Man, or is it not?

CUSINS: It is historically true. I loathe having to admit it. I repudiate your sentiments. I abhor your nature. I defy you in every possible way. Still, it is true. But it ought not to be true.

UNDERSHAFT: Ought! ought! ought! ought! ought! Are you going to spend your life saying ought, like the rest of our moralists? Turn your oughts into shalls, man. Come and make explosives with me. Whatever can blow men up can blow society up. The history of the world is the history of those who had courage enough to embrace this truth. Have you the courage to embrace it, Barbara?

LADY BRITOMART: Barbara: I positively forbid you to listen to your father's abominable wickedness. And you, Adolphus, ought to know better than to go about saying that wrong things are true. What does it matter whether they are true if they are wrong?

UNDERSHAFT: What does it matter whether they are wrong if they are true?

LADY BRITOMART (*rising*): Children: come home instantly. Andrew: I am exceedingly sorry I allowed you to call on us. You are wickeder than ever. Come at once.

BARBARA (*shaking her head*): It's no use running away from wicked people, mamma.

LADY BRITOMART: It is every use. It shews your disapprobation of them.

BARBARA: It does not save them.

LADY BRITOMART: I can see that you are going to disobey me. Sarah: are you coming home or are you not?

SARAH: I daresay it's very wicked of papa to make cannons; but I dont think I shall cut him on that account.

LOMAX (*pouring oil on the troubled waters*): The fact is, you know, there is a certain amount of tosh about this notion of wickedness. It doesnt work. You must look at facts. Not that I would say a word in favor of anything wrong; but then, you see, all sorts of chaps are always doing all sorts of things; and we have to fit them in somehow, dont you know. What I mean is that you cant go cutting everybody; and thats about what it comes to. (*Their rapt attention to his eloquence makes him nervous.*) Perhaps I dont make myself clear.

LADY BRITOMART: You are lucidity itself, Charles. Because Andrew is successful and has plenty of money to give to Sarah, you will flatter him and encourage him in his wickedness.

LOMAX (*unruffled*): Well, where the carcase is, there will the eagles be gathered, dont you know. (*To* UNDERSHAFT.) Eh? What?

UNDERSHAFT: Precisely. By the way, may I call you Charles?

LOMAX: Delighted. Cholly is the usual ticket.

UNDERSHAFT (*to* LADY BRITOMART): Biddy —

LADY BRITOMART (*violently*): Dont dare call me Biddy. Charles Lomax: you are a fool. Adolphus Cusins: you are a Jesuit. Stephen: you are a prig. Barbara: you are a lunatic. Andrew: you are a vulgar tradesman. Now you all know my opinion; and my conscience is

clear, at all events. (*She sits down with a vehemence that the rug fortunately softens.*)

UNDERSHAFT: My dear: you are the incarnation of morality. (*She snorts.*) Your conscience is clear and your duty done when you have called everybody names. Come, Euripides! It is getting late; and we all want to go home. Make up your mind.

CUSINS: Understand this, you old demon —

LADY BRITOMART: Adolphus!

UNDERSHAFT: Let him alone, Biddy. Proceed, Euripides.

CUSINS: You have me in a horrible dilemma. I want Barbara.

UNDERSHAFT: Like all young men, you greatly exaggerate the difference between one young woman and another.

BARBARA: Quite true, Dolly.

CUSINS: I also want to avoid being a rascal.

UNDERSHAFT (*with biting contempt*): You lust for personal righteousness, for self-approval, for what you call a good conscience, for what Barbara calls salvation, for what I call patronizing people who are not so lucky as yourself.

CUSINS: I do not call the poet in me recoils from being a good man. But there are things in me that I must reckon with. Pity —

UNDERSHAFT: Pity! The scavenger of misery.

CUSINS: Well, love.

UNDERSHAFT: I know. You love the needy and the outcast: you love the oppressed races, the negro, the Indian ryot, the underdog everywhere. Do you love the Japanese? Do you love the English?

CUSINS: No. Every true Englishman detests the English. We are the wickedest nation on earth; and our success is a moral horror.

UNDERSHAFT: That is what comes of your gospel of love, is it?

CUSINS: May I not love even my father-in-law?

UNDERSHAFT: Who wants your love, man? By what right do you take the liberty of offering it to me? I will have your due heed and respect, or I will kill you. But your love! Damn your impertinence!

CUSINS (*grinning*): I may not be able to control my affections, Mac.

UNDERSHAFT: You are fencing, Euripides. You are weakening: your grip is slipping. Come! try your last weapon. Pity and love have broken in your hand: forgiveness is still left.

CUSINS: No: forgiveness is a beggar's refuge. I am with you there: we must pay our debts.

UNDERSHAFT: Well said. Come! you will suit me. Remember the words of Plato.

CUSINS (*starting*): Plato! You dare quote Plato to me!

UNDERSHAFT: Plato says, my friend, that society cannot be saved until either the Professors of Greek take to making gunpowder, or else the makers of gunpowder become Professors of Greek.

CUSINS: Oh, tempter, cunning tempter!

UNDERSHAFT: Come! choose, man, choose.

CUSINS: But perhaps Barbara will not marry me if I make the wrong choice.

BARBARA: Perhaps not.

CUSINS (*desperately perplexed*): You hear!

BARBARA: Father: do you love nobody?

UNDERSHAFT: I love my best friend.

LADY BRITOMART: And who is that, pray?

UNDERSHAFT: My bravest enemy. That is the man who keeps me up to the mark.

CUSINS: You know, the creature is really a sort of poet in his way. Suppose he is a great man, after all!

UNDERSHAFT: Suppose you stop talking and make up your mind, my young friend.

CUSINS: But you are driving me against my nature. I hate war.

UNDERSHAFT: Hatred is the coward's revenge for being intimidated. Dare you make war on war? Here are the means: my friend Mr Lomax is sitting on them.

LOMAX (*springing up*): Oh I say! You dont mean that this thing is loaded, do you? My ownest: come off it.

SARAH (*sitting placidly on the shell*): If I am to be blown up, the more thoroughly it is done the better. Dont fuss, Cholly.

LOMAX (*to* UNDERSHAFT, *strongly remonstrant*): Your own daughter, you know!

UNDERSHAFT: So I see. (*To* CUSINS.) Well, my friend, may we expect you here at six tomorrow morning?

CUSINS (*firmly*): Not on any account. I will see the whole establishment blown up with its own dynamite before I will get up at five. My hours are healthy, rational hours: eleven to five.

UNDERSHAFT: Come when you please: before a week you will come at six and stay until I turn you out for the sake of your health. (*Calling.*) Bilton! (*He turns to* LADY BRITOMART, *who rises.*) My dear: let us leave these two young people to themselves for a moment. (BILTON *comes from the shed.*) I am going to take you through the gun cotton shed.

BILTON (*barring the way*): You cant take anything explosive in here, sir.

LADY BRITOMART: What do you mean? Are you alluding to me?

BILTON (*unmoved*): No, maam. Mr Undershaft has the other gentleman's matches in his pocket.

LADY BRITOMART (*abruptly*): Oh! I beg your pardon. (*She goes into the shed.*)

UNDERSHAFT: Quite right, Bilton, quite right: here you are. (*He gives* BILTON *the box of matches.*) Come, Stephen. Come, Charles. Bring Sarah. (*He passes into the shed.*)

(BILTON *opens the box and deliberately drops the matches into the fire-bucket.*)

LOMAX: Oh! I say. (BILTON *stolidly hands him the empty box.*) Infernal nonsense! Pure scientific ignorance! (*He goes in.*)

SARAH: Am I all right, Bilton?

BILTON: Youll have to put on list slippers, miss: thats all. Weve got em inside. (*She goes in.*)

STEPHEN (*very seriously to* CUSINS): Dolly, old fellow, think. Think before you decide. Do you feel that you are a sufficiently practical man? It is a huge undertaking, an enormous responsibility. All this mass of business will be Greek to you.

CUSINS: Oh, I think it will be much less difficult than Greek.

STEPHEN: Well, I just want to say this before I leave you to yourselves. Dont let anything I have said about right and wrong prejudice you against this great chance in life. I have satisfied myself that the business is one of the highest character and a credit to our country. (*Emotionally.*) I am very proud of my father. I — (*Unable to proceed, he presses* CUSINS' *hand and goes hastily into the shed, followed by* BILTON.)

(BARBARA *and* CUSINS, *left alone together, look at one another silently.*)

CUSINS: Barbara: I am going to accept this offer.

BARBARA: I thought you would.

CUSINS: You understand, dont you, that I had to decide without consulting you. If I had thrown the burden of the choice on you, you would sooner or later have despised me for it.

BARBARA: Yes: I did not want you to sell your soul for me any more than for this inheritance.

CUSINS: It is not the sale of my soul that troubles me: I have sold it too often to care about that. I have sold it for a professorship. I have sold it for an income. I have sold it to escape being imprisoned for refusing to pay taxes for hangmen's ropes and unjust wars and things that I abhor. What is all human conduct but the daily and hourly sale of our souls for trifles? What I am now selling it for is neither money nor position nor comfort, but for reality and for power.

BARBARA: You know that you will have no power, and that he has none.

CUSINS: I know. It is not for myself alone. I want to make power for the world.

BARBARA: I want to make power for the world too; but it must be spiritual power.

CUSINS: I think all power is spiritual: these cannons will not go off by themselves. I have tried to make spiritual power by teaching Greek. But the world can never be really touched by a dead language and a dead civilization. The people must have power; and the people cannot have Greek. Now the power that is made here can be wielded by all men.

BARBARA: Power to burn women's houses down and kill their sons and tear their husbands to pieces.

CUSINS: You cannot have power for good without having power for evil too. Even mother's milk nourishes murderers as well as heroes. This power which only tears men's bodies to pieces has never been so horribly abused as the intellectual power, the imaginative power, the poetic, religious power that can enslave men's souls. As a teacher of Greek I gave the intellectual man weapons against the common man. I now want to give the common man weapons against the intellectual man. I love the common people. I want to arm them against the lawyers, the doctors, the priests, the literary men, the professors, the artists, and the politicians, who, once in authority, are more disastrous and tyrannical than all the fools, rascals, and impostors. I want a power simple enough for common men to use, yet strong enough to force the intellectual oligarchy to use its genius for the general good.

BARBARA: Is there no higher power than that (pointing to the shell)?

CUSINS: Yes; but that power can destroy the higher powers just as a tiger can destroy a man: therefore Man must master that power first. I admitted this when the Turks and Greeks were last at war. My best pupil went out to fight for Hellas. My parting gift to him was not a copy of Plato's Republic, but a revolver and a hundred Undershaft cartridges. The blood of every Turk he shot — if he shot any — is on my head as well as on Undershaft's. That act committed me to this place for ever. Your father's challenge has beaten me. Dare I make war on war? I must. I will. And now, is it all over between us?

BARBARA (touched by his evident dread of her answer): Silly baby Dolly! How could it be!

CUSINS (overjoyed): Then you — you — you — Oh for my drum! (He flourishes imaginary drumsticks.)

BARBARA (angered by his levity): Take care, Dolly, take care. Oh, if only I could get away from you and from father and from it all! if I could have the wings of a dove and fly away to heaven!

CUSINS: And leave me!

BARBARA: Yes, you, and all the other naughty mischievous children of men. But I cant. I was happy in the Salvation Army for a moment. I escaped from the world into a paradise of enthusiasm and prayer and soul saving; but the moment our money ran short, it all came back to Bodger: it was he who saved our people: he, and the Prince of Darkness, my papa. Undershaft and Bodger: their hands stretch everywhere: when we feed a starving fellow creature, it is with their bread, because there is no other bread; when we tend the sick, it is in the hospitals they endow; if we turn from the churches they build, we must kneel on the stones of the streets they pave. As long as that lasts, there is no getting away from them. Turning our backs on Bodger and Undershaft is turning our backs on life.

CUSINS: I thought you were determined to turn your back on the wicked side of life.

BARBARA: There is no wicked side: life is all one. And I never wanted to shirk my share in whatever evil must be endured, whether it be sin or suffering. I wish I could cure you of middle-class ideas, Dolly.

CUSINS (gasping): Middle cl — ! A snub! A social snub to me! from the daughter of a foundling!

BARBARA: That is why I have no class, Dolly: I come straight out of the heart of the whole people. If I were middle-class I should turn my back on my father's business; and we should both live in an artistic drawing room, with you reading the reviews in one corner, and I in the other at the piano, playing Schumann: both very superior persons, and neither of us a bit of use. Sooner than that, I would sweep out the guncotton shed, or be one of Bodger's barmaids. Do you know what would have happened if you had refused papa's offer?

CUSINS: I wonder!

BARBARA: I should have given you up and married the man who accepted it. After all, my dear old mother has more sense than any of you. I felt like her when I saw this place — felt that I must have it — that never, never, never could I let it go; only she thought it was the houses and the kitchen ranges and the linen and china, when it was really all the human souls to be saved: not weak souls in starved bodies, sobbing with gratitude for a scrap of bread and treacle, but fullfed, quarrelsome, snobbish, uppish creatures, all standing on their little rights and dignities, and thinking that my father ought to be greatly obliged to them for making so much money for him — and so he ought. That is where salvation is really wanted. My father shall never throw it in my teeth again that my converts were bribed with bread. (*She is transfigured.*) I have got rid of the bribe of bread. I have got rid of the bribe of heaven. Let God's work be done for its own sake: the work he had to create us to do because it cannot be done except by living men and women. When I die, let him be in my debt, not I in his; and let me forgive him as becomes a woman of my rank.

CUSINS: Then the way of life lies through the factory of death?

BARBARA: Yes, through the raising of hell to heaven and of man to God, through the unveiling of an eternal light in the Valley of The Shadow. (*Seizing him with both hands.*)

Oh, did you think my courage would never come back? did you believe that I was a deserter? that I, who have stood in the streets, and taken my people to my heart, and talked of the holiest and greatest things with them, could ever turn back and chatter foolishly to fashionable people about nothing in a drawing room? Never, never, never, never: Major Barbara will die with the colors. Oh! and I have my dear little Dolly boy still; and he has found me my place and my work. Glory Hallelujah! (*She kisses him.*)

CUSINS: My dearest: consider my delicate health. I cannot stand as much happiness as you can.

BARBARA: Yes: it is not easy work being in love with me, is it? But it's good for you. (*She runs to the shed, and calls, childlike.*) Mamma! Mamma! (BILTON *comes out of the shed, followed by* UNDERSHAFT.) I want Mamma.

UNDERSHAFT: She is taking off her list slippers, dear. (*He passes on to* CUSINS.) Well? What does she say?

CUSINS: She has gone right up into the skies.

LADY BRITOMART (*coming from the shed and stopping on the steps, obstructing* SARAH, *who follows with* LOMAX. BARBARA *clutches like a baby at her mother's skirt*): Barbara: when will you learn to be independent and to act and think for yourself? I know as well as possible what that cry of 'Mamma, Mamma,' means. Always running to me!

SARAH (*touching* LADY BRITOMART's *ribs with her finger tips and imitating a bicycle horn*): Pip! pip!

LADY BRITOMART (*highly indignant*): How dare you say Pip! pip! to me, Sarah? You are both very naughty children. What do you want, Barbara?

BARBARA: I want a house in the village to live in with Dolly. (*Dragging at the skirt.*) Come and tell me which one to take.

UNDERSHAFT (*to* CUSINS): Six o'clock tomorrow morning, Euripides.

THE END

One of the earliest English remarks about comedy, Sir Philip Sidney's written about 1580, runs thus:

> Comedy is an imitation of the common errors of our life, which he repre-senteth in the most ridiculous and scornful sort that may be; so that it is impossible that any beholder can be content to be such a one.

Sidney is indebted to Italian commentators, who in turn are indebted to Roman commentators, and behind them are the Greeks, notably Aristotle. Along the way, of course, there are lots of variations, but the basic ideas may fairly be said to constitute the "classical" theory of comedy:

1. The characters are ignoble
2. Their actions arouse derision (rather than, say, terror or pity)
3. The spectators, if they have resembled the dramatis personae, leave the theater morally improved after seeing the absurdity of such behavior.

The "classical" theory, often stated before Sidney, has since been restated at least as often. Almost every comic dramatist who has commented on his work has offered it as his justification. Shaw, in a preface to his *Complete Plays*, put it thus:

> If I make you laugh at yourself, remember that my business as a classic writer of comedies is "to chasten morals with ridicule"; and if I some-times make you feel like a fool, remember that I have by the same action cured your folly, just as the dentist cures your toothache by pulling out your tooth. And I never do it without giving you plenty of laughing gas.

To begin with the laughing gas in *Major Barbara*: the first act suggests that the play is a drawing-room comedy, full of aristocratic people bouncing elegant lines off each other. (Lady Brit, of course, affects innocence, but she is accomplished at getting what she wants.) Sample:

> I am not a Pharisee, I hope; and I should not have minded his merely doing wrong things: we are none of us perfect. But your father didnt ex-actly do wrong things: he said them and thought them: that was what was so dreadful. He really had a sort of religion of wrongness. Just as one doesnt mind men practising immorality so long as they own that they are in the wrong by preaching morality; so I couldnt forgive Andrew for preaching immorality while he practised morality.

Another sample:

> CUSINS: Let me advise you to study Greek, Mr. Undershaft. Greek scholars are privileged men. Few of them know Greek; and none of them know anything else; but their position is unchallengeable. Other lan-guages are the qualifications of waiters and commercial travellers: Greek is to a man of position what the hallmark is to silver.

If Shaw had been content to write a comedy in the classical tradition, he would have contrived a plot which would probably have involved an unsuitable wooer of Barbara, maybe a rich old aristocrat, maybe a parvenu, maybe a for-tune hunter, who would finally be unmasked and then displaced by an ap-

propriately young and charming and socially acceptable bridegroom. But Shaw
turned to comedy as a propagandist. He had been deeply impressed by Ibsen's
plays, and he saw in the drama an opportunity to preach his economic ideas to
a wider audience than is normally reached by the pamphleteer. For Shaw, the
heart of Ibsen's plays lies in such a "discussion" as the one in A Doll's House,
where Nora explains to her husband that things are all wrong in their apparently happy marriage. (The interested reader is advised to look at Shaw's The
Quintessence of Ibsenism, especially the next to the last chapter, "The Technical Novelty," which insists that post-Ibsen plays must replace the old formula
of exposition-situation-unraveling with "exposition, situation, and discussion;
and the discussion is the test of the playwright.... The serious playwright
recognizes not only the main test of his highest powers, but also the real center
of his play's interest.")

What Shaw does, then, is introduce massive discussions into a comedy
that at first seems to be doing little more than spoofing Lady Brit and holding
her son Stephen up to rather obvious ridicule. Stephen is not merely an ass; he
is made to serve as a sort of straightman for Undershaft, who expounds at
length unconventional ideas about munitions, sin, power, and poverty. These
ideas require discussion because Shaw, unlike most comic writers, is not content with the traditional views. Comic playwrights usually criticize eccentric
behavior, and at least implicitly suggest that there is a reasonable norm,
known to all men of sense, from which fools depart. But because Shaw believed that society's norm is itself foolish, he devotes much of his play to ex-
pounding a new creed. Shaw reverses the old joke about the entire platoon
being out of step except Johnny; for Shaw, the deviant, Johnny, is in step, and
the rest of the platoon is laughably out of step. During the central part of
Major Barbara, then, Undershaft, the eccentric, is for Shaw the least laughable character. Even Barbara, the heroine, is exposed as a fool, though with
great tenderness, and is forced to shed her conventional illusions. So great is
the tenderness that as we see her world collapse, she seems almost a tragic
figure:

> I stood on the rock I thought eternal; and without a word of warning it
> reeled and crumbled under me.

But Undershaft dispels the tragedy, harshly but necessarily, with, "Come,
come, my daughter! dont make too much of your little tinpot tragedy....
Dont persist in that folly. If your old religion broke down yesterday, get a
newer and a better one for tomorrow."

Enough has been said to give some idea of the novelty of Shaw's comic
practice, however conventional his theory. But one should note, too, that in
one important way his practice is conventional: his plays have the stock quack
doctors, pompous statesmen, dragonlike matrons, and young lovers of traditional comedy. And in Major Barbara he even uses the ancient motif of the
foundling who proves to be a suitable husband for the heroine.

Something more, however, must be said of Undershaft. Having allowed Undershaft to triumph over Barbara, Shaw does not stop; very late in the play Undershaft himself is threatened with the loss of *his* illusions when Barbara and Adolphus Cusins will make their presence felt in the munitions factory. The play ends with the usual marriage, joy, and promise of a newly organized society; in its suggestion, however, that this new society is not a return to a sensible world that was lost before the play began (think, for example, of the end of *As You Like It*, where the duke is restored to his realm), but rather is the beginning of a totally new sort of world, it marks a departure from comic practice. Maybe that is why the end of the play has seemed to most audiences the least amusing part.

The Comic Rhythm

Susanne K. Langer

In Boswell's *Life of Doctor Johnson* we hear of a man who intended to be a philosopher but who failed because "cheerfulness was always breaking in." Susanne K. Langer is a philosopher, but she does not see cheerfulness as an enemy. She sees in comedy a dramatization of the basic biological patterns of persistence and growth, "human vitality holding its own in the world amid the surprises of unplanned coincidence."

The pure sense of life is the underlying feeling of comedy, developed in countless different ways. To give a general phenomenon one name is not to make all its manifestations one thing, but only to bring them conceptually under one head. Art does not generalize and classify; art sets forth the individuality of forms which discourse, being essentially general, has to suppress. The sense of life is always new, infinitely complex, therefore infinitely variable in its possible expressions. This sense, or "enjoyment" as Alexander would call it,[1] is the realization in direct feeling of what sets organic nature apart from inorganic: self-preservation, self-restoration, functional tendency, purpose. Life is teleological, the rest of nature is, apparently, mechanical; to maintain the pattern of vitality in a non-living universe is the most elementary instinctual purpose. An organism tends to keep its equilibrium amid the bombardment of aimless forces that beset it, to regain equilibrium when it has been disturbed, and to pursue a sequence of actions dictated by the need of keeping all its interdependent parts constantly renewed, their structure intact. Only organisms have needs; lifeless objects whirl or slide or tumble about, are shattered and scattered, stuck together,

piled up, without showing any impulse to return to some pre-eminent condition and function. But living things strive to persist in a particular chemical balance, to maintain a particular temperature, to repeat particular functions, and to develop along particular lines, achieving a growth that seems to be preformed in their earliest, rudimentary, protoplasmic structure.

That is the basic biological pattern which all living things share: the round of conditioned and conditioning organic processes that produces the life rhythm. When this rhythm is disturbed, all activities in the total complex are modified by the break; the organism as a whole is out of balance. But, within a wide range of conditions, it struggles to retrieve its original dynamic form by overcoming and removing the obstacle, or if this proves impossible, it develops a slight variation of its typical form and activity and carries on life with a new balance of functions — in other words, it adapts itself to the situation. A tree, for instance, that is bereft of the sunshine it needs by the encroachment of other trees, tends to grow tall and thin until it can spread its own branches in the light. A fish that has most of its tail bitten off partly overcomes the disturbance of its locomotion patterns by growing new tissue, replacing some of the tail, and partly adapts to its new condition by modifying the normal uses of its fins, swimming effectively without trying to correct the list of its whole body in the water, as it did at first.

[1] S. Alexander, *Space, Time and Deity*. See Vol. I, p. 12.

But the impulse to survive is not spent only in defense and accommodation; it appears also in the varying power of organisms to seize on opportunities. Consider how chimney swifts, which used to nest in crevasses among rocks, have exploited the products of human architecture, and how unfailingly mice find the warmth and other delights of our kitchens. All creatures live by opportunities, in a world fraught with disasters. That is the biological pattern in most general terms. . . .

Mankind has its rhythm of animal existence, too — the strain of maintaining a vital balance amid the alien and impartial chances of the world, complicated and heightened by passional desires. The pure sense of life springs from that basic rhythm, and varies from the composed well-being of sleep to the intensity of spasm, rage, or ecstasy. But the process of living is incomparably more complex for human beings than for even the highest animals; man's world is, above all, intricate and puzzling. The powers of language and imagination have set it utterly apart from that of other creatures. In human society an individual is not, like a member of a herd or a hive, exposed only to others that visibly or tangibly surround him, but is consciously bound to people who are absent, perhaps far away, at the moment. Even the dead may still play into his life. His awareness of events is far greater than the scope of his physical perceptions. Symbolic construction has made this vastly involved and extended world: and mental adroitness is his chief asset for exploiting it. The pattern of his vital feeling, therefore, reflects his deep emotional relation to those symbolic structures that are his realities, and his instinctual life modified in almost every way by thought — a brainy opportunism in face of an essentially dreadful universe.

This human life-feeling is the essence of comedy. It is at once religious and ribald, knowing and defiant, social and freakishly individual. The illusion of life which the comic poet creates is the oncoming future fraught with dangers and opportunities, that is, with physical or social events occurring by chance and building up the coincidences with which individuals cope according to their lights. This ineluctable future — ineluctable because its countless factors are beyond human knowledge and control — is Fortune. Destiny in the guise of Fortune is the fabric of comedy; it is developed by comic action, which is the upset and recovery of the protagonist's equilibrium, his contest with the world and his triumph by wit, luck, personal power, or even humorous, or ironical, or philosophical acceptance of mischance. Whatever the theme — serious and lyrical as in *The Tempest*, coarse slapstick as in the *Schwänke* of Hans Sachs, or clever and polite social satire — the immediate sense of life is the underlying feeling of comedy, and dictates its rhythmically structured unity, that is to say its organic form.

Comedy is an art form that arises naturally wherever people are gathered to celebrate life, in spring festivals, triumphs, birthdays, weddings, or initiations. For it expresses the elementary strains and resolutions of animate nature, the animal drives that persist even in human nature, the delight man takes in his special mental gifts that make him the lord of creation; it is an image of human vitality holding its own in the world amid the surprises of unplanned coincidence. The most obvious occasions for the performance of comedies are thanks or challenges to fortune. What justifies the term "Comedy" is not that the ancient ritual procession, the Comus, honoring the god of that name, was the source of this great art form — for comedy has arisen in many parts of the world, where the Greek god with his particular worship was unknown — but that the Comus was a fertility rite, and the god it celebrated a fertility god, a symbol of perpetual rebirth, eternal life. . . .

Because comedy abstracts, and reincarnates for our perception, the motion and rhythm of living, it enhances our vital feeling, much as the presentation of space in painting enhances our awareness of visual space. The virtual life on the stage is not diffuse and only half felt, as actual life usually is: virtual life, always moving visibly into the future, is intensified, speeded up, exaggerated; the exhibition of vitality rises to a breaking point, to mirth and laughter. We laugh in the theater at small incidents and drolleries which would hardly rate a chuckle offstage. It is not for such psychological reasons that we go there to be amused, nor are we bound by rules of politeness to hide our hilarity, but these trifles at which we laugh are really funnier *where they occur* than they would be elsewhere; they are employed in the play, not merely brought in casually. They occur where the tension of dialogue or other action reaches a high point. As thought breaks into speech — as the wave breaks into form — vitality breaks into humor.

Humor is the brilliance of drama, a sudden heightening of the vital rhythm. A good comedy, therefore, builds up to every laugh; a performance that has been filled up with jokes at the indiscretion of the comedian or of his writer may draw a long series of laughs, yet leave the spectator without any clear impression of a very funny play. The laughs, moreover, are likely to be of a peculiar sameness, almost perfunctory, the formal recognition of a timely "gag."

The amoral character of the comic protagonist goes through the whole range of what may be called the comedy of laughter. Even the most civilized products of this art — plays that George Meredith would honor with the name of "comedy," because they provoke "thoughtful laughter" — do not present moral distinctions and issues, but only the ways of wisdom and of folly. Aristophanes, Menander, Molière — practically the only authors this most exacting of critics admitted as truly comic poets — are not moralists, yet they do not flout or deprecate morality; they have, literally, "no use" for moral principles — that is, they do not use them. Meredith, like practically all his contemporaries, labored under the belief that poetry must teach society lessons, and that comedy was valuable for what it revealed concerning the social order.[2] He tried hard to hold its exposé of foibles and vindication of common sense to an ethical standard, yet in his very efforts to justify its amoral personages he only admitted their amoral nature, and their simple relish for life, as when he said: "The heroines of comedy are like women of the world, not necessarily heartless from being clear-sighted. . . . Comedy is an exhibition of their battle with men, and that of men with them. . . ."

There it is, in a nutshell: the contest of men and women — the most universal contest, humanized, in fact civilized, yet still the primitive joyful challenge, the self-preservation and self-assertion whose progress is the comic rhythm. . . .

The same impulse that drove people, even in prehistoric times, to enact fertility rites and celebrate all phases of their biological existence, sustains their eternal interest in comedy. It is in the nature of comedy to be erotic, risqué, and sensuous if not sensual, impious, and even wicked. This assures it a spontaneous emotional interest, yet a dangerous one: for it is easy and tempting to command an audience by direct stimulation of feeling and fantasy, not by artistic power. But where the formulation of feeling is really achieved, it probably reflects the whole development of mankind and man's world, for feeling is the intaglio image of reality. The sense of precariousness that is the typical tension of light comedy was undoubtedly developed in the eternal struggle with chance that every farmer knows only too well — with weather, blights, beasts, birds and beetles. The embarrassments, perplexities and mounting panic which characterize that favorite genre, comedy of manners, may still reflect the toils of ritual and taboo that complicated the caveman's existence. Even the element of aggressiveness in comic action serves to develop a fundamental trait of the comic rhythm — the deep cruelty of it, as all life feeds on life. There is no biological truth that feeling does not reflect, and that good comedy, therefore, will not be prone to reveal.

But the fact that the rhythm of comedy is the basic rhythm of life does not mean that biological existence is the "deeper meaning" of all its themes, and that to understand the play is to interpret all the characters as symbols and the story as a parable, a disguised rite of spring or fertility magic, performed four hundred and fifty times on Broadway. The stock characters are probably symbolic both in origin and in appeal. There are such independently symbolic

[2] His well-known little work is called *An Essay on Comedy, and the Uses of the Comic Spirit*. These uses are entirely non-artistic. Praising the virtues of "good sense" (which is whatever has survival value in the eyes of society), he says: "The French have a school of stately comedy to which they can fly for renovation whenever they have fallen away from it; and their having such a school is the main reason why, as John Stuart Mill pointed out, they know men and women more accurately than we do." And a few pages later: "The *Femmes Savantes* is a capital instance of the uses of comedy in teaching the world to understand what ails it. The French had felt the burden of this new nonsense [the fad of academic learning, new after the fad of excessive nicety and precision in speech, that had marked the *Précieuses*]; but they had to see the comedy several times before they were consoled in their suffering by seeing the cause of it exposed."

factors, or residues of them, in all the arts,[3] but their value for art lies in the degree to which

their significance can be "swallowed" by the single symbol, the art work. Not the derivation of personages and situations, but of the rhythm of "felt life" that the poet puts upon them, seems to me to be of artistic importance: the essential comic feeling, which is the sentient aspect of organic unity, growth, and self-preservation.

[3] E.g., the symbolization of the zodiac in some sacred architecture, of our bodily orientation in the picture plane, or of walking measure, a primitive measure of actual time, in music. But a study of such non-artistic symbolic functions would require a monograph.

Old and New Comedy

Northrop Frye

Professor Frye points out that the ancient form called New Comedy (essentially, boy gets girl; more profoundly, a movement toward rebirth of the sort that Mrs. Langer discusses in the previous essay) has dominated the comic theater for more than two thousand years. But he goes on to argue that another ancient form, Old Comedy (represented in this book by Aristophanes' *The Birds*), which is essentially a clash between personalities or representatives of social forces, which is inclined toward fantasy and mockery and argumentativeness, and which may conclude without a sense that an end has been achieved, may be the dominant form on the modern stage.

The Old and New Comedy forms in Greek literature are highly stylized and conventionalized forms, each the product of very specific cultural and historical conditions that can never recur. Each may be of course imitated in later ages: the *Comedy of Errors* adapts Plautus, and there is some imitation of Aristophanes in *The Knight of the Burning Pestle*. But more important than the possibility of imitation is the fact that the two Greek forms are species of larger dramatic genera. The *kind* of comedy they represent may and inevitably will recur, when a larger pattern of cultural and historical factors makes it possible.

I begin with New Comedy, as the more familiar, and as having something more like a continuous line of tradition. The distinguishing feature of New Comedy is the teleological plot: perhaps this feature had something to do with Aristotle's approval of it. As a rule the main theme of this plot is that of the alienated lover moving towards sexual fulfilment. New Comedy reaches a *telos* in its final scene, which is superficially marriage, and, more profoundly, a rebirth. A new society is created on the stage in the last moments of a typical New Comedy, when objections, oppositions, misunderstand-

ings and the schemes of rivals are all cleared out of the way. This newborn society is frequently balanced by a recognition scene and a theme of the restoring of a birthright, the recognition (*cognitio*) being connected with the secret of somebody's birth in the very common device of the foundling plot. Much simpler and more popular is the comedy in which a hero, after many setbacks, succeeds in doing something that wins him the heroine and a new sense of identity.

In such a structure the characters are essentially functions of the plot. However fully realized they may be, they are always organically related to the roles on which the plot turns, whether senex, parasite, bragging rival or whatever it is. The *commedia dell'arte* indicates with particular clarity how a group of stock characters related to a stock plot is the basis of the comic structures of Shakespeare and Molière, both of whom show many affinities with the *commedia dell'arte*. In Ben Jonson's "humour" theory the New Comedy conception of character as a plot-function is rationalized in a most ingenious way. The character as plot-function has something predictable at his basis: the "humour" is a character who is completely dominated by a predictable reaction. But predictability of response is also one of the main sources of the comic mood, as has been emphasized in most theories of comedy and laughter

Reprinted by permission of the publisher, Cambridge University Press, from *Shakespeare Survey* 22, edited by K. Muir.

down to Bergson. Thus the "humour" is the appropriate type of character for a New Comedy plot because in the humour comic structure and comic mood are unified.

The imagery and characterization of New Comedy belong to an extensive area of literary symbolism which I shall call Eros symbolism. Eros symbolism includes all the medieval poetry in which an alienated lover is stimulated by his love to make some gigantic achievement, whether his goal is explicitly sexual, as it is in *The Romaunt of the Rose,* or spiritual and sublimated, as it is in the *Purgatorio.* The two climaxes of the Eros quest we may call, following Milton, the *allegro* and the *penseroso* forms. The Biblical archetypes of Dante's quest are the journey of man towards the garden of Eden, the journey through the wilderness to the Promised Land, and the vision of the *hortus conclusus* of the Song of Songs which in its Christian form is the epiphany of the virgin mother and divine child. Here the transcendence of a sexual goal goes along with the vision of a divine childhood which is partly the poet's childhood as well, for Dante in Eden regains his generic childhood as a son of an unfallen Adam. In all these quests we notice the figure of the lonely old man who can see but not enter the sacred garden. This figure is represented by Moses in the Old Testament, by Joseph in the New, and by Virgil in Dante. He corresponds in New Comedy to the defeated or reconciled senex. In Shakespeare we notice how in *As You Like It* the quadruple marriage is contrasted with the melancholy Jaques, who goes off to consult a hermit, and how in *The Tempest* the festivities of Ferdinand and Miranda are an emotional contrast to the world-weariness of Prospero.

New Comedy develops two main forms, the romantic form of Shakespeare and the more realistic and displaced form of the Neo-Classical tradition, of which the greatest name is Molière. The more realistic such comedy becomes, the more it is in danger of becoming a sentimental domestic comedy, like the *comédie larmoyante* of the eighteenth century. A combination of realistic treatment and comic structure has a tendency to sentimentality inherent in it, as its theme approximates very closely the favourite rubric of the agony column: "Come home; all is forgiven." Molière avoids this by focusing nearly all the dramatic interest on a central senex or blocking figure, whose particular folly, whether avarice or snobbery or hypo-

chondria, keeps the tone well away from the sentimental. But in Sheridan and Goldsmith the effort to keep the texture dry and witty is more of a strain. The domestic virtues do not appear to have attracted the loyalty of a major dramatic genius, unless we wish to call Beethoven a major dramatic genius. *Fidelio* is a bachelor's tribute to the domestic virtues, but the extraordinary unevenness of the music indicates some doubts even in his mind. Naturally, too, anything in the nature of a "well-made play," like the plays of Scribe and Sardou, or in general of what Bernard Shaw called "Sardoodledom," belongs to the New Comedy tradition.

Eventually the New Comedy structure tends to desert the stage for the domestic novel, where a sentimental tone is easier to accommodate. The foundling plot reappears in *Tom Jones,* and reaches perhaps its culmination in Dickens. For in Dickens, while the story normally ends in marriage, a great deal is made of the mystery of birth. The production of the parents of the hero or heroine, even when they are bare names unrelated to the story, like the father of Oliver Twist or the parents of Little Nell, seems to be a feature of great importance. And, of course, the whole conception of characterization in Dickens is very close to that of the Jonsonian humour, except that the looser fictional form can find room for a greater number of peripheral characters who are not directly concerned in the central plot.

When drama revives in Great Britain towards the end of the nineteenth century, the formulas of New Comedy are used increasingly for purposes of parody, parody being the usual sign in literature that some conventions are getting worn out. We begin with parodies of foundling and mysterious-heir plots in Gilbert and Sullivan, notably in *Pinafore* and *The Gondoliers;* then we have Wilde's urbane treatment of the foundling plot in *The Importance of Being Earnest,* where the hero has to overcome a refusal to "marry into a waiting room, and contract an alliance with a parcel." Wilde is followed by Bernard Shaw, who was well aware of the extent to which some standard New Comedy devices, such as the hero's being attracted by a girl whom he does not know to be his sister, had already been parodied by Ibsen. Among Shaw's parodies of recognition scenes we may note the ingenious device that enables Undershaft to adopt his son-in-law as his successor in

Major Barbara, and the discovery in *Arms and the Man* that captain Bluntschli is of the highest social rank possible in his country, being an ordinary Swiss citizen, besides being made rich enough, by inheriting a hotel business, to upstage his rival Sergius. In the next generation, the writer who most closely followed the New Comedy structure as laid down by Plautus and Terence was P. G. Wodehouse. In other words, the teleological New Comedy structure seems to have dropped out of the centre of serious literature in the twentieth century.

In this situation writers of comedy clearly have to do something else, and what they are doing may be easier to understand if we think of Old Comedy, not simply as the form of Aristophanes, but as a genus of comedy — I should be inclined to suggest that it is *the* alternative genus — which is open to writers bored or inhibited by the other conventions. The structure of Old Comedy is dialectical rather than teleological, and its distinguishing feature is the *agon* or contest. This feature makes for a processional or sequential form, in which characters may appear without introduction and disappear without explanation. In this form characters are not functions of a plot, but vehicles or embodiments of the contest. For a dramatic contest is as a rule not simply between personalities as such, but between personalities as representatives of larger social forces. These forces may be those of a class struggle, as they are in Brecht, or they may be more concrete situations like a war or an election, or they may be psychological forces or attitudes of mind. Such a form is the appropriate one for introducing historical figures. We recall how Socrates and Euripides appear in Aristophanes: in Bernard Shaw, who shows the transition to Old Comedy conventions very clearly, we have the caricatures of Asquith and Lloyd George in *Back to Methuselah*; and this prepares the way for more recent plays about Churchill, the Pope, and various analogues of Hitler. Or such characters may come from literature: I think, as a random example, of Tennessee Williams's *Camino Real,* which begins with Don Quixote and Sancho Panza entering from the audience, in a way curiously reminiscent of *The Frogs.*

We notice in Aristophanes that while the *agon* may conclude with the victory of something the dramatist approves of, it may equally well be a victory of something patently absurd, as in *The Birds.* A comic structure based on a contest in which absurdity is the victor of the contest is clearly anti-teleological, the greatest possible contrast to the more idealistic New Comedy form. Although Aristophanes himself is a high-spirited writer, full of jokes and slapstick, the form he uses, in its larger context, is the appropriate form for black or absurd comedy. The darker tone latent in Old Comedy was recognized in Elizabethan times: Puttenham says, for example: "this bitter poem called the old *Comedy* being disused and taken away, the new *Comedy* came in place, more civil and pleasant a great deal." It was perhaps the more deeply sardonic tone of *Every Man Out of His Humour* that made Jonson speak of it as closer to Old Comedy, though it is still within the conventions of New Comedy in its structure. In our day the black comedy is normal, but half a century ago, when Chekhov showed characters slowly freezing in the grip of a dying class, many audiences found it difficult to believe that *The Cherry Orchard* or *The Three Sisters* were comedies at all.

New Comedy may go either in a romantic or in a realistic direction: the natural development of Old Comedy is towards fantasy, which now seems to us a peculiarly modern technique. Where characters are embodiments of social or psychological conflicts, the conception of the individual as defined by sanity, wakefulness, and ordinary experience is only one of many possible points of view. In New Comedy we are continually aware of the predominance of the chain of being: we notice this, for example, in the rigid social hierarchy of Shakespearian comedy, which the action of the comedy never essentially disturbs. Old Comedy, by contrast, may be called the drama of unchained being. In Aristophanes characters may be gods, as in *The Birds,* or the dead, as in *The Frogs,* or pure allegories, as in *Peace.* A similar tendency to introduce characters who are not coterminous with the bodies of individuals is marked in the theatre of the absurd, especially in Ionesco. One form of this is the archetypal characterization that we find, for instance, in *Waiting for Godot,* where the two main characters identify themselves with a number of representative figures, such as the two thieves crucified with Christ.

Waiting for Godot is also, in one of its aspects, a parody of the vaudeville dialogue, which bears much the same relation to Old Comedy that the *commedia dell'arte* does to

New Comedy. In more sophisticated versions of such dialogue, as we have it in Nichols and May, it becomes more clearly a verbal *agon*. When the contest is one of incident rather than words, we may have the loose sequential structure of some of the early Chaplin films, where there is a series of collisions between the hero and a number of unsympathetic antagonists, very similar in form to, for example, the last part of Aristophanes' *The Acharnians*. In New Comedy the essential meaning of the play, or what Aristotle calls its *dianoia*, is bound up with the revelation of the plot, but such a meaning may be crystallized in a number of sententious axioms that express reflexions arising from the various stages of the plot. Menander was famous for his sententious or proverbial utterances, one of which was quoted by St Paul: Terence was highly prized for the same quality in the Renaissance, and the same characteristic recurs in Shakespeare, as in the well-known line from *A Midsummer Night's Dream*: "The course of true love never did run smooth." Old Comedy is less sententious but more argumentative and conceptual than New Comedy, hence it can find a place for the long harangue or monologue, which tends to disrupt the action of a New Comedy, and so appears in it only as a technical *tour de force*, like the speech of Jaques on the seven ages of man. In Aristophanes we have the parabasis or direct address to the audience; in Shaw the parabasis is transferred to a preface which the audience is expected to read along with the play; and many recent comedies not only include but are based on monologue, as we see in several plays of Beckett and in Albee's *Zoo Story*.

Two other characteristics of Old Comedy may be more briefly mentioned. As we see in Aristophanes' use of a chorus, Old Comedy, because of its looser processional form, can be more spectacular and less purely verbal than New Comedy. In New Comedy, once we go beyond the incidental songs that we find in Shakespeare, music and spectacle tend to caricature the complications of the plot, as in *The Marriage of Figaro*. But Old Comedy is in its nature closer to musical comedy, and we notice again how the plays of Shaw, despite their intensely verbal texture, make surprisingly good musical comedies. Again, the fact that Old Comedy is less preoccupied with the game of love and the rituals of courtship make it a better medium for a franker and more explicit treatment of the

workings of the sexual instinct. Even the scurrility which is so conspicuous in Aristophanes recurs in *Mac Bird* and similar forms of undercover drama.

Of modern dramatists, perhaps T. S. Eliot shows most clearly the conflict between the two types of comedy. Eliot begins his dramatic efforts with the exuberant and superbly original *Sweeney Agonistes*, subtitled "Fragment of an Agon," where, besides the obvious and avowed influence of Aristophanes, many of the features noted above appear, such as the assimilation to musical comedy and vaudeville forms. When he settles down to write seriously for the stage, however, we get such confections as *The Confidential Clerk*, where the main influence is Euripides' *Ion*, usually taken as the starting point of New Comedy. But this play seems, in comparison with *Sweeney Agonistes*, a somewhat pedantic joke, an attempt to do over again what Oscar Wilde (and, for that matter, Gilbert) had already done with more freshness.

Shakespeare's comedies conform for the most part to a romantic development of New Comedy. But Shakespeare was a versatile experimenter, and there is at least one play which falls within the genus of Old Comedy as we have been dealing with it here. This play is, of course, *Troilus and Cressida*. Here the characters are well-known figures from history or literature; the structure is a simple sequential one, built up on the background movement of Helen from Greece to Troy and the foreground movement of Cressida in the reverse direction; the characters are both embodiments and prisoners of the social codes they adopt, and so far as the action of the play itself is concerned, the only clear victor of the contest is absurdity. The reasons why this play seems to us a peculiarly "modern" one should be clear by now.

New Comedy, especially in its more romantic or Shakespearian form, tends to be an ideal structure with strong analogies to religion. The sense in which Christianity is a divine comedy is a New Comedy sense: here history is a teleological drama of which the hero is Christ, and the heroine who becomes his bride is also a reborn society. Similar affinities between romantic New Comedy and religious myth may occur outside Christianity, as we see in *Sakuntala* and other Indian comedies. Old Comedy is a more existential form in which the central theme is mockery, which may include mockery of the gods, above or below. The presiding genius of

New Comedy is Eros, but the presiding genius of Old Comedy is more like Prometheus, a titanic power involved by his contempt for the gods in a chaotic world of absurdity and anguish. The fictional counterpart of New Comedy is the classical novel as it develops from Fielding to Henry James; the fictional counterpart of Old Comedy is the kind of satire that we have in Lucian, Apuleius, and more particularly Rabelais, where the theme of descent into a lower and more chaotic mode of existence occupies a prominent place. A hero may escape from this chaos, as Odysseus does from the cave of Polyphemus, or all the characters may remain involved in it. Such titles as *Huit Clos* and *Endgame* suggest that the latter is the more conventional form today. Whatever its conventions, the dramatic genus of Old Comedy is the one now established on our stage, and as we enter the age of anarchism it is likely to remain there.

The Rise and Fall of the Custard Pie

Richard Boston

> Richard Boston's recent essay on comedy is included here mainly for three reasons: first, it offers a fine modification to the prevailing view (most fully stated by Henri Bergson, and summarized in the introduction to this book) that comic figures usually act mechanically; second, it is one of the very few essays on comic movies that actually gets to some of the sources of their comedy; third, the essay is good reading.

Cinema specialists among my colleagues at the National Institute of Joke Research (a fine body of men, cruelly starved of funds) tell me that Mack Sennett invented what they call "face-pie contact." Ignoring the great weight of their authority, however, I prefer to believe a different, and apparently fallacious, version which has the delightful Mabel Normand enlivening a dull scene with a piece of improvisation that was to have incalculable consequences. In this account the recipient of that first, epoch-making pie was the face of Ben Turpin, and the cream of the jest, so to speak, must have been the moment when the pie was wiped away to reveal the Sartrean strabismus of that comedian's astonished and astonishing eyes.

After that nothing was ever quite the same again. An endless barrage of pies flew across the sets, studios, and screens of the world into the faces of policemen, firemen, bankers, men in top hats, men in bowler hats, tramps, or just anyone who happened to be around. "I figured up once," said Snub Pollard, "I have caught about 14,000 pies in my puss." (He was also hit by 600 automobiles.)

What did people laugh at before the custard pie? "Some hunchbacks, for instance, will excite laughter." Thus Bergson in 1900. "What is there comic about a rubicund nose?" he asks, "And why does one laugh at a Negro?" "A

Reprinted by permission of the author from the *Times Literary Supplement*, June 18, 1971.

man, running along the street, stumbles and falls: the passers-by burst out laughing." I can understand an audience laughing, helplessly, at Chaplin or Buster Keaton impersonating a man falling over, but whenever I have witnessed such a scene in real life it has invariably elicited from bystanders only sympathy and assistance. Perhaps this is one of those changes of taste, like no longer being able to laugh at the torments of Malvolio (though as recently as 1969 Raymond Durgnat was writing " . . . if you slip on a banana-skin, I find that highly comic. . ."). Laughter implies a withdrawal of sympathy from whatever is being laughed at. We laugh at Buster Keaton falling because we know that we needn't worry about his getting hurt, that we can withhold sympathy from him with a clear conscience, and that he will jump up like a rubber ball and start running again.

Those who don't find falling men, red noses, Negroes, and hunchbacks funny may also have certain reservations about the analysis Bergson makes on the assumption that they are. Fortunately these examples are not central to his case. Bergson's axiom — that the attitudes, gestures and movements of the human body are laughable in proportion to the amount they remind us of a machine — at first sight looks like an accurate anticipation of Keaton's style. There *is* something non-human about Keaton. That blank, expressionless face belongs to a statue rather than a living being, and when he walks the stiff, jerky movements of the arms and legs are more like those of a robot than a man. To quote James Agee:

> When he swept a semaphorelike arm to point, you could almost hear the electrical impulse in the signal block. When he ran from a cop his transitions from accelerating walk to easy jogtrot to brisk canter to headlong gallop to flogged-piston sprint — always floating, above this frenzy, the untroubled, untouchable face — were as distinct and as soberly in order as an automatic gearshift.

There is a scene in *The Navigator* which shows Keaton behaving in a completely automatic manner which would have had Bergson doubled up. Keaton puts on a deep-sea-diving suit and goes down on the sea-bed to do some repairs to the ship. Having put up a "Men at work" sign, he fills a bucket, underwater, washes his hands, and then *empties the bucket*.

On the other hand, in refutation of Bergson, the moments when Keaton is at his funniest are precisely those when he *ceases* to be machine-like; when, for example, he escapes from danger in a way that is not only intelligent, resourceful, graceful and unexpected but also totally human. Bergson's evolutionary view that it is witnessing a machine-like failure to adapt that causes laughter is contradicted every time an audience laughs at the marvellous ingenuity with which Keaton faces new and unexpected circumstances.

As in a dream, the world of silent comedy is one in which the normal laws of the universe have been suspended. Inanimate objects take on a life of their own: cars, garden rakes, ladders, wardrobes, folding beds, boats, pianos, planks of wood, hose-pipes, brick walls, and of course custard pies exist only to bring about man's downfall (or pratfall). It is a world in which, not quite in Emerson's sense, "Things are in the saddle and ride mankind." The presence of Keaton, Chaplin, Laurel and Hardy, Harold Lloyd, Ben Turpin, or Fatty Arbuckle ensures that things will fall apart, and neither the centre nor anything else can hold. In the crossfire of flying pies, crashing cars and headlong policemen, mere anarchy is loosed upon the world.

As in a dream, our normal waking feelings are suspended. The most appalling things can happen to screen comedians (or such animated characters as Tom and Jerry) without any sympathy being aroused even in the most tender-hearted. It is here that Chaplin, who moves in and out of reality, tends to leave people rather confused about his work. (Another reason is that opportunities to see his films are so rare.) Chaplin's incomparable gifts as a mime, his agility, his timing, his inventiveness, these are all recognized. What is hard to take is when he asks us at one moment to laugh as he is thrown down a flight of stairs, and at the next to weep when the girl rejects him. Chaplin's work is all flawed by this appeal for sympathy, which is precisely what the audience must withhold from any clown-figure. There are wonderful moments in Chaplin, but they are *only* moments because the comic vision is destroyed the moment we feel sorry for him. We never *pity* Keaton, and this is one reason why Keaton's reputation has gone up in recent years at the expense of Chaplin's. Nor do we pity Max Linder or Jacques Tati. We most certainly never pity Groucho, Harpo, or Chico.

The films of the great clown-comedians are also dream-like in their subversiveness. Everything that is repressed in the waking world is let out to run riot. They are subversive on a straight political level; the preferred targets of the pies are the faces of policemen, fathers-in-law, men in top hats, or any other emblem of authority or representative of capitalism. The bowler hats of Chaplin and Laurel and Hardy are as far as they ever manage to get by way of behaving like ordinary, orderly, respectable, middle-class people. *Duck Soup* was banned in Mussolini's Italy. Jacques Tati, in his early films anyway, is supremely an agent of chaos in the social order. There is a scene in *Les Vacances de Monsieur Hulot* where he is waiting for someone, alone, in an empty room. He starts, if I remember rightly, by straightening the angle of a picture on the wall. In a few minutes, with no assistance but the riding-crop tucked under his arm, he has reduced the room to a shambles.

The uptight Superegoist values of bourgeois respectability are directly confronted by the free libidinous clown in Renoir's *Boudu Sauvé des eaux*. A *clochard*, Boudu, beautifully played by the irresistibly repulsive Michel Simon, jumps in the Seine and is saved from drowning by a book-dealer, who takes the tramp into his own home, feeds him, has him washed and shaved, gives him smart clean clothes and accommodation. This Samaritan-like behaviour is rewarded by Boudu's climbing ape-like over the furniture, spitting on the carpet, wiping his shoes on the bedcovers, and seducing the man's wife. When Boudu is upbraided for this behaviour, he replies unanswerably that he didn't ask to be pulled out of the river. Still, he is a kind fellow at heart and sorry to have upset the book-dealer. He will no longer spit on the carpet. In an unforgettable image we see him take from a book case a precious, leatherbound volume, open it in the middle, spit into it, shut the book and replace it on the shelf.

Renoir's is a gentle vision, which is not how one could describe the Marx Brothers. I have said that one never pities them, and they themselves are pitiless. They attack government (*Duck Soup*), education (*Horse Feathers*), and high society (all the time). There is something pre-human about them. I imagine that *homo australopithecus* walked with something like Groucho's loose-limbed, close-to-the-ground stride; an upright posture has been adopted but options are being kept open on a return to the quadruped in case two legs turn out to be insufficient after all.

And Harpo's dumbness is not simply a physical matter. Rather he seems to have come from an age before the invention of language, a time when people communicated with a range of squeaks and grunts and the other noises that Harpo is able to whistle or hoot. Not that his dumbness in any way inconveniences him. A pair of scissors is all he needs to get the better of whoever he happens to come across, snipping off beards, ties, hat-brims, coat-tails, skirts, or anything else his wild eyes fall upon.

Groucho, by contrast, is all talk, and in his verbal assault on the universe (the refrain of one of his songs is, "Whatever it is, I'm against it") he is as all-conquering as Harpo is physically. It is a typical inversion of waking logic that the only people who ever get the better of fast-talking Groucho are Harpo, who uses no words, and Chico, whose grasp on language is at best tenuous. A good example is the scene in *A Night at the Opera* where Chico and Groucho are negotiating a contract. Whenever one of them objects to a clause it is torn off the top of the piece of paper. Finally there is only one clause left. As Chico makes to tear this up too, Groucho checks him by pointing out that they have to keep that because it's the sanity clause. Chico replies: "You can'ta fool me. Dere ain't no Santy Claus," and tears it up.

Or take the scene in *Duck Soup* where Groucho, as Rufus T. Firefly, President of Freedonia, offers Chico a job in his Cabinet.

GROUCHO: How'd you like a job in the Mint?
CHICO: No ... ah ... Haven't you got any other flavour?
GROUCHO: Just for that you don't get the job I was going to offer you.
CHICO: What was it?
GROUCHO: Secretary of War.
CHICO: All right. I take it.
(They shake hands.)

That Laurel and Hardy have the bodies of grown men and happen to wear suits and bowler hats does not for long disguise the fact that they are really babies. Only very small boys could revel for so long in pushing one another into pools of mud. The fact that they so often share a bed signifies not their homosexuality but their pre-sexuality. What could be more infantile than their total delight in destruction, than Laurel's obsession with eating, or his "cry" face, or Hardy's egocentricity?

The Marx Brothers, however, go back further even than infancy. Humour without a sanity clause — their films are often described as "crazy" or "mad" — takes them back into the world of dream, madness and pre-human archetypes. What they are most like is Trickster. Joan Westcott ("The Sculpture and Myths of Eshu-Elegba, the Yoruba Trickster," *Africa* 22, 1962, pages 336–354) describes the Trickster as "a creature of instinct and great energy" one of whose functions is as a "rule-breaker ... a spanner in the social works," which sounds much like Groucho. Paul Radin, writing of the Winnebago Trickster, describes his primary traits as "his voracious appetite, his wandering and his unbridled sexuality," a fair description of Harpo.

In the Winnebago Trickster myth which was collected by Sam Blowsnake of the Thunderbird clan in 1912 (see Paul Radin, *The Trickster: A Study in American Indian Mythology*), Trickster is able to change sex (cf. female impersonation in music hall and film comedy). His body is an assemblage of semi-autonomous units. His penis, for example, is carried in a box on his shoulder. On one occasion Trickster saw the Chief's daughter swimming on the opposite shore of a lake. He sent his penis swimming across the water to the other side where it lodged firmly in the girl and was only extracted with great difficulty.

Parts of Trickster's body can quarrel with one another. Trickster kills a buffalo with a knife held in his right hand. His left hand grabs the buffalo, and the right hand gets extremely cross. " 'Give that back to me, it's mine! Stop that or I will use my knife on you!' So spoke the right arm." The arms continue to quarrel, eventually fight and the left arm is badly cut.

Compare Trickster's behaviour with that of Harpo. In *Monkey Business* he sits down at the harp, plays a few unsatisfactory notes, looks disapprovingly at his left hand, unscrews it, throws it away, produces his real hand and starts playing properly. In the same film, in the Punch and Judy scene, he gives the illusion of being able to detach a whole leg. In all of his films it is a favourite gag of Harpo's to "give" his knee to other people. He also has a habit of putting his hand into other people's pockets — not always to steal things: often he seems unaware of which leg is his and which is someone else's. Like Trickster, Harpo is apparently able to communicate with animals, and his feeding habits are certainly more animal than human. "He's half goat," Chico explains. Harpo eats buttons, telephones, ties, and cigars with enjoyment.

Groucho too is Trickster-like in his inversions of logic and defiance of social norms. The beginning of the Winnebago Trickster myth is extraordinarily similar to the beginning of *Duck Soup*, but I will have to leave detailed comparison for some other time.

Though the Marx Brothers go furthest, there is something of Trickster to be found in all the great film comedians. But if I am right in thinking that behind them there is something archetypal, and therefore timeless, why is it apparently so difficult to make comedies at this particular time? For the dearth of funny films in recent years is undeniable.

The films of Jacques Tati may point to an answer. His first two films, made with low budgets in black and white, were among the funniest ever made. *Mon Oncle*, more lavish in scale, had hilarious moments but aroused doubts. These were confirmed by the enormously expensive *Playtime* (in which, by a set of curious chances, I myself acted a role) and now by his latest film, *Traffic*, which opened a couple of months ago in Paris.

The way in which the coming of sound ended an era of film comedy is well known. The same has happened again with the coming of wide screens, colour, stereophonic sound, and so on. Everything has become over-explicit, and the old economy, fluency, and ease are gone. Watching Tati at work one can see that he is highly inventive. I am not sure that one would guess this from his recent films. Every gag is painstakingly built up and has every drop squeezed from it as though it was some black-market delicacy in a time of severe food rationing. Compare this with the prodigality of the silent comedies. There are as many gags in five minutes of Keaton as in the whole of *Playtime*. But then people like Keaton, Chaplin, Harold Lloyd, and Laurel and Hardy made as many films in a year as Tati has made in his whole career (Max Linder made something like 400 films in less than ten years).

The prolific rate at which the early comedies were produced gave a freedom to improvise and experiment which is denied the expensive, cumbersome productions of today, when everything has to be done by the script, all carefully planned, and nothing left to the inspiration of the moment. For anything like the freedom of the classic comedies of the beginning of the century you have to look at hastily-produced, low-budget television comedies such as "Monty Python's Flying Circus."

Another reason for Tati's decline may be the subject matter. The rustic pastoral of *Jour de Fête* belongs to a completely different world from the urban industrialism of the three colour films. And there is not yet a comic vocabulary for dealing with this new world. The old images have gone stale or sour. There was quite a good pie fight in the Tony Curtis film *The Great Race*, but it looked more like an exercise in nostalgia than anything else. Keaton could get endless laughter out of situations involving motorcars speeding, turning over, crashing, or falling apart. It is harder to laugh at Tati's *Traffic*, which is altogether too much like the street outside the cinema. We are too aware of the slaughter on the roads, and of the way traffic is ruining our cities, to find cars funny any longer. In the same way it is now hard to see policemen as the comic figures the Keystone Kops were when we are conscious that the behaviour of the police in Chicago and Paris and other cities has gone so far beyond a joke. When it really is a mad, mad, mad, mad world, and anyone can see that for himself, the comedian is out of business.

At the end of James Sully's *Essay on Laugh-*

ter the author writes gloomily that "the most cheerful of men would perhaps hardly call the present a mirthful moment," and sees "the decline of popular mirth" as "only a part of a larger change, the disappearance of the spirit of play, of a full self-abandonment to the mood of light entertainment. . . . Where is the fun, where is the gaiety, in the football and the cricket matches of today?" If this complaint sounds depressingly familiar, there may be a grain of comfort to be drawn from the fact that Sully's book was published in 1902.

TRAGICOMEDY

THE CHERRY ORCHARD

Anton Chekhov

Translated by Stark Young

Anton Chekhov (1860–1904) received his medical degree from the University of Moscow in 1884, but he had already published some stories. His belief that his medical training assisted him in writing about people caused some people to find him cold, but on the whole the evidence suggests that he was a genial, energetic young man with considerable faith in reason and (as befitted a doctor) in science, and with very little faith in religion and in heroics. His major plays are *The Seagull* (1896), *Uncle Vanya* (1899), *Three Sisters* (1901), and, finally, *The Cherry Orchard* (1903), written during his last illness.

CHARACTERS

RANEVSKAYA, LYUBOFF ANDREEVNA, *a landowner*
ANYA, *her daughter, seventeen years old*
VARYA, *her adopted daughter, twenty-four years old*
GAYEFF, LEONID ANDREEVICH, *brother of Ranevskaya*
LOPAHIN, YERMOLAY ALEXEEVICH, *a merchant*
TROFIMOFF, PYOTR SERGEEVICH, *a student*
SEMYONOFF-PISHTCHIK, BORIS BORISOVICH, *a landowner*
CHARLOTTA IVANOVNA, *a governess*
EPIHODOFF, SEMYON PANTELEEVICH, *a clerk*
DUNYASHA, *a maid*
FIERS, *a valet, an old man of eighty-seven*
YASHA, *a young valet*
A PASSERBY *or* STRANGER
THE STATIONMASTER
A POST-OFFICE CLERK
VISITORS, SERVANTS

Scene: The action takes place on the estate of L. A. RANEVSKAYA.

Act I of the original production of *The Cherry Orchard* in 1904. (Photograph reproduced from J. L. Styan, *Chekhov in Performance*. Copyright 1971 by Cambridge University Press.)

ACT I

A room that is still called the nursery. One of the doors leads into ANYA's *room. Dawn, the sun will soon be rising. It is May, the cherry trees are in blossom but in the orchard it is cold, with a morning frost. The windows in the room are closed. Enter* DUNYASHA *with a candle and* LOPAHIN *with a book in his hand.*

LOPAHIN: The train got in, thank God! What time is it?

DUNYASHA: It's nearly two. (*Blows out her candle.*) It's already daylight.

LOPAHIN: But how late was the train? Two hours at least. (*Yawning and stretching.*) I'm a fine one, I am, look what a fool thing I did! I drove here on purpose just to meet them at the station, and then all of a sudden I'd overslept myself! Fell asleep in my chair. How provoking! — You could have waked me up.

DUNYASHA: I thought you had gone. (*Listening.*) Listen, I think they are coming now.

LOPAHIN (*listening*): No — No, there's the luggage and one thing and another. (*A pause.*) Lyuboff Andreevna has been living abroad five years. I don't know what she is like now — She is a good woman. An easy-going, simple woman. I remember when I was a boy about fifteen, my father, who is at rest — in those days he ran a shop here in the village — hit me in the face with his fist, my nose was bleeding — We'd come to the yard together for something or other, and he was a little drunk. Lyuboff Andreevna, I can see her now, still so young, so slim, led me to the washbasin here in this very room, in the nursery. "Don't cry," she says, "little peasant, it will be well in time for your wedding" — (*A pause.*) Yes, little peasant — My father was a peasant truly, and here I am in a white waistcoat and yellow shoes. Like a pig rooting in a pastry shop — I've got this rich, lots of money, but if you really stop and think of it, I'm just a peasant — (*Turning the pages of a book.*) Here I was reading a book and didn't get a thing out of it. Reading and went to sleep. (*A pause.*)

DUNYASHA: And all night long the dogs were not asleep, they know their masters are coming.

LOPAHIN: What is it, Dunyasha, you're so —

DUNYASHA: My hands are shaking. I'm going to faint.

LOPAHIN: You're just so delicate, Dunyasha. And all dressed up like a lady, and your hair all done up! Mustn't do that. Must know your place.

(*Enter* EPIHODOFF, *with a bouquet: he wears a jacket and highly polished boots with a loud squeak. As he enters he drops the bouquet.*)

EPIHODOFF (*picking up the bouquet*): Look, the gardener sent these, he says to put them in the dining room. (*Giving the bouquet to* DUNYASHA.)

LOPAHIN: And bring me some kvass.

DUNYASHA: Yes, sir. (*Goes out.*)

EPIHODOFF: There is a morning frost now, three degrees of frost (*sighing*) and the cherries all in bloom. I cannot approve of our climate — I cannot. Our climate can never quite rise to the occasion. Listen, Yermolay Alexeevich, allow me to subtend, I bought myself, day before yesterday, some boots and they, I venture to assure you, squeak so that it is impossible. What could I grease them with?

LOPAHIN: Go on. You annoy me.

EPIHODOFF: Every day some misfortune happens to me. But I don't complain, I am used to it and I even smile.

(DUNYASHA *enters, serves* LOPAHIN *the kvass.*)

EPIHODOFF: I'm going. (*Stumbling over a chair and upsetting it.*) There (*as if triumphant*), there, you see, pardon the expression, a circumstance like that, among others — It is simply quite remarkable. (*Goes out.*)

DUNYASHA: And I must tell you, Yermolay Alexeevich, that Epihodoff has proposed to me.

LOPAHIN: Ah!

DUNYASHA: I don't know really what to — He is a quiet man but sometimes when he starts talking, you can't understand a thing he means. It's all very nice, and full of feeling, but just doesn't make any sense. I sort of like him. He loves me madly. He's a man that's unfortunate, every day there's something or other. They tease him around here, call him twenty-two misfortunes —

LOPAHIN (*cocking his ear*): Listen, I think they are coming —

DUNYASHA: They are coming! But what's the matter with me — I'm cold all over.

LOPAHIN: They're really coming. Let's go meet them. Will she recognize me? It's five years we haven't seen each other.

DUNYASHA (*excitedly*): I'm going to faint this very minute. Ah, I'm going to faint!

(Two carriages can be heard driving up to the house. LOPAHIN *and* DUNYASHA *hurry out. The stage is empty. In the adjoining rooms a noise begins.* FIERS *hurries across the stage, leaning on a stick; he has been to meet* LYUBOFF ANDREEVNA, *and wears an old-fashioned livery and a high hat; he mutters something to himself, but you cannot understand a word of it. The noise offstage gets louder and louder. A voice: "Look! Let's go through here —"* LYUBOFF ANDREEVNA, ANYA *and* CHARLOTTA IVANOVNA, *with a little dog on a chain, all of them dressed for traveling,* VARYA, *in a coat and kerchief,* GAYEFF, SEMYONOFF-PISHTCHIK, LOPAHIN, DUNYASHA, *with a bundle and an umbrella,* SERVANTS *with pieces of luggage — all pass through the room.*)

ANYA: Let's go through here. Mama, do you remember what room this is?

LYUBOFF ANDREEVNA (*happily, through her tears*): The nursery!

VARYA: How cold it is, my hands are stiff. (*To* LYUBOFF ANDREEVNA.) Your rooms, the white one and the violet, are just the same as ever, Mama.

LYUBOFF ANDREEVNA: The nursery, my dear beautiful room — I slept here when I was little — (*Crying.*) And now I am like a child — (*Kisses her brother and* VARYA, *then her brother again.*) And Varya is just the same as ever, looks like a nun. And I knew Dunyasha — (*Kisses* DUNYASHA.)

GAYEFF: The train was two hours late. How's that? How's that for good management?

CHARLOTTA (*to* PISHTCHIK): My dog he eats nuts too.

PISHTCHIK (*astonished*): Think of that!

(*Everybody goes out except* ANYA *and* DUNYASHA.)

DUNYASHA: We waited so long — (*Taking off* ANYA's *coat and hat.*)

ANYA: I didn't sleep all four nights on the way. And now I feel so chilly.

DUNYASHA: It was Lent when you left, there was some snow then, there was frost, and now? My darling (*laughing and kissing her*), I waited so long for you, my joy, my life — I'm telling you now, I can't keep from it another minute.

ANYA (*wearily*): There we go again —

DUNYASHA: The clerk Epihodoff, proposed to me after Holy Week.

ANYA: You're always talking about the same thing — (*Arranging her hair.*) I've lost all my hairpins — (*She is tired to the point of staggering.*)

DUNYASHA: I just don't know what to think. He loves me, loves me so!

ANYA (*looks in through her door, tenderly*): My room, my windows, it's just as if I had never been away. I'm home! Tomorrow morning I'll get up, I'll run into the orchard — Oh, if I only could go to sleep! I haven't slept all the way, I was tormented by anxiety.

DUNYASHA: Day before yesterday, Pyotr Sergeevich arrived.

ANYA (*joyfully*): Petya!

DUNYASHA: He's asleep in the bathhouse, he lives there. I am afraid, he says, of being in the way. (*Taking her watch from her pocket and looking at it.*) Somebody ought to wake him up. It's only that Varvara Mikhailovna told us not to. Don't you wake him up, she said.

VARYA (*enter* VARYA *with a bunch of keys at her belt*): Dunyasha, coffee, quick — Mama is asking for coffee.

DUNYASHA: This minute. (*Goes out.*)

VARYA: Well, thank goodness, you've come back. You are home again. (*Caressingly.*) My darling is back! My precious is back!

ANYA: I've had such a time.

VARYA: I can imagine!

ANYA: I left during Holy Week, it was cold then. Charlotta talked all the way and did her tricks. Why did you fasten Charlotta on to me —?

VARYA: But you couldn't have traveled alone, darling; not at seventeen!

ANYA: We arrived in Paris, it was cold there

and snowing. I speak terrible French. Mama lived on the fifth floor; I went to see her; there were some French people in her room, ladies, an old priest with his prayer book, and the place was full of tobacco smoke — very dreary. Suddenly I began to feel sorry for Mama, so sorry, I drew her to me, held her close and couldn't let her go. Then Mama kept hugging me, crying — yes —

VARYA (*tearfully*): Don't — oh, don't —

ANYA: Her villa near Menton she had already sold, she had nothing left, nothing. And I didn't have a kopeck left. It was all we could do to get here. And Mama doesn't understand! We sit down to dinner at a station and she orders, insists on the most expensive things and gives the waiters rouble tips. Charlotta does the same. Yasha too demands his share; it's simply dreadful. Mama has her butler, Yasha, we've brought him here —

VARYA: I saw the wretch.

ANYA: Well, how are things? Has the interest on the mortgage been paid?

VARYA: How could we?

ANYA: Oh, my God, my God — !

VARYA: In August the estate is to be sold —

ANYA: My God — !

LOPAHIN (*looking in through the door and mooing like a cow*): Moo-o-o — (*Goes away.*)

VARYA (*tearfully*): I'd land him one like that — (*Shaking her fist.*)

ANYA (*embracing* VARYA *gently*): Varya, has he proposed? (VARYA *shakes her head.*) But he loves you — Why don't you have it out with him, what are you waiting for?

VARYA: I don't think anything will come of it for us. He is very busy, he hasn't any time for me — And doesn't notice me. God knows, it's painful for me to see him — Everybody talks about our marriage, everybody congratulates us, and the truth is, there's nothing to it — it's all like a dream — (*In a different tone.*) You have a brooch looks like a bee.

ANYA (*sadly*): Mama bought it. (*Going toward her room, speaking gaily, like a child.*) And in Paris I went up in a balloon!

VARYA: My darling is back! My precious is back! (DUNYASHA *has returned with the coffee pot and is making coffee.* VARYA *is standing by the door.*) Darling, I'm busy all day long with the house and I go around thinking things. If only you could be married to a rich man, I'd be more at peace too, I would go all by myself

to a hermitage — then to Kiev — to Moscow, and I'd keep going like that from one holy place to another — I would go on and on. Heavenly!

ANYA: The birds are singing in the orchard. What time is it now?

VARYA: It must be after two. It's time you were asleep, darling. (*Going into* ANYA'S *room.*) Heavenly!

YASHA (YASHA *enters with a lap robe and a traveling bag. Crossing the stage airily*): May I go through here?

DUNYASHA: We'd hardly recognize you, Yasha; you've changed so abroad!

YASHA: Hm — And who are you?

DUNYASHA: When you left here, I was like that — (*Her hand so high from the floor.*) I'm Dunyasha, Fyodor Kozoyedoff's daughter. You don't remember!

YASHA: Hm — You little peach! (*Looking around before he embraces her; she shrieks and drops a saucer;* YASHA *hurries out.*)

VARYA (*at the door, in a vexed tone*): And what's going on here?

DUNYASHA (*tearfully*): I broke a saucer —

VARYA: That's good luck.

ANYA (*emerging from her room*): We ought to tell Mama beforehand: Petya is here —

VARYA: I told them not to wake him up.

ANYA (*pensively*): Six years ago our father died, a month later our brother Grisha was drowned in the river, such a pretty little boy, just seven. Mama couldn't bear it, she went away, went away without ever looking back — (*Shuddering.*) How I understand her, if she only knew I did. (*A pause.*) And Petya Trofimoff was Grisha's tutor, he might remind —

FIERS (*enter* FIERS; *he is in a jacket and white waistcoat. Going to the coffee urn, busy with it*): The mistress will have her breakfast here — (*Putting on white gloves.*) Is the coffee ready? (*To* DUNYASHA, *sternly.*) You! What about the cream?

DUNYASHA: Oh, my God — (*Hurrying out.*)

FIERS (*busy at the coffee urn*): Oh, you good-for-nothing — ! (*Muttering to himself.*) Come back from Paris — And the master used to go to Paris by coach — (*Laughing.*)

VARYA: Fiers, what are you — ?

FIERS: At your service. (*Joyfully.*) My mistress is back! It's what I've been waiting for! Now I'm ready to die — (*Crying for joy.*)

(LYUBOFF ANDREEVNA, GAYEFF *and* SEMYO-NOFF-PISHTCHIK *enter;* SEMYONOFF-PISHTCHIK *is in a podyovka of fine cloth and sharovary.* GAYEFF *enters; he makes gestures with his hands and body as if he were playing billiards.*)

LYUBOFF ANDREEVNA: How is it? Let me remember — Yellow into the corner! Duplicate in the middle!

GAYEFF: I cut into the corner. Sister, you and I slept here in this very room once, and now I am fifty-one years old, strange as that may seem —

LOPAHIN: Yes, time passes.

GAYEFF: What?

LOPAHIN: Time, I say, passes.

GAYEFF: And it smells like patchouli here.

ANYA: I'm going to bed. Good night, Mama. (*Kissing her mother.*)

LYUBOFF ANDREEVNA: My sweet little child. (*Kissing her hands.*) You're glad you are home? I still can't get myself together.

ANYA: Good-by, Uncle.

GAYEFF (*kissing her face and hands*): God be with you. How like your mother you are! (*To his sister.*) Lyuba, at her age you were exactly like her.

(ANYA *shakes hands with* LOPAHIN *and* PISHTCHIK, *goes out and closes the door behind her.*)

LYUBOFF ANDREEVNA: She's very tired.

PISHTCHIK: It is a long trip, I imagine.

VARYA (*to* LOPAHIN *and* PISHTCHIK): Well, then, sirs? It's going on three o'clock, time for gentlemen to be going.

LYUBOFF ANDREEVNA (*laughing*): The same old Varya. (*Drawing her to her and kissing her.*) There, I'll drink my coffee, then we'll all go. (FIERS *puts a small cushion under her feet.*) Thank you, my dear. I am used to coffee. Drink it day and night. Thank you, my dear old soul. (*Kissing* FIERS.)

VARYA: I'll go see if all the things have come. (*Goes out.*)

LYUBOFF ANDREEVNA: Is it really me sitting here? (*Laughing.*) I'd like to jump around and wave my arms. (*Covering her face with her hands.*) But I may be dreaming! God knows I love my country, love it deeply, I couldn't look out of the car window, I just kept crying. (*Tearfully.*) However, I must drink my coffee.

Thank you, Fiers, thank you, my dear old friend. I'm so glad you're still alive.

FIERS: Day before yesterday.

GAYEFF: He doesn't hear well.

LOPAHIN: And I must leave right now. It's nearly five o'clock in the morning, for Kharkov. What a nuisance! I wanted to look at you — talk — You are as beautiful as ever.

PISHTCHIK (*breathing heavily*): Even more beautiful — In your Paris clothes — It's a feast for the eyes —

LOPAHIN: Your brother, Leonid Andreevich here, says I'm a boor, a peasant money grubber, but that's all the same to me, absolutely. Let him say it. All I wish is you'd trust me as you used to, and your wonderful, touching eyes would look at me as they did. Merciful God! My father was a serf; belonged to your grandfather and your father; but you, your own self, you did so much for me once that I've forgotten all that and love you like my own kin — more than my kin.

LYUBOFF ANDREEVNA: I can't sit still — I can't. (*Jumping up and walking about in great excitement.*) I'll never live through this happiness — Laugh at me, I'm silly — My own little bookcase — ! (*Kissing the bookcase.*) My little table!

GAYEFF: And in your absence the nurse here died.

LYUBOFF ANDREEVNA (*sitting down and drinking coffee*): Yes, may she rest in Heaven! They wrote me.

GAYEFF: And Anastasy died. Cross-eyed Petrushka left me and lives in town now at the police officer's. (*Taking out of his pocket a box of hard candy and sucking a piece.*)

PISHTCHIK: My daughter, Dashenka — sends you her greetings —

LOPAHIN: I want to tell you something very pleasant, cheerful. (*Glancing at his watch.*) I'm going right away. There's no time for talking. Well, I'll make it two or three words. As you know, your cherry orchard is to be sold for your debts; the auction is set for August twenty-second, but don't you worry, my dear, you just sleep in peace, there's a way out of it. Here's my plan. Please listen to me. Your estate is only thirteen miles from town. They've run the railroad by it. Now if the cherry orchard and the land along the river were cut up into building lots and leased for summer cottages, you'd have at the very lowest twenty-five thousand roubles per year income.

GAYEFF: Excuse me, what rot!

LYUBOFF ANDREEVNA: I don't quite understand you, Yermolay Alexeevich.

LOPAHIN: At the very least you will get from the summer residents twenty-five roubles per year for a two-and-a-half acre lot and if you post a notice right off, I'll bet you anything that by autumn you won't have a single patch of land free, everything will be taken. In a word, my congratulations, you are saved. The location is wonderful, the river's so deep. Except, of course, it all needs to be tidied up, cleared — For instance, let's say, tear all the old buildings down and this house, which is no good any more, and cut down the old cherry orchard —

LYUBOFF ANDREEVNA: Cut down? My dear, forgive me, you don't understand at all. If there's one thing in the whole province that's interesting — not to say remarkable — it's our cherry orchard.

LOPAHIN: The only remarkable thing about this cherry orchard is that it's very big. There's a crop of cherries once every two years and even that's hard to get rid of. Nobody buys them.

GAYEFF: This orchard is even mentioned in the encyclopedia.

LOPAHIN (glancing at his watch): If we don't cook up something and don't get somewhere, the cherry orchard and the entire estate will be sold at auction on the twenty-second of August. Do get it settled then! I swear there is no other way out. Not a one!

FIERS: There was a time, forty-fifty years ago when the cherries were dried, soaked, pickled, cooked into jam and it used to be —

GAYEFF: Keep quiet, Fiers.

FIERS: And it used to be that the dried cherries were shipped by the wagon-load to Moscow and to Kharkov. And the money there was! And the dried cherries were soft then, juicy, sweet, fragrant — They had a way of treating them then —

LYUBOFF ANDREEVNA: And where is that way now?

FIERS: They have forgotten it. Nobody remembers it.

PISHTCHIK (to LYUBOFF ANDREEVNA): What's happening in Paris? How is everything? Did you eat frogs?

LYUBOFF ANDREEVNA: I ate crocodiles.

PISHTCHIK: Think of it — !

LOPAHIN: Up to now in the country there have been only the gentry and the peasants, but now in summer the villa people too are coming in. All the towns, even the least big ones, are surrounded with cottages. In about twenty years very likely the summer resident will multiply enormously. He merely drinks tea on the porch now, but it might well happen that on this two-and-a-half acre lot of his, he'll go in for farming, and then your cherry orchard would be happy, rich, splendid —

GAYEFF (getting hot): What rot!

(Enter VARYA and YASHA.)

VARYA: Here, Mama. Two telegrams for you. (Choosing a key and opening the old bookcase noisily.) Here they are.

LYUBOFF ANDREEVNA: From Paris (Tearing up the telegrams without reading them.) Paris, that's all over —

GAYEFF: Do you know how old this bookcase is, Lyuba? A week ago I pulled out the bottom drawer and looked, and there the figures were burned on it. The bookcase was made exactly a hundred years ago. How's that? Eh? You might celebrate its jubilee. It's an inanimate object, but all the same, be that as it may, it's a bookcase.

PISHTCHIK (in astonishment): A hundred years — ! Think of it — !

GAYEFF: Yes — quite something — (Shaking the bookcase.) Dear, honored bookcase! I saluted your existence, which for more than a hundred years has been directed toward the clear ideals of goodness and justice; your silent appeal to fruitful endeavor has not flagged in all the course of a hundred years, sustaining (tearfully) through the generations of our family, our courage and our faith in a better future and nurturing in us ideals of goodness and of a social consciousness.

(A pause.)

LOPAHIN: Yes.

LYUBOFF ANDREEVNA: You're the same as ever, Lenya.

GAYEFF (slightly embarrassed): Carom to the right into the corner pocket. I cut into the side pocket!

LOPAHIN (glancing at his watch): Well, it's time for me to go.

YASHA (handing medicine to LYUBOFF ANDREEVNA): Perhaps you'll take the pills now —

PISHTCHIK: You should never take medicaments, dear madam — They do neither harm nor good — Hand them here, dearest lady. (*He takes the pillbox, shakes the pills out into his palm, blows on them, puts them in his mouth and washes them down with kvass.*) There! Now!

LYUBOFF ANDREEVNA (*startled*): Why, you've lost your mind!

PISHTCHIK: I took all the pills.

LOPAHIN: Such a glutton!

(*Everyone laughs.*)

FIERS: The gentleman stayed with us during Holy Week, he ate half a bucket of pickles — (*Muttering.*)

LYUBOFF ANDREEVNA: What is he muttering about?

VARYA: He's been muttering like that for three years. We're used to it.

YASHA: In his dotage.

(CHARLOTTA IVANOVNA *in a white dress — she is very thin, her corset laced very tight — with a lorgnette at her belt, crosses the stage.*)

LOPAHIN: Excuse me, Charlotta Ivanovna, I haven't had a chance yet to welcome you. (*Trying to kiss her hand.*)

CHARLOTTA (*drawing her hand away*): If I let you kiss my hand, 'twould be my elbow next, then my shoulder —

LOPAHIN: No luck for me today. (*Everyone laughs.*) Charlotta Ivanovna, show us a trick!

CHARLOTTA: No. I want to go to bed. (*Exit.*)

LOPAHIN: In three weeks we shall see each other. (*Kissing* LYUBOFF ANDREEVNA'S *hand.*) Till then, good-by. It's time. (*To* GAYEFF.) See you soon. (*Kissing* PISHTCHIK.) See you soon. (*Shaking* VARYA'S *hand, then* FIERS' *and* YASHA'S.) I don't feel like going. (*To* LYUBOFF ANDREEVNA.) If you think it over and make up your mind about the summer cottages, let me know and I'll arrange a loan of something like fifty thousand roubles. Think it over seriously.

VARYA (*angrily*): Do go on, anyhow, will you!

LOPAHIN: I'm going, I'm going — (*Exit.*)

GAYEFF: Boor. However, pardon — Varya is going to marry him, it's Varya's little fiancé.

VARYA: Don't talk too much, Uncle.

LYUBOFF ANDREEVNA: Well, Varya, I should be very glad. He's a good man.

PISHTCHIK: A man, one must say truthfully — A most worthy — And my Dashenka — says also that — she says all sorts of things — (*Snoring but immediately waking up.*) Nevertheless, dearest lady, oblige me — With a loan of two hundred and forty roubles — Tomorrow the interest on my mortgage has got to be paid —

VARYA (*startled*): There's not any money, none at all.

LYUBOFF ANDREEVNA: Really, I haven't got anything.

PISHTCHIK: I'll find it, somehow. (*Laughing.*) I never give up hope. There, I think to myself, all is lost, I am ruined and lo and behold — a railroad is put through my land and — they paid me. And then, just watch, something else will turn up — if not today, then tomorrow — Dashenka will win two hundred thousand — She has a ticket.

LYUBOFF ANDREEVNA: We've finished the coffee, now we can go to bed.

FIERS (*brushing* GAYEFF'S *clothes, reprovingly*): You put on the wrong trousers again. What am I going to do with you!

VARYA (*softly*): Anya is asleep. (*Opening the window softly.*) Already the sun's rising — it's not cold. Look, Mama! What beautiful trees! My Lord, what air! The starlings are singing!

GAYEFF (*opening another window*): The orchard is all white. You haven't forgotten, Lyuba? That long lane there runs straight — as a strap stretched out. It glistens on moonlight nights. Do you remember? You haven't forgotten it?

LYUBOFF ANDREEVNA (*looking out of the window on to the orchard*): Oh, my childhood, my innocence! I slept in this nursery and looked out on the orchard from here, every morning happiness awoke with me, it was just as it is now, then, nothing has changed. (*Laughing with joy.*) All, all white! Oh, my orchard! After a dark, rainy autumn and cold winter, you are young again and full of happiness. The heavenly angels have not deserted you — If I only could lift the weight from my breast, from my shoulders, if I could only forget my past!

GAYEFF: Yes, and the orchard will be sold for debt, strange as that may seem.

LYUBOFF ANDREEVNA: Look, our dear mother is walking through the orchard — In a white dress! (*Laughing happily.*) It's she.

GAYEFF: Where?

VARYA: God be with you, Mama!

LYUBOFF ANDREEVNA: There's not anybody, it only seemed so. To the right, as you turn to the summerhouse, a little white tree is leaning there, looks like a woman — (*Enter* TROFI-MOFF, *in a student's uniform, well worn, and glasses.*) What a wonderful orchard! The white masses of blossoms, the sky all blue.

TROFIMOFF: Lyuboff Andreevna! (*She looks around at him.*) I will just greet you and go immediately. (*Kissing her hand warmly.*) I was told to wait until morning, but I hadn't the patience —

(LYUBOFF ANDREEVNA *looks at him puzzled.*)

VARYA (*tearfully*): This is Petya Trofimoff —

TROFIMOFF: Petya Trofimoff, the former tutor of your Grisha — Have I really changed so?

(LYUBOFF ANDREEVNA *embraces him; and crying quietly.*)

GAYEFF (*embarrassed*): There, there, Lyuba.

VARYA (*crying*): I told you, Petya, to wait till tomorrow.

LYUBOFF ANDREEVNA: My Grisha — My boy — Grisha — Son —

VARYA: What can we do, Mama? It's God's will.

TROFIMOFF (*in a low voice, tearfully*): There, there —

LYUBOFF ANDREEVNA (*weeping softly*): My boy was lost, drowned — Why? Why, my friend? (*More quietly.*) Anya is asleep there, and I am talking so loud — Making so much noise — But why, Petya? Why have you lost your looks? Why do you look so much older?

TROFIMOFF: A peasant woman on the train called me a mangy-looking gentleman.

LYUBOFF ANDREEVNA: You were a mere boy then, a charming young student, and now your hair's not very thick any more and you wear glasses. Are you really a student still? (*Going to the door.*)

TROFIMOFF: Very likely I'll be a perennial student.

LYUBOFF ANDREEVNA (*kissing her brother, then* VARYA): Well, go to bed — You've grown older too, Leonid.

PISHTCHIK (*following her*): So that's it, we are going to bed now. Oh, my gout! I'm staying here — I'd like, Lyuboff Andreevna, my soul, tomorrow morning — Two hundred and forty roubles —

GAYEFF: He's still at it.

PISHTCHIK: Two hundred and forty roubles — To pay interest on the mortgage.

LYUBOFF ANDREEVNA: I haven't any money, my dove.

PISHTCHIK: I'll pay it back, my dear — It's a trifling sum —

LYUBOFF ANDREEVNA: Oh, very well, Leonid will give — You give it to him, Leonid.

GAYEFF: Oh, certainly, I'll give it to him. Hold out your pockets.

LYUBOFF ANDREEVNA: What can we do, give it, he needs it — He'll pay it back.

(LYUBOFF ANDREEVNA, TROFIMOFF, PISH-TCHIK *and* FIERS *go out.* GAYEFF, VARYA *and* YASHA *remain.*)

GAYEFF: My sister hasn't yet lost her habit of throwing money away. (*To* YASHA.) Get away, my good fellow, you smell like hens.

YASHA (*with a grin*): And you are just the same as you used to be, Leonid Andreevich.

GAYEFF: What? (*To* VARYA.) What did he say?

VARYA (*to* YASHA): Your mother has come from the village, she's been sitting in the servants' hall every since yesterday, she wants to see you —

YASHA: The devil take her!

VARYA: Ach, shameless creature!

YASHA: A lot I need her! She might have come tomorrow. (*Goes out.*)

VARYA: Mama is just the same as she was, she hasn't changed at all. If she could, she'd give away everything she has.

GAYEFF: Yes — If many remedies are prescribed for an illness, you may know the illness is incurable. I keep thinking, I rack my brains, I have many remedies, a great many, and that means, really, I haven't any at all. It would be fine to inherit a fortune from somebody, it would be fine to marry off our Anya to a very rich man, it would be fine to go to Yaroslavl and try our luck with our old aunt, the Countess. Auntie is very, very rich.

VARYA (*crying*): If God would only help us!

GAYEFF: Don't bawl! Auntie is very rich but she doesn't like us. To begin with, Sister married a lawyer, not a nobleman — (ANYA *appears at the door.*) Married not a nobleman and behaved herself, you could say, not very virtuously. She is good, kind, nice, I love her very much, but no matter how much you allow for the extenuating circumstances, you must admit she's a depraved woman. You feel it in her slightest movement.

VARYA (*whispering*): Anya is standing in the door there.

GAYEFF: What? (*A pause.*) It's amazing, something got in my right eye. I am beginning to see poorly. And on Thursday, when I was in the District Court —

(ANYA *enters.*)

VARYA: But why aren't you asleep, Anya?

ANYA: I don't feel like sleeping. I can't.

GAYEFF: My little girl — (*Kissing* ANYA's *face and hands.*) My child — (*Tearfully.*) You are not my niece, you are my angel, you are everything to me. Believe me, believe —

ANYA: I believe you, Uncle. Everybody loves you, respects you — But dear Uncle, you must keep quiet, just keep quiet — What were you saying, just now, about my mother, about your own sister? What did you say that for?

GAYEFF: Yes, yes — (*Putting her hand up over his face.*) Really, it's terrible! My God! Oh, God, save me! And today I made a speech to the bookcase — So silly! And it was only when I finished it that I could see it was silly.

VARYA: It's true, Uncle, you ought to keep quiet. Just keep quiet. That's all.

ANYA: If you kept quiet, you'd have more peace.

GAYEFF: I'll keep quiet. (*Kissing* ANYA's *and* VARYA's *hands.*) I'll keep quiet. Only this, it's about business. On Thursday I was in the District Court; well, a few of us gathered around and a conversation began about this and that, about lots of things; apparently it will be possible to arrange a loan on a promissory note to pay the bank the interest due.

VARYA: If the Lord would only help us!

GAYEFF: Tuesday I shall go and talk it over again. (*To* VARYA.) Don't bawl! (*To* ANYA.) Your mother will talk to Lopahin; of course, he won't refuse her . . . And as soon as you rest up, you will go to Yaroslavl to your great-aunt, the Countess. There, that's how we will move from three directions, and the business is in the bag. We'll pay the interest. I am convinced of that — (*Putting a hard candy in his mouth.*) On my honor I'll swear, by anything you like, that the estate shall not be sold! (*Excitedly.*) By my happiness, I swear! Here's my hand, call me a worthless, dishonorable man, if I allow it to come up for auction! With all my soul I swear it!

ANYA (*a quieter mood returns to her; she is happy*): How good you are, Uncle, how clever! (*Embracing her uncle.*) I feel easy now! I feel easy! I'm happy!

FIERS (FIERS *enters, reproachfully*): Leonid Andreevich, have you no fear of God? When are you going to bed?

GAYEFF: Right away, right away. You may go, Fiers. For this once I'll undress myself. Well, children, beddy bye — More details tomorrow, and now, go to bed. (*Kissing* ANYA *and* VARYA.) I am a man of the eighties — It is a period that's not admired, but I can say, nevertheless, that I've suffered no little for my convictions in the course of my life. It is not for nothing that the peasant loves me. One must know the peasant! One must know from what —

ANYA: Again, Uncle!

VARYA: You, Uncle dear, keep quiet.

FIERS (*angrily*): Leonid Andreevich!

GAYEFF: I'm coming, I'm coming — Go to bed. A double bank into the side pocket! A clean shot — (*Goes out,* FIERS *hobbling after him.*)

ANYA: I feel easy now. I don't feel like going to Yaroslavl; I don't like Great-aunt, but still I feel easy. Thanks to Uncle. (*Sits down.*)

VARYA: I must get to sleep. I'm going. And there was unpleasantness here during your absence. In the old servants' quarters, as you know, live only the old servants: Yephemushka, Polya, Yevstignay, well, and Karp. They began to let every sort of creature spend the night with them — I didn't say anything. But then I hear they've spread the rumor that I'd given orders to feed them nothing but beans. Out of stinginess, you see — And all that from Yevstignay — Very well, I think to myself. If that's the way it is, I think to myself, then you just wait. I call in Yevstignay — (*Yawning.*) He comes — How is it, I say, that you, Yevstignay — You're such a fool — (*Glancing at* ANYA.) Anitchka — (*A pause.*) Asleep! (*Takes* ANYA *by her arm.*) Let's go to bed — Come on! — (*Leading her.*) My little darling fell asleep! Come on — (*They* go. *Far away beyond the orchard a shepherd is playing on a pipe.* TROFIMOFF *walks across the stage and, seeing* VARYA *and* ANYA, *stops.*) Shh — She is asleep — asleep — Let's go, dear.

ANYA (*softly, half dreaming*): I'm so tired — All the bells! — Uncle — dear — And Mama and Uncle — Varya.

VARYA: Come on, my dear, come on. (*They go into* ANYA's *room.*)

TROFIMOFF (*tenderly*): My little sun! My spring!

ACT II

A field. An old chapel, long abandoned, with crooked walls, near it a well, big stones that apparently were once tombstones, and an old bench. A road to the estate of GAYEFF *can be seen. On one side poplars rise, casting their shadows, the cherry orchard begins there. In the distance a row of telegraph poles; and far, far away, faintly traced on the horizon, is a large town, visible only in the clearest weather. The sun will soon be down.* CHARLOTTA, YASHA *and* DUNYASHA *are sitting on the bench;* EPIHODOFF *is standing near and playing the guitar; everyone sits lost in thought.* CHARLOTTA *wears an old peak cap (fourrage); she has taken a rifle from off her shoulders and is adjusting the buckle on the strap.*

CHARLOTTA (*pensively*): I have no proper passport, I don't know how old I am — it always seems to me I'm very young. When I was a little girl, my father and mother traveled from fair to fair and gave performances, very good ones. And I did *salto mortale* and different tricks. And when Papa and Mama died, a German lady took me to live with her and began teaching me. Good. I grew up. And became a governess. But where I came from and who I am I don't know — Who my parents were, perhaps they weren't even married — I don't know. (*Taking a cucumber out of her pocket and beginning to eat it.*) I don't know a thing. (*A pause.*) I'd like so much to talk but there's not anybody. I haven't anybody.

EPIHODOFF (*playing the guitar and singing*): "What care I for the noisy world, what care I

for friends and foes." — How pleasant it is to play the mandolin!

DUNYASHA: That's a guitar, not a mandolin. (*Looking into a little mirror and powdering her face.*)

EPIHODOFF: For a madman who is in love this is a mandolin — (*Singing.*) "If only my heart were warm with the fire of requited love."

(YASHA *sings with him.*)

CHARLOTTA: How dreadfully these people sing — Phooey! Like jackals.

DUNYASHA (*to* YASHA): All the same what happiness to have been abroad.

YASHA: Yes, of course. I cannot disagree with you. (*Yawning and then lighting a cigar.*)

EPIHODOFF: That's easily understood. Abroad everything long since attained its complete development.

YASHA: That's obvious.

EPIHODOFF: I am a cultured man. I read all kinds of remarkable books, but the trouble is I cannot discover my own inclinations, whether to live or to shoot myself, but nevertheless, I always carry a revolver on me. Here it is — (*Showing a revolver.*)

CHARLOTTA: That's done. Now I am going. (*Slinging the rifle over her shoulder.*) You are a very clever man, Epihodoff, and a very terrible one; the women must love you madly. Brrrr-r-r-r! (*Going.*) These clever people are all so silly, I haven't anybody to talk with. I'm always alone, alone, I have nobody and — Who I am, why I am, is unknown — (*Goes out without hurrying.*)

EPIHODOFF: Strictly speaking, not touching on other subjects, I must state about myself, in passing, that fate treats me mercilessly, as a storm does a small ship. If, let us suppose, I am mistaken, then why, to mention one instance, do I wake up this morning, look and there on my chest is a spider of terrific size — There, like that. (*Showing the size with both hands.*) And also I take some kvass to drink and in it I find something in the highest degree indecent, such as a cockroach. (*A pause.*) Have you read Buckle? (*A pause.*) I desire to trouble you, Avdotya Feodorovna, with a couple of words.

DUNYASHA: Speak.

EPIHODOFF: I have a desire to speak with you alone — (*Sighing.*)

DUNYASHA (*embarrassed*): Very well — But bring me my cape first — by the cupboard — It's rather damp here —

EPIHODOFF: Very well — I'll fetch it — Now I know what I should do with my revolver — (*Takes the guitar and goes out playing.*)

YASHA: Twenty-two misfortunes! Between us he's a stupid man, it must be said. (*Yawning.*)

DUNYASHA: God forbid he should shoot himself. (*A pause.*) I've grown so uneasy, I'm always fretting. I was only a girl when I was taken into the master's house, and now I've lost the habit of simple living — and here are my hands white, white as a lady's. I've become so delicate, fragile, ladylike, afraid of everything — Frightfully so. And, Yasha, if you deceive me, I don't know what will happen to my nerves.

YASHA (*kissing her*): You little cucumber! Of course every girl must behave properly. What I dislike above everything is for a girl to conduct herself badly.

DUNYASHA: I have come to love you passionately, you are educated, you can discuss anything. (*A pause.*)

YASHA (*yawning*): Yes, sir — To my mind it is like this: If a girl loves someone, it means she is immoral. (*A pause.*) It is pleasant to smoke a cigar in the clear air — (*Listening.*) They are coming here — It is the ladies and gentlemen —

(DUNYASHA *impulsively embraces him.*)

YASHA: Go to the house, as though you had been to bathe in the river, go by this path, otherwise, they might meet you and suspect me of making a rendezvous with you. That I cannot tolerate.

DUNYASHA (*with a little cough*): Your cigar has given me the headache. (*Goes out.*)

(YASHA *remains, sitting near the chapel.* LYUBOFF ANDREEVNA, GAYEFF *and* LOPAHIN *enter.*)

LOPAHIN: We must decide definitely, time doesn't wait. Why, the matter's quite simple. Are you willing to lease your land for summer cottages or are you not? Answer in one word, yes or no? Just one word!

LYUBOFF ANDREEVNA: Who is it smokes those disgusting cigars out here — ? (*Sitting down.*)

GAYEFF: The railroad running so near is a great convenience. (*Sitting down.*) We made a trip to town and lunched there — Yellow in the side pocket! Perhaps I should go in the house first and play one game —

LYUBOFF ANDREEVNA: You'll have time.

LOPAHIN: Just one word! (*Imploringly.*) Do give me your answer!

GAYEFF (*yawning*): What?

LYUBOFF ANDREEVNA (*looking in her purse*): Yesterday there was lots of money in it. Today there's very little. My poor Varya! For the sake of economy she feeds everybody milk soup, and in the kitchen the old people get nothing but beans, and here I spend money — senselessly — (*Dropping her purse and scattering gold coins.*) There they go scattering! (*She is vexed.*)

YASHA: Allow me, I'll pick them up in a second. (*Picking up the coins.*)

LYUBOFF ANDREEVNA: If you will, Yasha. And why did I go in town for lunch — ? Your restaurant with its music is trashy, the tablecloths smell of soap — Why drink so much, Lyonya? Why eat so much? Why talk so much? Today in the restaurant you were talking a lot again, and all of it beside the point. About the seventies, about the decadents. And to whom? Talking to waiters about the decadents!

LOPAHIN: Yes.

GAYEFF (*waving his hand*): I am incorrigible, that's evident — (*To* YASHA, *irritably.*) What is it? — You are forever swirling around in front of us!

YASHA (*laughing*): I cannot hear your voice without laughing.

GAYEFF (*to his sister*): Either I or he —

LYUBOFF ANDREEVNA: Go away, Yasha. Go on —

YASHA (*giving* LYUBOFF ANDREEVNA *her purse*): I am going right away. (*Barely suppressing his laughter.*) This minute. (*Goes out.*)

LOPAHIN: The rich Deriganoff intends to buy your estate. They say he is coming personally to the auction.

LYUBOFF ANDREEVNA: And where did you hear that?

LOPAHIN: In town they are saying it.

GAYEFF: Our Yaroslavl aunt promised to send us something, but when and how much she will send, nobody knows —

LOPAHIN: How much will she send? A hundred thousand? Two hundred?

LYUBOFF ANDREEVNA: Well — maybe ten, fifteen thousand — we'd be thankful for that.

LOPAHIN: Excuse me, but such light-minded people as you are, such odd, unbusinesslike people, I never saw. You are told in plain Russian that your estate is being sold up and you just don't seem to take it in.

LYUBOFF ANDREEVNA: But what are we to do? Tell us what?

LOPAHIN: I tell you every day. Every day I tell you the same thing. Both the cherry orchard and the land have got to be leased for summer cottages, it has to be done right now, quick — The auction is right under your noses. Do understand! Once you finally decide that there are to be summer cottages, you will get all the money you want, and then you'll be saved.

LYUBOFF ANDREEVNA: Summer cottages and summer residents — it is so trivial, excuse me.

GAYEFF: I absolutely agree with you.

LOPAHIN: I'll either burst out crying, or scream, or faint. I can't bear it! You are torturing me! (To GAYEFF.) You're a perfect old woman!

GAYEFF: What?

LOPAHIN: A perfect old woman! (About to go.)

LYUBOFF ANDREEVNA (alarmed): No, don't go, stay, my lamb, I beg you. Perhaps we will think of something!

LOPAHIN: What is there to think about?

LYUBOFF ANDREEVNA: Don't go, I beg you. With you here it is more cheerful any-how — (A pause.) I keep waiting for something, as if the house were about to tumble down on our heads.

GAYEFF (deep in thought): Double into the corner pocket — Bank into the side pocket —

LYUBOFF ANDREEVNA: We have sinned so much —

LOPAHIN: What sins have you — ?

GAYEFF (puts a hard candy into his mouth): They say I've eaten my fortune up in hard candies — (Laughing.)

LYUBOFF ANDREEVNA: Oh, my sins — I've always thrown money around like mad, reck-lessly, and I married a man who accumulated nothing but debts. My husband died from champagne — he drank fearfully — and to my misfortune I fell in love with another man. I lived with him, and just at that time — it was my first punishment — a blow over the head: right here in the river my boy was drowned and I went abroad — went away for good, never to return, never to see this river again — I shut my eyes, ran away, beside myself, and he after me — mercilessly, brutally. I bought a villa near Menton, because he fell ill there, and for three years I knew no rest day or night, the sick man exhausted me, my soul dried up. And last year when the villa was sold for debts, I went to Paris and there he robbed me of everything, threw me over, took up with another woman; I tried to poison myself — so stupid, so shameful — And suddenly I was seized with longing for Russia, for my own country, for my little girl — (Wiping away her tears.) Lord, Lord, have mercy, forgive me my sins! Don't punish me any more! (Getting a telegram out of her pocket.) I got this today from Paris, he asks forgiveness, begs me to return — (Tears up the telegram.) That sounds like music somewhere. (Listening.)

GAYEFF: It is our famous Jewish orchestra. You remember, four violins, a flute and double bass.

LYUBOFF ANDREEVNA: Does it still exist? We ought to get hold of it sometime and give a party.

LOPAHIN (listening): Can't hear it — (Singing softly.) "And for money the Ger-mans will frenchify a Russian." (Laughing.) What a play I saw yesterday at the theatre, very funny!

LYUBOFF ANDREEVNA: And most likely there was nothing funny about it. You shouldn't look at plays, but look oftener at yourselves. How gray all your lives are, what a lot of idle things you say!

LOPAHIN: That's true. It must be said frankly this life of ours is idiotic — (A pause.) My father was a peasant, an idiot, he under-stood nothing, he taught me nothing, he just beat me in his drunken fits and always with a stick. At bottom I am just as big a dolt and idiot as he was. I wasn't taught anything, my handwriting is vile, I write like a pig — I am ashamed for people to see it.

LYUBOFF ANDREEVNA: You ought to get married, my friend.

LOPAHIN: Yes — That's true.

LYUBOFF ANDREEVNA: To our Varya, per-haps. She is a good girl.

LOPAHIN: Yes.

LYUBOFF ANDREEVNA: She comes from simple people, and she works all day long, but the main thing is she loves you. And you, too, have liked her a long time.

LOPAHIN: Why not? I am not against it — She's a good girl. (*A pause.*)

GAYEFF: They are offering me a position in a bank. Six thousand a year — Have you heard that?

LYUBOFF ANDREEVNA: Not you! You stay where you are —

FIERS (FIERS *enters, bringing an overcoat. To* GAYEFF): Pray, Sir, put this on, it's damp.

GAYEFF (*putting on the overcoat*): You're a pest, old man.

FIERS: That's all right — This morning you went off without letting me know. (*Looking him over.*)

LYUBOFF ANDREEVNA: How old you've grown, Fiers!

FIERS: At your service.

LOPAHIN: She says you've grown very old!

FIERS: I've lived a long time. They were planning to marry me off before your papa was born. (*Laughing.*) And at the time the serfs were freed I was already the head footman. I didn't want to be freed then, I stayed with the masters — (*A pause.*) And I remember, everybody was happy, but what they were happy about they didn't know themselves.

LOPAHIN: In the old days it was fine. At least they flogged.

FIERS (*not hearing*): But, of course. The peasants stuck to the masters, the masters stuck to the peasants, and now everything is all smashed up, you can't tell about anything.

GAYEFF: Keep still, Fiers. Tomorrow I must go to town. They have promised to introduce me to a certain general who might make us a loan.

LOPAHIN: Nothing will come of it. And you can rest assured you won't pay the interest.

LYUBOFF ANDREEVNA: He's just raving on. There aren't any such generals.

(TROFIMOFF, ANYA *and* VARYA *enter.*)

GAYEFF: Here they come.

ANYA: There is Mama sitting there.

LYUBOFF ANDREEVNA (*tenderly*): Come, come — My darlings — (*Embracing* ANYA *and* VARYA.) If you only knew how I love you both! Come sit by me — there — like that.

(*Everybody sits down.*)

LOPAHIN: Our perennial student is always strolling with the young ladies.

TROFIMOFF: It's none of your business.

LOPAHIN: He will soon be fifty and he's still a student.

TROFIMOFF: Stop your stupid jokes.

LOPAHIN: But why are you so peevish, you queer duck?

TROFIMOFF: Don't you pester me.

LOPAHIN (*laughing*): Permit me to ask you, what do you make of me?

TROFIMOFF: Yermolay Alexeevich, I make this of you: you are a rich man, you'll soon be a millionaire. Just as it is in the metabolism of nature, a wild beast is needed to eat up everything that comes his way; so you, too, are needed.

(*Everyone laughs.*)

VARYA: Petya, you'd better tell us about the planets.

LYUBOFF ANDREEVNA: No, let's go on with yesterday's conversation.

TROFIMOFF: What was it about?

GAYEFF: About the proud man.

TROFIMOFF: We talked a long time yesterday, but didn't get anywhere. In a proud man, in your sense of the word, there is something mystical. Maybe you are right, from your standpoint, but if we are to discuss it in simple terms, without whimsy, then what pride can there be, is there any sense in it, if man physiologically is poorly constructed, if in the great majority he is crude, unintelligent, profoundly miserable. One must stop admiring oneself. One must only work.

GAYEFF: All the same, you will die.

TROFIMOFF: Who knows? And what does it mean — you will die? Man may have a hundred senses, and when he dies only the five that are known to us may perish, and the remaining ninety-five go on living.

LYUBOFF ANDREEVNA: How clever you are, Petya!

LOPAHIN (*ironically*): Terribly!

TROFIMOFF: Humanity goes forward, perfecting its powers. Everything that's unattainable now will some day become familiar, understandable; it is only that one must work and must help with all one's might those who seek the truth. With us in Russia so far only a very few work. The great majority of the intelligentsia that I know are looking for nothing, doing nothing, and as yet have no capacity for work. They call themselves intelligentsia, are free and easy with the servants, treat the peasants like animals, educate themselves poorly, read nothing seriously, do absolutely nothing; about science they just talk and about art they understand very little. Every one of them is serious, all have stern faces; they all talk of nothing but important things, philosophize, and all the time everybody can see that the workmen eat abominably, sleep without any pillows, thirty or forty to a room, and everywhere there are bedbugs, stench, dampness, moral uncleanness — And apparently with us, all the fine talk is only to divert the attention of ourselves and of others. Show me where we have the day nurseries they are always talking so much about, where are the reading rooms? They only write of these in novels, for the truth is there are not any at all. There is only filth, vulgarity, orientalism — I am afraid of very serious faces and dislike them. I'm afraid of serious conversations. Rather than that let's just keep still.

LOPAHIN: You know I get up before five o'clock in the morning and work from morning till night. Well, I always have money, my own and other people's, on hand, and I see what the people around me are. One has only to start doing something to find out how few honest and decent people there are. At times when I can't go to sleep, I think: Lord, thou gavest us immense forests, unbounded fields and the widest horizons, and living in the midst of them we should indeed be giants —

LYUBOFF ANDREEVNA: You feel the need for giants — They are good only in fairy tales, anywhere else they only frighten us.

(At the back of the stage EPIHODOFF passes by, playing the guitar.)

LYUBOFF ANDREEVNA (lost in thought): Epihodoff is coming —
ANYA (lost in thought): Epihodoff is coming.
GAYEFF: The sun has set, ladies and gentlemen.
TROFIMOFF: Yes.
GAYEFF (not loud and as if he were declaiming): Oh, Nature, wonderful, you gleam with eternal radiance, beautiful and indifferent, you, whom we call Mother, combine in yourself both life and death, you give life and you take it away.

VARYA (beseechingly): Uncle!
ANYA: Uncle, you're doing it again!
TROFIMOFF: You'd better bank the yellow into the side pocket.
GAYEFF: I'll be quiet, quiet.

(All sit absorbed in their thoughts. There is only the silence. FIERS is heard muttering to himself softly. Suddenly a distant sound is heard, as if from the sky, like the sound of a snapped string, dying away, mournful.)

LYUBOFF ANDREEVNA: What's that?
LOPAHIN: I don't know. Somewhere far off in a mine shaft a bucket fell. But somewhere very far off.
GAYEFF: And it may be some bird — like a heron.
TROFIMOFF: Or an owl —
LYUBOFF ANDREEVNA (shivering): It's unpleasant, somehow. (A pause.)
FIERS: Before the disaster it was like that. The owl hooted and the samovar hummed without stopping, both.
GAYEFF: Before what disaster?
FIERS: Before the emancipation. (A pause.)
LYUBOFF ANDREEVNA: You know, my friends, let's go. Twilight is falling. (To ANYA.) You have tears in your eyes — What is it, my dear little girl? (Embracing her.)
ANYA: It's just that, Mama. It's nothing.
TROFIMOFF: Somebody is coming.

(A STRANGER appears in a shabby white cap, and an overcoat; he is a little drunk.)

THE STRANGER: Allow me to ask you, can I go straight through here to the station?
GAYEFF: You can. Go by that road.
THE STRANGER: I am heartily grateful to you. (Coughing.) The weather is splendid — (Declaiming.) Brother of mine, suffering brother — Go out to the Volga, whose moans — (To VARYA.) Mademoiselle, grant a hungry Russian man some thirty kopecks —

(VARYA is frightened and gives a shriek.)

LOPAHIN (angrily): There's a limit to everything.
LYUBOFF ANDREEVNA (flustered): Take this — Here's this for you — (Searching in her purse.) No silver — It's all the same, here's a gold piece for you —
THE STRANGER: I am heartily grateful to you. (Goes out. Laughter.)

VARYA (*frightened*): I'm going — I'm going — Oh, Mama, you poor little Mama! There's nothing in the house for people to eat, and you gave him a gold piece.

LYUBOFF ANDREEVNA: What is to be done with me, so silly? I shall give you all I have in the house. Yermolay Alexeevich, you will lend me some this once more! —

LOPAHIN: Agreed.

LYUBOFF ANDREEVNA: Let's go, ladies and gentlemen, it's time. And here, Varya, we have definitely made a match for you, I congratulate you.

VARYA (*through her tears*): Mama, that's not something to joke about.

LOPAHIN: Achmelia, get thee to a nunnery.

GAYEFF: And my hands are trembling; it is a long time since I have played billiards.

LOPAHIN: Achmelia, oh nymph, in thine orisons be all my sins remember'd —

LYUBOFF ANDREEVNA: Let's go, my dear friends, it will soon be suppertime.

VARYA: He frightened me. My heart is thumping so!

LOPAHIN: I remind you, ladies and gentlemen: August twenty-second the cherry orchard will be auctioned off. Think about that! — Think! —

(*All go out except* TROFIMOFF *and* ANYA.)

ANYA (*laughing*): My thanks to the stranger, he frightened Varya, now we are alone.

TROFIMOFF: Varya is afraid we might begin to love each other and all day long she won't leave us to ourselves. With her narrow mind she cannot understand that we are above love. To sidestep the petty and illusory, which prevent our being free and happy, that is the aim and meaning of our life. Forward! We march on irresistibly toward the bright star that burns there in the distance. Forward! Do not fall behind, friends!

ANYA (*extending her arms upward*): How well you talk! (*A pause.*) It's wonderful here today!

TROFIMOFF: Yes, the weather is marvelous.

ANYA: What have you done to me, Petya, why don't I love the cherry orchard any longer the way I used to? I loved it so tenderly, it seemed to me there was not a better place on earth than our orchard.

TROFIMOFF: All Russia is our orchard. The earth is immense and beautiful, and on it are many wonderful places. (*A pause.*) Just think, Anya: your grandfather, great-grandfather and all your ancestors were slave owners, in possession of living souls, and can you doubt that from every cherry in the orchard, from every leaf, from every trunk, human beings are looking at you, can it be that you don't hear their voices? To possess living souls, well, that depraved all of you who lived before and who are living now, so that your mother and you, and your uncle no longer notice that you live by debt, at somebody else's expense, at the expense of those very people whom you wouldn't let past your front door — We are at least two hundred years behind the times, we have as yet absolutely nothing, we have no definite attitude toward the past, we only philosophize, complain of our sadness or drink vodka. Why, it is quite clear that to begin to live in the present we must first atone for our past, must be done with it; and we can atone for it only through suffering, only through uncommon, incessant labor. Understand that, Anya.

ANYA: The house we live in ceased to be ours long ago, and I'll go away, I give you my word.

TROFIMOFF: If you have the household keys, throw them in the well and go away. Be free as the wind.

ANYA (*transported*): How well you said that!

TROFIMOFF: Believe me, Anya, believe me! I am not thirty yet, I am young, I am still a student, but I have already borne so much! Every winter I am hungry, sick, anxious, poor as a beggar, and — where has destiny not chased me, where haven't I been! And yet, my soul has always, every minute, day and night, been full of inexplicable premonitions. I have a premonition of happiness, Anya, I see it already —

ANYA (*pensively*): The moon is rising.

(EPIHODOFF *is heard playing on the guitar, always the same sad song. The moon rises. Somewhere near the poplars* VARYA *is looking for* ANYA *and calling:* "Anya! Where are you?")

TROFIMOFF: Yes, the moon is rising. (*A pause.*) Here is happiness, here it comes, comes always nearer and nearer, I hear its footsteps now. And if we shall not see it, shall not come to know it, what does that matter? Others will see it!

VARYA (*off*): Anya! Where are you?

TROFIMOFF: Again, that Varya! (*Angrily.*) It's scandalous!

ANYA: Well, let's go to the river. It's lovely there.

TROFIMOFF: Let's go. (*They go out.*)

VARYA (*off*): Anya! Anya!

ACT III

The drawing room, separated by an arch from the ballroom. A chandelier is lighted. A Jewish orchestra is playing — the same that was mentioned in Act II. Evening. In the ballroom they are dancing grand rond. The voice of SEMYONOFF-PISHTCHIK: *"Promenade à une paire!" They enter the drawing room; in the first couple are* PISHTCHIK *and* CHARLOTTA IVANOVNA; *in the second,* TROFIMOFF *and* LYUBOFF ANDREEVNA; *in the third,* ANYA *with the* POST-OFFICE CLERK; *in the fourth,* VARYA *with the* STATION-MASTER *et cetera —* VARYA *is crying softly and wipes away her tears while she is dancing.* DUNYASHA *is in the last couple through the drawing room.* PISHTCHIK *shouts: "Grand rond, balancez!" and "Les Cavaliers à genoux et remerciez vos dames!"*

FIERS *in a frock coat goes by with seltzer water on a tray.* PISHTCHIK *and* TROFIMOFF *come into the drawing room.*

PISHTCHIK: I am full-blooded, I have had two strokes already, and dancing is hard for me, but as they say, if you are in a pack of dogs, you may bark and bark, but you must still wag your tail. At that, I have the health of a horse. My dear father — he was a great joker — may he dwell in Heaven — used to talk as if our ancient line, the Semyonoff-Pishtchiks, were descended from the very horse that Caligula made a Senator — (*Sitting down.*) But here's my trouble: I haven't any money. A hungry dog believes in nothing but meat — (*Snoring but waking at once.*) And the same way with me — I can't talk about anything but money.

TROFIMOFF: Well, to tell you the truth, there is something of a horse about your figure.

PISHTCHIK: Well — a horse is a fine animal — You can sell a horse —

(*The sound of playing billiards comes from the next room.* VARYA *appears under the arch to the ballroom.*)

TROFIMOFF (*teasing*): Madam Lopahin! Madam Lopahin!

VARYA (*angrily*): A mangy-looking gentleman!

TROFIMOFF: Yes, I am a mangy-looking gentleman, and proud of it!

VARYA (*in bitter thought*): Here we have gone and hired musicians and what are we going to pay them with? (*Goes out.*)

TROFIMOFF (*to* PISHTCHIK): If the energy you have wasted in the course of your life trying to find money to pay the interest had gone into something else, you could very likely have turned the world upside down before you were done with it.

PISHTCHIK: Nietzsche — the philosopher — the greatest — the most celebrated — a man of tremendous mind — says in his works that one may make counterfeit money.

TROFIMOFF: And have you read Nietzsche?

PISHTCHIK: Well — Dashenka told me. And I'm in such a state now that I could make counterfeit money myself — Day after tomorrow three hundred and ten roubles must be paid — one hundred and thirty I've on hand — (*Feeling in his pockets, alarmed.*) The money is gone! I have lost the money! (*Tearfully.*) Where is the money? (*Joyfully.*) Here it is, inside the lining — I was in quite a sweat —

(LYUBOFF ANDREEVNA *and* CHARLOTTA IVANOVNA *come in.*)

LYUBOFF ANDREEVNA (*humming lazginka, a Georgian dance*): Why does Leonid take so long? What's he doing in town? (*To* DUNYASHA.) Dunyasha, offer the musicians some tea —

TROFIMOFF: In all probability the auction did not take place.

LYUBOFF ANDREEVNA: And the musicians came at an unfortunate moment and we planned the ball at an unfortunate moment — Well, it doesn't matter. (*Sitting down and singing softly.*)

CHARLOTTA (*gives* PISHTCHIK *a deck of cards*): Here is a deck of cards for you, think of some one card.

PISHTCHIK: I have thought of one.

CHARLOTTA: Now, shuffle the deck. Very good. Hand it here; oh, my dear Monsieur Pishtchik. *Ein, zwei, drei!* Now look for it, it's in your coat pocket —

PISHTCHIK (*getting a card out of his coat pocket*): The Eight of Spades, that's absolutely right! (*Amazed.*) Fancy that!

CHARLOTTA (*holding a deck of cards in her palm; to* TROFIMOFF): Tell me quick now, which card is on top?

TROFIMOFF: What is it? Well — the Queen of Spades.

CHARLOTTA: Right! (*To* PISHTCHIK.) Well? Which card's on top?

PISHTCHIK: The Ace of Hearts.

CHARLOTTA: Right! (*Strikes the deck against her palm; the deck of cards disappears.*) And what beautiful weather we are having today!

(*A mysterious feminine voice answers her, as if from under the floor: "Oh, yes. The weather is splendid, madame." "You are so nice, you're my ideal —" The voice: "Madame, you too please me greatly."*)

THE STATIONMASTER (*applauding*): Madam Ventriloquist, bravo!

PISHTCHIK (*amazed*): Fancy that! Most charming Charlotta Ivanovna — I am simply in love with you.

CHARLOTTA: In love? (*Shrugging her shoulders.*) Is it possible that you can love? *Guter Mensch aber schlechter Musikant.*

TROFIMOFF (*slapping* PISHTCHIK *on the shoulder*): You horse, you —

CHARLOTTA: I beg your attention, one more trick. (*Taking a lap robe from the chair.*) Here is a very fine lap robe — I want to sell it — (*Shaking it out.*) Wouldn't somebody like to buy it?

PISHTCHIK (*amazed*): Fancy that!

CHARLOTTA: *Ein, zwei, drei!*

(*She quickly raises the lowered robe, behind it stands* ANYA, *who curtseys, runs to her mother, embraces her and runs back into the ballroom amid the general delight.*)

LYUBOFF ANDREEVNA (*applauding*): Bravo, bravo — !

CHARLOTTA: Now again! *Ein, zwei, drei!*

(*Lifting the robe: behind it stands* VARYA, *she bows.*)

PISHTCHIK (*amazed*): Fancy that!

CHARLOTTA: That's all. (*Throwing the robe at* PISHTCHIK, *curtseying and running into the ballroom.*)

PISHTCHIK (*hurrying after her*): You little rascal — What a girl! What a girl! (*Goes out.*)

LYUBOFF ANDREEVNA: And Leonid is not here yet. What he's doing in town so long, I don't understand! Everything is finished there, either the estate is sold by now, or the auction didn't take place. Why keep it from us so long?

VARYA (*trying to comfort her*): Uncle has bought it, I am sure of that.

TROFIMOFF (*mockingly*): Yes.

VARYA: Great-aunt sent him power of attorney to buy it in her name and transfer the debt. She did this for Anya. And I feel certain, God willing, that Uncle will buy it.

LYUBOFF ANDREEVNA: Our Yaroslavl great-aunt has sent fifteen thousand to buy the estate in her name — She doesn't trust us, but that wouldn't be enough to pay the interest even — (*Covering her face with her hands.*) Today my fate will be decided, my fate —

TROFIMOFF (*teasing* VARYA): Madam Lopahin!

VARYA (*angrily*): Perennial student! You have already been expelled from the University twice.

LYUBOFF ANDREEVNA: But why are you angry, Varya? He teases you about Lopahin, what of it? Marry Lopahin if you want to, he is a good man, interesting. If you don't want to, don't marry him; darling, nobody is making you do it.

VARYA: I look at this matter seriously, Mama, one must speak straight out. He's a good man, I like him.

LYUBOFF ANDREEVNA: Then marry him. What there is to wait for I don't understand!

VARYA: But I can't propose to him myself, Mama. It's two years now; everyone has been talking to me about him, everyone talks, and he either remains silent or jokes. I understand. He's getting rich, he's busy with his own affairs, and has no time for me. If there were money, ever so little, even a hundred roubles, I would drop everything, and go far away. I'd go to a nunnery.

TROFIMOFF: How saintly!

VARYA (*to* TROFIMOFF): A student should be intelligent! (*In a low voice, tearfully.*) How homely you have grown, Petya, how old you've got. (*To* LYUBOFF ANDREEVNA, *no longer crying.*) It is just that I can't live without working, Mama. I must be doing something every minute.

YASHA (YASHA *enters. Barely restraining his laughter*): Epihodoff has broken a billiard cue! — (*Goes out.*)

VARYA: But why is Epihodoff here? Who allowed him to play billiards? I don't understand these people — (*Goes out.*)

LYUBOFF ANDREEVNA: Don't tease her, Petya; you can see she has troubles enough without that.

TROFIMOFF: She is just too zealous. Sticking her nose into things that are none of her business. All summer she gave us no peace, neither me nor Anya; she was afraid a romance would spring up between us. What business is that of hers? And besides I haven't shown any signs of it. I am so remote from triviality. We are above love!

LYUBOFF ANDREEVNA: Well, then, I must be beneath love. (*Very anxiously.*) Why isn't Leonid here? Just to tell us whether the estate is sold or not? Calamity seems to me so incredible that I don't know what to think, I'm lost — I could scream this minute — I could do something insane. Save me, Petya. Say something, do say. . . .

TROFIMOFF: Whether the estate is sold today or is not sold — is it not the same? There is no turning back, the path is all grown over. Calm yourself, my dear, all that was over long ago. One mustn't deceive oneself, one must for once at least in one's life look truth straight in the eye.

LYUBOFF ANDREEVNA: What truth? You see where the truth is and where the untruth is, but as for me, it's as if I had lost my sight, I see nothing. You boldly decide all important questions, but tell me, my dear boy, isn't that because you are young and haven't had time yet to suffer through any one of your problems? You look boldly ahead, and isn't that because you don't see and don't expect anything terrible, since life is still hidden from your young eyes? You are braver, more honest, more profound than we are, but stop and think, be magnanimous, have a little mercy on me, just a little. Why, I was born here. My father and mother lived here and my grandfather. I love this house, I can't imagine my life without the cherry orchard and if it is very necessary to sell it, then sell me along with the orchard — (*Embracing* TROFIMOFF *and kissing him on the forehead.*) Why, my son was

drowned here — (*Crying.*) Have mercy on me, good, kind man.

TROFIMOFF: You know I sympathize with you from the bottom of my heart.

LYUBOFF ANDREEVNA: But that should be said differently, differently — (*Taking out her handkerchief; a telegram falls on the floor.*) My heart is heavy today, you can't imagine how heavy. It is too noisy for me here, my soul trembles at every sound, I tremble all over and yet I can't go off to myself, when I am alone the silence frightens me. Don't blame me, Petya — I love you as one of my own. I should gladly have given you Anya's hand, I assure you, only, my dear, you must study and finish your course. You do nothing. Fate simply flings you about from place to place, and that's so strange — Isn't that so? Yes? And you must do something about your beard, to make it grow somehow — (*Laughing.*) You look funny!

TROFIMOFF (*picking up the telegram*): I do not desire to be beautiful.

LYUBOFF ANDREEVNA: This telegram is from Paris. I get one every day. Yesterday and today too. That wild man has fallen ill again, something is wrong again with him — He asks forgiveness, begs me to come, and really I ought to make a trip to Paris and stay awhile near him. Your face looks stern, Petya, but what is there to do, my dear, what am I to do, he is ill, he is alone, unhappy and who will look after him there, who will keep him from doing the wrong thing, who will give him his medicine on time? And what is there to hide or keep still about? I love him, that's plain. I love him, love him — It's a stone about my neck, I'm sinking to the bottom with it, but I love that stone and live without it I cannot. (*Pressing* TROFIMOFF's *hand.*) Don't think harshly of me, Petya, don't say anything to me, don't —

TROFIMOFF (*tearfully*): Forgive my frankness, for God's sake! Why, he picked your bones.

LYUBOFF ANDREEVNA: No, no, no, you must not talk like that. (*Stopping her ears.*)

TROFIMOFF: But he is a scoundrel, only you, you are the only one that doesn't know it. He is a petty scoundrel, a nonentity —

LYUBOFF ANDREEVNA (*angry but controlling herself*): You are twenty-six years old or twenty-seven, but you are still a schoolboy in the second grade!

TROFIMOFF: Very well!

LYUBOFF ANDREEVNA: You should be a man

— at your age you should understand people who love. And you yourself should love some-one — you should fall in love! (*Angrily.*) Yes, yes! And there is no purity in you; you are simply smug, a ridiculous crank, a freak —

TROFIMOFF (*horrified*): What is she saying!

LYUBOFF ANDREEVNA: "I am above love!" You are not above love, Petya, you are, as our Fiers would say, just a good-for-nothing. Imag-ine, at your age, not having a mistress — !

TROFIMOFF (*horrified*): This is terrible! What is she saying! (*Goes quickly into the ballroom, clutching his head.*) This is horri-ble — I can't bear it, I am going — (*Goes out but immediately returns.*) All is over between us. (*Goes out into the hall.*)

LYUBOFF ANDREEVNA (*shouting after him*): Petya, wait! You funny creature, I was joking! Petya! (*In the hall you hear someone running up the stairs and suddenly falling back down with a crash. You hear ANYA and VARYA scream but immediately you hear laughter.*) What's that?

ANYA (ANYA *runs in. Laughing*): Petya fell down the stairs! (*Runs out.*)

LYUBOFF ANDREEVNA: What a funny boy that Petya is — ! (*The STATIONMASTER stops in the center of the ballroom and begins to recite "The Sinner" by A. Tolstoi. They listen to him but he has recited only a few lines when the strains of a waltz are heard from the hall and the recitation is broken off. They all dance.* TROFIMOFF, ANYA, VARYA *and* LYUBOFF ANDREEVNA *come in from the hall.*) But, Petya — but, dear soul — I beg your forgive-ness — Let's go dance. (*She dances with* TROFI-MOFF. ANYA *and* VARYA *dance.* FIERS *enters, leaving his stick by the side door.* YASHA *also comes into the drawing room and watches the dancers.*)

YASHA: What is it, Grandpa?

FIERS: I don't feel very well. In the old days there were generals, barons, admirals dancing at our parties, and now we send for the post-office clerk and the stationmaster, and even they are none too anxious to come. Somehow I've grown feeble. The old master, the grand-father, treated everybody with sealing-wax for all sicknesses. I take sealing-wax every day, have done so for twenty-odd years or more; it may be due to that that I'm alive.

YASHA: You are tiresome, Grandpa. (*Yawn-ing.*) Why don't you go off and die?

FIERS: Aw, you — good-for-nothing! — (*Mut-tering.*)

(TROFIMOFF *and* LYUBOFF ANDREEVNA *dance in the ballroom and then in the drawing room.*)

LYUBOFF ANDREEVNA: *Merci.* I'll sit down awhile — (*Sitting down.*) I'm tired.

ANYA (ANYA *enters. Agitated*): And just now in the kitchen some man was saying that the cherry orchard had been sold today.

LYUBOFF ANDREEVNA: Sold to whom?

ANYA: He didn't say who to. He's gone.

(*Dancing with* TROFIMOFF, *they pass into the ballroom.*)

YASHA: It was some old man babbling there. A stranger.

FIERS: And Leonid Andreevich is still not here, he has not arrived. The overcoat he has on is light, midseason — let's hope he won't catch cold. Ach, these young things!

LYUBOFF ANDREEVNA: I shall die this min-ute. Go, Yasha, find out who it was sold to.

YASHA: But he's been gone a long time, the old fellow. (*Laughing.*)

LYUBOFF ANDREEVNA (*with some annoy-ance*): Well, what are you laughing at? What are you so amused at?

YASHA: Epihodoff is just too funny. An empty-headed man. Twenty-two misfortunes!

LYUBOFF ANDREEVNA: Fiers, if the estate is sold, where will you go?

FIERS: Wherever you say, there I'll go.

LYUBOFF ANDREEVNA: Why do you look like that? Aren't you well? You know you ought to go to bed —

FIERS: Yes — (*With a sneer.*) I go to bed and without me who's going to serve, who'll take care of things? I'm the only one in the whole house.

YASHA (*to* LYUBOFF ANDREEVNA): Lyuboff Andreevna, let me ask a favor of you, do be so kind! If you ever go back to Paris, take me with you, please do! It's impossible for me to stay here. (*Looking around him, and speaking in a low voice.*) Why talk about it? You can see for yourself it's an uncivilized country, an immoral people and not only that, there's the boredom of it. The food they give us in that kitchen is abominable and there's that Fiers, too, walking about and muttering all kinds of words that are out of place. Take me with you, be so kind!

PISHTCHIK (*enters*): Allow me to ask you — for a little waltz, most beautiful lady — (LYUBOFF ANDREEVNA *goes with him.*) Charming lady, I must borrow a hundred and eighty roubles from you — will borrow — (*dancing*) a hundred and eighty roubles — (*They pass into the ballroom.*)

YASHA (*singing low*): "Wilt thou know the unrest in my soul!"

(*In the ballroom a figure in a gray top hat and checked trousers waves both hands and jumps about; there are shouts of "Bravo, Charlotta Ivanovna!"*)

DUNYASHA (*stopping to powder her face*): The young lady orders me to dance — there are a lot of gentlemen and very few ladies — but dancing makes my head swim and my heart thump. Fiers Nikolaevich, the post-office clerk said something to me just now that took my breath away.

(*The music plays more softly.*)

FIERS: What did he say to you?
DUNYASHA: You are like a flower, he says.
YASHA (*yawning*): What ignorance — ! (*Goes out.*)
DUNYASHA: Like a flower — I am such a sensitive girl, I love tender words awfully.
FIERS: You'll be getting your head turned.

(EPIHODOFF *enters.*)

EPIHODOFF: Avdotya Feodorovna, you don't want to see me — It's as if I were some sort of insect. (*Sighing.*) Ach, life!
DUNYASHA: What do you want?
EPIHODOFF: Undoubtedly you may be right. (*Sighing.*) But of course, if one considers it from a given point of view, then you, I will allow myself so to express it, forgive my frankness, absolutely led me into a state of mind. I know my fate, every day some misfortune happens to me, but I have long since become accustomed to that, and so I look on my misfortunes with a smile. You gave me your word and, although I —
DUNYASHA: I beg you, we'll talk later on, but leave me now in peace. I'm in a dream now. (*Playing with her fan.*)
EPIHODOFF: I have a something wrong happens every day — I will allow myself so to express it — I just smile, I even laugh.
VARYA (*enters from the ballroom*): You are not gone yet, Semyon? What a really disrespectful man you are! (*To* DUNYASHA.) Get out of here, Dunyasha. (*To* EPIHODOFF.) You either play billiards and break a cue or you walk about the drawing room like a guest.

EPIHODOFF: Allow me to tell you, you cannot make any demands on me.
VARYA: I'm not making any demands on you, I'm talking to you. All you know is to walk from place to place but not do any work. We keep a clerk, but what for, nobody knows.
EPIHODOFF (*offended*): Whether I work, whether I walk, whether I eat, or whether I play billiards are matters to be discussed only by people of understanding and my seniors.
VARYA: You dare to say that to me! (*Flying into a temper.*) You dare? So I don't understand anything? Get out of here! This minute!
EPIHODOFF (*alarmed*): I beg you to express yourself in a delicate manner.
VARYA (*beside herself*): This very minute, get out of here! Get out! (*He goes to the door; she follows him.*) Twenty-two misfortunes! Don't you dare breathe in here! Don't let me set eyes on you! (EPIHODOFF *has gone out, but his voice comes from outside the door:* "I shall complain about you.") Ah, you are coming back? (*Grabbing the stick that* FIERS *put by the door.*) Come on, come — come on, I'll show you — Ah, you are coming? You are coming? Take that then — !

(*She swings the stick, at the very moment when* LOPAHIN *is coming in.*)

LOPAHIN: Most humbly, I thank you.
VARYA (*angrily and ironically*): I beg your pardon!
LOPAHIN: It's nothing at all. I humbly thank you for the pleasant treat.
VARYA: It isn't worth your thanks. (*Moving away, then looking back and asking gently.*) I haven't hurt you?
LOPAHIN: No, it's nothing. There's a great bump coming though.

(*Voices in the ballroom:* "Lopahin has come back." "Yermolay Alexeevich!")

PISTCHIK (*enters*): See what we see, hear what we hear — ! (*He and* LOPAHIN *kiss one another.*) You smell slightly of cognac, my dear, my good old chap. And we are amusing ourselves here too.
LYUBOFF ANDREEVNA (*enters*): Is that you, Yermolay Alexeevich? Why were you so long? Where is Leonid?
LOPAHIN: Leonid Andreevich got back when I did, he's coming.
LYUBOFF ANDREEVNA (*agitated*): Well, what? Was there an auction? Do speak!
LOPAHIN (*embarrassed, afraid of showing the*

joy he feels): The auction was over by four o'clock — We were late for the train, had to wait till half-past nine. (*Sighing heavily.*) Ugh, my head's swimming a bit!

(GAYEFF *enters; with his right hand he carries his purchases, with his left he wipes away his tears.*)

LYUBOFF ANDREEVNA: Lyona, what? Lyona, eh? (*Impatiently, with tears in her eyes.*) Quick, for God's sake —

GAYEFF (*not answering her, merely waving his hand; to* FIERS, *crying*): Here, take it — There are anchovies, some Kertch herrings — I haven't eaten anything all day — What I have suffered! (*The door into the billiard room is open; you hear the balls clicking and* YASHA's *voice: "Seven and eighteen!"* GAYEFF's *expression changes, he is no longer crying.*) I'm terribly tired. You help me change, Fiers. (*Goes to his room through the ballroom,* FIERS *behind him.*)

PISHTCHIK: What happened at the auction? Go on, tell us!

LYUBOFF ANDREEVNA: Is the cherry orchard sold?

LOPAHIN: It's sold.

LYUBOFF ANDREEVNA: Who bought it?

LOPAHIN: I bought it. (*A pause.* LYUBOFF ANDREEVNA *is overcome. She would have fallen had she not been standing near the chair and table.* VARYA *takes the keys from her belt, throws them on the floor in the middle of the drawing room and goes out.*) I bought it. Kindly wait a moment, ladies and gentlemen, everything is muddled up in my head, I can't speak — (*Laughing.*) We arrived at the auction, Deriganoff was already there. Leonid Andreevich had only fifteen thousand and Deriganoff right off bids thirty over and above indebtedness. I see how things are, I match him with forty thousand. He forty-five. I fifty-five. That is to say he raises it by fives, I by tens — So it ended. Over and above the indebtedness, I bid up to ninety thousand, it was knocked down to me. The cherry orchard is mine now. Mine! (*Guffawing.*) My God, Lord, the cherry orchard is mine! Tell me I'm drunk, out of my head, that I'm imagining all this — (*Stamps his feet.*) Don't laugh at me! If only my father and grandfather could rise from their graves and see this whole business, see how their Yermolay, beaten, half-illiterate Yermolay, who used to run around barefoot in winter, how that very Yermolay has bought an estate that nothing in the world can beat. I bought the estate where grandfather and father were slaves, where you wouldn't even let me in the kitchen. I am asleep, it's only some dream of mine, it only seems so to me — That's nothing but the fruit of your imagination, covered with the darkness of the unknown — (*Picking up the keys, with a gentle smile.*) She threw down the keys, wants to show she is not mistress any more — (*Jingling the keys.*) Well, it's all the same. (*The orchestra is heard tuning up.*) Hey, musicians, play, I want to hear you! Come on, everybody, and see how Yermolay Lopahin will swing the ax in the cherry orchard, how the trees will fall to the ground! We are going to build villas and our grandsons and great-grandsons will see a new life here — Music, play! (*The music is playing.* LYUBOFF ANDREEVNA *has sunk into a chair, crying bitterly.* LOPAHIN *reproachfully.*) Why, then, didn't you listen to me? My poor dear, it can't be undone now. (*With tears.*) Oh, if this could all be over soon, if somehow our awkward, unhappy life would be changed!

PISHTCHIK (*taking him by the arm, in a low voice*): She is crying. Come on in the ballroom, let her be by herself — Come on — (*Taking him by the arm and leading him into the ballroom.*)

LOPAHIN: What's the matter? Music, there, play up! (*Sarcastically.*) Everything is to be as I want it! Here comes the new squire, the owner of the cherry orchard. (*Quite accidentally, he bumps into the little table, and very nearly upsets the candelabra.*) I can pay for everything!

(*Goes out with* PISHTCHIK. *There is nobody left either in the ballroom or the drawing room but* LYUBOFF ANDREEVNA, *who sits all huddled up and crying bitterly. The music plays softly.* ANYA *and* TROFIMOFF *enter hurriedly.* ANYA *comes up to her mother and kneels in front of her.* TROFIMOFF *remains at the ballroom door.*)

ANYA: Mama — ! Mama, you are crying? My dear, kind, good Mama, my beautiful, I love you — I bless you. The cherry orchard is sold, it's not ours any more, that's true, true; but don't cry, Mama, you've your life still left you, you've your good, pure heart ahead of you — Come with me, come on, darling, away from here, come on — We will plant a new orchard, finer than this one, you'll see it, you'll understand; and joy, quiet, deep joy will sink into your heart, like the sun at evening, and you'll smile, Mama! Come, darling, come on!

ACT IV

The same setting as in Act I. There are neither curtains on the windows nor are there any pictures on the walls. Only a little furniture remains piled up in one corner as if for sale. A sense of emptiness is felt. Near the outer door, at the rear of the stage, is a pile of suitcases, traveling bags, and so on. The door on the left is open, and through it VARYA's *and* ANYA's *voices are heard.* LOPA-HIN *is standing waiting.* YASHA *is holding a tray with glasses of champagne. In the hall* EPIHODOFF *is tying up a box, offstage at the rear there is a hum. It is the peasants who have come to say good-by.* GAYEFF's *voice: "Thanks, brothers, thank you."*

YASHA: The simple folk have come to say good-by. I am of the opinion, Yermolay Alex-eevich, that the people are kind enough but don't understand anything.

(*The hum subsides.* LYUBOFF ANDREEVNA *enters through the hall with* GAYEFF; *she is not crying, but is pale, her face quivers, she is not able to speak.*)

GAYEFF: You gave them your purse, Lyuba. Mustn't do that! Mustn't do that

LYUBOFF ANDREEVNA: I couldn't help it! I couldn't help it!

(*Both go out.*)

LOPAHIN (*calling through the door after them*): Please, I humbly beg you! A little glass at parting. I didn't think to bring some from town, and at the station I found just one bottle. Please! (*A pause.*) Well, then, ladies and gentlemen! You don't want it? (*Moving away from the door.*) If I'd known that, I wouldn't have bought it. Well, then I won't drink any either. (YASHA *carefully sets the tray down on a chair.*) At least, you have some, Yasha.

YASHA: To those who are departing! Pleasant days to those who stay behind! (*Drinking.*) This champagne is not the real stuff, I can assure you.

LOPAHIN: Eight roubles a bottle. (*A pause.*) It's devilish cold in here.

YASHA: They didn't heat up today, we are leaving anyway. (*Laughing.*)

LOPAHIN: What are you laughing about?

YASHA: For joy.

LOPAHIN: Outside it's October, but it's sunny and still, like summer. Good for build-ing. (*Looking at his watch, then through the door.*) Ladies and gentlemen, bear in mind we have forty-six minutes in all till train time! Which means you have to go to the station in twenty minutes. Hurry up a little.

TROFIMOFF (*in an overcoat, entering from outside*): Seems to me it is time to go. The carriages are ready. The devil knows where my rubbers are. They've disappeared. (*In the door.*) Anya, my rubbers are not here! I can't find them.

LOPAHIN: And I have to go to Harkoff. I'm going on the same train with you. I'm going to live in Harkoff all winter. I've been dilly-dal-lying along with you, I'm tired of doing nothing. I can't be without work, look, I don't know what to do with my hands here, see, they are dangling somehow, as if they didn't belong to me.

TROFIMOFF: We are leaving right away, and you'll set about your useful labors again.

LOPAHIN: Here, drink a glass.

TROFIMOFF: I shan't.

LOPAHIN: It's to Moscow now?

TROFIMOFF: Yes. I'll see them off to town, and tomorrow to Moscow.

LOPAHIN: Yes — Maybe the professors are not giving their lectures. I imagine they are waiting till you arrive.

TROFIMOFF: That's none of your business.

LOPAHIN: How many years is it you've been studying at the University?

TROFIMOFF: Think of something newer. This is old and flat. (*Looking for his rubbers.*) You know, perhaps, we shall not see each other again; therefore, permit me to give you one piece of advice at parting! Don't wave your arms! Cure yourself of that habit — of arm waving. And also of building summer cottages, figuring that the summer residents will in time become individual landowners; figuring like that is arm waving too — Just the same, however, I like you. You have delicate soft fingers like an artist, you have a delicate soft heart —

LOPAHIN (*embracing him*): Good-by, my

dear boy. Thanks for everything. If you need it, take some money from me for the trip.

TROFIMOFF: Why should I? There's no need for it.

LOPAHIN: But you haven't any!

TROFIMOFF: I have. Thank you. I got some for a translation. Here it is in my pocket. (*Anxiously.*) But my rubbers are gone.

VARYA (*from another room*): Take your nasty things! (*Throws a pair of rubbers on to the stage.*)

TROFIMOFF: But what are you angry about, Varya? Hm — Why, these are not my rubbers.

LOPAHIN: In the spring I planted twenty-seven hundred acres of poppies and now I've made forty thousand clear. And when my poppies were in bloom, what a picture it was! So look, as I say, I've made forty thousand, which means I'm offering you a loan because I can afford to. Why turn up your nose? I'm a peasant — I speak straight out.

TROFIMOFF: Your father was a peasant, mine — an apothecary — and from that absolutely nothing follows. (LOPAHIN *takes out his wallet.*) Leave it alone, leave it alone — If you gave me two hundred thousand even, I wouldn't take it. I am a free man. And everything that you all value so highly and dearly, both rich man and beggars, has not the slightest power over me, it's like a mere feather floating in the air. I can get along without you, I can pass you by, I am strong and proud. Humanity is moving toward the loftiest truth, toward the loftiest happiness that is possible on earth and I am in the front ranks.

LOPAHIN: Will you get there?

TROFIMOFF: I'll get there. (*A pause.*) I'll get there, or I'll show the others the way to get there.

(*In the distance is heard the sound of an ax on a tree.*)

LOPAHIN: Well, good-by, my dear boy. It's time to go. We turn up our noses at one another, but life keeps on passing. When I work a long time without stopping, my thoughts are clearer, and it seems as if I, too, know what I exist for, and, brother, how many people are there in Russia who exist, nobody knows for what? Well, all the same, it's not that that keeps things circulating. Leonid Andreevich, they say, has accepted a position — he'll be in a bank, six thousand a year —

the only thing is he won't stay there, he's very lazy —

ANYA (*in the doorway*): Mama begs of you until she's gone, not to cut down the orchard.

TROFIMOFF: Honestly, haven't you enough tact to — (*Goes out through the hall.*)

LOPAHIN: Right away, right away — What people, really! (*Goes out after him.*)

ANYA: Has Fiers been sent to the hospital?

YASHA: I told them to this morning. They must have sent him.

ANYA (*to* EPIHODOFF, *who is passing through the room*): Semyon Panteleevich, please inquire whether or not they have taken Fiers to the hospital.

YASHA (*huffily*): This morning, I told Igor. Why ask ten times over!

EPIHODOFF: The venerable Fiers, according to my conclusive opinion, is not worth mending, he ought to join his forefathers. And I can only envy him. (*Putting a suitcase on a hatbox and crushing it.*) Well, there you are, of course. I knew it. (*Goes out.*)

YASHA (*mockingly*): Twenty-two misfortunes —

VARYA (*on the other side of the door*): Have they taken Fiers to the hospital?

ANYA: They have.

VARYA: Then why didn't they take the letter to the doctor?

ANYA: We must send it on after *them* — (*Goes out.*)

VARYA (*from the next room*): Where is Yasha? Tell him his mother has come, she wants to say good-by to him.

YASHA (*waving his hand*): They merely try my patience.

(DUNYASHA *has been busying herself with the luggage; now when* YASHA *is left alone, she goes up to him.*)

DUNYASHA: If you'd only look at me once, Yasha. You are going away — leaving me — (*Crying and throwing herself on his neck.*)

YASHA: Why are you crying? (*Drinking champagne.*) In six days I'll be in Paris again. Tomorrow we will board the express train and dash off out of sight; somehow, I can't believe it. *Vive la France!* It doesn't suit me here — I can't live here — Can't help that. I've seen enough ignorance — enough for me. (*Drinking champagne.*) Why do you cry? Behave yourself properly, then you won't be crying.

DUNYASHA (*powdering her face, looking into*

a small mirror): Send me a letter from Paris. I loved you, Yasha, you know, loved you so! I am a tender creature, Yasha!

YASHA: They are coming here. (*Bustling about near the suitcases, humming low.*)

(LYUBOFF ANDREEVNA, GAYEFF, ANYA *and* CHARLOTTA IVANOVNA *enter.*)

GAYEFF: We should be going. There is very little time left. (*Looking at* YASHA.) Who is it smells like herring!

LYUBOFF ANDREEVNA: In about ten minutes let's be in the carriage — (*Glancing around the room.*) Good-by, dear house, old Grandfather. Winter will pass, spring will be here, but you won't be here any longer, they'll tear you down. How much these walls have seen! (*Kissing her daughter warmly.*) My treasure, you are beaming, your eyes are dancing like two diamonds. Are you happy? Very?

ANYA: Very! It's the beginning of a new life, Mama!

GAYEFF (*gaily*): Yes, indeed, everything is fine now. Before the sale of the cherry orchard, we all were troubled, distressed, and then when the question was settled definitely, irrevocably, we all calmed down and were even cheerful — I'm a bank official. I am a financier now — Yellow ball into the side pocket, anyway, Lyuba, you look better, no doubt about that.

LYUBOFF ANDREEVNA: Yes. My nerves are better, that's true. (*They hand her her hat and coat.*) I sleep well. Carry out my things, Yasha. It's time. (*To* ANYA.) My little girl, we shall see each other again soon — I am going to Paris, I shall live there on the money your Yaroslavl great-aunt sent for the purchase of the estate — long live Great-aunt! But that money won't last long.

ANYA: Mama, you'll come back soon, soon — Isn't that so? I'll prepare myself, pass the examination at high school, and then I'll work, I will help you. We'll read all sorts of books together. Mama, isn't that so? (*Kissing her mother's hands.*) We'll read in the autumn evenings, read lots of books, and a new, wonderful world will open up before us — (*Daydreaming.*) Mama, do come —

LYUBOFF ANDREEVNA: I'll come, my precious. (*Embracing her daughter.*)

(LOPAHIN *enters with* CHARLOTTA *who is softly humming a song.*)

GAYEFF: Lucky Charlotta: she's singing!

CHARLOTTA (*taking a bundle that looks like a baby wrapped up*): My baby, bye, bye — (*A baby's cry is heard: Ooah, ooah — !* Hush, my darling, my dear little boy. (*Ooah, ooah — !*) I am so sorry for you! (*Throwing the bundle back.*) Will you please find me a position? I cannot go on like this.

LOPAHIN: We will find something, Charlotta Ivanovna, don't worry.

GAYEFF: Everybody is dropping us, Varya is going away. — All of a sudden we are not needed.

CHARLOTTA: I have no place in town to live. I must go away. (*Humming.*) It's all the same —

(PISHTCHIK *enters.*)

LOPAHIN: The freak of nature — !

PISHTCHIK (*out of breath*): Ugh, let me catch my breath — I'm exhausted — My honored friends — Give me some water —

GAYEFF: After money, I suppose? This humble servant will flee from sin! (*Goes out.*)

PISHTCHIK: It's a long time since I was here — Most beautiful lady — (*To* LOPAHIN.) You here — ? Glad to see you — a man of the greatest intellect — Here — Take it — (*Giving* LOPAHIN *some money.*) Four hundred roubles — That leaves eight hundred and forty I still owe you —

LOPAHIN (*with astonishment, shrugging his shoulders*): I must be dreaming. But where did you get it?

PISHTCHIK: Wait — I'm hot — Most extraordinary event. Some Englishmen came and found on my land some kind of white clay — (*To* LYUBOFF ANDREEVNA.) And four hundred for you — Beautiful lady — Wonderful lady — (*Handing over the money.*) The rest later. (*Taking a drink of water.*) Just now a young man was saying on the train that some great philosopher recommends jumping off roofs — "Jump!" he says, and "therein lies the whole problem." (*With astonishment.*) You don't say! Water!

LOPAHIN: And what Englishmen were they?

PISHTCHIK: I leased them the parcel of land with the clay for twenty-four years — And now, excuse me, I haven't time — I must run along — I'm going to Znoykoff's — To Kardamonoff's — I owe everybody — (*Drinking.*) I wish you well — I'll drop in on Thursday —

LYUBOFF ANDREEVNA: We are moving to

town right away, and tomorrow I'm going abroad —

PISHTCHIK: What? (*Alarmed.*) Why to town? That's why I see furniture — Suitcases — Well, no matter — (*Tearfully.*) No matter — Men of the greatest minds — those Englishmen — No matter — Good luck! God will help you — No matter — Everything in this world comes to an end — (*Kissing* LYUBOFF ANDREEVNA'S *hand.*) And should the report reach you that my end has come, think of that well-known horse and say: "There was once on earth a so and so — Semyonoff Pishtchik — The kingdom of Heaven be his." Most remarkable weather — yes — (*Going out greatly disconcerted, but immediately returning and speaking from the door.*) Dashenka sends her greetings! (*Goes out.*)

LYUBOFF ANDREEVNA: And now we can go. I am leaving with two worries. First, that Fiers is sick. (*Glancing at her watch.*) We still have five minutes —

ANYA: Mama, Fiers has already been sent to the hospital. Yasha sent him off this morning.

LYUBOFF ANDREEVNA: My second worry — is Varya. She is used to getting up early and working, and now without any work she is like a fish out of water. She has grown thin, pale and cries all the time, poor thing — (*A pause.*) You know this, Yermolay Alexeevich: I dreamed — of marrying her to you. And there was every sign of your getting married.(*Whispering to* ANYA, *who beckons to* CHARLOTTA; *both go out.*) She loves you, you are fond of her, and I don't know, don't know why it is you seem to avoid each other — I don't understand it!

LOPAHIN: I don't understand it either, I must confess. It's all strange somehow — If there's still time, I am ready right now even — Let's finish it up — and *basta*, but without you I feel I won't propose.

LYUBOFF ANDREEVNA: But that's excellent. Surely it takes only a minute. I'll call her at once.

LOPAHIN: And to fit the occasion there's the champagne. (*Looking at the glasses.*) Empty, somebody has already drunk them. (YASHA *coughs.*) That's what's called lapping it up —

LYUBOFF ANDREEVNA (*vivaciously*): Splendid! We'll go out — Yasha, *allez!* I'll call her — (*Through the door.*) Varya, drop everything and come here. Come on! (*Goes out with* YASHA.)

LOPAHIN (*looking at his watch*): Yes —

(*A pause. Behind the door you hear smothered laughter, whispering, finally* VARYA *enters.*)

VARYA (*looking at the luggage a long time*): That's strange, I just can't find it —

LOPAHIN: What are you looking for?

VARYA: I packed it myself and don't remember where. (*A pause.*)

LOPAHIN: Where do you expect to go now, Varvara Mikhailovna?

VARYA: I? To Regulin's. I agreed to go there to look after the house — As a sort of housekeeper.

LOPAHIN: That's in Yashnevo? It's nigh on to seventy miles. (*A pause.*) And here ends life in this house —

VARYA (*examining the luggage*): But where is it? Either I put it in the trunk, perhaps — Yes, life in this house is ended — it won't be any more—

LOPAHIN: And I am going to Harkoff now — By the next train. I've a lot to do. And I am leaving Epihodoff — on the ground here — I've hired him.

VARYA: Well!

LOPAHIN: Last year at this time it had already been snowing, if you remember, and now it's quiet, it's sunny. It's only that it's cold, about three degrees of frost.

VARYA: I haven't noticed. (*A pause.*) And besides our thermometer is broken — (*A pause. A voice from the yard through the door.*) Yermolay Alexeevich —

LOPAHIN (*as if he had been expecting this call for a long time*): This minute! (*Goes out quickly.*)

(VARYA, *sitting on the floor, putting her head on a bundle of clothes, sobs quietly. The door opens,* LYUBOFF ANDREEVNA *enters cautiously.*)

VARYA (*she is not crying any longer, and has wiped her eyes*): Yes, it's time, Mama. I can get to Regulin's today, if we are just not too late for the train — (*Through the door.*) Anya, put your things on! (ANYA, *then* GAYEFF *and* CHARLOTTA IVANOVNA *enter.* GAYEFF *has on a warm overcoat, with a hood. The servants gather, also the drivers.* EPIHODOFF *busies himself with the luggage.*) Now we can be on our way.

ANYA (*joyfully*): On our way!

GAYEFF: My friends, my dear, kind friends! Leaving this house forever, can I remain silent, can I restrain myself from expressing, as we say, farewell, those feelings that fill now my whole being —

ANYA (*beseechingly*): Uncle!

VARYA: Dear Uncle, don't!

GAYEFF (*dejectedly*): Bank the yellow into the side pocket — I am silent —

(TROFIMOFF *and then* LOPAHIN *enter.*)

TROFIMOFF: Well, ladies and gentlemen, it's time to go!

LOPAHIN: Epihodoff, my coat!

LYUBOFF ANDREEVNA: I'll sit here just a minute more. It's as if I had never seen before what the walls in this house are like, what kind of ceilings, and now I look at them greedily, with such tender love —

GAYEFF: I remember when I was six years old, on Trinity Day, I sat in this window and watched my father going to Church —

LYUBOFF ANDREEVNA: Are all the things taken out?

LOPAHIN: Everything, I think. (*Putting on his overcoat. To* EPIHODOFF.) Epihodoff, you see that everything is in order.

EPIHODOFF (*talking in a hoarse voice*): Don't worry, Yermolay Alexeevich!

LOPAHIN: Why is your voice like that?

EPIHODOFF: Just drank some water, swallowed something.

YASHA (*with contempt*): The ignorance —

LYUBOFF ANDREEVNA: We are going and there won't be a soul left here —

LOPAHIN: Till spring.

VARYA (*she pulls an umbrella out from a bundle, it looks as if she were going to hit someone;* LOPAHIN *pretends to be frightened*): What do you, what do you — I never thought of it.

TROFIMOFF: Ladies and gentlemen, let's get in the carriages — It's time! The train is coming any minute.

VARYA: Petya, here they are, your rubbers, by the suitcase. (*Tearfully.*) And how dirty yours are, how old — !

TROFIMOFF (*putting on the rubbers*): Let's go, ladies and gentlemen!

GAYEFF (*greatly embarrassed, afraid he will cry*): The train — The station — Cross into the side, combination off the white into the corner —

LYUBOFF ANDREEVNA: Let's go!

LOPAHIN: Everybody here? Nobody there? (*Locking the side door on the left.*) Things are stored here, it must be locked up, let's go!

ANYA: Good-by, house! Good-by, the old life!

TROFIMOFF: Long live the new life!

(*Goes out with* ANYA. VARYA *casts a glance around the room and, without hurrying, goes out.* YASHA *and* CHARLOTTA, *with her dog, go out.*)

LOPAHIN: And so, till spring. Out, ladies and gentlemen — Till we meet. (*Goes out.*)

(LYUBOFF ANDREEVNA *and* GAYEFF *are left alone. As if they had been waiting for this, they throw themselves on one another's necks sobbing, but smothering their sobs as if afraid of being heard.*)

GAYEFF (*in despair*): Oh, Sister, Sister —

LYUBOFF ANDREEVNA: Oh, my dear, my lovely, beautiful orchard! My life, my youth, my happiness, good-by!

ANYA (ANYA'*s voice, gaily, appealingly*): Mama — !

TROFIMOFF (TROFIMOFF'*s voice, gaily, excitedly*): Aaooch!

LYUBOFF ANDREEVNA: For the last time, just to look at the walls, at the window — My dear mother used to love to walk around in this room —

GAYEFF: Oh, Sister, Sister — !

ANYA (ANYA'*s voice*): Mama — !

TROFIMOFF (TROFIMOFF'*s voice*): Aaooch — !

LYUBOFF ANDREEVNA: We are coming! (*They go out.*)

(*The stage is empty. You hear the keys locking all the doors, then the carriages drive off. It grows quiet. In the silence you hear the dull thud of an ax on a tree, a lonely, mournful sound. Footsteps are heard. From the door on the right* FIERS *appears. He is dressed as usual, in a jacket and a white waistcoat, slippers on his feet. He is sick.*)

FIERS (*going to the door and trying the knob*): Locked. They've gone. (*Sitting down on the sofa.*) They forgot about me — No matter — I'll sit here awhile — And Leonid Andreevich, for sure, didn't put on his fur coat, he went off with his top coat — (*Sighing anxiously.*) And I didn't see to it — The young saplings! (*He mutters something that cannot be understood.*) Life has gone by, as if I hadn't lived at all — (*Lying down.*) I'll lie down awhile — You haven't got any strength, nothing is left, nothing — Ach, you — good-for-nothing — (*He lies still.*)

(*There is a far-off sound as if out of the sky, the sound of a snapped string, dying away, sad. A stillness falls, and there is only the thud of an ax on a tree, far away in the orchard.*)

At the end of *The Cherry Orchard*, the old servant Fiers, forgotten by the family he has long served, wanders onto the stage, locked within the house that is no longer theirs. Is he comic, in his mutterings, in his old maidish frettings about Leonid Andreevich's inadequate coat, and in his implicit realization that although he is concerned about the aristocrats the aristocrats are unconcerned about him? Or is he tragic, dying in isolation? Or neither? The comedy is scarcely uproarious; if there is humor in his realization that his life has been trivial, this humor is surely tinged with melancholy. And the "tragic" reading is also ambiguous: first, the text does not say that he dies; second, if it can be assumed that he dies, the death of an ill eighty-seven-year-old man can scarcely seem untimely; and third, Fiers does not seem particularly concerned about dying.

If this play ends with a death, then, it is not the sort of death that Byron had in mind when he said, "All tragedies are finished by a death, / All comedies are ended by a marriage." We are in the dramatic world that Shaw spoke of when he said that "the curtain no longer comes down on a hero slain or married: it comes down when the audience has seen enough of the life presented to it, . . . and must either leave the theatre or miss its last train." Chekhov insisted that *The Cherry Orchard* was a comedy, but what sort of comedy? In the latter part of the last act there is almost a proposal of marriage, but, typically, it never gets made. For two years everyone has joked about the anticipated marriage between Lopahin and Varya, but when these two are thrust together they are overcome by embarrassment, and the interview is dissipated in small talk. Not that (of course) a comedy must end with a marriage; marriage is only the conventional way of indicating a happy union, or reunion, that symbolizes the triumph of life. But in this play we *begin* with a reunion — the family is reunited in the ancestral home — and we end with a separation, the inhabitants scattering when the home is sold.

Another way of getting at *The Cherry Orchard* is to notice that in this play, although there are innumerable references to Time between the first speech, when Lopahin says "The train got in, thank God! What time is it?" and the last act, where there is much talk about catching the outbound train, Time does not function as it usually functions either in tragedy or in comedy. In tragedy we usually feel, If there had only been more time. . . . For example, in *Romeo and Juliet* Friar Laurence writes a letter to Romeo, explaining that Juliet will take a potion that will put her in a temporary, death-like trance, but the letter is delayed, Romeo mistakenly hears that Juliet is dead, and he kills himself. A few moments after his suicide Juliet revives. Had Friar

Laurence's message arrived on schedule, or had Romeo not been so quick to commit suicide, no great harm would have been done. In *King Lear*, Edmund repents that he has ordered a soldier to kill Cordelia, and a messenger hurries out to change the order, but he is too late.

If in tragedy we usually feel the pressure of time, in comedy there is usually a sense of leisure. Things are difficult now, but in the course of time they will work themselves out. Sooner or later people will realize that the strange goings-on are due to the existence of identical twins; sooner or later the stubborn parents will realize that they cannot forever stand in the way of young lovers; sooner or later the money will turn up and all will be well. In the world of comedy, one is always safe in relying on time. In *The Cherry Orchard*, Lopahin insists, correctly enough, that the family must act *now* if it is to save the orchard: "We must decide definitely, time won't wait." There is ample time to act on Lopahin's suggestion that the orchard be leased for summer houses, and the play covers a period from May to October, but the plan is not acted on because to the aristocrats any sort of selling is unthinkable, and although one Pishtchik is in the course of time miraculously redeemed from financial ruin by some Englishmen who discover and buy "some kind of white clay" on *his* land, time brings Mme. Ranevskaya and her brother Gayeff no such good fortune. So far as the main happenings in the play are concerned, time neither presses nor preserves; it only passes.

During the passage of time in this play, the orchard is lost (tragic?) and the characters reveal themselves to be funny (comic?). The loss of the orchard is itself a happening of an uncertain kind. It stands, partly, for the end of an old way of life. But if that way once included intelligent and gracious aristocrats, it also included slavery, and in any case it now is embodied in the irresponsible heirs we see on the stage, Mme. Ranevskaya and her brother Gayeff, along with their deaf and near-senile servant Fiers. For Gayeff the orchard is important chiefly because it lends prestige, since it is mentioned in the encyclopedia. Mme. Ranevskaya sees more to it. For her it is "all white" and it is "young again and full of happiness"; we are momentarily touched by her vision, but there is yet another way of seeing the orchard: for Trofimoff, a student who envisions a new society as an orchard for all men, the ancestral cherry orchard is haunted by the serfs of the bad old days. Moreover, although the orchard is much talked about, it seems to have decayed to a trivial ornament. Long ago its crop was regularly harvested, pickled, and sold, thus providing food and income, but now "nobody remembers" the pickling formula and nobody buys the crop. There seems to be some truth to Lopahin's assertion that "the only remarkable thing about this cherry orchard is that it's very big," and although one must point out that this remark is made by a despised merchant, Lopahin is neither a fool nor the "money grubber" that Gayeff thinks he is. Lopahin delights in nature put to use. He made "forty thousand clear" from poppies, "And when my poppies were in bloom, what a picture it was!" His enthusiasm for the flowers is undercut for us only a little, if at all, by the fact that they were of use to him and to others.

Lopahin's serious concern, whether for his poppies or for the future of the cherry orchard, contrasts interestingly with Mme. Ranevskaya's and with Gayeff's sporadic passion for the orchard. Mme. Ranevskaya says, "I can't imagine my life without the cherry orchard," and she doubtless means what she says, but that her words have not much relation to reality is indicated by her meaningless addition, "If it is very necessary to sell it, then sell me along with the orchard." After the orchard has been sold, Gayeff confesses, "everything is fine now. Before the sale of the cherry orchard, we all were troubled, distressed, and then when the question was settled definitely, irrevocably, we all calmed down and were even cheerful — I'm a bank official. . . . Lyuba, you look better, no doubt about that." His sister agrees: "Yes. My nerves are better, that's true. . . . I sleep well. Carry out my things, Yasha. It's time." She returns to her lover in Paris, Gayeff goes off to a job in the bank, and though we can imagine that the orchard will continue to be an occasional topic of conversation, we cannot imagine that the loss has in any way changed them. The play ends, but things will go on in the same way; neither a tragic nor a comic action has been completed.

The characters no less than the action are tragicomic. Their longings would touch the heart if only these people did not so quickly digress or engage in little actions that call their depth into doubt. Charlotta laments that she has no proper passport and that her deceased parents may not have been married: "Where I came from and who I am I don't know." And then, having touched on the mighty subject of one's identity, the subject that is the stuff of tragedy in which heroes endure the worst in order to know who they are, she begins to eat a cucumber, and somehow that simple and entirely necessary act diminishes her dignity — though it does not totally dissipate our glimpse of her alienation. In the same scene, when Epihodoff confesses that although he reads "all kinds of remarkable books" he "cannot discover [his] own inclinations," we hear another echo of the tragic hero's quest for self-knowledge, but we also hear an echo from the world of comedy, say of the pedant who guides his life by a textbook. Epihodoff, perhaps like a tragic hero, is particularly concerned with whether to live or to shoot himself, but this racking doubt is diminished by his prompt explanation that since he may someday decide on suicide, he always carries a revolver, which he proceeds to show to his listeners. Almost all of the characters bare their souls, but their slightly addled minds and their hungry bodies expose them to a gentle satirical treatment so that they evoke a curious amused pathos. One can, for example, sympathize with Mme. Ranevskaya's despair — but one cannot forget that she is scatterbrained and that domestic duties and local pieties occupy her mind only occasionally and that her disreputable lover in Paris means as much as the orchard she thinks she cannot live without. And when Gayeff says, "On my honor I'll swear, by anything you like, that the estate shall not be sold," we know that he has very little honor and even less ability to focus on the problem (mostly he takes refuge in thoughts about billiards, and somehow his habit of eating candy does not enhance his status in our eyes) and that the estate will be sold.

Finally, something must be said about the ambiguous treatment of the future. We know, from his correspondence, that Chekhov looked forward to a new and happier society. Russia, like much of the rest of Europe, was ceasing to be an agrarian society, but if the death throes were evident, one could not be so confident about the birth pangs. Something of the presence of two worlds is hinted at in the stage direction at the beginning of the second act, where we see the estate with its orchard, and also "in the distance a row of telegraph poles; and far, far away, faintly traced on the horizon, is a large town." The telegraph poles and the town silently represent the new industrial society, but Trofimoff the student speaks at length of the glorious possibilities of the future, and his speeches were sufficiently close to the bone for the censor to delete two passages sharply critical of the present. But we cannot take Trofimoff's speeches quite at face value. He is a student, but he is almost thirty and still has not received his degree. His speeches in Act II are moving, especially those on the need to work rather than to talk if the future is to be better than the past, but we cannot quite rid ourselves of the suspicion that Trofimoff talks rather than works. Certainly he is contemptuous of the merchant Lopahin, who delights in work. And, worse, Trofimoff frets too much about his overshoes, thinks he is "above love," and is so confounded by Mme. Ranevskaya's remark, "Imagine, at your age, not having a mistress," that he falls down a flight of stairs. None of these personal failings invalidates his noble view of the future; certainly none of them turns this view into a comic pipedream, and yet all of these things, along with a certain nostalgia that we feel for the past, do suffuse even his noblest statements about the future with a delicate irony that puts them, along with the much praised but totally neglected cherry orchard, firmly in the tragicomic world. One understands why Chekhov called the play a comedy, and one understands why Stanislavsky (who directed the first production and played the part of Gayeff) told Chekhov, "It is definitely not a comedy . . . but a tragedy." Perhaps neither of the men fully wanted to see the resonant ambiguities in the play.

HENRY IV

A Tragedy in Three Acts

Luigi Pirandello

English version by Edward Storer

Luigi Pirandello (1867–1936) was born in Sicily, the son of the owner of a profitable sulfur mine. Pirandello studied at Rome and then at Bonn, where in 1891 he received a doctorate for a thesis on Sicilian dialect. Back in Rome he wrote poetry, fiction, and literary criticism, and taught Italian at a teachers college. Troubles came thick: his family, and his wife's, suffered financial setbacks, and his wife became intermittently insane. But from 1917 onward he had great success in the theater with many of his forty or so plays. Among the best-known plays are *Right You Are (If You Think You Are)* (1917), *Six Characters in Search of an Author* (1921), and *Henry IV* (1922). In 1934 Pirandello was awarded the Nobel Prize. Curiously, this philosophic skeptic was a supporter of Italian fascism, and he gave his Nobel medal to be melted down for Mussolini's Abyssinian campaign.

CHARACTERS

HENRY IV
THE MARCHIONESS MATILDA SPINA
FRIDA, *her daughter*
CHARLES DI NOLLI, *the young* Marquis
BARON TITO BELCREDI
DOCTOR DIONYSIUS GENONI
HAROLD [FRANCO] ⎫
LANDOLPH [LOLO] ⎪ *The four private counselors*
ORDULPH [MOMO] ⎬ *(The names in brackets are*
BERTHOLD [FINO] ⎭ *nicknames)*
JOHN, *the old waiter*
THE TWO VALETS *in* Costume

A Solitary Villa in Italy in Our Own Time

Torch Theatre Production of *Henry IV*, London, 1939. (Photograph: Angus McBean. Harvard Theatre Collection.)

ACT I

*Salon in the villa, furnished and decorated
so as to look exactly like the throne room of
Henry IV in the royal residence at Goslar.
Among the antique decorations there are
two modern life-size portraits in oil painting.
They are placed against the back wall, and
mounted in a wooden stand that runs the
whole length of the wall. (It is wide and
protrudes, so that it is like a large bench.)
One of the paintings is on the right; the
other on the left of the throne, which is in
the middle of the wall and divides the
stand.*

The Imperial chair and Baldachin.

*The two portraits represent a lady and a
gentleman, both young, dressed up in carnival costumes: one as "Henry IV," the other
as the "Marchioness Matilda of Tuscany."
Exits to right and left.*

When the curtain goes up, the TWO
VALETS *jump down, as if surprised, from the
stand on which they have been lying, and go
and take their positions, as rigid as statues,
on either side below the throne with their
halberds in their hands. Soon after, from the
second exit, right, enter* HAROLD, LANDOLPH,
ORDULPH *and* BERTHOLD, *young men employed by the* MARQUIS CHARLES DI NOLLI *to
play the part of "Secret Counsellors" at the
court of "Henry IV." They are, therefore,
dressed like German knights of the XIth
century.* BERTHOLD, *nicknamed* FINO, *is just
entering on his duties for the first time. His
companions are telling him what he has to
do and amusing themselves at his expense.
The scene is to be played rapidly and
vivaciously.*

LANDOLPH (*to* BERTHOLD *as if explaining*):
And this is the throne room.

HAROLD: At Goslar.

ORDULPH: Or at the castle in the Hartz, if
you prefer.

HAROLD: Or at Wurms.

LANDOLPH: According as to what's doing, it
jumps about with us, now here, now there.

ORDULPH: In Saxony.

HAROLD: In Lombardy.

LANDOLPH: On the Rhine.

ONE OF THE VALETS (*without moving, just
opening his lips*): I say . . .

HAROLD (*turning round*): What is it?

FIRST VALET (*like a statue*): Is he coming in
or not? (*He alludes to* HENRY IV.)

ORDULPH: No, no, he's asleep. You needn't
worry.

SECOND VALET (*releasing his pose, taking a
long breath and going to lie down again on the
stand*): You might have told us at once.

FIRST VALET (*going over to* HAROLD): Have
you got a match, please?

LANDOLPH: What? You can't smoke a pipe
here, you know.

FIRST VALET (*while* HAROLD *offers him a
light*): No; a cigarette. (*Lights his cigarette
and lies down again on the stand.*)

BERTHOLD (*who has been looking on in
amazement, walking round in the room, regarding the costumes of the others*): I say
. . . this room . . . these costumes . . . Which
Henry IV is it? I don't quite get it. Is he
Henry IV of France or not? (*At this* LAN-
DOLPH, HAROLD, *and* ORDULPH, *burst out
laughing.*)

LANDOLPH (*still laughing; and pointing to*
BERTHOLD *as if inviting the others to make fun
of him*): Henry of France he says: ha! ha!

ORDULPH: He thought it was the king of
France!

HAROLD: Henry IV of Germany, my boy:
the Salian dynasty!

ORDULPH: The great and tragic Emperor!

LANDOLPH: He of Canossa. Every day we
carry on here the terrible war between Church
and State, by Jove.

ORDULPH: The Empire against the Papacy!

HAROLD: Antipopes against the Pope!

LANDOLPH: Kings against anti-kings!

ORDULPH: War on the Saxons!

HAROLD: And all the rebels Princes!

LANDOLPH: Against the Emperor's own sons!

BERTHOLD (*covering his head with his hands to protect himself against this avalanche of information*): I understand! I understand! Naturally, I didn't get the idea at first. I'm right then: these aren't costumes of the XVIth century?

HAROLD: XVIth century be hanged!

ORDULPH: We're somewhere between a thousand and eleven hundred.

LANDOLPH: Work it out for yourself: if we are before Canossa on the 25th of January, 1071 . . .

BERTHOLD (*more confused than ever*): Oh my God! What a mess I've made of it!

ORDULPH: Well, just slightly, if you supposed you were at the French court.

BERTHOLD: All that historical stuff I've swatted up!

LANDOLPH: My dear boy, it's four hundred years earlier.

BERTHOLD (*getting angry*): Good Heavens! You ought to have told me it was Germany and not France. I can't tell you how many books I've read in the last fifteen days.

HAROLD: But I say, surely you knew that poor Tito was Adalbert of Bremen, here?

BERTHOLD: Not a damned bit!

LANDOLPH: Well, don't you see how it is? When Tito died, the Marquis Di Nolli . . .

BERTHOLD: Oh, it was he, was it? He might have told me.

HAROLD: Perhaps he thought you knew.

LANDOLPH: He didn't want to engage anyone else in substitution. He thought the remaining three of us would do. But *he* began to cry out: "With Adalbert driven away . . .": because, you see, he didn't imagine poor Tito was dead; but that, as Bishop Adalbert, the rival bishops of Cologne and Mayence had driven him off . . .

BERTHOLD (*taking his head in his hand*): But I don't know a word of what you're talking about.

ORDULPH: So much the worse for you, my boy!

HAROLD: But the trouble is that not even we know who you are.

BERTHOLD: What? Not even you? You don't know who I'm supposed to be?

ORDULPH: Hum! "Berthold."

BERTHOLD: But which Berthold? And why Berthold?

LANDOLPH (*solemnly imitating* HENRY IV): "They've driven Adalbert away from me. Well then, I want Berthold! I want Berthold!" That's what he said.

HAROLD: We three looked one another in the eyes: who's got to be Berthold?

ORDULPH: And so here you are, "Berthold," my dear fellow!

LANDOLPH: I'm afraid you will make a bit of a mess of it.

BERTHOLD (*indignant, getting ready to go*): Ah, no! Thanks very much, but I'm off! I'm out of this!

HAROLD (*restraining him with the other two, amid laughter*): Steady now! Don't get excited!

LANDOLPH: Cheer up, my dear fellow! We don't any of us know who we are really. He's Harold; he's Ordulph; I'm Landolph! That's the way he calls us. We've got used to it. But who are we? Names of the period! Yours, too, is a name of the period: Berthold! Only one of us, poor Tito, had got a really decent part, as you can read in history: that of the Bishop of Bremen. He was just like a real bishop. Tito did it awfully well, poor chap!

HAROLD: Look at the study he put into it!

LANDOLPH: Why, he even ordered his Majesty about, opposed his views, guided and counselled him. We're "secret counsellors" — in a manner of speaking only; because it is written in history that Henry IV was hated by the upper aristocracy for surrounding himself at court with young men of the bourgeoise.

ORDULPH: Us, that is.

LANDOLPH: Yes, small devoted vassals, a bit dissolute and very gay . . .

BERTHOLD: So I've got to be gay as well?

HAROLD: I should say so! Same as we are!

ORDULPH: And it isn't too easy, you know.

LANDOLPH: It's a pity; because the way we're got up, we could do a fine historical reconstruction. There's any amount of material in the story of Henry IV. But, as a matter of fact, we do nothing. We have the form without the content. We're worse than the real secret counsellors of Henry IV; because certainly no one had given them a part to play — at any rate, they didn't feel they had a part to play. It was their life. They looked after their own interests at the expense of others, sold investitures and — what not! We stop here in this magnificent court — for what? — Just doing nothing. We're like so many puppets hung on the wall, waiting for some one to come and move us or make us talk.

HAROLD: Ah, no, old sport, not quite that! We've got to give the proper answer, you know. There's trouble if he asks you something and you don't chip in with the cue.

LANDOLPH: Yes, that's true.

BERTHOLD: Don't rub it in too hard! How the devil am I to give him the proper answer, if I've swatted up Henry IV of France, and now he turns out to be Henry IV of Germany? (The other three laugh.)

HAROLD: You'd better start and prepare yourself at once.

ORDULPH: We'll help you out.

HAROLD: We've got any amount of books on the subject. A brief run through the main points will do to begin with.

ORDULPH: At any rate, you must have got some sort of general idea.

HAROLD: Look here! (Turns him around and shows him the portrait of the MARCHIONESS MATILDA on the wall.) Who's that?

BERTHOLD (looking at it): That? Well, the thing seems to me somewhat out of place, anyway: two modern paintings in the midst of all this respectable antiquity!

HAROLD: You're right! They weren't there in the beginning. There are two niches there behind the pictures. They were going to put up two statues in the style of the period. Then the places were covered with those canvases there.

LANDOLPH (interrupting and continuing): They would certainly be out of place if they really were paintings!

BERTHOLD: What are they, if they aren't paintings?

LANDOLPH: Go and touch them! Pictures all right . . . but for him! (Makes a mysterious gesture to the right, alluding to HENRY IV.) . . . who never touches them! . . .

BERTHOLD: No? What are they for him?

LANDOLPH: Well, I'm only supposing, you know; but I imagine I'm about right. They're images such as . . . well — such as a mirror might throw back. Do you understand? That one there represents himself, as he is in this throne room, which is all in the style of the period. What's there to marvel at? If we put you before a mirror, won't you see yourself, alive, but dressed up in ancient costume? Well, it's as if there were two mirrors there, which cast back living images in the midst of a world which, as you well see, when you have lived with us, comes to life too.

BERTHOLD: I say, look here . . . I've no particular desire to go mad here.

HAROLD: Go mad, be hanged! You'll have a fine time!

BERTHOLD: Tell me this: how have you all managed to become so learned?

LANDOLPH: My dear fellow, you can't go back over 800 years of history without picking up a bit of experience.

HAROLD: Come on! Come on! You'll see how quickly you get into it!

ORDULPH: You'll learn wisdom, too, at this school.

BERTHOLD: Well, for Heaven's sake, help me a bit! Give me the main lines, anyway.

HAROLD: Leave it to us. We'll do it all between us.

LANDOLPH: We'll put your wires on you and fix you up like a first-class marionette. Come along! (They take him by the arm to lead him away.)

BERTHOLD (stopping and looking at the portrait on the wall): Wait a minute! You haven't told me who that is. The Emperor's wife?

HAROLD: No! The Emperor's wife is Bertha of Susa, the sister of Amadeus II of Savoy.

ORDULPH: And the Emperor, who wants to be young with us, can't stand her, and wants to put her away.

LANDOLPH: That is his most ferocious enemy: Matilda, Marchioness of Tuscany.

BERTHOLD: Ah, I've got it: the one who gave hospitality to the Pope!

LANDOLPH: Exactly: at Canossa!

ORDULPH: Pope Gregory VII!

HAROLD: Our bête noir! Come on! come on! (All four move toward the right to go out, when, from the left, the old servant JOHN enters in evening dress.)

JOHN (quickly, anxiously): Hss! Hss! Franco! Lolo!

HAROLD (turning round): What is it?

BERTHOLD (marvelling at seeing a man in modern clothes enter the throne room): Oh! I say, this is a bit too much, this chap here!

LANDOLPH: A man of the XXth century, here! Oh, go away! (They run over to him, pretending to menace him and throw him out.)

ORDULPH (heroically): Messenger of Gregory VII, away!

HAROLD: Away! Away!

JOHN (*annoyed, defending himself*): Oh, stop it! Stop it, I tell you!

ORDULPH: No, you can't set foot here!

HAROLD: Out with him!

LANDOLPH (*to* BERTHOLD): Magic, you know! He's a demon conjured up by the Wizard of Rome! Out with your swords! (*Makes as if to draw a sword.*)

JOHN (*shouting*): Stop it, will you? Don't play the fool with me! The Marquis has arrived with some friends . . .

LANDOLPH: Good! Good! Are there ladies too?

ORDULPH: Old or young?

JOHN: There are two gentlemen.

HAROLD: But the ladies, the ladies, who are they?

JOHN: The Marchioness and her daughter.

LANDOLPH (*surprised*): What do you say?

ORDULPH: The Marchioness?

JOHN: The Marchioness! The Marchioness!

HAROLD: Who are the gentlemen?

JOHN: I don't know.

HAROLD (*to* BERTHOLD): They're coming to bring us a message from the Pope, do you see?

ORDULPH: All messengers of Gregory VII! What fun!

JOHN: Will you let me speak, or not?

HAROLD: Go on, then!

JOHN: One of the two gentlemen is a doctor, I fancy.

LANDOLPH: Oh, I see, one of the usual doctors.

HAROLD: Bravo Berthold, you'll bring us luck!

LANDOLPH: You wait and see how we'll manage this doctor!

BERTHOLD: It looks as if I were going to get into a nice mess right away.

JOHN: If the gentlemen would allow me to speak . . . they want to come here into the throne room.

LANDOLPH (*surprised*): What? She? The Marchioness here?

HAROLD: Then this is something quite different! No play-acting this time!

LANDOLPH: We'll have a real tragedy: that's what!

BERTHOLD (*curious*): Why? Why?

ORDULPH (*pointing to the portrait*): She is that person there, don't you understand?

LANDOLPH: The daughter is the fiancée of the Marquis. But what have they come for, I should like to know?

ORDULPH: If he sees her, there'll be trouble.

LANDOLPH: Perhaps he won't recognize her any more.

JOHN: You must keep him there, if he should wake up . . .

ORDULPH: Easier said than done, by Jove!

HAROLD: You know what he's like!

JOHN: — even by force, if necessary! Those are my orders. Go on! Go on!

HAROLD: Yes, because who knows if he hasn't already wakened up?

ORDULPH: Come on then!

LANDOLPH (*going towards* JOHN *with the others*): You'll tell us later what it all means.

JOHN (*shouting after them*): Close the door there, and hide the key! That other door too. (*Pointing to the other door on right.*)

JOHN (*to the* TWO VALETS): Be off, you two! There! (*Pointing to exit right.*) Close the door after you, and hide the key!

(*The* TWO VALETS *go out by the first door on right.* JOHN *moves over to the left to show in:* DONNA MATILDA SPINA, *the young* MARCHIONESS FRIDA, DR. DIONYSIUS GENONI, *the* BARON TITO BELCREDI *and the young* MARQUIS CHARLES DI NOLLI, *who, as master of the house, enters last.*

DONNA MATILDA SPINA *is about 45, still handsome, although there are too patent signs of her attempts to remedy the ravages of time with make-up. Her head is thus rather like a Walkyrie. This facial make-up contrasts with her beautiful sad mouth. A widow for many years, she now has as her friend the* BARON TITO BELCREDI, *whom neither she nor anyone else takes seriously — at least so it would appear.*

What TITO BELCREDI *really is for her at bottom, he alone knows; and he is, therefore, entitled to laugh, if his friend feels the need of pretending not to know. He can always laugh at the jests which the beautiful* MARCHIONESS *makes with the others at his expense. He is slim, prematurely gray, and younger than she is. His head is bird-like in shape. He would be a very vivacious person, if his ductile agility (which among other things makes him a redoubtable swordsman) were not enclosed in a sheath of Arab-like laziness, which is revealed in his strange, nasal drawn-out voice.*

FRIDA, *the daughter of the* MARCHIONESS, *is 19. She is sad; because her imperious and too beautiful mother puts her in the shade,*

*and provokes facile gossip against her daugh-
ter as well as against herself. Fortunately for
her, she is engaged to the* MARQUIS CHARLES
DI NOLLI.

CHARLES DI NOLLI *is a stiff young man,
very indulgent towards others, but sure of
himself for what he amounts to in the
world. He is worried about all the responsibilities which he believes weigh on him. He
is dressed in deep mourning for the recent
death of his mother.*

DR. DIONYSIUS GENONI *has a bold rubicund
Satyr-like face, prominent eyes, a pointed
beard (which is silvery and shiny) and elegant manners. He is nearly bald. All enter
in a state of perturbation, almost as if afraid,
and all (except* DI NOLLI) *looking curiously
about the room. At first, they speak sotto
voce.)*

DI NOLLI (*to* JOHN): Have you given the
orders properly?

JOHN: Yes, my lord; don't be anxious about
that.

BELCREDI: Ah, magnificent! magnificent!

DOCTOR: How extremely interesting! Even in
the surroundings his raving madness — is perfectly taken into account!

DONNA MATILDA (*glancing round for her
portrait, discovers it, and goes up close to it*):
Ah! Here it is! (*Going back to admire it, while
mixed emotions stir within her.*) Yes . . . yes
. . . (*Calls her daughter* FRIDA.)

FRIDA: Ah, your portrait!

DONNA MATILDA: No, no . . . look again; it's
you, not I, there!

DI NOLLI: Yes, it's quite true. I told you so,
I . . .

DONNA MATILDA: But I would never have
believed it! (*Shaking as if with a chill.*) What
a strange feeling it gives one! (*Then looking at
her daughter.*) Frida, what's the matter? (*She
pulls her to her side, and slips an arm round
her waist.*) Come: don't you see yourself in
me there?

FRIDA: Well, I really . . .

DONNA MATILDA: Don't you think so? Don't
you, really? (*Turning to* BELCREDI.) Look at
it, Tito! Speak up, man!

BELCREDI (*without looking*): Ah, no! I shan't
look at it. For me, *a priori,* certainly not!

DONNA MATILDA: Stupid! You think you are
paying me a compliment! (*Turning to* DOCTOR

GENONI.) What do you say, Doctor? Do say
something, please!

DOCTOR (*makes a movement to go near to
the picture*).

BELCREDI (*with his back turned, pretending
to attract his attention secretly*): — Hss! No,
Doctor! For the love of Heaven, have nothing
to do with it!

DOCTOR (*getting bewildered and smiling*):
And why shouldn't I?

DONNA MATILDA: Don't listen to him! Come
here! He's insufferable!

FRIDA: He acts the fool by profession, didn't
you know that?

BELCREDI (*to the* DOCTOR, *seeing him go
over*): Look at your feet, Doctor! Mind where
you're going!

DOCTOR: Why?

BELCREDI: Be careful you don't put your
foot in it!

DOCTOR (*laughing feebly*): No, no. After all,
it seems to me there's no reason to be
astonished at the fact that a daughter should
resemble her mother!

BELCREDI: Hullo! Hullo! He's done it now;
he's said it.

DONNA MATILDA (*with exaggerated anger,
advancing towards* BELCREDI): What's the
matter? What has he said? What has he done?

DOCTOR (*candidly*): Well, isn't it so?

BELCREDI (*answering the* MARCHIONESS): I
said there was nothing to be astounded
at — and you are astounded! And why so, then,
if the thing is so simple and natural for you
now?

DONNA MATILDA (*still more angry*): Fool!
fool! It's just because it is so natural! Just
because it isn't my daughter who is there.
(*Pointing to the canvas.*) That is my portrait;
and to find my daughter there instead of me
fills me with astonishment, an astonishment
which, I beg you to believe, is sincere. I forbid you to cast doubts on it.

FRIDA (*slowly and wearily*): My God! It's
always like this . . . rows over nothing . . .

BELCREDI (*also slowly, looking dejected, in
accents of apology*): I cast no doubt on
anything! I noticed from the beginning that
you haven't shared your mother's astonishment; or, if something did astonish you, it was
because the likeness between you and the
portrait seemed so strong.

DONNA MATILDA: Naturally! She cannot

recognize herself in me as I was at her age; while I, there, can very well recognize myself in her as she is now!

DOCTOR: Quite right! Because a portrait is always there fixed in the twinkling of an eye: for the young lady something far away and without memories, while, for the Marchioness, it can bring back everything: movements, gestures, looks, smiles, a whole heap of things . . .

DONNA MATILDA: Exactly!

DOCTOR (continuing, turning towards her): Naturally enough, you can live all these old sensations again in your daughter.

DONNA MATILDA: He always spoils every innocent pleasure for me, every touch I have of spontaneous sentiment! He does it merely to annoy me.

DOCTOR (frightened at the disturbance he has caused, adopts a professional tone): Likeness, dear Baron, is often the result of imponderable things. So one explains that . . .

BELCREDI (interrupting the discourse): Somebody will soon be finding a likeness between you and me, my dear Professor!

DI NOLLI: Oh! let's finish with this, please! (Points to the two doors on the right, as a warning that there is someone there who may be listening.) We've wasted too much time as it is!

FRIDA: As one might expect when he's present. (Alludes to BELCREDI.)

DI NOLLI: Enough! The Doctor is here; and we have come for a very serious purpose which you all know is important for me.

DOCTOR: Yes, that is so! But now, first of all, let's try to get some points down exactly. Excuse me, Marchioness, will you tell me why your portrait is here? Did you present it to him then?

DONNA MATILDA: No, not at all. How could I have given it to him? I was just like Frida then — and not even engaged. I gave it to him three or four years after the accident. I gave it to him because his mother wished it so much . . . (Points to DI NOLLI.)

DOCTOR: She was his sister? (Alludes to HENRY IV.)

DI NOLLI: Yes, Doctor; and our coming here is a debt we pay to my mother who has been dead for more than a month. Instead of being here, she and I (indicating FRIDA) ought to be traveling together . . .

DOCTOR: . . . taking a cure of quite a different kind!

DI NOLLI: — Hum! Mother died in the firm conviction that her adored brother was just about to be cured.

DOCTOR: And can't you tell me, if you please, how she inferred this?

DI NOLLI: The conviction would appear to have derived from certain strange remarks which he made, a little before mother died.

DOCTOR: Oh, remarks! . . . Ah! . . . It would be extremely useful for me to have those remarks, word for word, if possible.

DI NOLLI: I can't remember them. I know that mother returned awfully upset from her last visit with him. On her death-bed, she made me promise that I would never neglect him, that I would have doctors see him, and examine him.

DOCTOR: Um! Um! Let me see! let me see! Sometimes very small reasons determine . . . and this portrait here then? . . .

DONNA MATILDA: For Heaven's sake, Doctor, don't attach excessive importance to this. It made an impression on me because I had not seen it for so many years!

DOCTOR: If you please, quietly, quietly . . .

DI NOLLI: — Well, yes, it must be about fifteen years ago.

DONNA MATILDA: More, more: eighteen!

DOCTOR: Forgive me, but you don't quite know what I'm trying to get at. I attach a very great importance to these two portraits . . . They were painted, naturally, prior to the famous — and most regrettable pageant, weren't they?

DONNA MATILDA: Of course!

DOCTOR: That is . . . when he was quite in his right mind — that's what I've been trying to say. Was it his suggestion that they should be painted?

DONNA MATILDA: Lots of the people who took part in the pageant had theirs done as a souvenir . . .

BELCREDI: I had mine done — as "Charles of Anjou!"

DONNA MATILDA: . . . as soon as the costumes were ready.

BELCREDI: As a matter of fact, it was proposed that the whole lot of us should be hung together in a gallery of the villa where the pageant took place. But in the end, everybody wanted to keep his own portrait.

DONNA MATILDA: And I gave him this portrait of me without very much regret . . . since his mother . . . (*Indicates* DI NOLLI.)

DOCTOR: You don't remember if it was he who asked for it?

DONNA MATILDA: Ah, that I don't remember . . . Maybe it was his sister, wanting to help out . . .

DOCTOR: One other thing: was it his idea, this pageant?

BELCREDI (*at once*): No, no, it was mine!

DOCTOR: If you please . . .

DONNA MATILDA: Don't listen to him! It was poor Belassi's idea.

BELCREDI: Belassi! What had he got to do with it?

DONNA MATILDA: Count Belassi, who died, poor fellow, two or three months after . . .

BELCREDI: But if Belassi wasn't there when . . .

DI NOLLI: Excuse me, Doctor; but is it really necessary to establish whose the original idea was?

DOCTOR: It would help me, certainly!

BELCREDI: I tell you the idea was mine! There's nothing to be proud of in it, seeing what the result's been. Look here, Doctor, it was like this. One evening, in the first days of November, I was looking at an illustrated German review in the club. I was merely glancing at the pictures, because I can't read German. There was a picture of the Kaiser, at some University town where he had been a student . . . I don't remember which.

DOCTOR: Bonn, Bonn!

BELCREDI: — You are right: Bonn! He was on horseback, dressed up in one of those ancient German student guild-costumes, followed by a procession of noble students, also in costume. The picture gave me the idea. Already someone at the club had spoken of a pageant for the forthcoming carnival. So I had the notion that each of us should choose for this Tower of Babel pageant to represent some character: a king, an emperor, a prince, with his queen, empress, or lady, alongside of him — and all on horseback. The suggestion was at once accepted.

DONNA MATILDA: I had my invitation from Belassi.

BELCREDI: Well, he wasn't speaking the truth! That's all I can say, if he told you the idea was his. He wasn't even at the club the

evening I made the suggestion, just as he (*meaning* HENRY IV) wasn't there either.

DOCTOR: So he chose the character of Henry IV?

DONNA MATILDA: Because I . . . thinking of my name, and not giving the choice any importance, said I would be the Marchioness Matilda of Tuscany.

DOCTOR: I . . . don't understand the relation between the two.

DONNA MATILDA: — Neither did I, to begin with, when he said that in that case he would be at my feet like Henry IV at Canossa. I had heard of Canossa of course; but to tell the truth, I'd forgotten most of the story; and I remember I received a curious impression when I had to get up my part, and found that I was the faithful and zealous friend of Pope Gregory VII in deadly enmity with the Emperor of Germany. Then I understood why, since I had chosen to represent his implacable enemy, he wanted to be near me in the pageant as Henry IV.

DOCTOR: Ah, perhaps because . . .

BELCREDI: — Good Heavens, Doctor, because he was then paying furious court to her! (*Indicates the* MARCHIONESS.) And she, naturally . . .

DONNA MATILDA: Naturally? Not naturally at all . . .

BELCREDI (*pointing to her*): She shouldn't stand him . . .

DONNA MATILDA: — No, that isn't true! I didn't dislike him. Not at all! But for me, when a man begins to want to be taken seriously, well . . .

BELCREDI (*continuing for her*): He gives you the clearest proof of his stupidity.

DONNA MATILDA: No, dear; not in this case; because he was never a fool like you.

BELCREDI: Anyway, I've never asked you to take me seriously.

DONNA MATILDA: Yes, I know. But with him one couldn't joke. (*Changing her tone and speaking to the* DOCTOR.) One of the many misfortunes which happen to us women, Doctor, is to see before us every now and again a pair of eyes glaring at us with a contained intense promise of eternal devotion. (*Bursts out laughing.*) There is nothing quite so funny. If men could only see themselves with that eternal look of fidelity in their faces! I've always thought it comic; then more even than now. But I want to make a confession — I can do so after twenty years or more. When I laughed at him then, it was partly out of fear. One might have almost believed a promise from those eyes of his. But it would have been very dangerous.

DOCTOR (*with lively interest*): Ah! ah! This is most interesting! Very dangerous, you say?

DONNA MATILDA: Yes, because he was very different from the others. And then, I am . . . well . . . what shall I say? . . . a little impatient of all that is pondered, or tedious. But I was too young then, and a woman. I had the bit between my teeth. It would have required more courage than I felt I possessed. So I laughed at him too — with remorse, to spite myself, indeed; since I saw that my own laugh mingled with those of all the others — the other fools — who made fun of him.

BELCREDI: My own case, more or less!

DONNA MATILDA: You make people laugh at you, my dear, with your trick of always humiliating yourself. It was quite a different affair with him. There's a vast difference. And you — you know — people laugh in your face!

BELCREDI: Well, that's better than behind one's back!

DOCTOR: Let's get to the facts. He was then already somewhat exalted, if I understand rightly.

BELCREDI: Yes, but in a curious fashion, Doctor.

DOCTOR: How?

BELCREDI: Well, cold-bloodedly so to speak.

DONNA MATILDA: Not at all! It was like this, Doctor! He was a bit strange, certainly; but only because he was fond of life: eccentric, there!

BELCREDI: I don't say he simulated exaltation. On the contrary, he was often genuinely exalted. But I could swear, Doctor, that he saw himself at once in his own exaltation. Moreover, I'm certain it made him suffer. Sometimes he had the most comical fits of rage against himself.

DOCTOR: Yes?

DONNA MATILDA: That is true.

BELCREDI (*to* DONNA MATILDA): And why? (*To the* DOCTOR.) Evidently, because that immediate lucidity that comes from acting, assuming a part, at once put him out of key with his own feelings, which seemed to him not exactly false, but like something he was

obliged to give the value there and then of — what shall I say — of an act of intelligence, to make up for that sincere cordial warmth he felt lacking. So he improvised, exaggerated, let himself go, so as to distract and forget himself. He appeared inconstant, fatuous, and — yes — even ridiculous, sometimes.

DOCTOR: And may we say unsociable?

BELCREDI: No, not at all. He was famous for getting up things: *tableaux vivants*, dances, theatrical performances for charity: all for the fun of the thing, of course. He was a jolly good actor, you know!

DI NOLLI: Madness has made a superb actor of him.

BELCREDI: — Why, so he was even in the old days. When the accident happened, after the horse fell . . .

DOCTOR: Hit the back of his head, didn't he?

DONNA MATILDA: Oh, it was horrible! He was beside me! I saw him between the horse's hoofs! It was rearing!

BELCREDI: None of us thought it was anything serious at first. There was a stop in the pageant, a bit of disorder. People wanted to know what had happened. But they'd already taken him off to the villa.

DONNA MATILDA: There wasn't the least sign of a wound, not a drop of blood.

BELCREDI: We thought he had merely fainted.

DONNA MATILDA: But two hours afterwards . . .

BELCREDI: He reappeared in the drawing-room of the villa . . . that is what I wanted to say . . .

DONNA MATILDA: My God! What a face he had. I saw the whole thing at once!

BELCREDI: No, no! that isn't true. Nobody saw it, Doctor, believe me!

DONNA MATILDA: Doubtless, because you were all like mad folk.

BELCREDI: Everybody was pretending to act his part for a joke. It was a regular Babel.

DONNA MATILDA: And you can imagine, Doctor, what terror struck into us when we understood that he, on the contrary, was playing his part in deadly earnest . . .

DOCTOR: Oh, he was there too, was he?

BELCREDI: Of course! He came straight into the midst of us. We thought he'd quite recovered, and was pretending, fooling, like all the rest of us ... only doing it rather better; because, as I say, he knew how to act.

DONNA MATILDA: Some of them began to hit him with their whips and fans and sticks.

BELCREDI: And then — as a king, he was armed, of course — he drew out his sword and menaced two or three of us ... It was a terrible moment, I can assure you!

DONNA MATILDA: I shall never forget that scene — all our masked faces hideous and terrified gazing at him, at that terrible mask of his face, which was no longer a mask, but madness, madness personified.

BELCREDI: He was Henry IV, Henry IV in person, in a moment of fury.

DONNA MATILDA: He'd got into it all the detail and minute preparation of a month's careful study. And it all burned and blazed there in the terrible obsession which lit his face.

DOCTOR: Yes, that is quite natural, of course. The momentary obsession of a dilettante became fixed, owing to the fall and the damage to the brain.

BELCREDI (to FRIDA and DI NOLLI): You see the kind of jokes life can play on us. (To DI NOLLI.) You were four or five years old. (To FRIDA.) Your mother imagines you've taken her place there in that portrait; when, at the time, she had not the remotest idea that she would bring you into the world. My hair is already grey; and he — look at him — (points to portrait) — ha! A smack on the head, and he never moves again: Henry IV for ever!

DOCTOR (seeking to draw the attention of the others, looking learned and imposing): — Well, well, then it comes, we may say, to this ...

(Suddenly the first exit to right, the one nearest footlights, opens, and BERTHOLD enters all excited.)

BERTHOLD (rushing in): I say! I say! (Stops for a moment, arrested by the astonishment which his appearance has caused in the others.)

FRIDA (running away terrified): Oh dear! oh dear! it's he, it's ...

DONNA MATILDA (covering her face with her hands so as not to see): Is it, is it he?

DI NOLLI: No, no, what are you talking about? Be calm!

DOCTOR: Who is it then?

BELCREDI: One of our masqueraders.

DI NOLLI: He is one of the four youths we keep here to help him out in his madness ...

BERTHOLD: I beg your pardon, Marquis ...

DI NOLLI: Pardon be damned! I gave orders that the doors were to be closed, and that nobody should be allowed to enter.

BERTHOLD: Yes, sir, but I can't stand it any longer, and I ask you to let me go away this very minute.

DI NOLLI: Oh, you're the new valet, are you? You were supposed to begin this morning, weren't you?

BERTHOLD: Yes, sir, and I can't stand it, I can't bear it.

DONNA MATILDA (to DI NOLLI excitedly): What? Then he's not so calm as you said?

BERTHOLD (quickly): — No, no, my lady, it isn't he; it's my companions. You say "help him out with his madness," Marquis; but they don't do anything of the kind. They're the real madmen. I come here for the first time, and instead of helping me ...

(LANDOLPH and HAROLD come in from the same door, but hesitate on the threshold.)

LANDOLPH: Excuse me?

HAROLD: May I come in, my Lord?

DI NOLLI: Come in! What's the matter? What are you all doing?

FRIDA: Oh God! I'm frightened! I'm going to run away. (Makes towards exit at left.)

DI NOLLI (restraining her at once): No, no Frida!

LANDOLPH: My Lord, this fool here ... (Indicates BERTHOLD.)

BERTHOLD (protesting): Ah, no thanks, my friends, no thanks! I'm not stopping here! I'm off!

LANDOLPH: What do you mean — you're not stopping here?

HAROLD: He's ruined everything, my Lord, running away in here!

LANDOLPH: He's made him quite mad. We can't keep him in there any longer. He's given orders that he's to be arrested; and he wants to "judge" him at once from the throne: What is to be done?

DI NOLLI: Shut the door, man! Shut the door! Go and close that door! (LANDOLPH goes over to close it.)

HAROLD: Ordulph, alone, won't be able to keep him there.

LANDOLPH: — My Lord, perhaps if we could announce the visitors at once, it would turn his thoughts. Have the gentlemen thought under what pretext they will present themselves to him?

DI NOLLI: — It's all been arranged! (*To the* DOCTOR.) If you, Doctor, think it well to see him at once. . . .

FRIDA: I'm not coming! I'm not coming! I'll keep out of this. You too, mother, for Heaven's sake, come away with me!

DOCTOR: — I say . . . I suppose he's not armed, is he?

DI NOLLI: — Nonsense! Of course not. (*To* FRIDA.) Frida, you know this is childish of you. You wanted to come!

FRIDA: I didn't at all. It was mother's idea.

DONNA MATILDA: And I'm quite ready to see him. What are we going to do?

BELCREDI: Must we absolutely dress up in some fashion or other?

LANDOLPH: — Absolutely essential, indispensable, sir. Alas! as you see . . . (*shows his costume*), there'd be awful trouble if he saw you gentlemen in modern dress.

HAROLD: He would think it was some diabolical masquerade.

DI NOLLI: As these men seem to be in costume to you, so we appear to be in costume to him, in these modern clothes of ours.

LANDOLPH: It wouldn't matter so much if he wouldn't suppose it to be the work of his mortal enemy.

BELCREDI: Pope Gregory VII?

LANDOLPH: Precisely. He calls him "a pagan."

BELCREDI: The Pope a pagan? Not bad that!

LANDOLPH: — Yes, sir, — and a man who calls up the dead! He accuses him of all the diabolical arts. He's terribly afraid of him.

DOCTOR: Persecution mania!

HAROLD: He'd be simply furious.

DI NOLLI (*to* BELCREDI): But there's no need for you to be there, you know. It's sufficient for the Doctor to see him.

DOCTOR: — What do you mean? . . . I? Alone?

DI NOLLI: — But they are there. (*Indicates the three young men.*)

DOCTOR: I don't mean that . . . I mean if the Marchioness . . .

DONNA MATILDA: Of course. I mean to see him too, naturally. I want to see him again.

FRIDA: Oh, why mother, why? Do come away with me, I implore you!

DONNA MATILDA (*imperiously*): Let me do as I wish! I came here for this purpose! (*To* LANDOLPH.) I shall be "Adelaide," the mother.

LANDOLPH: Excellent! The mother of the Empress Bertha. Good! It will be enough if her Ladyship wears the ducal crown and puts on a mantle that will hide her other clothes entirely (*To* HAROLD.) Off you go, Harold!

HAROLD: Wait a moment! And this gentleman here? . . . (*Alludes to the* DOCTOR.)

DOCTOR: — Ah yes . . . we decided I was to be . . . the Bishop of Cluny, Hugh of Cluny!

HAROLD: The gentleman means the Abbot. Very good! Hugh of Cluny.

LANDOLPH: — He's often been here before!

DOCTOR (*amazed*): — What? Been here before?

LANDOLPH: — Don't be alarmed! I mean that it's an easily prepared disguise . . .

HAROLD: We've made use of it on other occasions, you see!

DOCTOR: But . . .

LANDOLPH: Oh, no, there's no risk of his remembering. He pays more attention to the dress than to the person.

DONNA MATILDA: That's fortunate for me too then.

DI NOLLI: Frida, you and I'll get along. Come on, Tito!

BELCREDI: Ah no. If she (*indicates the* MARCHIONESS) stops here, so do I!

DONNA MATILDA: But I don't need you at all.

BELCREDI: You may not need me, but I should like to see him again myself. Mayn't I?

LANDOLPH: Well, perhaps it would be better if there were three.

HAROLD: How is the gentleman to be dressed then?

BELCREDI: Oh, try and find some easy costume for me.

LANDOLPH (*to* HAROLD): Hum! Yes . . . he'd better be from Cluny too.

BELCREDI: What do you mean — from Cluny?

LANDOLPH: A Benedictine's habit of the Abbey of Cluny. He can be in attendance on Monsignor. (*To* HAROLD.) Off you go! (*To* BERTHOLD.) And you too get away and keep out of sight all today. No, wait a bit! (*To* BERTHOLD.) You bring here the costumes he will give you. (*To* HAROLD.) You go at once and announce the visit of the "Duchess Adelaide" and "Monsignor Hugh of Cluny." Do you understand? (HAROLD *and* BERTHOLD *go off by the first door on the right.*)

DI NOLLI: We'll retire now. (*Goes off with* FRIDA, *left.*)

DOCTOR: Shall I be a *persona grata* to him, as Hugh of Cluny?

LANDOLPH: Oh, rather! Don't worry about that! Monsignor has always been received here with great respect. You too, my Lady, he will be glad to see. He never forgets that it was owing to the intercession of you two that he was admitted to the Castle of Canossa and the presence of Gregory VII, who didn't want to receive him.

BELCREDI: And what do I do?

LANDOLPH: You stand a little apart, respectfully: that's all.

DONNA MATILDA (*irritated, nervous*): You would do well to go away, you know.

BELCREDI (*slowly, spitefully*): How upset you seem! . . .

DONNA MATILDA (*proudly*): I am as I am. Leave me alone!

(BERTHOLD *comes in with the costumes.*)

LANDOLPH (*seeing him enter*): Ah, the costumes: here they are. This mantle is for the Marchioness . . .

DONNA MATILDA: Wait a minute! I'll take off my hat.

(*Does so and gives it to* BERTHOLD.)

LANDOLPH: Put it down there! (*Then to the* MARCHIONESS, *while he offers to put the ducal crown on her head.*) Allow me!

DONNA MATILDA: Dear, dear! Isn't there a mirror here?

LANDOLPH: Yes, there's one there. (*Points to the door on the left.*) If the Marchioness would rather put it on herself . . .

DONNA MATILDA: Yes, yes, that will be better. Give it to me! (*Takes up her hat and goes off with* BERTHOLD, *who carries the cloak and the crown.*)

BELCREDI: Well, I must say, I never thought I should be a Benedictine monk! By the way, this business must cost an awful lot of money.

DOCTOR: Like any other fantasy, naturally!

BELCREDI: Well, there's a fortune to go upon.

LANDOLPH: We have got there a whole wardrobe of costumes of the period, copied to perfection from old models. This is my special job. I get them from the best theatrical costumers. They cost lots of money. (DONNA MATILDA *re-enters, wearing mantle and crown.*)

BELCREDI (*at once, in admiration*): Oh magnificent! Oh, truly regal!

DONNA MATILDA (*looking at* BELCREDI *and bursting out into laughter*): Oh no, no! Take it off! You're impossible. You look like an ostrich dressed up as a monk.

BELCREDI: Well, how about the Doctor?

DOCTOR: I don't think I look so bad, do I?

DONNA MATILDA: No; the Doctor's all right . . . but you are too funny for words.

DOCTOR: Do you have many receptions here then?

LANDOLPH: It depends. He often gives orders that such and such a person appear before him. Then we have to find someone who will take the part. Women too . . .

DONNA MATILDA (*hurt, but trying to hide the fact*): Ah, women too?

LANDOLPH: Oh, yes; many at first.

BELCREDI (*laughing*): Oh, that's great! In costume, like the Marchioness?

LANDOLPH: Oh well, you know, women of the kind that lend themselves to . . .

BELCREDI: Ah, I see! (*Perfidiously to the* MARCHIONESS.) Look out, you know he's becoming dangerous for you.

(*The second door on the right opens, and* HAROLD *appears making first of all a discreet sign that all conversation should cease.*)

HAROLD: His Majesty, the Emperor!

(*The* TWO VALETS *enter first, and go and stand on either side of the throne. Then* HENRY IV *comes in between* ORDULPH *and* HAROLD, *who keep a little in the rear respectfully.*

HENRY IV *is about 50 and very pale. The hair on the back of his head is already grey; over the temples and forehead it appears blond, owing to its having been tinted in an evident and puerile fashion. On his cheek bones he has two small, doll-like dabs of color, that stand out prominently against the rest of his tragic pallor. He is wearing a penitent's sack over his regal habit, as at Canossa. His eyes have a fixed look which is dreadful to see, and this expression is in strained contrast with the sackcloth.* ORDULPH *carries the Imperial crown;* HAROLD, *the sceptre with eagle, and the globe with the cross.*)

HENRY IV (*bowing first to* DONNA MATILDA *and afterwards to the* DOCTOR): My Lady ... Monsignor ... (*Then he looks at* BELCREDI *and seems about to greet him too; when, suddenly, he turns to* LANDOLPH, *who has approached him, and asks him sotto voce and with diffidence.*) Is that Peter Damiani?

LANDOLPH: No, Sire. He is a monk from Cluny who is accompanying the Abbot.

HENRY IV (*looks again at* BELCREDI *with increasing mistrust, and then noticing that he appears embarrassed and keeps glancing at* DONNA MATILDA *and the* DOCTOR, *stands upright and cries out*): No, it's Peter Damiani! It's no use, father, your looking at the Duchess. (*Then turning quickly to* DONNA MATILDA *and the* DOCTOR *as though to ward off a danger.*) I swear it! I swear that my heart is changed towards your daughter. I confess that if he (*indicates* BELCREDI) hadn't come to forbid it in the name of Pope Alexander, I'd have repudiated her. Yes, yes, there were people ready to favor the repudiation: the Bishop of Mayence would have done it for a matter of one hundred and twenty farms. (*Looks at* LANDOLPH *a little perplexed and adds.*) But I mustn't speak ill of the bishops at this moment! (*More humbly to* BELCREDI.) I am grateful to you, believe me, I am grateful to you for the hindrance you put in my way! — God knows, my life's been all made of humiliations: my mother, Adalbert, Tribur, Goslar! And now this sackcloth you see me wearing! (*Changes tone suddenly and speaks like one who goes over his part in a parenthesis of astuteness.*) It doesn't matter: clarity of ideas, perspicacity, firmness and patience under adversity that's the thing. (*Then turning to all and speaking solemnly.*) I know how to make amend for the mistakes I have made; and I can humiliate myself even before you, Peter Damiani. (*Bows profoundly to him and remains curved. Then a suspicion is born in him which he is obliged to utter in menacing tones, almost against his will.*) Was it not perhaps you who started that obscene rumor that my holy mother had illicit relations with the Bishop of Augusta?

BELCREDI (*since* HENRY IV *has his finger pointed at him*): No, no, it wasn't I ...

HENRY IV (*straightening up*): Not true, not

true? Infamy! (*Looks at him and then adds.*) I didn't think you capable of it! (*Goes to the* DOCTOR *and plucks his sleeve, while winking at him knowingly.*) Always the same, Monsignor, those bishops, always the same!

HAROLD (*softly, whispering as if to help out the* DOCTOR): Yes, yes, the rapacious bishops!

DOCTOR (*to* HAROLD, *trying to keep it up*): Ah, yes, those fellows ... ah yes ...

HENRY IV: Nothing satisfies them! I was a little boy, Monsignor ... One passes the time, playing even, when, without knowing it, one is a king. — I was six years old; and they tore me away from my mother, and made use of me against her without my knowing anything about it ... always profaning, always stealing, stealing! ... One greedier than the other ... Hanno worse than Stephen! Stephen worse than Hanno!

LANDOLPH (*sotto voce, persuasively, to call his attention*): Majesty!

HENRY IV (*turning round quickly*): Ah yes ... this isn't the moment to speak ill of the bishops. But this infamy against my mother, Monsignor, is too much. (*Looks at the* MARCHIONESS *and grows tender.*) And I can't even weep for her, Lady ... I appeal to you who have a mother's heart! She came here to see me from her convent a month ago ... They had told me she was dead! (*Sustained pause full of feeling. Then smiling sadly.*) I can't weep for her; because if you are here now, and I am like this (*shows the sackcloth he is wearing*) it means I am twenty-six years old!

HAROLD: And that she is therefore alive, Majesty! ...

ORDULPH: Still in her convent!

HENRY IV (*looking at them*): Ah yes! And I can postpone my grief to another time. (*Shows the* MARCHIONESS *almost with coquetry the tint he has given to his hair.*) Look! I am still fair ... (*Then slowly as if in confidence.*) For you ... there's no need! But little exterior details do help! A matter of time, Monsignor, do you understand me? (*Turns to the* MARCHIONESS *and notices her hair.*) Ah, but I see that you too, Duchess ... Italian, eh? (*As much as to say "false"; but without any indignation, indeed rather with malicious admiration.*) Heaven forbid that I should show disgust or surprise! Nobody cares to recognize that obscure and fatal power which sets limits to our will. But I say, if one is born and one dies ... Did you want to be born, Monsignor? I didn't! And in both cases, independently of our wills, so many things happen we would wish didn't happen, and to which we resign ourselves as best we can! ...

DOCTOR (*merely to make a remark, while studying* HENRY IV *carefully*): Alas! Yes, alas!

HENRY IV: It's like this: When we are not resigned, out come our desires. A woman wants to be a man ... an old man would be young again. Desires, ridiculous fixed ideas of course — But reflect! Monsignor, those other desires are not less ridiculous: I mean, those desires where the will is kept within the limits of the possible. Not one of us can lie or pretend. We're all fixed in good faith in a certain concept of ourselves. However, Monsignor, while you keep yourself in order, holding on with both your hands to your holy habit, there slips down from your sleeves, there peels off from you like ... like a serpent ... something you don't notice: life, Monsignor! (*Turns to the* MARCHIONESS.) Has it never happened to you, my Lady, to find a different self in yourself? Have you always been the same? My God! One day ... How was it, how was it you were able to commit this or that action? (*Fixes her so intently in the eyes as almost to make her blanch.*) Yes, that particular action, that very one: we understand each other! But don't be afraid: I shall reveal it to none. And you, Peter Damiani, how could you be a friend of that man? ...

LANDOLPH: Majesty!

HENRY IV (*at once*): No, I won't name him! (*Turning to* BELCREDI.) What did you think of him? But we all of us cling tight to our conceptions of ourselves, just as he who is growing old dyes his hair. What does it matter that this dyed hair of mine isn't a reality for you, if it *is*, to some extent, for me? — you, you, my Lady, certainly don't dye your hair to deceive the others, nor even yourself; but only to cheat your own image a little before the looking-glass. I do it for a joke! You do it seriously! But I assure you that you too, Madam, are in masquerade, though it be in all seriousness; and I am not speaking of the venerable crown on your brows or the ducal mantle. I am speaking only of the memory you wish to fix in yourself of your fair complexion one day when it pleased you — or of your dark complexion, if you were dark: the fading image

of your youth! For you, Peter Damiani, on the contrary, the memory of what you have been, of what you have done, seems to you a recognition of past realities that remain within you like a dream. I'm in the same case too: with so many inexplicable memories — like dreams! Ah! ... There's nothing to marvel at in it, Peter Damiani! Tomorrow it will be the same thing with our life of today! (*Suddenly getting excited and taking hold of his sackcloth.*) This sackcloth here ... (*Beginning to take it off with a gesture of almost ferocious joy while the* THREE VALETS *run over to him, frightened, as if to prevent his doing so.*) Ah, my God! (*Draws back and throws off sackcloth.*) Tomorrow, at Bressanone, twenty-seven German and Lombard bishops will sign with me the act of deposition of Gregory VII! No Pope at all! Just a false monk!

ORDULPH (*with the other three*): Majesty! Majesty! In God's name! ...

HAROLD (*inviting him to put on the sackcloth again*): Listen to what he says, Majesty!

LANDOLPH: Monsignor is here with the Duchess to intercede in your favor. (*Makes secret signs to the* DOCTOR *to say something at once.*)

DOCTOR (*foolishly*): Ah yes ... yes ... we are here to intercede ...

HENRY IV (*repenting at once, almost terrified, allowing the three to put on the sackcloth again, and pulling it down over him with his own hands*): Pardon ... yes ... yes ... pardon, Monsignor: forgive me, my Lady. I swear to you I feel the whole weight of the anathema. (*Bends himself, takes his face between his hands, as though waiting for something to crush him. Then changing tone, but without moving, says softly to* LANDOLPH, HAROLD *and* ORDULPH.) But I don't know why I cannot be humble before that man there! (*Indicates* BELCREDI.)

LANDOLPH (*sotto voce*): But why, Majesty, do you insist on believing he is Peter Damiani, when he isn't, at all?

HENRY IV (*looking at him timorously*): He isn't Peter Damiani?

HAROLD: No, no, he is a poor monk, Majesty.

HENRY IV (*sadly with a touch of exasperation*): Ah! None of us can estimate what we do when we do it from instinct ... You perhaps, Madam, can understand me better than the others, since you are a woman and a Duchess. This is a solemn and decisive moment. I could, you know, accept the assistance of the Lombard bishops, arrest the Pope, lock him up here in the castle, run to Rome and elect an anti-Pope; offer alliance to Robert Guiscard — and Gregory VII would be lost! I resist the temptation; and, believe me, I am wise in doing so. I feel the atmosphere of our times and the majesty of one who knows how to be what he ought to be! a Pope! Do you feel inclined to laugh at me, seeing me like this? You would be foolish to do so; for you don't understand the political wisdom which makes this penitent's sack advisable. The parts may be changed tomorrow. What would you do then? Would you laugh to see the Pope a prisoner? No! It would come to the same thing: I dressed as a penitent, today; he, as prisoner tomorrow! But woe to him who doesn't know how to wear his mask, be he king or Pope! — Perhaps he is a bit too cruel! No! Yes, yes, maybe! — You remember, my Lady, how your daughter Bertha, for whom, I repeat, my feelings have changed (*turns to* BELCREDI *and shouts to his face as if he were being contradicted by him*) — yes, changed on account of the affection and devotion she showed me in that terrible moment . . . (*then once again to the* MARCHIONESS) . . . you remember how she came with me, my Lady, followed me like a beggar and passed two nights out in the open, in the snow? You are her mother! Doesn't this touch your mother's heart? Doesn't this urge you to pity, so that you will beg His Holiness for pardon, beg him to receive us?

DONNA MATILDA (*trembling, with feeble voice*): Yes, yes, at once . . .

DOCTOR: It shall be done!

HENRY IV: And one thing more! (*Draws them in to listen to him.*) It isn't enough that he should receive me! You know he can do *everything* — *everything* I tell you! He can even call up the dead. (*Touches his chest.*) Behold me! Do you see me? There is no magic art unknown to him. Well, Monsignor, my Lady, my torment is really this: that whether here or there (*pointing to his portrait almost in fear*) I can't free myself from this magic. I am a penitent now, you see; and I swear to you I shall remain so until he receives me. But you two, when the excommunication is taken

off, must ask the Pope to do this thing he can so easily do: to take me away from that; (*indicating the portrait again*) and let me live wholly and freely my miserable life. A man can't always be twenty-six, my Lady. I ask this of you for your daughter's sake too; that I may love her as she deserves to be loved, well disposed as I am now, all tender towards her for her pity. There: it's all there! I am in your hands! (*Bows.*) My Lady! Monsignor!

(*He goes off, bowing grandly, through the door by which he entered, leaving everyone stupefied, and the* MARCHIONESS *so profoundly touched, that no sooner has he gone than she breaks out into sobs and sits down almost fainting.*)

ACT II

Another room of the villa, adjoining the throne room. Its furniture is antique and severe. Principal exit at rear in the background. To the left, two windows looking on the garden. To the right, a door opening into the throne room.

Late afternoon of the same day.

DONNA MATILDA, *the* DOCTOR *and* BELCREDI *are on the stage engaged in conversation; but* DONNA MATILDA *stands to one side, evidently annoyed at what the other two are saying; although she cannot help listening, because, in her agitated state, everything interests her in spite of herself. The talk of the other two attracts her attention, because she instinctively feels the need for calm at the moment.*

BELCREDI: It may be as you say, Doctor, but that was my impression.

DOCTOR: I won't contradict you; but, believe me, it is only . . . an impression.

BELCREDI: Pardon me, but he even said so, and quite clearly. (*Turning to the* MARCHIONESS.) Didn't he, Marchioness?

DONNA MATILDA (*turning round*): What did he say? . . . (*Then not agreeing.*) Oh yes . . . but not for the reason you think!

DOCTOR: He was alluding to the costumes we had slipped on . . . Your cloak (*indicating the* MARCHIONESS), our Benedictine habits . . . But all this is childish!

DONNA MATILDA (*turning quickly, indignant*): Childish? What do you mean, Doctor?

DOCTOR: From one point of view, it is — I beg you to let me say so, Marchioness! Yet, on the other hand, it is much more complicated than you can imagine.

DONNA MATILDA: To me, on the contrary, it is perfectly clear!

DOCTOR (*with a smile of pity of the competent person towards those who do not understand*): We must take into account the peculiar psychology of madmen; which, you must know, enables us to be certain that they observe things and can, for instance, easily detect people who are disguised; can in fact recognize the disguise and yet believe in it; just as children do, for whom disguise is both play and reality. That is why I used the word childish. But the thing is extremely complicated, inasmuch as he must be perfectly aware of being an image to himself and for himself — that image there, in fact! (*Alluding to the portrait in the throne room, and pointing to the left.*)

BELCREDI: That's what he said!

DOCTOR: Very well then — An image before which other images, ours, have appeared: understand? Now he, in his acute and perfectly lucid delirium, was able to detect at once a difference between his image and ours: that is, he saw that ours were make-believes. So he suspected us; because all madmen are armed with a special diffidence. But that's all there is to it! Our make-believe, built up all round his, did not seem pitiful to him. While his seemed all the more tragic to us, in that he, as if in defiance — understand? — and induced by his suspicion, wanted to show us up merely as a joke. That was also partly the case with him, in coming before us with painted cheeks and hair, and saying he had done it on purpose for a jest.

DONNA MATILDA (*impatiently*): No, it's not that, Doctor. It's not like that! It's not like that!

DOCTOR: Why isn't it, may I ask?

DONNA MATILDA (*with decision but trembling*): I am perfectly certain he recognized me!

DOCTOR: It's not possible . . . it's not possible!

BELCREDI (*at the same time*): Of course not!

DONNA MATILDA (*more than ever determined, almost convulsively*): I tell you, he recognized me! When he came close up to speak to me — looking in my eyes, right into my eyes — he recognized me!

BELCREDI: But he was talking of your daughter!

DONNA MATILDA: That's not true! He was talking of me! Of me!

BELCREDI: Yes, perhaps, when he said . . .

DONNA MATILDA (*letting herself go*): About my dyed hair! But didn't you notice that he added at once: "or the memory of your dark hair, if you were dark"? He remembered perfectly well that I was dark — then!

BELCREDI: Nonsense! nonsense!

DONNA MATILDA (*not listening to him, turning to the* DOCTOR): My hair, Doctor, is really dark — like my daughter's! That's why he spoke of her.

BELCREDI: But he doesn't even know your daughter! He's never seen her!

DONNA MATILDA: Exactly! Oh, you never understand anything! By my daughter, stupid, he meant me — as I was then!

BELCREDI: Oh, this is catching! This is catching, this madness!

DONNA MATILDA (*softly, with contempt*): Fool!

BELCREDI: Excuse me, were you ever his wife? Your daughter is his wife — in his delirium: Bertha of Susa.

DONNA MATILDA: Exactly! Because I, no longer dark — as he remembered me — but *fair*, introduced myself as "Adelaide," the mother. My daughter doesn't exist for him: he's never seen her — you said so yourself! So how can he know whether she's fair or dark?

BELCREDI: But he said dark, speaking generally, just as anyone who wants to recall, whether fair or dark, a memory of youth in the color of the hair! And you, as usual, begin to imagine things! Doctor, you said I ought not to have come! It's she who ought not to have come!

DONNA MATILDA (*upset for a moment by* BELCREDI'S *remark, recovers herself. Then with a touch of anger, because doubtful*): No, no . . . he spoke of me . . . He spoke all the time to me, with me, of me . . .

BELCREDI: That's not bad! He didn't leave me a moment's breathing space; and you say he was talking all the time to you? Unless you think he was alluding to you too, when he was talking to Peter Damiani!

DONNA MATILDA (*defiantly, almost exceeding the limits of courteous discussion*): Who knows? Can you tell me why, from the outset, he showed a strong dislike for you, for you alone? (*From the tone of the question, the expected answer must almost explicitly be: "because he understands you are my lover."* BELCREDI *feels this so well that he remains silent and can say nothing.*)

DOCTOR: The reason may also be found in the fact that only the visit of the Duchess Adelaide and the Abbot of Cluny was announced to him. Finding a third person present, who had not been announced, at once his suspicions . . .

BELCREDI: Yes, exactly! His suspicion made him see an enemy in me: Peter Damiani! But she's got it into her head, that he recognized her . . .

DONNA MATILDA: There's no doubt about it! I could see it from his eyes, Doctor. You know, there's a way of looking that leaves no doubt whatever . . . Perhaps it was only for an instant, but I am sure!

DOCTOR: It is not impossible: a lucid moment . . .

DONNA MATILDA: Yes, perhaps . . . And then his speech seemed to me full of regret for his and my youth — for the horrible thing that happened to him, that has held him in that disguise from which he has never been able to free himself, and from which he longs to be free — he said so himself!

BELCREDI: Yes, so as to be able to make love to your daughter, or you, as you believe — having been touched by your pity.

DONNA MATILDA: Which is very great, I would ask you to believe.

BELCREDI: As one can see, Marchioness; so much so that a miracle-worker might expect a miracle from it!

DOCTOR: Will you let me speak? I don't work miracles, because I am a doctor and not a miracle-worker. I listened very intently to all he said; and I repeat that that certain analogical elasticity, common to all systematized delirium, is evidently with him much . . . what shall I say? — much relaxed! The elements, that is, of his delirium no longer hold together. It seems to me he has lost the equilibrium of his second personality and sudden recollections drag him — and this is very comforting — not from a state of incipient apathy, but rather from a morbid inclination

to reflective melancholy, which shows a . . . a very considerable cerebral activity. Very comforting, I repeat! Now if, by this violent trick we've planned . . .

DONNA MATILDA (*turning to the window, in the tone of a sick person complaining*): But how is it that the motor has not returned? It's three hours and a half since . . .

DOCTOR: What do you say?

DONNA MATILDA: The motor, Doctor! It's more than three hours and a half . . .

DOCTOR (*taking out his watch and looking at it*): Yes, more than four hours, by this!

DONNA MATILDA: It could have reached here an hour ago at least! But, as usual . . .

BELCREDI: Perhaps they can't find the dress . . .

DONNA MATILDA: But I explained exactly where it was! (*Impatiently.*) And Frida . . . where is Frida?

BELCREDI (*looking out of the window*): Perhaps she is in the garden with Charles . . .

DOCTOR: He'll talk her out of her fright.

BELCREDI: She's not afraid, Doctor; don't you believe it: the thing bores her rather . . .

DONNA MATILDA: Just don't ask anything of her! I know what she's like.

DOCTOR: Let's wait patiently. Anyhow, it will soon be over, and it has to be in the evening . . . It will only be the matter of a moment! If we can succeed in rousing him, as I was saying, and in breaking at one go the threads — already slack — which still bind him to this fiction of his, giving him back what he himself asks for — you remember, he said: "one cannot always be twenty-six years old, madam!" if we can give him freedom from this torment, which even *he* feels is a torment, then if he is able to recover at one bound the sensation of the distance of time . . .

BELCREDI (*quickly*): He'll be cured! (*Then emphatically with irony.*) We'll pull him out of it all!

DOCTOR: Yes, we may hope to set him going again, like a watch which has stopped at a certain hour . . . just as if we had our watches in our hands and were waiting for that other watch to go again. — A shake — so — and let's hope it'll tell the time again after its long stop. (*At this point the* MARQUIS CHARLES DI NOLLI *enters from the principal entrance.*)

DONNA MATILDA: Oh, Charles! . . . And Frida? Where is she?

DI NOLLI: She'll be here in a moment.

DOCTOR: Has the motor arrived?

DI NOLLI: Yes.

DONNA MATILDA: Yes? Has the dress come?

DI NOLLI: It's been here some time.

DOCTOR: Good! Good!

DONNA MATILDA (*trembling*): Where is she? Where's Frida?

DI NOLLI (*shrugging his shoulders and smiling sadly, like one lending himself unwillingly to an untimely joke*): You'll see, you'll see! ... (*Pointing towards the hall.*) Here she is! ... (BERTHOLD *appears at the threshold of the hall, and announces with solemnity.*)

BERTHOLD: Her Highness the Countess Matilda of Canossa! (FRIDA *enters, magnificent and beautiful, arrayed in the robes of her mother as "Countess Matilda of Tuscany," so that she is a living copy of the portrait in the throne room.*)

FRIDA (*passing* BERTHOLD, *who is bowing, says to him with disdain*): Of Tuscany, of Tuscany! Canossa is just one of my castles!

BELCREDI (*in admiration*): Look! Look! She seems another person ...

DONNA MATILDA: One would say it were I! Look! — Why, Frida, look! She's exactly my portrait, alive!

DOCTOR: Yes, yes ... Perfect! Perfect! The portrait, to the life.

BELCREDI: Yes, there's no question about it. She *is* the portrait! Magnificent!

FRIDA: Don't make me laugh, or I shall burst! I say, mother, what a tiny waist you had? I had to squeeze so to get into this!

DONNA MATILDA (*arranging her dress a little*): Wait! ... Keep still! ... These pleats ... is it really so tight?

FRIDA: I'm suffocating! I implore you, to be quick! ...

DOCTOR: But we must wait till it's evening!

FRIDA: No, no, I can't hold out till evening!

DONNA MATILDA: Why did you put it on so soon?

FRIDA: The moment I saw it, the temptation was irresistible ...

DONNA MATILDA: At least you could have called me, or have had someone help you! It's still all crumpled.

FRIDA: So I saw, mother; but they are old creases; they won't come out.

DOCTOR: It doesn't matter, Marchioness! The illusion is perfect. (*Then coming nearer and asking her to come in front of her daughter,*) *without hiding her.*) If you please, stay there, there ... at a certain distance ... now a little more forward ...

BELCREDI: For the feeling of the distance of time ...

DONNA MATILDA (*slightly turning to him*): Twenty years after! A disaster! A tragedy!

BELCREDI: Now don't let's exaggerate!

DOCTOR (*embarrassed, trying to save the situation*): No, no! I meant the dress ... so as to see ... You know ...

BELCREDI (*laughing*): Oh, as for the dress, Doctor, it isn't a matter of twenty years! It's eight hundred! An abyss! Do you really want to shove him across it (*pointing first to* FRIDA *and then to the* MARCHIONESS) from there to here? But you'll have to pick him up in pieces with a basket! Just think now: for us it is a matter of twenty years, a couple of dresses, and a masquerade. But, if, as you say, Doctor, time has stopped for and around him: if he lives there (*pointing to* FRIDA) with her, eight hundred years ago ... I repeat: the giddiness of the jump will be such, that finding himself suddenly among us ... (*The* DOCTOR *shakes his head in dissent.*) You don't think so?

DOCTOR: No, because life, my dear baron, can take up its rhythms. This — our life — will at once become real also to him; and will pull him up directly, wresting from him suddenly the illusion, and showing him that the eight hundred years, as you say, are only twenty! It will be like one of those tricks, such as the leap into space, for instance, of the Masonic rite, which appears to be heaven knows how far, and is only a step down the stairs.

BELCREDI: Ah! An idea! Yes! Look at Frida and the Marchioness, Doctor! Which is more advanced in time? We old people, Doctor! The young ones think they are more ahead; but it isn't true: we are more ahead, because time belongs to us more than to them.

DOCTOR: If the past didn't alienate us ...

BELCREDI: It doesn't matter at all! How does it alienate us? They (*pointing to* FRIDA *and* DI NOLLI) have still to do what we have accomplished, Doctor: to grow old, doing the same foolish things, more or less, as we did ... This is the illusion: that one comes forward through a door to life. It isn't so! As soon as one is born, one starts dying; therefore, he who started first is the most advanced of all. The youngest of us is father Adam! Look there: (*pointing to* FRIDA) eight hundred years younger than all of us — the Countess Matilda of Tuscany. (*He makes her a deep bow.*)

DI NOLLI: I say, Tito, don't start joking.

BELCREDI: Oh, you think I am joking? . . .

DI NOLLI: Oh course, of course . . . all the time.

BELCREDI: Impossible! I've even dressed up as a Benedictine . . .

DI NOLLI: Yes, but for a serious purpose.

BELCREDI: Well, exactly. If it has been serious for the others . . . for Frida, now, for instance. (*Then turning to the* DOCTOR.) I swear, Doctor, I don't yet understand what you want to do.

DOCTOR (*annoyed*): You'll see! Let me do as I wish . . . At present you see the Marchioness still dressed as . . .

BELCREDI: Oh, she also . . . has to masquerade?

DOCTOR: Of course! of course! In another dress that's in there ready to be used when it comes into his head he sees the Countess Matilda of Canossa before him.

FRIDA (*while talking quietly to* DI NOLLI *notices the* DOCTOR's *mistake*): Of Tuscany, of Tuscany!

DOCTOR: It's all the same!

BELCREDI: Oh, I see! He'll be faced by two of them . . .

DOCTOR: Two, precisely! And then . . .

FRIDA (*calling him aside*): Come here, Doctor! Listen!

DOCTOR: Here I am! (*Goes near the two young people and pretends to give some explanations to them.*)

BELCREDI (*softly to* DONNA MATILDA): I say, this is getting rather strong, you know!

DONNA MATILDA (*looking him firmly in the face*): What?

BELCREDI: Does it really interest you as much as all that — to make you willing to take part in . . . ? For a woman this is simply enormous! . . .

DONNA MATILDA: Yes, for an ordinary woman.

BELCREDI: Oh, no, my dear, for all women, — in a question like this! It's an abnegation.

DONNA MATILDA: I owe it to him.

BELCREDI: Don't lie! You know well enough it's not hurting you!

DONNA MATILDA: Well, then, where does the abnegation come in?

BELCREDI: Just enough to prevent you losing caste in other people's eyes — and just enough to offend me! . . .

DONNA MATILDA: But who is worrying about you now?

DI NOLLI (*coming forward*): It's all right. It's all right. That's what we'll do! (*Turning towards* BERTHOLD.) Here you, go and call one of those fellows!

BERTHOLD: At once! (*Exit.*)

DONNA MATILDA: But first of all we've got to pretend that we are going away.

DI NOLLI: Exactly! I'll see to that . . . (*to* BELCREDI) you don't mind staying here?

BELCREDI (*ironically*): Oh, no, I don't mind, I don't mind! . . .

DI NOLLI: We must look out not to make him suspicious again, you know.

BELCREDI: Oh, Lord! He doesn't amount to anything!

DOCTOR: He must believe absolutely that we've gone away. (LANDOLPH *followed by* BERTHOLD *enters from the right.*)

LANDOLPH: May I come in?

DI NOLLI: Come in! Come in; I say — your name's Lolo, isn't it?

LANDOLPH: Lolo, or Landolph, just as you like!

DI NOLLI: Well, look here: the Doctor and the Marchioness are leaving, at once.

LANDOLPH: Very well. All we've got to say is that they have been able to obtain the permission for the reception from His Holiness. He's in there in his own apartments repenting of all he said — and in an awful state to have the pardon! Would you mind coming a minute? . . . If you would, just for a minute . . . put on the dress again . . .

DOCTOR: Why, of course, with pleasure . . .

LANDOLPH: Might I be allowed to make a suggestion? Why not add that the Marchioness of Tuscany has interceded with the Pope that he should be received?

DONNA MATILDA: You see, he has recognized me!

LANDOLPH: Forgive me . . . I don't know my history very well. I am sure you gentlemen know it much better! But I thought it was believed that Henry IV had a secret passion for the Marchioness of Tuscany.

DONNA MATILDA (*at once*): Nothing of the kind! Nothing of the kind!

LANDOLPH: That's what I thought! But he

says he's loved her ... he's always saying it ... And now he fears that her indignation for this secret love of his will work him harm with the Pope.

BELCREDI: We must let him understand that this aversion no longer exists.

LANDOLPH: Exactly! Of course!

DONNA MATILDA (to BELCREDI): History says — I don't know whether you know it or not — that the Pope gave way to the supplications of the Marchioness Matilda and the Abbot of Cluny. And I may say, my dear Belcredi, that I intended to take advantage of this fact — at the time of the pageant — to show him my feelings were not so hostile to him as he supposed.

BELCREDI: You are most faithful to history, Marchioness ...

LANDOLPH: Well then, the Marchioness could spare herself a double disguise and present herself with Monsignor (indicating the DOCTOR) as the Marchioness of Tuscany.

DOCTOR (quickly, energetically): No, no! That won't do at all. It would ruin everything. The impression from the confrontation must be a sudden one, give a shock! No, no, Marchioness, you will appear again as the Duchess Adelaide, the mother of the Empress. And then we'll go away. This is most necessary: that he should know we've gone away. Come on! Don't let's waste any more time! There's a lot to prepare.

(Exeunt the DOCTOR, DONNA MATILDA, and LANDOLPH, right.)

FRIDA: I am beginning to feel afraid again.

DI NOLLI: Again, Frida?

FRIDA: It would have been better if I had seen him before.

DI NOLLI: There's nothing to be frightened of, really.

FRIDA: He isn't furious, is he?

DI NOLLI: Of course not! he's quite calm.

BELCREDI (with ironic sentimental affectation): Melancholy! Didn't you hear that he loves you?

FRIDA: Thanks! That's just why I am afraid.

BELCREDI: He won't do you any harm.

DI NOLLI: It'll only last a minute ...

FRIDA: Yes, but there in the dark with him ...

DI NOLLI: Only for a moment; and I will be near you, and all the others behind the door ready to run in. As soon as you see your mother, your part will be finished ...

BELCREDI: I'm afraid of a different thing: that we're wasting our time ...

DI NOLLI: Don't begin again! The remedy seems a sound one to me.

FRIDA: I think so too! I feel it! I'm all trembling!

BELCREDI: But, mad people, my dear friends — though they don't know it, alas — have this felicity which we don't take into account ...

DI NOLLI (interrupting, annoyed): What felicity? Nonsense!

BELCREDI (forcefully): They don't reason!

DI NOLLI: What's reasoning got to do with it, anyway?

BELCREDI: Don't you call it reasoning that he will have to do — according to us — when he sees her (indicates FRIDA) and her mother? We've reasoned it all out, surely!

DI NOLLI: Nothing of the kind: no reasoning at all! We put before him a double image of his own fantasy, or fiction, as the doctor says.

BELCREDI (suddenly): I say, I've never understood why they take degrees in medicine.

DI NOLLI (amazed): Who?

BELCREDI: The alienists!

DI NOLLI: What ought they to take degrees in, then?

FRIDA: If they are alienists, in what else should they take degrees?

BELCREDI: In law, of course! All a matter of talk! The more they talk, the more highly they are considered. "Analogous elasticity," "the sensation of distance in time!" And the first thing they tell you is that they don't work miracles — when a miracle's just what is wanted! But they know that the more they say they are not miracle-workers, the more folk believe in their seriousness!

BERTHOLD (who has been looking through the keyhole of the door on right): There they are! There they are! They're coming in here.

DI NOLLI: Are they?

BERTHOLD: He wants to come with them ... Yes! ... He's coming too!

DI NOLLI: Let's get away, then! Let's get away, at once! (To BERTHOLD.) You stop here!

BERTHOLD: Must I?

(Without answering him, DI NOLLI, FRIDA, and BELCREDI go out by the main exit, leaving BERTHOLD surprised. The door on *the right opens, and* LANDOLPH *enters first, bowing. Then* DONNA MATILDA *comes in, with mantle and ducal crown as in the first act; also the* DOCTOR *as the Abbot of Cluny.* HENRY IV *is among them in royal dress.* ORDULPH *and* HAROLD *enter last of all.)*

HENRY IV (*following up what he has been saying in the other room*): And now I will ask you a question: how can I be astute, if you think me obstinate?

DOCTOR: No, no, not obstinate!

HENRY IV (*smiling, pleased*): Then you think me really astute?

DOCTOR: No, no, neither obstinate, nor astute.

HENRY IV (*with benevolent irony*): Monsignor, if obstinacy is not a vice which can go with astuteness, I hoped that in denying me the former, you would at least allow me a little of the latter. I can assure you I have great need of it. But if you want to keep it all for yourself . . .

DOCTOR: I? I? Do I seem astute to you?

HENRY IV: No. Monsignor! What do you say? Not in the least! Perhaps in this case, I may seem a little obstinate to you. (*Cutting short to speak to* DONNA MATILDA.) With your permission: a word in confidence to the Duchess. (*Leads her aside and asks her very earnestly.*) Is your daughter really dear to you?

DONNA MATILDA (*dismayed*): Why, yes, certainly . . .

HENRY IV: Do you wish me to compensate her with all my love, with all my devotion, for the grave wrongs I have done her — though you must not believe all the stories my enemies tell about my dissoluteness!

DONNA MATILDA: No, no, I don't believe them. I never have believed such stories.

HENRY IV: Well, then are you willing?

DONNA MATILDA (*confused*): What?

HENRY IV: That I return to love your daughter again? (*Looks at her and adds, in a mysterious tone of warning.*) You mustn't be a friend of the Marchioness of Tuscany!

DONNA MATILDA: I tell you again that she has begged and tried not less than ourselves to obtain your pardon . . .

HENRY IV (*softly, but excitedly*): Don't tell me that! Don't say that to me! Don't you see the effect it has on me, my Lady?

DONNA MATILDA (*looks at him; then very softly as if in confidence*): You love her still?

HENRY IV (*puzzled*): Still? Still, you say? You know, then? But nobody knows! Nobody must know!

DONNA MATILDA: But perhaps she knows, if she has begged so hard for you!

HENRY IV (*looks at her and says*): And you love your daughter? (*Brief pause. He turns to the* DOCTOR *with laughing accents.*) Ah, Monsignor, it's strange how little I think of my wife! It may be a sin, but I swear to you that I hardly feel her at all in my heart. What is stranger is that her own mother scarcely feels her in her heart. Confess, my Lady, that she amounts to very little for you. (*Turning to the* DOCTOR.) She talks to me of that other woman, insistently, insistently, I don't know why! . . .

LANDOLPH (*humbly*): Maybe, Majesty, it is to disabuse you of some ideas you have had about the Marchioness of Tuscany. (*Then, dismayed at having allowed himself this observation, adds.*) I mean just now, of course . . .

HENRY IV: You too maintain that she has been friendly to me?

LANDOLPH: Yes, at the moment, Majesty.

DONNA MATILDA: Exactly! Exactly! . . .

HENRY IV: I understand. That is to say, you don't believe I love her. I see! I see! Nobody's ever believed it, nobody's ever thought it. Better so, then! But enough, enough! (*Turns to the* DOCTOR *with changed expression.*) Monsignor, you see? The reasons the Pope has had for revoking the excommunication have got nothing at all to do with the reasons for which he excommunicated me originally. Tell Pope Gregory we shall meet again at Brixen. And you, Madame, should you chance to meet your daughter in the courtyard of the castle of your friend the Marchioness, ask her to visit me. We shall see if I succeed in keeping her close beside me as wife and Empress. Many women have presented themselves here already assuring me that they were she. And I thought to have her — yes, tried sometimes — there's no shame in it, with one's wife! — But when they said they were Bertha, and they were from Susa, all of them — I can't think why — started laughing! (*Confidentially.*) Understand? — in bed — I undressed — so did she — yes, by God, undressed — a man and a woman — it's natural after all! Like that, we don't bother much about who we are. And one's dress is like a phantom that hovers always near one. Oh, Monsignor, phantoms in general are nothing more than trifling disorders of the spirit: images we cannot contain within the bounds of sleep. They reveal themselves even when we are awake, and they frighten us. I . . . ah . . . I am always afraid when, at night time, I see disordered images before me. Sometimes I am even afraid of my own blood pulsing loudly in my arteries in the silence of night, like the sound of a distant step in a lonely corridor! . . . But, forgive me! I have kept you standing too long already. I thank you, my Lady, I thank you, Monsignor. (DONNA MATILDA *and the* DOCTOR *go off bowing. As soon as they have gone,* HENRY IV *suddenly changes his tone.*) Buffoons, buffoons! One can play any tune on them! And that other fellow . . . Pietro Damiani! . . . Caught him out perfectly! He's afraid to appear before me again. (*Moves up and down excitedly while saying this; then sees* BERTHOLD, *and points him out to the other three* VALETS.) Oh, look at this imbecile watching me with his mouth wide open! (*Shakes him.*) Don't you understand? Don't you see, idiot, how I treat them, how I play the fool with them, make them appear before me just as I wish? Miserable, frightened clowns that they are! And you (*addressing the* VALETS) are amazed that I tear off their ridiculous masks now, just as if it wasn't I who had made them mask themselves to satisfy this taste of mine for playing the madman!

LANDOLPH — HAROLD — ORDULPH (*bewildered, looking at one another*): What? What does he say? What?

HENRY IV (*answers them imperiously*): Enough! enough! Let's stop it. I'm tired of it. (*Then as if the thought left him no peace.*) By God! The impudence! To come here along with her lover! . . . And pretending to do it out of pity! So as not to infuriate a poor devil already out of the world, out of time, out of life! If it hadn't been supposed to be done out of pity, one can well imagine that fellow wouldn't have allowed it. Those people expect others to behave as they wish all the time. And, of course, there's nothing arrogant in that! Oh, no! Oh, no! It's merely their way of thinking, of feeling, of seeing. Everybody has his own way of thinking; you fellows, too. Yours is that of a flock of sheep — miserable, feeble, uncertain . . . But those others take advantage of this and make you accept their way of thinking; or, at least, they suppose they do; because, after all, what do they succeed in imposing on you? Words, words which anyone can interpret in his own manner! That's the way public opinion is formed! And it's a bad look out for a man who finds himself labelled one day with one of these words which everyone repeats; for example "madman," or "imbecile." Don't you think it is rather hard for a man to keep quiet, when he knows that there is a fellow going about trying to persuade everybody that he is as he sees him, trying to fix him in other people's opinion as a "madman" — according to him? Now I am talking seriously! Before I hurt my head, falling from my horse . . . (*Stops suddenly, noticing the dismay of the* FOUR YOUNG MEN.) What's the matter with you? (*Imitates their amazed looks.*) What? Am I, or am I not, mad? Oh, yes! I'm mad all right! (*He becomes terrible.*) Well, then, by God, down on your knees, down on your knees! (*Makes them go down on their knees one by one.*) I order you to go down on your knees before me! And touch the ground three times with your foreheads! Down, down! That's the way you've got to be before madmen! (*Then annoyed with their facile humiliation.*) Get up, sheep! You obeyed me, didn't you? You might have put the strait jacket on me! . . . Crush a man with the weight of a word — it's nothing — a fly! all our life is crushed by the weight of words: the weight of the dead. Look at me here: can you really suppose that Henry IV is still alive? All the same, I speak, and order you live men about! Do you think it's a joke that the dead continue to live? — Yes, *here* it's a joke! But get out into the live world! — Ah, you say: what a beautiful sunrise — for us! All time is before us! — Dawn! We will do what we like with this day — . Ah, yes! To Hell with tradition, the old conventions! Well, go on! You will do nothing but repeat the old, old words, while you imagine you are living! (*Goes up to* BERTHOLD *who has now become quite stupid.*) You don't understand a word of this, do you? What's your name?

BERTHOLD: I? . . . What? . . . Berthold . . .

HENRY IV: Poor Berthold! What's your name here?

BERTHOLD: I . . . I . . . my name is Fino.

HENRY IV (*feeling the warning and critical glances of the others, turns to them to reduce them to silence*): Fino?

BERTHOLD: Fino Pagliuca, sire.

HENRY IV (*turning to* LANDOLPH): I've heard you call each other by your nick-names often enough! Your name is Lolo, isn't it?

LANDOLPH: Yes, sire ... (*Then with a sense of immense joy.*) Oh Lord! Oh Lord! Then he is not mad ...

HENRY IV (*brusquely*): What?

LANDOLPH (*hesitating*): No ... I said ...

HENRY IV: Not mad, any more. No. Don't you see? We're having a joke on those that think I am mad! (*To* HAROLD.) I say, boy, your name's Franco ... (*To* ORDULPH.) And yours ...

ORDULPH: Momo.

HENRY IV: Momo, Momo ... A nice name that!

LANDOLPH: So he isn't ...

HENRY IV: What are you talking about? Of course not! Let's have a jolly, good laugh! ... (*Laughs.*) Ah! ... Ah! ... Ah! ...

LANDOLPH — HAROLD — ORDULPH (*looking at each other half happy and half dismayed*): Then he's cured! ... he's all right! ...

HENRY IV: Silence! Silence! ... (*To* BERTHOLD.) Why don't you laugh? Are you offended? I didn't mean it especially for you. It's convenient for everybody to insist that certain people are mad, so they can shut up. Do you know why? Because it's impossible to hear them speak! What shall I say of these people who've just gone away? That one is a whore, another a libertine, another a swindler ... don't you think so? You can't believe a word he says ... don't you think so? — By the way, they all listen to me terrified. And why are they terrified, if what I say isn't true? Of course, you can't believe what madmen say — yet, at the same time, they stand there with their eyes wide open with terror! — Why? Tell me, tell me, why? — You see I'm quite calm now!

BERTHOLD: But, perhaps, they think that ...

HENRY IV: No, no, my dear fellow! Look me well in the eyes! ... I don't say that it's true — nothing is true, Berthold! But ... look me in the eyes!

BERTHOLD: Well ...

HENRY IV: You see? You see? ... You have terror in your own eyes now because I seem mad to you! There's the proof of it. (*Laughs.*)

LANDOLPH (*coming forward in the name of the others, exasperated*): What proof?

HENRY IV: Your being so dismayed because now I seem again mad to you. You have thought me mad up to now, haven't you? You feel that this dismay of yours can become terror too — something to dash away the ground from under your feet and deprive you of the air you breathe! Do you know what it means to find yourselves face to face with a madman — with one who shakes the foundations of all you have built up in yourselves, your logic, the logic of all your constructions? Madmen, lucky folk! construct without logic, or rather with a logic that flies like a feather. Voluble! Voluble! Today like this and tomorrow — who knows? You say: "This cannot be"; but for them everything can be. You say: "This isn't true!" And why? Because it doesn't seem true to you, or you, or you ... (*indicates the three of them in succession*) ... and to a hundred thousand others! One must see what seems true to these hundred thousand others who are not supposed to be mad! What a magnificent spectacle they afford, when they reason! What flowers of logic they scatter! I know that when I was a child, I thought the moon in the pond was real. How many things I thought real! I believed everything I was told — and I was happy! Because it's a terrible thing if you don't hold on to that which seems true to you today — to that which will seem true to you tomorrow, even if it is the opposite of that which seemed true to you yesterday. I would never wish you to think, as I have done, on this horrible thing which really drives one mad: that if you were beside another and looking into his eyes — as I one day looked into somebody's eyes — you might as well be a beggar before a door never to be opened to you; for he who does enter there will never be you, but someone unknown to you with his own different and impenetrable world ... (*Long pause. Darkness gathers in the room, increasing the sense of strangeness and consternation in which the four young men are involved.* HENRY IV *remains aloof, pondering on the misery which is not only his, but everybody's. Then he pulls himself up, and says in an ordinary tone.*) It's getting dark here ...

ORDULPH: Shall I go for a lamp?

HENRY IV (*ironically*): The lamp, yes the lamp! ... Do you suppose I don't know that as soon as I turn my back with my oil lamp to go to bed, you turn on the electric light for yourselves, here, and even there, in the throne room? I pretend not to see it!

ORDULPH: Well, then, shall I turn it on now?

HENRY IV: No, it would blind me! I want my lamp!

ORDULPH: It's ready here behind the door. (*Goes to the main exit, opens the door, goes out for a moment, and returns with an ancient lamp which is held by a ring at the top.*)

HENRY IV: Ah, a little light! Sit there around the table, no, not like that; in an elegant, easy, manner! . . . (*To* HAROLD.) Yes, you, like that! (*Poses him. Then to* BERTHOLD.) You, so! . . . and I, here! (*Sits opposite them.*) We could do with a little decorative moonlight. It's very useful for us, the moonlight. I feel a real necessity for it, and pass a lot of time looking up at the moon from my window. Who would think, to look at her that she knows that eight hundred years have passed, and that I, seated at the window, cannot really be Henry IV gazing at the moon like any poor devil? But, look, look! See what a magnificent night scene we have here: the emperor surrounded by his faithful counsellors! . . . How do you like it?

LANDOLPH (*softly to* HAROLD, *so as not to break the enchantment*): And to think it wasn't true! . . .

HENRY IV: True? What wasn't true?

LANDOLPH (*timidly as if to excuse himself*): No . . . I mean . . . I was saying this morning to him (*indicates* BERTHOLD) — he has just entered on service here — I was saying: what a pity that dressed like this and with so many beautiful costumes in the wardrobe . . . and with a room like that . . . (*Indicates the throne room.*)

HENRY IV: Well? what's the pity?

LANDOLPH: Well . . . that we didn't know . . .

HENRY IV: That it was all done in jest, this comedy?

LANDOLPH: Because we thought that . . .

HAROLD (*coming to his assistance*): Yes . . . that it was done seriously!

HENRY IV: What do you say? Doesn't it seem serious to you?

LANDOLPH: But if you say that . . .

HENRY IV: I say that — you are fools! You ought to have known how to create a fantasy for yourselves, not to act it for me, or anyone coming to see me; but naturally, simply, day by day, before nobody, feeling yourselves alive in the history of the eleventh century, here at the court of your emperor, Henry IV! You, Ordulph (*taking him by the arm*), alive in the castle of Goslar, waking up in the morning, getting out of bed, and entering straightway into the dream, clothing yourself in the dream that would be no more a dream, because you would have lived it, felt it all alive in you. You would have drunk it in with the air you breathed; yet knowing all the time that it was a dream, so you could better enjoy the privilege afforded you of having to do nothing else but live this dream, this far off and yet actual dream! And to think that at a distance of eight centuries from this remote age of ours, so colored and so sepulchral, the men of the twentieth century are torturing themselves in ceaseless anxiety to know how their fates and fortunes will work out! Whereas you are already in history with me . . .

LANDOLPH: Yes, yes, very good!

HENRY IV: . . . Everything determined, everything settled!

ORDULPH: Yes, yes!

HENRY IV: And sad as is my lot, hideous as some of the events are, bitter the struggles and troublous the time — still all history! All history that cannot change, understand? All fixed for ever! And you could have admired at your ease how every effect followed obediently its cause with perfect logic, how every event took place precisely and coherently in each minute particular! The pleasure, the pleasure of history, in fact, which is so great, was yours.

LANDOLPH: Beautiful, beautiful!

HENRY IV: Beautiful, but it's finished! Now that you know, I could not do it any more! (*Takes his lamp to go to bed.*) Neither could you, if up to now you haven't understood the reason of it! I am sick of it now. (*Almost to himself with violent contained rage.*) By God, I'll make her sorry she came here! Dressed herself up as a mother-in-law for me . . . ! And he as an abbot . . . ! And they bring a doctor with them to study me . . . ! Who knows if they don't hope to cure me? . . . Clowns . . . ! I'd like to smack one of them at least in the face: yes, that one — a famous swordsman, they say! . . . He'll kill me . . . Well, we'll see, we'll see! . . . (*A knock at the door.*) Who is it?

THE VOICE OF JOHN: Deo Gratias!

HAROLD (*very pleased at the chance for another joke*): Oh, it's John, it's old John, who comes every night to play the monk.

ORDULPH (*rubbing his hands*): Yes, yes! Let's make him do it!

HENRY IV (*at once, severely*): Fool, why? Just to play a joke on a poor old man who does it for love of me?

LANDOLPH (*to* ORDULPH): It has to be as if it were true.

HENRY IV: Exactly, as if true! Because, only so, truth is not a jest (*Opens the door and admits* JOHN *dressed as a humble friar with a roll of parchment under his arm.*) Come in, come in, father! (*Then assuming a tone of tragic gravity and deep resentment.*) All the documents of my life and reign favorable to me were destroyed deliberately by my enemies. One only has escaped destruction, this, my life, written by a humble monk who is devoted to me. And you would laugh at him! (*Turns affectionately to* JOHN, *and invites him to sit down at the table.*) Sit down, father, sit down! Have the lamp near you! (*Puts the lamp near him.*) Write! Write!

JOHN (*opens the parchment and prepares to write from dictation*): I am ready, your Majesty!

HENRY IV (*dictating*): "The decree of peace proclaimed at Mayence helped the poor and the good, while it damaged the powerful and the bad. (*Curtain begins to fall.*) It brought wealth to the former, hunger and misery to the latter . . ."

CURTAIN.

ACT III

The throne room so dark that the wall at the bottom is hardly seen. The canvases of the two portraits have been taken away; and, within their frames, FRIDA, dressed as the "Marchioness of Tuscany" and CHARLES DI NOLLI, as "Henry IV," have taken the exact positions of the portraits.

For a moment, after the raising of curtain, the stage is empty. Then the door on the left opens; and HENRY IV, holding the lamp by the ring on top of it, enters. He looks back to speak to the FOUR YOUNG MEN, who, with JOHN, are presumably in the adjoining hall, as at the end of the second act.

HENRY IV: No, stay where you are, stay where you are. I shall manage all right by myself. Good night! (*Closes the door and walks, very sad and tired, across the hall towards the second door on the right, which leads into his apartments.*)

FRIDA (*as soon as she sees that he has just passed the throne, whispers from the niche like one who is on the point of fainting away with fright*): Henry . . .

HENRY IV (*stopping at the voice as if someone had stabbed him traitorously in the back, turns a terror-stricken face towards the wall at the bottom of the room; raising an arm instinctively, as if to defend himself and ward off a blow*): Who is calling me? (*It is not a question, but an exclamation vibrating with terror, which does not expect a reply from the darkness and the terrible silence of the hall, which suddenly fills him with the suspicion that he is really mad.*)

FRIDA (*at his shudder of terror, is herself not less frightened at the part she is playing, and repeats a little more loudly*): Henry! . . . (*But, although she wishes to act the part as they have given it to her, she stretches her head a little out of the frame towards the other frame.*)

HENRY IV (*gives a dreadful cry; lets the lamp fall from his hands to cover his head with his arms, and makes a movement as if to run away*).

FRIDA (*jumping from the frame on to the stand and shouting like a mad-woman*): Henry! . . . Henry! . . . I'm afraid! . . . I'm terrified! . . .

(*And while* DI NOLLI *jumps in turn on to the stand and thence to the floor and runs to* FRIDA *who, on the verge of fainting, continues to cry out, the* DOCTOR, DONNA MATILDA, *also dressed as "Matilda of Tuscany,"* TITO BELCREDI, LANDOLPH, BERTHOLD *and* JOHN *enter the hall from the doors on the right and on the left. One of them turns on the light: a strange light coming from lamps hidden in the ceiling so that only the upper part of the stage is well lighted. The others without taking notice of* HENRY IV, *who looks on astonished by the unexpected inrush, after the moment of terror which still causes him to tremble, run anxiously to support and comfort the still shaking* FRIDA, *who is moaning in the arms of her fiancé. All are speaking at the same time.*)

DI NOLLI: No, no, Frida . . . Here I am . . . I am beside you!

DOCTOR (*coming with the others*): Enough! Enough! There's nothing more to be done! . . .

DONNA MATILDA: He is cured, Frida. Look! He is cured! Don't you see?

DI NOLLI (*astonished*): Cured?

BELCREDI: It was only for fun! Be calm!

FRIDA: No! I am afraid! I am afraid!

DONNA MATILDA: Afraid of what? Look at him. He was never mad at all! . . .

DI NOLLI: That isn't true! What are you saying? Cured?

DOCTOR: It appears so. I should say so . . .

BELCREDI: Yes, yes! They have told us so. (*Pointing to the* FOUR YOUNG MEN.)

DONNA MATILDA: Yes, for a long time! He has confided in them, told them the truth!

DI NOLLI (*now more indignant than astonished*): But what does it mean? If, up to a short time ago . . . ?

BELCREDI: Hum! He was acting, to take you in and also us, who in good faith . . .

DI NOLLI: Is it possible? To deceive his sister, also, right up to the time of her death?

HENRY IV (*remains apart, peering at one and now at the other under the accusation and the mockery of what all believe to be a cruel joke of his, which is now revealed. He has shown by the flashing of his eyes that he is meditating a revenge, which his violent contempt prevents him from defining clearly, as yet. Stung to the quick and with a clear idea of accepting the fiction they have insidiously worked up as true, he bursts forth at this point*): Go on, I say! Go on!

DI NOLLI (*astonished at the cry*): Go on! What do you mean?

HENRY IV: It isn't *your* sister only that is dead!

DI NOLLI: My sister? Yours, I say, whom you compelled up to the last moment, to present herself here as your mother Agnes!

HENRY IV: And was she not *your* mother?

DI NOLLI: My mother? Certainly my mother!

HENRY IV: But your mother is dead for me, *old and far away!* You have just got down now

from there. (*Pointing to the frame from which he jumped down.*) And how do you know whether I have not wept her long in secret, dressed even as I am?

DONNA MATILDA (*dismayed, looking at the others*): What does he say? (*Much impressed, observing him.*) Quietly! quietly, for Heaven's sake!

HENRY IV: What do I say? I ask all of you if Agnes was not the mother of Henry IV? (*Turns to* FRIDA *as if she were really the "Marchioness of Tuscany."*) You, Marchioness, it seems to me, ought to know.

FRIDA (*still frightened, draws closer to* DI NOLLI): No, no, I don't know. Not I!

DOCTOR: It's the madness returning. . . . Quiet now, everybody!

BELCREDI (*indignant*): Madness indeed, Doctor! He's acting again! . . .

HENRY IV (*suddenly*): I? You have emptied those two frames over there, and he stands before my eyes as Henry IV . . .

BELCREDI: We've had enough of this joke now.

HENRY IV: Who said joke?

DOCTOR (*loudly to* BELCREDI): Don't excite him, for the love of God!

BELCREDI (*without lending an ear to him, but speaking louder*): But they have said so (*pointing again to the* FOUR YOUNG MEN), they, they!

HENRY IV (*turning round and looking at them*): You? Did you say it was all a joke?

LANDOLPH (*timid and embarrassed*): No . . . really we said that you were cured.

BELCREDI: Look here! Enough of this! (*To* DONNA MATILDA.) Doesn't it seem to you that the sight of him (*pointing to* DI NOLLI), Marchioness, and that of your daughter dressed so, is becoming an intolerable puerility?

DONNA MATILDA: Oh, be quiet! What does the dress matter, if he is cured?

HENRY IV: Cured, yes! I am cured! (*To* BELCREDI.) Ah, but not to let it end this way all at once, as you suppose! (*Attacks him.*) Do you know that for twenty years nobody has ever dared to appear before me here like you and that gentleman? (*Pointing to the* DOCTOR.)

BELCREDI: Of course I know it. As a matter of fact, I too appeared before you this morning dressed . . .

HENRY IV: As a monk, yes!

BELCREDI: And you took me for Peter Damiani! And I didn't even laugh, believing, in fact, that . . .

HENRY IV: That I was mad! Does it make you laugh seeing her like that, now that I am cured? And yet you might have remembered that in my eyes her appearance now . . . (*Interrupts himself with a gesture of contempt.*) Ah . . . (*Suddenly turns to the* DOCTOR.) You are a doctor, aren't you?

DOCTOR: Yes.

HENRY IV: And you also took part in dressing her up as the Marchioness of Tuscany? To prepare a counter-joke for me here, eh?

DONNA MATILDA (*impetuously*): No, no! What do you say? It was done for you! I did it for your sake.

DOCTOR (*quickly*): To attempt, to try, not knowing . . .

HENRY IV (*cutting him short*): I understand. I say counter-joke, in his case (*indicates* BELCREDI) because he believes that I have been carrying on a jest . . .

BELCREDI: But excuse me, what do you mean? You say yourself you are cured.

HENRY IV: Let me speak! (*To the* DOCTOR.) Do you know, Doctor, that for a moment you ran the risk of making me mad again? By God, to make the portraits speak; to make them jump alive out of their frames . . .

DOCTOR: But you saw that all of us ran in at once, as soon as they told us . . .

HENRY IV: Certainly! (*Contemplates* FRIDA *and* DI NOLLI, *and then looks at the* MARCHIONESS, *and finally at his own costume.*) The combination is very beautiful . . . Two couples . . . Very good, very good, Doctor! For a madman, not bad! . . . (*With a slight wave of his hand to* BELCREDI.) It seems to him now to be a carnival out of season, eh? (*Turns to look at him.*) We'll get rid now of this masquerade costume of mine, so that I may come away with you. What do you say?

BELCREDI: With me? With us?

HENRY IV: Where shall we go? To the Club? In dress coats and with white ties? Or shall both of us go the Marchioness' house?

BELCREDI: Wherever you like! Do you want to remain here still, to continue — alone — what was nothing but the unfortunate joke of a day of carnival? It is really incredible, incredible how you have been able to do all this, freed from the disaster that befell you!

HENRY IV: Yes, you see how it was! The fact is that falling from my horse and striking my head as I did, I was really mad for I know not how long . . .

DOCTOR: Ah! Did it last long?

HENRY IV (*very quickly to the* DOCTOR): Yes, Doctor, a long time! I think it must have been about twelve years. (*Then suddenly turning to speak to* BELCREDI.) Thus I saw nothing, my dear fellow, of all that, after that day of carnival, happened for you but not for me: how things changed, how my friends deceived me, how my place was taken by another, and all the rest of it! And suppose my place had been taken in the heart of the woman I loved? . . . And how should I know who was dead or who had disappeared? . . . All this, you know, wasn't exactly a jest for me, as it seems to you . . .

BELCREDI: No, no! I don't mean that if you please. I mean after . . .

HENRY IV: Ah, yes? After? One day. (*Stops and addresses the* DOCTOR.) — A most interesting case, Doctor! Study me well! Study me carefully! (*Trembles while speaking.*) All by itself, who knows how, one day the trouble here (*touches his forehead*) mended. Little by little, I open my eyes, and at first I don't know whether I am asleep or awake. Then I know I am awake. I touch this thing and that; I see clearly again . . . Ah! — then, as *he* says (*alludes to* BELCREDI) away, away with this masquerade, this incubus! Let's open the windows, breathe life once again! Away! Away! Let's run out! (*Suddenly pulling himself up.*) But where? And to do what? To show myself to all, secretly, as Henry IV, not like this, but arm in arm with you, among my dear friends?

BELCREDI: What are you saying?

DONNA MATILDA: Who could think it? It's not to be imagined. It was an accident.

HENRY IV: They all said I was mad before. (*To* BELCREDI.) And you know it! You were more ferocious than any one against those who tried to defend me.

BELCREDI: Oh, that was only a joke!

HENRY IV: Look at my hair. (*Shows him the hair on the nape of his neck.*)

BELCREDI: But mine is grey too!

HENRY IV: Yes, with this difference: that mine went grey here, as Henry IV, do you understand? And I never knew it! I perceived it all of a sudden, one day, when I opened my eyes; and I was terrified because I understood at once that not only had my hair gone grey, but that I was all grey, inside; that everything had fallen to pieces, that everything was finished; and I was going to arrive, hungry as a wolf, at a banquet which had already been cleared away . . .

BELCREDI: Yes, but, what about the others? . . .

HENRY IV (*quickly*): Ah, yes, I know! They couldn't wait until I was cured, not even those, who, behind my back, pricked my saddled horse till it bled. . . .

DI NOLLI (*agitated*): What, what?

HENRY IV: Yes, treacherously, to make it rear and cause me to fall.

DONNA MATILDA (*quickly, in horror*): This is the first time I knew that.

HENRY IV: That was also a joke, probably!

DONNA MATILDA: But who did it? Who was behind us then?

HENRY IV: It doesn't matter who it was. All those that went on feasting and were ready to leave me their scrapings, Marchioness, of miserable pity, or some dirty remnant of remorse in the filthy plate! Thanks! (*Turning quickly to the* DOCTOR.) Now, Doctor, the case must be absolutely new in the history of madness; I preferred to remain mad — since I found everything ready and at my disposal for this new exquisite fantasy. I would live it — this madness of mine — with the most lucid consciousness; and thus revenge myself on the brutality of a stone which had dinted my head. The solitude — this solitude — squalid and empty as it appeared to me when I opened my eyes again — I determined to deck it out with all the colors and splendors of that far off day of carnival, when you (*looks at* DONNA MATILDA *and points* FRIDA *out to her*) — when you, Marchioness, triumphed. So I would oblige all those who were around me to follow, by God, at my orders that famous pageant which had been — for you and not for me — the jest of a day. I would make it become — for ever — no more a joke but a reality, the reality of a real madness: here, all in masquerade, with throne room, and these my four secret counsellors: secret and, of course, traitors. (*He turns quickly towards them.*) I should like to know what you have gained by revealing the fact that I was cured! If I am cured, there's no longer any need of you, and you will be discharged! To give anyone one's confidence . . . that is really the act of a

madman. But now I accuse you in my turn. (*Turning to the others.*) Do you know? They thought (*alludes to the* VALETS) they could make fun of me too with you. (*Bursts out laughing. The others laugh, but shamefacedly, except* DONNA MATILDA.)

BELCREDI (*to* DI NOLLI): Well, imagine that . . . That's not bad . . .

DI NOLLI (*to the* FOUR YOUNG MEN): You?

HENRY IV: We must pardon them. This dress (*plucking his dress*) which is for me the evident, involuntary caricature of that other continuous, everlasting masquerade, of which we are the involuntary puppets (*indicates* BELCREDI), when, without knowing it, we mask ourselves with that which we appear to be . . . ah, that dress of theirs, this masquerade of theirs, of course, we must forgive it them, since they do not yet see it is identical with themselves . . . (*Turning again to* BELCREDI.) You know, it is quite easy to get accustomed to it. One walks about as a tragic character, just as if it were nothing . . . (*imitates the tragic manner*) in a room like this . . . Look here, Doctor! I remember a priest, certainly Irish, a nice-looking priest, who was sleeping in the sun one November day, with his arm on the corner of the bench of a public garden. He was lost in the golden delight of the mild sunny air which must have seemed for him almost summery. One may be sure that in that moment he did not know any more that he was a priest, or even where he was. He was dreaming . . . A little boy passed with a flower in his hand. He touched the priest with it here on the neck. I saw him open his laughing eyes, while all his mouth smiled with the beauty of his dream. He was forgetful of everything . . . But all at once, he pulled himself together, and stretched out his priest's cassock; and there came back to his eyes the same seriousness which you have seen in mine; because the Irish priests defend the seriousness of their Catholic faith with the same zeal with which I defend the sacred rights of hereditary monarchy! I am cured, gentlemen: because I can act the madman to perfection, here; and I do it very quietly. I'm only sorry for you that have to live your madness so agitatedly, without knowing it or seeing it.

BELCREDI: It comes to this, then, that it is we who are mad. That's what it is!

HENRY IV (*containing his irritation*): But if

you weren't mad, both you and she (*indicating the* MARCHIONESS) would you have come here to see me?

BELCREDI: To tell the truth, I came here believing that you were the madman.

HENRY IV (*suddenly indicating the* MARCHIONESS): And she?

BELCREDI: Ah, as for her... I can't say. I see she is all fascinated by your words, by this *conscious* madness of yours. (*Turns to her.*) Dressed as you are (*speaking to her*), you could even remain here to live it out, Marchioness.

DONNA MATILDA: You are insolent!

HENRY IV (*conciliatingly*): No, Marchioness, what he means to say is that the miracle would be complete, according to him, with you here, who — as the Marchioness of Tuscany, you well know, — could not be my friend, save, as at Canossa, to give me a little pity...

BELCREDI: Or even more than a little! She said so herself!

HENRY IV (*to the* MARCHIONESS, *continuing*): And even, shall we say, a little remorse!...

BELCREDI: Yes, that too she has admitted.

DONNA MATILDA (*angry*): Now look here...

HENRY IV (*quickly, to placate her*): Don't bother about him! Don't mind him! Let him go on infuriating me — though the Doctor's told him not to. (*Turns to* BELCREDI.) But do you suppose I am going to trouble myself any more about what happened between us — the share you had in my misfortune with her (*indicates the* MARCHIONESS *to him and pointing* BELCREDI *out to her*) the part he has now in your life? This is my life! Quite a different thing from your life! Your life, the life in which you have grown old — I have not lived that life. (*To* DONNA MATILDA.) Was this what you wanted to show me with this sacrifice of yours, dressing yourself up like this, according to the Doctor's idea? Excellently done, Doctor! Oh, an excellent idea: — "As we were then, eh? and as we are now?" But I am not a madman according to your way of thinking, Doctor. I know very well that that man there (*indicates* DI NOLLI) cannot be me; because I am Henry IV, and have been, these twenty years, cast in this eternal masquerade. She has lived these years! (*Indicates the* MARCHIONESS.) She has enjoyed them and has become — look at her! — a woman I can no

longer recognize. It is so that I knew her! (*Points to* FRIDA *and draws near her.*) This is the Marchioness I know, always this one!... You seem a lot of children to be so easily frightened by me... (*To* FRIDA.) And you're frightened too, little girl, aren't you, by the jest that they made you take part in — though they didn't understand it wouldn't be the jest they meant it to be, for me? Oh miracle of miracles! Prodigy of prodigies! The dream alive in you! More than alive in you! It was an image that wavered there and they've made you come to life! Oh, mine! You're mine, mine, mine, in my own right! (*He holds her in his arms, laughing like a madman, while all stand still terrified. Then as they advance to tear* FRIDA *from his arms, he becomes furious, terrible and cries imperiously to his* VALETS.) Hold them! Hold them! I order you to hold them!

(*The* FOUR YOUNG MEN *amazed, yet fascinated, move to execute his orders, automatically, and seize* DI NOLLI, *the* DOCTOR, *and* BELCREDI.)

BELCREDI (*freeing himself*): Leave her alone! Leave her alone! You're no madman!

HENRY IV (*in a flash draws the sword from the side of* LANDOLPH, *who is close to him*). I'm not mad, eh! Take that, you!... (*Drives sword into him. A cry of horror goes up. All rush over to assist* BELCREDI, *crying out together.*)

DI NOLLI: Has he wounded you?

BERTHOLD: Yes, yes, seriously!

DOCTOR: I told you so!

FRIDA: Oh God, oh God!

DI NOLLI: Frida, come here!

DONNA MATILDA: He's mad, mad!

DI NOLLI: Hold him!

BELCREDI (*while they take him away by the left exit, he protests as he is borne out*): No, no, you're not mad! You're not mad. He's not mad!

(*They go out by the left amid cries and excitement. After a moment, one hears a still sharper, more piercing cry from* DONNA MATILDA, *and then, silence.*)

HENRY IV (*who has remained on the stage between* LANDOLPH, HAROLD *and* ORDULPH,

with his eyes almost starting out of his head,
terrified by the life of his own masquerade
which has driven him to crime.) Now, yes . . .
we'll have to (*calls his* VALETS *around him as*

if to protect him) here we are . . . together . . .
for ever!

CURTAIN.

Pirandello subtitled *Henry IV* "a tragedy," but it would be hard to find another tragedy in which there is as much talk about laughing, joking, and jests as there is in *Henry IV*. (There are, of course, comic scenes in Shakespeare's tragedies, but there is no talk *about* comedy in them.) Roughly speaking, until the middle of the nineteenth century most theories of laughter were of two sorts. One held that we laugh good-naturedly, in genial fellow-feeling, out of a spirit of play. An adult sees an infant, smiles affectionately, and the infant returns the smile and adds a giggle, stimulating the adult to even more genial feelings. This spirit of play allegedly can be seen also in persons splashing each other in the water, in the host smiling as he heaps food on a guest's plate, etc. The other theory holds that laughter is derisive, proceeding from a sense of superiority. We laugh at the child trying to walk because he does badly with effort what we do well and easily; we laugh at the pompous man slipping on a banana peel because his pretensions are knocked down as he suddenly assumes an ungainly posture, while we remain squarely on our feet in full control of ourselves. Similarly, we laugh at the lover who is blind to the faults that we clearly see in his beloved, and we laugh at the hen-pecked husband who is less than the man we are. The distinction between the two theories is easily seen in the distinction we make between laughing *with* someone and laughing *at* someone, though it should be added that the theories are often combined in various ways that blur the distinction.

From the middle of the nineteenth century to the present, another theory — not unknown earlier, but not often held — gains prominence, a theory holding that we laugh in order to escape from the sorrows of existence. Ancient literature and ancient history attest to man's perennial unhappiness, but the usual response was to lament it; in the last hundred years there has developed a sort of tragic comedy, a literature that laughs or jokes to fend off pain. In the introduction to this book something has been said about the triple blows delivered by Darwin, Marx, and Freud to man's heroic image of himself; here it need only be mentioned that Darwinism saw man not as a special creation but as a soulless animal that had evolved by means of "accidental variations"; Marxism saw him as the creature of economic forces; and Freudianism as the victim of infantile experiences. Still, despite his ignoble origin and his helplessness, man has reason and has aspirations unknown to the other animals. As the joke puts it, astronomically speaking man is nothing — but man is the astronomer. Of all the created things, man alone sees the ludicrousness and loathsomeness of life. His superiority to the rest of creation is his curse, for it painfully informs him that he is different from the rest and that despite his noble dreams, he is sentenced to the same ignoble end.

To make the point, one could quote the heavyweights at length, Dostoevsky and Kierkegaard, but fortunately it can also be made briefly:

> And if I laugh at any mortal thing,
> Tis that I may not weep.
>
> Byron, *Don Juan*

The comic alone is able to give us the strength to bear the tragedy of existence.

> Eugène Ionesco, *Notes and Counter Notes*

The laugh of laughs, the *risus purus*, the laugh laughing at the laugh, the beholding, the saluting of the highest joke, in a word the laugh that laughs — silence please — [is] at that which is unhappy.

> Samuel Beckett, *Watt*

Pirandello had much to be unhappy about: his parents lost their wealth in a flood that destroyed the family's profitable sulfur mine, his wife lost her dowry, and, worst, his wife became insanely suspicious of her husband, who was forced to lock himself in his room to assure her of his fidelity. But it would be unjust to Pirandello to suggest that his deep unhappiness was due simply to personal misfortunes; his unhappiness was that of a thinking man, not that of a mismatched husband. Something must be said of his thinking, which can be found not only in the plays and in his preface to *Six Characters in Search of an Author*, but also in an essay of 1908 entitled "Umorismo" ("Humor"). Reality is fluid, and beyond the grasp of reason. But man *has* reason, and he cannot tolerate a fluid, irrational world, so he sets up reasonable — but false — categories. He establishes laws, codes of ethics, religions, and other "communal lies," but in certain dreadful moments he may become aware that these creations are distortions of the unknowable reality. So great is the dread, however, that he clings to his illusory conceptions. Such is (in the words of the preface to *Six Characters*) "the inherent tragic conflict between life (which is always moving and changing) and form (which fixes it, immutable)." The "form" is, in Pirandello's terminology, a "mask," and we all have our masks. We think we have made ourselves into loyal citizens or rebels, virtuous husbands or libertines, etc., but whatever the mask, the face beneath it is a bundle of indeterminate instincts. A man wears the mask of an elderly Supreme Court judge, but the face, the real man, wishes to marry a girl of twenty-one. Instantly there is an outcry from respectable masks, demanding that the judge be subjected to a mental examination, so inconceivable is it, to these others, that an aged jurist should harbor such feelings. (The example is not from Pirandello but from contemporary American life, but Pirandello does have a play, *When One Is Somebody*, about a poet in late middle age who finds that he must choose between being the respected poet who has gained official recognition or the lyric poet whom the new generation applauds. So powerful is the pressure of society that he accepts the official honor and becomes an automaton.) Sometimes in a passionate moment the suffering face bursts through the mask, but usually the mask succeeds in confining the face, so great is the individual's dread of confessing that he has a face different from his mask. Most often man finds it best to play the game, to cherish the illusion that masks are faces. Men therefore greet each other politely, feign interest in one another's problems, and so forth. Moreover, the mask is adopted not merely to conceal the truth from one's fellows but even from oneself; a man lies to himself to protect himself from the horrifying truth of a meaningless or unknowable reality. To reject the illusions is to confront a reality that is maddening. It is also tragically comic: the gap between illusions or masks and reality or faces is so great that when seen it evokes not only lamentation but bitter laughter.

In "Umorismo" Pirandello quotes Machiavelli with approval: "If I sometimes laugh or sing, it is to have an outlet for tears." The mere comic writer, Pirandello says, will laugh at man's deception and self-deception, but the "humorist will see its serious and painful side." He will take the construction apart, but not merely to laugh at it; and even though he laughs, he will sympathize. Among the instances Pirandello cites is Copernicus' invention of the telescope. The telescope does not reveal the real nature of the universe, but it did demolish the cherished illusion that man's earth was the center of the universe. The loss of this illusion is, for some, dreadful, but the "humorist," with his interest in contradictions replies that if man can conceive of infinite distances, he can conceive of infinite grandeur too, and that is no small thing.

In *Henry IV* the masquerade that has been a trivial joke for the participants became a bitter joke, a reality, for the man whose head struck a stone and who was left with the insane belief that he was Henry IV. During his insanity, the illusions of the rest of the world meant nothing to him, and he succeeded in arresting time. Life outside went on, but his moment as Henry remained. Twenty years later, the woman he loved was no longer young and beautiful, but her daughter now resembled the mother of that earlier period, and for Henry the daughter is the beloved. Ordinarily, Pirandello says, the lover is comic: in the words of this play, men look at a woman "with that eternal look of fidelity in their faces! I've always thought it comic; then more than now." For Henry, twenty years later, the lover and beloved are unchanged. The parts that were initially played as a joke have given the madman a reality, a release from the world of flux. "The jest of the day" became "no more a joke but a reality, the reality of a real madness."

A meddling pretentious physician has a plan — which he calls a "trick" akin to a practical joke — to cure Henry of his madness and to bring him into the "real" world of the present. The man of science does not, of course, understand that the real world cannot be catalogued, and that what he thinks is the real world is a world of illusory constructions. Henry explains what the doctor's "real" world is. (The doctor is disguised as a clergyman.)

> We are all fixed in good faith in a certain concept of ourselves. However, Monsignor, while you keep yourself in order, holding on with both your hands to your holy habit, there slips down from your sleeves, there peels off from you . . . like a serpent . . . something you don't notice: life, Monsignor! (*Turns to the Marchioness*) Has it never happened to you, my Lady, to find a different self in yourself? Have you always been the same?

My god! One day . . . how was it, how was it you were able to commit this
or that action?

Nor does the doctor understand — so attached is he to his mask of know-it-
all — that real life is a horror. But Henry knows:

It's a terrible thing if you don't hold on to that which seems true to
you. . . . I would never wish you to think, as I have done, on this horrible
thing which really drives one mad: that if you were beside another and
looking into his eyes — as I one day looked into somebody's eyes — you
might as well be a beggar before a door never to be opened to you; for he
who does enter there will never be you, but someone unknown to you
with his own different and impenetrable world.

We may try to dismiss such skepticism with the same shrug we give to the
ancient paradox that a man cannot twice cross the same river: the man is
different, and so is the river. But the ancient paradox was not embodied in an
imaginative plot with such arresting characters. When at the end of the play
Henry IV, having killed a man because of the doctor's "trick" to bring Henry
back to "reality," gathers his servants about him with "Here we are . . . together . . . forever!" we do not feel that we are listening to ingenious paradoxes;
we feel that we are looking at an image of life. At the end of *Oedipus the King*
the chorus tells the audience to count no man happy until his life is over;
similarly, Henry's years of madness, real and feigned, culminate in an action
that forever deprives him of happiness.

THE GOOD WOMAN OF SETZUAN

Bertolt Brecht

Translated by Eric Bentley

Bertolt Brecht (1898–1956) was born in Germany of middle-class parents, attended public schools and then entered the University of Munich to study medicine, but after one year was drafted for military service in World War I and served as a medical orderly for about a year. At the end of the war he returned to a shattered Germany, and during most of the twenties he seems to have been more or less an anarchist; in any case, his earliest poems and plays (e.g., *The Threepenny Opera*, 1928) cannot be called Communist, though around 1928 he seems to have become a believer in Communism. With the rise of Hitler, Brecht left Germany (1933), spending most of the years 1933 to 1939 in Denmark, 1940 in Finland, and 1941 to 1948 in the United States. Most of his best-known plays (including *The Good Woman of Setzuan*, 1938–1941) were written during his fifteen years of exile. His return in 1948 to Germany — to East Berlin — was somewhat equivocal, for he obtained Austrian citizenship (1950) and arranged for the copyright to his work to be held by a publisher in West Berlin. He died suddenly, of a thrombosis, in 1956.

CHARACTERS

WONG, *a water seller*
THREE GODS
SHEN TE, *a prostitute, later a shopkeeper*
MRS. SHIN, *former owner of Shen Te's shop*
A FAMILY OF EIGHT (*husband, wife, brother, sister-in-law, grandfather, nephew, niece, boy*)
AN UNEMPLOYED MAN
A CARPENTER
MRS. MI TZU, *Shen Te's landlady*

YANG SUN, *an unemployed pilot, later a factory manager*
AN OLD WHORE
A POLICEMAN
AN OLD MAN
AN OLD WOMAN, *his wife*
MR. SHU FU, *a barber*
MRS. YANG, *mother of Yang Sun*
GENTLEMEN, VOICES, CHILDREN (*three*), etc.

The Württemburgische Staatstheater production of *The Good Woman of Setzuan*, directed by Peter Palitzsch, set by Gerd Richter, Stuttgart, 1965. (Photograph: Werner Schloske.)

PROLOGUE

At the gates of the half-Westernized city of Setzuan. Evening. WONG *the water seller introduces himself to the audience.*

WONG: I sell water here in the city of Setzuan. It isn't easy. When water is scarce, I have long distances to go in search of it, and when it is plentiful, I have no income. But in our part of the world there is nothing unusual about poverty. Many people think only the gods can save the situation. And I hear from a cattle merchant — who travels a lot — that some of the highest gods are on their way here at this very moment. Informed sources have it that heaven is quite disturbed at all the complaining. I've been coming out here to the city gates for three days now to bid these gods welcome. I want to be the first to greet them. What about those fellows over there? No, no, they *work*. And that one there has ink on his fingers, he's no god, he must be a clerk from the cement factory. *Those* two are another story. They look as though they'd like to beat you. But gods don't need to beat you, do they?

(THREE GODS *appear.*)

What about those three? Old-fashioned clothes — dust on their feet — they *must* be gods! (*He throws himself at their feet.*) Do with me what you will, illustrious ones!

FIRST GOD (*with an ear trumpet*): Ah! (*He is pleased.*) So we were expected?

WONG (*giving them water*): Oh, yes. And I *knew* you'd come.

FIRST GOD: We need somewhere to stay the night. You know of a place?

WONG: The whole town is at your service, illustrious ones! What sort of a place would you like?

(*The* GODS *eye each other.*)

FIRST GOD: Just try the first house you come to, my son.

WONG: That would be Mr. Fo's place.

FIRST GOD: Mr. Fo.

WONG: One moment! (*He knocks at the first house.*)

VOICE FROM MR. FO'S: No!

(WONG *returns a little nervously.*)

WONG: It's too bad. Mr. Fo isn't in. And his servants don't dare do a thing without his consent. He'll have a fit when he finds out who they turned away, won't he?

FIRST GOD (*smiling*): He will, won't he?

WONG: One moment! The next house is Mr. Cheng's. Won't he be thrilled!

FIRST GOD: Mr. Cheng.

(WONG *knocks.*)

VOICE FROM MR. CHENG'S: Keep your gods. We have our own troubles!

WONG (*back with the* GODS): Mr. Cheng is very sorry, but he has a houseful of relations. I think some of them are a bad lot, and naturally, he wouldn't like you to see them.

THIRD GOD: Are we so terrible?

WONG: Well, only with bad people, of course. Everyone knows the province of Kwan is always having floods.

SECOND GOD: Really? How's that?

WONG: Why, because they're so irreligious.

SECOND GOD: Rubbish. It's because they neglected the dam.

FIRST GOD (*to* SECOND): Sh! (*To* WONG.) You're still in hopes, aren't you, my son?

WONG: Certainly. All Setzuan is competing for the honor! What happened up to now is pure coincidence. I'll be back. (*He walks away, but then stands undecided.*)

SECOND GOD: What did I tell you?

THIRD GOD: It *could* be pure coincidence.

SECOND GOD: The same coincidence in Shun, Kwan, and Setzuan? People just aren't religious any more, let's face the fact. Our mission has failed!

FIRST GOD: Oh come, we might run into a good person any minute.

THIRD GOD: How did the resolution read? (*Unrolling a scroll and reading from it.*) "The world can stay as it is if enough people are found (*at the word "found" he unrolls it a little more*) living lives worthy of human beings." Good people, that is. Well, what about this

Bertolt Brecht, *The Good Woman of Setzuan,* © 1956, 1961 by Eric Bentley. Epilogue © 1965 by Eric Bentley. Originally published in *Parables for the Theatre: Two Plays by Bertolt Brecht,* translated by Eric Bentley. University of Minnesota Press, Minneapolis. © 1948 by Eric Bentley.

water seller himself? *He's* good, or I'm very much mistaken.

SECOND GOD: You're very much mistaken. When he gave us a drink, I had the impression there was something odd about the cup. Well, look! (*He shows the cup to the* FIRST GOD.)

FIRST GOD: A false bottom!

SECOND GOD: The man is a swindler.

FIRST GOD: Very well, count *him* out. That's one man among millions. And as a matter of fact, we only need one on *our* side. These atheists are saying, "The world must be changed because no one can *be* good and *stay* good." No one, eh? I say: let us find one — just one — and we have those fellows where we want them!

THIRD GOD (*to* WONG): Water seller, is it so hard to find a place to stay?

WONG: Nothing could be easier. It's just me. I don't go about it right.

THIRD GOD: Really?

(*He returns to the others. A* GENTLEMAN *passes by.*)

WONG: Oh dear, they're catching on. (*He accosts the* GENTLEMAN.) Excuse the intrusion, dear sir, but three gods have just turned up. Three of the very highest. They need a place for the night. Seize this rare opportunity — to have real gods as your guests!

GENTLEMAN (*laughing*): A new way of finding free rooms for a gang of crooks. (*Exit* GENTLEMAN.)

WONG (*shouting at him*): Godless rascal! Have you no religion, gentleman of Setzuan? (*Pause.*) Patience, illustrious ones! (*Pause.*) There's only one person left. Shen Te, the prostitute. She *can't* say no. (*Calls up to a window.*) Shen Te!

(SHEN TE *opens the shutters and looks out.*)

WONG: Shen Te, it's Wong. *They're* here, and nobody wants them. Will you take them?

SHEN TE: Oh, no, Wong, I'm expecting a gentleman.

WONG: Can't you forget about him for tonight?

SHEN TE: The rent has to be paid by tomorrow or I'll be out on the street.

WONG: This is no time for calculation, Shen Te.

SHEN TE: Stomachs rumble even on the Emperor's birthday, Wong.

WONG: Setzuan is one big dung hill!

SHEN TE: Oh, very well! I'll hide till my gentleman has come and gone. Then I'll take them. (*She disappears.*)

WONG: They mustn't see her gentleman or they'll know what she is.

FIRST GOD (*who hasn't heard any of this*): I think it's hopeless.

(*They approach* WONG.)

WONG (*jumping, as he finds them behind him*): A room has been found, illustrious ones! (*He wipes sweat off his brow.*)

SECOND GOD: Oh, good.

THIRD GOD: Let's see it.

WONG (*nervously*): Just a minute. It has to be tidied up a bit.

THIRD GOD: Then we'll sit down here and wait.

WONG (*still more nervous*): No, no! (*Holding himself back.*) Too much traffic, you know.

THIRD GOD (*with a smile*): Of course, if you *want* us to move.

(*They retire a little. They sit on a doorstep.* WONG *sits on the ground.*)

WONG (*after a deep breath*): You'll be staying with a single girl — the finest human being in Setzuan!

THIRD GOD: That's nice.

WONG (*to the audience*): They gave me such a look when I picked up my cup just now.

THIRD GOD: You're worn out, Wong.

WONG: A little, maybe.

FIRST GOD: Do people here have a hard time of it?

WONG: The good ones do.

FIRST GOD: What about yourself?

WONG: You mean I'm not good. That's true. And I don't have an easy time either!

(*During this dialogue, a* GENTLEMAN *has turned up in front of* SHEN TE's *house, and has whistled several times. Each time* WONG *has given a start.*)

THIRD GOD (*to* WONG, *softly*): Psst! I think he's gone now.

WONG (*confused and surprised*): Ye-e-es.

(*The* GENTLEMAN *has left now, and* SHEN TE *has come down to the street.*)

SHEN TE (*softly*): Wong!

(*Getting no answer, she goes off down the street.* WONG *arrives just too late, forgetting his carrying pole.*)

WONG (*softly*): Shen Te! Shen Te! (*To him-*

self.) So she's gone off to earn the rent. Oh dear, I can't go to the gods *again* with no room to offer them. Having failed in the service of the gods, I shall run to my den in the sewer pipe down by the river and hide from their sight!

(*He rushes off.* SHEN TE *returns, looking for him, but finding the* GODS. *She stops in confusion.*)

SHEN TE: You are the illustrious ones? My name is Shen Te. It would please me very much if my simple room could be of use to you.

THIRD GOD: Where is the water seller, Miss . . . Shen Te?

SHEN TE: I missed him, somehow.

FIRST GOD: Oh, he probably thought you weren't coming, and was afraid of telling us.

THIRD GOD (*picking up the carrying pole*): We'll leave this with you. He'll be needing it.

(*Led by* SHEN TE, *they go into the house. It grows dark, then light. Dawn. Again escorted by* SHEN TE, *who leads them through the half-light with a little lamp, the* GODS *take their leave.*)

FIRST GOD: Thank you, thank you, dear Shen Te, for your elegant hospitality! We shall not forget! And give our thanks to the water seller — he showed us a good human being.

SHEN TE: Oh, *I'm* not good. Let me tell you something: when Wong asked me to put you up, I hesitated.

FIRST GOD: It's all right to hesitate if you then go ahead! And in giving us that room you did much more than you knew. You proved that good people still exist, a point that has been disputed of late — even in heaven. Farewell!

SECOND GOD: Farewell!

THIRD GOD: Farewell!

SHEN TE: Stop, illustrious ones! I'm not sure you're right. I'd like to be good, it's true, but there's the rent to pay. And that's not all: I sell myself for a living. Even so I can't make ends meet, there's too much competition. I'd like to honor my father and mother and speak nothing but the truth and not covet my neighbor's house. I should love to stay with one man. But how? How is it done? Even breaking a few of your commandments, I can hardly manage.

FIRST GOD (*clearing his throat*): These thoughts are but, um, the misgivings of an unusually good woman!

THIRD GOD: Good-bye, Shen Te! Give our regards to the water seller!

SECOND GOD: And above all: be good! Farewell!

FIRST GOD: Farewell!

THIRD GOD: Farewell!

(*They start to wave good-bye.*)

SHEN TE: But everything is so expensive, I don't feel sure I can do it!

SECOND GOD: That's not in our sphere. We never meddle with economics.

THIRD GOD: One moment. (*They stop.*) Isn't it true she might do better if she had more money?

SECOND GOD: Come, come! How could we ever account for it Up Above?

FIRST GOD: Oh, there are ways. (*They put their heads together and confer in dumb show. To* SHEN TE, *with embarrassment.*) As you say you can't pay your rent, well, um, we're not paupers, so of course we *insist* on paying for our room. (*Awkwardly thrusting money into her hand.*) There! (*Quickly.*) But don't tell anyone! The incident is open to misinterpretation.

SECOND GOD: It certainly is!

FIRST GOD (*defensively*): But there's no law against it! It was never decreed that a god mustn't pay hotel bills!

(*The* GODS *leave.*)

I

A small tobacco shop. The shop is not as yet completely furnished and hasn't started doing business.

SHEN TE (*to the audience*): It's three days now since the gods left. When they said they wanted to pay for the room, I looked down at my hand, and there was more than a thousand silver dollars! I bought a tobacco shop with the money, and moved in yesterday. I don't own the building, of course, but I can pay the rent, and I hope to do a lot of good here. Beginning with Mrs. Shin, who's just coming across the square with her pot. She had the shop before me, and yesterday she dropped in to ask for rice for her children. (*Enter* MRS. SHIN. *Both women bow.*) How do you do, Mrs. Shin.

MRS. SHIN: How do you do, Miss Shen Te. You like your new home?

SHEN TE: Indeed, yes. Did your children have a good night?

MRS. SHIN: In that hovel? The youngest is coughing already.

SHEN TE: Oh, dear!

MRS. SHIN: You're going to learn a thing or two in these slums.

SHEN TE: Slums? That's not what you said when you sold me the shop!

MRS. SHIN: Now don't start nagging! Robbing me and my innocent children of their home and then calling it a slum! That's the limit! (*She weeps.*)

SHEN TE (*tactfully*): I'll get your rice.

MRS. SHIN: And a little cash while you're at it.

SHEN TE: I'm afraid I haven't sold anything yet.

MRS. SHIN (*screeching*): I've got to have it. Strip the clothes from my back and then cut my throat, will you? I know what I'll do: I'll dump my children on your doorstep! (*She snatches the pot out of* SHEN TE'*s hands.*)

SHEN TE: Please don't be angry. You'll spill the rice.

(*Enter an elderly* HUSBAND *and* WIFE *with their shabbily dressed* NEPHEW.)

WIFE: Shen Te, dear! You've come into money, they tell me. And we haven't a roof over our heads A tobacco shop. We had one too. But it's gone. Could we spend the night here, do you think?

NEPHEW (*appraising the shop*): Not bad!

WIFE: He's our nephew. We're inseparable!

MRS. SHIN: And who are these . . . ladies and gentlemen?

SHEN TE: They put me up when I first came in from the country. (*To the audience.*) Of course, when my small purse was empty, they put me out on the street, and they may be afraid I'll do the same to them. (*To the newcomers, kindly.*) Come in, and welcome, though I've only one little room for you — it's behind the shop.

HUSBAND: That'll do. Don't worry.

WIFE (*bringing* SHEN TE *some tea*): We'll stay over here, so we won't be in your way. Did you make it a tobacco shop in memory of your first real home? We can certainly give you a hint or two! That's one reason we came.

MRS. SHIN (*to* SHEN TE): Very nice! As long as you have a few customers too!

HUSBAND: Sh! A customer!

(*Enter an* UNEMPLOYED MAN, *in rags.*)

UNEMPLOYED MAN: Excuse me. I'm unemployed.

(MRS. SHIN *laughs.*)

SHEN TE: Can I help you?

UNEMPLOYED MAN: Have you any damaged cigarettes? I thought there might be some damage when you're unpacking.

WIFE: What nerve, begging for tobacco! (*Rhetorically.*) Why don't they ask for bread?

UNEMPLOYED MAN: Bread is expensive. One cigarette butt and I'll be a new man.

SHEN TE (*giving him cigarettes*): That's very important — to be a new man. You'll be my first customer and bring me luck.

(*The* UNEMPLOYED MAN *quickly lights a cigarette, inhales, and goes off, coughing.*)

WIFE: Was that right, Shen Te, dear?

MRS. SHIN: If this is the opening of a shop, you can hold the closing at the end of the week.

HUSBAND: I bet he had money on him.

SHEN TE: Oh, no, he said he hadn't!

NEPHEW: How d'you know he wasn't lying?

SHEN TE (*angrily*): How do you know he was?

WIFE (*wagging her head*): You're too good, Shen Te, dear. If you're going to keep this shop, you'll have to learn to say no.

HUSBAND: Tell them the place isn't yours to dispose of. Belongs to . . . some relative who insists on all accounts being strictly in order . . .

MRS. SHIN: That's right! What do you think you are — a philanthropist?

SHEN TE (*laughing*): Very well, suppose I ask you for my rice back, Mrs. Shin?

WIFE (*combatively, at* MRS. SHIN): So that's her rice?

(*Enter the* CARPENTER, *a small man.*)

MRS. SHIN (*who, at the sight of him, starts to hurry away*): See you tomorrow, Miss Shen Te! (*Exit* MRS. SHIN.)

CARPENTER: Mrs. Shin, it's you I want!

WIFE (*to* SHEN TE): Has she some claim on you?

SHEN TE: She's hungry. That's a claim.

CARPENTER: Are you the new tenant? And filling up the shelves already? Well, they're not yours till they're paid for, ma'am. I'm the carpenter, so I should know.

SHEN TE: I took the shop "furnishings included."

CARPENTER: You're in league with that Mrs. Shin, of course. All right. I demand my hundred silver dollars.

SHEN TE: I'm afraid I haven't got a hundred silver dollars.

CARPENTER: Then you'll find it. Or I'll have you arrested.

WIFE (whispering to SHEN TE): That relative: make it a cousin.

SHEN TE: Can't it wait till next month?

CARPENTER: No!

SHEN TE: Be a little patient, Mr. Carpenter, I can't settle all claims at once.

CARPENTER: Who's patient with me? (He grabs a shelf from the wall.) Pay up — or I take the shelves back!

WIFE: Shen Te! Dear! Why don't you let your . . . cousin settle this affair? (To CARPENTER.) Put your claim in writing. Shen Te's cousin will see you get paid.

CARPENTER (derisively): Cousin, eh?

HUSBAND: Cousin, yes.

CARPENTER: I know these cousins!

NEPHEW: Don't be silly. He's a personal friend of mine.

HUSBAND: What a man! Sharp as a razor!

CARPENTER: All right. I'll put my claim in writing. (Puts shelf on floor, sits on it, writes out bill.)

WIFE (to SHEN TE): He'd tear the dress off your back to get his shelves. Never recognize a claim. That's my motto.

SHEN TE: He's done a job, and wants something in return. It's shameful that I can't give it to him. What will the gods say?

HUSBAND: You did your bit when you took us in.

(Enter the BROTHER, limping, and the SISTER-IN-LAW, pregnant.)

BROTHER (to HUSBAND and WIFE): So this is where you're hiding out! There's family feeling for you! Leaving us on the corner!

WIFE (embarrassed, to SHEN TE): It's my brother and his wife. (To them.) Now stop grumbling, and sit quietly in that corner. (To SHEN TE.) It can't be helped. She's in her fifth month.

SHEN TE: Oh yes. Welcome!

WIFE (to the couple): Say thank you. (They mutter something.) The cups are there. (To SHEN TE.) Lucky you bought this shop when you did!

SHEN TE (laughing and bringing tea): Lucky indeed!

(Enter MRS. MI TZU, the landlady.)

MRS. MI TZU: Miss Shen Te? I am Mrs. Mi Tzu, your landlady. I hope our relationship will be a happy one. I like to think I give my tenants modern, personalized service. Here is your lease. (To the others, as SHEN TE reads the lease.) There's nothing like the opening of a little shop, is there? A moment of true beauty! (She is looking around.) Not very much on the shelves, of course. But everything in the gods' good time! Where are your references, Miss Shen Te?

SHEN TE: Do I have to have references?

MRS. MI TZU: After all, I haven't a notion who you are!

HUSBAND: Oh, we'd be glad to vouch for Miss Shen Te! We'd go through fire for her!

MRS. MI TZU: And who may you be?

HUSBAND (stammering): Ma Fu, tobacco dealer.

MRS. MI TZU: Where is your shop, Mr. . . . Ma Fu?

HUSBAND: Well, um, I haven't got a shop — I've just sold it.

MRS. MI TZU: I see. (To SHEN TE.) Is there no one else that knows you?

WIFE (whispering to SHEN TE): Your cousin! Your cousin!

MRS. MI TZU: This is a respectable house, Miss Shen Te. I never sign a lease without certain assurances.

SHEN TE (slowly, her eyes downcast): I have . . . a cousin.

MRS. MI TZU: On the square? Let's go over and see him. What does he do?

SHEN TE (as before): He lives . . . in another city.

WIFE (prompting): Didn't you say he was in Shung?

SHEN TE: That's right. Shung.

HUSBAND (prompting): I had his name on the tip of my tongue. Mr. . . .

SHEN TE (with an effort): Mr. . . . Shui . . . Ta.

HUSBAND: That's it! Tall, skinny fellow!

SHEN TE: Shui Ta!

NEPHEW (to CARPENTER): You were in touch with him, weren't you? About the shelves?

CARPENTER (surlily): Give him this bill. (He hands it over.) I'll be back in the morning. (Exit CARPENTER.)

NEPHEW (*calling after him, but with his eyes on* MRS. MI TZU): Don't worry! Mr. Shui Ta pays on the nail!

MRS. MI TZU (*looking closely at* SHEN TE): I'll be happy to make his acquaintance, Miss Shen Te. (*Exit* MRS. MI TZU.)

(*Pause.*)

WIFE: By tomorrow morning she'll know more about you than you do yourself.

SISTER-IN-LAW (*to* NEPHEW): This thing isn't built to last.

(*Enter* GRANDFATHER.)

WIFE: It's Grandfather! (*To* SHEN TE.) Such a good old soul!

(*The* BOY *enters.*)

BOY (*over his shoulder*): Here they are!

WIFE: And the boy, how he's grown! But he always could eat enough for ten.

(*Enter the* NIECE.)

WIFE (*to* SHEN TE): Our little niece from the country. There are more of us now than in your time. The less we had, the more there were of us; the more there were of us, the less we had. Give me the key. We must protect ourselves from unwanted guests. (*She takes the key and locks the door.*) Just make yourself at home. I'll light the little lamp.

NEPHEW (*a big joke*): I hope her cousin doesn't drop in tonight! The strict Mr. Shui Ta!

(SISTER-IN-LAW *laughs.*)

BROTHER (*reaching for a cigarette*): One cigarette more or less . . .

HUSBAND: One cigarette more or less.

(*They pile into the cigarettes. The* BROTHER *hands a jug of wine round.*)

NEPHEW: Mr. Shui Ta'll pay for it!

GRANDFATHER (*gravely, to* SHEN TE): How do you do?

(SHEN TE, *a little taken aback by the belatedness of the greeting, bows. She has the carpenter's bill in one hand, the landlady's lease in the other.*)

WIFE: How about a bit of a song? To keep Shen Te's spirits up?

NEPHEW: Good idea. Grandfather: you start!

SONG OF THE SMOKE

GRANDFATHER:
I used to think (before old age beset me)
    That brains could fill the pantry of the poor.
But where did all my cerebration get me?
    I'm just as hungry as I was before.
        So what's the use?
        See the smoke float free
        Into ever colder coldness!
        It's the same with me.

HUSBAND:
The straight and narrow path leads to disaster
    And so the crooked path I tried to tread.
That got me to disaster even faster.
    (They say we shall be happy when we're
        dead.)
        So what's the use?
        See the smoke float free
        Into ever colder coldness!
        It's the same with me.

NIECE:
You older people, full of expectation,
    At any moment now you'll walk the plank!
The future's for the younger generation!
    Yes, even if that future is a blank.
        So what's the use?
        See the smoke float free
        Into ever colder coldness!
        It's the same with me.

NEPHEW (*to the* BROTHER): Where'd you get that wine?

SISTER-IN-LAW (*answering for the* BROTHER): He pawned the sack of tobacco.

HUSBAND (*stepping in*): What? That tobacco was all we had to fall back on! You pig!

BROTHER: *You'd* call a man a pig because your wife was frigid! Did you refuse to drink it?

(*They fight. The shelves fall over.*)

SHEN TE (*imploringly*): Oh don't! Don't break everything! Take it, take it, take it all, but don't destroy a gift from the gods!

WIFE (*disparagingly*): This shop isn't big enough. I should never have mentioned it to Uncle and the others. When *they* arrive, it's going to be disgustingly overcrowded.

SISTER-IN-LAW: And did you hear our gracious hostess? She cools off quick!

(*Voices outside. Knocking at the door.*)

UNCLE'S VOICE: Open the door!

WIFE: Uncle! Is that you, Uncle?

UNCLE'S VOICE: Certainly, it's me. Auntie says to tell you she'll have the children here in ten minutes.

WIFE (*to* SHEN TE): I'll have to let him in.

SHEN TE (*who scarcely hears her*):
The little lifeboat is swiftly sent down
Too many men too greedily
Hold on to it as they drown.

I A

WONG's *den in a sewer pipe.*

WONG (*crouching there*): All quiet! It's four days now since I left the city. The gods passed this way on the second day. I heard their steps on the bridge over there. They must be a long way off by this time, so I'm safe. (*Breathing a sigh of relief, he curls up and goes to sleep. In his dream the pipe becomes transparent, and the GODS appear. Raising an arm, as if in self-defense.*) I know, I know, illustrious ones! I found no one to give you a room — not in all Setzuan! There, it's out. Please continue on your way!

FIRST GOD (*mildly*): But you did find someone. Someone who took us in for the night, watched over us in our sleep, and in the early morning lighted us down to the street with a lamp.

WONG: It was . . . Shen Te that took you in?

THIRD GOD: Who else?

WONG: And I ran away! "She isn't coming," I thought, "she just can't afford it."

GODS (*singing*):
O you feeble, well-intentioned, and yet feeble chap
Where there's need the fellow thinks there is no goodness!
When there's danger he thinks courage starts to ebb away!
Some people only see the seamy side!
What hasty judgment! What premature desperation!

WONG: I'm *very* ashamed, illustrious ones.

FIRST GOD: Do us a favor, water seller. Go back to Setzuan. Find Shen Te, and give us a report on her. We hear that she's come into a little money. Show interest in her goodness — for no one can be good for long if goodness is not in demand. Meanwhile we shall continue the search, and find other good people. After which, the idle chatter about the impossibility of goodness will stop!

(*The* GODS *vanish.*)

II

A knocking.

WIFE: Shen Te! Someone at the door. Where is she anyway?

NEPHEW: She must be getting the breakfast. Mr. Shui Ta will pay for it.

(*The* WIFE *laughs and shuffles to the door. Enter* MR. SHUI TA *and the* CARPENTER.)

WIFE: Who is it?

SHUI TA: I am Miss Shen Te's cousin.

WIFE: What?

SHUI TA: My name is Shui Ta.

WIFE: Her cousin?

NEPHEW: Her cousin?

NIECE: But that was a joke. She hasn't got a cousin.

HUSBAND: So early in the morning?

BROTHER: What's all the noise?

SISTER-IN-LAW: This fellow says he's her cousin.

BROTHER: Tell him to prove it.

NEPHEW: Right. If you're Shen Te's cousin, prove it by getting the breakfast.

SHUI TA (*whose regime begins as he puts out the lamp to save oil; loudly, to all present, asleep or awake*): Would you all please get dressed! Customers will be coming! I wish to open my shop!

HUSBAND: *Your* shop? Doesn't it belong to our good friend Shen Te?

(SHUI TA *shakes his head.*)

SISTER-IN-LAW: So we've been cheated. Where *is* the little liar?

SHUI TA: Miss Shen Te has been delayed. She wishes me to tell you there will be nothing she can do — now I am here.

WIFE (*bowled over*): I thought she was good!

NEPHEW: Do you have to believe *him*?

HUSBAND: I don't.

NEPHEW: Then do something.

HUSBAND: Certainly! I'll send out a search

party at once. You, you, you, and you, go out and look for Shen Te. (*As the* GRANDFATHER *rises and makes for the door.*) Not you, Grandfather, you and I will hold the fort.

SHUI TA: You won't find Miss Shen Te. She has suspended her hospitable activity for an unlimited period. There are too many of you. She asked me to say: this is a tobacco shop, not a gold mine.

HUSBAND: Shen Te never said a thing like that. Boy, food! There's a bakery on the corner. Stuff your shirt full when they're not looking!

SISTER-IN-LAW: Don't overlook the raspberry· tarts.

HUSBAND: And don't let the policeman see you.

(*The* BOY *leaves.*)

SHUI TA: Don't you depend on this shop now? Then why give it a bad name by stealing from the bakery?

NEPHEW: Don't listen to him. Let's find Shen Te. She'll give him a piece of her mind.

SISTER-IN-LAW: Don't forget to leave us some breakfast.

(BROTHER, SISTER-IN-LAW, *and* NEPHEW *leave.*)

SHUI TA (*to the* CARPENTER): You see, Mr. Carpenter, nothing has changed since the poet, eleven hundred years ago, penned these lines:

A governor was asked what was needed
To save the freezing people in the city.
He replied:
"A blanket ten thousand feet long
to cover the city and all its suburbs."

(*He starts to tidy up the shop.*)

CARPENTER: Your cousin owes me money. I've got witnesses. For the shelves.

SHUI TA: Yes, I have your bill. (*He takes it out of his pocket.*) Isn't a hundred silver dollars rather a lot?

CARPENTER: No deductions! I have a wife and children.

SHUI TA: How many children?

CARPENTER: Three.

SHUI TA: I'll make you an offer. Twenty silver dollars.

(*The* HUSBAND *laughs.*)

CARPENTER: You're crazy. Those shelves are real walnut.

SHUI TA: Very well. Take them away.

CARPENTER: What?

SHUI TA: They cost too much. Please take them away.

WIFE: Not bad! (*And she, too, is laughing.*)

CARPENTER (*a little bewildered*): Call Shen Te, someone! (*To* SHUI TA.) She's *good!*

SHUI TA: Certainly. She's ruined.

CARPENTER (*provoked into taking some of the shelves*): All right, you can keep your tobacco on the floor.

SHUI TA (*to the* HUSBAND): Help him with the shelves.

HUSBAND (*grins and carries one shelf over to the door where the* CARPENTER *now is*): Good-bye, shelves!

CARPENTER (*to the* HUSBAND): You dog! You want my family to starve?

SHUI TA: I repeat my offer. I have no desire to keep my tobacco on the floor. Twenty silver dollars.

CARPENTER (*with desperate aggressiveness*): One hundred!

(SHUI TA *shows indifference, looks through the window. The* HUSBAND *picks up several shelves.*)

CARPENTER (*to* HUSBAND): You needn't smash them against the doorpost, you idiot! (*To* SHUI TA.) These shelves were made to measure. They're no use anywhere else!

SHUI TA: Precisely.

(*The* WIFE *squeals with pleasure.*)

CARPENTER (*giving up, sullenly*): Take the shelves. Pay what you want to pay.

SHUI TA (*smoothly*): Twenty silver dollars.

(*He places two large coins on the table. The* CARPENTER *picks them up.*)

HUSBAND (*brings the shelves back in*): And quite enough too!

CARPENTER (*slinking off*): Quite enough to get drunk on.

HUSBAND (*happily*): Well, we got rid of *him!*

WIFE (*weeping with fun, gives a rendition of the dialogue just spoken*): "Real walnut," says he. "Very well, take them away," says his lordship. "I have three children," says he. "Twenty silver dollars," says his lordship. "They're no use anywhere else," says he. "Pre-cisely," said his lordship! (*She dissolves into shrieks of merriment.*)

SHUI TA: And now: go!

HUSBAND: What's that?

SHUI TA: You're thieves, parasites. I'm giving you this chance. Go!

HUSBAND (*summoning all his ancestral dignity*): That sort deserves no answer. Besides, one should never shout on an empty stomach.

WIFE: Where's that boy?

SHUI TA: Exactly. The boy. I want no stolen goods in this shop. (*Very loudly.*) I strongly advise you to leave! (*But they remain seated, noses in the air. Quietly.*) As you wish. (SHUI TA *goes to the door. A* POLICEMAN *appears.* SHUI TA *bows.*) I am addressing the officer in charge of this precinct?

POLICEMAN: That's right, Mr., um, what was the name, sir?

SHUI TA: Mr. Shui Ta.

POLICEMAN: Yes, of course, sir.

(*They exchange a smile.*)

SHUI TA: Nice weather we're having.

POLICEMAN: A little on the warm side, sir.

SHUI TA: Oh, a little on the warm side.

HUSBAND (*whispering to the* WIFE): If he keeps it up till the boy's back, we're done for. (*Tries to signal* SHUI TA.)

SHUI TA (*ignoring the signal*): Weather, of course, is one thing indoors, another out on the dusty street!

POLICEMAN: Oh, quite another, sir!

WIFE (*to the* HUSBAND): It's all right as long as he's standing in the doorway — the boy will see him.

SHUI TA: Step inside for a moment! It's quite cool indoors. My cousin and I have just opened the place. And we attach the greatest importance to being on good terms with the, um, authorities.

POLICEMAN (*entering*): Thank you, Mr. Shui Ta. It *is* cool!

HUSBAND (*whispering to the* WIFE): And now the boy *won't* see him.

SHUI TA (*showing* HUSBAND *and* WIFE *to the* POLICEMAN): Visitors, I think my cousin knows them. They were just leaving.

HUSBAND (*defeated*): Ye-e-es, we were . . . just leaving.

SHUI TA: I'll tell my cousin you couldn't wait.

(*Noise from the street. Shouts of "Stop, Thief!"*)

POLICEMAN: What's that?

(*The* BOY *is in the doorway with cakes and buns and rolls spilling out of his shirt. The* WIFE *signals desperately to him to leave. He gets the idea.*)

POLICEMAN: No, you don't! (*He grabs the* BOY *by the collar.*) Where's all this from?

BOY (*vaguely pointing*): Down the street.

POLICEMAN (*grimly*): So that's it. (*Prepares to arrest the* BOY.)

WIFE (*stepping in*): And *we* knew nothing about it. (*To the* BOY.) Nasty little thief!

POLICEMAN (*dryly*): Can you clarify the situation, Mr. Shui Ta?

(SHUI TA *is silent.*)

POLICEMAN (*who understands silence*): Aha. You're all coming with me — to the station.

SHUI TA: I can hardly say how sorry I am that my establishment . . .

WIFE: Oh, he saw the boy leave not ten minutes ago!

SHUI TA: And to conceal the theft asked a policeman in?

POLICEMAN: Don't listen to her, Mr. Shui Ta, I'll be happy to relieve you of their presence one and all! (*To all three.*) Out! (*He drives them before him.*)

GRANDFATHER (*leaving last, gravely*): Good morning!

POLICEMAN: Good morning!

(SHUI TA, *left alone, continues to tidy up.* MRS. MI TZU *breezes in.*)

MRS. MI TZU: You're her cousin, are you? Then have the goodness to explain what all this means — police dragging people from a respectable house! By what right does your Miss Shen Te turn my property into a house of assignation? — Well, as you see, I know all!

SHUI TA: Yes. My cousin has the worst possible reputation: that of being poor.

MRS. MI TZU: No sentimental rubbish, Mr. Shui Ta. Your cousin was a common . . .

SHUI TA: Pauper. Let's use the uglier word.

MRS. MI TZU: I'm speaking of her conduct, not her earnings. But there must have *been* earnings, or how did she buy all this? Several elderly gentlemen took care of it, I suppose. I repeat: this is a respectable house! I have tenants who prefer not to live under the same roof with such a person.

SHUI TA (*quietly*): How much do you want?

MRS. MI TZU (*he is ahead of her now*): I beg your pardon.

SHUI TA: To reassure yourself. To reassure your tenants. How much will it cost?

MRS. MI TZU: You're a cool customer.

SHUI TA (*picking up the lease*): The rent is high. (*He reads on.*) I assume it's payable by the month?

MRS. MI TZU: Not in her case.

SHUI TA (*looking up*): What?

MRS. MI TZU: Six months' rent payable in advance. Two hundred silver dollars.

SHUI TA: Six . . . ! Sheer usury! And where am I to find it?

MRS. MI TZU: You should have thought of that before.

SHUI TA: Have you no heart, Mrs. Mi Tzu? It's true Shen Te acted foolishly, being kind to all those people, but she'll improve with time. I'll see to it she does. She'll work her fingers to the bone to pay her rent, and all the time be as quiet as a mouse, as humble as a fly.

MRS. MI TZU: Her social background . . .

SHUI TA: Out of the depths! She came out of the depths! And before she'll go back there, she'll work, sacrifice, shrink from nothing. . . . Such a tenant is worth her weight in gold, Mrs. Mi Tzu.

MRS. MI TZU: It's silver we were talking about, Mr. Shui Ta. Two hundred silver dollars or . . .

(*Enter the* POLICEMAN.)

POLICEMAN: Am I intruding, Mr. Shui Ta?

MRS. MI TZU: This tobacco shop is well known to the police, I see.

POLICEMAN: Mr. Shui Ta has done us a service, Mrs. Mi Tzu. I am here to present our official felicitations!

MRS. MI TZU: That means less then nothing to me, sir. Mr. Shui Ta, all I can say is: I hope your cousin will find my terms acceptable. Good day, gentlemen. (*Exit.*)

SHUI TA: Good day, ma'am.

(*Pause.*)

POLICEMAN: Mrs. Mi Tzu a bit of a stumbling block, sir?

SHUI TA: She wants six months' rent in advance.

POLICEMAN: And you haven't got it, eh? (SHUI TA *is silent.*) But surely you can get it, sir? A man like you?

SHUI TA: What about a woman like Shen Te?

POLICEMAN: You're not staying, sir?

SHUI TA: No, and I won't be back. Do you smoke?

POLICEMAN (*taking two cigars, and placing them both in his pocket*): Thank you, sir — I see your point. Miss Te — let's mince no words — Miss Shen Te lived by selling herself. "What else could she have done?" you ask. "How else was she to pay the rent?" True. But the fact remains, Mr. Shui Ta, it is not respectable. Why not? A very deep question. But, in the first place, love — love isn't bought and sold like cigars, Mr. Shui Ta. In the second place, it isn't respectable to go waltzing off with someone that's paying his way, so to speak — it must be for love! Thirdly and lastly, as the proverb has it: not for a handful of rice but for love! (*Pause. He is thinking hard.*) "Well," you may say, "and what good is all this wisdom if the milk's already spilt?" Miss Shen Te is what she is. Is *where* she is. We have to face the fact that if she doesn't get hold of six months' rent pronto, she'll be back on the streets. The question then as I see it — everything in this world is a matter of opinion — the question as I see it is: *how* is she to get hold of this rent? How? Mr. Shui Ta: I don't know. (*Pause.*) I take that back, sir. It's just come to me. A husband. We must find her a husband!

(*Enter a little* OLD WOMAN.)

OLD WOMAN: A good cheap cigar for my husband, we'll have been married forty years tomorrow and we're having a little celebration.

SHUI TA: Forty years? And you still want to celebrate?

OLD WOMAN: As much as we can afford to. We have the carpet shop across the square. We'll be good neighbors, I hope?

SHUI TA: I hope so too.

POLICEMAN (*who keeps making discoveries*): Mr. Shui Ta, you know what we need? We need capital. And how do we acquire capital? We get married.

SHUI TA (*to* OLD WOMAN): I'm afraid I've been pestering this gentleman with my personal worries.

POLICEMAN (*lyrically*): We can't pay six months' rent, so what do we do? We marry money.

SHUI TA: That might not be easy.

POLICEMAN: Oh, I don't know. She's a good match. Has a nice, growing business. (*To the* OLD WOMAN.) What do you think?

OLD WOMAN (*undecided*): Well —

POLICEMAN: Should she put an ad in the paper?

OLD WOMAN (*not eager to commit herself*): Well, if *she* agrees —

POLICEMAN: I'll write it for her. *You* lend us a hand, and *we* write an ad for you! (*He chuckles away to himself, takes out his notebook, wets the stump of a pencil between his lips, and writes away.*)

SHUI TA (*slowly*): Not a bad idea.

POLICEMAN: "What . . . *respectable* . . . man . . . with small capital . . . widower . . . not excluded . . . desires . . . marriage . . . into flourishing . . . tobacco shop?" And now let's add: "Am . . . pretty . . ." No! . . . "Prepossessing appearance."

SHUI TA: If you don't think that's an exaggeration?

OLD WOMAN: Oh, not a bit. I've seen her.

(*The* POLICEMAN *tears the page out of his notebook, and hands it over to* SHUI TA.)

SHUI TA (*with horror in his voice*): How much luck we need to keep our heads above water! How many ideas! How many friends! (*To the* POLICEMAN.) Thank you, sir, I think I see my way clear.

III

Evening in the municipal park. Noise of a plane overhead. YANG SUN, *a young man in rags, is following the plane with his eyes: one can tell that the machine is describing a curve above the park.* YANG SUN *then takes a rope out of his pocket, looking anxiously about him as he does so. He moves toward a large willow. Enter two prostitutes, one the* OLD WHORE, *the other the* NIECE *whom we have already met.*

NIECE: Hello. Coming with me?

YANG SUN (*taken aback*): If you'd like to buy me a dinner.

OLD WHORE: Buy you a dinner! (*To the* NIECE.) Oh, we know him — it's the unemployed pilot. Waste no time on him!

NIECE: But he's the only man left in the park. And it's going to rain.

OLD WHORE: Oh, how do you know?

(*And they pass by.* YANG SUN *again looks about him, again takes his rope, and this time throws it round a branch of the willow tree. Again he is interrupted. It is the two prostitutes returning — and in such a hurry they don't notice him.*)

NIECE: It's going to pour!

(*Enter* SHEN TE.)

OLD WHORE: There's that *gorgon* Shen Te! That *drove* your family out into the cold!

NIECE: It wasn't her. It was that cousin of hers. She offered to pay for the cakes. I've nothing against her.

OLD WHORE: I have, though. (*So that* SHEN TE *can hear.*) Now where could the little lady be off to? She may be rich now but that won't stop her snatching our young men, will it?

SHEN TE: I'm going to the tearoom by the pond.

NIECE: Is it true what they say? You're marrying a widower — with three children?

SHEN TE: Yes. I'm just going to see him.

YANG SUN (*his patience at breaking point*): Move on there! This is a park, not a whorehouse!

OLD WHORE: Shut your mouth!

(*But the two prostitutes leave.*)

YANG SUN: Even in the farthest corner of the park, even when it's raining, you can't get rid of them! (*He spits.*)

SHEN TE (*overhearing this*): And what right have you to scold them? (*But at this point she sees the rope.*) Oh!

YANG SUN: Well, what are you staring at?

SHEN TE: That rope. What is it for?

YANG SUN: Think! Think! I haven't a penny. Even if I had, I wouldn't spend it on you. I'd buy a drink of water.

(*The rain starts.*)

SHEN TE (*still looking at the rope*): What is the rope for? You mustn't!

YANG SUN: What's it to you? Clear out!

SHEN TE (*irrelevantly*): It's raining.

YANG SUN: Well, don't try to come under this tree.

SHEN TE: Oh, no. (*She stays in the rain.*)

YANG SUN: Now go away. (*Pause.*) For one thing, I don't like your looks, you're bowlegged.

SHEN TE (*indignantly*): That's not true!

YANG SUN: Well, don't show 'em to me. Look, it's raining. You better come under this tree.

(*Slowly, she takes shelter under the tree.*)

SHEN TE: Why did you want to do it?

YANG SUN: You really want to know? (*Pause.*) To get rid of you! (*Pause.*) You know what a flyer is?

SHEN TE: Oh yes, I've met a lot of pilots. At the tearoom.

YANG SUN: You call *them* flyers? Think they know what a machine is? Just 'cause they have leather helmets? They gave the airfield director a bribe, that's the way *those* fellows got up in the air! Try one of them out sometime. "Go up to two thousand feet," tell them, "then let it fall, then pick it up again with a flick of the wrist at the last moment." Know what he'll say to that? "It's not in my contract." Then again, there's the landing problem. It's like landing on your own backside. It's no different, planes are human. Those fools don't understand. (*Pause.*) And I'm the biggest fool for reading the book on flying in the Peking school and skipping the page where it says: "We've got enough flyers and we don't need you." I'm a mail pilot with no mail. You understand that?

SHEN TE (*shyly*): Yes. I do.

YANG SUN: No, you don't. You'd never understand that.

SHEN TE: When we were little we had a crane with a broken wing. He made friends with us and was very good-natured about our jokes. He would strut along behind us and call out to stop us going too fast for him. But every spring and autumn when the cranes flew over the villages in great swarms, he got quite restless. (*Pause.*) I understand that. (*She bursts out crying.*)

YANG SUN: Don't!

SHEN TE (*quieting down*): No.

YANG SUN: It's bad for the complexion.

SHEN TE (*sniffing*): I've stopped.

(*She dries her tears on her big sleeve. Leaning against the tree, but not looking at her, he reaches for her face.*)

YANG SUN: You can't even wipe your own face. (*He is wiping it for her with his handkerchief. Pause.*)

SHEN TE (*still sobbing*): I don't know *anything*!

YANG SUN: You interrupted me! What for?

SHEN TE: It's such a rainy day. You only wanted to do . . . *that* because it's such a rainy day. (*To the audience.*)

In our country
The evenings should never be somber
High bridges over rivers
The gray hour between night and morning
And the long, long winter:
Such things are dangerous
For, with all the misery,
A very little is enough
And men throw away an unbearable life.

(*Pause.*)

YANG SUN: Talk about yourself for a change.

SHEN TE: What about me? I have a shop.

YANG SUN (*incredulous*): You have a shop, have you? Never thought of walking the streets?

SHEN TE: I did walk the streets. Now I have a shop.

YANG SUN (*ironically*): A gift of the gods, I suppose!

SHEN TE: How did you know?

YANG SUN (*even more ironical*): One fine evening the gods turned up saying: here's some money!

SHEN TE (*quickly*): One fine morning.

YANG SUN (*fed up*): This isn't much of an entertainment.

(*Pause.*)

SHEN TE: I can play the zither a little. (*Pause.*) And I can mimic men. (*Pause.*) I got the shop, so the first thing I did was to give my zither away. I can be as stupid as a fish now, I said to myself, and it won't matter.

I'm rich now, I said
I walk alone, I sleep alone
For a whole year, I said
I'll have nothing to do with a man.

YANG SUN: And now you're marrying one! The one at the tearoom by the pond?

(SHEN TE *is silent.*)

YANG SUN: What do you know about love?

SHEN TE: Everything.

YANG SUN: Nothing. (*Pause.*) Or d'you just mean you enjoyed it?

SHEN TE: No.

YANG SUN (*again without turning to look at her, he strokes her cheek with his hand*): You like that?

SHEN TE: Yes.

YANG SUN (*breaking off*): You're easily satisfied, I must say. (*Pause.*) What a town!

SHEN TE: You have no friends?

YANG SUN (*defensively*): Yes, I have! (*Change of tone.*) But they don't want to hear I'm still unemployed. "What?" they ask. "Is there still water in the sea?" You have friends?

SHEN TE (*hesitating*): Just a . . . cousin.

YANG SUN: Watch him carefully.

SHEN TE: He only came once. Then he went away. He won't be back. (YANG SUN *is looking away.*) But to be without hope, they say, is to be without goodness!

(*Pause.*)

YANG SUN: Go on talking. A voice is a voice.

SHEN TE: Once, when I was a little girl, I fell, with a load of brushwood. An old man picked me up. He gave me a penny too. Isn't it funny how people who don't have very much like to give some of it away? They must like to show what they can do, and how could they show it better than by being kind? Being wicked is just like being clumsy. When we sing a song, or build a machine, or plant some rice, we're being kind. You're kind.

YANG SUN: You make it sound easy.

SHEN TE: Oh, no. (*Little pause.*) Oh! A drop of rain!

YANG SUN: Where'd you feel it?

SHEN TE: Between the eyes.

YANG SUN: Near the right eye? Or the left?

SHEN TE: Near the left eye.

YANG SUN: Oh, good. (*He is getting sleepy.*) So you're through with men, eh?

SHEN TE (*with a smile*): But I'm not bow-legged.

YANG SUN: Perhaps not.

SHEN TE: Definitely not.

(*Pause.*)

YANG SUN (*leaning wearily against the willow*): I haven't had a drop to drink all day, I haven't eaten anything for *two* days. I couldn't love you if I tried.

(*Pause.*)

SHEN TE: I like it in the rain.

(*Enter* WONG *the water seller, singing.*)

THE SONG OF THE WATER SELLER IN THE RAIN

"Buy my water," I am yelling
And my fury restraining
For no water I'm selling
'Cause it's raining, 'cause it's raining!
  I keep yelling: "Buy my water!"
  But no one's buying
  Athirst and dying
  And drinking and paying!
  Buy water!
  Buy water, you dogs!

Nice to dream of lovely weather!
Think of all the consternation
Were there no precipitation
Half a dozen years together!
  Can't you hear them shrieking: "Water!"
  Pretending they adore me?
  They all would go down on their knees before me!
  Down on your knees!
  Go down on your knees, you dogs!

What are lawns and hedges thinking?
What are fields and forests saying?
"At the cloud's breast we are drinking!
And we've no idea who's paying!"
  I keep yelling: "Buy my water!"
  But no one's buying
  Athirst and dying
  And drinking and paying!
  Buy water!
  Buy water, you dogs!

(*The rain has stopped now.* SHEN TE *sees* WONG *and runs toward him.*)

SHEN TE: Wong! You're back! Your carrying pole's at the shop.

WONG: Oh, thank you, Shen Te. And how is life treating *you*?

SHEN TE: I've just met a brave and clever man. And I want to buy him a cup of your water.

WONG (*bitterly*): Throw back your head and open your mouth and you'll have all the water you need —

SHEN TE (*tenderly*):
I want *your* water, Wong
The water that has tired you so
The water that you carried all this way
The water that is hard to sell because
  it's been raining.

I need it for the young man over there — he's a flyer!

A flyer is a bold man:
Braving the storms
In company with the clouds
He crosses the heavens
And brings to friends in faraway lands
The friendly mail!

(*She pays* WONG, *and runs over to* YANG SUN *with the cup. But* YANG SUN *is fast asleep.*)

SHEN TE (*calling to* WONG, *with a laugh*): He's fallen asleep! Despair and rain and I have worn him out!

IIIA

WONG's *den. The sewer pipe is transparent, and the* GODS *again appear to* WONG *in a dream.*

WONG (*radiant*): I've seen her, illustrious ones! And she hasn't changed!
FIRST GOD: That's good to hear.
WONG: She loves someone.
FIRST GOD: Let's hope the experience gives her the strength to stay good!
WONG: It does. She's doing good deeds all the time.
FIRST GOD: Ah? What sort? What sort of good deeds, Wong?
WONG: Well, she has a kind word for everybody.
FIRST GOD (*eagerly*): And then?
WONG: Hardly anyone leaves her shop without tobacco in his pocket — even if he can't pay for it.
FIRST GOD: Not bad at all. Next?
WONG: She's putting up a family of eight.
FIRST GOD (*gleefully, to the* SECOND GOD): Eight! (*To* WONG.) And that's not all, of course!
WONG: She bought a cup of water from me even though it was raining.
FIRST GOD: Yes, yes, yes, all these smaller good deeds!
WONG: Even they run into money. A little tobacco shop doesn't make so much.
FIRST GOD (*sententiously*): A prudent gardener works miracles on the smallest plot.

WONG: She hands out rice every morning. That eats up half her earnings.
FIRST GOD (*a little disappointed*): Well, as a beginning . . .
WONG: They call her the Angel of the Slums — whatever the carpenter may say!
FIRST GOD: What's this? A carpenter speaks ill of her?
WONG: Oh, he only says her shelves weren't paid for in full.
SECOND GOD (*who has a bad cold and can't pronounce his n's and m's*): What's this? Not paying a carpenter? Why was that?
WONG: I suppose she didn't have the money.
SECOND GOD (*severely*): One pays what one owes, that's in our book of rules! First the letter of the law, then the spirit.
WONG: But it wasn't Shen Te, illustrious ones, it was her cousin. She called *him* in to help.
SECOND GOD: Then her cousin must never darken her threshold again!
WONG: Very well, illustrious ones! But in fairness to Shen Te, let me say that her cousin is a businessman.
FIRST GOD: Perhaps we should inquire what is customary? I find business quite unintelligible. But everybody's doing it. Business! Did the Seven Good Kings do business? Did Kung the Just sell fish?
SECOND GOD: In any case, such a thing must not occur again!

(*The* GODS *start to leave.*)

THIRD GOD: Forgive us for taking this tone with you, Wong, we haven't been getting enough sleep. The rich recommend us to the poor, and the poor tell us they haven't enough room.
SECOND GOD: Feeble, feeble, the best of them!
FIRST GOD: No great deeds! No heroic daring!
THIRD GOD: On such a *small* scale!
SECOND GOD: Sincere, yes, but what is actually *achieved*?

(*One can no longer hear them.*)

WONG (*calling after them*): I've thought of something, illustrious ones: Perhaps you shouldn't ask — too — much — all — at — once!

IV

The square in front of SHEN TE's *tobacco shop. Besides* SHEN TE's *place, two other shops are seen: the carpet shop and a barber's. Morning. Outside* SHEN TE's *the* GRAND-FATHER, *the* SISTER-IN-LAW, *the* UNEMPLOYED MAN, *and* MRS. SHIN *stand waiting.*

SISTER-IN-LAW: She's been out all night again.

MRS. SHIN: No sooner did we get rid of that crazy cousin of hers than Shen Te herself starts carrying on! Maybe she does give us an ounce of rice now and then, but can you depend on her? Can you depend on her?

(*Loud voices from the barber's.*)

VOICE OF SHU FU: What are you doing in my shop? Get out — at once!

VOICE OF WONG: But sir. They all let me sell . . .

(WONG *comes staggering out of the barber's shop pursued by* MR. SHU FU, *the barber, a fat man carrying a heavy curling iron.*)

SHU FU: Get out, I said! Pestering my customers with your slimy old water! Get out! Take your cup!

(*He holds out the cup.* WONG *reaches out for it.* MR. SHU FU *strikes his hand with the curling iron, which is hot.* WONG *howls.*)

SHU FU: You had it coming, my man!

(*Puffing, he returns to his shop. The* UNEMPLOYED MAN *picks up the cup and gives it to* WONG.)

UNEMPLOYED MAN: You can report that to the police.

WONG: My hand! It's smashed up!

UNEMPLOYED MAN: Any bones broken?

WONG: I can't move my fingers.

UNEMPLOYED MAN: Sit down. I'll put some water on it.

(WONG *sits.*)

MRS. SHIN: The water won't cost you anything.

SISTER-IN-LAW: You might have got a bandage from Miss Shen Te till she took to staying out all night. It's a scandal.

MRS. SHIN (*despondently*): If you ask me, she's forgotten we ever existed!

(*Enter* SHEN TE *down the street, with a dish of rice.*)

SHEN TE (*to the audience*): How wonderful to see Setzuan in the early morning! I always used to stay in bed with my dirty blanket over my head afraid to wake up. This morning I saw the newspapers being delivered by little boys, the streets being washed by strong men, and fresh vegetables coming in from the country on ox carts. It's a long walk from where Yang Sun lives, but I feel lighter at every step. They say you walk on air when you're in love, but it's even better walking on the rough earth, on the hard cement. In the early morning, the old city looks like a great heap of rubbish! Nice, though, with all its little lights. And the sky, so pink, so transparent, before the dust comes and muddies it! What a lot you miss if you never see your city rising from its slumbers like an honest old craftsman pumping his lungs full of air and reaching for his tools, as the poet says! (*Cheerfully, to her waiting guests.*) Good morning, everyone, here's your rice! (*Distributing the rice, she comes upon* WONG.) Good morning, Wong, I'm quite lightheaded today. On my way over, I looked at myself in all the shop windows. I'd love to be beautiful.

(*She slips into the carpet shop.* MR. SHU FU *has just emerged from his shop.*)

SHU FU (*to the audience*): It surprises me how beautiful Miss Shen Te is looking today! I never gave her a passing thought before. But now I've been gazing upon her comely form for exactly three minutes! I begin to suspect I am in love with her. She is overpoweringly attractive! (*Crossly, to* WONG.) Be off with you, rascal!

(*He returns to his shop.* SHEN TE *comes back out of the carpet shop with the* OLD MAN, *its proprietor, and his wife — whom we have already met — the* OLD WOMAN. SHEN TE *is wearing a shawl. The* OLD MAN *is holding up a looking glass for her.*)

OLD WOMAN: Isn't it lovely? We'll give you a reduction because there's a little hole in it.

SHEN TE (*looking at another shawl on the* OLD WOMAN's *arm*): The other one's nice too.

OLD WOMAN (*smiling*): Too bad there's no hole in that!

SHEN TE: That's right. My shop doesn't make very much.

OLD WOMAN: And your good deeds eat it all up! Be more careful, my dear. . . .

SHEN TE (*trying on the shawl with the hole*): Just now, I'm lightheaded! Does the color suit me?

OLD WOMAN: You'd better ask a man.

SHEN TE (*to the* OLD MAN): Does the color suit me?

OLD MAN: You'd better ask your young friend.

SHEN TE: I'd like to have your opinion.

OLD MAN: It suits you very well. But wear it this way: the dull side out.

(SHEN TE *pays up.*)

OLD WOMAN: If you decide you don't like it, you can exchange it. (*She pulls* SHEN TE *to one side.*) Has he got money?

SHEN TE (*with a laugh*): Yang Sun? Oh, no.

OLD WOMAN: Then how're you going to pay your rent?

SHEN TE: I'd forgotten about that.

OLD WOMAN: And next Monday is the first of the month! Miss Shen Te, I've got something to say to you. After we (*indicating her husband*) got to know you, we had our doubts about that marriage ad. We thought it would be better if you'd let *us* help you. Out of our savings. We reckon we could lend you two hundred silver dollars. We don't need anything in writing — you could pledge us your tobacco stock.

SHEN TE: You're prepared to lend money to a person like me?

OLD WOMAN: It's folks like you that need it. We'd think twice about lending anything to your cousin.

OLD MAN (*coming up*): All settled, my dear?

SHEN TE: I wish the gods could have heard what your wife was just saying, Mr. Ma. They're looking for good people who're happy — and helping me makes you happy because you know it was love that got me into difficulties!

(*The* OLD COUPLE *smile knowingly at each other.*)

OLD MAN: And here's the money, Miss Shen Te.

(*He hands her an envelope.* SHEN TE *takes it. She bows. They bow back. They return to their shop.*)

SHEN TE (*holding up her envelope*): Look, Wong, here's six months' rent! Don't you believe in miracles now? And how do you like my new shawl?

WONG: For the young fellow I saw you with in the park?

(SHEN TE *nods.*)

MRS. SHIN: Never mind all that. It's time you took a look at his hand!

SHEN TE: Have you hurt your hand?

MRS. SHIN: That barber smashed it with his hot curling iron. Right in front of our eyes.

SHEN TE (*shocked at herself*): And I never noticed! We must get you to a doctor this minute or who knows what will happen?

UNEMPLOYED MAN: It's not a doctor he should see, it's a judge. He can ask for compensation. The barber's filthy rich.

WONG: You think I have a chance?

MRS. SHIN (*with relish*): If it's really good and smashed. But is it?

WONG: I think so. It's very swollen. Could I get a pension?

MRS. SHIN: You'd need a witness.

WONG: Well, you all saw it. You could all testify.

(*He looks round. The* UNEMPLOYED MAN, *the* GRANDFATHER, *and the* SISTER-IN-LAW *are all sitting against the wall of the shop eating rice. Their concentration on eating is complete.*)

SHEN TE (*to* MRS. SHIN): You saw it yourself.

MRS. SHIN: I want nothing to do with the police. It's against my principles.

SHEN TE (*to* SISTER-IN-LAW): What about you?

SISTER-IN-LAW: Me? I wasn't looking.

SHEN TE (*to the* GRANDFATHER, *coaxingly*): Grandfather, *you'll* testify, won't you?

SISTER-IN-LAW: And a lot of good that will do. He's simple-minded.

SHEN TE (*to the* UNEMPLOYED MAN): You seem to be the only witness left.

UNEMPLOYED MAN: My testimony would only hurt him. I've been picked up twice for begging.

SHEN TE:
Your brother is assaulted, and you shut your
    eyes?
He is hit, cries out in pain, and you are silent?
The beast prowls, chooses and seizes his victim,
    and you say:

"Because we showed no displeasure, he has spared us."

If no one present will be a witness, I will. I'll say *I* saw it.

MRS. SHIN (*solemnly*): The name for that is perjury.

WONG: I don't know if I can accept that. Though maybe I'll have to. (*Looking at his hand.*) Is it swollen enough, do you think? The swelling's not going down?

UNEMPLOYED MAN: No, no, the swelling's holding up well.

WONG: Yes. It's *more* swollen if anything. Maybe my wrist is broken after all. I'd better see a judge at once.

(*Holding his hand very carefully, and fixing his eyes on it, he runs off.* MRS. SHIN *goes quickly into the barber's shop.*)

UNEMPLOYED MAN (*seeing her*): She is getting on the right side of Mr. Shu Fu.

SISTER-IN-LAW: You and I can't change the world, Shen Te.

SHEN TE: Go away! Go away all of you!

(*The* UNEMPLOYED MAN, *the* SISTER-IN-LAW, *and the* GRANDFATHER *stalk off, eating and sulking.*
To the audience.)

They've stopped answering
They stay put
They do as they're told
They don't care
Nothing can make them look up
But the smell of food.

(*Enter* MRS. YANG, YANG SUN'*s mother, out of breath.*)

MRS. YANG: Miss Shen Te. My son has told me everything. I am Mrs. Yang, Sun's mother. Just think. He's got an offer. Of a job as a pilot. A letter has just come. From the director of the airfield in Peking!

SHEN TE: So he can fly again? Isn't that wonderful!

MRS. YANG (*less breathlessly all the time*): They won't give him the job for nothing. They want five hundred silver dollars.

SHEN TE: We can't let money stand in his way, Mrs. Yang!

MRS. YANG: If only you could help him out!

SHEN TE: I have the shop. I can try! (*She embraces* MRS. YANG.) I happen to have two hundred with me now. Take it. (*She gives her the old couple's money.*) It was a loan but they said I could repay it with my tobacco stock.

MRS. YANG: And they were calling Sun the Dead Pilot of Setzuan! A friend in need!

SHEN TE: We must find another three hundred.

MRS. YANG: How?

SHEN TE: Let me think. (*Slowly.*) I know someone who can help. I didn't want to call on his services again, he's hard and cunning. But a flyer must fly. And I'll make this the last time.

(*Distant sound of a plane.*)

MRS. YANG: If the man you mentioned can do it. . . . Oh, look, there's the morning mail plane, heading for Peking!

SHEN TE: The pilot can see us, let's wave!

(*They wave. The noise of the engine is louder.*)

MRS. YANG: You know that pilot up there?

SHEN TE: Wave, Mrs. Yang! I know the pilot who will be up there. He gave up hope. But he'll do it now. One man to raise himself above the misery, above us all. (*To the audience.*)

Yang Sun, my lover:
Braving the storms
In company with the clouds
Crossing the heavens
And bringing to friends in faraway lands
The friendly mail!

IVA

In front of the inner curtain. Enter SHEN TE, *carrying* SHUI TA'*s mask. She sings.*

THE SONG OF DEFENSELESSNESS

In our country
A useful man needs luck
Only if he finds strong backers
Can he prove himself useful.
The good can't defend themselves and
Even the gods are defenseless.

Oh, why don't the gods have their own ammunition
And launch against badness their own expedition
Enthroning the good and preventing sedition

And bringing the world to a peaceful condition?

Oh, why don't the gods do the buying and selling
Injustice forbidding, starvation dispelling
Give bread to each city and joy to each dwelling?
Oh, why don't the gods do the buying and selling?

(*She puts on* SHUI TA's *mask and sings in his
voice.*)

You can only help one of your luckless brothers
By trampling down a dozen others.

Why is it the gods do not feel indignation
And come down in fury to end exploitation
Defeat all defeat and forbid desperation
Refusing to tolerate such toleration?

Why is it?

V

SHEN TE's *tobacco shop. Behind the counter,*
MR. SHUI TA, *reading the paper.* MRS. SHIN
*is cleaning up. She talks and he takes no no-
tice.*

MRS. SHIN: And when certain rumors get
about, what *happens* to a little place like this?
It goes to pot. *I* know. So, if you want my advice, Mr. Shui Ta, find out just what has been
going on between Miss Shen Te and that Yang
Sun from Yellow Street. And remember: a certain interest in Miss Shen Te has been expressed by the barber next door, a man with
twelve houses and only one wife, who, for that
matter, is likely to drop off at any time. A certain interest has been expressed. He was even
inquiring about her means and, if *that* doesn't
prove a man is getting serious, what would?
(*Still getting no response, she leaves with her
bucket.*)

YANG SUN'S VOICE: Is that Miss Shen Te's tobacco shop?

MRS. SHIN'S VOICE: Yes, it is, but it's Mr.
Shui Ta who's here today.

(SHUI TA *runs to the mirror with the short,
light steps of* SHEN TE, *and is just about to
start primping, when he realizes his mistake,
and turns away, with a short laugh. Enter*

YANG SUN. MRS. SHIN *enters behind him and
slips into the back room to eavesdrop.*)

YANG SUN: I am Yang Sun. (SHUI TA *bows.*)
Is Shen Te in?

SHUI TA: No.

YANG SUN: I guess you know our relationship?
(*He is inspecting the stock.*) Quite a place!
And I thought she was just talking big. I'll be
flying again, all right. (*He takes a cigar, solicits
and receives a light from* SHUI TA.) You think
we can squeeze the other three hundred out of
the tobacco stock?

SHUI TA: May I ask if it is your intention to
sell at once?

YANG SUN: It was decent of her to come out
with the two hundred but they aren't much use
with the other three hundred still missing.

SHUI TA: Shen Te was overhasty promising so
much. She might have to sell the shop itself to
raise it. Haste, they say, is the wind that blows
the house down.

YANG SUN: Oh, she isn't a girl to keep a man
waiting. For one thing or the other, if you take
my meaning.

SHUI TA: I take your meaning.

YANG SUN (*leering*): Uh, huh.

SHUI TA: Would you explain what the five
hundred silver dollars are for?

YANG SUN: Want to sound me out? Very
well. The director of the Peking airfield is a
friend of mine from flying school. I give him
five hundred: he gets me the job.

SHUI TA: The price is high.

YANG SUN: Not as these things go. He'll have
to fire one of the present pilots — for negligence. Only the man he has in mind isn't neg-
ligent. Not easy, you understand. You needn't
mention that part of it to Shen Te.

SHUI TA (*looking intently at* YANG SUN): Mr.
Yang Sun, you are asking my cousin to give up
her possessions, leave her friends, and place her
entire fate in your hands. I presume you intend
to marry her?

YANG SUN: I'd be prepared to.

(*Slight pause.*)

SHUI TA: Those two hundred silver dollars
would pay the rent here for six months. If you
were Shen Te wouldn't you be tempted to continue in business?

YANG SUN: What? Can you imagine Yang
Sun the flyer behind a counter? (*In an oily
voice.*) "A strong cigar or a mild one, worthy
sir?" Not in this century!

SHUI TA: My cousin wishes to follow the promptings of her heart, and, from her own point of view, she may even have what is called the right to love. Accordingly, she has commissioned me to help you to this post. There is nothing here that I am not empowered to turn immediately into cash. Mrs. Mi Tzu, the landlady, will advise me about the sale.

(*Enter* MRS. MI TZU.)

MRS. MI TZU: Good morning, Mr. Shui Ta, you wish to see me about the rent? As you know it falls due the day after tomorrow.

SHUI TA: Circumstances have changed, Mrs. Mi Tzu: my cousin is getting married. Her future husband here, Mr. Yang Sun, will be taking her to Peking. I am interested in selling the tobacco stock.

MRS. MI TZU: How much are you asking, Mr. Shui Ta?

YANG SUN: Three hundred sil —

SHUI TA: Five hundred silver dollars.

MRS. MI TZU: How much did she pay for it, Mr. Shui Ta?

SHUI TA: A thousand. And very little has been sold.

MRS. MI TZU: She was robbed. But I'll make you a special offer if you'll promise to be out by the day after tomorrow. Three hundred silver dollars.

YANG SUN (*shrugging*): Take it, man, take it.

SHUI TA: It is not enough.

YANG SUN: Why not? Why not? Certainly, it's enough.

SHUI TA: Five hundred silver dollars.

YANG SUN: But why? We only need three!

SHUI TA (*to* MRS. MI TZU): Excuse me. (*Takes* YANG SUN *on one side.*) The tobacco stock is pledged to the old couple who gave my cousin the two hundred.

YANG SUN: Is it in writing?

SHUI TA: No.

YANG SUN (*to* MRS. MI TZU): Three hundred will do.

MRS. MI TZU: Of course, I need an assurance that Miss Shen Te is not in debt.

YANG SUN: Mr. Shui Ta?

SHUI TA: She is not in debt.

YANG SUN: When can you let us have the money?

MRS. MI TZU: The day after tomorrow. And remember: I'm doing this because I have a soft spot in my heart for young lovers! (*Exit.*)

YANG SUN (*calling after her*): Boxes, jars and sacks — three hundred for the lot and the pain's over! (*To* SHUI TA.) Where else can we raise money by the day after tomorrow?

SHUI TA: Nowhere. Haven't you enough for the trip and the first few weeks?

YANG SUN: Oh, certainly.

SHUI TA: How much, exactly.

YANG SUN: Oh, I'll dig it up, even if I have to steal it.

SHUI TA: I see.

YANG SUN: Well, don't fall off the roof. I'll get to Peking somehow.

SHUI TA: Two people can't travel for nothing.

YANG SUN (*not giving* SHUI TA *a chance to answer*): I'm leaving *her* behind. No millstones round *my* neck!

SHUI TA: Oh.

YANG SUN: Don't look at me like that!

SHUI TA: How precisely is my cousin to live?

YANG SUN: Oh, you'll think of something.

SHUI TA: A small request, Mr. Yang Sun. Leave the two hundred silver dollars here until you can show me two tickets for Peking.

YANG SUN: You learn to mind your own business, Mr. Shui Ta.

SHUI TA: I'm afraid Miss Shen Te may not wish to sell the shop when she discovers that . . .

YANG SUN: You don't know women. She'll want to. Even then.

SHUI TA (*a slight outburst*): She is a human being, sir! And not devoid of common sense!

YANG SUN: Shen Te is a woman: she *is* devoid of common sense. I only have to lay my hand on her shoulder, and church bells ring.

SHUI TA (*with difficulty*): Mr. Yang Sun!

YANG SUN: Mr. Shui Whatever-it-is!

SHUI TA: My cousin is devoted to you . . . because . . .

YANG SUN: Because I have my hands on her breasts. Give me a cigar. (*He takes one for himself, stuffs a few more in his pocket, then changes his mind and takes the whole box.*) Tell her I'll marry her, then bring me the three hundred. Or let her bring it. One or the other. (*Exit.*)

MRS. SHIN (*sticking her head out of the back room*): Well, he has your cousin under his thumb, and doesn't care if all Yellow Street knows it!

SHUI TA (*crying out*): I've lost my shop! And he doesn't love me! (*He runs berserk through the room, repeating these lines incoherently.*

Then stops suddenly, and addresses MRS. SHIN.) Mrs. Shin, you grew up in the gutter, like me. Are we lacking in hardness? I doubt it. If you steal a penny from me, I'll take you by the throat till you spit it out! You'd do the same to me. The times are bad, this city is hell, but we're like ants, we keep coming, up and up the walls, however smooth! Till bad luck comes. Being in love, for instance. One weakness is enough, and love is the deadliest.

MRS. SHIN (emerging from the back room): You should have a little talk with Mr. Shu Fu, the barber. He's a real gentleman and just the thing for your cousin. (She runs off.)

SHUI TA:
A caress becomes a stranglehold
A sigh of love turns to a cry of fear
Why are there vultures circling in the air?
A girl is going to meet her lover.

(SHUI TA sits down and MR. SHU FU enters with MRS. SHIN.)

SHUI TA: Mr. Shu Fu?
SHU FU: Mr. Shui Ta.

(They both bow.)

SHUI TA: I am told that you have expressed a certain interest in my cousin Shen Te. Let me set aside all propriety and confess: she is at this moment in grave danger.
SHU FU: Oh, dear!
SHUI TA: She has lost her shop, Mr. Shu Fu.
SHU FU: The charm of Miss Shen Te, Mr. Shui Ta, derives from the goodness, not of her shop, but of her heart. Men call her the Angel of the Slums.
SHUI TA: Yet her goodness has cost her two hundred silver dollars in a single day: we must put a stop to it.
SHU FU: Permit me to differ, Mr. Shui Ta. Let us, rather, open wide the gates to such goodness! Every morning, with pleasure tinged by affection, I watch her charitable ministrations. For they are hungry, and she giveth them to eat! Four of them, to be precise. Why only four? I ask. Why not four hundred? I hear she has been seeking shelter for the homeless. What about my humble cabins behind the cattle run? They are at her disposal. And so forth. And so on. Mr. Shui Ta, do you think Miss Shen Te could be persuaded to listen to certain ideas of mine? Ideas like these?
SHUI TA: Mr. Shu Fu, she would be honored.

(Enter WONG and the POLICEMAN. MR. SHU FU turns abruptly away and studies the shelves.)

WONG: Is Miss Shen Te here?
SHUI TA: No.
WONG: I am Wong the water seller. You are Mr. Shui Ta?
SHUI TA: I am.
WONG: I am a friend of Shen Te's.
SHUI TA: An intimate friend, I hear.
WONG (to the POLICEMAN): You see? (To SHUI TA.) It's because of my hand.
POLICEMAN: He hurt his hand, sir, that's a fact.
SHUI TA (quickly): You need a sling, I see. (He takes a shawl from the back room, and throws it to WONG.)
WONG: But that's her new shawl!
SHUI TA: She has no more use for it.
WONG: But she bought it to please someone!
SHUI TA: It happens to be no longer necessary.
WONG (making the sling): She is my only witness.
POLICEMAN: Mr. Shui Ta, your cousin is supposed to have seen the barber hit the water seller with a curling iron.
SHUI TA: I'm afraid my cousin was not present at the time.
WONG: But she was, sir! Just ask her! Isn't she in?
SHUI TA (gravely): Mr. Wong, my cousin has her own troubles. You wouldn't wish her to add to them by committing perjury?
WONG: But it was she that told me to go to the judge!
SHUI TA: Was the judge supposed to heal your hand?

(MR. SHU FU turns quickly around. SHUI TA bows to SHU FU, and vice versa.)

WONG (taking the sling off, and putting it back): I see how it is.
POLICEMAN: Well, I'll be on my way. (To WONG.) And you be careful. If Mr. Shu Fu wasn't a man who tempers justice with mercy, as the saying is, you'd be in jail for libel. Be off with you!

(Exit WONG, followed by POLICEMAN.)

SHUI TA: Profound apologies, Mr. Shu Fu.
SHU FU: Not at all, Mr. Shui Ta. (Pointing to the shawl.) The episode is over?

SHUI TA: It may take her time to recover. There are some fresh wounds.

SHU FU: We shall be discreet. Delicate. A short vacation could be arranged. . . .

SHUI TA: First of course, you and she would have to talk things over.

SHU FU: At a small supper in a small, but high-class, restaurant.

SHUI TA: I'll go and find her. (*Exit into back room.*)

MRS. SHIN (*sticking her head in again*): Time for congratulations, Mr. Shu Fu?

SHU FU: Ah, Mrs. Shin! Please inform Miss Shen Te's guests they may take shelter in the cabins behind the cattle run!

(MRS. SHIN *nods, grinning.*)

SHU FU (*to the audience*): Well? What do you think of me, ladies and gentlemen? What could a man do more? Could he be less selfish? More farsighted? A small supper in a small but . . . Does that bring rather vulgar and clumsy thoughts into your mind? Ts, ts, ts. Nothing of the sort will occur. She won't even be touched. Not even accidentally while passing the salt. An exchange of ideas only. Over the flowers on the table — white chrysanthemums, by the way (*he writes down a note of this*) — yes, over the white chrysanthemums, two young souls will . . . shall I say "find each other"? We shall NOT exploit the misfortune of others. Understanding? Yes. An offer of assistance? Certainly. But quietly. Almost inaudibly. Perhaps with a single glance. A glance that could also — also mean more.

MRS. SHIN (*coming forward*): Everything under control, Mr. Shu Fu?

SHU FU: Oh, Mrs. Shin, what do you know about this worthless rascal Yang Sun?

MRS. SHIN: Why, he's the most worthless rascal . . .

SHU FU: Is he really? You're sure? (*As she opens her mouth.*) From now on, he doesn't exist! Can't be found anywhere!

(*Enter* YANG SUN.)

YANG SUN: What's been going on here?

MRS. SHIN: Shall I call Mr. Shui Ta, Mr. Shu Fu? He wouldn't want strangers in here!

SHU FU: Mr. Shui Ta is in conference with Miss Shen Te. Not to be disturbed.

YANG SUN: Shen Te here? I didn't see her come in. What kind of conference?

SHU FU (*not letting him enter the back room*): Patience, dear sir! And if by chance I have an inkling who you are, pray take note that Miss Shen Te and I are about to announce our engagement.

YANG SUN: What?

MRS. SHIN: You didn't expect that, did you?

(YANG SUN *is trying to push past the barber into the back room when* SHEN TE *comes out.*)

SHU FU: My dear Shen Te, ten thousand apologies! Perhaps you . . .

YANG SUN: What is it, Shen Te? Have you gone crazy?

SHEN TE (*breathless*): My cousin and Mr. Shu Fu have come to an understanding. They wish me to hear Mr. Shu Fu's plans for helping the poor.

YANG SUN: Your cousin wants to part us.

SHEN TE: Yes.

YANG SUN: And you've agreed to it?

SHEN TE: Yes.

YANG SUN: They told you I was bad. (SHEN TE *is silent.*) And suppose I am. Does that make me need you less? I'm low, Shen Te, I have no money, I don't do the right thing but at least I put up a fight! (*He is near her now, and speaks in an undertone.*) Have you no eyes? Look at him. Have you forgotten already?

SHEN TE: No.

YANG SUN: How it was raining?

SHEN TE: No.

YANG SUN: How you cut me down from the willow tree? Bought me water? Promised me money to fly with?

SHEN TE (*shakily*): Yang Sun, what do you want?

YANG SUN: I want you to come with me.

SHEN TE (*in a small voice*): Forgive me, Mr. Shu Fu, I want to go with Mr. Yang Sun.

YANG SUN: We're lovers you know. Give me the key to the shop. (SHEN TE *takes the key from around her neck.* YANG SUN *puts it on the counter. To* MRS. SHIN.) Leave it under the mat when you're through. Let's go, Shen Te.

SHU FU: But this is rape! Mr. Shui Ta!!

YANG SUN (*to* SHEN TE): Tell him not to shout.

SHEN TE: Please don't shout for my cousin, Mr. Shu Fu. He doesn't agree with me, I know, but he's wrong.

(*To the audience.*)

I want to go with the man I love
I don't want to count the cost
I don't want to consider if it's wise
I don't want to know if he loves me
I want to go with the man I love.

YANG SUN: That's the spirit.

(*And the couple leave.*)

V A

In front of the inner curtain. SHEN TE *in her wedding clothes, on the way to her wedding.*

SHEN TE: Something terrible has happened. As I left the shop with Yang Sun, I found the old carpet dealer's wife waiting on the street, trembling all over. She told me her husband had taken to his bed sick with all the worry and excitement over the two hundred silver dollars they lent me. She said it would be best if I gave it back now. Of course, I had to say I would. She said she couldn't quite trust my cousin Shui Ta or even my fiancé Yang Sun. There were tears in her eyes. With my emotions in an uproar, I threw myself into Yang Sun's arms, I couldn't resist him. The things he'd said to Shui Ta had taught Shen Te nothing. Sinking into his arms, I said to myself:

To let no one perish, not even oneself
To fill everyone with happiness, even oneself
Is so good

How could I have forgotten those two old people? Yang Sun swept me away like a small hurricane. But he's not a bad man, and he loves me. He'd rather work in the cement factory than owe his flying to a crime. Though, of course, flying *is* a great passion with Sun. Now, on the way to my wedding, I waver between fear and joy.

VI

The "private dining room" on the upper floor of a cheap restaurant in a poor section of town. With SHEN TE: *the* GRANDFA-THER, *the* SISTER-IN-LAW, *the* NIECE, MRS. SHIN, *the* UNEMPLOYED MAN. *In a corner, alone, a* PRIEST. *A* WAITER *pouring wine. Downstage,* YANG SUN *talking to his* MOTHER. *He wears a dinner jacket.*

YANG SUN: Bad news, Mamma. She came right out and told me she can't sell the shop for me. Some idiot is bringing a claim because he lent her the two hundred she gave you.

MRS. YANG: What did you say? Of course, you can't marry her now.

YANG SUN: It's no use saying anything to *her.* I've sent for her cousin, Mr. Shui Ta. He said there was nothing in writing.

MRS. YANG: Good idea. I'll go and look for him. Keep an eye on things.

(*Exit* MRS. YANG. SHEN TE *has been pouring wine.*)

SHEN TE (*to the audience, pitcher in hand*): I wasn't mistaken in him. He's bearing up well. Though it must have been an awful blow — giving up flying. I do love him so. (*Calling across the room to him.*) Sun, you haven't drunk a toast with the bride!

YANG SUN: What do we drink to?

SHEN TE: Why, to the future!

YANG SUN: When the bridegroom's dinner jacket won't be a hired one!

SHEN TE: But when the bride's dress will still get rained on sometimes!

YANG SUN: To everything we ever wished for!

SHEN TE: May all our dreams come true!

(*They drink.*)

YANG SUN (*with loud conviviality*): And now, friends, before the wedding gets under way, I have to ask the bride a few questions. I've no idea what kind of wife she'll make, and it worries me. (*Wheeling on* SHEN TE.) For example. Can you make five cups of tea with three tea leaves?

SHEN TE: No.

YANG SUN: So I won't be getting very much tea. Can you sleep on a straw mattress the size of that book? (*He points to the large volume the* PRIEST *is reading.*)

SHEN TE: The two of us?

YANG SUN: The one of you.

SHEN TE: In that case, no.

YANG SUN: What a wife! I'm shocked!

(*While the audience is laughing, his* MOTHER *returns. With a shrug of her shoulders, she tells* YANG SUN *the expected guest hasn't arrived. The* PRIEST *shuts the book with a bang, and makes for the door.*)

MRS. YANG: Where are *you* off to? It's only a matter of minutes.

PRIEST (*watch in hand*): Time goes on, Mrs. Yang, and I've another wedding to attend to. Also a funeral.

MRS. YANG (*irately*): D'you think we planned it this way? I was hoping to manage with one pitcher of wine, and we've run through two already. (*Points to empty pitcher. Loudly.*) My dear Shen Te, I don't know where your cousin can be keeping himself!

SHEN TE: My cousin?!

MRS. YANG: Certainly. I'm old-fashioned enough to think such a close relative should attend the wedding.

SHEN TE: Oh, Sun, is it the three hundred silver dollars?

YANG SUN (*not looking her in the eye*): Are you deaf? Mother says she's old-fashioned. And I say I'm considerate. We'll wait another fifteen minutes.

HUSBAND: Another fifteen minutes.

MRS. YANG (*addressing the company*): Now you all know, don't you, that my son is getting a job as a mail pilot?

SISTER-IN-LAW: In Peking, too, isn't it?

MRS. YANG: In Peking, too! The two of us are moving to Peking!

SHEN TE: Sun, tell your mother Peking is out of the question now.

YANG SUN: Your cousin'll tell her. If he agrees. I don't agree.

SHEN TE (*amazed, and dismayed*): Sun!

YANG SUN: I hate this godforsaken Setzuan. What people! Know what they look like when I half close my eyes? Horses! Whinnying, fretting, stamping, screwing their necks up! (*Loudly.*) And what is it the thunder says? They are su-per-flu-ous! (*He hammers out the syllables.*) They've run their last race! They can go trample themselves to death! (*Pause.*) I've got to get out of here.

SHEN TE: But I've promised the money to the old couple.

YANG SUN: And since you always do the wrong thing, it's lucky your cousin's coming. Have another drink.

SHEN TE (*quietly*): My cousin can't be coming.

YANG SUN: How d'you mean?

SHEN TE: My cousin can't be where I am.

YANG SUN: Quite a conundrum!

SHEN TE (*desperately*): Sun, I'm the one that loves you. Not my cousin. He was thinking of the job in Peking when he promised you the old couple's money —

YANG SUN: Right. And that's why he's bringing the three hundred silver dollars. Here — to my wedding.

SHEN TE: He is not bringing the three hundred silver dollars.

YANG SUN: Huh? What makes you think that?

SHEN TE (*looking into his eyes*): He says you only bought one ticket to Peking.

(*Short pause.*)

YANG SUN: That was yesterday. (*He pulls two tickets part way out of his inside pocket, making her look under his coat.*) Two tickets. I don't want Mother to know. She'll get left behind. I sold her furniture to buy these tickets, so you see . . .

SHEN TE: But what's to become of the old couple?

YANG SUN: What's to become of me? Have another drink. Or do you believe in moderation? If I drink, I fly again. And if you drink, you may learn to understand me.

SHEN TE: You want to fly. But I can't help you.

YANG SUN: "Here's a plane, my darling — but it's only got one wing!"

(*The WAITER enters.*)

WAITER: Mrs. Yang!

MRS. YANG: Yes?

WAITER: Another pitcher of wine, ma'am?

MRS. YANG: We have enough, thanks. Drinking makes me sweat.

WAITER: Would you mind paying, ma'am?

MRS. YANG (*to everyone*): Just be patient a few moments longer, everyone, Mr. Shui Ta is on his way over! (*To the WAITER.*) Don't be a spoilsport.

WAITER: I can't let you leave till you've paid your bill, ma'am.

MRS. YANG: But they know me here!

WAITER: That's just it.

PRIEST (*ponderously getting up*): I humbly take my leave. (*And he does.*)

MRS. YANG (*to the others, desperately*): Stay where you are, everybody! The priest says he'll be back in two minutes!

YANG SUN: It's no good, Mamma. Ladies and gentlemen, Mr. Shui Ta still hasn't arrived and the priest has gone home. We won't detain you any longer.

(*They are leaving now.*)

GRANDFATHER (*in the doorway, having for-*

gotten to put his glass down): To the bride! (*He drinks, puts down the glass, and follows the others.*)

(*Pause.*)

SHEN TE: Shall I go too?

YANG SUN: You? Aren't you the bride? Isn't this your wedding? (*He drags her across the room, tearing her wedding dress.*) If we can wait, you can wait. Mother calls me her falcon. She wants to see me in the clouds. But I think it may be St. Nevercome's Day before she'll go to the door and see my plane thunder by. (*Pause. He pretends the guests are still present.*) Why such a lull in the conversation, ladies and gentlemen? Don't you like it here? The ceremony is only slightly postponed — because an important guest is expected at any moment. Also because the bride doesn't know what love is. While we're waiting, the bridegroom will sing a little song. (*He does so.*)

THE SONG OF
ST. NEVERCOME'S DAY

On a certain day, as is generally known,
    One and all will be shouting: Hooray, hooray!
For the beggar maid's son has a solid-gold
    throne
    And the day is St. Nevercome's Day
On St. Nevercome's, Nevercome's, Nevercome's Day
    He'll sit on his solid-gold throne

Oh, hooray, hooray! That day goodness will
    pay!
That day badness will cost you your head!
And merit and money will smile and be funny
    While exchanging salt and bread
On St. Nevercome's, Nevercome's, Nevercome's Day
    While exchanging salt and bread

And the grass, oh, the grass will look down at
    the sky
And the pebbles will roll up the stream
And all men will be good without batting an
    eye
    They will make of our earth a dream
On St. Nevercome's, Nevercome's, Nevercome's Day
    They will make of our earth a dream

And as for me, that's the day I shall be
    A flyer and one of the best
Unemployed man, you will have work to do
    Washerwoman, you'll get your rest

On St. Nevercome's, Nevercome's, Nevercome's Day
    Washerwoman, you'll get your rest

MRS. YANG: It looks like he's not coming.

(*The three of them sit looking at the door.*)

VIA

WONG'S *den. The sewer pipe is again transparent and again the* GODS *appear to* WONG *in a dream.*

WONG: I'm so glad you've come, illustrious ones. It's Shen Te. She's in great trouble from following the rule about loving thy neighbor. Perhaps she's *too* good for this world!

FIRST GOD: Nonsense! You are eaten up by lice and doubts!

WONG: Forgive me, illustrious one, I only meant you might deign to intervene.

FIRST GOD: Out of the question! My colleague here intervened in some squabble or other only yesterday. (*He points to the* THIRD GOD *who has a black eye.*) The results are before us!

WONG: She had to call on her cousin again. But not even he could help. I'm afraid the shop is done for.

THIRD GOD (*a little concerned*): Perhaps we should help after all?

FIRST GOD: The gods help those that help themselves.

WONG: What if we *can't* help ourselves, illustrious ones?

(*Slight pause.*)

SECOND GOD: Try, anyway! Suffering ennobles!

FIRST GOD: Our faith in Shen Te is unshaken!

THIRD GOD: We certainly haven't found any *other* good people. You can see where we spend our nights from the straw on our clothes.

WONG: You might help her find her way by —

FIRST GOD: The good man finds his own way here below!

SECOND GOD: The good woman too.

FIRST GOD: The heavier the burden, the greater her strength!

THIRD GOD: We're only onlookers, you know.

FIRST GOD: And everything will be all right in the end, O ye of little faith!

(*They are gradually disappearing through these last lines.*)

VII

The yard behind SHEN TE's *shop. A few articles of furniture on a cart.* SHEN TE *and* MRS. SHIN *are taking the washing off the line.*

MRS. SHIN: If you ask me, you should fight tooth and nail to keep the shop.

SHEN TE: How can I? I have to sell the tobacco to pay back the two hundred silver dollars today.

MRS. SHIN: No husband, no tobacco, no house and home! What are you going to live on?

SHEN TE: I can work. I can sort tobacco.

MRS. SHIN: Hey, look, Mr. Shui Ta's trousers! He must have left here stark naked!

SHEN TE: Oh, he may have another pair, Mrs. Shin.

MRS. SHIN: But if he's gone for good as you say, why has he left his pants behind?

SHEN TE: Maybe he's thrown them away.

MRS. SHIN: Can I take them?

SHEN TE: Oh, no.

(*Enter* MR. SHU FU, *running.*)

SHU FU: Not a word! Total silence! I know all. You have sacrificed your own love and happiness so as not to hurt a dear old couple who had put their trust in you! Not in vain does this district — for all its malevolent tongues — call you the Angel of the Slums! That young man couldn't rise to your level, so you left him. And now, when I see you closing up the little shop, that veritable haven of rest for the multitude, well, I cannot, I cannot let it pass. Morning after morning I have stood watching in the doorway not unmoved — while you graciously handed out rice to the wretched. Is that never to happen again? Is the good woman of Setzuan to disappear? If only you would allow *me* to assist you! Now don't say anything! No assurances, no exclamations of gratitude! (*He has taken out his checkbook.*) Here! A blank check. (*He places it on the cart.*) Just my signature. Fill it out as you wish. Any sum in the world. I herewith retire from the scene, quietly, unob-

trusively, making no claims, on tiptoe, full of veneration, absolutely selflessly . . . (*He has gone.*)

MRS. SHIN: Well! You're saved. There's always some idiot of a man. . . . Now hurry! Put down a thousand silver dollars and let me fly to the bank before he comes to his senses.

SHEN TE: I can pay you for the washing without any check.

MRS. SHIN: What? You're not going to cash it just because you might have to marry him? Are you crazy? Men like him *want* to be led by the nose! Are you still thinking of that flyer? All Yellow Street knows how he treated you!

SHEN TE:
When I heard his cunning laugh, I was afraid
But when I saw the holes in his shoes, I loved him dearly.

MRS. SHIN: Defending that good-for-nothing after all that's happened!

SHEN TE (*staggering as she holds some of the washing*): Oh!

MRS. SHIN (*taking the washing from her, dryly*): So you feel dizzy when you stretch and bend? There couldn't be a little visitor on the way? If that's it, you can forget Mr. Shu Fu's blank check: it wasn't meant for a christening present!

(*She goes to the back with a basket.* SHEN TE's *eyes follow* MRS. SHIN *for a moment. Then she looks down at her own body, feels her stomach, and a great joy comes into her eyes.*)

SHEN TE: O joy! A new human being is on the way. The world awaits him. In the cities the people say: he's got to be reckoned with, this new human being! (*She imagines a little boy to be present, and introduces him to the audience.*) This is my son, the well-known flyer!

Say: Welcome
To the conqueror of unknown mountains and
　　unreachable regions
Who brings us our mail across the impassable
　　deserts!

(*She leads him up and down by the hand.*)

Take a look at the world, my son. That's a tree. Tree, yes. Say: "Hello, tree!" And bow. Like this. (*She bows.*) Now you know each other. And, look, here comes the water seller. He's a friend, give him your hand. A cup of fresh water for my little son, please. Yes, it *is* a warm day. (*Handing the cup.*) Oh dear, a police-man, we'll have to make a circle round *him*. Perhaps we can pick a few cherries over there in the rich Mr. Pung's garden. But we mustn't be seen. You want cherries? Just like children with fathers. No, no, you can't go straight at them like that. Don't pull. We must learn to be rea-sonable. Well, have it your own way. (*She has let him make for the cherries.*) Can you reach? Where to put them? Your mouth is the best place. (*She tries one herself.*) Mmm, they're good. But the policeman, we must run! (*They run.*) Yes, back to the street. Calm now, so no one will notice us. (*Walking the street with her child, she sings.*)

Once a plum — 'twas in Japan —
Made a conquest of a man
But the man's turn soon did come
For he gobbled up the plum

> (*Enter* WONG, *with a* CHILD *by the hand. He coughs.*)

SHEN TE: Wong!

WONG: It's about the carpenter, Shen Te. He's lost his shop, and he's been drinking. His children are on the streets. This is one. Can you help?

SHEN TE (*to the* CHILD): Come here, little man. (*Takes him down to the footlights. To the audience.*)

You there! A man is asking you for shelter!
A man of tomorrow says: what about today?
His friend the conqueror, whom you know,
Is his advocate!

(*To* WONG.) He can live in Mr. Shu Fu's cab-ins. I may have to go there myself. I'm going to have a baby. That's a secret — don't tell Yang Sun — we'd only be in his way. Can you find the carpenter for me?

WONG: I knew you'd think of something. (*To the* CHILD.) Good-bye, son, I'm going for your father.

SHEN TE: What about your hand, Wong? I wanted to help, but my cousin . . .

WONG: Oh, I can get along with one hand, don't worry. (*He shows how he can handle his pole with his left hand alone.*)

SHEN TE: But your right hand! Look, take this cart, sell everything that's on it, and go to the doctor with the money . . .

WONG: She's still good. But first I'll bring the carpenter. I'll pick up the cart when I get back. (*Exit* WONG.)

SHEN TE (*to the* CHILD): Sit down over here, son, till your father comes.

> (*The* CHILD *sits cross-legged on the ground. Enter the* HUSBAND *and* WIFE, *each dragging a large, full sack.*)

WIFE (*furtively*): You're alone, Shen Te, dear?

> (SHEN TE *nods. The* WIFE *beckons to the* NEPHEW *off-stage. He comes on with another sack.*)

WIFE: Your cousin's away? (SHEN TE *nods.*) He's not coming back?

SHEN TE: No. I'm giving up the shop.

WIFE: That's why we're here. We want to know if we can leave these things in your new home. Will you do us this favor?

SHEN TE: Why, yes, I'd be glad to.

HUSBAND (*cryptically*): And if anyone asks about them, say they're yours.

SHEN TE: Would anyone ask?

WIFE (*with a glance back at her husband*): Oh, someone might. The police, for instance. They don't seem to like us. Where can we put it?

SHEN TE: Well, I'd rather not get in any more trouble . . .

WIFE: Listen to her! The good woman of Setzuan!

> (SHEN TE *is silent.*)

HUSBAND: There's enough tobacco in those sacks to give us a new start in life. We could have our own tobacco factory!

SHEN TE (*slowly*): You'll have to put them in the back room.

> (*The sacks are taken off-stage, while the* CHILD *is alone. Shyly glancing about him, he goes to the garbage can, starts playing with the contents, and eating some of the scraps. The others return.*)

WIFE: We're counting on you, Shen Te!

SHEN TE: Yes. (*She sees the* CHILD *and is shocked.*)

HUSBAND: We'll see you in Mr. Shu Fu's cabins.

NEPHEW: The day after tomorrow.

SHEN TE: Yes. Now, go. Go! I'm not feeling well.

> (*Exeunt all three, virtually pushed off.*)

He is eating the refuse in the garbage can!
Only look at his little gray mouth!

(*Pause. Music.*)

As this is the world *my* son will enter
I will study to defend him.
To be good to you, my son,
I shall be a tigress to all others
If I have to.
And I shall have to.

(*She starts to go.*)

One more time, then. I hope really the last.

(*Exit* SHEN TE *taking* SHUI TA's *trousers.*
MRS. SHIN *enters and watches her with
marked interest. Enter the* SISTER-IN-LAW
and the GRANDFATHER.)

SISTER-IN-LAW: So it's true, the shop has
closed down. And the furniture's in the back
yard. It's the end of the road!
MRS. SHIN (*pompously*): The fruit of high living, selfishness, and sensuality! Down the primrose path to Mr. Shu Fu's cabins — with you!
SISTER-IN-LAW: Cabins? Rat holes! He gave
them to us because his soap supplies only went
moldy there!

(*Enter the* UNEMPLOYED MAN.)

UNEMPLOYED MAN: Shen Te is moving?
SISTER-IN-LAW: Yes. She was sneaking away.
MRS. SHIN: She's ashamed of herself, and no
wonder!
UNEMPLOYED MAN: Tell her to call Mr. Shui
Ta or she's done for this time!
SISTER-IN-LAW: Tell her to call Mr. Shui Ta
or *we're* done for this time.

(*Enter* WONG *and* CARPENTER, *the latter
with a* CHILD *on each hand.*)

CARPENTER: So we'll have a roof over our
heads for a change!
MRS. SHIN: Roof? Whose roof?
CARPENTER: Mr. Shu Fu's cabins. And we
have little Feng to thank for it. (FENG, *we find,
is the name of the* CHILD *already there; his* FA-
THER *now takes him. To the other two.*) Bow
to your little brother, you two!

(*The* CARPENTER *and the two new arrivals
bow to* FENG. *Enter* SHUI TA.)

UNEMPLOYED MAN: Sst! Mr. Shui Ta!

(*Pause.*)

SHUI TA: And what is this crowd here for,
may I ask?
WONG: How do you do, Mr. Shui Ta. This is
the carpenter. Miss Shen Te promised him
space in Mr. Shu Fu's cabins.
SHUI TA: That will not be possible.
CARPENTER: We can't go there after all?
SHUI TA: All the space is needed for other
purposes.
SISTER-IN-LAW: You mean we have to get
out? But we've got nowhere to go.
SHUI TA: Miss Shen Te finds it possible to
provide employment. If the proposition interests you, you may stay in the cabins.
SISTER-IN-LAW (*with distaste*): You mean
work? Work for Miss Shen Te?
SHUI TA: Making tobacco, yes. There are
three bales here already. Would you like to get
them?
SISTER-IN-LAW (*trying to bluster*): We have
our own tobacco! We were in the tobacco business before you were born!
SHUI TA (*to the* CARPENTER *and the* UNEM-
PLOYED MAN): You *don't* have your own tobacco. What about you?

(*The* CARPENTER *and the* UNEMPLOYED
MAN *get the point, and go for the sacks.
Enter* MRS. MI TZU.)

MRS. MI TZU: Mr. Shui Ta? I've brought
you your three hundred silver dollars.
SHUI TA: I'll sign your lease instead. I've decided not to sell.
MRS. MI TZU: What? You don't need the
money for that flyer?
SHUI TA: No.
MRS. MI TZU: And you can pay six months'
rent?
SHUI TA (*takes the barber's blank check from
the cart and fills it out*): Here is a check for ten
thousand silver dollars. On Mr. Shu Fu's account. Look! (*He shows her the signature on
the check.*) Your six months' rent will be in
your hands by seven this evening. And now, if
you'll excuse me.
MRS. MI TZU: So it's Mr. Shu Fu now. The
flyer has been given his walking papers. These
modern girls! In my day they'd have said she
was flighty. That poor, deserted Mr. Yang Sun!

(*Exit* MRS. MI TZU. *The* CARPENTER *and
the* UNEMPLOYED MAN *drag the three sacks
back on the stage.*)

CARPENTER (*to* SHUI TA): I don't know why I'm doing this for you.

SHUI TA: Perhaps your children want to eat, Mr. Carpenter.

SISTER-IN-LAW (*catching sight of the sacks*): Was my brother-in-law here?

MRS. SHIN: Yes, he was.

SISTER-IN-LAW: I thought as much. I know those sacks! That's our tobacco!

SHUI TA: Really? I thought it came from my back room! Shall we consult the police on the point?

SISTER-IN-LAW (*defeated*): No.

SHUI TA: Perhaps you will show me the way to Mr. Shu Fu's cabins?

(*Taking* FENG *by the hand,* SHUI TA *goes off, followed by the* CARPENTER *and his two older children, the* SISTER-IN-LAW, *the* GRANDFATHER, *and the* UNEMPLOYED MAN. *Each of the last three drags a sack. Enter* OLD MAN *and* OLD WOMAN.)

MRS. SHIN: A pair of pants — missing from the clothesline one minute — and next minute on the honorable backside of Mr. Shui Ta.

OLD WOMAN: We thought Miss Shen Te was here.

MRS. SHIN (*preoccupied*): Well, she's not.

OLD MAN: There was something she was going to give us.

WONG: She was going to help me too. (*Looking at his hand.*) It'll be too late soon. But she'll be back. This cousin has never stayed long.

MRS. SHIN (*approaching a conclusion*): No, he hasn't, has he?

VIIA

The Sewer Pipe: WONG *asleep. In his dream, he tells the* GODS *his fears. The* GODS *seem tired from all their travels. They stop for a moment and look over their shoulders at the water seller.*

WONG: Illustrious ones. I've been having a bad dream. Our beloved Shen Te was in great distress in the rushes down by the river — the spot where the bodies of suicides are washed up. She kept staggering and holding her head down as if she was carrying something and it was dragging her down into the mud. When I

called out to her, she said she had to take your Book of Rules to the other side, and not get it wet, or the ink would all come off. You had talked to her about the virtues, you know, the time she gave you shelter in Setzuan.

THIRD GOD: Well, but what do you suggest, my dear Wong?

WONG: Maybe a little relaxation of the rules, Benevolent One, in view of the bad times.

THIRD GOD: As for instance?

WONG: Well, um, good will, for instance, might do instead of love?

THIRD GOD: I'm afraid that would create new problems.

WONG: Or, instead of justice, good sportsmanship?

THIRD GOD: That would only mean more work.

WONG: Instead of honor, outward propriety?

THIRD GOD: Still more work! No, no! The rules will have to stand, my dear Wong!

(*Wearily shaking their heads, all three journey on.*)

VIII

SHUI TA's *tobacco factory in* SHU FU's *cabins. Huddled together behind bars, several families, mostly women and children. Among these people the* SISTER-IN-LAW, *the* GRANDFATHER, *the* CARPENTER, *and his* THREE CHILDREN. *Enter* MRS. YANG *followed by* YANG SUN.

MRS. YANG (*to the audience*): There's something I just *have* to tell you: strength and widom are wonderful things. The strong and wise Mr. Shui Ta has transformed my son from a dissipated good-for-nothing into a model citizen. As you may have heard, Mr. Shui Ta opened a small tobacco factory near the cattle runs. It flourished. Three months ago — I shall never forget it — I asked for an appointment, and Mr. Shui Ta agreed to see us — me and my son. I can see him now as he came through the door to meet us. . . .

(*Enter* SHUI TA *from a door.*)

SHUI TA: What can I do for you, Mrs. Yang?

MRS. Yang: This morning the police came to the house. We find you've brought an action for breach of promise of marriage. In the name of Shen Te. You also claim that Sun came by two hundred silver dollars by improper means.

SHUI TA: That is correct.

MRS. YANG: Mr. Shui Ta, the money's all gone. When the Peking job didn't materialize, he ran through it all in three days. I know he's a good-for-nothing. He sold my furniture. He was moving to Peking without me. Miss Shen Te thought highly of him at one time.

SHUI TA: What do *you* say, Mr. Yang Sun?

YANG SUN: The money's gone.

SHUI TA (*to* MRS. YANG): Mrs. Yang, in consideration of my cousin's incomprehensible weakness for your son, I am prepared to give him another chance. He can have a job — here. The two hundred silver dollars will be taken out of his wages.

YANG SUN: So it's the factory or jail?

SHUI TA: Take your choice.

YANG SUN: May I speak with Shen Te?

SHUI TA: You may not.

(*Pause.*)

YANG SUN (*sullenly*): Show me where to go.

MRS. YANG: Mr. Shui Ta, you are kindness itself: the gods will reward you! (*To* YANG SUN.) And honest work will make a man of you, my boy. (YANG SUN *follows* SHUI TA *into the factory.* MRS. YANG *comes down again to the footlights.*) Actually, honest work didn't agree with him — at first. And he got no opportunity to distinguish himself till — in the third week — when the wages were being paid . . .

(SHUI TA *has a bag of money. Standing next to his foreman — the former* UNEMPLOYED MAN — *he counts out the wages. It is* YANG SUN's *turn.*)

UNEMPLOYED MAN (*reading*): Carpenter, six silver dollars. Yang Sun, six silver dollars.

YANG SUN (*quietly*): Excuse me, sir. I don't think it can be more than five. May I see? (*He takes the foreman's list.*) It says six working days. But that's a mistake, sir. I took a day off for court business. And I won't take what I haven't earned, however miserable the pay is!

UNEMPLOYED MAN: Yang Sun. Five silver dollars. (*To* SHUI TA.) A rare case, Mr. Shui Ta!

SHUI TA: How is it the book says six when it should say five?

UNEMPLOYED MAN: I must've made a mistake, Mr. Shui Ta. (*With a look at* YANG SUN.) It won't happen again.

SHUI TA (*taking* YANG SUN *aside*): You don't hold back, do you? You give your all to the firm. You're even honest. Do the foreman's mistakes always favor the workers?

YANG SUN: He does have . . . friends.

SHUI TA: Thank you. May I offer you any little recompense?

YANG SUN: Give me a trial period of one week, and I'll prove my intelligence is worth more to you than my strength.

MRS. YANG (*still down at the footlights*): Fighting words, fighting words! That evening, I said to Sun: "If you're a flyer, then fly, my falcon! Rise in the world!" And he got to be foreman. Yes, in Mr. Shui Ta's tobacco factory, he worked real miracles.

(*We see* YANG SUN *with his legs apart standing behind the workers who are handing along a basket of raw tobacco above their heads.*)

YANG SUN: Faster! Faster! You, there, d'you think you can just stand around, now you're not foreman any more? It'll be your job to lead us in song. Sing!

(UNEMPLOYED MAN *starts singing. The others join in the refrain.*)

SONG OF THE EIGHTH ELEPHANT

Chang had seven elephants — all much the
    same —
But then there was Little Brother
The seven, they were wild, Little Brother, he
    was tame
And to guard them Chang chose Little
    Brother
      Run faster!
      Mr. Chang has a forest park
      Which must be cleared before tonight
      And already it's growing dark!

When the seven elephants cleared that forest
    park
Mr. Chang rode high on Little Brother
While the seven toiled and moiled till dark
    On his big behind sat Little Brother
      Dig faster!
      Mr. Chang has a forest park
      Which must be cleared before tonight
      And already it's growing dark!

And the seven elephants worked many an hour
    Till none of them could work another
Old Chang, he looked sour, on the seven he did
    glower

But gave a pound of rice to Little Brother
  What was that?
  Mr. Chang has a forest park
  Which must be cleared before tonight
  And already it's growing dark!

And the seven elephants hadn't any tusks
  The one that had the tusks was Little
    Brother!
Seven are no match for one, if the one has a
  gun!
  How old Chang did laugh at Little
    Brother!
    Keep on digging!
  Mr. Chang has a forest park
  Which must be cleared before tonight
  And already it's growing dark!

(*Smoking a cigar,* SHUI TA *strolls by.* YANG SUN, *laughing, has joined in the refrain of the third stanza and speeded up the tempo of the last stanza by clapping his hands.*)

MRS. YANG: And that's why I say: strength and wisdom are wonderful things. It took the strong and wise Mr. Shui Ta to bring out the best in Yang Sun. A real superior man is like a bell. If you ring it, it rings, and if you don't, it don't, as the saying is.

IX

SHEN TE's *shop, now an office with club chairs and fine carpets. It is raining.* SHUI TA, *now fat, is just dismissing the* OLD MAN *and* OLD WOMAN. MRS. SHIN, *in obviously new clothes, looks on, smirking.*

SHUI TA: No! I can NOT tell you when we expect her back.
OLD WOMAN: The two hundred silver dollars came today. In an envelope. There was no letter, but it must be from Shen Te. We want to write and thank her. May we have her address?
SHUI TA: I'm afraid I haven't got it.
OLD MAN (*pulling* OLD WOMAN's *sleeve*): Let's be going.
OLD WOMAN: She's got to come back some time!

(*They move off, uncertainly, worried.* SHUI TA *bows.*)

MRS. SHIN: They lost the carpet shop be-cause they couldn't pay their taxes. The money arrived too late.
SHUI TA: They could have come to me.
MRS. SHIN: People don't like coming to you.
SHUI TA (*sits suddenly, one hand to his head*): I'm dizzy.
MRS. SHIN: After all, you *are* in your seventh month. But old Mrs. Shin will be there in your hour of trial! (*She cackles feebly.*)
SHUI TA (*in a stifled voice*): Can I count on that?
MRS. SHIN: We all have our price, and mine won't be too high for the great Mr. Shui Ta! (*She opens* SHUI TA's *collar.*)
SHUI TA: It's for the child's sake. All of this.
MRS. SHIN: "All for the child," of course.
SHUI TA: I'm so fat. People must notice.
MRS. SHIN: Oh no, they think it's 'cause you're rich.
SHUI TA (*more feelingly*): What will happen to the child?
MRS. SHIN: You ask that nine times a day. Why, it'll have the best that money can buy!
SHUI TA: He must never see Shui Ta.
MRS. SHIN: Oh, no. Always Shen Te.
SHUI TA: What about the neighbors? There are rumors, aren't there?
MRS. SHIN: As long as Mr. Shu Fu doesn't find out, there's nothing to worry about. Drink this.

(*Enter* YANG SUN *in a smart business suit, and carrying a businessman's briefcase.* SHUI TA *is more or less in* MRS. SHIN's *arms.*)

YANG SUN (*surprised*): I guess I'm in the way.
SHUI TA (*ignoring this, rises with an effort*): Till tomorrow, Mrs. Shin.

(MRS. SHIN *leaves with a smile, putting her new gloves on.*)

YANG SUN: Gloves now! She couldn't be fleec-ing you? And since when did *you* have a private life? (*Taking a paper from the briefcase.*) You haven't been at your desk lately, and things are getting out of hand. The police want to close us down. They say that at the most they can only permit twice the lawful number of workers.
SHUI TA (*evasively*): The cabins are quite good enough.
YANG SUN: For the workers maybe, not for the tobacco. They're too damp. We must take over some of Mrs. Mi Tzu's buildings.
SHUI TA: Her price is double what I can pay.

YANG SUN: Not unconditionally. If she has me to stroke her knees she'll come down.

SHUI TA: I'll never agree to that.

YANG SUN: What's wrong? Is it the rain? You get so irritable whenever it rains.

SHUI TA: Never! I will never . . .

YANG SUN: Mrs. Mi Tzu'll be here in five minutes. You fix it. And Shu Fu will be with her. . . . What's all that noise?

(*During the above dialogue,* WONG *is heard off-stage, calling: "The good Shen Te, where is she? Which of you has seen Shen Te, good people? Where is Shen Te?" A knock. Enter* WONG.)

WONG: Mr. Shui Ta, I've come to ask when Miss Shen Te will be back, it's six months now. . . . There are rumors. People say something's happened to her.

SHUI TA: I'm busy. Come back next week.

WONG (*excited*): In the morning there was always rice on her doorstep — for the needy. It's been there again lately!

SHUI TA: And what do people conclude from this?

WONG: That Shen Te is still in Setzuan! She's been . . . (*He breaks off.*)

SHUI TA: She's been what? Mr. Wong, if you're Shen Te's friend, talk a little less about her, that's my advice to you.

WONG: I don't want your advice! Before she disappeared, Miss Shen Te told me something very important — she's pregnant!

YANG SUN: What? What was that?

SHUI TA (*quickly*): The man is lying.

WONG: A good woman isn't so easily forgotten, Mr. Shui Ta.

(*He leaves.* SHUI TA *goes quickly into the back room.*)

YANG SUN (*to the audience*): Shen Te pregnant? So that's why. Her cousin sent her away, so I wouldn't get wind of it. I have a son, a Yang appears on the scene, and what happens? Mother and child vanish into thin air! That scoundrel, that unspeakable . . . (*The sound of sobbing is heard from the back room.*) What was that? Someone sobbing? Who was it? Mr. Shui Ta the Tobacco King doesn't weep his heart out. And where does the rice come from that's on the doorstep in the morning? (SHUI TA *returns. He goes to the door and looks out into the rain.*) Where is she?

SHUI TA: Sh! It's nine o'clock. But the rain's so heavy, you can't hear a thing.

YANG SUN: What do you want to hear?

SHUI TA: The mail plane.

YANG SUN: What?!

SHUI TA: I've been told *you* wanted to fly at one time. Is that all forgotten?

YANG SUN: Flying mail is night work. I prefer the daytime. And the firm is very dear to me — after all it belongs to my ex-fiancée, even if she's not around. And she's not, is she?

SHUI TA: What do you mean by that?

YANG SUN: Oh, well, let's say I haven't altogether — lost interest.

SHUI TA: My cousin might like to know that.

YANG SUN: I might not be indifferent — if I found she was being kept under lock and key.

SHUI TA: By whom?

YANG SUN: By you.

SHUI TA: What could you do about it?

YANG SUN: I could submit for discussion — my position in the firm.

SHUI TA: You are now my manager. In return for a more . . . appropriate position, you might agree to drop the inquiry into your ex-fiancée's whereabouts?

YANG SUN: I might.

SHUI TA: What position *would* be more appropriate?

YANG SUN: The one at the top.

SHUI TA: My own? (*Silence.*) And if I preferred to throw you out on your neck?

YANG SUN: I'd come back on my feet. With suitable escort.

SHUI TA: The police?

YANG SUN: The police.

SHUI TA: And when the police found no one?

YANG SUN: I might ask them not to overlook the back room. (*Ending the pretense.*) In short, Mr. Shui Ta, my interest in this young woman has not been officially terminated. I should like to see more of her. (*Into* SHUI TA's *face.*) Besides, she's pregnant and needs a friend. (*He moves to the door.*) I shall talk about it with the water seller.

(*Exit.* SHUI TA *is rigid for a moment, then he quickly goes into the back room. He returns with* SHEN TE's *belongings: underwear, etc. He takes a long look at the shawl of the previous scene. He then wraps the things in a bundle, which, upon hearing a noise, he hides under the table. Enter* MRS. MI TZU *and* MR. SHU FU. *They put away their umbrellas and galoshes.*)

MRS. MI TZU: I thought your manager was here, Mr. Shui Ta. He combines charm with business in a way that can only be to the advantage of all of us.

SHU FU: You sent for us, Mr. Shui Ta?

SHUI TA: The factory is in trouble.

SHU FU: It always is.

SHUI TA: The police are threatening to close us down unless I can show that the extension of our facilities is imminent.

SHU FU: Shui Ta, I'm sick and tired of your constantly expanding projects. I place cabins at your cousin's disposal; you make a factory of them. I hand your cousin a check; you present it. Your cousin disappears; you find the cabins too small and start talking of yet more —

SHUI TA: Mr. Shu Fu, I'm authorized to inform you that Miss Shen Te's return is now imminent.

SHU FU: Imminent? It's becoming his favorite word.

MRS. MI TZU: Yes, what does it mean?

SHUI TA: Mrs. Mi Tzu, I can pay you exactly half what you asked for your buildings. Are you ready to inform the police that I am taking them over?

MRS. MI TZU: Certainly, if I can take over your manager.

SHU FU: What?

MRS. MI TZU: He's so efficient.

SHUI TA: I'm afraid I need Mr. Yang Sun.

MRS. MI TZU: So do I.

SHUI TA: He will call on you tomorrow.

SHU FU: So much the better. With Shen Te likely to turn up at any moment, the presence of that young man is hardly in good taste.

SHUI TA: So we have reached a settlement. In what was once the good Shen Te's little shop we are laying the foundations for the great Mr. Shui Ta's twelve magnificent super tobacco markets. You will bear in mind that though they call me the Tobacco King of Setzuan, it is my cousin's interests that have been served . . .

VOICES (off): The police, the police! Going to the tobacco shop! Something must have happened!

(Enter YANG SUN, WONG and the POLICE-MAN.)

POLICEMAN: Quiet there, quiet, quiet! (They quiet down.) I'm sorry, Mr. Shui Ta, but there's a report that you've been depriving Miss Shen Te of her freedom. Not that I believe all I hear, but the whole city's in an uproar.

SHUI TA: That's a lie.

POLICEMAN: Mr. Yang Sun has testified that he heard someone sobbing in the back room.

SHU FU: Mrs. Mi Tzu and myself will testify that no one here has been sobbing.

MRS. MI TZU: We have been quietly smoking our cigars.

POLICEMAN: Mr. Shui Ta, I'm afraid I shall have to take a look at that room. (He does so. The room is empty.) No one there, of course, sir.

YANG SUN: But I heard sobbing. What's that? (He finds the clothes.)

WONG: Those are Shen Te's things. (To crowd.) Shen Te's clothes are here!

VOICES (off, in sequence):
— Shen Te's clothes!
— They've been found under the table!
— Body of murdered girl still missing!
— Tobacco King suspected!

POLICEMAN: Mr. Shui Ta, unless you can tell us where the girl is, I'll have to ask you to come along.

SHUI TA: I do not know.

POLICEMAN: I can't say how sorry I am, Mr. Shui Ta. (He shows him the door.)

SHUI TA: Everything will be cleared up in no time. There are still judges in Setzuan.

YANG SUN: I heard sobbing!

IXA

WONG's den. For the last time, the GODS appear to the water seller in his dream. They have changed and show signs of a long journey, extreme fatigue, and plenty of mishaps. The FIRST no longer has a hat; the THIRD has lost a leg; all three are barefoot.

WONG: Illustrious ones, at last you're here. Shen Te's been gone for months and today her cousin's been arrested. They think he murdered her to get the shop. But I had a dream and in this dream Shen Te said her cousin was keeping her prisoner. You must find her for us, illustrious ones!

FIRST GOD: We've found very few good people anywhere, and even they didn't keep it up. Shen Te is still the only one that stayed good.

SECOND GOD: If she has stayed good.

WONG: Certainly she has. But she's vanished.

FIRST GOD: That's the last straw. All is lost!

SECOND GOD: A little moderation, dear colleague!

FIRST GOD (plaintively): What's the good of moderation now? If she can't be found, we'll have to resign! The world is a terrible place! Nothing but misery, vulgarity, and waste! Even the countryside isn't what it used to be. The trees are getting their heads chopped off by telephone wires, and there's such a noise from all the gunfire, and I can't stand those heavy clouds of smoke, and —

THIRD GOD: The place is absolutely unlivable! Good intentions bring people to the brink of the abyss, and good deeds push them over the edge. I'm afraid our book of rules is destined for the scrap heap —

SECOND GOD: It's people! They're a worthless lot!

THIRD GOD: The world is too cold!

SECOND GOD: It's people! They're too weak!

FIRST GOD: Dignity, dear colleagues, dignity! Never despair! As for this world, didn't we agree that we only have to find one human being who can stand the place? Well, we found her. True, we lost her again. We must find her again, that's all! And at once!

(*They disappear.*)

X

Courtroom. Groups: SHU FU *and* MRS. MI TZU; YANG SUN *and* MRS. YANG; WONG, *the* CARPENTER, *the* GRANDFATHER, *the* NIECE, *the* OLD MAN, *the* OLD WOMAN; MRS. SHIN, *the* POLICEMAN; *the* UNEMPLOYED MAN, *the* SISTER-IN-LAW.

OLD MAN: So much power isn't good for one man.

UNEMPLOYED MAN: And he's going to open twelve super tobacco markets!

WIFE: One of the judges is a friend of Mr. Shu Fu's.

SISTER-IN-LAW: Another one accepted a present from Mr. Shui Ta only last night. A great fat goose.

OLD WOMAN (*to* WONG): And Shen Te is nowhere to be found.

WONG: Only the gods will ever know the truth.

POLICEMAN: Order in the court! My lords the judges!

(*Enter the* THREE GODS *in judges' robes. We overhear their conversation as they pass along the footlights to their bench.*)

THIRD GOD: We'll never get away with it, our certificates were so badly forged.

SECOND GOD: My predecessor's "sudden indigestion" will certainly cause comment.

FIRST GOD: But he *had* just eaten a whole goose.

UNEMPLOYED MAN: Look at that! New judges.

WONG: New judges. And what good ones!

(*The* THIRD GOD *hears this, and turns to smile at* WONG. *The* GODS *sit. The* FIRST GOD *beats on the bench with his gavel. The* POLICEMAN *brings in* SHUI TA *who walks with lordly steps. He is whistled at.*)

POLICEMAN (*to* SHUI TA): Be prepared for a surprise. The judges have been changed.

(SHUI TA *turns quickly round, looks at them, and staggers.*)

NIECE: What's the matter now?

WIFE: The great Tobacco King nearly fainted.

UNEMPLOYED MAN: Look at that! New judges.

WONG: Does *he* know who they are?

(SHUI TA *picks himself up, and the proceedings open.*)

FIRST GOD: Defendant Shui Ta, you are accused of doing away with your cousin Shen Te in order to take possession of her business. Do you plead guilty or not guilty?

SHUI TA: Not guilty, my lord.

FIRST GOD (*thumbing through the documents of the case*): The first witness is the policeman. I shall ask him to tell us something of the respective reputations of Miss Shen Te and Mr. Shui Ta.

POLICEMAN: Miss Shen Te was a young lady who aimed to please, my lord. She liked to live and let live, as the saying goes. Mr. Shui Ta, on the other hand, is a man of principle. Though the generosity of Miss Shen Te forced him at times to abandon half measures, unlike the girl he was always on the side of the law, my lord. One time, he even unmasked a gang of thieves to whom his too trustful cousin had given shelter. The evidence, in short, my lord, proves that Mr. Shui Ta was *incapable* of the crime of which he stands accused!

FIRST GOD: I see. And are there others who could testify along, shall we say, the same lines?

(SHU FU *rises.*)

POLICEMAN (*whispering to* GODS): Mr. Shu Fu — a very important person.

FIRST GOD (*inviting him to speak*): Mr. Shu Fu!

SHU FU: Mr. Shui Ta is a businessman, my lord. Need I say more?

FIRST GOD: Yes.

SHU FU: Very well, I will. He is Vice President of the Council of Commerce and is about to be elected a Justice of the Peace. (*He returns to his seat.*)

(MRS. MI TZU *rises.*)

WONG: Elected! *He* gave him the job!

(*With a gesture the* FIRST GOD *asks who* MRS. MI TZU *is.*)

POLICEMAN: Another very important person. Mrs. Mi Tzu.

MRS. MI TZU: My lord, as Chairman of the Committee on Social Work, I wish to call attention to just a couple of eloquent facts: Mr. Shui Ta not only has erected a model factory with model housing in our city, he is a regular contributor to our home for the disabled. (*She returns to her seat.*)

POLICEMAN (*whispering*): And she's a great friend of the judge that ate the goose!

FIRST GOD (*to the* POLICEMAN): Oh, thank you. What next? (*To the Court, genially.*) Oh, yes. We should find out if any of the evidence is less favorable to the defendant.

(WONG, *the* CARPENTER, *the* OLD MAN, *the* OLD WOMAN, *the* UNEMPLOYED MAN, *the* SISTER-IN-LAW, *and the* NIECE *come forward.*)

POLICEMAN (*whispering*): Just the riffraff, my lord.

FIRST GOD (*addressing the "riffraff"*): Well, um, riffraff — do you know anything of the defendant, Mr. Shui Ta?

WONG: Too much, my lord.

UNEMPLOYED MAN: What don't we know, my lord.

CARPENTER: He ruined us.

SISTER-IN-LAW: He's a cheat.

NIECE: Liar.

WIFE: Thief.

BOY: Blackmailer.

BROTHER: Murderer.

FIRST GOD: Thank you. We should now let the defendant state his point of view.

SHUI TA: I only came on the scene when Shen Te was in danger of losing what I had understood was a gift from the gods. Because I did the filthy jobs which someone had to do, they hate me. My activities were restricted to the minimum, my lord.

SISTER-IN-LAW: He had us arrested!

SHUI TA: Certainly. You stole from the bakery!

SISTER-IN-LAW: Such concern for the bakery! You didn't want the shop for yourself, I suppose!

SHUI TA: I didn't want the shop overrun with parasites.

SISTER-IN-LAW: We had nowhere else to go.

SHUI TA: There were too many of you.

WONG: What about this old couple: Were *they* parasites?

OLD MAN: We lost our shop because of you!

OLD WOMAN: And we gave your cousin money!

SHUI TA: My cousin's fiancé was a flyer. The money had to go to *him*.

WONG: Did you care whether he flew or not? Did you care whether she married him or not? You wanted her to marry someone else! (*He points at* SHU FU.)

SHUI TA: The flyer unexpectedly turned out to be a scoundrel.

YANG SUN (*jumping up*): Which was the reason you made him your manager?

SHUI TA: Later on he improved.

WONG: And when he improved, you sold him to her? (*He points out* MRS. MI TZU.)

SHUI TA: She wouldn't let me have her premises unless she had him to stroke her knees!

MRS. MI TZU: What? The man's a pathological liar. (*To him.*) Don't mention my property to me as long as you live! Murderer! (*She rustles off, in high dudgeon.*)

YANG SUN (*pushing in*): My lord, I wish to speak for the defendant.

SISTER-IN-LAW: Naturally. He's your employer.

UNEMPLOYED MAN: And the worst slave driver in the country.

MRS. YANG: That's a lie! My lord, Mr. Shui Ta is a great man. He . . .

YANG SUN: He's this and he's that, but he is not a murderer, my lord. Just fifteen minutes before his arrest I heard Shen Te's voice in his own back room.

FIRST GOD: Oh? Tell us more!

YANG SUN: I heard sobbing, my lord!

FIRST GOD: But lots of women sob, we've been finding.

YANG SUN: Could I fail to recognize her voice?

SHU FU: No, you made her sob so often yourself, young man!

YANG SUN: Yes. But I also made her happy. Till he (*pointing at* SHUI TA) decided to sell her to you!

SHUI TA: Because you didn't love her.

WONG: Oh, no: it was for the money, my lord!

SHUI TA: And what was the money for, my lord? For the poor! And for Shen Te so she could go on being good!

WONG: For the poor? That he sent to his sweatshops? And why didn't you let Shen Te be good when you signed the big check?

SHUI TA: For the child's sake, my lord.

CARPENTER: What about *my* children? What did he do about them?

(SHUI TA *is silent.*)

WONG: The shop was to be a fountain of goodness. That was the gods' idea. You came and spoiled it!

SHUI TA: If I hadn't, it would have run dry!

MRS. SHIN: There's a lot in that, my lord.

WONG: What have you done with the good Shen Te, bad man? She *was* good, my lords, she was, I swear it! (*He raises his hand in an oath.*)

THIRD GOD: What's happened to your hand, water seller?

WONG (*pointing to* SHUI TA): It's all his fault, my lord, *she* was going to send me to a doctor — (*To* SHUI TA.) You were her worst enemy!

SHUI TA: I was her only friend!

WONG: Where is she then? Tell us where your good friend is!

(*The excitement of this exchange has run through the whole crowd.*)

ALL: Yes, where is she? Where is Shen Te? (*Etc.*)

SHUI TA: Shen Te . . . had to go.

WONG: Where? Where to?

SHUI TA: I cannot tell you! I cannot tell you!

ALL: Why? Why did she have to go away? (*Etc.*)

WONG (*into the din with the first words, but talking on beyond the others*): Why not, why not? Why did she have to go away?

SHUI TA (*shouting*): Because you'd all have torn her to shreds, that's why! My lords, I have

a request. Clear the court! When only the judges remain, I will make a confession.

ALL (*except* WONG, *who is silent, struck by the new turn of events*): So he's guilty? He's confessing! (*Etc.*)

FIRST GOD (*using the gavel*): Clear the court!

POLICEMAN: Clear the court!

WONG: Mr. Shui Ta has met his match this time.

MRS. SHIN (*with a gesture toward the judges*): You're in for a little surprise.

(*The court is cleared. Silence.*)

SHUI TA: Illustrious ones!

(*The* GODS *look at each other, not quite believing their ears.*)

SHUI TA: Yes, I recognize you!

SECOND GOD (*taking matters in hand, sternly*): What have you done with our good woman of Setzuan?

SHUI TA: I have a terrible confession to make: I am she! (*He takes off his mask, and tears away his clothes.* SHEN TE *stands there.*)

SECOND GOD: Shen Te!

SHEN TE: Shen Te, yes. Shui Ta *and* Shen Te. Both.

Your injunction
To be good and yet to live
Was a thunderbolt:
It has torn me in two
I can't tell how it was
But to be good to others
And myself at the same time
I could not do it
Your world is not an easy one, illustrious ones!
When we extend our hand to a beggar, he tears
  it off for us
When we help the lost, we are lost ourselves
And so
Since not to eat is to die
Who can long refuse to be bad?
As I lay prostrate beneath the weight of good
  intentions
Ruin stared me in the face
It was when I was unjust that I ate good meat
And hobnobbed with the mighty
Why?
Why are bad deeds rewarded?
Good ones punished?
I enjoyed giving
I truly wished to be the Angel of the Slums

But washed by a foster mother in the water of
    the gutter
I developed a sharp eye
The time came when pity was a thorn in my
    side
And, later, when kind words turned to ashes in
    my mouth
And anger took over
I became a wolf
Find me guilty, then, illustrious ones,
But know:
All that I have done I did
To help my neighbor
To love my lover
And to keep my little one from want
For your great, godly deeds, I was too poor, too
    small.

(*Pause.*)

FIRST GOD (*shocked*): Don't go on making
yourself miserable, Shen Te! We're overjoyed
to have found you!

SHEN TE: I'm telling you I'm the bad man
who committed all those crimes!

FIRST GOD (*using — or failing to use — his
ear trumpet*): The good woman who did all
those good deeds?

SHEN TE: Yes, but the bad man too!

FIRST GOD (*as if something had dawned*):
Unfortunate coincidences! Heartless neighbors!

THIRD GOD (*shouting in his ear*): But how is
she to continue?

FIRST GOD: Continue? Well, she's a strong,
healthy girl . . .

SECOND GOD: You didn't hear what she said!

FIRST GOD: I heard every word! She is confused, that's all! (*He begins to bluster.*) And
what about this book of rules — we can't renounce our rules, can we? (*More quietly.*)
Should the world be changed? How? By whom?
The world should *not* be changed! (*At a sign
from him, the lights turn pink, and music
plays.*)[1]

And now the hour of parting is at hand.
Dost thou behold, Shen Te, yon fleecy cloud?
It is our chariot. At a sign from me

'Twill come and take us back from whence we
    came
Above the azure vault and silver stars. . . .

SHEN TE: No! Don't go, illustrious ones!

FIRST GOD:
Our cloud has landed now in yonder field
From which it will transport us back to heaven.
Farewell, Shen Te, let not thy courage fail
    thee. . . .

(*Exeunt* GODS.)

SHEN TE: What about the old couple?
They've lost their shop! What about the water
seller and his hand? And I've got to defend myself against the barber, because I don't love
him! And against Sun, because I do love him!
How? How?

(SHEN TE's *eyes follow the* GODS *as they are
imagined to step into a cloud which rises and
moves forward over the orchestra and up beyond the balcony.*)

FIRST GOD (*from on high*): We have faith
in you, Shen Te!

SHEN TE: There'll be a child. And he'll have
to be fed. I can't stay here. Where shall I go?

FIRST GOD: Continue to be good, good
woman of Setzuan!

SHEN TE: I need my bad cousin!

FIRST GOD: But not very often!

SHEN TE: Once a week at least!

FIRST GOD: Once a month will be quite
enough!

SHEN TE (*shrieking*): No, no! Help!

(*But the cloud continues to recede as the*
GODS *sing.*)

VALEDICTORY HYMN

What rapture, oh, it is to know
    A good thing when you see it
And having seen a good thing, oh,
    What rapture 'tis to flee it

Be good, sweet maid of Setzuan
    Let Shui Ta be clever
Departing, we forget the man
    Remember your endeavor

Because through all the length of days
    Her goodness faileth never
Sing hallelujah! Make Shen Te's
    Good name live on forever!

SHEN TE: Help!

---

[1] The rest of this scene has been adapted for the
many American theatres that do not have "fly-
space" to lower things from ropes. The translation
in the first Minnesota edition, following the German
exactly, is reprinted here on page 566. [E.B.]

EPILOGUE

You're thinking, aren't you, that this is no right
Conclusion to the play you've seen tonight?[2]
After a tale, exotic, fabulous,
A nasty ending was slipped up on us.
We feel deflated too. We too are nettled
To see the curtain down and nothing settled.
How could a better ending be arranged?
Could one change people? Can the world be
    changed?
Would new gods do the trick? Will atheism?
Moral rearmament? Materialism?
It is for you to find a way, my friends,
To help good men arrive at happy ends.
You write the happy ending to the play!
There must, there must, there's got to be a
    way![3]

ALTERNATE ENDING FOR GERMAN PRODUCTION

FIRST GOD:
And now . . . (*He makes a sign and music is
    heard. Rosy light.*) let us return.
This little world has much engaged us.
Its joy and its sorrow have refreshed and pained
    us.
Up there, however, beyond the stars,
We shall gladly think of you, Shen Te, the
    good woman
Who bears witness to our spirit down below,
Who, in cold darkness, carries a little lamp!
Good-bye! Do it well!

(*He makes a sign and the ceiling opens. A
pink cloud comes down. On it the* THREE
GODS *rise, very slowly.*)

---

[2] *At afternoon performances:*
    We quite agree, our play this afternoon
    Collapsed upon us like a pricked balloon.
[3] When I first received the German manuscript of
Good Woman from Brecht in 1945 it had no
Epilogue. He wrote it a little later, influenced by
misunderstandings of the ending in the press on the
occasion of the Viennese première of the play. I
believe that the Epilogue has sometimes been spoken
by the actress playing Shen Te, but the actor playing
Wong might be a shrewder choice, since the audience has already accepted him as a kind of chorus.
On the other hand, it is not Wong who should
deliver the Epilogue: whichever actor delivers it
should drop the character he has been playing. [E.B.]

SHEN TE: Oh, don't, illustrious ones! Don't
go away! Don't leave me! How can I face the
good old couple who've lost their store and the
water seller with his stiff hand? And how can I
defend myself from the barber whom I do not
love and from Sun whom I do love? And I am
with child. Soon there'll be a little son who'll
want to eat. I can't stay here! (*She turns with a
hunted look toward the door which will let her
tormentors in.*)
FIRST GOD: You can do it. Just be good and
everything will turn out well!

(*Enter the witnesses. They look with surprise
at the judges floating on their pink cloud.*)

WONG: Show respect! The gods have ap-
peared among us! Three of the highest gods
have come to Setzuan to find a good human
being. They had found one already, but . . .
FIRST GOD: No "but"! Here she is!
ALL: Shen Te!
FIRST GOD: She has not perished. She was
only hidden. She will stay with you. A good
human being!
SHEN TE: But I need my cousin!
FIRST GOD: Not too often!
SHEN TE: At least once a week!
FIRST GOD: Once a month. That's enough!
SHEN TE: Oh, don't go away, illustrious ones!
I haven't told you everything! I need you
desperately!

(*The* GODS *sing.*)

THE TRIO OF THE VANISHING GODS ON THE CLOUD

Unhappily we cannot stay
More than a fleeting year.
If we watch our find too long
It will disappear.

Here the golden light of truth
With shadow is alloyed
Therefore now we ask your leave
To go back to our void.

SHEN TE: Help! (*Her cries continue through
the song.*)

Since our search is over now
Let us fast ascend!
The good woman of Setzuan
Praise we at the end!

(*As* SHEN TE *stretches out her arms to them
in desperation, they disappear above, smiling
and waving.*)

Earlier drama interested Brecht enormously, but he believed that it was obsolete and he devoted a fair amount of his time to trying to adapt it to the twentieth century. (His most popular play, *The Threepenny Opera*, is an adaptation of John Gay's *The Beggar's Opera*, and at the time of his death he was working on an adaptation of Shakespeare's *Coriolanus*. Accused of plagiarism, he replied that in literature as in life he did not recognize the idea of private property.)

Roughly speaking, earlier tragedy, as Brecht saw it, depicted a hero who, inevitably driven to the wall, performed some terrible deed and then became aware of all of its implications, thus achieving full understanding of himself and his fate. Interpreting Aristotle's comments on tragedy, Brecht went on to say that tragedy customarily sought to cause the audience to identify itself with the tragic hero and through the identification to undergo an emotional cleansing or catharsis. Here is one of Brecht's characteristically earthy and acerbic comments:

> The drama of our time still follows Aristotle's recipe for achieving what he calls catharsis (the spiritual cleansing of the spectator). In aristotelian drama the plot leads the hero into situations where he reveals his innermost being. All the incidents shown have the object of driving the hero into spiritual conflicts. It is a possibly blasphemous but quite useful comparison if one turns one's mind to the burlesque shows on Broadway, where the public, with yells of "Take it off!" forces the girls to expose their bodies more and more. The individual whose innermost being is thus driven into the open then of course comes to stand for Man with a capital M. Everyone (including every spectator) is then carried away by the momentum of the events portrayed, so that in a performance of *Oedipus* one has for all practical purposes an auditorium full of little Oedipuses, an auditorium full of Emperor Joneses for a performance of *The Emperor Jones*.*

Now, in opposition to what he called "aristotelian drama," drawing partly on German critical theories about the difference between drama and epic, Brecht developed the idea of "non-Aristotelian" or "epic drama." Whereas the usual play is set in the present and implies that what is happening on the stage happens *now*, to all of us, the epic traditionally is a story set in the past and is quite frankly about how things *used to be*. Because the reader of an epic, the argument goes, is a detached individual he is capable of using his mind critically, but the spectator at an aristotelian drama is part of a mob, his reason having been subordinated to a communal emotion. "Epic drama," then, in opposition to traditional aristotelian drama, seeks to create a detachment comparable to that which the epic creates. Brecht's word for this quality is V*erfremdung*, i.e., detachment, estrangement, alienation. The point of estranging the dramatic action from the audience is to make the audience regard it critically and thus see it more clearly, unobscured by emotional prejudices. To induce this estrangement, to shatter a sense of community between actors and audience, Brecht interrupted the action of his plays with such devices as songs,

* *Brecht on Theatre*, translated by John Willett (New York: Hill and Wang; London: Methuen & Co., 1964), p. 87.

addresses to the audience, and slogans projected onto the stage, and he insisted on highly stylized acting (Chaplin was one of his heroes) and unrealistic scenery. Brecht's ideal audience at an epic drama is critically aware of — not emotionally overcome by — what it sees on the stage. Brecht thus rejected tragedy of the sort that Yeats characterized as "a drowning and breaking of the dykes that separate man from man," and he insisted, in contrast to Yeats, that detachment is not limited to the spectator at a comedy.

Every play gives some image of the world; according to Brecht the aristotelian play shows a static world, for in the hero's agony it claims to reveal with increasing clarity how things inevitably are. The epic play, however, shows a dynamic or changing world, or a world that can be — must be — changed. (The direction in which Brecht wanted the change to go is clear enough; he was a Communist.)

> The dramatic [i.e., aristotelian] theatre's spectator says: Yes, I have felt like that too — Just like me — It's only natural — It'll never change — The sufferings of this man appall me, because they are inescapable — That's great art; it all seems the most obvious thing in the world — I weep when they weep, I laugh when they laugh.
>
> The epic theatre's spectator says: I'd never have thought it — That's not the way — That's extraordinary, hardly believable — It's got to stop — The sufferings of this man appall me, because they are unnecessary — That's great art: nothing obvious in it —I laugh when they weep, I weep when they laugh.*

Brecht put the distinctions between the two kinds of drama into the following tabular form, but one should keep in mind that he was talking about emphases, not utter opposites:†

DRAMATIC THEATRE	EPIC THEATRE
plot	narrative
implicates the spectator in a stage situation	turns the spectator into an observer, but
wears down his capacity for action	arouses his capacity for action
provides him with sensations	forces him to take decisions
experience	picture of the world
the spectator is involved in something	he is made to face something
suggestion	argument
instinctive feelings are preserved	brought to the point of recognition
the spectator is in the thick of it, shares the experience	the spectator stands outside, studies
the human being is taken for granted	the human being is the object of the inquiry
he is unalterable	he is alterable and able to alter

* *Brecht on Theatre*, p. 71.

† The list is reprinted from *Brecht on Theatre*, translated by John Willett, p. 37. Copyright © 1957, 1963 and 1964 by Suhrkamp Verlag, Frankfurt am Main.

This translation and notes © 1964 by John Willett. Reprinted by permission of Hill and Wang, Inc., and Methuen & Co. Ltd.

eyes on the finish	eyes on the course
one scene makes another	each scene for itself
growth	montage
linear development	in curves
evolutionary determinism	jumps
man as a fixed point	man as a process
thought determines being	social being determines thought
feeling	reason

It was with this scaffolding that Brecht built his plays. His interest was not in passionate tragic heroes who reveal their greatness when they assert themselves and do a deed of horror that affronts a mysterious metaphysical order that demands their life in expiation, but with the no less momentous issues of How do we survive? Must little people be imposed on? Above all, What is to be done? Such plays do not seek to evoke the woe or wonder that Shakespeare spoke of in connection with tragedy, for these emotions induce a sense of the inevitability of guilt and suffering, and send us out of the theater reconciled to the naturalness of our present condition. For Brecht, what is "natural" is not guilty actions but generous actions. (Brecht would argue that the following speech is counter-balanced by many other speeches because epic drama shows several sides, but it seems evident that the speech represents Brecht's own thinking.) Shen Te, the charitable prostitute, says in another version of *The Good Woman of Setzuan*:

> Why are you so bad?
> You tread on your fellow man.
> Isn't it a strain?
> Your veins swell with your efforts to be greedy.
> Extended naturally, a hand gives and receives with equal ease.

But somehow, according to Brecht, in our present (i.e., capitalistic) society, we find that we are forced into unnatural postures; Shen Te finds that she cannot continue to be charitable without the aid of a cruel "cousin" (she is so torn by the problem that she invents this person in order to protect herself from her own generous impulses). Moreover, in our society love itself must become savage: Shen Te so loves her child, and so fears that he may encounter a life of poverty, that she determines for his sake to be ruthless in her business dealings, and she determines also (further irony) to shield the child from knowledge of her activities so that he will grow up to be good — in a world in which goodness cannot survive.

These life-and-death issues are treated tragicomically. First, and least important, the play mingles gods and mortals, like Plautus' *Amphitryon*, a mixture which caused Plautus to introduce the word tragicomedy. And what gods they are, mouthing amiable pieties, getting a black eye when they intervene in a mortal quarrel, and finally, in a concluding scene that is funny and terrible, ascending to heaven on a cloud, singing, smiling, and waving to Shen Te, who is crying for help. More important, in this immensely earnest play that seeks to face some of the darkest facts of our life as it is, there are a good many comic figures and there is a good deal of wry wit. One example will have to suffice. Yang Sun wants to be sure that his wife will be frugal.

> YANG SUN: Can you sleep on a straw mattress the size of that book?
> SHEN TE: The two of us?
> YANG SUN: The one of you.
> SHEN TE: In that case, no.

More broadly, *The Good Woman of Setzuan*, like all comedies, calls attention to incongruity, but here the incongruity is not from some sort of unlovely behavior needlessly adopted in a smiling world where things will work out all right; rather, the incongruity is generosity in a corrupt world. Shen Te is funny in her persistent innocence and goodness — but she is not only funny, she is compelling (despite Brecht's theories?) and deeply sympathetic, as when she persists in loving the deceitful Yang Sun:

> SHEN TE:
> When I heard his cunning laugh, I was afraid
> But when I saw the holes in his shoes, I loved him dearly.

At the end, the play does not let us rest content, as tragedy and comedy in their different ways traditionally do. An epilogue invites us to work out a sequel:

> We feel deflated too. We too are nettled
> To see the curtain down and nothing settled.
> How could a better ending be arranged?
> Could one change people? Can the world be changed?
> Would new gods do the trick? Will atheism?
> Moral rearmament? Materialism?
> It is for you to find a way, my friends,
> To help good men arrive at happy ends.
> *You* write the happy ending to the play!
> There must, there must, there's got to be a way!

Probably Brecht assumed that Marx had shown us the way out: Change the economic basis of society and you will find a new human nature. Still, at rehearsals of his plays Brecht sometimes quoted his own Galileo: "I'm not trying to show that I'm in the right, but to find out whether."

WILD STRAWBERRIES

Ingmar Bergman

Translated by Lars Malmström and David Kushner

Ingmar Bergman, born in 1918, in Uppsala, Sweden, the son of a Lutheran clergyman, has said that for him "religious problems are continuously alive." Although he began his professional career as a stage actor and playwright, and he continued to be active in the theater until 1966 when he resigned as head of the Royal Dramatic Theater, his international fame is as a writer and director of films. His first screenplay, *Torment* (1944), established him as a writer of screenplays; the next year he directed his first film, *Crisis*. Among other major films in an extremely prolific career are *Smiles of a Summer Night* (1955), *The Seventh Seal* (1956), *Wild Strawberries* (1957), *The Silence* (1963), and *Persona* (1966).

CAST

PROFESSOR ISAK BORG	ISAK'S WIFE	CHARLOTTA
SARA	HER LOVER	ANGELICA
MARIANNE	AUNT	MRS. AKERMAN
EVALD	ALMAN	ANNA
AGDA	AKERMAN	THE TWINS
ANDERS	UNCLE ARON	HAGBART
VIKTOR	SIGFRID	BENJAMIN
ISAK'S MOTHER	SIGBRITT	PROMOTER
MRS. ALMAN		

Note: There are no cast listings for TIGER and JAKOB because the scene in which these characters appear (see pp. 598–599) did not appear in the finished film.

Top: Still photograph from *Wild Strawberries*, illustrating pages 601–602. (Reprinted from *Four Screenplays of Ingmar Bergman*, courtesy of Simon and Schuster, Inc.) *Bottom:* Still photograph from the filmscript of *Wild Strawberries*, illustrating Victor Sjöström as Professor Borg on page 602. (Photograph reproduced by permission of the publishers, Lorrimer Publishing, London.)

[*At the age of seventy-six, I feel that I'm much too old to lie to myself. But, of course, I can't be too sure. My complacent attitude towards my own truthfulness could be dishonesty in disguise, although I don't quite know what I might want to hide. Nevertheless, if for some reason I would have to evaluate myself, I am sure that I would do so without shame or concern for my reputation. But if I should be asked to express an opinion about someone else, I would be considerably more cautious. There is the greatest danger in passing such judgment. In all probability one is guilty of errors, exaggerations, even tremendous lies. Rather than commit such follies, I remain silent.*

As a result, I have of my own free will withdrawn almost completely from society, because one's relationship with other people consists mainly of discussing and evaluating one's neighbour's conduct. Therefore I have found myself rather alone in my old age. This is not a regret but a statement of fact. All I ask of life is to be left alone and to have the opportunity to devote myself to the few things which continue to interest me, however superficial they may be. For example, I derive pleasure from keeping up with the steady progress made in my profession (I once taught bacteriology), I find relaxation in a game of golf, and now and then I read some memoirs or a good detective story.

My life has been filled with work, and for that I am grateful. It began with a struggle for daily bread and developed into the continuous pursuit of a beloved science. I have a son living in Lund who is a physician and has been married for many years. He has no children. My MOTHER *is still living and quite active despite her advanced age (she is ninety-six). She lives in the vicinity of Huskvarna. We seldom see each other.*

My nine sisters and brothers are dead, but they left a number of children and grandchildren. I have very little contact with my relatives. My wife Karin died many years

ago. *Our marriage was quite unhappy. I am fortunate in having a good housekeeper.*

That is all I have to say about myself. Perhaps I ought to add that I am an old pedant, and at times quite trying, both to myself and to the people who have to be around me. I detest emotional outbursts, women's tears and the crying of children. On the whole, I find loud noises and sudden startling occurrences most disconcerting.

Later I will come back to the reason for writing this story, which is, as nearly as I can make it, a true account of the events, dreams and thoughts which befell me on a certain day.][1]

In the early morning of Saturday, the first of June, I had a strange and very unpleasant dream. I dreamed that I was taking my usual morning stroll through the streets. It was quite early and no human being was in sight. This was a bit surprising to me. I also noted that there were no vehicles parked along the kerbs. The city seemed strangely deserted, as if it were a holiday morning in the middle of summer.

The sun was shining brightly and made sharp black shadows, but it gave off no warmth. Even though I walked on the sunny side, I felt chilly.

The stillness was also remarkable. I usually stroll along a broad, tree-lined boulevard, and even before sunrise the sparrows and crows are as a rule extremely noisy. Besides, there is always the perpetual roar from the centre of the city. But this morning nothing was heard, the silence was absolute, and my footsteps echoed almost anxiously against the walls of the buildings. I began to wonder what had happened.

Just at that moment I passed the shop of a watchmaker-optometrist, whose sign had always been a large clock that gave the exact time. Under this clock hung a picture of a pair of giant eyeglasses with staring eyes. On my morning walks I had always smiled to myself at this slightly grotesque detail in the street scene.

To my amazement, the hands of the clock had disappeared. The dial was blank, and

[1] In the film, the scene in square brackets appears before the credits against shots of Isak in the library.

below it someone had smashed both of the eyes so that they looked like watery, infected sores.

Instinctively I pulled out my own watch to check the time, but I found that my old reliable gold timepiece had also lost its hands. I held it to my ear to find out if it was still ticking. Then I heard my heart beat. It was pounding very fast and irregularly. I was overwhelmed by an inexplicable feeling of frenzy.

I put my watch away and leaned for a few moments against the wall of a building until the feeling had passed. My heart calmed down and I decided to return home.

To my joy, I saw that someone was standing on the street corner. His back was towards me. I rushed up to him and touched his arm. He turned quickly and to my horror I found that the man had no face under his soft felt hat.

I pulled my hand back and in the same moment the entire figure collapsed as if it were made of dust or frail splinters. On the sidewalk lay a pile of clothes. The person himself had disappeared without a trace. I looked around in bewilderment and realized that I must have lost my way. I was in a part of the city where I had never been before.

I stood on an open square surrounded by high, ugly apartment buildings. From this narrow square, streets spread out in all directions. Everyone was dead; there was not a sign of a living soul.

High above me the sun shone completely white, and light forced its way down between the houses as if it were the blade of a razor-sharp knife. I was so cold that my entire body shivered.

Finally I found the strength to move again and chose one of the narrow streets at random. I walked as quickly as my pounding heart allowed, yet the street seemed to be endless.

Then I heard the tolling of bells and suddenly I was standing on another open square near an unattractive little church of red brick. There was no graveyard next to it and the church was surrounded on all sides by grey-walled buildings.

Not far from the church a funeral procession was wending its way slowly through the streets, led by an ancient hearse and followed by some old-fashioned hired carriages. These were pulled by pairs of meagre-looking horses, weighed down under enormous black

shabracks. I stopped and uncovered my head. It was an intense relief to see living creatures, hear the sound of horses trotting and church bells ringing. Then everything happened very quickly and so frighteningly that even as I write this I still feel a definite uneasiness.

The hearse was just about to turn in front of the church gate when suddenly it began to sway and rock like a ship in a storm. I saw that one of the wheels had come loose and was rolling towards me with a loud clatter. I had to throw myself to one side to avoid being hit. It struck the church wall right behind me and splintered into pieces.

The other carriages stopped at a distance but no one got out or came to help. The huge hearse swayed and teetered on its three wheels. Suddenly the coffin was thrown out and fell into the street. As if relieved, the hearse straightened and rolled on towards a side street, followed by the other carriages.

The tolling of the church bells had stopped and I stood alone with the overturned, partly smashed coffin. Gripped by a fearful curiosity, I approached. A hand stuck out from the pile of splintered boards. When I leaned forward, the dead hand clutched my arm and pulled me down towards the casket with enormous force. I struggled helplessly against it as the corpse slowly rose from the coffin. It was a man dressed in a frock coat.

To my horror, I saw that the corpse was myself. I tried to free my arm, but he held it in a powerful grip. All this time he stared at me without emotion and seemed to be smiling scornfully.

In this moment of senseless horror, I awakened and sat up in my bed. It was three in the morning and the sun was already reflecting from the rooftops opposite my window. I closed my eyes and I muttered words of reality against my dream — against all the evil and frightening dreams which have haunted me these last few years.

ISAK: My name is Isak Borg. I am still alive. I am seventy-six years old.[2] I really feel quite well.

(When I had muttered these words I felt calmer, drank a glass of water, and lay down to ponder on the day which was ahead of me. I knew immediately what I should do. I got

2 In the film, Isak is seventy-eight.

out of bed, pulled open the curtains, found the weather radiant, and breathed in the fine morning air. Then I put on my robe and went through the apartment (where the clocks were striking three) to the room of my old housekeeper. When I opened the door she sat up immediately, wide awake.)

AGDA: Are you ill, Professor?

ISAK: Listen, Miss Agda, will you please prepare some breakfast? I'm taking the car.

AGDA: You're taking the car, Professor?

ISAK: Yes, I'll drive down to Lund with my own two hands. I've never believed in aeroplanes.

AGDA: Dear Professor! Go back to sleep and I'll bring you coffee at nine o'clock and then we'll start at ten, as was decided.

ISAK: Very well then, I'll go without eating.

AGDA: And who's going to pack the frock coat?

ISAK: I'll do that myself.

AGDA: And what will become of me?

ISAK: Miss Agda, you can go with me in the car or take the aeroplane — that's up to you.

AGDA: For an entire year I've been looking forward to being present at the ceremony when you become a Jubilee Doctor, and everything was perfectly organised. Now you come and tell me that you're going to drive down instead of going by plane.

ISAK: The presentation is not until five o'clock, and if I leave at once I'll have fourteen hours in which to get there.

AGDA: Everything will be ruined that way. Your son will be waiting at Malmö airport. What will he say?

ISAK: You can make some explanation, Miss Agda.

AGDA: If you take the car, I won't be with you at the ceremony.

ISAK: Now listen, Miss Agda.

AGDA: You can take the car and drive there and destroy the most solemn day of my life . . .

ISAK: We are not married, Miss Agda.

AGDA: I thank God every night that we're not. For seventy-four years I have acted according to my own principles, and they won't fail me today.

ISAK: Is that your last word on this matter, Miss Agda?

AGDA: That is my last word. But I'll be saying a lot to myself about mean old gentlemen who think only of themselves and never about the feelings of others who have served them faithfully for forty years.

ISAK: I really don't know how I've been able to stand your immense hunger for power all these years.

AGDA: Just tell me and it can be ended tomorrow.

ISAK: Anyway, I'm going to drive, and you may do whatever the hell you want to. I'm a grown man and I don't have to put up with your bossiness.

(Our last words, I must admit, were spoken rather loudly, partly because of MISS AGDA's unruly temper and partly because I had gone to the bathroom, where I shaved and completed my morning toilet. When I came out of the bathroom, I found to my surprise that MISS AGDA was busy packing my frock coat and other necessities. She seemed to have come to her senses and I tried a friendly pat on her back to make her understand that I had forgiven her.)

ISAK: There is no one who can pack like you.

AGDA: Is that so.

ISAK: Old sourpuss.

(I was very angry that she didn't answer. True, my last words weren't very well chosen, but MISS AGDA has a way of being cross which would try the patience of a saint.)

AGDA: Should I boil a couple of eggs to go with the coffee, sir?

ISAK: Yes, thank you, that's very kind of you, Miss Agda. Thank you, dear Miss Agda.

(Without noticing my efforts to be nice in spite of everything, the old lady disappeared into the kitchen.)

ISAK: Jubilee Doctor! Damn stupidity. The faculty could just as well make me jubilee idiot. I'm going to buy something for the old sourpuss to sweeten her up a little. I hate people who are slow to forget. I can't even hurt a fly; how could I ever hurt Miss Agda?

(Then she appeared in the doorway.)

AGDA: Do you want toast?

ISAK: No, thank you for everything. Don't trouble yourself over me.

AGDA: Why are *you* sour?

(I didn't have time to answer before the door closed in my face. I dressed and went into the dining-room, where my breakfast was

waiting. The morning sun threw a bright stripe across the dining-room table. MISS AGDA *puttered about quietly with a coffee pot and poured steaming coffee into my personal cup.*)

ISAK: Won't you have a cup too?
AGDA: No, thanks.

(MISS AGDA *went over to water the flowers in the window and turned her back to me quite naturally but in a very definite way. Then the door of a nearby room opened and my daughter-in-law,* MARIANNE, *entered. She was still wearing pyjamas and was smoking a cigarette.*)

ISAK: May I ask why my esteemed daughter-in-law is out of bed at this hour of the morning?
MARIANNE: It's a little difficult to sleep when you and Miss Agda are shouting at each other loud enough to shake the walls.
ISAK: Surely no one here has been shouting.
AGDA: Of course not, no one here has been shouting.
MARIANNE: You're going by car to Lund.
ISAK: Yes, I think so.
MARIANNE: May I go with you?
ISAK: What? You want to go home?
MARIANNE: Yes, I want to go home.
ISAK: Home to Evald?
MARIANNE: That's it. You don't have to ask my reasons. If I could afford it, I would take the train.
ISAK: Of course you can go with me.
MARIANNE: I'll be ready in about ten minutes.

(MARIANNE *put out her cigarette in an ash tray on the table, went into her room and closed the door.* AGDA *brought another cup but said nothing. We were both surprised but had to remain silent about* MARIANNE's *sudden decision to go home to my son* EVALD. *Nevertheless, I felt obliged to shake my head.*)

AGDA: Good Lord!

([*Shortly after half past three, I drove my car out of the garage.* MARIANNE *came out through the front gate dressed in slacks and a short jacket (she is a stately young woman). I looked up towards the window to see if* AGDA *was standing there. She was. I waved to her but she did not wave back. Angrily I got*

into the car, slammed the door and started the engine.][3] *Silently we left the quiet, sleeping city.* MARIANNE *was about to light a cigarette.*)

ISAK: Please don't smoke.
MARIANNE: Of course.
ISAK: I can't stand cigarette smoke.
MARIANNE: I forgot.
ISAK: Besides, cigarette smoking is both expensive and unhealthy. There should be a law against women smoking.
MARIANNE: The weather is nice.
ISAK: Yes, but oppressive. I have a feeling that we'll have a storm.
MARIANNE: So do I.
ISAK: Now take the cigar. Cigars are an expression of the fundamental idea of smoking. A stimulant and a relaxation. A manly vice.
MARIANNE: And what vices may a woman have?
ISAK: Crying, bearing children, and gossiping about the neighbours.
MARIANNE: How old are you really, Father Isak?
ISAK: Why do you want to know?
MARIANNE: No real reason. Why?
ISAK: I know why you asked.
MARIANNE: Oh.
ISAK: Don't pretend. You don't like me and you never have.
MARIANNE: I know you only as a father-in-law.
ISAK: Why are you going home again?
MARIANNE: An impulse. That's all.
ISAK: Evald happens to be my son.
MARIANNE: Yes, I'm sure he is.
ISAK: So, it may not be so strange that I ask you.
MARIANNE: This is something which really does not concern you.
ISAK: Do you want to hear my opinion?

(*She provoked me with her unshakable calm and remoteness. Besides, I was very curious and a little worried.*)

ISAK: Evald and I are very much alike. We have our principles.
MARIANNE: You don't have to tell me.
ISAK: This *loan* for example. Evald got a loan from me with which to complete his studies. He was to have paid it back when he became a

3 The scene in square brackets does not appear in the finished film.

lecturer at the university. It became a matter of honour for him to pay it back at the rate of five thousand per year. Although I realise that it's difficult for him, a bargain is a bargain.

MARIANNE: For us it means that we can never have a holiday together and that your son works himself to death.

ISAK: You have an income of your own.

MARIANNE: . . . Especially when you're stinking rich and have no need for the money.

ISAK: A bargain is a bargain, my dear Marianne. And I know that Evald understands and respects me.

MARIANNE: That may be true, but he also hates you.

(Her calm, almost matter-of-fact tone startled me. I tried to look into her eyes, but she stared straight ahead and her face remained expressionless.)

ISAK: Evald and I have never coddled each other.

MARIANNE: I believe you.

ISAK: I'm sorry that you dislike me, because I rather like you.

MARIANNE: That's nice.

ISAK: Tell me, what do you really have against me?

MARIANNE: Do you want me to be frank?

ISAK: Please.

MARIANNE: You are an old egotist, Father. You are completely inconsiderate and you have never listened to anyone but yourself. All this is well hidden behind your mask of old-fashioned charm and your friendliness. But you are hard as nails, even though everyone depicts you as a great humanitarian. We who have seen you at close range, we know what you really are. You can't fool us. For instance, do you remember when I came to you a month ago? I had some idiotic idea that you would help Evald and me. So I asked to stay with you for a few weeks. Do you remember what you said?

ISAK: I told you that you were most cordially welcome.

MARIANNE: This is what you really said, but I'm sure you've forgotten: Don't try to pull me into your marital problems because I don't give a damn about them, and everyone has his own troubles.

ISAK: Did I say that?

MARIANNE: You said more than that.

ISAK: That was the worst, I hope.

MARIANNE: This is what you said, word for word: I have no respect for suffering of the soul, so don't come to me and complain. But if you need spiritual masturbation, I can make an appointment for you with some good quack, or perhaps with a minister, it's so popular these days.

ISAK: Did I say that?

MARIANNE: You have rather inflexible opinions, Father. It would be terrible to have to depend on you in any way.

ISAK: Is that so. Now, if I am honest, I must say that I've enjoyed having you around the house.

MARIANNE: Like a cat.

ISAK: Like a cat, or a human being, it's the same thing. You are a fine young woman and I'm sorry that you dislike me.

MARIANNE: I don't dislike you.

ISAK: Oh.

MARIANNE: I feel sorry for you.

(I could hardly keep from laughing at her odd tone of voice and lack of logic. She herself laughed, by the way, and it cleared the air a bit.)

ISAK: I really would like to tell you about a dream I had this morning.

MARIANNE: I'm not very interested in dreams.

ISAK: No, perhaps not.

(We drove for a while in silence. The sun stood high in the sky and the road was brilliantly white. Suddenly I had an impulse. I slowed down and swung the car into a small side road on the left, leading down to the sea. It was a twisting, forest road, bordered by piles of newly cut timber which smelled strongly in the heat of the sun. MARIANNE looked up, a bit surprised, but remained silent. I parked the car in a curve of the road.)

ISAK: Come, I'll show you something.

(She sighed quietly and followed me down the little hill to the gate. Now we could see the large yellow house set among the birch trees, with its terrace facing the bay. The house slept behind closed doors and drawn blinds.)

ISAK: Every summer for the first twenty years of my life we lived out here. There were ten of us children. Yes, you probably know that.

MARIANNE: What a ridiculous old house.

ISAK: It is an antique.

MARIANNE: Do people live here now?

ISAK: Not this summer.

MARIANNE: I'll go down to the water and take a dip if you don't mind. We have lots of time.

ISAK: I'll go over to the wild strawberry patch for a moment.

(*I suddenly found that I was speaking without a listener.* MARIANNE *was lazily making her way down to the beach.*)

ISAK: The old strawberry patch . . .

(*I went towards the house and immediately found the spot, but it seemed to be much smaller and less impressive than I had remembered. There were still many wild strawberries, however. I sat down next to an old apple tree that stood alone and ate the berries, one by one. I may very well have become a little sentimental. Perhaps I was a little tired and somewhat melancholy. It's not unlikely that I began to think about one thing or another that was associated with my childhood haunts.*

I had a strange feeling of solemnity, as if this were a day of decision. (It was not the only time that day that I was to feel that way.) The quietness of the summer morning. The calm bay. The birds' brilliant concert in the foliage. The old sleeping house. The aromatic apple tree which leaned slightly, supporting my back. The wild strawberries.

I don't know how it happened, but the day's clear reality flowed into dreamlike images. I don't even know if it was a dream, or memories which arose with the force of real events. I do not know how it began either, but I think it was when I heard the playing of a piano.

Astonished, I turned my head and looked at the house, a short distance up the hill. It had been transformed in a strange way. The façade, which only a few moments ago was so blind and shut, was now alive and the sun glittered on the open windows. White curtains swayed in the warm summer breeze. The gaudy awnings were rolled halfway down; smoke came from the chimney. The old summer-house seemed to be bursting with life. You could hear the music of the piano (it was something by Waldteufel), happy voices echoing through the open windows, laughter, footsteps, the cries of chil-

dren, the squeaking of the pump. Someone started to sing up there on the second floor. It was a strong, almost Italian bel-canto tenor. In spite of all this, not a human being was in sight. For a few moments the scene still had a feeling of unreality, like a mirage which could instantly evaporate and be lost in silence.

Suddenly I saw her. When I turned round after looking at the strangely transformed house I discovered her where she was kneeling in her sun-yellow cotton dress, picking wild strawberries. I recognized her immediately and I became excited. She was so close to me that I could touch her, but my lingering feeling of the evanescence of the situation prevented me from making her notice my presence. (I was amused. Mental image or dream or whatever this was, she looked just as I remembered her: a girl in a yellow summer dress, freckled and tanned and glowing with light-hearted young womanhood.)

I sat for a few minutes and silently looked at her. Finally I couldn't help calling out her name, rather quietly but nevertheless quite audibly. She didn't react. I tried once more, a little louder.)

ISAK: Sara . . . It's me, your cousin Isak . . . I've become a little old, of course, and do not quite look as I used to. But you haven't changed the slightest bit. Little cousin, can't you hear me?

(*She didn't hear me, but eagerly continued to pick the wild strawberries, putting them into a small straw basket. I understood then that one cannot easily converse with one's memories. This discovery did not make me particularly sad. I decided to keep quiet and hoped that this unusual and pleasant situation would last as long as possible.*

Then, a boy came strolling down the hill. He was already growing a small moustache despite the fact that he couldn't have been more than eighteen or nineteen years old. He was dressed in a shirt and trousers and wore his student's cap pushed way back on his head. He stepped right behind SARA, *took off his glasses and wiped them with a large white handkerchief. (I recognised him as my brother* SIGFRID, *one year older than myself. We shared many happy moments and troubles. He died, by the way, relatively young, of pyelitis. He was a lecturer in Slavic languages at Uppsala University.*)

SIGFRID: Good morning, sweet cousin. What are you doing?

SARA: Can't you see that I'm picking wild strawberries, stupid?

SIGFRID: And who shall be favoured with these tasty berries, plucked in the morning watch by a dulcet young maiden?

SARA: Oh you! Don't you know that Uncle Aron's birthday is today? I forgot to prepare a present for him. So, he gets a basket of wild strawberries. That's good enough, isn't it?

SIGFRID: I'll help you.

SARA: You know, Charlotta and Sigbritt have sewn a sampler for him and Angelica has baked a cake and Anna has painted a really pretty picture and Kristina and Birgitta have written a song which they'll sing.

SIGFRID: That's best of all, because Uncle Aron is stone deaf.

SARA: He will be very happy and you are stupid.

SIGFRID: And the nape of your neck is deuced pretty.

(SIGFRID *quickly bent over the girl and rather gallantly kissed her on her downy neck.* SARA *became rather annoyed.*)

SARA: You know that you're not allowed to do that.

SIGFRID: Who said so?

SARA: I said so. Besides, you are a particularly unbearable little snot who thinks he's something.

SIGFRID: I'm your cousin, and you're sweet on me.

SARA: On you!

SIGFRID: Come here and I'll kiss you on the mouth.

SARA: If you don't keep away I'll tell Isak that you try to kiss me all the time.

SIGFRID: Little Isak. I can beat him easily with one hand tied behind my back.

SARA: Isak and I are secretly engaged. You know that very well.

SIGFRID: Yes, your engagement is so secret that the whole house knows about it.

SARA: Could I help it if the twins ran around and blabbered everything?

SIGFRID: Then when are you going to get married? When are you going to get married?

When are you going to get married? When are you going to get married?

SARA: I'll tell you one thing, of your four brothers I can't decide which is the least vain. But I think it's Isak. In any case, he's the kindest. And you are the most awful, the most unbearable, the most stupid, the most idiotic, the most ridiculous, the most cocky — I can't think of enough names to call you.

SIGFRID: Admit that you're a little sweet on me.

SARA: Besides, you smoke smelly cigars.

SIGFRID: That's a man's smell, isn't it?

SARA: Besides, the twins, who know *everything*, say that you've done *rather* nasty things with the oldest Berglund girl. And she's not a *really nice* girl, the twins say. And I believe them.

SIGFRID: If you only knew how pretty you are when you blush like that. Now you must kiss me. I can't stand it any more. I'm completely in love with you, now that I think about it.

SARA: Oh, that's only talk. The twins say that you're crazy about girls. Is it really true?

(*Suddenly he kissed her hard and rather skilfully. She was carried away by this game and returned his kiss with a certain fierceness. But then she was conscious-stricken and threw herself down on the ground, knocking over the basket of wild strawberries. She was very angry and began crying with excitement.*)

SIGFRID: Don't scream. Someone might come.

SARA: Look at the wild strawberries, all spilled. And what will Isak say? He is so kind and really loves me. Oh, how sorry I am, oh, what you've done to me. You've turned me into a bad woman, at least *nearly*. Go away. I don't want to see you any more, at least not before breakfast. I have to hurry. Help me pick up the strawberries. And look, I've got a spot on my dress.

(*Then the gong suddenly sounded, announcing that breakfast was being served. The sound seemed to bring forth many human beings not far from where I stood, an astonished onlooker.*

The flag with the Swedish-Norwegian Union emblem went up and instantly stiffened against the light summer clouds, big brother HAGBART, *dressed in his cadet uniform, handled the ropes expertly. From the bath-house one could hear wild laughter, and through the louvered door tumbled two red-headed girls about thirteen years old, as identical as two wild strawberries. They laughed so hard they could hardly walk, and they whispered things to each other that were apparently both very secret and quite amusing.* SIGBRITT, *tall and lanky, with thick hair in heavy rolls across her forehead, came out carrying the baby's bassinet and placed it in the shadow of the arbour.* CHARLOTTA (*the diligent, self-sacrificing sister who carried the responsibilities of the household on her round shoulders*) *rushed out on the veranda and shouted to* SARA *and* SIGFRID *to hurry. Seventeen-year-old* BENJAMIN *dived out of some bushes, his pimply face red from the sun, and looked around with an annoyed expression.*[4] *In his hand he held a thick, open book.* ANGELICA (*the beauty of the family*) *came skipping out of the woods, joined the twins, and was immediately made part of some hilarious secret. Finally, fifteen-year-old* ANNA *came running out of the house, asked* HAGBART *about something, then raised her voice and started to shout for* ISAK. *I arose, surprised and worried, unable to answer her cry.*)

TWINS (*in unison*): I think that Isak is out fishing with Father and they probably can't hear the gong. And Father said, by the way, that we shouldn't wait to eat. That's what Father said, I definitely remember.

(*Oh, yes,* FATHER *and I were out fishing together. I felt a secret and completely inexplicable happiness at this message, and I stood for a long while wondering what I should do in this new old world which I was suddenly given the opportunity to visit.*

The rest of the family had entered the house and something was being discussed quite loudly inside. Only SIGBRITT'S *little child remained on the terrace, sleeping in the shadows of the tall lilac bushes. Curiosity overwhelmed me. I went slowly up the slope towards the house and soon found myself in the long, dark corridor which was connected with the foyer by glass doors. From there I had a good view into the large,*

sunlit dining-room with its white table already set for breakfast, the light furniture, the wallpaper, the figurines, the palms, the airy summer curtains, the scoured white wooden floor with its broad planks and blue rag rugs, the pictures and the sampler, the large, crownlike chandelier.

There they were now, my nine brothers and sisters, my AUNT *and* UNCLE ARON. *The only ones missing were* FATHER, MOTHER *and I.*

Everyone was standing behind his chair, with lowered head, and hands clenched together. AUNT *recited the prayer 'In Jesus's name to the table we go, Bless You for the food You bestow.' After which the whole troop sat down with much chatter and scraping of chairs. My aunt (a stately woman in her best years, endowed with a powerful sense of authority and a resonant voice) demanded silence.*)

AUNT: Benjamin will immediately go and wash his hands. How long is it going to take you to learn cleanliness?

BENJAMIN: I *have* washed my hands.

AUNT: Sigbritt, pass the porridge to Angelica and give the twins their portions. Your fingernails are coal-black. Pass me the bread, Hagbart. Who taught you to spread so much butter on the bread? Can you do that at the military academy? Charlotta, the salt-cellar is stopped up. How often have I told you that it shouldn't be left out in the open, because the salt gets humid.

BENJAMIN: I *have washed my hands*, but I have paint under my nails.

UNCLE ARON: Who has picked wild strawberries for me?

SARA: I have. (*Louder.*) I have.

AUNT: You have to speak up, my child. You know that Uncle Aron is a bit hard of hearing.

SARA (*thunderously*): I have!

ARON: Oh my, you remembered Uncle Aron's birthday. That was really very kind of you.

HAGBART: Couldn't Uncle Aron have a little drink for breakfast in honour of the day?

AUNT: A drink at breakfast when Father isn't home is completely out of the question.

TWINS (*in unison*): Uncle Aron has already had three drinks. I know. I know. We saw him at eight o'clock when we went down to the bath-house.

---

[4] In the film, Benjamin is seen jumping down from a tree.

AUNT: The twins should hold their tongues and eat. Besides, you haven't made your beds and as punishment you'll have to dry the dinner silverware. Benjamin must not bite his nails. Don't sit and jump on the chair, Anna. You aren't a child any more.

ANNA: I want to give Uncle Aron my picture, please, Auntie. Can't we give him our presents now, right away?

AUNT: Where is your picture?

ANNA: Here under the table.

AUNT: You'll have to wait until we've eaten.

SIGFRID: It's a very advanced work of art, I'd say. It's a picture of Tristan and Isolde, but you can't tell for sure which one is Tristan.

SARA: Oh, he always spoils things, the little fop! Now he's making Anna unhappy. See if she doesn't start to cry.

ANNA: Not at all. I can overlook Sigfrid's faults.

TWINS (together): By the way, what were Sara and Sigfrid up to in the wild strawberry patch this morning? We saw everything from the bath-house.

SIGBRITT: Calm down now, children!

CHARLOTTA: Someone should put gags on the twins.

AUNT: Twins, keep still or leave the table.

BENJAMIN: Doesn't a person have freedom of expression, eh?

SIGFRID: Shut up, you snotnoses.

ANGELICA: Sara is blushing, Sara is blushing, Sara is blushing.

TWINS: Sigfrid is blushing, too. Ha-ha! Sigfrid and Sara! Sigfrid and Sara! Sigfrid and Sara!

AUNT (thunderously): Quiet! We'll have quiet at the table!

ARON: What did you say? Of course we shall be happy.

(The TWINS snigger in the silence. SARA throws the porridge spoon at her tormentors.)

CHARLOTTA: But, Sara!

SARA: They're just lying! They're liars!

(SARA rose from the table so violently that her chair turned over. She stood hesitantly for a moment, her face red and tears splashing down her cheeks. Then she ran away furiously, throwing herself at the door and out into the hall.

She opened the glass door and disap-peared out on the porch, where I could hear her sobbing violently. Gentle CHARLOTTA came out of the dining-room and went past me on her way to console SARA.

I could hear their voices from the darkness of the foyer and I came closer stealthily. SARA sat on a red stool (which GRANDMOTHER once used, when she wanted to take off her rubber boots) while CHARLOTTA stood in front of her, patting her gently on the head. The miserable girl pressed her tear-stained face against CHARLOTTA's skirt over and over again. The tinted light from the stained-glass windows of the outer door painted the whole picture in a strange way.)

SARA: Isak is so refined. He is so enormously refined and moral and sensitive and he wants us to read poetry together and he talks about the after-life and wants to play duets on the piano and he likes to kiss only in the dark and he talks about sinfulness. I think he is extremely intellectual and morally aloof and I feel so worthless, and I am so worthless, you can't deny that. But sometimes I get the feeling that I'm much older than Isak, do you know what I mean? And then I think he's a child even if we are the same age, and then Sigfrid is so fresh and exciting and I want to go home. I don't want to be here all summer, to be a laughing stock for the twins and the rest of you — no, I don't want that.

CHARLOTTA: I'll talk to Sigfrid, I will! If he doesn't leave you alone, I'll see to it that he gets a few more chores to do. Father will arrange that without any trouble. He also thinks Sigfrid is nasty and needs a little work to keep him out of mischief.

SARA: Poor little Isak, he is so kind to me. Oh, how unfair everything is.

CHARLOTTA: Everything will work out for the best, you'll see. Listen, now they're singing for Uncle Aron.

SARA: Isn't it crazy to write a song for a deaf man! That's typical of the twins.

(Then two girlish voices sang a song that could be heard throughout the house. CHARLOTTA placed her arm around SARA's shoulders and SARA blew her nose quite loudly.

Both girls returned to the dining-room, where the mood had become very lively.[5]

[5] In the film, the girls do not return to the dining-room.

Uncle ARON *had arisen, his round perspiring face lit like a lantern, and he had tears in his eyes. He held a sheet of music before him while the twins stood nearby and sang with all their might. When they had finished everyone applauded, and Uncle* ARON *kissed them on the forehead and wiped his face with a napkin. My* AUNT *rose from the table and proposed a quadruple cheer. Everyone got up and hurrahed. Suddenly* ANNA *shouted and pointed out the window. Everyone turned to look.*)

ANNA: Look, here comes Father.

AUNT: Well, finally! Sigbritt, take out the porridge bowl and have it warmed. Charlotta, you bring up more milk from the cellar.

(*The women fussed around, but* SARA *ran out of the house, down the slope, and disappeared behind the small arbour which stood on the edge of the birch-tree pasture. I followed her with curiosity, but lost her. Suddenly I stood alone at the wild strawberry patch. A feeling of emptiness and sadness came over me. I was awakened by a girl's voice asking me something. I looked up.*

In front of me stood a young lady in shorts and a boy's checked shirt. She was very tanned and her blonde hair was tangled and bleached by the sun and the sea. She sucked on an unlit pipe, wore wooden sandals on her feet and dark glasses on her nose.)

SARA: Is this your shack?

ISAK: No, it isn't.

SARA: It's a good thing you're the truthful type. My old man owns the whole peninsula . . . including the shack.

ISAK: I lived here once. Two hundred years ago.

SARA Uh huh. Is that your jalopy standing up at the gate?

ISAK: It's my jalopy, yes.

SARA: Looks like an antique.

ISAK: It *is* an antique, just like its owner.

SARA: You've got a sense of humour about yourself, too. That's fantastic. Where are you heading, by the way? In which direction, I mean.

ISAK: I'm going to Lund.

SARA: What a fantastic coincidence. I'm on my way to Italy.

ISAK: I'd feel very honoured if you came along.

SARA: My name is Sara. Silly name, isn't it?

ISAK: My name is Isak. Rather silly too.

SARA: Weren't they married?

ISAK: Unfortunately not. It was Abraham and Sara.

SARA: Shall we take off?

ISAK: I have another lady with me. Here she comes. This is Sara, and this is Marianne. We'll have company to Lund. Sara is going to Italy but she has agreed to travel part of the way with us.

SARA: Now you're being ironic again, but it suits you.

(*We began walking towards the car.* MAR-IANNE *and I exchanged amused glances, the first contact between us. When we came to the car, two young men with round blond crew-cut heads popped up.*[6] *They were also wearing checked shirts, shorts, wooden sandals and sunglasses. Each carried a rucksack.*)

SARA: Hey, fellows. I've got a lift nearly all the way to Italy. This is Anders, and this one with the glasses is Viktor, called Vicke . . . and this is Father Isak.

VIKTOR: Hello.

ISAK: Hello.

ANDERS: How do you do, sir.

ISAK: Hello.

SARA: That cookie you're staring at so hard, her name is Marianne.

MARIANNE: Hello.

BOYS (*together*): Hello.

SARA: It's a pretty big car.

ISAK: Just jump in. There's room for everybody. We can put the baggage in the boot, if you don't mind.

(*We packed things away, and then we all got into the car. I drove carefully, leaving my childhood world behind.* SARA *took off her sunglasses and laughed. She was very much like her namesake of the past.*)

SARA: Of course I have to tell Isak that Anders and I are going steady. We are crazy about each other. Viktor is with us as a chaperon. That was decided by the old man. Viktor is also in love with me and is watching Anders like a madman. This was a brilliant idea of my old man. I'll probably have to seduce Viktor

---

[6] In the film, one of the young men has dark hair.

to get him out of the way. I'd better tell Isak
that I'm a virgin. That's why I can talk so brazenly.

(*I looked at her through the rear-view mirror.
She was sitting comfortably with her legs on
the backs of the folding seats.* ANDERS *had a
proprietary arm around her shoulders and
looked rather angry, for which I could hardly
blame him.* VIKTOR, *on the other hand,
seemed completely disinterested and stared
fixedly at the nape of* MARIANNE's *neck —
and whatever else he could glimpse of her
figure.*)

SARA: I smoke a pipe. Viktor says it's healthier. He's crazy about everything that's healthy.

(*No one answered, or considered any comment necessary. We continued our trip in a
silence which was by no means unpleasant,
just a little shy. The weather had become
quite warm, almost oppressive, and we had
opened all the windows. The road was broad
and straight. I was in a spirited mood. The
day had been full of stimulating surprises.*)

ISAK: I had a first love whose name was Sara.
SARA: She was like me, of course.
ISAK: As a matter of fact, she was rather like
you.
SARA: What happened to her?
ISAK: She married my brother Sigfrid and had
six children. Now she's seventy-five years old
and a rather beautiful little old lady.
SARA: I can't imagine anything worse than
getting old. Oh, excuse me. I think I said something stupid.

(*Her tone was so sincerely repentant that everyone burst into laughter. And then it happened.
We were on a broad, blind right curve. I
kept hard to the left and at that moment a
little black car came speeding straight towards us. I had time to see* MARIANNE *brace
her right hand against the windshield and I
heard* SARA *scream. Then I slammed on the
brakes with all my strength. Our big car
skidded to the left and went off the road
into a pasture. The black car disappeared
with a squeal, rolled over and fell into a
deep ditch to the right of the road. Startled,
we stared at one another; we had escaped
without a scratch. Some thick black tyre
tracks and several big marks on the road*

*surface were the only signs of the other car.
A short distance away, a couple of rotating
wheels stuck up from the ditch.
All of us began running towards it and
then stopped in astonishment. The overturned car's radio sang a morning hymn.
Two people crawled out of the ditch, a man
and a woman, in the midst of a violent quarrel which was on the verge of coming to
blows. When they saw us watching they immediately stopped and the man limped towards me.*)

ALMAN: How are you? There's nothing for
me to say. The blame is completely ours. We
have no excuses. It was my wife who was driving. Are you all right? Everyone safe and
sound? Thank God for that.

(*He mumbled nervously, took off his glasses
and put them on again, and looked at us with
frightened glances.*)

ALMAN: The would-be murderers should introduce themselves. Alman is my name. I'm an
engineer at the Stockholm electric power plant.
Back there is my wife, Berit. She used to be an
actress, and it was that fact we were discussing
when . . . when . . . when . . .

(*He interrupted himself with an artificial
laugh and waved at his wife. When she remained motionless, he took a few limping
steps towards her.*)

ISAK: How is your leg?
ALMAN: It's not from this. I've been crippled
for years. Unfortunately it's not only my leg
that's crippled, according to my wife. Come
here now, Berit, and make your apologies.

(*The woman mustered her courage. She
moved jerkily in spite of her rotund body.*)

BERIT: Please, pretty please forgive me, as
children say. It was my fault, everything. I was
just going to hit my husband when that curve
appeared. One thing is obvious: God punishes
some people immediately — or what do you
think, Sten? You're a Catholic.
ISAK: Perhaps we should take a look at your
car and see if we can't put it right side up again.
ALMAN: Please don't trouble yourself over
us. I beg of you.
BERIT: Shut up now, Sten darling. Some
people do have completely unselfish intentions,
even if you don't believe it.

ALMAN: My wife is a little nervous, I think. But we've had a shock. That's the word. A shock.

(*He laughed once more and tore off his glasses and put them on again. The young men had already jumped down into the ditch and were trying to lift the little car.* MARIANNE *ran back to our car and backed it down the road. With the help of a rope which I always carry in the boot, we succeeded in getting the other car on an even keel.* MR. ALMAN *suddenly cheered up, threw off his jacket and rolled up his shirt sleeves. Then he put his shoulder alongside* SARA, VIKTOR *and* ANDERS *and began to push.*)

BERIT: Now watch the engineer closely, see how he matches his strength with the young boys, how he tenses his feeble muscles to impress the pretty girl. Sten darling, watch out that you don't have a haemorrhage.

ALMAN: My wife loves to embarrass me in front of strangers. I let her — it's psychotherapy.

(*We towed and shoved and pushed and suddenly the little car was standing on the road. By then, of course, its radio had gone dead.* ALMAN *sat down behind the wheel of the dented car and got the motor started. The car had gone a few feet when one of the front wheels rolled off abruptly and slid far down into the ravine.*)

BERIT: A true picture of our marriage.

(ALMAN *stood hesitantly on the gleaming white road, perspiring nervously.* MARIANNE, *who had stayed out of the whole scene, was still sitting behind the wheel of our car. The youngsters sat down at the edge of the road. All of us were a little upset.*)

ISAK: I can't see any other way out. The lady and the gentleman must ride with us to the nearest petrol station. There you can telephone for help.

ALMAN: Don't trouble yourself over us. We'll have a refreshing walk. Won't we, Berit?

BERIT: With his leg. Dear Lord, that would be a scream.

ALMAN: In her delightful way my wife has just said thank you for both of us.

(*Silently we climbed into the car, which was suddenly completely filled.* (MARIANNE *drove; I sat beside her.* MR. *and* MRS. ALMAN *were on the folding seats. The three youngsters occupied the back seat.*) ALMAN *whistled some popular tune softly but soon fell silent. No one had any particular desire to converse.* MARIANNE *drove very calmly and carefully.*

Suddenly BERIT ALMAN *started to cry. Her husband carefully put his arm around her shoulders, but she drew away and pulled out a handkerchief, which she began tearing with her fingernails.*)

ALMAN: I can never tell if my wife is really crying or putting on an act. Dammit, I think these are real tears. Well, that's the way it is when you see death staring you in the face.

BERIT: Can't you shut up?

ALMAN: My wife has unusual powers of the imagination. For two years she made me believe that she had cancer and pestered all our friends with all kinds of imaginary symptoms, despite the fact that the doctors couldn't find anything the matter. She was so convincing that we believed her more than the doctors. That's pretty clever, admit it. It's such stuff that saints are made of! Look, now she's crying about a death scare. It's a pity we don't have a movie camera around. Lights! Action! Camera! It's a 'take,' as they say in the film world.

MARIANNE: It's understandable that you're upset, Mr. Alman, but how about leaving your wife alone for a little while?

ALMAN: A woman's tears are meant for women. Don't criticize a woman's tears — they're holy. You are beautiful, dear Miss whatever your name is. But Berit here is beginning to get a little shabby. That's why you can afford to defend her.

MARIANNE: Allow me to feel compassion for your wife for different reasons.

ALMAN: Very sarcastic! Still, you don't seem to be at all hysterical. But Berit is a genius at hysterics. Do you know what that means from my point of view?

MARIANNE: You're a Catholic, aren't you? That's what your wife said.

ALMAN: Quite right. That is my way of enduring. I ridicule my wife and she ridicules me. She has her hysterics and I have my Catholicism. But we need each other's company. It's only out of pure selfishness that we haven't murdered each other by now.[7]

[7] In the film, after Alman's speech, we see Isak looking out of the window of the car.

(BERIT *turned towards her husband and slapped his face. He dropped his glasses, which he had fortunately just taken off. His large nose swelled and began to bleed. His froglike mouth twitched spasmodically as if he were on the verge of tears, but he immediately got control of himself, pulled out a handkerchief and pressed it to his nose, blinked his eyes and laughed.* VIKTOR *leaned forward, picked up the glasses and slowly handed them to him.*)

ALMAN: Right on the beat. It's called syncopation, isn't it? Ha-ha! Isn't it comic? If I had a stop watch, I could have timed the explosion on the nose.

BERIT (*screams*): Shut up! Shut up! Shut up!

(MARIANNE *turned pale. She applied the brakes and slowly stopped the car.*)

MARIANNE: Maybe this is the terrible truth and maybe it's just what's called letting off steam. But we have three children in the car and for their sake may I ask the lady and the gentleman to get out immediately. There is a house back there; maybe they have a telephone. The walk won't be too strenuous.

(*All of us were silent after* MARIANNE'*s speech. Without another word,* STEN ALMAN *stepped out of the car. His face was ashen grey and his nose was still bleeding. His wife looked at us and suddenly made a heroic attempt to say something sincere.*)

BERIT: Forgive us if you can.

(*Then* BERIT *got out and stood by her husband, who had turned his back on us. He had pulled out a comb and a pocket mirror and was straightening the hair on his white scalp. His wife took his bloody handkerchief and blew her nose. Then she touched his elbow, but he was suddenly very tired and hung his head. They sat down close to each other by the road. They looked like two scolded schoolchildren sitting in a corner.*

MARIANNE *started the car, and we quickly drove away from this strange marriage.*

The petrol station between Gränna and Huskvarna lies on a hill with a wide view over a very beautiful, richly foliaged landscape. We stopped to fill up the tank and decided to have lunch at a hotel some kilometers farther south.

It was with mixed feelings that I saw this region again. First, because I began my medical practice here (incidentally, it lasted for fifteen years; I succeeded the local doctor). Second, because my old MOTHER *lives near here in a large house. She is ninety-six now and is generally considered a miracle of health and vitality, although her ability to move around has diminished considerably during the last few years.*

The petrol-station owner was a big, blond man with a broad face, abnormally large hands and long arms.)

AKERMAN: Ah ha! So the doctor is out driving. Shall it be a full tank? Well, well, so it is, and those are children and grandchildren, I know. Have you got the key to the petrol tank, Doctor?

ISAK: Hello, Henrik. You recognise me.

AKERMAN: Recognise! Doctor, you were there when I was born. And then you delivered all my brothers. And fixed our cuts and scratches and took care of us, as you did of everybody while you were a doctor around here.

ISAK: And things are going well for you?

AKERMAN: Couldn't be better! I'm married, you know, and I have heirs. (*Shouts.*) Eva!

(EVA *came out of the petrol-station. She was a young woman, gypsy-like, with long, thick hair and a generous smile. She was in an advanced stage of pregnancy.*)

AKERMAN: Here you see Dr. Borg himself in person. This is the man that Ma and Pa and the whole district still talk about. The world's best doctor.

(*I looked at* MARIANNE *who was standing to the side. She applauded somewhat sarcastically and bowed. The three youngsters were in the midst of a lively dispute and pointing in different directions.* EVA *stepped up and shook my hand.*)

AKERMAN: I suggest that we name our new baby for the doctor. Isak Akerman is a good name for a prime minister.

EVA: But what if it's a girl?

AKERMAN: Eva and I only make boys. Do you want oil and water too?

ISAK: Yes, thank you. And your father is well, in spite of his bad back?

AKERMAN: Well, it's getting a bit hard for the old man, you know, but the old lady is a little bombshell.

(The last was said in greatest confidence as we bent over the dip stick to see if we needed more oil. We did.)

AKERMAN: And now you'll be visiting *your* mother, eh, Doctor?

ISAK: I suppose so.

AKERMAN: She's a remarkable lady, your mother, although she must be at least ninety-five.

ISAK: Ninety-six.

AKERMAN: Well, well, how about that.

ISAK: How much is all this?

AKERMAN: Eva and I want it to be on the house.

ISAK: No, I can't allow that.

AKERMAN: Don't insult us, Doctor! We can do things in the grand manner, too, even if we live here in little Gränna.

ISAK: There isn't the slightest reason you should pay for my petrol. I appreciate your kindness, but . . .

AKERMAN: One remembers things, you know. One doesn't forget one's gratitude, and there are some things that can never be paid back.

(AKERMAN became a little serious and I a little sentimental. We looked at each other quite moved. EVA stepped up and stood beside her husband. She squinted in the sun and beamed like a big strawberry in her red dress.)

EVA *(like an echo)*: No, we don't forget. We don't forget.

AKERMAN: Just ask anybody in town or in the hills around here, and they remember the doctor and know what the doctor did for them.

(I looked around, but MARIANNE had disappeared. No, she had got into the car. The youngsters were still busy with their discussion.)

ISAK: Perhaps I should have remained here.

AKERMAN: I don't understand.

ISAK: What? What did you say, Henrik?

AKERMAN: You said that you should have stayed here, Doctor.

ISAK: Did I say that? Yes, perhaps. Thank you anyway. Send me word and I may come to be godfather for the new Akerman. You know where to reach me.

(I shook hands with them and we parted. MARIANNE called the youngsters and we continued our trip to the inn.)

Our lunch was a success. We had a large table on the open terrace and enjoyed a most magnificent view across Lake Vättern. The head waiter, one of my former patients, did everything to satisfy our slightest wish.

I became very lively, I must admit, and told the youngsters about my years as a country doctor. I told them humorous anecdotes which had a great deal of human interest. These were a great success (I don't think they laughed just out of politeness) and I had wine with the food (which was excellent) and cognac with my coffee.

ANDERS *suddenly rose and began to recite with both feeling and talent.)*

ANDERS: 'Oh, when such beauty shows itself in each facet of creation, then how beautiful must be the eternal source of this emanation!'

(None of us thought of laughing at him. He sat down immediately and emptied his coffee cup in embarrassment. SARA was the one who broke the silence.)

SARA: Anders will become a minister and Viktor a doctor.

VIKTOR: We swore that we wouldn't discuss God or science on the entire trip. I consider Anders' lyrical outburst as a breach of our agreement.

SARA: Oh, it was beautiful!

VIKTOR: Besides, I can't understand how a modern man can become a minister. Anders isn't a complete idiot.

ANDERS: Let me tell you, your rationalism is incomprehensible nonsense. And you aren't an idiot either.

VIKTOR: In my opinion the modern —

ANDERS: In my opinion —

VIKTOR: In my opinion a modern man looks his insignificance straight in the eye and believes in himself and his biological death. Everything else is nonsense.

ANDERS: And in my opinion modern man exists only in your imagination. Because man looks at his death with horror and can't bear his own insignificance.

VIKTOR: All right. Religion for the people. Opium for the aching limb. If that's what you want.

SARA: Aren't they fantastically sweet? I always agree with the one who's spoken last. Isn't this all extremely interesting?

VIKTOR *(angry)*: When you were a child

you believed in Santa Claus. Now you believe in God.

ANDERS: And you have always suffered from an astonishing lack of imagination.

VIKTOR: What do you think about it, Professor?

ISAK: Dear boys, you would receive my opinion with ironic indulgence, whatever I happened to say. That's why I'm keeping quiet.

SARA: Then think how very unlucky they are.

ISAK: No, Sara. They are very, very lucky.

(MARIANNE *laughed and lit my cigar. I leaned back in my chair and squinted at the light filtering down between the table umbrellas. The boys looked surprised as I began to recite.*)

ISAK: 'Where is the friend I seek everywhere? Dawn is the time of loneliness and care. When twilight comes, when twilight comes . . .' What comes after that, Anders?

MARIANNE: 'When twilight comes I am still yearning.'

ANDERS: 'Though my heart is burning, burning. I see His trace of glory . . .'

SARA: You're religious, aren't you, Professor?

ISAK: 'I see His trace of glory and power, In an ear of grain and the fragrance of flower . . .'

MARIANNE: 'In every sign and breath of air. His love is there. His voice whispers in the summer breeze . . .'

(*Silence.*)

VIKTOR: As a love poem, it isn't too bad.

SARA: Now I've become very solemn. I can become quite solemn for no reason at all.

(*I rose from the table.*)

ISAK: I want to pay a visit to my mother, who happens to live nearby. You can remain here and enjoy yourselves for a while. I'll be back soon.

MARIANNE: May I come with you?

ISAK: Of course. Goodbye for now, young friends.

(*I was in a good mood and felt very happy.* MARIANNE *suddenly took my arm and walked beside me. In passing, I patted her hand.*

The house was surrounded by an ancient, parklike garden and protected from onlookers by a wall as tall as a man. Inside, everything was quiet and somewhat unreal. The sky had clouded over, and the grey light sharpened the contours of the landscape so that it looked like a skillfully painted set in an old theatre.

In a little round drawing-room filled with storm-grey light and graced by light, delicate furniture, an old nurse in uniform sat embroidering. On the carpet next to her chair a fat white poodle lay looking at us with sleepy, lidded eyes. When the nurse saw us she immediately arose, smiling politely, to greet us and shake our hands. She introduced herself as SISTER ELISABET. *I asked her quietly how my mother was and if it was convenient for us to visit her.* SISTER ELISABET *answered that* MRS. BORG *was quite well and would be happy with our visit because she was usually rather lonely. I pointed out that it was unfortunate that my visits were rather infrequent, because of the difficult journey, and* SISTER ELISABET *said that she understood. After this hushed introduction, the Sister asked us to wait for a few minutes and disappeared into a nearby room.* MARIANNE *became a little nervous with all the solemnity and pulled out a cigarette from a crushed pack and was just about to light it.*)

ISAK: Please don't smoke. Mother hates the smell of tobacco and her senses are as sharp as those of an animal in the woods.

(*At the same moment,* SISTER ELISABET *returned and told us that we were welcome.*

The room was rather small and oddly irregular, but it had a lofty ceiling. On the walls hung many beautiful and expensive paintings. Heavy draperies covered the doors. In a corner stood a tall porcelain stove with a fire burning. At the room's only window stood an incongruous desk which did not harmonize with the other pieces of furniture. My MOTHER *was sitting in a big chair. She was dressed entirely in black and wore a small lace cap on her head. She was busy entering figures in a large blue ledger. When she recognised me, she immediately rose from her seat (although with some difficulty) and walked towards us with many small steps; she seemed to be shoving one foot in front of the other without her soles ever leaving the floor. She smiled cordially and stretched forth both her hands. I grasped them and then kissed her with a son's reverence.*)

MOTHER: I just sent a telegram to tell you that I was thinking about you today. Today is your big day. And then you come here!

ISAK: Well, I had a moment of inspiration, Mother!

MOTHER: Is that your wife standing back there, Isak? You will ask her to leave the room immediately. I refuse to talk with her. She has hurt us too much.

ISAK: Mother, darling, this is not Karin. This is Evald's wife, my daughter-in-law, Marianne!

MOTHER: Well, then, she can come here and greet me.

MARIANNE: How do you do, Mrs. Borg. (*Curtsies.*)

MOTHER: I've seen you in a photograph. Evald showed it to me. He was extremely proud of your beauty. By the way, why are you travelling this way?

MARIANNE: I've been in Stockholm, visiting.

MOTHER: Why aren't you home with Evald and taking care of your child?

MARIANNE: Evald and I don't have any children.

MOTHER: Isn't it strange with young people nowadays? I bore ten children. Will someone please bring me that large box standing over there.

(*She pointed at a brown cardboard box on a chair.* MARIANNE *picked it up and placed it on the desk in front of the old lady. Both of us helped lift the lid.*)

MOTHER: My mother lived in this house before me. And you children often visited here. Do you remember, Isak?

ISAK: I remember quite well.

MOTHER: In this box are some of your toys. I've tried to think which of you owned what.

(MOTHER *looked bewilderedly into the big box, as if she expected to find all her children there among the toys and things. Then she shook her head and looked up at* MAR-IANNE.)

MOTHER: Ten children, and all of them dead except Isak. Twenty grandchildren. None of them visits me except Evald, once a year. It's quite all right — I don't complain — but I have fifteen great-grandchildren whom I've never seen. I send letters and presents for fifty-three birthdays and anniversaries every year. I get kind thank-you notes, but no one visits me ex-cept by accident or when someone needs a loan. I am tiresome, of course.

ISAK: Don't look at it that way, Mother dear!

MOTHER: And then I have another fault. I don't die. The inheritance doesn't materialise according to the nice, neat schedules made up by smart young people.

(*She laughed sarcastically and shook her head. Then she pulled a doll out of the box. It was an old doll, with fine gold hair and a porcelain face (a little scratched) and a beautiful lace gown.*)

MOTHER: This doll's name is Goldcrown and it belonged to Sigbritt. She got it when she was eight years old. I sewed the dress myself. She never liked it much, so Charlotta took it over and cared for it. I remember it clearly.

(*She dropped the doll and picked up a little box of bright-coloured tin soldiers and poked in it with a small, sharp finger.*)

MOTHER: Hagbart's tin soldiers. I never liked his war games. He was shot while hunting moose. We never understood each other.

(*This she said in a matter-of-fact tone, completely without sentimentality. She threw the tin soldiers into the box and fished out a photograph.*)

MOTHER: Can you see who this is? This is Sigfrid when he was three years old and you when you were two, and here is Father and me. Good Lord, how one looked in those days. It was taken in 1883.

ISAK: May I see that picture?

MOTHER (*uninterested*): Yes, of course, you can have it. It's only trash. Here is a colouring book. Maybe it belonged to the twins, or perhaps to Anna or Angelica. I really don't know because all of them have put their names in the book. And then it says: 'I am Anna's best friend.' But Anna has written: 'I love Angelica.' and Kristina has scribbled: 'Most of all in the whole world I love Father best.' And Birgitta has added: 'I am going to marry Father.' Isn't that amusing? I laughed when I read it.

(MARIANNE *took the book from her and turned the pages. It was partly scribbled on and partly painted with great vitality and strong colours. The light in the small room grew dimmer as the sky darkened outside. In the distance the thunder was already rumbling in the sky.* MOTHER *picked up a toy locomotive and looked at it closely.*)

MOTHER: I think that this is Benjamin's locomotive because he was always so amused by trains and circuses and such things. I suppose that's why he became an actor. We quarrelled often about it because I wanted him to have an honest profession. And I was right. He didn't make it. I told him that several times. He didn't believe me, but I was right. It doesn't pay much to talk. Isn't it cold in here? The fire doesn't really warm.

ISAK: No, it isn't particularly cold.

(*She turned her head towards the darkened skies outside. The trees stood heavy, as if waiting.*)

MOTHER: I've always felt chilly as long as I can remember. What does that mean? You're a doctor? Mostly in the stomach. Here.

ISAK: You have low blood pressure.

MOTHER: Do you want me to ask Sister Elisabet to make some tea for us so we can sit down and talk for a while? Wouldn't that be . . .

ISAK: No, Mother, thank you. We don't want to trouble you any more. We've just had lunch and we're rather in a hurry.

MOTHER: Look here for a moment. Sigbritt's eldest boy will be fifty. I'm thinking of giving him my father's old gold watch. Can I give it to him, even though the hands have loosened? It is so difficult to find presents for those who have everything. But the watch is beautiful and it can probably be repaired.

(*She looked anxiously, appealingly, from* MARIANNE *to me and back to* MARIANNE. *She had opened the lid of the old gold watch and the blank dial stared at me. I suddenly remembered my early-morning dream: the blank clock face and my own watch which lacked hands, the hearse and my dead self.*)

MOTHER: I remember when Sigbritt's boy had just been born and lay there in his basket in the lilac arbour at the summerhouse. Now he will be fifty years old. And little cousin Sara, who always went around carrying him, cradling him, and who married Sigfrid, that no-good. Now you have to go so that you'll have time for all the things you must do. I'm very grateful for your visit and I hope we'll see each other sometime. Give my best regards to Evald. Goodbye.

(*She offered me her cheek and I bent down*

and kissed it. It was very cold but unbelievably soft and full of sharp little lines. MARIANNE *curtsied and my mother answered her gesture with an abstract smile.* SISTER ELISABET *opened the door as if she had been listening to us. In a few minutes we were out in the grey daylight, which hurt our eyes with its piercing sharpness.*

Once again MARIANNE *took my arm, and when she did so I was filled with gratitude towards this quiet, independent girl with her naked, observant face.*

When we reached the inn the youngsters were no longer there. The waitress told us that the young lady was waiting at the car. The head waiter stood nearby bowing and looking as if he had just had another of his old ulcer-attacks.

Sure enough, SARA *was leaning against the car looking as though she were ready to cry.*)

MARIANNE: Where are Anders and Viktor?

(SARA *pointed without answering. Down on the slope the boys stood glaring at each other with furious expressions on their faces. Every so often one of them would utter some terrible expletive at the other.*)

SARA: When you left they were talking away about the existence of God. Finally they got so angry that they began shouting at each other. Then Anders grabbed Viktor's arm and tried to twist it off, and Viktor said that was a pretty lousy argument for the existence of God. Then I said that I thought they could skip God and pay some attention to me for a while instead, and then they said that I could stop babbling because I didn't understand that it was a debate of principles, and then I said that whether there was a God or not, they were real wet blankets. Then I left and they ran down the hill to settle things because each of them insisted that the other had hurt his innermost feelings. So now they're going to slug it out.

(MARIANNE *put on a very wise countenance and started off to calm down the two debaters. I stepped into the car.* SARA *looked at the departing* MARIANNE *with envy.*)

SARA: Well, which one of the boys do *you* like the most?

ISAK: Which do you like best?

SARA: I don't know. Anders will become a minister. But he is rather masculine and warm, you know. But a minister's wife! But Viktor's funny in another way. Viktor will go far, you know.

ISAK: What do you mean by that?

SARA (*tired*): A doctor earns more money. And it's old-fashioned to be a minister. But he has nice legs. And a strong neck. But how *can* one believe in God!

(SARA *sighed and we sank into our own thoughts.*

MARIANNE *came up the hill bringing with her the two fighting cocks, barely reconciled. She sat down behind the wheel and we continued our trip.*

The sun shone white on the blue-black clouds which towered above the dark, gleaming surface of Lake Vättern. The breeze coming from the open side windows did not cool us any longer, and in the south summer lightning cut across the sky with thin, jagged scratches. Because of the approaching storm, and all the good food and wine, I became rather sleepy. I silently blessed my luck in having MARIANNE *beside me as a reliable chauffeur.*

ANDERS *and* VIKTOR *sat in sullen silence.* SARA *yawned again and again and blinked her eyes.*

I fell asleep, but during my nap I was pursued by dreams and images which seemed extremely real and were very humiliating to me.

I record these in the order in which they occurred, without the slightest intention of commenting on their possible meaning. I have never been particularly enthusiastic about the psychoanalytical theory of dreams as the fulfillment of desires in a negative or positive direction. Yet I cannot deny that in these dreams there was something like a warning, which bore into my consciousness and embedded itself there with relentless determination. I have found that during the last few years I glide rather easily into a twilight world of memories and dreams which are highly personal. I've often wondered if this is a sign of increasing senility. Sometimes I've also asked myself if it is a harbinger of approaching death.[8]

[8] In the film, as the dream sequence begins the following shots are seen:

Dissolve to the dark sky with large birds circling, wheeling and shrieking. Dissolve to more large birds flying among the tree tops. Dissolve to a basket of wild strawberries spilled on the grass.

Again I found myself at the wild strawberry patch of my childhood, but I was not alone. SARA *was there, and this time she turned her face towards mine and looked at me for a long time. I knew that I sat there looking old, ugly and ridiculous. A Professor Emeritus who was going to be made a Jubilee Doctor. The saddest thing about it was that although* SARA *spoke to me in a grieved and penetrating tone, I couldn't answer her except in stammered, one-syllable words. This, of course, increased the pain of my dream.*

Between us stood a little woven basket filled with strawberries; around us lay a strange, motionless twilight, heavy with dull expectations. SARA *leaned towards me and spoke in such a low voice that I had difficulty grasping her words.*)

SARA: Have you looked at yourself in the mirror, Isak? You haven't. Then I'll show you how you look.

(*She picked up a mirror that lay hidden under the small strawberry basket and showed me my face, which looked old and ugly in the sinking twilight. I carefully pushed away the looking glass and I could see that* SARA *had tears in her eyes.*)

SARA: You are a worried old man who will die soon, but I have my whole life before me . . . Oh, now you're offended.

ISAK: No, I'm not offended.

SARA: Yes, you are offended because you can't bear to hear the truth. And the truth is that I've been too considerate. One can easily be unintentionally cruel that way.

ISAK: I understand.

SARA: No, you don't understand. We don't speak the same language. Look at yourself in the mirror again. No, don't look away.

ISAK: I see.

SARA: Now listen. I'm about to marry your brother Sigfrid. He and I love each other, and it's all like a game. Look at your face now. Try to smile! All right, now you're smiling.

ISAK: It hurts.

SARA: You, a Professor Emeritus, ought to know why it hurts. But you don't. Because in spite of all your knowledge you don't really know anything.

(*She threw away the mirror and it shattered. The wind began to blow through the trees, and from somewhere the crying of a child could be heard. She arose immediately, drying her tears.)*

SARA: I have to go. I promised to look after Sigbritt's little boy.

ISAK: Don't leave me.

SARA: What did you say?

ISAK: Don't leave me.

SARA: You stammer so much that I can't hear your words. Besides, they don't really matter.

(I saw her run up to the arbour. The old house was draped in the grey twilight. She lifted the crying child and cradled it in her arms. The sky turned black above the sea and large birds circled overhead, screeching towards the house, which suddenly seemed ugly and poor. There was something fateful and threatening in this twilight, in the crying of the child, in the shrieking of the black birds. SARA cradled the baby and her voice, half singing, was very distant and sorrowful.)

SARA: My poor little one, you shall sleep quietly now. Don't be afraid of the wind. Don't be afraid of the birds, the jackdaws and the sea gulls. Don't be afraid of the waves from the sea. I'm with you. I'm holding you tight. Don't be afraid, little one. Soon it will be another day. No one can hurt you; I am with you; I'm holding you.

(But her voice was sorrowful and tears ran down her cheeks without end. The child became silent, as if it were listening, and I wanted to scream until my lungs were bloody.

Now I saw that a door had opened in the house and someone was standing there shouting for SARA. It was my brother SIGFRID.

She ran towards him, gave him the child, and they both disappeared into the house and closed the door.

Suddenly I noticed that the wind had died and the birds had flown away. All the windows in the house shone festively. Over the horizon stood a jagged moon, and music from a piano penetrated the stillness of the strawberry patch.

I went closer and pressed my face against the brightly lit dining-room window. An elegantly laid table stood before me and SARA sat behind the piano, playing. She was wearing an expensive but old-fashioned dress and her hair was piled on top of her head, which made her face look womanly and mature. Then SIGFRID entered the room and they both sat down immediately at the table. They laughed and joked and celebrated some kind of event. The moon rose higher in the heavens and the scene inside became obscure. I rapped on the window so that they would hear me and let me in. But they did not notice me; they were too preoccupied with each other.

On the window sill lay many splinters of glass, and in my eager attempt to get their attention I accidentally cut my hand.

Turning away, I was blinded by the moonlight, which threw itself against me with an almost physical force.

I heard a voice calling my name, and then I saw that the door had been opened. Someone was standing in the doorway and I recognised MR. ALMAN. He bowed politely though stiffly and invited me inside.

He led me down a short corridor and unlocked a narrow door. We entered a large windowless room with benches arranged like an amphitheatre. There sat about ten youngsters, amongst whom I immediately recognised SARA, ANDERS and VIKTOR. On one of the low walls hung a large blackboard, and on a work table in the centre of the room stood a microscope.

I realised that this was the hall where I used to hold my polyclinical lectures and examinations. ALMAN sat down and asked me to take a seat at the short end of the table. For a few moments he studied some papers in a dossier. The audience remained completely still.)

ALMAN: Do you have your examination book with you?

ISAK: Yes, of course. Here it is.

ALMAN: Thank you.

(I handed him the examination book and he flipped through it distractedly. Then he leaned forward and looked at me for a long time. After that he gestured towards the microscope.)

ALMAN: Will you please identify the bacteriological specimen in the microscope. Take your time.

(I arose, stepped up to the instrument and adjusted it. But whatever I did, I couldn't find any specimen. The only thing I saw was

my own eye, which stared back at me in an absurd enlargement.)

ISAK: There must be something wrong with the microscope.

(ALMAN *bent over and peered into it. Then he regarded me seriously and shook his head.)*

ALMAN: There is nothing wrong with the microscope.

ISAK: I can't see anything.

(*I sank down on the chair and wetted my lips. No one moved or said anything.)*

ALMAN: Will you please read this text.

(*He pointed to the blackboard which hung behind him. Something was printed on it in large crooked letters. I made a great effort to interpret what was written: INKE TAN MA-GROV STAK FARSIN LOS KRET FAJNE KASERTE MJOTRON PRESETE.)*

ALMAN: What does it mean?

ISAK: I don't know.

ALMAN: Oh, really?

ISAK: I'm a doctor, not a linguist.

ALMAN: Then let me tell you, Professor Borg, that on the blackboard is written the first duty of a doctor. Do you happen to know what this is?

ISAK: Yes, if you let me think for a moment.

ALMAN: Take your time.

ISAK: A doctor's first duty . . . a doctor's first duty . . . a doctor's . . . Oh, I've forgotten.

(*A cold sweat broke out on my forehead, but I still looked* ALMAN *straight in the eye. He leaned towards me and spoke in a calm, polite tone.)*

ALMAN: A doctor's first duty *is to ask forgiveness.*

ISAK: Of course, now I remember!

(*Relieved, I laughed but immediately became silent.* ALMAN *looked wearily at his papers and smothered a yawn.)*

ALMAN: Moreover, you are guilty of guilt.

ISAK: Guilty of guilt?

ALMAN: I have noted that you don't understand the accusation.

ISAK: Is it serious?

ALMAN: Unfortunately, Professor.

(*Next to me stood a table with a water de-*

canter. I poured a glass, but spilled a lot of it on the table and the tray.)

ISAK: I have a bad heart. I'm an old man, Mr. Alman, and I must be treated with consideration. That's only right.

ALMAN: There is nothing concerning your heart in my papers. Perhaps you wish to end the examination?

ISAK: No, no, for heaven's sake, no!

(ALMAN *arose and lit a small lamp which hung from a cord in the ceiling. Under the lamp (very brightly lit) sat a woman wrapped in a hospital robe and wearing wooden sandals on her feet.)*

ALMAN: Will you please make an anamnesis and diagnosis of this patient.

ISAK: But the patient is dead.

(*At that moment the woman arose and began laughing as if she had just heard a great joke.* ALMAN *leaned across the table and wrote something in my examination book.)*

ISAK: What are you writing in my book?

ALMAN: My conclusion.

ISAK: And that is . . .

ALMAN: That you're incompetent.

ISAK: Incompetent.

ALMAN: Furthermore, Professor Borg, you are accused of some smaller but nonetheless serious offences. (ISAK *remains silent.)* Indifference, selfishness, lack of consideration.

ISAK: No.

ALMAN: These accusations have been made by your wife. Do you want to be confronted by her?

ISAK: But my wife has been dead for many years.

ALMAN: Do you think I'm joking? Will you please come with me voluntarily. You have no choice in any case. Come!

(ALMAN *placed the examination book in his pocket, made a sign for me to follow him, opened the door and led me into a forest.*

The trunks of the trees stood close together. Twilight had almost passed. Dead trees were strewn on the ground and the earth was covered with decaying leaves. Our feet sank into this soft carpet with every step, and mud oozed up around them. From behind the foliage the moon shone steadily, like an inflamed eye, and it was as warm as inside a hothouse. ALMAN *turned around.)*

ALMAN: Watch out, Professor Borg. You'll find many snakes here.

(*Suddenly I saw a small, gleaming body which twisted around and disappeared in one of* ALMAN's *wet footsteps. I stepped swiftly aside but nearly trod on a large grey creature which pulled away. Wherever I looked, snakes seemed to well forth from the swampy, porous ground. Finally we arrived at a clearing in the forest, but we halted at the very edge. The moon shone in our eyes and we hid among the shadows of the trees. The clearing stretched out before us. It was overgrown with twisted roots. At one end a black cliff fell away into a body of water. On the sides, the trees stood lofty and lifeless, as if burdened by each other's enormous shadows. Then a giggling laugh was heard and I discovered a woman standing near the hill. She was dressed in a long black gown and her face was averted from us. She made movements with her hands, as if to ward off someone. She laughed continually and excitedly. A man stood half hidden, leaning against a tree trunk. His face, which I glimpsed, was large and flat, but his eyebrows were quite bushy and his forehead protruded over his eyes. He made gestures with his hand and said some unintelligible words, which made the woman laugh uncontrollably. Suddenly she became serious, and a harassed, discontented expression appeared on her face. She bent over and picked up a small purse. The man stretched out his hand and jokingly began to pull the pins out of her skilfully pompadoured hair. She pretended to be very angry and flailed the air around her furiously. This amused the man, who continued his game. When she finally walked away he followed and took hold of her shoulders. Petrified, she stopped and turned her pale, embittered face towards her pursuer. He muttered something and stretched out his other hand towards her breast. She moved away, but couldn't free herself. When she saw that she was caught, she began to twist and squirm as if the man's grip on her shoulders hurt intensely. The man continued to mutter incoherent words, as if to an animal. Suddenly she freed herself and ran with bent knees and a shuffling step in a semicircle. The man remained standing, waiting and breathless. He perspired heavily and wiped his face over and over again with the* back of his hand. The woman stopped as if exhausted and regarded the man, wide-eyed and gaping. She was also out of breath. Then she began running again but pretended to trip and fell on her hands and knees. Her large rump swayed like a black balloon over the ground. She lowered her face between her arms and began crying, rocking and swaying. The man knelt at her side, took a firm grasp of her hair, pulled her face upward, backward and forced her to open her eyes. He panted with effort the whole time. She teetered and nearly fell to the side, but the man straddled her and leaned over her heavily. Suddenly she was completely still, with closed eyes and a swollen, pale face. Then she collapsed, rolled over, and received the man between her open knees.*)

ALMAN: Many men forget a woman who has been dead for thirty years. Some preserve a sweet, fading picture, but *you* can always recall this scene in your memory. Strange, isn't it? Tuesday, May 1, 1917, you stood here and heard and saw exactly what that woman and that man said and did.

(*The woman sat up and smoothed her gown over her short, thick thighs. Her face was blank and almost distorted in its puffy slackness. The man had got up and was wandering around aimlessly with his hands hanging at his sides.*)

WOMAN: Now I will go home and tell this to Isak and I know exactly what he'll say: Poor little girl, how I pity you. As if he were God himself. And then I'll cry and say: Do you really feel pity for me? And he'll say: I feel infinitely sorry for you. And then I'll cry some more and ask him if he can forgive me. And then he'll say: You shouldn't ask forgiveness from me. I have nothing to forgive. But he doesn't mean a word of it, because he's completely cold. And then he'll suddenly be very tender and I'll yell at him that he's not really sane and that such hypocritical nobility is sickening. And then he'll say that he'll bring me a sedative and that he understands everything. And then I'll say that it's his fault that I am the way I am, and then he'll look very sad and will say that he is to blame. But he doesn't care about anything because he's completely cold.

(*She arose with effort and shook out her hair and began combing it and pinning it up in the same careful way that it was before. The man sat down on a stone a little further away. He smoked quietly. I couldn't see his gaze below the protruding eyebrows, but his voice was calm and scornful.*)

MAN: You're insane, the way you're carrying on.

(*The woman laughed and went into the forest.*

I turned around. ALMAN *had a strange, wry smile on his face. We stood quietly for a few moments.*)

ISAK: Where is she?
ALMAN: You know. She is gone. Everyone is gone. Can't you hear how quiet it is? Everything has been dissected, Professor Borg. A surgical masterpiece. There is no pain, no bleeding, no quivering.
ISAK: It is rather quiet.
ALMAN: A perfect achievement of its kind, Professor.
ISAK: And what is the penalty?
ALMAN: Penalty? I don't know. The usual one, I suppose.
ISAK: The usual one?
ALMAN: Of course. Loneliness.
ISAK: Loneliness?
ALMAN: Exactly. *Loneliness.*
ISAK: Is there no grace?
ALMAN: Don't ask me. I don't know anything about such things.

(*Before I had time to answer,* ALMAN *had disappeared, and I stood alone in the complete stillness of the moonlight and the forest.* [*Then I heard a voice quite close to me.*)

SARA: Didn't you have to go with them to get your father?

(*The girl stretched out her hand, but when she saw my face she immediately withdrew it.*)

ISAK: Sara . . . It wasn't always like this. If only you had stayed with me. If only you could have had a little patience.

(*The girl did not seem to hear what I was saying but began to look restless.*)

SARA: Hurry up.

(*I followed her as well as I could, but she moved so much more easily and faster than I.*)

ISAK: I can't run, don't you understand?
SARA: But hurry up.
ISAK: I can't see you any more.
SARA: But here I am.
ISAK: Wait for me.

(*She materialised for a moment and then she was gone. The moon disappeared into darkness and I wanted to cry with wild, childish sorrow, but I could not.*][9]

At that moment, I awoke. The car stood still and the storm was over, but it was still drizzling slightly. We were in the neighbourhood of the Strömsnäs Foundry, where the road wanders between rich forests on one side and river rapids on the other. Everything was completely silent. The three children had left the car and MARIANNE *sat quietly smoking a cigarette and blowing the smoke through the open window. Gusts of strong and pleasant odours came from the wet forest.*)

ISAK: What is this?
MARIANNE: The children wanted to get out for a moment and stretch their legs. They are over there.

(*She made a gesture towards a clearing near the river. All three were busy picking flowers.*)

ISAK: But it's still raining.
MARIANNE: I told them about the ceremony today, and they insisted on paying homage to you.
ISAK (*sighs*): Good Lord.
MARIANNE: Did you sleep well?
ISAK: Yes, but I dreamed. Can you imagine — the last few months I've had the most peculiar dreams. It's really odd.
MARIANNE: What's odd?
ISAK: It's as if I'm trying to say something to myself which I don't want to hear when I'm awake.
MARIANNE: And what would that be?
ISAK: That I'm dead, although I live.

(MARIANNE *reacted violently. Her gaze blackened and she took a deep breath. Throwing her cigarette out the window, she turned towards me.*)

---

9 The scene in square brackets does not appear in the print of the film distributed in England.

MARIANNE: Do you know that you and Evald are very much alike?

ISAK: You told me that.

MARIANNE: Do you know that Evald has said the very same thing?

ISAK: About me? Yes, I can believe that.

MARIANNE: No, about himself.

ISAK: But he's only thirty-eight years old.

MARIANNE: May I tell you everything, or would it bore you?

ISAK: I'd be grateful if you would tell me.

MARIANNE: It was a few months ago. I wanted to talk to Evald and we took the car and went down to the sea. It was raining, just like now. Evald sat where you are sitting and I drove....

EVALD: Can't you stop the windshield wipers?

MARIANNE: Then we won't be able to see the ocean.

EVALD: They're working so hard it makes me nervous.

MARIANNE (*shuts them off*): Very well.

(*They sit in silence for a few minutes, looking at the rain, which streams down the windshield quietly. The sea merges with the clouds in an infinite greyness. EVALD strokes his long, bony face and looks expectantly at his wife. He talks jokingly, calmly.*)

EVALD: So now you have me trapped. What did you want to say? Something unpleasant, of course.

MARIANNE: I wish I didn't have to tell you about it.

EVALD: I understand. You've found someone else.

MARIANNE: Now don't be childish.

EVALD (*mimicking her*): Now don't be childish. What do you expect me to think? You come and say in a funereal voice that you want to talk to me. We take the car and go down to the sea. It rains and it's hard for you to begin. Good Lord, Marianne, let's have it. This is an excellent moment for the most intimate confidence. But for heaven's sake, don't keep me dangling.

MARIANNE: Now I feel like laughing. What do you really think I'm going to say? That I've murdered someone, or embezzled the faculty funds? I'm pregnant, Evald.

EVALD: Oh, is that so.

MARIANNE: That's the way it is. And seeing how careless we've been recently, there isn't much to be surprised about, is there?

EVALD: And you're sure?

MARIANNE: The report on the test came yesterday.

EVALD: Oh. Oh, yes. So that was the secret.

MARIANNE: Another thing I want to tell you. I shall have this child.

EVALD: That seems to be clear.

MARIANNE: Yes, it is!

MARIANNE (*voice over*): We sat quietly for a long time, and I felt the hatred growing big and thick between us. Evald looked out through the wet window, whistled soundlessly and looked as if he were cold. Somewhere in my stomach I was shivering so hard that I could barely sit upright. Then he opened the door and got out of the car and marched through the rain down to the beach. He stopped under a big tree and stood there for a long while. Finally I also stepped out and went to him. His face and hair were wet and the rain fell down his cheeks to the sides of his mouth.

EVALD (*calmly*): You know that I don't want to have any children. You also know that you'll have to choose between me and the child.

MARIANNE (*looks at him*): Poor Evald.

EVALD: Please don't 'poor' me. I'm of sound mind and I've made my position absolutely clear. It's absurd to live in this world, but it's even more ridiculous to populate it with new victims and it's most absurd of all to believe that they will have it any better than us.

MARIANNE: That is only an excuse.

EVALD: Call it whatever you want. Personally I was an unwelcome child in a marriage which was a nice imitation of hell. Is the old man really sure that I'm his son? Indifference, fear, infidelity and guilt feelings — those were my nurses.

MARIANNE: All this is very touching, but it doesn't excuse the fact that you're behaving like a child.

EVALD: I have to be at the hospital at three o'clock and have neither the time nor the desire to talk any more.

MARIANNE: You're a coward!

EVALD: Yes, that's right. This life disgusts me and I don't think that I need a responsibility which will force me to exist another day longer than I want to. You know all that, and you know that I'm serious and that this isn't some kind of hysteria, as you once thought.

MARIANNE (*voice over*): We went towards

the car, he in front and I following. I had begun to cry. I don't know why. But the tears couldn't be seen in the rain. We sat in the car, thoroughly wet and cold, but the hatred throbbed in us so painfully that we didn't feel cold. I started the car and turned it towards the road. Evald sat fiddling with the radio. His face was completely calm and closed.

MARIANNE: I know that you're wrong.

EVALD: There is nothing which can be called right or wrong. One functions according to one's needs; you can read that in an elementary-school textbook.

MARIANNE: And what do we need?

EVALD: You have a damned need to live, to exist and create life.

MARIANNE: And how about you?

EVALD: My need is to be dead. Absolutely, totally dead.

(*I've tried to relate* MARIANNE's *story as carefully as possible. My reaction to it was very mixed. But my strongest feeling was a certain sympathy towards her for this sudden confidence, and when* MARIANNE *fell silent she looked so hesitant that I felt obliged to say something even though I wasn't very sure of my own voice.*)

ISAK: If you want to smoke a cigarette, you may.

MARIANNE: Thank you.

ISAK: Why have you told me all this?

(MARIANNE *didn't answer at once. She took her time lighting a cigarette and puffed a few times. I looked at her, but she turned her head away and pretended to look at the three youngsters, who had picked up some kind of soft drink which they shared in great amity.*)

MARIANNE: When I saw you together with your mother, I was gripped by a strange fear.

ISAK: I don't understand.

MARIANNE: I thought, here is his mother. A very ancient woman, completely ice-cold, in some ways more frightening than death itself. And here is her son, and there are light-years of distance between them. And he himself says that he is a living death. And Evald is on the verge of becoming just as lonely and cold — and dead. And then I thought that there is only coldness and death, and death and loneliness, all the way. Somewhere it must end.

ISAK: But you are going back to Evald.

MARIANNE: Yes, to tell him that I can't agree to his condition. I want my child; no one can take it from me. Not even the person I love more than anyone else.

(*She turned her pale, tearless face towards me, and her gaze was black, accusing, desperate. I suddenly felt shaken in a way which I had never experienced before.*)

ISAK: Can I help you?

MARIANNE: No one can help me. We are too old, Isak. It has gone too far.

ISAK: What happened after your talk in the car?

MARIANNE: Nothing. I left him the very next day.

ISAK: Haven't you heard from him?

MARIANNE: No. No, Evald is rather like you.

(*She shook her head and bent forward as if to protect her face. I felt cold; it had become quite chilly after the rain.*)

MARIANNE: Those two wretched people whom I made leave the car — what was their name again?

ISAK: I was just thinking about Alman and his wife. It reminded me of my own marriage.

MARIANNE: I don't want Evald and I to become like . . .

ISAK: Poor Evald grew up in all that.

MARIANNE: But we love each other.

(*Her last words were a low outburst. She stopped herself immediately and moved her hands towards her face, then stopped again. We sat quietly for a few moments.*)

ISAK: We must get on. Signal to the children.

(MARIANNE *nodded, started the motor and blew the horn.* SARA *came laughing through the wet grass, closely followed by her two cavaliers. She handed me a large bouquet of wild flowers wrapped in wet newspapers. All three of them had friendly, mocking eyes.* SARA *cleared her throat solemnly.*)

SARA: We heard that you are celebrating this day. Now we want to pay our respects to you with these simple flowers and to tell you that we are *very* impressed that you are so old and that you've been a doctor for fifty years. And we know, of course, that you are a *wise* and *venerable* old man. One who regards us youngsters with *lenience* and gentle irony. One who knows *all* about life and who has learned all the prescriptions by heart.

(*She gave me the flowers with a little mock curtsy and kissed my cheek. The boys bowed and laughed, embarrassed. I couldn't answer. I only thanked them very briefly and rather bluntly. The children probably thought that I had been hurt by their joke.*

After a few more hours' travel, we reached Lund. When we finally stopped at EVALD's *house, a small rotund woman ran out and approached us quickly. To my surprise and pleasure I discovered that it was* MISS AGDA.)

AGDA: So you did come. Evald and I had just given up hope. It's relaxing and convenient to drive, isn't it? Now, Professor, you'll have to put on your frock coat immediately. Hello, Marianne. I've prepared Evald for your arrival.

ISAK: So, Miss Agda, you came after all.

AGDA: I considered it my duty. But the fun is gone. There's nothing you can say that will make me feel different. Who are these young people? Are they going to the ceremony too?

MARIANNE: These are good friends of ours, and if there is any food in the kitchen, invite them in.

AGDA: And why shouldn't there be? I've had a lot of things to arrange here, believe me.

(EVALD *met us in the foyer. He was already dressed in evening clothes and seemed nervous. Everything was extremely confused, but* MISS AGDA *was a pillar of strength in the maelstrom. Without raising her voice, and dressed in her best dress (especially made for the occasion), she sent the children, the married couple, servants and an old professor in different directions. Within ten minutes, everything was in order.*

Just before that, EVALD, MARIANNE *and I had a chance to say hello. I wouldn't want to give the impression that our reunion was marked by overwhelming cordiality. This has never been the case in our family.*)

EVALD: Hello, Father. Welcome.

ISAK: Hello, Evald. Thank you. As you can see, I brought Marianne with me.

EVALD: Hello, Marianne.

MARIANNE: Can I take my things upstairs?

EVALD: Do you want to stay in the guest room as usual, Father?

ISAK: Thank you, that would be just fine.

EVALD: Let me take your suitcase. It's rather heavy.

ISAK: Thank you, I'll take it myself.

EVALD: Did you have a nice trip?

MARIANNE: Yes, thanks it's been pleasant.

EVALD: Who were those youngsters you had with you?

MARIANNE: Don't know. They're going to Italy.

EVALD: They looked rather nice.

ISAK: They are really very nice.

(*We had come to the second floor.* EVALD *politely opened the door to the guest room and I entered.* AGDA *came after us as if she were rolling on ball bearings, forced her way in and took the suitcase, putting it on a chair.*)

AGDA: I bought new shoelaces, and I took the liberty of bringing the white waistcoat to your evening dress if you should want to go to the banquet after the ceremony. And you forgot your razor blades, Professor.

(*She unpacked, murmuring sounds of worried concern. I didn't listen. Instead I listened to the conversation between* MARIANNE *and* EVALD *outside the half-closed door. Their voices were formal and faultlessly polite.*)

MARIANNE: No, I'll go tomorrow, so don't worry.

EVALD: Do you intend to stay in a hotel?

MARIANNE (*gay*): Why? We can share a bedroom for another night, if you have no objection. Help me to unpack.

EVALD: It was really nice to see you. And unexpected.

MARIANNE: I feel the same way. Are we going to the dinner afterwards, or what do you want to do?

EVALD: I'll just call Stenberg and tell him that I'm bringing a lady. He arranges such things.

(*The door was closed, so I couldn't hear any more of the conversation. I had sat down on the bed to take off my shoes.* MISS AGDA *helped me, but she wasn't very gracious.*

[*Oddly enough, there were three Jubilee Doctors that year. The dean's office had thoughtfully placed us three old men in a special room while the procession was arranged out in the large vestibule of the university hall. I happened to know one of the other two who were going to be honoured. He was an old schoolmate, the former Bishop* JAKOB HOVELIUS. *We greeted each other cordially and embraced. The third old man seemed rather atrophied and declined all conversation. It turned out that he was the former Professor of Roman Law,* CARL-ADAM TIGER *(a great fighter in his time and a man who, according to his students, really lived up to his name).)*

ISAK: How comforting it is to meet another old corpse. How are you nowadays, my dear Jakob?

JAKOB: I enjoy my leisure. But don't ask me if I do it *cum dignitate.*

ISAK: Do you know the third man to be honoured?

JAKOB: Of course. It's Carl-Adam Tiger, Professor of Roman Law.

ISAK: The Tiger! Good Lord!

JAKOB: He has three interests left in life. A thirty-year-old injustice, a goldfish, and his bowels.

ISAK: Do you think that we are like that?

JAKOB: What's your opinion? As Schopenhauer says somewhere, 'Dreams are a kind of lunacy and lunacy a kind of dream.' But life is also supposed to be a kind of dream, isn't it? Draw your own conclusion.

ISAK: Do you remember how in our youth we fought with each other on what we called the metaphysical questions?

JAKOB: How could I forget?

ISAK: And what do you believe now?

JAKOB: I'll tell you, I've ceased thinking about all that. One of these days, knowledge will be achieved.

ISAK: My, how surprised you'll be.

JAKOB: And you. But one has a right to be curious.

TIGER: Gentlemen, do you think I'd have time to make a small secret visit before the great farce begins?

ISAK: I don't know, Professor Tiger.

TIGER *(sighs)*: *In dubio non est agendum.* When in doubt, don't, as the old Romans used to say. I'll stay here.][10]

(THE FESTIVITIES

What should I describe? Trumpet fanfares, bells ringing, field-cannon salutes, masses of people, the giant procession from the univer-

sity to the cathedral, the white-dressed garland girls, royalty, old age, wisdom, beautiful music, stately Latin sentences which echoed off the huge vaults. The students and their girls, women in bright, magnificent dresses, this strange rite with its heavy symbolism but as meaningless as a passing dream. Then I saw SARA *with her two boys among the onlookers outside the cathedral. They waved to me and suddenly looked childishly happy and full of expectations. Among the lecturers was* EVALD, *tall and serious, disinterested and absent. Inside the church, I saw* MARIANNE *in her white dress and next to her sat* MISS AGDA, *pale and with her lips pressed tightly together. The ceremonial lecture was dull (as usual). The whole thing went on endlessly (as usual) and the garland girls had to go out and relieve themselves in the little silver pot in the sacristy. But we adults unfortunately had to stay where we were. As you know, culture provides us with these moments of refined torture.* PROFESSOR TIGER *looked as if he were dying, my friend the* BISHOP *fell asleep, and more than one of those present seemed ready to faint. Even our behinds, which have withstood long academic services, lectures, dusty dissertations and dull dinners, started to become numb and ache in silent protest.*

I surprised myself by returning to the happenings of the day, and it was then that I decided to recollect and write down everything that had happened. I was beginning to see a remarkable causality in this chain of unexpected, entangled events. At the same time, I couldn't escape recalling the BISHOP's *words: 'Dreams are a kind of lunacy and lunacy a kind of dream, but life is also supposed to be a dream, isn't it . . .'*

After the ceremony there was a banquet, but I really felt too tired to go. I took a cab home and found MISS AGDA *in my room busy making my bed the way I like (very high under my head and folded neatly at my feet). A heating pad was already connected and my sleeping pills stood on the table. Almost at once,* MISS AGDA *began helping me with my shoes and evening dress, and I felt a great warmth towards this extraordinary, faithful, thoughtful old woman. I would really have liked to become friends with her again, and I repented the morning's thoughtless utterances (which, I noticed, she had by no means forgotten).)*

---

[10] The scene in square brackets does not appear in the finished film.

ISAK: Did you enjoy the ceremony?
AGDA: Yes, thank you.
ISAK: Are you tired, Miss Agda?
AGDA: I won't deny it.
ISAK: Take one of my sleeping pills.
AGDA: No, thanks.
ISAK: Oh, Miss Agda, I'm sorry for this morning.
AGDA: Are you sick, Professor?
ISAK: No. Why?
AGDA: I don't know, but that sounds alarming.
ISAK: Oh really, is it so unusual for me to ask forgiveness?
AGDA: Do you want the water decanter on the table?
ISAK: No, thanks.

(*We pottered about for a while, silently.*)

AGDA: Thanks anyway.
ISAK: Oh, Miss Agda.
AGDA: What do you want, Professor?
ISAK: Don't you think that we who have known each other for two generations could drop formality and say '*du*' to each other?
AGDA: No, I don't really think so.
ISAK: Why not, if I may ask?
AGDA: Have you brushed your teeth, Professor?
ISAK: Yes, thanks.
AGDA: Now, I'll tell you. I beg to be excused from all intimacies. It's all right the way it is between us now.
ISAK: But, dear Miss Agda, we are old now.
AGDA: Speak for yourself, Professor. A woman has to think of her reputation, and what would people say if the two of us suddenly started to say '*du*' to each other?
ISAK: Yes, what would people say?
AGDA: They would ridicule us.
ISAK: Do you always act correctly?
AGDA: Nearly always. At our age one ought to know how to behave. Isn't that so, Professor?
ISAK: Good night, Miss Agda.
AGDA: Good night, Professor. I will leave the door ajar. And you know where I am if you should want something. Good night, Professor.
ISAK: Good night, Miss Agda.

(*I was just going to lie down in bed (I had been sitting on the edge in my old robe) when I heard singing and music from the garden. I thought I recognised the voices and walked over to the window and lifted the*

blinds. Down there under the trees I recognised my three companions from the trip. They sang to their heart's delight, and AN-DERS *accompanied them on his guitar.*)

SARA: Hey, Father Isak! You were fantastic when you marched in the procession. We were real proud that we knew you. Now we're going on.
ANDERS: We got a lift all the way to Hamburg.
VIKTOR: With a fifty-year-old deaconess. Anders is already sweet on the old girl.
ANDERS: Stop babbling!
VIKTOR: We came to say goodbye.
ISAK: Goodbye, and thank you for your company.
SARA: Goodbye, Father Isak. Do you know that it is really you I love, today, tomorrow and forever?
ISAK: I'll remember that.
VIKTOR: Goodbye, Professor.
ISAK: Goodbye, Viktor.
ANDERS: Goodbye, Professor. Now we have to run.
ISAK: Let me hear from you sometime.

(*Those last words I said to myself, and rather quietly. The children waved to me and were swallowed up by the summer night. I heard their laughter, and then they were gone.*
At the same moment, I heard voices out in the foyer. It was EVALD *and* MARIANNE. *They whispered out of consideration to me and I heard the rustle of* MARIANNE's *evening gown. I called to* EVALD. *He entered the room, but stopped at the door.*)

ISAK: Are you home already?
EVALD: Marianne had to change shoes. Her heel broke.
ISAK: So you are going to the dance?
EVALD: Yes, I suppose so.
ISAK: A-ha.
EVALD: How are you otherwise?
ISAK: Fine, thanks.
EVALD: How's the heart holding up?
ISAK: Excellently.
EVALD: Good night, and sleep well.

(*He turned and went through the door. I asked him to come back. He looked very surprised. I felt surprised myself, and confused. I didn't really know what to say.*)

ISAK: Sit down a moment.

EVALD: Is it something special?

(*He sat obediently on the chair near the bed. His starched shirt rustled and his hands hung a little tiredly across his knees. I realised that my son was becoming middle-aged.*)

ISAK: May I ask you what's going to happen between you and Marianne? (EVALD *shakes his head.*) Forgive my asking.

EVALD: I know nothing.

ISAK: It's not my business, but . . .

EVALD: What?

ISAK: But shouldn't . . .

EVALD: I have asked her to remain with me.

ISAK: And how will it . . . I mean . . .

EVALD: I can't be without her.

ISAK: You mean you can't live alone.

EVALD: I can't be without *her.* That's what I mean.

ISAK: I understand.

EVALD: It will be as she wants.

ISAK: And if she wants . . . I mean, does she want?

EVALD: She says that she'll think it over. I don't really know.

ISAK: Regarding that loan you had from me . . .

EVALD: Don't worry, you'll get your money.

ISAK: I didn't mean that.

EVALD: You'll get your money all right.

(EVALD *rose and nodded to me. Just then* MARIANNE *appeared in the door. She had on a very simple but extraordinarily beautiful white dress.*)

MARIANNE: How are you, Father Isak?

ISAK: Fine, thanks. Very well.

MARIANNE: I broke a heel, so we had to come home to change. Can I wear these shoes instead?

ISAK: They look fine.

(MARIANNE *came up to me. She smelled good and rustled in a sweet, womanly way. She leaned over me.*)

ISAK: Thanks for your company on the trip.

MARIANNE: Thank *you.*

ISAK: I like you, Marianne.

MARIANNE: I like you too, Father Isak.

(*She kissed me lightly on the cheek and disappeared. They exchanged a few words outside the door. I heard their steps on the stairs and then the door slamming in the foyer. I heard my heart and my old watch. I heard the tower clock strike eleven, with the light tones designating the four quarter hours and the heavier sounds marking the hour.*

Now it began to rain, not very hard, but quietly and evenly. A lulling sound. The street lamp swung on its cord and threw shadows on the light-coloured window blinds.

Whenever I am restless or sad, I usually try to recall memories from my childhood, to calm down. This is the way it was that night too, and I wandered back to the summerhouse and the wild strawberry patch and everything I had dreamed or remembered or experienced during this long day.[11]

I sat under the tree by the wild strawberry patch and it was a warm, sunny day with soft summer skies and a mild breeze coming through the birches. Down at the dock, my sisters and brothers were romping with UNCLE ARON. *My* AUNT *went by, together with* SARA: *They were laden with large baskets. Everyone laughed and shouted to each other and applauded when the red sail went up the mast of the old yacht (an ancient relic from the days of my parents' childhood; a mad impulse of our grandfather, the Admiral).* SARA *turned around and when she caught sight of me she put down her baskets and ran towards me.*)

SARA: Isak, darling, there are no wild strawberries left. Aunt wants you to search for your father. We will sail around the peninsula and pick you up on the other side.

ISAK: I have already searched for him, but I can't find either Father or Mother.

SARA: Your mother was supposed to go with him.

ISAK: Yes, but I can't find them.

SARA: I will help you.

(*She took me by the hand and suddenly we found ourselves at a narrow sound with deep, dark water. The sun shone brightly on the opposite side, which rose softly into a meadow. Down at the beach on the other side of the dark water a gentleman sat, dressed in*

[11] In the film, at the beginning of the dream sequence, the camera dissolves from Isak asleep to the family coming out of the summerhouse and the scene of the family down by the dock appears a little later during the conversation between Isak and Sara.

white with his hat on the back of his head and an old pipe in his mouth. He had a soft, blond beard and pince-nex. He had taken off his shoes and stockings and between his hands he held a long slender bamboo pole. A red float lay motionless on the shimmering water.

Farther up the bank sat my MOTHER. *She wore a bright summer dress and a big hat which shaded her face. She was reading a book.* SARA *dropped my hand and pointed to my parents. Then she was gone. I looked for a long time at the pair on the other side of the water. I tried to shout to them but not a word came from my mouth. Then my* FA-THER *raised his head and caught sight of*

me. He lifted his hand and waved, laughing. My MOTHER *looked up from her book. She also laughed and nodded.*

Then I saw the old yacht with its red sail. It cruised so smoothly in the mild breeze. In the prow stood UNCLE ARON, *singing some sentimental song, and I saw my brothers and sisters and* AUNT *and* SARA, *who lifted up* SIGBRITT's *little boy. I shouted to them, but they didn't hear me.*

I dreamed that I stood by the water and shouted towards the bay, but the warm summer breeze carried away my cries and they did not reach their destination. Yet I wasn't sorry about that; I felt, on the contrary, rather lighthearted.)

It is sometimes argued that although film can be violent, serious, and sad, it is inherently anti-tragic. If tragedy is chiefly concerned with man asserting himself and exhausting himself in some painfully constricting "boundary situation" (Hamlet called upon to revenge his father's death, King Lear forced to recognize his own lack of self-knowledge) and if comedy is chiefly concerned with man living most fully by getting along with his fellows in this not-too-bad world, the camera (it has been argued) is better suited to comedy because as it records trees, skies, rivers, crowds, even cups of hot coffee and people going to bed or getting out of bed, it gives us a sense of the abundance and vitality of life, of rich diversity and of ongoingness rather than of pressure and exhaustion and finality. There is probably a good deal to this view; in any case, although in Bergman's film *Wild Strawberries* we have a story about the movement toward death, it is wonderfully suffused with a sense of the continuing vitality or richness of ordinary life.

The gist of Bergman's story has clear affinities with tragic stories: a man, near to death, finds that he has made a mistake. Dr. Isak Borg at the start thinks that he withdrew from society for highly civilized reasons: when we express opinions about people, he says, we are likely to be "guilty of errors, exaggerations, even tremendous lies," and "rather than commit such follies, I remain silent. As a result, I have of my own free will withdrawn almost completely from society." (Here he is a true heir to those materialistic ideas of the late nineteenth century, such as Darwinism and Marxism, that substituted scientific certainties for religious and metaphysical certainties but soon left thoughtful men without confidence in anything, even in the distinction between the tragic and the comic, as the Theater of the Absurd demonstrates.) All that Dr. Borg asks of life "is to be left alone," to be allowed to continue his scientific studies, to play golf, and to read an occasional detective story. To keep life at a distance he developed, therefore, a somewhat courtly manner but life has a way of breaking in, and now, old, he finds he is troubled with dreams. The film begins with a dream of shattered eyeglasses, a watch without hands, a faceless man who turns out to be bodiless too, and a hearse carrying Dr. Borg's corpse. As he later puts it, his dreams tell him "that I'm dead, although I live." Moreover as the story progresses we learn that both his ninety-six-year-old mother and his thirty-eight-year-old son (who knows that he was an unwanted child) are also living a death-in-life.

But this dark story is transfused with something of the stuff of comedy. First, there is the doctor's moderately genial ironic attitude toward himself and others; even at the start, although he is mistaken about the reasons for his withdrawal, he nevertheless looks at himself with a sort of entertaining irony. Second, there are a good many scenes that are funny: the doctor and his house-keeper bicker as though they are a married couple, two children compose a song as a birthday present for a deaf uncle, an incipient divinity student argues with an incipient scientist about the existence of God and is reduced to twist-ing his rival's arm ("Viktor said that was a pretty lousy argument for the exist-ence of God"). Third, we are continually reminded, as comedy reminds us and as tragedy does not, of the business of pushing on through daily life: people smoke and eat (in tragedy does anyone eat except at a great banquet?) and even go to the bathroom: just before the bestowal of honorary degrees on three distinguished old men, one of them is said to have only three interests in life, "a thirty-year-old injustice, a goldfish, and his bowels," and this honorable old man at this ceremonious moment is anxious to get to the bathroom; "the gar-land girls had to go out and relieve themselves in the little silver pot in the sacristy. But we adults unfortunately had to stay where we were." Fourth, and most important, the story moves not only toward the doctor's self-recognition or anagnorisis, but toward his reunion with society, or with life.

This reunion is largely brought about through two women, his daughter-in-law Marianne and a young girl named Sara whom they meet by chance, and also through the doctor's memories of a young girl (also named Sara) to whom he was engaged but who did not marry him because even in his youth his seriousness and his refinement had something deathly in them. Through these women, and the two young men who accompany Sara, the ice around the doctor's heart begins to melt. For example, at the beginning of the film, talk-ing about a loan he had made to his son and which his son finds difficult to repay, the doctor matter-of-factly says, "A bargain is a bargain," but near the end of the story he is moved to alter the bargain — though his son interrupts him and his thoughts must go unspoken. (It is in tragedy that a bargain is a bargain, that actions have remorseless consequences; in comedy bad bargains have a way of dissolving, and in *Wild Strawberries* Borg's own bad bargain with life, so to speak, is dissolved, and he is given a second chance.)

This movement from death to life, from isolation to union — even though, of course, the life of a seventy-eight-year-old man will end relatively soon — is marked by such symbolic details as the transition from the faceless clock of his initial dream to the ticking watch and the striking clock near the end, and by such actions as his attempt to ease his son's debt and — comically — by his attempt to establish a more intimate relationship with his old housekeeper (but she firmly rejects his suggestion that now that forty years have passed, perhaps they can use the *du* [equivalent to the French *tu*] form of address). It is most effectively conveyed, however (putting aside the wonderful photography), through the gentle laughter that periodically recurs through the story. Laughter, of course, can be hostile, the derisive laughter we engage in when we feel superior. And in *Wild Strawberries* there are occasional artificial laughs, bitter laughs, and nervous laughs. But most of the laughter is social, shared by all concerned. Even its first occurrence is of this sort. Early, when the doctor says that he has enjoyed having Marianne around, she replies, somewhat bitterly, "like a cat"; he laughs, she joins in the laughter, and "it cleared the air a bit." This cleansing power of shared laughter, in *Wild Strawberries* usually stimulated by women or young people, manifests itself again and again. Amused by Sara and her two boyfriends, "Marianne and I exchanged amused glances, the first contact between us"; a little later "everyone burst into laughter"; later, moved by the generosity and affection of an old acquaintance, the doctor tells "humorous anecdotes which had a great deal of human interest. These were a great success (I don't think they laughed just out of politeness)." (We can note here that Dr. Borg is still reserved, still judging himself and others, but he is now far more humane, far more social.) Later, "Marianne laughed and lit my cigar," and this leads them to recite a poem together — another step in the doctor's union with society, a step made even more clear by the contrast provided by his mother's house, which is "protected from onlookers by a wall as tall as a man." Later, the last thing he hears from the three young people who have helped him to find a new self through contact with others is their laughter. Finally (to cut short what could be a long list) at the end of the film, when he has a vision of his father accompanied by his mother, fishing in a river, his father waves to him and laughs, and so does his mother. His last words are, "I felt . . . rather lighthearted."

This final vision, so different from the initial dream of the hearse and the clock without hands, is implicitly a vision of man in contact with the mysterious sources of life (man and woman on an idyllic riverbank, the man's fishing rod gracefully rising to the heavens) and is explicitly a vision of Dr. Borg's happy reunion with the past; the meanings join, to affirm that the past lives again in the present, and that the present itself — the life of Dr. Borg specifically — is not an isolated or dead moment but something vitally united with a vast world of people and things.

THE GAP

Eugène Ionesco

Translated by Rosette Lamont

Eugène Ionesco was born in 1912 in Rumania of a Rumanian father and a French mother. He spent his childhood in France and did not return to Rumania, or learn Rumanian, until he was 13. (He has said that his view of the world as a place where almost nothing can be known is partly due to the fact that until he was 13 he heard that Frenchmen were the bravest in the world, and after 13 he heard that Rumanians were the bravest.) After university training in Rumania, he taught French, but in 1939 he returned to France and worked for a publisher. He did not write his first play, *The Bald Soprano*, until about 1948, and he did not become well known as a dramatist until 1956, when a revival of *The Chairs* (1951) attracted critical attention. Other major plays are *The Lesson* (1950), *Amédée* (1953), *The Killer* (1957), *Rhinoceros* (1959), and *The King Dies* (1962). *The Gap* was written in 1962 and revised in 1965.

CAST OF CHARACTERS

THE FRIEND
THE ACADEMICIAN
THE ACADEMICIAN'S WIFE
THE MAID

Set: A rich bourgeois living room with artistic pretensions. One or two sofas, a number of armchairs, among which, a green, Régence style one, right in the middle of the room. The walls are covered with framed diplomas. One can make out, written in heavy script at the top of a particularly large one, "Doctor Honoris causa." This is followed by an almost illegible Latin inscription. Another equally impressive diploma states: "Doctorat honoris causa," again followed by a long, illegible text. There is an abundance of smaller diplomas, each of which bears a clearly written "doctorate."

A door to the right of the audience.

Jean Desailly as The Friend, Pierre Bertin as The Academician, and Madeleine Renaud as The Academician's Wife in the Theatre de France production directed by Jean-Louis Barrault, Paris, 1966. (Photograph: Bernand.)

As the curtain rises, one can see THE ACADE-
MICIAN'S WIFE *dressed in a rather crumpled
robe. She has obviously just gotten out of
bed, and has not had time to dress.* THE
FRIEND *faces her. He is well dressed: hat,
umbrella in hand, stiff collar, black jacket
and striped trousers, shiny black shoes.*

THE WIFE: Dear friend, tell me all.

THE FRIEND: I don't know what to say.

THE WIFE: I know.

THE FRIEND: I heard the news last night. I
did not want to call you. At the same time I
couldn't wait any longer. Please forgive me for
coming so early with such terrible news.

THE WIFE: He didn't make it! How terrible!
We were still hoping. . . .

THE FRIEND: It's hard, I know. He still had
a chance. Not much of one. We had to expect
it.

THE WIFE: I didn't expect it. He was always
so successful. He could always manage somehow, at the last moment.

THE FRIEND: In that state of exhaustion. You
shouldn't have let him!

THE WIFE: What can we do, what can we
do! . . . How awful!

THE FRIEND: Come on, dear friend, be
brave. That's life.

THE WIFE: I feel faint: I'm going to faint.
(*She falls in one of the armchairs.*)

THE FRIEND (*holding her, gently slapping
her cheeks and hands*): I shouldn't have
blurted it out like that. I'm sorry.

THE WIFE: No, you were right to do so. I had
to find out somehow or other.

THE FRIEND: I should have prepared you,
carefully.

THE WIFE: I've got to be strong. I can't help
thinking of him, the wretched man. I hope they
won't put it in the papers. Can we count on the
journalists' discretion?

THE FRIEND: Close your door. Don't answer
the telephone. It will still get around. You
could go to the country. In a couple of months,
when you are better, you'll come back, you'll go
on with your life. People forget such things.

THE WIFE: People won't forget so fast. That's
all they were waiting for. Some friends will feel

Reprinted by permission from *The Massachusetts
Review*, 10 (Winter 1969), © 1969 The Massachusetts Review, Inc.

sorry, but the others, the others. . . . (THE ACAD-
EMICIAN *comes in, fully dressed: uniform, chest
covered with decorations, his sword on his
side.*)

THE ACADEMICIAN: Up so early, my dear?
(*To* THE FRIEND.) You've come early too.
What's happening? Do you have the final re-
sults?

THE WIFE: What a disgrace!

THE FRIEND: You mustn't crush him like
this, dear friend. (*To* THE ACADEMICIAN.) You
have failed.

THE ACADEMICIAN: Are you quite sure?

THE FRIEND: You should never have tried to
pass the baccalaureate examination.

THE ACADEMICIAN: They failed me. The rats!
How dare they do this to me!

THE FRIEND: The marks were posted late in
the evening.

THE ACADEMICIAN: Perhaps it was difficult to
make them out in the dark. How could you
read them?

THE FRIEND: They had set up spotlights.

THE ACADEMICIAN: They're doing everything
to ruin me.

THE FRIEND: I passed by in the morning;
the marks were still up.

THE ACADEMICIAN: You could have bribed
the concierge into pulling them down.

THE FRIEND: That's exactly what I did. Unfortunately the police were there. Your name
heads the list of those who failed. Everyone's
standing in line to get a look. There's an awful
crush.

THE ACADEMICIAN: Who's there? The parents of the candidates?

THE FRIEND: Not only they.

THE WIFE: All your rivals, all your colleagues
must be there. All those you attacked in the
press for ignorance: your undergraduates, your
graduate students, all those you failed when you
were chairman of the board of examiners.

THE ACADEMICIAN: I am discredited! But I
won't let them. There must be some mistake.

THE FRIEND: I saw the examiners. I spoke
with them. They gave me your marks. Zero in
mathematics.

THE ACADEMICIAN: I had no scientific training.

THE FRIEND: Zero in Greek, zero in Latin.

THE WIFE (*to her husband*): You, a human-
ist, the spokesman for humanism, the author of

that famous treatise "The Defense of Poesy and Humanism."

THE ACADEMICIAN: I beg your pardon, but my book concerns itself with twentieth century humanism. (*To* THE FRIEND.) What about composition? What grade did I get in composition?

THE FRIEND: Nine hundred. You have nine hundred points.

THE ACADEMICIAN: That's perfect. My average must be all the way up.

THE FRIEND: Unfortunately not. They're marking on the basis of two thousand. The passing grade is one thousand.

THE ACADEMICIAN: They must have changed the regulations.

THE WIFE: They didn't change them just for you. You have a frightful persecution complex.

THE ACADEMICIAN: I tell you they changed them.

THE FRIEND: They went back to the old ones, back to the time of Napoleon.

THE ACADEMICIAN: Utterly outmoded. Besides, when did they make those changes? It isn't legal. I'm chairman of the Baccalaureate Commission of the Ministry of Public Education. They didn't consult me, and they cannot make any changes without my approval. I'm going to expose them. I'm going to bring government charges against them.

THE WIFE: Darling, you don't know what you're doing. You're in your dotage. Don't you recall handing in your resignation just before taking the examination so that no one could doubt the complete objectivity of the board of examiners?

THE ACADEMICIAN: I'll take it back.

THE WIFE: You should never have taken that test. I warned you. After all, it's not as if you needed it. But you have to collect all the honors, don't you? You're never satisfied. What did you need this diploma for? Now all is lost. You have your Doctorate, your Master's, your high school diploma, your elementary school certificate, and even the first part of the baccalaureate.

THE ACADEMICIAN: There was a gap.

THE WIFE: No one suspected it.

THE ACADEMICIAN: But *I* knew it. Others might have found out. I went to the office of the Registrar and asked for a transcript of my record. They said to me: "Certainly Professor, Mr. President, Your Excellency...." Then they looked up my file, and the Chief Registrar came

back looking embarrassed, most embarrassed indeed. He said: "There's something peculiar, very peculiar. You have your Master's, certainly, but it's no longer valid." I asked him why, of course. He answered: "There's a gap behind your Master's. I don't know how it happened. You must have registered and been accepted at the University without having passed the second part of the baccalaureate examination."

THE FRIEND: And then?

THE WIFE: Your Master's degree is no longer valid?

THE ACADEMICIAN: No, not quite. It's suspended. "The duplicate you are asking for will be delivered to you upon completion of the baccalaureate. Of course you will pass the examination with no trouble." That's what I was told, so you see now that I had to take it.

THE FRIEND: Your husband, dear friend, wanted to fill the gap. He's a conscientious person.

THE WIFE: It's clear you don't know him as I do. That's not it at all. He wants fame, honors. He never has enough. What does one diploma more or less matter? No one notices them anyway, but he sneaks in at night, on tiptoe, into the living room, just to look at them, and count them.

THE ACADEMICIAN: What else can I do when I have insomnia?

THE FRIEND: The questions asked at the baccalaureate are usually known in advance. You were admirably situated to get this particular information. You could also have sent in a replacement to take the test for you. One of your students, perhaps. Or if you wanted to take the test without people realizing that you already knew the questions, you could have sent your maid to the black market, where one can buy them.

THE ACADEMICIAN: I don't understand how I could have failed in my composition. I filled three sheets of paper. I treated the subject fully, taking into account the historical background. I interpreted the situation accurately... at least plausibly. I didn't deserve a bad grade.

THE FRIEND: Do you recall the subject?

THE ACADEMICIAN: Hum... let's see....

THE FRIEND: He doesn't even remember what he discussed.

THE ACADEMICIAN: I do... wait... hum.

THE FRIEND: The subject to be treated was the following: "Discuss the influence of Renaissance painters on novelists of the Third Republic." I have here a photostatic copy of your examination paper. Here is what you wrote.

THE ACADEMICIAN (*grabbing the photostat and reading*): "The trial of Benjamin: After Benjamin was tried and acquitted, the assessors holding a different opinion from that of the President murdered him, and condemned Benjamin to the suspension of his civic rights, imposing on him a fine of nine hundred francs. . . ."

THE FRIEND: That's where the nine hundred points come from.

THE ACADEMICIAN: "Benjamin appealed his case . . . Benjamin appealed his case. . . ." I can't make out the rest. I've always had bad handwriting. I ought to have taken a typewriter along with me.

THE WIFE: Horrible handwriting, scribbling and crossing out; ink spots didn't help you much.

THE ACADEMICIAN (*goes on with his reading after having retrieved the text his wife had pulled out of his hand*): "Benjamin appealed his case. Flanked by policemen dressed in zouave uniforms . . . in zouave uniforms. . . ." It's getting dark. I can't see the rest. . . . I don't have my glasses.

THE WIFE: What you've written has nothing to do with the subject.

THE FRIEND: Your wife's quite right, friend. It has nothing to do with the subject.

THE ACADEMICIAN: Yes, it has. Indirectly.

THE FRIEND: Not even indirectly.

THE ACADEMICIAN: Perhaps I chose the second question.

THE FRIEND: There was only one.

THE ACADEMICIAN: Even if there was only that one, I treated another quite adequately. I went to the end of the story. I stressed the important points, explaining the motivations of the characters, highlighting their behavior. I explained the mystery, making it plain and clear. There was even a conclusion at the end. I can't make out the rest. (*To* THE FRIEND.) Can you read it?

THE FRIEND: It's illegible. I don't have my glasses either.

THE WIFE (*taking the text*): It's illegible and I have excellent eyes. You pretended to write. Mere scribbling.

THE ACADEMICIAN: That's not true. I've even provided a conclusion. It's clearly marked here in heavy print: "Conclusion or sanction . . . Conclusion or sanction. . . ." They can't get

away with it. I'll have this examination rendered null and void.

THE WIFE: Since you treated the wrong subject, and treated it badly, setting down only titles, and writing nothing in between, the mark you received is justified. You'd lose your case.

THE FRIEND: You'd most certainly lose. Drop it. Take a vacation.

THE ACADEMICIAN: You're always on the side of the Others.

THE WIFE: After all, these professors know what they're doing. They haven't been granted their rank for nothing. They passed examinations, received serious training. They know the rules of composition.

THE ACADEMICIAN: Who was on the board of examiners?

THE FRIEND: For Mathematics, a movie star. For Greek, one of the Beatles. For Latin, the champion of the automobile race, and many others.

THE ACADEMICIAN: But these people aren't any more qualified than I am. And for composition?

THE FRIEND: A woman, a secretary in the editorial division of the review *Yesterday, the Day Before Yesterday, and Today.*

THE ACADEMICIAN: Now I know. This wretch gave me a poor grade out of spite because I never joined her political party. It's an act of vengeance. But I have ways and means of rendering the examination null and void. I'm going to call the President.

THE WIFE: Don't! You'll make yourself look even more ridiculous. (*To* THE FRIEND.) Please try to restrain him. He listens to you more than to me. (THE FRIEND *shrugs his shoulders, unable to cope with the situation.* THE WIFE *turns to her husband, who has just lifted the receiver off the hook.*) Don't call!

THE ACADEMICIAN (*on the telephone*): Hello, John? It is I . . . What? . . . What did you say? . . . But, listen, my dear friend . . . but, listen to me . . . Hello! Hello! (*Puts down the receiver.*)

THE FRIEND: What did he say?

THE ACADEMICIAN: He said . . . He said . . . , "I don't want to talk to you. My mummy won't let me make friends with boys at the bottom of the class." Then he hung up on me.

THE WIFE: You should have expected it. All is lost. How could you do this to me? How could you do this to me?

THE ACADEMICIAN: Think of it! I lectured at the Sorbonne, at Oxford, at American universities. Ten thousand theses have been written on my work; hundreds of critics have analyzed it. I hold an *honoris causa* doctorate from Amsterdam as well as a secret university Chair with the Duchy of Luxembourg. I received the Nobel Prize three times. The King of Sweden himself was amazed by my erudition. A doctorate *honoris causa, honoris causa* . . . and I failed the baccalaureate examination!

THE WIFE: Everyone will laugh at us!

(THE ACADEMICIAN *takes off his sword and breaks it on his knee*.)

THE FRIEND (*picking up the two pieces*): I wish to preserve these in memory of our ancient glory.

(THE ACADEMICIAN *meanwhile in a fit of rage is tearing down his decorations, throwing them on the floor, and stepping on them*.)

THE WIFE (*trying to salvage the remains*): Don't do this! Don't! That's all we've got left.

In *Notes and Counter Notes* Ionesco argues that "realism" is deceptive; what we see on the realistic stage is the world as "reason" sees it, but reason is a sort of systemized thinking — a highly selective vision — that is utterly unable to grasp the fluid, elusive reality. Take, the idea of "character." Reason has told us that there is such a thing as character, but what is character? Is there really a coherent self that can be understood by the scientific mind? Polonius says to Laertes, "This above all, to thine own self be true," but what *is* one's own self? Hamlet certainly does not know. He is eager to avenge his father, but he berates himself for not acting, and he wonders if he is a coward or villain rather than a loving son. The idea that a man has a character, a more or less coherent nature which we can understand through our reason, then, is itself perhaps a simplification of reality. Like Pirandello (see p. 525), Ionesco argues that reason cannot comprehend reality; it is merely an illusory device by which man simplifies an absurd world in order to make it bearable. But illusions are the traditional material of comic dramatists, and so reason — and the ridiculous behavior that it engenders — is one of Ionesco's chief subjects.

Fantasy is the weapon with which Ionesco seeks to bludgeon his audience out of its reason-induced illusions and into an awareness of the strangeness of the world. "The authentic nature of things, the truth," he has written "can only be revealed to us through fantasy." His characters at first provoke us to say, "People are not at all like that," and his situations (he scarcely has plots) are wildly improbable — as reason understands improbability. But his gross exaggerations — for example, farcical characters who speak idiotic clichés — serve, first, to make us see that people do indeed speak idiotic clichés, and second, to make us see that they do so because they are terrified of the anguish that would encompass them if they did not fend it off with neat verbal formulas. Without such formulas as "travel broadens us," "we learn from our mistakes," "children develop a sense of responsibility by having a dog," we can hardly stand life; certainly we would have serious doubts about why we bother to cope with foreign money, we would be driven to distraction by our mistakes, and we would kick the dog out. In short, things exist but cannot be justified; existence is absurd (the argument runs) and we hide this terrifying truth from ourselves by imposing on existence a vast mechanism of institutions, including language and traditions, which (though really only a sort of systematic madness) gives us the illusion that there is a meaningful pattern in life.

In *The Gap* a professor cannot tolerate a gap in his career because a gap means that the pattern is not complete, and if the pattern is not complete there may not really be a pattern at all. We have all agreed that college degrees mean something, or are important, and we have agreed that professors are learned men with degrees. Therefore, a man who holds a doctorate *must* have been awarded a baccalaureate earlier; anything else is unthinkable, for it calls the system into doubt, and we are horribly uncomfortable without the system. We *are* our degrees — and our car and our clothes and our children. If a degree is missing, a part of the person is missing, and the person himself becomes unsure of his identity. Not surprisingly Ionesco's professor has a habit of keeping his eye on his framed diplomas: "He sneaks in at night, on tiptoe, into the living room, just to look at them, and count them." The professor is farcical, of course, but the zany reduction of a man to a puppet-like figure gets across the point that we persistently relate the self to externals. The farcical characters thus are not merely farcical or sub-human, for they convey a sense of deep — and real — unhappiness. Ionesco's plays are filled with people who desperately depend on things: chairs in *The Chairs*, coffee cups in *Victims of Duty*, furniture in *The New Tenant* (note too in *The Gap* that the description of the furniture on the set is an embodiment of the protagonist's conception of himself), and eggs in *The Future Is in Eggs*.

The venerable doctor's failure to pass an undergraduate examination is not just a joke about the stupidity of professors; it is also a violent comment on the tissue of conventions that we have invented in order to allow us to have a sense of identity in an irrational world. At the end of the play, when the discredited professor begins to destroy his decorations, his wife salvages the remnants and states quite clearly the dependence of her identity on things: "Don't do this! Don't. That's all we've got left."

We all fail our examination (compare Dr. Borg in *Wild Strawberries*) because we all fend off a frightening irrational reality by taking comfort in simplifications. Ionesco forces us to examine ourselves. The stage direction at the end of *Jack* says, "All this must produce in the audience a feeling of embarrassment, awareness and shame." We are not allowed merely to laugh at the folly of others; we are forced at the same time to look into our own guilt. Is Ionesco's vision comic or tragic? The automatic behavior and the automatic language are traditional comic materials, but the anguish — farcical but felt — has affinities with tragedy. Ionesco himself has often said that for him the comic is tragic. He has even taken Bergson's famous description of the comic as the mechanical encrusted on the living (see the introduction to this book, p. 9) and found tragic implications in it:

At the start, you have "a little of something mechanical encrusted on the living." It's comic. But if the mechanical gets bigger and bigger and the living shrinks and shrinks, things become stifling and then tragic, because we get the impression that the world is slipping from our mental grasp.... The sorcerer's apprentice must have had this same anguished feeling of the world escaping his grasp. Perhaps it's also the image of what could happen in the near future. We are, now, no longer masters of the extraordinary machines we set in motion. Our planet could go up in smoke ... so they tell us.*

Both comedy and tragedy customarily have showed man at the end of his rope, but the attitude that the audience was to take toward tragic desperation was very different from the attitude it was to take toward comic desperation. In our time, however, the distinction has become blurred, partly because, as Thoreau said more than a hundred years ago, most of us live lives of quiet desperation. We can scarcely see ourselves as heroes, but we don't quite see ourselves as mere fools either.

*From *Conversations with Eugène Ionesco* by Claude Bonnefoy, p. 108. Translated by Jan Dawson. Holt, Rinehart and Winston, 1970. Reprinted by permission of the publisher.

THE EFFECT OF GAMMA RAYS ON MAN-IN-THE-MOON MARIGOLDS

Paul Zindel

Paul Zindel (born in 1936) has lived most of his life in New York. He has said that the depiction of the mother in *Marigolds*, written when he was twenty-five, is indebted to his own mother, and that the play as a whole owes something to his experience as a high school teacher of chemistry. Zindel has also written several books for children and two other plays. *Marigolds*, produced in 1970, won the Pulitzer Prize for Drama.

shortened version
↓

CHARACTERS

TILLIE, *The Girl*
"In front of my eyes, one part of the world was becoming another. Atoms exploding ... atom after atom breaking down into something new ... It would go on for millions of years ..."

BEATRICE, *The Mother*
"This long street, with all the doors of the houses shut and everything crowded next to each other ... And then I start getting afraid that the vegetables are going to spoil ... and that nobody's going to buy anything ..."

RUTH, *The Other Daughter*
"Well, they say I came out of my room ... and I started down the stairs, step by step ... and I heard the choking and banging on the bed ..."

NANNY
. . .

JANICE VICKERY
. . .

The Setting: A room of wood which was once a vegetable store — and a point of debarkation for a horse-drawn wagon to bring its wares to a small town.

But the store is gone, and a widow of confusion has placed her touch on everything. A door to NANNY'*s room leads off from this main room, and in front of the door hang faded curtains which allow ventilation in the summer. There is a hallway and a telephone. A heavy wood staircase leads to a landing with a balustrade, two doors, and a short hall.* BEATRICE *sleeps in one room;* TILLIE *and* RUTH *share the other.*

Objects which respectable people usually hide in closets are scattered about the main room: newspapers, magazines, dishes; empty

---

Sada Thompson as Beatrice, Amy Levitt as Ruth, and, in back, Pamela Payton-Wright as Tillie in the original production directed by Melvin Bernhardt, New York, 1970. (Photograph: Bert Andrews.)

bottles; clothes; suitcases; last week's sheets. Such carelessness is the type which is so perfected it must have evolved from hereditary processes; but in all fairness to the occupants, it can be pointed out that after twilight, when shadows and weak bulbs work their magic, the room becomes interesting.

On a table near the front left of the room is a small wire cage designed to hold a rabbit. Near this are several school books, notebook papers, and other weapons of high school children. A kitchen area, boasting a hot plate, has been carved near the bottom of the staircase, and the window, which was formerly the front of the vegetable store, is now mostly covered with old newspapers so that passers-by cannot see in. A bit of the clear glass remains at the top — but drab, lifeless drapes line the sides of the window.

ACT I

The lights go down slowly as music creeps in — a theme for lost children, the near misbegotten.

From the blackness TILLIE's VOICE *speaks against the music.*

TILLIE's VOICE: He told me to look at my hand, for a part of it came from a star that exploded too long ago to imagine. This part of me was formed from a tongue of fire that screamed through the heavens until there was our sun. And this part of me — this tiny part of me — was on the sun when it itself exploded and whirled in a great storm until the planets came to be.

(Lights start in.)

And this small part of me was then a whisper of the earth. When there was life, perhaps this part of me got lost in a fern that was crushed and covered until it was coal. And then it was a diamond millions of years later — it must have been a diamond as beautiful as the star from which it had first come.

TILLIE *(taking over from recorded voice)*: Or perhaps this part of me became lost in a terrible beast, or became part of a huge bird that flew above the primeval swamps.

And he said this thing was so small — this part of me was so small it couldn't be seen — but it was there from the beginning of the world.

And he called this bit of me an atom. And when he wrote the word, I fell in love with it.

Atom.

Atom.

What a beautiful word.

(The phone rings.)

BEATRICE *(off stage)*: Will you get that please?

(The phone rings again before BEATRICE *appears in her bathrobe from the kitchen.)*

No help! Never any help!

(She answers the phone.)

Hello? Yes it is. Who is this? . . . I hope there hasn't been any trouble at school . . . Oh, she's always been like that. She hardly says a word around here, either. I always say some people were born to speak and others born to listen . . .

You know I've been meaning to call you to thank you for that lovely rabbit you gave Matilda. She and I just adore it and it's gotten so big . . .

Well, it certainly was thoughtful. Mr. Goodman, I don't mean to change the subject but aren't you that delightful young man Tillie said hello to a couple of months back at the A & P? You were by the lobster tank and I was near the frozen foods? That delightful and handsome young man? . . . Why, I would very much indeed use the expression *handsome*. Yes, and . . .

Well, I encourage her at every opportunity at home. Did she say I didn't? Both my daughters have their own desks and I put 75-watt bulbs right near them . . . Yes . . . Yes . . . I think those tests are very much overrated, anyway, Mr. Goodman . . . Well, believe me she's nothing like that around this house . . .

Now I don't want you to think I don't appreciate what you're trying to do, Mr. Goodman, but I'm afraid it's simply useless. I've tried just everything, but she isn't a pretty girl — I mean, let's be frank about it — she's going to have her problems. Are you married, Mr. Goodman? Oh, that's too bad. I don't know what's the matter with women today letting a handsome young man like you get away . . .

Well, some days she just doesn't feel like going to school. You just said how bright she is, and I'm really afraid to put too much of a strain on her after what happened to her sister. You know, too much strain is the worst thing in this modern world, Mr. Goodman, and I can't afford to have another convulsive on my hands, now can I? But don't you worry about Matilda. There will be some place for her in this world. And, like I said, some were born to speak and

others just to listen . . . and do call again, Mr. Goodman. It's been a true pleasure speaking with you. Goodbye.

*(*BEATRICE *hangs up the phone and advances into the main room. The lights come up.)*

Matilda, that wasn't very nice of you to tell them I was forcibly detaining you from school. Why, the way that Mr. Goodman spoke, he must think I'm running a concentration camp. Do you have any idea how embarrassing it is to be accused of running a concentration camp for your own children?

Well, it isn't embarrassing at all.

That school of yours is forty years behind the times anyway, and believe me you learn more around here than that ugly Mr. Goodman can teach you!

You know, I really feel sorry for him. I never saw a man with a more effeminate face in my life. When I saw you talking to him by the lobster tank I said to myself, "Good Lord, for a science teacher my poor girl has got herself a Hebrew hermaphrodite." Of course, he's not as bad as Miss Hanley. The idea of letting her teach girl's gym is staggering.

And you have to place me in the embarrassing position of giving them a reason to call me at eight-thirty in the morning, no less.

TILLIE: I didn't say anything.

BEATRICE: What do you tell them when they want to know why you stay home once in a while?

TILLIE: I tell them I'm sick.

BEATRICE: Oh, you're sick all right, the exact nature of the illness not fully realized, but you're sick all right. Any daughter that would turn her mother in as the administrator of a concentration camp has got to be suffering from something very peculiar.

TILLIE: Can I go in today, Mother?

BEATRICE: You'll go in, all right.

TILLIE: Mr. Goodman said he was going to do an experiment —

BEATRICE: Why, he looks like the kind that would do his experimenting after sundown.

TILLIE: On radioactivity —

BEATRICE: On radioactivity? That's all that high school needs!

TILLIE: He's going to bring in the cloud chamber —

BEATRICE: Why, what an outstanding event. If you had warned me yesterday I would've gotten all dressed to kill and gone with you today. I love seeing cloud chambers being brought in.

TILLIE: You can actually see —

BEATRICE: You're giving me a headache.

TILLIE: Please?

BEATRICE: No, my dear, the fortress of knowledge is not going to be blessed with your presence today. I have a good number of exciting duties for you to take care of, not the least of which is rabbit droppings.

TILLIE: Oh, Mother, please . . . I'll do it after school.

BEATRICE: If we wait a minute longer this house is going to ferment. I found rabbit droppings in my bedroom even.

TILLIE: I could do it after Mr. Goodman's class. I'll say I'm ill and ask for a sick pass.

BEATRICE: Do you want me to chloroform that thing right this minute?

TILLIE: No!

BEATRICE: Then shut up.

(RUTH *comes to the top of the stairs. She is dressed for school, and though her clothes are simple she gives the impression of being slightly strange. Her hair isn't quite combed, her sweater doesn't quite fit, etc.*)

RUTH: Do you have Devil's Kiss down there?

BEATRICE: It's in the bathroom cabinet.

(RUTH *comes downstairs and goes to the bathroom door, located under the stairs. She flings it open and rummages in the cabinet.*)

RUTH: There's so much junk in here it's driving me crazy.

BEATRICE: Maybe it's in my purse . . . If you don't hurry up you'll be late for school.

RUTH: Well, I couldn't very well go in without Devil's Kiss, now could I?

BEATRICE: Doesn't anyone go to school these days without that all over their lips?

RUTH (*finding the lipstick*): Nobody I know, except Tillie, that is. And if she had a little lipstick on I'll bet they wouldn't have laughed at her so much yesterday.

BEATRICE: Why were they laughing?

RUTH: The assembly. Didn't she tell you about the assembly?

BEATRICE: Ruth, you didn't tell me she was in an assembly.

RUTH: Well, I just thought of it right now. How could I tell you anything until I think of

it — did you ever stop to consider that? Some crummy science assembly.

BEATRICE (*to* TILLIE): What is she talking about?

RUTH: I thought she'd tell the whole world. Imagine, right in front of the assembly, with everybody laughing at her.

BEATRICE: Will you be quiet, Ruth? *Why were they laughing at you?*

TILLIE: I don't know.

RUTH: You don't know? My heavens, she was a sight. She had that old jumper on — the faded one with that low collar — and a raggy slip that showed all over and her hair looked like she was struck by lightning.

BEATRICE: You're exaggerating . . .

RUTH: She was cranking this model of something —

TILLIE: The atom.

RUTH: This model of the atom . . . you know, it had this crank and a long tower so that when you turned it these little colored balls went spinning around like crazy. And there was Tillie, cranking away, looking weird as a coot . . . that old jumper with the raggy slip and the lightning hair . . . cranking away while some boy with glasses was reading this stupid speech . . . and everybody burst into laughter until the teachers yelled at them. And all day long, the kids kept coming up to me saying, "Is that really your sister? How can you bear it?" And you know, Chris Burns says to me — "She looks like the one that went to the looney doctors." I could have kissed him there and then.

BEATRICE (*taking a backscratcher*): Matilda, if you can't get yourself dressed properly before going to school you're never going to go again. I don't like the idea of everybody laughing at you, because when they laugh at you they're laughing at me. And I don't want you cranking any more . . . atoms.

RUTH (*putting the lipstick back in* BEATRICE'*s bag*): You're almost out of Devil's Kiss.

BEATRICE: If you didn't put so much on it would last longer.

RUTH: Who was that calling?

BEATRICE: Matilda turned me in to the Gestapo.

RUTH: Can I earn a cigarette this morning?

BEATRICE: Why not?

(BEATRICE *offers her the backscratcher along with a cigarette.*)

RUTH: Was it Mr. Goodman?

BEATRICE: Who?

RUTH (*lighting the cigarette*): The call this morning. Was it Mr. Goodman?

BEATRICE: Yes.

RUTH (*using the backscratcher on* BEATRICE, *who squirms with ecstasy*): I figured it would be.

BEATRICE: A little higher, please.

RUTH: There?

BEATRICE: Yes, *there* . . . Why did you figure it would be Mr. Goodman?

RUTH: Well, he called me out of sewing class yesterday — I remember because my blouse wasn't all buttoned — and he wanted to know why Tillie's out of school so much.

BEATRICE: Lower. A little lower . . . And what did you tell him?

RUTH: I wish you'd go back to Kools. I liked Kools better.

TILLIE (*gravely concerned*): What did you tell him?

RUTH: I told him you were ill, and he wanted to know what kind, so I told him you had leprosy.

TILLIE: You didn't!

RUTH: You should have seen his face. He was so cute. And I told him you had ringworm and gangrene.

BEATRICE: What did he say?

RUTH: And I told him you had what Mother's last patient had . . . whatchamacallit?

BEATRICE: Psoriasis?

RUTH: Yeah. Something like that.

TILLIE: Tell me you didn't, Ruth!

RUTH: O.K. I didn't . . . But I really did.

BEATRICE: He knew you were joking.

RUTH: And then I told him to go look up the *history* and then he'd find out. Whenever they go look up the history then they don't bother me anymore 'cause they think I'm crazy.

BEATRICE: Ruth —

RUTH: And I told him the disease you had was fatal and that there wasn't much hope for you.

BEATRICE: What kind of *history* is it?

RUTH: Just a little folder with the story of our lives in it, that's all.

BEATRICE: How did you ever see it?

RUTH: I read the whole thing last term when Miss Hanley dragged me into the record room because I didn't want to climb the ropes in gym and I told her my skull was growing.

BEATRICE: A little *lower*, please.

RUTH: Lower! Higher! I wish you'd make up your mind. If you'd switch back to Kools it might be worth it, but ugh! these are awful. You know, I really did think my skull was growing. Either that or a tumor. So she dragged me out of gym class, and she thought I couldn't read upside down while she was sitting opposite me with the history. But I could.

BEATRICE: What does it say?

RUTH: Oh, it says you're divorced and that I went crazy . . . and my father took a heart attack at Star Lake . . . and now you're a widow —

BEATRICE (*referring to the backscratching*): That's it! Hold it right there! Aaah!

RUTH: And it says that I exaggerate and tell stories and that I'm afraid of death and have nightmares . . . and all that stuff.

BEATRICE: And what else does it say?

RUTH: I can't remember everything you know. Remember this, remember that . . . remember this, that . . .

(*Go to dark. Music in.*)

TILLIE'S VOICE: Today I saw it. Behind the glass a white cloud began to form. He placed a small piece of metal in the center of the chamber and we waited until I saw the first one — a trace of smoke that came from nowhere and then disappeared. And then another . . . and another, until I knew it was coming from the metal. They looked like water-sprays from a park fountain, and they went on and on for as long as I watched.

And he told me the fountain of smoke would come forth for a long time, and if I had wanted to, I could have stayed there all my life and it would never have ended — that fountain, so close I could have touched it. In front of my eyes, one part of the world was becoming another. Atoms exploding, flinging off tiny bullets that caused the fountain, atom after atom breaking down into something new. And no one could stop the fountain. It would go on for millions of years — on and on, this fountain from eternity.

(*By the end of this speech, the lights are in to show* TILLIE *preparing boxes of dirt in which to plant seeds. The rabbit is in the cage near her, and* BEATRICE *is reading a newspaper on the other side of the room. She is sipping coffee from a huge coffee cup.*)

BEATRICE: I thought we had everything, but

leave it to you to think of the one thing we're missing . . .

(*She reads from the newspaper.*)

Twenty-two acres in Prince's Bay. Small pond. $6,000 . . . That's cheap. I'd take a look at it if I had any money . . .

What kind of seeds are they?

TILLIE: Marigolds. *They've been exposed to cobalt-60.*

BEATRICE: If there's one thing I've always wanted, it's been a living room planted with marigolds that have been exposed to cobalt-60. While you're at it, why don't you throw in a tomato patch in the bathroom?

TILLIE: Just let me keep them here for a week or so until they get started and then I'll transplant them to the backyard.

BEATRICE (*reading again*): Four-family house. Six and a half and six and a half over five and five. Eight garages. I could really do something with that. A nursing home . . .

Don't think I'm not kicking myself that I didn't finish that real estate course. I should have finished beauty school, too . . .

God, what I could do with eight garages . . .

(*There is a sound from beyond the curtained doorway.* BEATRICE *gestures in that direction.*)

You know, I'm thinking of getting rid of *that* and making this place into something.

TILLIE: Yes.

BEATRICE: I've been thinking about a tea shop. Have you noticed there aren't many of them around anymore?

TILLIE: Yes.

BEATRICE: And this is just the type of neighborhood where a good tea shop could make a go of it. We'd have a good cheesecake. You've got to have a good cheesecake . . .

(*She calculates.*)

Eight times ten — well, eight times eight, if they're falling down — that's sixty-four dollars a month from the garages alone . . . I swear money makes money.

(*There is a rustling at the curtains. Two thin and wrinkled hands push the curtains apart slowly and then the ancient face of* NANNY *appears. She negotiates her way through the curtains. She is utterly wrinkled and dried, perhaps a century old. Time has left her with*

a whisper of a smile — a smile from a soul half-departed. If one looked closely, great cataracts could be seen on each eye, and it is certain that all that can pierce her soundless prison are mere shadows from the outside world. She pervades the room with age.

NANNY *supports herself by a four-legged tubular frame which she pushes along in front of her with a shuffling motion that reminds one of a ticking clock. Inch by inch she advances into the room.* TILLIE *and* BEATRICE *continue speaking, knowing that it will be minutes before she is close enough to know they are there.*)

BEATRICE: What is cobalt-60?

TILLIE: It's something that causes . . . changes in seeds. Oh, Mother — he set the cloud chamber up just for me and he told me about radioactivity and half-life and he got the seeds for me.

BEATRICE (*her attention still on the newspaper*): What does half-life mean?

(NANNY *is well into the room as* TILLIE *replies.*)

TILLIE (*reciting from memory*): The half-life of Polonium-210 is one hundred and forty days.

The half-life of Radium-226 is one thousand five hundred and ninety years.

The half-life of Uranium-238 is four and one-half billion years.

BEATRICE (*putting away her newspaper*): Do you know you're giving me a headache?

(*Then, in a loud, horribly saccharine voice, she speaks to* NANNY *as if she were addressing a deaf year-old child.*)

LOOK WHO'S THERE! IT'S NANNY! NANNY CAME ALL THE WAY OUT HERE BY HERSELF!

I'm going to need a cigarette for this.

NANNY! YOU COME SIT DOWN AND WE'LL BE RIGHT WITH HER!

You know, sometimes I've got to laugh. I've got *this* on my hands and all you're worried about is planting marigolds.

I'VE GOT HOTSY WATER FOR YOU, NANNY. WOULD YOU LIKE SOME HOTSY WATER AND HONEY?

(NANNY *has seated herself at a table, smiling but oblivious to her environment.*)

I've never seen it to fail. Every time I decide to

have a cup of coffee I see that face at the curtains. I wonder what she'd do . . .

(*She holds pot of boiling water.*)

. . . if I just poured this right over her head. I'll bet she wouldn't even notice it.
NANNY'S GOING TO GET JUST WHAT SHE NEEDS!

(*She fills a cup for her and places a honey jar near her.*)

You know if someone told me when I was young that I'd end up feeding honey to a zombie, I'd tell them they were crazy.
SOMETHING WRONG, NANNY? OH, DID I FORGET NANNY'S SPOON? MERCY! MERCY! I FORGOT NANNY'S SPOON!

(*She gets a spoon and stands behind* NANNY.)

I'll give you a spoon, Nanny, I'll give you a spoon.

(*She makes a motion behind* NANNY'*s back as if she's going to smack her on the head with the spoon.*)

Matilda! Watch me give Nanny her spoon.
A SPOON FOR NANNY!

(*It manages to be slightly funny and* TILLIE *yields to a laugh, along with her mother.*)

Fifty dollars a week. Fifty dollars. I look at you, Nanny, and I wonder if it's worth it. I think I'd be better off driving a cab.
TAKE HONEY, NANNY. HONEY WITH HOTSY WATER!

You should have seen her daughter bring her here last week . . . I could have used you that day . . . She came in pretending she was Miss Career Woman of the Year. She said she was in real estate and *such a busy little woman,* such a busy little woman — she just couldn't give all the love and care and affection her little momsy needed anymore . . .

(*Then, with a great smile, she speaks right into* NANNY'*s uncomprehending face.*)

Nanny's quite a little cross to bear, now aren't you, Nanny dear? But you're a little better than Mr. Mayo was — with the tumor on his brain — or Miss Marion Minto with her cancer, or Mr. Brougham . . . what was his first name?
TILLIE: Alexander.

BEATRICE: Mr. Alexander Brougham with the worms in his legs.
WHY, NANNY'S QUITE SOME LITTLE GIRL, AREN'T YOU, NANNY? A GIRL DRINKING HER HOTSY AND HONEY! . . .
Cobalt-60. Ha! You take me for a fool, don't you?
TILLIE: No, Mother.
BEATRICE: Science, science, science! Don't they teach our misfits anything anymore? Anything decent and meaningful and sensitive? Do you know what I'd be now if it wasn't for this mud pool I got sucked into? I'd probably be a dancer. Miss Betty Frank, The Best Dancer of the Class of 19 . . . something. One minute I'm the best dancer in school — smart as a whip — the head of the whole crowd! And the next minute . . .
One mistake. That's how it starts. Marry the wrong man and before you know it he's got you tied down with two stones around your neck for the rest of your life.
When I was in that lousy high school I was one of the most respected kids you ever saw.
I used to wonder why people always said, "Why, just yesterday . . . why, just yesterday . . . why, just yesterday."
Before I knew what happened I lost my dancing legs and got varicose legs. Beautiful varicose legs. Do you know, everything I ever thought I'd be has exploded!
NANNY, YOU HURRY UP WITH THAT HONEY!
Exploded! You know, I almost forgot about everything I was supposed to be . . .
NANNY'S ALMOST FINISHED. ISN'T THAT WONDERFUL?
She's almost finished, all right.
NANNY'S DAUGHTER IS COMING TO SEE YOU SOON. WILL THAT MAKE NANNY HAPPY?
The day Miss Career Woman of the Year comes to visit again I think I'll drop dead. Nobody's too busy for anything they want to do, don't you tell me. What kind of an idiot do people take me for?
NANNY, YOU'RE SPILLING YOUR HOTSY! JESUS CHRIST!
You know, I ought to kick you right out and open that tea shop tomorrow.
Oh, it's coming. I can feel it. And the first thing I'll do is get rid of that rabbit.
TILLIE (*hardly listening*): Yes, Mother.

BEATRICE: You think I'm kidding?
TILLIE: No, I don't.
BEATRICE: You bet I'm not!

(*She rummages through some drawers in a chest.*)

I was going to do this a month ago.

(*She holds up a small bottle.*)

Here it is. Here's a new word for you.

(*She reads.*)

Trichloro . . . methane. Do you know what this is, Matilda? Well, it's chloroform!

(*She puts the bottle away.*)

I'm saving it for that Angora manure machine of yours. Speaking of manure machines, IS NANNY READY TO GO MAKE DUTY?

(*She starts helping* NANNY *out of the chair and props her up with the tubular frame.*)

NANNY IS ALWAYS READY FOR DUTY, AREN'T YOU NANNY? BECAUSE NAN-NY'S A GOODY-GOODY GIRL AND GOODY-GOODY GIRLS ALWAYS GET GOODY-GOODY THINGS. GOD LOOKS OUT FOR GOODY-GOODY GIRLS AND GIVES THEM HOTSY AND HONEY — RIGHT, NANNY?

(BEATRICE *sits down in the hall and watches* NANNY *make her way toward the bathroom. There is a pause as the woman's shuffling continues.*
    The lights go low on TILLIE, NANNY *becomes a silhouette, and the light remains on* BEATRICE. *She starts to read the paper again, but the shuffling gets on her nerves and she flings the paper down.*)

Half-life! If you want to know what a half-life is, just ask me. You're looking at the original half-life!
I got stuck with one daughter with half a mind; another one who's half a test tube; half a husband — a house half full of rabbit crap — and half a corpse!
That's what I call a half-life, Matilda! Me and cobalt-60! Two of the biggest half-*lifes* you ever saw!

(*The set goes to dark.*
    After a few seconds, the sound of some-one dialing a phone can be heard. As the
spot *comes up on her, we see* BEATRICE *holding the phone and struggling to get a cigarette.*)

BEATRICE (*on the phone*): Hello — Mr. Goodman, please . . . How would I know if he's got a class? . . . Hello, Mr. Goodman? Are you Mr. Goodman? . . . Oh, I beg your pardon, Miss Torgersen . . . Yes, I'll wait.

(*She lights her cigarette.*)

Couldn't you find him, Miss Torgersen? . . . Oh! Excuse me, Mr. Goodman. How are you? . . . I'll bet you'll never guess who this is — it's Mrs. Hunsdorfer — remember the frozen foods?

(*She laughs.*)

You know, Ruth told me she's your new secre-tary and I certainly think that's a delight. You were paying so much attention to Matilda that I'll bet Ruth just got jealous. She does things like that, you know. I hope she works hard for you, although I can't imagine what kind of work Ruth could be doing in that great big sci-ence office. She's a terrible snoop . . .

(*She takes a puff.*)

Your attendance? Isn't that charming. And the *cut* cards! Imagine. You trust her with . . . why, I didn't know she could type *at all* . . . imagine. Well . . . I'll . . . Of course, *too* much work isn't good for anyone, either. No wonder she's failing everything. I mean, I never knew a girl who failed everything regardless of what they were suffering from. I suppose I should say *recover-ing* from . . .
    Well, it's about the seeds you gave Matilda . . . Well, she's had them in the house for a week now and they're starting to grow. Now, she told me they had been subjected to radioactivity, and I hear such terrible things about radioactivity that I automatically associ-ate radioactivity with sterility, and it positively horrifies me to have those seeds right here in my living room. Couldn't she just grow plain marigolds like everyone else?

(*She takes a puff.*)

Oh . . .

(*Another big puff, forming a mushroom cloud.*)

It does sound like an interesting project, but . . .

(*The biggest puff yet.*)

No, I must admit that at this very moment I don't know what a *mutation* is . . .

(*She laughs uncomfortably.*)

Mr. Goodman . . . Mr. Goodman! I don't want you to think I'm not interested, but please spare me definitions over the phone. I'll go to the library next week and pick me out some little book on science and then I'll know all about mutations . . . No, you didn't insult me, but I just want you to know that I'm not *stupid* . . .

I just thought prevention was better than a tragedy, Mr. Goodman. I mean, Matilda has enough problems to worry about without *sterility* . . .

Well, I was just concerned, but you've put my poor mother's heart at ease. You know, really, our schools need more exciting young men like you, I really mean that. Really. Oh, I do. Goodbye, Mr. Goodman.

(*By the end of her talk on the phone, her face is left in a spotlight, and then the stage goes black. The music theme comes in, in a minor key, softly at first, but accentuated by increasingly loud pulses which transmute into thunder crashes.*

There is a scream heard from upstairs and we see the set in night shadows.

TILLIE *tears open her bedroom door and rushes into* BEATRICE'S *room.* RUTH *screams again.*)

TILLIE: Mother! She's going to have one!

(RUTH *appears on the landing and releases another scream which breaks off into gasps. She starts down the stairs and stops halfway to scream again. There is another tremendous thunder crash as* BEATRICE *comes out of her room, puts on the hall light, and catches the hysterical girl on the stairs.*)

BEATRICE (*shouting*): Stop it! Stop it, Ruth!
TILLIE (*at the top of the stairs*): She's going!
BEATRICE: Ruth! Stop it!
TILLIE: She's going to go!
BEATRICE (*Yelling at* TILLIE): Shut up and get back in your room!

(RUTH *screams.*)

You're not going to let yourself go, do you hear me, Ruth? You're not going to go!
RUTH: He's after me!

(*She screams, lightning and thunder crash follow.*)

BEATRICE: You were dreaming, do you hear me? Nobody's after you! Nobody!
TILLIE: I saw her eyes start to go back —
BEATRICE (*to* TILLIE): Get back in your room!

(*She helps* RUTH *down the rest of the stairs.*)

There, now, nobody's after you. Nice and easy. Breathe deeply . . . Did the big bad man come after my little girl?

(*She sits* RUTH *down and then puts both hands up to her own face and pulls her features into a comic mask.* RUTH *begins to laugh at her.*)

That big bad bogey man?

(*They both laugh heartily.*)

Now that wasn't so bad, was it?
RUTH: It was the dream, with Mr. Mayo again.
BEATRICE: Oh. Well, we'll just get you a little hot milk and —

(*A tremendous thunder crash throws the set into shadows.*)

Why, the electricity's gone off. Do you remember what happened to those candles?
RUTH: What candles?
BEATRICE: The little white ones from my birthday cake last year.
RUTH: Tillie melted them down for school a long time ago.
BEATRICE (*searching through drawers*): She had no right doing that.
RUTH: She asked you. She used them to attach a paper straw to a milk bottle with a balloon over it, and it was supposed to tell if it was going to rain.
BEATRICE (*finding a flashlight*): There! It works. I don't want her wasting anything of mine unless she's positive I won't need it. You always need candles.

(*She steers* RUTH *toward the couch as lightning flashes.*)

Why, Ruth — your skin just turned ice cold!

(*She rummages through one of the boxes and grabs a blanket.*)

This will warm you up . . . What's the matter?

RUTH: The flashlight —

BEATRICE: What's wrong with it?

RUTH: It's the same one I used to check on Mr. Mayo with.

BEATRICE: So it is. We don't need it.

RUTH: No, let me keep it.

(*Starting to laugh.*)

Do you want to know how they have it in the history?

BEATRICE: No, I don't.

RUTH: Well, they say I came out of my room . . .

(*She flashes the light on her room.*)

. . . And I started down the stairs, step by step . . . and I heard the choking and banging on the bed, and . . .

BEATRICE: I'm going back to bed.

RUTH: No!

BEATRICE: Well, talk about something nice, then.

RUTH: Oh, Mama, tell me about the wagon.

BEATRICE: You change so fast I can't keep up with you.

RUTH: Mama, *please* . . . the story about the wagon.

BEATRICE: I don't know anything about telling stories. Get those great big smart teachers of yours to do that sort of stuff.

RUTH: Tell me about the horses again, and how you stole the wagon.

BEATRICE: Don't get me started on that.

RUTH: Mama, *please* . . .

BEATRICE (*taking out a pack of cigarettes*): Do you want a cigarette?

RUTH (*taking one*): Leave out the part where they shoot the horses, though.

(*They both light up.*)

BEATRICE: Honey, you know the whole story —

RUTH: "Apples! Pears! *Cu* . . . cumbers!"

BEATRICE: No. It's "Apples! Pears! *Cucum* . . . bers!"

(*They say it together.*)

"Apples! Pears! Cu*cum* . . . bers!"

(*And they laugh.*)

RUTH: How did you get the wagon out without him seeing you?

BEATRICE: That was easy. Every time he got

home for the day he'd make us both some sandwiches — my mama had been dead for years — and he'd take a nap on the old sofa that used to be . . . there!

(*She points to a corner of the room.*)

And while he was sleeping I got the horses hitched up and went riding around the block waving to everyone.

RUTH: Oh, Mama, you didn't!

BEATRICE: Of course I did. I had more nerve than a bear when I was a kid. Let me tell you it takes nerve to sit up on that wagon every day yelling "Apples! . . .

(*Both together.*)

Pears! Cu*cum* . . . bers!"

(*They laugh again.*)

RUTH: Did he find out you took the wagon?

BEATRICE: Did he find out? He came running down the street after me and started spanking me right on top of the wagon — not hard — but it was so embarrassing — and I had one of those penny marshmallow ships in the back pocket of my overalls, and it got all squished. And you better believe I never did it again . . .

You would have loved him, Ruth, and gone out with him on the wagon . . . all over Stapleton yelling as loud as you wanted.

RUTH: "Apples! Pears! *Cu* . . . cumbers!"

BEATRICE: No!

RUTH: "Cu*cum* . . . bers!"

BEATRICE: My father made up for all the other men in this whole world, Ruth. If only you two could have met. He'd only be about seventy now, do you realize that? And I'll bet he'd still be selling vegetables around town. All that fun — and then I don't think I ever knew what really hit me.

RUTH: Don't tell about —

BEATRICE: Don't worry about the horses.

RUTH: What hit you?

BEATRICE: Well it was just me and Papa . . . and your father hanging around. And then Papa got sick . . . and I drove with him up to the sanatorium. And then I came home and there were the horses —

RUTH: Mother!

BEATRICE: And I had the horses . . . taken care of. And then Papa got terribly sick and he begged me to marry so that he'd be sure I'd be taken care of.

(She laughs.)

If he knew how I was taken care of he'd turn over in his grave.

And *nightmares!* Do you want to know the nightmare I used to have?

I never had nightmares over the fights with your father, or the divorce, or his thrombosis — he deserved it — I never had nightmares over any of that.

Let me tell you about my nightmare that used to come back and back:

Well, I'm on Papa's wagon, but it's newer and shinier, and it's being pulled by beautiful white horses, not dirty workhorses — these are like circus horses with long manes and tinsel — and the wagon is blue, shiny blue. And it's full — filled with yellow apples and grapes and green squash.

You're going to laugh when you hear this. I'm wearing a lovely gown with jewels all over it, and my hair is piled up on top of my head with a long feather in it, and the bells are ringing.

Huge bells swinging on a gold braid strung across the back of the wagon, and they're going DONG, DONG . . . DONG, DONG. And I'm yelling "APPLES! PEARS! CUCUM . . . BERS!"

RUTH: That doesn't sound like a nightmare to me.

BEATRICE: And then I turn down our street and all the noise stops. This long street, with all the doors of the houses shut and everything crowded next to each other, and there's not a soul around. And then I start getting afraid that the vegetables are going to spoil . . . and that nobody's going to buy anything, and I feel as though I shouldn't be on the wagon, and I keep trying to call out.

But there isn't a sound. Not a single sound. Then I turn my head and look at the house across the street. I see an upstairs window, and a pair of hands pull the curtains slowly apart. I see the face of my father and my heart stands still . . .

Ruth . . . take the light out of my eyes.

(A long pause.)

RUTH: Is Nanny going to die here?
BEATRICE: No.
RUTH: How can you be sure?
BEATRICE: I can tell.
RUTH: Are you crying?

BEATRICE: What's left for me, Ruth?
RUTH: What, Mama?
BEATRICE: What's left for me?

(The stage goes slowly to dark as the drizzling rain becomes louder and then disappears.

When the lights come up again NANNY is seated at the kitchen table with a bottle of beer and a glass in front of her. TILLIE comes in the front door with a box of large marigold plants and sets them down where they'll be inconspicuous. She gets the rabbit out of its cage, sits down near NANNY and gives her a little wave. BEATRICE suddenly appears at the top of the stairs and drops a stack of newspapers with a loud thud. She goes back into her room and lets fly another armful of junk.)

TILLIE: What are you doing?
BEATRICE: A little housecleaning, and you're going to help. You can start by getting rid of that rabbit or I'll suffocate the bastard.

(She takes a drink from a glass of whiskey.)

You don't think I will, do you? You wait and see. Where's Ruth? She's probably running around the schoolyard in her brassiere.

(She comes downstairs.)

TILLIE: Mother, they want me to do something at school.
BEATRICE: NANNY! DID YOU HEAR THAT? THEY WANT HER TO DO SOMETHING AT SCHOOL! ISN'T THAT MOMENTOUS, NANNY?

Well I want you to do something around here. Like get rid of that bunny. I'm being generous! I'll let you give it away. Far away. Give it to Mr. Goodman. I'd chloroform the thing myself, but that crazy sister of yours would throw convulsions for fifty years . . . and I hate a house that vibrates.

And get rid of those sterile marigolds. They stink!

HI, NANNY—HOW ARE YOU, HONEY? HOW WOULD YOU LIKE TO GO ON A LONG TRIP?

You see, everybody, I spent today taking stock of my life and I've come up with zero. I added up all the separate departments and the total reads zero . . .

zero zero zero zero zero zero zero
zero zero zero zero zero

zero zero zero
zero zero
zero

. . . And do you know how you pronounce that, with all your grammatical schoolin' and foolin'? You pronounce it o,o,o,o,O,O,O,O,O, O! o,o,o,o,O,O,O,O,O,O,O,O!

Right, Nanny? RIGHT, NANNY?

So, by the end of the week, you get rid of that cottontail compost heap and we'll get you a job down at the five-and-ten-cent store. And if you don't do so well with the public, we'll fix you up with some kind of machine. Wouldn't that be nice?

(RUTH *enters at a gallop, throwing her books down and babbling a mile a minute.*)

RUTH (*enthusiastically*): Can you believe it? I didn't, until Chris Burns came up and told me about it in Geography, and then Mr. Goodman told me himself during the eighth period in the office when I was eavesdropping. Aren't you so happy you could bust? Tillie? I'm so proud I can't believe it, Mama. Everybody was talking about it and nobody . . . well, it was the first time they all came up screaming about her and I said, "Yes, she's my sister!" I said it, "She's my sister! My sister! My *sister!*" Give me a cigarette.

BEATRICE: Get your hands off my personal property.

RUTH: I'll scratch your back later.

BEATRICE: I don't want you to touch me!

RUTH: Did he call yet? My God, I can't believe it, I just can't!

BEATRICE: Did who call yet?

RUTH: I'm not supposed to tell you, as Mr. Goodman's private secretary, but you're going to get a call from school.

BEATRICE (*to* TILLIE): What is she talking about?

TILLIE: I was in the Science Fair at school.

RUTH: Didn't she tell you yet? Oh, Tillie, how could you? She's fantastic, Mama! She's a finalist in the Science Fair. There were only five of them out of hundreds and hundreds. She won with all those plants over there. They're freaks! Isn't that a scream? Dr. Berg picked her himself. The principal! And I heard Mr. Goodman say she was going to be another Madam Pasteur and he never saw a girl do anything like that before and . . . so I told everybody, "Yes, she's my sister!" Tillie, "You're my sister!" I

said. And Mr. Goodman called the Advance and they're coming to take your picture. Oh, Mama, isn't it crazy? And nobody laughed at her, Mama. She beat out practically everybody and nobody laughed at her. "She's my sister," I said. "She's my sister!"

(*The telephone rings.*)

That must be him! Mama, answer it — I'm afraid.

(*Ring.*)

Answer it before he hangs up!

(*Ring.*)

Mama! He's gonna hang up!

(RUTH *grabs the phone.*)

Hello? . . . Yes . . .

(*Aside to* BEATRICE.)

It's him! . . . Just a minute, please . . .

(*Covering the mouthpiece.*)

He wants to talk to you.
BEATRICE: Who?
RUTH: The *principal*!
BEATRICE: Hang up.
RUTH: I told him you were here! Mama!

(BEATRICE *gets up and shuffles slowly to the phone.*)

BEATRICE (*finally, into the phone*): Yes? . . . I know who you are, Dr. Berg . . . I see . . . Couldn't you get someone else? There's an awfully lot of work that has to be done around here, because she's not as careful with her home duties as she is with man-in-the-moon marigolds . . .

Me? What would you want with me up on the stage? . . . The other mothers can do as they please . . . I would have thought you had enough in your *history* without . . . I'll think about it . . . Goodbye, Dr. Berg . . .

(*Pause, then screaming.*)

I SAID I'D THINK ABOUT IT!

(*She hangs up the phone, turns her face slowly to* RUTH, *then to* TILLIE, *who has her face hidden in shame in the rabbit's fur.*)

RUTH: What did he say?
BEATRICE (*flinging her glass on the floor*):

How could you do this to me? HOW COULD YOU LET THAT MAN CALL OUR HOME!

I have no clothes, do you hear me? I'd look just like you up on the stage, ugly little you!

DO YOU WANT THEM TO LAUGH AT US? LAUGH AT THE TWO OF US?

RUTH (*disbelievingly*): Mother . . . aren't you proud of her? Mother . . . it's an *honor*.

(TILLIE *breaks into tears and moves away from* BEATRICE. *It seems as though she is crushed, but then she halts and turns to face her mother.*)

TILLIE (*through tears*): But . . . nobody laughed at me.

(BEATRICE'*s face begins to soften as she glimpses what she's done to* TILLIE.)

BEATRICE: Oh, my God . . .

(TILLIE *starts toward her.* BEATRICE *opens her arms to receive her as music starts in and lights fade. A chord of finality punctuates the end of Act I.*)

ACT II

About two weeks later.

The room looks somewhat cheery and there is excitement in the air. It is early evening and preparations are being made for TILLIE *to take her project to the final judging of the Science Fair.*

TILLIE *has been dressed by her mother in clothes which are clean but too girlish for her awkwardness. Her hair has been curled, she sports a large bow, and her dress is a starched flair.*

RUTH *has dressed herself up as well. She has put on too much makeup, and her lipstick has been extended beyond the natural line of her lips. She almost appears to be sinister.*

A large three-panel screen stands on one of the tables. THE EFFECT OF GAMMA RAYS ON MAN-IN-THE-MOON MARIGOLDS is printed in large letters running across the top of the three panels. Below this on each panel there is a subtopic: THE PAST; THE PRESENT; THE FUTURE. *Additional charts and data appear below the titles.*

RUTH: The only competition you have to worry about is Janice Vickery. They say she caught it near Princess Bay Boulevard and it was still alive when she took the skin off it.

TILLIE (*taking some plants from* RUTH): Let me do that, please, Ruth.

RUTH: I'm sorry I touched them, really.

TILLIE: Why don't you feed Peter?

RUTH: Because I don't feel like feeding him . . . Now I feel like feeding him.

(*She gets some lettuce from a bag.*)

I heard that it screamed for three minutes after she put it in because the water wasn't boiling yet. How much talent does it take to boil the skin off a cat and then stick the bones together again? That's what I want to know. Ugh. I had a dream about that, too. I figure she did it in less than a day and she ends up as one of the top five winners . . . and you spend months growing atomic flowers.

TILLIE: Don't you think you should finish getting ready?

RUTH: Finish? This is it!

TILLIE: Are you going to wear that sweater?

RUTH: Look, don't worry about me. I'm not getting up on any stage, and if I did I wouldn't be caught dead with a horrible bow like that.

TILLIE: Mother put it —

RUTH: They're going to laugh you off the stage again like when you cranked that atom in assembly . . . I didn't mean that . . . The one they're going to laugh at is Mama.

TILLIE: What?

RUTH: I said the one they're going to laugh at is Mama . . . Oh, let me take that bow off.

TILLIE: It's all right.

RUTH: Look, just sit still. I don't want everybody making fun of you.

TILLIE: What made you say that about Mama?

RUTH: Oh, I heard them talking in the Science Office yesterday. Mr. Goodman and Miss Hanley. She's getting $12.63 to chaperon the thing tonight.

TILLIE: What were they saying?

RUTH: Miss Hanley was telling Mr. Goodman about Mama . . . when she found out you were one of the five winners. And he wanted to know if there was something wrong with Mama because she sounded crazy over the phone. And Miss Hanley said she *was* crazy and she always has been crazy and she can't wait to see what she looks like after all these years. Miss Hanley said her nickname used to be *Betty the Loon*.

TILLIE (*as* RUTH *combs her hair*): Ruth, you're hurting me.

RUTH: She was just like you and everybody thought she was a big weirdo. There! You look much better!

(*She goes back to the rabbit.*)

Peter, if anybody stuck you in a pot of boiling water I'd kill them, do you know that? . . .

(*Then to* TILLIE.)

What do they call boiling the skin off a cat? I call it murder, that's what I call it. They say it was hit by a car and Janice just scooped it up and before you could say *bingo* it was screaming in a pot of boiling water . . .

Do you know what they're all waiting to see? Mama's feathers! That's what Miss Hanley said. She said Mama blabs as though she was the Queen of England and just as proper as can be, and that her idea of getting dressed up is to put on all the feathers in the world and go as a bird. Always trying to get somewhere, like a great big bird.

TILLIE: Don't tell Mama, please. It doesn't matter.

RUTH: I was up there watching her getting dressed and sure enough, she's got the feathers out.

TILLIE: You didn't tell her what Miss Hanley said?

RUTH: Are you kidding? I just told her I didn't like the feathers and I didn't think she should wear any. But I'll bet she doesn't listen to me.

TILLIE: It doesn't matter.

RUTH: It doesn't matter? Do you think I want to be laughed right out of the school tonight, with Chris Burns there, and all? Laughed right out of the school, with your electric hair and her feathers on that stage, and Miss Hanley splitting her sides?

TILLIE: Promise me you won't say anything.

RUTH: On one condition.

TILLIE: What?

RUTH: Give Peter to me.

TILLIE (*ignoring her*): The taxi will be here any minute and I won't have all this stuff ready. Did you see my speech?

RUTH: I mean it. Give Peter to me.

TILLIE: He belongs to all of us.

RUTH: For me. All for me. What do you care? He doesn't mean anything to you anymore, now that you've got all those crazy plants.

TILLIE: Will you stop?

RUTH: If you don't give him to me I'm going to tell Mama that everybody's waiting to laugh at her.

TILLIE: Where are those typewritten cards?

RUTH: I MEAN IT! Give him to me!

TILLIE: Does he mean that much to you?

RUTH: Yes!

TILLIE: All right.

RUTH (*after a burst of private laughter*): Betty the Loon . . .

(*She laughs again.*)

That's what they used to call her, you know. Betty the Loon!

TILLIE: I don't think that's very nice.

RUTH: First they had Betty the Loon, and now they've got Tillie the Loon . . .

(*To rabbit.*)

You don't have to worry about me turning you in for any old plants . . .

How much does a taxi cost from here to the school?

TILLIE: Not much.

RUTH: I wish she'd give me the money it costs for a taxi — and for all that cardboard and paint and flowerpots and stuff. The only time she ever made a fuss over me was when she drove me nuts.

TILLIE: Tell her to hurry, please.

RUTH: By the way, I went over to see Janice Vickery's pot, that she did you know what in, and I started telling her and her mother about the worms in Mr. Alexander Brougham's legs, and I got thrown out because it was too near dinner time. That Mrs. Vickery kills me. She can't stand worms in somebody else's legs but she lets her daughter cook a cat.

TILLIE (*calling upstairs*): Mother! The taxi will be here any minute.

(BEATRICE *comes to the top of the stairs. Her costume is strange, but not that strange, by any means. She is even a little attractive tonight, and though her words say she is greatly annoyed with having to attend the night's function, her tone and direction show she is very, very proud.*)

BEATRICE: You're lucky I'm coming, without all this rushing me.

TILLIE: Mama, you look beautiful.

BEATRICE: Don't put it on too thick. I said I'd go and I guess there's no way to get out of it. Do you mind telling me how I'm supposed to get up on the stage? Do they call my name or what? And where are you going to be? If you ask me, they should've sent all the parents a mimeographed sheet of instructions. If this is supposed to be such a great event, why don't they do it right?

TILLIE: You just sit on the stage with the other parents before it begins.

BEATRICE: How long is this thing going to last? And remember, I don't care even if you do win the whole damn thing, I'm not making any speech. I can hold my own anywhere, but I hated that school when I went there and I hate it now . . . and the only thing I'd have to say is, what a pack of stupid teachers and vicious children they have. Imagine someone tearing the skin off a cat.

RUTH: She didn't tear it. She boiled it off.

BEATRICE: You just told me upstairs that girl tore the skin off with an orange knife and . . . do you know, sometimes you exasperate me?

(*To* TILLIE.)

If you've got all the plants in this box, I can manage the folding thing. Do you know I've got a headache from doing those titles? And you probably don't even like them.

TILLIE: I like them very much.

BEATRICE: Look, if you don't want me to go tonight, I don't have to. You're about as enthusiastic as a dummy about this whole thing.

TILLIE: I'm sorry.

BEATRICE: And I refuse to let you get nervous. Put that bow back in your hair.

RUTH: I took it out.

BEATRICE: What did you do that for?

RUTH (*taking the rabbit in her arms*): Because it made her look crazy.

BEATRICE: How would you know what's crazy or not? If that sweater of yours was any tighter it'd cut off the circulation in your chest.

(*Fussing over* TILLIE.)

The bow looks very nice in your hair. There's nothing wrong with looking proper, Matilda, and if you don't have enough money to look expensive and perfect, people like you for *trying* to look nice. You know, one day maybe you will be pretty. You'll have some nice features, when that hair revives and you do some tricks with makeup. I hope you didn't crowd the plants too close together. Did you find your speech?

TILLIE: Yes, Mother.

BEATRICE: You know, Matilda, I was wondering about something. Do you think you're really going to win? I mean, not that you won't be the best, but there's so much politics in school. Don't laugh, but if there's anyone who's an expert on that, it's me, and someday I'm going to write a book and blast that school to pieces. If you're just a little bit different in this world, they try to kill you off.

RUTH (*putting on her coat*): Tillie gave Peter to me.

BEATRICE: Oh? Then you inherited the rabbit droppings I found upstairs. What are you doing with your coat on?

RUTH: I'm going out to wait for the taxi.

BEATRICE: Oh, no you're not. You start right in on the rabbit droppings. Or you won't get another cigarette even if you scratch my back with an orange knife.

RUTH: I'm going down to the school with you.

BEATRICE: Oh, no you're not! You're going to keep company with that corpse in there. If she wakes up and starts gagging just slip her a shot of whiskey.

(*The taxi horn blows outside.*)

Quick! Grab the plants, Matilda —I'll get the big thing.

RUTH: I want to go! I promised Chris Burns I'd meet him.

BEATRICE: Can't you understand English?

RUTH: I've got to go!

BEATRICE: Shut up!

RUTH (*almost berserk*): I don't care. I'M GOING ANYWAY!

BEATRICE (*shoving* RUTH *hard*): WHAT DID YOU SAY?

TILLIE: Mother!

(*After a pause, the horn blows again.*)

BEATRICE: Hurry up with that box, Matilda, and tell him to stop blowing the horn. HURRY UP!

(TILLIE *reluctantly exits with the box of plants.*)

I don't know where you ever got the idea you were going tonight. Did you think nobody was going to hold down the fort? ...

Now you know how I felt all those years you and everybody else was running out whenever they felt like it — because there was always me to watch over the fifty-dollar-a-week corpse. If there's one thing I demand it's respect. I don't ask for anything from you but respect.

RUTH (*pathetically*): Why are you ashamed of me?

BEATRICE: I've been seen with a lot worse than you. I don't even know why I'm going to-night, do you know that? Do you think I give one goddam about the whole thing? ...

(*She starts to fold the large three-panel screen with the titles:* THE PAST, THE PRESENT, *and* THE FUTURE.

Do you want to know why I'm going? Do you really want to know why this once somebody else has to stick with that dried prune for a few minutes? Because this is the first time in my life I've ever felt just a little bit proud over something. Isn't that silly? Somewhere in the back of this turtle-sized brain of mine I feel just a little *proud*! Jesus Christ! And you begrudge me even that, you little bastard.

(*The taxi horn blows impatiently.*)

RUTH (*in a hard voice*): Hurry up. They're waiting for you ... They're *all* waiting for you.

BEATRICE (*carrying the folded screen so that* THE PAST *is face out in bold black letters*): I hope the paint is dry ... Who's waiting for me?

RUTH: Everybody ... including Miss Hanley. She's been telling all the teachers ... about you ... and they're all waiting.

BEATRICE: You're such a little liar, Ruth, do you know that? When you can't have what you want, you try to ruin it for everybody else.

(*She starts to the door.*)

RUTH: Goodnight, *Betty the Loon.*

(BEATRICE *stops as if she's been stabbed. The taxi horn blows several times as* BEATRICE *puts down the folding screen.*)

BEATRICE (*helplessly*): Take this thing.
RUTH: What for?

BEATRICE: Go with Matilda.
RUTH: I don't want to go now.
BEATRICE (*blasting*): GET OUT OF HERE!

RUTH (*after a long pause*): Now Tillie's going to blame it on me that you're not going — and take the rabbit back.

(*The taxi beeps again, as* RUTH *puts her coat on.*)

I can't help it what people call you.

(*She picks up the screen.*)

I'll tell Tillie you'll be down later, all right? ... Don't answer me. What do I care!

(RUTH *exits.*

BEATRICE *breaks into tears that shudder her body, and the lights go down slowly on her pathetic form. Music in.*

Suddenly a bolt of light strikes an area in the right stage — JANICE VICKERY *is standing in the spotlight holding the skeleton of a cat mounted on a small platform. Her face and voice are smug.*)

JANICE: *The Past:* I got the cat from the A.S.P.C.A. immediately after it had been killed by a high-altitude pressure system. That explains why some of the rib bones are missing, because that method sucks the air out of the animal's lungs and ruptures all cavities. They say it prevents cruelty to animals but I think it's horrible.

(*She laughs.*)

Then I boiled the cat in a sodium hydroxide solution until most of the skin pulled right off, but I had to scrape some of the grizzle off the joints with a knife. You have no idea how difficult it is to get right down to the bones.

(*A little gong sounds.*)

I have to go on to *The Present,* now — but I did want to tell you how long it took me to put the thing together. I mean, as it is now, it's extremely useful for students of anatomy, even with the missing rib bones, and it can be used to show basic anatomical aspects of many, many animals that are in the same family as felines. I suppose that's about the only present uses I can think for it, but it is nice to remember as an accomplishment, and it looks good on college applications to show you did something else in school besides dating.

(*She laughs, and a second gong sounds.*)

The Future: The only future plans I have for Tabby — my little brother asked the A.S.P.C.A. what its name was when he went to pick it up and they said it was called Tabby, but I think they were kidding him —

(*She laughs again.*)

I mean as far as future plans, I'm going to donate it to the science department, of course, and next year, if there's another Science Fair perhaps I'll do the same thing with a dog.

(*A third gong sounds.*)

Thank you very much for your attention, and I hope I win!

(JANICE *and her spotlight disappear as suddenly as they had arrived, and music returns as the lights come up slowly on* BEATRICE.

She has obviously been drinking and is going through a phone book. Finding her number, she goes to the phone and dials.)

BEATRICE (*into the phone*): I want to talk to the principal, please . . .
Well, you'll have to get him down off the stage . . .
It's none of your goddam business who I am! . . .
Oh, I see . . . Yes. I have a message for him and Mr. Goodman, and you, too . . . And this is for Miss Hanley, too . . .
Tell them Mrs. Hunsdorfer called to thank them for making her wish she was dead . . . Would you give them that message, please? . . . Thank you very much.

(*She hangs up the phone, pauses, then surveys the room. Her attention fixes on the store window covered with newspapers. The phone rings several times but she ignores it. She goes to the window and proceeds to rip the paper from it. That finished, she turns and surveys the room again. She goes to the kitchen table and rearranges its position. She spies a card table with school supplies and hurls them on the floor. Next, she goes to a bureau and rummages through drawers, finding tablecloths and napkins. She throws cloths on two or three tables and is heading*

toward the kitchen table when the phone rings again. The ringing triggers off something else she wants to do. She empties a cup filled with scraps of paper and finds a telephone number. She lifts the receiver off the ringing phone and hangs up immediately. She lifts the receiver again, checks to make sure there's a dial tone, and then dials the number on the scrap of paper.)

BEATRICE (*into the phone*): Hello. This is Mrs. Hunsdorfer . . . I'm sorry if I frightened you, I wouldn't want you to think Nanny had deceased or anything like that — I can imagine how terrible you'd feel if anything like that ever happened . . . Terrible tragedy that would be, Miss Career Woman of the Year . . .
Yes, I'll tell you why I'm calling. I want her out of here by tomorrow. I told you when you rolled her in here I was going to try her out for a while and if I didn't like her she was to get the hell out. Well I don't like her, so get her the hell out . . .
It's like this. I don't like the way she cheats at solitaire. Is that a good enough reason? . . . Fine. And if she's not out of here by noon I'll send her collect in an ambulance, you son of a bitch!

(*She slams down the phone and bursts into laughter. The laughter subsides somewhat as she pours herself another drink. She takes the drink to a chair and as she sits down her foot accidentally hits the rabbit cage. She gives the cage a little kick and then an idea strikes. She gets up and finds a large blue towel which she flings over her shoulder. She gets the bottle of chloroform and approaches the cage. Having reached a decision she picks up the cage and takes it upstairs.*
Music in and lights fade.
From the darkness a beam of light falls on TILLIE *in the same way* JANICE VICKERY *had been presented.*)

TILLIE (*deathly afraid, and referring to her cards*): *The Past:* The seeds were exposed to various degrees . . . of gamma rays from radiation sources in Oak Ridge . . .
Mr. Goodman helped me pay for the seeds . . . their growth was plotted against . . . time.

(*She loses her voice for a moment and then the first gong sounds.*)

The Present: The seeds which received little radiation have grown to plants which are normal in appearance. The seeds which received moderate radiation gave rise to mutations such as double blooms, giant stems, and variegated leaves. The seeds closest to the gamma source were killed or yielded dwarf plants.

(*The second gong rings.*)

The Future: After radiation is better understood, a day will come when the power from exploding atoms will change the whole world we know.

(*With inspiration.*)

Some of the mutations will be good ones — wonderful things beyond our dreams — and I believe, I believe this with all my heart, THE DAY WILL COME WHEN MANKIND WILL THANK GOD FOR THE STRANGE AND BEAUTIFUL ENERGY FROM THE ATOM.

(*Part of her last speech is reverberated electronically. Deep pulses of music are added as the light focuses on* TILLIE's *face.*
Suddenly there is silence, except for RUTH *picking up* TILLIE's *last words.*
The lights come up on the main set, and the room is empty.
RUTH *bursts in the front door. She is carrying the three-panel card and a shopping bag of plants, both of which she drops on the floor.*)

RUTH: MAMA! MAMA! She won! Mama! Where are you? She won!

(*She runs back to the front door and yells to* TILLIE.)

Hurry up! Hurry! Oh, my God, I can't believe it!

(*Then yelling upstairs.*)

Mama! Come on down! Hurry!

(TILLIE *comes in the front door, carrying the rest of her plants, and the large trophy.* RUTH *takes the trophy.*)

Give me that!

(*She starts upstairs.*)

Mama! Wait till you see this!

(BEATRICE *appears at the top of the stairs. She has been drinking a great deal, and clings fast to a bunch of old cheap curtains and other material.*)

Mama! She won . . .

(BEATRICE *continues mechanically on down the stairs.*)

Didn't you hear me? Tillie won the whole thing! . . . Mama? . . . What's the matter with you? What did you rip the paper off the windows for?

(BEATRICE *commences tacking up one of the curtains.*)

TILLIE: Mama? Are you going to open a . . . shop?

RUTH: What's the matter? Can't you even answer?

BEATRICE (*to* TILLIE): Hand me some of those tacks.

RUTH (*screaming*): I SAID SHE WON! ARE YOU DEAF?

BEATRICE: Ruth, if you don't shut up I'm going to have you put away.

RUTH: They ought to put *you* away, BETTY THE LOON!

(*There is a long pause.*)

BEATRICE: The rabbit is in your room. I want you to bury it in the morning.

RUTH: If you did anything . . . I'LL KILL YOU!

(*She runs upstairs.*)

TILLIE: Mother, you didn't kill it, did you?

BEATRICE: Nanny goes tomorrow. First thing tomorrow.

(*There is a cry from upstairs.*)

TILLIE: Ruth? Are you all right?

BEATRICE: I don't know what it's going to be. Maybe a tea shop. Maybe not.

(RUTH *appears in the doorway of her room. She is holding the dead rabbit on the blue towel. As she reaches the top of the stairs, she begins to moan deeply.*)

After school you're going to have regular hours. You'll work in the kitchen, you'll learn how to cook, and you're going to earn your keep, just like in any other business.

(TILLIE *starts slowly up the stairs toward* RUTH.)

TILLIE (*with great fear*): Mama . . . I think she's going to go.

(RUTH *commences to tremble.* TILLIE *speaks softly to her.*)

Don't go . . . don't go . . .

(RUTH'*s eyes roll in her head, and the trembling of her body becomes pronounced throbbing. She drops the rabbit with the towel covering it.*)

Help me! Mama! Help me!

BEATRICE: Snap out of it, do you hear me? RUTH, DON'T LET YOURSELF GO!

(*To* TILLIE.)

Help me get her downstairs!

(*By the time the trio reaches the bottom of the stairs,* RUTH *is consumed by a violent convulsion.* BEATRICE *holds her down and pushes* TILLIE *out of the way.*)

BEATRICE (*screaming*): Get the wooden spoon!

(TILLIE *responds as* BEATRICE *gets* RUTH *onto a sofa. The convulsion runs its course of a full minute, then finally subsides.* TILLIE *gets a blanket and covers* RUTH.)

TILLIE: Shall I call the doctor?

(*There is a long pause.*)

Shall I call the doctor?

BEATRICE: No. She'll be all right.

TILLIE: I think we should call him.

BEATRICE: I DIDN'T ASK YOU WHAT YOU THOUGHT! . . . We're going to need every penny to get this place open.

(BEATRICE *spreads a tablecloth on one of the tables and places a pile of old cloth napkins on it. She sits down and lights a cigarette.*)

TILLIE (*picking up the rabbit on the stairs*): I'd better bury him in the backyard.

(*She starts out.*)

BEATRICE: Don't bury the towel.

(TILLIE *stops, sobs audibly, then gets control.*)

TILLIE: I'll do it in the morning.

(*She gently lays the rabbit near the door. She tucks* RUTH *in on the couch and sits a few minutes by her sleeping sister.*

Music starts in softly as BEATRICE *continues folding napkins with her back to the others.*

There is the sound of someone at the curtained doorway, and NANNY *commences negotiating herself into the room. Slowly she advances with the tubular frame — unaware, desiccated, in some other land.*)

BEATRICE (*weakly*): Matilda?

TILLIE: Yes, Mama?

BEATRICE: I hate the world. Do you know that, Matilda?

TILLIE: Yes, Mama.

BEATRICE: I hate the world.

(*The lights have started down, the music makes its presence known, and a spot clings to* TILLIE. *She moves to the staircase and the rest of the set goes to black during the following speech. As she starts up the stairs her recorded voice takes over as in the opening of the play.*)

TILLIE'S VOICE: *The Conclusion:* My experiment has shown some of the strange effects radiation can produce . . . and how dangerous it can be if not handled correctly.

Mr. Goodman said I should tell in this conclusion what my future plans are and how this experiment has helped me make them.

For one thing, the effect of gamma rays on man-in-the-moon marigolds has made me curious about the sun and the stars, for the universe itself must be like a world of great atoms — and I want to know more about it.

But most important, I suppose, my experiment has made me feel important — every atom in me, in everybody, has come from the sun — from places beyond our dreams. The atoms of our hands, the atoms of our hearts . . .

(*All sound out.*

TILLIE *speaks the rest live — hopeful, glowing.*)

Atom.

Atom.

What a beautiful word.

THE END

Most plays deal, in one way or another, with families: Oedipus killed his father and married his mother; King Lear disowns one daughter and is tortured by two others; in *As You Like It* brothers are reconciled and young men and women become husbands and wives. To say that most plays deal with families is only, of course, to say that most plays deal with the impact of people on those nearest to them — parents and children, husbands and wives, brothers and sisters, people in love. To this generalization we can add the first paragraph of Tolstoy's *Anna Karenina*: "All happy families resemble one another; every unhappy family is unhappy in its own way." A debatable idea, of course, but one sees what Tolstoy means: when all of the relationships are right, happiness results, but since any one (or more) of the relationships may not be right (the father may be dominant, or weak, or a philanderer; the mother may be a nag, or a mouse, or a nymphomaniac) there are many special kinds of unhappiness.

Many twentieth-century plays about unhappy families are, by virtue of their abundant concern for young children, markedly different from classical plays about families, where such children scarcely exist. Shakespeare, for example, knowing that children should be seen as little as possible and not heard, wrote very few parts for immature children. (Romeo and Juliet are the chief exceptions, and even they are old enough to marry.) By the time adolescents came to be regarded as a fit subject for literature, i.e., for the contemplation of adults, the novel had become the dominant literary form, with its Oliver Twists and Holden Caulfields; but the drama — ever conservative — held back until about the middle of the twentieth century (with the notable exception of Ibsen), keeping traditional themes and plots: in tragedy, the fall of adults, in comedy, the obstacle race to the altar. But around the middle of the twentieth century the drama caught up with modern thinking and, especially in America where children are less likely than in Europe to continue to hold their parents' ideas and to move into their parents' jobs, the drama now at least occasionally is concerned with children, especially with their psychological states and their roles as victims of their elders.

Marigolds, like a number of other American plays, dramatizes a family unit in which an adult (here, the mother) violently impedes the children's achieving of self-fulfillment. The two daughters, Tillie and Ruth, more or less fall into two modern stage types of children, the Sensitive-but-Sane and the Psychotic. The play is fairly typical too in its relative plotlessness (it is basically a-day-in-the-life-of), its cinematic techniques (e.g., a voice against music, fadeouts), and its black comedy (the talk about psoriasis, boiling a cat, Nanny's bowels, and the somewhat entertaining presentation of the destructive demented mother) but it is almost unique in its final rhapsodic vision of a happy atomic world:

> But most important, I suppose, my experiment has made me feel important — every atom in me, in everybody, has come from the sun — from places beyond our dreams. The atoms of our hands, the atoms of our hearts . . .

Atom.

Atom.

What a beautiful word.

There is irony in the fact that Tillie, the girl who has this vision, is daily subjected to assaults by a desperate mother who does all she can to deny the girl's importance, but the speech itself is unironic, and by showing the freedom of Tillie's mind it provides a happy ending to a play that has shown a world of chaos. Somewhat unfashionably, Zindel takes science and the atom not as symbols of man's alienation and death, but as symbols of man's heavenly origin or his link with the sun, and with only a little exaggeration one can say that the play moves from the chaotic living room of the first stage direction, with its litter, through the mother's crazy dreams of an impossible new life as proprietor of a tea shop, to the uncorrupted daughter's joyful vision of a richly exciting world that shares a single life.

Comedy, Tragedy, and Tragicomedy

Cyrus Hoy

Professor Hoy's essay is chiefly not about a particular dramatic form but about a distinctive vision of the disparity between the ideal and the reality. This vision he finds in the profoundest comedies, which he argues are close to tragedies. He further pursues his argument in a book, *The Hyacinth Room*, which includes discussions of playwrights ranging from Euripides to Ionesco.

In one of the later incidents of the *Satyricon* of Petronius, the disreputable poet Eumolpus relates the story of the widow of Ephesus. It is a well-known tale; Jeremy Taylor related it, in his *Holy Dying*, in the mid-seventeenth century; and in our own time, Christopher Fry has made it the subject of a one-act play, A *Phoenix Too Frequent*. Briefly, the story goes like this: A married woman of Ephesus, famed for her virtue, determines, upon the death of her husband, to immure herself in his underground vault and end her life with his, for she finds her loss unendurable. She is accompanied by a devoted maid, and is hailed throughout the city as "the one true and brilliant example of chastity and love." The ladies spend five days in the tomb without food. At this point, the governor of the province orders some robbers to be crucified near the vault where the widow mourns. A soldier is placed on guard, to watch over the crosses, lest anyone take down a body for burial. When, the next night, he sees a light among the tombs, curiosity leads him to discover its source. Finding the lady weeping over the body of the dead man, he correctly surmises her intentions. Bringing his supper into the tomb, he sets about urging the mourner not to persist in useless grief, but she will not be dissuaded. Neither will she accept his offer of food. But the maid is framed of weaker stuff. She partakes of the soldier's food and drink, and thus refreshed,

sets about to assail her mistress's obstinacy ("What will you gain by all this, if you faint away with hunger, if you bury yourself alive, if you breathe out your undoomed soul before Fate calls for it?"). The lady's resolution is broken; she eats; and then, even as she has been persuaded to live, so is she persuaded to love. The soldier is young, handsome, and eloquent; and the maid, again, is helpful, pleading to her mistress to be gracious ("Wilt thou fight love even when love pleases thee?"). So, in Eumolpus's words, the lady and the soldier pass "not only their wedding night together, but the next and a third, of course shutting the door of the vault, so that any friend or stranger who came to the tomb would imagine that this most virtuous lady had breathed her last over her husband's body." But meanwhile, the parents of one of the crucified robbers, noting that the watch is ill-kept, come in the dark and make off with the body of their man. When the soldier discovers the loss, he is distraught; by the laws of Ephesus, his body must be fixed in the place of the stolen corpse. He explains to the lady what has happened, declaring that he will not wait for a court-martial, but will punish his own neglect with his own hand. It is now the lady's turn to urge the arguments against self-slaughter, and in doing so, she shows herself as practical as she was passionate. "Heaven forbid," she cries, "that I should look at the same moment on the dead bodies of two men whom I love. No, I would rather make a dead man useful, than send a live man to death." Whereupon she orders her hus-

Reprinted by permission of the author from the *Virginia Quarterly Review*.

band's body to be taken out of the coffin and fixed up on the empty cross. "The soldier," says Eumolpus in conclusion, "availed himself of this far-seeing woman's device, and the people wondered the next day by what means the dead man had ascended the cross."

The sailors to whom Eumolpus tells this sophisticated tale greet it with a roar of laughter, which is altogether as it should be, for the irony of the reversal on which the story turns derives from the fine display of the incongruity of human intention and human deed which the Ephesian Widow's tergiversations afford; and incongruity is the essence of comedy. The Widow of Ephesus's high-flown intentions end in an all too human surrender, and her tale is but further testimony to the sad truth that, though the spirit be willing, the flesh is weak. Boundless is the will to do good, but the power of performance is sadly limited; the elevated purpose issues but feebly in action; and the generally inadequate standard of human conduct makes a travesty of the ideals that nourish man's illusions about himself and what he can achieve. The discrepancy between the noble intention and the ignoble deed points directly to the most glaring incongruity in the human condition: that which exists between man as he is, and man as he might be, or as he thinks he might be. "Every man," says Conrad in *The Secret Sharer*, "sets up for himself secretly" an "ideal conception of [his] own personality" to which he would be faithful if he could. The extent to which he is able to keep faith with this ideal of self will go far toward determining his personal destiny. But everything must turn, finally, on the nature of the ideal conception. Is it humanly possible to be faithful to it? If so, is it worth the effort? The questions are relevant, because there is always the possibility that the pursuit of the ideal may turn out to be a delusion and a snare. In a world in which man's purposes are infirm, his knowledge imperfect, and his highest endeavors doomed to issue, ultimately, in death, it is safe to say that any effort to keep faith with the ideal is fated to meet with no more than partial success. The spectacle of man seeking, in despite of all the odds, to fulfill an ideal of self, to live up to his own best intentions, may be a deeply moving and ennobling one; but there comes a point at which the pity that we feel for the embattled idealist gives way to amusement at one who steadfastly refuses to recognize the conditions of his all too

human frailty. Tears turn to laughter as the tragic struggle ends in a rather grotesque effort to transcend the limits of mortality. In one sense it is deeply tragic that the Widow of Ephesus is not able to remain faithful to her ideal of virtuous bereavement; and the fact that she is not might be taken as all too symptomatic of the scurvy tricks that life plays on men and women, undermining their most pious intents, thwarting their most earnest desires, making sport generally of their finest gestures in the direction of heroic virtue. This is the great irony of life: that man can envision an ideal of good, can passionately desire to achieve it, and yet fails to live up to it. The failure can occasion either tears or laughter: tears in recognition of the fact that this is the way life is; laughter at the folly of those who fail to recognize that this is the way life is. The protagonists of tragedy and comedy alike are deficient in their knowledge of human limitations, of what they can hope to achieve and what it is the better part of wisdom not to attempt. In a word, they are lacking in self-knowledge. But there is this difference: that while the tragic protagonist's lack of self-knowledge leads to destruction, the comic protagonist's lack of self-knowledge leads instead to a rude awakening in which he is made aware — often cruelly so — of the truth about himself, and is left to live with it — often a fate worse than death. This at least is true of the protagonists of the greatest comedy: plays that probe so deeply into the irony of human fate as to bring them close upon tragedy. By comic protagonists in this sense I have in mind characters such as Jonson's Volpone, Shakespeare's Angelo in *Measure for Measure*, Molière's Alceste in *Le Misanthrope*, Chekhov's Uncle Vanya, Pirandello's Henry IV. Since all these characters are found in plays that are generally regarded as inhabiting the border regions between tragedy and comedy, and since the term "comedy" generally connotes either farce or comedy of manners, it will be best to label such characters "tragicomic," reserving the adjective "comic" for the Widow of Ephesus and her kind.

She is decidedly not tragic. When her noble intentions collapse, and she goes the way of all flesh, we are not moved to pity; we merely shake our heads knowingly. But her failure to fulfill her ideal of virtue, to remain faithful to her particular conception of self, is fraught with tragic potential. This will be clear if we turn to another lady, also possessed of an ideal of virtuous bereavement, and listen as she declares her intention — not, in this case, to immolate herself on her husband's tomb — but never to re-marry upon her husband's death.

> Nor earth to me give food, nor heaven light,
> Sport and repose lock from me day and night,
> To desperation turn my trust and hope,
> An anchor's cheer in prison be my scope,
> Each opposite that blanks the face of joy,
> Meet what I would have well, and it destroy,
> Both here and hence pursue me lasting strife,
> If once a widow ever I be wife.

The speaker here is, of course, the Player Queen in *Hamlet* (III,2,214 ff.), and in the presence of her, we are but one short step from tragedy; for the Player Queen, as everyone knows, is but a thin disguise for the real Queen Gertrude. The Player King responds to his wife's grandiloquence in respectful but guarded tones:

> I do believe you think what now you speak,
> But what we do determine oft we break.
> Purpose is but the slave to memory,
> Of violent birth but poor validity,

and he continues with a succession of epigrammatic couplets, each having reference to the discrepancy between human intention and deed:

> What to ourselves in passion we propose.
> The passion ending, doth the purpose lose.
>
> .   .   .
>
> Our wills and fates do so contrary run,
> That our devices still are overthrown;
> Our thoughts are ours, their ends none of our
>   own. . . .

Gertrude, viewing the scene, declares that "the lady doth protest too much," and her words have the ring of one who knows whereof she speaks. She has heard all this before, having presumably made similar protestations to the dead King Hamlet. Her ideal of self, if she can be truly said ever to have possessed one, has been shattered, and whatever the effect of this on Gertrude herself, it has precipitated the tragedy of her son.

What our argument comes to, then, is this: that in serious drama, comic or tragic, we are confronted with what is, at bottom, a single truth about the human condition. Man is possessed of an ideal of human conduct, but circumstances together with his own inherent failings conspire to make the belief that the ideal can be fulfilled a finally illusory one. But man persists in despite of all the odds, and in his persistence he may appear as nobly enduring, stubbornly unyielding, foolishly blind, or a combination of all three. The more forcibly and apparently these diverse qualities are linked in combination, the more surely sounds the note of tragicomedy.

As an example of the fully developed tragicomic protagonist, there is the figure of the already mentioned Angelo in Shakespeare's *Measure for Measure*. In the context of the play as a whole, Angelo cannot be viewed as the protagonist of *Measure for Measure*; that rôle clearly falls to the Duke Vincentio, and Angelo must be cast in the rôle of antagonist, both to the Duke and to Isabella. But in the context of the drama that goes forth within the soul of Angelo — which is all that I am concerned with here — Angelo, or the part of him which passes in public under this name, is engaged in desperate struggle with his baser self, his private devil. He is well named; and his name gives us the clue to what he aspires to be, which is nothing less than angelic. He would deny his bodily nature, with all that that implies, for in his ideal conception of himself, he sees himself as one beyond the reach of physical desire, as proof against the clamorous demands of human passion. Since the unique quality in the nature of man is precisely his duality, Angelo, in denying the sensual half of his being, is in effect denying his very humanity. In this respect, the comments made about him by the other characters in the play are instructive. The Duke, for instance, makes some penetrating observations on the character of his Deputy in I,3, when he visits the Friar's cell after his supposed departure from Vienna:

> Lord Angelo is precise;
> Stands at a guard with envy; scarce confesses
> That his blood flows; or that his appetite
> Is more to bread than stone: hence shall we
>   see,
> If power change purpose — what our seemers
>   be.
>
> (I,3,50 ff.)

And Lucio, the fantastic, characterizes him in similar terms for the benefit of Isabella in the following scene (I,4) — the only occasion in the play when the usually foul-mouthed courtier and the righteous Duke are in accord:

> Lord Angelo; a man whose blood
> Is very snow-broth; one who never feels
> The wanton stings and motions of the sense;
> But doth rebate and blunt his natural edge
> With profits of the mind, study and fast.
>   (I,4,57 ff.)

But the blood, the very seat of life, which Angelo has sought to deny, will assert itself in the end. "Blood, thou art blood," says Angelo in grim if belated acceptance of a truth he has sought long to ignore; and with that, the struggle that has been waged within him ends in the capitulation of his ideal self to his basest instincts. The angel and the devil have fought, and the devil has won. "Let's write 'good Angel' on the devil's horn, / 'Tis now the devil's crest," he says in conclusion (II,4,16–17). In striving to be more than man, he has ended a good deal less. Recognizing this truth, he puts it to use in the course of his temptation of Isabella later in the same scene (II,4,134–5): "Be that you are," he urges her, "That is, a woman; if you be more, you're none." But she will not be corrupted, and Angelo turns from persuasion to threats. If he cannot be an angel, he will be a very demon of the flesh: "I have begun, / And now I give my sensual race the rein," he announces, and then proceeds to state the terms on which Isabella can redeem her brother. His fall is complete, and thereafter he has forfeited any share in the divine — the angelic — nature which man might justly claim. One of the Duke's octosyllabic couplets near the end of III,2 notes with appropriate horror the infamy that is here:

> O, what may man within him hide,
> Though angel on the outward side.

And at the beginning of V,1, when the Duke refers Isabella to Angelo for justice, she calls him by his own name: "O worthy duke, / You bid me seek redemption of the devil." When the truth has been revealed, and he stands forth in his shame, he judges himself with unsparing severity; "immediate sentence . . . and sequent death" is all the grace he begs (V,1,369–70). And he is still craving "death more willingly than mercy" (" 'Tis my deserving, and I do entreat it") in the last lines that he speaks in the play (V,1,472–3). By then he is a strangely dignified and absurd figure: dignified for the manner in which he endures his shame, absurd in the willful blindness through which he has brought it on himself. He has been duped on every hand — by the Duke, by Isabella, by Mariana — he who has seemed to be so thoroughly in command both of himself and of events around him. His reputation for "gravity" (in which, as he admits himself in hushed tones on one occasion, he takes pride) falls from him, and he stands exposed: a singularly unsuccessful lecher, and that when he has reached years of discretion, too. Nothing less than the dignity of death could make him an object of tragic pity, and Shakespeare has denied him that, leaving him instead clutching the tatters of his unyielding pride, stubbornly reiterating his request for death as the only proper punishment for his offenses, and having it denied him. He is doomed not to get what he seeks. The incongruity that I have already stated to be of the essence of comedy is grimly apparent here in the incongruous distance that separates Angelo's pride from Angelo's shame — that separates Angelo as he is, and Angelo as he thinks he might have been, and this is surely the principal reason why *Measure for Measure* is one of Shakespeare's grimmest plays.

The grimness is intensified because Angelo's ideal of self-righteous virtue is such a false one: false both because virtue of the thoroughgoing kind that he has sought is beyond human achievement, and because it is not altogether desirable that it should be within human reach. He has shown himself lamentably ignorant in the knowledge of self, which is to say, in the knowledge of what a man is, and to what he can legitimately aspire. He has draped himself in a cloak of self-righteous virtue, and in it he cuts as ill a figure as does Malvolio in his cross-garters and yellow stockings. And the comparison does not end there, for Malvolio is but a shallower Angelo: more vain, and with even less to justify his vanity. Still, if we do not feel for Angelo the tragic pity that we accord a Hamlet or an Othello or a Lear, we do pity him nonetheless. His ideal is at once so right and so wrong: right because it is surely proper for man to aspire to virtue, wrong because it can never be proper for him to aspire to it self-righteously. It is wrong, too, in the sense that it is the wrong ideal for him. Angelo's ideal conception of self is an ascetic ideal, and in his blindness and his pride, he never sees that he is not the ascetic type. He is no more capable of asceticism than the Widow of Ephesus was of sacrificing herself to her husband's memory, or than the Player Queen — to say nothing of Queen Gertrude — was of refraining from a second marriage. He has deceived himself about human limitations generally, and his personal limitations in particular. And the final crushing irony is that the very things Angelo has sought most feverishly to avoid — the sensual, the physical, the passionate — are precisely the objects of his most secret longings. He is in the terrible position of one who is inwardly seeking the very things that his conscious will has pledged itself to avoid.

Angelo's position is terrible, but because he is a single figure, and that not the principal one, in a larger scene, we are not shown the full intensity of its terror. For that, we must turn to Greek tragedy, and to the *Bacchae* of Euripides. In the figure of Pentheus, the Theban king who opposes himself to Dionysus, we have the tragic extreme of the tragicomic Angelo, even as Malvolio is the comic extreme. Malvolio, Angelo, Pentheus: what these three very diverse characters have in common is what comedy, tragicomedy, and tragedy have in common. All three are possessed of an ideal of virtuous conduct which is more or less febrile as they are more or less tragic, but an ideal which nonetheless fails, all along the line, to square with the facts of life. In their virtuous zeal, they are dedicated to imposing their ideal of conduct upon the world that lies within their charge, be this the kingdom of Thebes, the city of Vienna, or the lower domestic regions of the Lady Olivia's house in Illyria; they are determined that, because they are virtuous, there shall be no more cakes and ale. All three are humiliated for their presumption. For Malvolio, the humiliation is an end in itself; for Angelo, it involves the shame of public exposure; for Pentheus, it is the prelude to a terrible death.

In seeking to prevent the introduction of Dionysiac rites into Thebes, Pentheus is by implication seeking to deny the existence of the Dionysiac principle in man, even as he has sought to deny its existence in himself. He would prohibit the women of Thebes from participating in the Bacchic ceremonies on Mount Cithaeron, which he is convinced are only a pretext for gatherings of lecherous men and lewd women, just as Angelo decrees that all "the houses of resort" in the suburbs of Vienna be pulled down. As guardians of the public morality, there is much to be said for both; the difficulty is that they would impose restrictions on the conduct of human life which mortal flesh is not able to endure. Seeking to realize a perhaps noble but illusory ideal of life, they are in fact enemies of life. Pompey, the part tapster, part bawd of *Measure for Measure*, says that if Angelo would enforce the laws against immorality in Vienna, he must "geld and splay all the youth in the city," which may be a sad comment on human nature, but is nonetheless true. And the case is even clearer in the *Bacchae*, where Pentheus stands forth as the open enemy of Dionysus, the god of earthly fertility. Pentheus, in his pride, like Angelo, would legislate human weakness out of existence; he would deliver mankind from the infirmities of the flesh by fiat; and he must inevitably pay the price of such presumption. The Chorus comments appropriately:

> They who in pride pretend
> Beyond man's limit, will lose what lay
> Close to their hand and sure.
>
> (lines 396–8)

And later in the same ode the Chorus speaks of the happiness of him who is

> Watchful to keep aloof both mind and heart
> From men whose pride claims more than mortals may.
>
> (lines 427–8)

The task that Pentheus has appointed himself is impossible for any man to accomplish; it is the more so for him, being the kind of man he is. For Pentheus, like Angelo, is fatally drawn to the very pleasures of human life which he seeks most fervently to deny, both in himself and others. Again the final, crushing — here altogether tragic — irony: the Dionysiac principle against which Pentheus has vowed eternal enmity is strong in him, so strong that through its operation the king is lured to his own destruction. There comes the terrible scene in which god and king confront each other. It is the measure of Pentheus's blindness that he fails throughout the play to recognize Dionysus as the god in person (just as he has refused to acknowledge Dionysus's deity), and he persists in mistaking the figure before him as a mere Bacchic priest. Bit by bit, as he and the god converse, Pentheus betrays an all too passionate interest in the details of the Bacchic revels, and the god is quick to seize upon this. Would the king care to view the revels at first hand, he asks; and Pentheus confesses that he would. It can be arranged, says the god, but the king must disguise himself as a bacchanal, lest he be recognized as an interloper. The king, who is by now altogether under the god's sway, consents; and he appears a little later clad in woman's clothes, thyrsus in hand and fawnskin draped about him, ready to go. Thus bedizened, the grave and dignified king is led by the god through the streets of Thebes, en route to Mount Cithaeron. Having been humiliated in the eyes of his people (shades of Malvolio in his cross garters and yellow stockings) he is ready for the slaughter at the hands of the bacchae, with his mother at their head.

The principle of fertility, of life, has asserted itself and triumphed, as it always does. The enemies of life have been vanquished, even as they always are, whether the enemies of life take the form of a Pentheus, an Angelo, or one of the wretched old men — the perpetual enemy of youth and vitality — who would prevent the marriage of the young lovers, and who are eternally appearing in comedy, from Menander through Plautus and Terence to the present. Comedy notoriously ends in marriage, even as tragedy typically ends in death; and the dance with which comedy traditionally closes — even such a sophisticated piece as *The Way of the World* has one — is something of an act of faith, an affirmation that life, in spite of its follies and its miseries, is worthwhile, and worthy to be perpetuated. Comedy implies, then, an acceptance of life, which implies as well an acceptance of man, and to accept man, one must be prepared to forgive all the weakness and the treachery and the downright depravity which, in spite of man's best intentions, he is continually guilty of. To accept and to forgive, one must be, above everything else, clear-sighted about what man is, and what can be properly expected of him. Only then will one refrain from asking the impossible, of himself and of others, and being plunged into the depths of tragic despair when the impossible is not achieved. Comedy is nothing if not hardheadedly realistic about the nature of man and the nature of human life; but it can also be compassionate in its forgiveness and its acceptance of human failings, because it recognizes the existence of these. That is why the burden of com-

edy, again and again, turns on the need for man to undeceive himself about the limitations of humanity, to see life for what it is, and to make the best of it.

For a fine demonstration of this double theme of acceptance and forgiveness in the terms of sheerest comedy, it is tempting to turn to the operatic stage, and da Ponte's libretto for Mozart's *Così fan tutte*. It is an elegant, rather cynical, and yet finally compassionate performance, and it stands squarely in the tradition of great comedy. We are confronted with two pairs of lovers: the sisters Fiordiligi and Dorabella, and their respective gallants, Guglielmo and Ferrando. The gentlemen have a cynical old bachelor friend, Don Alfonso, who assures them that, if their ladies are faithful, it is only because they have not had occasion to be otherwise. The lovers, in the fullness of their simplicity, laugh him to scorn; but then to vindicate their faith and prove the folly of Don Alfonso's suspicions, they agree to put their ladies to the test that he suggests. They announce to the sisters that they have been called to the wars, and bid them a tearful farewell, amid many protestations of eternal devotion and faith on both sides. After the lovers' departure, the sisters are prostrated with grief, Dorabella viewing her condition as especially terrible:

> Relentless infatuation which thrills my very soul and will not cease till I die of grief. What a wretched example of tragic love shall I give the Eumenides if I manage to live through the horrible sound of my own sighs,

she sings. But Don Alfonso promptly goes to work. The sisters have a maid, even as the Widow of Ephesus had, and Don Alfonso bribes this soubrette, named Despina, to introduce two friends into the presence of her mistresses as prospective lovers. The two new suitors are, of course, Guglielmo and Ferrando, disguised as Albanian noblemen. Despina complies, but the sisters are indignant that she should presume so much, and the lovers' proposals are scornfully rejected. They are sent away, but they return shortly, announcing that if the ladies will not be kind, they will not live; whereupon they drink a reportedly poisonous concoction, and fall to the ground. The sisters are distraught; they call a doctor who appears (it is Despina in disguise) and restores the lovers to life. The ladies are impressed at such devotion, but still faithful to their first vows at the conclusion of Act I. But in the second act, their fall is accomplished. First Dorabella gives way to the advances of Guglielmo, then Fiordiligi yields to the suit of Ferrando. When the lovers compare notes, and find that their respective mistresses have proved false, they are plunged into gloom; that "all those tears, promises, and sighs and vows" should be utterly forgotten in so short a time! They are dedicated to vengeance. But Don Alfonso takes them in hand with timely advice: women are weak, they must not be blamed; young, old, pretty or ugly, they all do it. And he makes them repeat with him: "*Così fan tutte!*" Meanwhile, the sisters are prepared to marry their Albanian suitors. The farce is played through to the end, until the lovers throw off their disguises and confront the ladies with their perfidy. The sisters are overcome with shame, and court their punishment in terms worthy of an Angelo: "punish my guilt with death. I see my faults too late. With that sword pierce this unworthy breast," they sing together. All turn on Don Alfonso, who has engineered the deception. He freely admits it, and justifies having done so, thus pointing the moral of the piece:

> I deceived you [addressing the sisters], but it was to undeceive your lovers, who will be wiser in future. Take my advice, join hands, you are betrothed. Kiss and be friends.

To the credit of them all, they have the wit to do just this, and the opera ends with a final chorus that sums up the wisdom which it is the special province of comedy to celebrate, even as it is the common purpose of comedy, tragedy, and tragicomedy to delineate the sundry consequences that follow when that wisdom is lacking:

> Happy the man who accepts life as it really is, and in all its ups and downs takes a reasonable view; who can laugh when others weep and finds peace in the midst of the world's tumult!

Comedy and Tragedy Transposed

Ellen Douglass Leyburn

Surveying mid-twentieth-century drama, Professor Leyburn suggests that absurd comedy has taken over from tragedy the presentation of rather sympathetic characters in extreme situations and that tragedy (e.g., the plays of Arthur Miller and Tennessee Williams), having been drained of grandeur, now tends to present the small, unsympathetic characters traditionally associated with comedy.

The remark of Socrates at the end of the *Symposium* that the genius of tragedy and comedy are the same has usually been taken as a joking paradox meant to round off gaily a night of talking and drinking. Yet its measure of truth has haunted responses to the supreme achievements in drama. The heightening of the tragedy of Lear by the Fool, "who labours to outjest his heart-struck injuries," on the one hand, and the deepening of the comedy of *Le Misanthrope* through the suffering of Alceste, on the other, are enough to make us pause before dismissing the remark of Socrates. Plato's jest, if indeed it be jest, seems nearer to the truth of what we find in postclassical drama than does Aristotle's strict separation of tragedy and comedy.

Nevertheless, we have had the feeling until recently that when we used the terms, we knew at least vaguely what they meant and could be understood by others when we used them to distinguish kinds of drama which were distinct even when they appeared in the same play. The assumption that tragedy is one dramatic mode and comedy another has been the foundation of all the varied and elaborate structures of definition of both genres. And the same assumption persists in the proliferation of analyses of the death of tragedy which have followed Joseph Wood Krutch's lament over the paralysis of tragic power in modern man in his much-quoted chapter called "The Tragic Fallacy," which

Reprinted by permission from *The Yale Review*. Copyright 1964 by Yale University.

appeared as long ago as the Twenties and fits the whole thesis of his book *The Modern Temper*. The very force of Krutch's indictment grows from his knowing so clearly what he thinks the demands of tragedy are and wherein modern drama is deficient. This clarity of conviction about the nature of tragedy is equally marked in more recent treatments of the same theme, such as William Van O'Connor's *Climates of Tragedy*, which appeared during the Second World War, and George Steiner's *The Death of Tragedy*, which has appeared still more recently. The same assurance marks criticism of comedy. However varied their definitions, the critics resemble each other in seeming to know what it is they are defining.

What I should like to suggest is that in modern drama comedy has so far invaded tragedy — and tragedy, comedy — that the terms have lost their old distinctness. Whereas comedy has for centuries displayed man's weakness, this now seems to be the function of tragedy — or of drama which is intended to arouse the emotions commonly called tragic, whatever new name we try to find for the plays of Tennessee Williams or Arthur Miller or John Osborne. Whereas tragedy has in earlier eras looked at man in "boundary situations," it is now the comedies of Beckett and Ionesco which show man in extremity; and the equally terrifying plays of Pinter and Duerrenmatt make use of grotesque comedy to reveal the precariousness of life and the condition of man confronted with pervasive evil. Duerrenmatt's

643

note on *The Visit* ends: "*The Visit of the Old Lady* is a wicked play, yet for this very reason it must not be presented wickedly, but most humanely, with sadness, not with anger, but also with humor, for nothing harms this comedy — which ends tragically — more than brutal seriousness." Tragedy and comedy seem to have shifted not only in perspective and in substance, but also in effect. Our responses are almost the reverse of what used to be the conventional attitudes to tragedy and comedy. We resist tragic identification with the miserable characters of most of our serious drama and look at them with the detachment which has hitherto seemed appropriate to critical comedy. Conversely, the comedies that end tragically compel us into a strange and unwilling empathy rather than into comic judgment: in the seemingly odd characters we recognize our most familiar selves, and in their fantastic plights, the very situations in which we are involved.

The dramatists of the absurd are clearly conscious of this interpenetration of tragedy and comedy and deliberately exploit its disturbing imaginative effect. Ionesco makes the illuminating statement: "Personally, I have never understood the distinctions that are made between the comic and the tragic. Since the comic is the intuition of the absurd, it seems to me more hopeless than the tragic. . . . The comic offers no escape . . . the comical is tragic, and the tragedy of man, derisory." Ionesco's assertion is highly characteristic not just of his own attitude, repeatedly expressed in comments on his plays, but also of the mood of much of the drama of the absurd besides his own. The writers of serious plays, on the contrary, seem unaware of the intrusion of comic elements into their pathetic worlds. They solemnly present their small characters and seem to demand for them the large emotional response aroused by tragedy. This unawareness confuses the artistic effect of their plays; but it is in itself an impressive demonstration of the pervasiveness of the interpenetration of tragedy and comedy which marks the drama of our time. The shifts in the nature of both tragedy and comedy reflect the convulsion of society and of man's sense of himself which characterizes the world which the dramatists inhabit.

Arthur Miller and Tennessee Williams are perhaps the most striking examples of contemporary dramatists who consider themselves writers of tragedies and yet have produced plays in which the themes and characters resemble those of earlier critical comedy. There are almost as many contradictions as theories among definitions of tragedy; but two criteria which are consistently used by critics with otherwise extremely diverse theories are that tragedy should have a hero with stature enough to make his suffering significant and that its course of action should produce enlightenment. Neither of these criteria is fulfilled, I think, by the plays of Williams and Miller. The protagonists arouse pity, but little admiration and little of the identification necessary for tragic terror; and in the rhythm of the plays the emphasis is largely on passion rather than on purpose and perception. On the other hand, both dramatists focus their plays on the very kind of human weakness which has hitherto been the subject of critical or realistic comedy. The self-deception of their leading characters is of the sort which earlier dramatists have held up to ridicule. It is the anomaly of a pathetic view of characters formerly seen as objects of satire which makes the difficulty for the traditionalist in responding to such plays according to the authors' intentions. The contradictory feelings which the characters evoke seem to me more important than their sheer inadequacy as tragic heroes so much stressed by Krutch and his followers. The discrepancy between expectation and event for such characters lacks the kind of irony which has been thought of as tragic; and of enlightenment there is little or none. *Death of a Salesman* and *A Streetcar Named Desire*, each the most successful play of its author, well illustrate all of these points.

It was in answer to the criticism of Willy Loman as a tragic hero that Miller wrote "Tragedy and the Common Man" to serve as introduction to a Viking Press edition of *Death of a Salesman*. His contention is that "the common man is as apt a subject for tragedy in its highest sense as kings were," a judgment with which in our day few would quarrel. It is not Willy's low station, but his low intelligence (or if intelligence seems too narrow a word, his lack of sheer force of being) which keeps his woes from affecting us as do those of Orestes, Hamlet, Medea, and Macbeth — the tragic figures of the past whom Miller cites. "Ineffectual" is the word which seems to characterize Willy both as salesman and as father. His constant need of bolstering from both Linda and Charley and his pitiful efforts to win the respect of Biff in order to feed his own self-esteem make it strange for Miller to say in reference to him that "the tragic hero is intent upon claiming his whole due as a personality," though Willy's personality is so small that the comment has a kind of unintentional irony. Even apart from the hallucinated scenes with Ben and the suggestions of actual insanity, Willy's characteristic state is bewilderment. He enters the play puzzled by his fruitless effort to reach his territory, and he leaves it persuading himself that Biff will be "magnificent . . . with twenty thousand dollars in his pocket." The lack of integrity which has made him teach Biff to steal seems to be the result of inability to distinguish truth from falsehood rather than of deliberate dishonesty. Biff, who for all his limitations comes much nearer to self-realization than his father does, tries to open Willy's eyes: "The man don't know who we are! The man is gonna know! (*To Willy*) We never told the truth for ten minutes in this house! . . . Pop! I'm a dime a dozen, and so are you!" But Biff's tears simply send Willy into a new "phony dream"; and the son's comment at his father's grave is: "Charley, the man didn't know who he was." This hardly fits Miller's conception of tragedy as "a man's total compulsion to evaluate himself justly." Rather, Willy's self-deception, although Miller treats it so as to win compassion, is of exactly the sort which has regularly marked the comic figure. Even his physical defects of fatness and flabbiness which make the salesman laugh at him and call him "walrus" and his loudmouthed over-heartiness of manner identify him with a long line of aging comic butts who have tried to convince an unbelieving world and themselves that they are "well liked." It is worth notice in passing that *A View from the Bridge* again depicts a man past middle age who has no power to "evaluate himself justly" and that in the later play sexual jealousy over a young girl brings the pathetic protagonist even nearer to one of the stereotypes of comedy.

The counterpart to the amorous old fool in traditional comedy has been the woman who tries to trade upon fading sexual attractiveness; and it is this forumula which Williams transmutes into the heartrending character of Blanche DuBois. Like Willy, she seeks and is given bolstering from the other characters; and Stella, like Linda in *Salesman*, not only gives the needed compliments but urges the other characters to tell Blanche how pretty her finery is and how fresh and attractive she looks. But Williams is more willing than Miller is to let harsh judgment of his weakling have expression in the play. Willy hears the voice of reality largely through the kindly tones of Charley, who does tell him to grow up, but endures his insults and gives him money under the fiction of weekly loans, whereas Blanche has to listen to the taunts of Stella's husband, whom she regards as "subhuman." Miller depends primarily on Willy's own self-revelation to show the audience the discrepancies between Willy as he is and Willy as he thinks he is. Williams, in contrast, uses the harsh judgment of Stanley not only to add to Blanche's misery, but also to enlighten the audience about her "lies and conceit and tricks." The conflict between the dream and the grim reality is thus accentuated through the hostility of the character who reveals the ugly truth. By giving Blanche a personal antagonist when she is already incapable of coping with her inner plight and has "run for protection . . . from under one leaky roof to another leaky roof — because it was storm — all storm, and [she] was — caught in the center," Williams intensifies her woe and provides the bitter irony of her seeking shelter under the roof of her sharpest critic. At the same time, the audience is made to see her partly through Stanley's eyes. He becomes a kind of satiric chorus within the play, which heightens the anomaly of our being asked to respond with tragic emotions to so wretched a figure as Blanche. But Stanley is far more than simply an interpreter. It is he who, through his cruel disillusioning of Mitch, makes Blanche lose what tenuous hold on reality she has had and brings about her final desolate departure to the mental hospital, still trying to enact the part of the gracious lady, depending on "the kindness of strangers."

Both of these plays are full of irony, even of the irony of fate; but we miss the grandeur which pits the tragic hero against his fate and leads to tragic irony. There is a strong element of the ludicrous which makes the plights of both Willy and Blanche more painful. Fate, in the form of the social order, does seem to have played a cruel joke on the simple-minded and well-meaning Willy Loman in giving him the false goals of success through personality and of getting away with whatever can be filched. In his refusal to be enlightened by Biff, he does seem to go off to his useless suicide as the dupe of a power he cannot combat. Blanche is equally the victim of a hideous practical joke. She is ridiculous in her effort to charm the naïve Mitch with her pretense of innocence. And in her case, the fate which finally tricks her takes the very palpable form of Stanley, though the state to which she has been reduced before the play begins can be called a joke played on her by fate in the form of the social order, just as society has largely represented fate for Willy. But both are too weak to achieve a tragic protest. Since they are simply victims, the irony leaves us uncomfortable at the advantage taken of weakness rather than filled with awe at heroic man confronting mysterious forces within him and without. The ambivalence of the response to both plays comes from the fact that the protagonists are self-deluded enough to seem appropriate objects of mockery; but they are too miserable and too sympathetically viewed by their creators to allow the audience to feel as comic the irony in what happens to them. Consequently, the plays present a seemingly double vision on the part of the playwrights and have a disconcertingly mixed effect.

This kind of apparently unintentional doubleness marks a great number of contemporary plays. It would be easy to link many other soberly treated characters, such as the disagreeable ones of John Osborne or the sentimentalized ones of William Inge, with the traditional figures of critical comedy. The plays of Williams and Miller seem more impressive demonstrations of the penetration of serious drama by comic types only because Williams and Miller seem to make larger tragic claims.

Since the writers of absurd comedy are highly conscious of the doubleness of their plays and use it with full artistic awareness and often with great artistic skill, their plays are much more profoundly disturbing than are those of the humorless writers of serious plays with weak heroes. The contradictions of pain and amusement in the best comedies of the absurd are evoked with clear intention and the most deliberate finesse. Ionesco is the playwright who has been most explicit about his conception of the theatre as the mirror of the contradictions of life: "I try to project on the stage my inner conflict (incomprehensible to myself) telling myself always that, the microcosm being the image of the macrocosm, it can be that this in-

terior world, broken, disarticulated, is in some way the mirror or the symbol of universal contradictions." It is the absurdity, the tragic comedy, of life itself of which these dramatists seek to make their plays the image. The surface effect of most of their plays is comic; but the vision which informs it is largely tragic. Martin Esslin in *The Theatre of the Absurd* quotes Pinter's comment: "The point about tragedy is that it is *no longer* funny." The writers of the "funny" plays of our time are concerned with the same ultimate questions about man's identity and his destiny which in earlier periods have led to the writing of tragedy. One after another of the plays of Beckett and Ionesco, of Pinter and Duerrenmatt, show man in extremity and posing ultimate questions about his very existence: who he is, why he lives, and why he suffers. Yet these plays which reach no comic resolution and raise ultimate rather than temporal questions are clearly comic in the sense of being outrageously funny. The farcical element in the dramaturgy, with its dependence on mime and music-hall slapstick devices, has been much discussed. My concern here is not with the arts the playwrights use to evoke laughter; but with the fact that the plays do evoke it and use it exactly to sharpen the terror. Comedy is an essential part of the situations presented and makes their desperateness more real. The seemingly meaningless repetitions of the dialogue — as skilful a use of language as the most florid passages in heroic drama, the clowning and dependence on farcical gesture, the monopolizing of the stage by objects, bear an organic relation to the absurd situations and are the very means by which the dramatists produce the feeling (to quote Ionesco again) that "in a space without space, all seems to be volatilized, all is *menaced* [my italics] . . . by an imminent, silent engulfment, in I know not what abyss, beyond day and beyond night." The plays as wholes present comic incongruity raised to tragic proportions and effecting in the audience tragic involvement and the tragic feelings of pity and terror. Because of the intense reality of these dramas and because they do raise more fundamental questions, the mixture of feelings they produce is nearer to the old tragic emotion than that of contemporary plays of solely tragic intention. Again, two very familiar plays offer proof of all the points suggested. W*aiting for Godot* and *The Chairs* are both funny and terrible.

The two tramps in Beckett's play are preoccupied with the question which confronts all men and has lately been asked more insistently perhaps than ever before: why live at all? Indeed, their recurrent attempts at suicide make one of the unifying repetitions in the circular motion of the play, if their painfully funny frustrations of action can be called motion. They debate the question of *The Myth of Sisyphus* and seem to stumble upon a measure of Camus's answer. For if they do not decide to live and protest, their very persistence in waiting constitutes a kind of protest. They differ from Camus, of course, in not being sure that Godot will *not* come in spite of their continually baffled hopes. This refusal quite to accept the logic of their own experience is part of what makes us enter into their situation with the kind of identification we accord to tragic characters. It does not require the constant reminders Beckett puts into their mouths that "We are all humanity," to make us recognize ourselves in their already battered state and in the beatings and subjection to physical infirmity within the play. We are drawn to them not just by their clowning and by our amusement at the brisk turns of stichomythia with which they try to amuse themselves. They are irresistibly appealing in their uneasy need of each other, in their very endurance of what we must endure. And we give them the kind of empathy which we withhold from Willy Loman and Blanche DuBois.

The old couple in *The Chairs* ask the still more elementary question of who we are. They show man not just at the limits of his being as man, but beyond identity; and yet in their need to affirm their identity, to leave some message, they too compel us to ally ourselves with them. The frenzy of their attempts to establish connection with the "real" invisible characters and their being crowded apart even from each other by the oppressive multiplication of chairs make vivid their inability to exist even before their suicide in the dank waters that surround their island. Their own progressive loss of the power of articulate speech and the inane babblings of the dumb orator whom they leave as their surrogate are the audible counterpart of the visual image. The laughter which Ionesco evokes by the farcical movement and by the ridiculous echoing "orphan-dworfan" speech, which finally becomes the "Arf ... arf ... arf" of helpless barking, makes the tragic effect much deeper than could a direct appeal to the pity and terror in which the search for identity involves us.

The shifting of ground in the realms of tragedy and comedy poses for contemporary critics an awkward problem of terminology. The old phrases like "mixed drama" and "tragicomedy," which sufficed to describe the combination in one play of known and recognizable modes, have little relevance to the strange new genres which seem to be evolving. Furthermore, while the serious plays with weak characters and the comic plays which move us tragically seem to be opposite and complementary parts of the same phenomenon, the dramatic rendering of the dislocation of our times, they are so different in substance and in effect that no one term could conceivably embrace both. The rather cumbersome phrase "Theatre of the Absurd," to which Esslin's book with that title has given wider currency, is useful for the funny plays of tragic import; *The Dark Comedy*, the title of the valuable study by J. L. Styan, which has appeared since this essay was first written, supplies another usable designation; but no new term seems to have been invented for the corresponding and opposite kind of plays which treat ridiculous characters pathetically. As we grope toward nomenclature and definition (a groping perhaps not unrelated to the struggles of Ionesco's characters with language) we come back broodingly to Plato's joke at the end of the *Symposium*: "the chief thing which he remembered was Socrates compelling the other two to acknowledge that the genius of comedy was the same with that of tragedy, and that the true artist in tragedy was an artist in comedy also. To this they were constrained to assent, being drowsy, and not quite following the argument."

King Lear or Endgame

Jan Kott

Translated by Boleslaw Taborski

Jan Kott, a Polish critic who now teaches at the State University of New York, Stonybrook, achieved some fame or notoriety a few years ago because his interpretation of *King Lear* helped to shape Peter Brook's production of the play in which the world was made to seem as bleak and loveless as the world of much contemporary Absurdist drama. In this essay Kott concentrates on that contemporary drama in which "tragic situations become grotesque" and which "offers no consolation whatsoever."

The book devoted to "Shakespeare and the new drama" has not yet been written. Perhaps it is too early for such a book to appear. But it is odd how often the word "Shakespearean" is uttered when one speaks about Brecht, Dürrenmatt, or Beckett. These three names stand, of course, for three different kinds of theatrical vision, and the word "Shakespearean" means something different in relation to each of them. It may be invoked to compare with Dürrenmatt's full-bloodedness, sharpness, lack of cohesion, and stylistic confusion; with Brecht's epic quality; or with Beckett's new *Theatrum mundi*. But every one of these three kinds of drama and theatre has more similarities to Shakespeare and medieval morality plays than to nineteenth-century drama, whether romantic, or naturalistic. Only in this sense can the new theatre be called anti-theatre.

A striking feature of the new theatre is its grotesque quality. Despite appearances to the contrary, this new grotesque has not replaced the old drama and the comedy of manners. It deals with problems, conflicts and themes of tragedy such as: human fate, the meaning of existence, freedom and inevitability, the dis-

crepancy between the absolute and the fragile human order. Grotesque means tragedy re-written in different terms. Maurice Regnault's statement: "the absence of tragedy in a tragic world gives birth to comedy" is only seemingly paradoxical. Grotesque exists in a tragic world. Both the tragic and the grotesque vision of the world are composed as it were of the same elements. In a tragic and grotesque world, situations are imposed, compulsory and inescapable. Freedom of choice and decision are part of this compulsory situation, in which both the tragic hero and the grotesque actor must always lose their struggle against the absolute. The downfall of the tragic hero is a confirmation and recognition of the absolute; whereas the downfall of the grotesque actor means mockery of the absolute and its desecration. The absolute is transformed into a blind mechanism, a kind of automaton. Mockery is directed not only at the tormentor, but also at the victim who believed in the tormentor's justice, raising him to the level of the absolute. The victim has consecrated his tormentor by recognizing himself as victim.

In the final instance tragedy is an appraisal of human fate, a measure of the absolute. The grotesque is a criticism of the absolute in the name of frail human experience. That is why tragedy brings catharsis, while grotesque offers no consolation whatsoever. "Tragedy," wrote Gorgias of Leontium, "is a swindle in which the swin-

From *Shakespeare Our Contemporary* by Jan Kott. Copyright © 1964 by Panstwowe Wydawnictvo Naukowe. Reprinted by permission of Doubleday & Company, Inc.

dler is more just than the swindled, and the swindled wiser than the swindler." One may travesty this aphorism by saying that grotesque is a swindle in which the swindled is more just than the swindler, and the swindler wiser than the swindled. Claire Zachanassian in Dürrenmatt's *Visit* is wiser than Anton Schill, but he is more just than she is. Schill's death, like Polonius's death in *Hamlet,* is grotesque. Neither Schill, nor the inhabitants of Güllen are tragic heroes. The old lady with her artificial breasts, teeth and limbs is not a goddess; she hardly even exists, she might almost have been invented. Schill and the people of Güllen find themselves in a situation in which there is no room for tragedy, but only for grotesque. "Comedy," writes Ionesco in his "Expérience du théâtre," "is a feeling of absurdity, and seems more hopeless than tragedy; comedy allows no way out of a given situation."[1]

The tragic and the grotesque worlds are closed, and there is no escape from them. In the tragic world this compulsory situation has been imposed in turn by the Gods, Fate, the Christian God, Nature, and History that has been endowed with reason and inevitability.

On the other side, opposed to this arrangement, there was always man. If Nature was the absolute, man was unnatural. If man was natural, the absolute was represented by Grace, without which there was no salvation. In the world of the grotesque, downfall cannot be justified by, or blamed on, the absolute. The absolute is not endowed with any ultimate reasons; it is stronger, and that is all. The absolute is absurd. Maybe that is why the grotesque often makes use of the concept of a mechanism which has been put in motion and cannot be stopped. Various kinds of impersonal and hostile mechanisms have taken the place of God, Nature and History, found in the old tragedy. The notion of absurd mechanism is probably the last metaphysical concept remaining in modern grotesque. But this absurd mechanism is not transcendental any more in relation to man, or at any rate to mankind. It is a trap set by man himself into which he has fallen.

The scene of tragedy has mostly been a natural landscape. Raging nature witnessed man's downfall, or — as in *King Lear* — played an active part in the action. Modern grotesque usually takes place in the midst of civilization. Nature has evaporated from it almost completely. Man is confined to a room and surrounded by inanimate objects. But objects have now been raised to the status of symbols of human fate, or situation, and perform a similar function to that played in Shakespeare by forest, storm, or eclipse of the sun. Even Sartre's hell is just a vast hotel consisting of rooms and corridors, beyond which there are more rooms and more corridors. This hell "behind closed doors" does not need any metaphysical aids.

Ionesco's hell is arranged on similar lines. A new tenant moves into an empty flat. Furniture is brought in. There is more and more furniture. Furniture surrounds the tenant on all sides. He is surrounded already by four wardrobes but more are brought in. He has been closed in by furniture. He can no longer be seen. He has been brought down to the level of inanimate objects and has become an object himself.

In Beckett's *Endgame* there is a room with a wheelchair and two dustbins. A picture hangs face to the wall. There is also a staircase, a telescope and a whistle. All that remains of nature is sand in the dustbins, a flea, and the part of man that belongs to nature: his body.

> HAMM: Nature has forgotten us.
> CLOV: There's no more nature.
> HAMM: No more nature! You exaggerate.
> CLOV: In the vicinity.
> HAMM: But we breathe, we change! we lose our hair, our teeth! Our bloom! Our ideals!
> CLOV: Then she hasn't forgotten us.
> (p. 16)[2]

It can easily be shown how, in the new theatre, tragic situations become grotesque. Such a classic situation of tragedy is the necessity of making a choice between opposing values. Antigone is doomed to choose between human and divine order; between Creon's demands, and those of the absolute. The tragedy lies in the very principle of choice by which one of the values must be annihilated. The cruelty of the absolute lies in demanding such a choice and in imposing a situation which excludes the possibility of a compromise, and where one of the al-

---

[1] E. Ionesco, "Expérience du théâtre," *Nouvelle Revue Française,* February 1958.

[2] All quotations from Beckett are given in the author's own translation. Page references in quotations from *Endgame* and *Act Without Words* apply to the Faber & Faber edition of 1958.

ternatives is death. The absolute is greedy and demands everything; the hero's death is its confirmation.

The tragic situation becomes grotesque when both alternatives of the choice imposed are absurd, irrelevant or compromising. The hero has to play, even if there is no game. Every move is bad, but he cannot throw down his cards. To throw down the cards would also be a bad move.

It is this situation that Dürrenmatt's Romulus finds himself in. He is the last emperor of a crumbling empire. He will not alter the course of history. History has made a fool of him. He can either die in a spectacular fashion, or lie on his bed and wait to be butchered. He can surrender, compose speeches, or commit suicide. In his position as the last Roman emperor, every one of these solutions is compromising and ridiculous. History has turned Romulus into a clown, and yet demands that he treat her seriously. Romulus has only one good move to make: consciously to accept the part of a clown and play it to the end. He can breed chickens. In this way the historical inevitability will have been made a fool of. The absolute will have been flouted.

Antigone is a tragedy of choice, *Oedipus* a tragedy of "unmerited guilt" and destiny. The gods loyally warn the protagonist that fate has destined him to be a patricide and his own mother's husband. The hero has full freedom of decision and action. The gods do not interfere; they just watch and wait until he makes a mistake. Then they punish him. The gods are just, and punish the hero for a crime he has indeed committed, and only after he has committed it. But the protagonist had to commit a crime. Oedipus wanted to cheat fate, but did not and could not escape it. He fell into a trap, made his mistake, killed his father and married his mother. What is to happen will happen.

The tragedy of Oedipus may, perhaps, be posed as a problem belonging to the theory of game. The game is just, i.e. at the outset both partners must have the same chances of losing or winning, and both must play according to the same rules. In its game with Oedipus fate does not invoke the help of the gods, does not change the laws of nature. Fate wins its game without recourse to miracles.

The game must be just, but at the same time must be so arranged that the same party always wins; so that Oedipus always loses.

Let us imagine an electronic computer, which plays chess and calculates any number of moves in advance. A man must play chess with an electronic computer, cannot leave or break the game, and has to lose the game. His defeat is just, because it is effected according to the rules of the game; he loses because he has made a mistake. But he could not have won.

A man losing the chess game with an electronic computer, whom he himself has fed with combinatorial analysis and rules, whom he himself has "taught" to play, is not a tragic hero any more. If he plays that chess game from the moment he was born until he dies, and if he has to lose, he will at most be the hero of a tragi-grotesque. All that is left of tragedy, is the concept of "unmerited guilt," the inevitable defeat, and unavoidable mistake. But the absolute has ceased to exist. It has been replaced by the absurdity of the human situation.

The absurdity does not consist in the fact that man-made mechanisms are in certain conditions stronger, and even wiser, than he. The absurdity consists in the fact that they create a compulsory situation by forcing him to a game in which the probability of his total defeat constantly increases. The Christian view of the end of the world, with the Last Judgement and its segregation of the just and the unjust, is pathetic. The end of the world caused by the big bomb is spectacular, but grotesque just the same. Such an end of the world is intellectually unacceptable, whether to Christians or to Marxists. It would be a silly ending.

The comparison between fate's game with Oedipus, and a game of chess with an electronic computer, is not precise enough. An automatic device to play chess, even if it could compute any number of moves, need not win all the time. It would simply more often win than lose. But among automatic devices that really exist one could find a much better example. There is a machine for a game similar to tossing coins for "heads or tails." I put a coin on the table the way I like, with "heads" or "tails" on top. The machine does not see the coin, but it is to make out how I have put it. If it gives the right answer, it wins. I inform the machine whether it has given the right answer. I put the coin again, and so on. After a time the machine begins to win by giving the right answers more and more often. It has memorized and learned my system; it has deciphered me as it were. It foresees that after three "heads" I will put two "tails." I change the system, and play using a different method. The blind machine learns this one too, and begins to win again. I am endowed with free will and have the freedom of choice. I can put "heads" or "tails." But in the end, like Oedipus, I must lose the game.

There is a move by which I do not lose. I do not put the coin on the table, I do not choose. I simply toss it. I have given up the system, and left matters to chance. Now the machine and I have even chances. The possibility of win and loss, of "heads" or "tails" is the same. It amounts to fifty-fifty. The machine wanted me to treat it seriously, to play rationally with it, using a system, a method. But I do not want to. It is I who have now seen through the machine's method.

The machine stands for fate, which acts on the principle of the law of averages. In order to have even chances with fate I must become fate myself; I must chance my luck; act with a fifty-fifty chance. A man who, when playing with the machine, gives up his free will and freedom of choice, adopts an attitude to fate similar to that which Dürrenmatt's Romulus adopted with regard to historical necessity. Instead of putting the coin with "heads" on top a hundred times in succession, or "heads" and "tails" in turn, or two "tails" after ten "heads," he would just toss the coin up. That kind of man most certainly is not a tragic hero. He has adopted a clownish attitude to fate. Romulus is such a man.

In modern tragedy fate, gods and nature have been replaced by history. History is the only frame of reference, the final authority to accept or reject the validity of human actions. It is unavoidable and realizes its ultimate aims; it is objective "reason," as well as objective "progress." In this scheme of things history is a theatre with actors, but without an audience. No one watches the performance, for everybody is taking part. The script of this grand spectacle has been composed in advance and includes a necessary epilogue, which will explain everything. But, as in the *commedia dell'arte*, the text has not been written down. The actors improvise and only some of them foresee correctly what will happen in the following acts. In this particular theatre the scene changes with the actors; they are constantly setting it up and pulling it down again.

Actors are often wrong, but their mistakes have been foreseen by the scenario. One might even say that mistakes are the basis of the script, and that it is thanks to them that the action unfolds. History contains both the past and the future. Actors from previous scenes keep coming back, repeating old conflicts, and want to play parts that are long since over. They needlessly prolong the performance and have to be removed from the stage. They arrived too late. Other actors have arrived too early and start performing a scene from the next act, without noticing that the stage is not yet ready for them. They want to speed up the performance, but this cannot be done: every act has to be performed in its proper order. Those who arrive too early are also removed from the stage.

It is these parts that nineteenth-century philosophy and literature considered tragic. For Hegel the tragic heroes of history were those who came too late. Their reasons were noble but one-sided. They had been correct in the previous era, in the preceding act. If they continue to insist on them, they must be crushed by history. La Vendée was for Hegel an example of historical tragedy. Count Henry in Krasinski's *Undivine Comedy* is a Hegelian tragic hero.

Those who came too early, striving in vain to speed up the course of history, are also history's tragic heroes. Their reasons, too, are one-sided; they will become valid only at the next historical phase, in the succeeding act. They failed to understand that freedom is only the conscious recognition of necessity. Consequently they were annihilated by historical necessity, which solves only those problems that are capable of solution. The Paris Commune is an example of this kind of historical tragedy. Pancrace in *Undivine Comedy* is a tragic hero of history thus conceived.

The grotesque mocks the historical absolute, as it has mocked the absolutes of gods, nature and destiny. It does so by means of the so-called "barrel of laughs," a popular feature of any fun-fair: a score or more of people try to keep their balance while the upturned barrel revolves round its axis. One can only keep one's balance by moving on the bottom of the barrel in the opposite direction to, and with the same speed as, its movement. This is not at all easy. Those who move too fast or too slow in relation to the barrel's movement are bound to fall. The barrel brings them up, then they roll downwards trying desperately to cling to the moving floor.

The more violent their gestures and their grip on the walls, the more difficult it is for them to get up, and the funnier they look.

The barrel is put in motion by a motor, which is transcendental in relation to it. However, one may easily imagine a barrel that is set in motion by the people inside it: by those who manage to preserve their balance and those who fall over. A barrel like this would be immanent. Its movements would, of course, be variable: sometimes it would revolve in one direction, sometimes in the other. It would be even more difficult to preserve one's balance in a barrel like this: one would have to change step all the time, move forward and backward, faster or slower. In such an immanent barrel many more people would fall over. But neither those who fall because they move too fast, nor those who fall because they move too slow, are tragic heroes. They are just grotesque. They will be grotesque even if there is no way out of this immanent barrel. The social mechanism shown in most of Adamov's plays is very much like the barrel of laughs.

The world of tragedy and the world of grotesque have a similar structure. Grotesque takes over the themes of tragedy and poses the same fundamental questions. Only its answers are different. This dispute about the tragic and grotesque interpretations of human fate reflects the everlasting conflict of two philosophies and two ways of thinking; of two opposing attitudes defined by the Polish philosopher Leszek Kolakowski as the irreconcilable antagonism between the priest and the clown. Between tragedy and grotesque there is the same conflict for or against such notions as eschatology, belief in the absolute, hope for the ultimate solution of the contradiction between the moral order and every-day practice. Tragedy is the theatre of priests, grotesque is the theatre of clowns.

This conflict between two philosophies and two types of theatre becomes particularly acute in times of great upheavals. When established values have been overthrown, and there is no appeal, to God, Nature, or History, from the tortures inflicted by the cruel world, the clown becomes the central figure in the theatre. He accompanies the exiled trio — the king, the nobleman and his son — on their cruel wanderings through the cold endless night which has fallen on the world; through the "cold night" which, as in Shakespeare's *King Lear*, "will turn us all to fools and madmen."

A GLOSSARY
OF DRAMATIC TERMS

Absurd, Theater of the. Drama of such writers as Eugène Ionesco and Samuel Beckett in France and Harold Pinter in England that imitates the absurdity of man's existence. "Everything, as I see it, is an aberration," Ionesco has said. Among the basic themes are man's loneliness in a world without God, man's inability to communicate, man's dehumanization at the hands of mass media, and man's impotence in the face of society and of death. Though the plays are serious, they may contain extravagantly comic scenes in depicting a reality that is absurd, illogical, senseless, a world of futility and meaningless clichés. In Ionesco's *The Chairs* (1951) an elderly couple rush about, filling a room with chairs for nonexistent visitors. Old age is a fact, but an absurdity, too, and old people are incomprehensible. At the end of *The Chairs*, an orator, who is to deliver a solemn talk about the truths of life, turns out to be deaf and dumb and merely makes unintelligible noises and gestures to the invisible crowd. Ionesco summarizes the theme of *The Chairs* (*The New York Times*, June 1, 1958): "I have tried to deal . . . with emptiness, with frustration, with this world, at once fleeting and crushing. The characters I have used are not fully conscious of their spiritual rootlessness, but they feel it instinctively and emotionally." One basis of man's inability to communicate, and one which the "Absurd" dramatists seize upon, is the corruption of language. The absurdity of trying to communicate by means of a debased language is dramatized by Ionesco in *The Bald Soprano* (1948), where the characters speak in clichés. Because the characters are incomprehensible and the happenings illogical and baffling, the spectators cannot simply sit back in ease, but are continually challenged to grasp the play's meaning. Consult M. Esslin, *The Theatre of the Absurd.*

act. A main division in drama or opera. Act divisions probably arose in Roman theory and derive ultimately from the Greek practice of separating episodes in a play by choral interludes, but Greek (and probably Roman) plays were performed without interruption, for the choral interludes were part of the plays themselves. The division of Elizabethan plays into five acts is often the work of editors rather than authors. No play of Shakespeare's was published in his lifetime with divisions into five acts. Today an act division is commonly indicated by lowering the curtain and turning up the houselights. A **scene** is a smaller unit, either: (1) a division with no change of locale or abrupt shift of time, or (2) a division consisting of an actor or a group of actors on the stage; according to the second definition, the departure or entrance of an actor changes the composition of the group and thus produces a new scene. In an entirely different sense, the scene is the locale where a work is set. The first speech in *Romeo and Juliet* informs the audience of the play's locale: "In fair Verona, where we lay our scene. . . ." Often the décor lets the spectator know where the play is set, but during the last hundred years playwrights have tended, for the convenience of readers, to write long stage directions describing the scene. Here is the beginning of the first stage direction in Shaw's *Candida*: "A fine morning in October 1894 in the north east quarter of London, a vast district miles away from the London of Mayfair and St James's, and much less narrow, squalid, fetid and airless in its slums. . . ."

action. (1) The physical movement of an actor, whether he is leaping into Ophelia's grave or speaking softly to himself. That talk is action is easily seen in the Bastard's remark (*King John*, II.i.466): "Zounds! I was never so bethumped with words / Since I first called my brother's father dad." (2) An incident in the plot, an episode. (3) Aristotle's statement that a drama is an "imitation of an action" (*praxis*) has provoked considerable controversy; recently there has been a tendency to regard this action as the motive underlying the outward deeds of the plot. Francis Fergusson says (in *The Human Image in Dramatic Literature*, p. 116), for example, that the action of *Oedipus the King* "is the quest for Laius's slayer, . . . which persists through the changing circumstances of the play." See above, pp. 3–5.

aesthetic distance, or **psychical distance.** The detachment between the receptor and the work of art. The concept is chiefly associated with Edward Bullough (see the essay in his *Aesthetics*, reprinted in Melvin Rader, *A Modern Book of Aesthetics*). Bullough explains that there must be some sort of psychical "distance" (gap) between our practical self (our personal needs) and the work of art. Thus, an old man who has been treated harshly by his children may be unable to divorce his personal feelings from *King Lear*. He may be too involved with the piece as life to see it as art. But "distance" does not mean that the receptor is totally detached or objective. Rather, he is detached from his usual personal involvements, and because of this detachment he can look with a new vigorous interest — he can look with a new sort of passion born of his new personality — at the work of art as art. Persons who do not understand the need for distance between themselves and a work, Bullough explains, commonly say that they do not wish to see a tragedy because there is enough suffering in real life. But the more sophisticated spectator at a tragedy realizes that as a picture is distanced by the frame, a play is distanced (the characters may speak verse, they perform behind footlights, and their deeds cohere to make a unified harmonious pattern); the feelings it evokes in him are not the feelings evoked by a roughly similar event in real life. In the theater we feel "rapturous awe" at what in life would be depressing. See also dramatic illusion, empathy, epic drama. Consult Oscar Budel, "Contemporary Theater and Aesthetic Distance," *PMLA*, 76 (1961), 277–291.

agon (Greek: *contest*). A debate in a Greek comedy. See p. 315. In the last few decades the term has been used (e.g., by Francis Fergusson, *The Idea of a Theater*) to designate a scene of conflict in tragedy, such as the agonizing struggle between Oedipus and Teiresias.

agroikos. See character.

alazon. See character.

alienation effect. See epic drama.

allegory. Frequently an allegory is a narrative wherein abstractions (e.g., virtue, fear) are made concrete (Mr. Virtue, Giant Fear), for the purpose of effectively communicating a moral, but in essence an allegory is merely a system of equivalents. Though allegory need not personify abstractions, allegoric drama almost always does. *Everyman* (c. 1500), an allegoric morality play includes among its dramatis personae Death, Good Deeds, Beauty, and of course, Everyman. But morality plays may also include allegoric castles (standing for strength or chastity), roses (standing for love or virtue), etc. Consult Bernard Spivack, *Shakespeare and the Allegory of Evil.*

anagnorisis, or **disclosure, discovery, recognition.** For Aristotle the "recognition" or "disclosure" seems to be merely a recognition of who is who, by such tokens as birthmarks, clothes, etc., but the term has been extended to include the tragic hero's recognition of himself and/or the essence of life. Thus Othello, having murdered his faithful wife, learns he was beguiled into thinking her dishonest, and finally recognizes himself as "one not easily jealous, but being wrought / Perplexed in the extreme"; and he exacts justice from himself by suicide. See pp. 6–7.

antecedent action. See plot.

anticlimax. A descent, the lines or happenings being markedly less important or less impressive than their predecessors. In melodrama, a decrease in tension may cause disappointment and loss of interest; in comedy, a sharp descent (the beautiful princess opens her mouth and sounds like a burlesque queen) may get a desirable laugh. On the desirability of a gradual decrease in tension in tragedy (i.e., a "quiet ending"), consult Max Beerbohm, "Last Acts," in *Around Theatres.*

antimasque. See masque.

arena stage. (1) In British usage, a stage with a back wall and with an audience on three sides. (2) In American usage, a playing space surrounded by spectators, **theater-in-the-round.** Proponents of arena staging (in the American sense) stress the intimacy afforded by having actors in the midst of the audience, but opponents suggest that at least for some plays the intimacy ought not to be very great. (See aesthetic distance.) It has been noted, too, that even in arena staging the audience normally feels set apart from the actors, for the audience is in the dark while the actors are in an illuminated playing area. Critics of arena staging cite the following difficulties: soliloquies, asides, and direct addresses are hard to deliver in such a theater; directors, aware that the back of an actor's head is not very expressive, tend to have the actors gyrate disturbingly and meaninglessly; entrances and exits are cumbersome; little use can be made of elevation and of groupings of actors.

arras. See Elizabethan playhouse.

aside. See soliloquy, convention.

bombast. From a word meaning "cotton stuffing"; rant, speech that is too inflated for the occasion. In Marlowe's *Tamburlaine* (c. 1587), Tamburlaine brags thus:

Our quivering lances, shaking in the air,
And bullets, like Jove's dreadful thunderbolts,
Enrolled in flames and fiery smoldering mists,
Shall threat the gods more than Cyclopian wars:
And with our sun-bright armor as we march,
Will chase the stars from Heaven and dim their
    eyes
That stand and muse at our admirèd arms.

bomolochos. See character.

bourgeois drama. A serious play with middle-class dramatis personae. There are a few Elizabethan tragedies of middle-class life, but bourgeois drama, with its emphasis on pathos, is more or less an eighteenth-century invention. Bourgeois dramas were written in the eighteenth and nineteenth centuries, apparently in response to the middle class's desire to see itself on the stage; the bourgeois by the eighteenth century regarded himself as a suitable replacement for the nobleman of earlier tragedy. Speaking generally, the characteristics of these plays are: middle-class dramatis personae, virtue in distress, sentimentality, and an unreasonably high moral tone. Eighteenth-century critics, not sure what to do with pathetic plays on middle-class life, used the terms *drame, drame bourgeois, comédie larmoyante* (tearful comedy), *tragédie bourgeoise, bürgerliches Trauerspiel* (bourgeois tragedy) interchangeably. (Note that a *comédie larmoyante* need not end happily, nor a *tragédie bourgeoise* end sadly.) In England, George Lillo's *The London Merchant* (1731), "a tale of private woe. A London 'prentice ruined," depicted an apprentice who murdered his benefactor. Bourgeois drama in the nineteenth century became melodrama in many hands and tragedy in Ibsen's hands. Consult Fred O. Nolte, *Early Middle Class Drama*; and Eric Auerbach, *Mimesis*, Ch. 17. On Ibsen as a bourgeois dramatist, consult Eric Bentley, *The Playwright as Thinker*. See domestic tragedy, sentimental, and pp. 230–233, 634–635.

box set. See realism.

braggart soldier. See character.

burlesque. Any imitation which, by distortion, aims to amuse. Its subject matter is sometimes said to be faults rather than vices, and its tone is neither shrill nor savage. Thus, in distinction from satire it can be defined as a comic imitation of a mannerism or a minor fault (either in style or subject-matter), contrived to arouse amusement rather than indignation. In the theater, a burlesque may be a play that amusingly criticizes another play by grotesquely imitating aspects of it, as Gay's *The Beggar's Opera* (1728) mimicked serious operas. In England, a burlesque may be a musical extravaganza in which fantasy has almost entirely ousted criticism. In America, burlesque (especially popular in the late nineteenth and first half of the twentieth century) is usually a sort of vaudeville or variety show stressing bawdy humor and sex. The sexual theme is most fully revealed in the striptease, introduced about 1920. Consult V. C. Clinton-Baddeley, *The Burlesque Tradition in the English Theater after 1660*; Gypsy Rose Lee, *The G-String Murders*. See comedy, satire.

catastrophe. See plot.

catharsis. Aristotle and countless followers said that tragedy evokes pity and fear, and that it produces in the spectator a catharsis (purgation, or, some scholars hold, purification) of these emotions: it drains or perhaps refines or modifies these emotions, and thus tragedy is socially useful. (Aristotle's *Poetics* is the subject of much controversy; one cannot with security assert that Aristotle said anything, without a counter-argument being offered. For various views of catharsis, consult F. L. Lucas, *Tragedy*, and Gerald F. Else's monumental *Aristotle's Poetics*.) For Brecht on catharsis, see p. 567.

character. (1) One of the dramatis personae, e.g., King Lear. (2) The personality of such a figure. Characters are sometimes divided into flat and **round characters**. The former have only one "side," representing a single trait (e.g., the faithful wife, the genial drunkard); the latter have many traits and are seen, as it were, from all sides, in the round. The behavior of flat characters is thoroughly predictable, that of round characters is sometimes unexpected though credible. A **stock character** is a type that recurs in many works. For example, from Greek comedy to the present there have been numerous braggart soldiers, stubborn fathers, jealous husbands. Northrop Frye finds four chief types of comic figures: (1) the *alazon,* the impostor, boaster, hypocrite; (2) the *eiron* (see irony), the man who deprecates himself and exposes the boaster; (3) the *bomolochos,* the buffoon, or more generally, the man who entertains by his mannerisms and talk; (4) the *agroikos,* the straightman who is the unwitting butt of humor. Each of these types appears in many dresses; the *alazon,* for example, is most commonly the braggart soldier (*miles gloriosus*), but he is also the pedant, the crank, or anyone who is full of ideas that have no relation to reality. (See *commedia dell'arte;* consult Northrop Frye, *Anatomy of Criticism,* pp. 171–176.) Stock characters are not limited to comedy; the proud tragic hero is a stock character, as are, for example, the cruel stepmother and the son who wishes to avenge his father. See also motivation, plot. Consult J. L. Styan, *The Elements of Drama,* Ch. 8.

chorus. In Greek drama, a group of performers who play a role, e.g., Old Men of Corinth. (The chorus leader is the *koryphaeus.*) In Aeschylus' *The Suppliants* (c. 490 B.C.), perhaps the earliest extant play, the chorus consists of the heroines, but in most Greek plays the chorus consists of subsidiary figures who comment rather helplessly on what is happening to the important people. Aeschylus reduced the chorus of fifty to twelve; Sophocles increased it to fifteen, where it remained. The Greek chorus, it is often said, is a sort of middle-man between the unusual main figures and the humdrum spectators. Elizabethan dramas occasionally had a chorus of one actor who, not a participant in the story, commented on it. The Chorus (or prologue) in Shakespeare's *Henry V* urges the audience to

Think when we talk of horses that you see them
Printing their proud hoofs i' the receiving earth;
For 'tis your thoughts that now must deck our
    kings,
Carry them here and there, jumping o'er times,
Turning the accomplishment of many years
Into an hour-glass: for the which supply,
Admit me Chorus to this history:

Who prologue-like your humble patience pray,
Gently to hear, kindly to judge, our play.

A **chorus character,** or *raisonneur,* however, such as Enobarbus in *Antony and Cleopatra,* is a character who participates in the story yet seems to be the author's mouthpiece, intelligently commenting (often with irony) on the actions of the other characters. But Alfred Harbage, in *As They Liked It,* skeptically and aptly calls such a figure "The Unreliable Spokesman." The use of the chorus, in one form or another, continues into our times, for example in T. S. Eliot's *Murder in the Cathedral,* whose "Chorus of Women of Canterbury," like a Greek chorus and like the audience, "are forced to bear witness"; and in Tennessee Williams' *The Glass Menagerie,* whose Tom Wingfield tells the audience he is "the narrator of the play, and also a character in it."

climax. See plot.

closet drama. A play suited only for reading, not for acting. Most nineteenth-century English poetic dramas (e.g., Coleridge's, Shelley's, Tennyson's) fit into this category, although Byron's plays have recently been moving out of the closet. Consult Moody Prior, *The Language of Tragedy.*

comedy. Most broadly, anything amusing—a literary work or a situation — is a comedy. More specifically, comedy is (in Dr. Johnson's words) "such a dramatic representation of human life, as may excite mirth." Dramatic comedies generally depict a movement from unhappiness to happiness, from (for example) young lovers frustrated by their parents to young lovers happily married. The unhappy situation is so presented that it entertains rather than distresses the spectator; it is ridiculous and/or diverting rather than painful.
Comic drama seems related to fertility rituals; it celebrates generation, renewal, variety (laughing away any narrow-minded persons who seek to limit life's abundance), and it celebrates man's triumphs over the chances of life. Irate parents and shipwrecks cannot prevent journeys from ending with lovers meeting. For the kinds of Greek comedy (Old, Middle, and New) see pp. 315–317. For the characters in Greek comedy, see character. Consult C. Hoy, *The Hyacinth Room; Theories of Comedy,* ed. P. Lauter; L. J. Potts, *Comedy.*

comedy of humors. A term sometimes applied to plays — notably those of Ben Jonson — wherein the characters, though somewhat individualized, obviously represent types or moods (the jealous husband, the witless pedant). A humor was a bodily liquid (blood [Latin: *sanguis*], phlegm, yellow bile, black bile) thought to control one's behavior. Allegedly, a proper mixture produced a well adjusted man, but a preponderance of any one humor produced a distorted personality. The old sense of the word survives in the phrase, "He is in a bad humor"; "sanguine," "phlegmatic," and "bilious" are also modern survivals of the old psychology of humors. **Humor characters** are common in **situational comedy;** they are engineered by a clever plot into a situation that displays their absurdity: the man who craves silence is confronted with a talkative woman; the coward is confronted by the braggart.

comic relief. Humorous episodes in tragedy, alleged to alleviate or lighten the tragic effect. Some comic scenes in tragedy, however, not only provide "relief" but enlarge the canvas of tragedy, showing us a fuller picture of life. The clown who brings Cleopatra the poisonous asp sets her tragedy against the daily world. Critics have increasingly noted that the comic scenes (such as the macabre comments of the gravediggers in *Hamlet*) often deepen rather than alleviate the tragic effect. See tragicomedy. Consult A. P. Rossiter, *Angel with Horns*, Ch. 14.

commedia dell'arte. Italian drama, more or less improvised, performed by professionals in Italy and abroad, mostly in the sixteenth century but still alive in the early eighteenth century. In contrast to the classically-inspired written drama (*commedia erudita*) performed by actors who memorized their lines, *commedia dell'arte* (perhaps best translated as "professional drama") employed sketches of plots (*scenario;* plural: *scenarii*) specifying entrances and exits and the gist of the dialogue; in performance these *scenarii* were fleshed out with stock bits of comic stage business (*lazzi*) or larger pieces of business (*burle*) such as practical jokes. (The singulars are *lazzo* and *burla.*) Thus a *scenario* may call for the *lazzo* of anger, or the *burla* of chasing a fly, and leave it to the actor to work out the swats and the smile when at last he munches the fly. Though these plays are said to have been improvised, the stock characters,

stock situations, and stock stage business make them something more — or less — than improvised. The chief characters — most of whom wore masks — are Pantalone, an elderly Venetian merchant wearing a little cap, a red jacket, loose trousers (hence our word "pants"), and slippers: his age, amours, and avarice make him ridiculous; Dottore, a Bolognese doctor wearing a black academic gown: his age and his pedantry make him ridiculous; Capitano, a soldier, ridiculous because a braggart and a coward; several servants called *zanne* (singular: *zanni*, from *Gianni*, "Johnny") including Arlecchino (later Harlequin), who in the sixteenth century wore patches that in the next century were represented by triangles or diamonds; Brighella, a rather cruel and crafty rogue; Pulcinella, noted for his resourcefulness and his disguises; Pedrolino, a naive valet who becomes the melancholy Pagliacci and Pierrot; Colombina, who later becomes Columbine and loves Harlequin. Further, there are usually four lovers, children of the two Old Men. Consult Allardyce Nicoll, *Masks, Mimes and Miracles*, and *The World of Harlequin*; and K. M. Lea, *Italian Popular Comedy*.

complication. See plot.

confidant (feminine: **confidante**). A character in whom a principal character confides, revealing his state of mind and often furthering the exposition. Horatio is Hamlet's confidant; Oenone is Phèdre's. Although Horatio and Oenone are memorable, the confidant is sometimes absurdly vapid; though the French defended the device as more plausible than the soliloquy, the confidant may be more trouble than he is worth. In *The Critic* (1779), Sheridan ridiculed it thus: "Enter Tilburina stark mad in white satin, and her confidante stark mad in white linen."

conflict. See plot.

convention. An unrealistic device that the public agrees to tolerate. Thus, a character in a drama may express his thoughts aloud and not be heard by other characters (the **aside**), or he may speak his thoughts aloud on the empty stage (the **soliloquy**). Italian characters (e.g., Desdemona and Iago) speak English, yet are understood to be speaking Italian. In motion pictures, one image fades out, another fades in, and through this convention the audience knows that there is a shift in time or place. More generally any character-type, any theme, or motif (e.g., the suspected butler) widely used in literature or drama is a convention. Consult Harry Levin, *Refractions*; M. C. Bradbrook, *Themes and Conventions of Elizabethan Tragedy*.

coup de théatre. A surprise, especially a striking turn of events in the plot. Consult Alan R. Thompson, *The Anatomy of Drama*.

Cruelty, Theater of. Antonin Artaud (1896–1948) used the term in 1933 to refer to a drama that, working rather like a plague, would shock man out of the bonds of his "logical" or "civilized" conceptions and would release the suppressed primitive or pre-logical powers within him, such as criminal instincts and erotic obsessions, revealing the "cruelty" or terrible mystery of existence. This drama, relying more on gestures, shapes, music, and light than on words (Artaud was immensely impressed by Balinese drama although he did not understand Indonesian) would bypass mere realism (i.e., psychology) and would make manifest the truly real supernatural, creating in the spectator a "kind of terror" or a purifying delirium. Artaud, a poet, actor, and director, published relatively little but his metaphysics and his emphasis on an anti-realistic theater in various ways have influenced Sartre, Camus, Beckett, Ionesco, Genet (consult the preface to *The Maids*) and others: language sometimes becomes gibberish, and madness and violence are presented in order to jolt the spectator out of his comfortable false view of man and of the universe — or, in less metaphysical plays, in order to reflect on the stage the cruelty of the modern world. Consult Artaud's *The Theater and Its Double*; several articles in *Tulane Drama Review*, 8 (Winter 1963); and the "Conclusion" in Jacques Guicharnaud and June Beckelman, *Modern French Theatre*.

denouement. See plot.

deus ex machina. Literally, a god out of a machine. (1) In Greek drama a god who descends by a crane-like arrangement and solves a problem in the story, thus allowing the play to end. It was much used by Euripides; Sophocles in his old age borrowed the idea and introduced

Heracles at the end of *Philoctetes* to induce the title-character to go to Troy. (2) Any unexpected and improbable device (e.g., an unexpected inheritance from a long-lost uncle in Australia) used to unknot a problem and thus conclude the work.

deuteragonist. See protagonist.

dialogue. The speech exchanged between characters, or, loosely, even the speech of a single character. Dialogue is sometimes contrasted to action, but Elizabeth Bowen aptly says that dialogue is what the characters *do* to each other, and Shaw aptly says that his plays are all talk just as Beethoven's symphonies are all music. **Stichomythia** is a special form of dialogue, wherein two speakers in a verbal duel thrust and parry in alternating lines. Example:

QUEEN:
Hamlet, thou hast thy father much offended.
HAMLET:
Mother, you have my father much offended.
QUEEN:
Come, come, you answer with an idle tongue.
HAMLET:
Go, go, you question with a wicked tongue.

See action, soliloquy. Consult J. L. Styan, *The Elements of Drama*, Chs. 1–2; and Eric Bentley, *The Life of the Drama*.

diction. (1) Choice of words, wording. Dr. Johnson objected to the "knife" ("an instrument used by butchers and cooks," he said) which Lady Macbeth says she will use to murder the King. "Words too familiar, or too remote," Johnson said, "defeat the purpose of a poet." Consult Moody Prior, *The Language of Tragedy*. (2) A performer's manner or style of speaking, including pronunciation and phrasing.

Dionysus. Greek god of wine, the phallus, the surge of growth, and (to join all these) irrational impulse. It is commonly held that Greek tragedy grew from choral celebrations in his honor; in any case, from the sixth century B.C. tragedies were performed in Athens at the **Great** (or **Greater,** or **City**) **Dionysia**, a festival in Dionysus' honor. (The Dionysiac origin is interestingly rejected by H. D. F. Kitto, in *Theatre Survey*, 1 [1960], 3–17.) Friedrich Nietzsche suggested in *The Birth of Tragedy* (1872) that Greek tragedy, usually considered calm and poised, was not the product of quiet minds. If tragedy, Nietzsche said, showed light and beauty (over which the god Apollo presided), it was nevertheless also indebted to Dionysus, who represented the frenzied, buried self-assertions of the mind. That is, Greek tragedy was the product of **Dionysian** ecstatic and violent self-assertion tamed by (or fused with) the **Apollonian** sense of reason, of moderation, and of external order. "Apollonian" is often associated with classicism, and "Dionysian" with romanticism.

domestic tragedy. A serious play showing the misfortunes (especially within the family) of a private citizen rather than of a man of high rank who is involved in events that shake a realm. See bourgeois drama. Consult Henry H. Adams, *English Domestic or Homiletic Tragedy 1575 to 1642.*

drama (from Greek *dran*: to do). (1) A play, a work that tells a story by means of impersonators. (2) The whole body of work written for the theater. (3) A serious but untragic play (see drame). (4) Events containing conflict, tension, surprise ("life is full of drama"; "the first act lacks drama"). See closet drama, comedy, melodrama, tragedy. A play is written by a **dramatist;** the art of writing plays is **dramaturgy.** A man who writes plays is also a **playwright.** (Note that the last syllable is not "-write" but "-wright," denoting a maker, as a shipwright is a maker of ships.) Consult Kenneth T. Rowe, *Write That Play*; Walter Kerr, *How Not to Write a Play*; Bernard Grebanier, *Playwriting.*

dramatic illusion. The state between delusion (the spectator thinks the world on the stage is real), and full awareness (the spectator never forgets he is looking at scenery and actors). In *A Midsummer Night's Dream*, Bottom fears that delusion will occur unless the audience is carefully warned: "Write me a prologue, and let the prologue seem to say we will do no harm with our swords, and that Pyramus is not killed indeed. And, for the more better assurance, tell them that I Pyramus am not Pyramus, but Bottom the Weaver. This will put them out of fear." See aesthetic distance.

George Henry Lewes (1817–1878) introduced into English dramatic criticism the term *optique du théâtre*, taken from the French actor François René Molé (1734–1802). A spectator must have this "theater view," this understanding of "scenic illusion," if he is to enjoy the theater; if he lacks it, he will complain that Hamlet ought to be speaking Danish (see convention). *Optique du théâtre* requires that we be given not reality but a symbolic representation of it. A stage miser should finger his gold differently from a real miser; a stage character must be heard, even though in real life the character he is playing might speak softly.

Staging that aims at delusion or a high degree of illusion is **representational staging.** Here the stage-characters eat real food on stage, speak with their backs to the audience, etc. (See naturalism, realism.) When David Belasco staged *The Governor's Lady* in 1912, he was representational, placing on the stage an exact duplicate of a particular (Child's) restaurant. On the other hand, **presentational staging** is antirealistic; in Thornton Wilder's *Our Town* (1938), a drugstore counter, for example, consisted of a board across the backs of two chairs. The staging in musical comedies, ballets, and puppet shows is, of course, presentational. Presentational staging is sometimes called **theatrical staging. Theatricalism,** by its unreality, continually reminds us that we are in the theater, not in the street. On theatricalism, see style. A derogatory way of saying a work is theatrical is to say it is **stagy.**

drame. A solemn but untragic play, especially an eighteenth-century play that, quietly glorifying the bourgeois virtues, preaches and appeals to the audience's emotions. See bourgeois drama. Consult Alan R. Thompson, *The Anatomy of Drama*, which classifies most naturalistic and realistic plays (e.g., Ibsen's and Chekhov's) as *drames.*

Elizabethan playhouse. The first permanent structure built in England for plays was The Theater, built outside the city limits of London in 1576 by James Burbage. It soon had several competitors, but little is known about any of these playhouses. The contract for one, The Fortune (built in 1600), survives; it tells us that the three-storied building was square, 80 feet on the outside, 55 feet on the inside. The stage was 43 feet broad and 27½ feet deep. It has been calculated that about 800 people (the **groundlings**) could stand around the three sides of the stage on the ground that was called the **yard,** and another 1500 could be seated in the three galleries. The other chief pieces of evidence concerning the physical nature of the theater are (1) the "De Witt drawing," which is really a copy of a sketch made by a visitor (c. 1596) to The Swan, and (2) bits of evidence that can be gleaned from the plays themselves, such as "Enter a Fairy at one door, and Robin Goodfellow at another." Conclusions vary and scholarly tempers run high; the following statements are not indisputable. Most theaters were polygonal or round structures (Shakespeare calls the theater a "wooden O") with three galleries; the yard was open to the sky. From one side a raised stage (or open **platform**) jutted into the middle. A sort of wooden canopy (the **heavens,** or the **shadow**) projected over the stage and in some theaters rested on two pillars; these pillars could conveniently serve as a hiding place for an actor supposed to be unseen by the other characters. At the rear of the stage there sometimes was a curtained alcove or booth, which when uncurtained might represent a room or a cave. The curtain is often called an **arras,** and it was probably behind this curtain that Polonius hid, only to be stabbed. At the rear of the stage (flanking the curtained space?) there were perhaps also two or three doors, through which entrances and exits were made. Probably the **tiring house** ("attiring house," i.e., dressing room) was behind the rear of the stage. Above the alcove or booth was an area that could be used for an **upper stage** (for example, in scenes of people standing on a city's walls); flanking the upper stage were windows, one of which may have served Juliet for her misnamed balcony scene. Some scholars argue that in a yet higher place were musicians, and at the very top — called the **top** — was an opening from which an actor could look; in *Henry VI, Part I,* Joan of Arc appears "on the top, thrusting out a torch burning." Most of the acting was done on the main stage (the platform), but the "inner stage," "upper stage," "windows," and "top" must have been useful occasionally (if they existed). The **cellar** (beneath the stage) was used, for example for the voice of the ghost in *Hamlet,* and for Ophelia's grave. Though some scenery was used, the absence of a front curtain precluded many elaborate scenic effects (much, however, could be done by carrying banners) and encouraged continuous action. The stage that was a battlefield could in an instant, by the

introduction of a throne, become a room in a palace. Two readable books are A. M. Nagler, *Shakespeare's Stage,* and C. Walter Hodges, *The Globe Restored.* Nagler (Ch. 12) also gives information about a second kind of Elizabethan theater — basically a platform at one end of a hall — that catered to a courtly group. Interesting specialized items on playhouses are in *Shakespeare Survey,* 1 and 12, ed. Allardyce Nicoll.

empathy. The projection of one's feelings into a perceived object. The Germans call it *Einfühlung* — "a feeling into." Vernon Lee, one of the formulators of the idea, claimed that when we say "the mountain rises" we do so not because the mountain rises (it doesn't) but because we have often raised our eyes, head, and total muscular structure to look at mountains or other tall objects. In perceiving a mountain, we merge (unawares) its image with the previously accumulated idea of rising. We are said to empathize with a character if we flinch at a blow directed at him, or if we feel bowed with his grief; if, in short, we *experience* as well as *see* his behavior. Empathy is often distinguished from **sympathy:** we empathize if we feel *with* the character; we sympathize if we feel *for* the character. See aesthetic distance. Consult Vernon Lee's essay in *A Modern Book of Aesthetics,* ed. Melvin Rader; Herbert S. Langfeld, *The Aesthetic Attitude.*

epic drama. Bertolt Brecht (1898–1956) labeled "aristotelian" most drama before his own. He held that it aimed at enthralling the spectators by building up to a climax, thus arousing and then purging their emotions. In contrast, Brecht said, epic drama (he borrowed the phrase from Erwin Piscator) aims at arousing the audience's detached thought; it teaches, keeping the spectators alert by preventing any emotional involvement. The epic drama (probably so-called because it resembles the epic in its abundance of loosely connected scenes and its tendency to deal with a society rather than merely with a few individuals) achieves this estrangement or **alienation effect** (German: *Verfremdungseffekt*) by many means: the epic play (e.g., Brecht's *The Good Woman of Setzuan,* or his *Mother Courage*) commonly consists of a series of loosely connected scenes rather than a tightly organized plot with a climax; the settings are not realistic but merely suggest the locale, and they are often changed in full view of the audience, preventing any entrancing illusion (a night scene may be done on an illuminated stage, again to prevent the audience from emotionally entering into the play); the actor may address the audience directly, sometimes in song, and he aims not at becoming the character but at presenting him, or, to put it differently, at making a comment on him, as we might do when we put aside a cigarette and say, "He said to me, '....'"; loudspeakers, films, and placards may be used, and the whole is something of a lecture-demonstration, aimed not at arousing and then quieting the audience's emotions, but at making things somewhat strange to the audience so that the audience will look sharply and will think. Consult Bertolt Brecht, "A Short Organum," in *Playwrights on Playwriting*, ed. Toby Cole; *Brecht on Theatre*, trans. John Willett; R. Gray, *Brecht*; *The Tulane Drama Review*, 6 (Sept. 1961). See pp. 567–569.

epilogue. (1) An appendix (usually a concluding address) to a play; (2) the actor who recites such an appendix (e.g., Rosalind, at the close of Shakespeare's *As You Like It*).

exposition. See plot.

expressionism. An anti-naturalistic movement chiefly associated with Germany just after World War I, but which was foreshadowed by Strindberg, notably in his trilogy, *To Damascus* (1898–1904), and in his *A Dream Play* (1902). Expressionism does not seek to present reality dispassionately imitated, but reality passionately felt. Thus, when Mr. Zero shakes his employer (in Elmer Rice's *The Adding Machine* [1923]), the office spins; when he is on trial, the walls of the courtroom veer crazily. Speaking broadly, expressionist plays (in addition to being unrealistic) usually (1) depict types or classes (Rice's Mr. Zero; the Man, the Woman, the Nameless One in Ernst Toller's *Man and Masses* [1921]), (2) employ dream sequences, (3) assume that society is responsible for man's troubles. In *The Emperor Jones*, Eugene O'Neill's concentration on a single figure representative of man (Jones) and his use of visions and unrealistic settings illustrate the first two points. Though Arthur Miller's *Death of a Salesman* (1949) is in many ways "realistic," it also is indebted to expressionism,

especially in the scenes involving Willy's memories. (Miller originally planned to call the play *The Inside of His Head*.) Note, too, the name of Miller's hero — Loman, i.e., low man. Consult John Willett, *Expressionism*.

farce. A sort of comedy based not on clever language or subtleties of character, but on broadly humorous situations (a man mistakenly enters the ladies' locker room), is lucidly defended by Eric Bentley in his introduction to *"Let's Get a Divorce" and Other Plays*, where he suggests that farce, like dreams, shows "the disguised fulfillment of repressed wishes." Farce is usually filled with surprise, with swift physical action, and with assault. The characters are physically and intellectually insensitive, and characterization is subordinated to plot. See also Bentley's *The Life of the Drama*. **Slapstick** (named for an implement made of two slats which resound when slapped against a posterior) is farce that relies on physical assault. Farce and slapstick are **low comedy,** as is comedy that depends on obscenity.

foil. A character who sets off another, as Laertes and Fortinbras — young men who, like Hamlet, have lost a father — help to set off Hamlet, or as a braggart soldier helps to set off a courageous one.

Greek and **Hellenistic theater.** The great age of the Greek drama was the fifth century B.C. The audience sat on wooden benches in tiers on a hillside, looking down at a flat circular dancing-place (the **orchestra**), in the middle of which was an altar to Dionysus; behind the dancing place was a playing-area, which logic (but no concrete evidence) suggests may have been slightly elevated; visible behind the playing-area was the *skene,* a wooden "scene-building" introduced about 458 B.C. that served as a background, as a place for actors to make entrances from and exits to, and as a dressing room. To speak of these elements in a little more detail: the seating-area, which held as many as 16,000 people, was the *theatron* ("seeing-place"); fan-shaped or horseshoe shaped, it swept around the orchestra in a segment a little greater than a semicircle. The chorus, entering by an aisle (*parodos*) at each side of the *theatron,* danced in the orchestra. The front (i.e., the façade) of the *skene* (or perhaps a temporary screen) and sometimes the playing-area in front of it seem to have been called the **proskenion.** Though the *skene's* façade perhaps suggested the front of a palace, there were further efforts at indicating locale: Sophocles is said to have invented scene-painting (a painted cloth or screen in front of the *skene?*), and there are allusions to *periaktoi,* upright prisms bearing a different decoration on each side. Apparently when a new locality in the same town was to be indicated, the *periaktos* at the right was turned, when an entirely new locality was to be indicated, both *periaktoi* were turned. Other machines were the **eccyclema,** a platform that was rolled out of the *skene* to indicate a scene indoors, and the **mechane,** a crane from which a god could descend or by means of which a character could soar through the air. (See *deus ex machina.)*

Plays were put on chiefly during two holidays, the **Lenaea** (Feast of the Wine-press) in January, and the **Great** (or **Greater,** or **City**) **Dionysia** in March or April. The Lenaea was chiefly associated with comedy, the Great Dionysia with tragedy. At the latter, on each of three mornings a tragic dramatist presented three tragedies and one satyr-play. The expense was born by a **choregus,** a rich citizen ordered by the state to assume the financial burden. See comedy, satyr-play, tragedy.

The **Hellenistic theater** (i.e., theaters of, say, the third and second centuries B.C. erected in towns to which Greek culture had been spread by Alexander's conquests) seems to have been much like the Greek theater, though now the *proskenion* is apparently more highly decorated, having pillars a few feet in front of it and being fitted with painted panels called *pinakes.* And the *skene,* now of stone rather than of wood, may have had projections at the sides (*paraskenia*) and an upper story (*episkenion*). The playing-area on this upper level is the *logeion.* Consult Margarete Bieber, *The History of the Greek and Roman Theater.*

hamartia. This Greek word is variously translated as "tragic flaw" or "error" or "shortcoming" or "weakness," and in many plays it *is* a flaw or even a vice such as *hybris* (also *hubris*) — Greek for overweening pride, arrogance, excessive confidence. But in other plays it is merely a misstep, such as a choice that turns out badly. Indeed, the tragic hero may be undone by his virtue — his courage, for example, when others are not merely prudent

but cowardly. See pp. 5–8. On *hamartia* and *hybris* see Richmond Lattimore, *Story Patterns in Greek Tragedy.*

happening. A kind of theatrical activity popular in the early 1960's, named for Allan Kaprow's *18 Happenings in 6 Parts* (1959). Instead of a conventional theater there is simply a place (art gallery, backyard), instead of actors who play roles there are participants, instead of a plot there are discontinuous actions or happenings. Sample: a man asks if Howard Saretta is in the audience; when there is no answer he sits down among the spectators, and someone else gets up, skips rope, washes his face, and then breaks a pair of eyeglasses. Often there is some violence directed against people (participants and audience) and against objects (here, against eyeglasses). Consult *Happenings,* ed. Michael Kirby; Susan Sontag, *Against Interpretation;* and A. Kaprow, *Art News* (May 1961).

high comedy. Intellectual rather than physical, it requires the close attention of a sophisticated audience, flourishing (says George Meredith in his *Essay on Comedy* [1877]) in a "society of cultivated men and women . . . wherein ideas are current, and the perceptions quick." Etherege, Wycherley, Congreve, and other playwrights of the decades following the Restoration of Charles II to the throne of England (1660) wrote **Restoration comedy,** high comedy of a particular sort, often called **comedy of manners** or **comedy of wit.** Their plays abound in witty **repartee** (what Dr. Johnson called "gay remarks and unexpected answers"), and often strike modern audiences as cynical. Restoration comedy has no precise terminal date, but can be said to end about 1700, with the development of sentimental comedy, plays of venerable parents and middle-class dutiful sons who love pure young things. Example: Richard Steele's *The Conscious Lovers* (1722). Consult Thomas H. Fujimura, *The Restoration Comedy of Wit;* Louis Kronenberger, *The Thread of Laughter;* Norman N. Holland, *The First Modern Comedies.*

hubris. See *hamartia.*

hybris. See *hamartia.*

imitation (Greek: *mimesis*). Not a pejorative term in much criticism, for it often implies a "making" or "re-creating" or "re-presenting" of a form in a substance not natural to it. Thus Michelangelo reproduced or imitated the form of Moses, in stone. For Aristotle, tragedy is the imitation (i.e., representation, re-creation) by means of words, gesture, music, and scenery, of an important action.

irony. Irony is of several sorts. **Socratic irony,** named for Socrates, who commonly feigned more ignorance than he possessed, denotes understatement. The *eiron* (see character) is the cunning fellow who plays the underdog. **Dramatic irony,** or **Sophoclean irony,** or **tragic irony** refers to a condition of affairs which is the tragic reverse of what the participants think. Thus, it is ironic that Macbeth kills Duncan, thinking he will achieve happiness; he later finds he loses all that makes life worth living. Oedipus accuses the blind prophet of corruption, but by the end of the play Oedipus learns (as the audience knew at the outset) that he himself is corrupt, that he has been mentally blind (ignorant) and that the prophet has had vision (knowledge). Oedipus meant what he said, but his words have proved to be ironic. (Aristotle's word for reversal is *peripeteia*.) We have dramatic irony, it can be said, when a speech or action is more fully understood by the spectators than by the characters. This sort of irony, based on misunderstanding, or partial knowledge, is common in tragedy, but comedy too has its misunderstandings; comic speeches or actions are ironic if they bring about the opposite of what is intended. More generally, the contrast implied in "irony" need be neither tragic nor comic; it is "ironic" that the strong man is overthrown by the weak man and that the liar unknowingly tells the truth. **irony of fate** (a phrase which H. W. Fowler's *Modern English Usage* aptly says is hackneyed), or **cosmic irony,** denotes the view that God, or fate, or some sort of supernatural figure, is amused to manipulate human beings as a puppeteer manipulates his puppets. Thus, by an irony of fate the messenger delivers the prisoner's pardon an instant too late. Consult Garnett G. Sedgewick, *Of Irony;* Alan R. Thompson, *The Dry Mock.*

liturgical drama. A play that is part of the church service or liturgy. In the tenth century the churchmen put on a playlet of a few lines as part of the Easter liturgy. The text is based on Mark 16:1–7: clerics dressed as the Three Marys approach the "tomb" of Christ (the altar) and are asked by a cleric, disguised as an angel, whom they seek. When they reply that they seek Christ, he tells them that Christ has risen and shows them the empty "tomb." The performers were all male, and the dialogue (in Latin) was chanted or sung; probably the gestures were stylized.

low comedy. See farce.

masque, mask, disguising. An entertainment (apparently derived from an ancient ritual) in the Renaissance court, wherein noblemen performed a dignified playlet, usually allegorical and mythological. The masque was lavishly produced, but its basic structure was generally simple: the masquers (costumed and masked noble performers) enter, supposedly having come from afar, they dance with the ladies of the court, and then they depart. Because the masquers are of the same rank as the ladies, and because performers and audience join in a dance, the masque is very close to the masked ball. Ben Jonson (1572–1637) popularized what he called the **antimasque** (a grotesque dance of monsters or clowns), performed by professionals representing chaos, who are dispelled by the courtly performers. ("Anti," from "antic," meaning "a grotesque caper" or "a fool," is sometimes written "ante" because the antimasque precedes the masque.) Consult Enid Welsford, *The Court Masque;* E. K. Chambers, *The Mediaeval Stage* and *The Elizabethan Stage.*

melodrama. Originally, in Renaissance Italy, an opera; later, a drama with occasional songs, or with music (*melos* is Greek for "song") expressing a character's thoughts, much as in films today. In the early nineteenth century plays with musical accompaniment became so stereotyped that the word acquired a second (and now dominant) meaning: a play wherein characters clearly virtuous or vicious are pitted against each other in sensational situations filled with suspense, until justice triumphs. The situations, not the characters, are exciting. The exotic horror (castles with dungeons) dominant in early nineteenth-century melodramas was often replaced later in the century by local horror (the cruel landlord), but whether exotic or local, melodrama is improbable, and virtue — unsullied by any touch of guilt — triumphs over unlikely circumstances. Melodrama is sometimes said to be tragedy with character left out (i.e., it contains serious happenings), but by virtue of its happy ending and its one-sided characters it can better be described as comedy with good-humor left out. Some critics use "melodrama" without any pejorative connotation to describe such serious, often sensational, plays as Emlyn Williams' *Night Must Fall* (1935), Robert Ardrey's *Thunder Rock* (1939), and Arthur Miller's *All My Sons*. Consult Robert B. Heilman, *Tragedy and Melodrama*.

miracle play. A medieval play on a Biblical episode or a saint's life. Consult Arnold Williams, *The Drama of Medieval England*.

morality play. A late medieval development, popular well into the sixteenth century, allegorically dramatizing some aspect of the moral life, including such characters as Everyman, Good Deeds, and Avarice. It usually showed the conflict between good and evil, or the way in which the Christian faces death. Consult Arnold Williams, *The Drama of Medieval England*; Bernard Spivack, *Shakespeare and the Allegory of Evil*.

motivation. Grounds in character and situation that make behavior plausible. Such grounds are not always present, even in great drama: when Othello asks why Iago "hath thus ensnared my soul," Iago replies, "Demand me nothing: what you know, you know." See character. Consult J. I. M. Stewart, *Character and Motive in Shakespeare*.

naturalism. Sometimes defined, like realism, as the portrayal of "a scientifically accurate, detached picture of life, including everything and selecting nothing." The spectator looking through the peephole of the proscenium, as a scientist looks through the eyepiece of a microscope, is to feel he is witnessing life rather than a symbolic representation of life. More commonly, however, "naturalism" alludes neither to a panoramic view nor to the detailed presentation of a narrow **slice of life** (French: *tranche de vie*), but to a particular attitude held by some writers since the middle of the nineteenth century. Though claiming to be dispassionate observers, they were influenced by evolutionary thought, and regarded man not as possessed of a soul and of free will, but as a creature determined by his heredity and environment. The movement in drama can be said to begin with the Goncourt Brothers' unsuccessful *Henriette Maréchal* (1865), but it is usual to say that the opening gun in the battle for naturalism was fired in Émile Zola's dramatization (1873) of his novel, *Thérèse Raquin*. Thérèse and her lover drown her husband, but are then so guilt-ridden that they poison themselves. In his preface Zola urged that the theater be brought "into closer relation with the great movement toward truth and experimental science which has since the last century been on the increase. . . . I have chosen characters who were completely dominated by their nerves and blood." In Paris, André Antoine opened his Théâtre Libre in 1887, devoting it mostly to plays showing the power of instincts and the influence of heredity and environment. These plays were staged as untheatrically as possible; for example, the actors turned their backs to the audience. In Germany, Otto Brahm opened the Freie Bühne in 1889, and in England J. T. Grein opened the Independent Theatre in 1891, both with Ibsen's *Ghosts* (1881), a play showing the destruction of a young man by inherited syphilis. Ibsen's greatness does not allow him to be pinned down by the label "naturalist," but he can be said to be naturalistic (among other things) by virtue of his serious interest in the effects of heredity and environment. Other dramatists who wrote naturalistic plays include August Strindberg (e.g., his *Miss Julie* [1888]) and Gerhart Hauptmann (early in his career, say, through *The Weavers* [1892]), and Eugene O'Neill (again, the early plays such as *The Rope* [1918] and *Diff'rent* [1920]). Note, however, that the major naturalistic writers usually are more than naturalistic; Strindberg's *Miss Julie*, for example, has a preface that talks about the influence of heredity and environment, and it deals with sordid aspects of reality, but it also has symbolic overtones, notably in Julie's and Jean's dreams. Consult Mordecai Gorelik, *New Theatres for Old*; *TDR: The Drama Review*, 13 (Winter 1968); and (for Strindberg, O'Neill, and the sources of their ideas) Oscar Cargill, *Intellectual America*.

obligatory scene. See *scène à faire*.

pathos. The quality that evokes pity. The pathetic is often distinguished from the tragic; in the former, the suffering is experienced by the passive and the innocent (especially women and children), while in the latter it is experienced by persons who act, struggle, and are in some measure responsible for their sufferings. Discussing Aeschylus' *The Suppliants*, H. D. F. Kitto says in *Greek Tragedy* (2nd ed.): "The Suppliants are not only pathetic, as the victims of outrage, but also tragic, as the victims of their own misconceptions." See bourgeois drama, and the afterword to Arthur Miller's *Death of a Salesman*, pp. 230–232.

peripeteia (anglicized to **peripety,** meaning **reversal**). The reversal occurs when an action produces the opposite of what was intended or expected, and it is therefore a kind of irony. In *Julius Caesar*, Brutus kills Caesar in order to free Rome from tyranny, but the deed introduces tyranny into Rome. (See irony, plot.)

pièce à thèse. A play with a thesis, a play in which the dramatist argues a point. Commonly the thesis is not about, say, the benevolence of God, but about the merits or defects of some social institution; a play dealing with a social institution may also be called a **problem play** or a **drama of ideas.** Some critics distinguish between the terms, saying that a problem play merely poses a social problem, as Galsworthy does in *Strife* (1909), while a thesis play propounds a solution. Shaw says that "The material of the dramatist is always some conflict of human feeling with circumstances"; when the circumstances are "human institutions" (e.g., divorce laws, penal codes) rather than unchanging facts of life (e.g., death), and the audience is forced to meditate on the value of the institutions, we have a problem play. Shaw's essay, "The Play of Ideas," is in *Shaw on Theatre*, ed. E. J. West. Consult also Walter Kerr, *How Not to Write a Play*, Ch. 5.

pièce bien faite, or **well-made play.** A play, with much suspense and with little depth of characterization, that relies on a cleverly constructed plot, first developing a situation, then building the crisis to a climax, and then resolving the business. The type, which perhaps can be described as melodrama with the fisticuffs left out, is chiefly associated with Victorien Sardou (1831–1908), but Sardou was indebted to Eugène Scribe (1791–1861). Shaw called their plays clockwork mice, and Sardoodledom, but the influence of Sardou on Shaw's hero, Ibsen, is undeniable. See plot, and consult Walter Kerr, *How Not to Write a Play*, Ch. 10; Eric Bentley, "Homage to Scribe," *What Is Theatre?*; C. E. Montague, *Dramatic Values*, pp. 63–74; *Camille and Other Plays*, ed. Stephen S. Stanton.

plot and **character.** The plot is sometimes the "story," the "narrative," but usually it is the happenings *as the author arranges them.* In *Hamlet*, for example, the story involves the poisoning of Hamlet's father, but Shakespeare omits this scene from his plot. Aristotle, in Chapter 6 of the *Poetics*, calls plot "the whole structure of the incidents," and he speaks of plot as the "soul of tragedy," thus making it more important than character. By character he means the personalities of the figures in the story. Menander (a Greek comic dramatist) is said to have told a friend that he had finished a comedy, though he had not yet written a line of dialogue; the anecdote implies that Menander had completed his idea of *what happens* (action) and in *what order* (plot), and he would find it easy then to write the lines of the characters necessary to this plot. The separation, however, between plot and character is misleading, for the two usually interplay. Although it is true that there may be much plot and little character (as in a thriller), in most great plays there is such a fusion between what is done and the personality of the doer that we feel the truth of Henry James's questions: "What is character but the determination of incident? What is incident but the illustration of character?" (See also character.)

Most plots entail a **conflict,** wherein the protagonist is somehow opposed. If he is opposed chiefly by another person rather than by a force such as Fate or God or by an aspect of himself, the opposing figure is the antagonist. The German critic, Gustav Freytag, in *Technique of the Drama* (1863), held that a play dramatizes "the rushing forth of will power from the depths of man's soul toward the external world," and "the coming into being of a deed and its consequences on the human soul." The five-act play, he said, commonly arranged such an action into a **pyramidal structure,** consisting of a **rising action,** a **climax,** and a **falling action.** The rising action begins with the **exposition,** in which is given essential information, especially about the **antecedent action** (what has occurred before this piece of action begins). The two gossiping servants who tell each other that after a year away in Paris the young master is coming home today with his new wife are giving the audience the exposition. The exposition in Shakespeare's *The Tempest* is almost ruthlessly direct: Prospero tells his naive daughter "I should inform thee farther," and for about one hundred and fifty lines he proceeds to tell her why she is on an almost uninhabited island. The action rises through a **complication** (the protagonist is opposed) to a high point or **crisis** or **climax** (a moment at which tension is high, and which is a decisive turning point). The falling action goes through a **reversal** (if a tragedy, the protagonist loses power), and then into a **catastrophe,** also called a **denouement** (unknotting) or resolution. (Aristotle's word for the reversal is *peripeteia,* anglicized to **peripety,** and translated as "irony of events," would in a comedy be a change from bad fortune to good, and the catastrophe would thus be happy.) The denouement frequently involves what Aristotle called an *anagnorisis* (recognition, disclosure, discovery). This recognition may be as simple as the identification of a long-lost brother by a birth mark, or it may involve a character's recognition of his own true condition. Shakespeare sometimes used a pyramidal structure, placing his climax neatly in the middle of what seems to us to be the third of five acts. In *Julius Caesar,* Brutus rises in the first half of the play, reaching his height in III.i, with the death of Caesar; but later in this scene he gives Marc Antony permission to speak at Caesar's funeral and thus sets in motion his own fall, which occupies the second half of the play. In *Macbeth,* the protagonist attains his height in III.i. ("Thou hast it now: King"), but he soon perceives that he is going downhill:

> I am in blood
> Stepped in so far that, should I wade no more,
> Returning were as tedious as go o'er.

Some works have a **double plot,** that is, two plots, usually with some sort of relation. For example, the **subplot** or **underplot** (the secondary narrative) might be a grotesque version of the serious main plot. In Shakespeare's *The Tempest,* the main plot and subplot both deal with usurpation. In *King Lear,* the main plot concerns Lear's relation to his daughters, while the parallel subplot concerns Gloucester's relation to his sons. For another aspect of the subplot, see comic relief; consult William Empson, *Some Versions of Pastoral,* Ch. 2. On plotting see *pièce bien faite* and *scène à faire.*

poetic justice. A term coined by Thomas Rymer in 1678, denoting the reward of the virtuous and the punishment of the vicious. Aristotle had said or implied that the tragic hero is undone partly by some sort of personal flaw — i.e., he is at least partly responsible for the suffering he later encounters. (See *hamartia,* and pp. 5–8.) "Poetic justice," with its idea that all characters reap the harvest of their just deserts, is a hardening of Aristotle's suggestion. Consult M. A. Quinlan, *Poetic Justice in the Drama.*

problem play. See *pièce à thèse.*

prologue. (1) A preface or introduction. For the Greeks the *prologos* was the first scene, which gave the exposition. Elizabethan prologues commonly summarize the plot, as the Chorus does in the prologue to *Romeo and Juliet,* but in the English theater of the late seventeenth century, the prologue was almost an independent verse essay spoken before the play began. Consult Autrey N. Wiley, *Rare Prologues and Epilogues 1642–1700.* (2) The actor who speaks a piece of the sort described above.

proscenium stage, or **picture-frame stage.** A playing-area framed in the front, and thus separated from the audience. This frame is the **proscenium arch** or the **proscenium;** the empty space it contains, sometimes filled with a curtain is the **proscenium opening.** Basically a **proscenium theater** has two rooms, one for the audience and another (with a hole in the mutual wall) for the performers. Such a theater is at least as old as the early seventeenth century, when the Farnese Theater was built in Parma. Consult Allardyce Nicoll, *The Development of the Theatre.*

protagonist. The chief figure in a play. In Greek the word means literally the "first contender," i.e., the chief actor (*protos:* first). The second role was given to the **deuteragonist,** the third to the **tritagonist.** The protagonist is commonly opposed by the **antagonist,** played by the deuteragonist. For the relationship between the protagonist and the antagonist, see plot.

realism. The reproduction of life, especially as it appears to the eye and ear; the illusion of nature. Usually it deals with ordinary men in ordinary situations, moving in scenery that closely imitates reality. In England, T. W. Robertson (1829–1871) insisted, for example, that doorknobs not be painted on the doors but be three-dimensional. Wings and a backcloth (i.e., projecting flats at the sides and a painted cloth at the rear) were increasingly replaced by the box set (a room with the front wall missing, containing real furniture) for interior scenes. Gas lighting, introduced to the stage about 1820, soon became capable of producing effects of sunlight, moonlight, etc. The dialogue, as well as the sets, came closer to what the senses perceive. Realistic plays (in prose, of course) avoided soliloquies, asides, and declamation. The great playwrights of the movement are Ibsen and Chekhov. As Mary McCarthy says of American realistic drama (*On the Contrary*), "realism is a depreciation of the real," for in "its resolve to tell the whole truth" it tends to deflate, to reveal human littleness. (It doesn't believe in exceptional, heroic people; when it treats the upper classes, it usually tends toward satire.) The oppressive box set of realistic plays, Miss McCarthy points out, "is the box or 'coffin' of average middle-class life opened at one end to reveal the corpse within." That realism shades into naturalism is clear; that in Ibsen it shades into symbolism is less obvious but is well demonstrated by John Northam, *Ibsen's Dramatic Method.* A simple example of Ibsen's symbolism: in *Hedda Gabler*, Hedda's hair is "not particularly ample," but Thea's is "unusually rich and wavy," suggesting Hedda's barrenness and Thea's fertility. Consult Mordecai Gorelik, *New Theatres for Old*; A. Nicholas Vardac, *Stage to Screen*, Chs. 4, 9; Ernest B. Watson, *Sheridan to Robertson*. In **selective realism,** some of the scenery (e.g., a window and a door) closely reproduces reality, but some (e.g., a framework *suggesting* a roof) does not.

Roman theater. A permanent theater was not built at Rome until the first century B.C. The plays of Plautus (254?–184 B.C.) and Terence

(190?–159? B.C.) were performed on temporary stages erected in the Circus Maximus and the Forum during holidays. In the permanent Roman theater, the enormous audience (40,000 or more) sat in a semicircle around a level space that was a vestige of what had been called the "orchestra" ("dancing place") of the Greek theater. Behind this vestige was the stage, running through what would have been the diameter of the circle. The long, slightly elevated stage was backed by a façade (painted to resemble two or three houses) with several doors through which actors made some of their exits and entrances, the others being made at the ends of the stage. Behind the façade was the dressing-room. The Roman theater, unlike the Greek and Hellenistic theaters, was a self-enclosed structure, built on level ground, not against a hillside. Consult Margarete Bieber, *The History of the Greek and Roman Theater.*

satire. A work ridiculing aspects of human behavior and seeking to arouse in the audience contempt for its object. Satirists almost always justify their attacks by claiming that satire is therapeutic. Shaw says, in the preface to his *Complete Plays*, "If I make you laugh at yourself, remember that my business as a classic writer of comedies is to 'chasten morals with ridicule'; and if I sometimes make you feel like a fool, remember that I have by the same action cured your folly." Satire, however, is sometimes distinguished from comedy on the grounds that satire aims to correct by ridiculing, while comedy aims simply to evoke amusement. Among notable satires are the plays of Aristophanes; Gay's *The Beggar's Opera* (1728); Brecht's *The Threepenny Opera* (1928); Kaufman, Ryskind, and Gershwin's *Of Thee I Sing* (1931) — though Kaufman himself has defined satire as "that which closes on Saturday night." See burlesque, comedy. Consult Dane F. Smith, *Plays about the Theatre in England from "The Rehearsal" in 1671 to the Licensing Act in 1737*; Northrop Frye, *Anatomy of Criticism.*

satyr-play. A piece in which there is a chorus of lewd satyrs (creatures half-man, the other half either horse or goat). The Greek tragic playwright of the fifth century B.C. presented three tragedies and a satyr-play for the dramatic festival. Apparently the satyr-play often burlesqued a hero, showing him in a ludicrous situation. Only one complete satyr-play (Euripides' *The Cyclops*) is extant; it travesties the legend of Odysseus' encounter with Polyphemus. Consult Philip W. Harsh, *A Handbook of Classical Drama*.

scene. Set act.

scenery. The carpentry and painted cloths (and projected images) used on a stage. Scenery may be used to conceal parts of the stage, to decorate, to imitate or suggest locales, to establish time or to evoke mood. For comments on early scenery, see Greek theater and Elizabethan playhouse. The Elizabethan public theater did not use much scenery. In *Twelfth Night*, when Viola asks "What country, friends, is this?" she is told "This is Illyria, lady," and the audience knows all that carpenters and painters can tell them. But even before Shakespeare's birth, Renaissance Italians had placed buildings, probably of lath and cloth, at the right and left of the stage. Behind the buildings, which were three-dimensional and were embellished with moldings, projected flat pieces cut and painted to look like other buildings at a distance, and behind these flat pieces were yet other flats, still smaller. On the symbolic use of scenery, see pp. 23–24.

scène à faire, or (in William Archer's translation of Francisque Sarcey's term) **obligatory scene.** "An obligatory scene [Archer says] is one which the audience (more or less clearly and consciously) foresees and desires, and the absence of which it may with reason resent." For example, a familiar legend may make a scene obligatory, or a dramatist may cause the audience to expect a certain scene. In *Hamlet* the play-within-the-play (III.ɪɪ) has been called such a scene: Hamlet has doubted the ghost, and we must see the ghost's words verified. Consult William Archer, *Play-making*.

Senecan tragedy. Any of the serious plays by the Roman author Seneca (4 B.C.–65 A.D.), or imitations of them. Of the ten extant Roman tragedies, nine are attributed to Seneca, and these were probably written not for the stage but for private readings. The heroes seem to us to be almost madmen, but perhaps they are to be regarded sympathetically as people over-

whelmed by passion. Seneca's influence on the Elizabethan dramatists was considerable; the **revenge play**, with it ghosts and its deranged hero who seeks vengeance, doubtless would have been different had Seneca not existed. Among the signs of Seneca's influence are: ghosts, revenge, deeds of horror (e.g., children stewed and served to their parents), occasional stoical speeches but a predominance of passionate speeches, use of stichomythia (see dialogue), a *nuntius* (messenger) who recites in a heightened style an off-stage happening (e.g., the wounded soldier in *Macbeth*, I.ɪ). But, of course, not every use of any of these characteristics is necessarily attributable to Seneca's influence. And there are differences: e.g., the horrors in Seneca are narrated, but in *King Lear* Gloucester is blinded on the stage. Consult F. L. Lucas, *Seneca and Elizabethan Tragedy*; Madeleine Doran, *Endeavors of Art*; Willard Farnham, *The Medieval Heritage of Elizabethan Tragedy*; Howard Baker, *Induction to Tragedy*, minimizes Seneca's influence.

sentimental. Generally a pejorative word in criticism, indicating a superabundance of tender emotion, a disproportionate amount of sentiment (feeling). It is sentimental to be intensely distressed because one has stepped on a flower. A character, say Hamlet, may display deep emotions, but they are sentimental only if they are in excess of what the situation warrants. More specifically, "sentimental" writing refers to writing wherein evil is facilely conquered, denied, overlooked, or bathed in a glow of forgiving tenderness. In the eighteenth century the ability to respond emotionally (usually tearfully) to acts of benevolence or malevolence was called **sensibility**. In its **sentimental drama** there is at the expense of reason an emphasis on tearful situations; man's benevolent emotions are overestimated, for he is assumed to be innately good, and villains reform, usually in bursts of repenting tears. There is little wit, the characters are usually of the middle class, and they demonstrate their virtue by weeping at the sight of distress. In his "Comparison between Sentimental and Laughing Comedy" (1772), Oliver Goldsmith attacked sentimental comedy, saying that in it:

> the virtues of private life are exhibited, rather than the vices exposed; and the distresses rather than the faults of mankind make our interest in the

piece.... Almost all the characters are good, ... and though they want humor, have abundance of sentiment and feeling. If they happen to have faults or foibles, the spectator is taught, not only to pardon, but to applaud them, in consideration of the goodness of their hearts; so that folly, instead of being ridiculed, is commended, and the comedy aims at touching our passions, without the power of being truly pathetic.

See bourgeois drama. Consult Ernest Bernbaum, *The Drama of Sensibility*; Arthur Sherbo, *English Sentimental Drama*.

slice of life. See naturalism.

sock and **buskin.** Performers of Latin comedy wore a light slipper or sandal called the *soccus*. The sock is either this piece of footwear or comedy itself. The high boot worn by Greek tragic actors was the **cothurnus** or **kothurnus**. In Hellenistic times it acquired a very thick sole, giving the performer the height appropriate to a great man. In English this footgear (or tragic drama in general) is called the buskin, apparently from Old French *broissequin*, from Middle Dutch *brosekin*, a small leather boot. Consult Margarete Bieber, *The History of the Greek and Roman Theater*.

soliloquy. A speech wherein a character utters his thoughts aloud while alone. An **aside** is a speech wherein a character expresses his thoughts in words audible to the spectators but supposedly unheard by the other stage characters present. Both were important conventions in Elizabethan drama and, later, in melodrama, but the late nineteenth century sought so vigorously to present on the stage the illusion of real life that both techniques were banished. They have, however, been revived in the twentieth century, e.g., in Eugene O'Neill's *Strange Interlude*, where the asides represent the characters' thoughts and unspoken desires. In **direct address,** a character turns from the world on the stage and speaks directly to the audience, telling it, for instance to watch closely. Consult Una Ellis-Fermor, *The Frontiers of Drama*, Ch. 6; George E. Duckworth, *The Nature of Roman Comedy*; Max Beerbohm, "Soliloquies in Drama," *Around Theatres*. The soliloquy, the aside, and direct address are all monologues, but more often a **monologue** is either a long speech delivered by one character, which may be heard but not interrupted by oth-

ers in his presence, or a performance by a single actor.

sound effect. An imitative noise, usually produced by simple machinery. Though a sound effect may be a mere imitation of nature, it may also be a richly symbolic suggestion. Chekhov's *The Cherry Orchard* (1904) concludes: "There is a far-off sound as if out of the sky, the sound of a snapped string, dying away, sad. A stillness falls, and there is only the thud of an ax on a tree, far away in the orchard." Consult Frank Napier, *Noises Off*.

spectacle. The last of Aristotle's six elements of drama, spectacle denotes what appeals to the eye, e.g., costume and scenery. Greek drama was splendidly costumed and made some use of scenery. Aeschylus especially seems to have contrived moments that caught the eye, such as Agamemnon's entrance in a chariot. The Elizabethan stage, though sparse in scenery, apparently was architecturally impressive, and doubtless military scenes were embellished with waving banners. In the Restoration, spectacle sometimes got the upper hand. Alexander Pope complained:

The play stands still; damn action and discourse,
Back fly the scenes, and enter foot and horse;
Pageants on pageants, in long order drawn,
Peers, heralds, bishops, ermine, gold, and lawn.

In the nineteenth century the development of gas light and then electric light made possible elaborate sunrises and twilights, and at the end of the century (especially in Russia) there was an emphasis on ensemble acting which gave a tableau-effect. Pictorial effects in late-nineteenth-century productions of Shakespeare were often achieved at the cost of Shakespeare's lines. At the very end of the century William Poel rejected spectacle and helped establish a trend to stage Shakespeare in what was thought to be an Elizabethan manner: an uncluttered stage, allowing the action to proceed rapidly. Consult James Laver, *Drama*; A. Nicholas Vardac, *Stage to Screen*, Chs. 3–4.

stage business. Minor physical action — including posture and facial expression — by a performer. Business ranges from headscratching to an addition Henry Irving made to *The Merchant of Venice*, II.vi: in Shakespeare's scene, Jessica and Lorenzo elope and the scene ends quietly; Irving added business in which Shylock entered, and knocked on the door of his empty house while the curtain fell. His successors amplified this business; Shylock entered the house, cried out, and reappeared, etc. Consult Arthur C. Sprague, *Shakespeare and the Actors*.

style. The mode of expression. Newman, talking of the writer's style, called it "a thinking out into language." This idea of "a thinking out" (but not into language) is applicable also to the style of the scene designer, the costume designer, etc. Kenneth Tynan in *Curtains* defines good style as "a happy consonance of manner with matter, of means with end, of tools with job." To **stylize** a play commonly means to present it with a noticeable artful manner rather than to present it realistically, though in fact realism itself is a style. A **stylized production** usually is presentational or anti-illusionistic rather than representational (see dramatic illusion). Consult George R. Kernodle, "Style, Stylization, and Styles of Acting," *Educational Theatre Journal*, 12 (1960), 251–261.

surrealism. A literary movement, especially vigorous in France in the 1920's and 1930's, that insisted that reality is grasped by the unconscious, the irrational, rather than by the conscious. The best art, it is held, is the dream. Among the forerunners were Alfred Jarry, whose *Ubu Roi* (1896) combined grotesque farce with anti-bourgeois satire, August Strindberg, whose *To Damascus* (three parts, 1898–1904) and *The Dream Play* (1902) had presented dream-like worlds, and Guillaume Apollinaire, whose *Breasts of Tiresias* (1917) was called a "*drame surréaliste*" (the first use of the word) by the author. Perhaps the chief surrealist dramatist is Jean Cocteau, notably in his *Orpheus* (1926), in which a glazier is an angel and a horse dictates prophetic words. Consult Georges E. Lemaître, *From Cubism to Surrealism in French Literature*.

suspense. Uncertainty, often characterized by anxiety. Suspense is usually a curious mixture of pain and pleasure, as Gwendolen, in Oscar Wilde's *The Importance of Being Earnest*, implies: "This suspense is terrible. I hope it will last." Most great art relies more heavily on suspense than on **surprise** (the unexpected). One can rarely sit twice through a play depending on

surprise; the surprise gone, the interest is gone. Suspense is usually achieved in part by **foreshadowing** — hints of what is to come. Dumas *fils* put it this way: "The art of the theater is the art of preparations." Coleridge, who held that Shakespeare gives us not surprise but expectation and then the satisfaction of perfect knowledge, once wrote: "As the feeling with which we startle at a shooting star, compared with that of watching the sunrise at the pre-established moment, such and so low is surprise compared with expectation." Thus, in *Hamlet*, the ghost does not pop up surprisingly, but satisfies the eager expectations that have been aroused by references to "this thing," "this dreaded sight," and "this apparition." Often, in fact, Shakespeare — like the Greek dramatists — used traditional stories; the audience presumably was not surprised by the deaths of Caesar and Brutus, and it enjoyed the suspense of anticipating them. Suspense is thus related to tragic irony. The tragic character moves closer and closer to his doom, and though he may be surprised by it, we are not; we are held by suspense. On surprise, consult David L. Grossvogel, *The Self-Conscious Stage in Modern French Drama* (reprinted in paperback as *Twentieth-Century French Drama*).

symbolism. Derived from Greek *symballein*, "to throw together," which thus suggests the essential quality of symbolism, the drawing together of two worlds; it presents the concrete material world of roses, toads, caves, stars, etc., and through them reveals an otherwise invisible world. As a noun, the original Greek word denoted half of something broken in two, and thus the word suggests not something that stands for something else, but something that is part of a larger unit.

Symbolism is often distinguished from allegory. Where the allegorist commonly invents a world (the author of *Everyman* [c. 1500] invents a figure called Everyman, who seeks aid from figures called Goods, Kindred, etc.) in order to talk about the real world, the symbolist commonly presents the phenomena of what we usually call the real world in order to reveal a "higher," eternal world of which the symbol is a part. The allegorist is free to invent any number of imaginary worlds to talk about the real world, but the symbolist feels that there is only one way by which he can present the "higher" real world he envisions. The everyday world is often considered by symbolists as a concrete but transient version of a more important realm, and the symbolist who presents, say, a rose, is (he might hold) speaking about a rose and also about the eternal beauty of womanhood in the only possible way.

In the second half of the nineteenth century there arose in France the so-called **Symbolist Movement,** but it must be emphasized that symbolism of a sort is probably as old as literature. An author's insistence on some object may cause us to regard it as more than its apparent nature. For example, the forest or greenwood in *As You Like It* suggests a benevolent nature that restores man to his best part. But on the whole Shakespeare's plays do not leave the world of sensible reality. The plays of the Symbolists do. The Symbolic writer presents a world that seems to be a dream world, a world that is not the usual world enriched, but a new world. In his preface to *The Dream Play* (1902), Strindberg says he "has tried to imitate the disconnected but seemingly logical form of the dream. Anything may happen.... The characters split, double, multiply, vanish, solidify, blur, clarify." A play is the expression of a "soul-state" (Stéphane Mallarmé's term) rather than an imitation of an external action. See *surrealism.*

The best naturalists (Ibsen, Chekhov, Strindberg, and Hauptmann) at times wrote symbolic works, but the chief Symbolic dramatists are the French (if we include the Belgian Maurice Maeterlinck) and William Butler Yeats. In Maeterlinck's *The Intruder* (1890) a blind old man sees with his soul the approach of Death. In *The Blind* (1890) a group of blind men are lost in a forest; their leader was a priest, but he has died. Maeterlinck occasionally said some of his plays were for marionettes, and though his statement is sometimes held to be a mildly self-deprecating joke, in fact there is much in the plays that belongs to the realm of impassive, other-worldly dolls, not surprising in the work of a writer who said he wished to study "man ... in the presence of eternity and mystery." Paul Claudel's *Tidings Brought to Mary* (written in 1892, revised in 1899 and 1912) was acted in 1912. Claudel, who said he had gained from Arthur Rimbaud (one of the leading Symbolists) "an almost physical impression of the supernatural," in this play envelops his medieval characters in a divine world, and dramatizes salvation. In Ireland, Yeats, who compared an artistic work to a magic talisman ("it entangles ... a part of the Divine essence") wrote verse plays of Irish supernatural creatures and heroes. In *On Baile's Strand* (1903), for instance, Cuchulain, the protagonist, is said to have been sired by a hawk. The bird imagery is insisted on; Cuchulain's associates are chicks and nestlings, and the Fool (who represents Cuchulain on another level) is delighted with feathers. Near the conclusion of the play, Cuchulain rushes out to fight the waves, literally doing what Hamlet spoke metaphorically of doing.

In Russia, Meyerhold in 1906 staged Ibsen's *Hedda Gabler* (1890) as symbolically as possible, turning what had been a naturalistic play into a vision suggestive of another world, something (in the words of a hostile critic) "halfway between metaphysics and ballet." (Consult Nikolai Gorchakov, *The Theater in Soviet Russia.*) For symbolism in the sense of richly suggestive images, consult Alan S. Downer, "The Life of Our Design: the Function of Imagery in the Poetic Drama," *The Hudson Review,* 2 (Summer 1949), 242–260. On the Symbolist Movement, consult William Butler Yeats, *Essays and Introductions;* Arthur Symons, *The Symbolist Movement in Literature;* *Yale French Studies,* No. 9; Eric Bentley, *The Playwright as Thinker;* John Gassner, *Form and Idea in the Modern Theatre.*

total theater. The idea that the theater should not try to imitate realistically an aspect of life but should embody a synthesis of all of the expressive arts, e.g., music, movement, speech, lighting, etc. The expression "total theater" probably is derived from Richard Wagner's *Gesamtkunstwerk,* "united" or "total artwork." Consult *Total Theatre,* ed. E. T. Kirby.

tragedy. For Aristotle, tragedy was a dramatic imitation (representation) of an "action of high importance." A Greek tragedy was serious, but it did not necessarily end unhappily. Aeschylus' *Eumenides,* for example, ends on a note of solemn joy. For us a tragedy is generally a play that faces evil, depicts suffering, and ends with death or (especially in the naturalistic tragedies since the latter part of the nineteenth century) ends with the hero alive but spiritually crushed. Tragedy's essence, Alfred North Whitehead says (*Science and the Modern World,* Ch. 1), resides not in unhappiness but "in the solemnity of the remorseless working of things." H. D. F. Kitto says (*The Greeks*, Ch. 4) that Greek tragedy — and perhaps one might add the great tragedy of other countries — was in part the product of intellectualism and humanism. Intellectualism let the Greeks see that human life must be lived within a great framework of what might be called the will of the gods, or Necessity: "Actions must have their consequences; ill-judged actions must have uncomfortable results." Humanism denied the Greeks an easy view of a heavenly life, and gave them an "almost fierce joy in life, the exultation in human achievement and in human personality." The tragic note, Kitto suggests, is produced by a tension between this unalterable framework and this passionate delight in life. Consult R. Sewall, *The Vision of Tragedy*; T. R. Henn, *The Harvest of Tragedy*; H. J. Muller, *The Spirit of Tragedy*.

tragicomedy. Renaissance critical theorists, embroidering on Aristotle's *Poetics*, assumed that tragedy dealt with noble (important) figures and ended with a death; comedy dealt with trivial (laughable) figures and ended with a celebration. A tragicomedy was some sort of mixture: high characters in a play ending happily, or a mingling of deaths and feasts, or, most often (as in many American films) threats of death which are happily — and unconvincingly — evaded. John Fletcher (1579–1625), who with his collaborator Francis Beaumont, wrote graceful dramas relying heavily on passionate outbursts and surprising turns of plot, defined a tragicomedy as a play that lacks deaths (and thus is no tragedy) but "brings some near it, which is enough to make it no comedy." One of the speakers in John Dryden's *Essay of Dramatick Poesie* (1668) says: "There is no theater in the world has anything so absurd as the English tragi-comedy; . . . here a course of mirth, there another of sadness and passion, and a third of honor and a duel: thus, in two hours and a half, we run through all the fits of Bedlam." Consult Eugene Waith, *The Pattern of Tragi-Comedy*. On what can roughly be called the bitter or ironic comedy of the nineteenth and twentieth centuries, consult K. S. Guthke, *Modern Tragi-comedy*; C. Hoy, *The Hyacinth Room*; and Eric Bentley, *The Life of the Drama*.

trilogy. A unit of three works. Though Greek tragic dramatists submitted three tragedies at a time, the plays are only a trilogy if they have an internal unity. Aeschylus' *Oresteia* (458 B.C.) is the only extant complete Greek trilogy; Sophocles' three plays on the Oedipus legend — *Antigone* (c. 422 B.C.), *Oedipus the King* (c. 425), and *Oedipus at Colonus* (c. 406) are not properly a trilogy because they were written at widely separated times and do not cohere into a consistent, unified whole. A modern trilogy: O'Neill's *Mourning Becomes Electra* (1931).

unity. Generally means something like "coherence," "congruence"; in a unified piece the parts work together and jointly contribute to the whole. The subplot of a play may parallel the main plot, or one character may be a foil to another. In any case, unity suggests "completeness" or "pattern" resulting from a controlling intelligence. In the *Poetics*, Aristotle had said that a tragedy should have a unified action, and he had mentioned that most tragedies cover a period of twenty-four hours. Italian critics, making his comments rigid, in the late sixteenth century established the **Three Unities** of Time, Place, and Action: a play (1) must not cover more than twenty-four hours, (2) must be set in one locale only, or, at worst, in various parts of a single city, and (3) must be either entirely tragic or entirely comic, rather than a mixture of (as Sir Philip Sidney said) "hornpipes and funerals." (Consult H. B. Charlton, *Castelvetro's Theory of Poetry*.) Actually, the time covered by Greek tragedies is vague; characters come from distant places in the space of relatively few lines. For example, in *Oedipus the King*, a shepherd, who lives in the "farthest" fields from Corinth, is sent for in line 863 and arrives in line 1108. Nor is unity of place invariable in Greek tragedy; there are violations of it in, for example, Aeschylus' *The Eumenides* and Sophocles' *Ajax*.

well-made play. See *pièce bien faite*.

To the student:

We, as publishers, realize that one way to improve education is to improve textbooks. We also realize that you, the student, have a large role in the success or failure of textbooks. Although teachers choose books to be used in the classroom, if the students do not buy and use books, those books are failures.

Usually only the teacher is asked about the quality of a text; his opinion alone is considered as revisions are written or as new books are planned. Now, Little, Brown would like to ask you about this book: how you liked or disliked it; why it was successful or dull; if it taught you anything. Would you fill in this form and return it to us at: Little, Brown and Co., College Division, 34 Beacon St., Boston, Mass. 02106. It is your chance to directly affect the publication of future textbooks.

Book title:_____ School:_____

Course title:_____ Course enrollment:_____

1. Did you like the book?_____

2. CONTENT: Was it too easy?_____

   Did you read all the selections?_____

   Which did you like most?_____

   Which did you like least?_____

3. FORMAT: Did you like the cover?_____

   Did you like the size?_____

   Did you like the margins?_____

   Did you like the illustrations?_____

   Did you like the type size?_____

(over)

4. Were the study questions, review summaries, or other pedagogical apparatus useful?_____

How should they be changed?_____

_____

5. INTRODUCTIONS: Are they useful?_____

How might they be improved?_____

_____

6. Do you feel the professor should continue to assign this book next year?

_____

7. Will you keep this book for your library?_____

8. Please add any comments or suggestions on how we might improve this book, in either content or format.

_____

_____

_____

_____

_____

9. May we quote you, either in promotion for this book, or in future publishing ventures?   _____yes   _____no

_____   _____
date   signature